SECOND EDITION

Strategic Brand Management

Building, Measuring, and Managing Brand Equity

Kevin Lane Keller

Amos Tuck School of Business
Dartmouth College

Prentice
Hall

Pearson Education International

Senior Editor: Wendy Craven
Editor-in-Chief: Jeff Shelstad
Assistant Editor: Melissa Pellerano
Editorial Assistant: Danielle Serra
Media Project Manager: Anthony Palmiotto
Marketing Manager: Michelle O'Brien
Marketing Assistant: Christine Genneken
Managing Editor (Production): John Roberts
Permissions Coordinator: Suzanne Grappi
Associate Director, Manufacturing: Vincent Scelta
Production Manager: Arnold Vila
Manufacturing Buyer: Michelle Klein
Photo Researcher: Teri Stratford
Image Coordinator: Valerie Gold
Cover Design: Blair Brown
Cover Illustration: George Abe
Full-Service Project Management: Compset
Printer/Binder: Hamilton

Credits and acknowledgments borrowed from other sources and reproduced, with permission, in this textbook appear on page 769.

This edition may be sold only in those countries to which it is consigned by Pearson Education International. It is not to be re-exported and it is not for sale in the U.S.A., Mexico, or Canada.

Pearson Education LTD.
Pearson Education Australia PTY, Limited
Pearson Education Singapore, Pte. Ltd
Pearson Education North Asia Ltd
Pearson Education, Canada, Ltd
Pearson Educación de Mexico, S.A. de C.V.
Pearson Education–Japan
Pearson Education Malaysia, Pte. Ltd
Pearson Education, Upper Saddle River, New Jersey

10 9 8 7 6 5 4 3 2 1
ISBN 0-13-110583-3

*This book is dedicated to my mother
and the memory of my father
with much love, respect, and admiration.*

Contents

PART III: PLANNING AND IMPLEMENTING BRAND MARKETING PROGRAMS

PART IV: MEASURING AND INTERPRETING BRAND PERFORMANCE

CHAPTER 8   Developing a Brand Equity Measurement and Management System   388

CHAPTER 9   Measuring Sources of Brand Equity: Capturing Customer Mindset   429

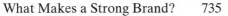

Prologue: Branding Is Not Rocket Science

Although the challenges in branding can be immense and difficult, branding is not necessarily rocket science. I should know. I am not a rocket scientist—but my dad was. He was a physicist in the Air Force for 20 years, working on various rocket fuels. Always interested in what I did, he once asked what the book was all about. I explained the concept of brand equity and how the book addressed how to build, measure, and manage it. He listened, paused, and remarked, "That's very interesting but, uh, that's not *exactly* rocket science."

He's right. Branding is not rocket science. In fact, it is an art and a science. There is always a creativity and originality component involved with marketing. Even if someone were to follow all the guidelines in the book—and all the guidelines were properly specified—the success or failure of a brand strategy would still depend largely on how exactly the guidelines were translated into a strategy and how this strategy was then implemented. Nevertheless, good marketing is all about improving the odds for success. The hope is that this book adds to the scientific aspect of branding, illuminating the subject and providing guidance to those who make brand-related decisions.

Preface

It is useful to answer a few questions to provide the reader and instructor with some background as to what this book is about, how it is different from other books about branding, who should read it, how the book is organized, what is new in this second edition, and how a reader can get the most out of using the book.

WHAT IS THE BOOK ABOUT?

This book deals with brands—why they are important, what they represent to consumers, and what should be done by firms to manage them properly. As many business executives now recognize, perhaps one of the most valuable assets that a firm has is the brands that the firm has invested in and developed over time. Although manufacturing processes and factory designs often can be duplicated, strongly held beliefs and attitudes established in the minds of consumers often cannot be so easily reproduced. The difficulty and expense of introducing new products, however, puts more pressure than ever on firms to skillfully launch their new products as well as manage their existing brands.

Although brands may represent invaluable intangible assets, creating and nurturing a strong brand poses considerable challenges. Fortunately, the concept of *brand equity*—the main focus of this book—can provide marketers valuable perspective and a common denominator to interpret the potential effects and tradeoffs of various strategies and tactics for their brands. Fundamentally, the brand equity concept stresses the importance of the role of the brand in marketing strategies. Brand equity relates to the fact that different outcomes result from the marketing of a product or service because of its brand name or some other brand element than if that same product or service did not have that brand identification. In other words, brand equity can be thought of as the marketing effects uniquely attributable to the brand. In a practical sense, brand equity represents the added value endowed to a product as a result of past investments in the marketing activity for a brand. Brand equity serves as the bridge between what happened to the brand in the past and what should happen to the brand in the future.

The chief purpose of this book is to provide a comprehensive and up-to-date treatment of the subjects of brands, brand equity, and strategic brand management. *Strategic brand management* involves the design and implementation of marketing programs and activities to build, measure, and manage brand equity. An important goal of the book is to provide managers with concepts and techniques to improve the long-term profitability of their brand strategies. The book incorporates current thinking and developments on these topics from both academics and industry participants. The book combines a comprehensive theoretical foundation with numerous practical insights to assist managers in their day-to-day and long-term brand decisions. Illustrative examples and case studies are based on brands marketed in the United States and all over the world.

Specifically, the book provides insights into how profitable brand strategies can be created by building, measuring, and managing brand equity. It addresses three important questions:

1. How can brand equity be created?
2. How can brand equity be measured?
3. How can brand equity be used to expand business opportunities?

In addressing these questions, the book is written to deliver a number of benefits. Readers will learn the following:

➤ The role of brands, the concept of brand equity, and the advantages of creating strong brands
➤ The three main ways to build brand equity by properly choosing brand elements, designing supporting marketing programs, and leveraging secondary associations
➤ Different approaches to measure brand equity and how to implement a brand equity measurement system
➤ Alternative branding strategies and how to devise brand hierarchies and brand portfolios
➤ The role of corporate brands, family brands, individual brands, and brand modifiers, and how they can be combined into sub-brands
➤ How to adjust branding strategies over time and geographic boundaries to maximize brand equity

WHAT IS DIFFERENT ABOUT THIS BOOK?

In writing this book, the objective was to satisfy three key criteria by which any marketing text can be judged:

➤ *Depth:* The material in the book had to be presented in the context of a conceptual framework that was comprehensive, internally consistent and cohesive, and well grounded in the academic and practitioner literature.
➤ *Breadth:* The book had to cover all those topics that practicing managers and students of brand management found interesting or important.
➤ *Relevance:* Finally, the book had to be well grounded in practice and easily related to past and present marketing activities, events, and case studies.

Although a number of excellent books have been written about brands, no book has really maximized these three dimensions to the greatest possible extent. Accordingly, this book set out to fill that gap by accomplishing three things. First, the book develops a framework that provides a definition of brand equity, identifies sources and outcomes of brand equity, and provides tactical guidelines as to how to build, measure, and manage brand equity. Recognizing the general importance of consumers and customers to marketing (i.e., the necessity of understanding and satisfying their needs and wants), this framework approaches branding from the perspective of the consumer and is referred to as *customer-based brand equity*. Second, besides these broad, fundamentally important branding topics, over 30 Science of Branding boxes provide in-depth treatment of cutting-edge ideas and concepts, and each chapter contains a Brand Focus appendix that delves into detail on specific, related branding topics such as brand audits, legal issues, brand crises, and corporate name changes. Finally, to maximize relevance, numerous examples are included to illuminate the discussion on virtually every topic, and over 100 Branding Briefs are included to provide more in-depth examination of certain topics or brands.

Thus, this book can help readers understand the important issues in planning and evaluating brand strategies, as well as provide appropriate concepts, theories, and other tools to make better branding decisions. The book identifies successful and unsuccessful brand marketers—and why they have been so. Readers will gain a greater appreciation of the range of issues covered in branding as well as a means to organize their thoughts about those issues.

WHO SHOULD READ THIS BOOK?

A wide range of people can benefit from reading this book:

➤ Students interested in increasing both their understanding of basic branding principles and their exposure to classic and contemporary branding applications and case studies

➤ Managers and analysts concerned with the effects of their day-to-day marketing decisions on brand performance

➤ Senior executives concerned with the longer-term prosperity of their brand franchises and product or service portfolios

➤ All marketers interested in new ideas with implications for marketing strategies and tactics

The perspective adopted in the book is relevant to any type of organization (public or private, large or small), and the examples provided cover a wide range of industries and geographies. To facilitate understanding of branding concepts across different settings, specific applications to industrial, high-tech, online, service, retailer, and small-business brands are reviewed in Chapters 1 and 15.

HOW IS THE BOOK ORGANIZED?

The book is divided into six major parts, adhering to the "three-exposure opportunity" approach to learning new material. Part I introduces branding concepts; Parts II, III, IV, and V provide all the specific details of those concepts; and Part VI summarizes and applies the concepts in various contexts. The specific chapters for each part and their contents are as follows.

Part I sets the stage for the book by providing the "big picture" of what strategic brand management is all about. The goal of these chapters is to provide a sense of the content and context of strategic brand management by identifying key branding decisions and suggesting some of the important considerations for those decisions. Specifically, Chapter 1 introduces some basic notions about brands and the role that they have played and are playing in marketing strategies. Chapter 1 defines what a brand is, why brands matter, and how anything can be branded and provides an overview of the strategic brand management process.

Part II addresses the topic of brand equity and provides a blueprint for the rest of the book. Chapter 2 introduces the concept of customer-based brand equity, outlines the customer-based brand equity framework, and summarizes guidelines for building, measuring, and managing customer-based brand equity. The first two chapters provide a useful overview of the scope and topics covered in the book. As such, they provide an excellent "top-line summary" for readers who want to sample the flavor of the book or who do not have the time to read all of the chapters. Chapter 3 develops a conceptual model of brand knowledge and addresses the critically important issue of competitive brand positioning.

Part III examines the three major ways to build customer-based brand equity, taking more of a "single product–single brand" perspective. Chapter 4 addresses the first way to build customer-based brand equity and how to choose brand elements (i.e., brand names, logos, symbols, slogans, and so forth) and the role they play in contributing to brand equity. Chapters 5 and 6 are concerned with the second way to build brand equity and how to optimize the marketing mix to create customer-based brand equity. Chapter 5 is concerned with product, pricing, and distribution strategies; Chapter 6 is devoted to the topic of creating integrated marketing communication programs to build brand equity. Although most readers are probably familiar with these "4 Ps" of marketing, it can be illuminating to consider them from the standpoint of brand equity and the effects of brand knowledge on consumer response to marketing mix activity and vice versa. Finally, Chapter 7 examines the third major way to build brand equity: leveraging secondary associations from other entities (e.g., companies, geographic regions, persons, other brands, and so on).

Part IV looks at how to measure customer-based brand equity. These chapters take a detailed look at what consumers know about brands, what marketers want them to know, and how marketers can develop measurement procedures to assess how well they are doing. Chapter 8 provides a big-picture perspective of these topics, introducing the brand value chain and examining how to develop and implement a brand equity measurement system. Chapter 9 examines approaches to measure customers' brand knowledge structures in order to be able to identify and quantify potential sources of brand equity. Chapter 10 examines how to measure potential outcomes of brand equity in terms of the major benefits a firm accrues from these sources of brand equity.

Part V addresses how to manage brand equity, taking a broader, "multiple product-multiple brand" perspective as well as a longer-term, multiple-market perspective to brands. Chapter 11 considers issues related to branding strategies (e.g., which brand elements a firm chooses to apply across the various products it sells) and how brand equity can be maximized across all the different brands and products that might be sold by a firm. Chapter 11 describes two important tools to help formulate branding strategies: the brand-product matrix and the brand hierarchy. Chapter 12 outlines the pros and cons of brand extensions and develops guidelines to facilitate the introduction and naming of new products and brand extensions. Chapter 13 considers how to reinforce, revitalize, and retire brands, examining a number of specific topics in managing brands over time, such as the advantages of maintaing brand consistency, the importance of protecting sources of brand equity, and tradeoffs between fortifying and leveraging brands. Chapter 14 examines the implications of differences in consumer behavior and the existence of different types of market segments on managing brand equity. Particular attention is paid to international issues and global branding strategies.

Finally, Part VI considers some implications and applications of the customer-based brand equity framework. Chapter 15 highlights managerial guidelines and key themes that emerged in earlier chapters of the book. The chapter also summarizes success factors for branding, applies the customer-based brand equity framework to address specific strategic brand management issues for different types of products (i.e., industrial goods, high-tech products, online brands, services, retailers, and small businesses), and relates the framework to several other popular views of brand equity.

REVISION STRATEGY FOR THE SECOND EDITION

The overarching goal of the revision of *Strategic Brand Management* was to preserve the aspects of the text that worked well but to improve it as much as possible and add new material as needed. The main objective of the second edition was to again maximize three dimensions: depth, breadth, and relevance. The customer-based brand equity framework that was the centerpiece of the first edition was retained but embellished in several significant ways. Given all the academic research progress that has been made in recent years as well as new market developments and events, the book required and was given some substantial updates.

Specifically, there were six objectives to the revision, as follows:

1. Overhaul the conceptual thrust of certain chapters.
2. Adopt a stronger technological and global perspective.
3. Update Branding Briefs and academic references.
4. Streamline chapters.
5. Update original cases and introduce new cases.
6. Provide better presentation of text material and stronger supplementary support.

Overhaul the Conceptual Thrust of Certain Chapters

A number of chapters reflect new thinking and concepts.

➤ *Chapter 1:* The chapter now formally introduces the strategic brand management process.
➤ *Chapter 2:* This chapter is now organized around the customer-based brand equity pyramid that describes the four steps (identity, meaning, response, and relationships) and six different types of core brand values (salience, performance, image, judgments, feelings, and resonance) necessary to build a brand. This detailed framework helps to provide more structure to the consumer brand knowledge topics as well as tie more directly into how to build brand equity, the thrust of the next four chapters.
➤ *Chapter 3:* New positioning material is included to further develop the book's unique competitive brand positioning model and the key concepts of points of parity and points of difference.
➤ *Chapter 6:* A new set of criteria is included on how to evaluate integrated marketing communication programs.

➤ *Chapter 7:* A revised framework for brand leverage is used as an organizing device.

➤ *Chapters 8, 9, and 10:* The material from Chapter 10 of the first edition has been combined with new material on the brand value chain to create a new Chapter 8 that provides a big-picture perspective on the theory and practice of measuring brand equity. The material on research techniques and approaches has been updated and augmented and placed in new Chapters 9 and 10.

➤ *Chapter 14:* To provide clearer focus, global brand management guidelines are presented in terms of the "Ten Commandments of Global Branding."

➤ *Chapter 15:* New summary comments and future branding priorities are included to provide contemporary perspectives.

Adopt a Stronger Technological and Global Perspective

Technology and online brands and concepts are highlighted throughout the book. Specifically, Chapter 1 introduces both high-tech and online brands as key branding applications. Special attention is paid to URLs and naming Web sites in Chapter 4; Web design and service issues in Chapter 5; and the Internet as a communication tool and brand builder in Chapter 6. Finally, Chapter 15 has detailed sections on how to build high-tech and online brands. In terms of global perspectives, besides Chapter 14, a stronger global flavor is found in the text examples and the Branding Briefs.

Update Branding Briefs and Academic References

Over half of the examples within the text and the 100-plus Branding Briefs have been replaced with more current material. The goal was to blend classic and contemporary examples, so some appropriate examples were retained from the first edition. The academic references throughout the book have also been brought up to date.

Streamline Chapters

Lengthy passages and examples have been edited. Each chapter includes a Brand Focus appendix that includes more detailed material or material that might disrupt the flow of the chapter. Examples include the history of branding in Chapter 1, brand audit guidelines in Chapter 2, private labels in Chapter 5, crisis marketing in Chapter 6, and corporate name changes in Chapter 13.

Update Original Cases and Introduce New Cases

To provide broader, more relevant coverage, the cases have been removed from the back of the book, updated, and placed in a separate casebook. Seven new cases that cover even more branding topics have also been included in the casebook: Starbucks, DuPont, Snapple, Accenture, Red Bull, MTV, and Yahoo.

Provide Better Presentation of Text Material and Stronger Supplementary Support

The text includes more schematics and figures that help to summarize key conceptual material. All critical figures are reprinted in the instructor's manual. The instructor's manual has been expanded to provide more help for classroom instruction and provide guidance for experiential learning.

HOW CAN A READER GET THE MOST OUT OF THIS BOOK?

Branding is a fascinating topic that has received much attention in the popular press. The ideas presented in the book will help readers interpret current branding developments. One good way to better understand branding and the customer-based brand equity framework is to apply the concepts and ideas that were presented in the book to current events or any of the more detailed branding issues or case studies presented in the Branding Briefs. The Discussion Questions at the end of the chapters often ask readers to pick a brand and apply one or more concepts from that chapter. Focusing on one brand across all of the questions—perhaps as part of a class project—permits some cumulative and integrated learning and is an excellent way to become more comfortable and facile with the material in the book.

Although it is a trite saying, this book truly belongs to the reader. As with most marketing, branding does not involve "right" or "wrong" answers, and readers should question things they do not understand or do not believe. This book is designed to facilitate your understanding of what is involved with strategic brand management and present some "best practice" guidelines. At the end of the day, however, what you get out of the book will be what you put into it and how you blend the ideas contained in these pages with what you already know or believe.

Acknowledgments

This book took longer to write and revise than I might have liked, but it would have taken even longer—and perhaps may not have even been finished—without the help and guidance of various people. I want to recognize and thank those and others who made valuable contributions to the completion of the book.

At Prentice Hall, Sandy Steiner, David Borkowsky, and Jim Boyd were enthusiastic supporters from start to finish. Paul Feyn helped to "seal the deal," Whitney Blake provided invaluable editorial guidance for both editions. The Prentice Hall team on the second edition was a huge help in the revision—many thanks to: Jeff Shelstad, Wendy Craven, Melissa Pellerano, Danielle Serra, Anthony Palmiotto, Suzanne Grappi, Teri Stratford, and John Roberts.

I have learned much about branding in my work with industry participants who have unique perspectives on what is working and not working (and why) in the marketplace, especially the executives who have participated in my seminars and workshops and MBA students who have taken my courses. Our discussions have enriched my appreciation for the challenges in building, measuring, and managing brand equity and the factors affecting the success and failure of brand strategies. I particularly want to thank the following individuals and others from their respective organizations at the time of our projects: Scott Bedbury and Jerome Conlon (Starbucks); Liz Dolan and Bill Zeitz (Nike); Meera Buck (Shell); Dennis Carter, Sally Fundakowski, Karen Alter, Ann Lewnes, and Ellen Konar (Intel); Norbert Krapp and Ann-Christin Wagemann (Beiersdorf); Steve Goldstein, Robert Hanson, James Capon, and Bobbi Silten (Levi Strauss); Jack Kowiak (Kodak); Jeff Manning (CMPB); Lconora Polonsky (Procter & Gamble); Charles Mangano (Merrill Lynch); Patrick Tickle (Terraspring); Jay Dean, Ed Lebar, Phil Buehler and Monika Sawicka (Young & Rubicam); Jim Schroer (Ford); Jim Murphy, Teresa Poggenpohl, and Brian Harvey (Accenture); Andy Bird (Unilever); Laurie Lang (Disney); David Sherbon (CDC); Peter Feigin (New York Knicks); John Copeland (Envision); K. K. Davey and Doss Struse (Knowledge Networks); Jon Coleman, Warren Kurtzman, and Chris Ackerman (Coleman Research); Jim Figura (Colgate-Palmolive); and John La Forgia, Kent Seltman, and Scott Swanson (Mayo Clinic).

I have benefited from the wisdom of my colleagues at the institutions where I have held academic positions: Dartmouth College, Duke University, the University of California at Berkeley, Stanford University, the Australian Graduate School of Management, and the University of North Carolina at Chapel Hill. Several individuals deserve special recognition. First and foremost, David Aaker from the University of California at Berkeley has been a research colleague, sounding board, and good friend for as long as I have been working in the branding area. I have learned much from him, and although it is tempting to say that he taught me all I know, that wouldn't explain my backhand (Dave, check the Epilogue—I'm still counting). Duke University's Richard Staelin and Jim Bettman helped to get me started and continue to serve as role models in every sense of the word. Northwestern University's Brian Sternthal and Harvard University's Stephen Greyser have been remarkably helpful to me over the years in all my teaching efforts. John Roberts from the Australian Graduate School of Management at the University of New South Wales has broadened my perspective on branding in a number of different, important ways. Finally, Stanford University's Jim Lattin has been a helpful resource on just about anything I could ever think of—he's as good a colleague as anyone could hope for.

Over the years, the doctoral students that I have advised have helped in a variety of useful ways in my branding pursuits, including Sheri Bridges (Wake Forest University), Christie Brown (University of Michigan), and Sanjay Sood (University of California at Los Angeles). Special thanks to Meg Campbell (University of Colorado at Boulder) and Jennifer Aaker (Stanford University) for especially detailed feedback on a draft of this second edition. I would also like to thank a group of talented reviewers who provided insightful feedback to early versions of the manuscript in its first or second edition.

Keith Richey provided incredibly detailed and perceptive research and writing assistance. Without his help, the book would not have been nearly as good, if the revision would have been finished at all. I owe him a tremendous debt of gratitude.

Finally, thanks go to my wife, Punam Anand Keller, and two daughters, Carolyn and Allison, for their understanding and patience. Being able to spend more time with them is my chief reward from finishing.

About the Author

 **Kevin Lane Keller** is the E. B. Osborn Professor of Marketing at the Amos Tuck School of Business Administration at Dartmouth College. Professor Keller received his B.A. in Mathematics and Economics from Cornell University in 1978, his M.B.A. from Carnegie-Mellon University's Graduate School of Industrial Administration in 1980, and his Ph.D. in Marketing from Duke University's Fuqua School of Business in 1986. At Dartmouth, he teaches an M.B.A. elective on strategic brand management and lectures in executive programs on that topic.

Previously, Professor Keller was on the faculty of the Graduate School of Business at Stanford University, where he also served as the head of the marketing group. Additionally, he has been on the marketing faculty of the Schools of Business Administration at the University of California at Berkeley and the University of North Carolina at Chapel Hill, has been a Visiting Professor at Duke University and the Australian Graduate School of Management, and has two years of industry experience as Marketing Consultant for Bank of America.

Professor Keller is acknowledged as one of the international leaders in the study of strategic brand management and integrated marketing communications. He is currently conducting a variety of studies that address strategies to build, measure, and manage brand equity. His advertising and branding research has been published in three of the major marketing journals—the *Journal of Marketing*, the *Journal of Marketing Research*, and the *Journal of Consumer Research*. He also sits on the Editorial Review Boards of those journals. With more than forty published papers, his research has been widely cited and has received numerous awards.

Actively involved with industry, he has worked on a host of different types of branding projects. He has served as brand confidant to marketers for some of the world's most successful brands, including Disney, Ford, Intel, Levi Strauss, Nike, Procter & Gamble, and Starbucks. Additional brand consulting activities have been with other top companies such as Accenture, AC Nielsen, Beiersdorf (Nivea), General Mills, Goodyear, Kodak, Mayo Clinic, MTV, the New York Knicks, Nordstrom, Shell Oil, Unilever, and Young & Rubicam. He is a Senior Marketing Consultant for Knowledge Networks and an academic trustee for the Marketing Science Institute. A popular speaker, he has conducted branding seminars to top executives in a variety of forums.

An avid sports, music, and film enthusiast, in his so-called spare time, he helps to manage and market one of Australia's great rock and roll treasures, The Church. Professor Keller lives in Etna, New Hampshire, with his wife, Punam (also a Tuck marketing professor), and his two daughters, Carolyn and Allison.

CHAPTER

1

Brands and Brand Management

PREVIEW

More and more firms and other organizations have come to the realization that one of their most valuable assets is the brand names associated with their products or services. In an increasingly complex world, individuals and businesses are faced with more and more choices but seemingly have less and less time to make those choices. The ability of a strong brand to simplify consumer decision making, reduce risk, and set expectations is thus invaluable. Creating strong brands that deliver on that promise, and maintaining and enhancing the strength of those brands over time, is thus a management imperative.

The purpose of this text is to assist those who seek a deeper understanding of how to achieve those branding goals. This advanced MBA-level text addresses the important branding decisions faced by individuals and organizations in their marketing. Its basic objectives are

1. To increase understanding of the important issues in planning, implementing, and evaluating brand strategies
2. To provide the appropriate concepts, theories, models, and other tools to make better branding decisions

Particular emphasis is placed on understanding psychological principles at the individual or organizational level so as to improve managerial decision making with respect to brands. The objective is for this book to be relevant for any type of organization, regardless of size, nature of business, or profit orientation.

Why does there need to be a special marketing text on brands? What does this book offer that is not covered in introductory or advanced marketing texts? Unfortunately, many of the important branding issues have been relatively neglected by these other texts. Moreover, although many of the traditional and well-established principles of brand management are still basically valid (e.g., defining target markets, establishing differentiated product positions), the context in which those principles must be applied to manage brands has dramatically changed. By putting more focus on the brand and accounting for these new developments, this book will provide students of marketing valuable knowledge, a broader perspective, and greater understanding of brand strategies and tactics. It will consider a host of marketing issues from the point of view of branding. In doing so, it will examine issues that one may have otherwise overlooked and will teach lessons that one may not have otherwise realized by practicing "marketing as usual."

With these goals in mind, this first chapter defines what a brand is. It considers the functions of a brand from the perspective of both consumers and firms and why brands are important to both. It considers what can and cannot be branded and identifies some strong brands. The chapter concludes with an overview of the concept of brand equity and the strategic brand management process. Brand Focus 1.0 at the end of the chapter traces some of the historical origins of branding.

WHAT IS A BRAND?

Branding has been around for centuries as a means to distinguish the goods of one producer from those of another. In fact, the word *brand* is derived from the Old Norse word *brandr,* which means "to burn," as brands were and still are the means by which owners of livestock mark their animals to identify them.[1] According to the American Marketing Association (AMA), a brand is a "name, term, sign, symbol, or design, or a combination of them, intended to identify the goods and services of one seller or group of sellers and to differentiate them from those of competition." Technically speaking, then, whenever a marketer creates a new name, logo, or symbol for a new product, he or she has created a brand.

It should be recognized that many practicing managers, however, refer to a brand as more than that—defining a brand in terms of having actually created a certain amount of awareness, reputation, prominence, and so on in the marketplace. In some sense, a distinction can thus be made between the AMA definition of a "small-*b* brand" and the industry practice of a "big-*b* brand"—that is, a "brand" versus a "Brand." It is important to recognize this distinction because disagreements about branding principles or guidelines often revolve around the definition of what is meant by a "brand."

Thus, the key to creating a brand, according to the AMA definition, is to be able to choose a name, logo, symbol, package design, or other attribute that identifies a product and distinguishes it from others. These different components of a brand that identify and differentiate it can be called *brand elements.* As Chapter 4 shows, brand elements come in many different forms. For example, consider the variety of brand name strategies that exist. In some cases, the company name is essentially used for all products (e.g., as with General Electric and Hewlett-Packard). In other cases, manufacturers assign individual brand names to new products that are unrelated to the company name (e.g., as with Procter & Gamble and their Tide, Pampers, Iams, and Pantene product brands). Retailers create their own brands based on their store name or some other means (e.g., Macy's has their own I.N.C., Charter Club, and Club Room brands).

The names themselves given to products come in many different forms.[2] There are brand names based on people (e.g., Estée Lauder cosmetics, Porsche automobiles, and Orville Redenbacher popcorn), places (e.g., Sante Fe cologne, Chrysler's New Yorker automobile, and British Airways), animals or birds (e.g., Mustang automobiles, Dove soap, and Greyhound buses), or other things or objects (e.g., Apple computers, Shell gasoline, and Carnation evaporated milk). There are brand names that use words with inherent product meaning (e.g., Lean Cuisine, JustJuice, and Ticketron) or that suggest important attributes or benefits (e.g., DieHard auto batteries, Mop & Glo floor cleaner, and Beautyrest mattresses). There are brand names that are made up and include prefixes and suffixes that sound scientific, natural, or prestigious (e.g., Intel microprocessors, Lexus automobiles, or Compaq computers). Similarly, other brand elements, such as brand logos and symbols, may be based on people, places, and things, abstract images, and so on in different ways. In sum, in creating a brand, marketers have many choices over the number and nature of the brand elements they choose to identify their products.

Brands Versus Products

It is important to contrast a brand and a product. According to Phillip Kotler, a well-regarded marketing academic, a *product* is anything that can be offered to a market for attention, acquisition, use, or consumption that might satisfy a need or want. Thus, a product may be a physical good (e.g., a cereal, tennis racquet, or automobile), service (e.g., an airline, bank, or insurance company), retail store (e.g., a department store, specialty store, or supermarket), person (e.g., a political figure, entertainer, or professional athlete), organization (e.g., a nonprofit organization, trade organization, or arts group), place (e.g., a city, state, or country), or idea (e.g., a political or social cause). This book adopts this broad definition of product. It discusses the role of brands in some of these different categories in more detail later in this chapter and in Chapter 15.

Kotler defines five levels to a product:[3]

1. The *core benefit level* is the fundamental need or want that consumers satisfy by consuming the product or service.
2. The *generic product level* is a basic version of the product containing only those attributes or characteristics absolutely necessary for its functioning but with no distinguishing features. This is basically a stripped-down, no-frills version of the product that adequately performs the product function.
3. The *expected product level* is a set of attributes or characteristics that buyers normally expect and agree to when they purchase a product.
4. The *augmented product level* includes additional product attributes, benefits, or related services that distinguish the product from competitors.
5. The *potential product level* includes all of the augmentations and transformations that a product might ultimately undergo in the future.

Figure 1-1 illustrates these different levels in the context of air conditioners and videocassette recorders. Kotler notes that competition within many markets essentially takes place at the product augmentation level because most firms can successfully build satisfactory products at the expected product level. Another well-respected marketing academic, Harvard's Ted Levitt, concurs and argues that "the new competition is not between what companies produce in their factories but between what they add to their factory output in the form of packaging, services, advertising, customer advice, financing, delivery arrangements, warehousing, and other things that people value."[4]

A brand is therefore a product, but one that adds other dimensions that differentiate it in some way from other products designed to satisfy the same need. These differences may be rational and tangible—related to product performance of the brand—or more symbolic, emotional, and intangible—related to what the brand represents. One marketing observer put it this way:

> More specifically, what distinguishes a brand from its unbranded commodity counterpart and gives it equity is the sum total of consumers' perceptions and feelings about the product's attributes and how they perform, about the brand name and what it stands for, and about the company associated with the brand.[5]

Extending our previous example, a branded product may be a physical good (e.g., Kellogg's Corn Flakes cereal, Prince tennis racquets, or Ford Taurus automobiles), a service (e.g., United Airlines, Bank of America, or Allstate insurance), a store (e.g., Bloomingdale's department store, Body Shop specialty store, or Safeway supermarket), a person (e.g., Bill Clinton, Julia Roberts, or Michael Jordan), a place (e.g., the city of London, state of California, or country of Australia), an organization (e.g., the Red

Level	Air Conditioner
1. Core benefit	Cooling and comfort.
2. Generic product	Sufficient cooling capacity (Btu per hour), an acceptable energy efficiency rating, adequate air intakes and exhausts, and so on.
3. Expected product	*Consumer Reports* states that for a typical large air conditioner, consumers should expect at least two cooling speeds, expandable plastic side panels, adjustable louvers, removable air filter, vent for exhausting air, power cord at least 60 inches long, R-22 HCFC refrigerant (less harmful to the earth's ozone layer than other types), one-year parts-and-labor warranty on the entire unit, and a five-year parts-and-labor warranty on the refrigeration system.[a]
4. Augmented product	Optional features might include electric touch-pad controls, a display to show indoor and outdoor temperatures and the thermostat setting, an automatic mode to adjust fan speed based on the thermostat setting and room temperature, a toll-free 800 number for customer service, and so on.
5. Potential product	Silent running, completely balanced throughout the room, and energy self-sufficient.

Level	Video Cassette Recorder
1. Core benefit	Convenient entertainment.
2. Generic product	Ability to record and play back television or video programs with adequate picture quality. Programmable.
3. Expected product	*Consumer Reports* states that for a typical VCR, consumers should expect a digital quartz tuner that receives 125 cable channels; ability to record at—and play tapes recorded at—SP, LP, and EP speeds; on-screen programming of eight events up to one year in advance with options for daily and weekly recording; power on when tape is inserted and auto rewind at end of tape; and one-year warranty on tape heads and other parts, three months on labor.[b]
4. Augmented product	Optional features might include hi-fi stereo sound, VCR Plus, and shuttle controls for easy backward and forward scanning.
5. Potential product	Voice-controlled programming; ability to edit out commercials.

[a]*Consumer Reports* 9, no. 6 (June 1994): 400–403.

[b]*Consumer Reports* 59, no. 3 (March 1994): 164–165.

FIGURE 1-1 Examples of Different Product Levels

Cross, American Automobile Association, or the Rolling Stones), or an idea (e.g., abortion rights, free trade, or freedom of speech).

Some brands create competitive advantages with product performance. For example, brands such as Gillette, Merck, Sony, 3M, and others have been leaders in their product categories for decades, due, in part, to continual innovation. Steady investments in research and development have produced leading-edge products, and sophisticated mass marketing practices have ensured rapid adoption of new technologies in

Coca-Cola's Branding Lesson

One of the classic marketing mistakes occurred in April 1985 when Coca-Cola replaced its flagship cola brand with a new formula. The motivation behind the change was primarily a competitive one. Pepsi-Cola's "Pepsi Challenge" promotion had posed a strong challenge to Coke's supremacy in the cola market. Starting initially in Texas, the promotion involved advertising and in-store sampling showcasing consumer blind taste tests between Coca-Cola and Pepsi-Cola. Invariably, Pepsi won these tests. Fearful that the promotion, if taken nationally, could take a big bite out of Coca-Cola's sales, especially among younger cola drinkers, Coca-Cola felt compelled to act.

Coca-Cola's strategy was to change the formulation of Coke to more closely match the slightly sweeter taste of Pepsi. To arrive at a new formulation, Coca-Cola conducted taste tests with an astounding number of consumers—190,000. The findings from this research clearly indicated that consumers "overwhelmingly" preferred the taste of the new formulation to the old one. Brimming with confidence, Coca-Cola announced the formulation change with much fanfare. Consumer reaction was swift but, unfortunately for Coca-Cola, negative. In Seattle, retired real estate investor Gay Mullins founded the "Old Cola Drinkers of America" and set up a hotline for angry

FIGURE A   Coca-Cola Packaging

consumers. A Beverly Hills wine merchant bought 500 cases of "Vintage Coke" and sold them at a premium. Meanwhile, back at Coca-Cola headquarters, roughly 1,500 calls a day and literally truckloads of mail poured in, virtually all condemning the company's actions. Finally, after several months of slumping sales, Coca-Cola announced that the old formulation would return as "Coca-Cola Classic" and join "new" Coke in the marketplace (see Figure A).

The New Coke debacle taught Coca-Cola a very important, albeit painful and public, lesson about its brand. Coke clearly is not just seen as a beverage or thirst-quenching refreshment by consumers. Rather, it seems to be viewed as more of an American icon, and much of its appeal lies not only in its ingredients but also in what it represents in terms of Americana, nostalgia, and its heritage and relationship with consumers. Coke's brand image certainly has emotional components, and consumers have a great deal of strong feelings for the brand. Although Coca-Cola made a number of other mistakes in introducing New Coke (e.g., both their advertising and packaging probably failed to clearly differentiate the brand and communicate its sweeter quality), their biggest slip was losing sight of what the brand meant to consumers in its totality. The *psychological* response to a brand can be as important as the *physiological* response to the product. At the same time, the American consumer also learned a lesson—just how much the Coke brand really meant to them. As a result of Coke's marketing fiasco, it is doubtful that either side will take the other for granted from now on.

Source: Patricia Winters, "For New Coke, 'What Price Success?' " *Advertising Age,* 20 March 1989, S1–S2.

the consumer market. Other brands create competitive advantages through non-product-related means. For example, Coca-Cola, Calvin Klein, Chanel No. 5, Marlboro, and others have become leaders in their product categories by understanding consumer motivations and desires and creating relevant and appealing images surrounding their products. Often these intangible image associations may be the only way to distinguish different brands in a product category.

Brands, especially strong ones, have a number of different types of associations, and marketers must account for all of them in making marketing decisions. The marketers behind some brands have learned this lesson the hard way. Branding Brief 1-1 describes the problems Coca-Cola encountered in the introduction of "New Coke" when they failed to account for all of the different aspects of the Coca-Cola brand image.

Not only are there many different types of associations to link to the brand, there are also many different means to create them. The entire marketing program can contribute to consumers' understanding of the brand and how they value it. As Interbrand's John Murphy puts it:

> Creating a successful brand entails blending all these various elements together in a unique way—the product or service has to be of high quality and appropriate to consumer needs, the brand name must be appealing and in tune with the consumer's perceptions of the product, the packaging, promotion, pricing and all other elements must similarly meet the tests of appropriateness, appeal, and differentiation.[6]

Category	Brands
Eating and drinking	Absolut, Betty Crocker, Birds Eye, Budweiser, Campbell's, Coca-Cola, Dannon, Gerber, Hershey, Kellogg's, Kraft, Marlboro, Miller Lite, Nabisco, Nutrasweet, Oscar Mayer, Perrier, Pillsbury, Sunkist, Swanson, Wrigley's
Dining and shopping	7–11, American Express, Hallmark, McDonald's, Montgomery Ward, Sears, Wal-Mart
Home	Frigidaire, General Electric, Hoover, Maytag, Owens-Corning Fiberglas, Reynolds Wrap, Rubbermaid, Saran Wrap, Styrofoam, Tide
Health and beauty	Band-Aid, Bayer, Burma Shave, Calvin Klein, Crest, Gillette, Ivory, Kleenex, Pampers, Revlon, Tampax, Tylenol
Apparel and footwear	Arrow, Chanel, DuPont, Keds, L'eggs, Levi's, Maidenform, Nike, Ralph Lauren
Information, sports, and entertainment	Barbie, CNN, Disney, ESPN, Elvis, Good Housekeeping, HBO, *Life,* MGM, NASCAR, network TV (ABC, NBC, CBS), *Playboy,* RCA, *Sesame Street,* Sony, *Time, Wall Street Journal*
Travel and transportation	Chevrolet, Federal Express, Ford, Goodyear, Greyhound, Harley-Davidson, Hertz, Holiday Inn, Jeep, Pan Am, Toyota, United Airlines, VW
Progress and ingenuity	3M, Apple, AT&T, IBM, Kodak, Microsoft, Motorola, Polaroid, Velcro, Xerox

FIGURE 1-2   100 Brands That Changed America (alphabetical citation)

By creating perceived differences among products through branding and developing a loyal consumer franchise, marketers create value that can translate to financial profits for the firm. The reality is that the most valuable assets that many firms have may not be tangible assets, such as plants, equipment, and real estate, but *intangible* assets such as management skills, marketing, financial, and operations expertise, and, most important, the brands themselves. Thus, a brand is a valued intangible asset that needs to be handled carefully. The next section examines some of the reasons why brands are so valuable. Figure 1-2 displays *Brand Marketing*'s list of the 100 brands that most changed America in the twentieth century.

WHY DO BRANDS MATTER?

An obvious question is, Why are brands important? What functions do they perform that make them so valuable to marketers? One can take a couple of perspectives to uncover the value of brands to both consumers and firms themselves. Figure 1-3 provides an overview of the different roles that brands play for these two parties.

Consumers
Identification of source of product
Assignment of responsibility to product maker
Risk reducer
Search cost reducer
Promise, bond, or pact with maker of product
Symbolic device
Signal of quality

Manufacturers
Means of identification to simplify handling or tracing
Means of legally protecting unique features
Signal of quality level to satisfied customers
Means of endowing products with unique associations
Source of competitive advantage
Source of financial returns

FIGURE 1-3   Roles That Brands Play

Consumers

As with the term *product,* this book uses the term *consumer* broadly to encompass all types of customers, including individuals as well as organizations. To consumers, brands provide important functions. Brands identify the source or maker of a product and allow consumers to assign responsibility to a particular manufacturer or distributor. Most important, brands take on special meaning to consumers. Because of past experiences with the product and its marketing program over the years, consumers learn about brands. They find out which brands satisfy their needs and which ones do not. As a result, brands provide a shorthand device or means of simplification for their product decisions.[7]

If consumers recognize a brand and have some knowledge about it, then they do not have to engage in a lot of additional thought or processing of information to make a product decision. Thus, from an economic perspective, brands allow consumers to lower search costs for products both internally (in terms of how much they have to think) and externally (in terms of how much they have to look around). Based on what they already know about the brand—its quality, product characteristics, and so forth—consumers can make assumptions and form reasonable expectations about what they may *not* know about the brand.

The meaning imbued in brands can be quite profound. The relationship between a brand and the consumer can be seen as a type of bond or pact. Consumers offer their trust and loyalty with the implicit understanding that the brand will behave in certain ways and provide them utility through consistent product performance and appropriate pricing, promotion, and distribution programs and actions. To the extent that consumers realize advantages and benefits from purchasing the brand, and as long as they derive satisfaction from product consumption, they are likely to continue to buy it.

These benefits may not be purely functional in nature. Brands can serve as symbolic devices, allowing consumers to project their self-image. Certain brands are associated with being used by certain types of people and thus reflect different values or traits. Consuming such products is a means by which consumers can communicate to others—or even to themselves—the type of person they are or would like to be. Pulitzer Prize–winning author Daniel Boorstein asserts that, for many people, brands serve the function that fraternal, religious, and service organizations used to serve—to help people define who they are and then help people communicate that definition to others. As Harvard's Susan Fournier notes:

> Relationships with mass [market] brands can soothe the "empty selves" left behind by society's abandonment of tradition and community and provide stable anchors in an otherwise changing world. The formation and maintenance of brand-product relationships serve many culturally-supported roles within postmodern society.[8]

Brands can also play a significant role in signaling certain product characteristics to consumers. Researchers have classified products and their associated attributes or benefits into three major categories: search goods, experience goods, and credence goods.[9] With *search goods*, product attributes can be evaluated by visual inspection (e.g., the sturdiness, size, color, style, weight, and ingredient composition of a product). With *experience goods*, product attributes—potentially equally important—cannot be assessed so easily by inspection, and actual product trial and experience is necessary (e.g., as with durability, service quality, safety, and ease of handling or use). With *credence goods*, product attributes may be rarely learned (e.g., insurance coverage). Because of the difficulty in assessing and interpreting product attributes and benefits with experience and credence goods, brands may be particularly important signals of quality and other characteristics to consumers for these type of products.[10]

Brands can reduce the risks in product decisions.[11] Consumers may perceive many different types of risks in buying and consuming a product:

➤ *Functional risk:* The product does not perform up to expectations
➤ *Physical risk:* The product poses a threat to the physical well-being or health of the user or others
➤ *Financial risk:* The product is not worth the price paid
➤ *Social risk:* The product results in embarrassment from others
➤ *Psychological risk:* The product affects the mental well-being of the user
➤ *Time risk:* The failure of the product results in an opportunity cost of finding another satisfactory product

Although there are a number of different means by which consumers handle these risks, certainly one way in which consumers cope is to buy well-known brands, especially those brands with which consumers have had favorable past experiences. Thus, brands can be a very important risk-handling device, especially in business-to-business settings where these risks can sometimes have quite profound implications.

In summary, to consumers, the special meaning that brands take on can change their perceptions and experiences with a product. The identical product may be evaluated differently by an individual or organization depending on the brand identification or attribution it is given. Brands take on unique, personal meanings to consumers that facilitate their day-to-day activities and enrich their lives. As consumers' lives become more complicated, rushed, and time starved, the ability of a brand to simplify decision making and reduce risk is invaluable.

Firms

Brands also provide a number of valuable functions to firms.[12] Fundamentally, they serve an identification purpose to simplify product handling or tracing for the firm. Operationally, brands help to organize inventory and accounting records. A brand also offers the firm legal protection for unique features or aspects of the product. A brand can retain intellectual property rights, giving legal title to the brand owner.[13] The brand name can be protected through registered trademarks, manufacturing processes can be protected through patents, and packaging can be protected through copyrights and designs. These intellectual property rights ensure that the firm can safely invest in the brand and reap the benefits of a valuable asset.

As noted earlier, these investments in the brand can endow a product with unique associations and meanings that differentiate it from other products. Brands can signal a certain level of quality so that satisfied buyers can easily choose the product again.[14] This brand loyalty provides predictability and security of demand for the firm and creates barriers of entry that make it difficult for other firms to enter the market. Although manufacturing processes and product designs may be easily duplicated, lasting impressions in the minds of individuals and organizations from years of marketing activity and product experience may not be so easily reproduced. In this sense, branding can be seen as a powerful means of securing a competitive advantage.

In short, to firms, brands represent enormously valuable pieces of legal property, capable of influencing consumer behavior, being bought and sold, and providing the security of sustained future revenues to their owner.[15] For these reasons, large earning multiples have been paid for brands in mergers or acquisitions, starting with the boom years of the mid-1980s. The merger and acquisition frenzy during this time resulted in Wall Street financiers seeking out undervalued companies from which investment or takeover profits could be made. One of the primary undervalued assets of these firms was their brands, given that they were off-balance-sheet items. Implicit in this Wall Street interest was a belief that strong brands resulted in better earnings and profit performance for firms, which, in turn, created greater value for shareholders.

For example, over the course of a short period of time in 1988, almost $50 billion changed hands in exchange for some well-known brands:[16]

➤ American food, tobacco, and drink manufacturer RJR Nabisco was the center of a vicious tug-of-war between its own management and various outsiders desiring to buy the company. Eventually, the brand was sold to leveraged buy-out specialists Kohlberg, Kravis, and Roberts for $30 billion.

➤ American food and tobacco manufacturer Philip Morris bought Kraft (home to Kraft cheese, Miracle Whip spread, Breyers ice cream, etc.) for $12.9 billion, or more than four times book value for tangible assets. An estimated $11.6 billion was for goodwill.[17] After the acquisition, Philip Morris substantially increased its intangible asset base and commenced systematically amortizing its assets.

➤ Grand Metropolitan, a U.K. food and drinks company, acquired Pillsbury (home to Pillsbury baking products, Green Giant frozen and canned vegetables, Burger King, etc.) for $5.5 billion, a 50 percent premium on the American firm's pre-bid value and several times the value of its tangible assets.

➤ Nestlé, a multinational powerhouse, acquired U.K.'s Rowntree (home to Kit Kat, After Eight, and Polo mints and other confectioneries) for $4.5 billion, more than five times its book value.

As these examples illustrate, the price premium paid for companies was often clearly justified on the basis of assumptions regarding the extra profits that could be extracted and sustained from their brands, as well as the tremendous difficulty and expense of creating similar brands from scratch. Thus, much of the recent interest in brands from senior management has been a result of these bottom-line financial considerations. For a typical fast-moving-consumer-goods (FMCG) company, the vast majority of its corporate value is made up by intangible assets and goodwill—net tangible assets may be as little as 10 percent of the total value (see Figure 1-4). Moreover, as much as 70 percent of their intangible assets can be made up by brands.

Sara Lee Corporation, sellers of Hanes underwear, Ball Park franks, Hanes hosiery, Kiwi shoe polish, and Coach leather products as well as their Sara Lee branded products, even took the dramatic step of outsourcing all their manufacturing operations to others. Becoming an "assetless" company through "de-verticalizing," according to Sara Lee CEO John Bryan, allowed the firm to concentrate on managing their brands.[18] Many other famous brands, such as Baskins-Robbins ice cream, Motorola cell phones, Samuel Adams beer, and Calvin Klein jeans, are no longer produced by the famous names themselves but by lesser-known companies on a contract basis.[19]

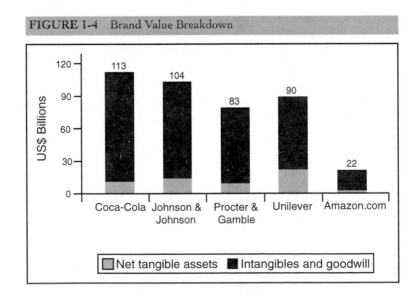

FIGURE 1-4   Brand Value Breakdown

CAN ANYTHING BE BRANDED?

Brands clearly provide important benefits to both consumers and firms. An obvious question, then, is, How are brands created? How do you "brand" a product? Although firms provide the impetus for brand creation through their marketing programs and other activities, ultimately *a brand is something that resides in the minds of consumers*. A brand is a perceptual entity that is rooted in reality, but it is also more than that, reflecting the perceptions and perhaps even the idiosyncrasies of consumers.

To brand a product it is necessary to teach consumers "who" the product is—by giving it a name and using other brand elements to help identify it—as well as what the product does and why consumers should care. In other words, to brand a product or service, it is necessary to give consumers a *label* for the product (i.e., "here's how you can identify the product") and to provide *meaning* for the brand to consumers (i.e., "here's what this particular product can do for you and why it is special and different from other brand name products"). Branding involves creating mental structures and helping consumers organize their knowledge about products and services in a way that clarifies their decision making and, in the process, provides value to the firm. *The key to branding is that consumers perceive differences among brands in a product category*. As noted earlier, brand differences often are related to attributes or benefits of the product itself. In other cases, however, brand differences may be related to more intangible image considerations.

Whenever and wherever consumers are deciding between alternatives, brands can play an important decision-making role. *Accordingly, marketers can benefit from branding whenever consumers are in a choice situation*. Given the myriad of choices consumers make each and every day, it is no surprise how pervasive branding has become. For example, consider how marketers have been able to brand what were once commodities. A *commodity* is a product presumably so basic that it cannot be physically differentiated in the minds of consumers. Over the years, a number of products that at one time were seen as essentially commodities have become highly differentiated as strong brands have emerged in the category.[20] Some notable examples (with brand pioneers in parentheses) are coffee (Maxwell House), bath soap (Ivory), flour (Gold Medal), beer (Budweiser), salt (Morton), oatmeal (Quaker), pickles (Vlasic), bananas (Chiquita), chickens (Perdue), pineapples (Dole), and even water (Perrier).

These former commodity products have become branded in various ways. The key success factor in each case, however, was that consumers became convinced that all the product offerings in the category were not the same and that meaningful differences existed. In some instances, such as with produce, marketers convinced consumers that a product was *not* a commodity and actually could vary appreciably in quality. In these cases, the brand was seen as assuring uniformly high quality in the product category on which consumers could depend. A recent example of this approach is Intel, which has spent vast sums of money on its "Intel Inside" promotion to brand its microprocessors or computer chips as delivering the highest level of performance (e.g., power) and safety (e.g., upgradability) possible (see Figure 1-5).

In other cases, because product differences were virtually nonexistent, brands have been created by image or other non-product-related considerations (e.g., as with

FIGURE 1-5   Intel Inside Logo

Perrier bottled mineral water). One of the best examples of branding a commodity in this fashion was by the California Raisin Advisory Board.

California Raisin Advisory Board

In the mid-1980s, the California Raisin Advisory Board was able to create some badly needed brand personality and image for their product on the basis of creative advertising. Raisins were seen as an undesirable, boring, and "wimpy" food with low top-of-mind awareness, so a new ad campaign was launched featuring the California Raisins—claymation raisin characters singing and dancing in sunglasses and white gloves to songs such as the Motown favorite "I Heard It Through the Grapevine." Intended to make raisins seem hip, different, and cool, the ad campaign ultimately boosted sales by 20 percent. Perhaps its greatest value, however, came in licensing opportunities. The characters' likenesses appeared on a host of products—toys, shirts, and so forth—whose sales were estimated initially to be 10 times greater than sales of the actual California raisins.[21]

The universality of branding can be recognized by looking at some different product applications. As noted previously, products can be defined broadly to include physical goods, services, retail stores, online businesses, people, organizations, places, or ideas. For each of these different types of products, the following sections review some basic considerations and provide illustrative examples. Some of these special cases are considered in more detail in Chapter 15.

Physical Goods

Physical goods are traditionally associated with brands and include many of the best-known and highly regarded consumer products (e.g., Coca-Cola, Kellogg's, Kodak, Marlboro, Sony, Mercedes-Benz, and Nescafé). As more and more different kinds of products are being sold or at least promoted directly to consumers, the adoption of modern marketing practices and branding has spread further.

The Pharmaceutical Industry

Prescription drugs are increasingly being branded and sold to consumers with traditional marketing tactics such as advertising and promotion.[22] In the 1990s, a host of prescription drugs became available over the counter and were backed by sizable marketing budgets (e.g., Pepcid, Tagamet, and Zantac heartburn remedies; Nicorette smoking cessation aid; and Rogain antibaldness drug).[23] In 2000, a number of brands received more than $100 million in ad support, including Merck's Vioxx arthritis treatment, Schering-Plough's Claritan antihistamine drug, and Pfizer's Viagra erectile dysfunction treatment.

More and more companies selling industrial or durable products to other companies are recognizing the benefits of developing strong brands. Brands have begun to emerge with certain types of physical goods that heretofore did not support brands. The remainder of this section considers the role of branding with industrial products as well as technologically intensive or "high-tech" products.

Business-to-Business Products

An increasing number of firms are recognizing the value of having a strong corporate brand in their business dealings with other firms. Business-to-business branding involves creating a positive image and reputation for the company as a whole. Creating such goodwill with business customers is thought to lead to greater selling opportunities and more profitable relationships. A strong brand can provide valuable reassurance to business customers who may be putting their company's fate—and perhaps their own careers—on the line. A strong business-to-business brand can thus provide a strong competitive advantage.

Business-to-business brands are often corporate brands, so understanding branding from that perspective becomes critical. The complexity of business-to-business branding lies in the many people involved, both on the company side and in terms of the many different market segments the company could be targeting. Such complexity requires adjustments in marketing programs and marketing communications. One challenge for many business-to-business brands is how to de-commoditize themselves to create product and service differences.

Eaton

Eaton Corporation is a global manufacturer of highly engineered products that serve industrial, vehicle, construction, commercial, aerospace and semiconductor markets (e.g., electrical power distribution and control equipment, truck drivetrain systems, engine components, and hydraulic products). Eaton's brand strategy is to emphasize their corporate name to a large extent, which takes on brand values such as innovation, performance, and integrity. Eaton does sell some product brands and has several subsidiaries, such as Cutler-Hammer.

High-Tech Products

Another example of the increasing realization of the important role that brands play in the marketing equation is with technologically intensive or high-tech products (e.g., computer-related products). Many technology companies have struggled with branding. Managed by technologists, they often lack any kind of brand strategy and, in the worst case, see branding as simply equal to naming their products. In many of these product markets, however, financial success is no longer driven by product innovation alone or by offering the latest and greatest product specifications and features. Marketing skills are playing an increasingly important role in the adoption and success of high-tech products.

> ### Intuit
>
> In discussing the origins of his company, Scott Cook, founder of Intuit, makers of the highly successful Quicken personal-finance software package, comments, "We started with the belief that it is a consumer market, not a technology market. We'd run it like Procter & Gamble."[24] Applying classic packaged-goods marketing techniques, Intuit first conducted extensive research with consumers and then designed a product to satisfy the unmet needs and wants of the market. Because their research revealed that most consumers did not like doing financial management and found it a necessary evil, Intuit designed the Quicken software package to offer two key benefits—ease of use and speed—that were not currently offered by other products in the market.

The rapid nature of the technology product life cycle causes unique branding challenges. Trust is critical, and customers often buy into companies as much as products. CEOs of technology companies often become a dominant component of the brand (e.g., Apple's Steve Jobs, Microsoft's Bill Gates, Cisco's John Chambers, Sun's Scott McNeely, and Oracle's Larry Ellison). Marketing budgets may be small, although adoption of packaged-goods marketing techniques by companies selling high-tech products has resulted in increased expenditures on mass market advertising. Branding Brief 1-2 describes some of the branding history at IBM.

Services

Although there have been strong service brands for years (e.g., American Express, British Airways, Hilton Hotels, Merrill Lynch, and, more recently, Federal Express), the pervasiveness and level of sophistication in branding services has accelerated in the past decade. Recent years have even seen corporate brand campaigns from professional service firms such as PricewaterhouseCoopers, KPMG, Ernst & Young, and Goldman Sachs. Citibank launched a $100 million ad campaign in 2000 with the tag line "Live richly." As Interband's John Murphy notes, "In the last 30 years, some of the greatest branding successes have come in the area of services." Branding Brief 1-3 describes the ascent of the Southwest Airlines brand.

One of the challenges in marketing services is that relative to products, they are more intangible and more likely to vary in quality depending on the particular person or people involved in providing the service. Consequently, branding can be particularly important to service firms to address potential intangibility and variability problems. Brand symbols may also be especially important because they help to make the abstract nature of services more concrete. Brands can help to identify and provide

IBM Learns How to Brand

IBM's experiences illustrate how important marketing and branding have become in the personal computer industry. IBM introduced its first PC in 1981 and built its market share to 41 percent by 1985. Three years later, however, its market share had dropped to 28 percent. Observers blamed much of IBM's lost sales on an unfocused marketing strategy that made the brand vulnerable to appeals from low-priced clone makers. Critics pointed to the complexity of IBM's branding strategy—there were too many brands, and too many of the product names were technical and consumer unfriendly. To improve its branding efforts, IBM established a centralized naming unit in 1988. The company also undertook extensive customer research, seeking input on issues from product design and features to appropriate brand names.

In 1993, IBM named Lou Gerstner as its CEO. The former RJR Nabisco CEO and former president of American Express set out to transform IBM from a lumbering hardware company to a nimble consumer-focused services firm. Another aspect of IBM's consumer focus was a renewed attention to advertising. The company consolidated its global advertising by firing 70 global agency partners and assigning Ogilvy & Mather the $500 million account in 1994.

Ogilvy & Mather (O&M) was chosen, in part, for its global presence and for its track record in building brands, as exemplified by its "brand stewardship" concept (see Chapter 8). O&M's first efforts were new campaigns in the fall of 1994 to launch the Aptiva models (IBM's replacements for its four-year-old PS/1 home and small-office PCs) featuring MTV-like graphics and the TV actor Paul Reiser. The ads ended with the tag line "There is a difference—IBM." Later ads used the tag line "Solutions for a Small Planet" and showed people in different parts of the world discussing the benefits they had derived from their IBM computers in their native tongues, with English subtitles added.

In 1997, IBM introduced the now-famous e-business concept with a television campaign designed by O&M. The distinctive campaign used a letterboxed format with a blue border, facilitating the branding of the ads. The company coined the term *e-business* and developed the familiar logo, which looks like a red "at" sign with the letter *e* instead of *a* in the center. It followed the original television campaign with a series of print ads documenting how IBM helped brick-and-mortar companies create e-businesses. The company also developed a Web site (ibm.com/e-business) that offers in-depth information about the e-business concept, including case studies and demonstrations. Between 1997 and 2000, IBM spent nearly $2 billion on marketing its e-business message.

IBM's hefty investment in marketing since 1994 enabled the company to make over its brand image. Peter Sealey, former marketing chief at Coca-Cola, praised IBM's brand strategy, saying, "Look at what IBM stood for six years ago. It was stuffy, white shirts, big iron. Now the company is accessible. It's a wonderful example of an institution recasting itself." With CEO Lou Gerstner's mandate for change and the help of consistently creative advertising, IBM successfully shed its old image as a mainframe manufacturer and transformed itself into a full-service computer solutions firm.

Sources: Greg Farrell, "Building a New Big Blue," *USA Today*, 22 November 1999; Tobi Elkin, "Branding Big Blue," *Advertising Age*, 28 February 2000.

Flying High with the Southwest Airlines Brand

Southwest Airlines, originally called Air Southwest, was founded by Texans Rollin King and Herb Kelleher in 1967. Southwest started as a commuter carrier with flights between Dallas, Houston, and San Antonio, but today it operates in 55 cities across the nation. Southwest is famous for its cheap fares and no-frills service. Seats on its plane are all the same class, and the in-flight service offers neither movies nor meals.

Southwest knew from an early stage that it could not differentiate on price alone, because competitors could easily muscle into the market with their own cheaper versions. To promote customer loyalty, the airline sought to create a unique flying experience for its customers. Early flights featured Jet Bunnies—flight attendants dressed in hot pants and go-go boots—who served beverages known as Love Potions and snacks called Love Bites. Southwest encouraged its pilots and cabin crew members to entertain the passengers with jokes and snappy patter during in-flight announcements. One of the company's early recruitment bulletins specified that applicants should have a sense of humor. Even CEO Herb Kelleher got into the act. On several occasions, Kelleher donned an Elvis Presley costume to meet passengers at the gate, and once on an Easter flight he served drinks and snacks while dressed in a bunny suit. Another passenger-pleasing feature of Southwest flights is the first-come, first-served open seating,

FIGURE A   Southwest Airlines Ad

whereby passengers are given numbered cards for boarding that reflect the order in which they arrived at the gate.

Southwest's advertising has always been informational, yet inflected with humor at the same time (see Figure A, for example). For several years, the airline has used as its tag line a clever play on the standard message from a captain telling passengers they are free to move about the plane's cabin. Southwest's version, which emphasizes its national route coverage, declares, "You are now free to move about the country." Recent ads highlighted Southwest's low fares with humorous television spots in which a character commits some social blunder, after which a voiceover asks, "Wanna Get Away?"

Today, Southwest is the nation's seventh-largest airline and holds the distinction of being the only low-fare airline to achieve long-term success. By offering a low-cost, convenient, and customer-friendly alternative to major carriers, Southwest attracted passengers in droves and, after its first profitable year in 1969, achieved profitability in each of the 28 years that followed.

Sources: Jane Woolridge, "Baby-Boom Airline Is Unknown, Cheap," *San Diego Union-Tribune*, 30 December 1984; Katrina Brooker, "The Chairman of the Board Looks Back," *Fortune*, 28 May 2001.

meaning to the different services provided by a firm. For example, branding has become especially important in financial services to help organize and label the myriad of new offerings in a manner that consumers can understand.

Branding a service can also be an effective way to signal to consumers that the firm has designed a particular service offering that is special and deserving of its own name. For example, British Airways not only branded their premium business class service as "Club Class" but also branded their regular coach service as "World Traveler," a clever way to communicate to their regular passengers that they are also special in some way and that their patronage is not taken for granted. Branding has clearly become a competitive weapon for services.

The Telecommunications Industry

Deregulation in the global telecommunications industry created increased competition among brands in the 1990s. AT&T, MCI, and Sprint waged a fierce battle for U.S. market share using traditional marketing tactics, including the introduction of various brands and sub-brands. For example, all three firms created discount savings plans to reward loyal callers, gave them descriptive names, and heavily advertised and promoted them (e.g., MCI's Friends and Family, AT&T's True USA Savings, and Sprint's Sense). Although the competitive ferocity in this market may have tarnished their brand images to some extent, AT&T, MCI, and Sprint have also been able to build brand equity at both the corporate and individual service offering levels through their branding strategies.

Retailers and Distributors

To the retailers or other channel members distributing products, brands provide a number of important functions. Brands can generate consumer interest, patronage, and loyalty in a store, and consumers learn to expect certain brands and products from a store. To the extent that "you are what you sell," brands help to create an image and establish a positioning for the store. Retailers can also create their own brand image by attaching unique associations to the quality of their service, their product assortment and merchandising, and their pricing and credit policy. Finally, the appeal and attraction of brands can permit higher price margins, increased sales volumes, and greater profits. These brand name products may come from manufacturers or other external sources or from the store itself.

Retailers can introduce their own brands by using their store name, creating new names, or some combination of the two. Thus, many distributors, especially in Europe, have actually introduced their own brands, which they sell in addition to—or sometimes even instead of—manufacturers' brands. These products, referred to as *store brands* or *private label* brands, offer another way for retailers to increase customer loyalty and generate higher margins and profits. In Britain, five or six grocery chains account for roughly half of the country's food and packaged-goods sales, led by Sainsbury and Tesco. Another top British retailer, Marks & Spencer, sells only its own-brand goods (under the label St. Michel). Several U.S. companies also emphasize their own brands.

Sears

Sears, Roebuck and Company became the United States' largest retailer by making household names of hard goods such as Craftsman tools, Kenmore appliances, Weatherbeater house paint, and DieHard auto batteries. Facing a sales slump in the 1980s, Sears enacted a number of different strategies, such as adopting an everyday low pricing strategy, closing their catalog business, organizing the store into seven "power formats" with their own distinct selling place and style, and aggressively selling more national brand name products such as Panasonic and Whirlpool. Sears also revamped its women's apparel offerings to move toward trendier fashions, better-trained and higher-quality service from salespeople, and slicker displays and presentations of clothes. Although "The Softer Side of Sears," as it was advertised, met with some initial success, earnings faded by the turn of the century. Late in 2001, Sears announced plans to abandon its traditional department store format and change the way it sold merchandise to try to create a unique position as neither a discounter nor a department store.[25]

Branding Brief 1-4 describes some of the branding developments at Wal-Mart. Chapter 5 considers store brands and private labels in greater detail.

Online Products and Services

The number of people with access to the Internet in the United States surpassed 50 percent of the population in 2001 as over 100 million Americans went online to send or receive e-mail or to access the Internet or World Wide Web. Other countries experienced similarly rapid adoption. The end of the twentieth century revealed an unprecedented head-long rush by new and existing businesses to create online Internet brands. Quickly, these businesses learned the complexities and challenges of building an online brand. Online brands came in many different forms, with business models based on selling information, products, experiences, and so on.

Many online brand marketers during this heady time made serious—and sometimes fatal—mistakes. In general, these marketers seemed to oversimplify the branding process, for example, equating flashy or unusual advertising with building a brand.

Branding the Wal-Mart Way

Wal-Mart, which first opened in Rogers, Arkansas, in 1962, currently has more than 1.2 million employees and operates 3,118 retail locations in America, with another 1,071 overseas. Wal-Mart's founder, Sam Walton, sought to build conveniently located retail outlets that offered wide selection, low prices, and quality customer service. Today, these outlets include the original Wal-Mart discount stores, Sam's Club warehouse stores, Wal-Mart Supercenters combination discount and grocery stores, and Neighborhood Markets mid-sized grocery stores. Wal-Mart is currently the largest retailer in the United States.

Wal-Mart's low prices have always been a key to pleasing consumers. The chain innovated the everyday-low-pricing strategy popular in many retail stores. The slogan "We Sell for Less. Always" illustrates Wal-Mart's dedication to underselling the competition. Its reputation for friendly service is another way the company creates customer satisfaction. At the entrances to its stores, Wal-Mart stations "people greeters" who welcome and assist customers. The company employs helpful and knowledgeable sales associates who are positioned throughout the store to answer questions and help customers find items. These gestures foster trust: According to a company survey that asked "What does Wal-Mart mean to you?" more customers responded "trust" than "low prices."

A less well-known contributor to the company's success is its implementation of sophisticated logistics. Sam Walton was something of a visionary when it came to logistics. He had the foresight to realize, as early as the 1960s, that the company growth he was striving for required the installation of advanced information systems to manage the volumes of merchandise. By 1998, Wal-Mart's computer database was second only to the Pentagon's in terms of capacity. One business writer recently proclaimed Wal-Mart to be "the king of store logistics."

Wal-Mart did not enjoy its usual level of success when it moved into e-commerce with the launch of Walmart.com in 1996. The original site offered a limited selection of products, but Wal-Mart waited to debut a fully expanded site until 1999. The bigger site was initially criticized for its sluggishness and poor customer service. In 2000, the company partnered with a Silicon Valley venture capital firm and made Walmart.com a separate company and retooled the Web site. Among the features added were in-store returns for items purchased on the Web site and more reliable delivery. In June 2001, Walmart.com debuted its Internet service provider, which offers unlimited Web access for less than $10 a month.

Wal-Mart today bears little resemblance to the Arkansas store that started it all. The company is an indelible part of the U.S. retail landscape and has expanded into South America and Europe. Wal-Mart's annual sales in 2000 reached a colossal $191 billion, earning the company the number two spot in the Fortune 500 ranking.

Sources: Wendy Zellner, "Someday, Lee, This May All Be Yours," *Business Week*, 15 November 1999; "Will WalMart.com Get It Right This Time?" *Business Week*, 6 November 2000; John Huey, "Discounting Dynamo: Sam Walton," *Time,* 7 December 1998; James Moore, "The Death of Competition," *Fortune*, 15 April 1999; Wendy Zellner, "Wal-Mart Spoken Here," *Business Week*, 23 June 1997; "Walmart.com to Start Internet Service," Associated Press, 2 June 2001; Mark Veverka, "Will Wal-Mart.com Steamroll the E-tailers?" *Barron's,* 23 October 2000.

Although such marketing efforts sometimes caught consumers' attention, more often than not they failed to create awareness of what products or services the brand represented, why those products or services were unique or different, and, most important, why consumers should buy the brand.

Online marketers quickly realized a number of realities of brand building. First, as with any brand, it is critical to create some unique aspects of the brand on some dimension important to consumers, such as convenience, price, variety, and so forth. At the same time, the brand needs to perform satisfactorily in other areas, such as customer service, credibility, and personality. In terms of the latter consideration, customers increasingly began to demand higher levels of service both during and after their Web site visits. As a consequence, to be competitive, many firms have had to improve their online service by making customer service agents available in real time, shipping products promptly and providing tracking updates, and adopting liberal return policies.[26] Such improvements have been critical to overcome the low customer service opinions that some consumers hold toward online businesses. Successful online brands were those that were well positioned and found unique ways to satisfy consumers' unmet needs.

Google

Founded in 1998 by two Stanford University Ph.D. students, search engine Google's name is a play on the word *googol*—the number represented by a 1 followed by 100 zeros—a reference to the huge amount of data online. With 25 million users worldwide generating 1,800 queries a second, the company has turned a profit by focusing on searches alone and not adding other services, as was the case with many other portals. By focusing on plain text, avoiding ads, and using sophisticated search algorithms, Google is seen as providing fast and reliable service. Google makes money from paid listings relevant to a searcher's query and from licensing their technology to firms such as Yahoo and the *Washington Post*.[27]

Online brands also learned the importance of off-line activities to draw customers to their Web site, and many of the most successful business ventures came from off-line brands leveraging their strong reputations and marketing muscle online. Homepage Web addresses, or URLs, began to appear on all related collateral and marketing material. Partnerships became critical as online brands developed networks of online partners and links. Online marketers began to target specific customer groups—often geographically widely dispersed—for which the brand could offer unique value propositions. Web site designs have begun to maximize the benefits of interactivity, customization, and timeliness and the advantages of being able to inform, persuade, and sell all at the same time. Branding Brief 1-5 describes how Amazon.com has built a strong online brand. Chapter 6 examines Web site and interactive advertising issues.

People and Organizations

Brands extend beyond products and services. People and organizations also can be viewed as brands. The naming aspect of the brand is generally straightforward in this case, and people and organizations also often have well-defined images understood and liked or disliked by others. This fact becomes particularly true when considering public figures such as politicians, entertainers, and professional athletes. All of these different public figures compete in some sense for public approval and acceptance and

Building the Amazon.com Brand

Jeffrey Bezos left his job on Wall Street as a hedge fund manager in 1994 to return to his home in suburban Seattle and found online retailer Amazon.com, despite the fact that he had no previous retail experience. Bezos did, however, have a vision of making Amazon.com "the earth's biggest bookstore." Within a year of opening, Amazon.com offered a selection of more than one million book titles, which made it the world's largest book broker.

In addition to offering unparalleled selection, Bezos wanted Amazon.com to provide a unique shopping experience and the highest level of customer service. He aimed for Amazon.com to be "the world's most customer-centric company." To this end, the site was designed so that when shoppers viewed a book title, a list of related titles that might interest them would instantly appear on the same Web page. For customers who submitted information on their favorite authors and subjects, Amazon.com sent periodic recommendations and reviews via e-mail. Another personal touch included the development of personalized front pages that opened whenever registered customers visited the site. Of these customized features, Bezos said, "We want Amazon.com to be the right store for you as an individual. If we have 4.5 million customers, we should have 4.5 million stores." To further promote goodwill among its customers, Amazon.com automatically upgraded many of its orders to priority shipping at no extra cost. These consumer-focused efforts yielded the desired results: In 1998, over 60 percent of orders on the site were from repeat customers.

Much of Amazon.com's early growth was credited to word-of-mouth sources such as testimonials from satisfied customers and media stories. Before long, Amazon.com had top-of-mind awareness among consumers looking to buy products online. As one industry analyst said in 1998, "When you think of Web shopping, you think of Amazon first." The company's ad spending was small compared with other dot-coms: During the fourth quarter of 1998, Amazon.com spent $3.7 million, most of which went to radio commercials. The company began advertising more extensively the following year, when it spent $50 million on a series of holiday-themed advertisements.

Once the bookselling strategy had proved successful, Amazon.com expanded into other product categories, such as CDs, videos, and gifts. Between 1998 and 2001, the site added numerous other product categories, including baby products, electronics, kitchen and housewares, tools and hardware, toys, and even barbecues. During that time, the company also expanded its global reach by establishing sister sites in the United Kingdom, Germany, France, Japan, Spain, and Austria. Bezos declared his company's intention of providing "the earth's biggest selection." With more than 29 million customers and almost $3 billion in annual sales in 2000, the Amazon.com brand is stronger than ever.

Sources: http://www.amazon.com; Alice Z. Cuneo, "Amazon Unleashes $50 Million for the Holidays," *Advertising Age*, 15 November 1999; Rachel Beck, "Amazon.com Moves Beyond Books and Music with Gift Shop, Video Launch," AP Newswire, 17 November 1998; Robert D. Hof, "Amazon.com: The Wild World of E-commerce," *Business Week*, 14 December 1998.

benefit from conveying a strong and desirable image. For example, well aware of her image, supermodel Cindy Crawford once commented that if she were to wear her hair up in a "high twist" on her TV show, *House of Style*, viewers would invariably write in and complain that they wanted her hair to look "normal" and "wanted Cindy to look like Cindy" (see Figure 1-6).[28]

Paul Newman

Legendary actor Paul Newman has translated his likable, down-to-earth image to a multi-million dollar business. Newman's Own was launched after many of his friends and neighbors wanted more of his own special-recipe salad dressing that he gave out as gifts. Since then, the brand has extended into pasta sauce, salsa, steak sauce, lemonade, and popcorn. Newman donates all profits, after taxes, for educational and charity purposes, totaling $100 million since 1982. He founded the Hole in the Wall Gang Camp to allow children with cancer or serious blood diseases a normal summer camp experience free of charge. With a corporate slogan of "Shameless Exploitation in Pursuit of the Common Good," it's not surprising that Newman would state on his Web site, "It started out as a joke and got out of control."

Branding Brief 1-6 describes how Martha Stewart made herself into a household brand name.

This is not to say that you only have to be well known or famous to be thought of as a brand. Anyone trying to build a career can be thought of as trying to create his

FIGURE 1-6   Cindy Crawford Brand

Martha Stewart Is a Brand

Martha Stewart started on her way to being the home advice expert she is today when she left her job as a stockbroker in 1972 to become a caterer. In 1979, she catered a party for a publishing house president who offered a book contract for her hostessing guide, *Entertaining*. The book, which is in its thirtieth printing and has sold more than 500,000 copies, launched the Martha Stewart franchise. Since then, Stewart has written 14 more books and published a series of more than 17 volumes called *The Best of Martha Stewart Living*. In 1995, Stewart began writing askMartha, a syndicated column that currently appears in more than 235 newspapers in the United States and Canada. The syndicated radio version of askMartha, which debuted in 1997, is now distributed to over 280 radio stations nationwide.

In addition to the flagship monthly magazine *Martha Stewart Living*, Stewart develops and stars in television programming such as the weekly syndicated show *Martha Stewart Living*, the Food Network program *From Martha's Kitchen*, and primetime holiday specials and also makes weekly appearances on *CBS This Morning*. Stewart's company, Martha Stewart Living Omnimedia, Inc., now controls a host of media and merchandise properties (see Figure A).

FIGURE A   The Martha Stewart Brand

Magazines
Martha Stewart Living
Martha Stewart Weddings
Martha Stewart Entertainment
Martha Stewart Clotheskeeping
Martha Stewart Baby
Martha Stewart Holiday

Books
Martha Stewart Entertaining
Martha Stewart Cooking
Martha Stewart Weddings
Martha Stewart Christmas

Television
Martha Stewart Living
From Martha's Kitchen

Newspapers/Radio
askMartha

Kmart/Zellers
Martha Stewart Everyday

Online
MarthaStewart.com
MarthasFlowers.com

Catalog
Martha by Mail

Sears/Canadian Tire
Paints

Product Mix at a Percentage of Revenue
Publishing: 62.6 %
Internet: 17.4%
Television: 11.4%
Merchandising: 8.6%

Source: Melanie Wells, "Overcooked: Low TV Ratings Are Eating into Martha Stewart's Multimedia Strategy," *Forbes,* 19 March 2001.

Martha Stewart branded apparel is a small but highly visible part of the company's product mix. In 1997, the company signed a licensing agreement with Kmart that brought Martha Stewart Everyday products to the struggling retailer. In its third year, the Martha Stewart Everyday line, which consists of bedding, bath, home and garden products, bakeware, housewares, and baby gifts, contributed $1 billion in sales. Annual sales at Kmart rose to $36 billion from $32 billion in those three years. A review of register data showed that shoppers purchasing Martha Stewart merchandise spent twice as much as the average $25 to $30 per visit.

In 1997, the company launched a Web site called marthastewart.com. The site makes available on the Web more than 1,500 products from the proprietary *Martha by Mail* catalog, and a partnership with Kmart's Bluelight.com enables shoppers to purchase Martha Stewart Everyday products online. Over the course of 2000, the number of average monthly visitors to the site increased nearly 50 percent, to 1.3 million, with revenues of the company's e-commerce segment growing 38 percent, to $50 million.

Part of Stewart's success is her ability to balance business savvy with credible homemaking advice. Stewart took her company public in 1999. True to form, Stewart served homemade breakfast fare consisting of scones, muffins, and orange juice in a tent outside the New York Stock Exchange to mark the occasion. Revenues for Martha Stewart Omnimedia grew 23 percent, to $286 million, in 2000. Since Stewart is the embodiment of her brand, it is essential for her to maintain a public presence if the company is to enjoy continued growth. Indeed, Stewart's profile remained high during 2001: She appeared on television as often as 21 times each week in some markets.

Sources: http://www.marthastewart.com; Terzah Ewing, "Queen for a Day: Martha Earns IPO Crown," *Wall Street Journal*, 20 October 1999; Melanie Wells, "Overcooked: Low TV Ratings Are Eating into Martha Stewart's Multimedia Strategy," *Forbes*, 19 March 2001; Calmetta Y. Coleman, "Grand Designs: Ms. Stewart's Advice for How to Improve Kmart," *Wall Street Journal*, 1 May 2000; Diane Brady, "Martha Inc.: Inside the Growing Empire of America's Lifestyle Queen," *Business Week*, 17 January 2000.

or her own brand. Certainly, one key for a successful career is that certain people (e.g., coworkers, superiors, or even important people outside the company) know who you are and what kind of person you are in terms of your skills, talents, attitude, and so forth. By building up a name and reputation in a business context, a person is essentially creating his or her own brand. The right awareness and image can be invaluable to the manner in which people treat you and interpret your words, actions, and deeds.[29]

Similarly, organizations often take on meanings through their programs, activities, and products. Nonprofit organizations such as the Sierra Club, the American Red Cross, Amnesty International, and UNICEF have increasingly emphasized marketing.

National Geographic

Founded in 1888 by 33 highly regarded scientists, National Geographic Society is a nonprofit scientific and educational membership organization with a mission related to "the increase and diffusion of geographic knowledge."[30] The distinctive yellow borders of the brand is one of the world's most recognizable brand symbols. The Society's products

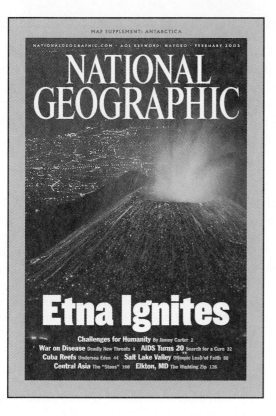

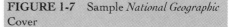

FIGURE 1-7   Sample *National Geographic* Cover

include *National Geographic* magazines, books, maps, television shows, and gift items (see Figure 1-7). The National Geographic Channel was launched in January 2001 to showcase the Society's stable of explorers, scientists, and photographers, and its Web site has won many awards. National Geographic Enterprises includes licensing, a catalog business, travel expeditions, e-commerce, and retail. These units oversee the merchandise related to the National Geographic brand worldwide. All National Geographic's net proceeds from licensing support vital exploration, conservation, research, and education programs. Like the manufacturer of any consumer product, National Geographic conducts surveys that examine perceptions of its image and reactions to possible new products. Moreover, it has developed a marketing database that records transactions, permits market segmentation and targeting analysis, and calculates the lifetime values of its customers.

Sports, Arts, and Entertainment

A special case of marketing people and organizations as brands is in the sports, arts, and entertainment industry. Sports marketing has become highly sophisticated in recent years, employing traditional packaged-goods techniques. No longer content to allow won-loss records to dictate attendance levels and financial fortunes, many sports teams are being marketed through a creative combination of advertising, promotions, sponsorship, direct mail, and other forms of communication. By building awareness,

BRANDING BRIEF 1-7

Building a Brand Winner with Manchester United

Manchester United, the wealthiest soccer club in the English league (the club is valued at $750 million) and one of the most popular sports organizations in the world, has a tradition of winning on the field and in the business world. The club was founded in 1878 and reached the pinnacle of sport with two consecutive English League titles in the 1950s. A tragic plane crash in 1958 that killed seven players brought the club international attention. In 1968, a rebuilt team won another European title. It was not until the 1990s, however, that Manchester United grew into its current role as one of the most popular and lucrative sports franchises in the world. In 1999, a year in which the team won a "treble"—three major English and European soccer titles—its stock market value surpassed $2 billion.

Television is credited with much of Manchester United's financial success. With the advent of satellite television, fans all over the world could enjoy live coverage of all the best matches. Soccer was already a global game played on every inhabited continent, but the game's visibility has never been higher as a result of this increased media coverage. One analyst described Manchester United's recent financial fortunes as follows: "Basically, they got really lucky. The success on the field has coincided with the success of soccer as pure media content." As one of the most successful club teams in the 1990s, Manchester United received a large share of this burgeoning media coverage.

The club's visibility, combined with its accomplishments, won it legions of foreign fans. In addition to roughly 7.3 million fans in Britain, Manchester United estimates it has 39 million fans worldwide. A recent survey showed that 79 percent of China's population had some awareness of the team. Though soccer is not nearly as popular in the United States as in other countries, American companies are showing an interest in Manchester United. In 2001, the club signed a $500 million, 13-year licensing deal with Nike. That same year, Manchester United forged a joint marketing agreement with the New York Yankees that involved sharing marketing information, selling licensed products from both teams, and developing sponsorships.

Sources: Bill Glauber, "Meet Manchester United Marketing," *Baltimore Sun*, 19 March 2001; Andy Dworkin, "Nike Scores Soccer Sponsorship," *Portland Oregonian*, 7 November 2000.

image, and loyalty, these sports franchises are able to meet ticket sales targets regardless of what their team's actual performance might turn out to be. Brand symbols and logos in particular have become important financial contributors to professional sports through licensing agreements. Branding Brief 1-7 describes how Manchester United built a powerhouse soccer team—and brand.

Branding plays an especially valuable function in the arts and entertainment industries (e.g., with movies, television, music, and books). These offerings are good examples of experience goods: Prospective buyers cannot judge quality by inspection and must use cues such as the particular people involved, the concept or rationale behind the project, word of mouth, and critical reviews.

Movie Sequels

A movie can be seen as a product in which the "ingredients" are the plots, actors, and director.[31] Certain movie titles, such as *Lethal Weapon*, *Batman*, *Scream*, and *Star Trek*, have established themselves as strong brands by combining all these ingredients into a formula that appeals to consumers and allows the studios to release sequels (essentially brand extensions) that rely on the initial popularity of the title. For years, some of the most valuable movie franchises have involved recurring characters or ongoing stories, and many of the successful movies in recent years have been sequels. Their success comes from the fact that moviegoers know from the title and the people involved (actors, producers, directors, etc.) that they can expect certain things—a classic application of branding. The force was certainly with *Star Wars*, which, before the new trilogy was launched in 1999, had amassed a staggering $7.2 billion in box office, video, and licensing revenue from the original trilogy (see Figure 1-8).[32]

The existence of a strong brand name in the entertainment industry is valuable because of the strong feelings that the names engender as a result of pleasurable past experiences. A new album release from Walter Becker and Donald Fagen would probably not have caused a ripple in the marketplace, but when *Two Against Nature* was hailed as coming from Steely Dan (their original band), the album won four Grammy awards and sold millions of copies. On the other hand, although Robert Plant and Jimmy Page's 1995 "Unledded" tour sold $33 million worth of tickets in North America and spawned album sales of about 1 million copies, observers believe that these were a fraction of what they could have sold if they had reunited as Led Zeppelin (their original band).

FIGURE 1-8   Branding *Star Wars*

Geographic Locations

Geographic locations, like products and people, also can be branded. In this case, the brand name is relatively fixed by the actual name of the location. The power of branding is in making people aware of the location and then linking desirable associations. Increased mobility of both people and businesses and growth in the tourism industry have contributed to the rise of place marketing. Cities, states, regions, and countries are now actively promoted through advertising, direct mail, and other communication tools. The goals of these types of campaigns are to create awareness and a favorable image of a location that will entice temporary visits or permanent moves from individuals and businesses alike.

Australia

Geographically isolated, but with many appealing and unusual features, the Australia Tourist Commission (ATC) has systematically marketed the country in recent years. Primarily targeting a younger age group, from 18 to 35 or perhaps even 44, the ATC believes that Australia's core brand values of "youthful, energetic, optimistic, stylish, genuine, open, and fun" and brand personality of "youthful, stylish, vibrant, and diverse" match the needs and wants of this target market well. A $100 million multimedia campaign launched in 1997 reflecting these core brand values was adapted slightly to suit differences in attitudes and behaviors in different regions and has been successful in attracting tourists and generating export earnings (see Figure 1-9).[33]

Branding Brief 1-8 describes some of the difficulties Great Britain has had with its image and the resulting implications.

FIGURE 1-9   Marketing Australia

Region/Country	Asia	United States	Japan	Europe
Australia's Attributes	Big nature, outdoors, city life	Fun, diversity, active, adventure, live it	Surprise, undiscovered, culture, lifestyle	Activity, relaxation, intriguing, enriching, diverse, powerful memories
Campaign	"Let the magic begin"	"Holiday"	"Country of surprises"	"The sooner you go the longer the memories . . ."
Message	Excitement, shopping, nightlife	Take a break from work and discover people and islands	Fast-paced, sophisticated, cosmopolitan, modern	Emotional, appealing, unique, travel now

Source: Brand Australia, video produced by the Australian Tourism Commission, 1997.

BRANDING BRIEF 1-8

Keep a Stiff Upper Lip? Britain's Imperially Flawed Image

If Great Britain were a brand, how would it sell? A report by advertising agency BMP DDB Needham in London addressed that question in the early 1990s with a study that ended as a harsh indictment of Britain's image abroad. The author of the agency's report, Anneke Elwes, compared Britain's image to that of a gentlemen's club—"aging, elitist, and a bastion of conservative and traditional values. . . . Its values are stuffy and male. . . . It is no longer aspirational or even relevant to a new generation." Ms. Elwes acknowledged that the theme of British-style tradition had been exploited by many advertisers, but that by exclusively marketing its past, Britain was failing to associate itself with progress.

In compiling the report, the agency carried out extensive group discussions with British men and women, teenagers, and foreign nationals living in Britain, as well as conducting surveys through its international offices in Western and Eastern Europe, the United States, India, Asia, Australia, and New Zealand. Although the impressions varied by region, collectively they suggested that Britain has an image problem. Some of these specific regional impressions were as follows:

- *Australasia:* Among Asian respondents, Britain was characterized by masculine reserve and arrogance and was seen as a "has-been, irrelevant" nation. Consumers in Australia and New Zealand viewed the country as unwilling to move with the times and associated Britain more with urban images of darkness, dirt, and overcrowding than with quaint pictures of country life.

- *Europe:* Western Europeans painted a kinder picture, based on positive images of London and the countryside. This positive response was tempered with opinions that the British were bad at cooking, dressing, industry, and "being European." Eastern Europeans respected Britain for being a strongly independent and self-confident island nation. For them, Britain also conjured up images of Rolls-Royce cars, the BBC, the British press, and universities.

- *America:* The report found that Americans had the most limited views of Britain. Croquet, tea time, Robin Hood, and James Bond were some of the more popular associations. Most knowledge about Britain in America came from films such as *Howard's End,* and the country was viewed as dull, conventional, and stuffy.

A report commissioned by the British Council in 1999 revealed similarly mixed attitudes toward Britain among young professionals from 13 diverse countries. The director of the council summarized the aim of the program as follows:

> Britain is respected but not seen as exciting. One of our aims is to show that Britain is not a country stuck in a time warp, that we're not just Shakespeare and Dickens. We want people to know that our fashion designers have taken Paris by storm and that our scientists cloned Dolly the sheep and invented Viagra.

The outbreaks of foot-and-mouth disease in 2000, which followed a prolonged scare over mad cow disease, damaged Britain's image further. These unfortunate developments led a planning director at advertising agency J. Walter Thompson to say, "The image of Britain is dreadful and it's going south."

Sources: Tara Parker-Pope, "Britain Suffers from Stuffy Image Abroad an Ad Agency Finds," *Wall Street Journal,* 4 January 1995, A8. Alessandra Galloni, "About Advertising: Britain: A Really Hard Sell," *Wall Street Journal Europe,* 30 March 2001; Gregory Katz, "Not-So-Jolly Old England," *Dallas Morning News,* 27 November 1999.

Branding a Cause: World Wildlife Fund

The World Wildlife Fund (WWF), founded in 1961, is today the world's largest private organization dedicated to nature conservation. The WWF boasts more than 4.7 million supporters in 100 countries. Its familiar panda logo represents its enduring efforts to protect that species.

In the United States, its annual budget does not allow for lavish marketing expenditures, so the WWF relies primarily on direct marketing campaigns to bring its message to the public and solicit contributions. One recent mailing offered recipients a chance to win one of several trips, including an African safari and an Alaskan cruise, in a sweepstakes.

The WWF also earns revenue through corporate partnerships. It offers four different business partnership options:

1. Conservation Partner: Major global sponsorship from multinational corporations; partners include Canon and Ogilvy & Mather.

2. Corporate Supporter: Financial or in-kind support from medium or large corporations; supporters include INRA and Delverde.

3. Corporate Club: Support from environmentally aware local businesses; only offered in Hungary, Russia, Poland, and United Arab Emirates.

4. Product Licensing: Corporate licensing agreements to use WWF trademarks. Groth AG manufactures WWF branded stamps and coins, and IBTT BV makes toy animals bearing the WWF panda logo.

To help spread its message, the WWF developed a Web site. The site contains pages for its national chapters, membership information, updates on current environmental issues, and information on special WWF projects. In 2000, the Web Marketing Association honored the site by naming it the best for any nonprofit organization on the Internet. In addition to its award-winning central Web site, the WWF developed a number of cause-specific Web sites, such as its Amazon rainforest relief site (www.worldwildlife.org/amazon), a site dedicated to its clean water campaign (www.panda.org/livingwaters), and a site dedicated to protecting the Arctic National Wildlife Refuge from oil drilling (www.worldwildlife.org/arctic-refuge).

The group changed its name to the Worldwide Fund for Nature in 1986, but is still known by the original World Wildlife Fund name in the United States and Canada. The original name and the accompanying acronym became a source of controversy when the WWF sued the World Wrestling Federation in 2001 over use of the initials WWF. The major point of contention was the similarity between the Web site addresses for the two organizations, since the World Wildlife URL was www.wwf.org and the World Wrestling Federation used www.wwf.com. The High Court in London decided in favor of the World Wildlife Fund, giving the wildlife group exclusive rights to the WWF initials and ordering the wrestling group to abandon its Web site address.

Source: http://www.wwf.org; "World Wrestling Federation Loses Court Case over Rights to WWF Name," Dow Jones Business News, 10 August 2001.

Ideas and Causes

Finally, numerous ideas and causes have become branded, especially by nonprofit organizations. These ideas and causes may be captured in a phrase or slogan and even be represented by a symbol (e.g., AIDS ribbons). By making the ideas and causes more visible and concrete, branding can provide much value. As Chapter 11 describes, cause marketing increasingly involves sophisticated marketing practices to attempt to inform or persuade consumers about the issues surrounding a cause.

rePlanet

Norwegian recycling giant Tomra Sytems ASA launched a chain of about 200 rePlanet kiosks in California. Brightly lit, clean, and convenient alternatives to traditional neighborhood recycling centers, their goal is to market recycling as an experience and to be the "Starbucks of the recycling business." Volume of recycled containers shot up by 60 percent at locations where the kiosks replaced old centers.[34]

Branding Brief 1-9 describes the activities of the World Wildlife Fund.

WHAT ARE THE STRONGEST BRANDS?

It is clear from the previous examples that virtually anything can be and has been branded. Which brands are the strongest, that is, the most well known or highly regarded? Figure 1-10 reveals *Business Week*'s ranking of the world's 25 most valuable brands based on Interbrand's brand valuation methodology (see Chapter 10).

Certainly some of the best-known brands can be found by simply walking down a supermarket aisle. It is also easy to identify a number of other brands with amazing staying power that have been market leaders in their respective categories for decades. For example, in ten major product categories, the number one U.S. brand from 1925 remains on top today: Kodak cameras and film, Goodyear tires, Nabisco crackers and cookies, Wrigley's chewing gum, Del Monte canned fruit, Gillette razors and blades, Ivory soap, Coca-Cola soft drinks, Campbell's soup, and Lipton tea. Similarly, many brands that were number one in the United Kingdom in 1933 also remain on top today: Hovis bread, *Stork* margarine, Kellogg's Corn Flakes, Cadbury's chocolates, Gillette razors, Schweppes mixers, Brooke Bond tea, Colgate toothpaste, and Hoover vacuum cleaners. These brands have evolved over the years and made a number of changes. In many cases, they barely resemble how they originally started. The Science of Branding 1-1 describes some of the branding principles that emerged from a study of early brand pioneers.

At the same time, there are a number of brands that have lost their market leadership and, in some cases, even their very existence! Winston, after years of dominance in the cigarette category, lost its leadership position to Marlboro in 1975 and now trails that brand by a large margin. Other seemingly invincible brands, such as Kodak, Levi-Strauss, General Motors, Montgomery Ward, Polaroid, and Xerox, have run into diffi-

Rank		2001 Brand Value ($ billions)	2000 Brand Value ($ billions)	Percent Change	Country of Ownership
1	Coca-Cola	68.95	72.54	−5	U.S.
2	Microsoft	65.07	70.20	−7	U.S.
3	IBM	52.75	53.18	−1	U.S.
4	GE	42.40	38.13	11	U.S.
5	Nokia	35.04	38.53	−9	Finland
6	Intel	34.67	39.05	−11	U.S.
7	Disney	32.59	33.55	−3	U.S.
8	Ford	30.09	36.37	−17	U.S.
9	McDonald's	25.29	27.86	−9	U.S.
10	AT&T	22.83	25.55	−11	U.S.
11	Marlboro	22.05	22.11	0	U.S.
12	Mercedes	21.73	21.11	3	Germany
13	Citibank	19.01	18.81	1	U.S.
14	Toyota	18.58	18.82	−1	Japan
15	Hewlett-Packard	17.98	20.57	−13	U.S.
16	Cisco Systems	17.21	20.07	−14	U.S.
17	American Express	16.92	16.12	5	U.S.
18	Gillette	15.30	17.36	−12	U.S.
19	Merrill Lynch	15.02	NA	NA	U.S.
20	Sony	15.01	16.41	−9	Japan
21	Honda	14.64	15.25	−4	Japan
22	BMW	13.86	12.97	7	Germany
23	Nescafé	13.25	13.68	−3	Switzerland
24	Compaq	12.35	14.60	−15	U.S.
25	Oracle	12.22	NA	NA	U.S.

FIGURE 1-10 *Business Week*'s Twenty-Five Most Valuable Global Brands

culties and seen their market preeminence challenged or even eliminated. Although in some cases these failures could be related to factors beyond the control of the firm, such as technological advances or shifting consumer preferences, in other cases the blame could probably be placed on the actions or inaction of the marketers behind these brands. Some of these marketers failed to account for changing market conditions and continued to operate with a "business as usual" attitude or, perhaps even worse, recognized that changes were necessary but were inadequate or inappropriate in their response.

The bottom line is that any brand—no matter how strong at any one point in time—is vulnerable and susceptible to poor brand management. The next section discusses why it is so difficult to manage brands in this modern-day environment. The Science of Branding 1-2 examines some of the academic developments in studying market leadership.

THE SCIENCE OF BRANDING 1-1

Entrepreneurs as Brand Builders

In her book *Brand New: How Entrepreneurs Earned Consumers' Trust from Wedgwood to Dell,* Harvard Business School professor Nancy Koehn examines innovative, successful entrepreneurs from different historical periods.[1] The six entrepreneurs she covers are Josiah Wedgwood, Henry Heinz, Marshall Field, Estée Lauder, Howard Schultz, and Michael Dell, each of whom built enduring brands from the ground up.

Each of the six achieved tremendous success in business by identifying emerging consumer needs and developing products and brands that met those needs. By focusing on the demand side of new markets, these entrepreneurs found unique ways of connecting with consumers. For example, Henry Heinz observed that industrialization was creating a vast array of consumables of widely varying quality, while urbanization was making it difficult for wives and mothers to produce canned and jarred foods at home. Heinz therefore decided to go into business manufacturing high-quality processed food that bore a recognizable symbol that customers would trust. He also employed advanced marketing techniques such as billboard advertising and point-of-sale displays to help raise awareness of his products. Within 15 years of its founding in 1876, total sales for the H.J. Heinz Company topped $1 million dollars. Today, Heinz is one of the largest food companies in the world, with annual sales of over $9 billion.

For modern entrepreneurs, a keen eye for identifying buyer demands and finding innovative ways of delivering to consumers is as indispensable as in Heinz's day. After traveling to Italy and observing the espresso bar coffee culture, Starbucks CEO Howard Schultz guessed that American consumers would enjoy drinking fresh, gourmet coffee if exposed to it in the right atmosphere. He also recognized that consumers were beginning to place higher value on customer service and were also seeking a "third place" between work and home. Few believed his coffee shops would succeed, but Schultz trusted his company's high-quality product and commitment to customer service, and Starbucks soon expanded all over the globe. Another modern entrepreneur, Michael Dell, founder of Dell computers, recognized a demand for customized computers and built a business model based on this demand. His direct-sales model enabled Dell to stay in close contact with consumers while keeping costs low, and the company became the number one computer seller in the country in 1999.

Koehn applauds these and the other entrepreneurs about which she writes for their broad view of the customer relationship. She writes, "These master brand builders all had deep respect for the way products fit into the lives of consumers" and identifies this fact as the "core" of their brands' success. She also believes that each of their stories provides valuable and timeless lessons for current managers to learn from:

> From Wedgwood to Dell, each entrepreneur was able to thrive during times of extraordinary social, economic, and technological transition. Because they succeeded in periods analogous to our time or indeed are succeeding today, they can help us understand what's happening in the information revolution.

[1] Nancy F. Koehn. *Brand New: How Entrepreneurs Earned Consumers' Trust from Wedgwood to Dell* (Boston: Harvard Business School Press, 2001).

Understanding Market Leadership

According to a study by New York University's Stern School of Business professor Peter Golder, over time, leading brands are more likely to lose their leadership position than retain it.[1] Golder evaluated more than 650 products in 100 categories and compared the category leaders from 1923 with the category leaders in 1997 (see Figure A). The study found that only 23 of the top brands in the 100 categories remained market leaders in 1997. Additionally, 28 percent of the leading brands in 1923 had failed by 1997. The clothing and fashion category experienced the greatest percentage of failures (67 percent) and had no brands that remained leaders in 1997. Leaders in the food and beverage category fared better, with 39 percent of brands maintaining leadership while only 21 percent failed.

One 1923 leader that did not maintain leadership was Underwood typewriters. Underwood's primary mistake was its lack of innovation. Rather than invest in research and development, Underwood followed a harvesting strategy that sought the highest margin possible for its products. By 1950, several competitors had already invested in computer technology, whereas Underwood only acquired a small computer firm in 1952. Subsequent developments in the market further damaged Underwood's position. Between 1956 and 1961, lower-priced foreign competitors more than doubled their share of manual typewriter sales. Additionally, sales of electric typewriters, which Underwood did not make, overtook sales of manual typewriters in the early 1960s. Olivetti acquired Underwood in the mid-1960s, and the brand name was dropped in the 1980s.

Golder uses Wrigley, which has dominated the chewing gum market for nine decades, as an example of a long-term leader. According to Golder, Wrigley's success is based on three factors: "maintaining and building strong brands, focusing on a single product, and being in a category that has not changed much." Wrigley has consistently marketed its brand with high-profile sponsorship and advertising. It also used subsidiaries to extend into new product categories such as sugarless gum and bubblegum, so as not to dilute the brand. Wrigley's sole focus on chewing gum enables the company to achieve maximum results in what is considered a mature category. During the 1990s, sales of Wrigley's products grew almost 10 percent annually. Finally, the chewing gum market is historically stable and uncomplicated. Still, Wrigley makes considerable investments in product and packaging improvement to maintain its edge.

One marketing expert was not surprised by the study's findings, noting that brands will decline if not properly cared for:

> If you don't invest in the brand as an asset like anything else . . . then you are going to lose market share and leadership. You have to maintain and replenish a brand or over time, it will die.[2]

Another paper by Golder and coauthor Gerard Tellis confirms this view that dedication to the brand is vital for sustained brand leadership.[3] The paper elucidates five factors for enduring market leadership (see Figure B).

---

[1] Peter N. Golder, "Historical Method in Marketing Research with New Evidence on Long-Term Market Share Stability," *Journal of Marketing Research* (May 2000): 156–172.

[2] Laurie Freeman, "Study: Leading Brands Aren't Always Enduring," *Advertising Age,* 28 February 2000.

[3] Gerard J. Tellis and Peter N. Golder, "First to Market, First to Fail? Real Causes of Enduring Market Leadership," *MIT Sloan Management Review,* 1 January 1996.

Category	1923 Leaders	1997 Leaders
Cleansers	Old Dutch	Comet Soft Scrub Ajax
Chewing Gum	Wrigley Adams	Wrigley's Bubble Yum Bubblicious
Motorcycles	Indian Harley-Davidson	Harley-Davidson Honda Kawasaki
5-Cent Mint Candies	Life Savers	Breath-Savers Tic Tac Certs
Peanut Butter	Beech-Nut Heinz	Jif Skippy Peter Pan
Razors	Gillette Gem Ever Ready	Gillette Bic Schick
Soft Drinks	Coca-Cola Cliquot Club Bevo	Coca-Cola Pepsi Dr. Pepper/Cadbury
Coffee	Arbuckle's Yuban White House Hotel Astor	Folger's Maxwell House Hills Bros.
Laundry Soap	Fels Naptha Octagon Kirkman	Tide Cheer Wisk
Cigarettes	Camel Fatima Pall Mall	Marlboro Winston Newport
Shoes	Douglas Walkover	Nike Reebok
Candy	Huyler's Loft Page & Shaw	Hershey M&M/Mars Nestlé
Jelly or Jam	Heinz	Smucker's Welch's Kraft

Source: Journal of Marketing Research/American Marketing Association.

FIGURE A   Brands Then and Now

Tellis and Golder identify the following five factors and rationale as the keys to enduring brand leadership.

Vision of the Mass Market
Companies with a keen eye for mass market tastes are more likely to build a broad and sustainable customer base. Though Pampers was not the market leader in the disposable diaper category during its first several years, it spent significantly on research and development in order to design an affordable and effective disposable diaper. Pampers quickly became the market leader.

Managerial Persistence
The "breakthrough" technology that can drive market leadership often requires the commitment of company resources over long periods of time. For example, JVC spent 21 years researching the VHS video recorder before launching it in 1976 and becoming a market leader.

Financial Commitment
The cost of maintaining leadership is high because of the demands for research and development and marketing. Companies that aim for short-term profitability rather than long-term leadership, as Rheingold Brewery did when it curtailed support of its Gablinger's light beer a year after the 1967 introduction of the product, are unlikely to enjoy enduring leadership.

Relentless Innovation
Due to changes in consumer tastes and competition from other firms, companies that wish to maintain leadership positions must continually innovate. Gillette, both a long-term leader and historically an innovator, typically has at least 20 shaving products on the drawing board at any given time.

Asset Leverage
Companies can become leaders in some categories if they hold a leadership position in a related category. For instance, Coca-Cola leveraged its success and experience with cola (Coke) and diet cola (Tab) to introduce Diet Coke in 1982. Within one year of its introduction, Diet Coke became the market leader.

Source: Gerard J. Tellis and Peter N. Golder, "First to Market, First to Fail? Real Causes of Enduring Market Lendership," *MIT Sloan Management Review,* 1 January 1996.

FIGURE B Factors Determining Enduring Leadership

BRANDING CHALLENGES AND OPPORTUNITIES

The reality is that although brands may be as important as ever to consumers, *brand management may be more difficult than ever*. Brand Focus 1.0 describes some of the historical origins of branding and brand management. Although there has been growing recognition of the value of brands, a number of developments have occurred in recent years that have significantly complicated marketing practices and pose challenges for brand managers (see Figure 1-11), as discussed next.[35]

Savvy customers
More complex brand families and portfolios
Maturing markets
More sophisticated and increasing competition
Difficulty in differentiating
Decreasing brand loyalty in many categories
Growth of private labels
Increasing trade power
Fragmenting media coverage
Eroding traditional media effectiveness
Emerging new communication options
Increasing promotional expenditures
Decreasing advertising expenditures
Increasing cost of product introduction and support
Short-term performance orientation
Increasing job turnover

FIGURE 1-11   Challenges to Brand Builders

Savvy Customers

Increasingly, consumers and businesses have become more experienced with marketing and more knowledgeable about how it works. A well-developed media market has resulted in increased attention paid to the marketing actions and motivations of companies. Consumer information and support exists in the form of consumer guides (e.g., *Consumer Reports*), online Web sites (e.g., Epinions.com), and so on. Many believe that it is more difficult to persuade consumers with traditional communications than it was in years gone by. As one marketer put it:

> The dollars that were spent on advertising in the 1950s and 1960s are still paying off. The advertising done 30 years ago for the Marlboro Man is still paying off all around the world. It was so cheap to get a large share of voice in the 1950s—it would be impossible to duplicate that now. There was also more receptivity in the marketplace. Now there is a more world-weary, seen-it-all attitude. People are more likely not to believe what they see on TV, to tune things out. The more you turn up the volume, the more people resist, and it becomes harder and harder to implant in peoples' minds that things are desirable.[36]

Other marketers believe that what consumers want from products and services and brands has changed. For example, Kevin Roberts of Saatchi and Saatchi argues that companies must transcend brands to create "trustmarks"—a name or symbol that emotionally binds a company with the desires and aspirations of its customers—and ultimately "lovemarks." He argues that it is not enough for a brand to be just respected.

> Pretty much everything today can be seen in relation to a love-respect axis. You can plot any relationship—with a person, with a brand—by whether it's based on love or based on respect. It used to be that a high respect rating

would win. But these days, a high love rating wins. If I don't love what you're offering me, I'm not even interested.

A passionate believer in the concept, Roberts reinforces the point that trustmarks belong to people and that an emotional connection is critical.[37]

Brand Proliferation

Another important change in the branding environment is the proliferation of new brands and products, in part spurred by the rise in line and brand extensions. As a result, a brand name may now be identified with a number of different products of varying degrees of similarity. Procter & Gamble's original Crest toothpaste, introduced in 1955, has been joined by a series of line extensions over the years, such as Crest Mint (1967), Advanced Formula Crest (1980), Crest Gel (1981), Crest Tartar Control (1985), Crest for Kids (1987), Crest Neat Squeeze (1991), Crest Baking Soda (1992), Crest for Sensitive Teeth (1994), and, in the last few years, Crest Whitening, Crest MultiCare, and Crest MultiCare Advanced Cleaning. Similarly, Coca-Cola now comes in diet, caffeine-free, and cherry-flavored forms. With so many brands having introduced extensions, there are few single (or "mono") product brands around, complicating the marketing decisions that have to be made.

Media Fragmentation

An important change in the marketing environment is the erosion or fragmentation of traditional advertising media and the emergence of interactive and nontraditional media, promotion, and other communication alternatives. For a number of reasons, marketers have become disenchanted with traditional advertising media, especially network television. First, the cost of network TV has risen dramatically in many countries. Since the mid-1970s, the price of network TV advertising in the United States has far outpaced the rate of inflation but without accompanying increases in audience size. Second, commercial breaks on network TV have become more cluttered as advertisers increasingly have decided to advertise with 15-second spots rather than the traditional 30- or 60-second spots. Third, the growth of independent stations and cable channels has resulted in a dramatic erosion of the network share of audience (from 91 percent in 1975 to under 60 percent by 2000). Fourth, the increase in remote controls, VCRs, and TV accessories such as TiVo—and the resulting zipping, zapping, grazing, and channel surfing, in the popular vernacular—has further reduced TV advertising effectiveness.[38]

For these and other reasons, the percentage of the communication budget devoted to advertising has shrunk over the years. In its place, marketers are spending more on nontraditional forms of communication and new and emerging forms of communication such as interactive, electronic media; sports and event sponsorship; in-store advertising; mini-billboards in transit vehicles, on parking meters, and in other locations; and product placement in movies.

Increased Competition

One reason marketers have been forced to use so many financial incentives or discounts is that the marketplace has become more competitive. Both demand-side and supply-side factors have contributed to the increase in competitive intensity. On the demand side, consumption for many products and services has flattened and hit the maturity stage, or even the decline stage, of the product life cycle. As a result, sales growth for brands can only be achieved at the expense of competing brands by taking away some of their market share.

On the supply side, new competitors have emerged due to a number of factors, such as the following:

➤ *Brand extensions:* As noted earlier, many companies have taken their existing brands and launched products with the same name into new categories. Many of these brands provide formidable opposition.

➤ *Deregulation:* Certain industries (e.g., telecommunications, financial services, health care, and transportation) have become deregulated, leading to increased competition from outside traditionally defined product-market boundaries.

➤ *Globalization:* Although firms have embraced globalization as a means to open new markets and potential sources of revenue, it has also resulted in an increase in the number of competitors in existing markets, threatening current sources of revenue.

➤ *Low-priced competitors:* Market penetration of generics, private labels, or low-priced "clones" imitating product leaders has increased on a worldwide basis. Retailers have gained power and often dictate what happens within the store. Their chief marketing weapon is price, and they have introduced and pushed their own brands and demanded greater compensation from trade promotions to stock and display national brands.

Increased Costs

At the same time that competition is increasing, the cost of introducing a new product or supporting an existing product has increased rapidly, making it difficult to match the investment and level of support that brands were able to receive in previous years. A.C. Nielsen and NPD have been jointly maintaining a database of trial and repeat trends for the average consumer products. Product trial, defined as a household buying a particular consumer packaged-goods product at least once during its introductory year, was around 15 percent in the latter half of the 1970s, but had dropped below 10 percent by the 1990s.[39]

Greater Accountability

Finally, marketers often find themselves responsible for meeting ambitious short-term profit targets because of financial market pressures and senior management imperatives. Stock analysts value strong and consistent earnings reports as an indication of the long-term financial health of a firm. As a result, marketing managers may find themselves in the dilemma of having to make decisions with short-term benefits but long-term costs (e.g., cutting advertising expenditures). Moreover, many of these same managers have experienced rapid job turnover and promotions and may not anticipate being in their current positions for very long. These different organizational pressures may encourage quick-fix solutions with perhaps adverse long-run consequences.

THE BRAND EQUITY CONCEPT

As the previous discussion points out, the complexity of both brand offerings and marketing communication options has significantly increased in recent years. A number of competitive challenges now exist for marketers. Some critics feel that the reaction by many marketers has been ineffective or, even worse, has further aggravated the problem. The remaining chapters present theories, models, and frameworks that accommodate and reflect these new developments in order to provide useful managerial guidelines and suggest promising new directions for future thought and research. In particular, a "common denominator" or unified conceptual framework based on the concept of brand equity is introduced as a tool to interpret the potential effects of various brand strategies.

One of the most popular and potentially important marketing concepts to arise in the 1980s was the concept of brand equity. The emergence of brand equity, however, has meant both good news and bad news to marketers. The good news is that it has raised the importance of the brand in marketing strategy, which heretofore had been relatively neglected, and provided focus for managerial interest and research activity. The bad news is that the concept has been defined a number of different ways for a number of different purposes (see Figure 1-12), resulting in some confusion and even frustration with the term. Through it all, no common viewpoint has emerged as to how brand equity should be conceptualized and measured.

Fundamentally, branding is about endowing products and services with the power of brand equity. Although a number of different specific views of brand equity may prevail, most observers are in agreement that brand equity should be defined in terms of marketing effects that are uniquely attributable to a brand. That is, brand equity relates to the fact that different outcomes result from the marketing of a product or service because of its brand than if that same product or service had not been identified by that brand. As a stark example of the transformational power of branding, consider the following.

Christie's Auctions

A May 2000 auction by Christie's East shows just how profoundly a brand can change people's opinions—and the prices they are willing to pay for products. Actress Judy Garland's slippers from *The Wizard of Oz*, which cost only $12.50 to make in 1938, sold for over $800,000! Actor Christopher Reeve's Superman suit fetched over $30,000, *Gilligan's Island*'s skipper hat sold for more than $8,000, and Penny Marshall's pajamas from *Laverne & Shirley* went for $1,500. Without such celebrity associations, it is doubtful that any of these items would cost more than a few hundred dollars at a flea market.

Branding is all about creating differences. Most marketing observers also agree with the following basic principles of branding and brand equity:

➤ Differences in outcomes arise from the "added value" endowed to a product as a result of past marketing activity for the brand.

➤ This value can be created for a brand in many different ways.

➤ Brand equity provides a common denominator for interpreting marketing strategies and assessing the value of a brand.

➤ There are many different ways in which the value of a brand can be manifested or exploited to benefit the firm (i.e., in terms of greater proceeds or lower costs or both).

Fundamentally, the brand equity concept stresses the importance of the role of the brand in marketing strategies. The concept of brand equity clearly builds on many previously identified principles about brand management. By virtue of the fact that it adapts current theorizing and research advances to address the new challenges in

The set of associations and behaviors on the part of the brand's customers, channel members, and parent corporation that permits the brand to earn greater volume or greater margins than it could without the brand name and that gives the brand a strong, sustainable, and differentiated advantage over competitors. (Marketing Science Institute)

The added value to the firm, the trade, or the consumer with which a given brand endows a product.[a] (Peter Farquhar, Claremont Graduate School)

A set of brand assets and liabilities linked to a brand, its name and symbol, that add to or subtract from the value provided by a product or service to a firm and/or to that firm's customers.[b] (David Aaker, University of California at Berkeley)

The sales and profit impact enjoyed as a result of prior years' marketing efforts versus a comparable new brand.[c] (John Brodsky, NPD Group)

Brand equity subsumes brand strength and brand value. Brand strength is the set of associations and behaviors on the part of a brand's customers, channel members, and parent corporation that permits the brand to enjoy sustainable and differentiated competitive advantages. Brand value is the financial outcome of management's ability to leverage brand strength via tactical and strategic actions in providing superior current and future profits and lowered risks.[d] (Raj Srivastava, University of Texas, and Allan Shocker, University of Minnesota)

The measurable financial value in transactions that accrues to a product or service from successful programs and activities.[e] (J. Walker Smith, Yankelovich Clancy Schulman)

Brand equity is the willingness for someone to continue to purchase your brand or not. Thus, the measure of brand equity is strongly related to loyalty and measures segments on a continuum from entrenched users of the brand to convertible users. (Market Facts)

Brands with equity provide "an ownable, trustworthy, relevant, distinctive promise to consumers." (Brand Equity Board)

[a]Peter Farquhar, "Managing Brand Equity," *Marketing Research* (September 1989): 1–11.

[b]David A. Aaker, *Managing Brand Equity* (New York: Free Press, 1991).

[c]John Brodsky, "Issues in Measuring and Monitoring" (paper presented at the ARF Third Annual Advertising and Promotion Workshop, February 5–6, 1991).

[d]Rajendra Srivastava and Allan D. Schocker, "Brand Equity: A Perspective on Its Meaning and Measurement," MSI Report 91-124 (Cambridge, MA: Marketing Science Institute, 1991).

[e]J. Walker Smith, "Thinking About Brand Equity and the Analysis of Customer Transactions" (paper presented at the ARF Third Annual Advertising and Promotion Workshop, February 5–6, 1991).

FIGURE 1-12   Definitions of Brand Equity

brand management created by a changing marketing environment, however, the concept of brand equity can provide potentially useful new insights. Chapters 2 and 3 in Part II of the book provide an important overview of this topic and provide a blueprint for the rest of the book. The remainder of the book addresses in much greater depth how to build brand equity (Chapters 4 to 7 in Part III), measure brand equity (Chapters 8 to 10 in Part IV), and manage brand equity (Chapters 11 to 14 in Part V). The concluding Chapter 15 in Part VI provides some additional applications and perspective. The remainder of this chapter provides an overview of the strategic brand management process that helps to pull all of these various concepts together.

STRATEGIC BRAND MANAGEMENT PROCESS

Strategic brand management involves the design and implementation of marketing programs and activities to build, measure, and manage brand equity. In this text, the *strategic brand management process* is defined as involving four main steps (see Figure 1-13):

1. Identifying and establishing brand positioning and values
2. Planning and implementing brand marketing programs
3. Measuring and interpreting brand performance
4. Growing and sustaining brand equity

The remainder of this section briefly highlights each of these four steps, which are examined in much more detail in the remainder of the book.[40]

Identifying and Establishing Brand Positioning and Values

The strategic brand management process starts with a clear understanding as to what the brand is to represent and how it should be positioned with respect to competitors, as outlined in Chapter 3. Kotler defines brand positioning as the "act of designing the company's offer and image so that it occupies a distinct and valued place in the target customer's mind." The goal is to locate the brand in the minds of consumers such that

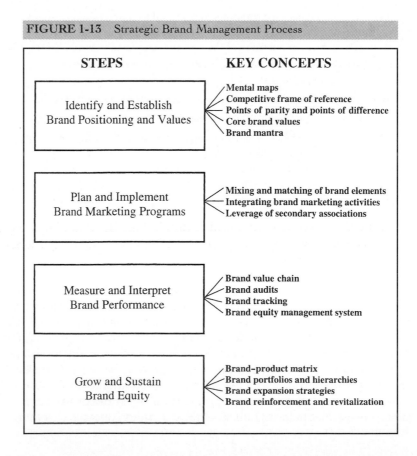

FIGURE 1-13 Strategic Brand Management Process

STEPS	KEY CONCEPTS
Identify and Establish Brand Positioning and Values	Mental maps Competitive frame of reference Points of parity and points of difference Core brand values Brand mantra
Plan and Implement Brand Marketing Programs	Mixing and matching of brand elements Integrating brand marketing activities Leverage of secondary associations
Measure and Interpret Brand Performance	Brand value chain Brand audits Brand tracking Brand equity management system
Grow and Sustain Brand Equity	Brand–product matrix Brand portfolios and hierarchies Brand expansion strategies Brand reinforcement and revitalization

the potential benefit to the firm is maximized. Competitive brand positioning is all about creating brand superiority in the minds of consumers. Fundamentally, positioning involves convincing consumers of the advantages of a brand vis-à-vis competitors, while at the same time alleviating concerns about any possible disadvantages.

Positioning often involves a specification of the appropriate core brand values and brand mantra. *Core brand values* are those set of abstract associations (attributes and benefits) that characterize a brand. To provide further focus as to what a brand represents, it is often useful to define a brand mantra, also known as a brand essence or core brand promise. A *brand mantra* is a short three- to five-word expression of the most important aspects of a brand and its core brand values. It can be seen as the enduring "brand DNA"—the most important aspects of the brand to the consumer and the company. Core brand values and a brand mantra are thus an articulation of the heart and soul of the brand.

Determining or evaluating a brand's positioning often benefits from a brand audit. A *brand audit* is a comprehensive examination of a brand, involving activities to assess the health of the brand, uncover its sources of equity, and suggest ways to improve and leverage that equity. A brand audit requires understanding sources of brand equity from the perspective of both the firm and the consumer. Chapter 3 describes the conceptual foundations of competitive brand positioning and provides detailed guidelines on how to develop such positioning strategies. Once the brand positioning strategy has been determined, the actual marketing program to create, strengthen, or maintain brand associations can be put into place.

Planning and Implementing Brand Marketing Programs

As Chapter 2 outlines, building brand equity requires creating a brand that consumers are sufficiently aware of and with which they have strong, favorable, and unique brand associations. In general, this knowledge-building process will depend on three factors:

1. The initial choices for the brand elements or identities making up the brand
2. The marketing activities and supporting marketing program and the manner by which the brand is integrated into them
3. Other associations indirectly transferred to the brand by linking it to some other entity (e.g., the company, country of origin, channel of distribution, or another brand)

Each of the three factors is discussed in turn in Part III of the book. Figure 1-14 provides a schematic overview of key concepts in building brand equity. Some important considerations are as follows.

Choosing Brand Elements
A number of options exist, and a number of criteria are relevant for choosing brand elements. As noted earlier, a brand element is visual or verbal information that serves to identify and differentiate a product. The most common brand elements are brand names, logos, symbols, characters, packaging, and slogans. Brand elements can be chosen to enhance brand awareness or facilitate the formation of strong, favorable, and unique brand associations. The best test of the brand-building contribution of brand elements is what consumers would think about the product or service if they knew only its brand name, associated logo, and so forth. Because different elements have different advantages, a subset or even all of the possible brand elements are often employed.

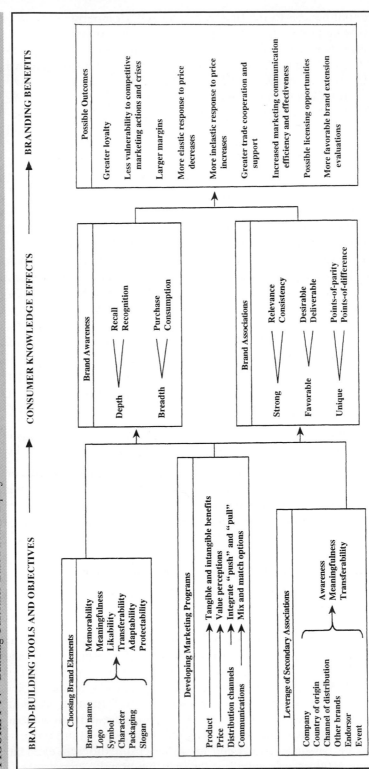

FIGURE 1-14   Building Customer-Based Brand Equity

Chapter 4 examines in detail the means by which the choice and design of brand elements can help to build brand equity.

Integrating the Brand into Marketing Activities and the Supporting Marketing Program

Although the judicious choice of brand elements can make some contribution to building brand equity, the primary input comes from the marketing activities related to the brand. Strong, favorable, and unique brand associations can be created in a variety of different ways by marketing programs. This text only highlights some particularly important marketing program considerations for building brand equity. Chapter 5 addresses new developments in designing marketing programs as well as issues in product strategy, pricing strategy, and channel strategy. Chapter 6 addresses issues in communications strategy.

Leveraging Secondary Associations

The third and final way to build brand equity is to leverage secondary associations. Brand associations may themselves be linked to other entities that have their own associations, creating secondary brand associations. In other words, a brand association may be created by linking the brand to another node or information in memory that conveys meaning to consumers. For example, the brand may be linked to certain source factors, such as the company (through branding strategies), countries or other geographic regions (through identification of product origin), and channels of distribution (through channel strategy), as well as to other brands (through ingredients or co-branding), characters (through licensing), spokespeople (through endorsements), sporting or cultural events (through sponsorship), or some other third-party sources (through awards or reviews).

Because the brand becomes identified with another entity, even though this entity may not directly relate to the product or service performance, consumers may *infer* that the brand shares associations with that entity, thus producing indirect or secondary associations for the brand. In essence, the marketer is borrowing or leveraging some other associations for the brand to create some associations of the brand's own and thus help build its brand equity. Chapter 7 describes the means of leveraging brand equity.

Measuring and Interpreting Brand Performance

To understand the effects of brand marketing programs, it is important to measure and interpret brand performance. A useful tool in that regard is the brand value chain. The *brand value chain* is a means to trace the value creation process for brands to better understand the financial impact of brand marketing expenditures and investments. Chapter 8 describes this planning tool, and Chapters 9 and 10 describe a number of measures to operationalize it.

The brand value chain helps to direct marketing research efforts. Profitable brand management requires successfully designing and implementing a brand equity measurement system. A *brand equity measurement system* is a set of research procedures designed to provide timely, accurate, and actionable information for marketers so that they can make the best possible tactical decisions in the short run and the best strategic decisions in the long run. As described in Chapter 8, implementing such a system involves two key

1. **Brand Audit**
   A. Brand inventory
   B. Brand exploratory

2. **Brand Value Chain**
   A. Brand equity sources
   B. Brand equity outcomes

3. **Brand Equity Management System**
   A. Brand equity charter
   B. Brand equity report
   C. Brand equity responsibilities

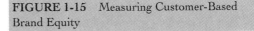

FIGURE 1-15   Measuring Customer-Based Brand Equity

steps: conducting tracking studies and implementing a brand equity management system. Figure 1-15 provides a schematic overview of key concepts in measuring brand equity.

Growing and Sustaining Brand Equity

Through the skillful design and implementation of marketing programs that capitalize on a well-conceived brand positioning, strong brand leadership positions can be obtained. Maintaining and expanding on that brand equity, however, can be quite challenging. Brand equity management concerns those activities that take a broader and more diverse perspective of the brand's equity—understanding how branding strategies should reflect corporate concerns and be adjusted, if at all, over time or over geographic boundaries or market segments. Managing brand equity involves managing brands within the context of other brands, as well as managing brands over multiple categories, over time, and across multiple market segments. Figure 1-16 provides a schematic overview of key concepts in managing brand equity.

Defining the Branding Strategy
The branding strategy of the firm provides the general guidelines as to which brand elements a firm chooses to apply across the products it offers. Two main tools in defining the corporate branding strategy are the brand–product matrix and the brand hierarchy. The brand–product matrix is a graphical representation of all the brands and products sold by the firm. The brand hierarchy reveals an explicit ordering of brands by displaying the number and nature of common and distinctive brand components across the firm's products. By capturing the potential branding relationships among the different products sold by the firm, a brand hierarchy is a useful means to graphically portray a firm's branding strategy. Chapter 11 reviews issues concerning branding strategies and the concepts of the brand–product matrix, brand portfolio, and brand hierarchy. Chapter 12 concentrates on the topic of brand extensions, in which an existing brand is used to launch a product in an existing category.

---

1. Define Brand Hierarchy
   A. Principle of simplicity $\longrightarrow$ Employ as few levels as possible
   B. Principle of relevance $\longrightarrow$ Create abstract associations relevant to as many
                                                         products as possible
   C. Principle of differentiation $\longrightarrow$ Differentiate individual products and brands
   D. Principle of prominence $\longrightarrow$ Adjust prominence to affect perceptions of product
                                                         distance
   E. Principle of commonality $\longrightarrow$ Link common products through shared brand
                                                         elements

---

2. Define Brand–Product Matrix
   A. Brand extensions $\longrightarrow$ Establish new equity and enhance existing equity
   B. Brand portfolio $\longrightarrow$ Maximize coverage and minimize overlap

---

3. Enhance Brand Equity over Time
   A. Brand reinforcement $\longrightarrow$ Innovation in product design, manufacturing, and
                                                merchandising
                            $\longrightarrow$ Relevance in user and usage imagery
   B. Brand revitalization $\longrightarrow$ "Back to basics" strategy
                            $\longrightarrow$ "Reinvention" strategy

---

4. Establish Brand Equity over Market Segments
   A. Identify differences in $\longrightarrow$ How they purchase and use products
      consumer behavior $\longrightarrow$ What they know and feel about different brands
   B. Adjust branding program $\longrightarrow$ Choice of brand elements
                                $\longrightarrow$ Nature of supporting marketing program
                                $\longrightarrow$ Leverage of secondary associations

FIGURE 1-16   Managing Customer-Based Brand Equity

Managing Brand Equity over Time

Effective brand management requires taking a long-term view of marketing decisions. Because consumers' responses to marketing activity depend on what they know and remember about a brand, short-term marketing mix actions, by changing brand knowledge, *necessarily* increase or decrease the success of future marketing actions. A long-term perspective of brand management recognizes that any changes in the supporting marketing program for a brand may, by changing consumer knowledge, affect the success of future marketing programs. Additionally, a long-term view results in proactive strategies designed to maintain and enhance customer-based brand equity over time in the face of external changes in the marketing environment and internal changes in a firm's marketing goals and programs. Chapter 13 outlines issues related to managing brand equity over time.

Managing Brand Equity over Geographic Boundaries, Cultures, and Market Segments

An important consideration in managing brand equity is recognizing and accounting for different types of consumers in developing branding and marketing programs. International issues and global branding strategies are particularly important in these decisions. Chapter 14 examines issues related to broadening of brand equity across market segments. In expanding a brand in this way, it is critical that equity is built by careful positioning and design and implementation of marketing programs that reflect the specific knowledge and behaviors of those market segments.

Review

This chapter began by defining a brand as a name, term, sign, symbol, or design, or some combination of these elements, intended to identify the goods and services of one seller or group of sellers and to differentiate them from those of competitors. The different components of a brand (i.e., brand names, logos, symbols, package designs and so forth) are defined as brand elements. Brand elements come in many different forms. A brand is distinguished from a product, which is defined as anything that can be offered to a market for attention, acquisition, use, or consumption that might satisfy a need or want. A product may be a physical good, service, retail store, person, organization, place, or idea.

A brand is a product, but one that adds other dimensions that differentiate it in some way from other products designed to satisfy the same need. These differences may be rational and tangible—related to product performance of the brand—or more symbolic, emotional, or intangible—related to what the brand represents. Brands themselves are valuable intangible assets that need to be managed carefully. Brands offer a number of benefits to customers and firms. The key to branding is that consumers perceive differences among brands in a product category. A number of examples were provided to show how virtually any type of product can be branded by giving the product a name and attaching meaning to it in terms of what the product has to offer and how it differs from competitors. A number of branding challenges and opportunities faced by present-day marketing managers were then outlined.

The chapter concluded by introducing the concepts of brand equity and the strategic brand management process and providing an overview and road map for the rest of the book. Brand positioning involves defining and establishing brand vision and positioning. Building brand equity depends on three main factors: (1) the initial choices for the brand elements or identities making up the brand, (2) the way the brand is integrated into the supporting marketing program, and (3) the associations indirectly transferred to the brand by linking the brand to some other entity (e.g., the company, country of origin, channel of distribution, or another brand). Measuring brand equity requires measuring aspects of the brand value chain and implementing a brand equity measurement system. Managing brand equity concerns those activities that take a broader and more diverse perspective of the brand's equity—understanding how branding strategies should reflect corporate concerns and be adjusted, if at all, over time or over geographic boundaries. Effectively managing brand equity includes defining the corporate branding strategy—by defining the brand hierarchy and brand–product matrix—and devising policy for brand fortification and leverage over time and over geographic boundaries.

Discussion Questions

1. What do brands mean to you? What are your favorite brands and why? Check to see how your perceptions of brands might differ from those of others.
2. Who do you think has the strongest brands? Why? What do you think of the *Business Week* list of the 25 strongest brands in Figure 1-10? Do you agree with the rankings? Why or why not?
3. Can you think of anything that cannot be branded? Pick an example that was not discussed in each of the categories provided (services; retailers and distributors; people and organizations; sports, arts, and entertainment) and describe how each is a brand.
4. Can you think of yourself as a brand? What do you do to "brand" yourself?
5. What do you think of the new branding challenges and opportunities that were listed? Can you think of any other issues?

B r a n d   F o c u s   1 . 0

Historical Origins of Branding

Branding, in one form or another, has been around for centuries.[41] The original motivation for branding was for craftsmen and others to identify the fruits of their labors so that customers could easily recognize them. Branding, or at least trademarks, can be traced back to ancient pottery and stonemason's marks, which were applied to handcrafted goods to identify their source. Pottery and clay lamps were sometimes sold far from the shops where they were made, and buyers looked for the stamps of reliable potters as a guide to quality. Marks have been found on early Chinese porcelain, on pottery jars from ancient Greece and Rome, and on goods from India dating back to about 1300 B.C.

In medieval times, potters' marks were joined by printers' marks, watermarks on paper, bread marks, and the marks of various craft guilds. In some cases, these were used to attract buyers loyal to particular makers, but the marks were also used to police infringers of the guild monopolies and to single out the makers of inferior goods. An English law passed in 1266 required bakers to put their mark on every loaf of bread sold, "to the end that if any bread bu faultie in weight, it may bee then knowne in whom the fault is." Goldsmiths and silversmiths were also required to mark their goods, both with their signature or personal symbol and with a sign of the quality of the metal. In 1597, two goldsmiths convicted of putting false marks on their wares were nailed to the pillory by their ears. Similarly harsh punishments were decreed for those who counterfeited other artisan's marks.

When Europeans began to settle in North America, they brought the convention and practice of branding with them. The makers of patent medicines and tobacco manufacturers were early U.S. branding pioneers. Medicine potions such as Swaim's Panacea, Fahnestock's Vermifuge, and Perry Davis' Vegetable Pain Killer became well known to the public prior to the Civil War. Patent medicines were packaged in small bottles and, because they were not seen as a necessity, were vigorously promoted. To further influence consumer choices in stores, manufacturers of these medicines printed elaborate and distinctive labels, often with their own portrait featured in the center.

Tobacco manufacturers had been exporting their crop since the early 1600s. By the early 1800s, manufacturers had packed bales of tobacco under labels such as Smith's Plug and Brown and Black's Twist. During the 1850s, many tobacco manufacturers recognized that more creative names—such as Cantaloupe, Rock Candy, Wedding Cake, and Lone Jack—were helpful in selling their tobacco products. In the 1860s, tobacco manufacturers began to sell their wares in small bags directly to consumers. Attractive-looking packages were seen as important, and picture labels, decorations, and symbols were designed as a result.

The history of branding in the United States since 1860 to its more modern developments from 1985 on (reviewed earlier in the chapter) can be divided into four main periods. We next consider some of the important developments in each.

EMERGENCE OF NATIONAL MANUFACTURER BRANDS: 1860 TO 1914

In the United States after the Civil War, a number of forces combined to make widely distributed, manufacturer-branded products a profitable venture:

➤ Improvements in transportation (e.g., railroads) and communication (e.g., the telegraph and telephone) made regional and even national distribution increasingly easy.

➤ Improvements in production processes made it possible to produce large quantities of high-quality products inexpensively.

➤ Improvements in packaging made individual (as opposed to bulk) packages that could be identified with the manufacturer's trademark increasingly viable.

➤ Changes in U.S. trademark law in 1879, the 1880s, and 1906 made it easier to protect brand identities.

➤ Advertising became perceived as a more credible option, and newspapers and magazines eagerly sought out advertising revenues.

➤ Retail institutions such as department and variety stores and national mail order houses served as effective middlemen and encouraged consumer spending.

➤ Population increased due to liberal immigration policies.

➤ Increasing industrialization and urbanization raised the standard of living and aspirations of Americans, although many products on the market still were of uneven quality.

➤ Literacy rose as the percentage of illiterate Americans dropped from 20 percent in 1870 to 10 percent in 1900.

All of these factors facilitated the development of consistent-quality consumer products that could be efficiently sold to consumers through mass market advertising campaigns. In this fertile branding environment, mass-produced merchandise in packages largely replaced locally produced merchandise sold from bulk containers. This change brought about the widespread use of trademarks. For example, Procter & Gamble made candles in Cincinnati and shipped them to merchants in other cities along the Ohio and Mississippi Rivers. In 1851, wharf hands began to brand crates of Procter & Gamble candles with a crude star. The firm soon noticed that buyers down river relied on the star as a mark of quality, and merchants refused the candles if the crates arrived without the mark. As a result, the candles were marked with a more formal star label on all packages and branded as "Star" and began to develop a loyal following.

The development and management of these brands was largely driven by the owners of the firm and their top-level management. For example, the first president of National Biscuit was involved heavily in the introduction in 1898 of Uneeda Biscuits, the first nationally branded biscuit. One of their first decisions was to create a pictorial symbol for the brand, the Uneeda biscuit slicker boy, who appeared in the supporting ad campaigns. H. J. Heinz built up the Heinz brand name through production innovations and spectacular promotions. Coca-Cola became a national powerhouse due to the efforts of Asa Candler, who actively oversaw the growth of the extensive distribution channel.

National manufacturers sometimes had to overcome resistance from consumers, retailers, wholesalers, and even employees from within their own company. To do so, these firms employed sustained "push" and "pull" efforts to keep both consumers and retailers happy and accepting of national brands. Consumers were attracted through the use of sampling, premiums, product education brochures, and heavy advertising. Retailers were lured by in-store sampling and promotional programs and shelf maintenance assistance.

As the use of brand names and trademarks spread, so did the practice of imitation and counterfeiting. Although the laws were somewhat unclear, more and more firms sought protection by sending their trademarks and labels to district courts for registration. Congress finally separated the registration of trademarks and labels in 1870 with the enactment of the country's first federal trademark law. Under the law, registrants were required to send a facsimile of their mark with a description of the type of goods on which it was used to the Patent Office in Washington, along with a $25 fee. One of the first marks submitted to the Patent Office under the new law was the Underwood devil, which was registered to William Underwood & Company of Boston on November 29, 1870, for use on "Deviled Entremets." By 1890, most countries had trademark acts, establishing brand names, labels, and designs as legally protectable assets.

DOMINANCE OF MASS MARKETED BRANDS: 1915 TO 1929

By 1915, manufacturer brands had become well established in the United States on both a regional and national basis. The next 15 years saw increasing acceptance and even admiration of manufacturer brands by consumers. The marketing of brands became more specialized under the guidance of functional experts in charge of production, promotion, personal selling, and other areas. This greater specialization led to more advanced marketing techniques. Design professionals were enlisted to assist in the process of trademark selection. Personal selling became more sophisticated as salesmen were carefully selected and trained to systematically handle accounts and seek out new businesses. Advertising combined more powerful creativity with more persuasive copy and slogans. Government and industry regulation came into place to reduce deceptive advertising. Marketing research became more important and influential in supporting marketing decisions.

Although functional management of brands had these virtues, it also presented problems. Because responsibility for any one brand was divided among two or more functional managers, as well as advertising specialists, poor coordination was always a potential problem. For example, the introduction of Wheaties cereal by General Mills was nearly sabotaged by the company's salesmen, who were reluctant to take on new duties to support the brand. Three years after the cereal's introduction and on the verge of its being dropped, a manager from the advertising department at General Mills decided to become a product champion for Wheaties, and the brand went on to great success in the following decades.

CHALLENGES TO MANUFACTURER BRANDS: 1930 TO 1945

The onset of the Great Depression in 1929 posed new challenges to manufacturer brands. Greater price sensitivity swung the pendulum of power in the favor of retailers, who pushed their own brands and dropped nonperforming manufacturer brands. Advertising came under fire as manipulative, deceptive, and tasteless and was increasingly being ignored by certain segments of the population. In 1938, the Wheeler Amendment gave power to the Federal Trade Commission (FTC) to regulate advertising practices. In response to these trends, manufacturers' advertising went beyond slogans and jingles to give consumers specific reasons why they should buy advertised products.

There were few dramatic changes in marketing of brands during this time. As a notable exception, Procter & Gamble put the first brand management system into place, whereby each of their brands had a manager assigned to only that brand who was responsible for its financial success. Other firms were slow to follow, however, and relied on their long-standing reputation for good quality—and a lack of competition—to sustain sales. During World War II, manufacturer brands became relatively scarce as resources were diverted to the war effort. Nevertheless, many brands continued to advertise and helped to bolster consumer demand during these tough times.

The Lanham Act of 1946 permitted federal registration of service marks (marks used to designate services rather than products) and collective marks such as union labels and club emblems.

ESTABLISHMENT OF BRAND MANAGEMENT STANDARDS: 1946 TO 1985

After World War II, the pent-up demand for high-quality brands led to an explosion of sales. Personal income grew as the economy took off, and market demand intensified as the rate of population growth exploded. Demand for national brands soared, fueled by a burst of new products and a receptive and growing middle class. Firm after firm during this time period adopted the brand management system.

In the brand management system, a brand manager took "ownership" of a brand. A brand manager was responsible for developing and implementing the annual marketing plan for his or her brand, as well as identifying new business opportunities. The brand manager might be assisted, internally, by representatives from manufacturing, the sales force, marketing research, financial planning, research and development, personnel, legal, and public relations and, externally, by representatives from advertising agencies, research suppliers, and public relations agencies.

Then, as now, a successful brand manager had to be a versatile jack-of-all-trades. For example, a marketing manager at Gillette once identified the following factors for being a successful brand manager:[42]

➤ A dedication to the brand, reflected in an effort to do what was best for the business

➤ An ability to assess a situation and see alternative solutions

➤ A talent for generating creative ideas and a willingness to be open to others' ideas

➤ An ability to make decisions in a highly ambiguous environment

➤ An ability to move projects through the organization

➤ Good communication skills

➤ A high energy level

➤ A capacity for handling many tasks simultaneously

Notes

1. Interbrand Group, *World's Greatest Brands: An International Review* (New York: John Wiley, 1992).

2. Ibid.; Adrian Room, *Dictionary of Trade Name Origins* (London: Routledge & Kegan Paul, 1982).

3. The second through fifth levels are based on a conceptualization in Theodore Levitt, "Marketing Success Through Differentiation—of Anything," *Harvard Business Review* (January–February 1980): 83–91.

4. Theodore Levitt, "Marketing Myopia," *Harvard Business Review* (July–August 1960): 45–56.

5. Alvin A. Achenbaum, "The Mismanagement of Brand Equity" (paper presented at the ARF Fifth Annual

Advertising and Promotion Workshop, February 1, 1993).

6. John Murphy, *Brand Strategy* (New York: Prentice-Hall, 1990), 4.

7. Jacob Jacoby, Jerry C. Olson, and Rafael Haddock, "Price, Brand Name, and Product Composition Characteristics as Determinants of Perceived Quality," *Journal of Consumer Research* 3, no. 4 (1971): 209–216; Jacob Jacoby, George Syzbillo, and Jacqueline Busato-Sehach, "Information Acquisition Behavior in Brand Choice Situations," *Journal of Marketing Research* 11 (1977): 63–69.

8. Susan Fournier, "Understanding Consumer-Brand Relationships," working paper 96-018, Harvard Business School, Boston, 1966, 3.

9. Philip Nelson, "Information and Consumer Behavior," *Journal of Political Economy* 78 (1970): 311–329; Michael R. Darby and Edi Karni, "Free Competition and the Optimal Amount of Fraud," *Journal of Law and Economics* 16 (April 1974): 67–88.

10. Allan D. Shocker and Richard Chay, "How Marketing Researchers Can Harness the Power of Brand Equity" (paper presented to the New Zealand Marketing Research Society, August 1992).

11. Ted Roselius, "Consumer Ranking of Risk Reduction Methods," *Journal of Marketing* 35 (January 1971): 56–61.

12. Leslie de Chernatony and Gil McWilliam, "The Varying Nature of Brands as Assets," *International Journal of Advertising* 8 (1989): 339–349.

13. Constance E. Bagley, *Managers and the Legal Environment: Strategies for the 21st Century*, 2nd ed. (St. Paul, MN: West Publishing, 1995).

14. Tulin Erdem, "Brand Equity as a Signaling Phenomenon," *Journal of Consumer Psychology* 7, no. 2 (1998): 131–157.

15. Charles Bymer, "Valuing Your Brands: Lessons from Wall Street and the Impact on Marketers" (paper presented at the ARF Third Annual Advertising and Promotion Workshop, February 5–6, 1991).

16. Interbrand Group, *World's Greatest Brands*.

17. Peter Farquhar, Julia Y. Han, and Yuji Ijiri, "Recognizing and Measuring Brand Assets,"

MSI Report 91-119 (Cambridge, MA: Marketing Science Institute, 1991).

18. James P. Miller, "Sara Lee Plans 'Fundamental Reshaping,'" *Wall Street Journal*, 16 September 1997, A1.

19. Kerry Dolan and Robyn Meredith, "Ghost Cars, Ghost Brands," *Forbes*, 30 April 2001, 106–112.

20. Levitt, "Marketing Success."

21. 1988 Harper's Index, *Harper's Magazine*, April 1989.

22. Yumiko Ono, "Prescription-Drug Makers Heighten Hard-Sell Tactics," *Wall Street Journal*, 29 August 1994, B1.

23. Pam Weisz, "Over-the-Counter Goes Under the Radar," *Brandweek*, 3 June 1996, 39–42.

24. Tom Clark, "Package-Goods Execs Flood into Software," *Advertising Age*, 16 May 1994, S4.

25. Kevin Kelly, "At Sears, the More Things Change . . . ," *Business Week*, 12 November 1990, 66–68; Kevin Kelly, "The Big Store May Be on a Roll," *Business Week*, 30 August 1993, 82–85; Susan Chandler, "Sears' Turnaround Is for Real—For Now," *Business Week*, 15 August 1994, 102–103; Mark Tatge, "The Harder Side of Sears," *Forbes*, 13 November 2000, 282–287; Amy Merrick, "Sears to Overhaul Stores, Change Format, Cut 5000 Jobs in Move to Boost Earnings," *Wall Street Journal*, 25 October 2001, B9.

26. Lorrie Grant, "Web Sites Look to Customer Service," *USA Today*, 29 September 1999, B3.

27. Jefferson Graham, "Googley-Eyed Over Success," *USA Today*, 27 August 2001, D3.

28. Cathy Horyn, "Absolute Cindy," *Vanity Fair*, August 1994, 76.

29. University professors are certainly aware of the power of the name as a brand. In fact, one reason why many professors choose to have students identify themselves on exams by student numbers of some type is so that they will not be biased in grading by their knowledge of the student that prepared it. Otherwise, it may be too easy to give higher grades to those students who the professor likes or, for whatever reason, expects to have done well on the exam.

30. Robert P. Parker, "If You Got It Flaunt It" (paper presented at the ARF Brand Equity Workshop, February 15–16, 1994).

31. Joel Hochberg, "Package Goods Marketing vs. Hollywood," *Advertising Age*, 20 January 1992.

32. Ben Pappas, "Star Bucks," *Forbes*, 17 May 1999, 53.

33. Nigel J. Morgan and Annette Pritchard, "Building Destination Brands: The Cases of Wales and Australia," *Journal of Brand Management* 7 (November 1999): 103–118.

34. Jim Carlton, "Recycling Redefined," *Wall Street Journal*, 6 March 2001, B1.

35. Allan D. Shocker, Rajendra Srivastava, and Robert Ruekert, "Challenges and Opportunities Facing Brand Management: An Introduction to the Special Issue," *Journal of Marketing Research* 31 (May 1994): 149–158.

36. B. G. Yovovich, "What Is Your Brand Really Worth?" *Adweek's Marketing Week,* 8 August 1988, 18–21.

37. Alan M. Webber, "Trust in the Future," *Fast Company* (September 2000): 210–220.

38. Alvin A. Achenbaum, "The Implication of Price Competition on Brands, Advertising and the Economy" (paper presented at the ARF Fourth Annual Advertising and Promotion Workshop, February 12–13, 1992). Zipping refers to the practice of fast-forwarding through ad breaks while watching taped TV programs; zapping refers to switching to other channels during commercial breaks while watching live TV programs. Channel grazing and surfing refer to watching a few minutes of one program, then of another, and so on.

39. Joel Rubinson, "Introduction to the Workshop" (presented at the ARF Fourth Annual Advertising and Promotion Workshop, February 12–13, 1992).

40. For discussion of other approaches to branding, see David A. Aaker, *Managing Brand Equity* (New York: Free Press, 1991); David A. Aaker, *Building Strong Brands* (New York: Free Press, 1996); David A. Aaker and Erich Joachimsthaler, *Brand Leadership* (New York: Free Press, 2000); Jean-Noel Kapferer, *Strategic Brand Management* (New York: Free Press, 1992); Scott M. Davis, *Brand Asset Management* (New York: Free Press, 2000); Frank Delano, *The OmniPowerful Brand* (New York: AMACOM, 1999); Linda Gorchels, *The Product Manager's Handbook* (Chicago: NTC Business Books, 1996); Duane Knapp, *The Brand Mindset* (New York: McGraw-Hill, 2000).

41. Much of this section is adapted from an excellent article by George S. Low and Ronald A. Fullerton, "Brands, Brand Management, and the Brand Manager System: A Critical-Historical Evaluation," *Journal of Marketing Research* 31 (May 1994): 173–190, and an excellent book by Hal Morgan, *Symbols of America* (New York: Viking, 1986).

42. Shirley Spence and Thomas Bonoma, "The Gillette Company: Dry Idea Advertising," Case 9-586-042 (Boston: Harvard Business School, 1986).

CHAPTER

Customer-Based Brand Equity

2

Review
Discussion Questions
Brand Focus 2.0   The Marketing Advantages of Strong Brands

PREVIEW

Chapter 1 introduced some basic notions about brands and the role that they have played and are playing in marketing strategies. The chapter concluded by observing that marketers are now faced with an increasing number of tactical options that must be efficiently and effectively applied to an increasing number of product variations for the brand. The concept of brand equity was identified as having the potential to provide guidance to marketers to help them make those decisions. Part II of the text explores brand equity and brand positioning and how to identify and establish brand positioning and values.

This chapter more formally examines the brand equity concept, introducing one particular view—the concept of customer-based brand equity—that will serve as the organizing framework for the rest of the book.[1] It considers the sources of customer-based brand equity and the outcomes or benefits that result from those sources. It then presents the customer-based brand equity model in detail and discusses some of the main implications of that model. Brand Focus 2.0 at the end of the chapter provides a detailed overview of the advantages of creating a strong brand. Chapter 3 concentrates on brand positioning.

CUSTOMER-BASED BRAND EQUITY

Two questions often arise regarding brands: What makes a brand strong? and How do you build a strong brand? To help answer both of these questions, this section introduces the customer-based brand equity (CBBE) model. This model incorporates recent theoretical advances and managerial practices in understanding and influencing consumer behavior. Although a number of useful perspectives concerning brand equity have been put forth, the CBBE model provides a unique point of view as to what brand equity is and how it should best be built, measured, and managed.

The CBBE model approaches brand equity from the perspective of the consumer—whether it be an individual or an organization. Understanding the needs and wants of consumers and devising products and programs to satisfy them are at the heart of successful marketing. In particular, two fundamentally important questions faced by marketers are: What do different brands mean to consumers? and How does the brand knowledge of consumers affect their response to marketing activity?

The basic premise of the CBBE model is that the power of a brand lies in what customers have learned, felt, seen, and heard about the brand as a result of their experiences over time. In other words, *the power of a brand lies in what resides in the minds of customers*. The challenge for marketers in building a strong brand is ensuring that customers have the right type of experiences with products and services and their accompanying marketing programs so that the desired thoughts, feelings, images, beliefs, perceptions, opinions, and so on become linked to the brand.

Customer-based brand equity is formally defined as the differential effect that brand knowledge has on consumer response to the marketing of that brand. A brand is said to have *positive* customer-based brand equity when consumers react more favorably to a product and the way it is marketed when the brand is identified than when it is not (e.g., when the product is attributed to a fictitious name or is unnamed). Thus, a brand with positive customer-based brand equity might result in consumers being more accepting of a new brand extension, less sensitive to price increases and withdrawal of advertising support, or more willing to seek the brand in a new distribution channel. On the other hand, a brand is said to have *negative* customer-based brand equity if consumers react less favorably to marketing activity for the brand compared with an unnamed or fictitiously named version of the product.

There are three key ingredients to this definition: (1) "differential effect," (2) "brand knowledge," and (3) "consumer response to marketing." First, brand equity arises from differences in consumer response. If no differences occur, then the brand name product can essentially be classified as a commodity or generic version of the product. Competition, most likely, would then just be based on price. Second, these differences in response are a result of consumers' knowledge about the brand, that is, what customers have learned, felt, seen, and heard about the brand as a result of their experiences over time. Thus, although strongly influenced by the marketing activity of the firm, brand equity ultimately depends on what resides in the minds of consumers. Third, the differential response by consumers that makes up the brand equity is reflected in perceptions, preferences, and behavior related to all aspects of the marketing of a brand (e.g., choice of a brand, recall of copy points from an ad, actions in response to a sales promotion, or evaluations of a proposed brand extension). Brand Focus 2.0 provides a detailed account of these advantages, as summarized in Figure 2-1.

The simplest way to illustrate what is meant by the concept of customer-based brand equity is to consider some of the typically observed results of product sampling or comparison tests. For example, with blind taste tests, one group of consumers samples a product without knowing which brand it is, whereas another group of consumers samples the product knowing which brand it is. Invariably, differences arise in the opinions of the two groups despite the fact that the two groups are consuming the same product.

Improved perceptions of product performance
Greater loyalty
Less vulnerability to competitive marketing actions
Less vulnerability to marketing crises
Larger margins
More inelastic consumer response to price increases
More elastic consumer response to price decreases
Greater trade cooperation and support
Increased marketing communication effectiveness
Possible licensing opportunities
Additional brand extension opportunities

FIGURE 2-1 Marketing Advantages of Strong Brands

For example, Larry Percy reports the results of a beer tasting experiment that showed how discriminating consumers could be when given the names of the well-known brands of the beer they were drinking, but how few differences consumers could detect when they did not know the brand names. Figure 2-2 displays the perceptual maps—visual tools to portray perceptual differences among brands expressed by consumers—that were derived from the two types of responses. As it turns out, even fairly knowledgeable consumers can have difficulty distinguishing different brands of beer.

When consumers report different opinions regarding branded and unbranded versions of identical products, it must be the case that knowledge about the brand, created by whatever means (e.g., past experiences, marketing activity for the brand), has somehow changed consumers' product perceptions. Examples of branded differences, such as was observed with the beer experiment, can be found with virtually every type of product—conclusive evidence that consumers' perceptions of the performance of a product are highly dependent on their impressions of the brand that goes along with it. In other words, clothes may seem to fit better, a car may seem to drive more smoothly, the wait in a bank line may seem shorter, and so on, depending on the particular brands involved.

Brand Equity as a Bridge

Thus, according to the customer-based brand equity model, the power of a brand lies in the minds of consumers or customers and what they have experienced and learned about the brand over time. Consumer knowledge drives the differences that manifest themselves in terms of brand equity. This realization has important managerial implications. In an abstract sense, according to this view, brand equity provides marketers with a vital strategic bridge from their past to their future.

Brands as a Reflection of the Past

All of the dollars spent each year on manufacturing and marketing products should not be considered so much as "expenses" but as "investments"—investments in what consumers learned, felt, experienced, and so forth about the brand. If not properly designed and implemented, these expenditures may not be good investments, in that the right knowledge structures may not have been created in consumers' minds, but they should be considered investments nonetheless. Thus, the *quality* of the investment in brand building is the most critical factor, not necessarily the *quantity* of investment, beyond some minimal threshold amount. In that sense, it is actually possible to "overspend" on brand building if money is not being spent wisely. Conversely, as will be evident throughout the book, there are examples of brands that are being considerably outspent but which amass a great deal of brand equity by judicious spending on marketing activities that create valuable, enduring memory traces in the minds of consumers.

Brands as Direction for the Future

At the same time, the brand knowledge that has been created over time by these marketing investments dictates appropriate and inappropriate future directions for the brand. Consumers will decide, based on their brand beliefs, attitudes, and so on, where they think the brand should go and grant permission (or not) to any marketing action or program. Thus, at the end of the day, the true value and future prospects of a brand rest with consumers and their knowledge about the brand.

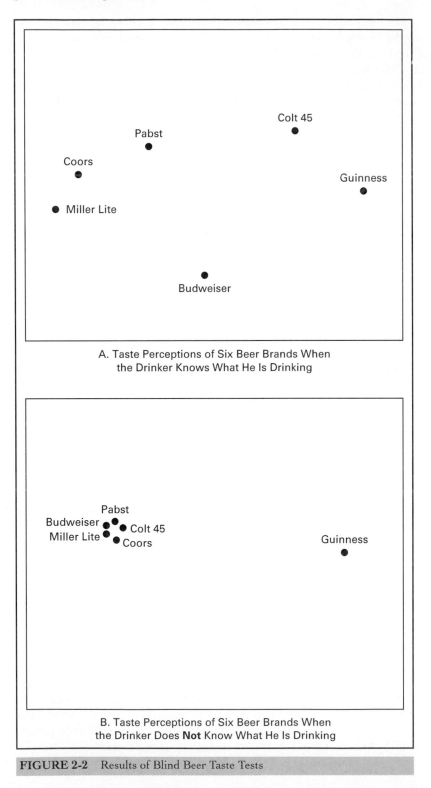

A. Taste Perceptions of Six Beer Brands When
the Drinker Knows What He Is Drinking

B. Taste Perceptions of Six Beer Brands When
the Drinker Does **Not** Know What He Is Drinking

FIGURE 2-2   Results of Blind Beer Taste Tests

No Logo

In her book *No Logo: Taking Aim at the Brand Bullies*, Naomi Klein details the aspects of global corporate growth that have led to widespread consumer backlash against brands. She explains the subject of her book as follows:

> The title *No Logo* is not meant to be read as a literal slogan (as in No More Logos!), or a post-logo logo (there is already a No Logo clothing line, I'm told). Rather, it is an attempt to capture an anti-corporate attitude I see emerging among many young activists. This book is hinged on a simple hypothesis: that as more people discover the brand-name secrets of the global logo web, their outrage will fuel the next big political movement, a vast wave of opposition squarely targeting those with very high name-brand recognition.

Klein first writes about the increasing occupation of free and open space by advertising. The author cites marketing campaigns that exist within schools and universities, among other examples of advertising encroaching on traditionally ad-free space. Klein asserts that as marketers compete for "eyeballs" using unconventional and unexpected means, fewer ad-free spaces remain, and consumer resentment builds. Klein then argues that the vast number of mergers and acquisitions in the past two decades, and the increasing number of brand extensions, has severely limited consumer choice and engendered additional consumer resentment.

Klein also examines the effect that the globalization of trade has had on workers. In addition to enumerating many of the exploitative effects globalization has had on workers in developing countries, she attributes job scarcity in developed countries to the fact that corporations seek cheap labor elsewhere. Klein also observes that as companies seek to reduce costs, they often divest their manufacturing operations and outsource production. The author argues that companies thus shifting from a production model to a marketing model are basically producing brands and nothing else. Klein quotes Phil Knight, founder of Nike, who summarized the marketing model position by saying, "There is no value in making things any more. The value is added by careful research, by innovation, and by marketing."

Klein ultimately details the numerous movements that have arisen to protest the growing power of corporations and the proliferation of branded space that accompanies this growth. The author highlights such anticorporate practices as "culture jamming" and "ad-busting," which serve to subvert and undermine corporate marketing by attacking the marketers on their own terms. For example, New York "guerilla artist" Jorge Rodriguez de Gerada uses existing billboard advertisements to create parodies that make the original message look ridiculous. Klein also discusses the formation of labor activist organizations such as Essential Action and the International Labour Organization, which perform labor monitoring and hold companies accountable for the treatment of their labor forces. Klein observes that the issues of corporate conduct are now highly politicized. As a result, Klein notes, "Political rallies, which once wound their predicable course in front of government buildings and consulates, are now just as likely to take place in front of the stores of the corporate giants."

Another observation Klein makes toward the end of the book serves as a note of caution for brand-based corporations. Referring to the public condemnation of brands such as Kathie Lee Gifford, the Gap, and Nike, Klein writes, "the fanatical obsession with logos extends not only to building them up, but also to tearing them down. Though on a vastly different scale, Nike's sweatshops are to labor reporting what O.J. Simpson's trial was to the legal beat." An inherent danger, then, of building a strong brand is that the public will be all the more eager to see the brand tarnished once unseemly facts surface.

Source: Naomi Klein, *No Logo: Taking Aim at the Brand Bullies* (New York: Picador, 1999).

In short, regardless of the particular definition adopted, the value to marketers of brand equity as a concept ultimately depends on how they use it. Brand equity can offer focus and guidance, providing marketers with a means to interpret their past marketing performance and design their future marketing programs. Everything the firm does can help to enhance or detract from brand equity. Those marketers who build strong brands have embraced the concept and use it to its fullest as a means of clarifying, communicating, and implementing their marketing actions. The process of creating such brand power is not without its critics, however, as described in the Science of Branding 2-1. The next section considers the issue of brand knowledge and CBBE in more detail. Branding Brief 2-1 describes the related concept of customer equity.

MAKING A BRAND STRONG: BRAND KNOWLEDGE

From the perspective of the CBBE model, brand knowledge is the key to creating brand equity, because it creates the differential effect that drives brand equity. What marketers need, then, is an insightful way to represent how brand knowledge exists in consumer memory. An influential model of memory developed by psychologists is helpful in that regard.[2] The *associative network memory model* views memory as consisting of a network of nodes and connecting links, in which nodes represent stored information or concepts and links represent the strength of association between this information or concepts. Any type of information can be stored in the memory network, including information that is verbal, visual, abstract, or contextual in nature.

Consistent with the associative network memory model, brand knowledge is conceptualized here as consisting of a brand node in memory with a variety of associations linked to it. In particular, brand knowledge can be characterized in terms of two components: brand awareness and brand image. *Brand awareness* is related to the strength of the brand node or trace in memory, as reflected by consumers' ability to identify the brand under different conditions.[3] Brand awareness is a necessary, but not always sufficient, step in building brand equity. Other considerations, such as the image of the brand, often come into play.

Brand image has long been recognized as an important concept in marketing.[4] Although there has not always been agreement on how to measure brand image,[5] one generally accepted view is that, consistent with an associative network memory model,

---

Defining Customer Equity

Some marketers espouse an alternative—but in many ways complementary—view to brand equity called *customer equity*. Blattberg and Deighton define customer equity in terms of the optimal balance between what is spent on customer acquisition versus what is spent on customer retention.[1] They calculate customer equity as follows.

> We first measure each customer's expected contribution toward offsetting the company's fixed costs over the expected life of that customer. Then we discount the expected contributions to a net present value at the company's target rate of return for marketing investments. Finally, we add together the discounted, expected contributions of all current contributions.

The authors offer the following observation:

> Ultimately, we contend that the appropriate question for judging new products, new programs, and new customer-service initiatives should not be, Will it attract new customers? or, Will it increase our retention rates? but rather, Will it grow our customer equity? The goal of maximizing customer equity by balancing acquisition and retention efforts properly should serve as the star by which a company steers its entire marketing program.

Blattberg and Deighton offer eight guidelines as a means of maximizing customer equity:

1. Invest in highest-value customers first.
2. Transform product management into customer management.
3. Consider how add-on sales and cross-selling can increase customer equity.
4. Look for ways to reduce acquisition costs.
5. Track customer equity gains and losses against marketing programs.
6. Relate branding to customer equity.
7. Monitor the intrinsic retainability of your customers.
8. Consider writing separate marketing plans—or even building two marketing organizations—for acquisition and retention efforts.

Rust, Zeithaml, and Lemon define customer equity as the discounted lifetime values of a firm's customer base.[2] According to their view, customer equity is made up of three components and key drivers:

- *Value equity:* Customers' objective assessment of the utility of a brand based on perceptions of what is given up for what is received. Three drivers of value equity are quality, price, and convenience.

- *Brand equity:* Customers' subjective and intangible assessment of the brand, above and beyond its objectively perceived value. Three key drivers of brand equity are customer brand awareness, customer brand attitudes, and customer perception of brand ethics.

- *Relationship equity:* Customers' tendency to stick with the brand, above and beyond objective and subjective assessments of the brand. Four key drivers of relationship equity are loyalty programs, special recognition and treatment programs, community-building programs, and knowledge-building programs.

These components' importance are proposed to vary by company and industry. For example, brand equity is assumed to matter more with low-involvement purchases involving simple decision processes (e.g., facial tissues), when the product is highly visible to others, when experiences associated with the product can be passed from one individual or generation to the next, or when it is difficult to evaluate the quality of a product or service prior to consumption. Value equity can be more important in business-to-business settings, whereas retention equity is more important for companies that sell a variety of products and services to the same customer.

[1]Robert C. Blattberg and John Deighton, "Manage Marketing by the Customer Equity Test," *Harvard Business Review* (July-August 1996).

[2]Roland T. Rust, Valarie A. Zeithamal, Katherine Lemon, *Driving Customer Equity* (New York: Free Press, 2000).

brand image can be defined as perceptions about a brand as reflected by the brand associations held in consumer memory.[6] In other words, brand associations are the other informational nodes linked to the brand node in memory and contain the meaning of the brand for consumers. Associations come in all forms and may reflect characteristics of the product or aspects independent of the product itself.

For example, consider Apple computers. If someone asked you what came to mind when you thought of Apple computers, what might you say? You might reply with associations such as "user friendly," "creative," "for desktop publishing," "used at many schools," and so forth. Figure 2-3 displays some commonly mentioned associations for Apple computers that consumers have expressed in the past. The associations that came to mind for you would make up your brand image for Apple. Through skillful marketing, Apple has been able to achieve a rich brand image made up of a host of brand associations in the minds of at least some consumers. Different consumers might think of different associations for Apple, although many associations are likely to be shared by a majority of consumers. In that sense, one can refer to "the" brand image of Apple, but at the same time, it must be recognized that this image may vary, perhaps

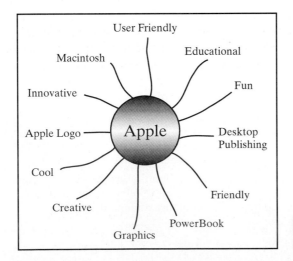

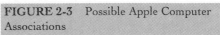

FIGURE 2-3   Possible Apple Computer Associations

even considerably, depending on the particular groups of consumers or market segments involved.

Other brands, of course, will be characterized by a different set of associations. For example, McDonald's marketing program attempts to create brand associations in consumers' minds to "quality," "service," "cleanliness," and "value." McDonald's rich brand image probably also includes strong associations to "Ronald McDonald," "golden arches," "for kids," and "convenient," as well as perhaps potentially negative associations such as "fast food." Coca-Cola's marketing program strives to link brand associations in consumers' minds to "refreshment," "taste," "availability," "affordability," and "accessibility." Whereas Mercedes-Benz has achieved strong associations to "performance" and "status," Volvo has created a strong association to "safety." Chapter 3 reviews in detail the different types of associations that can become linked to the brand. Chapter 9 outlines research techniques to measure these associations.

SOURCES OF BRAND EQUITY

What causes brand equity to exist? How do marketers create brand equity? *Customer-based brand equity occurs when the consumer has a high level of awareness and familiarity with the brand and holds some strong, favorable, and unique brand associations in memory.* In some cases, brand awareness alone is sufficient to result in more favorable consumer response, for example, in low-involvement decision settings where consumers are willing to base their choices merely on familiar brands. In most other cases, however, the strength, favorability, and uniqueness of the brand associations play a critical role in determining the differential response making up the brand equity. If the brand is perceived by consumers to be the same as a representative version of the product or service in the category, then consumer response to marketing for the brand would not be expected to vary from when the marketing is attributed to a fictitiously named or unnamed product or service. If the brand has some salient, unique associations, then consumer response should differ.

For branding strategies to be successful and brand equity to be created, consumers must be convinced that there are meaningful differences among brands in the product or service category. The key to branding is that consumers must *not* think that all brands in the category are the same. Thus, establishing a high level of brand awareness and a positive brand image in consumer memory—in terms of strong, favorable, and unique brand associations—produces the knowledge structures that can affect consumer response and produce different types of customer-based brand equity.

Brand Awareness

Brand awareness consists of brand recognition and brand recall performance. *Brand recognition* relates to consumers' ability to confirm prior exposure to the brand when given the brand as a cue. In other words, brand recognition requires that consumers can correctly discriminate the brand as having been previously seen or heard. For example, when consumers go to the store, is it the case that they will be able to recognize the brand as one to which they have already been exposed? *Brand recall* relates to consumers' ability to retrieve the brand from memory when given the product category, the needs fulfilled by the category, or a purchase or usage situation as a cue. In other words, brand recall requires that consumers correctly generate the brand from memory when given a relevant cue. For example, recall of Kellogg's Corn Flakes will depend on consumers' ability to retrieve the brand when they think of the cereal category or of what they should eat for breakfast or eat for a snack, either at the store (when making a purchase), at home (when making a consumption choice), or wherever.

As is the case with most information in memory, it is generally easier to recognize a brand than it is to recall it from memory. The relative importance of brand recall and recognition will depend on the extent to which consumers make product-related decisions with the brand present or not.[7] For example, if product decisions are made in the store, brand recognition may be more important because the brand will actually be physically present. Outside the store or in any situation where the brand is not present, on the other hand, it is probably more important that the consumer be able to actually recall the brand from memory. For this reason, brand recall is critical for service and online brands: Consumers must actively seek the brand and therefore be able to retrieve it from memory when appropriate.

Consequences of Brand Awareness

What are the advantages of creating a high level of brand awareness? Brand awareness plays an important role in consumer decision making for three main reasons.

Learning Advantages   The first way that brand awareness affects consumer decision making is by influencing the formation and strength of the brand associations that make up the brand image. A necessary condition for the creation of a brand image is that a brand node has been established in memory. The nature of that brand node should affect how easily different kinds of information can become attached to the brand in memory as brand associations. The first step in building brand equity is to register the brand in the minds of consumers, and the choice of brand elements may make that task easier or more difficult, as described in Chapter 4.

Consideration Advantages   Second, as suggested earlier, it is important that consumers think of and consider the brand whenever they are making a purchase for which the brand could potentially be acceptable, or whenever they are consuming a product whose needs the brand could potentially satisfy. In particular, raising brand awareness increases the likelihood that the brand will be a member of the *consideration set,* the handful of brands that receive serious consideration for purchase.[8] Much research has shown that consumers are rarely loyal to only one brand but instead have a set of brands that they would consider buying and another—possibly smaller—set of brands that they actually buy on a regular basis. Because consumers typically only consider a few brands for purchase, making sure that the brand is in the consideration set also means that *other* brands may be less likely to be considered or recalled. Research in psychology on "part-list cuing effects" has shown that recall of some information can inhibit recall of other information.[9] In a marketing context, that means that if a consumer thinks of going to Burger King for a quick lunch, he or she may be less likely to think of going to other types of fast food restaurants, such as Kentucky Fried Chicken or Taco Bell.[10]

Choice Advantages   The third advantage of creating a high level of brand awareness is that brand awareness can affect choices among brands in the consideration set, even if there are essentially no other associations to those brands. For example, consumers have been shown to adopt a decision rule to buy only more familiar, well-established brands in some cases.[11] Thus, in low-involvement decision settings, a minimum level of brand awareness may be sufficient for product choice, even in the absence of a well-formed attitude.[12] One influential model of attitude change and persuasion, the elaboration-likelihood model, is consistent with the notion that consumers may make choices based on brand awareness considerations when they have low involvement. Low involvement results when consumers lack either purchase motivation (e.g., when consumers don't care about the product or service) or purchase ability (e.g., when consumers do not know anything else about the brands in a category).[13]

1. *Consumer purchase motivation*. Although products and brands may be critically important to marketers, to many consumers in many categories, choosing a brand is not a life-or-death decision. For example, despite spending millions of dollars in TV advertising over the years to persuade consumers of product differences, one recent survey showed that 40 percent of consumers believed all brands of gasoline were about the same or did not know which brand of gasoline was best. A lack of perceived differences among brands in a category is likely to lead to consumers who are unmotivated regarding the brand choice process.

2. *Consumer purchase ability*. Consumers in some product categories just do not have the necessary knowledge or experience to be able to judge product quality even if they so desired. The obvious examples are products with a high degree of technical sophistication (e.g., telecommunications equipment involving state-of-the-art features). Yet, there are other instances with seemingly less complicated product specifications in which consumers still may lack the necessary ability to judge quality. Consider the college student who has not really had to cook or clean before on his or her own roaming the supermarket aisles for the first time. The reality is that product quality is often highly ambiguous and difficult to judge without a great deal of prior experience and expertise. In such cases, consumers will use whatever shortcut or heuristic they can come up with to make their decisions in the best manner possible. At times, they may end up simply choosing the brand with which they are most familiar and aware. We discuss the role of perceived quality in consumer decisions in greater detail later.

Establishing Brand Awareness

How do you create brand awareness? In the abstract, brand awareness is created by increasing the familiarity of the brand through repeated exposure, although this is generally more effective for brand recognition than for brand recall. That is, the more a consumer "experiences" the brand by seeing it, hearing it, or thinking about it, the more likely it is that the brand will become strongly registered in memory. Thus, anything that causes consumers to experience a brand name, symbol, logo, character, packaging, or slogan can potentially increase familiarity and awareness of that brand element. Examples include a wide range of communication options such as advertising and promotion, sponsorship and event marketing, publicity and public relations, and outdoor advertising. Moreover, it is important to visually and verbally reinforce the brand name with a full complement of brand elements (e.g., in addition to its name, Intel uses the Intel Inside logo and its distinctive symbol to enhance its awareness in multiple ways).

Although brand repetition increases the strength of the brand node in memory, and thus its recognizability, improving recall of the brand requires linkages in memory to appropriate product categories or other situational purchase or consumption cues. In particular, to build awareness, it is often desirable to develop a slogan or jingle that creatively pairs the brand and the appropriate category or purchase or consumption cues (and, ideally, the brand positioning as well, in terms of building a positive brand image). Additional use can be made of the other brand elements—logos, symbols, characters, and packaging.

The manner by which the brand and its corresponding product category are paired (e.g., as with an advertising slogan) will be influential in determining the strength of product category links. For brands with strong category associations (e.g., Ford cars), the distinction between brand recognition and recall may not matter much—consumers thinking of the category are likely to think of the brand. For brands that may not have the same level of initial category awareness (e.g., in competitive markets or when the brand is new to the category), it is more important to emphasize category links in the marketing program. Moreover, as will be discussed in Chapter 11, strongly linking the brand to the proper category or other relevant cues may become especially important over time if the product meaning of the brand changes (e.g., through brand extensions or mergers or acquisitions).

Many marketers have attempted to create brand awareness through so-called shock advertising with bizarre themes.[14] For example, online retailer Outpost.com used ads featuring gerbils shot through cannons, wolverines attacking marching bands, and preschoolers having the brand name tattooed on their foreheads. The problem with such approaches is that they invariably fail to create strong category links because the product is just not prominent enough in the ad, thus inhibiting brand recall. They also can generate a fair amount of ill will in the process. Often coming across as desperate measures, they rarely provide a foundation for long-term brand equity.

In short, brand awareness is created by increasing the familiarity of the brand through repeated exposure (for brand recognition) and strong associations with the appropriate product category or other relevant purchase or consumption cues (for brand recall).[15]

Brand Image

A positive brand image is created by marketing programs that link strong, favorable, and unique associations to the brand in memory. The definition of customer-based brand equity does not distinguish between the source of brand associations and the manner in which they are formed; all that matters is the resulting favorability, strength, and uniqueness of brand associations. This realization has important implications for building brand equity. Besides marketer-controlled sources of information, brand associations can also be created in a variety of other ways: by direct experience; from information communicated about the brand from the firm or other commercial or nonpartisan sources (e.g., *Consumer Reports* or other media vehicles) and word of mouth; and by assumptions or inferences from the brand itself (e.g., its name or logo) or from the identification of the brand with a company, country, channel of distribution, or some particular person, place, or event.

Marketers should recognize the influence of these other sources of information by both managing them as well as possible and adequately accounting for them in designing communication strategies. Consider how The Body Shop was able to build their brand equity.

The Body Shop
The Body Shop created a global brand image without using conventional advertising. Their strong associations to personal care and environmental concern occurred through their products (natural ingredients only, never tested on animals, etc.), packaging (simple, refillable, recyclable), merchandising (detailed point-of-sale posters, brochures, and displays), staff (encouraged to be enthusiastic and informative concerning environmental issues), sourcing policies (using small local producers from around the world), social action program (requiring each franchisee to run a local community program), and public relations programs and activities (taking visible and sometimes outspoken stands on various issues).

Strength of Brand Associations
Making sure that associations are linked sufficiently strongly to the brand will depend on how the marketing program and other factors affect consumers' brand experiences. Associations will vary in the strength of their connection to the brand node. Strength is a function of both the amount, or quantity, of processing that information receives as well as the nature, or quality, of that processing. The more deeply a person thinks about product information and relates it to existing brand knowledge, the stronger the resulting brand associations. Two factors facilitating the strength of association to any piece of information are the personal relevance of the information and the consistency with which this information is presented over time. The particular associations that are recalled and salient will depend not only on the strength of association, but also on the context in which the brand is considered and the retrieval cues that are present that can serve as reminders. This section considers the factors that, in general, affect the strength and recallability of a brand association. Chapters 4 through 7 provide more concrete guidelines.

As noted earlier, consumer beliefs about brand attributes and benefits can be formed in different ways. *Brand attributes* are those descriptive features that characterize a product or service. *Brand benefits* are the personal value and meaning that consumers attach to the product or service attributes. In general, the source of information creating the strongest brand attribute and benefit associations is direct experience. This type of information can be particularly influential in consumers' product decisions, as long as consumers are able to accurately interpret their experiences. As Figure 2-4 shows, according to at least one consumer survey, knowing what to expect from a product because of past experience was the most common reason for buying a particular brand. The next strongest associations are likely to be formed on the basis of word of mouth (friends, family, etc.) or other noncommercial sources of information (consumer unions, the popular press, etc.). Word of mouth is likely to be particularly important for restaurants, entertainment, banking, and personal services. Company-influenced sources of information, such as advertising, are often likely to create the weakest associations and thus may be the most easily changed.

To overcome this hurdle, marketing communication programs attempt to create strong brand associations and recalled communication effects through a variety of means, such as using creative communications that cause consumers to elaborate on brand-related information and relate it appropriately to existing knowledge, exposing consumers to communications repeatedly over time, and ensuring that many retrieval cues are present as reminders. Chapter 6 reviews in detail how integrated marketing communication programs can contribute to brand equity. Regardless, the entire marketing program and

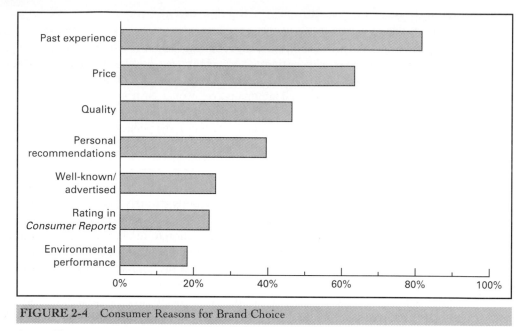

FIGURE 2-4   Consumer Reasons for Brand Choice

Source: The Roper Organization

all activities related to the brand will affect the strength of brand associations. Starbucks and Amazon.com are recent examples of companies that created amazingly rich brand images without the benefit of intensive advertising programs.

Favorability of Brand Associations

Choosing which favorable and unique associations to link to the brand requires careful analysis of the consumer and competition to determine the optimal positioning for the brand. Chapter 3 reviews important considerations involved in positioning and creating strong, favorable, and unique brand associations. In the most basic sense, favorable brand associations are created by convincing consumers that the brand possesses relevant attributes and benefits that satisfy their needs and wants, such that they form positive overall brand judgments. Thus, favorable associations for a brand are those associations that are desirable to consumers and are successfully delivered by the product and conveyed by the supporting marketing program for the brand (e.g., such that the brand is seen as highly convenient, reliable, effective, efficient, colorful, and so on).

In terms of desirability, how important or valued is the image association to the brand attitudes and decisions made by consumers? Desirability depends on three factors: (1) how *relevant* consumers find the brand association, (2) how *distinctive* consumers find the brand association, and (3) how *believable* consumers find the brand association. Creating a favorable association also requires that the firm be able to deliver on the desired association. In terms of deliverability, the main question is, What would be the cost or investment necessary and the length of time involved to create or change the desired association(s)? Deliverability also depends on three factors: (1) the actual or potential ability of the product to perform, (2) the current or future prospects of communicating that performance, and (3) the sustainability of the actual and communicated performance over time. Desirability and deliverability are reviewed in greater detail in Chapter 3.

Uniqueness of Brand Associations

Brand associations may or may not be shared with other competing brands. The essence of brand positioning is that the brand has a sustainable competitive advantage or "unique selling proposition" that gives consumers a compelling reason why they should buy that particular brand.[16] These differences may be communicated explicitly by making direct comparisons with competitors, or may be highlighted implicitly without stating a competitive point of reference. Furthermore, they may be based on product-related or non-product-related attributes or benefits. In fact, in many categories, non-product-related attributes, such as user type or usage situation, may more easily create unique associations (e.g., the rugged western image of Marlboro cigarettes or the rebellious nature of the Virginia Slims brand).

The existence of strongly held, favorably evaluated associations that are unique to the brand and imply superiority over other brands is critical to a brand's success. Yet, unless the brand faces no competition, it will most likely share some associations with other brands. Shared associations can help to establish category membership and define the scope of competition with other products and services.[17]

Research on noncomparable alternatives suggests that even if a brand does not face direct competition in its product category, and thus does not share product-related attributes with other brands, it can still share more abstract associations and face indirect competition in a more broadly defined product category.[18] Thus, although a railroad may not compete directly with another railroad, it still competes indirectly with other forms of transportation, such as airlines, cars, and buses. A maker of educational CD-ROM products may be implicitly competing with all other forms of education and entertainment, such as books, videos, television, and magazines. For these reasons, branding principles are now being used to market a number of different categories as a whole—for example, banks, furniture, carpets, bowling, and trains, to name just a few.

A product or service category can also be characterized by a set of associations that includes specific beliefs about any member in the category, as well as overall attitudes toward all members in the category. These beliefs might include many of the relevant product-related attributes for brands in the category, as well as more descriptive attributes that do not necessarily relate to product or service performance (e.g., the color of a product, such as red for ketchup). Certain attributes or benefits may be considered prototypical and essential to all brands in the category, and a specific brand may exist that is considered to be an exemplar and most representative of the product or service category.[19] For example, consumers might expect a running shoe to provide support and comfort and to be built well enough to withstand repeated wearings, and they may believe that Asics or some other leading brand best represents a running shoe. Similarly, consumers might expect an online retailer to offer easy navigation, a variety of offerings, reasonable shipping options, secure purchase procedures, responsive customer service, and strict privacy guidelines, and they may consider Amazon.com or some other market leader to be the best example of an online retailer.

Because the brand is linked to the product category, some category associations may also become linked to the brand, either in terms of specific beliefs or overall attitudes. Product category attitudes can be a particularly important determinant of consumer response. For example, if a consumer thinks that all brokerage houses are basically greedy and that brokers are in it for themselves, then he or she probably will have similarly unfavorable beliefs about and negative attitudes toward any particular brokerage house simply by virtue of its membership in the category. Thus, in almost all cases, some product category associations that are linked to the brand will also be shared with other brands in the category. Note that the strength of the brand associations to the product category is an important determinant of brand awareness.[20]

In short, to create the differential response that leads to customer-based brand equity, it is important that some of the strongly held brand associations are not only favorable but also unique. Unique brand associations are distinct associations not shared with competing brands. Beliefs about unique attributes and benefits for brands that consumers value more favorably than competitive brands can lead to a greater likelihood of the consumers choosing the former brands.

Thus, it is important to associate unique, meaningful *points of difference* to the brand to provide a competitive advantage and "reason why" consumers should buy it. For some brand associations, however, consumers only need to view them at least as favorably as competitors. That is, it may be sufficient that some brand associations are seen as roughly equal in favorability with competing brand associations, so that they function as *points of parity* in consumers' minds to negate potential points of difference for competitors. In other words, these associations are designed to provide "no reason why not" for consumers to choose the brand. Assuming that other brand associations are evident as points of difference, more favorable brand evaluations and a greater likelihood of choice should then result.

Not all brand associations will be deemed important and viewed favorably by consumers, nor will they be equally valued across different purchase or consumption situations. Moreover, not all brand associations will be relevant and valued in a purchase or consumption decision. The evaluations of brand associations may be situation or context dependent and vary according to the particular goals that consumers have in that purchase or consumption decision.[21] An association may be valued in one situation but not another.[22]

For example, the associations that might come to mind when consumers think of FedEx, a leading overnight delivery service, may be "fast," "dependable," and "convenient," with "purple and white packages and envelopes." Even though it is a strong brand association, the color of the packaging may matter little to most consumers when actually choosing an overnight delivery service, although it may perhaps play an important brand awareness function. On the other hand, fast, dependable, and convenient service may be more important in consumer choice, but even then only under certain situations. It may be that someone desires those benefits only when meeting an important deadline. If a consumer only needs a delivery "as soon as possible," then it may be that other less expensive options would be considered (e.g., the U.S. Postal Service's Express Mail).

Chapter 3 considers additional aspects of strength, favorability, and uniqueness of brand associations in terms of brand positioning and introduces the concepts of points of parity and points of difference more formally. The next section outlines a more complete version of the customer-based brand equity model.

BUILDING A STRONG BRAND: THE FOUR STEPS OF BRAND BUILDING

The previous section considered what makes a strong brand. This section considers in more detail how a strong brand is built or created. Building a strong brand, according to the CBBE model, can be thought of in terms of a sequence of steps, in which each step is contingent on successfully achieving the previous step. All the steps involve accomplishing certain objectives with customers-both existing and potential. The steps are as follows:

1. Ensure identification of the brand with customers and an association of the brand in customers' minds with a specific product class or customer need.
2. Firmly establish the totality of brand meaning in the minds of customers by strategically linking a host of tangible and intangible brand associations with certain properties.
3. Elicit the proper customer responses to this brand identification and brand meaning.
4. Convert brand response to create an intense, active loyalty relationship between customers and the brand.

These four steps represent a set of fundamental questions that customers invariably ask about brands—at least implicitly if not even explicitly—as follows (with corresponding brand steps in parentheses).

1. Who are you? (brand identity)
2. What are you? (brand meaning)
3. What about you? What do I think or feel about you? (brand responses)
4. What about you and me? What kind of association and how much of a connection would I like to have with you? (brand relationships)

There is an obvious ordering of the steps in this "branding ladder," from identity to meaning to responses to relationships. That is, meaning cannot be established unless identity has been created; responses cannot occur unless the right meaning has been developed; and a relationship cannot be forged unless the proper responses have been elicited.

Brand Building Blocks

Performing the four steps to create the right brand identity, brand meaning, brand responses, and brand relationship is a complicated and difficult process. To provide some structure, it is useful to think of sequentially establishing six "brand building blocks" with customers. To connote the sequencing involved, these brand building

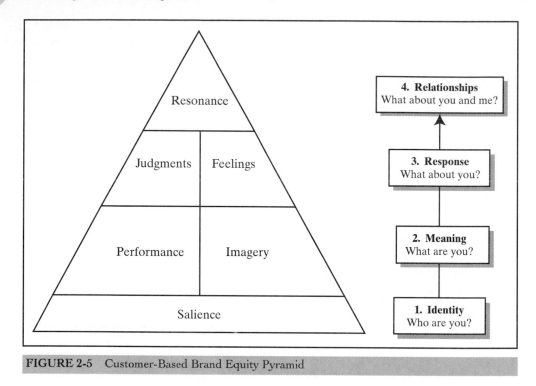

FIGURE 2-5   Customer-Based Brand Equity Pyramid

blocks can be assembled in terms of a brand pyramid. Creating significant brand equity involves reaching the pinnacle of the CBBE brand pyramid and will only occur if the right building blocks are put into place. The corresponding brand steps represent different levels of the CBBE brand pyramid. This brand-building process is illustrated in Figures 2-5 and 2-6, and each of these steps and corresponding brand building blocks and their subdimensions are examined in the following sections.

Brand Salience

Achieving the right brand identity involves creating brand salience with customers. *Brand salience* relates to aspects of the awareness of the brand, for example, how often and easily the brand is evoked under various situations or circumstances. To what extent is the brand top-of-mind and easily recalled or recognized? What types of cues or reminders are necessary? How pervasive is this brand awareness?

As defined previously, *brand awareness* refers to customers' ability to recall and recognize the brand, as reflected by their ability to identify the brand under different conditions. In other words, how well do the brand elements serve the function of identifying the product? Brand awareness is more than just customers knowing the brand name and having previously seen it, perhaps even many times. Brand awareness also involves linking the brand—the brand name, logo, symbol, and so forth—to certain associations in memory. In particular, building brand awareness involves helping customers to understand the product or service category in which the brand competes. There must be clear links regarding what products or services are sold under the brand

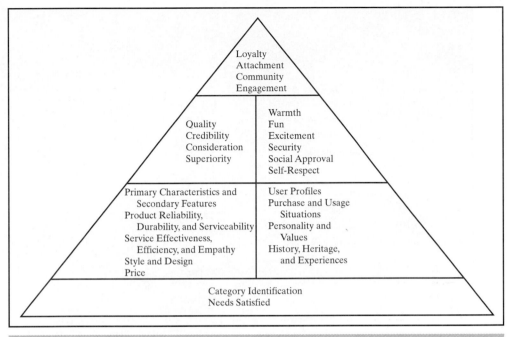

FIGURE 2-6   Subdimensions of Brand Building Blocks

name. At a broader, more abstract level, however, brand awareness also means making sure that customers know which of their "needs" the brand—through these products— is designed to satisfy. In other words, what basic functions does the brand provide to customers?

Breadth and Depth of Awareness

Creating brand awareness thus involves giving the product an identity by linking brand elements to a product category and associated purchase and consumption or usage situations. From a strategic standpoint, it is important to have high levels of brand awareness under a variety of conditions and circumstances. Brand awareness can be characterized according to depth and breadth. The *depth* of brand awareness concerns the likelihood that a brand element will come to mind and the ease with which it does so. For example, a brand that can be easily recalled has a deeper level of brand awareness than one that only can be recognized. The *breadth* of brand awareness concerns the range of purchase and usage situations in which the brand element comes to mind. The breadth of brand awareness depends to a large extent on the organization of brand and product knowledge in memory. To illustrate some of the issues involved, consider the breadth and depth of brand awareness for Tropicana orange juice (see Figure 2-7).

Tropicana

At the most basic level, it is necessary that consumers recognize the Tropicana brand when it is presented or exposed to them. Beyond that, consumers should think of Tropicana whenever they think of orange juice, particularly when they are considering a purchase in that category. Additionally, consumers ideally would think of Tropicana whenever they were

FIGURE 2-7   Tropicana Product Packaging

deciding which type of beverage to drink, especially when seeking a "tasty but healthy" beverage—some of the needs presumably satisfied by orange juice. Thus, consumers must think of Tropicana in terms of satisfying a certain set of needs whenever those needs arise. One of the challenges for any provider of orange juice in that regard is to link the product to usage situations outside of the traditional breakfast usage situation—hence the industry campaign to boost consumption of Florida orange juice that used the slogan "It's not just for breakfast anymore."

Product Category Structure

As suggested by the Tropicana example, to fully understand brand recall, it is important to appreciate *product category structure,* or how product categories are organized in memory. Typically, marketers assume that products are grouped at varying levels of specificity and can be organized in a hierarchical fashion.[23] Thus, in consumers' minds, a product hierarchy often exists, with product class information at the highest level, product category information at the second-highest level, product type information at the next level, and brand information at the lowest level.

The beverage market provides a good setting to examine issues in category structure and the effects of brand awareness on brand equity. Figure 2-8 contains a schematic depiction of one possible hierarchy that might exist in consumers' minds. According to this representation, consumers first distinguish between flavored or non-flavored beverages (i.e., water). Next, they distinguish between nonalcoholic and alcoholic flavored beverages. Nonalcoholic beverages are further distinguished in

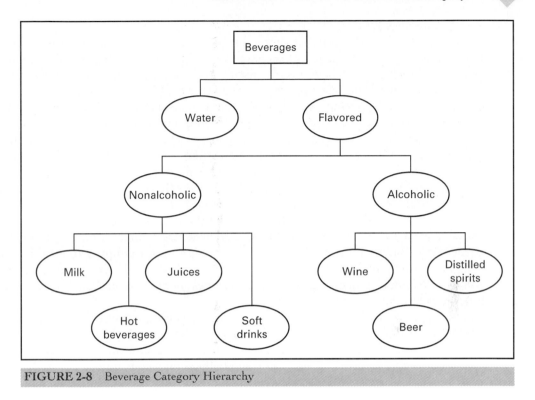

FIGURE 2-8   Beverage Category Hierarchy

consumers' minds by whether they are hot (e.g., coffee or tea) or cold (e.g., milk, juices, or soft drinks); alcoholic beverages are further distinguished by whether they are wine, beer, or distilled spirits. Even further distinctions are possible. For example, the beer category could be further divided into no-alcohol, low-alcohol (or "light"), and full-strength beers. Full-strength beers can be further distinguished along a number of different dimensions—by variety (e.g., ale or lager), by brewing method (e.g., draft, ice, or dry), by price and quality (e.g., discount, premium, or super-premium), and so on.

The organization of the product category hierarchy that generally prevails in memory will play an important role in consumer decision making. For example, consumers often make decisions in what could be considered a top-down fashion. Based on this simple representation, a consumer would first decide whether to have water or some type of flavored beverage. If the consumer chose a flavored drink, then the next decision would be whether or not to have an alcoholic or nonalcoholic drink, and so on. Finally, consumers might then choose the particular brand within the particular product category or product type in which they are interested. The depth of brand awareness would then relate to the likelihood that the brand came to mind, whereas the breadth of brand awareness would relate to the different types of situations in which the brand might come to mind. In general, soft drinks have great breadth of awareness in that they come to mind in a variety of different consumption situations. A consumer may consider drinking one of the different varieties of Coke virtually anytime, anywhere. Other beverages, such as alcoholic beverages, milk, and juices, have much more limited perceived consumption situations.

Strategic Implications

Understanding the product hierarchy has important implications for how to improve brand awareness, as well as how to properly position the brand (as will be addressed in Chapter 3). In terms of building awareness, in many cases, it is not only the depth of awareness that matters but also the breadth of awareness and properly linking the brand to various categories and cues in consumers' minds. In other words, it is important that the brand not only be top-of-mind and have sufficient "mind share," but it must also do so at the right times and places. Breadth is an oft-neglected consideration, even for brands that are category leaders. For many brands, the key question is not whether consumers can recall the brand but where they think of the brand, when they think of the brand, and how easily and often they think of the brand. In particular, many brands and products are ignored or forgotten during possible usage situations. As Chapter 13 shows, increasing the salience of the brand in those settings can be an effective means to drive consumption and increase sales volume. For example, tax preparer H&R Block launched a marketing campaign that attempted to establish the company in the minds of consumers as a "year-round financial services provider" that could provide help with mortgages, insurance, investments, banking, and financial planning services at any time and not just at tax time.[24]

In some cases, the best route for improving sales for a brand is not by improving consumer attitudes toward the brand but, instead, by increasing the breadth of brand awareness and situations in which consumers would consider using the brand. Consider the marketing challenges for Campbell's soup (see Figure 2-9).

FIGURE 2-9   Campbell's Product Portfolio

Campbell's Soup

Ads for Campbell's soup through the years have emphasized either taste (with their long-time advertising slogan "Mmm, Mmm, Good") or nutrition (with the advertising slogan "Never Underestimate the Power of Soup"). Part of Campbell's difficulty in increasing sales may lie not so much with the attitudinal considerations addressed by those ad campaigns as with memory considerations and the fact that people do not think of eating soup as often as they should for certain meal occasions. For example, although soup is often eaten as a side dish or appetizer when people dine at restaurants, it is probably often overlooked for more common dinner occasions at home. Creating a communication program for those consumers who already have a favorable attitude toward soup that will help them remember it in more varied consumption settings may be the most profitable way to grow the Campbell's soup franchise. Perhaps for this reason, Campbell Soup Company launched a $95 million ad campaign in 1999 aimed at convincing consumers that soup was "versatile" and "contemporary" in the hopes of expanding usage occasions.[25]

In other words, it may be harder to try to *change* existing brand attitudes than to *remind* people of their existing attitudes toward a brand in additional, but appropriate, consumption situations.

Summary

A highly salient brand is one that has both depth and breadth of brand awareness, such that customers always make sufficient purchases as well as always think of the brand across a variety of settings in which it could possibly be employed or consumed. Brand salience is an important first step in building brand equity, but is usually not sufficient. For many customers in many situations, other considerations, such as the meaning or image of the brand, also come into play. Creating brand meaning involves establishing a brand image and what the brand is characterized by and should stand for in the minds of customers. Although a myriad of different types of brand associations are possible, brand meaning broadly can be distinguished in terms of more functional, performance-related considerations versus more abstract, imagery-related considerations. Thus, brand meaning is made up of two major categories of brand associations that exist in customers' minds related to performance and imagery, with a set of specific subcategories within each. These brand associations can be formed directly (from a customer's own experiences and contact with the brand) or indirectly (through the depiction of the brand in advertising or by some other source of information, such as word of mouth). The next section describes the two main types of brand meaning—brand performance and brand imagery—and the subcategories within each of those two building blocks.

Brand Performance

The product itself is at the heart of brand equity, because it is the primary influence on what consumers experience with a brand, what they hear about a brand from others, and what the firm can tell customers about the brand in their communications. Designing and delivering a product that fully satisfies consumer needs and wants is a prerequisite for successful marketing, regardless of whether the product is a tangible good, service, organization, or person. To create brand loyalty and resonance, consumers' experiences with the product must at least meet, if not actually surpass, their expectations. As Chapter 1 noted, numerous studies have shown that high-quality brands tend to perform better financially (e.g., yielding higher returns on investment).

Brand performance relates to the ways in which the product or service attempts to meet customers' more functional needs. Thus, brand performance refers to the intrinsic properties of the brand in terms of inherent product or service characteristics. How well does the brand rate on objective assessments of quality? To what extent does the brand satisfy utilitarian, aesthetic, and economic customer needs and wants in the product or service category?

Brand performance transcends the ingredients and features that make up the product or service to encompass aspects of the brand that augment these characteristics. Any of these different performance dimensions can serve as a means by which the brand is differentiated. Often, the strongest brand positioning involves performance advantages of some kind, and it is rare that a brand can overcome severe deficiencies on these dimensions. The specific performance attributes and benefits making up functionality will vary widely by category. Nevertheless, there are five important types of attributes and benefits that often underlie brand performance, as follows:[26]

1. Primary ingredients and supplementary features
2. Product reliability, durability, and serviceability
3. Service effectiveness, efficiency, and empathy
4. Style and design
5. Price

Customers often have beliefs about the levels at which the primary ingredients of the product operate (e.g., low, medium, high, or very high). Additionally, they may have beliefs as to special, perhaps even patented, features or secondary elements of a product that complement these primary ingredients. Thus, some attributes are essential ingredients necessary for a product to work, whereas other attributes are supplementary features that allow for customization and more versatile, personalized usage. These types of attributes vary by product or service category:[27]

➤ *Some categories have few ingredients or features.* For bread, essential ingredients might include the grain and yeast flavors, texture, and nutrition content (in terms of complex carbohydrates, fiber, protein, iron, and vitamins and minerals), with few other distinguishing features.

➤ *Some products have many essential ingredients but few features.* For a toaster oven, essential ingredients might include a housing of plastic and metal; an oven pan, hinged crumb tray, and boiling grid; a clear glass door; 1200- to 1600-watt draw; and 2- to 3-foot power cord. Optional features might include safety features (such as automatic shut-off when the door is opened), a toast-ready bell, and certain settings.

➤ *Some products have numerous ingredients and features.* For a portable tape player or boom box, essential ingredients might include an AM/FM stereo radio, programmable CD player, and at least one cassette deck; at least two speaker drives; an ability to record from radio or CD player; an AC power cord; an ability to operate on batteries; and a telescoping antenna that pivots. Features might include a clock, extra bass, graphic equalizer, extra inputs/outputs, lights, and surround sound, plus extra features for the CD player and cassette deck.

As noted earlier, customers can view the performance of products or services in a broad manner. *Reliability* refers to the consistency of performance over time and from purchase to purchase. *Durability* refers to the expected economic life of the product. *Serviceability* refers to the ease of servicing the product if it needs repair. Thus, perceptions of product performance are affected by factors such as the speed, accuracy, and care of product delivery and installation; the promptness, courtesy, and helpfulness of customer service and training; and the quality of repair service and the time involved.

Customers often have performance-related associations that relate to the service interactions they have with brands. Along those lines, *service effectiveness* refers to how completely the brand satisfies customers' service requirements. *Service efficiency* refers to the manner by which these services are delivered in terms of speed, responsiveness, and so forth. Finally, *service empathy* refers to the extent to which service providers are seen as trusting, caring, and having the customer's interests in mind.

Consumers may have associations with the product that go beyond its functional aspects to more aesthetic considerations such as its size, shape, materials, and color involved. Thus, performance may also depend on sensory aspects such as how a product looks and feels, and perhaps even what it sounds or smells like.

Finally, the pricing policy for the brand can create associations in consumers' minds to the relevant price tier or level for the brand in the category, as well as to its corresponding price volatility or variance (in terms of the frequency or magnitude of discounts, etc.). In other words, the pricing strategy adopted for a brand can dictate how consumers categorize the price of the brand (e.g., as low, medium, or high priced) and how firm or flexible that price is seen (e.g., as frequently or infrequently discounted). Price is a particularly important performance association because consumers often have strong beliefs about the price and value of a brand and may organize their product category knowledge in terms of the price tiers of different brands.[28] Chapter 5 describes issues concerning price associations in greater detail.

Brand Imagery

The other main type of brand meaning involves brand imagery. Brand imagery deals with the extrinsic properties of the product or service, including the ways in which the brand attempts to meet customers' psychological or social needs. Brand imagery is how people think about a brand abstractly, rather than what they think the brand actually does. Thus, imagery refers to more intangible aspects of the brand. Imagery associations can be formed directly (from a consumer's own experiences and contact with the product, brand, target market, or usage situation) or indirectly (through the depiction of these same considerations as communicated in brand advertising or by some other source of information, such as word of mouth). Many kinds of intangibles can be linked to a brand, but four categories can be highlighted:

1. User profiles
2. Purchase and usage situations
3. Personality and values
4. History, heritage, and experiences

One set of brand imagery associations is the type of person or organization who uses the brand. This imagery may result in a profile or mental image by customers of actual users or more aspirational, idealized users. Associations of a typical or idealized brand user may be based on descriptive demographic factors or more abstract psychographic factors. Demographic factors might include the following:

➤ *Gender*. For example, Virginia Slims cigarettes and Secret deodorant have "feminine" associations, whereas Marlboro cigarettes and Right Guard deodorant have more "masculine" associations.

➤ *Age*. For example, Pepsi Cola, Powerade energy sports drink, and Fuji film position themselves as younger than Coke, Gatorade, and Kodak, respectively.

➤ *Race*. For example, Goya foods have a strong identification with the Hispanic market.

➤ *Income*. For example, during the 1980s, Sperry Topsider shoes, Polo shirts, and BMW automobiles became associated with yuppies—young, affluent, urban professionals.

Psychographic factors might include attitudes toward life, careers, possessions, social issues, or political institutions, for example, a brand user might be seen as iconoclastic or as more traditional and conservative. Branding Brief 2-2 describes how clothing retailer Abercrombie & Fitch has targeted a youthful lifestyle by blending trendy fashions, racy catalogs, and a hip store environment to achieve market success.

In a business-to-business setting, user imagery might relate to the size or type of organization. For example, Microsoft might be seen as an "aggressive" company, whereas Patagonia or Timberland might be seen as a "caring" company. User imagery may focus on more than characteristics of just one type of individual and center on broader issues in terms of perceptions of a group as a whole. For example, customers may believe that a brand is used by many people and therefore view the brand as "popular" or a "market leader."

A second set of associations is under what conditions or situations the brand could or should be bought and used. Associations of a typical purchase situation may be based on a number of different considerations, such as type of channel (e.g., seen as sold through department stores, specialty stores, or direct through the Internet or some other means), specific stores (e.g., Macy's, Foot Locker, or Fogdog.com), and ease of purchase and associated rewards (if any).

Similarly, associations of a typical usage situation may be based on a number of different considerations, such as particular time of the day, week, month, or year to use the brand; location to use the brand (e.g., inside or outside the home); and type of activity where the brand is used (e.g., formal or informal). For example, in terms of usage imagery, advertising for Snickers emphasizes that the candy bar is "packed with peanuts" and therefore "satisfies" as a healthy, filling snack. The third-largest U.S. hamburger chain, Wendy's, launched an ad campaign in 2001 to promote its new 1 a.m. closing time to try to capture the late-night market ("Eat Great, Even Late"). At the other end of the spectrum, Burger King began a marketing push for "burgers for breakfast" at the same time. For a long time, pizza chain restaurants had strong associations to their channels of distribution and the manner by which customers would purchase and eat the pizza—Domino's was known for delivery, Little Caesar for carryout, and Pizza Hut for dine-in service—although in recent years each of these major competitors has made inroads in the traditional markets of the others.

BRANDING BRIEF 2-2

Building a Hot Brand at Abercrombie & Fitch

Abercrombie & Fitch is today a staple in the clothing diet of teens and college students, but it was not always as popular. The company originated as an outdoor outfitter located in New York City, but it sold clothing exclusively by the time it was purchased by The Limited in 1988. Since coming to Abercrombie in 1992, CEO Michael Jeffries has transformed the company from a purveyor of conservative men's clothing into a hip casual clothes emporium for 14- to 24-year-olds. When Jeffries arrived at Abercrombie, the company had just 35 store locations, compared with more than 230 today.

Abercrombie's careful selection of its in-store sales force played a large role in building the brand's cachet. To ensure that its stores reflect the lifestyle of its core customer base, Abercrombie fills its sales staff rosters with good-looking college and high school students. The company recruits 75 percent of its salespeople, or "brand representatives," from college campuses near each store location. The visual appeal of the sales staff is of vital importance to creating the right in-store environment. "We're not interested in salespeople or clerks," said one Abercrombie & Fitch representative. "We're interested in finding people who represent the brand's lifestyle, which is the college lifestyle—leaders who have charisma, who portray the image of the brand."

FIGURE A   Sample Abercrombie & Fitch Catalog

The in-store environment of casual "cool" is painstakingly crafted. The employees are required to wear clothing purchased at the store with the 30 to 40 percent discounts offered them by Abercrombie. The employee clothing is coordinated to reflect the seasonal styles, and a shoe chart distributed to stores dictates which sneakers and sandals can be worn with which outfit. At the store entrances, embossed letters "A" and "F" mark spots for greeters to stand on. During peak shopping seasons, Abercrombie hires extra employees to come in after hours and do the restocking and inventory work that would otherwise clutter the sales floor and hamper the normal staff's ability to be cool and casual. According to an Abercrombie executive, greeters and sales staff "are not here [in stores] to fold clothes."

Another contributor to Abercrombie's success is its eye-catching advertising, featuring half-clad models of both sexes. One recent Abercrombie ad featured a completely naked couple sitting astride an elephant. The company also publishes a racy quarterly "magalog"—a catalog designed to look like a magazine—called the *A&F Quarterly* (see Figure A). The first 50 or so pages of the quarterly are devoted to depicting models in various states of undress. Complaints from parents and the Michigan attorney general prompted the company to check IDs of those intending to purchase the $6 magalog to ensure they are 18. The *A&F Quarterly* generated such a buzz that back issues of the magalog sold on eBay for as much as $32.

Source: Abigail Goodman, "Store Most Likely to Succeed," *Los Angeles Times*, 3 April 1999; Lauren Goldstein, "The Alpha Teenager," *Fortune*, 20 December 1999; Melanie Wells, "Anticlimax," *Forbes*, 20 March 2000.

Brands may also take on personality traits.[29] A brand, like a person, can be characterized as being "modern," "old-fashioned," "lively," or "exotic." Brand personality reflects how people feel about a brand as a result of what they think the brand is or does, the manner by which the brand is marketed, and so on. Brands may also take on values. Brand personality is often related to the descriptive usage imagery but also involves much richer, more contextual information. Five dimensions of brand personality (with corresponding subdimensions) that have been identified are sincerity (e.g., down-to-earth, honest, wholesome, and cheerful), excitement (e.g., daring, spirited, imaginative, and up-to-date), competence (e.g., reliable, intelligent, successful), sophistication (e.g., upper class and charming), and ruggedness (e.g., outdoorsy and tough).[30]

How does brand personality get formed? Although any aspect of the marketing program may affect brand personality, advertising may be especially influential because of the inferences consumers make about the underlying user or usage situation depicted in an ad. Advertisers may imbue a brand with personality traits through anthropomorphization and product animation techniques (e.g., California Raisins), personification through the use of brand characters (e.g., Jolly Green Giant), the creation of user imagery (e.g., the Mountain Dew "dudes"), and so on.[31] More generally, advertising may affect brand personality by the manner in which it depicts the brand, for example, the actors in an ad, the tone or style of the creative strategy, and the emotions or feelings evoked by the ad.

Although user imagery, especially as depicted by advertising, is a prime source of brand personality, user imagery and brand personality may not always be in agreement. In product categories where performance-related attributes are more central in consumer decisions (e.g., food products), brand personality and user imagery may be much less related. Differences may arise in other instances as well. For example, at one point in time, Perrier's brand personality was "sophisticated" and "stylish," whereas its actual user imagery was not as flattering or subdued but was seen more as "flashy" and "trendy."

In those categories in which user and usage imagery are important to consumer decisions, however, brand personality and user imagery are more likely to be related (e.g., for cars, beer, liquor, cigarettes, and cosmetics). Thus, consumers often choose and use brands that have a brand personality that is consistent with their own self-concept, although in some cases the match may be based on consumer's desired self-image rather than their actual image.[32] These effects may also be more pronounced for publicly consumed products than for privately consumed goods.[33] On the other hand, consumers who are high "self-monitors" (i.e., sensitive to how others see them) are more likely to choose brands whose personalities fit the consumption situation.[34]

Finally, brands may take on associations to their past and certain noteworthy events in the brand history. These types of associations may involve distinctly personal experiences and episodes or be related to past behaviors and experiences of friends, family, or others. Consequently, these types of associations may be fairly idiosyncratic across people, although sometimes exhibiting certain commonalties. Alternatively, these associations may be more public and broad-based and therefore be shared to a larger degree across people. For example, there may be associations to aspects of the marketing program for the brand, for example, the color of the product or look of its package, the company or person that makes the product and the country in which it is made, the type of store in which it is sold, the events for which the brand is a sponsor, and the people who endorse the brand. In either case, associations to history, heritage, and experiences involve more specific, concrete examples that transcend the generalizations that make up the usage imagery.

Summary

A number of different types of associations related to either performance and imagery may become linked to the brand. Regardless of the type involved, the brand associations making up the brand image and meaning can be characterized and profiled according to three important dimensions—strength, favorability, and uniqueness—that provide the key to building brand equity. Successful results on these three dimensions produce the most positive brand responses, the underpinning of intense and active brand loyalty.

To create brand equity, it is important that the brand have some strong, favorable, and unique brand associations *in that order*. In other words, it doesn't matter how unique a brand association is unless customers evaluate the association favorably, and it doesn't matter how desirable a brand association is unless it is sufficiently strong that customers actually recall it and link it to the brand. At the same time, as noted earlier, it should be recognized that not all strong associations are favorable, and not all favorable associations are unique.

Creating strong, favorable, and unique associations is a real challenge to marketers, but essential in terms of building customer-based brand equity. Strong brands typically have firmly established favorable and unique brand associations with consumers. Examples include Volvo and Michelin (safety), Intel (performance and compatibility), Marlboro (western imagery), Coke (Americana and refreshment), Disney (fun, magic, family entertainment), Nike (innovative products and peak athletic performance), and BMW (styling and driving performance).

Brand meaning is what helps to produce brand responses. *Brand responses* refers to how customers respond to the brand and all its marketing activity and other sources of information—that is, what customers think or feel about the brand. Brand responses can be distinguished according to brand judgments and brand feelings, that is, in terms of whether they arise from the "head" or from the "heart," as the following sections describe.

Brand Judgments

Brand judgments focus on customers' personal opinions and evaluations with regard to the brand. Brand judgments involve how customers put together all the different performance and imagery associations of the brand to form different kinds of opinions. Customers may make all types of judgments with respect to a brand, but in terms of creating a strong brand, four types of summary brand judgments are particularly important: quality, credibility, consideration, and superiority.

Brand Quality

Brand attitudes are defined in terms of consumers' overall evaluations of a brand.[35] Brand attitudes are important because they often form the basis for actions and behavior that consumers take with the brand (e.g., brand choice). Consumers' brand attitudes generally depend on specific considerations concerning the attributes and benefits of the brand. For example, consider Sheraton hotels. A consumer's attitude toward Sheraton depends on how much he or she believes that the brand is characterized by certain associations that matter to the consumer for a hotel chain (e.g., location convenience; room comfort, design, and appearance; service quality of staff; recreational facilities; food service; security; prices; and so on).

There are a host of attitudes that customers may hold toward brands, but the most important relate in various ways to the perceived quality of the brand. Other notable attitudes related to quality pertain to perceptions of value and satisfaction. In the annual EquiTrend survey by Total Research, consumers are asked to rate brands on a scale of 0 to 10, with 10 representing "outstanding/extraordinary quality," 5 representing "quite acceptable quality," and 0 representing "unacceptable/poor quality." Figure 2-10 shows the results of their first syndicated online consumer survey, which revealed 19 top "world class brands" in the U.S. market on the basis of perceived quality.

Brand Credibility

Customers may form judgments that transcend more specific brand quality concerns to consider broader issues related to the company or organization making the product or providing the service associated with the brand. In other words, customers may form judgments with respect to the company or organization behind the brand. As Chapter 11 describes, *brand credibility* refers to the extent to which the brand as a whole is seen as credible in terms of three dimensions: perceived expertise, trustworthiness, and likability. Is the brand seen as (1) competent, innovative, and a market leader (brand expertise); (2) dependable and keeping customer interests in mind (brand trustworthiness); and (3) fun, interesting, and worth spending time with (brand likability)? In other words, credibility concerns whether consumers see the company or

1. Waterford Crystal
2. Rolls-Royce Bentley
3. Craftsman Tools
4. Crayola Crayons and Markers
5. Bose Stereo & Speaker Systems
6. Discovery Channel
7. M&M's Candies
8. WD-40 Spray Lubricant
9. Philadelphia Brand Cream Cheese
10. Arm & Hammer Baking Soda
11. Reynolds Wrap Aluminum Foil
12. Harley-Davidson Motorcycles
13. Kodak Photographic Film
14. Neosporin Ointment
15. Heinz Ketchup
16. *National Geographic* Magazine
17. Master Lock Padlocks
18. Clorox Bleach
19. Reese's Peanut Butter Cups

Brands were rated according to quality by 27,000 U.S. consumers aged 15 or older in an online survey.

FIGURE 2-10 EquiTrend World-Class Brands

organization behind the brand as good at what they do, concerned about their customers, and just plain likable.

Brand Consideration

Eliciting favorable brand attitudes and perceptions of credibility is important but may be insufficient if customers do not actually seriously consider the brand for possible purchase or usage. As noted earlier, consideration is more than mere awareness and deals with the likelihood that customers will include the brand in the set of possible options of brands they might buy or use. Consideration depends in part on how personally relevant customers find the brand, that is, the extent to which customers view the brand as being appropriate and meaningful to themselves. Thus, customers often make an overall appraisal as to whether they have any personal interest in a brand and whether they would or should ever buy a brand. Brand consideration is a crucial filter in terms of building brand equity. No matter how highly regarded or credible a brand may be, unless the brand also receives serious consideration and is deemed relevant, customers will keep a brand at a distance and never closely embrace it. Brand consideration depends in large part on the extent to which strong and favorable brand associations can be created as part of the brand image.

Brand Superiority

Superiority relates to the extent to which customers view the brand as unique and better than other brands. In other words, do customers believe that the brand offers advantages that other brands cannot? Superiority is absolutely critical in terms of building intense and active relationships with customers and depends to a great degree on the number and nature of unique brand associations that make up the brand image.

Brand Feelings

Brand feelings are customers' emotional responses and reactions with respect to the brand. Brand feelings also relate to the social currency evoked by the brand. What feelings are evoked by the marketing program for the brand or by other means? How does the brand affect customers' feelings about themselves and their relationship with others? These feelings can be mild or intense and can be positive or negative.

The emotions evoked by a brand can become so strongly associated that they are accessible during product consumption or use. Researchers have defined *transformational advertising* as advertising designed to change consumer's perceptions of the actual usage experience with the product.[36] For example, Coast soap advertised its brand as the "eye-opener" in an attempt to change consumers' perceptions about what it feels like to use the product (i.e., "invigorating"). Pacific Bell ran a highly successful campaign in California in the mid-1980s that focused on the emotional rewards of calling someone on the telephone as opposed to more practical or functional reasons. Branding Brief 2-3 describes how Hallmark has engendered brand feelings with consumers.

The following are six important types of brand-building feelings.[37]

1. *Warmth:* Soothing types of feelings; the brand makes consumers feel a sense of calm or peacefulness. Consumers may feel sentimental, warmhearted, or affectionate about the brand.
2. *Fun*: Upbeat types of feelings; the brand makes consumers feel amused, lighthearted, joyous, playful, cheerful, and so on.
3. *Excitement:* A different form of upbeat feeling; the brand makes consumers feel energized and feel that they are experiencing something special. Brands that evoke feelings of excitement may result in consumers feeling a sense of elation, of "being alive," or being cool, sexy, or so on.
4. *Security:* The brand produces a feeling of safety, comfort, and self-assurance. As a result of the brand, consumers do not experience worry or concerns that they might have otherwise felt.
5. *Social approval*: The brand results in consumers having positive feelings about the reactions of others; that is, consumers feel that others look favorably on their appearance, behavior, and so on. This approval may be a result of direct acknowledgment of the consumer's use of the brand by others or may be less overt and a result of attribution of product use to consumers.
6. *Self-respect*: The brand makes consumers feel better about themselves; consumers feel a sense of pride, accomplishment, or fulfillment.

The first three types of feelings are experiential and immediate, increasing in level of intensity. The latter three types of feelings are private and enduring, increasing in level of gravity.

Although all types of customer responses are possible—driven from both the head and heart—ultimately what matters is how positive these responses are. Additionally, it is important that the responses are accessible and come to mind when consumers think of the brand. Brand judgments and feelings can only favorably affect consumer behavior if consumers internalize or think of positive responses in their encounters with the brand.

Eliciting Feelings for the Hallmark Brand

Hallmark was launched in 1910 when Joyce C. Hall distributed through the mail a number of postcards he had stored in two shoeboxes under his bed. From his room at the Kansas City YMCA, Hall sent packets containing a hundred of his postcards, along with invoices, to vendors throughout the Midwest. When a third of the vendors returned a check to him, Hallmark was in business. Hallmark quickly expanded into greeting cards, and over the course of the next 90 years moved into other categories such as wrapping paper, gifts, party decorations, and ornaments. The $4 billion company is today the leading greeting card company in the United States, with domestic market share exceeding 50 percent.

Hall demonstrated his knack for branding in 1928 when he began printing the Hallmark name on all cards the company produced. In 1932, the company became a pioneer in licensing when it struck an agreement with Disney to license Disney characters, the first licensing contract for either company. In 1944, the company added the slogan that appears on the back of every card, "When you care enough to send the very best."

FIGURE B   Sample Hallmark Store

One of the company's longest-lasting and highest-profile marketing programs is its sponsorship of the Hallmark Hall of Fame television series, which was introduced in 1951. The Hallmark Hall of Fame has won more Emmy awards than any other television program, including the first-ever Emmy given to a sponsor. A Hallmark executive explained the link between television programming and greeting cards, saying, "What we specialize in is emotional content, whether through greeting cards or movies."

The company initiated a relationship marketing program in 1990 when it began targeting female frequent customers, with the help of an extensive customer database, by sending personalized mailings filled with coupons, incentives, and information about new products. The mailings were designed to resemble the type of personal communication a woman might receive from a sister. The company then created an official loyalty program, called Gold Crown Card, that rewards frequent buyers with discounts and special incentives.

As competition from online greeting card companies such as Blue Mountain and americangreetings.com heated up in the late 1990s, Hallmark entered the e-commerce segment. Its initial Web site, launched in 1996, contained mostly corporate information. A revamped site, opened in 1999, featured free e-cards, a full catalog of gifts and other products, as well as an online calendar and address book that consumers could use to keep track of card and gift giving. To promote the site, Hallmark attached the URL (www.hallmark.com) to all its advertising and printed it on the backs of the billions of cards available in stores.

Sources: Kate Fitzgerald, "Hallmark Casts for New Role," *Advertising Age,* 29 August 1994; Kipp Cheng, "Hallmark.com Revamps Consumer-Targeted Site," *Adweek*, 24 May 1999; Carol Krol, "Hallmark Uses Loyalty Effort for Segmenting Consumers," *Advertising Age*, 1 February 1999; http://www.hallmark.com.

Brand Resonance

The final step of the model focuses on the ultimate relationship and level of identification that the customer has with the brand. *Brand resonance* refers to the nature of this relationship and the extent to which customers feel that they are "in sync" with the brand. Examples of brands with high resonance include Harley-Davidson, Apple, and eBay. Resonance is characterized in terms of intensity, or the depth of the psychological bond that customers have with the brand, as well as the level of activity engendered by this loyalty (e.g., repeat purchase rates and the extent to which customers seek out brand information, events, and other loyal customers). Specifically, brand resonance can be broken down into four categories:

1. Behavioral loyalty
2. Attitudinal attachment
3. Sense of community
4. Active engagement

The first dimension of brand resonance is behavioral loyalty in terms of repeat purchases and the amount or share of category volume attributed to the brand, that is, the "share of category requirements." In other words, how often do customers purchase a brand and how much do they purchase? For bottom-line profit results, the brand must generate sufficient purchase frequencies and volumes. The lifetime value of behaviorally loyal consumers can be enormous.[38] For example, a loyal General Motors customer could be worth $276,000 over his or her lifetime (assuming 11 or more vehicles bought and word-of-mouth endorsement that makes friends and relatives more likely to consider GM products). Similarly, experts have estimated that the lifetime value of a sophisticated computer user (defined as one who buys a new machine and software about every two years) is approximately $45,000. A nonsophisticated user who postpones purchases as long as possible was estimated to provide $25,000 in lifetime value.

Behavioral loyalty is necessary but not sufficient for resonance to occur.[39] Some customers may buy out of necessity—buying because the brand is the only product being stocked or readily accessible, the only one they can afford to buy, and so on. To create resonance, there also needs to be a strong personal attachment. Customers should go beyond having a positive attitude to viewing the brand as being something special in a broader context. For example, customers with a great deal of attitudinal attachment to a brand may state that they "love" the brand, describe it as one of their favorite possessions, or view it as a "little pleasure" that they look forward to.

Prior research has shown that mere satisfaction may not be enough.[40] Xerox found that if customer satisfaction was ranked on a scale of 1 (completely dissatisfied) to 5 (completely satisfied), customers who rated their products and services as "4"—and thus were satisfied—were six times more likely to defect to competitors than those customers who provided ratings of "5."[41] Similarly, loyalty guru Frederick Reichheld points out that although more than 90 percent of car buyers are satisfied or very satisfied when they drive away from the dealer's showroom, fewer than half buy the same brand of automobile the next time.[42] Creating greater loyalty requires deeper attitudinal attachment, which can be generated by developing marketing programs and products and services that fully satisfy consumer needs.

The brand may also take on broader meaning to the customer in terms of a sense of community.[43] Identification with a brand community may reflect an important social phenomenon whereby customers feel a kinship or affiliation with other people associated with the brand. These connections may involve fellow brand users or customers or may involve employees or representatives of the company. Branding Brief 2-4 profiles three company-initiated programs to help build brand communities.

Finally, perhaps the strongest affirmation of brand loyalty is when customers are willing to invest time, energy, money, or other resources in the brand beyond those expended during purchase or consumption of the brand. For example, customers may choose to join a club centered on a brand, receive updates, and exchange correspondence with other brand users or formal or informal representatives of the brand itself. They may choose to visit brand-related Web sites, participate in chat rooms, and so on. In this case, customers themselves became brand evangelists and ambassadors and help to communicate about the brand and strengthen the brand ties of others. Strong attitudinal attachment or social identity or both are typically necessary, however, for active engagement with the brand to occur.

BRANDING BRIEF 2-4

Building Brand Communities

APPLE

Apple encourages owners of its computers to form local Apple user groups. By 2001, there were over 600 groups, ranging in size from fewer than 25 members to over 1,000 members. The user groups provide Apple owners with opportunities to learn more about their computers, share ideas, and get product discounts, as well as sponsor special activities and events and perform community service. A visit to Apple's Web site helps customers find nearby user groups.

HARLEY-DAVIDSON

The world-famous motorcycle company sponsors the Harley Owners Group (HOG), which now numbers 550,000 members in over 1,200 chapters. The first-time buyer of a Harley-Davidson motorcycle gets a free one-year membership. HOG benefits include a magazine called *Hog Tales*, a touring handbook, emergency road service, a specially designed insurance program, theft reward service, discount hotel rates, and a Fly & Ride program enabling members to rent Harleys while on vacation. The company also maintains an extensive Web site devoted to HOG, which includes information on club chapters and events and features a special members-only section.

JEEP

In addition to the hundreds of local Jeep enthusiast clubs throughout the world, Jeep owners can convene with their vehicles in wilderness areas across America as part of the company's official Jeep Jamborees and Camp Jeep. Since the inaugural Camp Jeep in 1995, over 28,000 people have attended the three-day sessions, where they practice off-road driving skills and meet other Jeep owners. Jeep Jamborees bring Jeep owners and their families together for two-day off-road adventures in more than 30 different locations from spring through autumn each year.

In summary, brand relationships can be usefully characterized in terms of two dimensions: intensity and activity. *Intensity* refers to the strength of the attitudinal attachment and sense of community. In other words, how deeply felt is the loyalty? *Activity* refers to how frequently the consumer buys and uses the brand, as well as engages in other activities not related to purchase and consumption. In other words, in how many different ways does brand loyalty manifest itself in day-to-day consumer behavior? Branding Brief 2-5 describes some of MTV's branding efforts in creating resonance with its customers in the fiercely competitive cable television industry.

Building Resonance with the MTV Brand

Many of the cable television networks have created extensive marketing programs to build an identity for their channel and create loyalty and regular viewership. The competition in the cable TV industry to achieve sufficient "mind share" and loyalty with consumers is critically important in a marketplace where viewers can switch between channels with the flick of a dial or the push of a button. Cable television networks have built strong consumer franchises through extensive marketing programs that include Web sites, licensed products, and channel extension.

Viacom's MTV music television is one network that has gone beyond playing music videos to capture (and sell) the lifestyle of a generation. With the slogan "MTV. You'll never look at music the same way again," they began 24-hour programming of music videos introduced by personable "VJs" with their launch on August 1, 1981. The cable channel's rebellious and irreverent manner was the perfect formula to attract the 12- to 34-year-olds of that generation. Quickly embraced by America's youth, MTV became a powerful tool for advertisers who saw it as a means to reach and influence teenagers and young adults. Ads employing cutting-edge animation and cinematic techniques and whose artistic sensibility seamlessly merged with the elaborately produced music videos were created with MTV in mind. Through their programming, personalities, and promotions, MTV created an extremely desirable brand image with associations of "young," "hip," and "daring."

Unfortunately, most MTV viewers were in the habit of only watching for short periods of time as they journeyed around the dial. By the mid-1990s, MTV's ratings were suffering. To revitalize the brand and create the stable viewing patterns that advertisers desire, MTV made a number of changes, such as packaging music into more of a traditional show format and developing long-form programming that was not music based (e.g., *The Real World, Road Rules, The Tom Greene Show, Undressed,* and *Daria*). Additionally, MTV created greater viewer connection through activities surrounding their Times Square studio in New York City, contests such as "So You Want to Be a VJ," and on-air requests through their TRL show.

Riding a teen pop wave, MTV's ratings soared in the late 1990s. To capitalize on its popularity, 22 different regional versions of MTV have been launched in India, China, Taiwan, Australia, different parts of Europe, Russia, and Brazil and the rest of Latin America. Of the 116 million households who watch MTV every day, 70 million come from outside the United States. Although 60 percent of the total programming emanates from the United States, 70 percent of the music programming is local. The MTV name has also been used to introduce new merchandising products, movies, and media.

MTV's ability to create such strong resonance with its target market is a product of their rich set of brand values (e.g., musicality, credibility, personality, accessibility, interactivity, community, modernity, spontaneity, originality, and fluidity) and a well-conceived and executed marketing program to tap into those values. MTV faces a number of challenges going forward, such as cultivating and developing their brand equity, aligning their brand image with their Viacom siblings VH1 and Nickelodeon, and creating a distinct identity for their all-music spin-off, MTV2.

BRAND-BUILDING IMPLICATIONS

The importance of the customer-based brand equity model is in the road map and guidance it provides for brand building. It provides a yardstick by which brands can assess their progress in their brand-building efforts as well as a guide for marketing research initiatives. With respect to the latter, one CBBE application is in terms of brand tracking and providing quantitative measures of the success of brand-building efforts (see Chapter 8). Figure 2-11 contains a set of candidate measures for the six brand building blocks. The model also reinforces a number of important branding tenets, five of which are particularly noteworthy and are discussed in the following sections.

Customers Own Brands

The basic premise of the CBBE model is that the true measure of the strength of a brand depends on how consumers think, feel, and act with respect to that brand. In particular, the strongest brands will be those brands for which consumers become so attached and passionate that they, in effect, become evangelists or missionaries and attempt to share their beliefs and spread the word about the brand. *The key point to recognize is that the power of the brand and its ultimate value to the firm resides with customers.* It is through customers learning about and experiencing a brand that they end up thinking and acting in a way that allows the firm to reap the benefits of brand equity. Although marketers must take responsibility for designing and implementing the most effective and efficient brand-building marketing programs possible, the success of those marketing efforts ultimately depends on how consumers respond. This response, in turn, depends on the knowledge that has been created in their minds for those brands.

Don't Take Shortcuts with Brands

The CBBE model reinforces the fact that there are no shortcuts in building a brand. A great brand is not built by accident but is the product of carefully accomplishing—either explicitly or implicitly—a series of logically linked steps with consumers (see Figure 2-12). The more explicitly the steps are recognized and defined as concrete goals, the more likely it is that they will receive the proper attention and thus be fully realized, providing the greatest contribution to brand building. *The length of time to build a strong brand will therefore be directly proportional to the amount of time it takes to create sufficient awareness and understanding so that firmly held and felt beliefs and attitudes about the brand are formed that can serve as the foundation for brand equity.*

The brand-building steps may not be equally difficult. In particular, creating brand identity is a step that an effectively designed marketing program often can accomplish in a relatively short period of time. Unfortunately, this step is the one that many brand marketers tend to skip in their mistaken haste to quickly establish an image for the brand (as is evident by the numerous failed dot-com brands whose target market had no inkling as to what they did). As Chapter 3 describes, it is difficult for consumers to appreciate the advantages and uniqueness of a brand unless they have some sort of

FIGURE 2-11   Possible Measures of Brand Building Blocks

I.   Salience

What brands of product or service category can you think of?
   (using increasingly specific product category cues)
Have you ever heard of these brands?
Which brands might you be likely to use under the following situations . . . ?
How frequently do you think of this brand?

II.   Performance

Compared with other brands in the category, how well does this brand provide the
    basic functions of the product or service category?
Compared with other brands in the category, how well does this brand satisfy the
    basic needs of the product or service category?
To what extent does this brand have special features?
How reliable is this brand?
How durable is this brand?
How easily serviced is this brand?
How effective is this brand's service? Does it completely satisfy your requirements?
How efficient is this brand's service in terms of speed, responsiveness, and so forth?
How courteous and helpful are the providers of this brand's service?
How stylish do you find this brand?
How much do you like the look, feel, and other design aspects of this brand?
Compared with other brands in the category with which it competes, are this brand's
    prices generally higher, lower, or about the same?
Compared with other brands in the category with which it competes, do this brand's
    prices change more frequently, less frequently, or about the same amount?

III.   Imagery

To what extent do people you admire and respect use this brand?
How much do you like people who use this brand?
How well do the following words describe this brand: down-to-earth, honest, daring,
    up-to-date, reliable, successful, upper class, charming, outdoorsy?
What places are appropriate to buy this brand?
How appropriate are the following situations to use this brand?
Can you buy this brand in a lot of places?
Is this a brand that you can use in a lot of different situations?
To what extent does thinking of the brand bring back pleasant memories?
To what extent do you feel you grew up with the brand?

IV.   Judgments

Quality
What is your overall opinion of this brand?
What is your assessment of the product quality of this brand?
To what extent does this brand fully satisfy your product needs?
How good a value is this brand?

Credibility
How knowledgeable are the makers of this brand?
How innovative are the makers of this brand?
How much do you trust the makers of this brand?
To what extent do the makers of this brand understand your needs?
To what extent do the makers of this brand care about your opinions?
To what extent do the makers of this brand have your interests in mind?

(Continued)

FIGURE 2-11 *(Continued)*

Credibility (cont.)

How much do you like this brand?

How much do you admire this brand?

How much do you respect this brand?

Consideration

How likely would you be to recommend this brand to others?

Which are your favorite products in this brand category?

How personally relevant is this brand to you?

Superiority

How unique is this brand?

To what extent does this brand offer advantages that other brands cannot?

How superior is this brand to others in the category?

V. Feelings

Does this brand give you a feeling of warmth?

Does this brand give you a feeling of fun?

Does this brand give you a feeling of excitement?

Does this brand give you a feeling of security?

Does this brand give you a feeling of social approval?

Does this brand give you a feeling of self-respect?

VI. Resonance

Loyalty

I consider myself loyal to this brand.

I buy this brand whenever I can.

I buy as much of this brand as I can.

I feel this is the only brand of this product I need.

This is the one brand I would prefer to buy/use.

If this brand were not available, it would make little difference to me if I had to use another brand.

I would go out of my way to use this brand.

Attachment

I really love this brand.

I would really miss this brand if it went away.

This brand is special to me.

This brand is more than a product to me.

Community

I really identify with people who use this brand.

I feel like I almost belong to a club with other users of this brand.

This is a brand used by people like me.

I feel a deep connection with others who use this brand.

Engagement

I really like to talk about this brand to others.

I am always interested in learning more about this brand.

I would be interested in merchandise with this brand's name on it.

I am proud to have others know I use this brand.

I like to visit the Web site for this brand.

Compared with other people, I follow news about this brand closely.

It should be recognized that the core brand values at the bottom two levels of the pyramid—brand salience, performance, and imagery—are typically more idiosyncratic and unique to a product and service category than other brand values.

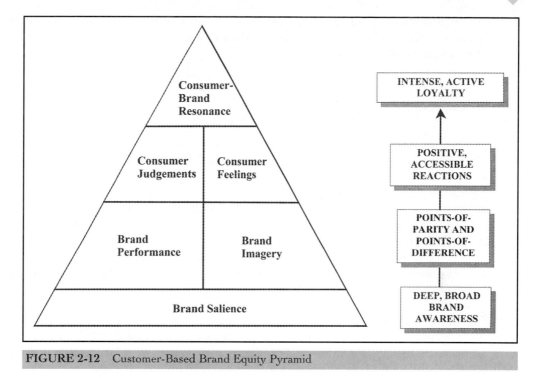

FIGURE 2-12   Customer-Based Brand Equity Pyramid

frame of reference as to what the brand is supposed to do and with whom or what it is supposed to compete. Similarly, it is difficult for consumers to achieve high levels of positive responses without having a reasonably complete understanding of the various dimensions and characteristics of the brand.

Finally, due to circumstances in the marketplace, it may be the case that consumers may actually start a repeated-purchase or behavioral loyalty relationship with a brand without having much underlying feelings, judgments, or associations. Nevertheless, these other brand building blocks will have to come into place at some point to create true resonance. That is, although the start point may differ, the same steps in brand building eventually must occur to create a truly strong brand.

Brands Should Have a Duality

One important point reinforced by the model is that a strong brand has a duality. A strong brand appeals to both the head *and* the heart. Thus, although there are perhaps two different ways to build loyalty and resonance-going up the left-hand side of the pyramid in terms of product-related performance associations and resulting judgments or going up the right-hand side in terms of non-product-related imagery associations and resulting feelings—strong brands often do both. *Strong brands blend product performance and imagery to create a rich, varied, but complementary set of consumer responses to the brand.* By appealing to both rational and emotional concerns, a strong brand provides consumers with multiple access points to the brand while reducing competitive vulnerability. Rational concerns can satisfy utilitarian needs, whereas emotional concerns can satisfy psychological or emotional needs. Combining the two allows brands to create a formidable brand position.

Brands Should Have Richness

The level of detail in the CBBE model highlights the number of possible ways to create meaning with consumers and the range of possible avenues to elicit consumer responses. Collectively, these various aspects of brand meaning and the resulting responses produce strong consumer bonds to the brand. The various associations making up the brand image may be reinforcing, helping to strengthen or increase the favorability of other brand associations, or may be unique, helping to add distinctiveness or offset some potential deficiencies. Strong brands thus have both breadth (in terms of duality) *and* depth (in terms of richness).

At the same time, brands should not necessarily be expected to score highly on all the various dimensions and categories making up each core brand value. Building blocks can have hierarchies in their own right. For example, with respect to brand awareness, it is typically important to first establish category identification in some way before considering strategies to expand brand breadth via needs satisfied or benefits offered. With brand performance, it is often necessary to first link primary characteristics and related features before attempting to link additional, more peripheral associations. Similarly, brand imagery often begins with a fairly concrete initial articulation of user and usage imagery that, over time, leads to broader, more abstract brand associations of personality, value, history, heritage, and experience. Brand judgments usually begin with positive quality and credibility perceptions that can lead to brand consideration and then perhaps ultimately to assessments of brand superiority. Brand feelings usually start with either experiential ones (i.e., warmth, fun, and excitement) or inward ones (i.e., security, social approval, and self-respect.) Finally, resonance again has a clear ordering, whereby behavioral loyalty is a starting point but attitudinal attachment or a sense of community is almost always needed for active engagement to occur.

Brand Resonance Provides Important Focus

As implied by the model construction, brand resonance is the pinnacle of the CBBE model and provides important focus and priority for decision making regarding marketing. Marketers building brands should use brand resonance as a goal and a means to interpret their brand-related marketing activities. The question to ask is, To what extent is marketing activity affecting the key dimensions of brand resonance—consumer loyalty, attachment, community, or engagement with the brand? Is marketing activity creating brand performance and imagery associations and consumer judgments and feelings that will support these brand resonance dimensions? In an application of the CBBE model, the marketing research firm Knowledge Networks found that brands that scored highest on loyalty and attachment dimensions were not necessarily the same ones that scored high on community and engagement dimensions (see Figure 2-13).

Rank Order	Brand Loyalty	Brand Attachment	Brand Community	Brand Engagement
1	Harley Davidson	Harley Davidson	Harley Davidson	Harley Davidson
2	Hershey's	Hershey's	Lifetime Television	Lifetime Television
3	Campbell's	Campbell's	Public Broadcasting	Lexus
4	Clorox	Discovery Channel	Fidelity Investments	Discovery Channel
5	Heinz	BMW	MSN	Public Broadcasting
6	Kodak	Wal-Mart	Lexus	Wal-Mart
7	Kraft	Public Broadcasting	Discovery Channel	BMW
8	Wal-Mart	Kraft	AOL.com	Dell
9	Duracell	Kodak	Chevrolet	Toyota
10	Discovery Channel	NBC	Hershey's	Fidelity Investments

FIGURE 2-13   Brand Rankings on Resonance Dimensions (United States, Fall 2001)

Yet, it must also be recognized that it is virtually impossible for consumers to experience an intense, active loyalty relationship with all the brands they purchase and consume. Thus, some brands will be more meaningful to consumers than others, in part because of the nature of their associated product or service, the characteristics of the consumer, and so on. In those cases in which it may be difficult to create a varied set of feelings and imagery associations, marketers might not be able to obtain the "deeper" aspects of brand resonance (e.g., active engagement). Nevertheless, by taking a broader view of brand loyalty, marketers may be able to gain a more holistic appreciation for their brand and how it connects to consumers. By defining the proper role for the brand, higher levels of brand resonance should be obtainable.

Review

Customer-based brand equity is the differential effect that brand knowledge has on consumer response to the marketing of that brand. A brand has positive customer-based brand equity when customers react more favorably to a product and the way it is marketed when the brand is identified than when it is not (e.g., when it is attributed to a fictitiously named or unnamed version of the product).

Brand knowledge can be defined in terms of an associative network memory model as a network of nodes and links wherein the brand node in memory has a variety of associations linked to it. Brand knowledge can be characterized in terms of two components: brand awareness and brand image. Brand awareness is related to the strength of the brand node or trace in memory, as reflected by consumers' ability to recall or recognize the brand under different conditions. Brand awareness can be characterized by depth and breadth. The depth of brand awareness relates to the likelihood that the brand can be recognized or recalled. The breadth of brand awareness relates to the variety of purchase and consumption situations in which the brand comes to mind. Brand image is defined as consumer perceptions of a brand as reflected by the brand associations held in consumers' memory.

Customer-based brand equity occurs when the consumer has a high level of awareness and familiarity with the brand and holds some strong, favorable, and unique brand associations in memory. In some cases, brand awareness alone is sufficient to result in more favorable consumer response—for example, in low-involvement decision settings where consumers are willing to base their choices merely on familiar brands. In other cases, the strength, favorability, and uniqueness of the brand associations play a critical role in determining the differential response making up the brand equity.

To create the differential response that leads to customer-based brand equity, it is important to associate unique, meaningful points of difference to the brand to provide a competitive advantage and a "reason why" consumers should buy it. For some brand associations, however, it may be sufficient that they are seen as roughly equally favorable with competing brand associations so that they function as points of parity in consumers' minds to negate potential points of difference for competitors. In other words, these associations are designed to provide consumers "no reason why not" to choose the brand. Assuming a positive brand image is created by marketing programs that link strong, favorable, and unique associations to the brand in memory, a number of benefits can result.

The CBBE model maintains that building a strong brand involves a series of logical steps: (1) establishing the proper brand identity, (2) creating the appropriate brand meaning, (3) eliciting the right brand responses, and (4) forging appropriate brand relationships with customers. Specifically, according to this model, building a strong brand involves establishing breadth and depth of brand awareness; creating strong, favorable, and unique brand associations; eliciting positive, accessible brand responses; and forging intense, active brand relationships. Achieving these four steps, in turn, involves establishing six brand building blocks: brand salience, brand performance, brand imagery, brand judgments, brand feelings, and brand resonance.

The strongest brands excel on all six of these dimensions and thus fully execute all four steps of building a brand. In the CBBE model, the most valuable brand building block, brand resonance, occurs when all the other core brand values are completely "in sync" with respect to customers' needs, wants, and desires. In other words, brand resonance reflects a completely harmonious relationship between customers and the brand. With true brand resonance, customers have a high degree of loyalty marked by a close relationship with the brand such that customers actively seek means to interact with the brand and share their experiences with others. Firms that are able to achieve resonance and affinity with their customers should reap a host of valuable benefits, such as greater price premiums and more efficient and effective marketing programs.

Thus, the basic premise of the CBBE model is that the true measure of the strength of a brand depends on how consumers think, feel, and act with respect to that brand.

Achieving brand resonance requires eliciting the proper cognitive appraisals and emotional reactions to the brand from customers. That, in turn, necessitates establishing brand identity and creating the right meaning in terms of brand performance and brand imagery associations. A brand with the right identity and meaning can result in a customer believing that the brand is relevant and "my kind of product." The strongest brands will be those brands for which consumers become so attached and passionate that they, in effect, become evangelists or missionaries and attempt to share their beliefs and spread the word about the brand.

Discussion Questions

1. Pick a brand. Attempt to identify its sources of brand equity. Assess its level of brand awareness and the strength, favorability, and uniqueness of its associations.
2. Which brands do you have the most resonance with? Why?
3. Can every brand achieve resonance with its customers? Why or why not?
4. Pick a brand. Assess the extent to which the brand is achieving the various benefits of brand equity.
5. Can you think of any other benefits of creating a strong brand? What might they be?

Brand Focus 2.0

The Marketing Advantages of Strong Brands[44]

Customer-based brand equity occurs when consumer response to marketing activity differs when consumers know the brand and when they do not. The actual nature of how that response differs will depend on the level of brand awareness and how favorably and uniquely consumers evaluate brand associations, as well as the particular marketing activity under consideration. A number of benefits can result from a strong brand, both in terms of greater revenue and lower costs.[44] For example, Ian Lewis from Time-Life categorizes the factors creating financial value for strong brands into two categories: factors related to growth (e.g., a brand's ability to attract new customers, resist competitive activity, introduce line extensions, and cross international borders) and factors related to profitability (e.g., brand loyalty, premium pricing, lower price elasticity, lower advertising/sales ratios, and trade leverage).[45]

This appendix considers in detail some of the benefits to the firm of having brands with a high level of awareness and a positive brand image.

GREATER LOYALTY AND LESS VULNERABILITY TO COMPETITIVE MARKETING ACTIONS AND CRISES

Prior research has demonstrated that different types of brand associations—if seen as favorable—can affect consumer product evaluations, perceptions of quality, and purchase rates.[46] This tendency may be especially apparent with difficult-to-assess "experience" goods[47] and as the uniqueness of brand associations increases.[48] In addition, familiarity with a brand has been shown to increase consumer confidence, attitude toward the brand, and purchase intention[49] and mitigate the potential negative impact of a negative trial experience.[50]

For these and other reasons, one characteristic of brands with a great deal of equity is that consumers feel great loyalty to the brand. For example, as noted in Chapter 1, at least some top brands have been market leaders for years despite the fact that there undoubtedly have been significant changes in both consumer attitudes and competitive activity over this period of time. Through it all, consumers have valued these brands—what they are and what they represent—sufficiently enough to stick with them and reject the overtures of competitors, creating a steady stream of revenues for the firm. Prior academic research in a variety of industry contexts also has found that brands with large market shares are more likely to have more loyal customers than brands with small market shares, a phenomenon dubbed *double jeopardy*.[51]

Brand loyalty is closely related to brand equity but is a distinct concept. Brand loyalty is often measured in a behavioral sense through the number of repeat purchases. Yet, a consumer may continually purchase for reasons not related to a strong preference for the brand, such as when the brand is prominently stocked or frequently promoted. Consumers may be in the habit of buying a particular brand without really thinking much about why. When confronted by a new or resurgent competitor providing compelling reasons to switch, consumers' ties to the brand may be tested for the first time.

The bottom line is that repeat buying is a necessary but not sufficient condition for being a brand-loyal buyer in an attitudinal sense: Someone can repeat buy but not be brand loyal. Brand loyalty is one of the many advantages of creating a positive brand image and of having brand equity. Thus, brand loyalty is related to, but distinct from, brand equity.

Returning to the benefits of brand equity, a brand with a positive brand image also is more likely to successfully weather a brand crisis or downturn in the brand's fortunes.[52] Perhaps the most compelling example of this fact is Johnson and Johnson's (J&J) Tylenol brand. Brand Focus 6.0 describes how J&J contended with a tragic product-tampering episode with their Tylenol pain reliever in the early 1980s. Despite having seen their market share drop from 37 percent to almost zero overnight and having Tylenol be written off as a brand with no future, J&J was able to regain virtually all lost Tylenol market share through the skillful handling of a marketing crisis and a good deal of brand equity.

The important lesson from J&J's Tylenol crisis is that effective handling of a marketing crisis requires swift and sincere actions. There must be an immediate admission that something has gone wrong and a an assurance that an effective remedy will be put in place. Most important, the greater the brand equity, the more likely it is that these statements will have the necessary credibility with consumers so that they will be both understanding and patient as the firm sets out to solve the crisis. Without some underlying brand equity, however, even the best-laid plans for recovery may fall short to a suspicious or unknowing public.[53] Finally, it should also be recognized that even if there is not a crisis per se, a strong brand offers some protection in the case of a marketing downturn or when the brand's fortunes fall.

LARGER MARGINS

Brands with positive customer-based brand equity can command a price premium.[54] Moreover, consumers should also have a fairly inelastic response to price increases and elastic responses to price decreases or discounts for the brand over time.[55] Consistent with this reasoning, research has shown that consumers loyal to a brand are less likely to switch in the face of price increases and more likely to increase the quantity of the brand purchased in the face of price decreases.[56] In a competitive sense, brand leaders draw a disproportionate amount of share from smaller-share competitors.[57] At the same time, prior research has demonstrated that market leaders are relatively immune to price competition from these small-share brands.[58]

In an analysis of consumer goods manufacturers from the extensive PIMS database, Boulding, Lee, and Staelin found that by providing unique and positive messages, a firm could insulate itself from future price competition, as witnessed by less negative future price elasticities. Conversely, they also found that nonunique messages could decrease future differentiation; for example, price promotions for firms that priced above the industry average led to more negative future price elasticities.[59]

The results of a study by the marketing research firm Intelliquest exploring the role of brand name and price in the decision purchase of business computer buyers is enlightening in that regard.[60] Survey respondents were asked, "What is the incremental dollar value you would be willing to pay over a 'no-name' clone computer brand?" IBM commanded the greatest price premium, followed by Compaq and Hewlett-Packard.

Some brands had negative brand equity; they actually received negative numbers. Clearly, according to this study, brands have specific meaning in the personal computer market that consumers value and will pay for.

At the same time, many firms have learned the hard way that consumers will not pay price premiums that exceed their perceptions of the value of a brand. Perhaps the most vivid illustration of this fact was the experience of Marlboro, Philip Morris's leading cigarette brand.[61] Branding Brief 2-6 describes how Philip Morris was forced to drop their prices on Marlboro so that they were more in line with discount and store brands that were gaining increased market share at Marlboro's expense. Although the Marlboro price discounts led to short-term profitability declines, they also led to regained market share that put the brand on stronger footing over the longer haul.

Two important lessons emerged from the Marlboro episode. First, strong brands can command price premiums. Once Marlboro's price difference entered a more acceptable range, consumers were then willing to pay the still-higher price to be able to buy Marlboro, and the sales of the brand started to increase. Second, strong brands cannot command an excessive price premium. The clear signal sent to marketers everywhere by Philip Morris's experience with Marlboro is that price hikes without corresponding investments in the value of the brand may increase the vulnerability of the brand to lower-priced competition. In these cases, consumers may be willing to "trade down" because they no longer can justify to themselves that the higher-priced brand is worth it.

Although much of the popular press attempted to exploit Marlboro's actions to proclaim that "brands were dead," nothing could have been further from the truth. In fact, a more accurate interpretation of the whole episode is that it showed that new brands were entering the scene, as evidenced by the ability of discount brands to create their own brand equity on the basis of strong consumer associations to "value." At the same time, existing brands, if properly managed, can command loyalty, enjoy price premiums, and still be extremely profitable. Chapter 5 reviews pricing strategies and discount policies to build brand equity.

GREATER TRADE COOPERATION AND SUPPORT

Marketers often do not sell directly to consumers. In these cases, middlemen in the form of wholesalers, retailers, and other parties play an important role in the selling of the product. The activities of these members of the channels of distribution can thus facilitate or inhibit the success of the brand. If the brand has a positive brand image with consumers, it is more likely to receive favorable treatment from the trade.

Specifically, a brand with a positive brand image is more likely to have retailers and other middlemen respond to the wishes of consumers and actively promote and sell the brand.[62] Recognizing the likelihood of this consumer demand, channel members are also less likely to require any marketing push from the manufacturer and are more likely to be receptive to any marketing overtures that do arise from the manufacturer to stock, reorder, and display the brand.[63] Thus, they should be more likely to pass through trade promotions, demand smaller slotting allowances, give more favorable shelf space or position, and so on.

In short, brands with positive customer-based brand equity are more likely to receive greater trade cooperation and support. This treatment might translate into more prominent and desirable shelf placements or store locations, more attractive promotional offers and displays, and so on. Given that many consumer decisions are

---

Marlboro's Price Drop

On April 2, 1993, or "Marlboro Friday," Philip Morris dropped a bombshell in the form of a three-page announcement: "Philip Morris USA . . . announced a major shift in business strategy designed to increase market share and grow long-term profitability in a highly price sensitive market environment." Quoting tobacco unit President and CEO William I. Campbell, the statement continued, "We have determined that in the current market environment caused by prolonged economic softness and depressed consumer confidence, we should take those steps necessary to grow our market share rather than pursue rapid income growth rates that might erode our leading market-place position." Specifically, Philip Morris announced four major steps:

1. An extensive retail promotional program.
2. Greatly expanded spending and attention to the Marlboro Adventure Team continuity program begun in October 1992. Presented to consumers through direct mail and advertising, the program worked much like a catalog: Consumers who saved empty Marlboro packs could send them to Philip Morris in return for free merchandise.
3. An increased effort to take share in the discount cigarette market with a new push behind the company's low-priced Basic brand (although Philip Morris sold 48 percent of the premium cigarettes, they only held a 19 percent share of the discount market).
4. A major promotional cut in the price of Marlboro (roughly 40 to 50 cents a pack), which was expected to decrease earnings in Philip Morris's most profitable unit by 40 percent.

The fourth proposed action caught the eye of marketers and Wall Street alike. The action was justified by the results of a month-long test in Portland, Oregon, the previous December in which a 40-cent decrease in pack price had increased market share by 4 points. The stock market reaction to the announcement was swift. By day's end, Philip Morris's stock price had declined from $64.12 to $49.37, a 23 percent drop that represented a one-day loss of $13 billion in shareholder equity! There was a ripple effect in the stock market, with significant stock price declines for other consumer goods companies with major brands (e.g., Sara Lee, Kellogg's, General Mills, and Procter & Gamble). The Dow Jones Industrial Average dropped 68.63 points, 30 points attributable to Philip Morris alone. A company that took one of the biggest hits was Coca-Cola, whose shareholders lost $5 billion in paper in the days following "Black Friday." Feeling that the stock market was overreacting, the Coca-Cola Company went to great pains to explain to the financial community that the marketing situation faced by their brands differed from the Marlboro situation. Branding Brief 2–7 contains some of the comparisons they made in their presentation to analysts.

A number of factors probably provided the impetus for why Marlboro felt compelled to cut prices so dramatically. The economy certainly was still sluggish coming out of a recession. Private label or store brand cigarettes had been increasing in quality and were receiving more attention from customers and retailers. A prime consideration suggested by many was related to Philip Morris's hefty price increases. These price hikes had often occurred two to three times a year and had been above the rate of inflation (as much as 10 percent in a year). The 80 cents to $1 difference between premium brands and discount brands that was prevailing at that time was thought to have resulted in steady sales increases for the discount brands. The growth in sales of those brands came at the expense of Marlboro market share, which had dropped to 22 percent and was further projected to decline to 18 percent if Philip Morris had made no changes.

By cutting the difference between discount cigarettes and Marlboro to roughly 40 cents, Philip Morris was able to woo back many customers. Within nine months after the price drop, their market share increased to almost 27 percent, eventually rising to almost 30 percent. Nevertheless, the lower prices had adverse profit implications, and by year end, analysts had estimated that the strategy had cut Philip Morris's domestic tobacco unit's earnings by $2.3 billion to $2.84 billion.[1]

To maintain the long-term sales growth and profitability of the Marlboro brand, Philip Morris has since expanded their marketing programs by introducing a new continuity program called Marlboro Country Store (offering Western wear such as boots, cowboy hats, belt buckles, denim shirts, and leather jackets, discreetly stenciled with the Marlboro brand logo); test marketing a new, shorter (15-millimeter) cigarette called Express for time-pressed and price-conscious consumers; and by slowly and carefully nudging up prices (a 4-cent increase in November 1992 seemed to be basically ignored by consumers). Subsequent marketing programs introduced a "Marlboro Unlimited" promotion in which 2,000 couples could win $1,000 cash and a five days' outdoor vacation in the western United States aboard a train brightly painted in the red and white colors of the cigarette pack.

---

[1]Laura Zinn, "The Smoke Clears at Marlboro," *Business Week*, 31 January 1994, 76–77.

made in the store, the possibility of additional marketing push by retailers is important. Chapter 5 describes how marketers can work with retailers to maximize their brand equity.

INCREASED MARKETING COMMUNICATION EFFECTIVENESS

A host of advertising and communication benefits may result from creating awareness of and a positive image for a brand. These benefits can be seen by considering the manner in which a consumer responds to marketing communications and how the marketing communications program for a brand with a great deal of equity may be processed differently by consumers as a result. One well-established view of consumer response to marketing communications is hierarchy of effects models. These models assume that consumers move through a series of stages or mental states on the basis of marketing communications—for example, exposure to, attention to, comprehension of, yielding to, retention of, and behaving on the basis of a marketing communication.

A brand with a great deal of equity already has created some knowledge structures in consumers' minds. The existence of these mental associations is extremely valuable because they increase the likelihood that consumers will pass through various stages of the hierarchy. For example, consider the effects of a positive brand image on the persuasive ability of advertising. As a result of having established brand awareness and strong, favorable, and unique brand associations, consumers may be more likely

Soft Drinks Are Not Cigarettes

In the aftermath of the Marlboro price reduction announcement on April 2, 1993, Coca-Cola's stock took a beating, losing an astounding $5 billion in value. From a high of 45⅜ the previous September, the stock had declined to 38, an almost two-year low. Apparently, the stock market felt that the pressures that had forced Marlboro to cut prices and lowered their profits were also being faced by Coca-Cola and others.

On April 21, Coca-Cola scheduled a meeting with top financial analysts to dispel what they believed were misconceptions about their brand. Led by Roberto Goizueta, chairman and chief executive officer, the theme of the Coca-Cola presentation was "Soft Drinks Are Not Cigarettes." During the course of their talk, Coca-Cola management made the following points:[1]

- Soft drink consumption had been steadily increasing in the United States. Cigarette consumption had been declining.

- The retail price of a pack of Marlboros more than tripled between 1980 and 1992, leaving room for discounters to undercut the brand. On the other hand, the average retail price of Coca-Cola had remained virtually unchanged during this same period (around 2 cents per ounce).

- Major cigarette makers, by selling both brand name and private label products, cannibalized their own sales and were their own worst enemy. Coca-Cola had no private label business in the United States.

- The discount market for cigarettes increased from virtually nothing to 30 percent of U.S. sales in 1992. Private label soft drinks, on the other hand, accounted for only 8.7 percent of U.S. sales in 1992, a figure that was actually lower than 20 years ago.

- More than 80 percent of Coca-Cola's earnings came from outside the United States, thus reducing their exposure to private label competitors in the United States.

Spreading the word concerning these differences seemed to help. Within a month, Coca-Cola's stock had increased to 42, just about where it had been at the time of the Marlboro announcement.

---

[1] Arthur M. Louis, "Coca-Cola's Stock Rescue Operation," *San Francisco Chronicle*, 1 June 1993, C1.

to notice an ad, may more easily learn about the brand and form favorable opinions, and may retain and act on these beliefs over time.

Academic research has shown that familiar, well-liked brands are less susceptible to "interference" and confusion from competitive ads,[64] are more responsive to creative strategies such as humor appeals,[65] and are less vulnerable to negative reactions due to concentrated repetition schedules.[66] In addition, panel diary members who were highly loyal to a brand increased purchases when advertising for the brand increased.[67] Other advantages associated with more advertising include increased likelihood of being the focus of attention and increased "brand interest."[68]

Because strong brand associations exist, lower levels of repetition may be necessary. For example, in a classic study of advertising weights, Anheuser-Busch ran a carefully conducted field experiment in which they varied the amount of Budweiser advertising shown to consumers in different matched test markets.[69] Seven different advertising expenditure levels were tested, representing increases and decreases from the previous advertising expenditure levels: minus 100 percent (no advertising), minus 50 percent, 0 percent (same level), plus 50 percent, plus 100 percent (double the level of advertising), plus 150 percent, and plus 200 percent. These expenditure levels were run for one year and revealed that the "no advertising" level resulted in the same amount of sales as the current program. In fact, the 50 percent cut in advertising expenditures actually resulted in an increase in sales. The experimental results are consistent with the notion that strong brands such as Budweiser do not require the same advertising levels, at least over a short period of time, as a less well-known or well-liked brand.[70]

Similarly, because of existing brand knowledge structures, consumers may be more likely to notice sales promotions, direct mail offerings, or other sales-oriented marketing communications and respond favorably. For example, several studies have shown that promotion effectiveness is asymmetric in favor of a higher-quality brand.[71] Chapter 6 outlines how to develop integrated marketing communication programs to build and capitalize on brand equity.

POSSIBLE LICENSING OPPORTUNITIES

A strong brand often has associations that may be desirable in other product categories. To capitalize on this value, a firm may choose to license its name, logo, or other trademark item to another company for use on their products and merchandise. Traditionally, licensing has been associated with characters such as Garfield the cat, Barney the dinosaur, and Disney's Mickey Mouse, or celebrities and designers such as Martha Stewart, Ralph Lauren, and Tommy Hilfiger. Recently, more conventional brands such as Caterpillar, Harley Davidson, Coca-Cola, and others have licensed their brands.

The rationale for the licensee (i.e., the company obtaining the rights to use the trademark) is that consumers will pay more for a product because of the recognition and image lent by the trademark. For example, one marketing research study showed that consumers would pay $60 for cookware licensed under the Julia Child name as opposed to only $40 for the identical cookware bearing the Sears name.[72]

The rationale for the licensor (i.e., the company behind the trademark) relates to profits, promotion, and legal protection. In terms of profits, a firm can expect an average royalty of about 5 percent of the wholesale price of each product, ranging from 2 percent to 10 percent depending on the circumstances involved. Because there are no manufacturing or marketing costs, these revenues translate directly to profits. Licensing is also seen as a means to enhance the awareness and image of the brand. Linking the trademarks to other products may broaden its exposure and potentially increase the strength, favorability, and uniqueness of brand associations. Finally, licensing may provide legal protection for trademarks. Licensing the brand for use in certain product categories prevents other firms or potential competitors from legally using the brand name to enter those categories. For example, Coca-Cola entered licensing agreements in a number of product areas, including radios, glassware, toy trucks, and clothes, in part as legal protection. As it turns out, their licensing program has been so successful they have subsequently introduced a catalog sent directly to consumers that offers a myriad of products bearing the Coca-Cola name for sale.

Despite the potential benefits from licensing related to profitability, image enhancement, or legal protection, there are certainly risks too. A trademark can become overexposed if marketers adopt a saturation policy. Consumers do not necessarily know the motivation or marketing arrangements behind a product and can become confused or even angry if the brand is licensed to a product that seemingly bears no relation. Moreover, if the product fails to live up to consumer expectations, the brand name could become tarnished. Chapter 7 discusses the pros and cons of licensing and its effect on brand equity in more detail.

ADDITIONAL BRAND EXTENSION OPPORTUNITIES

A *brand extension* is when a firm uses an established brand name to enter a new market. Extensions can be classified into two general categories. A *line extension* is when a current brand name is used to enter a new market segment in the existing product class (e.g., with new varieties, new flavors, and new sizes). For example, Colgate has introduced a number of different varieties of toothpaste that come in different flavors (e.g., Winterfresh gel), have different ingredients (e.g., Colgate with Baking Soda), or provide a specific benefit (e.g., Tartar Control Colgate). A *category extension* is when the current brand name is used to enter a different product class. For example, Swiss Army Brands capitalized on the success and precision image of their knives to introduce watches, sunglasses, writing instruments, travel gear, and cutlery.

A brand with a positive image allows the firm to introduce appropriate new products as brand extensions. There are many advantages to introducing new products as extensions. An extension allows the firm to capitalize on consumer knowledge of the parent brand to raise the awareness of and suggest possible associations for the brand extension. Thus, extensions can potentially provide the following benefits to facilitate new product acceptance: reducing the risk perceived by customers and distributors, decreasing the cost of gaining distribution and trial, increasing the efficiency of promotional expenditures, avoiding the cost (and risk) of developing new names, allowing for packaging and labeling efficiencies, and permitting consumer variety seeking.

Besides facilitating new product acceptance, extensions can also provide "feedback" benefits to the parent brand and the company as a whole. Extensions may enhance the parent brand image by improving the strength, favorability, and uniqueness of brand associations and by improving perceptions of company credibility (in terms of perceived expertise, trustworthiness, or likability). Extensions may also help to convey the broader meaning of the brand to consumers, clarifying the core benefit proposition and business definition of the company. Finally, extensions may also bring new customers into the brand franchise and increase market coverage.

Academic research has validated many of these assumptions. Studies have shown that well-known and well-regarded brands can extend more successfully and into more diverse categories than other brands.[73] In addition, the amount of brand equity has been shown to be correlated with the highest- or lowest-quality member in the product line for vertical product extensions.[74] Research has also shown that positive symbolic associations may be the basis of these evaluations, even if overall brand attitude itself is not necessarily high.[75]

Brands with varied product category associations through past extensions have been shown to be especially extendable.[76] As a result, introductory marketing programs for extensions from an established brand may be more efficient than other such programs.[77] Several studies have indicated that extension activity has aided (or at least did not dilute) brand equity for the parent brand.

For instance, brand extensions strengthened parent brand associations, and "flagship brands" were highly resistant to dilution or other potential negative effects caused by negative experiences with an extension.[78] Research has also found evidence of an ownership effect, whereby current owners generally had more favorable responses to brand line extensions.[79] Finally, extensions of brands that have both high familiarity and positive attitudes have been shown to receive higher initial stock market reactions than other brands.[80]

Chapter 12 provides a conceptual model of how consumers evaluate brand extensions and presents a number of guidelines for marketers to maximize extension success and its effect on brand equity.

OTHER BENEFITS

Finally, brands with positive customer-based brand equity may provide other advantages to the firm not directly related to the products themselves, such as helping the firm to attract better employees, generate greater interest from investors, and garner more support from shareholders. In terms of the latter, several research studies have shown that brand equity can be directly related to corporate stock price (see the Science of Branding 10–2).[81]

Notes

1. Kevin Lane Keller, "Conceptualizing, Measuring, and Managing Customer-Based Brand Equity," *Journal of Marketing* (January 1993): 1–29.
2. John R. Anderson, *The Architecture of Cognition* (Cambridge, MA: Harvard University Press, 1983); Robert S. Wyer Jr. and Thomas K. Srull, "Person Memory and Judgment," *Psychological Review* 96, no. 1 (1989): 58–83.
3. John R. Rossiter and Larry Percy, *Advertising and Promotion Management* (New York: McGraw-Hill, 1987).
4. Burleigh B. Gardner and Sidney J. Levy, "The Product and the Brand," *Harvard Business Review* (March-April 1955): 33–39.
5. Dawn Dobni and George M. Zinkhan, "In Search of Brand Image: A Foundation Analysis," in *Advances in Consumer Research*, Vol. 17, eds. Marvin E. Goldberg, Gerald Gorn, and Richard W. Pollay (Provo, UT: Association for Consumer Research, 1990), 110–119.
6. H. Herzog, "Behavioral Science Concepts for Analyzing the Consumer," in *Marketing and the Behavioral Sciences*, ed. Perry Bliss (Boston: Allyn and Bacon, 1963), 76–86; Joseph W. Newman, "New Insight, New Progress for Marketing," *Harvard Business Review* (November-December, 1957): 95–102.
7. James R. Bettman, *An Information Processing Theory of Consumer Choice* (Reading, MA: Addison-Wesley, 1979); Rossiter and Percy, *Advertising and Promotion Management*.
8. William Baker, J. Wesley Hutchinson, Danny Moore, and Prakash Nedungadi, "Brand Familiarity and Advertising: Effects on the Evoked Set and Brand Preference," in *Advances in Consumer Research*, Vol. 13, ed. Richard J. Lutz (Provo, UT: Association for Consumer Research, 1986), 637–642; Prakash Nedungadi, "Recall and Consumer Consideration Sets: Influencing Choice without Altering Brand Evaluations," *Journal of Consumer Research* 17 (December 1990): 263–276.
9. For example, see Henry L. Roediger, "Inhibition in Recall from Cuing with Recall Targets," *Journal of Verbal Learning and Verbal Behavior* 12 (1973): 644–657; and Raymond S. Nickerson, "Retrieval Inhibition from Part-Set Cuing: A Persisting

Enigma in Memory Research," *Memory and Cognition* 12 (November 1984): 531–552.

10. In an interesting twist, it is also the case that consumers would be more likely to recall closely related brands in the category, for example, Wendy's. See Prakash Nedungadi, "Recall and Consumer Consideration Sets."

11. Jacob Jacoby, George J. Syzabillo, and Jacqeline Busato-Schach, "Information Acquisition Behavior in Brand Choice Situations," *Journal of Consumer Research* 3 (1977): 209–216; Ted Roselius, "Consumer Ranking of Risk Reduction Methods," *Journal of Marketing* 35 (January 1977): 56–61.

12. James R. Bettman and C. Whan Park, "Effects of Prior Knowledge and Experience and Phase of the Choice Process on Consumer Decision Processes: A Protocol Analysis," *Journal of Consumer Research* 7 (December 1980): 234–248; Wayne D. Hoyer and Steven P. Brown, "Effects of Brand Awareness on Choice for a Common, Repeat-Purchase Product," *Journal of Consumer Research* 17 (September 1990): 141–148; C. W. Park and V. Parker Lessig, "Familiarity and Its Impact on Consumer Biases and Heuristics," *Journal of Consumer Research* 8 (September 1981): 223–230.

13. Richard E. Petty and John T. Cacioppo, *Communication and Persuasion* (New York: Springer-Verlag, 1986).

14. "Advertisers Often Take Bizarre Approaches," *Newsday*.

15. Joseph W. Alba and J. Wesley Hutchinson, "Dimensions of Consumer Expertise," *Journal of Consumer Research* 13 (March 1987): 411–453.

16. David A. Aaker, "Positioning Your Brand," *Business Horizons* 25 (May/June 1982): 56–62; Al Ries and Jack Trout, *Positioning: The Battle for Your Mind* (New York, McGraw-Hill, 1979); Yoram Wind, *Product Policy: Concepts, Methods, and Strategy* (Reading, MA: Addison-Wesley, 1982).

17. Deborah J. MacInnis and Kent Nakomoto, "Factors That Influence Consumers' Evaluations of Brand Extensions," working paper, Karl Eller School of Management, University of Arizona, 1991; Mita Sujan and James R. Bettman, "The Effects of Brand

Positioning Strategies on Consumers' Brand and Category Perceptions: Some Insights from Schema Research," *Journal of Marketing Research* 26 (November 1989): 454–467.

18. James R. Bettman and Mita Sujan, "Effects of Framing on Evaluation of Comparable and Noncomparable Alternatives by Expert and Novice Consumers," *Journal of Consumer Research* 14 (September 1987): 141–154; Michael D. Johnson, "Consumer Choice Strategies for Comparing Noncomparable Alternatives," *Journal of Consumer Research* 11 (December 1984): 741–753; C. Whan Park and Daniel C. Smith, "Product Level Choice: A Top-Down or Bottom-Up Process?" *Journal of Consumer Research* 16 (December 1989): 289–299.

19. Joel B. Cohen and Kanul Basu, "Alternative Models of Categorization: Towards a Contingent Processing Framework," *Journal of Consumer Research* 13 (March 1987): 455–472; Prakash Nedungadi and J. Wesley Hutchinson, "The Prototypicality of Brands: Relationships with Brand Awareness, Preference, and Usage," in *Advances in Consumer Research*, Vol. 12, eds. Elizabeth C. Hirschman and Morris B. Holbrook (Provo, UT: Association for Consumer Research, 1985), 489–503; Eleanor Rosch and Carolyn B. Mervis, "Family Resemblance: Studies in the Internal Structure of Categories," *Cognitive Psychology* 7 (October 1975): 573–605; James Ward and Barbara Loken, "The Quintessential Snack Food: Measurement of Prototypes," in *Advances in Consumer Research*, Vol. 13, ed. Richard J. Lutz (Provo, UT: Association for Consumer Research, 1986), 126–131.

20. Nedungadi and Hutchinson, "The Prototypicality of Brands"; Ward and Loken, "The Quintessential Snack Food."

21. George S. Day, Allan D. Shocker, and Rajendra K. Srivastava, "Customer-Oriented Approaches to Identifying Products-Markets," *Journal of Marketing* 43 (Fall 1979): 8–19.

22. K. E. Miller and J. L. Ginter, "An Investigation of Situational Variation in Brand Choice Behavior and Attitude," *Journal of Marketing Research* 16 (February 1979): 111–123.

23. Mita Sujan and Christine Dekleva, "Product Categorization and Inference Making: Some Implications for Comparative Advertising," *Journal of Consumer Research*, 14 (December 1987): 372–378.

24. Thomas A. Fogarty, "A Company for All Seasons," *USA Today*, 13 January 2000, B3.

25. Stephanie Thompson, "Campbell Tries to Stir Soup Sales with $95 Million," *Advertising Age*, 11 October 1999.

26. David Garvin, "Product Quality: An Important Strategic Weapon," *Business Horizons* 27 (May-June): 40–43; Philip Kotler, *Marketing Management*, 10th ed. (Upper Saddle River, NJ: Prentice-Hall, 2000).

27. These attributes are found in *Consumer Reports* reviews in 1994.

28. Robert C. Blattberg and Kenneth J. Wisniewski, "Price-Induced Patterns of Competition," *Marketing Science* 8 (Fall 1989): 291–309.

29. Joseph T. Plummer, "How Personality Makes a Difference," *Journal of Advertising Research* 24 (December 1984/January 1985): 27–31.

30. See Jennifer Aaker, "Dimensions of Brand Personality," *Journal of Marketing Research* 34 (August 1997): 347–357.

31. Aaker, "Dimensions of Brand Personality"; Susan Fournier, "Consumers and Their Brands: Developing Relationship Theory in Consumer Research," *Journal of Consumer Research* 24, no. 3 (1997): 343–373.

32. M. Joseph Sirgy, "Self Concept in Consumer Behavior: A Critical Review," *Journal of Consumer Research* 9 (December 1982): 287–300.

33. Timothy R. Graeff, "Consumption Situations and the Effects of Brand Image on Consumers' Brand Evaluations," *Psychology & Marketing* 14, no. 1 (1997): 49–70; Timothy R. Graeff, "Image Congruence Effects on Product Evaluations: The Role of Self-Monitoring and Public/ Private Consumption," *Psychology & Marketing* 13, no. 5 (1996): 481–499.

34. Jennifer L. Aaker, "The Malleable Self: The Role of Self-Expression in Persuasion," *Journal of Marketing Research* 36, no. 2 (1999): 45–57.

35. William L. Wilkie, *Consumer Behavior*, 2nd ed. (New York, John Wiley & Sons, 1990).

36. William D. Wells, "How Advertising Works," unpublished paper, 1980; Christopher P. Puto and William D. Wells, "Informational and Transformational Advertising: The Differential Effects of Time," in *Advances in Consumer Research*, Vol. 11, ed. Thomas C. Kinnear (Ann Arbor, MI: Association for Consumer Research, 1983), 638–643; Stephen J. Hoch and John Deighton, "Managing What Consumers Learn from Experience," *Journal of Marketing* 53 (April 1989): 1–20.

37. Lynn R. Kahle, Basil Poulos, and Ajay Sukhdial, "Changes in Social Values in the United States during the Past Decade," *Journal of Advertising Research* (February/March 1988): 35–41.

38. Greg Farrell, "Marketers Put a Price on Your Life," *USA Today*, 7 July 1999, 3B.

39. Arjun Chaudhuri and Morris B. Holbrook, "The Chain of Effects from Brand Trust and Brand Affect to Brand Performance: The Role of Brand Loyalty," *Journal of Marketing* 65 (April 2001): 81–93.

40. Thomas A. Stewart, "A Satisfied Customer Is Not Enough," *Fortune*, 21 July 1997, 112–113.

41. Thomas O. Jones and W. Earl Sasser Jr. "Why Satisfied Customers Defect," *Harvard Business Review* (November-December 1995): 88–99.

42. Fredrick Reichheld, *The Loyalty Effect: The Hidden Force Behind Growth, Profits, and Lasting Value* (Boston: Harvard Business School Press, 1996).

43. James H. McAlexander, John W. Schouten, and Harold F. Koenig, "Building Brand Community," *Journal of Marketing* 66 (January 2002): 38–54; Albert Muniz and Thomas O'Guinn, "Brand Community," *Journal of Consumer Research* 27 (March 2001): 412–432.

44. Brand Focus 2.0 is based in part on Steven Hoeffler and Kevin Lane Keller, "The Marketing Advantages of Strong Brands," working paper (UNC, 2002).

45. Ian M. Lewis, "Brand Equity or Why the Board of Directors Needs Marketing

Research" (paper presented at the ARF Fifth Annual Advertising and Promotion Workshop, February 1, 1993).

46. Peter A. Dacin and Daniel C. Smith, "The Effect of Brand Portfolio Characteristics on Consumer Evaluations of Brand Extensions," *Journal of Marketing Research* 31 (May 1994): 229–242; George S. Day and Terry Deutscher, "Attitudinal Predictions of Choices of Major Appliance Brands," *Journal of Marketing Research* 19 (May 1982), 192–198; W. B. Dodds, K. B. Monroe, and D. Grewal, "Effects of Price, Brand, and Store Information on Buyers' Product Evaluations," *Journal of Marketing Research* 28 (August 1991): 307–319; France Leclerc, Bernd H. Schmitt, and Laurette Dube, "Foreign Branding and Its Effects on Product Perceptions and Attitudes," *Journal of Marketing Research* 31, no. 5 (1994): 263–270; Akshay R. Rao and K. B. Monroe, "The Effects of Price, Brand Name, and Store Name on Buyers' Perceptions of Product Quality: An Integrative Review," *Journal of Marketing Research* 26 (August 1989): 351–357.

47. B. Wernerfelt, "Umbrella Branding as a Signal of New Product Quality: An Example of Signaling by Posting a Bond," *Rand Journal of Economics* 19, no. 3 (1988): 458–466; Tullin Erdem, "An Empirical Analysis of Umbrella Branding," *Journal of Marketing Research* 35, no. 8 (1998): 339–351.

48. Fred M. Feinberg, Barbara E. Kahn, and Leigh McAllister, "Market Share Response When Consumers Seek Variety," *Journal of Marketing Research* 29 (May 1992): 227–237.

49. Michel Laroche, Chankon Kim, and Lianxi Zhou, "Brand Familiarity and Confidence as Determinants of Purchase Intention: An Empirical Test in a Multiple Brand Context," *Journal of Business Research* 37 (1996): 115–120.

50. Robert E. Smith, "Integrating Information from Advertising and Trial," *Journal of Marketing Research* 30 (May 1993): 204–219.

51. Andrew S. C. Ehrenberg, Gerard J. Goodhardt, and T. Patrick Barwise, "Double Jeopardy Revisited," *Journal of Marketing* 54 (July 1990): 82–91.

52. Rohini Ahluwalia, Robert E. Burnkrant, and H. Rao Unnava, "Consumer Response to Negative Publicity: The Moderating Role of Commitment," *Journal of Marketing Research* 37 (May 2000): 203–214; Narij Dawar and Madam M. Pillutla, "Impact of Product-Harm Crises on Brand Equity: The Moderating Role of Consumer Expectations," *Journal of Marketing Research* 37 (May 2000): 215–226.

53. Susan Caminit, "The Payoff from a Good Corporate Reputation," *Fortune*, 10 February 1992, 74–77.

54. Deepak Agrawal, "Effects of Brand Loyalty on Advertising and Trade Promotions: A Game Theoretic Analysis with Empirical Evidence," *Marketing Science* 15, no. 1 (1996): 86–108; Chan Su Park and V. Srinivasan, "A Survey-Based Method for Measuring and Understanding Brand Equity and its Extendability," *Journal of Marketing Research* 31 (May 1994): 271–288; Raj Sethuraman, "A Model of How Discounting High-Priced Brands Affects the Sales of Low-Priced Brands," *Journal of Marketing Research* 33 (November 1996): 399–409.

55. Hermann Simon, "Dynamics of Price Elasticity and Brand Life Cycles: An Empirical Study," *Journal of Marketing Research* 16 (November 1979): 439–452; K. Sivakumar and S. P. Raj, "Quality Tier Competition: How Price Change Influences Brand Choice and Category Choice," *Journal of Marketing* 61 (July 1997): 71–84.

56. Lakshman Krishnamurthi and S. P. Raj, "An Empirical Analysis of the Relationship between Brand Loyalty and Consumer Price Elasticity," *Marketing Science* 10, no. 2 (Spring 1991): 172–183.

57. Greg M. Allenby and Peter E. Rossi, "Quality Perceptions and Asymmetric Switching between Brands," *Marketing Science* 10 (Summer 1991): 185–204; Rajiv Grover and V. Srinivasan, "Evaluating the Multiple Effects of Retail Promotions on Brand Loyal and Brand Switching Segments," *Journal of Marketing Research* 29 (February 1992): 76–89; Gary J. Russell and Wagner A. Kamakura, "Understanding Brand Competition Using Micro and Macro

Scanner Data," *Journal of Marketing Research* 31 (May 1994): 289–303.

58. Albert C. Bemmaor and Dominique Mouchoux, "Measuring the Short-Term Effect of In-Store Promotion and Retail Advertising on Brand Sales: A Factorial Experiment," *Journal of Marketing Research* 28 (May 1991): 202–214; Robert C. Blattberg and Kenneth J. Wisniewski, "Price-Induced Patterns of Competition," *Marketing Science* 8 (Fall 1989): 291–309; Randolph E. Bucklin, Sunil Gupta, and Sangman Han, "A Brand's Eye View of Response Segmentation in Consumer Brand Choice Behavior," *Journal of Marketing Research* 32 (February 1995): 66–74; Sivakumar and Raj, "Quality Tier Competition."

59. William Boulding, Eunkyu Lee, and Richard Staelin, "Mastering the Mix: Do Advertising, Promotion, and Sales Force Activities Lead to Differentiation?" *Journal of Marketing Research* 31 (May 1994): 159–172. See also Vinay Kanetkar, Charles B. Weinberg, and Doyle L. Weiss, "Price Sensitivity and Television Advertising Exposures: Some Empirical Findings," *Marketing Science* 11 (Fall 1992): 359–371.

60. Kyle Pope, "Computers: They're No Commodity," *Wall Street Journal*, 15 October 1993, B1.

61. Ira Teinowitz, "Marlboro Friday: Still Smoking," *Advertising Age*, 28 March 1994, 24.

62. Peter S. Fader and David C. Schmittlein, "Excess Behavioral Loyalty for High-Share Brands: Deviations from the Dirichlet Model for Repeat Purchasing," *Journal of Marketing Research* 30, no. 11 (1993): 478–493; Rajiv Lal and Chakravarthi Narasimhan, "The Inverse Relationship between Manufacturer and Retailer Margins: A Theory," *Marketing Science* 15, no. 2 (1996): 132–151.

63. David B. Montgomery, "New Product Distribution: An Analysis of Supermarket Buyer Decisions," *Journal of Marketing Research* 12, no. 3 (1978): 255–264.

64. Robert J. Kent and Chris T. Allen, "Competitive Interference Effects in Consumer Memory for Advertising: The Role of Brand Familiarity," *Journal of Marketing* 58 (July 1994): 97–105.

65. Amitava Chattopadyay and Kunal Basu, "Humor in Advertising: The Moderating Role of Prior Brand Evaluation," *Journal of Marketing Research* 27 (November 1990): 466–476; D. W. Stewart and David H. Furse, *Effective Television Advertising: A Study of 1000 Commercials* (Lexington, MA: D.C. Heath, 1986); M. G. Weinburger and C. Gulas, "The Impact of Humor in Advertising: A Review," *Journal of Advertising* 21, no. 4 (1992): 35–60.

66. Margaret Campbell and Kevin Lane Keller, "The Moderating Effect of Brand Knowledge on Ad Repetition Effects," working paper (UC-Boulder, 2002).

67. S. P. Raj, "The Effects of Advertising on High and Low Loyalty Consumer Segments," *Journal of Consumer Research* 9 (June 1982): 77–89.

68. Ravi Dhar and Itamar Simonson, "The Effect of the Focus of Comparison on Consumer Preferences," *Journal of Marketing Research* 29 (November 1992): 430–440; Karen A. Machleit, Chris T. Allen, and Thomas J. Madden, "The Mature Brand and Brand Interest: An Alternative Consequence of Ad-Evoked Affect," *Journal of Marketing* 57 (October 1993): 72–82; Itamar Simonson, Joel Huber, and John Payne, "The Relationship between Prior Brand Knowledge and Information Acquisition Order," *Journal of Consumer Research* 14 (March 1988): 566–578.

69. Russell L. Ackoff and James R. Emshoff, "Advertising Research at Anheuser-Busch, Inc. (1963–1968)," *Sloan Management Review* (Winter 1975): 1–15.

70. These results should be interpreted carefully, however, as they do not suggest that large advertising expenditures did not play an important role in creating equity for the brand in the past, or that advertising expenditures could be cut severely without some adverse sales consequences at some point in the future.

71. See Robert C. Blattberg, Richard Briesch, and Edward J. Fox, "How Promotions Work," *Marketing Science* 14 (1995): G122-

G132. See also Bart J. Bronnenberg and Luc Wathieu, "Asymmetric Promotion Effects and Brand Positioning," *Marketing Science* 15, no. 4 (1996): 379–394. This study show how the relative promotion effectiveness of high- and low-quality brands depends on their positioning along both price and quality dimensions.

72. Frank E. James, "I'll Wear the Coke Pants Tonight; They Go Well with My Harley-Davidson Ring," *Wall Street Journal*, 6 June 1985.

73. David A. Aaker and Kevin Lane Keller, "Consumer Evaluations of Brand Extensions," *Journal of Marketing* 54, no. 1 (1990): 27–41; Kevin Lane Keller and David A. Aaker, "The Effects of Sequential Introduction of Brand Extensions," *Journal of Marketing Research* 29 (February 1992): 35–50; A. Rangaswamy, P. R. Burke, and T. A. Oliva, "Brand Equity and the Extendibility of Brand Names," *International Journal of Research in Marketing* 10, no. 3 (1993): 61–75.

74. Taylor Randall, Karl Ulrich, and David Reibstein, "Brand Equity and Vertical Product Line Extent," *Marketing Science* 17, no. 4 (1998): 356–379.

75. Srinivas K. Reddy, Susan Holak, and Subodh Bhat, "To Extend or Not to Extend: Success Determinants of Line Extensions," *Journal of Marketing Research* 31, no. 5 (1994): 243–262; C. Whan Park, Sandra Milberg, and Robert Lawson, "Evaluation of Brand Extensions: The Role of Product Feature Similarity and Brand Concept Consistency," *Journal of Consumer Research* 18, no. 9 (1991): 185–193; Susan M. Broniarcysyk and Joseph W. Alba, "The Importance of the Brand in Brand Extension," *Journal of Marketing Research* 31, no. 5 (1994): 214–228.

76. Peter A. Dacin and Daniel C. Smith, "The Effect of Brand Portfolio Characteristics on Consumer Evaluations of Brand Extensions," *Journal of Marketing Research* 31 (May 1994): 229–242; Keller and Aaker, "The Effects of Sequential Introduction of Brand Extensions"; Daniel A. Sheinin and Bernd H. Schmitt, "Extending Brands with New Product Concepts: The Role of Category Attribute Congruity, Brand Affect, and Brand Breadth," *Journal of Business Research* 31 (1994): 1–10.

77. Roger A. Kerin, Gurumurthy Kalyanaram, and Daniel J. Howard, "Product Hierarchy and Brand Strategy Influences on the Order of Entry Effect for Consumer Packaged Goods," *Journal of Product Innovation Management* 13 (1996): 21–34.

78. Maureen Morrin, "The Impact of Brand Extensions on Parent Brand Memory Structures and Retrieval Processes," *Journal of Marketing Research* 36 (November 1999): 517–525; John Roedder, Barbara Loken, and Christopher Joiner, "The Negative Impact of Extensions: Can Flagship Products Be Diluted?" *Journal of Marketing* 62 (January 1998): 19–32; Daniel A. Sheinin, "The Effects of Experience with Brand Extensions on Parent Brand Knowledge," *Journal of Business Research* 49 (2000): 47–55.

79. Amna Kirmani, Sanjay Sood, and Sheri Bridges, "The Ownership Effect in Consumer Responses to Brand Line Stretches," *Journal of Marketing* 63 (January 1999): 88–101.

80. Vicki R. Lane and Robert Jacobson, "Stock Market Reactions to Brand Extension Announcements: The Effects of Brand Attitude and Familiarity," *Journal of Marketing* 59, no. 1 (1995): 63–77.

81. D. A. Aaker and R. Jacobson, "The Financial Information Content of Perceived Quality," *Journal of Marketing Research* 31, no. 5 (1994): 191–201; D. A. Aaker and R. Jacobson, "The Value Relevance of Brand Attitude in High-Technology Markets," *Journal of Marketing Research*, 38 (November 2001): 485–493; M. E. Barth, M. Clement, G. Foster, and R. Kasznik, "Brand Values and Capital Market Valuation," *Review of Accounting Studies* 3 (1998): 41–68.

CHAPTER

Brand Positioning and Values

PREVIEW

The first two chapters have provided some perspective on branding and described the concept of customer-based brand equity. Customer-based brand equity was defined as the differential effect that brand knowledge has on customer response to the marketing of that brand. According to this definition, brand knowledge in consumers' minds is central to the creation and management of brand equity. Brand knowledge was conceptualized in terms of a brand node in memory with brand associations, varying in strength, connected to it. Brand equity is then a function of the level of brand awareness and the strength, favorability, and uniqueness of brand associations.

The customer-based brand equity (CBBE) model lays out a series of steps for building a strong brand: (1) Establish the proper brand identity, (2) create the appropriate brand meaning, (3) elicit positive brand responses, and (4) forge strong brand relationships with customers. The CBBE model maintains that six brand building blocks—brand salience, brand performance, brand imagery, brand judgments, brand feelings, and brand resonance—provide the foundation for successful brand development.

As outlined in Chapter 1, the first step in the strategic brand management process is to identify and establish brand positioning and brand values. Accordingly, this chapter builds on the notions introduced in Chapter 2 to first consider how to define desired or ideal brand knowledge structures in terms of how to position a brand. Positioning involves identifying and establishing points of parity and points of difference to establish the right brand identity and to create the proper brand image.[1] Next, the chapter reviews how to identify and establish core brand values and a brand mantra. Part III (Chapters 4 through 7) then describes specific marketing actions that the firm can take based on this brand strategy to build brand equity. Brand Focus 3.0 at the end of the chapter highlights some important issues in conducting brand audits, a research approach to help formulate brand positioning.

IDENTIFYING AND ESTABLISHING BRAND POSITIONING

The CBBE model provides a blueprint for the steps involved in building a strong brand. To better operationalize the model, several strategic decisions must be made about the specific nature of the brand building blocks involved. To guide those decisions, it is necessary to define the brand positioning, described in this section, as well as a set of core brand values and brand mantra, described in the next section.

Basic Concepts

The CBBE model describes the process, in general, by which brand knowledge structures should be built to create brand equity. Critical to this view is the creation of strong, favorable, and unique brand associations as part of the brand meaning. This section considers in greater detail how marketers might determine *desired* brand meaning or positioning, that is, what they would like consumers to know about the brand as opposed to what they might currently know. Determining the desired brand knowledge structures involves positioning a brand.

Brand positioning is at the heart of marketing strategy. Kotler defines brand positioning as the "act of designing the company's offer and image so that it occupies a distinct and valued place in the target customer's minds."[2] Thus, positioning, as the name implies, involves finding the proper "location" in the minds of a group of consumers or market segment so that they think about a product or service in the "right" or desired way. Positioning is all about identifying the optimal location of a brand and its competitors in the minds of consumers to maximize potential benefit to the firm. A good brand positioning helps to guide marketing strategy by clarifying what a brand is all about, how it is unique and how it is similar to competitive brands, and why consumers should purchase and use the brand.

According to the CBBE model, deciding on a positioning requires determining a frame of reference (by identifying the target market and the nature of competition) and the ideal points-of-parity and points-of-difference brand associations. In other words, it is necessary to decide (1) who the target consumer is, (2) who the main competitors are, (3) how the brand is similar to these competitors, and (4) how the brand is different from these competitors. These four ingredients are each discussed in turn. Branding Brief 3-1 describes some of the positioning problems that PepsiCo had in launching their new Pepsi One soft drink.

Target Market

Identifying the consumer target is important because different consumers may have different brand knowledge structures and thus different perceptions and preferences for the brand. Without this understanding, it may be difficult to be able to state which brand associations should be strongly held, favorable, and unique. A number of considerations are important in defining and segmenting a market and choosing target market segments. A few are highlighted here.

A *market* is the set of all actual and potential buyers who have sufficient interest in, income for, and access to a product. In other words, a market consists of all consumers with sufficient motivation, ability, and opportunity to buy a product. *Market segmentation* involves dividing the market into distinct groups of homogeneous consumers who have similar needs and consumer behavior and thus require similar marketing mixes. Defining a market segmentation plan involves tradeoffs between costs and benefits. The more finely segmented the market, the greater the likelihood that the firm will be able to implement marketing programs that meet the needs of consumers in any one segment. The advantage of a more positive consumer response from a customized marketing program, however, can be offset by the greater costs from a lack of standardization.

Segmentation Bases

Figures 3-1 and 3-2 display some possible segmentation bases for consumer and industrial markets, respectively. In general, these bases can be classified as *descriptive* or customer-oriented (related to what kind of person or organization is the customer) versus *behavioral* or product-oriented (related to how the customer thinks of or uses the brand or product).

Behavioral segmentation bases are often most valuable in understanding branding issues because they have clearer strategic implications. For example, defining a benefit segment makes it clear what should be the ideal point of difference or desired benefit with which to establish the positioning. Take the toothpaste market. One research study uncovered four main segments:[3]

1. *The Sensory Segment:* Seeking flavor and product appearance
2. *The Sociables:* Seeking brightness of teeth
3. *The Worriers:* Seeking decay prevention
4. *The Independent Segment:* Seeking low price

BRANDING BRIEF 3-1

Arriving at One Good Positioning for Pepsi One

In 1998, Pepsi introduced a new diet cola called Pepsi One—in reference to the one calorie contained in the drink—after investing millions in research and development, design, and marketing. Pepsi waited patiently for the key ingredient, an artificial sweetener named acesulfame potassium (Ace-K), to be approved by the FDA. The design team spent an estimated 37,000 hours working out the look of the silver can, which de-emphasized the word "Pepsi" in favor of a large "ONE" running down the side of the can in bold black type. The company set a marketing budget of over $100 million for the year following the Pepsi One launch in October 1998.

Pepsi originally positioned Pepsi One as a full-flavored yet healthy alternative to regular colas and targeted 20- to 30-year-old men who did not like the taste of diet colas. The company purposely avoided attaching the word "diet" to the drink because of the negative associations of the diet cola category and its 5 percent market share decline (to 24 percent) since 1990, but initial advertising failed to describe exactly what Pepsi One was and how it was different from Diet Pepsi. Pepsi One was launched with an advertising campaign that featured the Oscar-winning actor Cuba Gooding Jr. as spokesperson. The first slogan for the beverage was "Only one has it all," which was

FIGURE A   Pepsi One Brand Launch

later changed to "True cola taste. One calorie." In 1999, Pepsi replaced Cuba Gooding Jr. with MTV personality Tom Green and added the phrase "Tasted more like regular cola" to Pepsi One cans.

Only 18 months after the launch, Pepsi had achieved a mere 0.8 percent market share in the carbonated soft drinks category, less than half the predicted result. The company cited the poorly defined positioning as one reason for the lack of success. One executive said, "We didn't explain it [Pepsi One] as well as we needed to. There's some confusion as to what Pepsi One is." Phil Marineau, Pepsi's North American Chief at the time, said consumers did not understand "why this [Pepsi One] was different than other diet drinks."

In early 2000, the company again changed the advertising message to include more information about Pepsi One's taste and the "breakthrough sweetener" Ace-K. The new ads also drew direct comparisons to Coca-Cola Classic and used the tag line "Too good to be one calorie . . . but it is." Later that year, Pepsi changed gears again by adding a new celebrity spokesperson, *Sex and the City* actress Kim Cattrall. Pepsi also increased its ad spending for Pepsi One in 2001 when market share remained at 1999 levels. Critics noted that the last new soft drink to be a big hit was Diet Coke in 1982, and warned that "as long as Pepsi has two diet colas on the market, consumers will likely remain confused."

Sources: Cathleen Egan, "PepsiCo Brings Back Actress Catrall for Pepsi One Ad," Dow Jones News Service, 22 August 2001; Nikhil Deogun. "PepsiCo Tweaks Its Ad Approach to Get People to Try Pepsi One," *Wall Street Journal*, 20 April 1999; Betsy McKay, "PepsiCo Tries to Clarify Pepsi One's Image," *Wall Street Journal*, 25 February 2000.

Behavioral
User status
Usage rate
Usage occasion
Brand loyalty
Benefits sought

Demographic
Income
Age
Sex
Race
Family

Psychographic
Values, opinions, and attitudes
Activities and lifestyle

Geographic
International
Regional

FIGURE 3-1   Consumer Segmentation Bases

Nature of Good
Kind
Where used
Type of buy

Buying Condition
Purchase location
Who buys
Type of buy

Demographic
SIC code
Number of employees
Number of production workers
Annual sales volume
Number of establishments

FIGURE 3-2 Business-to-Business Segmentation Bases

Given this market segmentation scheme, marketing programs could be put into place to attract one or more segments. For example, Close-Up initially targeted the first two segments, whereas Crest primarily concentrated on the third segment. Leaving no stone unturned, Beecham's Aquafresh went after all three of these segments, designing the toothpaste to have three stripes to dramatize each of the three different product benefits. With the success of multipurpose toothpastes such as Colgate Total, virtually all brands now offer products that emphasize multiple benefits. Branding Brief 3-2 describes a benefit segmentation plan for gasoline buyers devised by Mobil. Figure 3-3 contains a psychographic breakdown by one leading research firm that cuts across product categories and divides the U.S. population into eight major groups with differing core values.

Often, the underlying rationale for descriptive segmentation bases involves behavioral considerations. For example, marketers may choose to segment a market on the basis of age and target a certain age group, but the underlying reason why that age group may be an attractive market segment may be because they are particularly heavy users of the product, are unusually brand loyal, or are most likely to seek the benefit that the product is best able to deliver. Figure 3-4 shows differences in attitudes and behaviors for several different cultural groups. In some cases, however, broad demographic descriptors may mask important underlying differences.[4] A fairly specific target market of "women aged 35 to 44" may contain a number of very different segments who may require totally different marketing mixes (e.g., think Amy Grant vs. Courtney Love).

The main advantage of demographic segmentation bases is that the demographics of traditional media vehicles are generally well known from consumer research; as a result, it has been easier to buy media on that basis. Branding Brief 3-3 describes how marketers have gone after the teen market. With the growing importance of nontraditional media and other forms of communication, as well as the capability to build databases to profile customers on a behavioral and media usage basis, however, this advantage has become less important. For example, online Web sites can now target

Dividing Up Gasoline Buyers

In the 1950s, oil companies offered trading stamps, glasses, windshield washing services, and other incentives to differentiate their brands. In recent years, however, gasoline marketing has been based primarily on attracting customers with low prices. In an attempt to break out of the sometimes vicious and unprofitable price wars that resulted, Mobil interviewed 2,000 customers to gain new insights into what gasoline customers wanted. According to their study, only 20 percent of Mobil's customers bought gasoline based solely on price. The surveys led the company to conclude that many motorists would forsake gasoline discounters in favor of a "quality buying experience."

Specifically, Mobil's research turned up five primary purchasing groups, labeled the Road Warriors, True Blues, Generation F3 Drivers (for *fuel, food,* and *fast*), Homebodies, and Price Driven. Different groups exhibited different needs and spending habits: The Price Driven group spent no more than $700 annually, whereas the biggest spenders, the Road Warriors and True Blues, averaged at least $1,200 a year (see Figure A). Mobil decided to target these big spenders, as well as Generation F3 Drivers (because Mobil felt many of them were destined to become Road Warriors).

With a 10 percent share of the U.S. market, Mobil overtook Shell in 1995 to become the leading gasoline seller. In 1996, Mobil introduced "Friendly Serve," a program that harked back to the days when gas stations provided full service at no extra cost. Mobil instructed its gas station attendants to approach customers and offer to pump gas and wash windows free of charge. The program, designed to improve customer loyalty, enabled Mobil to increase prices.

FIGURE A Mobile Gasoline Buyer Segmentation Plan

Taxonomy at the Pump: Mobil's Five Types of Gasoline Buyers

Road Warriors:	True Blues:	Generation F3:	Homebodies:	Price Driven:
Generally higher-income middle-aged men who drive 25,000 to 50,000 miles a year . . . buy premium with a credit card . . . purchase sandwiches and drinks from the convenience store . . . will sometimes wash their cars at the carwash.	Usually men and women with moderate to high incomes who are loyal to a brand and sometimes to a particular station . . . frequently buy premium gasoline and pay in cash.	(for fuel, food and fast): Upwardly mobile men and women—half under 25 years of age—who are constantly on the go . . . drive a lot and snack heavily from the convenience store.	Usually housewives who shuttle their children around during the day and use whatever gasoline station is based in town or along their route of travel.	Generally aren't loyal to either a brand or a particular station, and rarely buy the premium line . . . frequently on tight budgets . . . efforts to woo them have been the basis of marketing strategies for years.
16% of buyers	**16% of buyers**	**27% of buyers**	**21% of buyers**	**20% of buyers**

Mobil provided another convenience for consumers when it introduced the Mobil Speedpass technology in 1997. Speedpass picked up where credit card payments at pumps left off by enabling customers to pay electronically by waving a transponder, which drivers attach to their keychains, in front of the pump. Speedpass could also be used to pay for items from mini-marts at Mobil stations.

Sources: Allanna Sullivan, "Mobil Bets Drivers Pick Cappuccino over Low Prices," *Wall Street Journal*, 1 January 1995, B1; Leah Rickard, "Mobil Pumps Up Image for Friendlier Service," *Advertising Age*, 6 February 1995, 8; Peter Fritsch, "Mobil Aims to Turn Its Gasoline Pumps into Express Lanes," *Wall Street Journal*, 19 February 1997.

such previously hard-to-reach markets as African Americans (NetNoir.com), Hispanics (Quepasa.com), Asian Americans (AsianAvenue.com), college students (Collegeclub.com), and homosexuals (PlanetOut.com).

Criteria

A number of criteria have been offered to guide segmentation and target market decisions, such as the following:[5]

➤ *Identifiability:* Can segment identification be easily determined?

➤ *Size:* Is there adequate sales potential in the segment?

➤ *Accessibility:* Are specialized distribution outlets and communication media available to reach the segment?

➤ *Responsiveness:* How favorably will the segment respond to a tailored marketing program?

The obvious overriding consideration in defining market segments is profitability. In many cases, profitability can be related to behavioral considerations. For example, Baldinger analyzes the implications of a brand loyalty segmentation scheme with four segments dubbed "Loyals," "Rotators," "Deal Selectives," and "Price Drivens." Along these lines, Market Facts research supplier has developed a conversion model to measure the strength of the psychological commitment between brands and consumers and their openness to change.[6] To determine the ease with which a consumer can be converted to another choice, the model assesses commitment based on factors such as consumer attitudes toward and satisfaction with current brand choices in a category and the importance of the decision to select a brand in the category.

The model segments *users* of a brand into four groups based on strength of commitment, from low to high, as follows:

1. *Convertible:* On the threshold of change; highly likely to switch brands
2. *Shallow:* Not ready to switch, but may be considering alternatives
3. *Average:* Comfortable with their choice; unlikely to switch in the future
4. *Entrenched:* Staunchly loyal; unlikely to change in the foreseeable future

The model also classifies *nonusers* of a brand into four other groups based on their openness to trying the brand, from low to high, as follows:

1. *Strongly Unavailable:* Strongly prefer their current brand
2. *Weakly Unavailable:* Preference lies with their current brand, although not strongly
3. *Ambivalent:* As attracted to the "other" band as to their current choice
4. *Available:* Prefer the "other" brand but have not yet switched

Category	Description
Up and Comers	
New Visionaries	See themselves as innovative and competitive. Focused on improvement and getting ahead.
Nouveau Nesters	Live for today. Ambitious but not worried about the future because they are self-confident and creative.
Go-getters	More established young households. Have become more practical and stressed, yet maintain competitive spirit, sense of fun.
Wired	Mostly young, single males. Active and involved. Strong technology affinity.
Young Materialists	
Rhythm and Youth	Stressed with information overload, trying to make ends meet. Not planning too far into the future.
Young and Restless	Aspiring students obsessed with style, status, and the good life.
Cynical Disconnectors	Mostly males. Want good things in life, yet have no plan to get there.
Stressed by Life	
Urban Strugglers	Primarily single mothers in ethnically diverse neighborhoods. Just getting by, yet trying to do best for their families. Feel overwhelmed. Focused on kids.
Rainbow Seekers	Optimistic, want to build a good life despite limited resources. Working and planning for better life for their kids.
Urban Romantics	Still want fun and excitement. Balancing child care, own needs. Result: stressed.
New Traditionalists	
Overbooked Moms	Many tasks, activities are juggled in these households. Plan, but constantly must improvise. Active and social, yet stressed as they try to do everything.
Heartwarmers	Family focused, but strivers, who plan and work for long-term goals.
Players	Want everyone in family to have active, fun life. Do a lot, much without stress. Active, involved, and pleasure-oriented.
Band Leaders	Younger families, focused on values. Many family activities out of the home.
All Americans	Slightly older families, in control of lives and achieving active family goals.
Family Limiteds	
The Blands	Focused totally on family to exclusion of strong interest or connection to rest of the world. Busy with family duties, wish for "a little more time" for themselves.
The Can't Be Bothered	Younger families, somewhat overextended financially. Put family before all else. Want things that make their lives easy, but have little interest in self-development or community.

(Continued)

FIGURE 3-3 Psychographic Breakdown of U.S. Population

Category	Description
Family Limiteds *(cont.)*	
Ships in the Harbor	Happy group, content with families, yet cautious in views of rest of the world.
Homebodies	Use family as retreat from scary, nasty world. Favor traditional family values.
Detached Introverts	
Loners	Suspicious, with limited resources, these households are averse to technology, yet wish for finer things (boat, faster car). Have little to do with world at large.
Hermits	Somewhat aimless. Educated, but passively watch TV at home and coast.
Internet Introverts	Inactive, middle-aged men who, despite higher incomes, have low self-image. Enamoured of technology and Internet, which is where they live their lives.
Technicians	Success drive, but not social. Few interests outside work.
Fence Builders	Conservative planners, focused on financial success. Low involvement or interest in social or cultural activities.
Renaissance Elders	
Self-Discovering Nesters	Still involved in growth, adventure, and enhancing life as they age. Consider themselves creative and ambitious.
Prime Timers	Successful older households reaping fruits of well-managed life. Progressive in values. Have little stress in their lives.
Satisfied Seniors	Maintain and plan family with strong sense of spirituality and community. Homes and families are top priorities. Vital and involved in their communities.
Comfortable Twilighters	Empty nesters with traditional values. Comfortable and secure, while staying connected to the world. Maintaining their health is a key focus.
Calm Retireds	Active, involved households, somewhat more male. Educated and capable of managing their retirements well.
Retired From Life	
Carefree Traditionals	Conservative, spiritual, focused on home and family to exclusion of the rest of the world, which they distrust.
Rooted in the Past	Also conservative and home-focused, but much more connected to the wider world through avid news readership. Are active and still value style and status in material possessions. Skeptical of new technology and somewhat cynical.
Complacent Seniors	A bit overburdened by the world, skeptical of modern innovations and feeling overwhelmed by information.

Source: Yankelovich.

FIGURE 3-3   *(Continued)*

	Agreements with Statements about Eating and Grocery Shopping				
	≥ General Market (%)	Total Anglo; (%)	Total African American (%)	Total Hispanic (%)	Total Asian; (%)
I prefer to use sugar rather than sugar substitutes	52	49	56	69	50
We're mainly a meat and potatoes family	39	38	34	59	21
I collect recipes	35	36	32	37	27
No matter how busy I get I eat the right foods	35	30	36	65	48
I exercise regularly	34	33	34	43	31
I'm worried about becoming overweight	28	24	27	62	28
I often overindulge	20	19	22	33	18
My family and I eat a lot of fast food	11	8	19	27	12

Source: MSR&C Ethnic Market Report, 1996.

FIGURE 3-4   Illustrative Example of Ethnic Differences

Figure 3-5 illustrates an application of the conversion model to the carbonated soft drink market in the summer of 1991. Market Facts defines the near-term potential of a brand and its future health as the difference between the Available Nonuser and Convertible User segments. On that basis, Market Facts believed that growth potential was found for several noncola soft drinks and later reported some confirmatory market evidence.

Nature of Competition

It is difficult to disentangle target market decisions from decisions concerning the nature of competition for the brand because they are often so closely related. In other words, deciding to target a certain type of consumer often, at least implicitly, defines the nature of competition because certain firms have also decided to target that segment in the past (or plan to do so in the future) or because consumers in that segment already may look to certain brands in their purchase decisions. Other issues can be raised, however, in defining the nature of competition and deciding which products and brands are most likely to be seen as close substitutes. For example, the nature of competition may depend on the channels of distribution chosen. Competitive analysis considers a whole host of factors—including the resources, capabilities, and likely intentions of various other firms—to choose markets where consumers can be profitably serviced (see also Chapter 11).[7]

One lesson stressed by many marketing strategists is not to be too narrow in defining competition. Often, competition may occur at the benefit level rather than the attribute

Targeting Teens

There are currently more than 30 million kids in the United States between the ages of 12 and 19. That number will grow to 35 million by 2010, at which point the teen population will be the largest in American history. According to Forrester Research, the average American teenager has almost $60 of weekly disposable income. Roughly 20 percent of U.S. teens have bank accounts and credit cards, and the same percentage invests in stocks or funds. Teens have lots of money to spend, but they are discerning about how and when they spend it. To capture the attention and dollars of the teen market, retailers are integrating disparate aspects of the teenage lifestyle into their locations and marketing.

One popular method for attracting the attention of teens is a "magalog"—a catalog designed to resemble a magazine. Magalogs showcase the company's products, of course, but they also feature travel articles, celebrity interviews, fashion spreads, short stories, home decorating tips, and other magazine-style items of interest to teens. Mass retailer Target launched a back-to-school magalog in 2000 that contained a profile on pop singer Macy Gray, an article about life at a Hawaiian high school, and a pictorial featuring neon-pink electronic products. Nancy Carruth, Target's director of advertising management, stated that the goal of the magalog is "to get the brand and merchandise in front of [teens] without being in their face." Clothing retailer Abercrombie & Fitch publishes a risqué magalog that features topless models (both male and female) cavorting in a minimum amount of A&F clothing. The relative absence of product in the A&F magalog confirms one retail executive's view that "the catalog is now more of a marketing tool than a selling tool."

Music is another essential element of the teen lifestyle that retailers are incorporating. Many magalogs contain music reviews, and retailers develop store "soundtracks" that customers can purchase. American Eagle, a clothing retailer, gives CDs to customers who spend over a certain amount. The Internet is another area of vital importance to teenagers. One-third of Americans aged 16 to 22 purchased items over the Internet in 2000. In addition to changing purchasing behavior, the Internet is changing teens' media habits. The drop in average hours of television watched among U.S. teens from 19 to 17 hours is attributed to the influx of the Internet into American households. To capitalize on the teen Internet trend, retailers are developing "lifestyle portals" that contain e-commerce features but also entertainment such as games, music, and chat rooms. For example, American Eagle developed an online "AE-Zine" that features such teen-oriented fare as a summer reading list, streaming video of American Eagle commercials, horoscopes, actor profiles, and CD reviews.

Sources: "The Young Survey," *The Economist*, 23 December 2000; Amy Barrett, "To Reach the Unreachable Teen," *Business Week*, 18 September 2000; http://www.ae.com.

FIGURE 3-5 Market Facts' Conversion Model Applied to Carbonated Soft Drinks

	Coca-Cola	Pepsi Cola	Diet Coke	Diet Pepsi	Dr Pepper	7 UP	Sprite	Minute Maid	Orange Crush	Mountain Dew
Users (%)										
Entrenched	4	4	1	1	3	1	1	0	—	—
Average	21	19	10	9	13	8	6	2	3	4
Shallow	12	9	7	4	4	5	6	3	2	2
Convertible	3	2	2	2	1	1	2	1	1	1
Total Users (%)	40	34	20	16	21	15	14	6	6	7
Nonusers (%)										
Available	2	4	1	3	4	6	6	4	6	3
Ambivalent	9	12	6	7	12	17	15	10	13	10
Weakly Unavailable	11	13	9	11	15	22	20	18	19	16
Strongly Unavailable	38	37	64	63	48	40	45	61	56	64
Total Nonusers (%)	60	66	80	84	79	85	86	94	94	93
Near-Term Potential	−1	+2	−1	+1	+3	+5	+4	+3	+5	+2

At the core of Market Facts' conversion model is a religion-based theory of how human commitment is formed. The model segments consumers according to the strength of their attachment to a particular brand. The direction of the difference between the sizes of the Available and Convertible segments is a strong indicator of future brand health.

level. Thus, a luxury good with a strong hedonic benefit (e.g., stereo equipment) may compete as much with a vacation as with other durable goods (e.g., furniture).

Baskin-Robbins

In the late 1990s, Baskin-Robbins set out on a $100 million face-lift because, as one executive put it, "If we do not transform this brand quickly, the greater risk is that the Baskin-Robbins brand won't be fit to compete in the 21st century." Remodeled stores displayed a new décor and a reallocation of space to more promiently feature growth products such as frozen coffee drinks and blended frozen-fruit smoothies. In sprucing up its image, Baskin-Robbins hoped to become a stronger competitor to Starbucks, Jamba Juice, TCBY, and the plethora of other snack chains—not just Dairy Queen, as perhaps in years gone by. As one franchise owner put it, "We're competing with bagel shops, Boston Market stores, McDonald's, and all the other food opportunities out there."[8]

As noted in Chapter 2, products are often organized in consumers' minds in a hierarchical fashion such that competition can be defined at a number of different levels. Take Fresca (a grapefruit—flavored soft drink) as an example: At the product type level, it competes with noncola, flavored soft drinks; at the product category level, it competes with all soft drinks; and at the product class level, it competes with all beverages. The target and competitive frame of reference chosen will dictate the breadth of brand awareness and the situations and types of cues that should become closely related to the brand. Recognizing the nature of different levels of competition has important implications for the desired brand associations, as described next.

Points of Parity and Points of Difference

Once the appropriate competitive frame of reference for positioning has been fixed by defining the customer target market and nature of competition, the basis of the positioning itself can be defined. Arriving at the proper positioning requires establishing the correct points-of-difference and points-of-parity associations.[9]

Points-of-Difference Associations

Points of difference (PODs) are strong, favorable, and unique brand associations for a brand. They may be based on virtually any type of attribute or benefit association. All that ultimately matters for an attribute or benefit association to become a point of difference is that it becomes a strong, favorable, and unique association in the minds of consumers. That is, PODs are attributes or benefits that consumers strongly associate with a brand, positively evaluate, and believe that they could not find to the same extent with a competitive brand. Although a myriad of different types of brand associations are possible candidates to become points of difference, according to the CBBE model, brand associations can be broadly classified in terms of either functional, performance-related considerations or abstract, imagery-related considerations.

The concept of PODs has much in common with several other well-known marketing concepts. For example, it is similar to the notion of *unique selling proposition* (USP), a concept pioneered by Rosser Reeves and the Ted Bates advertising agency in the

1950s. The original idea behind USP was that advertising should give consumers a compelling reason to buy a product that competitors could not match. With this approach, the emphasis in designing ads was placed on communicating a distinctive, unique product benefit (i.e., the ad message or claims) and not on the creative (i.e., the ad creative or execution). In other words, USP emphasized *what* was said in an ad as opposed to *how* it was said. As a result, ads singlemindedly hammered home the key consumer benefit.

Anacin

One notable—albeit widely disliked—example of applying the USP principle was an ad for Anacin aspirin. The ad schematically showed three boxes in the skull of a headache sufferer. In turn, a pounding hammer, a coiling spring, and a crackling lightening bolt were relieved by little bubbles of Anacin making their way up from the user's stomach, as the announcer stated: "Are you looking for fast, fast, fast relief? Then take Anacin. Anacin stops headache pain fast, relieves tension fast, and calms jittery nerves fast. Anacin—for fast, fast, *fast* relief." In 1954, American Home Products backed these Anacin ads with a lavish media budget. Although disliked, the message got through, and the brand gained considerable market share.

A related positioning concept is *sustainable competitive advantage* (SCA), which relates, in part, to a firm's ability to achieve an advantage in delivering superior value in the marketplace for a prolonged period of time.[10] Although the SCA concept is somewhat broader than points of difference—SCAs could be based on business practices such as human resource policies—it also emphasizes the importance of differentiating products in some fashion. Thus, the concept of points of difference is closely related to unique selling proposition and sustainable competitive advantage and maintains that a brand must have some strong, favorable, and unique associations to differentiate itself from other brands.

Consumers' actual brand choices often depend on the perceived uniqueness of brand associations. Creating strong, favorable, and unique associations is a real challenge to marketers, but essential in terms of competitive brand positioning. Swedish retailer Ikea took a luxury product—home furnishings and furniture—and made it a reasonably priced alternative for the mass market. Ikea supports its low prices by having customers serve, deliver, and assemble the products themselves. Ikea also gains a point of difference through its product offerings. As one commentator noted, "Ikea built their reputation on the notion that Sweden produces good, safe, well-built things for the masses. They have some of the most innovative designs at the lowest cost out there."[11] As another example, consider Subaru.

Subaru

By 1993, Subaru was selling only 104,000 cars annually in the United States, down 60 percent from their earlier peak. Cumulative U.S. losses approached $1 billion. Advertised as "Inexpensive and Built to Stay That Way," Subaru was seen as a me-too car that was undifferentiated from Toyota, Honda, and all their followers. To provide a clear, distinct image, Subaru decided to sell only all-wheel-drive in its passenger cars. After upgrading its luxury image—and increasing its price—Subaru sold over 175,000 cars by 2000.

Points of difference may involve performance attributes (e.g., the fact that Kraft Singles cheese has 5 ounces of milk) or performance benefits (e.g., the fact that Magnavox's electronic products have "consumer friendly" technological features, such as television sets with a button to help locate misplaced remotes and "Smart Sound" to automatically level out spikes in television volume). In other cases, PODs involve imagery associations (e.g., the western imagery of Marlboro cigarettes or the fact that British Airways is advertised as the "world's favourite airline"). Many top brands attempt to create a point of difference on "overall superior quality," whereas a positioning strategy adopted by a number of other firms is to create a point of difference for their brands as the "low-cost provider" of a product or service. Thus, a host of different types of PODs are possible.

Points-of-Parity Associations

Points of parity (POPs), on the other hand, are those associations that are not necessarily unique to the brand but may in fact be shared with other brands. These types of associations come in two basic forms: category and competitive. *Category points of parity* are those associations that consumers view as being necessary to be a legitimate and credible offering within a certain product or service category. In other words, they represent necessary—but not necessarily sufficient—conditions for brand choice. In terms of the discussion of product levels from Chapter 1, these attribute associations are minimally at the generic product level and most likely at the expected product level. Thus, consumers might not consider a bank truly a "bank" unless it offered a range of checking and savings plans; provided safety deposit boxes, travelers checks, and other such services; had convenient hours and automated teller machines; and so forth. Category POPs may change over time because of technological advances, legal developments, and consumer trends, but the attributes and benefits that function as category POPs can be seen as the "greens fees" to play the marketing game.

Note that category POPs become especially critical when a brand launches a brand extension into a new category. In fact, the more dissimilar the extension category, the more important it is to make sure that category POPs are sufficiently well established. The implications of this realization for the introductory marketing program for an extension are clear. In many cases, consumers might have a clear understanding of the extension's intended point of difference by virtue of its use of an existing brand name. Where consumers often need reassurance, however, and what should often be the focus of the marketing program, is whether the extension also has the necessary points of parity.

Nivea

Nivea became a leader in the skin cream category by creating strong points of difference on the benefits of "gentle," "protective," and "caring." As they leveraged their brand equity into categories such as deodorants, shampoos, and cosmetics (Figure 3-6), Nivea found it necessary to establish category points of parity before they could promote their brands' points of difference. Nivea's points of difference of gentle, protective, and caring were of little value unless consumers believed that its deodorant was strong enough, its shampoo

FIGURE 3-6 Nivea Product Packaging

would produce beautiful enough hair, and its cosmetics would be colorful enough. Once points of parity were established, Nivea's heritage and other associations could be introduced as compelling points of difference.

Competitive points-of-parity associations are those associations designed to negate competitors' points of difference. In other words, if in the eyes of consumers, the brand association designed to be the competitor's point of difference (e.g., a product benefit of some type) is as strongly held for the target brand as for competitor's brands *and* the target brand is able to establish another association as strong, favorable, and unique as part of its point of difference, then the target brand should be in a superior competitive position. In short, if a brand can "break even" in those areas where their competitors are trying to find an advantage *and* can achieve advantages in some other areas, the brand should be in a strong—and perhaps unbeatable—competitive position. For example, consider the introduction of Miller Lite beer (see Figure 3-7).[12]

Miller Lite

When Philip Morris bought Miller Brewing, their flagship High Life brand was not competing particularly well, leading the company to decide to introduce a light beer. The initial advertising strategy for Miller Lite was to assure parity with a necessary and important consideration in the category by stating that it "tastes great" while at the same time creating a point of difference with the fact that it contained one-third less calories (96 calories versus 150 calories for conventional 12-ounce full-strength beer) and was thus "less filling."

FIGURE 3-7   Miller Lite Brand Positioning

As is often the case, the point of parity and point of difference were somewhat conflicting, as consumers tend to equate taste with calories. To overcome potential consumer resistance to this notion, Miller employed credible spokespeople, primarily popular former professional athletes who would presumably not drink a beer unless it tasted good. These ex-jocks were placed in amusing situations in ads where they debated the merits of Miller Lite as to which of the two product benefits—"tastes great" or "less filling"—was more descriptive of the beer, creating valuable points of parity *and* points of difference. The ads ended with the clever tag line "Everything you've always wanted in a beer . . . and less."[13]

Points of Parity versus Points of Difference

To achieve a point of parity on a particular attribute or benefit, a sufficient number of consumers must believe that the brand is "good enough" on that dimension. There is a "zone" or "range of tolerance or acceptance" with POPs. It does not have to be the case that the brand is *literally* seen as equal to competitors, but consumers must feel that the brand does sufficiently well on that particular attribute or benefit so that they do not consider it to be a negative or a problem. Assuming consumers feel that way, they may then be willing to base their evaluations and decisions on other factors potentially more favorable to the brand. Points of parity are thus easier to achieve than points of difference, where the brand must demonstrate clear superiority.

Often, the key to positioning is not so much in achieving a point of difference as in achieving necessary or competitive points of parity.

SnackWell's.
One of the most successful new products in the last decade, SnackWell's was a pioneer in reduced-fat snacks (see Figure 3-8). Many competitors followed, however, so in the late 1990s, Nabisco launched a new campaign to reflect the product's changing market realities. One ad featured an attractive, swimsuit-clad young couple cavorting on a beach. During their tryst, however, the woman fantasizes about escaping to savor some SnackWell's cookies. A voiceover proclaimed, "Passion. Desire. Devotion. Nah, it goes beyond that," as a handful of glowing peanut butter chip cookies gently tumbled in the background. In explaining why the ad didn't even mention that the product had half the fat of a "regular version," a Nabisco executive commented, "Consumers hear SnackWell's and they know

FIGURE 3-8   SnackWell's Product Packaging

that we'll deliver low fat." To set the product apart, "we really want to emphasize taste." A later ad for coconut cream sandwich cookies contained the tag line "Being So Bad Was Never So Good."

Other examples of the importance of creating POPs abound. Branding Brief 3-4 describes how CNN has attempted to reposition itself away from the image of "Crisis News Network."

POSITIONING GUIDELINES

The concepts of points of difference and points of parity can be invaluable tools to guide positioning. A number of considerations come into play in conducting positioning analysis and deciding on the desired PODs and POPs and the resulting brand image. Two key issues in arriving at the optimal competitive brand positioning are (1) defining and communicating the competitive frame of reference and (2) choosing and establishing points of parity and points of difference.[14] Brand Focus 3.0 at the end of the chapter provides some research insight into the brand positioning process.

Defining and Communicating the Competitive Frame of Reference

A starting point in defining a competitive frame of reference for a brand positioning is to determine category membership. Membership indicates the products or sets of products with which a brand competes. Choosing to compete in different categories

BRANDING BRIEF 3-4

Tonight at 9, Crisis at CNN

Turner Broadcasting's Cable News Network (CNN) revolutionized television programming in many ways. Introduced in 1980, CNN slowly built a following by combining detailed 24-hour-a-day news coverage, live broadcasts, and expert analysis and commentary. With its sister network, Headline News, CNN's up-to-the minute and in-depth newscasts reach more than 80 million American households and are available to more than one billion viewers worldwide.

CNN's rating have soared whenever a crisis or breaking news story occurred. During the early weeks of the Persian Gulf War in January 1991, CNN achieved a daily 24-hour average rating of 7, which corresponded with 4 million viewers. Unfortunately, after the war ended, CNN's ratings dropped back to their normal, prewar average. This cycle repeated itself during O.J. Simpson's "white Bronco" low-speed chase and his subsequent trial. As a result of this ratings trend, CNN came to be known as the "Crisis News Network."

In analyzing their positioning, it could be argued that although CNN has strong points of difference on the basis of "in depth" and "up-to-the-minute," it may lack necessary points of parity. For example, it may also need to convey that it has as interesting and enjoyable programming as other cable channels, which would be worth viewing regardless of the particular current events involved. Consistent with this reasoning, CNN has moved beyond its regularly scheduled news shows (e.g., *Daybreak, Newsday,* and *PrimeNews*) and established varied programming such as interview and talk shows (e.g., *Larry King Live* and *Crossfire*) and specialized news shows (e.g., *Lou Dobbs Moneyline, CNN Sports Tonite,* and *Showbiz Today*).

The prolonged 2000 election controversy gave CNN a sixfold ratings boost over its 1999–2000 season average as it outpaced its rivals Fox News and MSNBC in terms of viewers. This surge was not enough to prevent a decline in ad revenues during 2000, which was compounded by the fact that CNN was over its programming budget for the year. In January of that year, CNN laid off 10 percent of its workforce.

To retain viewers in between crises, CNN added new call-in talk shows to its primetime lineup, including *The Spin Room,* a point-counterpoint show featuring the conservative Tucker Carlson and liberal Bill Press, and *The Point with Greta Van Susteren,* a show featuring the network's popular legal analyst, who eventually ended up leaving the network in a contract dispute. "It's about being live and alive," said CNN's U.S. network general manager Sid Bedingfield. "More live reporting, more live interviewing, more live debriefs." CNN management felt confident that the focus on live television would stem the network's ratings slide.

Sources: Sally Beatty, "CNN to Lay Off 400, Redefine Broadcast Roles," *Wall Street Journal*, 18 January 2001; Sally Beatty, "CNN Priority Is to Hold Viewers Between Crises," *Wall Street Journal*, 14 November 2000; Joe Flint, "CNN's Ratings Decline as Rivals Lure Away Its Viewers," *Wall Street Journal*, 31 March 2000.

often results in different competitive frames of reference and thus different POPs and PODs (see Branding Brief 3-5).

Communicating category membership informs the consumer about the goals that they might achieve by using a product or service. For highly established products and services, category membership is not a focal issue. Target customers are aware that Coca-Cola is a leading brand of soft drink, that Kellogg's Corn Flakes is a leading brand of cereal, McKinsey is a leading strategy consulting firm, and so on.

There are many situations, however, in which it is important to inform consumers of a brand's category membership. Perhaps the most obvious situation is the introduction of new products, where the category membership is not always apparent. This uncertainty can be especially true for high-tech products.

Personal Digital Assistants

When personal digital assistants (PDAs) were first introduced, the product could have been positioned as either a computer accessory or a replacement for an appointment book. Motorola Envoy's failure could be attributed in part to the lack of a clearly defined competitive set. By contrast, Palm Pilot, a product that performed many of the same tasks as Envoy, achieved considerable success by claiming membership in the electronic organizer category. More recently, BlackBerry has extended that category to encompass e-mail while offering a more traditional keyboard, thus serving as a substitute to some extent for laptop computers (see Figure 3-9). As these handheld devices continue to offer new features and services, their competitive frames of reference will continue to evolve.

Situations also exist in which consumers know a brand's category membership but may not be convinced that the brand is a true, valid member of the category. In such cases, alerting consumers to a brand's category membership is warranted. For example, consumers may be aware that Sony produces computers, but they may not be certain whether Sony computers are in the same "class" as IBM, Dell, and Compaq. In this instance, it might be useful to reinforce category membership.

Brands are sometimes affiliated with categories in which they do not hold membership rather than with the one in which they do. This approach is a viable way to highlight a brand's point of difference from competitors, provided that consumers know the brand's actual membership. For example, Bristol-Myers Squibb ran commercials for its Excedrin aspirin acknowledging Tylenol's perceived consumer acceptance for aches and pains, but touting their brand as "The Headache Medicine." With this approach, however, it is important that consumers understand what the brand stands for, and not just what it is *not*, as evidenced by the following experience.

Zima

Zima was launched in 1994 by Adolph Coors Company in the midst of the New Age beverage craze. Zima was defined almost entirely by what it was not: not a beer and not a wine cooler. The colorless beverage was supported by an introductory ad campaign in which a mysterious pitchman in a white suit and black hat described the product as, "It'z a secret.

Competitive Frames of Reference for FedEx

Consider the possible positioning options for FedEx, the U.S. market share leader in the overnight delivery service (ONDS) category. Within the ONDS category, FedEx created strong, favorable, and unique associations to the consumer benefits of being the fastest and most dependable delivery service around (as reinforced by their introductory slogan, "When it absolutely, positively has to be there overnight"). This association provided a key point of difference to traditional mail deliveries by the United States Postal Service (which would typically take two or more days depending on the destination involved), as well as other ONDS carriers who found it difficult, at least initially, to match FedEx's high level of service quality.

If FedEx were to define its competition as other brands in the ONDS category, then it might continue to design marketing programs to enhance its associations with speed and reliability. On the other hand, what other forms of competition does FedEx face? As a market leader, it could be argued that its competition comes to a large extent from other types of products that can satisfy needs similar to those satisfied by FedEx. For example, consider fax machines or e-mail. It certainly would be true that many documents that would have been sent by overnight delivery—and most likely by FedEx—a few years ago can now be sent more quickly and easily via a fax machine or as an e-mail attachment.

In that sense, some of FedEx's stiffest competition may come from other forms of document transmission and delivery. In the case of fax machines and e-mails, FedEx's key point of difference of "speedy delivery" is rendered meaningless by their instantaneous capabilities, suggesting that other points of difference are necessary. On the other hand, the confidence and risk reduction of sending a document by FedEx may still be relevant when competing with fax delivery. Although a fax may not find its way to the intended person in a timely manner, FedEx may be more likely to "hit the right mark." Similarly, e-mails also lack confirmation, so that it is unclear whether a message was properly received. Thus, FedEx may decide to emphasize security and confidentiality as compared with fax machines and e-mails. Along those lines, note that the company's heavily promoted tracking capabilities may actually help it to compete with both types of their main competitors—other ONDS carriers as well as alternative delivery forms such as fax machines and e-mail.

Finally, perhaps FedEx's greatest growth opportunity is with Internet commerce. However, at least initially, UPS has been able to gain more of that market due to its aggressive pricing and consumers' willingness to wait an extra day or two to save money.

Source: David Field, "FedEx Not Ready to Abandon Shipping," *USA Today*, 20 October 1999, B3.

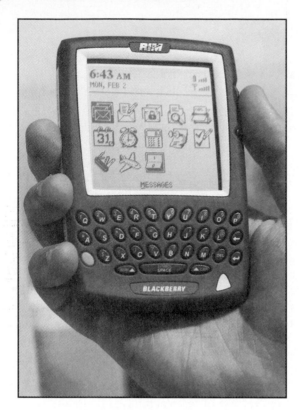

FIGURE 3-9 Positioning BlackBerry

It'z zomething different." Although the ads created some mystique, they never made it clear what Zima actually was. As one former executive of the company noted, "You couldn't tell whether you should be pounding it down or sipping it over ice." Compounding the problem was a quirky taste that many consumers did not like. Repeat sales stalled, and Coors management came to the realization that Zima was perhaps destined to be a niche brand. They subsequently launched the ad campaign "A Few Degrees Cooler" to reinforce Zima's product uniqueness.[15]

The preferred approach to positioning is to inform consumers of a brand's membership before stating its point of difference in relation to other category members. Presumably, consumers need to know what a product is and what function it serves prior to assessing whether it dominates the brands against which it competes. For new products, separate marketing programs are generally needed to inform consumers of membership and to educate them about a brand's point of difference. For brands with limited resources, this implies the development of a marketing strategy that establishes category membership prior to one that states a point of difference. Brands with greater resources can develop concurrent marketing programs in which one features membership and the other the point of difference. Efforts to inform consumers of membership and points of difference in the same ad, however, are often not effective.

Occasionally, a company will undertake to straddle two frames of reference.

BMW

When BMW first made a strong competitive push into the U.S. market in the early 1980s, it positioned the brand as being the only automobile that offered both luxury *and* performance. At that time, American luxury cars were seen by many as lacking performance, and American performance cars were seen as lacking luxury. By relying on the design of their cars, their German heritage, and other aspects of a well-designed marketing program, BMW was able to simultaneously achieve (1) a point of difference on luxury and a point of parity on performance with respect to performance cars and (2) a point of difference on luxury and a point of parity on performance with respect to performance cars. The clever slogan "The Ultimate Driving Machine" effectively captured the newly created umbrella category—luxury performance cars.

Although a straddle positioning often is attractive as a means of reconciling potentially conflicting consumer goals, it carries an extra burden. If the points of parity and points of difference with respect to both categories are not credible, the brand may not be viewed as a legitimate player in *either* category. Many early PDAs that unsuccessfully tried to straddle categories ranging from pagers to laptop computers provide a vivid illustration of this risk.

There are three main ways to convey a brand's category membership: communicating category benefits, comparing to exemplars, and relying on the product descriptor.

To reassure consumers that a brand will deliver on the fundamental reason for using a category, benefits are frequently used to announce category membership. Thus, industrial motors might claim to have power, and analgesics might announce their efficacy. These benefits are presented in a manner that does not imply brand superiority but merely notes that the brand possesses these properties as a means to establish category POPs. To provide supporting rationale so that consumers believe that a brand has the benefits that imply membership in a category, performance and imagery associations can be used. A cake mix might attain membership in the cake category by claiming the benefit of great taste and might support this benefit claim by possessing high-quality ingredients (performance) or by showing users delighting in its consumption (imagery).

Exemplars—well-known, noteworthy brands in a category—can also be used to specify a brand's category membership. For example, Wheaties introduced a presweetened cereal by telling consumers that if they liked Frosted Flakes, they should try Wheaties Honey Gold. The idea was not to compete with Frosted Flakes, but to tell consumers in an efficient way that Wheaties Honey Gold is a member of the "adult presweetened" cereal category. When Tommy Hilfiger was an unknown designer, advertising announced his membership as a great American designer by associating him with Geoffrey Beene, Stanley Blacker, Calvin Klein, and Perry Ellis, who were recognized members of that category.

The product descriptor that follows the brand name is often a very compact means of conveying category origin. For example, USAir changed its name to USAirways, according to CEO Stephen Wolf, as part of the airline's attempted transformation from a regional one with a poor reputation to a strong national or even international brand. The argument was that other major airlines had the word *airlines or* airways in their names rather than *air,* which was felt to be typically associated with smaller, regional carriers.[16] Consider the following examples.

➤ Ford Motor Company invested more than $1 billion on a radical new 2004 model named the X-Trainer that combines the attributes of an SUV, a minivan, and a station wagon. To communicate its unique position—and to avoid association with its Explorer and Country Squire models—the vehicle will be designated a "sports wagon."[17]

➤ When Campbell's launched their V-8 Splash beverage line, they deliberately avoided including the word "carrot" in the brand name despite the fact that it was the main ingredient. The name was chosen to convey healthful benefits but to avoid the negative perception of carrots.[18]

➤ California's prune growers and marketers have attempted to establish an alternative name for their product, "dried plums," because prunes were seen by the target market of 35- to 50-year-old women as "a laxative for old people."[19]

➤ SureBeam Corporation has a patented method of food irradiation that involves exposing foods to controlled levels of ionizing radiation to kill most pathogens, including potentially deadly strains of *E. coli* bacteria. But despite the FDA's blessing and the fact that the process might prevent some of the 5,000-plus food-safety-related deaths each year, SureBeam has to avoid the word *irradiation* because many Americans associate it with radioactivity. Consequently, the firm adopted their corporate name to be used as the ingredient brand, asking consumers in ads to look for the SureBeam seal.[20]

The product descriptor is often critical with new technology products. When Silicon Graphics introduced a low-cost version of their famed 3-D workstations, they chose to label the product as a "desktop workstation" to communicate its affordability as well as its power and functionality in an effort to broaden its potential market. Similarly, when IBM rebranded their multibillion-dollar server product line as the eSeries, they created four different sets of brands and products within the line. Although three of the series had clear designations—zSeries mainframe servers, pSeries Unix servers, and xSeries Intel servers—the designation for their iSeries integrated application servers (formerly the highly successful AS/400) did not necessarily provide clear category membership either within the IBM product line or with respect to its server competitors.

Although it is important to establish a brand's category membership, it is usually not sufficient for effective brand positioning. Although such efforts can help to grow the category, if many firms engage in category-building tactics, the result may be consumer confusion. For example, at the peak of the dot-com boom, a host of dot-coms advertised their category membership. Ameritrade, E*TRADE, Datek, and others advertised that they had lower commission rates on stock trades than conventional brokerage firms; Pets.com, Petopia, and other pet food supply companies promoted their vast array of pet supplies; and so on. A sound positioning strategy requires the specification not only of the category in which a brand holds membership, but also how a brand dominates other members of its category. Developing compelling points of difference is thus critical to effective brand positioning, as discussed next.

Choosing Points of Parity and Points of Difference

Points of parity are driven by the needs of category membership (to create category POPs) and the necessity of negating competitors' PODs (to create competitive POPs).

In terms of choosing points of difference, broadly, the two most important considerations are that consumers find the POD desirable and believe that the firm has the capabilities to deliver on it. If both of these considerations are satisfied, the POD has the potential to become a strong, favorable, and unique brand association. Both of these broad considerations have a number of specific criteria, as follows.

Desirability Criteria.   As noted in Chapter 2, there are three key desirability criteria for PODs—relevance, distinctiveness, and believability—that must be assessed from a consumer perspective. Only by satisfying these three criteria will the POD be sufficiently desirable to consumers to have the potential to serve as a viable positioning alternative.

➤ *Relevance:* Target consumers must find the POD personally relevant and important. Relevance considerations can be easily overlooked. For example, in the early 1990s, a number of brands in different product categories (colas, dish washing soaps, beer, deodorant, gasoline, etc.) introduced clear versions of their products to better differentiate themselves. Although "clear" perhaps signaled natural, pure, and lightness to consumers initially, a proliferation of clear versions of products that did not reinforce these other associations blurred its meaning. The "clear" association has not seemed to be of enduring value or to be sustainable as a point of difference. In many cases, these brands have experienced declining market share or disappeared altogether.

➤ *Distinctiveness:* Target consumers must find the POD distinctive and superior. When entering a category in which there are established brands, the challenge is to find a viable basis for differentiation. A frequent occurrence is that the point of difference selected is one on which a brand dominates its competition and not one that is important to consumers. Along these lines, several analgesic brands, including Aleve, have found limited demand for the claim that their brand was long lasting or that infrequent dosing was required. Most consumers place more importance on fast relief than long-lasting relief. Indeed, long lasting may imply slow acting—just the opposite of what is desired.

➤ *Believability:* Target consumers must find the POD believable and credible. A brand must offer a compelling reason for choosing it over the other options that might be considered. Perhaps the simplest approach is to point to a unique attribute of the product. Thus, Mountain Dew may argue that it is more energizing than other soft drinks and support this claim by noting that it has a higher level of caffeine. On the other hand, when the point of difference is abstract or image based, support for the claim may reside in more general associations to the company that have been developed over time. Thus, Chanel No. 5 perfume may claim to be the quintessential elegant, French perfume and support this claim by noting the long association between Chanel and haute couture.

Deliverability Criteria.   Chapter 2 also highlighted three key deliverability criteria: feasibility, communicability, and sustainability. If these are satisfied, the positioning has the potential to be enduring.

➤ *Feasibility:* The first factor affecting deliverability is performance potential in terms of the actual or potential ability of the product to perform at the level stated. In other words, it must be feasible for the firm—in terms of affordability, resources necessary, time horizon involved, and so forth—to actually create the POD. The product and marketing must be designed in a way to support the desired association. Does communicating the desired association involve real changes to the product itself or just perceptual ones as to how the consumer thinks of the product or brand? It is obviously easier to convince consumers of some fact about the brand that they were unaware of or may have overlooked than to make changes in the product *and* convince consumers of these changes.

➤ *Communicability:* The second factor affecting deliverability is the current or future prospects of communicating information to create or strengthen the desired associations. The key issue here is consumers' perceptions of the brand and the resulting brand associations. It is very difficult to create an association that is not consistent with existing consumer knowledge or that consumers, for whatever reason, have trouble believing in. The communicability of a brand association can depend on many things, but perhaps the most important one is whether consumers can be given a compelling reason why the brand will deliver the desired benefit. In other words, what factual, verifiable evidence or "proof points" can be given as support so that consumers will actually believe in the brand and its desired associations?

➤ *Sustainability:* The final factor affecting the deliverability of a brand association is the sustainability of the actual and communicated performance over time. Is the positioning preemptive, defensible, and difficult to attack? Is it the case that the favorability of a brand association can be reinforced and strengthened over time? If these are the case, the positioning is likely to last for years. Sustainability depends on internal commitment and use of resources as well as external market forces.

Establishing Points of Parity and Points of Difference

Creating a strong, competitive brand positioning requires establishing the right points of parity and points of difference. The difficulty in doing so, however, is that many of the attributes or benefits that make up the POPs or PODs are negatively correlated. That is, if consumers mentally rate the brand highly on one particular attribute or benefit, they also rate it poorly on another important attribute. For example, it might be difficult to position a brand as "inexpensive" and at the same time assert that it is "of the highest quality." Figure 3-10 displays some other examples of negatively correlated attributes and benefits. Moreover, individual attributes and benefits often have positive *and* negative aspects. For example, consider a long-lived brand that is seen as having a great deal of heritage. Heritage could be seen as a positive attribute because it can suggest experience, wisdom, and expertise. On the other hand, it could also be easily seen as a negative attribute because it might imply being old-fashioned and not contemporary and cutting-edge.

Unfortunately, consumers typically desire to maximize *both* of the negatively correlated attributes and benefits. The challenge is that competitors often are trying to achieve their point of difference on an attribute that is negatively correlated with the point of difference of the target brand. Much of the art and science of marketing is how to deal with tradeoffs, and positioning is no different. The best approach clearly is to

Low price vs. high quality
Taste vs. low calories
Nutritious vs. good tasting
Efficacious vs. mild
Powerful vs. safe
Strong vs. refined
Ubiquitous vs. exclusive
Varied vs. simple

FIGURE 3-10 Examples of Negatively Correlated Attributes and Benefits

develop a product or service that performs well on both dimensions. Thus, the ability of BMW to establish their straddle positioning image of "luxury and performance" was due in large part to product design and the fact that the car was considered both luxurious and high-performance. Similarly, Gore-Tex was able to overcome the seemingly conflicting product image of "breathable" and "waterproof" through technological advances. Several additional ways exist to address the problem of negatively correlated POPs and PODs. The following three approaches are listed in increasing level of effectiveness—but also increasing level of difficulty.

Separate the Attributes   An expensive but sometimes effective approach is to launch two different marketing campaigns, each one devoted to a different brand attribute or benefit. These campaigns may either run concurrently or sequentially. For example, Head & Shoulders met success in Europe with a dual campaign in which one ad emphasized its dandruff removal efficacy while another ad emphasized the appearance and beauty of hair after its use. The hope is that consumers will be less critical when judging the POP and POD benefits in isolation because the negative correlation might be less apparent. The downside to such an approach is that two strong campaigns have to be developed—not just one. Moreover, by not addressing the negative correlation head-on, consumers may not develop as positive associations as desired.

Leverage Equity of Another Entity   In the Miller Lite example discussed earlier, the brand "borrowed" or leveraged the equity of well-known and well-liked celebrities to lend credibility to one of the negatively correlated benefits. Brands can potentially link themselves to any kind of entity that possesses the right kind of equity—a person, other brand, event, and so forth—as a means to establish an attribute or benefit as a POP or POD. Self-branded ingredients may also lend some credibility to a questionable attribute in consumers' minds. Borrowing equity, however, is neither costless nor riskless. Chapter 7 reviews these considerations in detail and outlines the pros and cons of leveraging equity.

Redefine the Relationship   Finally, another potentially powerful but often difficult way to address the negative relationship between attributes and benefits in the minds of consumers is to convince them that in fact the relationship is positive. This redefinition can be accomplished by providing consumers a different perspective and suggesting that they may be overlooking or ignoring certain factors or other considerations.

Apple Computers
When Apple Computers launched the Macintosh, its key point of difference was "user friendly." Although many consumers valued ease of use—especially those who bought personal computers for the home—one drawback with the association was that customers who bought personal computers for business applications inferred that if a personal computer was easy to use, then it also must not be very powerful—a key choice consideration in that market. Recognizing this potential problem, Apple ran a clever ad campaign with the tag line "The power to be your best," in an attempt to redefine what a powerful computer meant. The message behind the ads was that because Apple was easy to use, people in fact did just that—they used them!—a simple but important indication of "power." In

FIGURE 3-11   Apple Brand Positioning

other words, the most powerful computers were ones that people actually used. (See Figure 3-11.)

Although difficult to achieve, such a strategy can be powerful because the two associations can become mutually reinforcing. The challenge is to develop a credible story with which consumers can agree.

Updating Positioning over Time

The previous section described some positioning guidelines that are especially useful for launching a new brand. With established brands, competitive forces often dictate shifts in positioning strategy over time. Branding Brief 3-6 describes how the two major U.S. political parties have applied branding principles and changed their positioning over time. The credit card wars provide another illustration.

Visa and American Express

Visa's POD in the credit card category is that it is the most widely available card, which underscores the category's main benefit of convenience. American Express, on the other hand, has built the equity of its brand by highlighting the prestige associated with the use of its card. Having established their PODs, Visa and American Express now compete by attempting to blunt each other's advantage to create POPs. Along these lines, Visa offers gold and platinum cards to enhance the prestige of its brand and advertises "It's

Positioning Politicians

The importance of marketing has not been lost on politicians, and, although there a number of different ways to interpret their words and actions, one way to interpret campaign strategies is from a brand equity perspective. For example, consultants to political candidates stress the importance of having "high name ID" or, in other words, a high level of brand awareness. In major races, at least 90 percent is desired. They also emphasize "positives-negatives"—voters' responses when asked if they think positively or negatively of a candidate.[1] A 3:1 ratio is desired (and 4:1 is seen as even better). This measure corresponds to a brand attitude in marketing terms.

The importance of positioning a political candidate can be seen by examining George Bush's textbook presidential campaign of 1988. Bush had been vice president for eight years under Ronald Reagan and was perceived by many as a moderate Republican. His Democratic opponent, on the other hand, the governor of Massachusetts, Michael Dukakis, was seen by many as being a traditional Democrat. The goal of Bush's campaign was to move Bush to the center of the political spectrum and make him a "safe" choice, a person who combined compassion with toughness and who was experienced and presidential in stature. The Republican campaign objective with Dukakis, on the other hand, was to make him seem liberal and move him to the left, emphasizing the risk of change. In terms of actual policies, the Republican strategy could be viewed as a classic application of positioning principles. Their goal was to create a point of difference on traditional Republican issues such as defense, the economy (and taxes), and crime and create a point of parity—thus negating their opponent's point of difference—on traditional Democratic issues such as the environment, education, and abortion rights.

The actual campaign was a fully integrated modern communications program, skillfully blending public relations and media news coverage with paid advertising. Campaign messages were researched carefully by focus groups and other means. Bush's convention speech and the line "a thousand points of light" became the centerpiece for several ads. Many ads were soft, positive spots, designed to combat Bush's "nerd" or "wimp" image or to portray Bush's career as a number of successful missions, leading up to the penultimate job of president. Other ads were hard-hitting negative spots, designed to attack Dukakis's image on the environment (in the famous Boston harbor spot), crime (in the equally famous prison furloughs ad that became associated with convict Willie Horton), the economy (in ads blasting the success of the "Massachusetts Miracle"), and defense (in the famous tank ride ad, taken off the air from a news sound bite, showing Dukakis riding a tank with a helmet on and gesturing thumbs up, perhaps looking a bit too much like *Mad* magazine's Alfred E. Neuman).

As a result of this well-designed and well-executed campaign, by the time of the election, Bush's ratio of positives to negatives had dramatically shifted to 60 percent to 20 percent. Equally important, on those key Democratic issues that were to be their points of difference, the Republicans were able to break even. For example, when voters were asked in exit polls which presidential candidate would be better for the environment, they were almost equally split between the two candidates. Having successfully achieved these points of parity and points of difference in the minds of the voters, Bush won in a landslide.

Although the Republicans ran a near flawless campaign in 1988, that was not the case in 1992. The new Democratic candidate, Bill Clinton, was a fierce campaigner who ran a very focused campaign designed to create a key point of difference on one main issue—the economy. Rather than attempting to achieve a point of parity on this issue, Bush, who was running for reelection, campaigned on other issues such as family values. By conceding a key point of difference to the Democrats and failing to create a compelling one of his own, Bush and the Republicans were defeated handily. Failing to learn from their mistakes, the Republicans ran a meandering campaign in 1996 that failed to achieve points of parity or points of difference. Not surprisingly, their presidential candidate, Bob Dole, lost decisively to the incumbent Bill Clinton.

The closeness of the 2000 election between Al Gore and George W. Bush reflected the failure of either candidate to create a strong point of difference with the electorate. In an interesting study during the middle of the race, brand consultant Landor examined the images of the candidates and compared them to various companies. Bush was seen as tougher, more straightforward and even glamorous, whereas Gore came across as kinder. Within the Republican faithful, Bush was seen to have much in common with IBM, Xerox, and Hewlett-Packard, whereas Gore's Democratic followers found him more closely aligned with Yahoo!, Alta Vista, and Lycos. Landor head Allen Adamson concluded that both men were like "classic brands that need to reinvent themselves. . . . Bush is like a line extension of a brand, former President Bush . . . and so much of Gore's success in the marketplace comes from the Clinton brand . . . he's got to totally re-launch himself."[2]

---

[1]Typically, the pollsters employ five-point scales to the question "Do you think positively or negatively of the candidate?" The bottom two points and top two points are collapsed together to reflect negative and positive opinions, respectively.

[2]"Gore and Bush Are Like Classic Brands," *New York Times*, 25 July 2000, B8.

Everywhere You Want to Be" in aspirational settings that reinforce exclusivity and acceptability. On the other hand, American Express has substantially increased the number of vendors that accept American Express cards and created other value enhancements through their "Do More" program to reduce Visa's advantage on this dimension.

Updating positioning involves two main issues. The first is how to deepen the meaning of the brand to tap into core brand values or other, more abstract considerations (*laddering*). The second is how to respond to competitive challenges that threaten an existing positioning (*reacting*).

Laddering
Although identifying PODs to dominate competition on benefits that are important to consumers provides a sound way to build an initial position, once the target market attains a basic understanding of how the brand relates to alternatives in the same category, it may be necessary to deepen the meanings associated with the brand

positioning. It is often useful to explore underlying consumer motivations in a product category to uncover the relevant associations. For example, Maslow's hierarchy maintains that consumers have different priorities and levels of needs.[21] From lowest to highest priority, they are as follows:

1. Physiological needs (food, water, air, shelter, sex)
2. Safety and security needs (protection, order, stability)
3. Social needs (affection, friendship, belonging)
4. Ego needs (prestige, status, self-respect)
5. Self-actualization (self-fulfillment).

According to Maslow, higher-level needs become relevant once lower-level needs are satisfied.

Marketers have also recognized the importance of higher-level needs. For example, means-end chains have been devised as a way of understanding higher-level meanings of brand characteristics.[22] A means-end chain takes the following structure: Attributes (descriptive features that characterize a product) lead to benefits (the personal value and meaning attached to product attributes), which, in turn, lead to values (stable and enduring personal goals or motivations).[23] In other words, a consumer chooses a product that delivers an attribute (A) that provides benefits or has certain consequences (B/C) that satisfy values (V). For example, in a study of salty snacks, one respondent noted that a flavored chip (A) with a strong taste (A) would mean that she would eat less (B/C), not get fat (B/C), and have a better figure (B/C), all of which would enhance her self-esteem (V).

Laddering thus involves a progression from attributes to benefits to more abstract values or motivations. In effect, laddering involves repeatedly asking what the implication of an attribute or benefit is for the consumer. Failure to move up the ladder may reduce the strategic alternatives available to a brand. For example, P&G introduced low-sudsing Dash detergent to attract consumers who used front-loading washing machines. Many years of advertising Dash in this manner made this position impenetrable by other brands. Dash was so associated with front-loaders, however, that when this type of machine went out of fashion, so did Dash. This outcome occurred despite the fact that Dash was among P&G's most effective detergents, and despite significant efforts to reposition the brand.

Some attributes and benefits may lend themselves to laddering more easily than others. For example, the Betty Crocker brand appears on a number of different baking products and thus is characterized by the physical warmth associated with baking. Such an association makes it relatively easy to talk about emotional warmth and the joy of baking or the good feelings that might arise from baking for others. Similarly, Nivea skin cream has well-entrenched benefits of being "caring," "gentle," and "protective" for the skin. Such a product foundation makes it easier to associate these same values with family relationships or friendships.

Thus, some of the strongest brands deepen their points of difference to create benefit and value associations, for example, Volvo and Michelin (safety and peace of mind), Intel (performance and compatibility), Marlboro (western imagery), Coke (Americana and refreshment), Disney (fun, magic, family entertainment), Nike (innovative products and peak athletic performance), and BMW (styling and driving performance). As a brand becomes associated with more and more products and moves up the product hierarchy, the brand's meaning will become more abstract. At the same time, it is important that the proper category membership and POPs and PODs exist in the minds of consumers for the particular products sold. After a consideration of how to react to competitor's actions, the following section discusses the related topic of core brand values. Chapter 11 addresses some additional issues in evolving the meaning of corporate brands over time.

Reacting

Competitive actions are often directed toward eliminating points of difference to make them points of parity or to strengthen or establish new points of difference. Often competitive advantages exist for only a short period of time before competitors attempt to match them. For example, when Goodyear introduced their Run-Flat tires (which allowed tires to keep going for up to 50 miles at a speed of 55 mph after a tire puncture or blowout) in the mid-1990s, Michelin quickly responded with their Zero Pressure tire, which offered the same consumer benefit. When a competitor challenges an existing POD or attempts to overcome a POP, there are essentially three main options for the target brand—from no reaction to moderate to significant reactions.

➤ *Do nothing.* If the competitive actions seem unlikely to recapture a POD or create a new POD, then the best reaction is probably to just stay the course and continue brand-building efforts.

➤ *Go on the defensive.* If the competitive actions appear to have the potential to disrupt the market some, then it may be necessary to take a defensive stance. One way to defend the positioning is to add some reassurance in the product or advertising to strengthen POPs and PODs.

➤ *Go on the offensive.* If the competitive actions seem potentially quite damaging, then it might be necessary to take a more aggressive stance and reposition the brand to address the threat. One approach might be to launch a product extension or ad campaign that fundamentally changes the meaning of the brand.

Deciding the severity of the competitive threat and the appropriate competitive stance can benefit from a brand audit, as described in Brand Focus 3.0 at the end of the chapter. Essentially, the intent of the audit in this case would be to assess competitive actions in terms of how they would affect POPs and PODs according to the desirability and deliverability criteria listed previously.

DEFINING AND ESTABLISHING BRAND VALUES

Brand positioning describes how a brand can effectively compete against a specified set of competitors in a particular market. In many cases, however, brands span multiple product categories and therefore may have multiple distinct—yet related—positionings. As brands evolve and expand across categories, it is often useful to define a set of core brand values to capture the important dimensions of the brand meaning and what the brand represents. It is also often useful to synthesize the core brand values to a core brand promise or brand mantra that reflects the essential "heart and soul" of the brand. Both concepts are described next.

Core Brand Values

Core brand values are those set of abstract associations (attributes and benefits) that characterize the 5 to 10 most important aspects or dimensions of a brand. Core brand values can serve as an important foundation for the brand strategy in numerous ways. In particular, core brand values can serve as the basis of brand positioning in terms of how they relate to points of parity and points of difference.

Core brand values can be identified through a structured process. The first step is to create a detailed mental map of the brand. A *mental map* accurately portrays in detail all salient brand associations and responses for a particular target market (e.g., brand users). Mental maps must reflect the reality of how the brand is actually perceived by consumers in terms of their beliefs, attitudes, opinions, feelings, images, and experiences. The CBBE brand pyramid from Chapter 2 helps to highlight some of the types of associations and responses that may emerge from the creation of a mental map. Chapter 9 describes some of the various research techniques that can be used to construct the mental map. One of the simplest means to get consumers to create a mental map is by asking consumers for their top-of-mind brand associations (e.g., "When you think of this brand, what comes to mind?").

Next, brand associations are grouped into categories according to how they are related, often with two to four associations per category. Each category is labeled to be as descriptive as possible as a core brand value. For example, in response to a Nike brand probe, consumers may list Michael Jordan, Tiger Woods, Andre Agassi, and Lance Armstrong, which could be summarized by the label "top athletes." There may be as few as 3 to 5 or maybe even as many as 10 to 12 different core brand values. In assembling core brand values, the challenge is to maximize the coverage of the mental map to include all relevant associations while making sure each core brand value is as distinct as possible. Figure 3-12 displays the mental map and core brand values of the New York Knickerbockers professional basketball team, as well as its brand mantra, which is described next.

Brand Mantras

To provide further focus as to what a brand represents, it is often useful to define a brand mantra.[24] A brand mantra is highly related to branding concepts such as "brand essence" or "core brand promise" used by others. A *brand mantra* is an articulation of the "heart and soul" of the brand. Brand mantras are short, three- to five-word phrases that capture the irrefutable essence or spirit of the brand positioning and brand values. Their purpose is to ensure that all employees within the organization and all external marketing partners understand what the brand most fundamentally is to represent with consumers so that they can adjust their actions accordingly.

Brand mantras are powerful devices. They can provide guidance as to what products to introduce under the brand, what ad campaigns to run, where and how the brand should be sold, and so on. The influence of brand mantras, however, can extend beyond these tactical concerns. Brand mantras may even guide the most seemingly unrelated or mundane decisions, such as the look of a reception area, the way phones are answered, and so on. In effect, brand mantras are designed to create a mental filter to screen out brand-inappropriate marketing activities or actions of any type that may have a negative bearing on customers' impressions of a brand.

Core Brand Values
An incomparable event, scene, and energy
Uniquely authentic
Relentless, resourceful, and tough
Championship caliber
A vital part of New York City
Unlimited in its possibilities

Brand Mantra
An intensely passionate, professional, unparalleled New York City experience.

FIGURE 3-12 Positioning the New York Knickerbockers Brand

Brand mantras are important for a number of reasons. First, any time a consumer or customer encounters a brand—in any way, shape, or form—his or her knowledge about that brand may change, and as a result, the equity of the brand is affected. Given that a vast number of employees, either directly or indirectly, come into contact with consumers in a way that may affect consumer knowledge about the brand, it is important that their words and actions consistently reinforce and support the brand meaning. Many employees or marketing partners (e.g., ad agency members) who potentially could help or hurt brand equity may be far removed from the marketing strategy formulation and may not even recognize their role in influencing equity. The existence and communication of a brand mantra signals the importance of the brand to the organization and an understanding of its meaning as well as the crucial role of employees and marketing partners in its management. It also provides memorable shorthand as to what are the crucial considerations of the brand that should be kept most salient and top-of-mind.

Designing a Brand Mantra

What makes for a good brand mantra? McDonald's brand philosophy of "Food, Folks, and Fun" captures their brand essence and core brand promise. Two high-profile and successful examples of brand mantras come from two powerful brands, Nike and Disney, as described in Branding Briefs 3-7 and 3-8. Brand mantras must economically communicate what the brand is and what the brand is *not*. The Nike and Disney examples show the power and utility of having a well-designed brand mantra. They also help to suggest what might characterize a good brand mantra. Both examples are essentially structured the same way, with three words, as follows:

	EMOTIONAL MODIFIER	DESCRIPTIVE MODIFIER	BRAND FUNCTIONS
Nike	Authentic	Athletic	Performance
Disney	Fun	Family	Entertainment

These brand mantras can be broken down into three terms. The *brand* functions term describes the nature of the product or service or the type of experiences or benefits that the brand provides. This may range from concrete language, where the term just reflects the product category itself, to more abstract notions, as with Nike and Disney, where the term relates to higher-order experiences or benefits that may be delivered by a variety of different products. The *descriptive* modifier is a way to circumscribe the business functions term to further clarify its nature. Thus, Nike's performance is not just any kind (e.g., not artistic performance) but only *athletic* performance; Disney's entertainment is not just any kind (e.g., not adult-oriented entertainment) but only *family* entertainment. Combined, the brand function term and descriptive modifier help to delineate the brand boundaries. Finally, the *emotional* modifier provides another qualifier in terms of how the brand delivers these benefits. In other words, what is the qualitative nature of what the brand does? How exactly does it provide benefits and in what way? This term provides further delineation and clarification.

Brand mantras don't necessarily have to follow this exact structure, but whatever structure is adopted, it must be the case that the brand mantra clearly delineates what the brand is supposed to represent and therefore, at least implicitly, what it is *not*. Several additional points about brand mantras are worth noting. First, brand mantras derive their power and usefulness from their collective meaning. Other brands may be strong on one, or perhaps even a few, of the brand associations making up the brand mantra. For the brand mantra to be effective, no other brand should singularly excel on *all* dimensions. Part of the key to both Nike's and Disney's success is that for years, no other competitor could really deliver on the promise suggested by their brand mantras as well as those brands. Second, brand mantras typically are designed to capture the

Nike Brand Mantra

A brand with a keen sense of what it represents to consumers is Nike. Nike has a rich set of associations with consumers, revolving around such considerations as its innovative product designs, its sponsorships of top athletes, its award-winning advertising, its competitive drive, and its irreverent attitude. Internally, Nike marketers adopted a three-word brand mantra of "authentic athletic performance" to guide their marketing efforts. Thus, in Nike's eyes, its entire marketing program—its products and how they are sold—must reflect those key brand values conveyed by the brand mantra.

Nike's brand mantra has had profound implications for its marketing. In the words of ex-Nike marketing gurus Scott Bedbury and Jerome Conlon, the brand mantra provided the "intellectual guard rails" to keep the brand moving in the right direction and to make sure it did not get off track somehow. From a product development standpoint, Nike's brand mantra has affected where it has taken the brand. Over the years, Nike has expanded its brand meaning from "running shoes" to "athletic shoes" to "athletic shoes and apparel" to "all things associated with athletics (including equipment)." Each step of the way, however, it has been guided by its "authentic athletic performance" brand mantra. For example, as Nike rolled out its successful apparel line, one important hurdle for the products was that they could be made innovative enough to truly benefit top athletes. At the same time, the company has been careful to avoid using the Nike name to brand products that do not fit with the brand mantra (e.g., causal shoes).

When Nike has experienced problems with its marketing program, it has often been a result of its failure to figure out how to translate their brand mantra to the marketing challenge at hand. For example, in going to Europe, Nike experienced several false starts until realizing that "authentic athletic performance" has a different meaning over there and, in particular, has to involve soccer in a major way, among other things. Similarly, Nike stumbled in developing their All Conditions Gear (ACG) outdoors shoes and clothing sub-brand in translating their brand mantra into a less competitive arena.

brand's points of difference, that is, what is unique about the brand. Other aspects of the brand positioning—especially the brand's points of parity—may also be important and may need to be reinforced in other ways (e.g., those defined as core brand values).

Implementing a Brand Mantra

Brand mantras should be developed at the same time as the brand positioning. As noted earlier, brand positioning typically is a result of an in-depth examination of the brand through some form of brand audit or other activities (as described in Brand Focus 3.0). Brand mantras may benefit from the learning gained from those activities but, at the same time, require more internal examination and involve input from a wider range of company employees and marketing staff. Part of this internal exercise is actually to determine the different means by which each and every employee currently

---

Disney Brand Mantra

Disney's development of its brand mantra was in response to its incredible growth through licensing and product development during the mid-1980s. In the late 1980s, Disney became concerned that some of its characters (Mickey Mouse, Donald Duck, etc.) were being used inappropriately and becoming overexposed. To investigate the severity of the problem, Disney undertook an extensive brand audit. As part of a brand inventory, it first compiled a list of all Disney products that were available (licensed and company manufactured) and all third-party promotions (complete with point-of-purchase displays and relevant merchandising) from stores across the country and all over the world. At the same time, Disney launched a major consumer research study—a brand exploratory—to investigate how consumers felt about the Disney brand. The results of the brand inventory revealed some potentially serious problems: The Disney characters were on so many products and marketed in so many ways that in some cases it was difficult to discern what could have been the rationale behind the deal to start with. The consumer study only heightened Disney's concerns. Because of the broad exposure of the characters in the marketplace, many consumers had begun to feel that Disney was exploiting its name. In some cases, consumers felt that the characters added little value to products and, worse yet, involved children in purchase decisions that they would typically ignore.

Because of their aggressive marketing efforts, Disney had written contracts with many of the "park participants" for co-promotions or licensing arrangements. Disney characters were selling everything from diapers to cars to McDonald's hamburgers. Disney learned in the consumer study, however, that consumers did not differentiate between all of the product endorsements. "Disney was Disney" to consumers, whether they saw the characters in films, records, theme parks, or consumer products. Consequently, *all* products and services that used the Disney name or characters had an impact on Disney's brand equity. Consumers reported that they resented some of these endorsements because they felt that they had a special, personal relationship with the characters and with Disney that should not be handled so carelessly.

As a result of their brand audit, Disney moved quickly to establish a brand equity team to better manage the brand franchise and more carefully evaluate licensing and other third-party promotional opportunities. One of the mandates of this team was to ensure that a consistent image for Disney-reinforcing its key brand associations—was conveyed by all third-party products and services. To facilitate this supervision, Disney adopted an internal brand mantra of "fun family entertainment" to serve as a screen for proposed ventures. Opportunities that were presented that were not consistent with the brand mantra—no matter how appealing—were rejected. For example, Disney was approached to co-brand a mutual fund in Europe that was designed for families as a way for parents to save for the college expenses of their children. The opportunity was declined despite the consistent "family" association because Disney believed that a connection with the financial community or banking suggested other associations that were inconsistent with their brand image (mutual funds are rarely intended to be entertaining).

affects brand equity and how he or she can contribute in a positive way to a brand's destiny.

Procedurally, the brand positioning can often be summarized in a few sentences or a short paragraph that suggests the ideal core brand values that should be held by consumers. Based on these brand values, a brainstorming session can attempt to identify different possible combinations of words as brand mantra candidates. A number of characteristics seem to distinguish brand mantras. To arrive at the final brand mantra, the following considerations should come into play.

➤ *Communicate:* A good brand mantra should define the category (or categories) of business for the brand and set the brand boundaries. It should also clarify what is unique about the brand.

➤ *Simplify:* An effective brand mantra should be memorable. As a result, it should be short, crisp, and vivid. In many ways, a three-word mantra is ideal because it is the most economical way to convey the brand positioning. There are times, however, when more words—in the form of clarifying the business functions or the nature of the modifiers—may be necessary.

➤ *Inspire:* Ideally, the brand mantra should also stake out ground that is personally meaningful and relevant to as many employees as possible. Brand mantras can do more than inform and guide; they can also inspire if the brand values tap into higher-level meaning with employees as well as consumers.

Regardless of exactly how many words make up the mantra, however, *there will always be a level of meaning beneath the brand mantra itself that will need to be articulated.* Virtually any word is inherently ambiguous enough that multiple interpretations are possible. Consequently, it becomes important to explain in greater detail just what is meant by each word or term in the mantra. For example, *fun, family,* and *entertainment* in Disney's brand mantra could each take on multiple meanings such that Disney felt the need to drill deeper with the mantra to provide a stronger foundation. Two or three short phrases were therefore added later to clarify each of the three words.

INTERNAL BRANDING

Core brand values and brand mantras point out the importance of *internal branding—*making sure that members of the organization are properly aligned with the brand and what it represents. Much of the branding literature has taken an *external* perspective, focusing on strategies and tactics that firms should take to build or manage brand equity with customers. Without question, at the heart of all marketing activity is the positioning of a brand and the essence of its meaning with consumers. In terms of strategic and tactical importance, properly positioning a brand is essential to creating a strong brand.

Equally important, however, is positioning the brand internally, that is, the manner by which the brand positioning is explained and communicated internally.[25] With service companies especially, an up-to-date and deep understanding of the brand by virtually all employees is critical. In the past, comparatively little attention was paid to an

Internal Branding Insights

CHRIS MACRAE

Macrae defines brand reality as "organizing branding so that employees are uniquely proud of the company's brand leadership and passionately aligned to branding this through activities they work on individually and in teams, processes, creativity spaces and knowledge webs..The concept of brand reality argues for an inclusive view of marketing organization in which all employees are as productively motivated as possible to serve the company's continuous purpose and to build value which the world would miss if the company did not exist."[1]

HAMISH PRINGLE AND WILLIAM GORDON

The central tenet of Pringle and Gordon's argument is that there can be a significant improvement in business performance by recognizing that good manners—how a company manages its brand promise—must occur in every encounter that takes place between the customer and the organization.[2] Specifically, they argue that good manners must occur on four dimensions that characterize all customer experiences:

- *Rational experiences (what goes on):* Good behaviors need to be repeatable and rewarded; the individual who performs well should be a hero in the organization.
- *Emotional experiences (how customers feel):* Both the customer and employee should enjoy the experience, boosting the self-confidence of each (in a non-egotistical way).
- *Political experiences (why it is right for the customer):* This dimension is all about real value created through entrepreneurial behavior (taking measured risks for customers) and resulting in a sense of fairness all around.
- *Spiritual experiences (where it leads customers):* Being (as opposed to having or doing), altruisim, and creating myths or legends of great experiences for the customer.

THOMAS GAD

In developing the concept of "4-D branding," Gad argues that to understand a brand fully, to live it and enable customers to live it, means creating a distinctive Brand Code.[3] He defines Brand Code as the genetic programming that creates brands, that is, the "business DNA." The Brand Code determines the characteristics of the business: what it looks like, how it feels, how it behaves—not just what it is, but who it is and what makes it unique. According to Gad, creating a Brand Code requires using the following four-dimensional model to understand the strengths and weaknesses of a brand in terms of a "brand mind space" (as illustrated with the IKEA brand):

- *Functional dimension:* The perception of the benefit of the product or service associated with the brand ("IKEA gives me good contemporary design and function and good value for the money.")

- *Social dimension:* The ability to create indentification with a group ("Buying at IKEA makes me seem savvy; it shows that I appreciate value for money and like good contemporary design.")

- *Spiritual dimension:* The perception of global or local responsibility ("IKEA drives the democratic process in the world, both by the way they work and by giving more people opportunity to create a better everyday life.")

- *Mental dimension:* The ability to support the individual mentally ("IKEA engages me in doing some of the work myself; I also get inspiration and ideas.")

NICHOLAS IND

Ind argues that a participatory approach can enhance employee commitment, improve service standards, and focus effort to deliver business goals.[4] He maintains that "living the brand" can be achieved by building meaning, purpose, and values into the organization to foster a culture of enthusiastic employee participation. He offers a number of suggestions as to how organizations can empower and enthuse their employees to create "brand champions." His main themes are as follows: Employees flourish in organizations where they identify with the brand; organizations flourish when the brand has relevance and creates meaning; purpose and values are not created—they exist, and the issue is how well they are articulated and embedded; brand clarity creates freedom; brands come to life when the boundaries between the internal and external blur; and stories and myths are important for sustaining brands. He concludes that living the brand requires brand ideas that are capable of being imaginative, authentic, courageous, and empowering.

[1]Chris Macrae, "Brand Reality Editorial," *Journal of Marketing Management* 15 (1999): 1–24.

[2]Hamish Pringle and William Gordon, *Brand Manners: How to Create the Self-Confident Organization to Live the Brand* (New York: John Wiley & Sons, 2001).

[3]Thomas Gad, *4-D Branding: Cracking the Corporate Code of the Network Economy* (Upper Saddle River, NJ: Financial Times Prentice-Hall, 2000).

[4]Nicholas Ind, *Living the Brand: How to Transform Every Member of Your Organization into a Brand Champion* (London: Kogan Page, 2001).

internal perspective to consider what steps firms should take to be sure their employees and marketing partners appreciate and understand basic branding notions and how they can affect and help—or hurt—the equity of their particular brands. Recently, though, a number of authors have provided insight into this important topic (see the Science of Branding 3-1), and a number of companies have put forth initiatives to improve their internal branding.

Hewlett Packard

Five months after arriving at Hewlett-Packard in July 1999, new president Carly Fiorina showed 200 top managers a video of customers talking about how incoherent HP had become. Salesmen from a dozen business units sometimes called on one account. From now on, she vowed, HP had to present one face to the consumer.[26]

Chapter 8 describes brand charters as a means to communicate internally and to marketing partners. Besides brand mantras, companies need to engage in continual open dialogue with their employees. Branding should be perceived as participatory. Some firms have pushed B2E (business-to-employee) programs through corporate intranets and other means. For example, Ford Motor Company offered its American employees free personal computers to help them get online. Their chairman sends weekly "Let's Chat" notes to provide employees updates and to help establish dialogue. Ford also offers a number of online training programs for their employees. Walt Disney is seen as so successful at internal branding and having employees support their brand that they teach seminars on the "Disney Style" of creativity, service, and loyalty for employees from other companies. Internal branding consultancy firm Trium engages clients in a number of activities to help "brand" employees.[27] For example, it conducts modules regarding key brand characteristics in order to help form personal associations with the words (e.g., what it means to be "trustworthy," "responsive," "unselfish," or "innovative" to personalize the brand).

In short, internal branding is a critical management priority. Successful internal branding requires a mixture of resources and processes, all designed to inform and inspire employees to maximize their mutually beneficial contribution to brand equity.

Review

Determining the desired brand knowledge structures involves positioning a brand in the minds of consumers. According to the customer-based brand equity model, deciding on a positioning requires determining a frame of reference (by identifying the target market and the nature of competition) and the ideal points-of-parity and points-of-difference brand associations. Determining the proper competitive frame of reference depends on understanding consumer behavior and the consideration sets that consumers adopt in making brand choices. Points of difference are those associations that are unique to the brand that are also strongly held and favorably evaluated by consumers. Determining points-of-difference associations that are strong, favorable, and unique is based on desirability and deliverability considerations, which are combined to determine the resulting anticipated levels of sales and costs that might be expected with the positioning. Points of parity, on the other hand, are those associations that are not necessarily unique to the brand but may in fact be shared with other brands. Category point-of-parity associations are those associations that consumers view as being necessary to be a legitimate and credible product offering within a certain category. Competitive point-of-parity associations are those associations designed to negate competitor's points of differences. Deciding on these four ingredients will then determine the brand positioning and dictate the desired brand knowledge structures.

A broader set of considerations is also useful for positioning, especially for a more developed brand that spans multiple categories. A mental map accurately portrays in detail *all* salient brand associations and responses for a particular target market (e.g., brand users). Core brand values are those set of abstract associations (attributes and benefits) that characterize the 5 to 10 most important aspects or dimensions of a brand. Core brand values can serve as an important foundation for the brand strategy in numerous ways. In particular, core brand values can serve as the basis of brand positioning in terms

Positioning a New Jeep Product

Jeep's heritage as a military utility vehicle greatly influences the design of its models. The company is the only automaker to design each of its vehicles to withstand a trip on the Rubicon Trail in California and Nevada, which is a Mecca for off-road enthusiasts. Yet most SUV owners do not use the vehicles off-road, and consumers are increasingly selecting SUVs that offer smoother on-road driving than Jeep models. Between 1997 and 2000, Jeep's share of the SUV segment dropped to 14 percent from 19 percent, while the SUV category's share of the U.S. light-vehicle market grew from 16 percent to 20 percent.

As part of an effort to broaden its consumer base, Jeep developed a replacement for the longstanding Cherokee model called the Jeep Liberty. Jeep engineered the Liberty, which debuted in 2001, to pass the Rubicon test, but also to appeal more to women and younger buyers. With the Liberty, the company aspired to achieve a duality that combined rugged features with comfort considerations. The Liberty features a smoother ride thanks to a carlike independent front suspension. It also boasts a more curved body than the boxy Cherokee, as well as a roomier and more refined interior than its predecessor. The Liberty also comes in a two-wheel drive model, which is less expensive than the traditional 4×4.

Advertising for the car focused on "urban situations" rather than strictly off-road settings. The ads, which touted the vehicle as "the next great Jeep idea," featured cityscapes as well as rugged outdoor scenes. The Liberty was an instant hit with consumers. In July 2001, one month after the launch, sales of the vehicle rose 24 percent, to 10,562 units.

Jeep conceived of the consumer-friendly Liberty in part as a way to prevent the company's rugged off-road performers from deterring consumers who just want a large vehicle to get around town in. At the same time, however, some worried that the wider appeal of the Liberty would hurt Jeep's image in the eyes of off-road devotees. One four-wheel enthusiast referred to the Liberty as "a little too Fisher-Price for me." Another off-roader scoffed at the idea of a Jeep being offered without four-wheel drive, calling the very notion "an insult to the Jeep name." Yet Jeep was clearly ready to embrace new customers in order to rebuild its market share, and also seemed ready to follow the Liberty with additional mass-appeal models. Thomas R. Marinelli, vice president in charge of Jeep marketing, said that future Jeep models might be tamer still. "My feeling is you don't need every single model to be able to go all the way," he said.

Sources: Jeffrey Ball, "The Softer Side of Jeep," *Wall Street Journal,* 24 April 2001; Jonathan Walsh, "Drive Buys: 2002 Jeep Liberty," *Wall Street Journal,* 22 June 2001; "Wrap: Chrysler July Sales Down 3%; Jeep Liberty Sales Up," Dow Jones News Service, 1 August 2001.

of how they relate to points of parity and points of difference. Finally, a brand mantra is an articulation of the "heart and soul" of the brand. Brand mantras are short, three- to five-word phrases that capture the irrefutable essence or spirit of the brand positioning and brand values. Their purpose is to ensure that all employees within the organization as well as all external marketing partners understand what the brand most fundamentally is to represent with consumers so that they can adjust their actions accordingly.

The concepts discussed in this chapter are powerful tools to guide positioning. Brand Focus 3.0 describes a number of considerations that come into play in conducting positioning analysis and deciding on the desired brand image.[28] As outlined there, a *brand audit* is a consumer-focused exercise that involves a series of procedures to assess the health of the brand, uncover its sources of brand equity, and suggest ways to improve and leverage its equity. A brand audit requires understanding sources of brand equity from the perspective of both the firm and the consumer. From the perspective of the firm, it is necessary to understand exactly what products and services are currently being offered to consumers and how they are being marketed and branded. From the perspective of the consumer, it is necessary to dig deeply into the minds of consumers and tap their perceptions and beliefs to uncover the true meaning of brands and products.

The brand audit consists of two steps: the brand inventory and the brand exploratory. The purpose of the *brand inventory* is to provide a complete, up-to-date profile of how all the products and services sold by a company are marketed and branded. Profiling each product or service requires that the associated brand elements be identified as well as the supporting marketing program. The *brand exploratory* is research activity directed to understanding what consumers think and feel about the brand to identify sources of brand equity.

Once the brand positioning strategy has been determined, the actual marketing program to create, strengthen, or maintain brand associations can be put into place. Chapters 4 through 7 in Part III of the text describe some of the important marketing mix issues in designing supporting marketing programs. Branding Bricf 3-9 describes some positioning challenges for the Jeep brand.

Discussion Questions

1. Apply the categorization model to a product category other than beverages. How do consumers make decisions whether or not to buy the product, and how do they arrive at their final brand decision? What are the implications for brand equity management for the brands in the category? How does it affect positioning, for example?

2. Pick a brand. Describe its breadth and depth of awareness.

3. Pick a category basically dominated by two main brands. Evaluate the positioning of each brand. Who are their target markets? What are their main points of parity and points of difference? Have they defined their positioning correctly? How might it be improved?

4. Can you think of any negatively correlated attributes and benefits other than those listed in Figure 3-10? Can you think of any other strategies to deal with negatively correlated attributes and benefits?

5. Think of one of your favorite brands. Can you come up with a brand mantra to capture its positioning?

Brand Focus 3.0

Brand Audit Guidelines

To learn what consumers know about brands and products so that the company can make informed strategic positioning decisions, marketers should first conduct a brand audit to profile consumer knowledge structures. A *brand audit* is a comprehensive examination of a brand in terms of its sources of brand equity. In accounting, an audit involves a systematic inspection of accounting records involving analyses, tests, and confirmations.[29] The outcome of an accounting audit is an assessment of the financial health of the firm. An outside accounting firm serves as the auditor and checks the accuracy, fairness, and general acceptability of accounting records, rendering their opinion in the form of a report.

A similar concept has been suggested for marketing. A marketing audit has been defined as a "comprehensive, systematic, independent, and periodic examination of a company's—or business unit's—marketing environment, objectives, strategies, and activities with a view of determining problem areas and opportunities and recommending a plan of action to improve the company's marketing performance."[30] The marketing audit process has been characterized as a three-step procedure in which the first step is agreement on objectives, scope, and approach; the second step is data collection; and the third and final step is report preparation and presentation. Thus, the marketing audit is an internally, company-focused exercise to make sure that marketing operations are efficient and effective.

A brand audit, on the other hand, is a more externally, consumer-focused exercise that involves a series of procedures to assess the health of the brand, uncover its sources of

brand equity, and suggest ways to improve and leverage its equity. A brand audit requires understanding the sources of brand equity from the perspective of both the firm and the consumer. From the perspective of the firm, it is necessary to understand exactly what products and services are currently being offered to consumers and how they are being marketed and branded. From the perspective of the consumer, it is necessary to dig deeply into the minds of consumers and tap their perceptions and beliefs to uncover the true meaning of brands and products.

The brand audit can be used to set strategic direction for the brand. Are the current sources of brand equity satisfactory? Do certain brand associations need to be strengthened? Does the brand lack uniqueness? What brand opportunities exist and what potential challenges exist for brand equity? As a result of this strategic analysis, a marketing program can be put into place to maximize long-term brand equity. A brand audit should be conducted whenever important shifts in strategic direction are contemplated. Moreover, conducting brand audits on a regular basis (e.g., annually) allows marketers to keep their fingers on the pulse of their brands so that they can be more proactively and responsively managed. As such, brand audits are particularly useful background for managers as they set up their marketing plans.

Brand audits can have profound implications on the strategic direction for brands and their resulting performance.[31] As a result of a brand audit, luxury goods marketer Alfred Dunhill refined its classic "English" appeal—which has been especially valuable in Asia—to also take on more of a dynamic, international flavor. In Europe, the results of a brand audit led Polaroid to decide to try to change their conventional photography image to emphasize the "fun side" of their cameras. Polaroid learned from research that their cameras could be seen as a social stimulant and catalyst, provoking fun moments in people's lives, a theme that was picked up in advertising and which suggested the creation of new distribution strategies.

The brand audit consists of two steps: the brand inventory and the brand exploratory. Each is discussed in turn. The appendix concludes by highlighting a brand audit of the Jose Cuervo brand performed a few years ago.

BRAND INVENTORY

The purpose of the *brand inventory* is to provide a current, comprehensive profile of how all the products and services sold by a company are marketed and branded. Profiling each product or service requires that all associated brand elements be identified as well as the supporting marketing program. In other words, it is necessary to catalogue the following for each product or service sold: the names, logos, symbols, characters, packaging, slogans, or other trademarks used; and the inherent product attributes or characteristics of the brand and the pricing, communications, distribution policies, and any other relevant marketing activity related to the brand. This information should be summarized in both visual and verbal form.

The outcome of the brand inventory should be an accurate, comprehensive, and timely profile of how all the products and services sold by a company are branded in terms of which brand elements are employed (and how) and the nature of the supporting marketing program. As part of the brand inventory, it is also advisable to profile competitive brands, in as much detail as possible, in terms of their branding and marketing efforts. Such information is useful in determining points of parity and points of difference.

Rationale

The brand inventory is a valuable first step in the brand audit for several reasons. First, it helps to suggest what consumers' current perceptions *may* be based on. In other words, consumer associations are typically—although not necessarily always—rooted in the reality of how products and services are branded according to the particular brand elements employed and the *intended* meaning attached to them through the supporting marketing program. Thus, the brand inventory provides useful information for interpreting follow-up research activity such as the brand exploratory that collects actual consumer perceptions toward the brand.

Although the brand inventory is primarily a descriptive exercise, some useful analysis can be conducted too, and the brand inventory may provide some initial insights into how brand equity may be better managed. For example, the consistency of all the different product or services sharing a brand name can be assessed. Are the different brand elements used on a consistent basis or are there many different variations and versions of the brand name, logo, and so forth for the same product—perhaps for no obvious reason— depending on which geographic market it is being sold in, which market segment it is being targeted to, and so forth? Similarly, are the supporting marketing programs logical and consistent across related brands? As firms expand their products geographically and extend them into other categories, it is common for deviations—sometimes significant in nature—to emerge in the appearance of brands and how they are being marketed across markets and products. A thorough brand inventory should be able to reveal the extent of brand consistency.

At the same time, a brand inventory can reveal a lack of perceived differences among different products sharing the brand name—for example, as a result of line extensions—that are designed to differ on one or more key dimensions. Creating sub-brands with distinct positions is often a marketing priority, and a brand inventory may help to uncover undesirable redundancy and overlap that could potentially lead to consumer confusion or retailer resistance.

BRAND EXPLORATORY

Although the supply-side view of the brand as revealed by the brand inventory is useful, *actual* consumer perceptions, of course, may not necessarily reflect the consumer perceptions that were intended to be created by the marketing program. Thus, the second step of the brand audit is to provide detailed information as to what consumers think of the brand by means of the brand exploratory, particularly in terms of brand awareness and the strength, favorability, and uniqueness of brand associations. The *brand exploratory* is research activity directed to understanding what consumers think and feel about the brand and its corresponding product category in order to identify sources of brand equity.

Preliminary Activities

Several preliminary activities are useful for the brand exploratory. First, in many cases, a number of prior research studies may exist and be relevant. It is important to dig through company archives to uncover reports that may have been buried, and perhaps even long forgotten, but which contain insights and answers to a number of important questions or suggest new questions that may still need to be posed. These studies should be carefully reviewed and summarized as to the insights they yield into sources and outcomes of brand equity.

Second, it is also useful to interview internal personnel to gain an understanding of their beliefs about consumer perceptions for the brand and competitive

brands. Past and current marketing managers may be able to share some wisdom not necessarily captured in prior research reports.

The diversity of opinion that typically emerges from these internal interviews about the brand serves several functions, for example, increasing the likelihood that useful insights or ideas will be generated, as well as pointing out any inconsistencies or misconceptions that may exist internally for the brand. Although these preliminary activities may yield some useful findings and suggest certain hypotheses, they are often incomplete. As a result, additional research is often required to better understand how customers shop for and use products and services and what they think of various brands. To allow a broad range of issues to be covered and to permit certain issues to be pursued in greater depth, the brand exploratory often employs qualitative research techniques. Chapter 9 reviews a number of these different approaches, as summarized in Figure 3-13.

Interpreting Qualitative Research

In choosing the range of possible qualitative research techniques to include in the brand exploratory, Gardner and Levy note:

> The emphasis in such research must necessarily be given to skill in interpretation and to reaching a coherent picture of the brand. The researchers must allow their respondents sufficient self-expression so that the data are rich in complex evaluations of the brand. In this way, the consumer's thoughts and feelings are given precedence rather than the preconceptions of the researchers, although these are present too in hypotheses and questions.[32]

Levy identifies three criteria by which a qualitative research program can be classified and judged: direction, depth, and diver-

Free association
Adjective ratings and checklists
Projective techniques
Photo sorts
Bubble drawings
Story telling
Personification exercises
Role playing

Source: Judie Lannon and Peter Cooper, "Humanistic Advertising: A Holistic Cultural Perspective," *International Journal of Advertising* 2 (1983): 195–213.

FIGURE 3-13   Summary of Qualitative Techniques

sity.[33] For example, any projective technique varies in terms of the nature of the stimulus information involved (e.g., related to the person or the brand), the extent to which responses are more superficial and concrete in meaning versus deeper and more abstract in meaning (and thus requiring more interpretation), and how it relates to the information gathered by other projective techniques.

In Figure 3-13, the tasks at the top of the list (e.g., free associations) involve very specific questions whose answers may be easier to interpret. The tasks on the bottom of the list (e.g., personification exercises and role playing) involve potentially much richer questions but ones that are also much harder to interpret. According to Levy, the more specific the question, the narrower the range of information given by the respondent. When the stimulus information in the question is open-ended and responses are freer or less constrained, the information provided tends to be greater. The more abstract and symbolic the research technique that is employed, however, the more important it is to follow up with probes and other questions that explicitly reveal the motivation and reasons behind consumers' responses.

Ideally, qualitative research conducted as part of the brand exploratory should vary in direction and depth as well as in the diversity of the techniques involved. Regardless of which techniques are actually employed, the challenge with qualitative research is to provide accurate interpretation—going beyond what consumers explicitly state to determine what they implicitly mean.

Conducting Quantitative Research

Qualitative research is suggestive, but a more definitive assessment of the depth and breadth of brand awareness and the strength, favorability, and uniqueness of brand associations often requires a quantitative phase of research. Chapter 9 reviews a number of different quantitative approaches to provide better approximations of consumer brand knowledge structures.

The guidelines for the quantitative phase of the exploratory are relatively straightforward. All potentially salient associations identified by the qualitative research phase should be assessed according to strength, favorability, and uniqueness. Both specific brand beliefs and overall attitudes and behaviors should be examined to reveal potential sources and outcomes of brand equity. Additionally, the depth and breadth of awareness of the brand should be assessed by employing various cues. Typically, it is necessary to conduct similar types of research for competitors to better understand their sources of brand equity and how they compare with the target brand.

Much of the discussion of qualitative and quantitative measures has concentrated on associations to the brand name element of the brand—for example, what do consumers think about the brand when given its name as a probe? Other brand elements could and should be studied in the brand exploratory because they may trigger other meanings and facets of the brand. Consumers can be asked what inferences they make about the brand on the basis of the product packaging, logo, or other attribute alone—for example, "What would you think about the brand on the basis of its packaging alone?" Specific aspects of the brand elements could be explored—for example, the label on the package or the shape of the package itself—to uncover their role in creating brand associations and thus sources of brand equity. The more it is the case that other brand elements are present and visible when consumers make brand and product decisions (e.g., at the point of purchase), the more important it is to employ all relevant brand elements as stimuli. In the process of examining other brand elements, it is also important to determine which of these elements most effectively represents and symbolizes the brand as a whole.

BRAND POSITIONING AND THE SUPPORTING MARKETING PROGRAM

The brand exploratory should uncover the current knowledge structures for the core brand and its competitors as well as determine the desired brand awareness and brand image and the necessary points of parity and points of difference with respect to competitors. Moving from the current brand image to the desired brand image typically involves decisions to add new associations, strengthen existing ones, or weaken or eliminate unde-

sirable ones in the minds of consumers. John Roberts, a leading marketing academic in Australia, sees the challenge in achieving the ideal positioning for a brand as being able to achieve congruence among what customers currently believe about the brand (and thus find credible), what customers will value in the brand, what the firm is currently saying about the brand, and where the firm would like to take the brand (see Figure 3-14).

A number of different internal management personnel can be part of the planning and positioning process (e.g., brand, marketing research, and production managers), as can relevant outside marketing partners (e.g., ad agency representatives). Once marketers have a good understanding from the brand audit of current brand knowledge structures for their target consumers and have decided on the desired brand knowledge structures for optimal positioning, additional research still may be necessary to test the viability of alternative tactical programs to achieve that positioning. A number of different possible marketing programs may exist that, at least on the surface, may be able to achieve the same goals, and additional research may be useful to assess their relative effectiveness and efficiency.

JOSE CUERVO APPLICATION

To illustrate how brand audits can be conducted, it is instructive to highlight some considerations from a brand audit of Jose Cuervo conducted in the mid-1990s.

Background

Produced in the town of Tequila in Jalisco, Mexico, Jose Cuervo was the world's first tequila. José Antonio de Cuervo, the first tequila producer, obtained a grant for land from the King of Spain in 1758, before Mexico had become an independent republic. In 1795, King Carlos IV of Spain transferred the deed to the second José Cuervo,

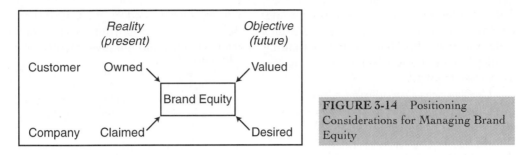

FIGURE 3-14   Positioning Considerations for Managing Brand Equity

José Maria Guadalupe Cuervo, and granted him the first concession to commercially produce tequila. This José Cuervo immediately built his distillery to produce the "wine of the earth"—tequila. Cuervo Especial (Gold) became the world's best-selling tequila.

The tequila share of the $40 billion spirits market grew from 1.6 percent in 1986 to 3.6 percent in 1993 due to the popularity of margaritas. Forty-two percent of all tequila was consumed in margaritas, which was the number one on-premise bar drink. Weekly consumption occasions averaged 1.3, however, which was less than the average for all spirits (1.7). The main drinking alternative to tequila was typically beer. Jose Cuervo had over half of the total market, and their sales were especially strong in the premium (95 percent market share) and super-premium (65 percent market share) segments.

Cuervo's primary target audience has been young adults of legal drinking age who are male or female (evenly divided), single or married, upper and upper middle class, with some university education, adventurous and willing to try new experiences, and urban. With social drinking an integral part of their lives, they are seen as young, energetic, and enthusiastic.

Marketing Activities

Cuervo was marketed largely through in-store merchandising and displays and on-premise themed events and promotions.

For example, mid-1990s on-premise event promotions revolved around Cinco de Mayo, beach volleyball matches, Ultimate Frisbee competitions, Halloween, "Wild Life Society" bar-specific events, and so forth. Advertising had proven difficult for the brand because there was no well-defined user image. Cuervo Gold ads featured modern, abstract Mexican art with a simple brand message of "Jose Cuervo. Primo Tequila." Cuervo 1800 ads featured classic, historical Mexican art with a stronger product message.

In 1996, the company spent millions acquiring an 8-acre island and resort in the British Virgin Islands—the Republic of Cuervo! Cuervo asked for a seat as the 192nd member of the General Assembly of the United Nations and sought permission from Atlanta Olympic organizers to send a beach volleyball team. They promoted an accompanying sweepstakes and the entire program with PR and on their Web site.

In evaluating any aspect of their marketing program, the basic question was always the same: Is it Cuervo?

Situation

Jose Cuervo faced a number of issues in the mid-1990s. In terms of threats, competitive intensity had increased from both traditional tequila makers and private labels. Nontequila margaritas that were wine or malt based had also been introduced. Consumers appeared to be increasingly price sensitive.

The core market—California—was maturing. Cuervo was also well aware of Bacardi's sales slide and loss of leadership (see Branding Brief 13-3) and wanted to be sure not to follow in their footsteps.

Cuervo was considering a number of possible new product extensions but was concerned about their potential effects. Would there be a loss in the Cuervo "magic"? Would there be confusion in the Cuervo personality? Would consumers have difficulty knowing what was the "real stuff"? There was also concern about the Cuervo brand and product portfolio and whether it was properly optimized. Management felt that there needed to be a long-term perspective to avoid short-term sacrifices. As one executive put it, "We don't want to surrender our brand credentials at a border check point we never meant to cross."

Brand Inventory

The brand inventory reviewed a number of aspects of the marketing program. Jose Cuervo's brand and product portfolio could be characterized as follows (in increasing levels of price and quality—see Figure 3-15).

➤ *Jose Cuervo Margaritas:* 11% proof pre-mixed margaritas (akin to a cooler) sold in four-packs, with Classic Lime, Melon, Mango, Moonlight, Pink Cad, Raspberry, and Strawberry flavors.

➤ *Jose Cuervo Authentic Margaritas:* 18% proof (full-strength) pre-mixed margaritas sold in regular and party size bottles, with Classic Lime, Strawberry, and Moonlight flavors.

➤ *Jose Cuervo Blanc (White) Tequila:* With the distinctive flavor of agave.

➤ *Cuervo Especial (Gold) Tequila:* Made from a blend of selected high-quality tequilas. Priced at around $15 a bottle, it commanded a 10 percent to 15 percent price premium over White.

➤ *Cuervo 1800 Tequila:* A unique combination of anejo (aged) tequila specially blended with other fine Cuervo tequilas to create a distinct smoothness. Typically priced at a little over $20.

➤ *Cuervo Tradicional Tequila:* 100% blue agave tequila sold in limited quantities of individually numbered bottles.

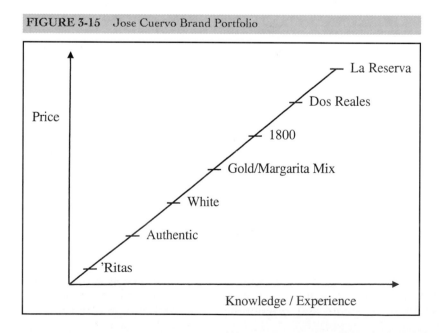

FIGURE 3-15   Jose Cuervo Brand Portfolio

Jose Cuervo also sold The Perfect Margarita Mix in assorted flavors under the Jose Cuervo brand

Brand Exploratory

The brand exploratory concentrated on uncovering consumer perceptions of the various Cuervo and competitive brands.

Cuervo's Mexican heritage had established the brand as the "real thing" to many drinkers—but with a certain amount of "magic." In general, key Cuervo brand associations were "fun," "party experience," "active," "casual," and "social." A dichotomy existed, however, between the different products (see Figure 3-16).

➤ *Tequila-based drinks:* These products, such as their Cuervo Gold flagship brand, had a more masculine and serious partying image, with associations such as "potent," "impact," "rough-tough," and "established." This side of the brand was characterized by shots and slammers. The brand personality was young and spirited—a catalyst to make any social occasion fun. It was seen as suited for serious partying. (See Figure 3-17.)

➤ *Pre-mixed margaritas and margarita drinks:* These products had a more feminine and socially acceptable image, with associations such as "light," "relaxing," "mild-mannered," and "hip." They were seen as fun to drink and a refreshing way to unwind.

Cuervo Gold was about "quality," "leadership," and "potency." Margaritas as a drink were seen less that way and more as an "everyday fun drink." A perceptual map was developed based on consumer perceptions of key Cuervo brands as well as other major brands of spirits (see Figure 3-18).

Recommendations

A number of recommendations emerged from the Jose Cuervo brand audit, some of which were later adopted, as follows.

Distinguish Cuervo Margarita and Tequila Brands

In general, the brand portfolio and hierarchy needed to be clarified and improved at both the upper and lower ends. At the lower end of the price/quality ladder, there was not a clear distinction between the two types of pre-mixed margaritas. The packaging was

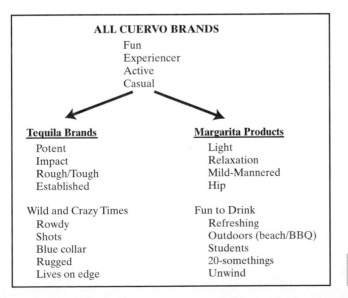

FIGURE 3-16   Jose Cuervo Brand Images

The Cuervo Gold Loyalist

He/She

- Is civilized, but with a streak of goofiness.
- Drinks Cuervo Gold straight, shooters, slammers/poppers, or on the rocks occasionally when he/she is in the right mood, environment, or with goofier friends. (Or at least he/she used to at college.)
- Is an activist in just about everything. Not a "shrink back" person. Sky diver, volley-baller, skier, scuba diver, surfer, dune buggy rider, dirt biker, hang glider, etc. Some may even play tennis and golf, but wouldn't tell their goofier friends.
- Is not intimidated by noisy, crowded bars. In fact, likes to hang out in them. Will whoop and holler in public, given half a chance. Has fun noticeably; may be a secret cowboy.
- Has business clothes, of course, but prefers jeans, beachwear, shorts, flip flops, ski vest, cowboy boots, and "lucky" hat. Isn't formal, except when being flamboyant or extravagant.
- Drinks straight (occasionally) to show some "macho" attitudes, but also to show he knows the real, legitimate, good stuff.
- Would accept Jack Daniels, Wild Turkey, or Yukon Jack straight if they are out of Cuervo Gold.
- Wants any products with legitimate, clear credentials.
- Likes the good things: Porsche, Rolex, tickets to the Grateful Dead, one beach that no one has ever heard of, Tony Lama boots, the opposite sex, Jerry Lee Lewis records, Rock 'n Roll Trivia, Cuervo Gold.
- Has "different" parties. Underwater Margarita party, drinks from water pistols, water coolers full of Blue Margaritas, Strawberry Margaritas from I.V. bottles and stands, etc. Goes out a lot.
- Knows how to defeat his/her beeper, doesn't live with parents, probably hard to find on a Friday afternoon.
- Either never eats sushi, or eats it three times a week.
- Orders "happy hour" house Margarita with a shot of Cuervo Gold on the side.
- Is not as worried about the negative aspects of tequila as the research department or the ad agency.

The Cuervo Gold Loyalist is an active, highly social person who enjoys life in a noticeable way, in front of others. Verbally advocates his/her favorite things, defends his/her favorite things, and is probably not neutral about *your* favorite things. As such, he/she often is the in-market spokesperson for Cuervo Gold when neither we, the trade, nor the advertising is present. Goes out often where he/she talks about us in a positive life-style way, often attributing things to us out of his/her personal folklore. May be a frequent consumer, and is certainly a frequent advocate.

FIGURE 3-17   The Cuervo Gold Brand User

---

virtually identical, and the Jose Cuervo name was prominently displayed on both. The risk was that the "not full strength" margaritas would—literally and figuratively—dilute the Cuervo brand image. One possible solution would be to rename Margaritas as 'Ritas to distinguish it from the full-strength Authentics brand and to also downplay the Cuervo name by reducing its prominence on the package. (The short name was actually used by many distributors and fit with its "not full strength" image.) Different flavor

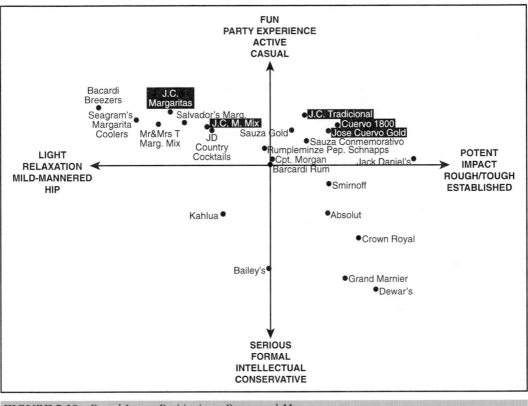

FIGURE 3-18   Brand Image Positionings: Perceptual Map

names for Authentics could also produce greater separation. In terms of Authentics, its name also probably needed to receive more emphasis than Jose Cuervo, but the packaging could be changed to make it look more like a tequila product (and less like 'Ritas).

Distinguish Cuervo 1800

At the higher end of the price/quality ladder, Cuervo 1800 was virtually indistinguishable from Cuervo Gold perceptually. To better round out the brand portfolio, it would make sense to make 1800 more distinct. An obvious approach to do so would be to make it more upscale through product extensions, communications, and the like. In this way, Cuervo 1800 would enter a different competitive space and minimize the overlap with Cuervo Gold. More generally,

there also needed to be a broader brand migration strategy to help move people up the price/quality ladder such that Cuervo could experience greater loyalty and higher price margins.

Generate Greater Consumer Demand

Although the promotions and events were typically quite creative, advertising support for Cuervo was not particularly well distinguished. Advertising needed to be improved to better reflect brand values. More generally, marketing communication programs needed to be sure to increase on-premise brand call and off-premise brand sales. Efforts also could be made to facilitate consumption of margaritas (the only cocktail routinely consumed with food).

Selectively Introduce Brand Extensions

Much opportunity existed at the high end of the market for more expensive, premium tequila brands. In fact, Cuervo's first new entry in this market became La Reserva de la Familia de Jose Cuervo, a 100% blue agave tequila aged for at least three years. Costing $75, La Reserva was introduced in a limited edition (4,000) in specially designed bottles to commemorate the 200th anniversary of the Cuervo brand.

Notes

1. Much of this chapter is based on Kevin Lane Keller, Brian Sternthal, and Alice Tybout, "Competitive Brand Positioning: Developing Brand Positionings to Maximize Profits," (*Harvard Business Review,* forthcoming).
2. Phillip Kotler, *Marketing Management*, 11th ed. (Upper Saddle River, NJ: Prentice-Hall, 2003).
3. Russell I. Haley, "Benefit Segmentation: A Decision-Oriented Research Tool," *Journal of Marketing* 32 (July 1968): 30–35.
4. Also, it may be the case that the actual demographic specifications given do not fully reflect consumer's underlying perceptions. For example, when the Ford Mustang was introduced, the intended market segment was much younger than the ages of the customers who actually bought the car. Evidently, these consumers felt or wanted to feel younger psychologically than they really were.
5. Ronald Frank, William Massey, and Yoram Wind, *Market Segmentation* (Englewood Cliffs, NJ: Prentice-Hall, 1972).
6. Chip Walker, "How Strong Is Your Brand?" *Marketing Tools* (January/February 1995): 46–53.
7. A complete treatment of this material is beyond the scope of this chapter. Useful reviews can be found in any good marketing strategy text. For example, see Chapter 3 of Donald R. Lehmann and Russell S. Winer, *Product Management* (Englewood Cliffs, NJ: Prentice-Hall, 1994).
8. Stacy Kravetz, "Baskin-Robbins Scoops Up a New Look," *Wall Street Journal*, 4 September 1977, B-1.
9. The concept of "points of parity" and "points of difference" and many of the other ideas and examples in this section were first developed by Northwestern University's Brian Sternthal and further refined in collaboration with Northwestern University's Alice Tybout.
10. John Czepiel, *Competitive Marketing Strategy* (Englewood Cliffs, NJ: Prentice-Hall, 1992).
11. Richard Heller, "Folk Fortune," *Forbes*, 4 September 2000, 66-69.
12. Brian Sternthal, "Miller Lite Case," Kellogg Graduate School of Management, Northwestern University.
13. Interestingly, when Miller Lite was first introduced, the assumption was that the relevant motivation underlying the benefit of "less filling" for consumers was that they could drink more beer. Consequently, Miller targeted heavy users of beer with a sizable introductory ad campaign concentrated on mass-market sports programs. As it turned out, the initial research showed that the market segment they attracted was more the moderate user—older and upscale. Why? The brand promise of "less filling" is actually fairly ambiguous. To this group of consumers, "less filling" meant that they could drink beer and stay mentally and physically agile (sin with no penalty!). From Miller's standpoint, attracting this target market was an unexpected but happy outcome because it meant that there would be less cannibalization with their more mass-market High Life brand. To better match the motivations of this group, there were some changes in the types of athletes in the ads, such as using ex-bull fighters to better represent mental and physical agility.
14. Brian Sternthal and Alice Tybout, D. Iacobucci, Ed., *Kellogg on Marketing*, (Chichester, NY: Wiley, 2001).
15. Richard A. Melcher, "Why Zima Faded So Fast," *Business Week*, 10 March 1997, 110–114.

16. David Field, "Airline Tries Loftier Name," *USA Today*, 10 March 1997, B7.

17. Keith Naughton, "Ford's 'Perfect Storm,'" *Newsweek*, 17 September 2001, 48–50.

18. Elizabeth Jensen, "Campbell's Juice Scheme: Stealth Health," *Wall Street Journal*, 18 April 1997, B6.

19. "Wrinkle for the Prune Industry," *Los Angeles Times*, 21 December 1999.

20. Shelly Branch, "Irradiated Food by Any Other Name Might Just Win Over Consumers," *Wall Street Journal*, 14 August 2001, B1.

21. Abraham Maslow, *Motivation and Personality*, 2nd ed. (New York: Harper & Row, 1970).

22. Thomas J. Reynolds and Jonathan Gutman, "Laddering Theory: Method, Analysis, and Interpretation," *Journal of Advertising Research* (February/March 1988): 11–31.

23. Marco Vriens and Frenkel Ter Hofstede, "Linking Attributes, Benefits, and Consumer Values," *Marketing Research* (Fall 2000): 3–8.

24. Kevin Lane Keller, "Brand Mantras: Rationale, Criteria, and Examples," *Journal of Marketing Management* 15 (1999): 43–51.

25. Stan Maklan and Simon Knox, *Competing on Value* (Upper Saddle River, NJ: Financial Times Prentice-Hall, 2000).

26. Quentin Hardy, "Backstabbing Carly," *Forbes*, 11 June 2001, 55.

27. Noah Hawley, "Creating Corporate Mini-Me's," *Business 2.0*, 27 June 2000, 135

28. Philip Kotler, *Marketing Management*, 10th ed. (Upper Saddle River, NJ: Prentice-Hall, 2000).

29. Sidney Davidson, James Schindler, Clyde P. Stickney, and Roman Weil, *Financial Accounting: An Introduction to Concepts, Methods, and Uses* (Hinsdale, IL: Dryden Press, 1976).

30. Phillip Kotler, William Gregor, and William Rogers, "The Marketing Audit Comes of Age," *Sloan Management Review* 18, no. 2, Winter 1977, 25–43.

31. Laurel Wentz, "Brand Audits Reshaping Images," *Ad Age International* (September 1996): 38–41.

32. Burleigh B. Gardner and Sidney J. Levy, "The Product and the Brand," *Harvard Business Review* (March–April 1955): 33–39.

33. Sidney J. Levy, "Dreams, Fairy Tales, Animals, and Cars," *Psychology and Marketing* 2, no. 2 (Summer 1985): 67–81.

C H A P T E R

Choosing Brand Elements to Build Brand Equity

PREVIEW

Brand elements, sometimes called brand identities, are those trademarkable devices that serve to identify and differentiate the brand. The main brand elements are brand names, URLs, logos, symbols, characters, spokespeople, slogans, jingles, packages, and signage. Independent of the decisions made about the product and how it is marketed, brand elements can be chosen in a manner to build as much brand equity as possible. That is, according to the customer-based brand equity model, brand elements can be chosen to enhance brand awareness; facilitate the formation of strong, favorable, and unique brand associations; or elicit positive brand judgments and feelings. The test of the brand-building ability of brand elements is what consumers would think or feel about the product *if* they only knew about its brand name, associated logo, and other characteristics. A brand element that provides a positive contribution to brand equity, for example, would be one for which consumers assumed or inferred certain valued associations or responses.

This chapter considers how different brand elements can be chosen to build brand equity. After describing the general criteria for choosing brand elements, it considers specific tactical issues for each of the different types of brand elements. The chapter concludes by addressing how a marketer should choose an optimal set of brand elements to build brand equity. Brand Focus 4.0 at the end of the chapter highlights some legal issues for branding.

CRITERIA FOR CHOOSING BRAND ELEMENTS

In general, there are six criteria in choosing brand elements (as well as more specific choice considerations in each case, as shown in Figure 4-1):

1. Memorability
2. Meaningfulness
3. Likability
4. Transferability
5. Adaptability
6. Protectability

The first three criteria—memorability, meaningfulness, and likability—can be characterized as "brand building" in nature and concern how brand equity can be built through the judicious choice of a brand element. The latter three, however, are more "defensive" in nature and are concerned with how the brand equity contained in a brand element can be leveraged and preserved in the face of different opportunities and constraints. The following sections briefly consider each of these general criteria.

Memorability

A necessary condition for building brand equity is achieving a high level of brand awareness. Toward that goal, brand elements can be chosen that are inherently memorable and therefore facilitate recall or recognition in purchase or consumption settings.

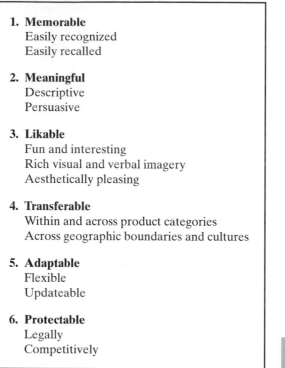

1. **Memorable**
   Easily recognized
   Easily recalled

2. **Meaningful**
   Descriptive
   Persuasive

3. **Likable**
   Fun and interesting
   Rich visual and verbal imagery
   Aesthetically pleasing

4. **Transferable**
   Within and across product categories
   Across geographic boundaries and cultures

5. **Adaptable**
   Flexible
   Updateable

6. **Protectable**
   Legally
   Competitively

FIGURE 4-1   Criteria for Choosing Brand Elements

In other words, the intrinsic nature of certain names, symbols, logos, and the like—their semantic content, visual properties, and so on—may make them more attention getting and easy to remember and therefore contribute to brand equity. For example, naming a brand of propane gas cylinders "Blue Rhino" and reinforcing it with a powder-blue mascot with a distinctive yellow flame is likely to stick in the minds of consumers.[1]

Meaningfulness

Besides choosing brand elements to build awareness, brand elements can also be chosen whose inherent meaning enhances the formation of brand associations. Brand elements may take on all kinds of meaning, varying in descriptive, as well as persuasive, content. For example, Chapter 1 described how brand names could be based on people, places, animals or birds, or other things or objects. Two particularly important dimensions or aspects of the meaning of a brand element are the extent to which it conveys the following:

➤ *General information about the nature of the product category*. In terms of descriptive meaning, to what extent does the brand element suggest something about the product category? How likely would it be that a consumer could correctly identify the corresponding product category or categories for the brand based on any one particular brand element? In a related question, does the brand element seem credible in the product category? In other words, is the content of a brand element consistent with what consumers would expect to see from a brand in that product category?

➤ *Specific information about particular attributes and benefits of the brand.* In terms of persuasive meaning, to what extent does the brand element suggest something about the particular kind of product that the brand would likely be, for example, in terms of key attributes or benefits? Does it suggest something about a product ingredient or the type of person who might use the brand?

Likability

The associations suggested by a brand element may not always be related to the product. Thus, brand elements can be chosen that are rich in visual and verbal imagery and inherently fun and interesting. Independent of its memorability and meaningfulness, how aesthetically appealing do consumers find the brand element? Is it inherently likable, both visually, verbally, and in other ways? In other words, independent of the particular product or service, how much would consumers like the brand element? The Science of Branding 4-1 outlines how marketing aesthetics can be applied to brand elements.

In terms of these first three criteria, a memorable, meaningful, and likable set of brand elements offers many advantages. Because consumers often do not examine much information in making product decisions, it is often desirable that brand elements be easily recognized and recalled and inherently descriptive and persuasive. Moreover, memorable or meaningful brand names, logos, symbols, and so on reduce the burden on marketing communications to build awareness and link brand associations. The different associations that arise from the likability and appeal of the brand elements also may play a critical role in the equity of a brand, especially when few other product-related associations exist. Often, the less concrete the possible product benefits are, the more important is the creative potential of the brand name and other brand elements to capture intangible characteristics of a brand. Branding Brief 4-1 describes how PepsiCo introduced their new Code Red soft drink.

Transferability

The fourth general criterion concerns the transferability of the brand element—in both a product category and geographic sense. First, to what extent can the brand element add to the brand equity of new products sharing the brand elements introduced either within the product class or across product classes? In other words, how useful is the brand element for line or category extensions? In general, the less specific the name, the more easily it can be transferred across categories. For example, Amazon connotes a massive South American river and therefore as a brand can be appropriate for a variety of different types of products, whereas Toys"R"Us obviously does not permit the same flexibility.

Second, to what extent does the brand element add to brand equity across geographic boundaries and market segments? To a large extent this depends on the cultural content and linguistic qualities of the brand element. For example, one of the main advantages of nonmeaningful names (e.g., Exxon) is that they translate well into other languages since they have no inherent meaning. The mistakes that even top companies have made in translating their brand names, slogans, and packages into other languages and cultures over the years have become legendary. Figure 4-2 lists some well-known global branding mishaps. Companies must review all their brand elements for cultural meaning before introducing the brand into a new market.[2]

THE SCIENCE OF BRANDING 4-1

Brand Design and Aesthetics

Schmitt and Simonson explore the importance and applications of "marketing aesthetics," a concept with many branding implications.[1] They refer to marketing aesthetics as "the marketing of sensory experiences in corporate or brand output that contributes to the organization's or brand's identity." They approach marketing aesthetics from three perspectives: product design, communications research, and spatial design. They argue that aesthetics offers tangible value to organizations by creating loyalty, allowing for premium pricing, cutting through information clutter, affording protection from competitive attacks, and saving costs and increasing productivity. The following provides a brief overview to this line of thinking.

Aesthetics strategy is defined as "the strategic planning and implementation of identity elements that provide sensory experiences and aesthetic gratification to the organization's multiple constituents." They describe the basic rationale for this approach as follows:

> Customers do not have direct access to an organizations' or a brand's culture, missions, strategies, values, to the "private self" of the organization or the brand. However, customers do see the public face of the organization or brand—its expressions. This public face is projected through multiple identity elements with various aesthetic styles and themes. It is never seen in its totality, but the various perceptions are integrated into overall customer impressions.

Thus, according to their approach, the styles and themes of design elements are the vehicle of how corporate expressions affect customer impressions, as follows.

Style refers to a distinctive quality or form, a manner of expression. Style is composed of primary elements, including sight (color, shape, line, pattern, and typeface), sound (loudness, pitch, and meter), touch (material and texture), taste, and smell. Key strategic issues in style creation are whether to juxtapose design elements and when styles should be adapted or abandoned. Four perceptual dimensions are identified to evaluate corporate or brand identity-related styles: complexity ("minimalism" vs. "ornamentalism"), representation ("realism" vs. "abstraction"), perceived movement ("dynamic" vs. "static"), and potency ("loud/strong" vs. "soft/weak"). The authors argue that to be effective, styles must be combined with themes that express an organization's or brand's private self succinctly and directly.

Themes refer to the content, the meaning, and the projected image of an identity. Themes can provide customers with mental anchors and reference points to allow them to put an organization in a wider context and to distinguish its position. Themes are expressed most pointedly if (1) they are used as prototypical expressions of an organization's core values or mission or of a brand's character, (2) they are repeated and adapted over time, and (3) they are developed into a system of interrelated ideas. Themes can be expressed in a variety of ways: as corporate brand names, symbols, narratives, slogans or jingles, concepts, or combinations of elements. Decisions regarding themes revolve around the use of one theme or multiple themes, theme variation or isolation, integration of verbal and visual information, and adapting or abandoning themes.

[1] Bernd H. Schmitt and Alex Simonson, *Marketing Aesthetics: The Strategic Management of Brands, Identity, and Image* (New York: Free Press, 1997).

Branding a New Soft Drink

When Pepsi-Cola's total volume increased a mere tenth of a percent in 2000, the company quickly sought to boost sales by launching the first line extension of its popular Mountain Dew drink since Diet Mountain Dew debuted in 1988. A cross-functional team composed of 35 people from seven Pepsi departments worked on developing the new product. The team considered several possibilities: Dew H20 bottled water, Dew Unplugged decaf Mountain Dew, a Mountain Dew sports drink, and a new Dew flavor. The company settled on creating a new flavor, and within 10 months, instead of the usual 2 years it takes Pepsi to develop a new product, launched a bright red cherry-flavored beverage called Mountain Dew Code Red (see Figure A).

For the launch, Pepsi used radio and outdoor advertising, as well as sampling and in-store merchandising. To build buzz for Code Red, the company sent free samples to 4,000 select consumers, such as hip-hop producer Jermaine Dupri and radio DJ Funkmaster Flex. The drink was heavily sampled at marquee sporting events such as the NCAA Final Four and ESPN's 2001 winter X Games. Pepsi also developed a special Web site for the brand that featured an interactive game called "Mission: Code Red 2." Additionally, Pepsi marketed Code Red to urban consumers. When research revealed that urban and

FIGURE A   Code Red Product Packaging

ethnic focus groups preferred the name Code Red to Wild Cherry Mountain Dew, Pepsi stuck with the former. The company also developed an ad campaign titled "Crack the Code" that used graffiti-art design elements and an urban setting.

Code Red attracted a rabid fan base. According to A.C. Nielsen, Code Red tested in the top 5 percent of all new product concepts ever tested among teens. The drink was also popular in the high-tech community. Two programmers who discovered a computer virus named it "Code Red" after the beverage they used to maintain late hours in front of their monitors. The virus eventually infected more than 700,000 computers. Pepsi sent the pair five cases of Code Red in appreciation for the free publicity.

Within two months of its May 2000 launch, Code Red was the fifth-best-selling soft drink sold at convenience stores and gas stations (Mountain Dew is number one). This signaled tremendous success, considering that the drink came in only two single-serve sizes and the muted marketing campaign at the time did not yet include television spots. Though the drink was launched midway through the second quarter of 2000, Pepsi credited the Code Red launch with helping to boost net sales 20 percent to $962 million that quarter. One bottler exclaimed, "It's flown off the shelves for us."

Sources: www.mountaindew.com; Hillary Chura, "Pepsi-Cola's Code Red Is White Hot," *Advertising Age,* 27 August 2001; Maureen Tkacik and Betsy McKay, "Code Red: PepsiCo's Guerilla Conquest," *Wall Street Journal,* 17 August 2001; Abigail Klingbeil, "The Making of a Brand," Gannett News Service, 29 June 2001.

Adaptability

The fifth consideration concerns the adaptability of the brand element over time. Because of changes in consumer values and opinions, or simply because of a need to remain contemporary, brand elements often must be updated over time. The more adaptable and flexible the brand element, the easier it is to update it. For example, logos and characters can be given a new look or a new design to make them appear more modern and relevant.

Protectability

The sixth and final general consideration concerns the extent to which the brand element is protectable—both in a legal and competitive sense. In terms of legal considerations, it is important to (1) choose brand elements that can be legally protected on an international basis, (2) formally register them with the appropriate legal bodies, and (3) vigorously defend trademarks from unauthorized competitive infringement. The necessity of legally protecting the brand is dramatized by the billions of dollars in losses in the United States alone from unauthorized use of patents, trademarks, and copyrights.

A closely related consideration is the extent to which the brand element is competitively protectable. Even if a brand element can be protected legally, it still may be the case that competitive actions can take away much of the brand equity provided by the brand elements themselves. If a name, package, or other attribute is too easily copied, much of the uniqueness of the brand may disappear. For example, consider the ice beer category. Although Molson Ice was one of the early entries in the category, its pioneering advantage from a branding standpoint was quickly lost when Miller Ice and what later became Bud Ice were introduced. Thus, it is important to reduce the likelihood that competitors can imitate the brand by creating a derivative based on salient prefixes or suffixes of the name, emulating the package look, or other actions.

1. When Braniff translated a slogan touting its upholstery, "Fly in leather," it came out in Spanish as "Fly naked."
2. Coors put its slogan, "Turn it loose," into Spanish, where it was read as "Suffer from diarrhea."
3. Chicken magnate Frank Perdue's line, "It takes a tough man to make a tender chicken," sounds much more interesting in Spanish: "It takes a sexually stimulated man to make a chicken affectionate."
4. Why Chevy Nova never sold well in Spanish-speaking countries: *No va* means "it doesn't go" in Spanish.
5. When Pepsi started marketing its products in China, they translated their slogan, "Pepsi Brings You Back to Life," pretty literally. The slogan in Chinese really meant "Pepsi Brings Your Ancestors Back from the Grave."
6. When Coca-Cola first shipped to China, they named the product something that when pronounced sounded like "Coca-Cola." The only problem was that the characters used meant "Bite the wax tadpole." They later changed to a set of characters that mean "Happiness in the mouth."
7. A hair products company, Clairol, introduced the "Mist Stick," a curling iron, into Germany only to find out that *mist* is slang for manure in German.
8. When Gerber first started selling baby food in Africa, they used the same packaging as in the United States, with the cute baby on the label. Later they found out that in Africa, companies routinely put pictures on the label of what's inside because most people can't read.
9. Japan's Mitsubishi Motors had to rename its Pajero model in Spanish-speaking countries because the term related to masturbation.
10. Toyota Motor's MR2 model dropped the number in France because the combination sounded like a French swearword.

FIGURE 4-2   Ten Global Branding Mishaps

OPTIONS AND TACTICS FOR BRAND ELEMENTS

The value of choosing brand elements strategically to build brand equity can be seen by considering the advantages of having chosen "Apple" as the name for a personal computer. Apple was a simple but well-known word that was distinctive in the product category—factors facilitating the development of brand awareness. The meaning of the name also gave the company a "friendly shine" and warm brand personality. Moreover, the name could be reinforced visually with a logo that could easily transfer across geographic and cultural boundaries. Finally, the name could serve as a platform for sub-brands (e.g., as with the Macintosh), aiding the introduction of brand extensions. Thus, as the Apple example illustrates, the judicious choice of a brand name can make an appreciable contribution to the creation of brand equity.

What would an ideal brand element be like? Consider brand names—perhaps the most central of all brand elements. Ideally, a brand name would be easily remembered, highly suggestive of both the product class and the particular benefits that served as the basis of its positioning, inherently fun or interesting, rich with creative potential, transferable to a wide variety of product and geographic settings, enduring in meaning and relevant over time, and strongly protectable both legally and competitively.

Unfortunately, it is difficult to choose a brand name—or any brand element, for that matter—that would satisfy all of these different criteria. For example, as noted earlier, the more meaningful the brand name, the more likely it is that the brand name will not be very transferable to other cultures due to translation problems. Moreover, brand names are generally less adaptable over time. Because it is virtually impossible to find one brand element that will satisfy all the choice criteria, multiple brand elements are typically employed. The following sections outline in detail the major considerations for each type of brand element. The chapter concludes by discussing how to put all of this together to design a set of brand elements to build brand equity.

Brand Names

The brand name is a fundamentally important choice because it often captures the central theme or key associations of a product in a very compact and economical fashion. Brand names can be an extremely effective shorthand means of communication. Whereas the time it takes consumers to comprehend marketing communications can range from a half a minute (for an advertisement) to potentially hours (for a sales call), the brand name can be noticed and its meaning registered or activated in memory within just a few seconds.

Because the brand name becomes so closely tied to the product in the minds of consumers, however, it is also the most difficult brand element for marketers to subsequently change. Consequently, brand names are often systematically researched before being chosen. The days when Henry Ford II could name his new automobile the "Edsel" after the name of a family member seem to be long gone. Is it difficult to come up with a brand name? Ira Bachrach, a well-known branding consultant, notes that although there are 140,000 words in the English vocabulary, the average American only recognizes 20,000 words; his consulting company, NameLab, sticks to the 7,000 words that make up the vocabulary of most TV programs and commercials. Although that may sound like a lot of choices, each year tens of thousands of new brands are registered as legal trademarks. In fact, arriving at a satisfactory brand name for a new product can be a painfully difficult and prolonged process. After realizing that most of the desirable brand names are already legally registered, many a frustrated executive has lamented that "all of the good ones are taken."

In some ways, this difficulty should not be surprising. Any parent can probably sympathize with how hard it can be to choose a name for a child, as evidenced by the thousand of babies born each year without names because their parents have not decided on—or perhaps not agreed upon—a name yet. It is rare that naming a product can be as easy as it was for Ford when it introduced the Taurus automobile. "Taurus" was the code name given to the car during its design stage because the chief engineer's and product manager's wives were both born under that astrological sign. As luck would have it, upon closer examination, the name turned out to have a number of desirable characteristics. Consequently, it was chosen as the actual name for the car, saving thousands of dollars in additional research and consulting expenses.

Naming Guidelines

Selecting a brand name for a new product is certainly an art and a science. This section provides some general guidelines for choosing a name. It focuses on developing a completely new brand name for the product; Chapter 12 considers how a company can use existing brand or company names in various ways to name new products. Figure 4-3 displays the different types of possible brand names according to identity experts Landor Associates. As with any brand element, brand names must be chosen with the

I. Descriptive
Describes function literally; generally unregisterable
Examples: Singapore Airlines, Global Crossing

II. Suggestive
Suggestive of a benefit or function
Examples: marchFIRST, Agilent Technologies

III. Compounds
Combination of two or more, often unexpected, words
Examples: redhat

IV. Classical
Based on Latin, Greek, or Sanskrit.
Example: Meritor

V. Arbitrary
Real words with no obvious tie-in to company
Example: Apple

VI. Fanciful
Coined words with no obvious meaning
Example: avanade

FIGURE 4-3 Landor's Brand Name Taxonomy

six general criteria in mind. After outlining some more specific naming criteria, this chapter describes the process by which a name should be chosen.

Brand Awareness   In general, it is believed that brand awareness is improved the extent to which brand names are chosen that are simple and easy to pronounce or spell; familiar and meaningful; and different, distinctive, and unusual.[3]

First, to enhance brand recall, it is desirable for the brand name to be simple and easy to pronounce or spell. Simplicity reduces consumers' cognitive effort to comprehend and process the brand name. Short names often facilitate recall because they are easy to encode and store in memory (e.g., Aim toothpaste, Raid pest spray, Bold laundry detergent, Suave shampoo, Off insect repellent, Jiff peanut butter, Ban deodorant, and Bic pens). Longer names can be shortened to ease recallability. For example, over the years Chevrolet cars have also become known as "Chevy," Budweiser beer has also become known as "Bud," and Coca-Cola has also become known as "Coke."

Ease of pronunciation is critical to obtain valuable repeated word-of-mouth exposure that helps to build strong memory links. Pronunciation also affects entry into consideration sets and the willingness of consumers to order or request the brand orally. Rather than risk the embarrassment of mispronouncing a difficult name (as might be the case with such potentially difficult-to-pronounce names as Hyundai automobiles, Fruzen Gladje ice cream, or Faconnable clothing), consumers may just avoid pronouncing it altogether. Clearly, it is a challenge to build brand equity for a brand with a difficult-to-pronounce name because so much of the initial marketing efforts have to be devoted to simply educating consumers as to the proper way to pronounce the name. In the case of Wyborowa imported Polish vodka (pronounced Vee-ba-rova), management actually resorted to running a print ad to help consumers pronounce the brand name—a key factor of consumer behavior for success in the distilled spirits category.

Ideally, the brand name should have a clear, understandable, and unambiguous pronunciation and meaning. The way a brand is pronounced can affect its meaning. One research study showed that certain hypothetical products that had brand names that were acceptable in both English and French (e.g., Vaner, Randal, and Massin) were perceived as more "hedonic" (i.e., providing much pleasure) and better liked when pronounced in French than in English.[4] Consumers may take away different perceptions of the brand if ambiguous pronunciation of its name results in different meanings.

Honda Precis

Research showed that the interpretation of the Honda Precis brand varied depending on how consumers thought it was pronounced.[5] The name was meant to imply that the car was "precise and accurate." If consumers thought it was pronounced PREE-sus, they were more likely to think of it as an economy car (the intended positioning); on the other hand, if they thought it was pronounced PRAY-see, they were more likely to think of it as a luxury or sports car. If they thought it was pronounced PRAY-sus, they were more likely to think of it as a family car.

Pronunciation problems may arise from not conforming to linguistic rules. Although Honda chose the name "Acura" because it was associated with words connoting precision in several languages, they initially had some trouble with consumer pronunciation of the name (pronounced AK-yur-a) in the American market, perhaps in part because they chose not to use the phonetically simpler English spelling of Accura (with a double *c*).

To improve pronounceability and recallability, many marketers seek a desirable cadence and pleasant sound in their brand names.[6] For example, brand names may use alliteration (repetition of consonants, such as in Coleco), assonance (repetition of vowel sounds, such as in Ramada Inn), consonance (repetition of consonants with intervening vowel change, such as in Hamburger Helper), or rhythm (repetition of pattern of syllable stress, such as in Better Business Bureau). Some words employ onomatopoeia-words composed of syllables that when pronounced generate a sound strongly suggestive of the word's meaning (e.g., Sizzler steak house, Cap'n Crunch cereal, Ping golf clubs, or Schweppes carbonated beverages).

A second consideration to enhance brand recall is that the brand name should be familiar and meaningful so that it is able to tap into existing knowledge structures. Brand names may be concrete or abstract in their meaning. As pointed out in Chapter 1, all types of categories of objects can be used to form a name (e.g., people, places, animals, birds, or different kinds of inanimate objects). Because these objects already exist in memory in verbal and visual form, less learning has to occur. Links can be more easily formed to the object name and product, increasing memorability.[7]

One research study of hypothetical brand names showed that "high-imagery" brand names, (e.g., Ocean, Frog, Plant, and Paper) were significantly more memorable across a variety of recall and recognition measures than "low-imagery" words (e.g., History, Truth, Moment, and Memory).[8] Thus, when a consumer sees an ad for the first time for a car called "Neon," the fact that the consumer already has the word stored in memory should make it easier to encode the product name and thus improve its recallability. In fact, Chrysler chose that name for its new car because it also connoted "young, youthful, and vibrant," fitting the desired image for the product.

To help create strong brand-category links and aid brand recall, the brand name may also be chosen to suggest the product or service category (e.g., JuicyJuice 100 percent fruit juices, Ticketron ticket selling service, and *Newsweek* weekly news magazine). Brand elements that are highly descriptive of the product category or its attribute and benefits, however, may be potentially quite restrictive.[9] For example, it may be difficult to introduce a soft drink extension for a brand called JuicyJuice!

Although choosing a simple, easy to pronounce, familiar, and meaningful brand name can improve recallability, to improve brand recognition, on the other hand, it is important that brand names be different, distinctive, and unusual. As Chapter 2 noted, recognition depends on consumers' ability to discriminate between brands, and more complex brand names are more easily distinguished. The distinctiveness of a brand name is a function of its inherent uniqueness as well as its uniqueness in the context of other competing brands in the product category. Distinctive words may be seldom-used or atypical words for the product category (e.g., Apple computers), unusual combinations of real words (e.g., Toys"R"Us), or completely made-up words (e.g., Xerox or Exxon). Even made-up brand names, however, have to satisfy prevailing linguistic rules and convention (e.g., try to pronounce names without vowels such as Blfft, Xgpr, or Msdy!).

Note that cultural differences may exist in brand name memorability and recall. In one study, Chinese speakers were more likely to recall names presented as brand names in visual rather than spoken recall, whereas English speakers were more likely to recall the names in spoken rather than visual recall, suggesting that mental representations of verbal information in Chinese are coded primarily in a visual manner, whereas verbal information in English is coded primarily in a phonological manner.[10] Another study showed that a match between peripheral features of a brand name (i.e., "script" aspects, such as the type of font employed, or "sounds" aspects, such as how the name is pronounced) and the associations or meaning of the brand resulted in more positive brand attitudes than a mismatch: Chinese native speakers were affected primarily by script matching, whereas English native speakers' attitudes were primarily affected by sound matching. These results were interpreted in terms of structural differences between logographic systems (such as Chinese, where characters stand for concepts and not sounds) and alphabetic systems (such as English, where the writing of a word is a close cue of its pronunciation) and their resulting visual and phonological representations in memory.[11]

As with all brand choice criteria, tradeoffs must be recognized. Even if a distinctive brand name is advantageous for brand recognition, it also has to be seen as credible and desirable in the product category. A notable exception is Smuckers jelly, which has tried to turn the handicap of its distinctive—but potentially dislikable—name into a positive through its slogan, "With a Name Like Smuckers, It Has to Be Good!"

Brand Associations   Although choosing a memorable name is valuable, it is often necessary for the brand to have broader meaning to consumers than just the product category it is in. Because the brand name is a compact form of communication, the

ColorStay lipsticks
Head & Shoulders shampoo
Close-Up toothpaste
SnackWell reduced fat snacks
DieHard auto batteries
Mop & Glo floor wax
Lean Cuisine low-calorie frozen entrees
Shake'n Bake chicken seasoning
Sub-Zero refrigerators and freezers
Cling-Free static buildup remover

FIGURE 4-4   Sample Suggestive Brand Names

explicit and implicit meaning that consumers extract from the name can be critical. In particular, the brand name may be chosen to reinforce an important attribute or benefit association that makes up its product positioning (see Figure 4-4).

PowerBook

In 1989, Apple had just introduced a heavy, ineffective portable computer that had failed in the marketplace. Needing a name for their new line of portables, they turned to name consultant Lexicon. Using focus groups of users of competitive products, Lexicon began working with the terms *laptop* and *notebook*. PowerBook became the winner because it combined two things that are very common but are typically not used together: "book," a small product that holds a lot of information, and "power." Lexicon's linguists even liked the sounds of the brand name and how it would relate to the product positioning, asserting that the *p* in *power* would bring to mind compactness and speed, and the *b* in *book* would suggest dependability.[12]

Besides performance-related considerations, brand names also can be chosen to communicate more abstract considerations. For example, brand names may be intangible or emotion-laden to arouse certain feelings (e.g., Joy dishwashing liquid, Caress soap, and Obsession perfumes).

A descriptive brand name should make it easier to link the reinforced attribute or benefit.[13] That is, it should be easier to communicate to consumers that a laundry detergent "adds fresh scent" to clothes if it were given a name such as "Blossom" than if it were given a neutral, nonsuggestive name such as "Circle."[14] Although brand names chosen to reinforce the initial positioning of a brand may facilitate the linkage of that brand association, they may also make it harder to link new associations to the brand if it later has to be repositioned.[15] For example, if a brand of laundry detergent were to be initially named Blossom and positioned as "adding fresh scent," it may be more difficult to attempt to later reposition the product, if necessary, and add a new brand association, for example, that the product "fights tough stains." Consumers may find it more difficult to accept or just too easy to forget the new positioning when the brand name continues to remind them of other product considerations.

With sufficient time and the proper marketing programs, however, the restrictive nature of suggestive names sometimes can be overcome. For example, consider Compaq computers. When two former Texas Instruments engineers were considering the name for their new line of portable personal computers, they chose the name "Compaq" because it suggested a small computer. Through subsequent introductions of "bigger" personal computers, advertising campaigns, and other marketing activity, Compaq has been able to transcend the initial positioning suggested by its name. Similarly, Johnson & Johnson Baby Shampoo was also able to transport its "gentleness" association to a more adult audience when they were forced to reposition in the 1970s when the birth rate declined. Nevertheless, it must be recognized that such marketing maneuvers can be a long and expensive process. Imagine the difficulty of repositioning brands such as "I Can't Believe It's Not Butter" or "Gee, Your Hair Smells Terrific!" Thus, it is important when choosing a meaningful name to consider the possible contingencies of later repositioning and the necessity of having to link other associations at some point that become relevant or desirable with consumers.

Meaningful names are not restricted to only real words. Consumers can extract meaning, if they so desire, even from made-up or "fanciful" brand names. For example, one study of computer-generated brand names containing random combinations of syllables found that "whumies" and "quax" were found to remind consumers of a breakfast cereal and that "dehax" reminded them of a laundry detergent.[16] Thus, consumers were able to extract at least some product meaning from these essentially arbitrary names when instructed to do so. Nevertheless, the likelihood of consumers extracting meaning out of highly abstract names will depend on their motivation to do so. In many cases, consumers may not be so inclined.

Made-up brand names, however, are generally devised more systematically. Fictitious words are typically based on combinations of morphemes. A *morpheme* is the smallest linguistic unit having meaning. There are 6,000 morphemes in the English language, including real words (e.g., "man") as well as prefixes, suffixes, or roots. For example, Compaq computer's name comes from a combination of two morphemes indicating "computers and communication" and a "small, integral object." The use of the less common morpheme "paq" as an ending—instead of pak, pac, or pach—was an attempt to suggest something scientific and unusual. Similarly, Nissan's Sentra automobile is a combination of two morphemes suggesting "central" and "sentry."[17] By combining carefully chosen morphemes, it is possible to construct brand names that actually have some relatively easily inferred or implicit meaning.

A number of linguistic issues could be raised with brand names. Figure 4-5 contains an overview of different categories of linguistic characteristics, with definitions and examples. Even individual letters can contain meaning that may be useful in developing a new brand name. The letter *X* has become much more common in recent years (e.g., ESPN's X Games, Nissan's Xterra SUV, and the WWF's short-lived XFL) because *X* is now seen to represent "extreme," "on-the-edge," and "youth"—that is, "what's alternative, what's next, and what's new."[18] Even the sounds of letters can take on meaning. For example, some words begin with phonemic elements called *plosives* (i.e., the letters *b, c, d, g, k, p,* and *t*), whereas others use *sibilants* (i.e., sounds like *s* and soft *c*). Plosives escape from the mouth more quickly than sibilants and are hasher and more direct. Consequently, they are thought to make names more specific and less abstract and be more easily recognized and recalled.[19] One survey of the top 200 brands in *Marketing and Media Decision*'s lists for the years 1971 to 1985 found a preponderance of brand names using plosives.[20] On the other hand, because sibilants have a softer sound, they tend to conjure up romantic, serene images and are often found

Characteristics	Definitions and/or Examples
Phonetic Devices	
Alliteration	Consonant repetition (Coca-Cola)
Assonance	Vowel repetition (Kal Kan)
Consonance	Consonant repetition with intervening vowel changes (Weight Watchers)
Masculine rhyme	Rhyme with end-of-syllable stress (Max Pax)
Feminine rhyme	Unaccented syllable followed by accented syllable (American Airlines)
Weak/imperfect/slant rhyme	Vowels differ or consonants similar, not identical (Black & Decker)
Onomatopoeia	Use of syllable phonetics to resemble the object itself (Wisk)
Clipping	Product names attenuated (Chevy)
Blending	Morphemic combination, usually with elision (Aspergum, Duracell)
Initial plosives	/b/, /c-hard/, /d/, /g-hard/, /k/, /p/, /q/, /t/ (Bic)
Orthographic Devices	
Unusual or incorrect spellings	Kool-Aid
Abbreviations	7 UP for Seven Up
Acronyms	Amoco
Morphologic Devices	
Affixation	Jell-O
Compounding	Janitor-in-a-Drum
Semantic Devices	
Metaphor	Representing something as if it were something else (Arrid); simile is included with metaphor when a name describes a likeness and not an equality (AquaFresh)
Metonymy	Application of one object or quality for another (Midas)
Synecdoche	Substitution of a part for the whole (Red Lobster)
Personification/pathetic fallacy	Humanizing the nonhuman, or ascription of human emotions to the inanimate (Betty Crocker)
Oxymoron	Conjunction of opposites (Easy-Off)
Paranomasia	Pun and word plays (Hawaiian Punch)
Semantic appositeness	Fit of name with object (Bufferin)

FIGURE 4-5 Brand Name Linguistic Characteristics

with products such as perfumes (e.g., Cie, Chanel, and Cerissa).[21] One study found a relationship between certain characteristics of the letters of brand names and product features: As consonant hardness and vowel pitch increased in hypothetical brand names for toilet paper and household cleansers, consumer perception of the harshness of the product also increased.[22]

Brand names are not restricted to letters alone. Alphanumeric brand names contain one or more numbers in either digit form (e.g., "5") or in written form (e.g., "five").[23] Alphanumeric brand names may include a mixture of letters and digits (e.g., WD-40), a mixture of words and digits (e.g., Formula 409), or mixtures of letters or words and numbers in written form (e.g., Saks Fifth Avenue). Alphanumeric brand names may also be used to designate generations or relationships in a product line in terms of particular product models (e.g., BMW's 3, 5, and 7 series). Paiva and Costa found that alphanumeric brand names often were associated with technology, although the particular perceptions depended on a number of factors, including the visual or aural aspects of the name, the actual numbers that were used in the name, and the words or letters that, along with the number(s), comprised the brand name.

Naming Procedures

A number of different procedures or systems have been suggested for naming new products (see Figure 4-6 for the approach recommended by John Murphy of the top naming firm Interbrand). Although some differences exist, most systems for developing brand names can be seen as basically adopting a procedure something along the following lines.

1.   In general, the first step in selecting a brand name for a new product is to define the branding objectives in terms of the six general criteria noted earlier. It is particularly important to define the ideal meaning that the brand should take. It is also necessary to recognize the role of the brand within the corporate branding hierarchy and how the brand should relate to other brands and products (as will be discussed in Chapter 11). In many cases, existing brand names may be used, at least in part. Finally, the role of the brand within the entire marketing program must be understood, as well as having an in-depth description of the target market.

2.   With the strategic branding direction in place, the second step involves generating as many names and concepts as possible. Any potential source of names can be used: company management and employees; existing or potential customers (including retailers or suppliers if relevant); ad agencies, professional name consultants, or specialized computer-based naming companies; and so on. Tens, hundreds, or even thousands of names may result from this step.

3.   Next, the names must be screened based on the branding objectives and marketing considerations identified in step 1, as well as just common sense, to produce a more manageable list. For example, General Mills starts by eliminating the following:
   - Names that have unintentional double meaning
   - Names that are patently unpronounceable, already in use, or too close to an existing name
   - Names that have obvious legal complications
   - Names that represent an obvious contradiction of the positioning

They next have in-depth evaluation sessions with management personnel and marketing partners to narrow the list down to a handful of names. Often, a quick-and-dirty legal search may be conducted to help screen out legal "problem childs."

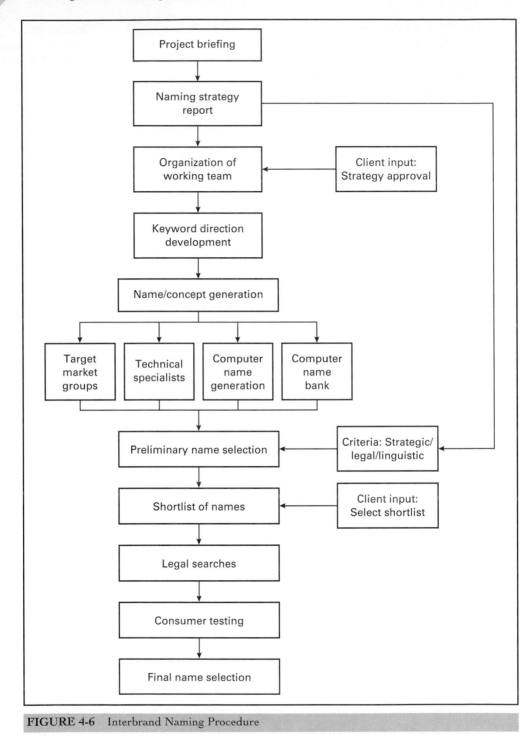

FIGURE 4-6   Interbrand Naming Procedure

4.   The fourth step involves collecting more extensive information on each of the final 5 to 10 or so names. Before spending large amounts of money on consumer research, it is usually advisable to do an extensive international legal search. Because of the costs involved, searches are sometimes done on a sequential basis, only testing in a new country those names that survived the legal screen from the previous country.

5.   Next, consumer research is often conducted to confirm management expectations as to the memorability and meaningfulness of the names. Consumer testing can take all forms. Many firms attempt to simulate the actual marketing program for the brand and consumer's likely purchase experiences as much as possible.[24] Thus, consumers may be shown the product and its packaging, price, or promotion so that they understand the rationale for the brand name and how it will be used. Realistic three-dimensional packages as well as concept boards or animatic advertising may also be shown. Multiple samples of consumers may have to be surveyed depending on the target markets involved (e.g., to capture differences in regional or ethnic appeal). The effects of the brand name with repeated exposure and when spoken versus when written can also be factored in.

6.   Finally, based on all of the information collected from the previous step, management can choose the name that maximizes the firm's branding and marketing objectives and then formally register the name.

In conducting the consumer research and selecting a brand name, it should be recognized that there will almost always be at least some potentially negative associations in some country or another. In most cases, however, assuming these associations were not severe, they would disappear or dissipate after the onset of the initial marketing launch. Similarly, brand names often are initially disliked in part because of their lack of familiarity or, in the case of a name change, because they represent a deviation from the norm. In assessing the potential impact of a new brand name, it is important to separate these temporal considerations from more enduring effects.

URLs

URLs (Uniform Resource Locators) are used to specify locations of pages on the Web, and are also commonly referred to as *domain names*. Anyone wishing to own a specific URL must register and pay for the name with a service such as Register.com. In recent years, as companies clamored for space on the Web, the number of registered URLs increased dramatically. From May to September 2000, the number of registered domain names nearly doubled to 17 million. By April 2000 every three-letter combination was registered. By September 2000, 98 percent of the words in a typical English dictionary had been registered. The rate of URL registrations reached 84,000 per day, or roughly one per second. The sheer volume of registered URLs often makes it necessary for companies to use coined words for new brands if they wish to have a Web site for the brand. For example, when Andersen Consulting selected a new name, it chose the coined word "Accenture" in part because the URL www.accenture.com had not been registered.

Another issue facing companies with regard to URLs is protection of their brands from unauthorized use in domain names.[25] For example, Nike would not approve of its name appearing in the URL of a fictitious fan site www.nikerules.com. To protect its brand from unauthorized use in a URL, a company can either sue the current owner of the URL for copyright infringement, buy the name from the current owner, or register all conceivable variations of its brand as domain names ahead of time. According to Gartner Inc., the average Global 2000 company had at least 300 registered URLs in 2001. Large companies are now carefully monitoring the Web for unauthorized use of their brands.

Caterpillar

Heavy machinery manufacturer Caterpillar assigned its trademark counsel, Gene Bolmarcich, the task of protecting the company's brand online. Caterpillar has 600 registered URLs, and Bolmarcich estimates that he spends 95 percent of his time protecting Caterpillar's name online. During the spring of 2000, the company reclaimed some 50 URLs by firing off cease-and-desist letters to companies registering names such as CAT that infringed on Caterpillar's copyright. Caterpillar also guards against infringement overseas by registering its name in 10 countries. But, Bolmarcich says, "You can't ever fully defend yourself."

In November 2000, ICANN, the agency that controls the Internet's address system, announced seven new domain suffixes. The addition of two new domains, .biz and .info, during the fall of 2001 provided new URL possibilities. These new domains complicated matters, however, for big companies that devoted considerable time and money to securing URLs in the three main domains, .com, .net, and .org. Caterpillar's Bolmarcich lamented this problem, saying, "They just threw .biz and .info at us, and now we have to register all these domain names ourselves or fight the same battle again in these new domain spaces." Even individuals are having to fight to protect their names. In 2001, former football star Joe Montana filed a suit seeking $5 million in damages from a man selling adult material from a Web site called Joemontanafanclub.com. The man, who claimed to have never heard of Joe Montana, eventually closed the Web site.

Brand recall is critical for URLs because, at least initially, consumers must remember the URL to be able to get to the site. At the peak of the Internet boom, investors paid $7.5 million for Business.com, $2.2 million for Autos.com, and $1.1 million for Bingo.com. Many of these "common noun" sites failed, however, and were criticized, among other things, as being too generic in name. During this time, many firms adopted names that started with a lowercase e or i and ended in "net," "systems," or, especially, "com." Many of these names became liabilities after the Internet bubble burst, forcing firms such as Internet.com to revert to a more conventional name, INTMedia Group. Yahoo, however, was able to create a memorable brand and URL (see Figure 4-7).

Yahoo!

Jerry Yang and David Filo named their Internet portal (created as a Stanford University thesis project) "Yahoo!" after thumbing through the dictionary for words that began with "ya," the universal computing acronym for "yet another." Filo stumbled upon *yahoo,* which brought back fond childhood memories of his father calling him "little yahoo." Liking the name, they created a more complete acronym: "Yet another hierarchical officious oracle."[26]

FIGURE 4-7   Yahoo! Brand Communications

Typically, for an existing brand, the main URL is a straightforward and maybe even literal translation of the brand name (www.shell.com), although there are some exceptions and variations. Figure 4-8 contains some URL naming advice from one industry expert.

Logos and Symbols

Although the brand name typically is the central element of the brand, visual brand elements often play a critical role in building brand equity, especially in terms of brand awareness. Logos have a long history as a means to indicate origin, ownership, or association. For example, families and countries have used logos for centuries to visually represent their names (e.g., the Hapsburg eagle of the Austro-Hungarian Empire).

There are many types of logos, ranging from corporate names or trademarks (i.e., word marks) written in a distinctive form, on one hand, to entirely abstract logos, which may be completely unrelated to the word mark, corporate name, or corporate activities, on the other hand.[27] Examples of brands with strong word marks (and no accompanying logo separate from the name) include Coca-Cola, Dunhill, and Kit-Kat. Examples of abstract logos include the Mercedes star, Rolex crown, CBS eye, Nike swoosh, and the Olympic rings. These non-word mark logos are also often called *symbols*.

1. *Get started now.* Don't leave your brand name and visual identity until the last minute. Bring in expert advice as early as possible. Like lawyers and accountants, branding consultants are paid to keep secrets. The more time they have to work with even limited information about your gestating brand, the better.
2. *Keep it as simple as possible.* The key criteria for any URL are that it be short, easy to spell, and understandable. Yes, we know that's easy to say in a world where most such names are registered by megacorporations or unemployed cybersquatters. However, there are still plenty of untried letter combinations out there.
3. *Avoid clichés.* Stay away from prefixes and suffixes that fail to differentiate you. The Net is saturated with names that use *cyber-, net-, -tech, -digi-, sys-,* and their ilk; using these terms can also shorten the life of a name. People can look at a name and date it the way they do a vintage wine: "Ah, yes, that looks and sounds like a mid-'90s."
4. *Avoid the .com.* These days, a Web site is a cost of entry. Why highlight the fact that you're a Web company when within three years most business will be conducted over the Web anyway? Investing in .com as part of your company name is shortsighted and could work against you in the longer term.
5. *Avoid the descriptive.* Sure, a descriptive name lets you own a space on the Internet. It's a great short-term strategy for building brand recognition fast, and it capitalizes on search-engine-driven random inquiries for your product or service. Wine.com is clever for online wine, but what happens when they want to get into beers and spirits? Descriptive is limiting, and limiting is bad.
6. *Create a unique personality.* Ask.com could have left it at that. A Web site devoted to answering questions is a masterstroke in itself. Yet the builders of this brand went further, and imbued it with the avuncular, dignified, and human character of Jeeves. Although Jeeves is little more than a digital hook on which to hang a brand personality, it works. It resonates, it's distinctive, and it sticks in the mind.
7. *Go for unexpected combinations.* Coined associative, coined descriptive, and possibly real arbitrary names represent the best bet for future domain name availability. Unexpected combinations of real words evoke an image immediately, providing a stronger foundation for brand building. *Fogdog* means nothing to most people, so online, it means everything its owners want it to mean.
8. *Reinvent a real word.* Using a real word in its traditional sense is limiting. But using it to mean something completely different? Now we're talking. It's not exactly a new tactic: What does *apple* have to do with technology or *shell* to do with petroleum? Bear in mind, however, that you'll have to work especially hard at building consumer expectations if your name has nothing to do with your product.
9. *Make new words.* Sometimes there just isn't the Internet room available; all the best words in the category are taken, with only uninspiring or limiting words left. In such cases, creating a new word may be the answer. *Expedia* isn't in the dictionary, but with a bit of brand-building support, it can easily become recognized as a site to aid the business traveler. When naming Hewlett-Packard's new test and measurement spin-off company, we eventually settled on *Agilent,* to represent a company that needs to remain agile and responsive to its market to survive. It's an invented word, but with the right marketing support, people get it.
10. *Ensure that your brand promise equates with your ability to deliver.* That's the best overall advice we can give. Any site with a memorable and differentiated name will pull in browsers. But if the content or architecture disappoints or your follow-up service fails to deliver, then no amount of memorability will help you.

FIGURE 4-8 Some URL Guidelines

Source: Clay Timon, "10 Tips for Naming," *Business 2.0,* March 2000, p. 151

Many logos fall between these two extremes. Often logos are devised as symbols to reinforce or embellish the brand meaning in some way. Some logos are literal representations of the brand name, enhancing brand awareness (e.g., the Arm and Hammer, American Red Cross, and Apple logos). Logos can be quite concrete or pictorial in nature (e.g., the American Express centurion, Land o' Lakes butter Indian, the Morton salt girl with umbrella, and Ralph Lauren's polo player). Certain elements of the product or company can become a symbol (e.g., the Goodyear blimp, McDonald's golden arches, and the Playboy bunny).

The importance of logos and symbols can be seen from the results of a study that asked 150 consumers their impressions of companies based on their names alone and also when their logos were present. As Figure 4-9 shows, the results could differ fairly dramatically depending on the company involved. Clearly, logos have meaning and associations that change consumer perceptions of the company. Like brand names, logos can acquire associations through their inherent meaning as well as through the supporting marketing program. In terms of inherent meaning, even fairly abstract logos can have different evaluations depending on the shapes involved. As with names, abstract logos can be quite distinctive and thus recognizable. Nevertheless, because abstract logos may lack the inherent meaning present with a more concrete logo, one of the dangers of an abstract logo is that consumers may not understand what the logo is intended to represent without a significant marketing initiative to explain its meaning.

Henderson and Cote conducted a comprehensive empirical analysis of 195 logos that were calibrated on 13 different design characteristics in terms of their ability to achieve different communication objectives. They interpreted their findings as suggesting that (1) high-recognition logos (which also have low false recognition and high positive affect) should be very natural, very harmonious, and moderately elaborate; (2) low-investment logos that are intended to create a false sense of knowing and positive affect should be less natural and very harmonious; and (3) high-image logos intended to create strong positive affect without regard to recognition should be moderately elaborate and natural but with high harmony.[28] In other words, more complex and elaborate logos are better at maintaining viewer interest and liking, logos with uniformity along a single dimension are more likely to be falsely recognized, and familiar logos are better liked than unfamiliar logos.[29]

Benefits

Because of their visual nature, logos and symbols are often easily recognized and can be a valuable way to identify products, although a key concern is how well they become linked in memory to the corresponding brand name and product to boost brand recall. That is, consumers may recognize certain symbols but be unable to link them to any specific product or brand.

Another branding advantage of logos is their versatility: Because logos are often nonverbal, they can be updated as needed over time and generally transfer well across cultures. Because logos are often abstract, without much product meaning, they can be relevant and appropriate in a range of product categories. For example, corporate brands often develop logos because their identity may be needed on a wide range of products, although perhaps in a subordinate way as a means to endorse different subbrands. Logos can allow the corporate brand to play a more explicit secondary role for these various products.

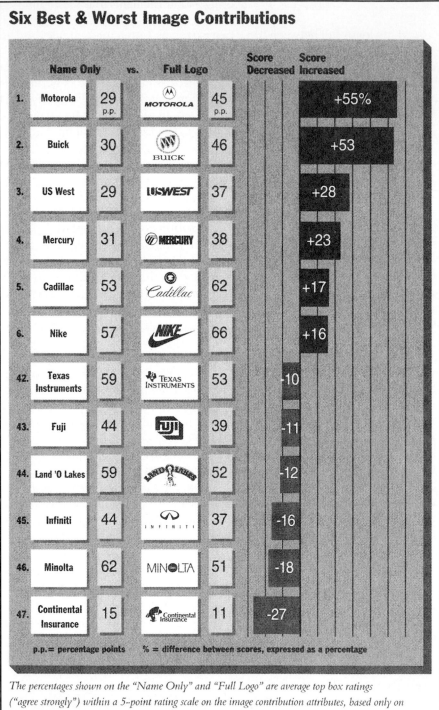

FIGURE 4-9   Brand Evaluations with and without Logos

Source: Alvin H. Schechter, "Measuring the Value of Corporate and Brand Logos," *Design Management Journal,* Winter, 1993.

Abstract logos are often useful when the use of the full brand name is restricted in some way. National Westminster Bank in the United Kingdom, for example, created a triangular device as a logo in part because the name itself was long and cumbersome and the logo could more easily appear as an identification device on check books, literature, signage, and promotional material.[30] Thus, logos and symbols can be particularly important in services because of their intangible, abstract nature. For example, many insurance firms use symbols of strength (e.g., the Rock of Gibraltar for Prudential and the stag for Hartford), security (e.g., the "good hands" of Allstate and the hard hat of Fireman's Fund), or some combination of the two (e.g., the castle for Fortis).

In the telecommunication industry, Sprint capitalized on an early ad campaign to create a powerful symbol. In introductory TV ads, Sprint demonstrated their fiber optic system by showing that someone could literally hear a pin drop over the phone. Later Sprint ads used the concept of a "pin drop" as a metaphor both visually and verbally to reinforce its early heritage, communicate a still important product benefit (sound quality), and signal an important corporate image dimension (innovation).

Similarly, Memorex has used a shattered glass—introduced in earlier TV ads featuring Ella Fitzgerald and others—as a symbol to reinforce the audio reproduction qualities of its audio tape and communicate and signal other qualities of the brand.

Finally, unlike brand names, logos can be easily changed over time to achieve a more contemporary look. For example, Burger King, the United States' second-largest hamburger chain, added blue to its logo to make it more eye-catching, and used slanted graphics to represent speed. Employee uniforms and stores were also updated as part of the makeover (see Figure 4-10). John Deere revamped its deer trademark for the first time in 32 years in 2000, making the animal appear to be leaping up rather than landing (see Figure 4-11). The change was intended to "convey a message of strength and agility with a technology edge."[31]

In updating logos, however, it is important to make gradual changes that do not lose sight of the inherent advantages of the logo. In the 1980s, the trend for many firms was to create more abstract, stylized versions of their logos. In the process, some of the meaning, and thus equity, residing in these logos was lost. Recognizing the logo's potential contribution to brand equity, some firms in the 1990s reverted to a more traditional look for their symbols (e.g., Prudential's Rock of Gibralter logo was changed back from black-and-white slanted lines to a more faithful rendition) or even brought back old symbols that had been tossed aside all together (e.g., Lincoln-Mercury's cougar). To hearken back to their historic past and to reflect their engineering and design prowess, the Chrysler winged badge replaced the Pentastar as a symbol of the brand. The wings, intended to symbolize freedom and flying, were found on the first Chrysler manufactured in 1924. Regardless of the reason why, changing a logo is not cheap. According to Allen Adamson, managing director of the corporate identity firm Landor Associates, creating a symbol or remaking an old one for a big brand "usually costs $1 million."[32]

Characters

Characters represent a special type of brand symbol—one that takes on human or real-life characteristics. Brand characters typically are introduced through advertising and can play a central role in these and subsequent ad campaigns and package designs.

FIGURE 4-10   New Burger King Brand Identity

FIGURE 4-11   New Deere Brand Logo

Like other brand elements, brand characters come in many different forms. Some brand characters are animated (e.g., Pillsbury's Poppin' Fresh Doughboy, the Keebler Elves, and numerous cereal characters such as Tony the Tiger, Toucan Sam, and Cap'n Crunch), whereas others are live-action figures (e.g., the Marlboro Cowboy, the Maytag Repairman, or Ronald McDonald). The 1990s saw the introduction of such notable characters as the Budweiser frogs, the Pets.com sock puppet, the SoBe lizard, and the AFLAC duck. Branding Brief 4-2 describes how Buddy Lee became an integral part of the Lee brand. Figure 4-12 contains a more complete list of some popular brand characters through the years.

Green Giant

One of the most powerful brand characters ever introduced is Pillsbury's Jolly Green Giant (see Figure 4-13).[33] His origin can be traced back to the 1920s, when the Minnesota Valley Canning Company placed a green giant on the label of a new variety of sweet, large English peas as a means to circumvent trademark laws that prevented them from naming the product "Green Giant." Ad Agency Leo Burnett used the Jolly Green Giant character in print ads beginning in 1930 and in TV ads beginning in the early 1960s. At first, TV ads featured an actor wearing green body make-up and a suit of leaves. Later, the ads moved to full animation. Creatively, the ads have been very consistent. The Green Giant is always in the background, with his features obscure, and only says "Ho-Ho-Ho." He moves very little, doesn't walk, and never leaves the "valley." The Green Giant has been introduced into international markets, following basically the same set of rules. The Little Sprout character was introduced in 1973 to bring a new look to the brand and allow for more flexibility. Unlike the Green Giant, the Little Sprout is a chatterbox, often imparting valuable product information. The Green Giant brand has enormous equity to Pillsbury, and they have found that using the name and character on a new product has been an effective signal to consumers that the product is "wholesome" and "healthy."

Benefits

Brand characters can provide a number of brand equity benefits. Because they are often colorful and rich in imagery, they tend to be attention getting. Consequently, brand characters can be quite useful for creating brand awareness. Brand characters can help brands break through the marketplace clutter as well as help to communicate a key product benefit. For example, Maytag's Lonely Repairman has helped to reinforce their key "reliability" product association. Perhaps a more common image enhancement is related to brand personality and just the sheer likability of the brand. The human element of brand characters can help to create perceptions of the brand as being fun, interesting, and so forth. The ability of a consumer to have a relationship with a brand may be easier when the brand literally has a humanistic character. As a result of the meaning and various feelings that can become attached to them, popular characters often are valuable licensing properties, providing direct revenue and additional brand exposure (see Chapter 7). Finally, because brand characters do not typically have direct product meaning, they may also be transferred relatively easily across product categories. For example, Aaker notes that "the Keebler's elf identity (which combines a sense of home style baking with a touch of magic and fun) gives the brand

Buddy Lee Sells Lee Dungarees

Lee Jeans faced a significant image perception problem in the late 1990s. Though the brand was popular among women aged 35 and above, the trendsetting teenage audience did not think Lee jeans were cool. Research revealed that 17- to 22-year-old males respected the brand for one thing, however: durability. Lee's agency, Fallon McElligott, tested logos and tag lines from Lee's archives. The word *dungarees* appealed to youths, as did a tagline from the 1940s, "Can't Bust 'Em." Buddy Lee, a vintage doll used to promote Lee jeans at points of sale from 1921 to 1962 (see Figure A), drew the biggest response from the tested audience. Most respondents thought Buddy Lee was cool; some even likened him to a character on *The Simpsons* or *South Park*. Fallon synthesized this information to develop Lee Dungarees and introduced the $10 million "Buddy Lee Challenge" campaign in 1998.

The introduction attempted to emulate the evolution of a pop culture trend by starting with a "phantom campaign" intended to bring leading-edge consumers to the brand. Fallon mounted unbranded Buddy Lee posters in 15 domestic markets and produced a six-minute biography parody film called *The Buddy Lee Story* that aired in late-night slots on channels popular with young adults. The agency also developed

FIGURE A   Buddy Lee

three unbranded Web sites intended to look like the homemade Web pages of "villains" that were later to appear with Buddy Lee in advertising. Fallon e-mailed the URLs of the three Web sites to a list of more than 200,000 consenting consumers. The various components of the phantom campaign did not connect to the Lee brand in any obvious way. Lisa Seward, Fallon's media director, explained, "We did what was necessary for kids to discover the brand on their own, not to give it to them in a prefabricated box."

Once leading-edge consumers were given sufficient exposure to Buddy Lee, Lee Dungarees were officially launched in mainstream media with on-site sponsorship of ESPN's X Games and a teaser campaign featuring television ads designed to look like movie trailers with Buddy Lee, "Man of Action," as the star. The teaser campaign was followed by a full-scale launch that included glossy print ads and television spots on a host of networks. The ads featured Buddy Lee battling the villains from the three Web sites mentioned earlier. The villains, played by cartoonish actors (one dressed like a caveman, for example), do battle with Buddy Lee but cannot "bust" him.

The Buddy Lee Challenge campaign was credited with changing perception of Lee Jeans and making it a sought-after label among young consumers. A tracking study showed that perceptions that the brand was "cool to wear" increased 10 points within a year of the launch, to 35 percent. Additionally, Lee received more than four times as many orders from retailers as anticipated for the Dungarees line. Most significantly, Lee gained 3 percent market share in jeans during 1998.

Sources: Eric Schmuckler, "Plan of the Year," *Mediaweek,* 24 May 1999; Kim Cross, "Jean Therapy," *Business 2.0,* 23 January 2001.

latitude to extend into other baked goods—and perhaps even into other types of food where homemade magic and fun might be perceived as a benefit."[34]

Cautions

There are some cautions and drawbacks to using brand characters. Brand characters can be so attention getting and well liked that they dominate other brand elements and actually *dampen* brand awareness.

Eveready

When Ralston Purina introduced their drumming pink bunny that "kept going . . . and going . . . and going" in ads for their Eveready Energizer battery, many consumers were so captivated by the character that they paid little attention to the name of the advertised brand. As a result, they often mistakenly believed that the ad was for Eveready's chief competitor, Duracell. Consequently, Eveready found it necessary to add the pink bunny as a reminder to their packages, promotions, and other marketing communications to create stronger brand links.

Characters often must be updated over time so that their image and personality remains relevant to the target market. The Campbell Soup kids have become more "buff" over time—taller, trimmer, and more athletic. Aunt Jemima has also lost some weight over the years and has a much different and contemporary look—she no longer wears a bandanna but sports a perky perm, pearl earrings, and a white collar instead.[35]

Brand	Character	Category
AFLAC	Duck	Insurance
Aunt Jemima	Aunt Jemima	Prepared foods
Bartles & Jaymes	Frank Bartle, Ed Jayme	Alcoholic beverages
Borden	Elsie the Cow	Dairy products
Bounty	Rosie the Waitress	Paper towels
Budweiser	Lizards	Alcoholic beverages
Butterworth	Mrs. Butterworth	Pancake syrup
California Raisins	Dancin' Raisins	Produce
Cap'n Crunch	Cap'n Crunch	RTE cereals
Cheetos	Chester Cheeta	Cheese snacks
Chicken of the Sea	Mermaid	Canned fish
Columbian	Juan Valdez	Coffee
Denny's	The Corlick Sisters	Food service
Domino's Pizza	Bad Andy	Food service
Dunkin' Donuts	Donut Man	Food service
Embassy Suites	Garfield	Hotel
Energizer	Bunny	Batteries
Fancy Feast	Fancy Feast Cat	Pet food
Froot Loops	Toucan Sam	RTE cereals
Fruit of the Loom	Fruit Guys	Underwear
Frosted Flakes	Tony the Tiger	RTE cereals
Green Giant	Green Giant/Little Sprout	Vegetables
Hamburger Helper	Helping Hand	Prepared foods
Hathaway Shirts	Man with eye-patch	Apparel
Hawaiian Punch	Punchy	Soft drinks
Hush Puppies	Hush Puppies puppy	Apparel
Isuzu	Joe Isuzu ("The Liar")	Automobiles
Keebler	Keebler Elves	Cookies and crackers
Kool-Aid	Kool-Aid Kid	Soft drinks
Kraft Macaroni'n'Cheese	"Elizabeth"	Prepared foods
Lipton	Sir Thomas Lipton	Tea
Lucky Charms	Leprechaun	RTE cereals
Marlboro	Marlboro Cowboy	Cigarettes
Maytag	Maytag Repairman	Household appliances
McDonald's	Ronald McDonald	Food service
Merrill Lynch	Merrill Lynch Bull	Financial services
Metropolitan	Peanuts characters	Insurance
Michelin	Michelin Man	Tires
Mr. Clean	Mr. Clean	Floor cleaner
Monster.com	Monster	Online job search
Morton Salt	Girl with umbrella	Salt
New Yorker magazine	Eustace Tilley	Publications
Nine-Lives	Morris the Cat	Pet food
NTHSA	Vince & Larry	Highway safety
Owens-Corning	Pink Panther	Insulation

(Continued)

FIGURE 4-12   Some Notable Past and Present Brand Characters

Brand	Character	Category
Palmolive	Madge the Manicurist	Dishwashing liquid
Pepperidge Farm	Clarence	Cookies and crackers
Peter Pan	Peter Pan	Peanut butter
Pets.com	Sock puppet	Online pet supplies
Planters	Mr. Peanut	Nuts
Pillsbury	Poppin' Fresh (doughboy)	Refrigerated dough
Qantas	Qantas Koala	Airline
RCA	Nipper the dog	Audio-video equipment
Rice Krispies	Snap, Crackle, & Pop	RTE cereals
Schweppes	Commander Whitehead	Beverages
Seven-Up	Seven-Up Spots	Soft drinks
Snuggle	Snuggle Bear	Fabric softener
Star-Kist	Charlie the Tuna	Canned fish
Sugar Pops	Dig'um the Frog	RTE cereals
Taco Bell	Chihuahua	Food service
Tanqueray	Mr. Jenkins	Gin
Trix	Trix Rabbit	RTE cereals
Union 76	Murph	Gasoline
Vlasic	Stork	Pickles

RTE = ready-to-eat.
Many thanks to University of Michigan's Christie Brown for helping to put together this list.

FIGURE 4-12   *(Continued)*

Recently, Michelin launched a newer, slimmer version of their famous tubby Michelin Man (whose real name is Bibendum) to mark his hundredth year. A company press release notes, "Thinner and smiling, Bibendum will look like the leader he is, with an open and reassuring manner." Over a 50-year period, there have been over 200 different "Breck Girls" who have appeared in ads for the shampoo, including such well-known actresses as Cybill Shepherd, Jaclyn Smith, Kim Basinger, and Brooke Shields.[36]

In general, the more realistic the brand character, the more important it is to keep it up-to-date. One advantage of fictitious or animated characters is that their appeal can be more enduring and timeless than real people.

Barbie

In 1998, at the age of 38, the world's best-selling toy, the Barbie doll, underwent major plastic surgery on her body for the first time. To create a "less graduated profile," the operation gave her a wider waist, slimmer hips, and a reduction in her bustline. According to Mattel, the new look reflected changing times and tastes. As children demanded greater realism, the slimmer, more lifelike body enabled Mattel to give Barbie, according to a company spokesperson, "a more contemporary look that fits into today's trendy clothes, such as hip-huggers." Barbie also got a new face—to replace the "Superstar" face from 1977—with a closed mouth, more natural-looking soft and straight hair in streaks and multiple colors, less makeup, and a finer nose. Barbie is a $2 billion brand, with the average

FIGURE 4-13 The Jolly Green Giant

American girl owning eight Barbies and more than one billion dolls already sold around the world at a rate of two every second.[37]

Branding Brief 4-3 describes the efforts by General Mills to evolve the Betty Crocker character over time.

Slogans

Slogans are short phrases that communicate descriptive or persuasive information about the brand. Slogans often appear in advertising but can play an important role on packaging and in other aspects of the marketing program. For example, Snickers' "Hungry? Snickers Really Satisfies" slogan appears in ads and on the candy bar wrapper itself. Slogans are powerful branding devices because, like brand names, they are an extremely efficient, shorthand means to build brand equity. Slogans can function as useful "hooks" or "handles" to help consumers grasp the meaning of a brand in terms of what the brand is and what makes it special. They are an indispensable means of summarizing and translating the intent of a marketing program in a few short words or phrases. For example, State Farm Insurance's "Like a Good Neighbor, State Farm Is There" has been used for decades as a slogan to represent the brand's dependability and friendship.

Updating Betty Crocker

In 1921, Washburn Crosby Company, makers of Gold Medal flour, launched a picture puzzle contest. The contest was a huge success—the company received 30,000 entries—and several hundred contestants sent along requests for recipes and advice about baking. To handle those requests, the company decided that they needed to create a spokesperson. They chose the name Betty Crocker because "Betty" was a popular, friendly sounding name and "Crocker" was a reference to William G. Crocker, a well-liked, recently retired executive. The company merged with General Mills in 1928, and the newly merged company introduced the *Betty Crocker Cooking School of the Air* as

FIGURE A Betty Crocker through the Years

BETTY CROCKER MAKEOVER

1936 1955 1965 1968

1972 1980 1986 1996

a national radio program. During this time, Betty was given a voice and her signature began to appear on nearly every product that the company produced.

In 1936, the Betty Crocker portrait was drawn by artist Neysa McMein as a composite of some of the home economists at the company. Prim and proper, Betty was shown with pursed lips, a hard stare, and graying hair. The appearance of Betty Crocker has been updated a number of times over the years (see Figure A), and her appearance has become more friendly (although she has never lost her reserved look.) Prior to getting a makeover in 1986, Betty Crocker was seen as honest and dependable, friendly and concerned about customers, and a specialist in baked goods, but also out-of-date, old and traditional, a manufacturer of "old standby products," and not particularly contemporary or innovative. The challenge was to give Betty a look that would attract younger consumers but not alienate older ones who remembered her as the stern homemaker of the past. There needed to be a certain fashionableness about her—not too dowdy and not too trendy, since the new look would need to last for 5 to 10 years. Her look also needed to be relevant to working women. Finally, for the first time, Betty Crocker's look was also designed to appeal to men, given the results of a General Mills study that showed that 30 percent of American men sometimes cooked for themselves.

A few years later, Betty Crocker received an Information Age update. This ultra-modern Betty Crocker, the current model, is the work of a committee that selected images of 75 women of many different races to create a computerized composite. The makeover seems to have taken—although Betty Crocker is now close to 75, she doesn't look a day over 35! Although the Betty Crocker name is on 200 or so products, her visual image has been largely replaced by the red spoon symbol and signature on package fronts and basically appears only on cookbooks and in advertising.

Source: "FYI Have You Seen This Person?" *Minneapolis-St. Paul Star Tribune,* 11 October 2000.

Benefits

Slogans can be devised in a number of different ways to help build brand equity. Some slogans help to build brand awareness by playing off the brand name in some way (e.g., "My Doctor Said Mylanta," or "Step Up to the Mic" for Micatin). Other slogans build brand awareness even more explicitly by making strong links between the brand and the corresponding product category by combining both entities in the slogan (e.g., "If You're Not Wearing Dockers, You're Just Wearing Pants"). Most important, slogans can help to reinforce the brand positioning and desired point of difference (e.g., "Nothing Runs Like a Deere," "It's Hard to Stop a Trane," and "Help Is Just Around the Corner. True Value Hardware"). For market leaders, slogans often employ "puffery" in which the brand is praised with subjective opinions, superlatives, and exaggerations (e.g., Keebler's "Uncomparably Good"; Anheuser-Busch's "When You've Said Budweiser, You've Said It All"; and Bayer's "Bayer Works Wonders").

Slogans often become closely tied to advertising campaigns and can be used as tag lines to summarize the descriptive or persuasive information conveyed in the ads. For example, DeBeers diamonds' "A Diamond Is Forever" tag line communicates the intended ad message that diamonds bring eternal love and romance and never lose value. Slogans can be more expansive and more enduring, however, than just ad tag lines. Campaign-specific tag lines may be used to help reinforce the message of a particular campaign instead of the brand slogan for a certain period of time. For example, Nike has used ad tag lines such as "I Can" and "What Are You Getting Ready For?" for ad campaigns instead of their well-known brand slogan, "Just Do It." Such substitutions can be a means to emphasize that the ad campaign represents a departure of some kind from the message conveyed by the brand slogan or just a means to give the brand slogan a rest so that it remains fresh.

Designing Slogans

Some of the most powerful slogans are those that contribute to brand equity in multiple ways. Slogans can play off the brand name in a way to build both awareness *and* image (e.g., "Get Certain. Get Certs" for Certs breath mints; "Maybe She's Born With It, Maybe Its Maybelline" for Maybelline cosmetics; or "The Big Q Stands for Quality" for Quaker State motor oil). Slogans also can contain meaning that is relevant in both a product-related *and* non-product-related sense. For example, consider the Champion sportswear slogan, "It Takes a Little More to Make a Champion." The slogan could be interpreted in terms of product performance, as meaning that Champion sportswear is made with a little extra care or with extra-special materials, but also could be interpreted in terms of user imagery as meaning that Champion sportswear is associated with top athletes. This combination of superior product performance and aspirational user imagery is a powerful platform on which to build brand image and equity. Benetton has an equally strong slogan on which to build brand equity ("United Colors of Benetton") but, as Branding Brief 4-4 describes, they have not always taken full advantage of it.

Updating Slogans

Some slogans become so strongly linked to the brand that it becomes difficult to subsequently introduce new ones (take the slogan quiz in Figure 4-14 and check the accompanying footnote to see how many slogans you can correctly identify). For example, Miller Lite beer has struggled to find a successor to its memorable "Tastes Great . . . Less Filling" slogan. After the failure of the controversial "Made by Dick" ads with their sometimes bizarre renditions of the "Miller Time" refrain, the company attempted to return to its roots to some extent with more conventional—but still humorous—interpretations of the Miller Time theme. Timex watches finally gave up trying to replace its classic "Takes a Licking and Keeps on Ticking" and has returned to the tag line in its advertising. Seven Up tried a number of different successors to its popular "Uncola" slogan—including "Freedom of Choice," "Crisp, and Clean and No Caffeine," "Don't You Feel Good About 7 UP," and "Feels So Good Coming Down"—before finally arriving at the somewhat edgy "Make 7 UP Yours."

Thus, a slogan that becomes so strongly identified with the brand can potentially box it in. Successful slogans can take on lives of their own and become public catch phrases (as with Wendy's "Where's the Beef?" in the 1980s and Budweiser's "Whassup?!" and Bud Light's "Yes I Am" and "I Love You, Man" in the 1990s), but there can also be a down side to this success: They can quickly become overexposed and lose specific brand or product meaning.

Once a slogan achieves such a high level of recognition and acceptance, it may still contribute to brand equity, but probably as more of a reminder of the brand. Consumers are probably unlikely to consider what the slogan means in a thoughtful way after seeing or hearing it too many times. At the same time, a potential difficulty

Benetton's Brand Equity Management

One of the world's top clothing manufacturers (with global sales of $2.4 billion), Benetton has experienced some ups and downs in managing its brand equity. Benetton built a powerful brand by creating a broad range of basic and colorful clothes that appealed to a wide range of consumers. Their corporate slogan, "United Colors of Benetton," would seem to almost perfectly capture their desired image and positioning. It embraces both product considerations (the colorful character of the clothes) and user considerations (the diversity reflected by the people who wore the clothes), providing a strong platform for the brand. Benetton's ad campaigns reinforced this positioning by showing people from a variety of different racial backgrounds wearing a range of different-colored clothes and products.

Benetton's ad campaigns switched directions, however, in the 1980s by addressing controversial social issues. Created in-house by famed designer Oliverio Toscani, Benetton print ads and posters featured such unusual and sometimes disturbing images as a white child wearing angel's wings alongside a black child sporting devil's horns; a priest kissing a nun; an AIDS patient and his family in the hospital moments before his death; and, in an ad run only once, 56 close-up photos of male and female genitalia. In 1994, Benetton launched a $15 million ad campaign in newspapers and billboards in 110 countries featuring the torn and bloodied uniform of a dead Bosnian soldier. In 2000, a campaign titled "We, On Death Row" showcased American death row inmates with pictures of the prisoners and details about their crimes and length of incarceration.

Critics have labeled these various campaigns as gimmicky "shock" advertising and accused Benetton of exploiting sensitive social issues to sell sweaters. One fact is evident. Although these new ad campaigns may be appreciated by and effective with a certain market segment, they are certainly more "exclusive" in nature—distancing the brand from many other consumers—than the early Benetton ad campaigns, which were strikingly inviting to consumers and "inclusive" in nature. Not surprisingly, the ad campaigns were not always well received by its retailers and franchise owners. The ad displaying the dead Bosnian soldier received an especially hostile reaction throughout Europe. In the United States, some of Benetton's more controversial ads have been rejected by the media, and Benetton's U.S. retailers commissioned their own campaign from TBWA/Chiat/Day ad agency in an attempt to create their own, more sophisticated image for the brand. After the death row ads debuted, Sears pulled the brand from its shelves. Response from U.S. consumers was equally negative: American sales of Benetton products shrunk by 50 percent to $52 million between 1993 and 2000. By 2001, the number of Benetton stores in the United States dropped to 150 from 600 in 1987.

One critic said, "Benetton's ad strategy is morally condemnable, legally untenable, and economically extremely damaging." Benetton responds that it is only "highlighting social problems" and that it will "continue to collaborate on dramatic issues" because "it's in our philosophy."

Sources: Leigh Gallagher, "About Face," *Forbes,* 19 March 2001; Michael McCarthy, "Benetton in Spotlight," *USA Today,* 16 February 2002, B3.

1. _____ Reach Out and Touch Someone
2. _____ Have It Your Way
3. _____ Just Do It
4. _____ When It Absolutely, Positively Has to Be There Overnite
5. _____ Drivers Wanted
6. _____ Don't Leave Home Without It
7. _____ Like a Rock
8. _____ Where's the Beef?
9. _____ The Ultimate Driving Machine
10. _____ When You Care Enough to Send the Very Best
11. _____ Mmm Mmm Good
12. _____ The Wonder Drug That Works Wonders
13. _____ No More Tears
14. _____ Melts in Your Mouth, Not in Your Hands
15. _____ We Try Harder
16. _____ Army of One
17. _____ Where Do You Want to Go Today?
18. _____ Diamonds Are Forever
19. _____ Breakfast of Champions
20. _____ Nobody Doesn't Like _____

Answers: (1) Bell Telephone; (2) Burger King; (3) Nike; (4) Federal Express; (5) Volkswagen; (6) American Express; (7) Chevrolet; (8) Wendy's; (9) BMW; (10) Hallmark; (11) Campbell's; (12) Bayer; (13) Johnson's Baby Shampoo; (14) M&M's; (15) Avis; (16) U.S. Army; (17) Microsoft; (18) DeBeers; (19) Wheaties; and (20) Sara Lee.

FIGURE 4-14   Famous Slogans Quiz

arises if the slogan continues to convey some product meaning that the brand no longer needs to reinforce. In this case, by not facilitating the linkage of new, desired brand associations, the slogan can become restrictive and fail to allow the brand to be updated as much as desired or necessary.

Because slogans are perhaps the easiest brand element to change over time, there is more flexibility in managing them. In changing slogans, however, as with changing other brand elements, it is important to do the following:

1. Recognize how the slogan is contributing to brand equity, if at all, through enhanced awareness or image.
2. Decide how much of this equity enhancement, if any, is still needed.
3. Retain as much as possible the needed or desired equities still residing in the slogan while providing whatever new twists of meaning are needed to contribute to equity in other ways.

In many cases, moderate modifications of an existing slogan may prove more fruitful than introducing a new slogan with a completely new set of meanings. For example, Dockers switched their slogan from the well-received "Nice Pants" to "One Leg at a Time" in the late 1990s before reverting to the previous slogan when recognizing that equity had been given up.

Jingles

Jingles are musical messages written around the brand. Typically composed by professional songwriters, they often have enough catchy hooks and choruses to become almost permanently registered in the minds of listeners—sometimes whether they want them to or not! During the first half of the nineteenth century, when broadcast advertising was confined primarily to radio, jingles became important branding devices. Figure 4-15 contains a few famous brand jingles—sing along if you want (and can remember)!

Jingles can be thought of as extended musical slogans and in that sense can be classified as a brand element. Because of their musical nature, however, jingles are not nearly as transferable as other brand elements. Jingles can communicate brand benefits, but they often convey product meaning in a nondirect and fairly abstract fashion given their musical foundation. The potential associations that might occur for the brand from jingles are probably most likely to relate to feelings and personality and other such intangibles. Jingles are perhaps most valuable in terms of enhancing brand awareness. Often, the jingle will repeat the brand name in clever and amusing ways that allow consumers multiple encoding opportunities. Because of their catchy nature, consumers are also likely to mentally rehearse or repeat the jingle even after seeing or hearing the ad, providing even additional encoding opportunities and increasing memorability.

A well-known jingle can serve as a foundation for advertising for years. As an example, in the United States, the familiar "Give Me a Break" jingle for Kit Kat candy bars has been sung in ads by professionals and everyday people since 1988 and has helped to propel the brand to the sixth best-selling chocolate candy bar. Similarly, after two decades as the centerpiece of their ad campaign, there was an uproar when the U.S. Army switched from their familiar "Be All That You Can Be" to "Army of One." Finally, Intel's distinctive three-second, four-note sound signature to their own or co-op ads echoes the company's slogan ("In-tel In-side"). Although seemingly simple, the first note alone is a mix of 16 sounds, including a tambourine and a hammer striking a brass pipe.[38]

Packaging

Packaging involves the activities of designing and producing containers or wrappers for a product. Like other brand elements, packages have a long history. Early humans used leaves and animal skin to cover and carry food and water. Glass containers first appeared in Egypt as early as 2000 B.C. Later, the French emperor Napoleon awarded 12,000 francs to the winner of a contest to find a better way to preserve food, leading to the first crude method of vacuum-packing.[39]

From the perspective of both the firm and consumers, packaging must achieve a number of objectives:[40]

➤ Identify the brand
➤ Convey descriptive and persuasive information
➤ Facilitate product transportation and protection
➤ Assist at-home storage
➤ Aid product consumption

To achieve the marketing objectives for the brand and satisfy the desires of consumers, the aesthetic and functional components of packaging must be chosen correctly. Aesthetic considerations relate to a package's size and shape, material, color,

I'd Like to Buy the World a Coke
(Coca-Cola)
I'd like to buy the world a home
And furnish it with love
Grow apple trees and honey bees
And snow-white turtle doves
I'd like to teach the world to sing
In perfect harmony
I'd like to buy the world a Coke
And keep it company
That's the real thing

I'd like to teach the world to sing
In perfect harmony
And I'd like to buy the world a Coke
And keep it company
It's the real thing
Coke is
(Repeat)

Be a Pepper
(Dr Pepper)
I drink Dr Pepper, and I'm proud
I used to be alone in a crowd
But now you look around these days
There seems to be a Dr Pepper crowd

Oh, You're a Pepper
I'm a Pepper, he's a Pepper, she's a
Pepper, we're a Pepper
Wouldn't you like to be a Pepper, too
I'm a Pepper, he's a Pepper, she's a Pepper
If you drink Dr Pepper, you're a Pepper, too

Us Peppers are an interesting breed
An original taste is what we need
Ask any Pepper and he'll say
Only Dr Pepper tastes that way

I'm a Pepper, he's a Pepper, she's a
Pepper, we're a Pepper
Wouldn't you like to be a Pepper, too
Be a Pepper, drink Dr Pepper . . .
(Repeat)

The Dogs Kids Love to Bite
(Armour Hot Dogs)
Hot dogs, Armour hot dogs
What kinds of kids eat Armour hot dogs
Fat kids, skinny kids, kids who climb on
rocks
Tough kids, sissy kids
Even kids with chicken pox
Love hot dogs, Armour hot dogs
The dogs kids love to bite!

Pickin' it up on the old banjo
Put on the mustard, and away we go
When men bite dog, it's news they say
But when kids bite dogs they yell hooray!
For hot dogs,
Armour hot dogs
The dogs kids love to bite!

If You've Got the Time
(Miller High Life)
If you've got the time
We've got the beer
Miller beer
Miller tastes too good to hurry through

But when it's time to relax
Miller stands clear
Beer after beer
If you've got the time, you've got the time
We've got the beer
Miller beer

This Bud's for You
(Budweiser)
This Bud's for you
And you and you and you
This Bud's for you

FIGURE 4-15 Popular Jingles

text, and graphics. Innovations in printing processes now permit eye-catching and appealing graphics that convey elaborate and colorful messages on the package at the "moment of truth" at the point of purchase.[41] Functionally, structural design is crucial. For example, packaging innovations with food products over the years have resulted in packages being resealable, tamperproof, and more convenient to use (e.g., easy to hold, easy to open, or squeezable). Changes in canning have made vegetables crunchier, and special wraps have extended the life of refrigerated food.[42] Despite all of the recent attention to food packaging, opportunities remain because consumers still report many problems with in-home use or storage. In a recent survey, consumers complained about food packages that stick, rip, or don't protect their contents. Out of frustration, some consumers were actually even doing their own repackaging at home.[43]

Benefits

Packaging can have important brand equity benefits for a company. Often, one of the strongest associations that consumers have with a brand relates to the look of its packaging. For example, if you ask the average consumer what comes to mind when they think of Heineken beer, a common response is "green bottle." The package appearance can become an important means of brand recognition. Moreover, the information conveyed or inferred from the package can build or reinforce valuable brand associations.

Structural packaging innovations can create a point of difference that permits a higher margin. New packages can also expand a market and capture new market segments.

V-8

Although V-8 had been a big seller for Campbell, consumer research found that soft sales among a younger target market was partly a result of the fact that these consumers simply did not shop the canned-good aisles where the brand was being stocked. Consequently, Campbell experimented by putting V-8 juice in cartons and six-packs so that they could be stocked in the more accessible refrigerator and beverage sections. Sales jumped 15 percent as a result.[44]

Packaging changes can have immediate impact on sales. For example, sales of the Heath candy bar increased 25 percent after its wrapper was redone. Similarly, Rice-A-Roni's sales increased 20 percent in the first year after a packaging revitalization. One of the major packaging trends of recent years is to make both bigger and smaller packaged versions of products (as well as portions) to appeal to new market segments.[45] Jumbo products have been successfully introduced with hot dogs, pizzas, English muffins, frozen dinners, and beer. For example, Pillsbury's introduction of their Grand biscuits—40 percent larger than their existing offerings—was the most successful new product in the company's 126-year history.

Packaging at the Point of Purchase

Package design also has become more important in recent years as brand proliferation continues and advertising is seen as becoming less cost-effective. Packaging can be a means of having strong appeal on the shelf and standing out from the clutter. The importance of packaging at the point of purchase can be seen by recognizing that the average supermarket shopper may be exposed to 15,000 to 20,000 products in a shopping visit that lasts less than 30 minutes and during which many purchases may be unplanned. For many consumers, the first encounter with a new brand may be on the supermarket shelf or in the store. Because few product differences exist in some categories, packaging innovations can provide at least a temporary edge on competition. For these reasons, packaging has been seen as a particularly cost-effective way to build brand equity.[46] Along these lines, packaging is sometimes called the "last five seconds of marketing" as well as "permanent media" or "the last salesman."

Consumer exposure to packaging is not restricted to the point of purchase and moments of consumption, because brand packages often play a starring role in advertising. One survey of 200 TV commercials in 10 mass-market product categories indicated that the package was featured, on average, in roughly 12 seconds of a 30-second spot.[47] Newer products, or variations or updates of older ones, tended to feature the package longer, a sensible advertising strategy for brands with marketing objectives to build brand recognition. Print ads also often prominently display the package.

Packaging Innovations

In mature markets especially, package innovations can provide a short-term sales boost. For example, packaging innovations such as the 2-liter jug bottle and the 12-pack carton helped soft drink makers experience steady 5 percent to 7 percent growth in the 1980s. With the rate of growth of the soft drink industry slowing down to 2 percent to 3 percent in the 1990s, soft drink makers sought new packaging innovations to fuel additional growth. As a result, Pepsi-Cola introduced the 24-pack Cube, 12-ounce resealable bottles, 8-ounce Pepsi Mini cans, and the wide-mouth, 1-liter Big Slam bottle. Even the traditional look of Pepsi's packaging, which had not been changed since 1973, was updated in a $500 million global redesign, eventually arriving at space-age blue packaging with updated graphics.

Not to be outdone, Coca-Cola returned to some of its brand heritage to feature their patented contour Coke bottle, originally introduced in 1915.[48] New "impact" graphics were added to the Coke can itself, featuring a newly opened bottle with liquid fizzing from the top. The Diet Coke can was redesigned to make it more "confident and sociable" by dropping the red wave that used to travel the length of the can and adding two new features—circular bubbles and a stylized soda fountain glass design—and rebalancing the four colors. Finally, Sprite's late-1990s sales ascendance was fueled in part by its green plastic bottle with dimples, which is reminiscent of a glass Sprite bottle from the 1960s.

Packaging innovations such as Snapple's widemouth glass bottle have also contributed to strong market performance for other beverages. Arizona's iced teas and fruit drinks in oversize (24-ounce), pastel-colored cans with a Southwestern motif became a $300 million brand in a few years with no marketing support beyond point-of-purchase and rudimentary outdoor ads, designed in-house.[49]

Package Design

For all these reasons, package design has been elevated in its importance and has now become an integral part of product development and launch. As with the choice of a brand name, package design has become a more sophisticated process. In the past, package design was often an afterthought, and colors, materials, and so forth were often chosen fairly arbitrarily. For example, legend has it that the color of the famous Campbell's soup can had its origins in one executive at the company liking the look of the red and white uniforms of Cornell University's football team!

These days, specialized package designers bring artistic techniques and scientific skills to package design in an attempt to meet the marketing objectives for a brand. These consultants conduct detailed analyses to break down the package into a number of different elements. They decide on the optimal look and content of each element and the proper packaging hierarchy in terms of which elements should be dominant in any one package (e.g., the brand name, illustration, or some other graphical element) and how the elements should relate. When brand extensions are introduced, these designers can also decide which elements should be shared across packages and which elements should differ (and how). The Science of Branding 4-2 describes the activities of Landor Associates, one of the leading package design and image management firms in the world.

Designers often refer to the "shelf impact" of a package—the visual effect that the package has at the point of the purchase when seen in the context of other packages in the category. For example, "bigger and brighter" packages are not always better when competitors' packages are also factored in.[50] Although some information is legally required on packages (e.g., nutrition information for food packages), a number of decisions can be made about design elements to improve brand awareness and facilitate the formation of brand associations.

Perhaps one of the most important visual design elements for a package is its color. Some package designers believe that consumers have a "color vocabulary" when it comes to products and expect certain types of products to have a particular look. For example, it is believed that it would be difficult to sell milk in anything but a white carton, club soda in anything but a blue package, and so forth. At the same time, certain brands are thought to have "color ownership" such that it would be difficult for other brands to use a similar look. One leading design executive outlined the following brand color palate:[51]

Red: Ritz crackers, Folgers coffee, Colgate toothpaste, and Coca-Cola soft drinks

Orange: Tide laundry detergent, Wheaties cereal, and Stouffer's frozen dinners

Yellow: Kodak film, Juicy Fruit chewing gum, Cheerios cereal, Lipton tea, and Bisquick biscuit mix

Green: Del Monte canned vegetables, Green Giant frozen vegetables, and 7 UP lemon-lime soft drink

Blue: IBM computers, Windex cleaner, Downy fabric softener, and Pepsi-Cola soft drinks

Packaging color can affect consumer's perceptions of the product itself.[52] For example, consumers ascribe sweeter taste to orange drinks the darker the orange shade of the can or bottle. Researchers at Derni Corporation found that when they changed the color of the packaging of their Barrelhead Sugar-Free Root Beer from beige to blue, people were more likely to agree that it "tasted like old-fashioned root

Brand Makeover Experts: Landor Associates

Landor Associates, one of the premier image consultants and strategic designers in the world, called the ferryboat *Kalmath,* anchored on Pier 5 in San Francisco, home for years. Although the firm has since moved into more spacious headquarters, Landor has retained the ferryboat as a symbol of the creativity and innovation that it feels it brings to its marketing assignments. Landor has provided a wide range of services to a varied list of clients. Some of the professional services Landor provides include corporate image management; naming systems; corporate, brand, and retail identity systems design; identity systems documentation; consumer research; retail space planning; brand value analysis; product positioning; communication strategies; corporate positioning; signage systems development; and corporate culture integration.

Specifically, Landor has provided the name and graphic identity for Touchstone Pictures, Saturn automobiles, and Dollar Rent A Car; devised packaging for Miller Genuine Draft; created the Cotton Mark—the first commodity product to add value through strategic branding; has redone packages for brands such as Coca-Cola, Maxwell House, V-8, Hawaiian Punch, Jergens soaps and lotions, and Oral-B; has created a branding and packaging system for 3M, General Electric, Birds Eye, Lean Cuisine, and Black & Decker; and has defined corporate identity for numerous airlines, including British Airways.

Several notable examples of how Landor helped to create "breakaway brands," along with the description and rationale of its efforts, are as follows:

- *KFC:* Colonel Sanders is *the* brand driver for KFC. Landor's new brand identity brought him back more prominently than ever, with his friendly smile offering a warm welcome and the promise of his personal touch. Bold use of KFC's red equity adds appetite appeal and visual impact

- *Energizer e^2:* Energizer recently introduced e^2, a line of super-premium batteries using new titanium technology. Working from the brand driver of "advanced technology for the next century," Landor's e^2 design employs a large asymmetrical package shape and subtly futuristic graphics to showcase the batteries' unique look and to herald the next revolution in exceptional battery performance and professional quality.

- *Physique:* For Procter & Gamble's Physique new ultra-premium, unisex hair care line, Landor developed the packaging based on the "science of style" brand driver. Landor's sleek, silver design brings prestige imagery to supermarket shelves. The scientific and artful images of the sigma and ellipse are subtly futuristic, suggesting the high style benefits and leading-edge technology behind the brand.

beer served in frosty mugs." Similarly, marketers of Miller High Life beer struggled for years with the fact that a clear bottle made their beer seem less hearty than the market leader, Budweiser, which was sold in a dark bottle (despite the fact that the actual Miller High Life beer was darker than Budweiser). They finally resorted to an ad campaign to try to correct the misperception.

Color is thus a critical element of packaging. Recent years have seen a rise in the use of blue as the look or even name for companies (e.g., Blue Martini, Jet Blue, Bluefly), perhaps because blue "suggests stature and professionalism" and "is cool, hip and relevant to technology" and therefore is a "safe choice."[53] Purple also came on strong as a "funky alternative" and therefore was embraced by many new-economy firms. In addition to the specific product inferences signaled by the color and other packaging design elements, it is also important that any other associations conveyed by the packaging be consistent with information conveyed by other aspects of the marketing program. In particular, as will be pointed out in Chapter 6, packaging should be designed in some cases to directly reinforce advertising in certain ways.

Packaging Changes

Although packaging changes can be expensive, they can be cost-effective compared with other marketing communication costs. Packages are changed for a number of reasons.[54] Packaging may be upgraded to signal a higher price, to more effectively sell products through new or shifting distribution channels (e.g., Kendall Oil redid its package to make it more appealing to do-it-yourselfers when it found more of its sales coming from supermarkets and hardware stores rather than service stations), or when there is a significant product line expansion that would benefit from a common look (e.g., as with Planter's nuts, Weight Watchers foods, or Stouffer's frozen foods). Package redesign may also accompany a new product innovation to signal changes to consumers. For example, when Procter & Gamble introduced Liquid Tide laundry detergent, the company felt that the 10 percent market share that the brand achieved was helped by the addition of a well-received drip-proof spout and bottle cap package design.[55]

Perhaps the most common reason for package redesign is that the old package just looks outdated. Under these circumstances, it is important not to lose the key package equities that have been built up. Packaging often has some unique graphic features that have achieved a high level of awareness and preference. The need to create a more contemporary look must be reconciled with the need to preserve existing packaging equities. In 1997, British Airways hoped for a more international look by adding Delft pottery, Chinese calligraphy, and other ethnic designs on the tail fins of many of its planes. A hostile public response led the company to make plans to return the Union Jack.[56] They are not alone in experiencing a consumer backlash to packaging.

Campbell's Soup

During a brand-wide label redesign in mid-1994, Campbell Soup eliminated the bright yellow decal from its vegetable soup cans that spelled out to consumers that it was actually alphabet macaroni soup inside. With a new label containing a splashy photo of the alphabet soup, the company figured the familiar yellow blimp with red lettering was not necessary. Sales of Campbell's seventh highest seller, however, plummeted 20 percent as a result, and thousands of consumers asked why the decal was dropped. Needless to say, the decal was quickly returned to the package, supported by an ad campaign announcing its return.

Packaging changes have accelerated in recent years as marketers have sought to gain an advantage wherever possible. As one Coca-Cola ad executive noted, "There's no question the crowded marketplace has inspired companies to change their boxes more often, and there's greater use of promotional packages to give the appearance that things are changing." In making a packaging change, it is thus important to recognize its effect on the original or current customer franchise for the brand.[57] To identify or confirm key package equities, it is often necessary to conduct consumer research.

Milk-Bone

When Nabisco set out to redesign the package for its 86-year old Milk-Bone brand of dog biscuits, it asked some of its loyal customers, as part of a research study, to draw the package from memory. Most people drew the dog bone shape that was the brand's logo correctly but had some difficulty drawing the head of the dog that appeared on the front of the package despite its prominent placement there. These people also tended to ignore other packaging elements that informed them of the biscuits' nutritional and teeth-cleaning advantages all together. The researchers interpreted the findings to mean that the Milk-Bone brand did not necessarily signify "clean teeth" to consumers as much as "love and affection." They also concluded that the brand's key packaging equity was wrapped up in the dog, the biscuit, and the bone shape. As a result, the package was redesigned by removing much of the informational clutter, placing the dog bone logo higher and more prominent on the box; and making the dog, which previously was shown staring off blankly into space, appear more engaging by having it look straight ahead, as if at the consumer. The package redesign was thought to have contributed to a halt in the sales erosion that the brand had been experiencing.[58]

If packaging recognition is a critical consumer success factor for the brand, however, packaging changes must be conducted especially carefully. If changed too significantly, consumers may not recognize the package when confronted with it in the store.

The importance of packaging is reflected in the fact that some marketing observers refer to it as the "fifth P" of the marketing mix. Packaging can play an important role in building brand equity directly through points of difference created by functional or aesthetic elements of the packaging or indirectly through the reinforcement of brand awareness and image. Figure 4-16 contains the recommendations of one expert on how to create packaging with high impact.[59]

FIGURE 4-16 Guidelines for Creating High-Impact Packaging

---

1. *Know your consumer*. Get inside your consumer's head and heart to learn about what motivates the purchase.
2. *Take the big-picture approach*. Packages that are most effective borrow ideas from a wide range of other product categories. They look at all forms of packaging and put the best ideas together in unique ways.
3. *Understand that package aesthetics and function are both critical*. The package has to grab consumers' attention in a sea of competing messages-but it also has to work well so that consumers will buy again.
4. *Know your distribution channels*. How do retailers view your package? How are channels changing? Which retailers like which package configurations?
5. *Educate management*. Make sure senior management recognizes the importance of packaging.

PUTTING IT ALL TOGETHER

The previous discussion highlighted some key considerations for brand names, URLs, logos, symbols, characters, slogans, jingles, and packages. Each of these different brand elements can play a different role in building brand equity. Conceptually, it is necessary to "mix and match" these different brand elements to maximize brand equity. That is, as noted earlier and summarized in Figure 4-17, each brand element has certain strengths and weaknesses. Thus, marketers must "mix" brand elements by choosing different brand elements to achieve different objectives. At the same time, marketers must "match" brand elements by making sure that certain brand elements are chosen to reinforce each other by shared meaning. For example, research has shown that meaningful brand names that are visually represented through logos are easier to remember than without such reinforcement.[60]

The entire set of brand elements can be thought of making up the *brand identity*. Brand identity reflects the contribution of all brand elements to awareness and image. The cohesiveness of the brand identity depends on the extent to which the brand elements are consistent. Ideally, brand elements would be chosen that support other brand elements and that could easily be incorporated into other aspects of the brand and marketing program. Some strong brands have a number of valuable brand elements that directly reinforce each other. For example, consider Charmin toilet tissue.

FIGURE 4-17   Critique of Brand Element Options

Criterion	Brand Element				
	Brand Names and URLs	Logos and Symbols	Characters	Slogans and Jingles	Packaging and Signage
Memorability	Can be chosen to enhance brand recall and recognition	Generally more useful for brand recognition	Generally more useful for brand recognition	Can be chosen to enhance brand recall and recognition	Generally more useful for brand recognition
Meaningfulness	Can reinforce almost any type of association, although sometimes only indirectly	Can reinforce almost any type of association, although sometimes only indirectly	Generally more useful for non-product-related imagery and brand personality	Can convey almost any type of association explicitly	Can convey almost any type of association explicitly
Likability	Can evoke much verbal imagery	Can provoke visual appeal	Can generate human qualities	Can evoke much verbal imagery	Can combine visual and verbal appeal
Transferability	Can be somewhat limited	Excellent	Can be somewhat limited	Can be somewhat limited	Good
Adaptability	Difficult	Can typically be redesigned	Can sometimes be redesigned	Can be modified	Can typically be redesigned
Protectability	Generally good, but with limits	Excellent	Excellent	Excellent	Can be closely copied

Phonetically, the name itself probably conveys softness. The brand character, Mr. Whipple, and the brand slogan, "Please Don't Squeeze the Charmin," also help to reinforce the key point of difference for the brand of "softness."

Brand names characterized by rich, concrete visual imagery often can yield powerful logos or symbols. For example, Cutty Sark has used their schooner sailing ship as a logo on all types of merchandise. L'eggs pantyhose is sold in an egg-shaped package that directly reinforces the name. Wells Fargo, a large California-based bank, has a brand name rich in Western heritage that can be exploited throughout their marketing program. Wells Fargo has adopted a stagecoach as a symbol and has named individual services to be thematically consistent, for example, creating investment funds under the Stagecoach Funds brand umbrella.

Review

Brand elements are those trademarkable devices that serve to identify and differentiate the brand. The main brand elements are brand names, URLs, logos, symbols, characters, slogans, jingles, and packages. Brand elements can be chosen to both enhance brand awareness and facilitate the formation of strong, favorable, and unique brand associations.

In choosing and designing brand elements, six criteria are particularly important. First, brand elements can be chosen to be inherently memorable, both in terms of brand recall and recognition. Second, brand elements can be chosen to be inherently meaningful such that they convey information about the nature of the product category or particular attributes and benefits of a brand, or both. The brand element may even reflect brand personality, user or usage imagery, or feelings for the brand. Third, the information conveyed by brand elements does not necessarily have to relate to the product alone and may simply be inherently appealing or likable. Fourth, brand elements can be chosen to be transferable within and across product categories (i.e., to support line and brand extensions) and across geographic and cultural boundaries and market segments. Fifth, brand elements can be chosen to be adaptable and flexible over time. Finally, brand elements must be chosen that are legally protectable and, as much as possible, competitively defensible. Brand Focus 4.0 outlines some of the key legal considerations in protecting the brand.

The chapter reviewed a number of considerations for each type of brand element. Because different brand elements have different strengths and weaknesses it is important to "mix and match" brand elements to maximize their collective contribution to brand equity. Brand elements are "mixed" by choosing different brand elements to achieve different objectives. Brand elements are "matched" by designing some brand elements to be mutually reinforcing and to share some meaning.

Discussion Questions

1. Pick a brand. Identify all of its brand elements and assess their ability to contribute to brand equity according to the choice criteria identified in this chapter.
2. What are your favorite brand characters? Do you think they contribute to brand equity in any way? How? Can you relate their effects to the customer-based brand equity model?

3. What are some other examples of slogans not listed in the chapter that make strong contributions to brand equity? Why? Can you think of any "bad" slogans? Why do you consider them to be so?

4. Choose a package of any supermarket product. Assess its contribution to brand equity. Justify your decisions.

5. Can you think of some general guidelines to help marketers mix and match brand elements? Can you ever have "too many" brand elements? Which brand do you think does the best job of mixing and matching brand elements?

B r a n d   F o c u s   4 . 0

Legal Branding Considerations

According to Dorothy Cohen, under common law, "a 'technical' trademark is defined as any fanciful arbitrary, distinctive, and non-descriptive mark, word, letter, number, design, or picture that denominates and is affixed to goods; it is an inherently distinctive trade symbol that identifies a product."[61] She maintains that *trademark strategy* involves proper trademark planning, implementation, and control, as follows.

➤ *Trademark planning* requires selecting a valid trademark, adopting and using the trademark, and engaging in search and clearance processes.

➤ *Trademark implementation* requires effectively using the trademark in enacting marketing decisions, especially with respect to promotional and distributional strategies.

➤ *Trademark control* requires a program of aggressive policing of a trademark to ensure its efficient usage in marketing activities, including efforts to reduce trademark counterfeiting and to prevent the trademark from becoming generic, as well as instituting suits for infringement of the trademark.

This appendix highlights a few key legal branding considerations. For more comprehensive treatments, it is necessary to consider other sources.[62]

COUNTERFEIT AND IMITATOR BRANDS

Why is trademark protection of brand elements such as brand names, logos, and symbols such an important brand management priority? Counterfeiting alone costs U.S. companies an astounding $200 billion a year, and an estimated 5 percent of products sold world-wide are phony. Virtually any product is fair game for illegal counterfeiting or questionable copycat mimicking—from Nike apparel to Windows 95 software, and from Similac baby formula to ACDelco auto parts.[63] Pirated products from China, Vietnam, and Russia, in particular, have flooded global markets. In China alone, copyright infringement costs Western businesses an estimated $16 billion in sales annually. Some 20 percent of Western brand name products sold in China are counterfeit. Procter & Gamble claims that counterfeiters sold $150 million worth—or 15 percent of its total 2000 Chinese sales—of products bearing P&G logos. Volkswagen discovered that almost two-thirds of the car parts sold to VW owners are fake. In China, 94 percent of all software units are believed to be counterfeit, compared with 24 percent in the United States.

In addition, some products attempt to gain market share by imitating successful brands. These copycat brands may mimic any one of the possible brand elements, such as brand names or packaging. For example, Calvin Klein's popular Obsession perfume and cologne has had to withstand imitators such as Compulsion, Enamoured, and Confess, whose package slogan proclaimed, "If you like Obsession, you'll love Confess." Many copycat brands are put forth by retailers as store brands, putting national brands in the dilemma of protecting their trade dress by cracking down on some of their best customers. Complicating matters is the fact that if challenged, many private labels contend, with some justification, that they should be permitted to continue labeling and packaging practices that have come to identify entire categories of products rather than a single national brand.[64] In other words, certain packaging looks may become a necessary point of parity in a product category.

A common victim of brand cloning, Contac cold medication underwent its first packaging overhaul in 33 years to better prevent knockoffs as well as update its image. Many national brand manufacturers are also responding through legal action. For national brands, the key is proving that brand clones are misleading consumers, who may think that they are buying national brands. The burden of proof is to establish that an appreciable number of reasonably acting consumers are confused and mistaken in their purchases.[65] In such cases, many factors might be considered by courts in determining likelihood of confusion, such as the strength of the national brand's mark, the relatedness of the national brand and brand clone products, the similarity of the marks, evidence of actual confusion, the similarity of marketing channels used, the likely degree of buyer care, the brand clone's intent in selecting the mark, and the likelihood of expansion of the product lines.

Simonson provides an in-depth discussion of these issues and methods to assess the likelihood of confusion and "genericness" of a trademark. He stresses the importance of recognizing that consumers may vary in their level or degree of confusion and that it is difficult as a result to identify a precise threshold level above which confusion occurs. He also notes how survey research methods must accurately reflect the consumers' state of mind when engaged in marketplace activities.[66]

HISTORICAL AND LEGAL PRECEDENCE

Simonson and Holbrook have made some provocative observations about and connections between appropriation and dilution, making the following points.[67] They begin

by noting that legally, a brand name is a "conditional-type property"—protected only after it has been used in commerce to identify products (goods or services) and only in relation to those products or to closely related offerings. To preserve a brand name's role in identifying products, the authors note, federal law protects brands from actions of others that may tend to cause confusion concerning proper source identification.

By contrast with the case of confusion, Simonson and Holbrook identify *trademark appropriation* as a developing area of state law that can severely curtail even those brand strategies that do not "confuse" consumers. They define appropriation in terms of enhancing the image of a new offering via the use of some property aspect of an existing brand; that is, appropriation resembles theft of an intangible property right. They note that the typical argument to prevent imitations is that even in the absence of confusion, a weaker brand will tend to benefit by imitating an existing brand name.

Simonson and Holbrook continue:

> Protection from "dilution"—a weakening or reduction in the ability of a mark to clearly and unmistakably distinguish the source—arose in 1927 when a legal ruling declared that "once a mark has come to indicate to the public a constant and uniform source of satisfaction, its owner should be allowed the broadest scope possible for the 'natural expansion of his trade' to other lines or fields of enterprise."

They observe that two brand-related rights followed: (1) the right to preempt and preserve areas for brand extensions and (2) the right to stop the introduction of similar or identical brand names even in the absence of consumer confusion so as to protect a brand's image and distinctiveness from being diluted.

Dilution can occur in three ways: blurring, tarnishment, and cybersquatting. *Blurring* happens when the use of an existing mark by a different company in a different category alters the "unique and distinctive significance" of that mark. *Tarnishment* is when a different company employs the mark in order to degrade its quality, such as in the context of a parody or satire. *Cybersquatting* occurs when an unaffiliated party purchases an Internet "domain name consisting of the mark or name of a company for the purpose of relinquishing the right to that domain name to the legitimate owner for a price."[68]

New American laws register trademarks for only 10 years (instead of 20); to renew trademarks, firms must prove they are using the name and not just holding it in reserve. The Trademark Law Revision Act of 1988 allowed entities to apply for a trademark based on their "intent to use" it within 36 months, eliminating the need to have an actual product in the works. To determine legal status, marketers must search trademark registrations, brand name directories, phone books, trade journals and advertisements, and so forth. As a result, the pool of potentially available trademarks has shrunk. In 1996, 200,000 trademark applications were filed with the U.S. Patent and Trademark Office, including a large number filed by foreign companies from Canada, Germany, Britain, and Japan.[69]

Figure 4-18 describes some broad guidelines concerning trademark protection. The remainder of this appendix describes some of the particular issues involved with two important brand elements: brand names and packaging.

FIGURE 4-18 Protecting Trademarks

A number of experts have put forth advice and checklists concerning trademark protection. Among the guidelines that have been suggested include the following:

1. Register the trademark formally; also any symbol or stylized use of it and color.
2. Whenever the trademark appears in print, make sure that it stands out from the surrounding text. To do this, always capitalize the first letter of your trademark and perhaps use italics or bold print.
3. Always follow the trademark with a generic or dictionary name.
4. Always use the trademark as an adjective, never as a noun; never pluralize the trademark; never use it in the possessive; never use it as a verb.
5. Never "fool around" with the spelling of the trademark.
6. Maintain a consistent visual identity for the trademark; do not allow a proliferation of different graphic treatments.
7. Use appropriate registration marks.
8. Educate all personnel on proper trademark use, especially secretaries, distributors, dealers, and others who might promote it or otherwise frequently use it.
9. Challenge each misuse of the trademark, particularly by others in the marketplace.
10. Maintain thorough records of "due diligence" in correctly using and protecting the trademark.

Sources: Based on material found in Jack Alexander, "What's in a Name? Too Much, Said the FCC," *Sales & Marketing Management* (January 1989): 75–78; and John M. Murphy, *Brand Strategy* (London: Prentice-Hall, 1990), Chapter 14.

TRADEMARK ISSUES CONCERNING NAMES

Without adequate trademark protection, brand names can become legally declared generic, as was the case with *vaseline, victrola, cellophane, escalator,* and *thermos.* For example, when Bayer set out to trademark the "wonder drug" acetylsalicyclic acid, they failed to provide a "generic" term or common descriptor for the product and provided only a trademark, *aspirin.* Without any other option available in the language, the trademark became the common name for the product. In 1921, a U.S. District Court ruled that Bayer had lost all its rights in the trademark. Other brand names have struggled to retain their legal trademark status, for example, Band Aids, Kleenex, Scotch Tape, Q-Tips, and Jello. Xerox spends $100,000 a year explaining that you don't "Xerox" a document, you photocopy it.[70]

Legally, the courts have created a hierarchy for determining eligibility for registration. In descending order of protection, these categories are as follows (with examples in parentheses):

1. Fanciful (Kodak)
2. Arbitrary (Camel)
3. Suggestive (Eveready)
4. Descriptive (Ivory)
5. Generic (Aspirin)

Thus, fanciful names are the most easily protected, but at the same time are less suggestive or descriptive of the product itself, suggesting the type of tradeoff involved in choosing brand elements. Generic terms are never protectable. Marks that are difficult to protect include those that are surnames, descriptive terms, or geographic names or those that relate to a functional product feature. Marks that are not inherently distinctive and thus are not immediately protectable may attain trademark protection if they acquire secondary meaning.

Secondary meaning refers to a mark gaining a meaning other than the older (primary) meaning. The secondary meaning must be the meaning the public usually attaches to the mark and that indicates the association between the mark and goods from a single source. Secondary meaning is usually proven through extensive advertising, distribution, availability, sales volume, length and manner of use, and market share.[71] Secondary meaning is necessary to establish trademark protection for descriptive marks, geographic terms, and personal names.

TRADEMARK ISSUES CONCERNING PACKAGING

In general, names and graphic designs are more legally defensible than shapes and colors. The issue of legal protection of the color of packaging for a brand is a complicated one. One federal appeals court in San Francisco ruled that companies cannot get trademark protection for a product's color alone.[72] The court ruled against a small Chicago manufacturer that makes green-gold padding used by dry cleaners and garment makers on machines that press clothes; the manufacturer had filed suit against a competitor that had started selling padding of the same hue. In rejecting protection for the color alone, the court said manufacturers with distinctively colored products can rely on existing law that protects "trade dress" related to the overall appearance of the product: "Adequate protection is available when color is combined in distinctive patterns or designs or combined in distinctive logos."

Color is one factor, but not a determinative one, under a trade dress analysis. This ruling differed from a landmark ruling in 1985 arising from a suit by Owens-Corning

Fiberglas Corporation, which sought to protect the pink color of its insulation. A Washington court ruled in the corporation's favor. Other courts have made similar rulings, but at least two other appeals courts in other regions of the country have subsequently ruled that colors cannot be trade-marked. Note that these trademark rulings apply only when color is not an integral part of the product. However, given the lack of uniform trademark protection across the United States, companies planning a national campaign may have to rely on the harder-to-prove trade dress arguments.

Notes

1. "Blue Rhino Tries Horning in on Propane Business," *USA Today*, 27 August 1996, 22. Blue Rhino seeks the lion share of the replacement sales for the propane tanks of backyard gas grills by promising consumers convenience, safety, and reliability.
2. Cacile Rohwedder, "Global Products Require Name Finders," *Wall Street Journal*, 11 April 1996, B8.
3. An excellent overview of the topic, some of which this section draws on, can be found in Kim R. Robertson, "Strategically Desirable Brand Name Characteristics," *Journal of Consumer Marketing* 6, no. 4 (1989): 61–71.
4. Frances Leclerc, Bernd H. Schmitt, and Laurette Dube, "Foreign Branding and Its Effects on Product Perceptions and Attitudes," *Journal of Marketing Research* 31 (May 1994): 263–270. See also M. V. Thakor and B. G. Pacheco, "Foreign Branding and Its Effect on Product Perceptions and Attitudes: A Replication and Extension in a Multicultural Setting," *Journal of Marketing Theory and Practice* (Winter 1997): 15–30.
5. Ronald Alsop, "Firms Create Unique Names, But Are They Pronounceable?" *Wall Street Journal*, 2 April 1987, B1.
6. Eric A. Yorkston, "Construction through Deconstruction: A Compositional Approach to Brand Name Development," UMI microform 9971805 (Ann Arbor, MI: Bell & Howell, 2000).
7. Robert N. Kanungo, "Effects of Fittingness, Meaningfulness, and Product Utility," *Journal of Applied Psychology* 52 (1968): 290–295.
8. Kim R. Robertson, "Recall and Recognition Effects of Brand Name Imagery," *Psychology and Marketing* 4 (1987): 3–15.
9. Kevin Lane Keller, Susan Heckler, and Michael J. Houston, "The Effects of Brand Name Suggestiveness on Advertising Recall," *Journal of Marketing* 62 (January 1998): 48–57.
10. Bernd Schmitt, Y. Pan, Y. Nader, and T. Tavassoli, "Language and Consumer Memory: The Impact of Linguistic Differences between Chinese and English," *Journal of Consumer Research* 21, no. 12 (1994): 419–431.
11. Y. Pan and B. Schmitt, "Language and Brand Attitudes: Impact of Script and Sound Matching in Chinese and English," *Journal of Consumer Psychology* 5, no. 3 (1996): 263–277.
12. Alex Frankel, "Name-o-rama," *Wired*, June 1997, 94.
13. William L. Moore and Donald R. Lehmann, "Effects of Usage and Name on Perceptions of New Products," *Marketing Science* 1, no. 4 (1982): 351–370.
14. Keller, Heckler, and Houston, "Effects of Brand Name Suggestiveness on Advertising Recall."
15. Ibid.
16. Robert A. Peterson and Ivan Ross, "How to Name New Brands," *Journal of Advertising Research* 12, no. 6 (December 1972): 29–34.
17. Robert A. Mamis, "Name Calling," *Inc.*, July 1984.
18. Michael McCarthy, "Xterra Discovers Extra Success," *USA Today*, 26 February 2001, 4B.
19. Bruce G. Vanden Bergh, Janay Collins, Myrna Schultz, and Keith Adler, "Sound Advice on Brand Names," *Journalism Quarterly* 61, no. 4 (1984): 835–840.
20. Bruce G. Vanden Bergh, Keith Adler, and Lauren Oliver, "Linguistic Distinction among Top Brand Names," *Journal of*

Advertising Research (August/September 1987): 39–44.

21. Daniel L. Doeden, "How to Select a Brand Name," *Marketing Communications* (November 1981): 58–61.

22. Timothy B. Heath, Subimal Chatterjee, and Karen Russo, "Using the Phonemes of Brand Names to Symbolize Brand Attributes," in *The AMA Educator's Proceedings: Enhancing Knowledge Development in Marketing*, eds. William Bearden and A. Parasuraman (Chicago: American Marketing Association, August 1990).

23. Much of this passage is based on Teresa M. Paiva and Janeen Arnold Costa, "The Winning Number: Consumer Perceptions of Alpha-Numeric Brand Names," *Journal of Marketing* 57 (July 1993): 85–98.

24. John Murphy, *Brand Strategy* (Upper Saddle River, NJ: Prentice-Hall, 1990), 79.

25. Matt Hicks, "Order Out of Chaos," *eWeek*, 1 July 2001.

26. Rachel Konrad, "Companies Resurrect Abandoned Names, Ditch '.com,' " CNET News.com, 13 November 2000.

27. Murphy, *Brand Strategy*.

28. Pamela W. Henderson and Jospeh A. Cote, "Guidelines for Selecting or Modifying Logos," *Journal of Marketing* 62, no. 2 (1998): 14–30.

29. See also Chris Janiszewski and Tom Meyvis, "Effects of Brand Logo Complexity, Repetition, and Spacing on Processing Fluency and Judgment," *Journal of Consumer Research* 28 (June 2001): 18–32.

30. Murphy, *Brand Strategy*.

31. Michael McCarthy, "More Firms Flash New Badge," *USA Today*, 4 October 2000, B3.

32. Ibid.

33. Cyndee Miller, "The Green Giant: An Enduring Figure Lives Happily Ever After," *Marketing News*, 15 April 1991, 2.

34. David A. Aaker, *Building Strong Brands* (New York: Free Press, 1996), 203.

35. Yukimo Ono, "Aunt Jemima Brand Hires Gladys Knight," *Wall Street Journal*, 16 September 1994, B3.

36. Charles Goodrum and Helen Dalyrmple, *Advertising in America* (New York: Harry N. Abrams, 1990).

37. Lisa Bannon, "Top-Heavy Barbie Is Getting Body Work at Hands of Mattel," *Wall Street Journal*, 17 November 1997, A1.

38. Dirk Smillie, "Now Hear This," *Forbes*, 25 December 2000, 234.

39. Nancy Croft, "Wrapping Up Sales," *Nation's Business* (October 1985): 41–42.

40. Susan B. Bassin, "Value-Added Packaging Cuts through Store Clutter," *Marketing News*, 26 September 1988, 21.

41. Raymond Serafin, "Packaging Becomes an Art," *Advertising Age*, 12 August 1985, 66.

42. Trish Hall, "New Packaging May Soon Lead to Food That Tastes Better and Is More Convenient," *Wall Street Journal*, 21 April 1986, 25.

43. "Food Packages Rile Consumers," *Wall Street Journal*, 11 November 1987.

44. Susan Spillman, "Right Package Is Vital to Wrap Up More Sales," *USA Today*, 13 February 1993, B1.

45. Eben Shapiro, "Portions and Packages Grow Bigger and Bigger," *Wall Street Journal*, 12 October 1993, B1.

46. Alecia Swasy, "Sales Lost Their Vim? Try Repackaging," *Wall Street Journal*, 11 October 1989, B1.

47. "Packaging Plays Starring Role in TV Commercials," *Marketing News*, 30 January 1987.

48. Eleena de Lisser, "Pepsi Puts Spotlight on New Packaging," *Wall Street Journal*, 11 August 1993, B1.

49. Gerry Khermouch, "John Ferolito, Don Vultaggio," *Brandweek*, 14 November 1995, 57.

50. For interesting discussion, see Margaret C. Campbell and Ronald C. Goodstein, "The Moderating Effect of Perceived Risk on Consumers' Evaluations of Product Incongruity: Preference for the Norm," *Journal of Consumer Research* 28 (December 2001): 439–449.

51. Michael Purvis, president of Sidjakov, Berman, and Gomez, as quoted in Carla Marinucci, "Advertising on the Store Shelves," *San Francisco Examiner*, 20 October 1986, C1–C2.

52. Lawrence L. Garber Jr., Raymond R. Burke, and J. Morgan Jones, "The Role of Package Color in Consumer Purchase Consideration

and Choice," MSI Report 00–104 (Cambridge, MA: Marketing Science Institute, 2000); Ronald Alsop, "Color Grows More Important in Catching Consumers' Eyes," *Wall Street Journal*, 29 November 1984, 37.

53. Susan Carey, "American Companies Are Blue and It's Not Just the Stock Market," *Wall Street Journal*, 30 August 2001, A1

54. Bill Abrams and David P. Garino, "Package Design Gains Stature as Visual Competition Grows," *Wall Street Journal*, 14 March 1979, 48.

55. Amy Dunkin, "Want to Wake Up a Tired Old Package? Repackage It," *Business Week*, 15 July 1985, 130–134.

56. Melanie Wells, "Face-lift Fever," *Forbes*, 15 November 1999, 58.

57. Garber, Burke, and Jones, "Role of Package Color."

58. Pam Weisz, "Repackaging," *Brandweek*, 27 February 1995, 25–27.

59. James W. Peters, "Five Steps to Packaging That Sells," *Brand Packaging* 3, no. 4 (July/August 1999): 3.

60. Terry L. Childers and Michael J. Houston, "Conditions for a Picture Superiority Effect on Consumer Memory," *Journal of Consumer Research* 11 (September 1984): 551–563; Kathy A. Lutz and Richard J. Lutz, "Effects of Interactive Imagery on Learning: Application to Advertising," *Journal of Applied Psychology* 62, no. 4 (1977): 493–498.

61. Dorothy Cohen, "Trademark Strategy," *Journal of Marketing* 50 (January 1986): 61–74; Dorothy Cohen, "Trademark Strategy Revisited," *Journal of Marketing* 55 (July 1991): 46–59.

62. For example, see Judy Zaichowsky, *Defending Your Brand Against Imitation* (Westpoint, CO: Quorom Books, 1995).

63. David Stipp, "Farewell, My Logo," *Fortune*, 27 May 1996, 128–140.

64. Paul F. Kilmer, "Tips for Protecting Brand from Private Label Lawyer," *Advertising Age*, 5 December 1994, 29.

65. Greg Erickson, "Seeing Double," *Brandweek*, 17 October 1994, 31–35.

66. Itamar Simonson, "Trademark Infringement from the Buyer Perspective: Conceptual Analysis and Measurement Implications," *Journal of Public Policy & Marketing* 13, no. 2 (Fall 1994): 181–199.

67. Alex Simonson and Morris Holbrook, "Evaluating the Impact of Brand-Name Replications on Product Evaluations," working paper, Marketing Department, Seton Hall University, 1994.

68. J. Thomas McCarthy, *McCarthy on Trademarks and Unfair Competition*, 4th ed., Deerfield, IL: Clark Boardman Callaghan, 1996

69. Alex Frankel, "Name-o-rama," *Wired*, June 1997, 94.

70. Constance E. Bagley, *Managers and the Legal Environment: Strategies for the 21st Century*, 2nd ed. (Minneapolis, MN: West Publishing, 1995).

71. Garry Schuman, "Trademark Protection of Container and Package Configurations—A Primer," *Chicago Kent Law Review* 59 (1982): 779–815.

72. Junda Woo, "Product's Color Alone Can't Get Trademark Protection," *Wall Street Journal*, 5 January 1994, B8.

CHAPTER 5

Designing Marketing Programs to Build Brand Equity

PREVIEW

Although the judicious selection of brand elements and the resulting brand identity can make an important contribution to customer-based brand equity, the primary input comes from marketing activities related to the brand and the corresponding marketing program. This chapter considers how marketing activities in general and product, pricing, and distribution strategies in particular can build brand equity—that is, enhance brand awareness, improve the brand image, elicit positive brand responses, and increase brand resonance. Chapter 6 considers how marketers can create integrated marketing communication programs to build brand equity.

In both of these chapters, the focus is on marketing activities from a branding perspective. The question is how marketing programs should be optimally designed to build brand equity. This chapter also considers how the brand itself can be effectively integrated into the marketing program to maximize the creation of brand equity. To obtain a broader perspective on marketing activities, however, it is necessary to consult a basic marketing management text, as well as the specific references noted in these chapters.[1] The analysis begins by considering some of the new developments in designing marketing programs. After next reviewing product, pricing, and channel strategies, this chapter concludes by considering the important topic of private labels in Brand Focus 5.0.

NEW PERSPECTIVES ON MARKETING

The strategy and tactics behind marketing programs have changed dramatically in recent years as firms have dealt with the enormous shifts of the "new economy" in their external marketing environment. As outlined in Chapter 1, changes in the economic, technological, political-legal, sociocultural, and competitive environments have forced marketers to embrace new approaches and philosophies. Kotler identifies five major drivers of this new economy:[2]

➤ Digitalization and connectivity (through Internet, intranet, and mobile devices)
➤ Disintermediation and reintermediation (via new middlemen of various sorts)
➤ Customization and customerization (through tailored products and by providing customers ingredients to make products themselves)
➤ Industry convergence (through the blurring of industry boundaries)
➤ New customer and company capabilities (see Figure 5-1)

These shifts and changes have a number of implications for the practice of brand management. As the Science of Branding 5-1 describes, marketers are increasingly abandoning the mass-market practices that built brand powerhouses in the 1950s, 1960s, and 1970s to implement new approaches. Interestingly, in many cases, these approaches can be seen as a throwback to marketing practices from over a century ago. As one marketing observer noted:

During the last 50 years, marketers designed and honed a blueprint for building brands and selling on a mass-market scale. With Procter & Gamble leading the way, companies developed products with a value proposition: whiter whites, cleaner teeth, good to the last drop! They refined the appeal in test

Consumers
A substantial increase in customer power
A greater variety of available goods and services
A great amount of information about practically anything
A greater ease in interacting and in placing and receiving orders
An ability to chat with strangers and compare notes on products and services

Companies
Can operate a powerful new information and sales channel with augmented geographic
  reach to inform and promote their company and its products
Can collect fuller and richer information about their markets, customers, prospects,
  and competitors
Can facilitate two-way communication with their customers and prospects, and facilitate
  transaction efficiency
Can send ads, coupons, promotion, and information by e-mail to customers and prospects
  who give them permission
Can customize their offerings and services to individual customers
Can improve their purchasing, recruiting, training, and internal and external communication

FIGURE 5-1   The New Capabilities of the New Economy

markets, then rolled out national ads pounding home the value message. In this top-down model, the all-knowing maker defined the brand and sold it via mass outlets with repetitive ads. It's a model fit for the scrap heap. . . .

The back-to-the-future replacement for top-down thinking is the general store of, say, the 1890's. The store owner knew his customers, because they lived nearby. He knew their kids' ages, their food and clothing tastes, what they did in their leisure time. He was, in essence, their personal shopping agent, and the store was both a brand and a trusted friend. Top marketers believe that's the model for future stores and brands—in the physical world and even more so on the Web.[3]

The rapid expansion of the Internet has brought the need for personalized marketing into sharp focus. Many maintain that the new economy celebrates the power of the individual consumer.[4] According to one writer, "the worry for big brand owners is that this [individualism] is leading to a fragmentation of brands as people try to express their individuality by moving away from the mass market."[5]

Personalizing Marketing

To adapt to the increased consumer desire for and competitive forces impelling toward personalization, marketers are embracing concepts such as experiential marketing, one-to-one marketing, and permission marketing.

Experiential Marketing
Experiential marketing promotes a product by not only communicating a product's features and benefits but also connecting it with unique and interesting

Understanding Modern Marketing

Leaders in marketing thought are always challenging marketing conventions in order to create a deeper appreciation and understanding of what marketing should and should not be doing.

In their thought-provoking book *Radical Marketing,* Sam Hill and Glenn Rifkin instruct readers on how to develop and employ "radical marketing" programs.[1] To provide lessons and examples, the authors explore famous brands that were built with the help of unconventional and rule-bending marketing, such as Harley-Davidson, Snap-on Tools, the Grateful Dead, and Harvard Business School. The Grateful Dead, for example, built a grassroots following by embracing and catering to their fan base with a relentless touring schedule of live concerts, encouraging fans to record and share recordings of these live concerts, and developing creative and popular merchandise tie-ins. Today, the incorporated Grateful Dead Productions does annual business of over $100 million, despite the fact that the original band no longer exists. Another radical marketer, Snap-on Tools, did not market its 80-year-old brand until 1994, preferring instead to build lasting bonds with customers through the personal contact its dealers and service centers provide.

According to Hill and Rifkin, the following are the 10 Rules of Radical Marketing:

1. *The CEO must own the marketing function.* CEOs of radical marketers do not delegate the marketing function; they are de facto chief marketing officers.

2. *Make sure the marketing department starts small and stays small and flat.* CEOs cannot stay in touch with marketing if levels of bureaucracy are built between them and the market.

3. *Get out of the head office and face-to-face with the people who matter most—the customers.* Radical marketers gather data and conduct research directly, listening to customers and getting close to them.

4. *Use market research cautiously.* Radical marketers utilize direct consumer research and testing, and only as a supplement to, not a substitute for, understanding their consumers.

5. *Hire only passionate missionaries.* If employees do not believe in their company, they will have difficulty convincingly marketing it.

6. *Love and respect your customers.* Viewing customers as individuals and not statistics is crucial to radical marketers. Every interaction with customers is an opportunity to learn from them about how the brand can be improved.

7. *Create a community of consumers.* Radical marketers create opportunities for their customers to come together, such as events and clubs.

8. *Rethink the marketing mix.* Rather than traditional and expensive advertising, radical marketers often prefer "micro-marketing" such as one-to-one or targeted communication.

9. *Celebrate uncommon sense.* Radical marketers seldom follow formulas and tend to act contrary to traditional wisdom.

10. *Be true to the brand.* Radical marketers never waver from reinforcing the integrity of the brand. Quality must never be sacrificed for the sake of savings or convenience.

In his book *The End of Marketing as We Know It,* Sergio Zyman proclaims, "Marketing is a strategic activity and discipline focused on the endgame of getting more consumers to buy your product more often so that your company makes more money."[2] He criticizes mass marketing practices for ignoring the fact that in today's "consumer democracy" there are simply too many choices. He maintains that marketers will have to place their emphasis on such considerations as sales, conversion rates, targeting customers, and creating value for shareholders. Zyman stresses the importance of thoroughly understanding consumers and developing intelligent positionings with a strong bottom-line focus.

In a similar vein, David Aaker and Erich Joachimsthaler, in their book *Brand Leadership,* maintain that the classic brand management system in marketing is outdated and needs to be replaced by what they call the *brand leadership paradigm.*[3] According to the authors, this paradigm involves moving from tactical to strategic management, from a limited to a broad focus, and from sales to brand identity as a driver of strategy. In terms of strategic management, the brand leadership paradigm emphasizes a strategic and visionary perspective, more senior and stable brand managers, and brand equity as a conceptual model and as a measurement focus. A broad focus entails emphasis on multiple products and markets, and a category focus entails complex brand architectures, a global perspective, and integrated marketing efforts with internal as well as external audiences.

These critics and others raise a number of valid and useful points. At the same time, they can themselves be criticized for sometimes exaggerating their positions, albeit to make a point. Perhaps the biggest criticism, however, that can be levied at some of these works, such as Zyman's treatise, is that they often are attacking an already obsolete and outdated marketing perspective that is no longer really practiced. The reality is that marketers in the new economy are increasingly embracing new approaches and updating old approaches: Those that do not simply do not survive in today's challenging marketing environment.

---

[1]Sam Hill and Glenn Rifkin, *Radical Marketing* (New York: Harper Business, 1999).

[2]Sergio Zyman, *The End of Marketing As We Know It* (New York: HarperCollins, 2000).

[3]David Aaker and Erich Joachimsthaler, *Brand Leadership: The Next Level of the Brand Revolution* (New York: Free Press, 2000).

experiences. One marketing commentator describes experiential marketing by writing, "The idea is not to sell something, but to demonstrate how a brand can enrich a customer's life."[6]

Pine and Gilmore, pioneers on the topic, argue that we are on the threshold of the "Experience Economy," a new economic era in which all businesses must orchestrate memorable events for their customers.[7] They make the following assertions:

➤ If you charge for stuff, then you are in the *commodity business.*
➤ If you charge for tangible things, then you are in the *goods business.*
➤ If you charge for the activities you perform, then you are in the *service business.*
➤ If you charge for the time customers spend with you, then and only then are you in the *experience* business.

Citing examples from a range of companies from Disney to AOL, they maintain that saleable experiences come in four varieties: entertainment, education, aesthetic, and escapist.

Columbia University's Bernd Schmitt describes how experiential marketing differs from traditional marketing in several distinct ways.[8] Experiential marketing

➤ Focuses on customer experience
➤ Focuses on the consumption situation
➤ Views customers as rational and emotional animals
➤ Uses eclectic methods and tools

Schmitt underscores the importance of experiential marketing: "The degree to which a company is able to deliver a desirable customer experience—and to use information technology, brands, and integrated marketing communication and entertainment to do so—will largely determine its success in the global marketplace of the new millennium."

Schmitt details five different types of experiences—sense, feel, think, act, and relate—that are becoming increasingly vital to consumers' perceptions of brands. He also describes how various "experience providers" (such as communications, visual/verbal identity and signage, product presence, co-branding, spatial environments, electronic media, and salespeople) can be used as part of a marketing campaign to create these experiences. In describing the increasingly more demanding consumer, Schmitt writes, "Customers want to be entertained, stimulated, emotionally affected and creatively challenged." Figure 5-2 lists Schmitt's 10 rules for successful experiential marketing.

Large corporations are catching on to the experiential marketing trend.[9] Coca-Cola was one of the first major companies to invest heavily in an experiential marketing program. In the late 1990s, it cut its sports sponsorship budget in half and reinvested in experience-based activities, such as developing a Coca-Cola Experience section at Atlanta's Turner Field baseball stadium. In the section, spectators can drink Coke beverages, mix and mingle, and watch the game from a preferred vantage point. At the 2001 Super Bowl, Budweiser unveiled an improved version of its Bud World traveling road show. Bud World features three experiences: the "World of Budweiser," a tour of the company's 136-year history; the "BudVision" stadium-seating theater that shows a film highlighting aspects of the brand, from hops fields in Idaho to NASCAR races; and the "Bud Brew House," where visitors receive instruction about brewing from authentic Anheuser-Busch brewmasters. Finally, as part of its sponsorship of the U.S. Open tennis tournament, Lincoln developed an interactive Lincoln American Luxury Immersion at the United States Tennis Association's New York headquarters. As a result of the project, Lincoln collected 30,000 leads and saw purchase consideration rise 47 percent.

One-to-One Marketing

Don Peppers and Martha Rogers have popularized the concept of *one-to-one marketing*.[10] In rationalizing their approach, Peppers and Rogers cite a number of trends in the marketing environment, such as a shift from transaction-based marketing to relationship marketing, advances in communication technologies (Internet), and a continued fragmentation of mass media. With this changing environment as a backdrop, the

1. Experiences don't just happen; they need to be planned. In that planning process, be creative; use surprise, intrigue and, at times, provocation. Shake things up.
2. Think about the customer experience first—and then about the functional features and benefits of your brand.
3. Be obsessive about the details of the experience. Traditional satisfaction models are missing the sensory, gut-feel, brain blasting, all-body, all-feeling, all-mind "EJ" experience. (EJ = *Exultate Jubilate*.) Let the customer delight in exultant jubilation!
4. Find the "duck" for your brand. More than five years ago, I stayed for the first time in the Conrad Hotel in Hong Kong. In the bathroom on the rim of the bathtub they had placed a bright yellow rubber duck with a red mouth. I fell in love with the idea (and the duck) immediately. It's the one thing that I always remember when I think about the hotel—and it becomes the starting point of remembering the entire hotel experience. Every company needs to have a duck for its brand. That is, a little element that triggers, frames, summarizes, stylizes the experience.
5. Think consumption situation, not product, e.g., "grooming in the bathroom" not "razor"; "casual meal" not "hot dog"; and "travel" not "transportation." Move along the sociocultural dimension.
6. Strive for "holistic experiences" that dazzle the senses, appeal to the heart, challenge the intellect, are relevant to people's lifestyles and provide relational, i.e., social identity, appeal.
7. Profile and track experiential impact with the "Experiential Grid." Profile different types of experiences (Sense, Feel, Think, Act, and Relate) across experience providers (logos, ads, packaging, advertising, Web sites, etc.)
8. Use methodologies eclectically. Some methods may be quantitative (questionnaire analyses or logit); others qualitative (a day in the life of the customer). Some may be verbal (focus group); others visual (digital camera techniques). Some may be conducted in artificial lab settings; others in pubs or cafes. Anything goes! Be explorative and creative, and worry about reliability, validity and methodological sophistication later.
9. Consider how the experience changes when extending the brand—into new categories, onto the Web, around the globe. Ask yourself how the brand could be leveraged in a new category, in an electronic medium, in a different culture through experiential strategies.
10. Add dynamism and "Dionysianism" to your company and brand. Most organization and brand owners are too timid, too slow, and too bureaucratic. The term "Dionysian" is associated with the ecstatic, the passionate, the creative. Let this spirit breathe in your organization, and watch how things change.

Source: Reprinted from Bernd H. Schmitt, *Experiential Marketing: How to Get Customers to Sense, Feel, Act, and Relate to Your Company and Brands* (New York: Free Press, 1999).

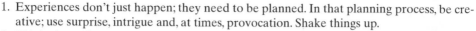

FIGURE 5-2   Guidelines for Experiential Marketing

basic rationale of one-to-one marketing is that consumers help to add value by providing information to marketers; marketers add value, in turn, by taking that information and generating rewarding experiences for consumers. In doing so, the firm is able to create switching costs, reduce transaction costs, and maximize utility for consumers, all helping to build strong, profitable relationships. One-to-one marketing is thus based on several fundamental concepts:

➤ Focus on individual consumers through consumer databases—"We single out consumers."

➤ Respond to consumer dialogue via interactivity—"The consumer talks to us."

➤ Customize products and services—"We make something unique for him or her."

Another tenet of one-to-one marketing is the importance of treating different consumers differently because of their different needs, different value to the firm (current as well as future or lifetime value), and so on. In particular, Peppers and Rogers stress the importance of devoting more marketing effort to the most valuable consumers.

Peppers and Rogers identify several examples of brands that practice one-to-one marketing, such as Avon, Owens-Corning, Amway, and Nike.[11] They note how Ritz-Carlton hotels use databases to store consumer preferences so that if a customer makes a special request in one of its hotels, it is already known when he or she stays in another. For example, if a customer requests "a glass of white wine with an ice cube" from room service while staying at the Ritz in San Francisco, room service at the Ritz in New York City would know to add an ice cube if the customer requested a glass of white wine there too. As another example, MCI's Friends and Family long-distance service allowed customers to create unique, personalized calling circles. The investment in time and energy to do so meant that MCI's customers were less likely to switch on the basis of competitors' offers.

Peppers and Rogers also provide an example of a localized version of one-to-one marketing. After having ordered flowers at a local florist for his or her mother, a customer might then receive a postcard "reminding him that he had sent roses and star lilies last year and that a phone call would put a beautiful arrangement on her doorstop again for her birthday this year." Although such reminders can be helpful, marketers must not assume that customers always want to repeat their behaviors. For example, what if the flowers were a doomed, last-chance attempt to salvage a failing relationship—a reminder under such circumstances may not be so welcome!

Permission Marketing

Permission marketing, the practice of marketing to consumers only after gaining their express permission, is gaining popularity as a tool with which companies can break through the clutter and build customer loyalty. A pioneer on the topic, Seth Godin, estimates that each American receives about 3,000 marketing messages daily.[12] He maintains that marketers can no longer employ "interruption marketing" in terms of mass media campaigns featuring magazines, direct mail, billboards, radio and television commercials and the like, because consumers have come to expect—but not necessarily appreciate—these interruptions. By contrast, Godin asserts, consumers appreciate receiving marketing messages they gave permission for: "The worse the clutter gets, the more profitable your permission marketing efforts become."

Given the large number of marketing communications that bombard consumers every day, Godin argues that if marketers want to attract a consumer's attention, they first need to get his or her permission with some kind of inducement—a free sample, a sales promotion or discount, a contest, and so on. By eliciting consumer cooperation in this manner, marketers can *potentially* develop stronger relationships with consumers so that they will wish to receive further communications in the future. Those relationships will only develop, however, if marketers respect consumers' wishes and if consumers express a willingness to become more involved with the brand.[13]

Permission marketing is capturing marketers' interest because of the powerful technology that now exists on the Internet. With the help of large databases and advanced software, companies can store gigabytes of customer data and process this information in order to send targeted, personalized marketing messages to customers.

Godin identifies five steps to effective permission marketing:

1. Offer the prospect an incentive to volunteer.
2. Offer the interested prospect a curriculum over time, teaching the consumer about the product or service being marketed.
3. Reinforce the incentive to guarantee that the prospect maintains the permission.
4. Offer additional incentives to get more permission from the consumer.
5. Over time, leverage the permission to change consumer behavior toward profits.

Godin also offers four tests of permission marketing (see Figure 5-3). According to Godin, effective permission marketing works because it is "anticipated, personal, and relevant." For example, Columbia House—a classic permission marketer—sends its club members a monthly music selection, something the members anticipate and that is relevant to them. The selection is personal because it represents a category of music that the member has specified as a preference. If the member chooses not to keep the selection, he or she simply returns it.

Permission marketing on the Web is typified by Amazon.com. With customer permission, Amazon uses database software to track its customers' purchase habits and send them personalized marketing messages. Each time a customer purchases something from Amazon.com, he or she receives a follow-up e-mail containing information about other products that might interest him or her based on that purchase. For example, if a customer buys a book, Amazon might send an e-mail containing a list of titles by the same author or of titles also purchased by customers who bought the original title. With just one click, the customer can get more detailed information. Amazon also sends periodic e-mails to customers informing them of new products, special offers, and sales. Each message is tailored to the individual customer based on past purchases and specified preferences.

Permission marketing can be seen as a developing the "consumer dialogue" component of one-to-one marketing in more detail. One drawback to permission market-

---

FIGURE 5-3 Four Tests for Permission Marketing

1. Does every single marketing effort you create encourage a learning relationship with your customers? Does it invite customers to "raise their hands" and start communicating?
2. Do you have a permission database? Do you track the number of people who have given you permission to communicate with them?
3. If consumers gave you permission to talk to them, would you have anything to say? Have you developed a marketing curriculum to teach people about your products?
4. Once people become customers, do you work to deepen your permission to communicate with those people?

Source: Reprinted from Seth Godin, *Permission Marketing: Turning Strangers into Friends, and Friends into Customers* (New York: Simon & Schuster, 1999).

ing, however, is that it presumes that consumers know what they want to some extent. In many cases, consumers have undefined, ambiguous, or conflicting preferences, such that it might be difficult for them to be expressed. Thus, in operationalizing permission marketing, it is important to recognize that consumers may need to be given guidance and assistance in forming and conveying their preferences. In that regard, "participatory marketing" may be a more appropriate term and concept to employ, because marketers and consumers need to work together to find out how the firm can best satisfy consumer goals.

Reconciling the New Marketing Approaches

These various new approaches and others help to reinforce a number of important marketing concepts and techniques. From a branding point of view, they are particularly useful means of thinking how to both elicit positive brand responses and create brand resonance to build customer-based brand equity. One-to-one, permission, and experiential marketing are all potentially effective means of getting consumers more actively involved with a brand. According to the CBBE model, however, the different approaches emphasize different aspects of brand equity. For example, one-to-one and permission marketing can be seen as particularly effective at creating stronger behavioral loyalty and attitudinal attachment. Experiential marketing, on the other hand, would seem to be particularly effective at establishing brand imagery and tapping into a variety of different feelings as well as helping to build brand communities. Despite potentially different areas of emphasis, all three approaches can be seen as a means of building stronger consumer-brand bonds.

One implication of these new marketing approaches is that the traditional "marketing mix" concept and the notion of the "4 Ps" of marketing—product, price, place (or distribution), and promotion (or marketing communications)—in many cases may not fully describe modern marketing programs. There are many activities that do not necessarily fit neatly into one of those designations. Nevertheless, firms still have to make decisions about what exactly they are going to sell, how (and where) they are going to sell it, and at what price. In other words, firms must still devise product, pricing, and distribution strategies as part of their marketing programs. The specifics of how those strategies are set, however, have changed considerably. These topics and some of the newer developments are discussed next, with the topic of communication strategy being addressed in Chapter 6.

PRODUCT STRATEGY

The product itself is at the heart of brand equity because it is the primary influence on what consumers experience with a brand, what they hear about a brand from others, and what the firm can tell customers about the brand in their communications. In other words, at the heart of a great brand is invariably a great product. Designing and delivering a product or service that fully satisfies consumer needs and wants is a prerequisite for successful marketing, regardless of whether the product is a tangible good, service, or organization. To create brand loyalty, consumers' experiences with the product must at least meet, if not actually surpass, their expectations. As Chapter 2 noted, numerous studies have shown that high-quality brands tend to perform better financially, for example, yielding higher returns on investment.[14]

This section considers two topics: how consumers form their opinions of the quality and value of a product, and the importance of taking a broad perspective through relationship marketing in formulating product strategy and offerings.

Perceived Quality and Value

Perceived quality has been defined as customers' perception of the overall quality or superiority of a product or service relative to relevant alternatives and with respect to its intended purpose. Thus, perceived quality is a global assessment based on customer perceptions of what constitutes a quality product and how well the brand rates on those dimensions. Achieving a satisfactory level of perceived quality has become more difficult as continual product improvements over the years have led to heightened consumer expectations regarding the quality of products.[15]

Much research attention has been devoted to understanding how consumers form their opinions about perceived quality. The specific attributes or benefits that become associated with favorable evaluations and perceptions of product quality can vary from category to category. Nevertheless, consistent with the CBBE model from Chapter 2, prior research has identified the following general dimensions of product quality.[16]

➤ *Performance:* Levels at which the primary characteristics of the product operate (e.g., low, medium, high, or very high)
➤ *Features:* Secondary elements of a product that complement the primary characteristics
➤ *Conformance quality:* Degree to which the product meets specifications and is absent of defects
➤ *Reliability:* Consistency of performance over time and from purchase to purchase
➤ *Durability:* Expected economic life of the product
➤ *Serviceability:* Ease of servicing the product
➤ *Style and design:* Appearance or feel of quality

Consumer beliefs along these dimensions often underlie perceptions of the quality of the product that, in turn, can influence attitudes and behavior toward a brand.

Brand Intangibles

As noted in Chapter 2, product quality depends not only on functional product performance but on broader performance considerations as well. For example, product quality may also be affected by factors such as the speed, accuracy, and care of product delivery and installation; the promptness, courtesy, and helpfulness of customer service and training; and the quality of repair service. Branding Brief 5-1 describes how Gateway expanded their brand meaning in part through an emphasis on customer service.

As also pointed out in Chapter 2, brand attitudes may not necessarily be based only on product performance but may also depend on more abstract product imagery, such as the symbolism or personality reflected in the brand. These "augmented" aspects of a product are often crucial to its equity. Finally, as noted in Chapter 3, in

Expanding the Gateway Brand

In the midst of fierce price wars in the PC industry, Gateway announced in early 1999 that it would begin focusing on services in an effort to improve margins. These services included seminars and training, Internet access, Web site hosting, online applications, customer integration, financing, planning and consulting, and customer support and warranty services. In an effort labeled "Beyond the Box," the company began bundling these services along with its PCs. Gateway also created incentives for its sales representatives by offering them higher commissions for selling services than for selling plain PCs. The emphasis on selling services had an immediate effect on profits: Between 1998 and 1999, sales grew 37 percent and net income nearly tripled.

Training became one of Gateway's largest new service areas. For PC buyers, Gateway offers a number of seminars and training courses on the Web, in its Gateway Country stores, and on CD-ROM. For businesses, Gateway offers seminars at its Gateway Country stores, as well as online and CD-ROM training in the areas of office productivity, e-commerce, workplace safety, and managerial skills. Online customers can choose to pay $99 for unlimited access to more than 450 courses on topics such as home and office applications, Web site development, and e-commerce basics. More

FIGURE A   Gateway Brand

complicated course topics, such as IT certification and network administration, are more costly.

Other popular services include Gateway's Custom Integration Service (CIS) for small and large businesses and broadband Internet access, which Gateway provides in partnership with AT&T@Home. CIS provides software and hardware integration, as well as customized products and support. In addition to its Internet access and Web hosting services, Gateway offers domain name registration, custom Web site design, and e-commerce tools.

Beyond-the-box sales grew 150 percent, to $1.8 billion in 2000 from $800 million in 1999. In the words of CEO Ted Waitt, the beyond-the-box strategy "helped shield us from the cyclical downswings that buffeted the industry throughout most of 2000."

Sources: http://www.gateway.com; Elizabeth Corcoran, "Gateway 2005," *Forbes,* 8 March 1999; Katrina Booker, "I Built This Company, I Can Save It," *Fortune,* 30 April 2001; Gary McWilliams, "Waitt List: Gateway Co-Founder Starts Comeback Plan with a Restatement," *Wall Street Journal,* 1 March 2001.

numerous instances consumer evaluations may not correspond to the perceived quality of the product and may be formed by less thoughtful decision making, such as simple heuristics and decision rules (e.g., regarding brand reputation or product characteristics such as color or scent).

Marketers thus must take a broad, holistic approach to building brand equity. Consistent with this observation, the Science of Branding 5-2 describes how McKinsey's 3-D marketing model offers suggestions as to how firms can go beyond mere functional considerations.

Total Quality Management and Return on Quality

Reflecting the importance of product quality, a number of firms have embraced concepts such as *quality function deployment* (QFD) and *total quality management* (TQM) to direct their efforts to maximize the quality of their products. Proponents of TQM adhere to a number of general tenets (see Figure 5-4).[17] TQM principles have provided some useful structure and guidance to marketing managers interested in improving product quality. In practicing TQM, however, some firms have run into implementation problems because they became overly focused—perhaps even obsessed—with processes and *how* they were doing business, losing sight of the needs and wants of customers and *why* they were doing business. In some cases, companies were able to successfully achieve benchmarks against top quality standards—but only by incurring prohibitive increases in costs at the same time. For example, scientific equipment maker Varian totally embraced TQM principles but found itself losing money as it became inwardly focused, rushing to meet production schedules and deadlines that it now feels may not have been that important to its customers to begin with.

In a reaction to this somewhat myopic behavior, some companies now concentrate their efforts on *return on quality* (ROQ). Adherents of ROQ advocate improving quality only on those dimensions that produce tangible customer benefits, lower costs, or increased sales.[18] This bottom-line orientation forces companies to make sure that the quality of the product offerings is in fact the quality consumers actually want, leading to recommendations such as those found in Figure 5-5.

McKinsey's 3-D Marketing

McKinsey Consulting has put forth an approach to marketing that they have dubbed *3-D marketing*. 3-D marketing proposes three product or service benefit dimensions and four factors that contribute to innovative marketing. Specifically, 3-D marketers communicate three types of benefits:

1. *Functional benefits:* Product and performance attributes; value; quality; and so forth
2. *Process benefits:* Ease of access to product information; broad product selection; simplified/assisted decision making; convenient transactions; automatic product replenishment; and so forth
3. *Relationship benefits:* Value based on personalized service; strong emotional relevance; information sharing that creates value exchange; differentiated loyalty rewards; and so forth

McKinsey argues that whereas traditional marketing typically communicates functional benefits, in an increasingly crowded marketplace, marketers must employ experiential marketing tactics and differentiate their products or services by communicating benefits from among the other two dimensions: "By improving the fuller customer experience, companies can keep consumers happier and hold on to them longer."

McKinsey's research revealed that companies with 3-D marketing programs performed better than traditional marketers in terms of shareholder value and profits. One such company, American Airlines, developed a 3-D marketing portfolio beginning in the 1980s. McKinsey cites American Airline's AAdvantage rewards program, the original and now the largest airline loyalty program, as a pioneering relationship benefit. The company has built on this benefit by adding incentives and services to the AAdvantage program, such as car rental discounts, credit card co-branding, and partner alliances. The program also includes process benefits, such as phone service and preferred treatment at airports, as well as functional benefits such as free upgrades. American Airlines has delivered more consistent profits and shareholder returns than its two largest competitors, United and Delta.

McKinsey cautions that a rapidly expanding 3-D portfolio risks eroding brand equity if the added benefits are not connected with the core of the brand. They applaud American Express for weaving a "Golden Thread" through its 3-D portfolio that ensures that each added benefit links back to the essence of the brand. American Express serves three customer segments (basic, gold, and platinum) and within each segment offers a wide variety of benefits from each of the functional, process, and relationship dimensions (e.g., travel insurance, instant card replacement, membership rewards). The company makes certain that its added benefits are always tied together with the Golden Thread—the "Membership Has Its Rewards" concept.

McKinsey recommends making use of advanced technology to build a "backbone" for the 3-D marketing program. Mass customization and customer relationship marketing are identified as two ways to deliver benefits to consumers with the help of technology. Finally, McKinsey advises marketers to invest in the areas of the 3-D portfolio that have the greatest impact and yield the best results financially. This approach will help companies reduce costs and maximize the effectiveness of their 3-D marketing programs.

Source: David Court, Tom French, Tim McGuire, and Michael Partington, "Marketing in Three Dimensions: The New Challenge for Marketers," McKinsey & Company, 1999.

1. Quality must be perceived by customers.
2. Quality must be reflected in every company activity, not just in company products.
3. Quality requires total employee commitment.
4. Quality requires high-quality partners.
5. Quality can always be improved.
6. Quality improvement sometimes requires quantum leaps.
7. Quality does not always cost more.
8. Quality is necessary but may not be sufficient.
9. A quality drive cannot save a poor product.

FIGURE 5-4 TQM Tenets

Value Chain

Consumers often combine quality perceptions with cost perceptions to arrive at an assessment of the value of a product. In considering consumer value perceptions, it is important to realize that costs are not restricted to the actual monetary price but may reflect opportunity costs of time, energy, and any psychological involvement in the decision that consumers might have.[19]

From a firm's perspective, it is therefore necessary to take a broad view of value creation. Harvard's Michael Porter has proposed the *value chain* as a strategic tool for identifying ways to create more customer value.[20] He views firms as a collection of activities that are performed to design, produce, market, deliver, and support products. The value chain identifies five primary value-creating activities (inbound logistics,

FIGURE 5-5 Guidelines for "Return on Quality" Strategies

1. *Start with an effective quality program.* Companies that don't have the basics, such as process and inventory controls and other building blocks, will find a healthy return on quality elusive.
2. *Calculate the cost of current quality initiatives.* Costs of warranties, problem prevention, and monitoring activities all count.
3. *Determine what key factors retain customers—and what drives them away.* Conduct detailed surveys. Forecast market changes, especially quality and new product initiatives of competitors.
4. *Focus on quality efforts most likely to improve customer satisfaction at a reasonable cost.* Figure the link between each dollar spent on quality and its effect on customer retention and market share.
5. *Roll out successful programs after pilot-testing the most promising efforts and cutting the ones that don't have a big impact.* Closely monitor results. Build word of mouth by publicizing success stories.
6. *Improve programs continually.* Measure results against anticipated gains. Beware of the competition's initiative and don't hesitate to revamp programs accordingly. Quality never rests.

Source: Reprinted from David Greising, "Quality: How to Make It Pay," *Business Week,* 8 August 1994, 54–59.

operations, outbound logistics, marketing and sales, and service) and four support activities that occur throughout these primary activities (firm infrastructure, human resources management, technology development, and procurement). According to Porter, firms can achieve competitive advantages by improving performance and reducing costs in any or all of these value-creating activities. He also emphasizes the importance of effectively managing core business processes and cross-functional integration and cooperation.

Porter notes how firms can create competitive advantages by partnering with other members of the value chain (e.g., suppliers as well as distributors) to improve the performance of the customer value-delivery system. For example, Procter & Gamble works closely with retailers such as Wal-Mart to ensure that P&G brands can be quickly and efficiently distributed to stores. P&G created a well-staffed office in Bentonville, Arkansas—site of Wal-Mart's headquarters—to better coordinate these efforts. From a branding perspective, these various activities are potentially a means of creating strong, favorable, and unique brand associations that can serve as sources of brand equity.

Relationship Marketing

Product strategies must therefore transcend the actual product or service to create stronger bonds with consumers and maximize brand resonance. This broader set of activities is sometimes called *relationship marketing*. With relationship marketing, marketers attempt to transcend the simple purchase exchange process with consumers to make more meaningful and richer contacts. Relationship marketing attempts to provide a more holistic, personalized brand experience to create stronger consumer ties. In other words, relationship marketing attempts to expand both the depth and breadth of brand-building marketing programs. The new approaches to marketing reviewed earlier (experiential, permission, and one-to-one marketing) can all be seen as means of creating stronger consumer-brand relationships.

Relationship marketing is based on the premise that current customers are the key to long-term brand success. The importance of customer retention can be seen by some of the benefits it provides:[21]

➤ Acquiring new customers can cost five times more than the costs involved in satisfying and retaining current customers.

➤ The average company loses 10 percent of its customers each year.

➤ A 5 percent reduction in the customer defection rate can increase profits by 25 percent to 85 percent, depending on the industry.

➤ The customer profit rate tends to increase over the life of the retained customer.

A number of topics in this and other chapters can be related to relationship marketing. This section considers three important relationship marketing issues: mass customization, aftermarketing, and loyalty programs.

Mass Customization

The concept behind mass customization, namely, making products to fit the customer's exact specifications, is an old one, but the advent of digital-age technology enables companies to offer customized products on a previously unheard-of scale. Via the Internet, customers can communicate their preferences directly to the manufacturer, who can, by using a sophisticated production line, assemble the product for a price comparable to that of a noncustomized item. Dell Computers is now a classic example of the power of mass customization. Dell's built-to-order computers, sold directly by the company on the Internet or over the phone, helped make it the most successful computer manufacturer of the 1990s. Mass customization is being widely used by fashion marketers.

Levi's

Levi's made measure-to-fit women's jeans under the Personal Pair banner starting in 1994. Recently, Levi's developed the Original Spin program, which uses computers in Levi's store locations to help customers design their own pair of jeans. First, customers enter a booth where a computer leads them through a 3-D Body Scan that creates personalized measurements within seconds. Next, using the Original Spin computer terminals provided in the store, customers choose from a range of cuts, styles, colors, and fabrics that represent hundreds of different pairs of jeans available for purchase. Although they encountered some financial problems, Levi's was expected to continue their customization thrust in the future.

In an age defined by the pervasiveness of mass-market goods, mass customization enables consumers to distinguish themselves with even basic purchases. "Customization addresses the need for individuality," said an analyst with Fallon McElligott advertising. "We seek experiences and products that have our stamp, our seal as part of the look." For example, Nike enables customers to put their own personalized message on a pair of shoes with the NIKEiD program. At the NIKEiD Web site, visitors can make a customized shoe by selecting the size, width, and color scheme and affixing an eight-character personal ID to their creation.

Mass customization can offer supply-side benefits too. Inventory can be reduced, saving warehouse space and the expense of keeping track of everything and of having to discount leftover merchandise.[22] Among the companies offering customized versions of their products are Mattel, which produces the "My Design" Barbie "friends" with customizable clothing, skin color, hair styles, and personalities; Procter & Gamble, which sells customized coffee over the Internet with its Millstone brand; and General Nutrition Center (GNC), which has put machines at a dozen of its Live Well stores that custom-mix daily vitamins, shampoo, and lotions. An Internet company named digiCHOICE offers a selection of thousands of custom products representing hundreds of categories.

Mass customization has its limitations, however, because not every product is easily customized and not every product demands customization. But even makers of expensive and production-intensive goods are looking for ways to employ mass customization. John Deere uses complexity theory to provide customized tractors for commercial farmers.[23] In 1999, Ford CEO Jacques Nasser spoke of making mass customization a priority for the company: "Different customers want different things, and we want to suit their needs." After the company rolled out the Ford Focus, Ford teamed with auto-customizing companies to test possible mass customization opportunities.

Mass customization is not restricted to products: Many service organizations such as banks are developing customer-specific services and trying to improve the personal nature of their service experience (e.g., more service options, more customer-contact personnel, and longer service hours). In support of these types of activities, academic researchers Rust, Moorman, and Dickson provide evidence suggesting that service firms should, on average, allocate *fewer* resources to traditional quality programs, productivity programs, and efficiency programs and allocate *more* resources to service-oriented revenue expansion initiatives such as customer satisfaction programs, customer retention and loyalty programs, customer relationship management (CRM) programs, and customer equity programs.[24]

Mass customization can be especially powerful with Internet sites. For example, Procter & Gamble launched Reflect.com, a customizable beauty product site. The site attracts more than 400,000 visitors a month. As one executive noted, "Personal preferences are being accommodated in a way that hasn't been possible before because consumers have been limited to products made for the masses. It's not a revolutionary concept. It's just that we can do it for every woman, not just the elite customer."[25]

Aftermarketing

As with brand awareness, both purchase *and* consumption issues should be reflected in product strategies to achieve the desired brand image. Much marketing activity is devoted to finding ways to encourage trial and repeat purchases by consumers. Perhaps the strongest and potentially most favorable associations, however, result from actual product experience.

Unfortunately, not enough marketing attention is typically devoted to finding new ways for consumers to truly appreciate the advantages and potential capabilities of products. Perhaps in response to that oversight, one notable trend in marketing is the growing importance of *aftermarketing,* that is, those marketing activities that occur *after* customer purchase. Innovative design, thorough testing, quality production, and effective communication—through mass customization or any other means—are without question the most important considerations in enhancing product consumption experiences that build brand equity. In many cases, however, they may only be necessary and not sufficient conditions for brand success, and other means to enhance consumption experiences may need to be employed as well.

For example, instruction manuals for many products are too often an afterthought, put together by engineers who use overly technical terms and convoluted language.[26] As a result, consumers' initial product experiences may be frustrating or, even worse, unsuccessful. In many cases, even if consumers are able to figure out how to make the product perform its basic functions, many more advanced features—highly desirable and potentially unique to the brand—may not be fully appreciated by consumers. In other words, if a consumer cannot set the clock on his or her VCR, what difference does it make if it has 14-day multiple programmability?

To enhance consumers' consumption experiences, it is important to develop user manuals that clearly and comprehensively describe both what the product potentially can do for consumers and how consumers can realize these product benefits. To achieve these goals, user manuals increasingly may need to utilize multimedia formats (e.g., employing video, CD-ROM, or computer diskettes) to graphically, succinctly, and persuasively portray product functions and benefits. Intuit, makers of the Quicken personal finance management software package, routinely sends their researchers home with first-time buyers to check that their software is easy to install and to identify any sources of problems that might arise.

Aftermarketing, however, involves more than the design and communication of product instructions. As one expert in the area notes, "The term 'aftermarketing' describes a necessary new mind-set that reminds businesses of the importance of building a lasting relationship with customers, to extend their lifetimes. It also points to the crucial need to better balance the allocation of marketing funds between conquest activities (like advertising) and retention activities (like customer communication programs)."[27] Creating stronger ties with consumers can be as simple as creating a well-designed customer service department, easily accessible by a toll-free 800 phone number or via the Web. Examples of seven specific activities to nurture loyalty and build relationships with customers are summarized in Figure 5-6.

Aftermarketing can also involve the sale of related, complementary products that are ingredients, help to make up a system, or in any other way enhance the value of the core product. Printer manufacturers such as Hewlett-Packard derive much of their revenue from high-margin postpurchase items such as ink-jet cartridges, laser toner cartridges, and paper specially designed for PC printers. Analysts estimate that the average owner of a home PC printer spends twice as much on consumables over the lifetime of the machine than on the machine itself.[28]

Loyalty Programs

Loyalty or frequency programs have become one popular means by which marketers can create stronger ties to customers.[29] The purpose of frequency marketing has been defined as "identifying, maintaining, and increasing the yield from a firm's 'best' customers through long-term, interactive, value-added relationships." Firms in all different kinds of industries—most notably in the airlines industry—have established loyalty programs through different mixtures of specialized services, newsletters, premiums, and incentives. Often these loyalty programs involve extensive co-branding arrangements or brand alliances.

American Airlines

In 1981, American Airlines founded the first airline loyalty program, called AAdvantage. This frequent-flier program rewarded the airline's top customers with free trips and

---

FIGURE 5-6 Seven Aftermarketing Activities

1. Establishing and maintaining a customer information file (tracking all current, potential, inactive, and past customers)
2. "Blueprinting" customer contacts (identifying and characterizing points of interaction with customers in search of "moments of truth")
3. Analyzing customer feedback (explore the nature of satisfaction and dissatisfaction)
4. Conducting customer satisfaction surveys (to also signal interest in customer's reactions)
5. Formulating and managing communication programs (sending customers proprietary magazine or newsletters)
6. Hosting special customer events or programs (celebrating relationships with the brand)
7. Identifying and reclaiming lost customers (one of the best sources for new customers)

Source: Reprinted from Terry Vavra, *Aftermarketing: How to Keep Customers for Life through Relationship Marketing* (Chicago: Irwin Professional Publishers, 1995).

upgrades based on mileage flown. By recognizing customers for their patronage and giving them incentives to bring their business to American Airlines, the airline hoped to increase loyalty among its passengers. The program was an instant success, and other airlines quickly followed suit. Today, more than 100 frequent-traveler programs exist, but American Airlines still has the largest, with membership of 43 million. American Airlines averages almost 11,000 new members daily. In 2001, more than 70 million U.S. travelers were enrolled in an airline loyalty program.

Many businesses besides airlines introduced loyalty programs in the intervening years. In 1991, American Express started its Membership Rewards program, which gives cardholders points based on the amount they charge. The points can be redeemed for a variety of items, including airline tickets, jewelry, and electronics. American Express states that customer spending on the card increases an average of 25 percent in the first year of enrollment. Also in 1991, Safeway, the third-largest grocer in the United States, started the Safeway Savings Club. Any shopper could apply for membership in the club, which earned its members discounts on certain marked items in stores. Within a year of its debut, the Safeway Savings Club had 1.2 million members. Starwood Hotels launched an aggressive frequent guest program backed by a $50 million ad campaign in 1999.[30]

Loyalty programs have been adopted by a wide range of industries because they often yield results.[31] As one marketing executive said, "Loyalty programs reduce defection rates and increase retention. You can win more of a customer's purchasing share." The value created by the loyalty program creates switching costs for consumers, reducing price competition among brands. Some tips for building effective loyalty programs follow:[32]

➤ *Know your audience.* Most loyalty marketers employ sophisticated databases and software to determine which customer segment to target with a given program. It is important to target customers whose purchasing behavior can be changed by the program.

➤ *Change is good.* Marketers must constantly update the program to attract new customers and prevent other companies in their category from developing "me-too" programs. "Any loyalty program that stays static will die," said one executive.

➤ *Listen to your best customers.* Suggestions and complaints from top customers must be carefully considered, because they can lead to improvements in the program. Since they typically represent a large percentage of business, top customers must also receive better service and more attention.

➤ *Engage people.* It is important to make customers want to join the program. This includes making the program easy to use and offering immediate rewards when customers sign up. Once they become members, customers must be made to "feel special," for example, by sending them birthday greetings, special offers, or invitations to special events.

Summary

The product is at the heart of brand equity. Products must be designed, manufactured, marketed, sold, delivered, and serviced in a way to create a positive brand image with strong, favorable, and unique brand associations; elicit positive brand responses in terms of favorable judgments and feelings; and foster greater degrees of brand resonance. Product strategy entails choosing both tangible and intangible benefits to be embodied by the product and its surrounding marketing activities that are desired by consumers as well as deliverable by the marketing program. A range of possible associations can become linked to the brand—some functional and performance related and some abstract and imagery related. Perceived quality and perceived value are particularly important brand associations that often drive consumer decisions.

Because of the importance of loyal customers, relationship marketing has become a branding priority. Consequently, consumers' actual product experiences and after-marketing activities have taken on increased importance in building customer-based brand equity. Those marketers who will be most successful at building CBBE will take the necessary steps to make sure they fully understand their customers and how they can deliver superior value before, during, and *after* purchase.

PRICING STRATEGY

Price is the one revenue-generating element of the traditional marketing mix, and price premiums are one of the most important brand equity benefits of creating brand awareness and strong, favorable, and unique brand associations. This section considers the different kinds of price perceptions that consumers might form and different pricing strategies that the firm might adopt to build brand equity.

Consumer Price Perceptions

The pricing policy for the brand can create associations in consumers' minds to the relevant price tier or level for the brand in the category, as well as to its corresponding price volatility or variance (in terms of the frequency or magnitude of discounts, etc.). In other words, the pricing strategy can dictate how consumers categorize the price of the brand (e.g., as low, medium, or high priced) and how firm or flexible consumers see that price (e.g., as frequently or infrequently discounted).

Consumers often rank brands according to price tiers in a category.[33] For example, Figure 5-7 shows the price tiers that resulted from a study of the ice cream market.[34] In that market, as the figure shows, there is also a relationship between price and quality. Within any price tier, as the figure also shows, there is a range of acceptable prices, called *price bands*. The price bands provide managers with some indication of the flexibility and breadth they can adopt in pricing their brands within a particular price tier.

Besides these descriptive "mean and variance" price perceptions, consumers may have price perceptions that have more inherent product meaning. In particular, in many categories, consumers may infer the quality of a product on the basis of its price. As noted earlier, consumers may combine their perceptions of the quality of the product with their perceptions of the price of the product to arrive at an assessment of its perceived value. Consumer associations of perceived value are often an important factor in their decisions. Accordingly, many marketers have adopted *value-based pricing strategies*—attempting to sell the right product at the right price—to better meet consumer wishes, as described in the next section.

Consumers' perceptions of value should obviously exceed the cost to the company of making and selling the product. As Chapter 2 pointed out, consumers are willing to pay a premium for certain brands because of what those brands represent to them. Based on tangible or intangible considerations, consumers place a value on the unique

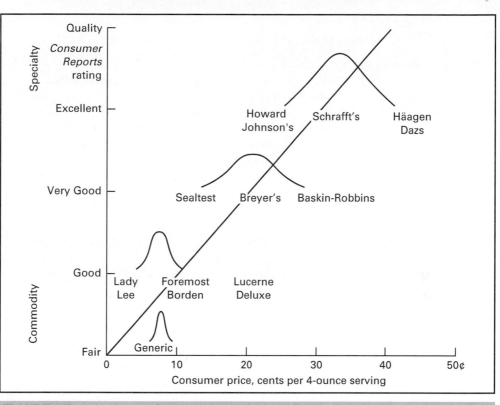

FIGURE 5-7   Price Tiers in the Ice Cream Market

aspects of a brand that justifies a higher price in their minds. For example, at one time, Hitachi and General Electric (GE) jointly owned a factory in England that made identical televisions for the two companies. The only difference was the brand name on the television. Nevertheless, the Hitachi televisions sold for a $75 premium over the GE televisions. Moreover, Hitachi sold twice as many sets as GE despite the higher price.[35] Similarly, industry analysts believe that Mondavi wines command higher prices than wines of similar quality from other producers because of the name and what it means to consumers.[36]

In short, price has complex meaning and can play multiple roles to consumers. The Science of Branding 5-3 provides insight into how consumers perceive and process prices as part of their shopping behavior. From a branding perspective, it is important to understand all price perceptions that consumers have for a brand. As part of this understanding, it is necessary to uncover quality and value inferences and any price premiums that exist.

Setting Prices to Build Brand Equity

Choosing a pricing strategy to build brand equity involves determining the following:

➤   A method or approach for how current prices will be set
➤   A policy or set of guidelines for the depth and duration of promotions and discounts over time

Understanding Consumer Price Perceptions

Many economists assume that consumers are "price takers" and take prices at face value, or as given. However, as Ofir and Winer note, consumers and customers often actively process price information, interpreting prices in terms of their knowledge from prior purchasing experience, formal communications (e.g., advertising), informal communications (e.g., friends or family members), and point-of-purchase or online information. Consumer purchase decisions are based on consumers' perceived prices, however, not the marketer's stated value. Understanding how consumers arrive at their perceptions of prices is thus an important marketing priority

Much prior research has shown that surprisingly few consumers can recall specific prices of products accurately, although they may have fairly good knowledge of the range of prices involved. When examining or considering an observed price, however, consumers often compare it with internal frames of reference (pricing information from memory) or external frames of reference (e.g., a posted "regular retail price"). Internal reference prices occur in many possible types, such as the following:

- "Fair price" (what product should cost)
- Typical price
- Last price
- Upper-bound price (most consumer would pay)
- Lower-bound price (least consumer would pay)
- Competitive prices
- Expected future price
- Usual discounted price

When consumers evoke one or more of these frames of reference, their perceived price can vary from the stated price. Most research on reference prices have found that "unpleasant surprises," such as when the stated price is higher than the perceived price, have a greater impact on purchase likelihood than pleasant surprises.

Consumer perceptions of prices are also affected by alternative pricing strategies. For example, research has shown that a relatively more expensive item can be seen as less expensive by breaking the price down into smaller units (e.g., a $500 annual membership is seen as more expensive than "less than $50 a month"). Research has also shown that one reason why prices often end with the number nine (e.g., $49.99) is that consumers process prices in a left-to-right manner rather than holistically or by rounding. Even the competitive environment has also been shown to affect consumer price judgments: Deep discounts (EDLP) can lead to lower perceived prices over time than frequent, shallow discounts (high-low pricing), even if the averages are the same.

Clearly, consumer perceptions of price are complex and depend on the pricing context involved.

Sources: Chezy Ofir and Russell S. Winer, "Pricing: Economic and Behavioral Models," in *Handbook of Marketing*, eds. Bart Weitz and Robin Wensley (New York, NY: Sage Publications; 2002): 5–86; Peter R. Dickson and Alan G. Sawyer, "The Price Knowledge and Search of Supermarket Shoppers," *Journal of Marketing* (July 1990): 42–53; Gurumurthy Kalyanaram and Russell S. Winer, "Empirical Generalizations from Reference Research," *Marketing Science* (Fall 1995): 161–169; John T. Gourville, "Pennies-a-Day: The Effect of Temporal Reframing on Transaction Evaluation," *Journal of Consumer Research* (March 1998): 395–408; Mark Stiving and Russell S. Winer, "An Empirical Analysis of Price Endings with Scanner Data," *Journal of Consumer Research* (June 1997): 57–68; Joseph W. Alba, Carl F. Mela, Terence A. Shimp, and Joel E. Urbany, "The Effect of Discount Frequency and Depth on Consumer Price Judgments," *Journal of Consumer Research* (September 1999): 99–114.

There are many different approaches to setting prices that depend on a number of considerations. This section highlights a few of the most important issues as they relate to brand equity.[37]

Factors related to the costs of making and selling products and the relative prices of competitive products are important determinants of the optimal pricing strategy. Increasingly, however, firms are placing greater importance on consumer perceptions and preferences in developing their pricing strategy. Many firms now are employing a value-pricing approach to set prices and an everyday-low-pricing approach to determine their discount pricing policy over time. This section describes both approaches in turn.

Value Pricing

The objective of *value pricing* is to uncover the right blend of product quality, product costs, and product prices that fully satisfies the needs and wants of consumers and the profit targets of the firm. As a concept, marketers have employed value pricing in various ways for years. Its increased adoption as a pricing strategy in recent years, however, is a result of an increased level of competition among brands and more-demanding customers. With a more debt-burdened and cost-conscious consumer base, many firms have found it more difficult to raise prices than in previous years.[38] Chapter 2 described consumer defections from Marlboro to lower-priced private label cigarettes as a result of sustained price hikes. Other brands have also met with resistance to higher prices from consumers—often for the first time in their history.

In this challenging new climate, several firms have been successful by adopting a value-pricing strategy. For example, Wal-Mart's slogan "We Sell for Less" describes the pricing strategy that has allowed them to become the world's largest retailer. Southwest Airlines combined low fares with no-frills—but friendly—service to become a powerful force in the airline industry. Taco Bell reduced operating costs enough to lower prices for many of the items on their menu to under $1, sparking an industry-wide trend in fast foods. The success of these and other firms has dramatized the potential benefits of implementing a value-pricing strategy.

As might be expected, there are a number of opinions regarding the keys for success in adopting a value-based pricing approach. In general, an effective value-pricing strategy should strike the proper balance among the following:

➤ Product design and delivery
➤ Product costs
➤ Product prices

In other words, the right kind of product has to be made the right way and sold at the right price. The chapter next considers issues related to each of these three areas. Branding Brief 5-2 describes an eight-step process for making better pricing decisions.

Product Design and Delivery   The first key is the proper design and delivery of the product. Product value can be enhanced through many types of well-conceived and executed marketing programs, such as those covered in this and other chapters of the book. Proponents of value pricing point out that the concept does *not* mean selling

---

Eight Steps to Better Pricing

Robert J. Dolan, a well-known academic pricing expert, describes pricing as "managers' biggest marketing headache." To relieve this headache, Dolan recommends that managers focus on the process of pricing rather than the results. He suggests that managers can make improvements to the pricing process by following these eight steps:

1. *Assess what value your customers place on a product or service.* Rather than basing pricing decisions on product cost, companies should determine the product's value to the customer.

2. *Look for variation in the way customers value the product.* Customers often vary in how and why they use the product, leading different customers to value the product differently. Companies can customize prices to take advantage of these different values.

3. *Assess customers' price sensitivity.* Companies should determine the price elasticity (percent change in quantity sold given a 1 percent change in price) for its products in three areas: customer economics, customer search and usage, and the competitive situation.

4. *Identify an optimal pricing structure.* Rather than a fixed price, companies can decide to offer discounts based on quantity purchased or use bundle pricing to sell a combination of products. The different pricing structures can be analyzed to determine the optimal one.

5. *Consider competitors' reactions.* In order to avoid costly price wars, companies must consider the long-term effects of price decisions in terms of the competition.

6. *Monitor prices realized at the transaction level.* Though a product may have a single list price, it may have many possible final prices due to discounts and rebates. Additionally, the real net revenue from a product is affected by factors such as customer returns and damage claims. The real price of a product must account for these elements.

7. *Assess customers' emotional response.* A customer's emotional response to a price can have long-term effects that outweigh the short-term economic impact of a sale.

8. *Analyze whether the returns are worth the cost to serve.* High cost-to-serve customers do not necessarily pay high prices, just as customers who spend little do not always receive low-cost service. Where possible, companies should aim to get customers to spend in accordance with the cost of serving them.

Source: Robert J. Dolan, "How Do You Know When the Price Is Right?" *Harvard Business Review* (September–October 1995).

---

stripped-down versions of products at lower prices. Consumers are willing to pay premiums when they perceive added value in products and services.

Japanese Automakers

By combining high performance at lower prices, Japanese luxury cars such as Lexus and Infiniti have been able to create strong value perceptions and sales in the United States against their American and European competitors. Auto critics cheered when the 1997 Camry was introduced and reviewed as roomier, smoother, faster, and quieter—and cheaper! In response, Honda held the line on its 1998 Accord, its chief Camry competitor, while also adding more standard equipment, relying on manufacturing and engineering innovations to cut costs. Both models still commanded $2,000 to $3,000 price premiums over comparable American makes.

Branding Brief 5-3 describes how Louis Vuitton Moet Hennessey (LVMH) is able to command luxury prices.

Some companies actually have been able to *increase* prices in some cases by introducing new or improved "value-added" products. In certain categories, marketers have been able to couple product innovations and improvements with higher prices that strike an acceptable balance to at least some market segments. Examples of such additions range from new flavors and bottle designs for iced teas to newly designed toothbrushes with special features such as rippled bristles and handles with tiny shock absorbers to lavishly packaged facial tissues with aroma and lotion.

When Gillette introduced the Mach III, it priced the cartridges at a 50 percent premium over its then-priciest blade, SensorExcel, despite the prevailing deflationary climate. The price increase did not deter customers, and Gillette reached its highest market share, 71 percent, since 1962. Dr Scholl's used biomechanics to develop a new shoe-insert pad as a remedy for leg and back pain. Although twice as expensive as existing inserts, it was the market leader in 1999.[39] Many products have been able to combine product improvements that provide consumers greater convenience with higher prices. Hefty One-Zip sandwich, freezer, and food-storage bags, featuring more convenient "sliding tab" technology, command a 15 percent premium over the older "tongue in groove" technology.[40]

With the advent of the Internet, many critics predicted that the ability of extensive, assisted online consumer searches would result in only low-cost providers surviving. The reality has been that the advantages of creating strong brand differentiation have led to price premiums for brands sold online just as much as when sold offline. For example, although undersold by numerous book and music sellers online, Amazon.com was able to maintain market leadership, eventually forcing low-priced competitors such as Books.com and others out of business.[41]

Product Costs   The second key to a successful value-pricing strategy is to lower costs as much as possible. Meeting cost targets invariably requires additional cost savings through productivity gains, outsourcing, material substitution (less expensive or less wasteful materials), product reformulations, process changes (automation or other factory improvements), and so on.[42] As one marketing executive put it:

> The customer is only going to pay you for what he perceives as real value-added. When you look at your overhead, you've got to ask yourself if the customer is really willing to pay for that. If the answer is no, you've got to figure out how to get rid of it or you're not going to make money.[43]

For example, by investing in efficient manufacturing technology, Sara Lee was able to maintain adequate margins for years on its L'eggs women's hosiery with minimal price increases. The combination of low prices and the strong L'eggs brand image resulted in an almost 50 percent market share.[44] At the same time, cost reductions cannot sacrifice quality.

BRANDING BRIEF 5-3

Selling Luxury at Louis Vuitton Moet Hennessey

Luxury leather goods maker Louis Vuitton was established in Paris in 1855. For more than a century and a half, the company made quality hand-crafted luggage and other leather goods. It remained a small, family-controlled company until the 1970s, when French businessman Henry Racamier married a Vuitton heiress and rapidly expanded and diversified the business. When Racamier took over in 1977, the company had only two shops in France and had combined sales of less than $50 million. By the mid-1980s, the company had 95 stores across the globe and reached revenues topping $500 million.

In 1987, the merger of Louis Vuitton with famed French spirits, champagne, and perfume group Moet-Hennessey marked a new era of consolidation in the luxury-goods industry. The newly formed Louis Vuitton Moet Hennessey (LVMH) instantly became the world's largest luxury-goods company, raking in $4 billion in revenues in 1991. The company continued to grow in the 1990s by acquiring a number of other luxury-goods companies, including fashion label Christian Lacroix and shoe designer Berluti in 1993, TAG Heuer watchmaker in 1999, and the Donna Karan brand in 2000. Today, LVMH has a portfolio of 50 luxury brands and is the number one worldwide seller of champagne, cognac, and fashion and leather goods, and the number three worldwide seller of perfumes and cosmetics. The company's revenues topped $10 billion in 2000.

Here are some of the famous luxury brands LVMH controls:

Champagne, Wine, Cognac, and Brandy
Moet & Chandon
Dom Perignon
Hennessey

Fashion
Berluti
Christian Lacroix
Givenchy
Louis Vuitton
Donna Karan

Fragrances
Christian Dior
Givenchy

Cosmetics
Hard Candy
Fresh
Urban Decay

Watches
Ebel
Tag Heuer

LVMH also owns several business and financial media publications, including *La Tribune* newspaper and two art magazines. The company owns all or part of a number of retail franchises, including the Sephora chain of cosmetic stores, DFS Group duty-free shops, Miami Cruiseline Services duty-free shops, and French department stores Le Bon Marche. Other businesses the company owns include auction houses Phillips, de Pury & Luxembourg, and Etude Tajan; Omas luxury pens; and a development capital business called LV Capital. LVMH maintains an Internet presence (www.lvmh.com), but its Web site is mostly informational. It does, however, feature an e-commerce site called eLuxury, which debuted in June 2000 and in which LVMH is a principal investor. The site strives to maintain an "exclusive" image by prohibiting advertising, providing editorial content on trends, travel, and entertainment, and partnering with more than 60 luxury brands.

LUXURY PRICING, LVMH STYLE

LVMH has consistently pursued a luxury pricing strategy, which means high markups, limited availability, and few if any markdowns. When asked by a reporter whether the Louis Vuitton store in Paris would have a post-Christmas sale, the company's president, Yves Carcelle, answered in the negative, saying "That would devalue the brand." Louis Vuitton sells its products only through a global network of company-owned stores. This keeps margins high and allows the company to maintain control of its products through every step in the channel. Bernard Arnault explained, "If you control your factory, you control your quality; if you control your distribution, you control your image." Today, LVMH maintains a global network of 1,286 stores, a 28 percent increase over 1999. Its 284 Louis Vuitton stores and 461 Sephora locations comprise over half of the stores in this network.

Recently, Louis Vuitton has built several flagship concept stores, located on high-fashion avenues around the world, such as Rodeo Drive and Fifth Avenue. These stores sell an estimated average of $1,800 per square foot. Some of the best-selling stores sell as much as $8,000 per square foot. Because maintaining an upscale image is vital to a luxury brand, LVMH devotes over 10 percent of annual sales to promotion and advertising. The company advertises its brands primarily in fashion and lifestyle publications. Some of the leading brands sponsor major international events with luxury cachet, as Louis Vuitton does by sponsoring the America's Cup. Because image is an essential part of marketing luxury goods, LVMH is careful to evaluate every advertising and promotional opportunity for consistency with the image of its brands. As a result, the company manages a portfolio of luxury brands unparalleled in both size and sales.

Sources: William Echikson, "Luxury Steals Back," *Fortune,* 16 January 1995; http://www.lvmh.com; http://www.eluxury.com; Thomas Kamm, "Latest Fashion," *Wall Street Journal,* 28 December 1987; Lisa Marsh, "LVMH Thinks of Vuitton Globally, Acts on 5 Ave," *New York Post,* 5 December 2000; Joshua Levine, "Liberté, Fraternité—But to Hell with Égalité!" *Forbes,* 2 June 1997.

Delta

Delta Airline's $1.6 billion cost-cutting efforts in 1995 were a disaster, resulting in the airline dropping to last place among the 10 largest carriers in on-time performance and struggling with customer complaints about ticketing delays, dirty planes, and mishandled bags. Morale among Delta employees slipped too. Admitting that they "cut too deeply," Delta took a number of steps to restore its quality of service, such as refurbishing planes and its Crown Room club rooms and hiring additional customer service staff.[45]

Product Prices   The final key to a successful value-pricing strategy is to understand exactly how much value consumers perceive in the brand and thus to what extent they will pay a premium over product costs. A number of techniques are available to estimate these consumer value perceptions (see Chapter 10 for a review). Perhaps the most straightforward approach involves directly asking consumers their perceptions of price and value in different ways.

The price suggested by estimating perceived value can often be used as a starting point in determining actual marketplace prices, adjusting by cost and competitive considerations as necessary. For example, General Motors's Cadillac division has used "target pricing" to arrive at the prices of its luxury cars. GM marketers determined the optimal price based on assumptions about the consumer and then figured out how to make the car at the right cost to ensure the necessary profit.[46] Similarly, to halt a precipitous slide in market share for its flagship 9-Lives brand, the pet products division of H.J. Heinz took a new tack in its pricing strategy. The company found from research that consumers wanted to be able to buy cat food at the price of "four cans for a dollar," despite the fact that its cat food cost between 29 and 35 cents per can. As a result, Heinz reshaped its product packaging and redesigned their manufacturing processes to be able to hit the necessary cost, price, and margin targets. Despite lower prices, profits for the brand doubled. Consumer-driven pricing strategies can thus lead to better marketing solutions.

Transrapid

Engineers designing the new magnetically levitated Transrapid train (which was being developed to run between major cities in Germany at a speed of 300 miles per hour) were planning to have trains departing every 10 minutes. Consumer research, however, revealed that the value to consumers increased significantly when planned departure frequency was cut from every 60 to between every 20 to 30 minutes but was much less when cut to every 10 minutes. Because costs were considerably higher at a 10-minute frequency, the decision was made to run the trains at 20-minute intervals, saving hundreds of millions of dollars.[47]

Summary   From a brand equity perspective, it is important that consumers find the price of the brand appropriate and reasonable given the benefits that they feel they accrue. To achieve the proper balance of perceived value, there is always tension between lowering prices on the one hand and increasing consumer perceptions of product quality on the other hand. Academic researchers Lehmann and Winer believe that although price reductions are more commonly employed to improve perceived value, in reality they are often more expensive than adding value through various brand-building marketing activities.[48] Their argument is that the lost revenue from a lower margin on each item sold is often much greater than the additional cost of value-added activities, primarily because many of these costs are fixed and spread over *all* the units sold, as opposed to the *per unit* reductions that result from lower prices.

At the same time, it should be recognized that different consumers may have different value perceptions and therefore could—and most likely should—receive different prices. Price segmentation involves setting and adjusting prices for appropriate market segments. In part because of wider adoption of the Internet, firms are increasingly employing yield management principles such as those adopted by airlines to price products differently to different market segments according to their different demand and value perceptions.[49]

In short, a successful value-pricing strategy requires skillful decisions in a number of areas. As one commentator noted:

> The delivery of value to the customer is the nexus at which all aspects of commerce converge. It calls for a clear understanding of customer needs, superior product design, intelligent application of technology, relentless focus on quality, cost control, and productivity—and a pugnacious insistence on one—upping the competition. This is the most basic test of business effectiveness. Those who don't pass it may not be with us when the value decade is done.[50]

Everyday Low Pricing

Everyday low pricing (EDLP) has received increased attention as a means of determining the nature of price discounts and promotions over time. EDLP eschews the sawtooth, whiplash pattern of alternating price increases and decreases or discounts in favor of establishing a more consistent set of "everyday" base prices on products. In many cases, these EDLP prices are based on the value-pricing considerations noted previously.

In the early 1990s, Procter & Gamble made a well-publicized conversion to EDLP (see Branding Brief 5-4). By reducing list prices on half of its brands and eliminating many temporary discounts, P&G reported that it saved $175 million in 1991, or 10 percent of its previous year's profits. Advocates of EDLP argue that maintaining consistently low prices on major items every day helps build brand loyalty, fend off private label inroads, and reduce manufacturing and inventory costs.[51]

Even strict adherents of EDLP, however, see the need for some types of price discounts over time. Well-conceived, timely sales promotions can provide important financial incentives to consumers and induce sales. As part of revenue-management systems or yield-management systems, many firms have been using sophisticated models and software to determine the optimal schedule for markdowns and discounts.[52] If that is the case, why do firms seek greater price stability? Manufacturers can be hurt by an overreliance on trade and consumer promotions and the resulting fluctuations in prices for several reasons.

As has been well documented, trade discounts rose considerably in past years in both breadth and depth. For example, the percentage of the total marketing communications expenditures devoted to trade promotions increased dramatically in the last several decades, from one-third to almost one-half of the budget total, and the extent of the average price discount, which previously was only 4 percent, became around 10 percent to 15 percent. Unfortunately, many of these trade promotion dollars are not always passed along as savings to consumers.[53] For example, although trade promotions are only supposed to result in discounts on products for a certain length of time and in a certain geographic region, that is not always the case. With *forward buying,* retailers order more product than they plan to sell during the promotional period so that they can later obtain a bigger margin by selling the remaining goods at the regular price after the promotional period has expired. With *diverting,* retailers pass along or sell the discounted products to retailers outside the designated selling area.

Although these practices may seem to provide some financial benefits to the retailer, critics argue that they can produce a false economy. Often overlooked are

Procter & Gamble Launches Value Pricing

In 1991, Procter & Gamble shifted from a discount- and promotion-driven pricing strategy to an everyday-low-pricing (EDLP) strategy. There were a number of problems with the old pricing system. First, many retailers didn't pass the discounts on to customers. Some retailers engaged in forward buying and diverting tactics-stocking up on huge quantities and selling them after the discount expired or in regions that were not even "on deal." Second, consumers became conditioned to buying brands only when they were discounted or on special. Even worse, consumers were looking to private label substitutes to obtain even lower prices. In order to stimulate sales, the frequency and depth of discounts kept increasing until at one point, 17 percent of all products sold by P&G, on average, were on deal. Escalating discounts and deals with the trade created cost whiplashes, and the company was making 55 daily prices on 80 or so brands, which necessitated reworking every third order.

P&G's solution to these problems was to implement its EDLP value-pricing strategy, although it faced several challenges in making the strategy successful. First, P&G could not deliver everyday low prices without incurring everyday costs. To reduce costs, P&G implemented a number of changes. The company cut overhead according to four simple guidelines: Change the work, do more with less, eliminate work, and reduce costs that cannot be passed on to consumers. P&G simplified the distribution chain to make restocking more efficient through continuous product replenishment. The company also scaled back its product portfolio by eliminating 25 percent of their stock-keeping units.

EDLP reduced list prices by 12 to 24 percent on nearly all of P&G's U.S. brands and drastically reduced the use of coupons and trade promotions, cutting spending on the two by 40 percent. In their place, P&G put greater emphasis on brand-building advertising and marketing communications (totaling $3 billion in 1994). P&G also spent more than ever on research and development (over $1 billion in 1994) and halved the time to market for new products on a global basis. Moreover, P&G also improved its relationships with retailers and was rated in a national survey of retailers as the consumer goods company most helpful in making retailers more efficient.

P&G has come a long way from its previous high-price/high-cost strategy. By 1993, nearly all its brands were value priced. Some retailers, such as Vons, resisted value pricing by threatening to drop some P&G products, but soon came to appreciate the benefits. Market share in some product categories slipped, although P&G's market share in two-thirds of the 40-plus categories in which it competed rose between 1992 and 1993. As P&G encountered difficulties in the late 1990s, however, it altered the value-pricing strategy in some segments and reinstated price promotions.[1]

Sources: Alecia Swasy, "In a Fast-Paced World, Procter & Gamble Sets Its Store in Old Values," *Wall Street Journal,* 21 September 1989, A1; Zachary Schiller, "The Marketing Revolution at Procter & Gamble," *Business Week,* 25 July 1988, 72; Bill Saporito, "Behind the Tumult at P&G," *Fortune,* 7 March 1994, 74–82; Zachary Schiller, "Procter & Gamble Hits Back," *Business Week,* 19 July 1993, 20–22; Zachary Schiller, "Ed Artzt's Elbow Grease Has P&G Shining," *Business Week,* 10 October 1994, 84–86; Zachary Schiller, "Make It Simple," *Business Week,* 9 September 1996, 96–104; "Executive Update: Value Pricing Plan Helps Push Products," *Investor's Business Daily,* 30 August 1995.

[1]For an interesting analysis, see Kusum L. Ailawadi, Donald R. Lehmann, and Scott A. Neslin, "Market Response to a Major Policy Change in the Marketing Mix: Learning from P&G's Value Pricing Strategy," *Journal of Marketing* 65, no. 1 (2001): 71–89.

the extra expenses involved due to additional warehouse facilities, shipping costs, overhead costs, and so forth. In justifying their switch to EDLP, Procter & Gamble argued that only 30 percent of their trade promotion dollars actually reached consumers in the form of lower prices—35 percent was thought to be lost in the form of higher retailer costs, while another 35 percent was thought to be taken as direct profits by the retailers. By reducing both the number of trade discounts as well as their wholesale list prices, P&G attempted to leave retailers in approximately the same net profitability position but to restore the price integrity of their brands in the process. From the manufacturer's perspective, these retailer practices created production complications: Factories had to run overtime because of excess demand during the promotion period but had slack capacity when the promotion period ended, costing manufacturers millions. On top of it all, on the demand side, many marketers felt that the see-saw of high and low prices on products actually trained consumers to wait to buy the brand until it was discounted or on special, thus eroding its perceived value. By creating a brand association to "discount" or "don't pay full price," brand equity was diminished.

Summary

To build brand equity, marketers must determine strategies for setting prices and adjusting them, if at all, over the short and long run. Increasingly, these decisions will reflect consumer perceptions of value. The benefits delivered by the product and its relative advantages with respect to competitive offerings, among other factors, will determine what consumers see as a fair price. Value pricing strikes a balance among product design, product costs, and product prices. Everyday low pricing is a complementary pricing approach to determine the nature of price discounts and promotions over time that maintains consistently low, value-based prices on major items on a day-to-day basis.

CHANNEL STRATEGY

The manner by which a product is sold or distributed can have a profound impact on the resulting equity and ultimate sales success of a brand. *Marketing channels* are defined as "sets of interdependent organizations involved in the process of making a product or service available for use or consumption."[54] Channel strategy involves the design and management of intermediaries such as wholesalers, distributors, brokers, and retailers. This section considers how channel strategy can contribute to brand equity.[55]

Channel Design

A number of possible channel types and arrangements exist. Broadly, they can be classified into direct and indirect channels. *Direct channels* involve selling through personal contacts from the company to prospective customers by mail, phone, electronic means, in-person visits, and so forth. *Indirect channels* involve selling through third-party intermediaries such as agents or broker representatives, wholesalers or distributors, and retailers or dealers.

Much research has considered the pros and cons of selling through various channels. Although the decision ultimately depends on the relative profitability of the different options, some more specific guidelines have been proposed. For example, one study for industrial products suggests that direct channels may be preferable when the following are true:[56]

➤ Product information needs are high.
➤ Product customization is high.
➤ Product quality assurance is important.
➤ Purchase lot size is important.
➤ Logistics are important.

On the other hand, this study suggests that indirect channels may be preferable when

➤ A broad assortment is essential.
➤ Availability is critical.
➤ After-sales service is important.

Exceptions to these generalities exist, especially depending on the market segments involved.

It is rare that a manufacturer will use only a single type of channel. More likely, it will be the case that a hybrid channel design with multiple channel types will be employed.[57]

Avon

Avon, which sold its cosmetics through individual salespeople for 116 years, entered JCPenney department stores beginning in 2001 through in-store shops. These centers carry a new line, called beComing, with six different types of products, including color cosmetics, skin care, fragrance, and aromatherapy. Dubbed "mass-tige" cosmetics, they feature sleek packaging and are priced higher than drugstore brands but lower than department store cosmetics. The in-store beComing shops are built around an "assisted open selling" concept in which customers can browse the racks or seek help from "beauty lifestyle" consultants trained by Avon. In addition to in-store shops, Avon also embarked on a live online selling effort, Avon.com, to complement its direct sales force of 500,000 U.S. sales representatives.[58]

In designing a hybrid channel system, the risk is having too many channels (leading to conflict among channel members or a lack of support) or too few channels (resulting in market opportunities being overlooked). Therefore, in general, the goal is to maximize channel coverage and effectiveness while minimizing channel cost and conflict. Because both direct and indirect channels are often used, it is worthwhile to consider the brand equity implications of the two major channel design types.

Indirect Channels

Although indirect channels can consist of a number of different types of intermediaries, this discussion concentrates on retailers. Retailers tend to have the most visible and direct contact with customers and therefore have the greatest opportunity to affect brand equity. Retailers come in many forms. Consumers may have associations to any one retailer on the basis of a number of factors, such as the retailer's product assortment, pricing and credit policy, and quality of service. Through the products and brands they stock, the means by which they sell, and so on, retailers strive to create their own brand equity by establishing awareness and strong, favorable, and unique associations.

At the same time, retailers can have a profound influence on the equity of the brands they sell, especially in terms of the brand-related services that they can support or help to create. Moreover, the interplay between a store's image and the brand images of the products it sells is an important one. Chapter 7 examines how the brand image of a retailer can be "transferred" to the products it sells. That is, because of the knowledge and associations that consumers have regarding retailers, consumers infer or make certain assumptions about the products they sell, such as "this store only sells good-quality, high-value merchandise, so this particular product must also be good quality and high value." Chapter 15 describes how retailers can build their own brand image and equity. This section considers how the marketing activity of retailers can directly affect the brand equity of the products they sell.

Push and Pull Strategies

Beside indirect means of image transfer, retailers can directly affect the equity of the brands they sell. The actions retailers take in stocking, displaying, and selling products can enhance or detract from brand equity, suggesting that manufacturers must take an active role in helping retailers add value to their brands.

Yet, at the same time, a battle has emerged in recent years between manufacturers and retailers making up their channels of distribution. Because of factors such as greater competition for shelf space among what many retailers feel are increasingly undifferentiated brands, retailers have gained in power and are now in a better position to set the terms of trade with manufacturers. Increased power means that retailers can command more frequent and lucrative trade promotions. Increasingly, supermarket retailers are demanding compensation to stock a new brand in the form of cash payments for the shelf space itself (slotting allowances), introductory deals (e.g., one free with three), postponed billing or extended credit (dating), payment for retailer advertising or promotion in support of the new brand, and so on.[59] Even after stocking brands, retailers can later require generous trade promotions to keep them on the shelf. Outside the supermarket, department stores are requiring that suppliers guarantee their stores' profit margin and insist on cash rebates if the guarantee is not met.[60] For all these reasons, manufacturers are vulnerable to retailers' actions.

Oakley

In April 2001, Italian sunglass maker Luxottica acquired Sunglass Hut International, which was Oakley Incorporated's biggest distributor of its core sunglasses products. Sunglasses accounted for about 75 percent of Oakley's overall sales of $425 million in fiscal year 2000. About one-third of those sunglasses were sold via Sunglass Hut stores. When Luxottica announced after the purchase that it would order about one-sixth of what had been expected—in order to provide preference to its own brands, such as Ray-Ban-Oakley's projected revenues dropped sharply, sending its stock price into a steep plunge.[61]

Retailers have thus increased their power over manufacturers. One way for manufacturers to regain some of their lost power is by creating strong brands through some of the brand-building tactics described in this book, for example, by selling innovative and unique products—properly priced and advertised—that consumers demand. In this way, consumers may ask or even pressure retailers to stock and promote manufacturers' products. By devoting marketing efforts to the end consumer, a manufacturer is said to employ a *pull strategy,* since consumers use their buying power and influence on retailers to "pull" the product through the channel. Alternatively, marketers can devote their selling efforts to the channel members themselves, providing direct incentives for them to stock and sell products to the end consumer. This approach is called a *push strategy,* since the manufacturer is attempting to reach the consumer by "pushing" the product through each step of the distribution chain.

Although certain brands seem to emphasize one strategy more than another (e.g., push strategies are usually associated with more selective distribution, and pull strategies with broader, more intensive distribution), in general, the most successful branding programs often skillfully blend push and pull strategies. For example, when Goodyear Tire & Rubber introduced its Aquatred tire, an all-season radial designed to provide better traction on wet roads, it was priced 10 percent higher than Goodyear's previous top-of-the line mass-market tire. Nevertheless, Goodyear was able to sell 2 million Aquatreds in the first two years of its introduction by combining strong merchandising support to tire dealers and a persuasive advertising campaign directed to consumers.[62]

Channel Support

A number of different services potentially provided by channel members can enhance the value to consumers of purchasing and consuming a brand name product (see Figure 5-8). Although firms are increasingly attempting to provide some of the

FIGURE 5-8   Services Provided by Channel Members

Marketing research	Gathering information necessary for planning and facilitating interactions with customers
Communications	Developing and executing communications about the product and service
Contact	Seeking out and interacting with prospective customers
Matching	Shaping and fitting the product/service to the customer's requirements
Negotiations	Reaching final agreement on price and other terms of trade
Physical distribution	Transporting and storing goods (inventory)
Financing	Providing credit or funds to facilitate the transaction
Risk-taking	Assuming risks associated with getting the product or service from firm to customer
Service	Developing and executing ongoing relationships with customers, including maintenance and repair

Source: Reprinted from Donald Lehmann and Russell Winer, *Product Management* (Burr Ridge, IL: Irwin, 1994).

services themselves through such means as toll-free 800 numbers and Web sites, establishing a "marketing partnership" with retailers may nevertheless be critical to ensure proper channel support and the execution of these various services. Two aspects of such a partnership involve retail segmentation activities and cooperative advertising programs.

Retail Segmentation   A manufacturer can initiate a number of marketing and merchandising programs to assist retailers' selling efforts. One important realization in developing these programs is that retailers have to be treated as if they were "customers" too. Because of their different marketing capabilities and needs, retailers may need to be divided into segments or even treated individually in designing the optimal marketing program so that they will provide the necessary brand support. In other words, different retailers may need to be given different product mixes, special delivery systems, customized promotions, or even their own branded version of the products.

For example, Shugan refers to *branded variants* as branded items that are not directly comparable to other items carrying the same brand name.[63] Branded variants can be found in a diverse set of durable and semi-durable goods categories.[64] Manufacturers create branded variants in many ways, including changes in color, design, flavor, options, style, stain, motif, features, and layout. Branded variants are a means to reduce retail price competition because they make direct price comparisons by consumers difficult. Thus, different retailers may be given different items or models of the same brand to sell. Shugan and his colleagues show that as the manufacturer of a product offers more branded variants, a greater number of retail stores carry the product, and these stores offer higher levels of retail service for these products.[65]

Cooperative Advertising   One relatively neglected means of increasing channel support is through better-designed and implemented cooperative advertising programs. Traditionally, with co-op advertising, a manufacturer pays for a portion of the advertising that a retailer runs to promote the manufacturer's product and its availability in the retailer's place of business. Manufacturers generally share the cost of advertising run by the retailer on a percentage business (usually 50–50), up to a certain limit. To be eligible to receive co-op funds, the retailer usually must follow the manufacturer's stipulations as to the nature of brand exposure in the ad. The total amount of cooperative advertising funds the manufacturer provides to the retailer is usually based on a percentage of dollar purchases made by the retailer from the manufacturer.[66]

The rationale behind cooperative advertising for manufacturers is that it concentrates some of the communication efforts at a local level where they may potentially have more relevance and selling impact with consumers. Unfortunately, the brand image communicated through co-op ads is not as tightly controlled as when the manufacturer runs its own ads, and there is a danger that the emphasis in a co-op ad may be on the store or on a particular sale it is running rather than on the brand. Perhaps even worse, there is also a danger that a co-op ad may communicate a message about the brand that runs counter to its desired image.

Some manufacturers are attempting to gain better control over their cooperative advertising by providing greater assistance to retailers. For example, Goodrich created an image ad for its tires that could be recut to plug various local dealerships at the same time. Rubbermaid has collaborated with big retailers such as Wal-Mart and Home Depot to find ad approaches that achieve the best of both worlds—allowing Rubbermaid to create more awareness and loyalty for its brand while creating sales momentum for the retailer in the same ad.[67]

Increasingly, it would seem desirable to achieve synergy between the manufacturer's own ad campaigns for a brand and its corresponding co-op ad campaigns with retailers. The challenge in designing effective co-op ads will continue to be how to strike a balance between pushing the brand while selling the store at the same time. In that sense, cooperative advertising will have to live up to its name, and manufacturers will have to get involved in the design and execution of retailer's campaigns rather than just handing over money or supplying generic, uninspired ads.

Summary   In eliciting channel support, manufacturers must be creative in how they develop marketing and merchandising programs aimed at the trade or any other channel members. In doing so, it is important to consider how channel activity can encourage trial purchase and communicate or demonstrate product information to build brand awareness and strong, favorable, and unique brand associations and to elicit positive brand responses. Branding Brief 5-5 describes how Nickelodeon skillfully combined push and pull strategies to build brand equity for a popular new cartoon series.

Direct Channels

For some of the reasons noted previously, manufacturers may choose to sell directly to consumers. Chapter 6 describes some general issues surrounding direct marketing in terms of how it fits into the marketing communications mix. This section considers some of the brand equity issues regarding selling through direct channels.

Company-Owned Stores
To gain control over the selling process and build stronger relationships with customers, some manufacturers are introducing their own retail outlets, as well as selling their product directly to customers through various means. These channels can take many forms. The most extensive form involves company-owned stores. Hallmark, Goodyear, and others have sold their own products in their own stores for years. Recently, a number of firms—including some of the biggest marketers around—have set up their own stores:

➤   In December 1994, after the Federal Trade Commission amended a 16-year ban on the jeans maker selling its own wares, Levi Strauss began to open up Original Levi's Stores in the United States and abroad, located mostly in downtown areas and upscale suburban malls. Over 1,000 stores now exist, and a flagship store was opened in San Francisco in 1999.[68]

➤   Nike Town stores stock essentially all of the products Nike sells. Each store consists of a number of individual shops or pavilions that feature shoes, clothes, and equipment for a different sport (e.g., tennis, jogging, biking, or water sports) or different lines within a sport (e.g., there might be three basketball shops and two tennis shops). Each shop develops its

Blending Push and Pull at Brand Launch

Nickelodeon's marquee cartoon, *SpongeBob SquarePants*, is a big hit with kids of all ages (see Figure A). The show stars a rectangular sea-dwelling sponge named SpongeBob who dresses like a human. This simple premise has propelled the cartoon to ratings success and spawned a host of licensed products. *SpongeBob*'s success from a marketing standpoint was a result of both push and pull phenomena.

The push strategy was a key to *SpongeBob*'s early success. Nickelodeon launched the show gradually, starting with a preview after the annual Kids Choice Awards in May 1999. The show was also heavily promoted with spots airing on Nickelodeon. These pushes were followed by various prelaunch pull activities, such as outdoor advertising in key markets. Nickelodeon targeted the college demographic with a Webcast preview of a *SpongeBob* episode that also gave away SpongeBob T-shirts. Ruth Sarlin, vice president of brand marketing at the time, explained, "By the time the show launched, we had our audience pretty keyed into wanting to watch it." Within a year, *SpongeBob* episodes were getting higher ratings than the heavyweight *Pokemon* cartoons on Saturday mornings. By 2001, *SpongeBob* was the second-rated children's show, behind Nickelodeon's *Rugrats*. Each month during that year, more than 28 million viewers tuned in to watch *SpongeBob*. One-third of this audience was over the age of 18.

FIGURE A   SpongeBob SquarePants

Thanks to this success, SpongeBob was the subject of several lucrative licensing and cross-promotional deals. Starting in 2001, SpongeBob and his friend Patrick Starfish were featured in a series of got milk? print and television advertisements. One television ad featured SpongeBob attempting to get a milk mustache but failing to keep one on his face because of his porous nature. Also that year, Burger King and Nickelodeon signed a cross-promotional agreement that put SpongeBob toys in Kids Meals. Additionally, Target Stores licensed SpongeBob for a vast array of merchandise, including school supplies, apparel, and toys. Target supported its new merchandise with television and print ads, as well as promotional activities such as in-store appearances by a SpongeBob costumed character. Target also made SpongeBob the grand marshal of the Target Grand Prix auto race.

Source: Mary Wagner, " 'SpongeBob Square Pants': Ruth Sarlin," *Advertising Age*, 26 June 2000.

own concepts based on lights, music, temperature, and unique multimedia displays. (See Figure 5-9.)

➤ The Disney Store, started in 1987, sells exclusive Disney branded merchandise, ranging from toys and videos to collectibles and clothing, priced from $3 to $3,000. Disney views the stores as an extension of the "Disney experience," referring to customers as "guests" and employees as "cast members." Disney also recently opened its first Walt Disney Gallery to sell only high-end merchandise and plans to attach these boutiques to some of their existing specialty stores.

A number of other brands have created their own stores, such as Bang & Olufsen audio equipment, OshKosh B'Gosh children's wear, Warner Bros. entertainment, and Speedo Authentic Fitness swimwear. Even Dr. Martens—best known for its thick-soled lace-up boots—opened a five-story 13,957-square-foot store in London, trying to transform the brand into a lifestyle brand.

Company stores provide many benefits.[69] Primarily, they are a means to showcase the brand and all of its different product varieties in a manner not easily achieved through normal retail channels. For example, Nike might find its products spread all through department stores and athletic specialty stores. These products may not be displayed in a logical, coordinated fashion, and certain product lines may not even be stocked. By opening its own stores, Nike can effectively put its best foot forward by showing the depth, breadth, and variety of Nike branded products. These types of stores can provide the added benefit of functioning as a test market to gauge consumer response to alternative product designs, presentations, and prices, allowing firms to keep their fingers on the pulse of consumers' shopping habits.

One issue with company stores, of course, is potential conflict with existing retail channels and distributors. In many cases, however, these stores can be seen as a means of bolstering brand image and building brand equity rather than as direct sales devices. For example, Nike views its stores as essentially advertisements and tourist attractions. Nike reports that research studies have confirmed that Nike Town stores enhanced the Nike brand image by presenting the full scope of Nike's sports and fitness lines to customers and "educating them" on the value, quality, and benefits of Nike products. The research also revealed that although only about 25 percent of visitors actually made a

FIGURE 5-9   Nike Town

purchase at a Nike Town store, 40 percent of those who did not buy during their visit eventually purchased Nike products from some other retailer.

These manufacturer-owned stores can also be seen as a means of hedging bets with retailers who continue to push their own labels. With one of its main suppliers, JCPenney, pushing its own Arizona brand of jeans, Levi's can protect its brand franchise to some extent by establishing its own distribution channel. Nevertheless, many retailers and manufacturers are dancing around the turf issue, avoiding head-on clashes in establishing competitive distribution channels. Manufacturers in particular have been careful to stress that their stores are not a competitive threat to their retailers but rather "showcases" that can help sell merchandise for any retailer carrying their brand.[70] Branding Brief 5-6 describes some of Mattel's channel conflict issues.

Other Means

Besides creating their own stores, some marketers—such as Nike, Polo, and Levi Strauss (with Dockers)—are attempting to create their own shops within major department stores. Procter & Gamble has created informational and promotional electronic kiosks for Oil of Olay; and Diageo, seller of Smirnoff vodka and Bell's whiskey, has created in-house drink zones in Sainsbury and Tesco in the United Kingdom. These approaches can offer the desirable dual benefits of appeasing retailers—and perhaps even benefiting from the retailer's brand image—while at the same time allowing the

Managing Channel Conflict at Mattel

In 1999, Mattel moved into the e-commerce sector when it began selling select products from its Fisher-Price infant and preschool toys online. The move raised eyebrows among retailers, who were worried that the e-commerce sales would take away from their business. Retailers grew more displeased when Mattel started selling Barbie toys and apparel on its Barbie.com site in September 2000 (see Figure A). In addition to selling Barbie merchandise on Barbie.com, Mattel mailed its first Barbie catalog to some 4 million households that month. One top toy retail executive said, "We're supposed to be partners and this is obviously competitive." Retailers were particularly upset because the simultaneous unveiling of the e-commerce-enhanced Barbie.com and the launch of the catalog came just before the holiday shopping season.

Mattel insisted its site was designed more as a "self-funding marketing and advertising tool" that built relationships with parents and children than as a device for direct competition. At the time of the Barbie.com launch, Christina DeRosa, vice president of Web site and media content for Mattel's Barbie division, said, "We've been at the fore

FIGURE A Barbie

front of marketing for 40 years, so we have to be at the forefront of this new medium." DeRosa added, "The Internet has become a very compelling part of a girl's life. When that happens to your consumer base you have to think about it." The site was an instant hit: During its first month of operation as an e-commerce portal, Barbie.com attracted 548,000 unique visitors.

Mattel could not afford to alienate retailers, since half of the company's revenue came from only five store chains. To appease retailers, Mattel voluntarily limited the number of products available on Barbie.com and in the catalog. Mattel pointed out that in addition to toys and apparel, the site offered less widely available items, such as Barbie brand bath and body creams, home furnishings, and books, that would not cannibalize retail sales. To drive traffic to stores, Mattel printed information about the nearest retailers according to zip code in each catalog and included a store locator on Barbie.com. Additionally, Mattel did not advertise the e-commerce features of its site. Finally, the company assured retailers that online and catalog sales would account for less than 1 percent of Barbie's overall sales in 2000.

Source: Lisa Bannon, "Selling Barbie Online May Pit Mattel vs. Stores," *Wall Street Journal*, 17 November 2000.

firm to retain control over the design and implementation of the product presentation at the point of purchase.

Finally, another channel option is to sell directly to consumers via phone, mail, or electronic means. Retailers have sold their goods through catalogs for years. Direct selling, a long-time successful strategy for brands such as Mary Kay and Tupperware, is being increasingly used by many mass marketers, especially those that also sell through their own retail stores. Sony introduced *Sony Style* magazine as a means of providing customers detailed information on a full range of its products and also developed a Sony style website and company store. These vehicles not only help to sell products but also contribute to brand equity by increasing consumer awareness of the range of products associated with a brand and increasing consumer understanding of the key benefits of those products. As Chapter 6 describes, although direct marketing efforts can be executed in many ways (such as catalogs, videos, or physical sites), they all represent an opportunity to engage in a dialogue and establish a relationship with consumers.

Web Strategies

One lesson from the dot-com boom and bust is the advantage of having both a physical "bricks and mortars" channel as well as a virtual, online retail channel. The Boston Consulting Group concluded that multichannel retailers were able to acquire customers at half the cost of Internet-only retailers, citing a number of advantages for the multichannel retailers:[71]

➤ They have market clout with suppliers.
➤ They have established distribution and fulfillment systems (e.g., L.L.Bean and Land's End).
➤ They can cross-sell between Web sites and stores (e.g, The Gap and Barnes & Noble).

Many of these same advantages are realized by multichannel product manufacturers. For example, Gateway sells its computers through catalogs and the Web but also through 300 Gateway Country stores.

Charles Schwab

In 1996, Schwab created its Internet trading firm, eSchwab, becoming an online leader. Customers complained, however, that they were dealing with two Schwabs: an online business that emphasized low prices, and a parent company that offered deeper services. Consequently, Schwab integrated eSchwab into its core business and announced a new commission structure. Although approximately two-thirds of Charles Schwab's online customers are recruited through its physical branches, more than half of all transactions are generated online.

Recognizing the power of integrated channels, many Internet-based companies are engaging in "physical world" activities to boost their brand. For example, Yahoo! opened a promotional store in New York's Rockefeller Center, and estyle.com launched a semiannual mail order catalog. Integrated channels allow consumers to shop when and how they want. For example, one research study suggested that nearly 50 percent of the most sophisticated shoppers found items they wanted online but purchased them in stores.[72]

Summary

Channels are the means by which firms distribute their products to consumers. Channel strategy to build brand equity involves designing and managing direct and indirect channels to build brand awareness and improve the strength, favorability, and uniqueness of brand associations. Direct channels can enhance brand equity by allowing consumers to better understand the depth, breadth, and variety of the products associated with the brand as well as any distinguishing characteristics. Indirect channels can influence brand equity through the actions taken and support given to the brand by intermediaries such as retailers and the transfer of any associations that these intermediaries might have to the brand.

Direct and indirect channels offer varying advantages and disadvantages that must be thoughtfully combined to both sell products in the short run as well as maintain and enhance brand equity in the long run. As is often the case with branding, the key is to mix and match channel options so that they collectively realize these goals. Thus, it is important to assess each possible channel option in terms of its direct effect on product sales and brand equity as well as its indirect effect through interactions with other channel options.

In many cases, future winning channel strategies will be those that can develop "integrated shopping experiences" that combine physical stores, Internet, telephone, and catalogs. For example, consider the variety of channels by which Nike sells its shoes, apparel, and equipment products:

➤ *Retail:* Nike products are sold in retail locations such as shoe stores, sporting goods stores, department stores, and clothing stores.

➤ *Branded Nike Town stores:* Nike Town stores, located in prime shopping avenues in metropolitan centers around the globe, offer a complete range of Nike products and serve as showcases for the latest fashions.

➤ *Niketown.com:* Nike's e-commerce site allows consumers to place Internet orders for a range of products.

➤ *Catalog retailers:* Nike's products appear in numerous shoe, sporting goods, and clothing catalogs.

➤ *Outlet stores:* Outlet stores feature discounted Nike merchandise.

➤ *Specialty stores:* Nike equipment from product lines such as Nike Golf and Nike Hockey are often sold through specialty stores such as golf pro shops or hockey equipment suppliers.

➤ *All Conditions Gear (ACG) stand-alone stores:* The first of these stores, which sell Nike's ACG outdoor products, opened in 2000 at the Canyons ski resort in Utah.

Review

This chapter considered new approaches to designing marketing programs as well as issues regarding the development of product, pricing, and distribution strategies to build brand equity.

Relationship marketing involves marketing activities that deepen and broaden how consumers think and act toward the brand. Experiential, one-to-one, and permission marketing are all means of getting consumers more actively involved with the product or service. Mass customization, aftermarketing, and loyalty programs are also ways to help create holistic, personalized buying experiences.

In terms of product design, both tangible and intangible considerations are important. Successful brands often create strong and favorable associations to both functional and symbolic benefits. Although perceived quality is often at the heart of brand equity, it is important to recognize the range of different possible associations that may become linked to the brand.

In terms of pricing strategies, it is important for marketers to fully understand consumer perceptions of value for the brand. Increasingly, firms are adopting value-based pricing strategies to set prices and everyday-low-pricing strategies to guide their discount pricing policy over time. Value-based pricing strategies attempt to properly balance product design and delivery, product costs, and product prices. Everyday-low-pricing strategies attempt to establish a stable set of "everyday" prices and only introduce price discounts very selectively.

In terms of channel strategies, it is important to appropriately match brand and store images to maximize the leverage of secondary associations; integrate push strategies for retailers with pull strategies for consumers; and consider a range of direct and indirect distribution options.

The following chapter considers how to develop integrated marketing communication programs to build brand equity.

Discussion Questions

1. Have you had any experience with a brand that has done a great job with relationship marketing, permission marketing, experiential marketing, or one-to-one marketing? What did the brand do? Why was it effective? Could others learn from that?

2. Think about the products you own. Assess their product design. Critique their aftermarketing efforts. Are you aware of all of the products' capabilities? Identify a product whose benefits you feel you are not fully capitalizing on. How might you suggest improvements?

3. Choose a product category. Profile all the brands in the category in terms of pricing strategies and perceived value. If possible, review the brands' pricing histories. Have these brands set and adjusted prices properly? What would you do differently?
4. Take a trip to a department store. Evaluate the in-store marketing effort. Which categories or brands seem to be receiving the biggest in-store push? What unique in-store merchandising efforts do you see?
5. Take a trip to a supermarket. Observe the extent of private label brands. In which categories do you think private labels might be successful? Why?

B r a n d   F o c u s   5 . 0

Private Label Strategies and Responses

This appendix considers the issue of private labels or store brands. After portraying private label branding strategies, it describes how major manufacturer's brands have responded to their threat.

PRIVATE LABELS

Although different terms and definitions are possible, this book defines *private labels* as products marketed by retailers and other members of the distribution chain. Private labels can be called *store brands* when they actually adopt the name of the store itself in some way (e.g., Safeway Select). Private labels should not be confused with *generics,* whose simple black and white packaging typically provides no information as to who made the product. Private label brands typically cost less to make and sell than the national or manufacturer brands with which they compete. Thus, the appeal to consumers of buying private labels and store brands often is the cost savings involved; the appeal to retailers of selling private labels and store brands is that their gross margin is often 25 percent to 30 percent—nearly twice that of national brands.

The history of private labels is one of many ups and downs. The first private label grocery products in the United States were sold by the Great Atlantic and Pacific Tea Company (later known as A&P), which was founded in 1863. During the first half of the twentieth century, a number of store brands were successfully introduced. Under competitive pressure from the sophisticated mass marketing practices adopted by large packaged-goods companies in the 1950s, pri-

vate labels fell out of favor with consumers. The recession of the 1970s, however, saw the successful introduction of low-cost, basic-quality, and minimally packaged generic products that appealed to bargain-seeking consumers. During the subsequent economic upswing, though, the lack of perceived quality eventually hampered sales of generics, and many consumers returned yet again to national or manufacturer's brands.

Because the appeal of private labels to consumers has traditionally been their lower cost, the sales of private labels generally have been highly correlated with personal disposable income. To better compete in today's marketplace, private label makers have begun improving quality and expanding the variety of their private label offerings to include premium products. In recognition of the power of bold graphics, supermarket retailers have been careful to design attractive, upscale packages for their own premium branded products. Because of these and other actions, private label sales have recently made some major inroads in new markets. This appendix examines how private labels have achieved this growth and studies some particularly successful examples as well as how some major brands have fought back.

PRIVATE LABEL STATUS

In the United States, private label goods have accounted for roughly 20 percent of all units sold in grocery stores and nearly 15 percent of total supermarket dollar volume. In other countries, these percentages are often quite higher. For example, private labels in the United Kingdom make up over a third of sales at grocery stores, in part because the grocery industry is more concentrated there. The five largest grocery chains make up almost two-thirds of sales in the United Kingdom (but only two-fifths of sales in the United States). Two of the large U.K. grocery chains are Tesco and Sainsbury. Tesco has two major labels: Tesco Own and the 50 percent lower priced Tesco Value. Sainsbury's slogan and the basis for its positioning in the United Kingdom is "Good Food Costs Less," which it has capitalized on to introduce a wide range of supermarket food products.

Private label appeal is widespread. In supermarkets, private label sales have always been strong in product categories such as dairy goods, vegetables, and beverages. More recently, private labels have been successful in previously "untouchable" categories such as cigarettes, disposable diapers, and cold remedies. One study indicated that although the 17 percent of households who shop primarily on the basis of price and are classified as "heavy" private label buyers account for 42 percent of total private labels sales, nearly one-third of *all* consumers now regularly buy some private label goods. In fact, users of private labels in bottled water and diapers are even more upscale (with average incomes of $25,000 to $55,000) and older (with average ages in the 30s) than buyers of national brands in those categories.

Nevertheless, some categories have not seen a strong private label presence. Many shoppers, for example, still seem unwilling to trust their hair, complexion, or dental care to store brands. Private labels also have been relatively unsuccessful in categories such as tuna fish, baby food, and beer. One implication that can be drawn from this pattern of product purchases is that consumers are being more selective in what they buy, no longer choosing to buy only national

brands. For less-important products in particular, consumers seem to feel "that top-of-the-line is unnecessary and good is good enough."[73] Categories that are particularly vulnerable to private label advances are those in which there is little perceived quality differences among brands in the eyes of a sizable group of consumers, for example, over-the-counter pain relievers, bottled water, plastic bags, paper towels, dairy products, and soft drinks.

PRIVATE LABEL BRANDING STRATEGY

Although the growth of private labels has been interpreted by some as a sign of the decline of brands, it could easily be argued that the *opposite* conclusion may in fact be more valid: Private label growth could be seen in some ways as a consequence of cleverly designed branding strategies. In terms of building brand equity, the key point of difference for private labels in consumers' eyes has always been "good value," a desirable and transferable association across many product categories. As a result, private labels can be extremely broad, and their name can be applied across many different products.

As with national brands, implementing a value-pricing strategy for private labels requires determining the right price and product offering. For example, one reported rule of thumb is that the typical "no-name" product has to sell for at least 15 percent less than a national brand, on average, to be successful. The challenge for private labels has been to determine the appropriate product offering. Specifically, to achieve the necessary points of parity, or even to create their own points of difference, private labels have been improving quality, and as a result are now aggressively positioning against even national brands. Many supermarket chains have introduced their own premium store brands, such as Safeway Select, Von's Royal Request, and Ralph's Private Selection.

For example, A&P positioned their premium Master Choice brand to fill the void between the mass-market national brands and the upscale specialty brands that they sell. They have used the brand across a wide range of products, such as teas, pastas, sauces, and salad dressings. Sellers of private labels are also adopting more extensive marketing communication programs to spread the word about their brands. For example, A&P produces a glossy Master Choice insert and uses Act Media shopping carts, freezer vision, instant coupon machines, and a television advertising campaign in selling its America's Choice brand. Branding Brief 5-7 describes how Loblaws has been successful at creating its own brands.

Three companies that have successfully established their own private labels to compete with national packaged-goods giants are Paragon, Cott, and Perrigo. Paragon, spun off from Weyerhaeuser, is a half-billion dollar player in the diaper business. It has made significant inroads into Procter & Gamble's sales by combining a high-quality product with competitive prices. Toronto-based Cott has been around for 40-some years, selling its own cola with the slogan "It's Cott to be Good." In the early 1990s, it became a private label supplier of cola for Safeway Select, President's Choice, and Master's Choice. Cott quickly gained 1 percent of this huge $30 billion market. Cott uses syrup supplied by RC Cola in its cola product and employs a top design firm in its packaging.[74] Finally, Perrigo, another private label supplier and producer, has grown to become a major player in the $3 billion private label health and beauty aids business. Perrigo's approach is sell look-alike products, or "knockoffs," at lower prices by not advertising and doing little original research. Instead, Perrigo's chemists simply take apart major brands and then put them back together again with a slight twist in

ingredients, when necessary, to avoid patent infringement.[75]

MAJOR BRAND RESPONSE TO PRIVATE LABELS

Branding Brief 5-6 described Procter & Gamble's value-pricing program, which is one strategy to combat competitive inroads from private labels and other brands. Other major national brands also have been successful at fending off private labels. For example, H.J. Heinz retained more than 50 percent market share in the ketchup category for years. Heinz's ingredients for success include a distinctive, slightly sweet-tasting product; a carefully monitored price gap with competitors; and aggressive packaging, product development, and promotional efforts, as evidenced by their introduction in years past of a squeezable, "no drips" bottle, flavored and colored (Blastin' Green) ketchup, and "hipper" advertising. As suggested by this example, the general approach adopted by Heinz and others to stay a step ahead of private label and other competitors is to emphasize both innovation and relevance throughout their marketing program (see Chapter 13).

To compete with private labels, a number of different tactics have been adopted by marketers of major national or manufacturer brands, as follows (see Figure 5-10). First, marketers of major brands have attempted to decrease costs and reduce price to negate the primary point of difference of private labels and achieve a critical point of parity. In many categories, prices of major brands had crept up to a point at which price premiums over private labels were 30 percent to 50 percent, or even 100 percent. In those categories in which consumers make frequent purchases, the cost savings of "trading down" to a private label brand were therefore quite substantial. For example, before Marlboro dropped its

---

Building Brands at Loblaws

Loblaws is Canada's largest food distributor. Loblaws's business success is attributable to a number of strategic considerations, as follows.

- *Real estate strategy:* In 1985, Loblaws embarked on a five-year, $1.26 billion capital expenditure program designed to upgrade existing units and to add new units. This money was spent to build new combination stores, build and refurbish supermarkets, acquire franchise businesses, and build wholesaling and servicing elements. Loblaws also sought out and willingly paid for prime store locations.

- *Store design strategy:* To more profitably manage their stores, Loblaws divided its 1,200 stores into four formats: no frills (under 20,000 square feet), conventional supermarkets (between 18,000 and 35,000 square feet), superstores (between 60,000 and 80,000 square feet), and combination stores or "SuperCentres" (between 100,000 and 140,000 square feet). Each format was designed and run differently to better meet the needs of its target market segment.

- *Procurement strategy:* Loblaws organized procurement, which contributes 80 percent of the costs of goods sold, through a company it formed called Intersave. Intersave consolidated retail and wholesale; centralized finance, real estate, and procurement activities; and installed state-of-the-art computer systems to gather product movement, profitability, and merchandise information.

- *Branding strategy:* Loblaws decided that a successful house brand or private label was one way to ensure customer loyalty to the chain itself. Loblaws followed many basic branding principles in getting its branding program off the ground, as described next.

In 1978, Loblaws was the first store in Canada to introduce generics, reflecting a carefully crafted strategy to build an image of quality and high value in six areas:

1. Product selection (fancy-grade products)
2. Quality testing
3. Packaging (bright, upbeat colors)
4. Advertising (print, billboard, and TV media)
5. Displays (color-coordinated)
6. Guarantees

By 1983, Loblaws carried over 500 generic products that accounted for 10 percent of store sales. This success was due to innovative marketing, low costs, and a large network of suppliers. Whereas generics were restricted to major product categories that provided volume necessary for the program to be successful, other categories presented different opportunities. In 1984 Loblaws chose to introduce a private label brand, President's Choice, that was designed to offer unique value through exceptional quality and moderate prices. These categories ranged from basic supermarket categories such as chocolate chip cookies, colas, and cereals to more exotic categories such as Devonshire custard from England and gourmet Russian mustard. The chocolate chip cookie had a higher percentage of chips (40

FIGURE A Sample *Insider's Report*

percent) than other brands and used real butter. The cookie's high quality was evidenced by the fact that it was rated as the best in its category by *Consumer Reports*. These products also used distinctive and attractive packaging with modern lettering and colorful labels and names ("decadent" cookies, "ultimate" frozen pizza, "and "too good to be true" peanut butter).

In terms of marketing communications, Loblaws consolidated its budget. Even though its advertising/sales ratio (3 percent) was less than half that of major brands, it was able to put into place a strong promotional program with much in-store merchandising. Loblaws also introduced its *Insider's Report*, a quarterly publication featuring its own store brands and offering consumers shopping tips (see Figure A). By 1989, approximately 2200 No Name brands and 700 President's Choice brands made up 30 percent of Loblaws's total sales while earning an average of 15 percent higher margin than the major brands. Approximately 200 new store brands were being introduced annually, with three-quarters of them being successful (as compared with a 10 percent or so success rate for major brands). Some Loblaws stores carry up to 40 percent private label goods, and President's Choice products can now be found in more than 17 supermarket chains representing 1,700 stores.

Sources: Mary L. Shelman and Ray A. Goldberg, "Loblaw Companies Limited," Case 9–588–039 (Boston: Harvard Business School, 1994); Gordon H. G. McDougall and Douglas Snetsinger, "Loblaws," in *Marketing Challenges*, 3rd ed., eds. Christopher H. Lovelock and Charles B. Weinberg (New York: McGraw-Hill, 1993), 169–185; "President's Choice Continues Brisk Pace," *Frozen Food Age*, March 1998.

Decrease costs
Cut prices
Increase R&D expenditures to improve products and
    identify new product innovations
Increase advertising and promotion budgets
Eliminate stagnant brands and extensions and concen-
    trate efforts on smaller number of brands
Introduce discount "fighter" brands
Supply private label makers
Track store brands' growth and compete market-by-
    market

FIGURE 5-10 Major Brand Response to Private Labels

prices, a smoker who purchased, on average, 10 packs of cigarettes a week could have saved over $500 a year by switching from a premium brand such as Marlboro that cost $2 a pack to a private label brand that only cost $1 a pack.

In instances in which major brands and private labels are on a more equal footing with regard to price, major brands often compete well because of other favorable brand perceptions that consumers might have. For example, when StarKist cut prices on its tuna to only five cents higher than private labels, it was able to slice the private label share in the category in half (from 20 percent to 10 percent) because of the positive image its brand had with consumers. Marketers of major brands have cut prices on older brands to make them more appealing. Procter & Gamble cut prices on a number of old standbys (e.g., Joy dishwashing detergent, Era laundry detergent, Luvs disposable diapers, and Camay beauty soap) by 12 percent to 33 percent, shifting them into the mid-tier level of pricing. Miller Brewing Company dropped prices on its Miller High Life brand by 20 percent, while also reviving the old "Miller Time" advertising theme, increasing sales 20 percent as a result.

It should be noted that one problem faced by marketers of major brands is that it can be difficult to actually lower prices even if they so desire. Supermarkets may not pass along the wholesale price cuts they are given. Moreover, marketers of major brands may not want to alienate retailers by attacking their store brands too forcefully, especially in zero-sum categories in which their brands could be easily replaced. For example, for their Luvs brand of diapers, P&G eliminated jumbo packs, streamlined package designs, simplified printing, and trimmed promotions, increasing retail margins from 3.3 percent to 8.6 percent as a result. Nevertheless, faced with margins on store brand diapers of 8 percent to 12 percent, the Safeway supermarket chain still chose to drop the Luvs brand altogether.

Besides these various pricing moves to achieve points of parity, marketers of major brands have used other tactics to achieve additional points of difference to combat the threat of private labels. They have increased R&D expenditures to improve products and identify new product innovations. They have increased advertising and promotion budgets. They have also tracked store brand growth more closely than in the past and are competing on a market-by-market basis. Marketers of major brands have also adjusted their brand portfolios. They have eliminated stagnant brands and extensions and concentrated their efforts on smaller numbers of brands. They have introduced discount "fighter" brands that are specially designed and promoted to compete with private labels.

One controversial move by some marketers of major brands is to actually supply private label makers. For example, Ralston Purina, Borden, ConAgra, and Heinz have all admitted to supplying products—sometimes lower in quality—to be used for private labels. Other marketers, however, criticize this "if you can't beat 'em, join 'em" strategy, maintaining that these actions, if revealed, may create confusion or even reinforce a perception by consumers that all brands in a category are essentially the same.

FUTURE DEVELOPMENTS

Many marketers feel that the brands most endangered by the rise of private labels are second-tier brands that have not been as successful at establishing a clear identity as market leaders have. For example, in the laundry detergent category, the success of a private label brand such as Wal-Mart's Ultra Clean is more likely to come at the expense of brands such as Oxydol, All, or Fab rather than market leader Tide. Highly priced, poorly differentiated and undersupported brands thus are especially vulnerable to private label competition.

At the same time, retailers will need the quality and image that go along with well-researched, efficiently manufactured, and professionally marketed major brands, if nothing else because of the wishes of consumers. When A&P let store brands soar to 35 percent of their dry grocery sales mix in the 1960s, many shoppers defected. The private label share of their product mix now is 18 percent.

Notes

1. Philip Kotler, *Marketing Management*, 11th ed. (Upper Saddle River, NJ: Prentice-Hall, 2003).
2. Ibid.
3. Greg Farrell, "Marketers Get Personal," *USA Today*, 19 July 1999, B9.
4. Christopher Locke, Rick Levine, Doc Searls, and David Weinberger, *The Cluetrain Manifesto: The End of Business as Usual* (Cambridge, MA: Perseus Press, 2000).
5. Richard Tomkins, "Fallen Icons," *Financial Times,* 1 February 2000.
6. Peter Post, "Beyond Brand—The Power of Experience Branding," *ANA/The Advertiser*, October/November 2000.
7. B. Joseph Pine and James H. Gilmore, *The Experience Economy: Work Is Theatre and Every Business a Stage* (Cambridge, MA: Harvard University Press, 1999).
8. Bernd H. Schmitt, *Experiential Marketing: How to Get Customers to Sense, Feel, Think, Act, and Relate to Your Company and Brands* (New York: Free Press, 1999).
9. Dan Hanover, "Are You Experienced?" *Promo*, 28 February 2001.
10. Don Peppers and Martha Rogers, *The One to One Future: Building Relationships One Customer at a Time* (New York: Doubleday, 1997); Don Peppers and Martha Rogers, *Enterprise One to One: Tools for Competing in the Interactive Age* (New York: Doubleday, 1999); Don Peppers and Martha Rogers, *The One to One Fieldbook: The Complete Toolkit for Implementing a 1 to 1 Marketing Program* (New York: Doubleday, 1999).
11. Don Peppers and Martha Rogers, "Welcome to the 1:1 Future," *Marketing Tools*, 1 April 1994.
12. Seth Godin, *Permission Marketing: Turning Strangers into Friends, and Friends into Customers* (New York: Simon & Schuster, 1999).
13. Susan Fournier, Susan Dobscha, and David Mick, "Preventing the Premature Death of Relationship Marketing," *Harvard Business Review* (January–February 1998): 42–51.
14. David A. Aaker and Robert Jacobson, "The Strategic Role of Product Quality," *Journal of Marketing* (October 1987): 31–44.

15. Stratford Sherman, "How to Prosper in the Value Decade," *Fortune*, 30 November 1992, 91

16. David Garvin, "Product Quality: An Important Strategic Weapon," *Business Horizons* 27 (May–June 1985): 40–43; Philip Kotler, *Marketing Management*, 10th ed. (Upper Saddle River, NJ: Prentice-Hall, 2000).

17. Kotler, *Marketing Management*, 11th ed.

18. David Greising, "Quality: How to Make It Pay," *Business Week*, 8 August 1994, 54–59; Roland T. Rust, Anthony J. Zahorik, and Timothy L. Keiningham, "Return on Quality (ROQ): Making Service Quality Financially Accountable," MSI Report 94–106 (Cambridge, MA: Marketing Science Institute, 1994).

19. Kotler, *Marketing Management*, 11th ed.

20. Michael E. Porter, *Competitive Advantage* (New York: Free Press, 1985).

21. Frederick F. Reichheld, *The Loyalty Effect* (Boston: Harvard Business School Press, 1996), as summarized in Philip Kotler, *Marketing Management*, 11th ed.

22. Chris Woodyard, "Mass Production Gives Way to Mass Customization," *USA Today*, 16 February 1998, 3B.

23. Paul Roberts, "John Deere Runs on Chaos," *Fast Company*, November 1998, 164–173.

24. Roland T. Rust, Christine Moorman, and Peter R. Dickson, "Getting Returns from Service Quality: Is the Conventional Wisdom Wrong?" MSI Report 00–120 (Cambridge, MA: Marketing Science Institute, 2000).

25. Evantheia Schibsted, "What Your Breakfast Reveals about You," *Business 2.0*, 20 March 2001, 80.

26. Lourdes Lee Valeriano, "Loved the Present! Hated the Manual!" *Wall Street Journal*, 15 December 1994, B1.

27. Terry Vavra, *Aftermarketing: How to Keep Customers for Life through Relationship Marketing* (Chicago: Irwin Professional Publishers, 1995).

28. Lee Gomes, "Computer-Printer Price Drop Isn't Starving Makers," *Wall Street Journal*, 16 August 1996.

29. "Loyal, My Brand, to Thee," *Promo*, 1 October 1997; Arthur Middleton Hughes, "How Safeway Built Loyalty—Especially among Second-Tier Customers," *Target Marketing*, 1 March 1999; Laura Bly, "Frequent Fliers Fuel a Global Currency," *USA Today*, 27 April 2001.

30. Christina Binkley, "Hotels Raise the Ante in Business-Travel Game," *Wall Street Journal*, 2 February 1999, B1.

31. James L. Heskett, W. Earl Sasser Jr., and Leonard A. Schlesinger, *The Service Profit Chain* (New York: Simon & Schuster, 1997).

32. Grahame R. Dowling and Mark Uncles, "Do Customer Loyalty Programs Really Work?" *Sloan Management Review* (Summer 1997): 71–82.

33. Robert C. Blattberg and Kenneth Wisniewski, "Price-Induced Patterns of Competition," *Marketing Science* 8 (Fall 1989): 291–309.

34. Elliot B. Ross, "Making Money with Proactive Pricing," *Harvard Business Review* (November–December 1984): 145–155.

35. Norman Berry, "Revitalizing Brands," *Journal of Consumer Marketing* 5, no. 3 (1988): 15–20.

36. Sally Lieberman, "Mondavi Uncorks New Wine, Stock," *San Francisco Examiner*, 2 May 1993, E1.

37. For a more detailed and comprehensive treatment of pricing strategy, see Thomas T. Nagle, *The Strategy and Tactics of Pricing* (Englewood Cliffs, NJ: Prentice-Hall, 1987); and Kent B. Monroe, *Pricing: Making Profitable Decisions*, 2nd ed. (New York: McGraw-Hill, 1990).

38. Yumiko Ono, "Companies Find That Consumers Continue to Resist Price Boosts," *Wall Street Journal*, 8 March 1994, B8.

39. William C. Symonds, " 'Build a Better Mousetrap' Is No Claptrap," *Business Week*, 1 February 1999, 47.

40. Dean Starkman, "Hefty's Plastic Zipper Bag Is Rapping Rivals," *Wall Street Journal*, 2 February 1999, B1.

41. Peter Coy, "The Power of Smart Pricing," *Business Week*, 10 April 2000, 600–164.

42. Allan J. Magrath, "Eight Timeless Truths about Pricing," *Sales & Marketing Management* (October 1989): 78–84.

43. Thomas J. Malott, CEO of Siemens, which makes heavy electrical equipment and

motors, quoted in Stratford Sherman, "How to Prosper in the Value Decade," *Fortune*, 30 November 1992, 90–103.

44. Christopher Power, "Value Marketing," *Business Week*, 11 November 1991, 132–140.

45. Martha Brannigan and Eleena de Lisser, "Cost Cutting at Delta Raises the Stock Price but Lowers the Service," *Wall Street Journal*, 20 June 1996, A1, A8.

46. Christopher Farrell, "Stuck! How Companies Cope When They Can't Raise Prices," *Business Week*, 15 November 1993, 146–150.

47. Hermann Simon and Ulf Munack, "Setting the Right Price, at Internet Speed," *Brandweek*, 21 August 2000, 28–30.

48. Donald Lehmann and Russell Winer, *Product Management* (Burr Ridge, IL: Irwin, 1994).

49. Amy Cortese, "Goodbye to Fixed Pricing?" *Business Week*, 4 May 1998, 71–84.

50. Sherman, "How to Prosper in the Value Decade."

51. Richard Gibson, "Broad Grocery Price Cuts May Not Pay," *Wall Street Journal*, 7 May 1993, B1.

52. Amy Merrick, "Retailers Try to Get Leg Up on Markdowns with New Software," *Wall Street Journal*, 7 August 2001, A1, A6.

53. Zachary Schiller, "Not Everyone Loves a Supermarket Special," *Business Week*, 17 February 1992, 64–66.

54. Kotler, *Marketing Management*, 10th ed.

55. For a more detailed and comprehensive treatment of channel strategy, see Louis W. Stern and Adel I. El-Ansary, *Marketing Channels*, 5th ed. (Upper Saddle River, NJ: Prentice-Hall, 1996).

56. V. Kasturi Rangan, Melvyn A. J. Menezes, and E. P. Maier, "Channel Selection for New Industrial Products: A Framework, Method, and Applications," *Journal of Marketing* 56 (July 1992): 69–82.

57. Rowland T. Moriarty and Ursula Moran, "Managing Hybrid Marketing Systems," *Harvard Business Review* 68 (1990): 146–155.

58. Mercedes Cardona, "Becoming a Store Brand," *Advertising Age*, 10 September 2001, 70; Emily Nelson and Ann Zimmerman, "Avon Goes Store to Store," *Wall Street Journal*, 18 September 2000, B1.

59. William M. Weilbacher, *Brand Marketing* (Lincolnwood, IL: NTC Business Books, 1993), 53.

60. Laura Bird and Wendy Bounds, "Stores' Demands Squeeze Apparel Companies," *Wall Street Journal*, 15 July 1997, B1.

61. Anne Marie Squeo, "Oakley Lowers Financial Forecast after Sunglass Hut Cuts Order," *Wall Street Journal*, 3 August 2001, B3.

62. Farrell, "Stuck!"

63. Steven M. Shugan, "Branded Variants," *Research in Marketing*, AMA Educators' Proceedings, Series no. 55, (Chicago: American Marketing Association, 1989), 33–38.

64. Shugan cites alarm clocks, answering machines, appliances, baby items, binoculars, dishwashers, luggage, mattresses, microwaves, sports equipment, stereos, televisions, tools, and watches as examples.

65. Mark Bergen, Shantanu Dutta, and Steven M. Shugan, "Branded Variants: A Retail Perspective," *Journal of Marketing Research* (February 1995): 9.

66. George E. Belch and Michael A. Belch, *Introduction to Advertising and Promotion* (Chicago: Irwin, 1995).

67. Raju Narisetti, "Joint Marketing with Retailers Spreads," *Wall Street Journal*, 24 October 1996.

68. Bill Richards, "Levi-Strauss Plans to Open 200 Stores in 5 Years, with Ending of FTC Ban," *Wall Street Journal*, 22 December 1994, A2.

69. Mary Kuntz, "These Ads Have Windows and Walls," *Business Week*, 27 February 1995, 74.

70. Elaine Underwood, "Store Brands," *Brandweek*, 9 January 1995, 22–27.

71. "The Real Internet Revolution," *The Economist*, 21 August 1999, 53–54.

72. Don Peppers and Martha Rogers, "The 'Store' Is Everywhere," *Business 2.0*, 6 February 2001, 72.

73. Chip Walker, "What's In a Name," *American Demographics*, February 1991, 54.

74. Patricia Sellers, "Brands: It's Thrive or Die," *Fortune*, 23 August 1993, 52–56.

75. Gabriella Stern, "Cheap Imitation: Perrigo's Knockoffs of Name-Brand Drugs Turn into Big Sellers," *Wall Street Journal*, 15 July 1993, A1, A9.

C H A P T E R

Integrating Marketing Communications to Build Brand Equity

Review
Discussion Questions
Brand Focus 6.0 Weathering a Brand Crisis: The Tylenol Experience
Brand Focus 6.1 Coordinating Media to Build Brand Equity

PREVIEW

The previous chapter described how various marketing activities and product, price, and distribution strategies can contribute to brand equity. This chapter considers the final and perhaps most flexible element of marketing programs. *Marketing communications* are the means by which firms attempt to inform, persuade, and remind consumers—directly or indirectly—about the brands that they sell. In a sense, marketing communications represent the voice of the brand and are a means by which the brand can establish a dialogue and build relationships with consumers. Although advertising is often a central element of a marketing communications program, it is usually not the only element—or even the most important one—for building brand equity. Figure 6-1

FIGURE 6-1 Marketing Communication Options

Media advertising
TV
Radio
Newspaper
Magazines

Direct response advertising
Mail
Telephone
Broadcast media
Print media
Computer-related
Media-related

Online advertising
Web sites
Interactive ads

Place advertising
Billboards and posters
Movies, airlines, and lounges
Product placement
Point of purchase

Point-of-purchase advertising
Shelf talkers
Aisle markers
Shopping cart ads
In-store radio or TV

Trade promotions
Trade deals and buying allowances
Point-of-purchase display allowances
Push money
Contests and dealer incentives
Training programs
Trade shows
Cooperative advertising

Consumer promotions
Samples
Coupons
Premiums
Refunds and rebates
Contests and sweepstakes
Bonus packs
Price-offs

Event marketing and sponsorship
Sports
Arts
Entertainment
Fairs and festivals
Cause-related

Publicity and public relations

Personal selling

displays some of the commonly used marketing communication options for the consumer market.

Although advertising and other communication options can play different roles in the marketing program, one important purpose of all marketing communications is to contribute to brand equity. According to the customer-based brand equity model, marketing communications can contribute to brand equity by creating awareness of the brand; linking strong, favorable, and unique associations to the brand in consumers' memory; eliciting positive brand judgments or feelings; and facilitating a stronger consumer-brand connection and brand resonance. In addition to forming the desired brand knowledge structures, marketing communication programs can provide incentives that elicit the differential response that makes up customer-based brand equity.

Thus, perhaps the simplest—but most useful way—to judge advertising or any other communication option is by its ability to achieve the desired brand knowledge structures and elicit the differential response that makes up brand equity. For example, how well does a proposed ad campaign contribute to awareness or to creating, maintaining, or strengthening certain brand associations? Does a sponsorship cause consumers to have more favorable brand judgments and feelings? To what extent does a promotion encourage consumers to buy more of a product? At what price premium? Along these lines, Figure 6-2 displays a simple three-step model for judging the effectiveness of advertising or any communication option to build brand equity.

The flexibility of marketing communications lies in part with the number of different ways that they can contribute to brand equity. At the same time, brand equity provides the focus for how different marketing communication options should best be designed and implemented. Accordingly, this chapter considers how to optimally develop marketing communication programs to build brand equity. The assumption is that the other elements of the marketing program have been properly put into place. Thus, the optimal brand positioning has been defined—especially in terms of the desired target market—and product, pricing, and distribution and other marketing program decisions have been made.

To help address the complexity of designing marketing communication programs, the chapter begins by reviewing a simple information processing model of communica-

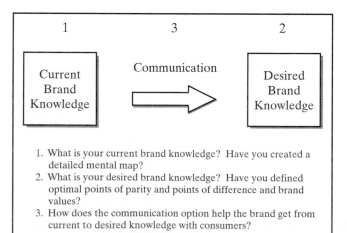

1. What is your current brand knowledge? Have you created a detailed mental map?
2. What is your desired brand knowledge? Have you defined optimal points of parity and points of difference and brand values?
3. How does the communication option help the brand get from current to desired knowledge with consumers?

FIGURE 6-2 Simple Test For Marketing Communication Effectiveness

tions. To provide necessary background, it next evaluates the major communication options in terms of their role in contributing to brand equity and some of their main costs and benefits. The chapter concludes by considering how to mix and match communication options—that is, how to employ a range of communication options in a coordinated or integrated fashion—to build brand equity. For the sake of brevity, this chapter will not consider a number of specific but important marketing communication issues such as media scheduling, budget estimation techniques, and research approaches.[1] Brand Focus 6.0 considers some marketing communication issues for handling a marketing crisis.

INFORMATION PROCESSING MODEL OF COMMUNICATIONS

A number of different models have been put forth over the years to explain communications and the steps involved in the persuasion process—recall the discussion on the hierarchy of effects model from Brand Focus 2.0. For example, William McGuire, an influential social psychologist from Yale, maintains that for a person to be persuaded by any form of communication (a TV advertisement, newspaper editorial, classroom lecture, etc.), the following six steps must occur[2]:

1. *Exposure:* A person must see or hear the communication.
2. *Attention:* A person must notice the communication.
3. *Comprehension:* A person must understand the intended message or arguments of the communication.
4. *Yielding:* A person must respond favorably to the intended message or arguments of the communication.
5. *Intentions:* A person must plan to act in the desired manner of the communication.
6. *Behavior:* A person must actually act in the desired manner of the communication.

The difficulty of creating a successful marketing communication program can be seen by recognizing that each of the six steps must occur for a consumer to be persuaded. If there is a breakdown or failure in any step along the way, then successful communication will not result.

For example, consider the potential pitfalls in launching a new advertising campaign:

1. A consumer may not be exposed to an ad because the media plan missed the mark.
2. A consumer may not notice an ad because of a boring and uninspired creative strategy.
3. A consumer may not understand an ad because of a lack of product category knowledge or technical sophistication or because of a lack of awareness and familiarity about the brand itself.
4. A consumer may fail to respond favorably and form a positive attitude because of irrelevant or unconvincing product claims.
5. A consumer may fail to form a purchase intention because of a lack of an immediate perceived need.
6. A consumer may fail to actually buy the product because of a failure to remember anything from the ad when confronted with the available brands in the store.

To show how fragile the whole communication process is, assume that the probability of *each* of the six steps being successfully accomplished is 50 percent—most likely an extremely generous assumption. The laws of probability suggest that the probability of *all* six steps successfully occurring, assuming they are independent events, would be $0.5 \times 0.5 \times 0.5 \times 0.5 \times 0.5 \times 0.5$, which equals 1.5625 percent. If the probability of each step occurring, on average, was a perhaps more reasonable 10 percent, then the joint probability of all six events occurring would be .0001. In other words, only 1 in 10,000! No wonder advertisers sometimes lament the limited power of advertising.

One implication of the information processing model is that to increase the odds for a successful marketing communications campaign, marketers must attempt to increase the likelihood that *each* step occurs. For example, from an advertising standpoint, the ideal ad campaign would ensure that

1. The right consumer is exposed to the right message at the right place and at the right time.
2. The creative strategy for the advertising causes the consumer to notice and attend to the ad but does not distract from the intended message.
3. The ad properly reflects the consumer's level of understanding about the product and the brand.
4. The ad correctly positions the brand in terms of desirable and deliverable points of difference and points of parity.
5. The ad motivates consumers to consider purchase of the brand.
6. The ad creates strong brand associations to all of these stored communication effects so that they can have an effect when consumers are considering making a purchase.

Clearly, marketing communication programs must be designed and executed carefully if they are to have the desired effects on consumers. The following section presents an overview and critique of the major marketing communication options: broadcast, print, direct response, online, and place advertising media; consumer and trade promotions; event marketing and sponsorship; publicity and public relations; and personal selling.

OVERVIEW OF MARKETING COMMUNICATION OPTIONS

Advertising

Advertising can be defined as any paid form of nonpersonal presentation and promotion of ideas, goods, or services by an identified sponsor. Advertising plays an important and often controversial role in contributing to brand equity. Although advertising is recognized as a powerful means of creating strong, favorable, and unique brand associations and eliciting positive judgments and feelings, it is controversial because the specific effects of advertising are often difficult to quantify and predict. Nevertheless, a number of studies using very different approaches have shown the power of advertising to affect brand sales.

For example, the American Association of Advertising Agencies has compiled a list of some of the studies demonstrating the productivity of advertising expenditures. Analyses of advertising effects using the PIMS (Profit Impact of Marketing Strategy) database of 750 consumer businesses in a variety of industries showed that firms which increased advertising during a recessionary period gained one-half to a full market share point coming out of a recession, whereas those firms who cut their advertising budget only gained two-tenths of a share point.[3]

Other comprehensive studies also document the power of advertising. For example, an analysis of the effects of advertising on sales using Nielsen's single-source database of 142 packaged-goods brands from 1991 to 1992 revealed that around half of the time, advertising worked. Specifically, 70 percent of the ad campaigns in the sample boosted sales immediately, although the effect was only strong in 30 percent of the cases. Forty-six percent of campaigns appeared to yield a long-term sales boost. Additional analyses revealed other interesting study findings:[4]

➤ Increased sales could come from a single advertisement.

➤ "Blitz campaigns" with concentrated exposure schedules could suffer from diminished returns, such that ads shown less frequently over a longer period of time were more effective.

➤ Advertising was more likely to increase both sales and profits than "money-off" sales promotions, which almost always lost money.

Another comprehensive study of advertising effectiveness conducted by a major research supplier, Information Resources Inc., using a different database reinforces these findings and provides several additional observations as to how advertising, as well as promotion, works (see The Science of Branding 6-1).[5]

Besides these broad-based empirical studies, numerous case studies point to the power of advertising, even during difficult economic times. For example, during the summer of 2001, Home Depot found their sales surging 16 percent in the face of a sluggish economy when they invested in a heavy product push with advertising featuring paint, appliances, and energy-savers such as thermostats.[6] Coca-Cola, Red Lobster, Heinz, and Gillette also chose to step up their ad spending during this time and similarly experienced sales increases. These experiences echoed those of other brands from prior times who chose to invest in advertising during an economic recession or downturn. For example, during the 1989–1991 recession, brands such as Jif peanut butter, Bud Light beer, and L'Oreal all increased advertising expenditures and thus their market share as a result.

Given the complexity of designing advertising—the number of strategic roles it might play, the sheer number of specific decisions involved, and its complicated effect on consumers—a comprehensive set of detailed managerial guidelines is difficult to provide. Different advertising media clearly have different strengths, however, and therefore are best suited to play certain roles in a communication program. Figure 6-3 provides a breakdown of national advertising spending by major advertising media, and Figure 6-4 summarizes the advantages and disadvantages of the main advertising media. This section highlights some key issues about each type of advertising medium in turn.

Television

Television is generally acknowledged as the most powerful advertising medium because it allows for sight, sound, and motion and reaches a broad spectrum of consumers. Virtually all American households have televisions, and the amount of time that television sets are on each day, on average, is a staggering seven hours. The wide reach of TV advertising translates to low cost per exposure. From a brand equity perspective, TV advertising has two particularly important strengths. First, TV advertising can be an effective means of vividly demonstrating product attributes and persuasively explaining their corresponding consumer benefits. Second, TV advertising can be a

Understanding the Effects of Advertising

Information Resources Inc. (IRI) provides a unique, in-depth examination into how advertising works. IRI uses a single-source testing service called BehaviorScan. Single-source research suppliers track behavior of individual households from TV sets to checkout counters in supermarkets in test markets across the United States. Consumers in test markets who sign up to be members of IRI's "Shoppers Hotline" panel agree to have microcomputers record when the TV set is on and to which station it is tuned and to have electronic scanners record UPC codes of their household purchases at supermarkets. IRI has the capability to send different commercials to different preselected homes to test the effects of advertising copy and weights. BehaviorScan can also test the effects of store feature, displays, coupons, and so forth.

In 1989, IRI reviewed the results of 389 research studies conducted over the previous seven years and offered the following general principles concerning advertising and promotion effectiveness:

- *TV advertising weight alone is not enough.* Only roughly half of heavy TV advertising plans have a measurable effect on sales, although when they do have an effect it is often large. The success rate is higher for new products or line extensions than for established brands.

- *TV advertising is more likely to work when there are changes in copy or media strategy.* Examples are a new copy strategy or an expanded target market.

- *When advertising is successful in increasing sales, its impact lasts beyond the period of peak spending.* Recent evidence shows that the long-term positive effects of advertising last up to two years after peak spending. Moreover, the long-term incremental sales generated are approximately double the incremental sales observed in the first year of an advertising spending increase.

- *About 20 percent of advertising plans pay out in the short term.* However, when the long-term effect of advertising is considered, it is likely that most advertising plans that show a significant effect in a split cable experiment would pay out.

- *Promotions almost always have a measurable impact on sales. However, the effect is usually purely short term.*

- *Payout statistics on promotions are dismal.* Roughly 16 percent of trade promotions are profitable. Furthermore, promotions' effects are often purely short term, except for new products.

- *These statistics on advertising and promotion payouts show that many brands are overspending on marketing support.* Many classes of spending can be reduced at an increase in profits.

- *Allocating marketing funds involves a continuous search for marketing programs that offer the highest return on the marketing dollar.* Tradeoffs between advertising, trade promotions, and consumer promotions can be highly profitable when based on reliable evaluation systems that measure this productivity at any point in time.

- *The current trend toward promotion spending is not sound from a marketing productivity standpoint.* When the strategic disadvantages of promotions are included (that is, losing control to the trade and training consumers to buy only on deal), then the case is compelling for a reevaluation of current practices and the incentive systems responsible for this trend.

Leonard M. Lodish, Magid Abraham, Stuart Kalmenson, Jeanne Livelsberger, Beth Lubetkin, Bruce Richardson, and Mary Ellen Stevens, "How T.V. Advertising Works: A Meta Analysis of 389 Real World Split Cable T.V. Advertising Experiments," *Journal of Marketing Research* (May 1995): 125–239; Magid Abraham and Leonard Lodish, "Advertising Works," *Information Resources, Inc.* (1989).

	Expenditures (billions of $)	**Percentage of Total**
TV	52.7	22
Radio	19.4	8
Newspaper	49.4	21
Magazines	12.3	5
Yellow Pages	13.3	6
Internet	3.4	1
Direct response	44.7	19
Other	40.0	17
Total	141.7	

Source: Tom Duncan, *IMC: Using Advertising and Promotion to Build Brands* (Boston: McGraw-Hill, 2002).

FIGURE 6-3 U.S. Marketing Communication Expenditures, 2001

compelling means for dramatically portraying non-product-related user and usage imagery, brand personality, and so on.

Sprite

A struggling brand, Sprite was relaunched in 1994 as a mainstream brand with a clever ad campaign that proclaimed, "Image Is Nothing. Thirst Is Everything. Obey Your Thirst." Ads featuring hip-hoppers and rappers targeted urban markets and young males. Sprite is now the leader of the lemon-lime soft drink market segment and the number six soft drink brand overall; the company credits its straightforward, honest advertising message with connecting with teens.[7]

On the other hand, television advertising has its drawbacks. Because of the fleeting nature of the message and the potentially distracting creative elements often found in a TV ad, product-related messages and the brand itself can be overlooked by consumers while viewing a TV ad. Moreover, the large number of ads and nonprogramming material on television creates clutter that makes it easy for consumers to ignore or forget ads. Another important disadvantage of TV ads is the high cost of production and placement. Even though the price of TV advertising has skyrocketed, the share of the prime time audience for the major networks has steadily declined. By any number of measures, the effectiveness of any one ad, on average, has diminished. For example, Video Storyboards reported that the number of viewers who reported that they paid attention to TV ads dropped significantly in the last decade.

Nevertheless, properly designed and executed TV ads can affects sales and profits. For example, over the years, one of the most consistently successful TV advertisers has been Apple. Their "1984" ad for the introduction of their Macintosh personal computer—portraying a stark Orwellian future with a feature film look—only ran once on TV but is one of the best-known ads ever. In the years that followed, Apple advertising successfully created awareness and image for a series of products, most recently with their acclaimed "Think Different" campaign. Branding Brief 6-1 describes how Skechers used advertising and clever marketing in getting its brand off the ground. Each year, the American Marketing Association awards "Effies" to those

Medium	Advantages	Disadvantages
Television	Mass coverage	Low selectivity
	High reach	Short message life
	Impact of sight, sound, and motion	High absolute cost
	High prestige	High production costs
	Low cost per exposure	Clutter
	Attention getting	
	Favorable image	
Radio	Local coverage	Audio only
	Low cost	Clutter
	High frequency	Low attention-getting capabilities
	Flexible	Fleeting message
	Low production costs	
	Well-segmented audiences	
Magazines	Segmentation potential	Long lead time for ad placement
	Quality reproduction	Visual only
	High information content	Lack of flexibility
	Longevity	
	Multiple readers	
Newspapers	High coverage	Short life
	Low cost	Clutter
	Short lead time for placing ads	Low attention-getting capabilities
	Ads can be placed in interest sections	Poor reproduction quality
	Timely (current ads)	Selective reader exposure
	Reader controls exposure	
	Can be used for coupons	
Direct response	High selectivity	High cost per contact
	Reader controls exposure	Poor image (junk mail)
	High information content	Clutter
	Opportunities for repeat exposures	
Interactive	Customized and personalized	Nonobtrusive
	In-depth information	Often lacks emotionality
	Can be engaging	
Outdoor	Location specific	Short exposure time requires short ad
	High repetition	Poor image
	Easily noticed	Local restrictions

Source: Reprinted from George E. Belch and Michael A. Belch, *Introduction to Advertising and Promotion*, 3rd ed. (Homewood, IL: Irwin, 1995).

FIGURE 6-4   Advertising Media Characteristics

Skechers

Robert Greenberg presided over the rise of one of the hottest shoe brands of the 1980s, L.A. Gear. After its sales grew to more than $900 million and it became the number three sneaker brand in 1990, L.A. Gear quickly lost its appeal and dropped out of sight. In 1992, Greenberg and his son Michael set out to create a new shoe brand, which they called Skechers after street slang for a person who cannot sit still. As with L.A. Gear, Greenberg based the brand on inexpensive copycat versions of popular shoe styles. Skechers originated as a line of utility boots imported from the Asian company that supplied Wolverine and Caterpillar footwear. Sales were tepid, and in 1996 Skechers introduced a line of women's sneakers. The women's shoes were a big hit, and sales reached $115 million by 1997.

As Skechers grew, it ramped up its copycat design strategy. When the latest fashions hit New York, Milan, and Paris, designers at the company would develop "approximate" styles that hit stores within three months. Skechers rolled out hundreds of different sneaker, sandal, and loafer designs each year, many priced as low as $50. When a certain model became a hit, the company would produce many different styles to capitalize on the trend. For example, the popular Energy sole comes in over 100 upper styles and colors. All told, the company has about 1,000 shoe styles in production.

The company takes great pains to create a hip, Generation Y-oriented image for the brand. Robert Greenberg describes Skechers as "a marketing company that happens to be in the shoe business" and readily admits that "I could not be Skechers without advertising." The company commits 10 percent of revenues to advertising, well above the percentages for many of its competitors. Skechers does not attempt to compete with performance shoes from Nike, Reebok, and Adidas. Instead, the company's advertising positions Skechers as a lifestyle brand. The ads feature young people hanging out in casual settings, not exercising or playing. Though the company uses Britney Spears to endorse the brand in Europe, the company employs celebrity endorsements domestically only for the Skechers Collection line of men's casual dress shoes. Michael Greenberg explained, "We [don't] want to paint the brand as too bubblegum."

In 2000, Skechers launched its biggest advertising effort in its history, a national TV campaign that the company estimated would reach more than 80 percent of the U.S. population. That same year, the company added 120 in-store shops at various retailers, which augment the dozens of branded stores it operates. These ambitious moves helped the company achieve tremendous growth. Revenue for 2000 increased 60 percent, to $675 million, while net income rose 121 percent, to $44 million.

Sources: Melanie Wells, "Sole Survivors," *Forbes*, 6 August 2001; Anna Rachmansky, "Skechers Post Record Gains," *Footwear News*, 5 March 2001; Claude Solnik, "Skechers Whips Up High Profits during Second Quarter," *Footwear News*, 7 August 2000; "Skechers Wants Retail to Tap into Its Fountain of Youth," *SportStyle*, 1 February 1999.

brands whose advertising campaigns have had a demonstrable impact on sales and profits. Branding Brief 6-2 discusses some of the 2001 winners. Finally, Figure 6-5 displays two recent rankings of "the greatest TV ads of all time."

Guidelines   In designing and evaluating an ad campaign, it is important to distinguish the *message strategy* or positioning of an ad (i.e., what the ad attempts to convey about the brand) from its *creative strategy* (i.e., how the ad expresses the brand claims). Designing effective advertising campaigns is both an art and a science: The artistic aspects relate to the creative strategy of the ad and its executional information; the scientific aspects relate to the message strategy of the ad and the brand claim information it contains. Thus, as Figure 6-6 describes, the two main concerns in devising an advertising strategy are as follows:

➤ Defining the proper positioning to maximize brand equity
➤ Identifying the best creative strategy to communicate or convey the desired positioning

Chapter 3 described a number of issues with respect to positioning strategies to maximize brand equity. Creative strategies can be broadly classified as either *informational* (i.e., elaborating on a specific product-related attribute or benefit) or *transformational* (i.e., portraying a specific non-product-related benefit or image).[8] These two general categories each encompasses several different specific creative approaches. Regardless of which general creative approach is taken, however, certain motivational or "borrowed interest" devices are often employed to attract consumers' attention and raise their involvement with an ad. These devices include the presence of cute babies, frisky puppies, popular music, well-liked celebrities, amusing situations, provocative sex appeals, or fear-inducing threats. Such techniques are thought to be necessary in the tough new media environment characterized by low-involvement consumer processing and much competing ad and programming clutter.

Unfortunately, these attention-getting tactics are often *too* effective and distract from brand or product claims. Thus, the challenge in arriving at the best creative strategy is figuring out how to break through the clutter to attract the attention of consumers but still be able to deliver the intended message at the same time.

Nissan
Nissan spent $330 million between 1996 and 1998 on an attention-grabbing campaign featuring an action figure driving his sporty car to pick up a Barbie-like girlfriend while the Van Halen cover of the Kinks classic "You Really Got Me" blared in the background. Although *Time* magazine named it the best campaign of 1996, sales slipped. Nissan replaced the ad with a testimonial-style campaign featuring Jerry P. Hirshberg, the company's chief designer. In the ads, shot against a simple black backdrop, Hirshberg appeared dressed in casual clothes and spoke to an off-camera listener about the unique features of Nissan cars. While the new campaign did not earn high creative marks, car sales rose 5 percent in 2000 and light-truck sales soared 21 percent.[9]

What makes an effective TV ad? Fundamentally, a TV ad should contribute to brand equity in some demonstrable way, for example, by enhancing awareness, strengthening a key association or adding a new association, or eliciting a positive consumer response. In applying the consumer information processing model, six criteria were

The American Marketing Association's
2001 Effie Awards for Best Advertising

Each year, the American Marketing Association (AMA) recognizes the most effective marketing programs with its Effie Awards. A panel of marketing professionals judges entries based on strategy, execution, and marketplace impact. Here are a few of the winners from the 2001 Effies.

NISSAN XTERRA

The 2000 launch campaign for the new Nissan Xterra sport utility vehicle won the Grand Effie for best in show. The campaign, created by TBWA/Chiat/Day, Los Angeles, consisted of television, print, and billboard advertising. The television component of the campaign used action shots of the Xterra alternating with scenes of men participating in action sports such as mountain biking and kayaking. The campaign led to stronger Xterra sales than the company anticipated, which in turn helped Nissan post a $2.3 billion profit in 2001, compared with a $6.4 billion loss in 2000.

BREATHE RIGHT

CNS Inc., manufacturers of Breathe Right nasal strips, and agency Campbell Mithun created the "On the Nose" campaign that won the Health Aids/Over-the-Counter category at the 2001 Effies. The campaign, aimed at raising awareness and sales of adult-sized nasal strips, included television and print advertising as well as direct marketing and sales promotion. According to CNS, the campaign led to a retail sales increase of 10 percent for the Breathe Right strips. Additionally, the campaign helped raise unaided brand awareness by 63 percent and increased unaided advertising awareness by 50 percent.

IBM

IBM and Ogilvy & Mather were awarded a Gold award in the Computer Software category for the "Software Evangelist" campaign. The campaign, designed to promote IBM's e-business software, included television and print ads. It also marked the first time IBM touted itself as a software provider. The campaign tag line was "It's a different kind of world. You need a different kind of software." The campaign helped IBM become the number one provider of "middleware"—a "fundamental building block for e-business"—and contributed to the company's $13 billion in software revenue during 2000.

CENSUS 2000

Kang & Lee and the Bravo Group won the Gold award in the Government/Institutional advertising category for their campaign "Census 2000. This Is Your Future. Don't Leave It Blank." Kang & Lee developed TV, print, and outdoor ads that targeted Asian and Middle-Eastern Americans representing 14 diverse ethnic groups. The Bravo Group developed ads that targeted the different nationalities and races that compose the Hispanic community. The campaign helped achieve a national response rate of 67 percent for the 2000 census, well above the projected 61 percent and the first rate increase in two decades.

Source: http://www.effie.org.

FIGURE 6-5 Fifty Greatest Commercials of All Time according to *TV Guide* and *Time Entertainment Weekly*

		TV Guide			Time Entertainment Weekly	
Rank	*Brand*	*Ad Title*	*Year*	*Brand*	*Ad Title*	*Year*
1	Apple Computer	"1984"	1984	Energizer	"Escape of the Bunny"	1989
2	Alka-Seltzer	"Spicy Meatballs"	1969	Federal Express	"Fast-Paced World"	1981
3	Volkswagen	"Funeral"	1969	American Tourister	"Gorilla"	1980
4	Volkswagen	"Snowplow"	1963	Alka Seltzer	"Spicy Meatball"	1969
5	Federal Express	"Fast-Paced World"	1981	Wendy's	"Russian Fashion Show"	1985
6	American Tourister	"Gorilla"	1970	Isuzu	"Joe Usuzu/Liar"	1985
7	Coca-Cola	"Mean Joe Greene"	1979	Coke	"Mean Joe Greene"	1979
8	Miller Lite	"Everything You Always Wanted in a Beer—and Less	1975	Partnership for a Drug Free America	"Fried Egg"	1987
9	Wendy's	"Fluffy Bun"	1984	Cracker Jack	"Train"	1965
10	Life Cereal	"Three Brothers"	1971	Rice Krispies	"Vesti"	1969
11	Partnership for a Drug-Free America	"Fried Egg"	1987	California Milk Board	"Aaron Burr"	1993
12	Coca-Cola	"Hilltop"	1971	Jell-O	"Weird Harold"	1973
13	California Milk Board	"Aaron Burr"	1993	California Raisins	"Lunchbox"	1986
14	Alka-Seltzer	"Prison"	1970	Hallmark	"100th Birthday"	1990
15	Benson & Hedges	"The Dis-Advantages"	1966	Benson & Hedges	"The Dis-Advantages"	1966
16	Keep America Beautiful	"Crying Indian"	1971	Nike	"Hang Time"	1989
17	Cracker Jack	"Train"	1965	Chevrolet	"Boy Meets Impala"	1958
18	Nike	"Bo Diddley"	1989	Marlboro	"Foggy Morning"	1967
19	Energizer Batteries	"Bunny"	1989	Diet Pepsi	"Apartment 10G"	1987
20	Lyndon B. Johnson for President	"Daisy"	1964	AT&T	"Joey Called"	1981
21	Pepsi	"Security Camera"	1996	MCI	"Parents"	1982

(Continued)

FIGURE 6-5 (Continued)

	TV Guide			Time Entertainment Weekly		
Rank	Brand	Ad Title	Year	Brand	Ad Title	Year
22	ESPN	"This is *Sportcenter*"	1995	Sunsweet Prunes	"Today the Pits"	1967
23	Xerox	"Monks"	1975	Dannon	"Old Russians"	1977
24	Pepsi	"Archeology"	1985	McDonald's	"Clean"	1971
25	Levi's	"The 501 Blues"	1984	Maypo	"Marky Maypo"	1956
26	California Raisins	"Lunchbox"	1986	Department of Transportation	"Crashing Glasses"	1983
27	Timex	"Acapulco Diver"	1962	Ikea	"Dining Room"	1994
28	Nike	"If You Let Me Play"	1995	Life	"Three Brothers"	1971
29	Little Caesars	"Training Camp"	1995	Levi's	"Doctors"	1996
30	Bartles & Jaymes	"Yuppies"	1986	Coke	"Max/Interview"	1987
31	Dannon	"Old Russians"	1977	Meow Mix	"Singing Cat"	1972
32	Marlboro	"Marlboro Man"	1962	Polaroid	"Onestep/Sun System"	1977
33	American Motors	"Driving School"	1968	Nissan	"Toys"	1996
34	MCI	"Parents"	1982	Wilkins Instant Coffee	"Cannon Shot"	1957
35	Union Carbide	"Chick"	1967	Dunkin' Donuts	"Time to Make the Donuts"	1982
36	Cheer	"Diva"	1988	Little Caesars	"High Chair"	1991
37	Dunkin' Donuts	"Time to Make the Donuts"	1982	Pepsi	"Security Camera"	1996
38	Hallmark	"Dance Card"	1991	Keep America Beautiful	"Crying Indian"	1971
39	McDonald's	"Showdown"	1993	Chanel No. 5	"Marilyn"	1994
40	Pepsi	"Ray Charles"	1990	American Express	"Rags to Riches"	1994
41	Diet Pepsi	"Apartment 10G"	1987	Volkswagen	"Ronnie & Jonnie"	1972
42	Wendy's	"Russian Fashion Show"	1985	Hush Puppies	"Ventilated Hush Puppies"	1988
43	Jeep	"Snow Covered"	1994	Brylcreem	"Girl in Tube"	1966
44	Eastman Kodak	"Daddy's Little Girl"	1989	Bic	"Flick Your Bic"	1974
45	Nissan	"Toys"	1996	Nike	"Munoz"	1995
46	Sunsweet Prunes	"Today the Pits"	1967	Quisp and Quake	"Quisp vs. Quake"	1965
47	McDonald's	"Clean Up"	1971	Cheer Detergent	"Handkerchief"	1987
48	Taco Bell	"Romeo & Juliet"	1998	Trix	"First Rabbit"	1959
49	Isuzu	"Joe Isuzu/Liar"	1985	Mentos	"The Freshmaker"	1992
50	Budweiser	"Frogs"	1995	The Veg-O-Matic	"It Slices, It Dices"	Late 1950s

Define Positioning to Establish Brand Equity
Competitive frame of reference
   Nature of competition
   Target market
Point-of-parity attributes or benefits
   Necessary
   Competitive
Point-of-difference attributes or benefits
   Desirable
   Deliverable

Identify Creative Strategy to Communicate Positioning Concept
Informational (benefit elaboration)
   Problem-solution
   Demonstration
   Product comparison
   Testimonial (celebrity or unknown consumer)
Transformational (imagery portrayal)
   Typical or aspirational usage situation
   Typical or aspirational user of product
   Brand personality and values
Motivational ("borrowed interest" techniques)
   Humor
   Warmth
   Sex appeal
   Music
   Fear
   Special effects

Source: Based on an insightful framework put forth in John R. Rossiter and Larry Percy, *Advertising and Promotion Management,* 2nd ed. (New York: McGraw-Hill, 1997).

FIGURE 6-6 Factors in Designing Effective Advertising Campaigns

identified as success factors for advertising: consumer targeting, the ad creative, consumer understanding, brand positioning, consumer motivation, and ad memorability.

Although managerial judgment using criteria such as these can and should be employed in evaluating advertising, research also can play a productive role. Advertising strategy research is often invaluable in clarifying communication objectives, target markets, and positioning alternatives. To evaluate the effectiveness of message and creative strategies, *copy testing* is often conducted, in which a sample of consumers is exposed to candidate ads and their reactions are gauged in some manner. There are many different ways to copy test an ad, depending on decisions in areas such as the following:[10]

➤ Type of advertisement used (e.g., mock-up or finished ad)
➤ Frequency of exposure (e.g., single or multiple)
➤ How the ad is shown (e.g., isolated, in ad clutter, or in a program or magazine)

➤ Where the exposure occurs (e.g., in a shopping center facility, at home on TV or through mail, or in a theater)

➤ How sample respondents are obtained (e.g., prerecruited or not)

➤ Geographic scope (e.g., one city or many)

Besides these methodological or data collection issues, perhaps the most important decision in copy testing is what type or types of measures to use to judge the ad (e.g., based on recall, recognition, persuasion, behavior, or a combination of these).

Unfortunately, copy-testing results may vary considerably depending on what decisions are made in these different areas. Consequently, the results of an ad copy test must be interpreted as only one possible data point that should be combined with managerial judgment and other information in evaluating the merits of an ad. Copy testing is perhaps most useful when managerial judgment reveals some fairly clear positive *and* negative aspects to an ad and is therefore somewhat inconclusive. In this case, copy-testing research may shed some light on how these various conflicting aspects "net out" and collectively affect consumer processing. Regardless, copy-testing results should not be seen as a means of making a "go" or "no go" decision; ideally, they should play a diagnostic role in helping to understand *how* an ad works. As an example of the potential fallibility of pretesting, consider NBC's experiences with the popular TV series *Seinfeld*.

Seinfeld

In October 1989, *The Seinfeld Chronicles*, as it was called then, was shown to several groups of viewers in order to gauge the show's potential, like most television pilot projects awaiting final network approval. The show tested badly—very badly. The summary research report noted that "no segment of the audience was eager to watch the show again." The reaction to Seinfeld himself was "lukewarm" because his character was seen as "powerless, dense, and naïve." The test report also concluded that "none of the supports were particularly liked and viewers felt that Jerry needed a better back-up ensemble." Despite the weak reaction, NBC decided to go ahead with what became one of the most successful television shows of the 1990s. Although they later also changed their testing methods, NBC's experience reinforces the limitations of testing and the dangers of relying on single numbers.[11]

Future prospects In the new computer era, the future of television and traditional mass marketing advertising is uncertain. As Edwin L. Artzt, then chairman and CEO of Procter & Gamble, once noted, "From where we stand today, we can't be sure that ad—supported TV programming will have a future in the world being created—a world of video-on-demand, pay-per-view and subscription television."[12] Other advertisers warn of eventually bypassing ad agencies via interactive shopping channels, CD-ROM catalogs, multimedia kiosks, and online services.[13] Nevertheless, at least for some, the power of TV ads remains. As one advertising executive put it, "Nothing competes with prime time television when it comes to communicating with a mass audience. Other mediums can't entertain and inform in the same captivating way."

Radio

Radio is a pervasive medium: 96 percent of all Americans 12 years and older listen to the radio daily and, on average, over 20 hours a week. Perhaps the main advantage to radio is flexibility—stations are very targeted, ads are relatively inexpensive to produce and place, and short closings allow for quick responses. For example, AT&T uses radio to target African American consumers.[14] African Americans spend an average of 4 hours every day listening to the radio, far more time than the national average of 2.8 hours. As the centerpiece of its 2000 multimedia campaign, AT&T sponsored a live radio broadcast of a Destiny's Child concert that included a promotion through which listeners could win a trip to New Orleans. Radio is a particularly effective medium in the morning and can effectively complement or reinforce TV ads. Radio also enables companies to achieve a balance between broad and localized market coverage.

Obvious disadvantages of radio, however, are the lack of visual image and the relatively passive nature of consumer processing that results. Nevertheless, as Branding Brief 6-3 shows, several brands have effectively built brand equity with radio ads. What makes an effective radio ad?[15] Radio has been less studied than other media. Because of its low-involvement nature and limited sensory options, radio advertising often must be fairly focused. For example, the advertising pioneer David Ogilvy believes four factors are critical:[16]

1. Identify your brand early in the commercial.
2. Identify it often.
3. Promise the listener a benefit early in the commercial.
4. Repeat it often.

Nevertheless, radio ads can be extremely creative. The lack of visual images is seen by some as a plus because they feel that the clever use of music, sounds, humor, and other creative devices can tap into the listener's imagination in a way to create powerfully relevant and liked images.

Print

Print media offer a stark contrast to broadcast media. Most important, because of their self-paced nature, magazines and newspapers can provide detailed product information. At the same time, the static nature of the visual images in print media makes it difficult to provide dynamic presentations or demonstrations. Another disadvantage of print advertising is that it can be a fairly passive medium.

In general, the two main print media-magazines and newspapers—have many of the same advantages and disadvantages. Magazines are particularly effective at building user and usage imagery. Newspapers, however, are more timely and pervasive. Daily newspapers are read by roughly three-fourths of the population and tend to be used a lot for local (especially retailer) advertising. On the other hand, although advertisers have some flexibility in designing and placing newspaper ads, poor reproduction quality and short shelf lives can diminish some of the possible impact of newspaper advertising as compared with magazine advertising.

Although print advertising is particularly well-suited to communicate product information, it can also effectively communicate user and usage imagery. One famous print ad campaign is the "Portraits" series by American Express that featured brilliant shots by famed photographer Annie Leibovitz of celebrity cardholders such as Tom Seaver, Ray Charles, and couples such as Jessica Tandy and Hume Cronyn in unique, attention-getting poses. Launched in 1987, the strategy behind the "Membership Has Its Privileges" campaign, created by ad agency Ogilvy & Mather, was to attempt image

Building Brands through the Radio Airwaves

Radio may be seen as a less glamorous media than television, but that does not mean it cannot be used for effective advertising, as the following examples attest.

MOTEL 6

One notable radio ad campaign is for Motel 6, the nation's largest budget motel chain, which was founded in 1962 when the "6" stood for $6 a night. After finding its business fortunes hitting bottom in 1986 with an occupancy rate of only 66.7 percent, Motel 6 made a number of marketing changes, including the launch of a radio campaign of humorous 60-second ads featuring folksy contractor-turned-writer Tom Bodett. Containing the clever tag line "We'll leave the light on for you," the ad campaign is credited with a rise in occupancy and a revitalization of the brand that continues to this day.

WENDY'S

Wendy's uses local radio ad buys exclusively, taking advantage of the flexibility of radio advertising by enabling its field marketing managers to customize the lengths and tag lines of radio spots. The company also supplements its national marketing campaign with local promotions. As one Wendy's executive notes, "Whenever there are promotional extensions, we can really see that transactions are increasing in stores where we made the radio buys."

AT&T

AT&T recently turned to radio advertising to increase 1-800-CALL-ATT's share of collect calls among teens and twenty-somethings. AT&T chose the medium because young people often listen to the radio away from home when they are likely to need to make collect calls. Radio advertising allowed AT&T to target the markets with the strongest collect call usage, while at the same time achieving national coverage. Karen Milke, AT&T's media director, said, "Network [national] radio maximizes our efficiency, and spot [local] radio allows us to emphasize our best potential markets." AT&T uses tracking studies to measure daily collect call usage across the country. This information can be broken down to the zip code level, which AT&T uses to determine which markets to target and also to measure the success of local radio campaigns.

PEPSI

Pepsi is a radio marketer that uses celebrity endorsers, such as Busta Rhymes, to promote its Mountain Dew brand in radio spots. Pepsi also carefully chooses which local stations and which DJs to air its commercials with. Charlee Taylor-Hines, Pepsi's director of urban and ethnic marketing, said, "Being on the stations with the most street credibility says you know what's happening."

Source: Radio Advertising Bureau, "Radio Is Everyone [advertising supplement]" (Irving, TX: Radio Avertising Bureau).

building in print and to dramatize the product benefits in TV—the reverse of the typical use of these media by most advertisers.[17]

Other brands, such as Calvin Klein, Tommy Hilfiger, and Guess, have also created strong nonproduct associations through print advertising. Some brands attempt to communicate both product benefits and user or usage imagery in their print advertising, for example, car makers such as Ford, Lexus, and Volvo or cosmetics makers such as Maybelline and Revlon.

One of the longest running and perhaps most successful print ad campaigns ever is for Absolut vodka.

Absolut

In 1980, Absolut was a tiny brand, selling 12,000 cases a year. Research conducted at that time had pointed out a number of liabilities for the brand: The name was seen as too gimmicky, the bottle shape was ugly and bartenders found it hard to pour, shelf prominence was limited, and there was no credibility for a vodka brand made in Sweden. Michel Roux, president of Carillon (Absolut's importer), and TBWA (Absolut's New York ad agency) decided to use the oddities of the brand—its quirky name and bottle shape—to create brand personality and communicate quality and style in a series of creative print ads. Each ad in the campaign visually depicts the product in an unusual fashion and verbally reinforces the image with a simple, two-word headline using the brand name and some other word in a clever play on words. For example, the first ad showed the bottle prominently displayed, crowned by an angel's halo, with the headline "Absolut Perfection" appearing at the bottom of the page. Follow-up ads explored various themes (e.g., seasonal, geographic, celebrity artists) but always attempted to put forth a fashionable, sophisticated, and contemporary image. By 1991, Absolut had become the leading imported vodka, and worldwide sales in 2000 exceeded $3 billion.

Guidelines What makes an effective print ad? Although the evaluation criteria noted earlier for television advertising basically apply, print advertising has some special requirements and rules. For example, research on print ads in magazines reveals that it is not uncommon for two-thirds of a magazine audience to not even notice any one particular print ad, and for only 10 percent or so of the audience to read much of the copy of any one ad. Many readers only glance at the most visible elements of a print ad, making it critical that an ad communicate clearly, directly, and consistently in the ad illustration and headline. Figure 6-7 contains some important creative guidelines for print ads that can be summarized in terms of three simple criteria: clarity, consistency, and branding.[18]

Direct Response

In contrast to advertising in traditional broadcast and print media, which typically communicates to consumers in a nonspecific and nondirective manner, *direct response* refers to the use of mail, telephone, and other nonpersonal contact tools to communicate with or solicit a response from specific customers and prospects. Direct response can take many forms and is not restricted to solicitations by mail, telephone, or even within traditional broadcast and print media. For example, frustrated with a poor response to their catalogs, Macy's spent $1 million to mail 500,000 teenagers a CD-ROM that contained both pop hits as well as back-to-school fashions. Videocassettes

In judging the effectiveness of a print ad, in addition to considering the communication strategy (e.g., target market, communication objectives, and message strategy) the following questions should be answered affirmatively concerning the executional elements:

1. Is the message clear at a glance? Can you quickly tell what the advertisement is all about?
2. Is the benefit in the headline?
3. Does the illustration support the headline?
4. Does the first line of the copy support or explain the headline and illustration?
5. Is the ad easy to read and follow?
6. Is the product easily identified?
7. Is the brand or sponsor clearly identified?

Source: Philip Ward Burton and Scott C. Purvis, *Which Ad Pulled Best?* 5th ed. (Lincolnwood, IL: NTC Business Books, 1987).

FIGURE 6-7   Print Ad Evaluation Criteria

have become an increasingly affordable means to market directly.[19] Soloflex has been selling its home-gym products via video since 1983 and reports that sales are twice that from using conventional brochures.[20]

One increasingly popular means of direct marketing is *infomercials.*[21] In a marketing sense, an infomercial attempts to combine the sell of commercials with the draw of educational information and entertainment. As such, infomercials can be thought of as a cross between a sales call and a television ad. Infomercials can vary in length but are often 30-minute video programs that are made at the cost of $250,000 to $500,000. A number of individuals have become famous with late-night channel switchers for pitching various wares (e.g., Tony Robbins, Victoria Principal, and Kathy Smith). Increasingly, companies selling products that are complicated, technologically advanced, or simply require a great deal of explanation are turning to infomercials, such as Callaway Golf, Carnival Cruises, Mercedes, Microsoft, Philips Electronics, Universal Studios, and even the online job search site Monster.com.[22]

Guidelines   Direct marketing has consistently outgrown every media spending category since 1986. This steady growth is a function of technological advances (e.g., the ease of setting up toll-free 800 numbers), changes in consumer behavior (e.g., increased need for convenience), and the needs of marketers (e.g., the desire to avoid wasteful communications to nontarget customers or customer groups). The advantage of direct response is that it facilitates the establishment of relationships with consumers by marketers. Branding Brief 6-4 describes some of the trend-setting direct response campaigns as judged by the Direct Marketing Association with their 2000 Echo Awards.[23]

Direct communications through newsletters, catalogs, electronic home pages, and so forth allow marketers to explain to consumers new developments with their brands on an ongoing basis, as well as allow consumers to provide feedback to marketers as to their likes and dislikes and specific needs and wants. By learning more about customers, marketers can fine-tune marketing programs to offer the right products to the right customers at the right time. In fact, direct marketing is often seen as a key component of relationship marketing—an important marketing trend reviewed in Chapter 5.

Direct Marketing Association 2000 Echo Award Winners

The Echo Awards, given out annually by the Direct Marketing Association, honor the most effective direct marketing campaigns, based on consumer response and marketing creativity. Some of the 2000 Echo Award winners included the following.

PEOPLEPC: DIAMOND AWARD FOR BEST IN SHOW

The OgilvyOne agency in New York developed a direct response television and radio campaign for client PeoplePC. PeoplePC is a subscription computer service that for a monthly fee offers an Internet account, a new name-brand PC every three years, and the necessary software, service, and support. The television ad featured a humorous pseudo-CEO, played by a child actor, going over the details of the service with hand-drawn pie charts and other visual aids. More than 800,000 consumers called the PeoplePC 800 number during the first year of the campaign.

ORANGE: USPS GOLD MAILBOX AWARD FOR BEST DIRECT MAIL CAMPAIGN

British telecom company Orange and direct response agency DP&A developed a high-tech mailing for its new technology called "Wildfire." The Wildfire mailing featured digital voice technology that created a "talking package" that greets the recipient with the message "Hello. I'm Wildfire. Brought to you by Orange." when the package is opened. The voice then gives a four-sentence description of Wildfire's key feature, namely, new phone technology that combines speech recognition software with mobile phones to create a "virtual personal assistant." The recipient is then instructed to play the included CD-ROM to learn more about Wildfire. The CD-ROM, narrated by Monty Python alumnus John Cleese, explains and demonstrates Wildfire's features in detail. This mailing culled a 55.3 percent response rate, more than four times Orange's target rate.

BANK OF NEW ZEALAND: GOLD AWARD

Bank of New Zealand won three Gold awards for financial service direct mail campaigns designed by Aim Direct. One campaign was designed to inform farmers about Bank of New Zealand's agricultural banking expertise. The campaign used multiple mailings, one of which contained a bottle of weed killer that symbolized that the bank's revolving credit account "Kills Loans Fast!" This mailing was credited with adding $14 million to the bank's revenues. A mailing in the shape of a toolbox, which resulted in $20 million additional revenues, informed farmers that the bank's customized fixed-rate term loans were "The ultimate tool for your farm." The third campaign consisted of 335 invitations to the America's Cup sailing competition in Auckland, which were mailed to premier clients and partners. The invitations were packaged in a canvas envelope that resembled the bag sails are stored in, and a follow-up mailing consisted of a brochure attached to a miniature paddle. The America's Cup campaign garnered a 100 percent response rate.

Sources: http://www.the-dma.org; Jonathan Boorstein, "Agent Orange," *Direct,* 15 September 1999; "International Gold Winners," *Advertising Age,* 16 October 2000.

As the name suggests, the goal of direct response is to elicit some type of behavior from consumers; as such, it is easy to measure the effects of direct marketing efforts—people either respond or they do not. The disadvantages to direct response, however, are the intrusiveness and clutter involved. To implement an effective direct marketing program, three critical ingredients are (1) developing an up-to-date and informative list of current and potential future customers, (2) putting forth the right offer in the right manner, and (3) tracking the effectiveness of the marketing program.

To improve the effectiveness of direct marketing programs, many marketers are embracing database marketing. Regardless of the particular means of direct marketing, marketers can potentially benefit from database marketing to create targeted communication and marketing programs tailored to the needs and wants of specific consumers. Database marketers collect names and information from consumers regarding their attitudes and behavior and compile it in a comprehensive database. Aside from ordering products, names and information can be collected from consumers in a variety of ways—for example, by sending in a coupon, filling out a warranty card, or entering a sweepstakes.

Database marketing is generally thought to be more effective at helping firms to retain existing customers than to attract new ones. As a rule of thumb, many marketers believe that database marketing makes more sense the higher the price of the product and the more often it is bought. Database marketing pioneers include a number of financial services firms and airlines. Even packaged-goods companies, however, are exploring the possible benefits of database marketing. For example, Procter & Gamble created a database to market their Pampers disposable diaper, allowing P&G to send out "individualized" birthday cards for babies and reminder letters to parents to move their child up to the next size.[24] Database management tools will become a priority to marketers as they attempt to track the lifetime value of customers. Along those lines, Branding Brief 6-5 describes some issues concerning customer relationship marketing.

Online

The end of the twentieth century was the dawn of interactive, online marketing communications. With the growth of the Internet, marketers scrambled to build a presence in cyberspace. The approaches that companies adopted vary widely. Reviewing all the guidelines for online marketing communications is beyond the scope of this text.[25] This section concentrates on two crucial online brand-building tools: Web sites and interactive ads.

Web sites   The main advantages to marketing on the Web are the low cost and the level of detail and degree of customization it offers. By capitalizing on its interactive nature, marketers can construct Web sites that allow for any consumer to choose the brand information that is relevant to his or her needs or desires. As such, interactive marketing can allow for solid relationship building. In creating these online information sources for consumers at company Web sites, it is important to deliver timely and reliable information. Web sites must be updated frequently and offer as much customized information as possible, especially for existing customers.

Because consumers often go online to seek information rather than be entertained, some of the more successful Web sites are those that are able to convey expertise in a consumer-relevant area. For example, Web sites such as P&G's Pampers.com and General Mills's Cheerios.com offer baby and parenting advice. Web sites can store

Branding via Customer Relationship Management

Customer relationship marketing (CRM) refers to a company's use of data systems and applications to track consumer activity and manage customer interactions with the company. As described by an article in MIT's *Sloan Management Review*:

> CRM synthesizes all of a company's customer 'touchpoints'—including e-mail, call centers, retail stores, and sales reps—to support subsequent customer interactions as well as to inform financial forecasts, product design, and supply-chain management.

For instance, CRM can help customer service representatives give better service by enabling them to instantly view and analyze pertinent information such as the customer's entire purchase record or the availability of product replacements and to determine the most cost-efficient course for both parties.

CRM projects usually involve the installation of sophisticated hardware and complicated software. A typical CRM implementation for a medium-sized business costs over $100,000 after the costs of data storage servers, software licenses, installation, and integration are totaled. For major corporations, the cost of software sophisticated enough to handle the necessary volume of customers, made by companies such as Siebel Systems or PeopleSoft, can run as much as $5,000 per user for the license. In 2001, the median annual CRM budget exceeded $1 million and the average project took four years to implement. Once they have CRM systems in place, companies expect to harness the data-mining power of the system to trim costs or increase profits and make back their investment.

As an alternative to expensive in-house CRM systems, several companies are marketing Web-based CRM applications that are considerably cheaper and easier to use. Salesforce.com, UpShot, Commence, and others offer software hosted on their own servers that companies contract to use for a monthly fee. A high-speed Internet connection allows user companies to remotely input customer information and conduct analyses without incurring the cost of purchasing, installing, and maintaining a CRM system. The cost of using these subscription services is typically in the low five figures.

Experts agree, however, that technology is only part of the CRM equation. If the company intends on building a relationship, it must do more than mine a customer's data in order to extract more money from that customer. As with the generic customer service example cited earlier, CRM can be used to increase value for both the company and the customer. As one marketing executive cautioned, "CRM isn't a bad idea, but companies should be sure to take their customers' point of view into account." In other words, employing the proper human touch is as important as installing the best CRM system.

Sources: Larry Yu, "Successful Customer Relationship Management," *MIT Sloan Management Review*, 1 July 2001; Kevin Ferguson, "Closer Than Ever: CRM Software Keeps You and Your Customer Ultra-Cozy," *Business Week*, 12 May 2001.

company and product information, press releases, advertising and promotional information, and so on as well as links to partners and key vendors.

Ragu

Ragu attempts to provide useful information updated regularly to bring browsers back. Their "Mama's Cucina" site offers Italian phrases and lessons, recipes, coupons, and sweepstakes. They claim "Mama's Cucina" is designed to be the Internet's family kitchen, with lots of interesting and fun information about food and the old country.

Many Web marketers collect names and addresses for a database and conduct e-mail surveys and online focus groups. A decent Web site that can sustain viewer interest can be built for less than $150,000 but can also cost more. Designing Web sites requires creating eye-catching pages that can sustain browsers' interest, employing the latest technology, and effectively communicating the corporate message. One top designer notes that it is important that users feel as if they have just entered a new, cohesive world, requiring that different pages and content areas within a site have consistent design elements, colors, and placement. Web site design is crucial because if consumers do not have a positive experience, it may be very difficult to entice them back in the highly competitive and cluttered online world.

To spread the word about their Web sites, advertisers adopt a number of approaches. For example, Zima prints its Web address on bottles and buys electronic billboards at other popular Web sites. Marketing on the Web will clearly change dramatically as its technology changes. Improved audio and video capabilities will allow for advertising with more impact, and advances in software that ensure secure transactions will drive more online sales. Traditional print and broadcast ads, however, may not translate well to a high-tech media form. The challenge will be to entertain people but still communicate desired information.

Interactive Ads   A number of potential advantages exist for Web advertising: It is accountable because software can track which ads went to which sales; it is nondisruptive, so it doesn't interrupt consumers; and it can target consumers so that only the most promising prospects are contacted, who could then seek as much or as little information as they desired.[26] Unfortunately, there are also many disadvantages. Many consumers find it easy to ignore banner ads. From 1995 to 2001, the click-through rate for banner ads slipped from 40 percent to 0.5 percent. Too many ads were uninspired as advertisers struggled to learn how to use the medium. Efforts to create more attention through pop-up or pop-under ads that generate mini-windows, however, often infuriated consumers.

As a result, attention has turned to "skyscraper" ads (tall, skinny oblong boxes at the side of a Web page) and "rectangle" ads (boxes much larger than banners). Bigger than banner ads, these types of ads can be spiced up with animation and add-ons such as pull-down menus as a means of providing a direct brand message that does not require a click through. Increasingly, Web ads are becoming closer to traditional form of advertising, as with streaming Web ads. BMW created a series of made-for-the-Web movies using well-known directors such as Guy Ritchie and actors such as Madonna. Ford and General Motors both created online videogames to promote their cars. For example, Ford's game for its Escape small sport utility vehicle allowed players to steer the vehicle through a race course on the moon. Users could then e-mail the game to friends and issue a challenge to beat their score.[27]

As a manifestation of permission marketing, e-mail ads in general—often including advanced features such as personalized audio messages, color photos, and streaming video—have increased in popularity. To promote a new line of clubs, Chipshot.com sent e-mails to its customers that included streaming video and an audio message and found that the multimedia message produced double the results of standard e-mail. E-mail ads often receive response rates of 20 percent to 30 percent at a cost less than that of banner ads. Tracking these response rates, marketers can fine-tune their messages. The key, as with direct advertising, is to create a good customer list.

Volvo

In 2000, Volvo developed an Internet-only launch for its new S60 sedan. The company signed an exclusive deal with America Online that placed banner ads for the car in prime locations on the AOL portal. The ads led viewers to a special Website, called revolvolution.com, where they could learn more about the vehicle, configure a car to their tastes, and request a quote from a nearby dealer. Though over one million consumers visited the site, dealers across the nation were disappointed with the customer response, in part due to an uncompetitive lease rate and a budget crunch that precluded use of other media. Volvo replaced the Internet-only launch with an integrated campaign that included Web, wireless, television, and print advertising.[28] (See Figure 6-8.)

FIGURE 6-8   Volvo S60

Place

The last category of advertising is also often called "nontraditional," "alternative," or "support" advertising because it has arisen in recent years as a means to complement more traditional advertising media. *Place advertising*, also called out-of-home advertising, is a broadly defined category that captures advertising outside traditional media. Increasingly, ads and commercials are showing up in unusual spots, sometimes as parts of experiential marketing programs. The rationale often given is that because traditional advertising media—especially television advertising—are seen as becoming less effective, marketers are better off reaching people in other environments, such as where they work, play, and, of course, shop. Some of the options available include billboards; movies, airlines, and lounges; product placement; and point-of-purchase advertising.

Billboards and Posters   In 1925, Burma-Shave placed a set of four billboards in sequence along roads nationwide with the following jingle:

> Shave the modern way.
> Fine for the skin.
> Druggists have it.
> Burma-Shave.

The success of Burma-Shave billboards convinced marketers that consumers would notice and remember simple messages conveyed in "unexpected" places. Billboards have been transformed over the years and now employ colorful, digitally produced graphics, backlighting, sounds, movement, and unusual—even three-dimensional-images to attract attention. Billboards do not even necessarily have to stay in one place. Marketers can buy ad space on billboard-laden trucks that are driven continuously all day in marketer-selected areas. For example, Oscar-Mayer sends six "Wienermobiles" traveling across the United States each year to increase brand exposure and goodwill.

Billboard-type poster ads are now showing up everywhere. Transit ads on buses, subways, and commuter trains—around for years—have now become a valuable means to reach working women. Street furniture (bus shelters, kiosks, and public areas) has become a fast-growing area. Goodyear, whose brand-emblazoned blimp enjoyed clear skies for over 50 years, has been subsequently joined by Fuji, Met Life, Monster.com, Blockbuster Video, and others in sponsoring a blimp. Advertisers now can buy space in stadiums and arenas and on garbage cans, bicycle racks, parking meters, airport luggage carousals, elevators, gasoline pumps, the bottom of golf cups, airline snacks, and supermarket produce in the form of tiny labels on apples and bananas. Leaving no stone unturned, advertisers can even buy space in toilet stalls and above urinals, which, according to research studies, office workers visit an average of three to four times a day for roughly four minutes per visit.[29] Figure 6-9 displays ten of the most successful outdoor advertisers.

Movies, Airlines, Lounges, and Other Places   Increasingly, advertisers are placing traditional TV and print ads in unconventional places.[30] Companies such as Whittle Communication and Turner Broadcasting have tried placing TV and commercial programming in classrooms, airport lounges, and other public places. Airlines now offer media-sponsored audio and video programming that accepts advertising (e.g., *USA Today Sky Radio* and *National Geographic Explorer*) and include catalogs in seat

U.S. Army posters (1992)[a]
Volkswagen and Burma-Shave (1993)
Nike (1994)
San Diego Zoo (1995)
Nissan (1996)
Coca-Cola (1997)
Levi's (1998)
Budweiser (1999)
Ford (2000)
Chevrolet (2001)

[a]Year of induction is listed in parentheses.

FIGURE 6-9   Obie Hall of Fame Winners (as selected by the Outdoor Advertising Association of America)

pockets for leading mail order companies (e.g., High Street Emporium). Movie theater chains such as the 271-theater Cineplex Odeon now run 30-, 60-, or 90-second ads. Although the same ads that also appear on TV or in magazines often appear in these unconventional places, many advertisers believe it is important to create specially designed ads for these out-of-home exposures to better meet consumer expectations.

Product Placement   Many major marketers pay fees of $50,000 to $100,00 and even higher so that their products can make cameo appearances in movies and on television, with the exact amount depending on the amount and nature of the brand exposure. This practice got a boost in 1982 when—after Mars declined an offer for use of its M&M's brand—the sales of Reese's Pieces increased 65 percent after prominently appearing in the blockbuster movie *E.T.: The Extraterrestrial.*[31] Placement is not restricted to movies. Contestants who want to use a phone call as a lifeline on ABC's *Who Wants to Be a Millionaire* do so courtesy of "our friends at AT&T," according to host Regis Philbin. Contestants in CBS's *Survivor* reality-TV series competed for Doritos tortilla chips, the use of Cingular Wireless mobile-phone service, and a trunk of goods from Target stores. The hosts of ABC's *The View* were paid to "spontaneously" plug Campbell's soups during the talk show.

Product placements can be combined with special promotions to publicize a brand's entertainment tie-ins. For example, BMW complemented product placement in the James Bond film *Goldeneye* with an extensive direct mail and advertising campaign to help launch their Z3 roadster. Some firms benefit from product placement at no cost by supplying their product to the movie company in return (e.g., Nike does not pay to be in movies but often supplies shoes, jackets, and bags) or simply because of the creative demands of the storyline (e.g., the central character in the film *Castaway*, played by Tom Hanks, was a FedEx pilot; as a result, the brand played a prominent role in the plot development without having to pay a cent).[32] To test the effects of product placement, marketing research companies such as CinemaScore conduct viewer exit surveys to determine which brands actually were noticed during movie showings.

Point of Purchase   A myriad of possibilities have emerged in recent years as ways to communicate with consumers at the point of purchase. In-store advertising includes ads on shopping carts, cart straps, aisles, or shelves, as well as promotion options such as in-store demonstrations, live sampling, and instant coupon machines. Point-of-purchase radio provides FM-style programming and commercial messages to 6,500 food stores and 7,900 drugstores nationwide. Programming includes a store-selected music format, consumer tips, and commercials.

The appeal of point-of-purchase advertising lies in the fact that numerous studies have shown that consumers in many product categories make the bulk of their final brand decisions in the store. For example, according to a study by ActMedia, which places ads in 7,000 supermarkets nationwide, 70 percent of all buying decisions are made in the store. In-store media are designed to increase the number and nature of spontaneous and planned buying decisions.

Guidelines   Nontraditional or place media present some interesting options for marketers to reach consumers in new ways. Ads now can appear virtually anyplace where consumers have a few spare minutes or even seconds and thus enough time to notice them. The main advantage of nontraditional media is that a very precise and—because of the nature of the setting involved—captive audience often can be reached in a cost-effective manner. Because out-of-home ads must be quickly processed, however, the message must be simple and direct. In fact, outdoor advertising is often called the "15-second sell." Thus, strategically, out-of-home advertising is often more effective at enhancing awareness or reinforcing existing brand associations than at creating new ones.

The challenge with nontraditional media is demonstrating their reach and effectiveness through credible, independent research. Another worry with nontraditional media is consumer backlash against overcommercialization. Perhaps because of the sheer pervasiveness of advertising, however, consumers seem to be less bothered by nontraditional media now than in the past. For example, unlike Europeans, Americans resisted the notion of on-screen advertising in movie theaters and videos.[33] Yet, almost half of all theaters now run ads, albeit often bigger and more cinematic than their small-screen companions.

Consumers must be favorably affected in some way to justify the marketing expenditures for nontraditional media, and some firms offering ad placement in supermarket checkout lines, fast food restaurants, physicians' waiting rooms, health clubs, and truck stops have suspended business at least in part because of a lack of consumer interest. The bottom line, however, is that there will always be room for creative means of placing the brand in front of consumers. The possibilities are endless. For example, who could have guessed that RJR Nabisco would distribute sandals with the word *Camel* carved onto the bottom of their soles so that beachgoers could leave "Camel tracks" in the sand to help promote its cigarette![34]

Promotion

Sales promotions can be defined as short-term incentives to encourage trial or usage of a product or service.[35] Sales promotions can be targeted at either the trade or at end consumers. Like advertising, sales promotions come in all forms. Whereas advertising typically provides consumers a *reason* to buy, sales promotions offer consumers an *incentive* to buy. Thus, sales promotions are designed to do the following:

➤   Change the behavior of the trade so that they carry the brand and actively support it

➤   Change the behavior of consumers so that they buy a brand for the first time, buy more of the brand, or buy the brand earlier or more often

1. *Type:* What type of promotion should be used?
   Immediate vs. delayed value
   Price cut vs. added value
2. *Product scope:* To what pack sizes or models should the promotion apply?
   Multiple or selective
   More or less popular
   In-line or out-of-line
3. *Market scope:* In which geographic markets should the promotion be offered?
   National or regional
4. *Timing:* When should the promotion be offered and for how long?
   When to promote (in- or off-season)
   When to announce (early or later)
   Duration (long or short)
   Frequency (high or low)
5. *Discount rate:* What explicit or implicit discount should the promotion include?
   Deep or shallow
6. *Terms:* What terms of sale should be attached to the promotion?
   Tight or loose

Source: Adapted from John A. Quelch, "Note on Sales Promotion Design," Teaching Note N-589–021 (Boston: Harvard Business School, 1988).

FIGURE 6-11 Issues in Designing Sales Promotions

Consumer Promotions

Consumer promotions are designed to change the choices, quantity, or timing of consumers' product purchases. Although consumer sales promotions come in all forms, a distinction has been made between customer franchise building promotions (e.g., samples, demonstrations, and educational material) and non-customer franchise building promotions (e.g., price-off packs, premiums, sweepstakes, and refund offers).[36] Customer franchise building promotions are promotions that are seen as enhancing the attitudes and loyalty of consumers toward a brand—in other words, those promotions that affect brand equity. For example, sampling is seen as a means of creating strong, relevant brand associations while also perhaps kick-starting word of mouth among consumers. Sampling is increasingly being done at the point of use (i.e., when consumers might actually use the product) as marketers become more precise in what, where, and how they deliver samples to maximize brand equity. For example, as part of a sampling program, aerobics instructors at Bally's Fitness Clubs handed out Dove body wash, deodorant, and face cloths to students at the end of their classes before they showered.[37]

Thus, sales promotions increasingly are being judged by their ability to contribute to brand equity as well as generate sales. Branding Brief 6-6 describes some award winners for the best promotions of 2000. As reflected by these examples, creativity is as critical to promotions as to advertising or any other form of marketing communications. Gillette's promotion in which one fan was picked to shoot a three-pointer for $1 million at the NCAA basketball championship resulted in 2 million fans—who had to

The Promotion Marketing Association's Reggie Awards

The Promotion Marketing Association (PMA) bestows Reggie Awards to recognize "superior promotional thinking, creativity, and execution across the full spectrum of promotional marketing." Some of the recent award-winning companies and their promotions are highlighted here.

CBS (*SURVIVOR*)

To promote its reality-TV series *Survivor,* CBS spent a total of $5 million on advertising and on-air promotion. The campaign won PMA's "Super Reggie" campaign-of-the-year award. "We were more involved in *Survivor* than any other show launched on the network," said Anne O'Grady, senior vice president of marketing and events for CBS. "It was a marketing project from the start."

In addition to television, print, and billboard advertising, CBS partnered with major advertisers to create *Survivor*-themed promotional advertising. Companies such as Reebok, Budweiser, and Pontiac created custom advertising for the show. Reebok used two contestants who were voted off the island in the early stages of the show in an ad.

Other channels owned by Viacom, the parent company of CBS, supplied on-air promotion for *Survivor*. Viacom television networks such as MTV, VH1, and UPN and each of the 165 stations in the Infinity radio network aired promotions and advertising for the show. Radio was a big part of CBS's promotional effort; the show's producer, Mark Burnett, and its host, Jeff Probst, gave roughly 700 interviews before and during the first season.

CBS even worked *Survivor* into the content of its news programs. For example, an episode of *48 Hours* dealing with the topic of fame and what people do to achieve it featured interviews with two *Survivor* contestants. CBS took to the Internet to promote the hit series. It sent more than 30,000 e-mails touting the show to users of its proprietary Web site iWon. Its own Web site, CBS.com, offered extra footage and content from the show as well as merchandise. The *Survivor* portion of CBS's Web site accounted for half of the traffic during the show's first season.

PILLSBURY/ALBERTSON'S

Packaged-foods maker Pillsbury teamed with Albertson's grocery stores, one of its largest accounts, to sponsor the Big Brothers Big Sisters of America Decorate a Cookie Day. In 35 Albertson's locations, participants in the Big Brothers Big Sisters program decorated cookies to enter into a drawing for free passes to Universal Studios Hollywood. The Pillsbury Doughboy mascot was on hand to oversee the proceedings at each location. Pillsbury took advantage of the occasion to promote its refrigerated dough products, as well as build awareness for new products such as Toaster Bagel Shoppe, Prepared Frozen Biscuits, and Progresso Soups with Real Steak. Both Pillsbury and Albertson's donated a percentage of sales to Big Brothers Big Sisters.

The program was promoted through "Ready Set Go" recipe booklets that were distributed at Albertson's, local cable television spots, ads in Albertson's circulars, billboard advertising, and in-store point-of-purchase displays. Universal Studios helped promote the Decorate a Cookie program by distributing $10 coupons for Albertson's.

Both Pillsbury and Albertson's experienced 10 percent sales increases during the 2000 holiday season. The two companies contributed a total of $170,000 to Big Brothers Big Sisters.

Sources: http://www.pmalink.org; Sonia Reyes, "Targeting Kids and Cookies," *Brandweek*, 12 March 2001; "Super Marketing: Farmer Jack, Albertson's and Pillsbury Win *Promo*'s First Grocery Promotion Awards," *Promo*, 1 July 2001.

buy a Gillette product to enter—signing up.[38] Gillette has devised similar promotions in other sports, such as baseball and golf.

Promotion strategy must reflect the attitudes and behavior of consumers. The last decade or so has seen a steady decrease in the percentage of coupons redeemed by consumers: The redemption rate was 3.5 percent in 1983, but dropped to only 1.3 percent in 2000.[39] Although there are a number of possible explanations, certainly one contributing factor is the large amount of coupon clutter. In 2000, marketers distributed 330 billion coupons valued at nearly $200 billion, about 85 percent of which were in Sunday newspapers. As a result, one area of promotional growth is in-store coupons, which marketers have increasingly turned to as redemption rates of traditional out-of-store coupons slip.

Trade Promotions

Trade promotions often come in the form of financial incentives or discounts given to retailers, distributors, and other members of the trade to stock, display, and facilitate in other ways the sale of a product (e.g., through slotting allowances, point-of-purchase displays, contests and dealer incentives, training programs, trade shows, and cooperative advertising). Trade promotions are typically designed to either secure shelf space and distribution for a new brand or to achieve more prominence on the shelf and in the store. Shelf and aisle positions in the store are important because they affect the ability of the brand to catch the eye of the consumer—placing a brand on a shelf at eye level may double sales compared with placing it on the bottom shelf.[40]

Because of the large amount of money spent on trade promotions, there is increasing pressure to make trade promotion programs more effective, as suggested by the following commentary:

Increasingly the answer that glues the two into a workable partnership is account-specific promotions, tailored to each retailer, with budgets carved up to suit each market's demands. Manufacturers are decentralizing promotions, giving more responsibility for trade budgets to field salesmen. Big companies are setting up internal departments to implement and track these myriad local promotions; mid-size and smaller companies who can't afford the infrastructure are turning to outside services.[41]

Additionally, as noted in Chapter 5, some firms are attempting to substitute consumer-oriented promotions and advertising that can build the brand in a way to satisfy retailers and manufacturers. For example, since 1992, Procter & Gamble has run brand-specific TV and direct mail advertising customized for Wal-Mart, Kmart, Target, and other retailers.

Event Marketing and Sponsorship

Event marketing refers to public sponsorship of events or activities related to sports, art, entertainment, or social causes. Although the origin of event marketing can be traced back to philanthropic activities from over a century ago, many observers identify mega-events in the mid-1980s, such as the 1984 Summer Olympics, Statue of Liberty Centennial, and Live Aid concert, as arousing marketer's interest in sponsorship in the United States.[42] According to the International Events Group, event sponsorship has grown rapidly in recent years, to total $24.6 billion globally in 2001. As Figure 6-12 shows, the vast majority of event expenditures go toward sports. Once employed mostly by cigarette, beer, and auto companies, sports marketing is now being embraced by virtually every type of company. Moreover, virtually every sport—from sled dog racing to fishing tournaments and from tractor pulls to professional beach volleyball—now receives corporate backing of some kind.[43] Branding Brief 6-7 describes auto-racing sponsorship with NASCAR.

Rationale

Event sponsorship provides a different kind of communication option for marketers. By becoming part of a special and personally relevant moment in consumers' lives, sponsors' involvement with events can broaden and deepen their relationship with their target market. Marketers report a number of reasons why they sponsor events:

➤ *To identify with a particular target market or lifestyle:* Marketers can link their brands to events popular with either a select or broad group of consumers. Customers can be targeted geographically, demographically, psychographically, or behaviorally according to

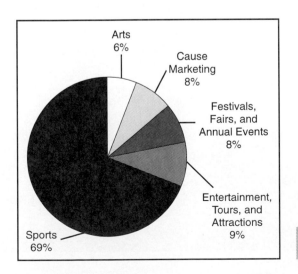

FIGURE 6-12 North American Sponsorship Spending by Property Type

Building Sponsorship Resonance with Nascar

The National Association for Stock Car Auto Racing (NASCAR), founded in 1947 by stock-car promoter Bill France, descended from amateur dirt-track car racing in the South. Modern-day NASCAR races, with 200,000-capacity stadiums, 200 mph speeds, Fortune 500 sponsors, and nationally televised coverage, bear little resemblance to the races during NASCAR's first official season, when former bootleggers driving hot rods vied for $1,000 purses. NASCAR eventually outgrew its provincial roots in the South by holding races in northern cities like Detroit and significantly improving racetrack facilities, but not until the sport reached a national television audience with a CBS broadcast of the entire Daytona 500 in 1979 did NASCAR racing truly become a big-ticket event. The broadcast exceeded all expectations and earned a 10.5 rating, which corresponded with 15 million viewers.

The NASCAR audience continued to grow from that point. Between 1990 and 1999, NASCAR attendance rose 65 percent, and TV ratings were up 40 percent between 1993 and 1999. In 1998, a poll showed that 47 percent of the American public had an interest in watching NASCAR racing. As audience interest grew, corporations became increasingly interested in affiliating themselves with NASCAR. In 1971, R.J. Reynolds ushered in the era of corporate sponsorship when it paid $100,000 to sponsor the Winston Cup Series because tobacco companies were prohibited from advertising

FIGURE A   NASCAR

on television. Corporate sponsorship of NASCAR events and race teams totaled almost $500 million in 1998. In 2001, major corporations paid between $5 million and $10 million to sponsor a racing team. Sponsoring companies include Canon, Eastman Kodak, Gillette, and McDonald's; sponsoring brands include Tide, Country Time, Purex, and Kellogg's Corn Flakes (see Figure A).

Perhaps the main appeal to NASCAR sponsors is the large amount of exposure time for their brands, because the cars, visible for much of the event, are typically emblazoned with the brand logo. Moreover, NASCAR fans are an attractive audience to corporate sponsors because they tend to support NASCAR sponsors, more so than is the case for fans of other sports. For example, respondents to a Performance Research survey had unaided awareness of more than 200 companies that sponsored NASCAR in some capacity, and identified only 1 percent of the companies incorrectly. Of these respondents, 60 percent said they trusted sponsors' products, compared with 30 percent of NFL fans. Finally, the research revealed that more than 40 percent of NASCAR fans switch brands when a company becomes a sponsor.

Today's NASCAR audience is also appealing to corporate sponsors because of its considerable gender and economic diversity: 40 percent of fans have annual income exceeding $50,000, and 39 percent of the audience is female. NASCAR races are becoming prized programming among television networks. In 1998, NASCAR races were broadcast on five networks: CBS, ABC, ESPN, TBS, and TNN. In 1999, NASCAR signed a $2.4 billion deal that gave television rights to NBC and Fox from 2001 through 2006. This deal increased NASCAR's annual television rights earnings from $110 million to $400 million.

In recent years, NASCAR has expanded its reach beyond the racetrack with an interactive Web site (www.nascar.com), a $20 million entertainment complex and museum called Daytona USA, the NASCAR Thunder chain of retail stores, and a restaurant called the NASCAR Café. In order to reach younger fans, NASCAR sponsored a 30-city summer concert tour in 1999 called "NASCAR Rocks."

Sources: Robert G. Hagstrom, *The NASCAR Way* (New York: John Wiley & Sons, 1998); Keith Dunnavant, "NASCAR: Unsafe at This Speed?" *Business Week*, 1 November 1999; Joe Flint, "NBC, Fox Secure 8-Year TV Pact for NASCAR Races," *Wall Street Journal*, 11 November 1999; Kate Fitzgerald, "NASCAR Rolls in Rock," *Advertising Age*, 14 June 1999.

events. In particular, events can be chosen based on attendees' attitudes and usage regarding certain products or brands. Lincoln sponsors tennis tournaments because of a belief that tennis players are prime customers for its product. Similarly, Subaru believed there was a match between skiing events and potential buyers of its four-wheel-drive vehicles.

➤ *To increase awareness of the company or product name:* Sponsorship often offers sustained exposure to a brand, a necessary condition to build brand recognition. By skillfully choosing sponsorship events or activities, identification with a product and thus brand recall can be enhanced. For example, Dutch Boy sponsors an "In the Paint" graphic in televised NBA coverage to update key game statistics (as hoop fans know, the area within the foul lines on a basketball court is referred to as "the paint"), and AT&T sponsors a long-distance shootout during NBA All Star Weekend as a contest to identify the best professional three-point shooter.

➤ *To create or reinforce consumer perceptions of key brand image associations:* Events themselves have associations that help to create or reinforce brand associations. For example, Anheuser-Busch chose to have Bud Light become a sponsor of the Ironman and other triathlons because it wanted a "healthy" image for the beer and did not want it to be seen as a beer for wimps. In some cases, the product itself may be used at an event, providing demonstration of its abilities. For example, Seiko has been the official timer of the Olympics for years. As part of Motorola's 1996 Olympic sponsorship in Atlanta, it donated 10,000 two-way radios, 6,000 pagers, 1,500 computer modems, and 1,200 cellular phones.

➤ *To enhance corporate image dimensions:* Sponsorship is seen as a soft sell and as a means to improve perceptions that the company is likable, prestigious, and so forth. It is often hoped that consumers will credit the company for its sponsorship and favor it in later product choices.

➤ *To create experiences and evoke feelings:* Events can be included as part of an experiential marketing program. The feelings engendered by an exciting or rewarding event may indirectly link to the brand. Marketers can also use the Web to provide further event support and additional experiences. For example, spirits marketer Kahlua sponsored a tour of clubs in major U.S. cities featuring dance mixes by six popular DJs and then offered streaming music, tour info, and a CD compilation on its Web site. American Express launched its Blue card through an outdoor concert in New York's Central Park featuring Sheryl Crow, among others.

➤ *To express commitment to the community or on social issues:* Often called *cause-related marketing,* these sponsorships involve corporate tie-ins with nonprofit organizations and charities (see Chapter 11). An early pioneer in this area, American Express supported more than 70 causes in 18 countries with $8.6 million in donations from 1981 to 1986, ranging from the preservation of the national bird of Norway to the protection of the Italian coastline. As another example, Colgate-Palmolive has sponsored the Starlight Foundation, which grants wishes to young people who are critically ill, for years.

➤ *To entertain key clients or reward key employees:* Many events have lavish hospitality tents and other special services or activities that are only available for sponsors and their guests. Involving clients with the event in these and other ways can engender goodwill and establish valuable business contacts. From an employee perspective, events can build participation and morale or be used as an incentive. For example, when John Hancock, as part of its Winter Olympic sponsorship in 1994, offered trips to Lillehammer, Norway, as a reward for agents who generated $100,000 in commissions, twice the number of agents qualified than in years past.

➤ *To permit merchandising or promotional opportunities:* Many marketers tie in contests or sweepstakes, in-store merchandising, and direct response or other marketing activities with their event. When Sprint sponsored the World Cup in 1994, its related activities included long-distance calling cards picturing soccer stars, a geography program for Latin American schools tied to game results, and discounts on long-distance calls for soccer-related businesses and local soccer groups.[44]

Despite these potential advantages, there are a number of potential disadvantages to sponsorship. The success of an event can be unpredictable and out of the control of the sponsor. For example, the hopes of Kodak as sponsor of the Great American Balloonfest were blown away when bad weather hampered the planned set of events. There can be much clutter in sponsorship. Finally, although many consumers will credit sponsors for providing necessary financial assistance to make an event possible, some consumers may still resent the commercialization of events through sponsorship.

Guidelines

Developing successful event sponsorship involves choosing the appropriate events, designing the optimal sponsorship program, and measuring the effects of sponsorship on brand equity.[45]

Choosing Sponsorship Opportunities   Because of the huge amount of money involved and the number of event opportunities that exist, many marketers are becoming more strategic about the events with which they will get involved and the manner by which they will do so. As it is, the sophistication in marketing events in the United States lags behind many countries in Europe and elsewhere where restricted media options have spawned greater sponsorship activity over the years.

There are a number of potential guidelines for choosing events (see Chapter 7). Fundamentally, the marketing objectives and communication strategy that have been defined for the brand must be met by the event. Thus, the audience delivered by the event must match the target market of the brand. Moreover, the event must have sufficient awareness, possess the desired image, and be capable of creating the desired effects with that target market. Of particular concern is whether consumers make favorable attributions to the sponsor for its event involvement. An "ideal event" might be one whose audience closely matches the ideal target market, that generates much favorable attention, that is unique but not encumbered with many sponsors, that lends itself to ancillary marketing activities, and that reflects or even enhances the brand or corporate image of the sponsor.

Of course, rather than linking themselves to an event, some sponsors create their own. The cable sports network ESPN created the X Games to capture youth-oriented activities (e.g., road-luge racing, in-line skating, skateboarding, bungee jumping, and sky surfing) that appealed to a market segment not as easily attracted to traditional sports. More and more firms are also using their names to sponsor the arenas, stadiums, and other venues that actually hold the events. Staples is paying $100 million over 20 years to name the downtown Los Angeles arena where the NBA Lakers and Clippers and the NHL Kings play and where concerts and other events are also held. Although stadium naming rights can command high fees, it should be recognized that its direct contribution to building brand equity is primarily in creating brand recognition—not brand recall—and typically would be expected to do little for brand image except perhaps to convey a certain level of scope and size.

Designing Sponsorship Programs   Many marketers believe that it is the marketing program accompanying a sponsorship that ultimately determines its success. A sponsor can strategically identify itself at an event in a number of ways, including banners, signs, and programs. For more significant and broader impact, however, sponsors typically supplement such activities with samples, prizes, advertising, retail promotions, publicity, and so forth. Marketers often note that from at least two to three times the amount of the sponsorship expenditure should be spent on related marketing activities.

David D'Allesandro, CEO of John Hancock, believes the key to successful sponsorship is leveraging the event so that it goes beyond simple calculations such as cost-per-thousand TV advertising exposures. John Hancock uses sponsorships to entertain big clients, attract new customers, inspire current salespeople, recruit new salespeople, and raise employee morale. For Hancock, D'Allesandro believes the best events are either very big in scope, like the Olympics, or very localized, like a youth hockey clinic with an Olympian.

Measuring Sponsorship Activities   There are two basic approaches to measuring the effects of sponsorship activities: The *supply-side* method focuses on potential exposure to the brand by assessing the extent of media coverage, and the *demand-side* method focuses on reported exposure from consumers.

Supply-side methods attempt to approximate the amount of time or space devoted to the brand in media coverage of an event. For example, the number of seconds that the brand is clearly visible on a television screen or the column inches of press clippings covering an event that mention the brand can be estimated. This measure of potential impressions delivered by an event sponsorship is then translated into an equivalent value in advertising dollars according to the fees associated with actually advertising in the particular media vehicle.

John Hancock

In 1991, John Hancock calculated that the value of press coverage of the college football bowl that it sponsored—which included 7,829 stories and some TV reports—was worth $1.1 million. Broadcast of the game by the CBS network included approximately 60 minutes of exposure to the brand in the four-hour telecast, which, when combined with the company's pregame promotions, added another $4 million in value. All told, Hancock believed the financial benefit of the sponsorship, based on the amount of coverage and what Hancock would have to pay for the same amount of ad space in print or commercial time on TV, was $5.1 million. Given that the total cost of the sponsorship was $1.6 million (which included $1 million sponsorship fees, $500,000 in TV rights fees, 10.5 minutes of paid commercial time during the TV broadcast, and $100,000 for various charity scholarships and a game banquet in the host city of El Paso), John Hancock believed the sponsorship was effective.[46]

Although supply-side exposure methods provide quantifiable measures, their validity can be questioned. The difficulty lies in the fact that equating media coverage with advertising exposure ignores the content of the respective communications that consumers receive. The advertiser uses media space and time to communicate a strategically designed message. Media coverage and telecasts only expose the brand and don't necessarily embellish its meaning in any direct way. Although some public relations professionals maintain that positive editorial coverage can be worth 5 to 10 times the advertising equivalency value, it is rare that sponsorship affords the brand such favorable treatment. As one group of critics noted:

Equating incidental visual and audio exposures with paid advertising time is, we feel, questionable at best. A commercial is a carefully crafted persuasive declaration of a product's virtues. It doesn't compete for attention with the actual on-camera action of a game or race. A 30-second exposure of a billboard in the background can't match the value of 30 seconds in which the product is the only star.[47]

An alternative measurement approach is the demand-side method, which attempts to identify the effects that sponsorship has on consumers' brand knowledge structures. Thus, tracking or custom surveys can explore the ability of the event sponsorship to affect awareness, attitudes, or even sales.

Event spectators can be identified and surveyed after the event to measure recall of the event's sponsor as well as attitudes and intentions toward the sponsor as a result. For example, a survey by DDB Needham in 1992 indicated that 22 of 37 Olympic sponsors created no connection in consumer minds with the event.[48] A random survey of viewers who watched 10 or so hours of television coverage of the 1993 U.S. Open tennis tournament found that only 7 percent knew who sponsored the men's singles title (Nissan Motor Corporation's Infiniti brand) and only 14 percent knew who sponsored the women's singles title (Bristol-Meyer's Clairol brand).

Public Relations and Publicity

Public relations and publicity relate to a variety of programs and are designed to promote or protect a company's image or its individual products. *Publicity* refers to nonpersonal communications such as press releases, media interviews, press conferences, feature articles, newsletters, photographs, films, and tapes. *Public relations* may also involve such things as annual reports, fund-raising and membership drives, lobbying, special event management, and public affairs.

The marketing value of public relations got a big boost in 1983 when public relations firm Burson-Marsteller's skillful handling of Johnson & Johnson's Tylenol product tampering incident was credited with helping to save the brand. Brand Focus 6.0 provides a comprehensive account of that landmark campaign. Around that time, politicians also discovered the power of campaign sound bites that were picked up by the press as a means of broad, cost-efficient candidate exposure.

Marketers now recognize that although public relations is invaluable during a marketing crisis, it also needs to be a routine part of any marketing communications program. Even companies that primarily use advertising and promotions can benefit from well-conceived and well-executed publicity. For example, when Heinz launched its new EZ Squirt kids' condiments, an extensive PR effort resulted in 4,000 news stories and a 5 percent increase in market share before advertising even hit the airwaves.

Buzz Marketing

Occasionally, a product enters the market with little fanfare yet is still able to attract a strong customer base. Something about the product attracts a core group of consumers, who are eager to spread word of the product among their peers. News travels in this fashion until enough tongues are wagging to constitute a "buzz" about the brand. Increasingly, companies are attempting to create consumer word of mouth through various techniques often called *buzz marketing*.[49] Krispy Kreme is an example of a brand that benefited from the buzz created by word-of-mouth publicity, rather than advertising, in the promotion of its product. Primarily with the aid of rave reviews from satisfied customers, the company gradually grew from a single donut shop in Winston-Salem, North Carolina, into one of the hottest franchises in America. The buzz surrounding the brand was readily apparent when Krispy Kreme saw shares from its April 2000 initial public offering increase 75 percent during the first day of trading.

Krispy Kreme built its reputation over 70 years by serving its donuts to an ever-widening group of customers. Established companies do not have the luxury of time, so they often attempt to catalyze the buzz marketing effect for new product introductions. One popular method is to allow consumers who are likely to influence other consumers "discover" the product in the hopes that they will pass a positive endorsement on to their peers. To this end, in 2000 Chrysler seeded rental car companies in trendy Miami with its retro-styled PT Cruiser in order to build buzz about the car. A variation on this method is to hire influencers to promote the product, as Piaggio USA did when it hired a street team of models to drive its Vespa scooters around Los Angeles and talk up the brand.

Buzz marketing works well when the marketing message appears to originate with an independent source and not with the brand. Because consumers are become increasingly skeptical and wary of traditional advertising, buzz marketers seek to expose consumers to their brands in a unique and innocuous fashion. One approach is to enlist genuine consumers able to give authentic-seeming endorsements of the brand. An ad executive with Bates USA explained the goal of this strategy: "Ultimately, the brand benefits because an accepted member of the social circle will always be more credible than any communication that could ever come directly from the brand."[50]

Some criticize buzz marketing as "a form of cultural corruption" in which marketers are actually creating the culture at a fundamental level. Critics claim that buzz marketing's interference in consumer's lives is insidious because the pitch cannot always be detected. Another potential problem with buzz marketing is that it requires a buzz-worthy product. As one marketing expert said, "The bad news is that [buzz marketing] only works in high-interest product categories." In spite of these drawbacks, experts predicted that buzz marketing would retain its appeal for marketers. Said one ad executive, "The biggest problem with buzz marketing in the next 24 months will be the glut of people trying to do it."[51] Branding Brief 6-8 describes how the film *The Blair Witch Project* was successfully marketed in this way.

Author and former Silicon Valley marketing executive Emanuel Rosen developed the following guidelines to help marketers avoid buzz marketing pitfalls in their advertising:[52]

➤ *Keep it simple.* Simple messages spread across social networks more easily.
➤ *Tell us what's new.* The message must be relevant and newsworthy for people to want to tell others about it.
➤ *Don't make claims you can't support.* Making false claims will kill buzz or, worse, lead to negative buzz.
➤ *Ask your customers to articulate what's special about your product or service.* If customers can explain why they like the product or service, they can then communicate this to others.
➤ *Start measuring buzz.* This can help determine which strategies generate the most buzz.
➤ *Listen to the buzz.* Monitoring consumer reaction can yield insights such as how to improve the product or service.

Personal Selling

Personal selling involves face-to-face interaction with one or more prospective purchasers for the purpose of making sales. Personal selling represents a communication option with

Generating a Buzz for *The Blair Witch Project*

The Blair Witch Project, an independent film made on a meager $35,000 budget (see Figure A), became an unexpected mainstream blockbuster thanks in no small part to the Internet. Of course, the groundbreaking nature of the frightening film deserves a lot of credit, but a carefully crafted Internet marketing strategy was vital to the film's success. With the help of a creative Web site and a viral marketing campaign designed to fuel word-of-mouth endorsements, buzz for the *Blair Witch Project* rapidly built up and propelled box office totals above $140 million.

Before the film had been picked up by a studio, the film's directors, Daniel Myrick and Eduardo Sanchez, created a Web site that presented the fictional disappearances depicted in the movie as fact. Artisan Entertainment, the studio that bought the film for $1.1 million after its debut at the Sundance Film Festival, continued to use the Internet as the primary marketing medium for the film. It redesigned the Web site to include fake photographs, police reports, and a history of the Blair Witch, and relaunched blairwitch.com on April Fool's Day 1999. While the buzz was simmering as a result of the site, the studio screened the movie at 40 college campuses, where wired students were likely to spread word of the Blair Witch to others.

FIGURE A   *The Blair Witch Project*

Rather than breaking the trailer on television, Artisan chose the entertainment Web site Ain't It Cool News to air the trailer first. When the trailer made it to MTV, the *Blair Witch* Web site address figured prominently on the screen. Artisan frequently added new links and features to the site, enticing surfers to return again and again. By the end of 1999, blairwitch.com had attracted more than 180 million page hits and over 20 million unique visitors. One Artisan executive described the Internet strategy as follows:

"Most people use the Internet as a promotional tool to provide information about a movie. We used it as a tool to establish the Blair Witch phenomenon. On the Internet, its easy to establish your own reality."

It cost only $1.5 million to get the Internet strategy off the ground, and marketing expenditures for the movie totaled $25 million, or less than half the marketing budget for a typical blockbuster. From its humble roots, the *Blair Witch Project* grew into a franchise complete with sequels, videos, merchandise, and comic books and spawned unaffiliated spoofs. The movie also changed attitudes in Hollywood about Internet marketing. Describing the effect of the *Blair Witch* phenomenon, Artisan home entertainment marketing chief Naomi Pollock said, "There probably won't be a single film from now on where the head of the studio won't ask, 'So what's our Internet strategy?' "

Unfortunately, Artisan was unable to replicate the success of the original with its sequel *Blair Witch II: Book of Shadows*. The sequel, which one critic called both "terrible" and "boring," managed to take in only $26 million at the box office. One of the reasons the original was such a success—word-of-mouth testimonials spreading rapidly via the Internet—actually *diminished* the audience in the case of *Blair Witch II*. Word spread rapidly in chat rooms, movie news sites, and e-mail messages that the sequel did not live up to the original. As a result, the movie barely covered its production costs.

Source: Michael McCarthy, "The Blair Web Project," *Adweek*, 15 November 1999.

---

pros and cons almost exactly the opposite of advertising. Specifically, the main advantages to personal selling are that a detailed, customized message can be sent to customers and that feedback can be gathered to help close the sale. Prospective customers can be identified, and tailored solutions can be offered. Products often can be demonstrated with customer involvement as part of the sales pitch for the brand. Personal selling can also be beneficial after the sale to handle customer problems and ensure customer satisfaction. The main disadvantages to personal selling are the high cost involved and its lack of breadth. For many mass-market products, personal selling would be cost prohibitive.[53]

Personal selling practices have changed in recent years in recognition of the importance of achieving competitive parity or even superiority with sales and customer service. According to a *Business Week* cover story, "smart selling" means focusing the entire company on its customers, including changing how salespeople are hired, trained, and paid.[54] These commentators believe that the keys to better selling are to

➤ *Rethink training.* Forget high-pressure, slam-dunk selling. Sales reps need new skills: They must learn to become customer advocates whose detailed knowledge of their customers' businesses helps them spot sales opportunities and service problems.

➤ *Get everyone involved.* Salespeople should no longer act solo. Everyone in a company, from product designers to plant managers and financial officers, must be a part of selling to and serving customers.

➤ *Inspire from the top.* Chief executives and top managers must frequently and visibly lead the smart-selling charge in their companies. Having the boss call regularly on customers and lead sales training sessions is a must.

➤ *Change the motivation.* Salespeople need constant recognition—but not in the form of the old-fashioned commission. That can be an incentive to scoring a quick sales hit. Instead, include measures of long-term customer satisfaction in calculating compensation.

➤ *Forge electronic links.* Use computerized marketing and distribution technology to track relationships with customers, make sure the right products get to the right stores at the right times, and make order-taking easy. It all adds up to high-tech intimacy.

➤ *Talk to your customers.* Make frequent phone calls, assign a company employee to a customer's plant, or drop notes to frequent shoppers. Customers like the attention, and the added communication makes for better intelligence gathering.

DEVELOPING INTEGRATED MARKETING COMMUNICATION PROGRAMS

The strategies behind marketing communication programs have changed dramatically over the years. Branding Brief 6-9 describes the integrated marketing program behind the Lincoln LS launch. The previous sections examined in depth the various communication options available to marketers. This section considers how to develop an integrated marketing communication (IMC) program in terms of the optimal range of options that should be chosen and the relationships among those options. The main theme that is developed in this discussion is that marketers should "mix and match" communication options to build brand equity—that is, choose a variety of different communication options that share common meaning and content but also offer different, complementary advantages.

Mixing Communication Options

Establishing brand awareness and a positive brand image in consumers' minds produces the knowledge structures that can affect consumer response and generate customer-based brand equity. One implication of the conceptualization of customer-based brand equity is that the *manner* in which brand associations are formed does not matter—only the resulting favorability, strength, and uniqueness of brand associations. In other words, if a consumer has an equally strong and favorable brand association from Rolaids antacids to the concept "relief" because of exposure to a "problem-solution" television ad that concludes with the tag line "Rolaids spells relief" *or* because of knowledge that Rolaids sponsors the "Rolaids Relief Pitcher of the Year" award for major league baseball, the impact in terms of customer-based brand equity should be identical *unless* additional associations are created (e.g., "advertised on television") or existing associations are affected in some way (e.g., "speed or potency of effects").

Thus, from the perspective of customer-based brand equity, marketers should evaluate *all* possible communication options available to create knowledge structures according to effectiveness criteria as well as cost considerations. This broad view of brand-building activities is especially relevant when considering marketing communication strategies to improve brand awareness. As noted in Chapter 2,

Integrated Communications: Launching the Lincoln LS

In 1999, Ford's Lincoln Mercury division debuted the Lincoln LS, a brand-new luxury performance sedan that used the same platform as the Jaguar S Class (see Figure A). The LS was designed to appeal to a younger set of buyers than the typical over-50 Lincoln owners. It was sportier than the flagship Lincoln Town Car and drew favorable comparisons in the auto press to BMW, Audi, and Lexus sedans. In order to get middle-aged adults interested in buying the LS, Lincoln division embarked on a massive $90 million integrated marketing campaign that attempted to alter perceptions of the company as a stodgy luxury car maker for old people.

FIGURE A Lincoln LS

The first component of the integrated marketing campaign was an internal launch to get dealers informed and excited about the LS. Lincoln spent an estimated $6 million on a dealer education event held at a U.S. naval base called Treasure Island in San Francisco Bay. The event was geared toward educating Lincoln dealers about the new car and also about the new, younger group of prospective customers. For dealers unable to attend, Lincoln embarked on a five-city road show that oriented dealers to the new car. Lincoln sent every dealer an elegant black box containing vital marketing materials, including a video of the TV advertising, a CD-ROM featuring the Internet campaign, sample print and direct mail advertising, and the product catalog.

Lincoln also developed extensive external marketing support for the LS launch. As part of a grassroots effort, Lincoln invited more than 4,000 opinion-making consumers to attend glitzy road shows throughout America. The company worked a sponsorship deal with traveling circus/theater/ballet show Cirque du Soleil, and invited potential customers to attend exclusive performances by the troupe during a special eight-city mini-tour. Finally, Lincoln supported the launch with an ambitious and innovative print and television ad campaign. Lincoln's launch promotion worked: It sold all the LS sedans it made in 1999–30,000 cars—and nearly 40 percent of LS buyers had never set foot in a Lincoln showroom prior to shopping for the car.

Sources: Andre Mouchard, "Lincoln-Mercury Enjoys Resurgence," *Winnipeg Free Press*, 29 October 1999; Jim Rogers, "Marketers of the Year: Concept Campaign," *Adweek*, 11 October 1999.

brand awareness is closely related to brand familiarity and can be viewed as a function of the number of brand-related exposures and experiences that have been accumulated by the consumer.[55] Thus, *anything* that causes the consumer to notice and pay attention to the brand can increase brand awareness, at least in terms of brand recognition. Obviously, the visibility of the brand in many sponsorship activities suggests that these activities may be especially valuable for enhancing brand recognition.

To enhance brand recall, however, more intense and elaborate processing of the brand may be necessary so that stronger brand links to the product category are established to improve memory performance. Similarly, because brand associations can be created in the abstract in many different ways, *all* of the possible marketing communication options reviewed earlier in this chapter should be considered to create the desired brand image and knowledge structures.

Consistent with this view, Schultz, Tannenbaum, and Lauterborn conceptualize integrated marketing communications in terms of contacts.[56] They define a *contact* as any information-bearing experience that a customer or prospect has with the brand, the product category, or the market that relates to the marketer's product or service. According to these authors, a person can come in contact with a brand in numerous ways:

> For example, a contact can include friends' and neighbors' comments, packaging, newspaper, magazine, and television information, ways the customer or prospect is treated in the retail store, where the product is shelved in the store, and the type of signage that appears in retail establishments. And the contacts do not stop with the purchase. Contacts also consist of what friends, relatives, and bosses say about a person who is using the product. Contacts include the type of customer service given with returns or inquiries, or even the types of letters the company writes to resolve problems or to solicit additional business. All of these are customer contacts with the brand. These bits and pieces of information, experiences, and relationships, created over time, influence the potential relationship among the customer, the brand, and the marketer.

Figure 6-13 displays a detailed "brand contact map" developed by the leading Australian financial service firm AMP to show all the different ways that people could be exposed to different aspects of its brand.

Determining Optimal Mix

In making the final decision as to how much and what kinds of marketing communications are necessary, economic theory would suggest placing dollars into a marketing communication budget and across communication options according to marginal revenue and cost. For example, the communication mix would be optimally distributed when the last dollar spent on each communication option generated the same return. Because such information may be difficult to obtain, other models of budget allocation emphasize more observable factors such as stage of brand life cycle, objectives and budget of the firm, product characteristics, size of budget, and media strategy of competitors. These factors are typically contrasted with the different characteristics of the media.

FIGURE 6-13   AMP Brand Contact Map

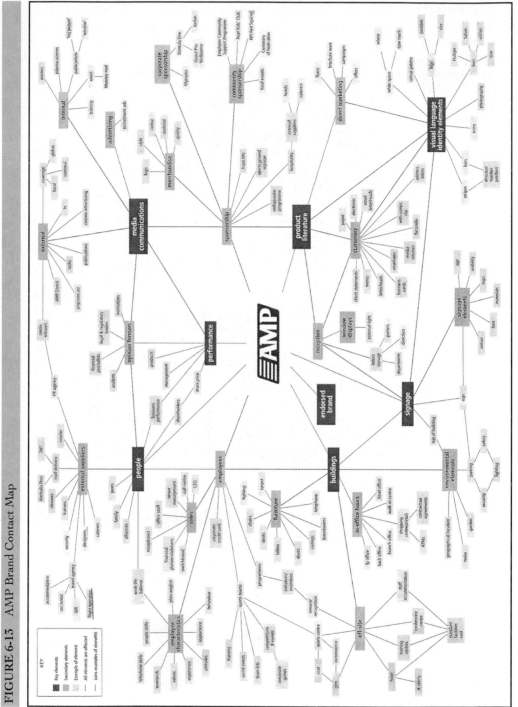

Map created by and provided courtesy of Karl Sergeant and AMP Corporate Brand Management group.

For example, marketing communication budgets tend to be higher when there is low channel support, much change in the marketing program over time, many hard-to-reach customers, more complex customer decision making, differentiated products and nonhomogeneous customer needs, and frequent product purchases in small quantities.[57] Personal selling tends to become a more dominant element in the communication mix when the brand has a high unit value, is technical in nature, requires demonstration, must be tailored to the specific needs of customers, and is purchased infrequently or involves a trade-in; when the firm has a limited communications budget; and when customers are easily identified.[58]

Besides these efficiency considerations, different communication options also may be chosen to target different market segments. For example, advertising may attempt to bring new customers into the market or attract competitor's customers to the brand, whereas promotions may attempt to reward loyal users of the brand, or vice versa.

Matching Communication Options

There are many ways to create IMC programs. A number of considerations come into play when holistically evaluating an IMC program, that is, when considering responses to a set of communications across a group of consumers. This discussion assumes that the marketer has already thoroughly researched the target market and fully understands who they are—their perceptions, attitudes, and behaviors—and therefore knows exactly what needs to be done with them in terms of communication objectives.

In assessing the collective impact of an IMC program, the overriding goal is to create the most effective and efficient communication program possible. Toward that goal, six relevant criteria can be identified:

1. Coverage
2. Contribution
3. Commonality
4. Complementarity
5. Versatility
6. Cost

The following sections consider each criterion in turn.

Coverage

Coverage relates to the proportion of the audience that is reached by each communication option employed, as well as how much overlap exists among communication options. In other words, to what extent do different communication options reach the designated target market and the same or different consumers making up that market? As Figure 6-14 shows, the unique aspects of coverage relate to the "main effects"; the common aspects relate to the "interaction effects."

The unique aspect of coverage relates to the inherent communication ability of a marketing communication option, as suggested by the second criterion (i.e., contribution). To the extent that there is some overlap in communication options, however,

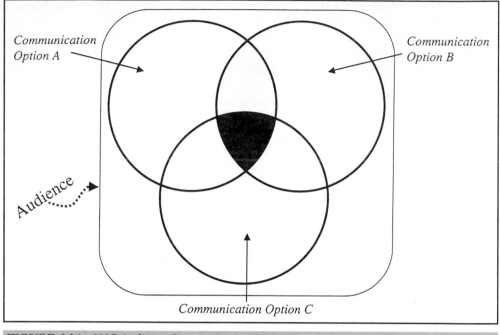

FIGURE 6-14   IMC Audience Communication Option Overlap

The circles represent the market segments reached by various communication options. The shaded portion represents the area of overlap among communication options.

marketers must decide how to optimally design their communication program to reflect the fact that consumers may already have some communication effects in memory prior to exposure to any particular communication option. In terms of its effect on brand knowledge, a communication option may either reinforce associations and strengthen linkages that are also the focus of other communication options or address other associations and linkages that are *not* the focus of other communication options, as suggested by the third and fourth criteria (i.e., commonality and complementarity). Moreover, if less than perfect overlap exists—which is almost always the case—a communication option may be designed to reflect the fact that consumers may or may not have seen other communication options, as suggested by the fifth criterion (i.e., versatility). Finally, all of these considerations must be offset by their cost, as suggested by the sixth criterion.

Contribution

Contribution relates to the inherent ability of a marketing communication to create the desired response and communication effects from consumers *in the absence of exposure to any other communication option*. In other words, contribution relates to the "main effects" of a marketing communication option in terms of how it affects consumers' processing of a communication and the resulting outcomes. As noted earlier, marketing communications can play many different roles (e.g., building awareness, enhancing image, eliciting responses, inducing sales), and the contribution of any marketing communication option will depend on how well it plays that role. Also as noted earlier, much prior research has considered this aspect of communications, generating conceptual guidelines and evaluation criteria in the process. Given that overlap with communication options exist, however, other factors must be considered, as follows.

Commonality

Regardless of which communication options are chosen, the entire marketing communication program should be coordinated to create a consistent and cohesive brand image in which brand associations share content and meaning. The consistency and cohesiveness of the brand image is important because the image determines how easily existing associations and responses can be recalled and how easily additional associations and responses can become linked to the brand in memory.

Commonality relates to the extent to which *common* associations are reinforced across communication options, that is, the extent to which information conveyed by different communication options shares meaning. Most definitions of IMC emphasize only this criterion. For example, Burnett and Moriarty define integrated marketing communications as the "practice of unifying all marketing communication tools—from advertising to packaging—to send target audiences a consistent, persuasive message that promotes company goals."[59]

In general, information that is consistent in meaning is more easily learned and recalled than unrelated information—though the unexpectedness of information inconsistent in meaning with the brand sometimes can lead to more elaborate processing and stronger associations than consistent information.[60] Nevertheless, with inconsistent associations and a diffuse brand image, consumers may overlook some associations or, because they are confused about the meaning of the brand, form less strong and less favorable new associations.

Therefore, in the long run, different communication elements should be designed and combined so that they work effectively together to create a consistent and cohesive brand image. As branding expert Larry Light states: "The total brand experience must be a result of an integrated, focused, strategically sound, differentiated, consistent, branded marketing program. Inconsistency, instead of integration, leads to uncertainty. Yet, uncertainty and inconsistency do seem to be the result of a lot of today's marketing practices."[61]

Note also that there may actually be memory advantages to using multiple communication options to create positive brand images. The *encoding variability principle* in psychology argues that presenting information in varied contexts causes information to be encoded in slightly different ways. As a result, multiple retrieval routes are formed in memory, each of which converges on the to-be-remembered information, thereby enhancing recall.[62] In other words, multiple ways of learning information provide multiple cues for recalling information, thereby improving memory performance. Thus, the encoding variability principle suggests that an IMC program, by employing multiple communication elements, may be an effective way to create, maintain, or strengthen brand associations in memory.

The more abstract the association to be created or reinforced by marketing communications, the more likely it would seem that it could be effectively reinforced in different ways across heterogeneous communication options.[63] For example, if the desired association is "contemporary," then there may be a number of different ways to make a brand seem modern and relevant. On the other hand, if the desired association is a concrete attribute (e.g., "rich chocolate taste"), then it may be difficult to convey in communication options that do not permit explicit product statements (e.g., sponsorship).

Finally, another commonality issue is the extent of executional consistency across communication options—that is, the extent to which non-product-related information is conveyed in different communication options. The more coordinated that executional information is, the more likely it is that this information can serve as a retrieval cue to other communication effects.[64] In other words, if a symbol is established in one communication option (e.g., a feather in a TV ad for a deodorant to convey mildness and softness), then it can be used in other communications to help trigger the knowledge, thoughts, feelings, and images stored in memory from exposure to a previous communication.

Complementarity

Communication options are often more effective when used in tandem. *Complementarity* relates to the extent to which *different* associations and linkages are emphasized across communication options. For example, research has shown that promotions can be more effective when combined with advertising.[65] In both cases, the awareness and attitudes created by advertising campaigns can improve the success of more direct sales pitches. Thus, the ideal marketing communication program would ensure that the communication options chosen are mutually compensatory and reinforcing to create desired consumer knowledge structures.

Different brand associations may be most effectively established by capitalizing on those marketing communication options best suited to eliciting a particular consumer response or establishing a particular type of brand association. For example, some media are demonstrably better at generating trial than engendering long-term loyalty (e.g., sampling or other forms of sales promotion). As part of the highly successful "Drivers Wanted" campaign, VW used television to introduce a story line that it continued and embellished on its Web site. Brand Focus 6.1 describes how communication options may need to be explicitly tied together to capitalize on complementarity to build brand equity.

Versatility

Versatility refers to the extent that a marketing communication option is robust and effective for different groups of consumers. There are two types of versatility: communication and consumer. The reality of any IMC program is that when consumers are exposed to a particular marketing communication, some consumers will have already been exposed to other marketing communications for the brand, whereas other consumers will not have had any prior exposure. The ability of a marketing communication to work at two levels—effectively communicating to consumers who have or have not seen other communications—is critically important. That is, some communications will be ineffective unless consumers have already been exposed to other communications. For example, mass advertising or some type of awareness-creating communication is often seen as a necessary condition for personal selling. A marketing communication option is deemed robust when it achieves its desired effect *regardless* of consumers' past communication history.

Besides this communication versatility, communication options may also be judged in terms of their broader consumer versatility, that is, in terms of how communications affect consumers who vary on dimensions other than their communication history, especially on dimensions such as brand or product knowledge or processing goals. In other words, how well does one particular marketing communication option inform or persuade depending on the different market segments involved? Communications directed at primarily creating brand awareness (e.g., sponsorship) may be more robust by virtue of their simplicity.

There would seem to be two possible means of achieving this dual communication ability:

1. *Multiple information provision strategy:* Providing different information within a communication option to appeal to the different types of consumers. An important issue here is how information that is designed to appeal to one target market of consumers will be processed by other consumers and target markets. Issues of information overload, confusion, and annoyance may come into play if communications become burdened with a great deal of detail.

2. *Broad information provision strategy:* Providing information that is rich or ambiguous enough to work regardless of prior consumer knowledge. The important issue here is how potent or successful that information can be made. By attempting to appeal to the lowest common denominator, the information may lack precision and sufficient detail to have any meaningful impact on consumers. To be successful, consumers with disparate backgrounds will have to find information in the communication sufficiently relevant to satisfy their goals given their product or brand knowledge or communications history.

Cost

Finally, evaluations of marketing communications on all of the preceding criteria must be weighed against their cost to arrive at the most effective *and* efficient communication program.

Using IMC Choice Criteria

The IMC choice criteria can provide some guidance for designing and implementing integrated marketing communication programs. To do so, however, involves evaluating communication options, establishing priorities and tradeoffs, and executing the final design and implementation.

Evaluating Communication Options

Marketing communication options or communication types can be judged according to the response and communication effects that they can create as well as how they rate on the IMC choice criteria. Different communication types and options have different strengths and weaknesses and raise different issues. Several points about the IMC choice criteria ratings are worth noting. First, there are not necessarily any inherent differences across communication types for contribution and complementarity because each communication type, if properly designed, can play a critical and unique role in achieving communication objectives. Similarly, all marketing communications are seemingly expensive, although some differences in market prices with respects to cost per thousands can prevail. Communication types vary, however, in terms of their breadth and depth of coverage as a result of the audiences that they can deliver. Communication types also differ in terms of commonality and versatility according to the number of modalities involved: The more modalities available with a communication type, the greater its potential commonality and versatility.

Arriving at a final mix requires, in part, decisions on priorities and tradeoffs among the IMC choice criteria, discussed next.

Establishing Priorities and Tradeoffs

Deciding on which IMC program to adopt, after the various marketing communication options have been profiled, will depend in part on how the choice criteria are ranked. In addition to setting priorities, decisions must be made concerning tradeoffs because the IMC choice criteria themselves are related.

Priorities will depend in part on the objectives of the marketing communication program (e.g., short-run vs. long-run concerns) and the marketing program in general, which, in turn, depend on a host of factors beyond the scope of this chapter. A number of possible tradeoffs can be identified with the IMC choice criteria, primarily dealing with the three factors that are concerned with overlaps in coverage.

➤ Commonality and complementarity will often be inversely related. The more that various marketing communication options emphasize the same brand attribute or benefit, all else being equal, the less they can effectively emphasize other attributes and benefits.

➤ Versatility and complementarity will also often be inversely related. The more a marketing communication program maximizes complementarity in content, the less critical is the versatility of any communication option. In other words, the more a communication program accounts for differences in consumers across communication options, the less necessary it is that any one communication is designed to appeal to different consumer groups.

➤ Commonality and versatility, on the other hand, do not share an obvious relationship; it may be possible, for example, to develop a sufficiently abstract message (e.g., "Brand X is contemporary") that can be effectively reinforced across multiple communication types (e.g., advertising, interactive, sponsorship, promotions).

Executing Final Design and Implementation

Once the broad strategic guidelines are put into place, specific executional details of each communication option must be determined, and the specific parameters of the media plan must be put into place. In terms of the former, communication options must be developed as creatively as possible to maximize the probability that they will achieve their desired objectives. In terms of the latter, decisions must be made about the concentration and continuity of the different communication options in the IMC plan. *Concentration* refers to the amount of communications that consumers receive. Consumers may be exposed to a varying amount of the same or different communications. *Continuity* refers to the distribution of those exposures in terms of how massed or diffused they are.

Review

This chapter provided conceptual frameworks and managerial guidelines for how marketing communications can be integrated to enhance brand equity. The chapter addressed this issue from the perspective of customer-based brand equity, which maintains that brand equity is fundamentally determined by the brand knowledge created in consumers' minds by the supporting marketing program. A number of basic communication options were reviewed (broadcast, print, direct response, online, and place advertising media; consumer and trade promotions; event marketing and sponsorship; publicity and public relations; and personal selling) in terms of basic characteristics as well as success factors for effectiveness. The chapter also provided criteria as to how different communication options should be combined to maximally build brand equity.

Two key implications emerge from this discussion. First, from the perspective of customer-based brand equity, all possible communication options should be evaluated in terms of their ability to affect brand equity. In particular, the CBBE concept provides a common denominator by which the effects of different communication options can be evaluated: Each communication option can be judged in terms of the effectiveness and efficiency by which it affects brand awareness and by which it creates, maintains, or strengthens favorable and unique brand associations. Different communication options have different strengths and can accomplish different objectives. Thus, it is important to employ a mix of different communication options, each playing a specific role in building or maintaining brand equity.

The second important insight that emerges from the conceptual framework is that the marketing communication program should be put together in a way such that the whole is greater than the sum of the parts. In other words, as much as possible, there should be a match among certain communication options so that the effects of any one communication option are enhanced by the presence of another option.

FIGURE 6-15   General Marketing Communication Guidelines

---

1. *Be analytical:* Use frameworks of consumer behavior and managerial decision making to develop well-reasoned communication programs.
2. *Be curious:* Better understand customers by using all forms of research, and always be thinking of how you can create added value for consumers.
3. *Be single-minded:* Focus your message on well-defined target markets (less can be more).
4. *Be integrative:* Reinforce your message through consistency and cuing across all communication options and media.
5. *Be creative:* State your message in a unique fashion; use alternative promotions and media to create favorable, strong, and unique brand associations.
6. *Be observant:* Keep track of competition, customers, channel members, and employees through monitoring and tracking studies.
7. *Be patient:* Take a long-term view of communication effectiveness to build and manage brand equity.
8. *Be realistic:* Understand the complexities involved in marketing communications.

In closing, the basic message of this chapter is simple: Advertisers need to evaluate marketing communication options strategically to determine how they can contribute to brand equity. To do so, advertisers need some theoretical and managerial guidelines by which they can determine the effectiveness and efficiency of various communication options both singularly and in combination with other communication options. Figure 6-15 provides the author's philosophy concerning the design, implementation, and interpretation of marketing communication strategies.

Discussion Questions

1. Pick a brand and gather all its marketing communication materials. How effectively has the brand mixed and matched marketing communications? Has it capitalized on the strengths of different media and compensated for their weaknesses at the same time? How explicitly has it integrated its communication program?
2. What do you see as the role of the Internet for building brands? How would you evaluate the Web site for a major brand, for example, Nike, Disney, or Levi's?
3. From a current issue of *Newsweek* or *Time* magazine, decide which print ad you feel is the best and which ad you feel is the worst based on the criteria described in this chapter.
4. Pick up a Sunday newspaper and look at the coupon supplements. How are they building brand equity, if at all? Try to find a good example and a poor example of brand-building promotions.
5. Choose a popular event. Who sponsors it? How are they building brand equity with their sponsorship? Are they integrating the sponsorship with other marketing communications?

Brand   Focus   6 . 0

Weathering a Brand Crisis: The Tylenol Experience

BUILDING THE TYLENOL BRAND

Tylenol has been a true marketing success story.[66] Originally introduced by McNeil Laboratories as a liquid alternative to aspirin for children, it achieved nonprescription status when McNeil was bought by Johnson & Johnson (J&J) in 1959. J&J's initial marketing plan promoted a tablet form of the product for physicians to prescribe as a substitute for aspirin when allergic reactions occurred. Tylenol consists of acetaminophen, a drug as effective as aspirin in the relief of pain and fever but without the stomach irritation that often accompanies aspirin. Backed by this selective physician push, sales for the brand grew slowly but steadily over the course of the next 15 years. By 1974, sales reached $50 million, or 10 percent of the analgesic market. In defending its turf from the competitive entry of Bristol-Myers' low-priced, but heavily promoted, competitor Datril, J&J recognized the value of advertising Tylenol directly to consumers.

Thanks also to the successful introduction of a line extension, Extra-Strength Tylenol in tablet and capsule form, the brand's market share had risen to 37 percent of the pain reliever market by 1982. As the largest single brand in the history of health and beauty aids, Tylenol was used by 100 million Americans. The brand contributed 8 percent to J&J's sales but almost twice that percentage in terms of net profits to the company. Advertising support for the brand was heavy. A $40 million media campaign was scheduled for 1982 that used two different messages. The "hospital campaign" employed testimonials from people who had been given Tylenol in the hospital and reported that they had grown to trust it. The ad concluded with the tag line "Trust Tylenol—hospitals do." The "hidden camera" campaign showed subjects who had been unobtrusively filmed while describing the symptoms of their headache, trying Extra-Strength Tylenol as a solution and vowing to use it again based on its effectiveness. These ads concluded with the tag line "Tylenol . . . the most potent pain reliever you can buy without a prescription."

THE TYLENOL CRISIS

All of this success came crashing to the ground with the news in the first week of October 1982 that seven people had died in the Chicago area after taking Extra-Strength Tylenol capsules that turned out to contain cyanide poison. Although it quickly became evident that the problem was restricted to that area of the country and had almost certainly been the work of some deranged person outside the company, consumer confidence was severely shaken. Most marketing experts believed that the damage to the reputation of the Tylenol brand was irreparable and that it would never fully recover. For example, well-known advertising guru Jerry Della Femina was quoted in the *New York Times* as saying, "On one day, every single human being in the country thought that Tylenol might kill them. I don't think there are enough advertising dollars, enough marketing men, to change that. . . . You'll not see the name Tylenol in any form within a year." Tylenol's comeback from these seemingly insurmountable odds has become a classic example of how best to handle a marketing crisis.

THE TYLENOL RECOVERY

Within the first week of the crisis, J&J issued a worldwide alert to the medical community, set up a 24-hour toll-free telephone number, recalled and analyzed sample batches of the product, briefed the Food and Drug Administration, and offered a $100,000 reward to apprehend the culprit of the tampering. During the week of October 5, J&J began a voluntary withdrawal of the brand by repurchasing 31 million bottles with a retail value of $100 million. The company stopped advertising, and all communications with the public were in the form of press releases. To monitor consumer response to the crisis, J&J started to conduct weekly tracking surveys with 1,000 consumer respondents. Ultimately, the company spent a total of $1.5 million for marketing research in the fourth quarter of 1982. The following week of October 12, it introduced a capsule exchange offer, promoted in half-page press announcements in 150 major markets across the country, inviting the public to mail in bottles of capsules to receive tablets in exchange. Although well intentioned, this offer met with poor consumer response.

During the week of October 24, J&J made its return to TV advertising with the goals of convincing Tylenol users that they could continue to trust the safety of Tylenol products as well as encouraging the use of the tablet form until tamper—resistant packaging was available. The spokesperson for the ad was Dr. Thomas N. Gates, the company's medical director, whose deep, reassuring voice exuded confidence and control. Looking calmly straight into the camera, he stated:

> You're all aware of the recent tragic events in which Extra-Strength Tylenol capsules were criminally tampered with in limited areas after they left our factories. This act damages all of us—you the American public because you have made Tylenol a trusted part of your healthcare and we who make Tylenol because we've worked hard to earn that trust. We will now work even harder to keep it. We have voluntarily withdrawn all Tylenol capsules from the shelf. We will reintroduce capsules in tamper-resistant containers as quickly as possible. Until then, we urge all Tylenol capsule users to use the tablet form and we have offered to replace your capsules with tablets. Tylenol has had the trust of the medical profession and 100 million Americans for over 20 years. We value that trust too much to let any individual tamper with it. We want you to continue to trust Tylenol.

The heavy media schedule for this ad ensured that 85 percent of the market viewed the ad at least four times during this week.

On November 11, 1982, six weeks after the poisonings and after intense behind-the-scenes activity, the chairman of J&J announced during a live teleconference with 600 news reporters throughout the United States the return of Tylenol capsules to the market in a new, triple-seal package that was regarded as virtually tamperproof. To get consumers to try the new packaging, the largest program of couponing in commercial history was undertaken. On November 28, 1982, 60 million coupons offering a free Tylenol product (valued up to $2.50) were distributed in Sunday newspapers nationwide. Twenty million more coupons were distributed the following Sunday. By the end of December, 30 percent of the coupons that had been issued had been redeemed. Accompanying these consumer marketing efforts, J&J also engaged in a number of activities to enlist the support of retailers in the form of trade promotions, sales calls, and so forth.

Convinced that market conditions were now stable enough to commence regular advertising, J&J's ad agency developed three ad executions using the testimony of loyal Tylenol users with the goal of convincing consumers that they could continue to use Tylenol with confidence. The first ad

execution contained excerpts of consumers' reaction to the tampering incident, the second ad brought back a Tylenol supporter from an ad campaign run before the tampering incident to reassert her trust in Tylenol, and the third ad used the testimony of a Tylenol user who reasoned that she could still trust the product because hospitals still used it. The recall scores for two of the commercials were among the highest ever recorded by ASI, a well-known marketing research firm that conducted the ad testing for J&J. The return to advertising was accompanied by additional coupon promotional offers to consumers.

Incredibly, by February 1983, sales for Tylenol had almost fully returned to the lofty pretampering sales levels the brand had enjoyed six months earlier. Figure 6-16 displays the Tylenol sales growth with respect to management actions during this period. Decades later, the brand is virtually a $1 billion brand, with extensions into

FIGURE 6-16   Tylenol Sales Growth

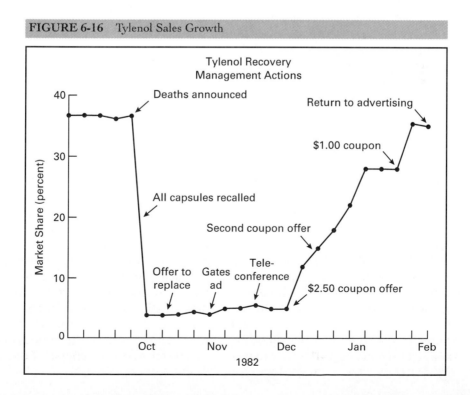

cough and cold remedies. The next-largest pain reliever competitor has only half the market share of Tylenol. Clearly, J&J's skillful handling of an extremely difficult situation was a major factor in the brand's comeback. Another important factor, however, was the equity of the brand and its strong and valuable "trust" association built up over the years prior to the incident. The feelings of trust engendered by the brand helped to speed the brand recovery, a fact certainly evident to J&J (note the number of times the word *trust* appears in the initial Gates ad—five times).

CRISIS MARKETING GUIDELINES

Not all brands have handled their crises as well. Although Exxon spent millions of dollars advertising its gasoline and crafting its brand image over the years, it had essentially ignored marketing its corporate identity and image. This decision came back to haunt the company in the weeks following March 24, 1989. That morning, the tanker *Exxon Valdez* hit a reef in Prince William Sound, Alaska, resulting in some 11,000,000 gallons of oil spilling into the waters off the Alaska shoreline. The oil spill wreaked devastation on the fish and wildlife of some 1,300 square miles of the previously unspoiled area. Top Exxon officials declined to comment publicly for almost a week after the incident, and the public statements that were eventually made sometimes appeared to contradict information from other sources involved in the situation (e.g., regarding the severity of the spill) or assigned blame for the slow clean-up efforts to other parties, such as the U.S. Coast Guard. Exxon received withering negative press and was the source of countless jokes on late-night talk shows. In frustration and anger, some of Exxon's consumers began literally to tear

up their Exxon credit cards. On April 3, ten days after the accident, Exxon's chairman ran an open letter to the public in the form of a full-page message expressing the company's concern and justifying its actions to address the situation.[67]

Marketing managers must assume that at some point in time, some kind of brand crisis will arise. Diverse brands such as Jack in the Box restaurants, Firestone tires, E.F. Hutton brokerage firms, USAir airlines, and Suzuki Samurai sport utility vehicles have all experienced a serious, potentially crippling brand crisis. In general, the more that brand equity and a strong corporate image have been established—especially with respect to corporate credibility and trustworthiness—the more likely it is that the firm can weather the storm. Careful preparation and a well-managed crisis management program, however, are also critical. Most experts would agree that the Exxon incident is a good example of how *not* to handle a brand crisis. As Johnson & Johnson's nearly flawless handling of the Tylenol product tampering incident suggests, the two keys to effectively managing a crisis is that the response by the firm should be seen by consumers as both swift *and* sincere, as follows.

Swiftness

The longer it takes a firm to respond to a marketing crisis, the more likely it is that consumers can form negative impressions as a result of unfavorable media coverage or word of mouth. Perhaps even worse, consumers may find out that they do not really like the brand that much after all and permanently switch to alternative brands or products. For example, Perrier was forced to halt production worldwide and recall all of their existing bottles in February 1994 when traces of benzene, a known carcinogen, was found in excessive quantities in the bottled water. Over the course of the next few weeks, several explanations were offered as to how the contamination occurred, creating confusion and skepticism. Perhaps even more damaging, the product itself was off the shelves until May 1994. Despite an expensive relaunch featuring ads and promotions, the brand struggled to regain lost market share, and a full year later found its sales less than half of what they once had been. Part of the problem was that during the time the product was unavailable, consumers and retailers found satisfactory substitutes (e.g., waters such as Saratoga and San Pellegrino). With its key "purity" association tarnished (the brand had been advertised as the "Earth's First Soft Drink" and "It's Perfect. It's Perrier."), the brand had no other compelling points of difference over these competitors.[68] Finally, compounding the problems arising from their marketing crisis, the brand was gaining an increasingly stodgy image and was seen as much more appealing to the over-45 consumer market and much less appealing to those consumers under 25 years old. Eventually, the company was taken over by Nestlé SA.

Sincerity

Swift actions must also come across as sincere to consumers. The more sincere the response by the firm—in terms of public acknowledgment of the severity of the impact on consumers and the firm's willingness to take whatever steps are necessary and feasible to solve the crisis—the less likely it is that consumers will form negative attributions regarding the firm's be-

havior. For example, although Gerber had established a strong image of trust with consumers, baby food is a product category characterized by an extremely high level of involvement and need for reassurance. When consumers reported finding shards of glass in some jars of its baby food, Gerber tried to reassure the public that there were no problems in its manufacturing plants but adamantly refused to have its baby food withdrawn from grocery stores. Some consumers clearly found Gerber's response unsatisfactory because the brand's market share slumped from 66 percent to 52 percent within a couple of months. As one company official admits, "Not pulling our baby food off the shelf gave the appearance that we aren't a caring company."[69]

Brand crises are difficult to manage because, despite a firm's best efforts, it is difficult to be in control of the situation. To some extent, the firm is at the mercy of public sentiment and media coverage, which it can attempt to direct and influence but which sometimes can take on a life of their own. Swift and sincere words and actions, however, often can go a long way toward defusing the situation. As one commentator notes:

> No one strategy works in every crisis. There are too many variables—the news play, the marketplace, public sympathy or antipathy, whether the company cleans house as well as its image. . . Reality still counts. But simple honesty—'We've got a problem and we're doing X, Y, and Z about it'—is inevitably the last resort.[70]

Brand   Focus   6.1

Coordinating Media to Build Brand Equity

In developing effective integrated marketing communications programs, marketing communications must sometimes be explicitly tied together to create or enhance brand equity. This appendix, after reviewing the nature of the problem, proposes alternative strategies as solutions.

FACTORS CREATING WEAK BRAND LINKS

For brand equity to be built, it is critical that the communication effects created by advertising be linked to the brand. Often, such links are difficult to create. For example, TV ads often do not "brand" well; that is, weak links may exist from the communication effects created by a TV ad to knowledge about the brand in memory. The three main reasons for this are competitive clutter, ad content and structure, and lack of consumer involvement. The following sections examine these factors.

Competitive Clutter

Competing ads in the product category can create interference and consumer confusion as to which ad goes with which brand.[71] Numerous instances can be found in which consumers mix up competing ads and brands. For example, Eveready introduced a clever ad campaign in 1989 for their Energizer batteries that featured a pink toy bunny that kept on "going . . . and going . . . and going." Unfortunately, consumer research by Video Storyboard discovered that

of the people in their annual survey who named this popular commercial as their favorite of the year, 40 percent mistakenly attributed it to Eveready's main competitor, Duracell—only 60 percent correctly identified it as an Energizer ad! To exacerbate this interference problem, it is often the case that competing ads appear in the same media vehicle because they typically target the same consumers. For example, an analysis of one week of prime time television advertising found that of the 57 commercials that ran in an average hour, 24, or 42 percent, faced at least one competitor running an ad during that same time period.[72]

Ad Content and Structure

Factors related to the content and structure of the ad itself can result in weak links from the brand to communication effects created by ad exposure. For example, advertisers have a vast range of creative strategies and techniques at their disposal to improve consumer motivation and lead to greater involvement and enhanced ad processing on their part. Although these "borrowed interest" tactics may effectively grab consumers' attention for an ad, the resulting focus of attention and processing may be directed in a manner that does *not* create strong brand associations. For example, when the popular actor James Garner was advertising for Polaroid, marketing research surveys routinely noted that many interview respondents mistakenly attributed his promotion to Kodak, its chief competitor. Moreover, when these attention-getting creative tactics are employed, the position and prominence of the brand in the ad are often downplayed. Delaying brand identification or providing few brand mentions in an ad may also raise processing intensity but result in attention directed away from the brand. Furthermore, limited brand exposure time in the ad allows little opportunity for elaboration of existing brand knowledge, also contributing to weak brand links.[73]

Consumer Involvement

In certain circumstances, consumers may not have any inherent interest in the product or service category or may lack knowledge of the specific brand (e.g., in the case of a low-share brand or a new market entry). The resulting decrease in consumer motivation and ability to process translates to weaker brand links. Similarly, a change in advertising strategy to target a new market segment or add a new attribute, benefit, or usage association to the brand image may also fail to produce strong brand links because consumers lack the ability to easily relate this new advertising information to existing brand knowledge.[74]

STRATEGIES TO STRENGTHEN COMMUNICATION EFFECTS

Thus, for a variety of reasons, consumers may fail to correctly identify advertising with the advertised brand or, even worse, incorrectly attribute advertising to a competing brand. In these cases, advertising worked in the sense that communication effects—ad claims and executional information, as well as cognitive and affective responses by consumers to that information—were stored in memory. Yet advertising failed in the sense that these communication effects were not accessible when critical brand-related decisions were made.

To address this problem, one common tactic marketers employ to achieve ad and point-of-purchase congruence and improve ad recall is to make the brand name and package information prominent in the ad. Unfortunately, this increase in brand emphasis means that communication effects and brand associations that can potentially affect brand evaluations are less likely to be able to be created by the ad and stored in consumer memory. In other words, although consumers are better able to recall the advertised brand with this tactic, there is *less* other information about the brand to actually recall. Three potentially more effective strategies are brand signatures, ad retrieval cues, and media interactions, as follows.

Brand Signatures

Perhaps the easiest way to increase the strength of brand links to communication effects is to create a more powerful and compelling brand signature. The *brand signature* is the manner by which the brand is identified at the conclusion of a TV or radio ad or displayed within a print ad. The brand signature must creatively engage the consumer and cause him or her to pay more attention to the brand itself and, as a consequence, increase the strength of brand associations created by the ad. An effective brand signature often dynamically and stylistically provides a seamless connection to the ad as a whole. For example, the famous "Got Milk?" campaign always displayed that tag line or slogan in a manner fitting the ad (e.g., in flames for the "yuppie in hell" ad or in primary school print for the "school lunchroom bully" ad). As another example, the introductory Intel Inside ad campaign always ended with a swirling image from which the Intel Inside logo dramatically appeared, in effect stamping the end of the ad with Intel Inside in an "in your face" manner.

Ad Retrieval Cues

An effective tactic to improve consumer's motivation and ability to retrieve communication effects when making a brand-related decision is to use advertising retrieval cues. An *advertising retrieval cue* is visual or verbal information uniquely identified with an ad that is evident when consumers are making a product or service decision. The purpose is to maximize the probability that consumers who have seen or heard the cued ad will retrieve from long-term memory the communication effects that were stored from earlier processing of that ad. Ad retrieval cues may consist of a key visual, a catchy slogan, or any unique advertising element that serves as an effective reminder to consumers. For example, in an attempt to remedy the problem they had with mistaken attributions, Quaker Oats placed a photograph of the "Mikey" character from the popular Life cereal ad on the front of the package. More recently, Eveready featured a picture of their pink bunny character on the packages for their Energizer batteries to reduce consumer confusion with Duracell.

Ad retrieval cues can be placed in the store (e.g., on the package or as part of a shelf talker or some other point-of-purchase device), combined with a promotion (e.g., with a free-standing insert coupon), included as part of a Yellow Pages directory listing, or embedded in any marketing communication option where recall of communication effects can be advantageous to marketers. By using ad retrieval cues, greater emphasis can be placed in the ad on supplying persuasive information and creating positive associations so that consumers have a reason *why* they should purchase the brand. Ad retrieval cues allow for creative freedom in ad execution because the brand and package need not be the centerpiece of the ad. The effectiveness of ad retrieval cues depends on how many communication effects are potentially retrievable and how likely these communication effects are to be retrieved from memory with only the brand as a cue, as compared with the executional information making up the ad retrieval cue. An ad retrieval cue is most effective when many communication effects are stored in memory but are only weakly associated to the brand because of one or more of the various factors noted previously.

Media Interactions

Other strategies besides ad retrieval cues may be employed to maximize the brand equity arising from TV advertising. Print and radio reinforcement of TV ads (in which the video and audio components of a TV ad serve as the basis for the respective type of ads) can be an effective means to leverage existing communication effects from TV ad exposure and more strongly link them to the brand. Cueing a TV ad with an explicitly linked radio or print ad can create similar or even enhanced processing outcomes that can substitute for additional TV ad exposures. Moreover, a potentially useful, although rarely employed, media strategy is to run explicitly linked print or radio ads *prior* to the accompanying TV ad. The print and radio ads in this case function as teasers and increase consumer motivation to process the more complete TV ad consisting of both audio and video components.

As another strategy, different combinations of TV ad excerpts within a campaign (e.g., 15-second spots consisting of highlights from longer 30- or 60-second spots for those campaigns characterized by only one dominant ad, or umbrella ads consisting of highlights from a pool of ads for those campaigns consisting of multiple ad executions) and across campaigns over time (e.g., including key elements from past ad campaigns that are strongly identified with the brand as part of the current ad campaign) may be particularly helpful for strengthening dormant associations and facilitating the formation of consumer evaluations of and reactions to the ads and their linkage to the brand.

TV ADS OVER TIME

The basic rationale for these different strategies is that TV ads should not be considered as discrete units that are created for a particular ad campaign and therefore run for a certain length of time before being replaced by a new ad campaign. Rather, TV ads should be thought of more broadly as consisting of different ingredients or pieces of information that advertisers might choose to combine in different ways over time to improve their brand-building abilities. The most important ingredients are those identifiable visual scenes, characters, symbols, and verbal phrases or slogans that can serve as cues or reminders of communication effects created by a single TV ad, an ad campaign with multiple TV ads, or a previous ad campaign.

Combining these ingredients to leverage communication effects over time offers several potential benefits. First, it can help to maintain the strength of unique and favorable brand associations. In particular, without such reminders, the heritage of a brand and its original associations may become weakened because the ad campaign is not being currently aired or a new ad campaign is using different appeals or creative strategies to reposition or modernize the brand. Second, it can facilitate the formation of favorable attitudes by consumers toward the advertising and brand. In other words, consumers may be likely to say, "I like the ads for that brand." As noted previously, these attitudes toward the ad can favorably affect brand evaluations, especially for low-involvement consumer decisions.

Note that an implicit issue in this discussion is the optimal continuity to have with advertising and communication campaigns over time. Congruity theory would suggest that a moderate amount of change is appropriate.[75] Too little change may not be noticed by consumers and thus have no effect. On the other hand, more dramatic changes in brand positioning may confuse consumers and result in them still continuing to think of the brand in the "old way." Because of strong associations already in memory, consumers may either fail to incorporate new ad information into their brand knowledge structures or fail to retrieve new ad information when making later product or service decisions. In many cases, a moderate change in creative (e.g., retaining the current positioning but communicating it with a new creative) may be the most effective way to maintain or enhance the strength of brand associations. If the favorability or uniqueness of brand associations are deficient in some way, however, then a more severe change in positioning emphasizing different points of parity or points of difference may be necessary.

Notes

1. To obtain a broader perspective, it is necessary to consult good advertising texts such as George E. Belch and Michael A. Belch, *Introduction to Advertising and Promotion*, 3rd ed. (Homewood, IL: Irwin, 1995); Rajeev Batra, John G. Meyers, and David A. Aaker, *Advertising Management*, 5th ed. (Upper Saddle River, NJ: Prentice-Hall, 1996); or John R. Rossiter and Larry Percy, *Advertising and Promotion Management* (New York: McGraw-Hill, 1987).

2. William J. McGuire, "The Nature of Attitudes and Attitude Change," in *The Handbook of Social Psychology, 2nd Ed.,* Eds. G. Lindzey and E. Aronson (Reading, Mass: Addison-Wesley, 1969), Vol. 3, 136–314.

3. Alexander L. Biel, "Converting Image into Equity," in *Brand Equity and Advertising*, eds. David A. Aaker and Alexander L. Biel (Hillsdale, NJ: Lawrence Erlbaum Associates, 1993), 67–82.

4. "How to Turn Junk Mail into a Goldmine— Or Perhaps Not," *The Economist*, 1 April 1995, 51–52.

5. Leonard M. Lodish, Magid Abraham, Stuart Kalmenson, Jeanne Livelsberger, Beth Lubetkin, Bruce Richardson, and Mary Ellen Stevens, "How T.V. Advertising Works: A Meta Analysis of 389 Real World Split Cable T.V. Advertising Experiments," *Journal of Marketing Research* 32 (May 1995): 125–139; Magid Abraham and Leonard Lodish, *Advertising Works: A Study of Advertising Effectiveness and the Resulting Strategies and Tactical Implications* (Chicago: Information Resources Inc., 1989).

6. Lorrie Grant, "Home Depot Sales Soar 16%," *USA Today*, 15 August 2001, B1.

7. Noreen O'Leary, "A Not-So-New Attitude," *Brandweek*, 11 December 2000, 44.

8. Rossiter and Percy, *Advertising and Promotion Management*.

9. Luisa Kroll, "Speed Bump," *Forbes*, 30 April 2001.

10. Batra, Meyers, and Aaker, *Advertising Management*, 5th ed.

11. Max Robins, "Seinfeld Aces Ultimate Test," *TV Guide*, 81.

12. Edwin L. Artzt, speech given at the American Association of Advertising Agencies convention, Greenbrier, VA, May 1994.

13. John Flinn, "Advertising's New Age," *San Francisco Chronicle*, 23 October 1994, B14.

14. Radio Advertising Bureau, "Radio Is Everyone [advertising supplement]" (Irving, TX: Radio Avertising Bureau).

15. For a comprehensive overview, see Bob Schulberg, *Radio Advertising: The Authoritative Handbook*, (Lincolnwood, IL: NTC Business Books, 1990).

16. David Ogilvy, *Ogilvy on Advertising* (New York: Vintage Books, 1983).

17. Judith Graham, "AmEx 'Portraits' Stresses Values," *Advertising Age*, 1 January 1990, 12.

18. For more discussion on these guidelines, see Philip Ward Burton and Scott C. Purvis, eds., *Which Ad Pulled Best?* 5th ed. (Lincolnwood IL: NTC Business Books, 1987).

19. Yumiko Ono, "Direct Marketers Press Fast-Forward on Using Videotapes as Costs Decline," *Wall Street Journal*, 31 October 1994, A8.

20. Julia Reed, "Ads Where You Least Expect Them," *U.S. News and World Report*, 9 March 1987, 46.

21. Kevin Goldman, "P&G Experiments with an Infomercial," *Wall Street Journal*, 8 July 1994, B9.

22. Jim Edwards, "The Art of the Infomercial," *Brandweek,* 3 September 2001, 14–19.

23. "1996 Echo Awards-Spotting the Trendsetters," *Direct Marketing* 59, no. 7 (November 1996): 10–17.

24. "How to Turn Junk Mail into a Goldmine"; Gary Levin, "Going Direct Route," *Advertising Age*, 11 November 1991, 37.

25. See Jakki J. Mohr, *Marketing of High-Technology Products and Innovations* (Upper Saddle River, NJ: Prentice-Hall, 2001); Ward Hanson, *Principles of Internet Marketing* (Cincinnati, OH: South-Western College Publishing, 1999); and Eloise Coupey, *Marketing and the Internet* (Upper Saddle River, NJ: Prentice-Hall, 2001).

26. "Banner-Ad Blues," *The Economist*, 24 February 2001, 63–64.

27. Suzanne Vranica, "GM Is Joining Online Videogame Wave," *Wall Street Journal*, 26 July 2001, B11.

28. Suzanne Vranica, "Volvo Campaign Tests New Media Waters," *Wall Street Journal*, 16 March 2001; Karen Lundegaard, "Volvo's Web-Only Vehicle Launch Ends Amid Ford Unit's Questioning of Tactic," *Wall Street Journal*, 11 January 2001.

29. Jeff Pelline, "New Commercial Twist in Corporate Restrooms," *San Francisco Chronicle*, 6 October 1986.

30. Chuck Stogel, "Quest for the Captive Audience," *Superbrands 1992*, 106–107.

31. David T. Friendly, "Selling It at the Movies," *Newsweek*, 4 July 1983, 46.

32. Joanne Lipman, "Product Placement Can Be Free Lunch," *Wall Street Journal*, 25 November 1991; John Lippman and Rick Brooks, "Hot Holiday Flick Pairs FedEx, Hanks," *Wall Street Journal*, 11 December 2001, B1.

33. Scott Hume and Marcy Magiera, "What Do Moviegoers Think of Ads?" *Advertising Age*, 23 April 1990, 4.

34. *Consumer Reports*, December 1982, 752–755.

35. For an excellent summary of issues related to the type, scope, and tactics of sales promotions design, see John A. Quelch, "Note on Sales Promotion Design," Teaching Note N-589-021 (Boston: Harvard Business School, 1988).

36. Michael L. Ray, *Advertising and Communication Management* (Upper Saddle River, NJ: Prentice-Hall, 1982).

37. Geoffrey Fowler, "When Free Samples Become Saviors," *Wall Street Journal*, 14 August 2001, B1.

38. Chris Roush, "A Sports Marketer with a Mean Curve," *Business Week*, 12 September 1994, 96.

39. Mathew Kinsman, "Coupons: Bad Is Good," *Promo*, 1 April 2001, 71.

40. Rossiter and Percy, *Advertising and Promotion Management*.

41. Eric Hollreiser, "Trading Up from Tactics to Strategy in the Trade Game," *Brandweek*, 3 October 1994, 26–33.

42. See Peggy Cunningham, Shirley Taylor, and Carolyn Reeder, "Event Marketing: The Evolution of Sponsorship from Philanthropy to Strategic Promotion," Conference on Historical Analysis & Research in Marketing, 1993, 407–425.

43. Michael Oneal and Peter Finch, "Nothing Sclls Like Sports," *Business Week*, 31 August 1987, 48–53.

44. Roush, "Sports Marketer."

45. The Association of National Advertisers has a useful source, *Event Marketing: A Management Guide*, which is available by contacting them at 155 East 44th Street, New York, NY 10017.

46. Michael J. McCarthy, "Keeping Careful Score on Sports Tie-Ins," *Wall Street Journal*, 24 April 1991, B1.

47. William L. Shankin and John Kuzma, "Buying That Sporting Image," *Marketing Management* (Spring 1992): 65.

48. Jim Crimmins, "Most Sponsorships Waste Money," *Advertising Age*, 21 June 1993, S-2.

49. Gerry Khermouch, "Buzz Marketing," *Business Week,* 30 July 2001; Catherine Valenti, "Some Brands Thrive without Advertising," ABCNews.com, 23 August 2001.

50. Gerry Khermouch, "Buzz Marketing: Suddenly This Stealth Strategy Is Hot," *Business Week,* 30 July 2001, 50.

51. Ibid.

52. Emanual Rosen, *The Anatomy of Buzz* (New York: Currency, 2000).

53. John Quelch, "Communications Policy," Teaching Note 5–585–021 (Boston: Harvard Business School, 1984).

54. Christopher Power, "Smart Selling," *Business Week*, 3 August 1992, 46–52.

55. Joseph W. Alba and J. Wesley Hutchinson, "Dimensions of Consumer Expertise," *Journal of Consumer Research* 13 (March 1987): 411–453.

56. Don E. Schultz, Stanley I. Tannenbaum, and Robert F. Lauterborn, *Integrated Marketing Communications* (Lincolnwood, IL: NTC Business Books, 1993).

57. Thomas C. Kinnear and Kenneth L. Bernhardt, *Principles of Marketing*, 2nd ed. (Glenview, IL: Scott Foresman, 1986).

58. Philip L. Kotler, *Marketing Management*, 9th ed. (Upper Saddle River, NJ: Prentice-Hall, 1997).

59. John Burnett and Sandra Moriarty, *Introduction to Marketing Communications: An Integrated Approach* (Upper Saddle River, NJ: Prentice-Hall, 1998).

60. Susan E. Heckler and Terry L. Childers, "The Role of Expectancy and Relevancy in Memory for Verbal and Visual Information: What Is Incongruency?" *Journal of Consumer Research* 18 (March 1992): 475–492; Michael J. Houston, Terry L. Childers, and Susan E. Heckler, "Picture-Word Consistency and the Elaborative Processing of Advertisements," *Journal of Marketing Research* 24 (November 1987): 359–369; Thomas K. Srull and Robert S. Wyer, "Person Memory and Judgment," *Psychological Review* 96, no. 1 (1989): 58–83.

61. Larry Light, "Bringing Research to the Brand Equity Process" (paper presented at the ARF Brand Equity Workshop, February 15–16, 1994).

62. For example, see Daniel R. Young and Francis S. Belleza, "Encoding Variability, Memory Organization, and the Repetition Effect," *Journal of Experimental Psychology: Learning, Memory, and Cognition* 8, no. 6 (1982): 545–559; and H. Rao Unnava and

Robert E. Burnkrant, "Effects of Repeating Varied Ad Executions on Brand Name Memory," *Journal of Marketing Research* 28 (November 1991): 406–416.

63. Michael D. Johnson, "Consumer Choice Strategies for Comparing Noncomparable Alternatives," *Journal of Consumer Research* 11 (December 1984): 741–753.

64. Julie A. Edell and Kevin Lane Keller, "The Information Processing of Coordinated Media Campaigns," J*ournal of Marketing Research,* 26 (May 1989): 149–163; Julie Edell and Kevin Lane Keller, "Analyzing Media Interactions: Print Reinforcement of Television Advertising Campaigns," working paper, Fuqua School of Business, Duke University (2002).

65. William T. Moran, "Insights from Pricing Research," in *Pricing Practices and Strategies*, ed. E. B. Bailey (New York: The Conference Board, 1978), 7–13.

66. J.A. Deighton, "Features of Good Integration: Two Cases and Some Generalizations," in *Integrated Communications: The Search for Surgery in Communication Voices,* ed. J. Moore and E. Thorsen (Hillsdale, NJ: Lawrence Erlbaum Associations, 1996).

67. Nancy Langford and Steven A. Greyser, "Exxon: Communications after Valdez," Case 9–593–014 (Boston: Harvard Business School, 1995).

68. Stephen A. Greyser and Norman Klein, "The Perrier Recall: A Source of Trouble," Case 9–590–104 (Boston: Harvard Business School, 1990); Stephen A. Greyser and Norman Klein, "The Perrier Relaunch," Case Supplement 9–590–130 (Boston: Harvard Business School, 1990).

69. Ronald Alsop, "Enduring Brands Hold Their Allure by Sticking Close to Their Roots," *Wall Street Journal Centennial Edition*, 1989.

70. Leslie Savan, "Selling a Sullied Product," *San Francisco Chronicle*, 17 August 1986 5.

71. Raymond R. Burke and Thomas K. Srull, "Competitive Interference and Consumer Memory for Advertising," *Journal of Consumer Research* 15 (June 1988): 55–68; Kevin Lane Keller, "Memory Factors in Advertising: The Effect of Advertising Retrieval Cues on Brand Evaluations," *Journal of Consumer Research* 14 (December 1987): 316–333; Kevin Lane Keller, "Memory and Evaluations in Competitive Advertising Environments," *Journal of Consumer Research* 17 (March 1991): 463–476; Robert J. Kent and Chris T. Allen, "Competitive Interference Effects in Consumer Memory for Advertising: The Role of Brand Familiarity," *Journal of Marketing* 58 (July1994): 97–105.

72. Joe Mandese, "Rivals' Ads Cluttering TV," *Advertising Age*, 14–20 October 1991.

73. David Walker and Michael J. von Gonten, "Explaining Related Recall Outcomes: New Answers from a Better Model," *Journal of Advertising Research* 29 (1989): 11–21.

74. Kevin Lane Keller, Susan Heckler, and Michael J. Houston, "The Effects of Brand Name Suggestiveness on Advertising Recall," *Journal of Marketing* 62 (January 1998): 48–57.

75. Joan Meyers-Levy and Alice M. Tybout, "Schema Congruity as a Basis for Product Evaluation," *Journal of Consumer Research* 16 (June 1989): 39–54.

CHAPTER

7

Leveraging Secondary Brand Knowledge to Build Brand Equity

PREVIEW

The previous chapters described how brand equity could be built through the choice of brand elements (Chapter 4) or through marketing program activities and product, price, distribution, and marketing communication strategies (Chapters 5 and 6). This chapter considers the third means by which brand equity can be built—namely, through the leverage of related or "secondary" brand associations. That is, brands themselves may be linked to other entities that have their own knowledge structures in the minds of consumers. Because of these linkages, consumers may assume or infer that some of the associations or responses that characterize the other entities may also be true for the brand. Thus, in effect, some associations or responses become transferred from other entities to the brand. In other words, the brand essentially borrows some brand knowledge and, depending on the nature of those associations and responses, perhaps some brand equity from other entities.

This indirect approach to building brand equity is referred to as *leveraging secondary brand knowledge* for the brand. Secondary brand knowledge may be quite important if existing brand associations or responses are deficient in some way. In other words, secondary associations can be leveraged to create strong, favorable, and unique associations or positive responses that may otherwise not be present. Secondary brand knowledge can also be an effective means to reinforce existing associations and responses in a fresh and different way.

This chapter considers the different means by which secondary brand knowledge can be created by linking the brand to the following:

1. Companies (e.g., through branding strategies)
2. Countries or other geographic areas (e.g., through identification of product origin)
3. Channels of distribution (e.g., through channel strategy)
4. Other brands (e.g., through co-branding)
5. Characters (e.g., through licensing)
6. Spokespersons (e.g., through endorsements)
7. Events (e.g., through sponsorship)
8. Other third-party sources (e.g., through awards or reviews)

The first three entities reflect source factors: who makes the product, where the product is made, and where it is purchased. The remaining entities deal with related people, places, or things.

As an example of some of the issues involved, suppose that Salomon—makers of alpine and cross-country ski bindings, ski boots, and skis—decided to introduce a new tennis racquet called "The Avenger." Although Salomon has been selling safety bindings for skis since 1947, much of Salomon's growth was fueled by its diversification into ski boots and the introduction of a revolutionary new type of ski called the monocoque. Salomon's innovative, stylish, and top-quality products have led to strong leadership positions. In creating the marketing program to support the new Avenger tennis racquet, Salomon could attempt to leverage secondary brand knowledge in a number of different ways, as follows.

➤ Salomon could leverage associations to the corporate brand by sub-branding the product—for example, by calling it Avenger by Salomon. Consumers' evaluations of the new product extension would be influenced by the extent to which consumers held favorable associations about Salomon as a company or brand because of their skiing products *and* felt that such knowledge was predictive of a tennis racquet that the company made.

➤ Salomon could try to rely on its European origins (it is headquartered near Lake Annecy at the foot of the Alps), although such a location would not seem to have much relevance to tennis.

➤ Salomon could also try to sell through upscale, professional tennis shops and clubs in a hope that these retailers' credibility would rub off on the Avenger brand.

➤ Salomon could attempt to co-brand by identifying a strong ingredient brand for their grip, frame, or strings (e.g., as Wilson did by incorporating Goodyear tire rubber on the soles of its ProStaff Classic tennis shoes).

➤ Although it is doubtful that a licensed character could be effectively leveraged, Salomon obviously could attempt to find one or more top professional players to endorse the racquet or could choose to become a sponsor of tennis tournaments or even the entire professional ATP men's or WTA women's tennis tour.

➤ Salomon could attempt to secure and publicize favorable ratings from third-party sources (e.g., *Tennis* magazine).

Thus, independent of the associations created by the racquet itself, its brand name, or any other aspects of the marketing program, Salomon may be able to build equity by linking the brand to these other entities in these various ways. This chapter first considers the nature of brand knowledge that can be leveraged or transferred from other entities and the process by which this is done. It then considers in detail each of the eight different means of leveraging secondary brand knowledge. The chapter concludes by considering the special topic of Olympic sponsorship in Brand Focus 7.0.

CONCEPTUALIZING THE LEVERAGING PROCESS

Linking the brand to some other entity—some source factor or related person, place, or thing—may create a new set of associations from the brand to the entity as well as affect existing brand associations. Both effects are discussed next.

Creation of New Brand Associations

By making a connection between the brand and another entity, consumers may form a mental association from the brand to this other entity and, consequently, to any or all associations, judgments, feelings, and the like linked to that entity. In general, this secondary brand knowledge is most likely to affect evaluations of a new product when consumers lack either the motivation or ability to judge product-related concerns. In other words, when consumers either don't care much about choosing a particular brand or don't feel that they possess the knowledge to choose the appropriate brand, they may be more likely to make brand decisions on the basis of such secondary considerations as what they think, feel, or know about the country from which the product came, the store in which the product is sold, and so forth.

Effects on Existing Brand Knowledge

Linking the brand to some other entity may not only create new brand associations to the entity but may also affect existing brand associations. The basic mechanism involved with these indirect effects of leveraging secondary brand knowledge is as follows. Consumers have some knowledge of an entity (e.g., varying degrees of awareness, thoughts, feelings, images, beliefs, perceptions, opinions). When a brand is identified as being linked to that entity, consumers may infer that some of the particular associations, judgments, or feelings that characterize the entity may also characterize the brand. A number of different theoretical mechanisms from psychology predict such an inferencing effect. For example, such reasoning by consumers could merely be a result of "cognitive consistency" considerations—in other words, in the minds of consumers, if it is true for the entity, then it must be true for the brand.

In terms of conceptualizing this inferencing process more formally, three factors are particularly important in predicting the extent of leverage that might result from linking the brand to another entity in some manner:

1. *Awareness and knowledge of the entity:* If consumers have no familiarity with or knowledge of the secondary entity, then obviously there is nothing that can be transferred. Ideally, consumers would be aware of the entity, hold some strong, favorable, and perhaps even unique associations regarding the entity, and have positive judgments and feelings about the entity.

2. *Meaningfulness of the knowledge of the entity:* Given that the entity evokes some potentially positive associations, judgments, or feelings, to what extent is this knowledge deemed relevant and meaningful for the brand? The meaningfulness of this knowledge may vary depending on the brand and product context. Some associations, judgments, or feelings may seem relevant to and valuable for the brand, whereas other knowledge may seem to consumers to have little connection.

3. *Transferability of the knowledge of the entity:* Assuming that some potentially useful and meaningful associations, judgments, or feelings exist regarding the entity and could possibly be transferred to the brand, to what extent will this knowledge actually become linked to brand? Thus, a key issue is the extent to which associations will in fact become strong, favorable, and unique, and judgments and feelings will become positive in the context of the brand.

In other words, the basic questions about transferring secondary knowledge from another entity are: What do consumers know about the other entity? and Does any of this knowledge affect what they think about the brand when it becomes linked or associated in some fashion with this other entity? Theoretically, any aspect of knowledge may be inferred from other entities to the brand. In general, it may be more likely for judgments or feelings to transfer from the entity than more specific associations. Many specific associations are likely to be seen as irrelevant or too strongly linked to the original entity to transfer to the brand.

The process by which knowledge such as associations from another entity can be transferred to a brand is discussed in detail in the context of brand extensions in Chapter 12. As is pointed out there, the inferencing process depends largely on the strength of the linkage or connection in consumers' minds between the brand and other entity. The more consumers see similarity of the entity to the brand, the more likely it is that consumers will infer similar knowledge about the brand.

Guidelines

Choosing to emphasize source factors or a particular person, place, or thing should be based on consumers' awareness of that entity, as well as how the associations, judgments, or feelings for the entity might possibly become linked to the brand or affect existing brand associations. Leveraging secondary brand knowledge may be a means of creating an important point of difference versus competitors or a necessary or competitive point of parity.

Entities may be chosen for which consumers have some or even a great deal of similar associations. A *commonality* leveraging strategy makes sense when consumers have associations in memory to another entity that are congruent with desired brand associations. For example, consider a country such as New Zealand, which is known for having more sheep than people. A New Zealand sweater manufacturer that positioned its product on the basis of its "New Zealand wool" presumably could more easily establish strong and favorable brand associations because New Zealand may already mean "wool" to many people.

On the other hand, there may be times when entities are chosen that represent a departure for the brand because there are few if any common or similar associations. Such *complementarity* branding strategies can be strategically critical in terms of delivering the desired position. The challenge here is to ensure means of transferability such that the less congruent knowledge for the entity has either a direct or indirect effect on existing brand knowledge. This may require skillfully designed marketing programs that overcome initial consumer confusion or skepticism. For example, when Buick signed Tiger Woods as an endorser, many questioned as to whether consumers would find a fit or consistency and, if not, how much value the endorsement would add to the Buick brand.

Even if consumers buy into the association one way or another, leveraging secondary brand knowledge may be risky because some control of the brand image is given up. The source factors or related person, place, or thing will undoubtedly have a host of other associations, of which only some smaller set will be of interest to the marketer. Managing the transfer process so that only the relevant secondary knowledge becomes linked to the brand may be difficult. Moreover, this knowledge may change over time as consumers learn more about the entity, and these new associations, judgments, or feelings may or may not be advantageous for the brand.

The following sections consider some of the main ways by which secondary brand knowledge can become linked to the brand.

COMPANY

The branding strategies adopted by the company that makes a product or offers a service are an important determinant of the strength of association from the brand to the company and any other existing brands. Three main branding options exist for a new product:

1. Create a new brand
2. Adopt or modify an existing brand
3. Combine an existing and new brand

Existing brands may be related to the corporate brand (e.g., Nokia) or a specific product brand (e.g., Nokia 8290 digital phone) and may involve names, logos, symbols, and so forth. To the extent that the brand is linked to another existing brand, as with options 2 and 3, then knowledge about the other brand may also become linked to the brand. In particular, a corporate or family brand can be a source of much brand equity. For example, as discussed in Chapter 11, a corporate brand may evoke associations of common product attributes, benefits, or attitudes; people and relationships; programs and values; and corporate credibility.

Leveraging a corporate brand may not always be useful, however, depending on the awareness and image involved. For example, Beatrice once attempted to create a corporate brand umbrella over some of the diverse products it sold at the time, such

BRANDING BRIEF 7-1

Fueling Credibility at Shell

To raise its profile as a consumer-focused company in the United States, Shell launched a $50 million advertising campaign entitled "Count on Shell." The campaign was the most expensive marketing program in the company's history and was also its first corporate image campaign in over 15 years. "Count on Shell" attempted to position the company as customer friendly and knowledgeable about important issues facing motorists.

Shell developed print and television advertising that contained driving safety information reinforced by dramatic scenes and illustrations. For example, one television ad demonstrated how a driver could avoid being trapped underwater in a car. The ad explained that if the driver could not get out through the window, he or she must wait until the car fills with water and the pressure on both sides of the door is equalized before opening the door and exiting the vehicle. Another ad instructed viewers to avoid braking hard after a tire blowout. In the ad, a driver averts an accident by not braking while a voiceover intones, "In the blink of an eye, this man will have to resist a basic human impulse. Can you?"

The company supplemented its television ads by distributing 30 million free booklets called "Driving Dangers." One such pamphlet was titled "Crash Course" and contained information on what motorists can do to help others in the event of a crash. Joe Kilgore, executive director of Ogilvy & Mather's Houston offices (Shell's agency for the campaign), explained that the "Count on Shell" campaign reconnected with traditional Shell advertising:

"People remember Shell as the kind of company that used to give them a lot of information. Shell had a foothold there, so it decided to take advantage of it."

In the year following the "Count on Shell" launch, Shell received more than 5,000 e-mails, letters, and phone calls from consumers for whom the educational advertising worked. One woman detailed how Shell's advice helped her avoid a crash when her tire blew out on an icy Alaskan road.

Another aspect of the "Count on Shell" campaign was a series of ads that touted Shell's technological advances in areas other than fuel. An ad featuring a professional snowboarder demonstrating tricks explained that Shell manufactures resins used in the making of a snowboard. Another ad showed a baby in diapers and conveyed the message that Shell polymers hold the diaper together. "This corporate campaign allows us to let more people know about the benefits Shell is providing," said Ogilvy & Mather's Kilgore. "The company wants to put a lot of information out there so people won't see Shell as a one-dimensional company."

The "Count on Shell" campaign had a positive effect on earnings from the sale of Shell Oil products in the United States, which rose to $264 million in 2000 from $98 million the previous year. Following the campaign's success in the United States, Shell exported it to 12 other countries.

Sources: http://www.shell.com; Greg Hassell, "Shell Oil Begins $50 Million Ad Campaign Stressing Safety Information," *Knight-Ridder Tribune Business News*, 6 February 1998; Allanna Sullivan, "Shell Taps into Harsh Realities to Build Warm, Fuzzy Feelings," *Wall Street Journal*, 18 February 1999.

as Hunt Wesson foods, Stiffel lamps, and Orville Redenbacher popcorn. An expensive ad campaign uniting the products around the theme "You've Known Us All Along" failed to connect with consumers. In fact, in some cases, large companies are deliberately introducing new brands in an attempt to convey a "smaller" image.[1] For example, Gallo created two folksy farmers, Ed Bartles and Frank Jaymes, to sell their wine cooler product. Philip Morris's Miller unit has used its Plank Road Brewery brand to introduce Icehouse and Red Dog beers. Philip Morris also invented a whole new tobacco company to market a new discount cigarette, Dave's. Promotional material read:

> Down in Concord, North Carolina, there's a guy named Dave. Dave is an entrepreneur who believes in the value of homemade products and the concept of offering folks quality cigarettes at the right price. . . . Dave guarantees, "If you don't like 'em, I'll eat 'em."

Chapter 11 considers the pros and cons of various branding strategies, including corporate and family branding strategies, and examines how different types of brand associations may potentially be linked to a new product by using an existing brand in some way to brand the new product.

Finally, it should be recognized that brands and companies are often unavoidably linked to the category and industry in which they compete, sometimes with adverse consequences. Some industries are characterized by fairly divided opinions, but consider the challenges faced by a brand in the oil and gas industry, which consumers generally view in a negative light. By virtue of membership in the category in which it competes, an oil company may expect to face a potentially suspicious or skeptical public *regardless* of what it does. Along those lines, Branding Brief 7-1 examines how Shell Oil developed its corporate image campaign, "Count on Shell."

COUNTRY OF ORIGIN AND OTHER GEOGRAPHIC AREAS

Besides the company that makes the product, the country or geographic location from which it is seen as originating may also become linked to the brand and generate secondary associations.[2] Many countries have become known for expertise in certain product categories or for conveying a particular type of image. As noted by many, the world is becoming a "cultural bazaar" where consumers can pick and choose brands originating in different countries based on their beliefs about the quality of certain types of products from certain countries or the image that these brands or products communicate. Thus, a consumer from anywhere in the world may choose to wear Italian suits, exercise in American athletic shoes, listen to a Japanese compact disc player, drive a German car, or drink English beer. Choosing brands with strong national ties may reflect a deliberate decision to maximize product utility and communicate self-image based on what consumers believe about products from those countries.

Thus, a number of brands are able to create a strong point of difference in part because of consumers' identification of and beliefs about the country of origin. For example, consider the following strongly linked brands and countries:

Levi's jeans—United States

Nike athletic shoes—United States

Coca-Cola soft drink—United States

Marlboro cigarettes—United States

Chanel perfume—France

Foster's beer—Australia

Barilla pasta—Italy

Dewar's whiskey—Scotland

Kikkoman soy sauce—Japan

Bertolli olive oil—Italy

Gucci shoes and purses—Italy

Mont Blanc pens—Switzerland

BMW—Germany

In attacking the European market, Timberland deliberately employed an "Americana" appeal that was different from how the brand was marketed in the United States. Specifically, the ad agency chose to emphasize a "brash, potent, in your face" approach that it felt best represented the way to sell America in Europe, whereas the U.S. ads were much more "spiritual" and featured "moody landscapes and moody young people."[3] Similarly, BellSouth billed itself as an all-American brand in building its "footprint" as a one-stop telecommunications shop in Latin America, proclaiming in one ad, "Our origins date back to Alexander Graham Bell, the inventor of the telephone; year after year, consumers in the U.S. rank us the company that serves them best."[4]

Other geographic associations besides country of origin are possible, such as states, regions, and cities. Establishing a geographic or country-of-origin association can be done in different ways. The location can actually be embedded in the brand name (e.g., Idaho potatoes, Maine blueberries, California peaches, Irish Spring soap, or South African Airways) or combined with a brand name in some way (e.g., Bailey's Irish Cream). Alternatively, the location may become the dominant theme in brand advertising (e.g., Foster's or Coors beer). Some countries have even created advertising campaigns to promote their products. For example, Puerto Rico advertises the quality of its rums. Other countries have developed and advertised labels or seals for their products. Branding Brief 7-2 describes New Zealand's attempt to create a brand, "The New Zealand Way."

Because it is typically a legal necessity for the country of origin to appear visibly somewhere on the product or package, associations to the country of origin almost always have the potential to be created at the point of purchase and to affect brand decisions there. The question really becomes one of relative emphasis and the role of country of origin or other geographic regions throughout the marketing program. Becoming strongly linked to a country of origin or specific geographic region is not without potential disadvantages. Events or actions associated with the country may color people's perceptions. For example, strong connections to a country may pose problems if the firm desires to move production elsewhere.

Waterford

Waterford Wedgwood PLC's famous, ornate crystal had been promoted as the ultimate in Irish handmade luxury for decades. Ads called Waterford "the ambassador of a nation" and attributed its brilliance to "deep, prismatic cutting that must be done entirely by skilled hands rather than machines." Because of cost considerations, Waterford had to confront the issue of shifting production out of Ireland and using machines to make some lines. Waterford was encouraged to make such a move because of consumer research in the United States—home to more than 70 percent of Waterford's crystal sales—that indicated

Selling Brands the New Zealand Way

In 1991, New Zealand set out to create "The New Zealand Way" (NZW) brand. The key objective of the New Zealand Brand Campaign was to build a strong national umbrella brand that added value to the marketing of New Zealand-origin products and services by differentiating New Zealand branded products and services in international markets; raising the awareness of New Zealand's unique values and personality; and utilizing the promotional activities of the New Zealand Tourism Board, Tradenz (a government trade development board), and manufacturers to heighten the profile of branded New Zealand products and services. The NZW brand was designed to position a broad range of the country's tourism and trade products and services at the forefront of world markets.

The focal point for communicating the personality and meaning of the NZW brand was to be the brand design and the campaign that was to be built around it. The three components of the NZW brand design were the brand logo, a descriptor word or short phrase (e.g., *quality*), and the slogan, "The New Zealand Way." The descriptor words were to allow users of the NZW brand to customize it to suit their marketing program. Any words or short phrases could be licensed as descriptors as long as they were seen as compatible with the overall personality of the NZW brand, described shortly. The campaign to launch and support the NZW brand included a range of promotional techniques, such as public relations, direct marketing, and events in key geographic markets.

The desired associations for the NZW brand to be created by the campaign were as follows:

- *Quality excellence:* Epitomized by the consistent delivery of products and services that meet and exceed the expectations of the customer
- *Environmental responsibility:* Reinforced by New Zealand's leadership in the efficient and sustainable use of environmental resources and delivery of fresh and natural products
- *Innovation:* Characterized by the unique personality of New Zealanders, who seek out new solutions and disregard the ingrained and inhibiting conventions of the country's trading partners
- *Contemporary values:* Reflected in the positioning of its products and services at the forefront of contemporary market trends and requirements
- *Honesty, integrity, and openness:* Personified in the business practices, lifestyles, and character of New Zealanders
- *Achievement:* Reflected in the endeavors and outstanding accomplishments of New Zealanders in business, sports, and the arts

By 1998, more than 170 companies were licensed to use the New Zealand Way fern brand. Goods produced by these companies accounted for more than $4 billion, or 20 percent, of New Zealand's foreign exchange earnings that year. Noting the success of the New Zealand Way campaign, other countries, such as Scotland, developed their own national product branding strategies.

that what mattered to its customers there was the Waterford label and not where the crystal was made per se. Nevertheless, many retailers worried that such a move could destroy the precious brand image that Waterford had built.

Finally, the favorability of a country-of-origin association must be considered both from a domestic and foreign perspective. In the domestic market, country-of-origin perceptions may stir consumers' patriotic notions or remind them of their past. As international trade grows, consumers may view certain brands as symbolically important of their own cultural heritage and identity. Patriotic appeals have been the basis of marketing strategies all over the world. Patriotic appeals, however, can lack uniqueness and even be overused. For example, during the Reagan administration in the 1980s, a number of different U.S. brands in a diverse range of product categories (e.g., cars, beer, clothing) used pro-American themes in their advertising, perhaps diluting the efforts of all as a result. Tragically, the events of September 11, 2001, raised the visibility of patriotic appeals once again.

CHANNELS OF DISTRIBUTION

Chapter 5 described how members of the channels of distribution can directly affect the equity of the brands they sell by the supporting actions that they take. It also was noted that retail stores can indirectly affect the brand equity of the products they sell by influencing the nature of associations that are inferred about these products on the basis of the associations linked to the retail stores in the minds of consumers. This section considers how retail stores can indirectly affect brand equity through this "image transfer" process.

Because of associations to product assortment, pricing and credit policy, quality of service, and so on, retailers have their own brand images in consumers' minds. Retailers create these associations through the products and brands they stock, the means by which they sell them, and so forth. To more directly shape their image, many retailers aggressively advertise and promote directly to customers. Given that a store has some associations in the minds of consumers, these associations may be linked to the products they sell or affect existing brand associations for these products in some way. For example, a consumer may infer certain characteristics about a product on the basis of where it is sold, for example, "If it is sold by Nordstrom, it must be good quality." The same brand may be perceived differently depending on whether it is sold in a store seen as prestigious and exclusive or in a store seen as designed for bargain shoppers and having more mass appeal.

The transfer of store image associations can be either positive or negative for a brand. For many high-end brands, a natural growth strategy is to expand their customer base by tapping new channels of distribution. Such strategies can be dangerous, however, depending on how existing customers and retailers react. When Levi Strauss & Company decided to expand the distribution channels for its Levi's jeans in the early 1980s beyond department and specialty shops to include mass-market chains Sears and Penney's, RH Macy's decided to drop the brand because it felt the brand's image had been cheapened.

OshKosh B'Gosh

In the early 1990s, OshKosh B'Gosh faced a dilemma as it sought to increase sales of its trendy children's overalls, cotton separates, and dress clothes. Part of its strategy involved

Calvin Klein and Warnaco's Battle of the Brands

From a humble start as a designer of women's coats, Calvin Klein bred a fashion empire with the help of savvy, high-image, and often risqué marketing created by his in-house CRK Advertising team. Calvin Klein started the designer jeans craze in the late 1970s with ads that featured a teenaged Brooke Shields claiming that nothing came between her and her Calvins. Ads in 1985 for Obsession perfume depicted a provocative "pseudo-orgy," and the fragrance quickly became the number two seller in the country. Klein touched off a scandal and an FBI investigation in 1995 when many of his jeans ads were labeled pornographic and exploitative because they contained revealing images of underage models. Through success and scandal, Calvin Klein remained one of the foremost names in American fashion.

Calvin Klein's business success was fueled in part by licensing of his name for a variety of products other than the seasonal designer clothing that made Calvin Klein a household name. For every $3,000 dress sold at Saks Fifth Avenue, many more pairs of $50 jeans, $14 cotton briefs, and $40 bottles of perfume bearing the familiar CK logo pass through checkout lines at department stores across the globe. Calvin Klein and his team do the design work for their products, while licensees take care of the logistics of manufacturing, distribution, and retail contracts. Although licensing his name led to millions in profits, it also reduced the control Calvin Klein had over his brand.

In a move that set off a highly publicized legal dispute, Calvin Klein sued jeanswear licensee Warnaco in June 2000 for "improper sales" to discounters such as Costco and Sam's Club. Calvin Klein alleged that by "producing jeans and underwear expressly for downmarket discount stores," the licensee was "cheapening" the Calvin Klein brand. In particular, Klein found fault with Warnaco's decision to sell CK underwear to low-cost retailer JCPenney. Other major Calvin Klein retail accounts, such as Dillard's and Federated Department stores, were angered by this decision and threatened to slow or halt future orders of CK underwear. The suit claimed that Warnaco had been pushing CK merchandise into other low-cost retailers without permission.

A month after Klein's filing, Warnaco countersued, charging Calvin Klein with violating the license agreement. Linda Wachner, CEO of Warnaco, defended her company's sales to discounters by saying, "[Calvin Klein] gets a full list every year of every account and every shipment, of every dollar." Warnaco's countersuit also accused Calvin Klein of trade libel and bad-faith dealing, claiming the designer had failed to attend a design meeting for over a year.

The two sides settled as the case was going to trial in 2001, and the license agreement remained intact. Warnaco agreed not to sell CK jeanswear and underwear to JCPenney, but was allowed to continue selling to discount retailers Costco, Sam's Club, and B.J.'s at "dramatically reduced volume." Other terms of the settlement effectively gave Calvin Klein more control over Warnaco's dealings with the brand.

Sources: Teri Agins, "Calvin Klein, Warnaco Settle Their Bitter Feud," *Wall Street Journal*, 23 January 2001; Teri Agins and Rebecca Quick, "Illegal Briefs?" *Wall Street Journal*, 1 June 2000.

expanding its distribution from existing upscale department and specialty stores to include Sears and Penney's stores.[5] Some of the company's department store customers reacted negatively, objecting that, because of competitive pressure from lower-priced chain stores, they were forced to reduce their prices on OshKosh items to remain competitive, cutting into their margins. To keep these customers happy, OshKosh decided to offer department stores some exclusive, higher-margin items. Although there was some decrease in volume from disgruntled department store buyers, OshKosh felt that this loss was more than made up by volume from the new mass-market outlets. Because of its strong relationship with consumers and perceived commitment to quality, OshKosh believes that its brand image was not tarnished in the process.

Branding Brief 7-3 describes the fierce battle between Calvin Klein and Warnaco that revolved largely on the issue of the appropriateness of retail distribution for the Calvin Klein brand.

CO-BRANDING

As noted previously, a new product can become linked to an existing corporate or family brand that has its own set of associations through a brand extension strategy. An existing brand can also leverage associations by linking itself to other existing brands from the same or different company. *Co-branding*—also called brand bundling or brand alliances—occurs when two or more existing brands are combined into a joint product or are marketed together in some fashion.[6] A special case of this strategy is ingredient branding, which is discussed in the next section.[7]

Co-branding has been around for years; for example, Betty Crocker paired with Sunkist Growers in 1961 to successfully market a lemon chiffon cake mix.[8] Interest in co-branding as a means of building brand equity has increased in recent years. For example, Leaf Specialty's Heath toffee candy bar has not only been extended into several new products—for example, Heath Sensations (bite-sized candies) and Heath Bits and Bits of Brickle (chocolate-covered and plain toffee baking products)—but also has been licensed to a variety of vendors, such as Dairy Queen (with its Blizzard drink), Ben & Jerry's (with their ice cream products), Nestlé (with their ice cream bar), and Pillsbury (with their cake frosting).[9] Figure 7-1 displays some supermarket examples of co-branding. In the credit card market, co-branding often involves three brands (e.g., Shell Chase Bank MasterCard). With airlines, brand alliances can involve a host of brands, such as United Airlines, Lufthansa, SAS, and Singapore Airlines.

Figure 7-2 summarizes the main advantages and disadvantages of co-branding and licensing. The main advantage to co-branding is that a product may be uniquely and convincingly positioned by virtue of the multiple brands involved. Co-branding can create more compelling points of difference or points of parity, or both, for the brand than might have been otherwise feasible. As a result, co-branding can generate greater sales from the existing target market as well as open additional opportunities with new consumers and channels. Co-branding can reduce the cost of product introduction because two well-known images are combined, accelerating potential adoption. Co-branding also may be a valuable means to learn about consumers and how other companies approach them. In poorly differentiated categories especially, co-branding may be an important means of creating a distinctive product.

Aunt Jemima oatmeal waffles with Quaker oatmeal
Beech-Nut baby foods with Chiquita bananas
Ben & Jerry's Heath Bar Crunch ice cream
Fat Free Cranberry Newtons with Ocean Spray
    cranberries
Kellogg's Pop-Tarts with Smuckers fruit filling
Pillsbury's Oreo Bars baking mix and frosting
Reese's Peanut Butter Puffs cereal
Post Raisin Bran with Sun-Maid raisins
Archway cookies with Kellogg's All-Bran
Nestlé's Cheerios cookie bars
M&M Cookie Bars baking mix
Smuckers Dove ice cream sauce
Brach's Hi-C candy
Yoplait Trix yogurt

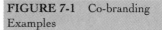

FIGURE 7-1   Co-branding Examples

Healthy Choice

When Kellogg's partnered with ConAgra to introduce a new line of cereal under ConAgra's popular Healthy Choice brand name, Kellogg's conducted research to see how a co-branded line would fit its business. The company found that the Healthy Choice name would "cut through the clutter" in the cereal market, quickly establish a level of credibility in nutrition, and overcome a lot of the initial hurdles associated with a new cereal.[10]

The potential disadvantages of co-branding are the risks and lack of control that arise from becoming aligned with another brand in the minds of consumers. Consumer expectations about the level of involvement and commitment with co-brands are likely to be high. Unsatisfactory performance thus could have negative repercussions for the brands involved. If the other brand is one that has entered into a number of co-branding

Advantages
Borrow needed expertise
Leverage equity you don't have
Reduce cost of product introduction
Expand brand meaning into related categories
    Broaden meaning
    Increase access points
Source of additional revenue

Disadvantages
Loss of control
Risk of brand equity dilution
Negative feedback effects
Lack of brand focus and clarity
Organizational distraction

FIGURE 7-2   Advantages and Disadvantages of Co-branding and Licensing

arrangements, there also may be a risk of overexposure that would dilute the transfer of any association. It may also result in distraction and a lack of focus on existing brands.

Guidelines

The Science of Branding 7-1 provides some additional insight as to how consumers evaluate co-branded products. To create a strong co-brand, it is important that both brands entering the agreement have adequate brand awareness; sufficiently strong, favorable, and unique associations; and positive consumer judgments and feelings. Thus, a necessary but not sufficient condition for co-branding success is that the two brands separately have some brand equity. The most important requirement is that there is a logical fit between the two brands such that the combined brand or marketing activity maximizes the advantages of the individual brands while minimizing the disadvantages. For example, Fisher-Price and Compaq teamed up to introduce a set of jointly branded Wonder Tools software and computer accessories targeting kids and their parents. Reflecting the complementarity of the strategy, ads stressed, "Nobody Knows Fun Like Fisher-Price, Nobody Knows Computers Like Compaq."[11] Crayola and Hallmark Entertainment jointly branded a series of children's videos, tapping into their images of fun for kids and wholesome family values, respectively. Not all such co-branding arrangements, however, seem to make as much sense.

Swatch

Some eyebrows were raised when DaimlerChrysler AG's Mercedes Benz unit agreed to manufacture a "Swatchmobile," named after SMH's colorful and fashionable lines of Swatch watches.[12] Personally championed by SMH's charismatic chairman, Nicolas Hayek, the Smart Car, as it came to be known, was designed to be small (less than 10 feet long) and low cost (under $10,000). The car combined the three most important features of Swatch watches—"affordability," "durability," and "stylishness"—with an important feature of a Mercedes Benz automobile—"safety and security in a crash." A number of critics believed the Mercedes Benz image could suffer if the car was unsuccessful, which was a very possible outcome given the fact that many products bearing the Swatch name (e.g., Swatch branded clothes, bags, telephones, pagers, and sunglasses) saw disappointing sales or were dropped altogether. Swatch sold its share of the Smart Car business to DaimlerChrysler in 1998. The Smart Car became very popular in Europe, however, selling 102,000 units in 2000.

Besides these strategic considerations, co-branding ventures must be entered into and executed carefully. Branding Brief 7-4 describes some of General Mills's co-branding and licensing experiences. Fundamentally, there must be the right kind of fit in values, capabilities, and goals in addition to an appropriate balance of brand equity. Executionally, there must be detailed plans to legalize contracts, make financial arrangements, and coordinate marketing programs. As one executive at Nabisco put it, "Giving away your brand is a lot like giving away your child—you want to make sure everything is perfect." The financial arrangement between brands may vary, although one common approach involves a licensing fee and royalty from the brand that is more involved in the production process.

More generally, brand alliances, such as with co-branding, involve a number of decision factors, such as the following:[13]

Understanding Brand Alliances

Brand alliances, in which two brands are combined in some way as part of a product or some other aspect of the marketing program, come in all forms.[1] Prior research has explored the effects of co-branding, ingredient branding strategies, and advertising alliances.

CO-BRANDING

Park, Jun, and Shocker compare co-brands to the notion of "conceptual combinations" in psychology.[2] A conceptual combination (e.g., "apartment dog") consists of a modifying concept, or "modifier" (e.g., *apartment*) and a modified concept, or "header" (e.g., *dog*). In general, research in psychology has shown that the modified concept plays the more important role in a person's impression of the composite. Experimentally, Park and his colleagues explored the different ways that Godiva (associated with expensive, high-calorie boxed chocolates) and Slim-Fast (associated with inexpensive, low-calorie diet food) could introduce a chocolate cake mix separately or together through a co-brand. They found that the co-branded version of the product was better accepted than if either brand attempted to extend individually into the cake mix category.

They also found that consumers' impressions of the co-branded concept were driven by the header brand (e.g., Slim-Fast chocolate cake mix by Godiva was seen as lower calorie than if the product was called Godiva chocolate cake mix by Slim-Fast; the reverse was true for associations of richness and luxury). Similarly, consumers' impressions of Slim-Fast after exposure to the co-branded concept were more likely to change when it was the header brand than when it was the modifier brand. Their findings show how carefully selected brands can be combined to overcome potential problems of negatively correlated attributes (e.g., rich taste and low calories).

Simonin and Ruth found that consumers' attitudes toward a brand alliance could influence subsequent impressions of each partner's brands (such that spillover effects existed), but that these effects also depended on other factors such as product fit or compatibility and brand fit or image congruity.[3] Brands less familiar than their partners contributed less to an alliance but experienced stronger spillover effects than their more familiar partners. Relatedly, Voss and Tansuhaj found that consumer evaluations of an unknown brand from another country were more positive when a well-known domestic brand was used in an alliance.[4]

Finally, Levin and Levin explored the effects of dual branding, which they defined as a marketing strategy in which two brands (usually restaurants) share the same facilities while providing consumers with the opportunity to use either one or both brands.[5] They found that when two brands were linked through a dual-branding arrangement and both brands were described by the same set of attributes, then the effect of dual branding was to reduce or eliminate the contrast effects. When two brands were linked through a dual-branding arrangement and the target brand was less well specified than the context brand, then the effect of dual branding was to increase assimilation effects.

INGREDIENT BRANDING

Desai and Keller conducted a laboratory experiment to consider how ingredient branding affected consumer acceptance of an initial line extension, as well as the ability of the brand to introduce future category extensions.[6] Two particular types of line extensions, defined as brand expansions, were studied: (1) *slot filler expansions*, in which the level of one existing product attribute changed (e.g., a new type of scent in Tide detergent) and (2) *new attribute expansions*, in which an entirely new attribute or characteristic was added to the product (e.g., cough relief liquid added to LifeSavers candy). Two types of ingredient branding strategies were examined by branding the target attribute ingredient for the brand expansion with either a new name as a *self-branded ingredient* (e.g., Tide with its own EverFresh scented bath soap) or an established, well-respected name as a *co-branded ingredient* (e.g., Tide with Irish Spring scented bath soap). The results indicated that with slot filler expansions, although a co-branded ingredient facilitated initial expansion acceptance, a self-branded ingredient led to more favorable subsequent extension evaluations. With more dissimilar new attribute expansions, however, a co-branded ingredient led to more favorable evaluations of both the initial expansion and the subsequent extension.

Venkatesh and Mahajan derived an analytical model based on bundling and reservation price notions to help formulate optimal pricing and partner selection decisions for branded components.[7] In an experimental application in the context of a university computer store selling 486-class laptop computers, they showed that at the bundle level, an all-brand Compaq PC with Intel 486 commanded a clear price premium over other alternatives. The relative brand strength of the Intel brand, however, was shown to be stronger in some sense than that of the Compaq brand.

ADVERTISING ALLIANCES

Samu, Krishnan, and Smith showed that the effectiveness of advertising alliances for new product introductions depended on the interactive effects of three factors: the degree of complementarity between the featured products, the type of differentiation strategy (common versus unique advertised attributes with respect to the product category), and the type of ad processing (top-down or bottom-up) that an ad evoked (e.g., the explicitness of the ad headline).[8]

[1] Akshay R. Rao, "Strategic Brand Alliances," *Journal of Brand Management* 5, no. 2 (1997): 111–119; Akshay R. Rao, L. Qu, and Robert W. Ruekert, "Signaling Unobservable Product Quality through a Brand Ally," *Journal of Marketing Research* (May 1999): 258–268; Allen D. Shocker, Raj K. Srivastava, and Robert W. Ruekert, "Challenges and Opportunities Facing Brand Management: An Introduction to the Special Issue," *Journal of Marketing Research* 31, no. 5 (1994): 149–158.

[2] C. Whan Park, Sung Youl Jun, and Allan D. Shocker, "Composite Branding Alliances: An Investigation of Extension and Feedback Effects," *Journal of Marketing Research* (November 1996): 453–467.

[3] B. L. Simonin and Julie A. Ruth, "Is a Company Known by the Company It Keeps? Assessing the Spillover Effects of Brand Alliances on Consumer Brand Attitudes," *Journal of Marketing Research* 35, no. 2 (1998): 30–42.

[4] Kevin E. Voss and P. Tansuhaj, "A Consumer Perspective on Foreign Market Entry: Building Brands through Brand Alliances," *Journal of International Consumer Marketing* 11, no. 2 (1999): 39–58.

[5] P. Levin and A. M. Levin, "Modeling the Role of Brand Alliances in the Assimilation of Product Evaluations," *Journal of Consumer Psychology* 9, no. 1 (2000): 43–52.

[6] Kalpesh Desai and Kevin Lane Keller, "The Effects of Brand Expansions and Ingredient Branding Strategies on Host Brand Extendibility," *Journal of Marketing*, 66 (January 2002), 73–93.

[7] R. Venkatesh and Vijay Mahajan, "Products with Branded Components: An Approach for Premium Pricing and Partner Selection," *Marketing Science* 16, no. 2 (1997): 146–165.

[8] S. Samu, H. Shanker Krishnan, and Robert E. Smith, "Using Advertising Alliances for New Product Introduction: Interactions between Product Complementarity and Promotional Strategies," *Journal of Marketing* 63, no. 1 (1999): 57–74.

Co-branding and Licensing at General Mills

General Mills, a consumer-goods giant that began as a single flour mill in 1877, has traditionally forged licensing and co-branding partnerships as part of its marketing program (see Figure A). General Mills partners with other leading brands to create new co-branded products, as it did with Pac-Man in the 1980s, or forges licensing agreements with other marketers, as when Honey Nut Cheerios in the early 1990s included Topps trading cards featuring members of the TV show *Beverly Hills 90210*. The aim is for the licensor and the licensee to benefit from these agreements as a result of the shared equity, increased awareness for the licensor, and greater sales for the licensee.

Some current exclusive co-brand partnerships include Cocoa Puffs made with Hershey's Cocoa, Betty Crocker Sunkist Lemon Bars, and Pop-Secret Homestyle Extra Butter microwave popcorn made with real Land O'Lakes butter. Current licensed products include Reese's Puffs, Hawaiian Punch Fruit Snacks, and Pokemon Rolls. Some ongoing product promotion licenses include free *Who Wants to be a Millionaire* games in boxes of General Mills cereals, and free die-cast NASCAR models in Wheaties boxes.

General Mills also licenses its own brands to other companies for use with a diverse range of products. Since 1987, General Mills has licensed the Betty Crocker

FIGURE A   Example of General Mills Co-branded Products

name and likeness for use with cookbooks, cookware, and other products related to food preparation. More recently, the company has licensed some of its other brand names, such as Wheaties and Cheerios. General Mills partnered with publisher Simon & Schuster to produce a series of Cheerios books aimed at young readers. The books, which include interactive counting games that encourage the use of actual Cheerios, are among the top sellers in the Little Simon imprint of Simon & Schuster. The company also forged an agreement with toy company Hasbro to develop plastic Cheerios dispensers molded in shapes such as cell phones. Other Cheerios licensed products include a toy tractor-trailer and a line of children's place settings. General Mills also licensed its Wheaties brand to sports memorabilia marketer Asset Marketing Services for a series of collectible miniature Wheaties boxes bearing classic "Wheaties Champions." The company is developing plans for other licensing deals involving products such as Lucky Charms and Cocoa Puffs. General Mills's 2001 acquisition of Pillsbury from parent Diageo PLC gave it an additional licensing tool, the Pillsbury Doughboy.

General Mills carefully selects each license opportunity to ensure that it fits with the overall brand image of the company. Leigh Ann Schwarzkopf, manager of trademark licensing for General Mills, said "You can really screw up your relationship with your consumers if [the tie between brand and product] becomes meaningless." Because licensing its brands constitutes only a small percentage of General Mills's annual profit, the company's "primary objective is to enhance our brand equity," said Kim Walter, the company's director of publishing and licensing.

Sources: http://www.what.com; Jennifer Franklin, "Big G Builds Brands by Books and Baseball," *Minneapolis-St. Paul CityBusiness,* 17 March 2000; "Cheerios Getting Zip from '90210,'" *Entertainment Marketing Letter,* 1 January 1993.

➤ What capabilities do you not have?

➤ What resource constraints are you faced with (people, time, money, etc.)?

➤ What growth goals or revenue needs do you have?

In assessing a joint branding opportunity, the following questions should be considered:

➤ Is it a profitable business venture?

➤ How does it help to maintain or strengthen brand equity?

➤ Is there any possible risk of dilution of brand equity?

➤ Does it offer any extrinsic advantages (e.g., learning opportunities)?

One of the highest-profile brand alliances is that of Disney and McDonald's, which has the exclusive global rights for 10 years in the fast food industry to promote everything from Disney movies and videos to TV shows and theme parks. McDonald's has brand partnerships with a number of brands, including Fisher-Price toys for its Happy Meals.

Ingredient Branding

A special case of co-branding is *ingredient branding,* which involves creating brand equity for materials, components, or parts that are necessarily contained within other branded products. Some successful ingredient brands include Dolby noise reduction,

Gore-Tex water-resistant fibers, Teflon nonstick coatings, Stainmaster stain-resistant fibers, and Scotchgard fabrics. Some popular ingredient-branded products are Betty Crocker baking mixes with Hershey's chocolate syrup, Lunchables lunch combinations with Taco Bell tacos, and Lay's potato chips made with KC Masterpiece barbecue sauce. Ingredient brands attempt to create sufficient awareness and preference for their product such that consumers will not buy a "host" product that does not contain the ingredient.

From a consumer behavior perspective, branded ingredients are often seen as a signal of quality. In a provocative study, Carpenter, Glazer, and Nakamoto found that the inclusion of a branded attribute (e.g., "Alpine Class" fill for a down jacket) significantly affected consumer choices even when consumers were explicitly told that the attribute was not relevant to their choice.[14] Clearly, consumers inferred certain quality characteristics as a result of the branded ingredient. The uniformity and predictability of ingredient brands can reduce risk and reassure consumers. As a result, ingredient brands can become industry standards to consumers such that they would not buy a product that did not contain the ingredient. In other words, ingredient brands can become in effect a category point of parity. Consumers do not necessarily have to know exactly how the ingredient works—just that it adds value.

Ingredient branding has become more prevalent as mature brands seek cost-effective means to differentiate themselves on the one hand, and potential ingredient products seek means to expand their sales opportunities on the other hand. To illustrate the range of alternatives involved with ingredient branding, consider the copy from a recent Singapore Airlines magazine ad, which prominently features both co-branded and self-branded ingredients in promoting one of their service offerings:

> **SINGAPORE AIRLINES NEW RAFFLES CLASS: BUSINESS IN A CLASS OF ITS OWN**
> Singapore Airlines has searched the world to bring you the finest business class in the sky. Top French design house, *Givenchy*, has created a cabin of contemporary elegance. And, for the ultimate in comfort, our new *Ultimo* seats from Italy are electrically controlled, offering luxurious legroom as well as personal privacy screens—a world first. In-seat laptop power is on hand for those who need to work; whereas those who prefer to relax can enjoy *KrisWorld*, your in-flight entertainment system, with over 60 entertainment options. And for the first time in the sky, you can enjoy blockbuster movies with *Dolby Headphone* surround sound. In addition our *World Gourmet Cuisine*—created by an international panel of acclaimed chefs—brings you a dining experience reminiscent of fine earth-bound restaurants, complemented by in-flight service even other airlines talk about.

Thus, as in this example, one product may contain a number of different branded ingredients. Ingredient brands are not restricted to just products and services. For example, RadioShack has established strategic alliances with Sprint, Compaq, RCA, Microsoft, and others that let the manufacturers set up kiosks within many of RadioShack's 7,100 stores in the United States.

Advantages and Disadvantages

The pros and cons of ingredient branding are similar to those of co-branding.[15] From the perspective of the firm making and supplying the ingredient, the benefit of branding its products as ingredients is that by creating consumer pull, greater sales can be generated at a higher margin than would have otherwise occurred. Additionally, there may be more stable and broader customer demand and better long-term supplier-buyer relationships. Enhanced revenues may accrue from having two revenue streams—the direct revenue from the cost of the supplied ingredients, as well as the possible extra revenue from the royalty rights paid to display the ingredient brand.

From the standpoint of the manufacturer of the host product, the benefit is in leveraging the equity from the ingredient brand to enhance its own brand equity. For example, Delicious Cookie Company has leveraged some better-known and well-liked brands such as Land O'Lakes butter, Skippy peanut butter, Chiquita bananas, Musselman's apple sauce, and Heath toffee candy bars to establish brand equity for its own cookies. On the demand side, the host product brands may achieve access to new product categories, different market segments, and more distribution channels than they otherwise could have expected. On the supply side, the host product brands may be able to share some production and development costs with the ingredient supplier.

Ingredient branding is not without its risks and costs. The costs of a supporting marketing communication program can be high-advertising to sales ratios for consumer products often surpass 5 percent—and many suppliers are relatively inexperienced at designing mass media communications that may have to contend with inattentive consumers and noncooperative middlemen. As with co-branding, there is a loss of control because marketing programs for the supplier and manufacturer may have different objectives and thus may send different signals to consumers. Some manufacturers may be reluctant to become supplier dependent or may not believe that the branded ingredient adds value, resulting in a loss of possible accounts. Manufacturers may resent any consumer confusion as to what is the "real brand" if the branded ingredient gains too much equity. Finally, the sustainability of the competitive advantage may be somewhat uncertain because brands that follow may benefit from consumers' increased understanding of the role of the ingredient. As a result, follower brands may not have to communicate the importance of the ingredient as much as why their particular ingredient brand is better than the pioneer or other brands.

Guidelines

Ingredient branding programs build brand equity in some of the same ways that conventional branding programs do. An example is Nutrasweet.

Nutrasweet

Monsanto launched an intensive marketing program to create awareness of and an image for its patented aspartame artificial sweetener, Nutrasweet, as a sugar substitute for foods and beverages. The Nutrasweet brand consists of a name to communicate two key associations to consumers—"nutritious" and "sweet"—as well as a symbol of a red swirl. An extensive advertising campaign was launched to communicate the natural benefits of Nutrasweet and establish a key point of parity. Another important aspect of the branding program was the stipulation that all products containing Nutrasweet were required to bear the brand name and symbol. Although Nutrasweet's patent expired in December 1992,

Ingredient Branding the Dupont Way

Perhaps one of the most successful ingredient brand marketers of all times is DuPont, which was founded in Delaware as a black-powder manufacturer in 1802 by Frenchman E. I. duPont de Nemours. Over the years, the company introduced a number of innovative products for use in markets ranging from apparel to aerospace. Many of the company's innovations, such as Lycra and Stainmaster fabrics, Teflon coating, and Kevlar fiber, became household names as ingredient brands in consumer products manufactured by many other companies.

Early on, DuPont learned an important branding lesson the hard way. Because the company did not protect the name of its first organic chemical fiber, nylon, it was not trademarkable and became generic. In total, DuPont now sells over 30,000 products across 1,500 different product lines, and uses 2,000 unique brands and 15,000 different brand registrations to support these products. In the pursuit of new innovations, the company has more than 40 research and customer service labs in the United States, and more than 35 in 11 other countries. Several recent ingredient brands include Supro isolated soy proteins, used in food products, and RiboPrinter genetic fingerprinting technology. A key question that DuPont constantly confronts is whether to brand a product as an ingredient brand. To address this question, DuPont typically applies several criteria, both quantitative and qualitative.

On the quantitative side, DuPont has a model that estimates the return on investment of promoting a product as an ingredient brand. Inputs to the model include brand resource allocations such as advertising and trade support, while outputs relate to favorability ratings and potential sales. The goal of the model is to determine whether branding an ingredient can be financially justified, especially in industrial markets. On the qualitative side, DuPont assesses how an ingredient brand can help a product's positioning. If competitive and consumer analyses reveal that conveying certain associations would boost sales, DuPont is more likely to brand the ingredient. For example, one reason that DuPont launched its stain-resistant carpet fiber under the ingredient brand Stainmaster was that the company felt a "tough" association would be highly valued in the market.

DuPont maintains that an appropriate, effective ingredient branding strategy leads to a number of competitive advantages, such as higher price premiums (often as much as 20 percent), enhanced brand loyalty, and increased bargaining power with other members of the value chain. DuPont employs both push and pull strategies to create its ingredient brands. Consumer advertising creates consumer pull by generating interest in the brand and a willingness to specifically request it. Extensive trade support in the form of co-op advertising, training, and trade promotions creates push by fostering a strong sense of loyalty to DuPont from other members of the value chain. This loyalty helps DuPont negotiate favorable terms from distributors and leads to increased cooperation when new products are introduced.

One of its greatest success stories is probably Lycra, the super-stretching polymer invented in DuPont labs in 1959.[1] Generically known as *spandex,* Lycra got its start as an ingredient for girdles. Lycra's use has expanded steadily since its invention, from bathing suits in the 1970s to bicyclists' pants and aerobic outfits in the 1980s. More recently, nylon-Lycra bike shorts and exercise wear have became fashionable as everyday wear, especially with young adults.

In building the brand, DuPont has applied its well-known formula for success—one part product development and one part consumer marketing. Over the years, DuPont scientists have invented new versions of Lycra that have expanded the uses for the versatile fiber. Originally too bulky for lightweight items, finer Lycra versions have since been developed that can be knitted or woven into delicate fabrics and lightweight items such as panty hoses and dresses. Mastering new and often difficult-to-make versions has made Lycra synonymous with the freedom of movement that comes from spandex. As one sportswear maker puts it, "I wouldn't buy any spandex that wasn't from DuPont." To reach consumers, DuPont actively advertises the benefits of Lycra in a print advertising campaign with the tag line, "Nothing Moves Like Lycra." It has also teamed up with the industry trade group, Cotton Inc., to develop a "Made with Cotton and Lycra" logo for clothes tags.

The success of these efforts can be seen by the results of a recent DuPont study in which consumers said they would pay 20 percent more for a wool-Lycra skirt than for an all-wool version. Despite losing its original patent years ago, DuPont owns two-thirds of the worldwide spandex market with the Lycra brand.

---

[1]Monica Roman, "How DuPont Keeps 'Em Coming Back for More," *Business Week,* 20 August 1990, 68.

much equity had been created with consumers before that time. The success of the branding program is evident in research by a potential competitor, Alberto-Culver, that revealed that about 95 percent of sweetener users knew what Nutrasweet was, whereas only 10 percent were familiar with the generic term *aspartame*.

What are the requirements for successful ingredient branding? Branding Brief 7-5 describes ingredient branding efforts at DuPont, which has successfully introduced a number of such brands. In general, four tasks must be accomplished:

1. Consumers must first perceive that the ingredient matters to the performance and success of the end product. Ideally, this intrinsic value would be easily visible or experienced.
2. Consumers must then be convinced that not all ingredient brands are the same and that the ingredient is superior. Ideally, the ingredient would have an innovation or some other substantial advantage over existing alternatives.
3. A distinctive symbol or logo must be designed to clearly signal to consumers that the host product contains the ingredient. Ideally, the symbol or logo would function essentially as a "seal" and would be simple and versatile—such that it could appear virtually anywhere—and credibly communicate quality and confidence to consumers.
4. Finally, a coordinated push and pull program must be put into place such that consumers understand the importance and advantages of the branded ingredient. Often this will involve consumer advertising and promotions and, sometimes in collaboration with manufacturers, retail merchandising and promotion programs. As part of the push strategy, some communication efforts may also need to be devoted to gaining the cooperation and support of manufacturers or other channel members.

LICENSING

Licensing involves contractual arrangements whereby firms can use the names, logos, characters, and so forth of other brands to market their own brands for some fixed fee. Essentially, a firm is "renting" another brand to contribute to the brand equity of its own product. Because it can be a shortcut means of building brand equity, licensing has gained in popularity in recent years—North American retail sales of licensed products jumped from $4 billion in 1977 to $72 billion in 1997.[16]

Entertainment licensing has also become big business in recent years. Successful licensors include movie titles and logos (e.g., *Star Wars, Jurassic Park,* and *The Lion King*), comic strip characters (e.g., Garfield and Peanuts characters), television and cartoon characters (e.g., from *Sesame Street, Rugrats, Teletubbies,* and *the Simpsons*). Every summer, marketers spend millions of dollars in movie tie-ins as marketers look for the next blockbuster franchise. Even athletes participate in the action. Boxer George Foreman signed an astounding $27.5 million-a-year licensing deal with housewares company Salton in December 1999 to use his name on food preparation products such as the popular Lean Mean Low Fat Grilling Machine. Perhaps the champion of licensing is Walt Disney. Branding Brief 7-6 describes some of its licensing practices and strategies.

Licensing can be quite lucrative for the licensor. Licensing has long been an important business strategy for designer apparel and accessories. Designers such as Donna Karan, Calvin Klein, Pierre Cardin, and others command large royalties for the rights to use their name on a variety of merchandise such as clothing, belts, ties, and luggage. Over the course of three decades, Ralph Lauren became the world's most successful designer, creating a $5 billion dollar business licensing his Ralph Lauren, Double RL, and Polo brands to many different kinds of products (see Figure 7-3). Everyone seems to get into the act with licensing. Sports licensing of clothing apparel and other products has grown considerably to become a multibillion dollar business. Even the Rolling Stones released a line of 80 licensed goods (including T-shirts, ties, and a credit card) that were sold at concerts during their Voodoo Lounge tour, via home shopping shows, on computer networks, and through a 16-page catalog.

Hello Kitty

A huge success in Japan, Hello Kitty's whiskered, marshmallow-like head became a schoolgirls' favorite by appearing on notebooks, book bags, barrettes, and so forth. The Tokyo creator, Sanrio Company, decided to capitalize on its success through an extensive licensing program that found success even with adults, primarily women. New products included Hello Kitty wedding telegrams, e-mail programs, boxer shorts, ties, guitars, golf bags, and toasters. Daihatsu Motor Company even sold 1,200 limited-edition $7,245 Hello Kitty cars with Kitty-patterned upholstery and a speedometer decorated with the Kitty logo (at 20 kph, she is sleeping; at 60 kph, she is smiling; at 80 kph, she is sweating bullets). Over half of licensed sales now come from grown-ups.[17]

Guidelines

One danger in licensing is that manufacturers can get caught up in licensing a brand that might be popular at the moment but is really only a fad and produces short-lived sales. Because of multiple licensing arrangements, licensed entities easily can become

Licensing the Disney Way

The Walt Disney Company is routinely recognized as having one of the strongest brands in the world. Much of its success lies in its flourishing television, movie, theme park, and other entertainment ventures. These different vehicles have created a host of well-loved characters and a reputation for quality entertainment. Disney Consumer Products is designed to keep the Disney name and characters fresh in the consumer's mind through seven business areas in the following ways:

1. *Merchandising licensing:* Selectively authorizing the use of Disney characters on high-quality merchandise
2. *Publishing:* Telling the Disney story in books, magazines, comics, and art
3. *Music and audio:* Playing favorite Disney songs and stories on tape and compact disc
4. *Computer software:* Programming Disney "fun" into home computers and computer game systems
5. *Educational production:* Casting the characters in award-winning films for schools and libraries
6. *The Disney Store:* Bringing the Disney magic to premium shopping centers in the United States and overseas
7. *Catalog marketing:* Offering Disney and Disney-quality products via top catalogs

The pervasiveness of these product offerings is staggering: All in all, over 3 billion entertainment-based impressions of Mickey Mouse are received by children every year, equivalent to 10 million impressions a day.

Disney believes that the fact that its characters have appeared on quality merchandise for years has added greatly to their popularity. The philosophy of Walt Disney, the founder of the company, was to present his characters in toys with real play value or in high-quality merchandise that would then extend the fun of the filmed entertainment and enhance the company's reputation for excellence. The first hand-made Mickey Mouse appeared in 1930. Disney started licensing its characters for toys made by Mattel in the 1950s. Disney Licensing is now responsible for some 3,000 contracts for 16,000 products with top manufacturers worldwide. Disney licenses its standard characters (Mickey, Minnie, Donald, Goofy, and Pluto) and filmed entertainment (e.g., theatrical releases such as *Aladdin, The Lion King,* and *Toy Story,* and TV properties such as *Duck Tales* and *Madeline*). In 2000, retail sales for Disney-licensed products totaled $13 billion, which amounted to 70 percent of revenue for Disney Consumer Products.

To capitalize on the popularity of its characters, Disney has developed a family of brands for Disney-licensed products, each one featuring Mickey Mouse, Minnie Mouse, or some other classic Disney character. Each brand was created for a special age group and distribution channel. The brand combines the name and character into a specially designed logo. Each can be used in a wide range of product categories, including apparel and accessories, toys, home furnishings, social expressions/novelties, sporting goods, and gifts.

Artists in Licensing's Creative Resources department work closely with manufacturers on all aspects of product marketing, including design, prototyping, manufacturing, packaging, and advertising. At each step, care is taken to ensure that the products are faithful to the look and personality of the characters. To protect and enhance the value of its brands, Disney issues a thick notebook of standards of brand identities for Disney licensing that specifies color treatment of the logo; proper use of secondary graphic elements or trade dress (distinctive color schemes, shapes, images, background patterns, or typography) in packaging, retail signage, or other communications; minimum unobstructed surrounding area; artwork reproduction procedures; use of the brand name outside the logo; and the Disney copyright notice. Disney maintains a team of employees who strictly interpret these guidelines, fiercely guarding the image of the characters.

One of Disney's most successful licensed characters is Winnie the Pooh. Disney has three separate Winnie the Pooh product lines: the familiar "red shirt" Pooh from Disney movies; the 100 Acre Collection, a more upscale line comprising products that typically sell in department stores; and the Classic Pooh line based on the original illustrations from A. A. Milne's *Winnie the Pooh* books. Pooh products, which existed since Disney's 1966 animated short *Winnie the Pooh and the Honey Tree,* have recently become a virtual goldmine. Between 1995 and 1998, the total licensing market for Winnie the Pooh grew from $390 million to $3.3 billion. By 2000, Pooh products generated an estimated $6 billion in sales for Disney. By comparison, Disney's other core characters—Mickey, Minnie, Goofy, Donald Duck, and Pluto—grew only 20 percent over the same period. In 2001, Disney bought the rights to Winnie the Pooh and all the related characters for $340 million and no longer has to pay licensing fees to the group of former rights holders.

Source: Bruce Orwall, "Disney's Magic Transformation?" *Wall Street Journal,* 4 October 2000.

overexposed and wear out quickly as a result. Licensed merchandise sales of Barney products hit a $500 million jackpot in 1993 but faded significantly the following year before making a comeback in 1996. Sales of Izod Lacoste, with its familiar alligator crest, peaked at $450 million in 1982 but dwindled to an estimated $150 million in shirt sales in 1990 after the brand became overexposed and discount priced.[18]

Teenage Mutant Ninja Turtles

First introduced in 1988, Teenage Mutant Ninja Turtles products were licensed for better or worse to more than a hundred businesses and generated an estimated $1 billion in sales in 1991 for products bearing the turtle name, ranging from conventional souvenirs and T-shirts to more exotic alternatives such as vanilla-flavored pizza candy and even pork rinds! After this high-water mark, however, sales of licensed Teenage Mutant Ninja Turtles merchandise dropped to $100 million in 1993.

Firms are taking a number of steps to protect themselves in their licensing agreements, especially those firms that have little brand equity of their own and rely on the image of their licensor.[19] For example, firms are obtaining licensing rights to a broad range of licensed entities—some of which are relatively more enduring in nature—to diversify their risk. Licensees are developing unique new products and sales and

Licensees: Apparel and Accessories

Infants and toddlers
  Schwab
Lauren (women's apparel)
  Jones Apparel Group
Polo jeans
  Sun Apparel
Men's tailored clothing
  Pietrafesa
Chaps men's clothing
  Peerless Clothing
Women's jewelry
  Carolee Design
Gloves
  Swany
  Elmer Little
Eyewear
  Safilo
  Optique Du Monde

Chaps men's sportswear
  Warnaco
Hoisery
  Hot Sox
Small leather goods and belts
  RL Leather Goods
Fragrance
  Cosmair
Scarves
  Echo
Handbags and luggage
  Wathne
Underwear and intimates
  Sara Lee
  Playtex
Footwear
  Rockport
  Reebok

Licensees: Home Collection

Sheets, towels, and bedding
  Westpoint Stevens
China, crystal, and home fragrance
  Pentland
Bathroom rugs
  Newmark
Wallpaper, fabrics, and rugs
  Folia
Table linens
  Audrey Table Linens

Blankets, pillows, and bedding accessories
  Pillowtex
Flatwear
  Reed & Barton
Furniture
  Henredon
Paint
  Sherwin-Williams
Area rugs
  Shyam Ahuja

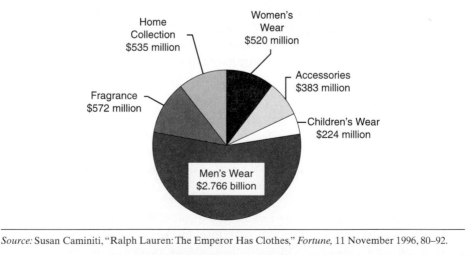

Home Collection $535 million

Women's Wear $520 million

Fragrance $572 million

Accessories $383 million

Children's Wear $224 million

Men's Wear $2.766 billion

Source: Susan Caminiti, "Ralph Lauren: The Emperor Has Clothes," *Fortune,* 11 November 1996, 80–92.

FIGURE 7-3   Ralph Lauren's $5 Billion Empire (1996)

marketing approaches so that their sales are not merely a function of the popularity of other brands. Some firms conduct marketing research to ensure the proper match of product and licensed entity or to provide more precise sales forecasts for effective inventory management.

Corporate trademark licensing—one of the fastest-growing segments of the licensing industry—is the licensing of company names, logos, or brands for use on various, often unrelated products.[20] For example, in the depths of a financial crisis a number of years ago, Harley-Davidson chose to license its name—synonymous with motorcycles and a certain lifestyle—to a polo shirt, gold ring, and even a wine cooler. Other seemingly narrowly focused brands such as Jeep, Caterpillar, Deere, and Jack Daniels have also entered a broad portfolio of licensing arrangements. Standards & Poors and Dow Jones now license their trademarks to manufacturers of financial products and to the exchanges where the products trade.

In licensing their corporate trademarks, firms may have different motivations, including generating extra revenues and profits, protecting their trademarks, increasing their brand exposure, or enhancing their brand image. The profit appeal can be enticing because there are no inventory expenses, accounts receivables, manufacturing expenses, and so forth. In an average deal, a licensee pays a corporation a royalty of about 5 percent of the wholesale price of each product, although the actual percentage can vary from 2 percent to 10 percent. As noted in Chapter 5, some firms now sell licensed merchandise through their own catalogs.

As with any co-branded arrangement, however, the risk is that the product will not live up to the reputation established by the brand. Inappropriate licensing can potentially dilute brand meaning with consumers and marketing focus within the organization. When Eddie Bauer, in the midst of a retailing slump in November 2000, announced a two-year licensing deal with Compaq for special-edition Compaq Presario 1400 notebooks computers sporting a distinctive trim, one industry analyst complained, "Their business has been terribly disappointing—their entire focus should be unrelentingly on their merchandise assortment."[21]

CELEBRITY ENDORSEMENT

Using well-known and admired people to promote products is a widespread phenomenon with a long marketing history. Even former U.S. president Ronald Reagan was a celebrity endorser, pitching several different products, including cigarettes, during his acting days. Some American actors or actresses who refuse to endorse products in the United States are willing to do so in Japan (e.g., Arnold Schwarzenegger for Aramin V-drink, Meg Ryan for Dingo autos, Leonardo DiCaprio for Suzuki Wagon R, Jodie Foster for Morinaga Caffe Late, and Harrison Ford for Honda Legend). The rationale behind these strategies is that a famous person can

> draw attention to a brand
>
> and shape the perceptions of the brand by virtue of the inferences that consumers make based on the knowledge they have about the famous person.

Consequently, in choosing a celebrity endorser, it is important for the celebrity to be well enough known that the awareness, image, and responses for the brand may be improved. In particular, a celebrity endorser should have a high level of visibility and a rich set of potentially useful associations, judgments, and feelings.[22] Ideally, a celebrity endorser would be seen as credible in terms of expertise, trustworthiness, and likability or attractiveness, as well as having specific associations that carry potential product relevance.

Q Ratings

Marketing Evaluations/TvQ Inc. conducts surveys to determine "Q ratings" for a broad range of entertainers and other public figures (e.g., TV performers, news and sports anchors and reporters, athletes, models). Each performer is rated on the following scale: "One of My Favorites," "Very Good," "Good," "Fair," "Poor," and "Never Seen or Heard of Before." The sum of the "Favorite" through "Poor" scores is "Total Familiar." The "One of My Favorites" score is an absolute measure of appeal or popularity, since it is based on 100 percent. Because some performers are not very well known and would have a low "Favorite" score, the Q rating is a ratio of the "Favorite" score to the "Familiar" score. It addresses the question, How appealing is he or she among those who do know him or her? Q ratings are used to reflect the potential of lesser-known personalities and provide an equivalent basis for comparison with more established personalities. Figure 7-4 displays some of Marketing Evaluation's recent Q ratings for popular entertainers

A number of different brands have created strong associations to celebrities that have served as sources of brand equity. For example, actress Candace Bergen appeared in over 100 commercials for Sprint and helped to give the brand a smart, feisty, and irreverent image before being replaced by TV actress Sela Ward. Similarly, Lee Iacocca was seen as a feisty, patriotic symbol for Chrysler automobiles while he was chairman there. Down-to-earth sportscaster John Madden has been a long-time pitchman for Ace Hardware.

Dave Thomas and Wendy's

Founder and chairman Dave Thomas was an effective pitchman for his Wendy's restaurant chain because of his down-home, unpretentious, folksy style and strong product focus. Recognized by over 90 percent of adult consumers, he appeared in hundreds of commercials over a 12-year period. A heart attack scare in 1997 forced Wendy's executives to contemplate "life after Dave"—a scary prospect given their belief that "nothing else builds traffic and moves product as well" and a reality they had to face with his death on January 8, 2002.[23]

Potential Problems

There are a number of potential problems with linking a celebrity endorser to a brand. First, celebrity endorsers can be overused by endorsing so many products that they lack any specific product meaning or are just seen as overly opportunistic or insincere. Over the years, comedian Bill Cosby has pitched for Jell-O, E.F. Hutton, Ford Motor Company, Coca-Cola, Texas Instruments, and Kodak, among others. More recently, teen pop singer Britney Spears appeared in ads or promotions for Pepsi, Clairol, McDonald's, Skechers, Polaroid, Sweet16.com, Youtopia.com, and Got Milk? within a one-year span. It could be argued that Michael Jordan, as talented a basketball player and as likable a person as he might be, loses effectiveness as an endorser when he is associated with so many brands and products, starring in ads for Nike athletic shoes,

	Familiarity (%)	Q Score (%)
Harrison Ford	85	51
Robin Williams	90	51
Mel Gibson	84	50
Tom Hanks	89	50
Bill Cosby	90	44
Sean Connery	84	44
Bill Goldberg	20	43
Jack Nicholson	81	42
Clint Eastwood	85	42
Michael Jordan	86	42
James Earl Jones	76	42
John Travolta	89	39
Will Smith	78	39
Whoopi Goldberg	87	38
Ron Howard	76	38
Shemar Moore	22	38
Michael Richards	69	37
Tim Allen	94	37
Roma Downey	60	37
Kim Zimmer	23	36
Nicholas Cage	76	36
Eddie Murphy	90	36
George Clooney	78	36
Helen Hunt	75	36
Paul Newman	80	36

Source: Marketing Evaluations/TvQ, Inc., Summer 1998 Performer Q Study.

FIGURE 7-4   Q Ranking of Perfomers (Among Population Aged 6 Years and Older)

Gatorade sports drink, Bijan fragrances, Hanes underwear, McDonald's restaurants, Ball Park Franks, Rayovac batteries, Wheaties cereal, and MCI WorldCom long distance telecommunications. He even supported his own brand in the form of Michael Jordan men's cologne and, later, the Nike subsidiary Jordan brand. Branding Brief 7-7 describes Tiger Woods's numerous endorsement activities.

Second, there must be a reasonable match between the celebrity and the product.[24] Many past endorsements would seem to fail this test. A classic mismatch occurred when the CEO of Bristol-Myers insisted on using his favorite Western actor, rugged John Wayne, as the spokesperson for Datril pain reliever. Tennis star John McEnroe was the spokesperson for Bic disposable razors despite his ubiquitous two-day stubble on the tennis court. George C. Scott, an Oscar winner for his patriotic movie portrayal of Patton, seemed to be a curious choice to endorse the French Renault car. Some potentially better matches in recent years include singer Tina Turner for Hanes Resilience panty hose, actor Paul Hogan of *Crocodile Dundee* fame for Subaru's line of Outback sports utility vehicles, and Lance Armstrong for Bristol-Myers Squibb's cancer medicines.

Third, celebrity endorsers can get in trouble or lose popularity, diminishing their marketing value to the brand. The Beef Council's advertising strategy of employing celebrity

Aiming for the Endorsement Sweet Spot with Tiger Woods

Athletes can be a particularly effective group for endorsing athletic products, beverages, and apparel. One of the premier athlete endorsers is professional golfer Tiger Woods. Woods was a star even before turning pro in 1996, and his early success on the pro tour earned him a number of endorsement offers. Within a month of losing his amateur status, Tiger had won a tournament and inked deals with Nike and Titleist worth a combined $60 million. In 2000, at the age of 24, Tiger became the all-time career earnings leader for the Professional Golfers Association (PGA). His success on the course has been rivaled only by his success in business: Woods earned an estimated $45 million from endorsements in 2000, second only to Michael Jordan, who earned $69 million, among all American athletes. Today, Woods endorses products from a number of companies:

Titleist/Cobra (5 year, $20 million)	Asahi
Nike (5 year, $100 million)	General Mills
Buick (5 year, $25 million)	*Golf Digest*
Rolex (5 year, $7 million)	EA Sports
American Express (5 year, $13 million)	CBS Sportsline
TLC Laser Eye Centers ($2 million)	Radica Games
All Star Café	Executive Jet

With his exceptional and exciting play, Tiger has had a measurable impact on golf's television audience and helped raise the prize money stakes for the entire game. After Tiger broke the scoring record at the Masters tournament in 1997, ratings for the final rounds at the four major tournaments collectively rose 56 percent by 2000. Consequently, TV networks are spending more money on PGA events: Total prizes averaged $3.2 million per event, an 87 percent increase between 1997 and 2000. Although endorsement spending by golf companies remained unchanged during that interval, spending from nongolf companies increased over 200 percent.

In 2000, Woods signed a blockbuster $100 million contract to endorse Nike products over the next five years. Nike Golf president Bob Wood expressed Tiger's value to the company when he said, "His representation is enough to reinforce everything we want to say about ourselves—competitiveness, excellence, and a desire to be better." One reason Nike was so enthusiastic is that their fledging golf division grew from $100 million to $250 million from 1996 to 2000 during Tiger Woods's first five-year contract. Nike also gained instant exposure when Tiger changed to Nike golf balls from Titleist, since television cameras repeatedly focused in on the new balls, which prominently feature a swoosh. Recalling the abundance of coverage the switch received, Nike Golf's Bob Wood said, "It was like winning the lottery."

At the time of the Nike signing, Tiger's father Earl Woods proclaimed, "This contract will be chump change compared to the next one, because Tiger is only going to get bigger and better." Since golfers' careers span decades, Tiger's earning potential is not expected to decrease any time soon. *ESPN Magazine* estimates that over the course of his lifetime, Woods's earnings from playing, endorsements, and appearance fees will total $6 billion. Tiger donates some of his earnings to the Tiger Woods Foundation, which provides minorities with opportunities to participate in golf.

Sources: Greg Johnson, "Woods Cautious Approach to the Green," *Los Angeles Times,* 26 July 2000; "Woods Gets a Ringing Endorsement," Associated Press, 19 September 2000.

---

actors and actresses as spokespeople in the mid-1980s backfired when actress Cybill Shepard admitted in a magazine article that she did not actually eat much red meat and the other spokesperson, actor James Garner, underwent quintuple-bypass heart surgery. Thus, linking the brand to a celebrity results in a certain lack of control; a number of spokespeople over the years have run into legal difficulties, personal problems, or controversies of some form that diminished their marketing value (e.g., as was the case with athletes Mike Tyson and O. J. Simpson, entertainer Michael Jackson, and others).

Fourth, many consumers feel that celebrities are only doing the endorsement for the money and do not necessarily believe in or even use the endorsed brand. Even worse, some consumers feel that the salaries for celebrities to appear in commercials add a significant and unnecessary cost to the brand. In reality, celebrities often do not come cheap and can demand literally millions of dollars to endorse a brand. Celebrities also can be difficult to work with and may not willingly follow the marketing direction of the brand. Tennis player Andre Agassi tried Nike's patience when—at the same time he was advertising for Nike—he appeared in commercials for the Canon Rebel camera. In these ads, he looked into the camera and proclaimed "Image Is Everything"—the antithesis of the "authentic athletic performance" positioning that is the foundation of the Nike brand equity.

Finally, as noted in Chapter 6, celebrities may distract attention from the brand in ads such that consumers notice the stars but have trouble remembering the advertised brand. For example, Susan Lucci appeared on Video Storyboards' top 10 endorser list in 1993. Unfortunately, only 15 percent of those surveyed knew she was promoting Fords—75 percent had no idea and, even worse, 10 percent thought she was representing rivals Chevrolet or Plymouth. Similar confusion has prevailed in the soft drink category, where, at one time, so many brands were using celebrities that consumers virtually needed a scorecard to keep track.

Guidelines

To overcome these problems, celebrity spokespeople must be evaluated, selected, and used strategically. First, it is important to choose a well-known and well-defined celebrity whose associations are relevant to the brand and likely to be transferable. In discussing Andre Agassi's role as a Nike endorser, Nike CEO Phil Knight made the following observation.[25]

> What's interesting about tennis is not hitting the ball back and forth across the net but the personalities. We've been pleased that we've always had interesting personalities endorsing our products. Andre certainly has a lot of flair and has created a lot of interest. It's surprising even to me how he's transcended the sport.

NASCAR driver Jeff Gordon has been an effective pitchman for a variety of brands, including Pepsi, Ray-Ban sunglasses, Close-Up toothpaste, and Edy's ice cream, because his good looks and self-effacing manner appeal to a wide segment of consumers who buy his endorsed products in support.

Thus, there must be a logical fit between the brand and person.[26] To reduce confusion or dilution, the celebrity ideally would not be linked to a number of other brands or overexposed. After winning Olympic gold in 1984, Mary Lou Retton appeared in commercials for so many brands that one marketing critic wearily complained, "I've seen more of her in the past year than I have of my mother—and I love my mother more!"[27] To broaden the appeal and reduce the risks of linking to one celebrity, some marketers have employed several celebrities. In the case of Tommy Hilfiger, multiple celebrities are used to reach multiple audiences (see Figure 7-5).

Second, the celebrity must be used in the advertising and communication program in a creative fashion that highlights the relevant associations and encourages their transfer. For example, comedian Jerry Seinfeld's popular commercials for American Express used the same unflappable charm and knack for finding himself in unusual situations that he displayed on his TV show. Finally, marketing research must be undertaken to help identify potential endorser candidates and facilitate the development of the proper marketing program, as well as track their effectiveness.

FIGURE 7-5 Tommy Hilfiger Celebrity Segmentation

Target	Products	Sales	Celebrity and Pitch
"Stylish Career Females" (18–35)	Casual knitwear for weekends and work	$405 million	Rebecca Romijn-Stamos TV ads featured *Sports Illustrated* cover girl driving cross-country as she waxed eloquent above American spirit.
"Workaday Natty Males" (18–45)	Casual work clothes, fragrances	$800 million	Lenny Kravitz Retro rocker's Freedom tour was named after the fragrance.
"Teenyboppers" (13 to early 20s)	Jeans	$230 million	Britney Spears Teen heartthrob's "Baby One More Time" tour was endorsed by the company.
"Socially Aware Set" (20 something females)	Women's wear, fragrances	$100 million-plus (fragrance)	Jewel Lilith Fair veteran went out on her own with Hilfiger Spirit tour. Company also sponsored Lilith Fair, promised to promote breast cancer research
"Sports Fanatics" (males, 24–45)	Golf clothing	$25 million-plus	David Toms Open champion and potential rising star.

Source: Rob Wherry, "Tommy in Tatters," *Forbes,* 7 February 2000, 56.

BRANDING BRIEF 7-8

Event Sponsorship at Visa

Back in 1985, Visa and MasterCard were seen as essentially identical products that faced stiff competition from other brands, particularly American Express, which had a strong and desirable image with consumers. Visa set out to create a differentiating and enduring perception of its brand as the best payment system for all types of purchases. Visa was positioned as the brand with superior acceptance by virtue of hard-hitting comparative ads with American Express. The "It's Everywhere You Want to Be" campaign featured interesting, unique, and prestigious locations where consumers might expect American Express to be accepted but where consumers were told to "bring your Visa card, because they don't take American Express." In terms of event marketing, Visa aligned itself with high-profile events (sporting events, concert tours, etc.) that similarly did not take American Express and backed up their sponsorships with additional comparative advertising campaigns.

Starting in 1988, the Olympics became Visa's biggest event association. Visa's Olympic involvement has helped to reinforce their desired positioning as a high-quality, globally accepted product. Visa's Olympic support and sponsorship were reinforced in many ways. Ads for the 1992 Olympic Games focused on how tough the competition would be at the Games, "but not as tough as the sellers at the ticket window if you don't have your Visa card." To support Olympic fund-raising, cardholder transactions were tied to Visa donations to certain Olympic teams in several countries. Visa also provided direct financial support to certain Olympic teams. Visa's "Olympics of the Imagination" brought school children from all over the world to the Olympics as part of an art competition tied into the Olympics. Visa adopted similar activities for the 1996 Olympic Games in Atlanta.

The effects of these sponsorship and other communication efforts have been dramatic. Research has shown that Visa is now perceived as more widely accepted than other cards and, as a result, as the card of choice for personal and family shopping, personal travel and entertainment, and even international travel, a former American Express stronghold.

SPORTING, CULTURAL, OR OTHER EVENTS

Chapter 6 described in detail the rationale for event marketing and sponsorship and provided guidelines on how to choose the appropriate event, design the optimal sponsorship program, and measure the effects of sponsorship on brand equity. The chapter noted that event marketing was a means of creating or reinforcing consumer perceptions of key associations. Events have their own set of associations that may become linked to a sponsoring brand under certain conditions.

The main means by which an event can transfer associations is on the basis of various dimensions of credibility. A brand may seem more likable or perhaps even trustworthy or expert by virtue of becoming linked to an event. For example, Branding Brief 7-8 describes how event sponsorship has played an important role in building brand equity for Visa credit cards.[28]

Sponsored events can contribute to brand equity by becoming associated to the brand and improving brand awareness, adding new associations, or improving the strength, favorability, and uniqueness of existing associations. The extent to which this transfer takes place will depend on which events are selected and how the sponsorship program is designed and integrated into the entire marketing program to build brand equity. Brand Focus 7.0 discusses sponsorship strategies for the Olympics Games.

THIRD-PARTY SOURCES

Finally, it should be noted that secondary associations can be created in a number of different ways by linking the brand to various third-party sources. For example, the *Good Housekeeping* seal has been seen as a mark of quality for decades (offering product replacement or refunds for defective products for up to two years from purchase). Endorsements from leading magazines (e.g., *PC* magazine), organizations (e.g., American Dental Association), and experts (e.g., film critic Roger Ebert) can obviously improve perceptions of and attitudes toward brands. Third-party sources can also have an effect at a more local level.

> **Pet Food**
> Pharmaceutical companies have wooed doctors for years to prescribe their drugs. In the $10 billion pet food category, the growth has been with the superpremium "high science" or "designer" brands, which promise higher-quality and more nutritious ingredients based on "pioneering research in animal nutrition" tailored to a pet's "life stage" or age. Many pet owners purchase brands and products on the basis of the recommendations of veterinarians. Recognizing veterinarians' power, Colgate's Hill's Science Diet and Procter & Gamble's Iams brands have targeted vets via funding for university research and nutrition courses, sales commissions on office sales, and other means.[29]

In another example of local third-party sources, with cigarette vending machines disappearing in many cities, tobacco companies increasingly have targeted bartenders at bars that attract young, hip drinkers as a means of interacting with customers. They justify the thousands of dollars spent on a single bar by the fact that a loyal cigarette smoker can spend more than $100,000 over his or her lifetime. As part of the deal, bar owners promise to use bar supplies displaying the sponsoring brand's name and, in some cases, to not sell or promote rival brands. Brown & Williamson, which spends $30 million a year on its bar program nationwide, tested its effectiveness by polling bargoers and comparing their impressions of its Lucky Strike brand to those who weren't exposed to the promotion. They found an "enormous improvement" as a result of the program.[30]

Third-party sources may be seen as especially credible sources. As a result, they are often featured in advertising campaigns and selling efforts. J.D. Powers and Associates' well-publicized Customer Satisfaction Index helped to cultivate an image of quality for Japanese automakers in the 1980s, with a corresponding adverse impact on the quality image of their U.S. rivals. In the 1990s, they began to rank quality in other industries, such as airlines, credit cards, rental cars, and phone service, and top-rated brands in these categories began to feature their awards in ad campaigns.

Review

This chapter considered the process by which other entities can be leveraged to create secondary associations. These other entities include source factors such as the company that makes a product, where the product is made, and where it is purchased, as well as related people, places, or things. By linking the brand to other entities with their own set of associations, consumers may expect that some of these same associations also characterize the brand. Thus, independent of how a product is branded, the nature of the product itself, and its supporting marketing program, brand equity can be created by "borrowing" it from other sources. Creating secondary associations in this fashion may be quite important if the corresponding brand associations are deficient in some way. Secondary associations may be especially valuable as a means to link favorable brand associations that can serve as points of parity or to create unique brand associations that can serve as points of difference in positioning a brand.

Eight different ways to leverage secondary associations to build brand equity are by linking the brand to (1) the company making the product, (2) the country or some other geographic location in which the product originates, (3) retailers or other channel members who sell the product, (4) other brands, including ingredient brands, (5) licensed characters, (6) famous spokespeople or endorsers, (7) events, and (8) third-party sources. In general, the extent to which any of these entities can be leveraged as a source of equity depends on consumer knowledge of the entity and how easily the appropriate associations or responses to the entity transfer to the brand. In general, global credibility or attitudinal dimensions may be more likely to transfer than specific attribute and benefit associations, although the latter can be transferred too. Linking the brand to other entities, however, is not without risk. Some control is given up, and managing the transfer process so that only the relevant secondary associations become linked to the brand may be difficult.

Discussion Questions

1. The Boeing Company makes a number of different types of aircraft for the commercial airline industry, for example, the 727, 747, 757, 767, and 777 jet models. Is there any way for Boeing to adopt an ingredient branding strategy with its jets? How? What would be the pros and cons?
2. After winning major championships, star players often complain about their lack of endorsement offers. Similarly, after every Olympics, a number of medal-winning athletes lament their lack of commercial recognition. From a branding perspective, how would you respond to the complaints of these athletes?
3. Think of the country in which you live. What image might it have with consumers in other countries? Are there certain brands or products that are highly effective in leveraging that image in global markets?
4. Which retailers have the strongest image and equity in your mind? Think about the brands they sell. Do they contribute to the equity of the retailer? Conversely, how does that retailer's image help the image of the brands it sells?
5. Pick a brand. Evaluate how it leverages secondary associations. Can you think of any ways that the brand could more effectively leverage secondary brand knowledge?

Brand Focus 7.0

Going for Corporate Gold at the Olympics

Competition at the Olympics is not restricted to just the athletes. A number of corporate sponsors also vie to make their sponsorship dollars earn the highest return possible.[31] Corporate sponsorship is a significant part of the business side of the Olympic Games. Sponsorships contributed 34 percent of the revenue of the 1992 and 1996 Games. Some of the world's largest and most visible companies, including McDonald's, Coca-Cola, Visa, and Kodak, signed sponsorship deals for as much as $50 million to sponsor the 2002 and 2004 Olympics.

Corporate sponsorship of the Olympics exploded with the commercial success of the 1984 Summer Games in Los Angeles. Many international sponsors (e.g., Fuji) realized positive image building and increased market share. In Atlanta in 1996, top-tier "Worldwide" corporate sponsors spent $40 million for the rights to display all Olympic logos and exclusive rights to the five-ring logo in their ads and on their packaging and to secure prime access to tickets, hotel rooms, athletes, cultural events, and the hospitality village. Centennial Olympic Games Partners had the same access as Worldwide Sponsors but could only use the Atlanta Games and U.S. Team logos. Centennial Olympic Game Sponsors provided services to the Games and could negotiate event tickets and access to athletes.

In addition to the 40 sponsors, there were an additional 75 suppliers and another 125 or so licensees. Besides direct expenditures, firms spent hundreds of millions more on related marketing efforts. Coca-Cola's total Olympic-related expenditure reportedly topped $500 million and included funding for the torch relay and a mega-retail promotion, Coke's Red Hot Olympic Summer. AT&T was the official "presenter" of the 21-acre tent-filled commercial showcase, Centennial Olympic Park (which included Bud World and the Swatch Pavilion) and erected a giant communications center in the Olympic Village.

Olympic sponsorship is controversial in terms of its marketing impact. For example, despite the fact that Hilton was the official hotel of the 1992 Summer Games, only 8 percent of consumers were aware of the sponsorship just weeks after the Olympics ended. Even worse, 9 percent thought the sponsor was Holiday Inn. Similarly, Kellogg also was a 1992 sponsor, but only 20 percent of consumers named Kellogg's Corn Flakes as a brand sponsor while 35 percent named Wheaties. In 1996, licensees fell short of their goal of $1 billion in total sales.

In some cases, sponsorship confusion may be due to ambush marketing. In ambush marketing, advertisers attempt to falsely give consumers the impression that they are Olympic sponsors by means such as running Olympic-themed ads that publicize other forms of sponsorship (sponsoring a national team, network telecast, etc.), identifying the brand as an official supplier, or using current or former Olympians as endorsers. For example, to retaliate against Visa's ads stressing their exclusive Olympic acceptability, American Express ran ads that focused on their card's presence in Olympic host cities. To improve the marketing effectiveness of sponsorship, the Olympic Committee has vowed to fight ambush marketing as well as attempted to reduce the number of sponsors to avoid clutter.

Following the scandal surrounding Salt Lake City's bid for the 2002 Winter Olympics, where it was revealed that organizers gave cash and gifts to some 30 International Olympic Committee (IOC) members, many criticized the Games for being overcommercialized. The scandal generated feelings of disillusionment from fans and compounded image problems resulting from drug use and poor sportsmanship in past Olympics. A survey conducted soon after the scandal broke revealed that 39 percent of people felt more negatively about the Games than in the past.

To counteract the negative perceptions, the IOC launched an image campaign to promote the 2000 Games. The ads, which ran in 200 countries, reflected the "core values of the Olympic movement" by featuring footage of former Olympic champions such as Jesse Owens, as well as unsung heroes. The $150 million campaign featured Internet advertising, six television spots, six radio spots, and four different print ads, one of which detailed how corporate sponsors contribute to the Games.

The scandal caused some corporations to reconsider their role in the games. An executive for Miller Brewing—which has not been a sponsor of the Games—said, "The Olympics, quite frankly, have never been more overpriced or overvalued." Sponsorship remained a big part of the 2000 Sydney Games, but some major sponsors toned down their Olympic ad blitz in order to seem less opportunistic and commercial. Instead of purchasing space on 50 billboards, as the company did for the 1996 Atlanta Games, Kodak dressed 35 actors like rolls of film and had them walk around the venue. Goodyear changed the logo on its blimp to display the Australian greeting "G'Day" on one side and "Good Luck" on the other. Even the typically brash marketer Nike adopted a more subtle approach to advertising at the Sydney Games. When the company wrapped a highly visible 30-story downtown building with images of Australian athletes, it used an undersized swoosh that measured only a few stories.

In 2001, the U.S. Olympic Committee (USOC) developed an advertising campaign to convey a "wholesome" image of the Olympics to Americans. The USOC hired Goodby Silverstein & Partners to create ads that targeted younger viewers and emphasized the Olympic ideals of fair play, honesty, and passion for sport. In another attempt to generate excitement for the Games among America's youth, the USOC developed a line of apparel such as baseball caps, fleece vests, and jackets. Officials anticipated that the 2002 Winter Olympics in Salt Lake City would restore domestic interest in the Games because they would take place on American soil.

Nevertheless, Olympic sponsorship remains highly controversial. Many corporate sponsors continue to believe that their Olympic sponsorship yields many significant benefits, creating an image of goodwill for their brand, serving as a platform to enhance awareness and communicate messages, and affording numerous opportunities to reward employees and entertain clients. Other criticize the event as horribly overcommercialized, citing the Atlanta Summer Games as an example. In any case, as suggested in Chapter 6, it is clear that the success of Olympic sponsorship-like any sports sponsorship—depends in large part on how well the sponsorship is executed and incorporated into the entire marketing plan.

Notes

1. Suen L. Hwang, "Philip Morris Makes Dave's—but Sh! Don't Tell," *Wall Street Journal*, 2 March 1995, B1.
2. Wai-Kwan Li and Robert S. Wyer Jr., "The Role of Country of Origin in Product Evaluations: Informational and Standard-of-Comparison Effects," *Journal of Consumer Psychology* 3, no. 2 (1994): 187–212.
3. Sarah Ellison, "U.K. Firm Touts Timberland as U.S. Icon," *Wall Street Journal*, 6 February 2001, B13.
4. Stephanie Mehta, "BellSouth Pushes Harder in Latin America," *Wall Street Journal*, 24 May 1999, B10.
5. Julia Flynn Siler, "OshKosh B'Gosh May Be Risking Its Upscale Image," *Business Week*, 25 July 1991, 140.
6. Akshay R. Rao and Robert W. Ruekert, "Brand Alliances as Signals of Product Quality," *Sloan Management Review* (Fall 1994): 87–97; Akshay R. Rao, Lu Qu, and Robert W. Ruekert, "Signalling Unobservable Product Quality through Brand Ally," *Journal of Marketing Research*, 36(2), May 1999, 258–268.
7. Robin L. Danziger, "Cross Branding with Branded Ingredients: The New Frontier" (paper presented at the ARF Fourth Annual Advertising and Promotion Workshop, February 1992).
8. Kim Cleland, "Multimarketer Melange an Increasingly Tasty Option on the Store Shelf," *Advertising Age*, 2 May 1994, S-10.
9. Teresa Gubbins, "Spinoffs Carry Popular Products All Over the Store," *Dallas Morning News*.
10. Betsy Spethmann and Karen Benezra, "Co-brand or Be Damned," *Brandweek*, 21 November 1994, 21–24. Eventually this product was discontinued, another casuality in the highly competitive cereal market.
11. This product was not a success in part because kids, who made up the target market, seemed to be more than happy to use their parents' computers, for better or for worse.
12. http://www.swatch.com; Kevin Helliker, "Can Wristwatch Whiz Switch Swatch Cachet to an Automobile?" *Wall Street Journal*, 4 March 1994, A1; Audrey Choi and Margaret Studer, "Daimler-Benz's Mercedes Unit to Build a Car with Maker of Swatch Watches," *Wall Street Journal*, 23 February 1994, A14; Beth Demain Reigber, "DaimlerChrysler Smarts as BMW Mini Looms," Dow Jones Newswire, 20 June 2001.
13. Based in part on a talk by Nancy Bailey, "Using Licensing to Build the Brand" (Brand Masters conference, 7 December 2000).
14. Gregory S. Carpenter, Rashi Glazer, and Kent Nakamoto, "Meaningful Brands from Meaningless Differentiation: The Dependence on Irrelevant Attributes," *Journal of Marketing Research* (August 1994): 339–350.
15. Donald G. Norris, "Ingredient Branding: A Strategy Option with Multiple Beneficiaries," *Journal of Consumer Marketing* 9, no. 3 (1992): 19–31.
16. Philip Kotler, *Marketing Management: Analysis, Planning, Implementation, and Control*, 10th ed. (Englewood Cliffs, NJ: Prentice-Hall, 2000).
17. Yumiko Ono, "Kitty-Mania Grips Grown-Ups in Japan," *Wall Street Journal*, 15 December 1998, B1.
18. Teri Agins, "Izod Lacoste Gets Restyled and Repriced," *Wall Street Journal*, 22 July 1991, B1.
19. Udayan Gupta, "Licensees Learn What's in a Pop-Culture Name: Risk," *Wall Street Journal*, 8 August 1991, B2.
20. Frank E. James, "I'll Wear the Coke Pants Tonight; They Go Well with My Harley-Davidson Ring," *Wall Street Journal*, 6 June 1985, 31.
21. Robert Berner, "The Name of the Game Is—The Name," *Business Week*, 27 November 2000, 12.
22. Grant McCracken, "Who Is the Celebrity Endorser? Cultural Foundations of the Endorsement Process," *Journal of Consumer Research* 16 (December 1989): 310–321.
23. John Grossman, "Dave Thomas' Recipe for Success," *Sky*, November 2000, 103–107; Bruce Horvitz, "Wendy's Icon Back at Work," *USA Today*, 31 March 1997, B1-B2.

24. Shekhar Misra and Sharon E. Beatty, "Celebrity Spokesperson and Brand Congruence," *Journal of Business Research* 21 (1990): 159–173.

25. Doug Smith, "Always the Showman; Now a Winner," *USA Today*, 11 January 1985, 1C–2C.

26. Misra and Beatty, "Celebrity Spokesperson and Brand Congruence."

27. Roderick Townley, "Is That Winning Smile Losing Its Charm?" *TV Guide*, 28 June 1986, 41–42.

28. Janet Soderstrom, "Brand Equity. It's Everywhere You Want to Be" (talk given at Branding Conference, San Francisco, California, 26 October 1995).

29. Tara Parker-Pope, "Why the Veterinarian Really Recommends That 'Designer' Chow," *Wall Street Journal*, 3 November 1997, A1, A10.

30. Suein Hwang, "Tobacco Companies Enlist the Bar Owner to Push Their Goods," *Wall Street Journal*, 21 April 1999, A1, A6.

31. Vanessa O'Connell, "Marketers Try to Burnish Olympics' Image," *Wall Street Journal*, 9 April 2001; Melanie Wells, "Rivals Wait in Wings as Olympic Sponsors Waffle," *USA Today*, 15 March 1999; Michael McCarthy, "Olympic Ads to Stress 'Core Values,'" *USA Today*, 20 December 1999; Bruce Horowitz, "Sponsors Scale Back Ad Blitz," *USA Today*, 26 September 2000; Bruce Horowitz, "Sponsors Warm Up a Year Before Games," *USA Today*, 19 July 1995, 1B-2B; Olympic Partnership, *Sports Illustrated* special advertising section.

Developing a Brand Equity Measurement and Management System

PREVIEW

The previous six chapters, which made up Parts II and III of the text, described various strategies and approaches to building brand equity. The next three chapters, which make up Part IV, take a detailed look at what consumers know about brands, what marketers want them to know, and how marketers can develop measurement procedures to assess how well they are doing.

The CBBE model provides guidance as to how brand equity can be measured. Given that customer-based brand equity is defined as the differential effect that knowledge about the brand—in terms of brand awareness and strong, favorable, and unique brand associations—has on customer response to the marketing of that brand, there would seem to be two basic approaches to measuring brand equity. An indirect approach could assess potential sources of customer-based brand equity by identifying and tracking consumers' brand knowledge structures. A direct approach, on the other hand, could measure customer-based brand equity by assessing the actual impact of brand knowledge on consumer response to different elements of the marketing program.

The two general approaches are complementary, and both can and should be employed by marketers. In other words, for brand equity to provide a useful strategic function and guide marketing decisions, marketers must fully understand the sources of brand equity, how they affect outcomes of interest (e.g., sales), and how these sources and outcomes change, if at all, over time. Chapter 3 provided a framework for conceptualizing consumers' brand knowledge structures. Chapter 9 uses this information and reviews research methods to measure sources of brand equity (e.g., the depth and breadth of brand awareness and strength, favorability, and uniqueness of brand associations). Chapter 10 reviews research methods to measure outcomes of brand equity (e.g., seven key benefits that potentially may result from creating these sources of brand equity).

Before getting into the specifics of how to measure sources and outcomes of brand equity in those two chapters, this chapter first provides some big-picture perspectives of how to think about brand equity measurement and management. Specifically, it considers how to develop and implement a brand equity measurement system. A *brand equity measurement system* is a set of research procedures designed to provide timely, accurate, and actionable information on brands for marketers so that they can make the best possible tactical decisions in the short run and strategic decisions in the long run. The goal in developing a brand equity measurement system is to be able to achieve a full understanding of the sources and outcomes of brand equity and be able, as much as possible, to relate the two.

The ideal brand equity measurement system would provide complete, up-to-date, and relevant information on the brand and all its competitors to relevant decision makers within the organization. Introducing a brand equity measurement system requires two critical steps: designing brand tracking studies and establishing a brand equity management system. This chapter examines these two steps in detail.

Crucial to the development of such a system, however, is an understanding of how brand equity or value gets created. Toward that goal, this chapter first presents a model of brand equity or value creation. The brand value chain is a means by which marketers can trace the value creation process for their brands to better understand the financial impact of their marketing expenditures and investments. Based in part on the CBBE model developed in Chapter 2, it offers a holistic, integrated approach to understanding how to capture the value created by brands. Brand Focus 8.0 describes how the Mayo Clinic has developed a brand equity measurement and management system.

THE BRAND VALUE CHAIN

To understand how to design and implement a brand equity measurement and management system, it is important to take a broader perspective than just the CBBE model. The *brand value chain* is a structured approach to assessing the sources and outcomes of brand equity and the manner by which marketing activities create brand value.[1] The brand value chain recognizes that numerous individuals within an organization can potentially affect brand equity and must be cognizant of relevant branding effects. Different individuals, however, make different brand-related decisions and need different types of information. Accordingly, the brand value chain provides insights to support brand managers, chief marketing officers, and managing directors and chief executive officers.

The brand value chain has several basic premises. Fundamentally, it assumes that the value of a brand ultimately resides with customers. Based on this insight, the model next assumes that the brand value creation process begins when the firm invests in a marketing program targeting actual or potential customers. The marketing activity associated with the program then affects the customer mindset with respect to the brand—what customers know and feel about the brand. This mindset, across a broad group of customers, then results in certain outcomes for the brand in terms of how it performs in the marketplace—the collective impact of individual customer actions regarding how much and when they purchase, the price that they pay, and so forth. Finally, the investment community considers this market performance and other factors such as replacement cost and purchase price in acquisitions to arrive at an assessment of shareholder value in general and a value of the brand in particular.

The model also assumes that a number of linking factors intervene between these stages. These linking factors determine the extent to which value created at one stage transfers or "multiplies" to the next stage. Three sets of multipliers moderate the transfer between the marketing program and the subsequent three value stages: the program multiplier, the customer multiplier, and the market multiplier. The brand value chain model is summarized in Figure 8-1. This section describes the model ingredients (i.e., the value stages and multiplying factors) in more detail and provides examples of both positive and negative multiplier effects.

Value Stages

Brand value creation begins with marketing activity by the firm that influences customers in a way affecting how the brand performs in the marketplace and thus how it is valued by the financial community.

Marketing Program Investment

Any marketing program investment that potentially can be attributed to brand value development, either intentional or not, falls into this first value stage. Chapters 4 to 7 outlined many such marketing activities. Specifically, some of the bigger marketing

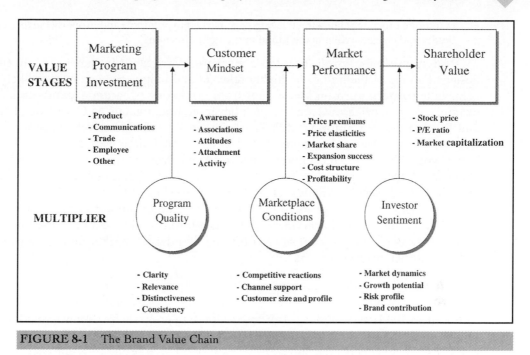

FIGURE 8-1   The Brand Value Chain

expenditures relate to product research, development, and design; trade or intermediary support; and marketing communications (e.g., advertising, promotion, sponsorship, direct and interactive marketing, personal selling, publicity, and public relations). The extent of financial investment committed to the marketing program, however, does not guarantee success in terms of brand value creation. In the 1990s, Miller Brewing spent over $2.5 billion in measured advertising in an effort to reestablish its brand portfolio, but launched questionable, ineffective campaigns. Anheuser-Busch, Heineken, and Corona were therefore able to steal key market positions and become the leading growth brands, dominating the beer category as a result. The ability of a marketing program investment to transfer or multiply farther down the chain will thus depend on qualitative aspects of the marketing program via the program multiplier.

Program Multiplier   The ability of the marketing program to affect the customer mindset will depend on the quality of that program investment. As outlined in earlier chapters, there are a number of different means to judge the quality of a marketing program. Four particularly important factors are as follows:

1. *Clarity:* How much clarity is evident in the marketing program? Do consumers properly interpret and evaluate the meaning conveyed by brand marketing?
2. *Relevance:* How relevant is the marketing program to customers? Do consumers feel that the brand is one that should receive serious consideration?
3. *Distinctiveness:* How unique or distinctive is the marketing program from those offered by competitors? How creative or differentiating is the marketing program?
4. *Consistency:* How consistent and well integrated is the marketing program? Do all aspects of the marketing program combine to create the biggest impact with customers? Does the

marketing program relate effectively to past marketing programs and properly balance continuity and change, evolving the brand in the right direction?

Not surprisingly, a well-integrated marketing program that has been carefully designed and implemented to be highly relevant and unique to customers is likely to achieve a greater return on investment from marketing program expenditures. For example, despite being outspent by such beverage brand giants as Coca-Cola, Pepsi, and Budweiser, the California Milk Processor Board was able to reverse a decades-long decline in consumption of milk in California through their well-designed and executed "got milk?" campaign. On the other hand, numerous marketers have found that expensive marketing programs do not necessarily produce sales unless they are well conceived. For example, brands such as Michelob, Reebok, 7 Up and others have seen their sales slide in recent years despite sizable marketing support because of poorly targeted and delivered marketing campaigns. More broadly, several dot-coms succeeded in wasting a great deal of cash through ill-advised marketing programs that failed to attract many customers.

Customer Mindset

As described in Chapter 2, a judicious marketing program investment could result in a number of different customer-related outcomes. Essentially, the issue is, in what ways have customers been changed as a result of the marketing program? How have those changes manifested themselves in the customer mindset? Remember that the customer mindset includes everything that exists in the minds of customers with respect to a brand: thoughts, feelings, experiences, images, perceptions, beliefs, attitudes, and so forth.

As will be reviewed in Chapter 9, a host of different approaches and measures are available to assess value at this stage. Nevertheless, five dimensions have emerged from prior research and are also highlighted in the CBBE model as particularly important measures of the customer mindset:

1. *Brand awareness:* The extent and ease with which customers recall and recognize the brand and can identify the products and services with which it is associated.

2. *Brand associations:* The strength, favorability, and uniqueness of perceived attributes and benefits for the brand. Brand associations often represent key sources of brand value, because they are the means by which consumers feel brands satisfy their needs.

3. *Brand attitudes:* Overall evaluations of the brand in terms of its quality and the satisfaction it generates.

4. *Brand attachment:* How loyal the customer feels toward the brand. A strong form of attachment, *adherence,* refers to the consumer's resistance to change and the ability of a brand to withstand bad news (e.g., a product or service failure). In the extreme, attachment can even become addiction.

5. *Brand activity:* The extent to which customers use the brand, talk to others about the brand, seek out brand information, promotions, and events, and so on.

An obvious hierarchy exists in the dimensions of value: Awareness supports associations, which drive attitudes that lead to attachment and activity. Brand value is created at this stage when customers have (1) a high level of awareness; (2) strong, favorable, and unique brand associations; (3) positive brand attitudes; (4) intense brand attachment and loyalty; and (5) a high degree of brand activity. Creating the right customer mindset can be critical in terms of building brand equity and value. AMD and Cyrix found that achieving performance parity with Intel's microprocessors did not reap initial benefits in 1998 when original equipment manufacturers were reluctant to adopt the new chips because of their lack of a strong brand image with consumers. Moreover, success with consumers or customers may not translate to success in the marketplace unless other conditions also prevail. The ability of this customer mindset to create value at the next stage depends on external factors designated the customer multiplier, as follows.

Customer Multiplier   The extent to which value created in the minds of customers affects market performance depends on various contextual factors external to the customer. Three such factors are as follows:

1. *Competitive superiority:* How effective are the quantity and quality of the marketing investment of other competing brands
2. *Channel and other intermediary support:* How much brand reinforcement and selling effort is being put forth by various marketing partners
3. *Customer size and profile:* How many and what types of customers (e.g., profitable or not) are attracted to the brand

The value created in the minds of customers will translate to favorable market performance when competitors fail to provide a significant threat, when channel members and other intermediaries provide strong support, and when a sizable number of profitable customers are attracted to the brand.

The competitive context faced by a brand can have a profound effect on its fortunes. For example, both Nike and McDonald's benefited in the 1990s from the marketing woes of their main rivals, Reebok and Burger King, respectively. Both of these latter brands have suffered from numerous repositionings and management changes. On the other hand, MasterCard has had to contend for the past decade with two strong, well-marketed brands in Visa and American Express and consequently has faced an uphill battle gaining market share. As another example, Clorox found its initially successful entry into the detergent market thwarted by competitive responses once major threats such as P&G entered (e.g., via Tide with Bleach). Similarly, Arm & Hammer's expansive brand extension program met major resistance in categories such as deodorants when existing competitors fought back.

Market Performance

As Chapter 2 explained, the customer mindset affects how customers react or respond in the marketplace in a variety of ways. Six key outcomes of that response are as follows. The first two dimensions relate to price premiums and price elasticities. How much extra are customers willing to pay for a comparable product because of its brand? And how much does their demand increase or decrease when the price rises or falls? A third dimension is market share, which measures the success of the marketing program to drive brand sales. Taken together, the first three dimensions determine the direct revenue stream attributable to the brand over time. Brand value is created with higher market shares, greater price premiums, and more elastic responses to price decreases and inelastic responses to price increases.

The fourth dimension is brand expansion, the success of the brand in supporting line and category extensions and new product launches into related categories. Thus, this dimension captures the ability to add enhancements to the revenue stream. The fifth dimension is cost structure or, more specifically, savings in terms of the ability to reduce marketing program expenditures because of the prevailing customer mindset. In other words, because customers already have favorable opinions and knowledge about a brand, any aspect of the marketing program is likely to be more effective for the same expenditure level; alternatively, the same level of effectiveness can be achieved at a lower cost because ads are more memorable, sales calls more productive, and so on. When combined, these five factors lead to brand profitability, the sixth dimension.

In short, brand value is created at this stage by building profitable sales volumes through a combination of these dimensions. The ability of the brand value created at this stage to reach the final stage in terms of stock market valuation again depends on external factors, this time according to the market multiplier.

Market Multiplier   The extent to which the value engendered by the market performance of a brand is manifested in shareholder value depends on various contextual factors external to the brand itself. Financial analysts and investors consider a host of factors in arriving at their brand valuations and investment decisions. Among these considerations are the following:

➤ *Market dynamics:* What are the dynamics of the financial markets as a whole (e.g., interest rates, investor sentiment, or supply of capital)?

➤ *Growth potential:* What are the growth potential or prospects for the brand and the industry in which it operates? For example, how helpful are the facilitating factors and how inhibiting are the hindering external factors that make up the firm's economic, social, physical, and legal environment?

➤ *Risk profile:* What is the risk profile for the brand? How vulnerable is the brand likely to be to those facilitating and inhibiting factors?

➤ *Brand contribution:* How important is the brand as part of the firm's brand portfolio and all the brands it has?

The value created in the marketplace for the brand is most likely to be fully reflected in shareholder value when the firm is operating in a healthy industry without serious environmental hindrances or barriers and when the brand contributes a significant portion of the firm's revenues and appears to have bright prospects. The obvious examples of brands that benefited from a strong market multiplier—at least for a while—are the numerous dot-com brands, such as Priceline, eToys, and so on. The huge premium placed on their (actually negative) market performance, however, quickly dissipated. On the other hand, many firms have lamented what they perceive as undervaluation by the market. For example, repositioned companies such as Corning have found it difficult to realize what they viewed as their true market value due to lingering investor perceptions from their past (i.e., Corning's heritage in dishes versus its more recent emphasis on optical fiber).

Shareholder Value
Based on all available current and forecasted information about a brand as well as many other considerations, the financial marketplace then formulates opinions and

makes various assessments that have very direct financial implications for the brand value. Three particularly important indicators are the stock price, the price/earnings multiple, and overall market capitalization for the firm.

Illustrations

Three simple examples help illustrate how the brand value chain can operate.

Starbucks

Figure 8-2 shows how Starbucks created value in its corporate brand during the period from 1993 to 1999. Specifically, although Starbucks increased its advertising budget some during this time, its main marketing investment was in market expansion and an increase in the number of outlets—and thus potential consumption opportunities for consumers. As one marketing observer noted, "Despite its lack of national advertising, Starbucks has become a household word by turning coffee into a ubiquitous attitude product . . . and by expanding the brand beyond its traditional roots—strategically placed, extremely fragrant coffee shops—into airplanes, restaurants, hotels, supermarkets and other venues."[2] Another commentary noted, "Starbucks' growth has come with virtually no use of traditional media advertising; the chain has relied on in-store marketing initiatives and word of mouth to develop brand cachet."[3] Founder Howard Schultz noted, "The marketing of Starbucks is not only what people see on the outside. The cost of internal marketing is quite high, but it is the key to our success."[4] Because of Starbucks's superior product and service delivery, the expansion investment enhanced the customer mindset.

Figure 8-2 also displays Young & Rubicam's BrandAsset Valuator (BAV) ratings of brand strength (i.e., brand relevance and differentiation) and stature (i.e., brand esteem and knowledge) as perceived by consumers (described in Brand Focus 10.0). Brand strength and stature bear a strong relationship to the five dimensions of the customer mindset identified earlier. Starbucks experienced a steady improvement in consumer perceptions during this period. This increasingly favorable customer mindset led to greater sales and a higher stock price and market capitalization.

Thus, Starbucks's marketing investment appeared to pay clear financial dividends. Starbucks was able to create so much brand value in part because of the positive

---

FIGURE 8-2 Brand Value Chain Analysis for Starbucks

	1993	**1997**	**1999**
Advertising (LNA millions)	3.73	13.48	12.24
Number of outlets	272	1412	2498
BAV strength	0.59	1.5	1.8
BAV stature	2.4	6.7	10.1
Sales (revenue) (millions—net)	—	975.4	1680.1
Stock price	2.78	9.59	12.13
Market capitalization (millions)	621	3034	4445

BAV, BrandAsset Valuator; LNA, Leading National Advertisers.

multipliers it experienced. Starbucks's program multiplier was positive because of the relevance and distinctiveness of its product offerings. The company also maintained great consistency during this period of time. Its customer multiplier was positive because of the lack of any strong competitive reactions, the strong channel support it provided itself due to its retail presence, and its single-minded customer focus on coffee lovers during this time. As one research analyst said during this period, "It's a foregone conclusion that Starbucks owns the specialty coffee market nationally. . . . No one wants to take them head on."[5] Another analyst noted, "Local competition among coffee stores is intense, but Starbucks is the only one out there that has a national level of recognition and awareness."[6] Finally, the market multiplier was equally positive due to Starbucks's corporate branding strategy and favorable financial market conditions.

Miller Brewing

In contrast, consider Miller Brewing. As noted earlier, the company spent $1.5 billion on measured advertising during the 1990s but still managed to lose share. Why? Its multipliers were primarily negative. Its ad campaigns were highly distinctive but, unfortunately, also largely irrelevant to its customer base because they unsuccessfully attempted to tap into the 21- to 25-year-old male psyche. A writer from the *Washington Post* called one of Miller's ad efforts during this time "quite possibly the worst ad campaign of the decade."[7] One ad executive experienced in beer marketing noted, "Beer industry veterans looked at Miller Lite's 'Dick' campaign and said, 'This has no chance of working,' It violated every convention in the business. You don't have to be stupid and insulting to be breakthrough."[8]

New ad campaigns for Miller Lite, Miller Genuine Draft, and Miller High Life came and went, creating program inconsistency. Besides a weak program multiplier, Miller encountered stiff competition from well-funded and well-conceived marketing programs from Anheuser-Busch, Coors, and Heineken, all of which gained share during this period. Moreover, Miller's distributors became disenchanted, contributing to a weak customer multiplier. "The company has to make wholesale changes. Advertising has to improve," said one distributor during this period. "It can't get worse."[9]

Not surprisingly, Miller's financial performance suffered, and a new management team was put into place. As the 1990s came to a close, industry bible *Advertising Age* offered a stinging criticism of Miller's marketing efforts: "The broader question is when—and whether—someone at Miller can get a grasp on what's happening to the damaged public perceptions of these two fine brands and turn things around. The hops in Lite may be choice, but nothing about the marketing at Miller can now be called smooth."[10] Figure 8-3 shows how brand value deteriorated despite huge investments because of the adverse effects the marketing program had on the customer mindset, which the decline in BAV ratings documents.

Reebok

A one-time market share leader in the United States in the late 1980s—by a considerable amount—Reebok has struggled to remain a player in the athletic shoe and clothing market. The 1990s got off to a rough start for the company. As *Business Week* observed in 1993, "Ever since Nike usurped the company as the top maker of athletic

	1993	**1997**	**1999**
Advertising (LNA millions)	170.4	227.5	133.5
BAV strength	0.86	0.83	0.76
BAV stature	14.5	13.9	13.2
Sales (revenue) (millions—net)	1650	1810	1770
Stock price	—	1.75	2.25
Market capitalization (millions)	1400	590	790

BAV, BrandAsset Valuator; LNA, Leading National Advertisers.

FIGURE 8-3 Brand Value Chain Analysis for Miller Brewing

shoes in 1989, Reebok has been flailing wildly in attempts to get back on top. Half a dozen ad campaigns have fizzled. It has been plagued by poor designs. And it missed a key fashion shift toward outdoors shoes that began a couple of years ago. Reebok also means to overhaul what CEO Fireman acknowledges has been until now a 'chaotic' marketing effort."[11]

But the remainder of the decade was no better for Reebok. The brand was seen as out of touch by women and largely irrelevant by kids—two of its key target markets. A cutback in R&D resulted in less stylish shoes, leading one analyst to comment, "Reebok shoes started to look like they belonged on the shelf of an orthopedic patient."[12] Reebok continued on a wandering path characterized by inconsistent marketing, high management turnover, and a bloated product lineup. As former president Roberto Muller noted, "There's been no consistency. It's still such a great brand that if they pick any strategy and stick with it, you will have a successful company. But lately it's been like Argentina and its ministers: for years they've been changing who runs the show and so they've got 4000 percent devaluation."[13] As a result, customer mindset as measured by BAV failed to recover and in fact slightly declined.

The brand value chain shows how Reebok's lack of support, both in quantitative and qualitative terms, led to a slide in its image with consumers and, ultimately, to a severe drop in its brand value. (see Figure 8-4). Specifically, a failure to maintain marketing investments at a competitive level and declining program and customer multipliers combined to result in a sharp decrease in market performance and shareholder value.

Implications

According to the brand value chain, marketers create value first through shrewd investments in their marketing program and then by maximizing, as much as possible, the program, customer, and market multipliers that translate that investment into bottom-line financial benefits. The brand value chain thus provides a structured means for managers to understand where and how value is created and where to look to improve that process. Certain stages will be of greater interest to different members of the organization. Brand and category marketing managers are likely to be comparatively more interested in the customer mindset and the impact of the marketing program on customers. Chief marketing officers (CMOs), on the other hand, are likely to be comparatively more interested in market performance and the impact of customer mindset on

	1993	1997	1999
Advertising (LNA millions)	56.3	53.4	10.2
BAV strength	2.26	1.94	1.96
BAV stature	22.2	19.0	20.0
Sales (revenue) (millions—net)	2894	3644	2900
Stock price	30.0	28.8	8.2
Market capitalization (millions)	2510	1625	460

BAV, BrandAsset Valuator; LNA, Leading National Advertisers.

FIGURE 8-4   Brand Value Chain Analysis for Reebok

actual market behaviors. Finally, a managing director or CEO is likely to be comparatively more interested in shareholder value and the impact of market performance on investment decisions.

The brand value chain has a number of implications. First, value creation begins with the marketing program investment. Therefore, a necessary—but not sufficient—condition for value creation is a well-funded, well-designed, and well-implemented marketing program. It is rare that marketers can get something for nothing. Second, value creation, from a marketing perspective, involves more than the initial marketing investment. Each of the three multipliers can increase or decrease market value as it moves from stage to stage. In other words, value creation also involves ensuring that value transfers from stage to stage. Unfortunately, in many cases, factors that can inhibit value creation may be largely out of the hands of the marketer (e.g., investors' industry sentiment). Recognizing the uncontrollable nature of these factors is important to help put in perspective the relative success or failure of a marketing program to create brand value. Just as sports coaches cannot be held accountable for unforeseen circumstances such as injuries to key players and financial hardships that make it difficult to attract top talent, so marketers cannot necessarily be held accountable for certain market forces and dynamics.

Third, as is outlined in the following two chapters, the brand value chain provides a detailed road map for tracking value creation that can facilitate marketing research and intelligence efforts. Each of the stages and multipliers has a set of measures by which it can be assessed. In general, there are three main sources of information, and each source of information taps into one value stage and one multiplier. The first stage, the marketing program investment, is straightforward and can come from the marketing plan and budget. Customer mindset and the program multiplier can both be assessed by quantitative and qualitative customer research. Market performance and the customer multiplier can both be captured through market scans and internal accounting records. Finally, shareholder value and the market multiplier can be estimated through investor analysis and interviews.

There are many possible modifications to the brand value chain that can expand its relevance and applicability. First, a number of feedback loops are possible. For example, stock prices can have an important effect on employee morale and motivation. Second, in some cases, the value creation may not occur sequentially as depicted. For example, stock analysts may react to an ad campaign for the brand—either personally or in recognition of public acceptance—and factor those reactions directly into their investment assessments. Third, some marketing activity may have only very diffuse effects that are manifested over the long term. For example, cause–related or social responsibility marketing activity might affect customer or investor sentiment slowly over time. Fourth, it should be recognized that both the mean and variance of some of the measures of the brand value chain could matter. For example, in terms of the customer mindset, a niche brand may receive very high marks but only across a very narrow range of customers.

DESIGNING BRAND TRACKING STUDIES

The brand value chain provides a big-picture perspective as to how brand equity or value can be created. Combined with the CBBE model, it provides guidance as to how to position a brand and how well the marketing program has achieved that positioning. Chapter 3 described the concept of brand audits, a means to provide in-depth information and insights that are essential for setting long-term strategic direction for the brand. Brand audits thus are an invaluable guide in positioning a brand. In terms of more short-term tactical considerations, less-detailed brand-related information should be collected as a result of conducting ongoing tracking studies. *Tracking studies* involve information collected from consumers on a routine basis over time. Such studies typically employ quantitative measures to provide marketers with current information as to how their brands and marketing programs are performing on a number of key dimensions identified by the brand audit or other means. Tracking studies are a means of applying the brand value chain to understand where, how much, and in what ways brand value is being created, thus offering invaluable information about how well a positioning has been achieved.

Tracking studies play an important function for managers by providing consistent baseline information to facilitate their day-to-day decision making. As more marketing activity surrounds the brand (e.g., new products are introduced as brand extensions, an increasing variety of communication options are incorporated into marketing communications programs supporting the brand, etc.), it becomes difficult and expensive to research each marketing action. Tracking studies provide valuable diagnostic insights into the collective effects of a host of marketing activities on the customer mindset, market outcomes, and perhaps even shareholder value. Regardless of how few or how many changes are made in the marketing program over time, it is important to monitor the health of the brand and its equity so that proper adjustments can be made if necessary.

A number of issues must be addressed in implementing a brand equity tracking system. This chapter addresses what measures should be employed in tracking studies, how tracking studies should be implemented, and how tracking studies should be interpreted.

What to Track

Figure 2-12 provided a detailed list of potential measures that correspond to the customer-based brand equity model, all of which are candidates for tracking. Chapter 9 reviews a number of quantitative measures of brand knowledge structures that also may be useful for tracking purposes. This section provides some general guidelines for tracking and considers several additional types of measures that may be usefully employed in tracking. In that spirit, it should be recognized that it is usually necessary to customize tracking surveys to address the specific issues faced by the brand or brands in question. To a great extent, each brand faces a unique situation that must be reflected in different types of questions in its tracking survey.

Product-Brand Tracking

Tracking an individual branded product involves measuring brand awareness and image for the particular brand. In terms of brand awareness, both recall and recognition measures should be collected. In general, awareness measures should move from more general to more specific questions. Thus, it may make sense to first ask consumers what brands come to mind in certain situations, to next ask for recall of brands on the basis of various product category cues, and to then finish with tests of brand recognition (if necessary).

As with brand awareness, it is usually desirable that a range of more general to more specific measures be employed in brand tracking surveys to measure brand image, especially in terms of specific perceptions (i.e., what consumers think characterizes the brand) and evaluations (i.e., what the brands mean to consumers). A number of specific brand associations typically exist for the brand, depending on the richness of consumer knowledge structures, which could potentially be tracked over time.

The most important specific brand associations are those performance and imagery beliefs that serve as the basis of the brand positioning in terms of key points of parity and points of difference with competitive brands, for example, attributes and benefits such as convenience and ease of use. Certainly those specific brand associations that make up the potential sources of brand equity should be assessed on the basis of strength, favorability, and uniqueness *in that order*. Unless associations are strong enough that they are likely to be recalled, their favorability does not matter, and unless associations are sufficiently favorable to be considerations in making a decision, uniqueness does not matter. Ideally, measures of all three dimensions would be collected, but perhaps for only certain associations and only some of the time (e.g., favorability and uniqueness may only be measured once a year for three to five key associations).

Given that brands often compete at the augmented product level (see Chapter 1), it is important to measure *all* associations that may distinguish competing brands. Thus, measures of specific, "lower-level" brand associations should include all potential sources of brand equity (performance and imagery attributes and benefits). Because they often represent key points of parity or points of difference, it is particularly important to track benefit associations. To better understand any changes in benefit beliefs for a brand, however, it may be necessary to also measure the corresponding attribute beliefs that underlie those benefits. In other words, changes in descriptive attribute beliefs may help to explain changes in more evaluative benefit beliefs for a brand.

At the same time, it is also important to track more general, "higher-level" judgments, feelings, and other outcome-related measures. Chapter 10 outlines various measures of consumer attitudes, intentions, and behaviors regarding brands. After asking for their overall opinions, consumers can be asked if they have changed their attitudes, intentions, or behavior in recent weeks or months and, if so, why they did so.

Branding Brief 8-1 provides an illustrative example of a simple tracking survey for McDonald's (see Figure 8-5).

Sample Brand Tracking Survey

Assume that McDonald's was interested in designing a short tracking survey to be conducted over the phone. How might you set it up? Although there are a number of different types of questions, it might take the following form.

We are conducting a short phone interview concerning consumer opinions about quick-service or "fast food" restaurant chains.

BRAND AWARENESS AND USAGE

   a. What brands of quick-service restaurant chains are you aware of?

   b. At which brands of quick-service restaurant chains would you consider eating?

   c. Have you eaten in a quick-service restaurant chain in the last week? Which ones?

   d. If you were to eat in a quick-service restaurant tomorrow for lunch, which one would you go to?

   e. What if instead it were for dinner? Where would you go?

   f. Finally, what if instead it were for breakfast? Where would you go?

   g. Which are your favorite quick-service restaurant chains?

We want to ask you some general questions about a particular quick-service restaurant chain, McDonald's.

Have you heard of this restaurant? [Establish familiarity.]

Have you eaten at this restaurant? [Establish trial.]

When I say McDonald's, what are the first associations that come to your mind? Anything else?

BRAND JUDGMENTS

We are interested in your overall opinion of McDonald's.

   a. How favorable is your attitude toward McDonald's?

   b. How well does McDonald's satisfy your needs?

   c. How likely would you be to recommend McDonald's to others?

   d. How good a value is McDonald's?

   e. Is McDonald's worth a premium price?

   f. What do you like best about McDonald's?

   g. What is most unique about McDonald's?

   h. To what extent does McDonald's offer advantages that other brands cannot?

   i. To what extent is McDonald's superior to other brands in the quick-service restaurant category?

   j. Compared to other brands in the quick-service restaurant category, how well does McDonald's satisfy your basic needs?

We now want to ask you some questions about McDonald's as a company. Please indicate your agreement with the following statements.

McDonald's is . . .

a. Innovative

b. Knowledgeable

b. Trustworthy

c. Likable

d. Concerned about their customers

e. Concerned about society as a whole

f. Likable

h. Admirable

BRAND PERFORMANCE

We now would like to ask some specific questions about McDonald's. Please indicate your agreement with the following statements.

McDonald's . . .

a. Is convenient to eat at

b. Provides quick, efficient service

c. Has clean facilities

d. Is for the whole family

e. Has delicious food

f. Has a varied menu

g. Has friendly, courteous staff

h. Offers fun promotions

i. Has a stylish and attractive look

j. Has high-quality food

BRAND IMAGERY

a. To what extent do people you admire and respect eat at McDonald's?

b. How much do you like people who eat at McDonald's?

c. How well do each of the following words describe this brand?

Down-to-earth, honest, daring, up-to-date, reliable, successful, upper class, charming, out-doorsy

d. Is McDonald's a restaurant that you can use in a lot of different situations?

e. To what extent does thinking of McDonald's bring back pleasant memories?

f. To what extent do you feel you grew up with McDonald's?

BRAND FEELINGS

Does McDonald's give you a feeling of . . .

a. Warmth?

    b. Fun?

    c. Excitement?

    d. Security?

    e. Social approval?

    f. Self-respect?

BRAND RESONANCE

    a. I consider myself loyal to McDonald's.

    b. I buy McDonald's whenever I can.

    c. I would go out of my way to eat at McDonald's.

    d. I really love McDonald's.

    e. I would really miss McDonald's if it went away.

    f. McDonald's is special to me.

    g. McDonald's is more than a product to me.

    h. I really identify with people who eat at McDonald's.

    i. I feel a deep connection with others who eat at McDonald's.

    j. I really like to talk about McDonald's to others.

    k. I am always interested in learning more about McDonald's.

    l. I would be interested in merchandise with the McDonald's name on it.

    m. I am proud to have others know I eat at McDonald's.

    n. I like to visit the Web site for McDonald's.

    o. Compared to other people, I follow news about McDonald's closely.

Corporate or Family Brand Tracking

    In the case of a family or corporate brand, some additional questions may be warranted. Although many of these types of questions could be included in tracking studies for individual products for the brand, there may also be justification for tracking the corporate or family brand separately or concurrently (or both) with individual products. Besides the measures of corporate credibility identified in Chapter 2, other specific measures of corporate brand associations are possible, including some of the following (illustrated with the GE corporate brand):

➤   How well managed is GE?

➤   How easy is it to do business with GE?

➤   How concerned is GE with its customers?

➤   How approachable is GE?

➤   How accessible is GE?

➤   How much do you like doing business with GE?

The actual questions used should reflect the level and nature of experience that the particular group of respondents would be likely to have had with the company.

    A number of firms track corporate image. As an example, DuPont has tracked the following broad measures of corporate image:[14]

FIGURE 8-5 McDonald's: A Global Brand Powerhouse

➤ Outstanding American companies (unaided)
➤ Outstanding companies on 11 different attributes (unaided)
➤ Rating on those attributes
➤ Outstanding companies in eight different industries (unaided)
➤ Association with those industries
➤ Ratings in associated industries
➤ Familiarity with products and services
➤ Likelihood of investing in stock
➤ Feeling about friend accepting employment

When a brand is identified with multiple products, as with a corporate or family branding strategy, one important issue is which particular products the brand reminds consumers of. An important related consideration is which particular products are most influential in affecting consumer perceptions about the brand. To identify which products are most closely linked to the brand, consumers could be probed as to which products they associate with the brand on an unaided basis (e.g., "What products come to mind when you think of the Nike brand?") or an aided basis by listing sub-brand names (e.g., "Are you aware of Nike Air Flight basketball shoes? Nike Challenge Court tennis apparel? Nike Air Max running shoes?"). To better understand the dynamics between the brand and its corresponding products, consumers can be probed as to their relationship ("There are many different products associated with Nike. Which ones are most important to you in formulating your opinion about the brand?").

Global Tracking

If tracking involves diverse geographic markets—especially if both developing and developed countries are involved—then it may be necessary to have a broader set of background measures to put the brand development in those markets in the right perspective. These brand context measures would presumably not need to be collected frequently, but could provide useful explanatory information (see Figure 8-6 for some representative measures).

FIGURE 8-6   Brand Context Measures

Economic Indicators
Gross domestic product
Interest rates
Unemployment
Average wage
Disposable income
Home ownership and housing debt
Exchange rates, share markets, and balance
    of payments

Retail
Total spent in supermarkets
Change year to year
Growth in house brand

Technology
Computer at home
Modem
Access to and use of Internet
Phones
Mobile phones
Microwaves
Freezers
Television

Personal Attitudes and Values
Confidence
Security
Family
Environment
Traditional values
Foreigners vs. sovereignty

Media Indicators
Media consumption: total time spent
    watching TV, consuming other media
Advertising expenditure: total, by media
    and by product category

Demographic Profile
Population profile: age, sex, income,
    household size
Geographic distribution
Ethnic and cultural profile

Other Products and Services
Transport: own car—how many
Best description of car
Motorbike
Home ownership or renting
Domestic trips overnight in last year
International trips in last two years

Attitude to Brands and Shopping
Buy on price
Like to buy new things
Country of origin or manufacture
Prefer to buy things that have been
    advertised
Importance of familiar brands

How to Conduct Tracking Studies

One question with these tracking studies is, Which elements of the brand should be used? In general, the brand name is always used in tracking, but, as noted in Chapter 4, it may also make sense to employ other brand elements, such as a logo or symbol, in probing brand structures, especially if these elements can play a visible and important role in the decision process. Conducting tracking studies also requires decisions in terms of who to track, as well as when and where to track.

Who to Track

As Chapter 3 noted, there are a number of possible segmentation schemes that can be profitably incorporated into tracking approaches. Tracking often concentrates on current customers, but it can also be informative to monitor nonusers of the brand or even of the product category as a whole (e.g., to suggest potential segmentation strategies). It often can be insightful to track those customers loyal to the brand versus those who are loyal to other brands or who switch among brands. Among current customers of the brand, it is often informative to distinguish between heavy and light users of the brand. Dividing up the market typically requires different questionnaires (or at least sections of a questionnaire) to better capture the specific issues associated with each segment.

Alka Seltzer

Miles Laboratory collects much data on the image of its flagship product, Alka Seltzer. The data have revealed marked differences in the product image for users versus nonusers. For example, users of Alka Seltzer regard effervescence as a highly convenient feature of the brand. In contrast, nonusers regard effervescence as highly *in*convenient. Desired benefits for Alka Seltzer also vary by type of user. Heavy users claim "efficacy" and "speed of relief" as the most valued attributes. Light users, on the other hand, value "gentleness" and "no side effects" more highly. Recognizing that effervescence is a key source of the brand equity for Alka Seltzer, it is tracked closely. Because of the strategic importance of this association, the company deliberated carefully before introducing a liquid gel version of the product and keenly watched subsequent consumer reaction.

Other types of customers can be monitored too. For example, it is often useful to track channel members and other intermediaries closely to understand their perceptions and actions toward the brand. Of particular interest is their image of the brand and the manner by which they feel they may be or could be helping or hurting its equity. Retailers can be asked direct questions such as, "Do you feel that products in your store sell faster if they have [the brand name] on it? Why?" Similarly, it also may be important to track employees (e.g., salespeople) to better understand their beliefs about the brand and how they feel they currently are contributing to its equity or possibly could contribute to its equity in the future. Such tracking may be especially important with service organizations, where employees play profound roles in affecting brand equity.

When and where to track

It is necessary to decide how frequently tracking information should be collected. One useful tracking approach for monitoring brand associations involves *continuous tracking studies,* in which information is collected from consumers on a continual basis over time. The advantage of continuous tracking is that it smoothes out aberrations or unusual marketing activities or events (e.g., a splashy new ad campaign or an unlikely occurrence in the marketing environment) to provide a more representative set of baseline measures.

There are a host of different ways to conduct these types of studies. The frequency of such tracking studies, in general, depends on the frequency of product purchase (durable goods are typically tracked less frequently because they are purchased less often) and on the consumer behavior and marketing activity in the product category. Many companies conduct a certain number of interviews of different consumers every week—or even every day—and assemble the results on a rolling or moving average basis for monthly or quarterly reports.

Millward Brown

Marketing research tracking pioneer Millward Brown usually interviews 50 to 100 people a week and looks at the data with moving averages trended over time in their Advanced Tracking Program. Typically, these involve short interviews (10 to 20 minutes in length, on the phone or Web) covering the client brand and competitive set. Data are usually collected on brand preferences and perceptions, ad awareness, and recall and reaction, as well as on demographics and usage. A short (12-minute) interview for a typical consumer product administered over the phone to 50 nationally representative consumers weekly can cost roughly $125,000 to $150,000 annually, depending on modality.[15]

When the brand has more stable and enduring associations, tracking can be conducted on a less frequent basis. Nevertheless, even if it were the case that the marketing of a brand may not appreciably change over time, it is still important to track brands because competitive entries can change consumer perceptions of the dynamics within the market. For example, when MCI entered the telecommunications market, it took on the persona of a "young, brash guy, just out of school, aggressively making his mark." As a result, in the eyes of consumers, AT&T took on much more of the persona of an "older, conservative banker type, staid and traditional in conducting business," even though its marketing program had not changed.

Finally, on a global basis, it is important to recognize the stage of the product or brand life cycle in deciding on the frequency of tracking: Opinions of consumers in mature markets may not change much, whereas emerging markets may shift quickly and perhaps in unpredictable ways.

How to Interpret Tracking Studies

For tracking measures to yield actionable insights and recommendations, they must be as reliable and sensitive as possible. One problem with many traditional measures of marketing phenomena is that they do not change much over time. Although this stability may reflect the fact that the underlying levels of brand awareness; the strength, favorability, and uniqueness of brand associations; the valence of brand judgments and feelings; and the intensity and activity of brand loyalty do not change much, in other cases it may be that one or more of those dimensions may have changed to some extent but that the measures themselves are not sensitive enough to detect these more subtle shifts. To develop sensitive tracking measures, it may be necessary to phrase questions in a comparative (e.g., "compared to other brands, how much. . .") or temporal (e.g., "compared to one month or one year ago, how much. . .") manner.

Another challenge in interpreting tracking studies is to decide on appropriate cutoffs. For example, what is a sufficiently high level of brand awareness? When are brand associations sufficiently strong, favorable, and unique? How positive should brand judgments and feelings be? What are reasonable expectations for the amount of brand resonance? To some extent, these targets need to be driven by competitive considerations and the nature of the category. In some low-involvement categories (e.g., lightbulbs), it may be difficult to carve out a distinct image, unlike higher-involvement products (e.g., cars or computers). Along these lines, it may be important to allow for and monitor the number of respondents who indicate that they "don't know" or have "no response" with respect to the brand tracking measures: The more of these types of answers that are evident, the less consumers would seem to care.

One of the most important tasks in conducting brand tracking studies is to identify the determinants of brand equity.[16] Of the brand associations that potentially can serve as sources of brand equity, which ones actually influence consumer attitudes and behavior and create value for the brand? Marketers must identify the real value drivers for a brand—that is, those tangible and intangible points of difference that influence and determine consumers' product and brand choices. Similarly, the marketing activities that have the most effective impact on brand knowledge need to be identified, especially with respect to consumer exposure to advertising and other communication mix elements. Carefully monitoring and relating key sources and outcome measures of brand equity should help to address these issues. The CBBE model and brand value chain suggest many possible links and paths that can be explored for their impact on brand equity.

ESTABLISHING A BRAND EQUITY MANAGEMENT SYSTEM

Brand tracking studies, as well as brand audits, can provide a huge reservoir of information concerning how to best build and measure brand equity. Nevertheless, the potential value of these research efforts will not be realized unless proper internal structures and procedures are put into place within the organization to capitalize on the usefulness of the brand equity concept and the information that is collected with respect to it. Although a brand equity measurement system does not ensure that "good" decisions about the brand will always occur, it should increase the likelihood that they do and, if nothing else, should at least decrease the likelihood that "bad" decisions about the brand will be made.

Embracing the concept of branding and brand equity, many firms constantly review how the concept can be best factored into the organization. Interestingly, perhaps one of the biggest threats to brand equity comes from *within* the organization and the fact that too many marketing managers remain on the job for only a limited period of time. As a result of these short-term assignments, marketing managers may adopt a short-term perspective, leading to an overreliance on quick-fix sales-generating tactics such as line and category extensions, sales promotions, and so forth. Because these managers lack an understanding and appreciation of the brand equity concept, some critics maintain that they are essentially running the brand "without a license."

To counteract these and other potential forces within an organization that may lead to ineffective long-term management of brands, internal branding has become a top priority, as noted in Chapter 3. As part of these efforts, a brand equity management system must be put into place. A *brand equity management system* is defined as a set of organizational processes designed to improve the understanding and use of the brand equity concept within a firm. Three major steps should be taken organizationally to implement a brand equity management system: creating brand equity charters, assembling brand equity reports, and defining brand equity responsibilities. The following subsections discuss each of these in turn.

Brand Equity Charter

The first step in establishing a brand equity management system is to formalize the company view of brand equity into a document, the *brand equity charter,* that provides relevant guidelines to marketing managers within the company as well as key marketing partners outside the company (e.g., ad agency personnel). This document should do the following:

➤ Define the firm's view of the brand equity concept and explain why it is important.

➤ Describe the scope of key brands in terms of associated products and the manner by which they have been branded and marketed (as revealed by historical company records as well as the most recent brand inventory).

➤ Specify what the actual and desired equity is for a brand at all relevant levels of the brand hierarchy, for example, at both the corporate level and at the individual product level (as outlined in Chapter 11). A range of relevant associations should be defined, including those that constitute points of parity and points of difference as well as core brand values and the brand mantra or core brand promise.

➤ Explain how brand equity is measured in terms of the tracking study and the resulting brand equity report (described shortly).

➤ Suggest how brand equity should be managed in terms of some general strategic guidelines (e.g., stressing clarity, relevance, distinctiveness, and consistency in marketing programs over time).

➤ Outline how marketing programs should be devised in terms of some specific tactical guidelines (e.g., ad evaluation criteria, brand name choice criteria).

➤ Specify the proper treatment of the brand in terms of trademark usage, packaging, and communications.

Although parts of the brand equity charter may not change from year to year, it should nevertheless be updated on an annual basis to provide decision makers with a current brand profile and to identify new opportunities and potential risks for the brand. As new products are introduced, brand programs are changed, and other marketing initiatives take place, they should be reflected adequately in the brand equity charter. Many of the in-depth insights that emerge from brand audits belong in the charter.

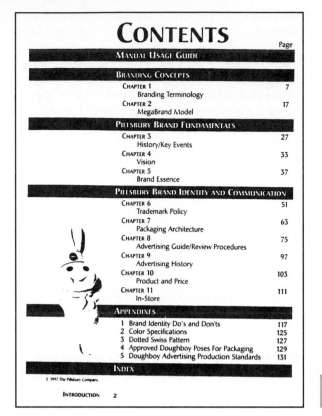

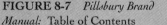

FIGURE 8-7 *Pillsbury Brand Manual:* Table of Contents

Figure 8-7 displays the table of contents for the Pillsbury brand manual. Another brand with a well-conceived brand charter is GE.

General Electric

GE has an "identity program document" that defines the GE brand as it should appear in all GE marketing communications. After providing a short history of branding and the importance of brands, the document summarizes research concerning the value of the GE brand; identifies the brand's core promise ("better living"), personality, and values; and provides guidelines as to how the brand should be managed. Guidelines stress consistency and discipline and are summarized by a checklist of questions that force GE marketing decision makers to specify key product features and sales propositions and how they relate to the core benefit promise of "better living" as exemplified in their slogan, "We Bring Good Things to Life."

Brand Equity Report

The second step in establishing a successful brand equity management system is to assemble the results of the tracking survey and other relevant performance measures for the brand into a *brand equity report* to be distributed to management on a regular basis (monthly, quarterly, or annually). Much of the information relevant to the report may already exist within or be collected by the organization. Yet the information may have been presented to management in disjointed chunks such that a holistic under-standing was not possible. The brand equity report attempts to effectively integrate all these different measures.[17]

The brand equity report should provide descriptive information as to *what* is hap-pening with a brand as well as diagnostic information as to *why* it is happening. It should include all relevant internal and external measures of brand performance and sources and outcomes of brand equity. In particular, one section of the report should summarize consumers' perceptions of key attribute or benefit associations, prefer-ences, and reported behavior as revealed by the tracking study. Another section of the report should include more descriptive market-level information such as the following:

➤ Product shipments and movement through channels of distribution
➤ Relevant cost breakdowns
➤ Price and discount schedules where appropriate
➤ Sales and market share information broken down by relevant factors (e.g., geographic region, type of retail account or customer)
➤ Profit assessments

These measures can provide insight into the market performance component of the brand value chain.

With advances in computer technology, it will be increasingly easy for firms to place the information that makes up the brand equity report online so that it can be accessible to managers through the firm's intranet or some other means. For example, NFO Market Mind has developed a brand management database system that inte-grates continuous consumer tracking survey data, media weight (or cost) data, ware-house sales and retail scan data, and PR and editorial content. Ocean Spray Cranberries has developed its own approach to distributing brand equity information.

> **Ocean Spray Cranberries**
> Assisted by Duke University's John McCann and John Gallagher, Ocean Spray Cranberries created a "Marketplace Insight Web" that, as described on its home page, was designed to "provide access to consumer and customer insights which help decision makers better understand and influence the marketplace. Content covers products, markets, accounts, and the marketing mix elements which impact our business." The first-level menu of the system allows users to link to additional information on advertising, coupons, distribution, pricing, trade promotion, products, markets, and retailers. In each case, relevant research informa-tion is presented with additional links for cross-reference or to elaborate on technical or definitional aspects of the research. For example, the Advertising Insights link has further links to video versions of all of the company's TV ads, as well as the original ASI copy test results and quarterly top-line reports from the Millward Brown continuous tracking studies. The site is password-protected so that only designated outside parties can access relevant information. Thus, Ocean Spray's Marketplace Insight Web allows marketing decision mak-ers to instantaneously obtain brand-relevant data and background information.

Brand Equity Responsibilities

To develop a brand equity management system that will maximize long-term brand equity, organizational responsibilities and processes with respect to the brand must be clearly defined. Brands need constant, consistent nurturing to grow. Weak brands often suffer from a lack of discipline, commitment, and investment in brand building. This section considers internal issues related to assigning responsibilities and duties for properly managing brand equity, as well as external issues related to the proper roles of marketing partners.

Overseeing Brand Equity

To provide central coordination, a position entitled Vice President or Director of Strategic Brand Management or Brand Equity Management should be established within the organization. The person in that position would be responsible for overseeing the implementation of the brand equity charter and brand equity reports to make sure that, as much as possible, product and marketing actions across divisions and geographic boundaries are performed in a way that reflects the spirit of the brand equity charter and the substance of the brand equity report so as to maximize the long-term equity of the brand. A natural place to house such oversight duties and responsibilities is in a corporate marketing group that has a senior management reporting relationship.

Scott Bedbury, who helped direct the Nike and Starbucks brands during some of their most successful years, is emphatic about the need for "top-down brand leadership."[18] He advocates the addition of a chief brand officer (CBO) who reports directly to the CEO of the company and who

➤ *Is an omnipresent conscience whose job is to champion and protect the brand—the way it looks and feels—both inside and outside the company.* The CBO recognizes that the brand is the sum total of everything a company does and strives to ensure that all employees understand the brand and its values, creating "brand disciples" in the process.

➤ *Is an architect and not only helps build the brand but also plans, anticipates, researches, probes, listens, and informs.* Working with senior leadership, the CBO helps envision not just what works best for the brand today but also what can help drive it forward in the future.

➤ *Determines and protects the voice of the brand over time by taking a long-term (two to three years) perspective.* The CBO can be accountable for brand-critical and corporate-wide activities such as advertising, positioning, corporate design, corporate communications, and consumer or market insights.

Even strong brands need to be watched carefully to prevent managers from overconfidently believing that it is acceptable to "make one little mistake" or "let it slide" with respect to the equity of the brand. A number of top companies (e.g., Colgate-Palmolive, Canada Dry, Quaker Oats, Pillsbury, Coca-Cola, and Nestlé Foods) have already created such brand equity gatekeepers for some or all of their brands.[19]

IBM

IBM put a team in place to be in charge of the research that involved brand equity. Their task has been to discover what associations existed for the corporate brand and then determine which ones were undesirable and therefore should be pruned and which were desirable and should be nurtured in order to take the brand image to where the firm wanted it to be in the future. This group has had input into a wide variety of areas—including the general "look and feel" of products—to ensure that the products reinforced the brand equity as much as possible. The team also has had responsibility for communicating the brand equity message throughout IBM's many divisions and arbitrating any disputes that might arise among groups concerning brand equity.

Branding expert Bedbury also advocates periodic brand development reviews (full-day meetings quarterly or even half-day meetings monthly) for brands in difficult circumstances. As part of a brand development review, he suggests the following topics and activities:[20]

➤ *Review brand-sensitive material.* For example, brand strength monitors or tracking studies, brand audits, and focus groups, as well as less formal personal observations or "gut feelings" should all be reviewed.

➤ *Review the status of key brand initiatives.* Because brand initiatives involve strategic thrusts to either strengthen a weakness in the brand or to exploit an opportunity to grow the brand in a new direction, customer perceptions may change as a result and therefore need to be assessed.

➤ *Review brand-sensitive projects.* For example, evaluate advertising campaigns, corporate communications, sales meeting agendas, and important human resources programs (recruitment, training, and retention that profoundly affect the organization's ability to embrace and project brand values).

➤ *Review new product and distribution strategies with respect to core brand values.*

➤ *Resolve brand positioning conflicts.*

One of the important roles taken by senior management is the determination of marketing budgets and where and how company resources will be allocated within the organization. It is important that a brand equity management system be able to inform and provide input to decision makers so that they are able to recognize the short-term and long-term ramifications of their decisions for brand equity. Decisions concerning which brands to invest in and whether to implement brand-building marketing programs or instead to leverage brand equity through brand extensions, reduced communication expenditures, and so forth should reflect the current and desired state of the brand as revealed through brand tracking and other measures.

Organizational Design and Structures

In a general sense, the marketing function must be organized within the firm in a way that optimizes brand equity. Several trends have emerged in organizational design and structure that reflect the growing recognition of the importance of the brand and the challenges of managing its equity carefully. For example, an increasing number of firms are embracing brand management. Firms from more and more industries—such as the automobile, health care, pharmaceutical, and computer software and hardware industries—are introducing brand managers into their organizations. Often, they have hired managers from top packaged-goods companies, adopting some of the same marketing practices with respect to brands as a result. Interestingly, packaged-goods companies continue to evolve the brand management system, as discussed in Branding Brief 8-2.

In considering the future of brand management, Hulbert, Berthon, and Pitt make several observations and forecasts:[21]

➤ It is incumbent upon the whole organization to become committed to a focus on the customer, and brands will increasingly be seen as a means to that end.

Category Management at Procter & Gamble

Procter & Gamble, pioneers of the brand management system, and several other top firms have made a significant shift in recent years to incorporate category management.[1] Previously, senior management at P&G included a handful of divisional marketing vice presidents, who were responsible for 3 to 6 product categories and 12 to 18 brands. With the company's new category emphasis starting in the late 1980s, a general manager was assigned to each of the 40 or so product categories in which P&G competed (e.g., laundry detergents, dishwashing detergents, and specialty products; see Figure A) and given direct profit responsibility. The duties of individual brand managers, however, were essentially unchanged.

Although in some ways P&G's new organizational structure is counter to management trends toward downsizing the organization and reducing management levels, the company cites a number of advantages.[2] By fostering internal competition among brand managers, the traditional brand management system created strong incentives to excel. These inducements came at the cost of internal coordination, however, because brand managers sometimes contested corporate resources (ad spending dollars, manufacturing capacity, etc.) and failed to synchronize their programs. Whereas a smaller-share category might have been relatively neglected before (e.g., in product categories such as "hard surface cleaners"), the new scheme was designed to ensure that all categories would receive adequate resources. Thus, category management was seen as a means to provide better management of brand portfolios to increase the

FIGURE A Procter & Gamble's Brand Portfolio

similarity, where appropriate, as well as the differences among brands in categories. As academic validation, Zenor provides a game theoretic analysis and empirical demonstration of the profit advantages of coordinating prices and other marketing activity for a firm's different products and brands through category management.[3]

Another often-cited rationale for placing more emphasis on category management is the increasing power of the trade. Because the retail trade has tended to think in terms of product categories and the profitability derived from different departments and sections of their stores, P&G felt it only made sense for it to deal with the trade along similar lines. Retailers such as Wal-Mart and regional grocery chains such as Dominick's have embraced category management themselves as a means to define a particular product category's strategic role within the store (e.g., in terms of its ability to generate store traffic or help provide a particular consumer image) and to address such operating issues as logistics, the role of private label products, and the tradeoffs between offering product variety and avoiding inefficient duplication.[4]

---

[1]Zachary Schiller, "The Marketing Revolution at Procter & Gamble," *Business Week*, 25 July 1988, 72–76; Laurie Freeman, "P&G Widens Power Base: Adds Category Managers," *Advertising Age*.

[2]John Byrne, "The Horizontal Corporation," *Business Week*, 20 December 1993, 76–81.

[3]Michael J. Zenor, "The Profit Benefits of Category Management," *Journal of Marketing Research* 31 (May 1994): 202–213.

[4]Gerry Khermouch, "Brands Overboard," *Brandweek*, 22 August 1994, 25–39.

➤ Marketing must become far more active in the initiation and driving of innovation.

➤ Information technology's role as a vehicle of analysis will increasingly be supplemented by its ability to enable and maintain large-scale customer and consumer interaction and conversation.

➤ To be effective, the onus for ownership and management of change in brands and the brand management system will increasingly shift to senior management.[20]

Many firms are thus attempting to redesign their marketing organizations to better reflect the challenges faced by their brands (see The Science of Branding 8-1). At the same time, because of changing job requirements and duties, the traditional marketing department is disappearing from a number of companies that are exploring other ways to conduct their marketing functions through business groups, multidisciplinary teams, and so on.[22] The goal in these new organizational schemes is to improve internal coordination and efficiencies as well as external focus with respect to retailers and consumers. Although these are laudable goals, clearly one of the challenges with these new designs is to ensure that the equity of brands is preserved and nurtured and not neglected due to a lack of oversight. Branding Brief 8-3 describes General Motors's struggles to better manage the equity of its brands.

With a multiple-product, multiple-market organization, the difficulty often lies in making sure that both place and product are in balance. As one commentator noted:

As companies grow more global, they keep running into the same basic management dilemma. . . . Is it better to be organized by product line or geography? NCR Corp, Ford Motor Co., Procter & Gamble Co., and several others have spent fortunes transforming themselves from one to the other. But taken too far, either model can spark fresh headaches. In the product model,

Global Brand Leadership

In their book *Brand Leadership*, David A. Aaker and Erich Joachimsthaler discuss the principles of building a leading global brand. The authors draw a distinction between a global brand and a leading global brand:

"The priority should be developing not global brands (although such brands might result) but rather global brand leadership—that is, strong brands in all markets, backed by effective, proactive global brand management."

In particular, they recommend four key steps to become a global brand leader: (1) Support a common global brand planning process, (2) stimulate the sharing of insights and best practices across countries, (3) assign managerial responsibility for brands in order to create cross-country synergy and fight local bias, and (4) execute brilliant brand-building programs.

SUPPORTING A GLOBAL BRAND PLANNING PROCESS

A common global brand planning process requires a uniform template for branding decisions at all levels and in every aspect of the corporation. This template ensures that the presentation of the brand is consistent across all markets. As the authors note, "A common brand planning process is a cornerstone for creating synergy and leverage across the global marketplace. Without it, the organization will remain splintered and fragmented."

SHARING INSIGHTS AND BEST PRACTICES

Because consumer tastes differ dramatically from market to market and from country to country, global brand leaders often rely on shared insights and best practices to help keep the marketing program consistently effective in all markets. The authors recommend that companies develop "(1) a global mechanism to detect and capture first-hand observations of effective best practices, (2) a way to communicate best practices to those who could benefit from them, and (3) an easy-to-use method to access an inventory of best practices when needed."

The authors describe how companies can implement formal methods for sharing best practices. For example, Frito-Lay conducts a biannual market university attended by marketing directors and general managers from around the globe. The curriculum includes case studies on successful marketing programs in different countries and encourages employees to share their knowledge and experience. Sony sends executives to different international markets to search for new best practices and to educate about existing ones. Companies can also provide incentives for employees to share information and insights. For example, American Management Systems tracks employee insights and best practices and includes these data in annual performance reviews.

ASSIGNING MANAGERIAL RESPONSIBILITY

Local managers often believe that insights and best practices from other markets would not work in their market. Assigning managerial responsibility for the brand can remedy this issue. Aaker and Joachimsthaler recommend "a centralized brand management system that dictates a global brand strategy." This centralized system can follow one of four possible models of global management structure: a business management team, a brand champion, a global brand manager, or a global brand team. Business management teams are led by top-level executives who "regard brands as the key asset in their business." The authors note how Procter & Gamble employed the business management team approach in the 1990s. Each of P&G's eleven product categories was run by a global team that oversaw R&D, manufacturing, and marketing. The brand champion is typically a senior executive—perhaps the CEO—who must approve all brand-related decisions. Nestlé employs brand champions who manage each of its 12 major brands. The global brand manager structure consists of an individual from middle management responsible for the brand strategy. The global brand team also looks after brand strategy, but is composed of managers from different markets.

EXECUTING BRAND-BUILDING PROGRAMS

Once the brand planning, best-practice sharing program, and management structure of the organization have been put in place, the company must execute brand-building programs to strengthen and nurture the brand.

Source: David A. Aaker and Erich Joachimsthaler, *Brand Leadership* (New York: Free Press, 2000).

businesses can reap efficiencies by standardizing manufacturing, introducing products around the world faster, coordinating prices better, and eliminating overlapping plants. Yet, companies typically find that tilting too far away from a geographic model slows their decision-making, reduces their pricing flexibility and can impair their ability to tailor products to the needs of specific customers.[23]

Like much in marketing and branding, achieving the proper balance is the goal, in order to maximize the advantages and minimize the disadvantages of either approach.

Managing Marketing Partners

Because the performance of a brand also depends on the actions taken by outside suppliers and marketing partners, these relationships must be managed carefully. Increasingly, firms have been consolidating their marketing partnerships and reducing the number of their outside suppliers. This trend has been especially apparent with global advertising accounts, where a number of firms have placed most, if not all, of their business with one agency (e.g., Colgate-Palmolive with Young & Rubicam, IBM with Ogilvy & Mather, and Reebok with Leo Burnett). A number of factors affect the decision of how many outside suppliers to hire in any one area, for example, cost efficiencies, organizational leverage, and creative diversification. From a branding perspective, one advantage of dealing with a single major supplier such as an ad agency is the potentially greater consistency that might be produced in the understanding and treatment of a brand.

Other marketing partners can also play an important role. For example, Chapter 5 described the importance of channel members and retailers in enhancing brand equity and the need for cleverly designed push programs.

General Motors's Branding Challenges

In the early 1920s, Alfred P. Sloan of the General Motors Corporation decreed that his company would not make a single, universal automobile—as did his main competitor, Ford, with its Model T—but would instead offer a line of automobiles: "A car for every purse and purpose." This philosophy led to the creation of the Cadillac, Oldsmobile, Buick, Pontiac, and Chevrolet divisions. Thus, GM's branding strategy traditionally has been to create different divisions and automobiles that would appeal to distinct market segments on the basis of price, product design, user imagery, and so forth.

Over the years, the marketing overlap between the five main GM divisions slowly increased and their distinctiveness diminished as each division attempted to offer cars for "everybody." Finally, by the mid-1980s, GM offered many of its basic body types under multiple brand names. For example, under pressure to reduce costs, GM sold one body type (the J-body) under *five* different brand names, with only minor physical differentiation. In fact, advertisements for Cadillac in the 1980s actually stated "Motors for a Cadillac may come from other divisions, including Buick and Oldsmobile." Not only were the cars sold in the same basic type of distribution channel, but in some cases, more than one GM brand could be sold through the same dealership (e.g., Oldsmobile and Cadillac).

General Motors brands seemed to lack innovation and relevance. In 1988, Oldsmobile attempted to break from their recent past with a lavish, $100 million-plus ad campaign. With the theme "This Is Not Your Father's Oldsmobile," each ad featured an icon from the 1960s—such as *Star Trek*'s William Shatner, TV game-show host Monty Hall, the Beatle's Ringo Starr, astronaut Scott Carpenter, and actress Priscilla Presley—paired with one of his or her children. The ads showed the celebrity parent being driven away in an Oldsmobile by his or her child. With the average age of an Oldsmobile buyer being 51 years, the purpose of the ads was to redefine user and usage imagery and make the brand relevant for a new market. Although the ads were among the best remembered of the year—especially among the target consumers aged 35 to 44—sales continued to slide even after the campaign was introduced. Ultimately, it was withdrawn from the air. Critics faulted the campaign for drawing attention to the dowdiness of the brand's image and the fact that Oldsmobile's models really hadn't changed all that much. Subsequent efforts to revive the brand similarly stuttered.

Recognizing that consumer confusion over product design, brand image, and the marketing of the different brands was hampering sales, GM set out in 1990 to draw sharper differences in the marketplace among its nameplates. At the same time, a corporate image ad campaign was launched to dispel customer concerns of slipping GM quality—and motivate their own 608,000 employee workforce—through ads touting "Putting Quality on the Road."

The different divisions attempted to clear up their blurry images by adopting new brand positions:

Division	Brand Positioning
Chevrolet	Value-priced entry level
Saturn	One-price, customer-oriented service
Pontiac	Sporty, performance-oriented cars for young people
Oldsmobile	Medium-priced larger cars
Buick	Premium and "near-luxury" cars
Cadillac	Top-of-the-line standard of luxury

In layman's terms, Chevrolet was supposed to build lower-price, quality cars; Pontiac was to concentrate on performance; Olds was supposed to excel in engineering; Buick was to emphasize highway comfort; and Cadillac was to represent the best. GM went back to basics to regain some of its lost equity. For example, GM abandoned attempts to make the Chevrolet brand look trend-setting and foreign and returned to images of "America, hot dogs, and apple pie" through the highly successful "Heartbeat of America" ad campaign.

Turning around the divisions has been a challenge for GM. Despite improved performances from Pontiac and the newly introduced Saturn division (the bottom and top of the lines), other divisions struggled. Chevrolet was criticized by some as having too many overlapping products—from a $7,000 Geo Metro to a $65,000 Corvette ZR-1—and a muddled marketing strategy. General Motors has also experienced problems with its aging Buick and Cadillac divisions. For example, Cadillac suffered from intense foreign competition and a disastrous foray with the downsized Cimarron model (see Chapter 12). Cadillac sales, which reached a peak of over 350,000 cars in 1978, dipped to roughly 175,000 in 1995. The average age of Cadillac buyers at that time was 65, but the average age of the entry-level luxury car owner was about 44. This younger market segment did not view Cadillac as a symbol of American affluence and success to as great an extent as their parents did. To attract younger consumers, Cadillac introduced the entry-level Catera, a clone of the Opel Omega MV6 sold by GM in Europe. Cadillac also targeted younger consumers with their older Seville models. To retain existing older customers, however, Cadillac only did a modest makeover of their Sedan de Ville models—redesigned primarily to satisfy their most loyal customers—and retained the expansive Fleetwood models. Similar demographic problems plagued the Buick line, causing one dealer to complain, "Our customers are going out the back door and nobody's coming in the front door."[1]

As a result, GM's U.S. market share dropped from 46 percent to 32 percent between 1980 and 1996. To combat this erosion of market share, General Motors adopted a brand management approach, called Brandscape, whereby each of 65 different GM car models received separate and distinct branding efforts under the direction of a different brand manager. In this brand management system, the brand manager was responsible for vehicle style and personality, advertising, pricing, promotion, and other marketing decisions. The brand management program enabled each model to target a specific consumer segment. For example, the Buick LeSabre was designed for "people seeking security, comfort, safety, and peace of mind." GM indicated that the shift to brand management would enable the company to "chase the needs of the customer" rather than "chase the competition."

The brand management program also involved establishing separate identities for each of GM's six car divisions: Buick, Cadillac, Chevrolet, Oldsmobile, Pontiac-GMC, and Saturn. Under the old corporate structure, divisions often competed against each other for the same customers. As a result, the distinction between divisions grew less obvious, particularly in the case of Buick, Oldsmobile, and Pontiac. Brand management aimed to sharpen the contrast between divisions and reduce sales cannibalization. Between 2000 and 2006, GM planned to release a new or "refreshed" product every 28 days, on average. The result, claimed the company, would be greater differentiation among brands.

Some criticized GM for adopting the brand management model, which was initially developed at packaged-goods giant Procter & Gamble. "You can't sell cars like a box of soap," said one industry expert. Another industry executive criticized the tag line for the Pontiac Bonneville by saying, " 'Luxury with Attitude' sounds an awful lot like 'Tide with Bleach.' " Still, executives at GM insisted the packaged-goods model worked with cars. "There's a high degree of overlap between a packaged-goods company and General Motors," said Jeffrey Cohen, brand manager at GMC Jimmy.

The switch to brand management was not altogether uniform. The Oldsmobile line was intended as a brand management test piece. GM aimed to target younger consumers in order to reduce Oldsmobile's average buyer's age, which was 62 in 1996. The switch to brand management yielded models like the Oldsmobile Intrigue, a sleek sedan introduced in the 1997 model year and backed by a $50 million campaign. GM significantly downplayed the presence of the Oldsmobile name on the Intrigue by affixing it to the car in only one location: on the dashboard. As a result, claimed an auto industry analyst, despite the fact that "the Intrigue is one of the best cars on the road . . . no one knows where to buy it." Unable to attract younger buyers and drifting away from their traditional older customer base, sales at Oldsmobile fell toward 300,000 vehicles per year, down from over 1 million annually in the 1980s. In 2000, GM announced plans to cut the Oldsmobile line entirely.

In the case of some other GM models, the brand management concept seemed to lack enforcement. One writer cited the Cadillac Escalade as an example of "brand management without backbone." In 1998, Cadillac introduced the Escalade, a ritzier version of the GMC Yukon Denali. Up to that point, however, GMC had been GM's luxury truck division and Cadillac had never made a truck. Robert Zarrella, GM's North American president and champion of the brand management program until he was relieved of his position in 2001, admitted that the Escalade introduction was not representative of brand management, but rather about "doing something fast and making a lot of money."

The immediate results of GM's brand management program were not promising: Market share fell to 29.5 percent in 2000. One automotive-marketing executive summarized the results of the program by stating the company "made almost no progress . . . in terms of changing the perception of GM brands." Following Robert Zarella's departure, GM began to move away from the brand management concept of separate and distinct models. In 2001, both Cadillac and Chevrolet developed advertising campaigns that focused on their umbrella brands. Additionally, GM allocated a greater percentage of its $2.8 billion annual advertising budget for overall brand marketing. "The lesson is that divisional positioning has to be king," said John G. Middlebrook, GM's general manager for brand marketing and corporate advertising. This means that individual models and advertising will reinforce each division's positioning, such as "American value" for Chevrolet and "Art and Science" for Cadillac.

Sources: Jeff Green, "The Carmakers 'Soap' Sell, So Far," *Brandweek*, 24 January 2000; John McElroy, "GM's Brand Management Might Work," *Automotive Industries*, 1 September 1996; Charles Child, "GM Brand Management Talk Is Cheap," *Automotive News*, 8 March 1999; David Welch, "Consumers to GM: You Talking to *Me*?" *Business Week*, 19 June 2000; Lawrence Ulrich, "With His Departure, General Motors' Chief Leaves behind Brand-Management Style," *Detroit Free Press,* 14 November 2001; Betsy Spethmann, "Not Your Father's Marketing Plan," *Promo,* 1 July 1997; Alfred P. Sloan, *My Years with General Motors* (Garden City, NY: Doubleday & Company, 1964), 67, as quoted in William M. Weilbacher, *Brand Marketing: Building Winning Brand Strategies That Deliver Value and Customer Satisfaction* (Lincolnwood, IL: NTC Business Books, 1993); Adrian B. Ryans, Roger A. More, and John S. Hulland, "Profitable Multibranding," working paper, Western Business School, University of Western Ontario: Please; Jerry Flint, "'A Brand Is Like a Friend,'" *Forbes*, 14 November 1988, 267–270; Mark Landler, "Shirley Young: Pushing GM's Humble-Pie Strategy," *Business Week*, 11 June 1990, 52–53; Neal Templin, "Chevy, a Bit Rusty and Slowing Down, Finds Itself Boxed in by GM's Problems," *Wall Street Journal*, 24 April 1992, B1.

[1]Oscar Suris, "Cadillac's Sedan de Ville Spurns Youth," *Wall Street Journal*, 10 August 1993, B1; Gabriella Stern, "As Old Cadillac Buyers Age, the GM Division Fights to Halt Slippage," *Wall Street Journal*, 25 August 1995, A1; Gabriella Stern, "Buick Confronts Its Fuddy-Duddy Image," *Wall Street Journal*, 19 June 1995, B1.

Review

The brand value chain is a means to trace the value creation process for brands to better understand the financial impact of brand marketing expenditures and investments. Taking the customer's perspective of the value of a brand, the brand value chain assumes that the brand value creation process begins when the firm invests in a marketing program targeting actual or potential customers. Any marketing program investment that potentially can be attributed to brand value development falls into this category, for example, product research, development, and design; trade or intermediary support; and marketing communications.

The marketing activity associated with the program then affects the customer mindset with respect to the brand—what customers know and feel about the brand. The customer mindset includes everything that exists in the minds of customers with respect to a brand: thoughts, feelings, experiences, images, perceptions, beliefs, attitudes, and so forth. Consistent with the customer-based brand equity model, five key dimensions that are particularly important measures of the customer mindset are brand awareness, brand associations, brand attitudes, brand attachment, and brand activity or experience.

The customer mindset affects how customers react or respond in the marketplace in a variety of ways. Six key outcomes of that response are price premiums, price elasticities, market share, brand expansion, cost structure, and brand profitability. Based on all available current and forecasted information about a brand, as well as many other considerations, the financial marketplace then formulates opinions and makes various assessments that have direct financial implications for the value of the brand. Three particularly important indicators are the stock price, the price/earnings multiple, and overall market capitalization for the firm.

The model also assumes that a number of linking factors intervene between these stages. These linking factors determine the extent to which value created at one stage transfers or "multiplies" to the next stage. Thus, there are three sets of multipliers that moderate the transfer between the marketing program and the subsequent three value stages: the program multiplier, the customer multiplier, and the market multiplier.

Managing Brands at Ogilvy & Mather

Ogilvy & Mather (O&M), one of the world's largest advertising agencies, manages its clients' brands by a five-step process called *brand stewardship*. The five steps are as follows:

1. Information gathering
2. The Brand Audit
3. The Brand Probe
4. The BrandPrint
5. The Brand Check

The first step is information gathering, in which all existing knowledge of the brand is reviewed (facts about product details, consumers, competition, and the marketing environment). The second step is the Brand Audit, which is defined as an "exhaustive effort to set down, in black and white, the intangible cluster of feelings, impressions, connections, opinions, flashes of memory, hopes, and satisfactions . . . and yes, criticisms and disappointments . . . which blend together to form the consumer's perception of your Brand." The audit is based on the information gathered in step 1. The final version of the audit becomes the raw material for the BrandPrint, which is step 4.

If O&M is unable to answer the brand audit questions from existing sources of information, it commissions research to provide the insight and understanding necessary to be able to complete the brand audit. The Brand Probe is described as a four-stage research program that explores the thoughts and attitudes of a wide sample of interested people (brand-loyal consumers, representatives from the client and agency, and other marketing companies working with the agency).

After this preliminary research is completed, O&M writes the BrandPrint, which the agency defines as "a vivid statement of the unique relationship that exists between the consumer and a brand." According to O&M, a good BrandPrint should be "distinctive, linked, clear, colloquial, colorful, appealing, and flexible in use." The BrandPrint is used in the fifth step as a tool to guide marketing, and especially advertising, decisions. The sixth and final step is the Brand Check, conducted once a year, to ensure that "every aspect of a brand, its product performance, its physical characteristics, its packaging, all its communications, etc. reflect the nature of and remain true to the brand consumer relationship as articulated in the BrandPrint."

As is clear from this description, Ogilvy is in the forefront of bringing branding issues and perspectives to the development of advertising and other communications.

Ogilvy & Mather, internal documents on brand stewardship.

A brand equity measurement system is defined as a set of research procedures designed to provide timely, accurate, and actionable information for marketers regarding brands so that they can make the best possible tactical decisions in the short run as well as strategic decisions in the long run. Implementing a brand equity measurement system involves two steps: designing brand tracking studies and establishing a brand equity management system.

Brand audits can be used to set the strategic direction for the brand (see Brand Focus 3.0). As a result of this strategic analysis, a marketing program can be put into place to maximize long-term brand equity. Tracking studies employing quantitative measures can then be conducted to provide marketers with current information as to how their brands are performing on the basis of a number of key dimensions identified by the brand audit. Tracking studies involve information collected from consumers on a routine basis over time and provide valuable tactical insights into the short-term effectiveness of marketing programs and activities. Whereas brand audits measure "where the brand has been," tracking studies measure "where the brand is now" and whether marketing programs are having their intended effects.

Three major steps must occur as part of a brand equity management system. First, the company view of brand equity should be formalized into a document, the brand equity charter. This document serves a number of purposes: It chronicles the company's general philosophy with respect to brand equity; summarizes the activity and outcomes related to brand audits, brand tracking, and so forth; outlines guidelines for brand strategies and tactics; and documents proper treatment of the brand. The charter should be updated annually to identify new opportunities and risks and to fully reflect information gathered by the brand inventory and brand exploratory as part of any brand audits. Second, the results of the tracking surveys and other relevant outcome measures should be assembled into a brand equity report that is distributed to management on a regular basis (monthly, quarterly, or annually). The brand equity report should provide descriptive information as to *what* is happening to a brand as well as diagnostic information as to *why* it is happening. Finally, senior management must be assigned to oversee how brand equity is treated within the organization. The people in that position would be responsible for overseeing the implementation of the brand equity charter and brand equity reports to make sure that, as much as possible, product and marketing actions across divisions and geographic boundaries are performed in a way that reflects the spirit of the charter and the substance of the report so as to maximize the long-term equity of the brand.

An alternative—albeit complementary—view of how firms should incorporate the brand equity concept into their marketing research and planning is described in Branding Brief 8-4, which examines how one of the world's best ad agencies, Ogilvy & Mather, incorporates branding issues in the services they provide their clients.

Discussion Questions

1. Pick a brand. Try to do an informal brand value chain analysis. Can you trace how the brand value is created and transferred? What are the roles of the multipliers?
2. Choose Starbucks, Reebok, or Miller. Update and supplement the brand value chain analysis presented in this chapter. What does the analysis suggest about the brand's fortunes in recent years?

3. A few years ago, Disney entered into a long-term agreement with McDonald's that included, among other things, joint promotions. From Disney's perspective and what you know about the two brands, was this the right decision? Is there any downside? Would you have wanted to conduct any research to inform the decision? What kind?

4. Consider the McDonald's tracking survey presented in Branding Brief 8-1. What might you do differently? What questions would you change or drop? What questions might you add? How might this tracking survey differ from those used for other products?

5. Can you develop a tracking survey for the Mayo Clinic? (See Brand Focus 8.0.) How might it differ from the McDonald's tracking survey?

Brand   Focus   8 . 0

Understanding and Managing the Mayo Clinic Brand

DESCRIPTION

Mayo Clinic was founded in the late 1800s by Dr. William Worral Mayo and his two sons, who later pioneered the "group practice of medicine" by inviting other physicians to work with them in Rochester, Minnesota.[24] The Mayos believed that "two heads are better than one and three are even better." From this beginning on the frontier, Mayo Clinic grew to be a worldwide leader in patient care, research, and education. A not-for-profit institution, Mayo Clinic became renowned for its world-class specialty care. In addition to the original facilities in Rochester, Mayo later built clinics in Jacksonville, Florida, and Scottsdale, Arizona, during the 1980s. More than 600,000 patients are cared for in Mayo's inpatient and outpatient practice annually.

Mayo Clinic has earned a reputation as a world-class research center. Most medical staff participate in research projects. Perhaps the most well-known research result was the discovery of cortisone, which brought Mayo Clinic Drs. Edward Kendall and Phillip Hench the Nobel Prize in medicine in 1950. Mayo Clinic also maintains a focus on education. It operates the Mayo Graduate School of Medicine, one of the world's largest graduate education centers, which trains physicians in more than 100 specialties. It also confers M.D.s through the Mayo Medical School, offers seven different Ph.D. programs at the Mayo Graduate School, trains students in 23 allied health programs at the Mayo School of Health Sciences, and annually offers more than 150 continuing education courses for physicians, nurses, and other medical professionals.

BRAND EVALUATION

In 1996, Mayo undertook a brand equity study and conducted both quantitative and qualitative studies, including 16 focus groups in eight cities. The quantitative studies found that overall awareness of the Mayo Clinic in the United States was 84.3 percent, and was more than 90 percent among respondents above age 45. One of the questions in the survey asked, "Suppose your health plan or personal finances permitted you to go anywhere in the U.S. for a serious medical condition which required highly specialized care, to which one institution would you prefer to go?" Mayo Clinic was the most popular choice, earning 15.4 percent of the responses, compared with 5.3 percent for the next most frequently mentioned medical center. The study found that consumers' strongest brand associations with Mayo were (1) scientific research, (2) cancer treatment, and (3) cardiac care. The study also revealed that word of mouth is influential in selecting highly specialized medical care, and that one-third of all respondents know at least one Mayo Clinic patient.

When asked for their thoughts and feelings about the brand, focus group participants' responses indicated five major types of associations: integrity, leadership, professionalism, a commitment to health and healing, and exclusivity. Pertaining to integrity, respondents remarked on Mayo Clinic's longevity, its heritage, the wisdom of its staff, and trust in the institution. For leadership, participants noted the clinic's modernity, premium quality, and international prestige. Perceptions that the clinic staff held high standards, were intellectually sophisticated, and efficient contributed to the association with professionalism. The association of a commitment to health and healing came from the Mayo Clinic's reputation for medical discoveries, preventive medicine, and tangible results.

The research did not find any negative features of the Mayo Clinic brand. Some focus group participants outside the Midwest expressed misperceptions such as Mayo being only for the rich and famous. The research also showed that Mayo Clinic is known for tertiary care rather than primary family care. Thus, these respondents said the clinic was "not like me."

CONCLUSIONS AND ACTIONS

From the study, Mayo concluded that its brand equity "is precious and powerful." This equity is expressed by the Mayo Clinic brand essence, as follows.

As perceived by patients and consumers, Mayo Clinic's Brand Essence has four key components:

1. *Excellence:* The best medical, personal, and technical expertise in patient care and education
2. *Care:* Compassionate patient care and education resulting in physical, mental, and emotional well-being
3. *Cooperation:* Care and education in cooperative and inclusive relationships among colleagues and with the patient, the patient's family, and consumers
4. *Enlightenment (Wisdom):* Commitment to pioneering knowledge, insight, and truth through research and education

By living out these standards fully and consistently, the Mayo Clinic has engendered in patients and consumers a sense of confidence, safety, hope, and serenity.

The importance of word-of-mouth referrals indicated that a satisfied national patient base is vital to maintaining Mayo's level of preference. Mayo Clinic realized that while it had an overwhelmingly positive image, it was vital to develop guidelines that protected the brand. In 1999, the clinic created the Office of Brand Management to be the "institutional clearinghouse for ongoing knowledge about external perceptions of Mayo Clinic and its related activities." The Office of Brand Management is responsible for the protection and enhancement of the Mayo Clinic brand and was charged with developing brand management guidelines and a positioning statement implementing a branding system, and with building awareness of brand management within the Mayo organization.

The Office of Brand Management also provides leadership and guidance for the Brand Management Support Team, which has the following responsibilities:

➤ Monitoring perceptions of the Mayo Clinic brand
➤ Conducting new research to examine opportunities for Mayo brand extensions and potential risks
➤ Implementing Foundation-wide educational programs about the value and essence of the Mayo Clinic brand
➤ Providing brand management support to project proponents from all Foundation entities

The Office of Brand Management established guidelines regarding application of the Mayo Clinic brand to products and services. Each new and existing Mayo Clinic branded product, service, or business relationship must meet the following criteria:

➤ A product, service, or relationship using the "Mayo" or "Mayo Clinic" brand name must be owned by Mayo or be under Mayo's full control.

➤ Use of the Mayo Clinic name solely to assure success or name recognition of a service, product, or relationship is not appropriate.

➤ The Mayo Clinic brand is not to be used in a manner that trivializes the name or institution.

➤ The Mayo Clinic brand will not be shared, leased, or sold to another party for use on products, services, facilities, or relationships in a manner inconsistent with these principles and criteria.

The brand management measures taken by Mayo Clinic work to ensure that the clinic's brand equity is preserved, as well as allow the Mayo Clinic to continue to accomplish its mission of providing "the best care to every patient every day through integrated clinical practice, education and research."

Notes

1. Kevin Lane Keller and Don Lehmann, "The Brand Value Chain: Optimizing Strategic and Financial Brand Performance," working paper. Dartmouth College, 2002. See also R. K. Srivastava, T. A. Shervani, and L. Fahey, "Market-Based Assets and Shareholder Value," *Journal of Marketing* 62, no. 1 (1998): 2–18; and M. J. Epstein and R. A. Westbrook, "Linking Actions to Profits in Strategic Decision Making," *MIT Sloan Management Review* (Spring 2001): 39–49. In terms of related empirical insights, see Manoj K. Agrawal and Vithala Rao, "An Empirical Comparison of Consumer-Based Measures of Brand Equity," *Marketing Letters* 7, no. 3 (1996): 237–247; and Walfried Lassar, Banwari Mittal, and Arun Sharma, "Measuring Customer-Based Brand Equity," *Journal of Consumer Marketing* 12, no. 4 (1995): 11–19.

2. Adrienne W. Fawcett, "The Marketing 100: Starbucks: Scott Bedbury," *Advertising Age,* 30 June 1997, S18.

3. Louise Kramer, "Brand Man Bedbury Departing Starbucks," *Advertising Age,* 18 May 1998, 1.

4. Alice Z. Cuneo, "Starbucks' Word-of-Mouth Wonder," *Advertising Age,* 7 March 1994.

5. Kim Murphy, "More Than Coffee: A Way of Life," *Los Angeles times Magazine,* 22 September 1996, 8.

6. Seana Browder, "Starbucks Does Not Live by Coffee Alone," *Business Week,* 5 August 1996, 76.

7. Paul Farhi, "Canning an Ad Campaign," *Washington Post,* 25 April 1999, H1.

8. Ira Teinowitz, "New Miller CEO Gives Agencies a Chance," *Advertising Age,* 12 April 1999, 3.

9. Ibid., 3.

10. "No Debate: Miller Aching," *Advertising Age,* 22 March 1999, 26.

11. Geoffrey Smith, "Can Reebok Regain Its Balance?" *Business Week,* 20 December 1993, 108.

12. Ron Stodghill II, "Rebound For Reebok," *Time Magazine,* 27 August 2001, 42.

13. "Bok in the Saddle Again," *Business Week,* 8 February 1999, 26.

14. John B. Frey, "Measuring Corporate Reputation and Its Value" (paper presented at the Marketing Science Conference at Duke University, March 17, 1989).

15. Personal correspondence, Nigel Hollis.

16. Na Woon Bong, Roger Marshall, and Kevin Lane Keller, "Measuring Brand Power: Validating a Model for Optimizing Brand Equity," *Journal of Product and Brand Management* 8, no. 3 (1999): 170–184.

17. Joel Rubinson, "Brand Strength Means More Than Market Share" (paper presented at the ARF Fourth Annual Advertising and Promotion Workshop, New York, 1992).

18. Scott Bedbury, *A New Brand World* (New York: Viking Press, 2002).

19. Betsy Spethman, "Companies Post Equity Gatekeepers," *Brandweek,* 2 May 1994, 5.

20. Bedbury A., *New Brand World.*

21. J. M. Hulbert, P. Berthon, and L. F. Pitt, "Brand Management Prognostications," *Sloan Management Review* (Winter 1998): 53–65.

22. "The Death of the Brand Manager," *The Economist*, 9 April 1994, 67–68.

23. Joann S. Lubin, "Place versus Product: It's Tough to Choose a Management Model," *Wall Street Journal*.

24. This appendix was prepared with the assistance and cooperation of Mayo's John La Forgia, Kent Seltman, and Scott Swanson. Sources include http://www.mayoclinic.org; and "Mayo Clinic Brand Management," internal document, 1999.

9

Measuring Sources of Brand Equity: Capturing Customer Mindset

PREVIEW

Understanding the current and desired brand knowledge structures of consumers is vital to effectively building and managing brand equity. As Gardner and Levy note in a classic marketing article:

> The image of a product associated with the brand may be clear-cut or relatively vague; it may be varied or simple; it may be intense or innocuous. Sometimes the notions people have about a brand do not seem very sensible or relevant to those who know what the product is "really" like. But they all contribute to the customer's deciding whether or not the brand is "for me." These sets of ideas, feelings, and attitudes that consumers have about brands are crucial to them in picking and sticking to ones that seem most appropriate.[1]

Ideally, marketers would be able to construct detailed "mental maps" of consumers to understand exactly what exists in their minds concerning brands—all their thoughts, feelings, perceptions, images, beliefs, and attitudes toward different brands. These mental blueprints would then provide managers with strategic and tactical guidance to help them make brand decisions. Unfortunately, these brand knowledge structures are not easily measured because they reside only in consumers' minds.

Nevertheless, effective brand management requires a thorough understanding of the consumer. Brand Focus 9.0 describes several potentially powerful tools to research consumers. Often a simple insight into how consumers think of or use products and the particular brands in a category can result in profitable changes in the marketing program. As a result, many large companies conduct exhaustive research studies (or brand audits, as described in Chapter 3) to learn as much as possible about consumers. Consequently, a number of detailed, sophisticated research techniques and methods have been developed to help marketers better understand consumer knowledge structures. Branding Brief 9-1 describes the lengths to which marketers have gone in the past to learn about consumers. Much has been written on the topic of consumer behavior. This chapter highlights some of the important considerations that are critical to the measurement of brand equity.[2] Figure 9-1 outlines some general considerations in understanding consumer behavior.

According to the brand value chain, sources of brand equity arise from the customer mindset. In general, measuring sources of brand equity requires that the brand manager fully understand how customers shop for and use products and services and, most important, what customers know, think, and feel about various brands. In particular, measuring sources of customer-based brand equity requires measuring various aspects of brand awareness and brand image that potentially can lead to the differential customer response that creates brand equity. To some extent, consumer reactions to a brand may be based on their "gestalt" knowledge. In other words, consumers may have a holistic view of brands that is difficult to divide into component parts. Yet, in many cases, consumers' perceptions of a brand can be isolated and assessed in greater detail. The remainder of this chapter describes both qualitative and quantitative approaches to identify potential sources of brand equity, that is, to capture the customer mindset.

Digging Beneath the Surface
to Understand Consumer Behavior

Most consumer research relies on surveys to obtain consumers' reported beliefs, attitudes, and behavior. However, useful marketing insights sometimes emerge from unobtrusively observing consumer behavior rather than talking to consumers. In many instances, consumer behavior that is observed differs from the behavior that consumers report in surveys.[1] For example, Hoover became suspicious when people claimed in surveys that they vacuumed their houses for an hour each week. To check, the company installed timers in certain models and exchanged them for the same models in consumers' homes. The timers showed that people actually spent only a little over *half* an hour vacuuming each week. People were exaggerating the amount. One researcher analyzed household trash to determine the types and quantities of food that people consumed, finding that people really don't have a very good idea of how much and what types of food they eat and tend to overestimate. Similarly, much research has shown that people report that they eat healthier food than would appear to be case if you opened their cabinets!

DuPont commissioned marketing studies to uncover personal pillow behavior for its Dacron Polyester unit, which supplies filling to pillow makers and sells its own Comforel brand. One challenge: People don't give up their old pillows. Thirty seven percent of one sample described their relationship with their pillow as like "an old married couple," and an additional 13 percent characterized it as like a "childhood friend." They found that people fell into distinct groups in terms of pillow behavior: stackers (23 percent), plumpers (20 percent), rollers or folders (16 percent), cuddlers (16 percent), and smashers, who pound their pillows into a more comfy shape (10 percent). Women were more likely to plump while men were more likely to fold. The prevalence of stackers led the company to sell more pillows packaged as pairs, as well as to market different levels of softness or firmness.[2]

Much of this type of research has its roots in ethnography, the anthropological term for the study of cultures in their natural surroundings. The intent behind these in-depth, observational studies is for consumers to drop their guard and provide a more realistic portrayal of who they are rather than who they would like to be. On the basis of ethnographic research that uncovered consumers' true feelings, ad campaigns have been created for a Swiss chocolate maker with the theme "The True Confessions of a Chocaholic" (because chocolate lovers often hid stashes all though the house), for Tampax Tampons with the theme "More Women Trust Their Bodies to Tampax" (because teen users wanted the freedom to wear body-conscious clothes), and for Crisco shortening with the theme "Recipe for Success" (because people often baked pies and cookies in a celebratory fashion).

---

[1]John Koten, "You Aren't Paranoid If You Feel Someone Eyes You Constantly," *Wall Street Journal*, 2 March 1985.

[2]Susan Warren, "Pillow Talk: Stackers Outnumber Plumpers; Don't Mention Drool," *Wall Street Journal*, 8 January 1998, B1.

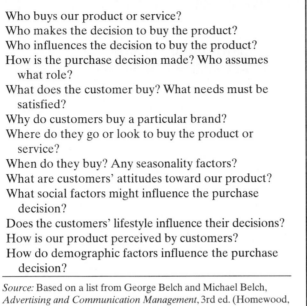

Who buys our product or service?

Who makes the decision to buy the product?

Who influences the decision to buy the product?

How is the purchase decision made? Who assumes what role?

What does the customer buy? What needs must be satisfied?

Why do customers buy a particular brand?

Where do they go or look to buy the product or service?

When do they buy? Any seasonality factors?

What are customers' attitudes toward our product?

What social factors might influence the purchase decision?

Does the customers' lifestyle influence their decisions?

How is our product perceived by customers?

How do demographic factors influence the purchase decision?

Source: Based on a list from George Belch and Michael Belch, *Advertising and Communication Management*, 3rd ed. (Homewood, IL: Irwin, 1995).

FIGURE 9-1   Understanding Consumer Behavior

QUALITATIVE RESEARCH TECHNIQUES

As Chapter 3 noted, a number of different types of associations can become linked to a brand. For example, consider the possible attribute and benefit beliefs that might exist for Levi's 501 brand of jeans (Figure 9-2). The Science of Branding 9-1 describes some of the basic ideas behind and applications of the associative network model of memory, which, as Chapter 2 noted, is a useful theoretical means of representing these associations.

There are also many different ways to uncover the types of associations linked to the brand and their corresponding strength, favorability, and uniqueness. Qualitative research techniques are often employed to identify possible brand associations and sources of brand equity. *Qualitative research techniques* are relatively unstructured measurement approaches whereby a range of possible consumer responses is permitted. Because of the freedom afforded both researchers in their probes and consumers in their responses, qualitative research can often be a useful first step in exploring consumer brand and product perceptions.

Qualitative research has a long history in marketing. Ernest Dichter, one of the early pioneers in consumer psychoanalytic research, first applied these research principles in a study for Plymouth automobiles in the 1930s.[3] His research revealed the important—but previously overlooked—role that women played in the automobile purchase decision. Based on his consumer analysis, a new print ad strategy was employed for Plymouth that highlighted a young couple gazing admiringly at a Plymouth automobile under the headline "Imagine Us in a Car Like That." His subsequent work had an important impact on a number of different ad campaigns.[4] Some of Dichter's assertions were fairly controversial. Based on his research, Dichter argued

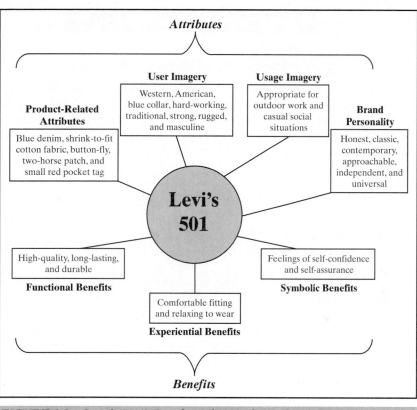

FIGURE 9-2   Sample Levi's Brand Attribute and Benefit Associations

that women used Ivory soap to wash away their sins before a date. He also equated convertibles with mistresses and suggested "Putting a Tiger in the Tank" for Exxon, resulting in a long-running and successful ad campaign.

This section next reviews a number of qualitative research techniques that can be employed to identify sources of brand equity. Branding Brief 9-2 describes one provocative technique, and Branding Brief 9-3 examines some practical issues in conducting focus groups.

Free Association

The simplest and often most powerful way to profile brand associations involves free association tasks whereby subjects are asked what comes to mind when they think of the brand without any more specific probe or cue than perhaps the associated product category (e.g., "What does the Rolex name mean to you?" or "Tell me what comes to mind when you think of Rolex watches."). The primary purpose of free association tasks is to identify the range of possible brand associations in consumers' minds, but they may also provide some rough indication of the relative strength, favorability, and uniqueness of brand associations, as follows.[5]

Coding free association responses in terms of the order of elicitation—early or late in the sequence—can yield at least a rough measure of strength.[6] For example, if many

Understanding Consumer Memory

The associative network memory model views memory as consisting of a network of nodes and connecting links. According to this model, recall or retrieval of information occurs through a concept called *spreading activation*. At any point in time, an information node may be a source of activation because it is either presented external information (e.g., when a person reads or hears a word or phrase) or retrieves internal information currently being processed (e.g., when a person thinks about some concept). A particular node in memory is activated, and activation spreads from that node to other nodes connected to it in memory. When the activation of a particular node exceeds a threshold level, the contents of that node are recalled. The spread of activation depends on the number and strength of the links connected to the activated node: Concepts connected to the activated node whose linkages have the greatest strength will receive the most activation.

As a result of spreading activation, the strength and organization of brand associations will be important determinants of the information that can be recalled about the brand to influence consumer response and brand-related decisions. Research in psychology provides some useful insights into some factors affecting association strength. In general, the strength of an association depends on how information is initially processed as it enters consumers' memory and where it is actually located as a result. Psychologists refer to these two processes as memory *encoding* and *storage*. Encoding processes can be characterized according to the amount, or *quantity,* of processing that information receives (i.e., how much a person thinks about the information) and the nature, or *quality,* of the processing that information receives (i.e., the manner in which a person thinks about the information). The quantity and quality of processing are important determinants of the strength of an association. Prior research has shown that a number of factors affect the quantity and quality of encoding processes, the accessibility of information from memory, and the ability of consumers to recall or retrieve brand associations.[1] Some of those factors are briefly highlighted here.[2]

QUALITY AND QUANTITY OF PROCESSING

In terms of qualitative considerations, in general, the more attention that is placed on the meaning of information during encoding, the stronger the resulting associations in memory will be.[3] Thus, when a consumer actively thinks about and "elaborates" on the significance of product or service information, stronger associations are created in memory. Another key determinant of the strength of a newly formed association is the content, organization, and strength of existing brand associations in memory. All else being equal, it will be easier for consumers to create an association to new information when extensive, relevant knowledge structures already exist in memory. One reason why personal experiences create such strong brand associations is that information about the product is likely to be related to existing knowledge because of its self-relevance.

To illustrate the issues involved, consider the brand associations that might be created by a new TV ad campaign employing a popular celebrity endorser designed to create a new benefit association for a well-known brand. For example, assume Bruce Springsteen and the classic rock anthem "Born to Run" were used to promote the "thrill" and "timeless appeal" of driving a Chevrolet. A number of different scenarios characterize how consumers might process such an ad:

- Some consumers might barely notice the ad, such that the amount of processing devoted to the ad is extremely low, resulting in weak to nonexistent brand associations.

- The ad might catch the attention of other consumers, resulting in sufficient processing, but these consumers might devote most of the ad thinking about the song and wondering why Springsteen decided to endorse a Chevy (and whether he actually drove one), resulting in strong associations to Springsteen but not to Chevrolet.

- Finally, another group of consumers might not only notice the ad but might think of how they had a wrong impression of Chevy and that it is "different" from the way they thought and that it looked fun to drive. The endorsement by Springsteen in this case helps to transfer and create some positive associations to the brand.

In addition to congruency or consistency with existing knowledge, the ease with which new information can be integrated into established knowledge structures clearly depends on the nature of that information, in terms of characteristics such as its inherent simplicity, vividness, and concreteness.

In terms of quantitative considerations, repeated exposure to information provides greater opportunity for processing and thus the potential for stronger associations. Recent advertising research in a field setting, however, suggests that qualitative considerations and the manner or style of consumer processing engendered by an ad are generally more important than the cumulative total of ad exposures per se.[4] In other words, high levels of repetition for an uninvolving, unpersuasive ad are unlikely to have as much sales impact as lower levels of repetition for an involving, persuasive ad.

In short, a number of factors affect the strength of brand associations. Perhaps the two most important factors are the relevance of the brand information and the consistency with which that brand information is presented to consumers at any one point in time, as well as over time.

RECALL OF BRAND ASSOCIATIONS

According to the associative network memory model, the strength of a brand association increases both the likelihood that that information will be accessible and the ease with which it can be recalled by spreading activation. Accessible, recalled information is important because it can create the differential response that makes up customer-based brand equity. Successful recall of brand information by consumers does not depend only on the initial associative strength of that information in memory, however, but also on other considerations. Three such factors are particularly important.

First, the presence of *other* product information in memory can produce interference effects and reduce the accessibility of similar brand information in memory. In particular, the presence of other information in memory may cause the target information to be either overlooked or confused with this other information. Second, the time since exposure to information at encoding affects the strength of a new association: The longer the time delay, the weaker the association. The time elapsed since the last exposure opportunity, however, has been generally shown to only produce gradual decay. That is, cognitive psychologists believe that memory is extremely durable, so that once information becomes stored in memory, its strength of association decays very slowly.[5] Third, the number and type of external retrieval cues that are available will be key factors affecting memory accessibility. That is, information may be "available" in memory (i.e., potentially recallable) but may not be "accessible" from memory (i.e., able to be recalled) without the proper retrieval cues or reminders. Thus, the particular associations for a brand that are salient and come to mind depend on the context in which the brand is considered. The more cues linked to a piece of information, however, the greater the likelihood that the information can be recalled.

[1]John R. Anderson, *The Architecture of Cognition* (Cambridge, MA: Harvard University Press, 1983).

[2]For additional discussion, see John G. Lynch Jr. and Thomas K. Srull, "Memory and Attentional Factors in Consumer Choice: Concepts and Research Methods," *Journal of Consumer Research* 9 (June 1982): 18–36; and Joseph W. Alba, J. Wesley Hutchinson, and John G. Lynch Jr., "Memory and Decision Making," in *Handbook of Consumer Theory and Research*, eds. Harold H. Kassarjian and Thomas S. Robertson (Englewood Cliffs, NJ: Prentice-Hall, 1992), 1–49.

[3]Fergus I. M. Craik and Robert S. Lockhart, "Levels of Processing: A Framework for Memory Research," *Journal of Verbal Learning and Verbal Behavior* 11 (1972): 671–684; Fergus I. M. Craik and Endel Tulving, "Depth of Processing and the Retention of Words in Episodic Memory," *Journal of Experimental Psychology* 104, no. 3 (1975): 268–294; Robert S. Lockhart, Fergus I. M. Craik, and Larry Jacoby, "Depth of Processing, Recognition, and Recall," in *Recall and Recognition*, ed. John Brown (New York: John Wiley & Sons, 1976).

[4]Magid Abraham and Leonard Lodish, *Advertising Works: A Study of Advertising Effectiveness and the Resulting Strategies and Tactical Implications* (Chicago: Information Resources Inc., 1989).

[5]Elizabeth F. Loftus and Gregory R. Loftus, "On the Permanence of Stored Information in the Human Brain," *American Psychologist* 35 (May 1980): 409–420.

consumers mention "fast and convenient" as one of their first associations when given "McDonald's restaurants" as a probe, then it is likely that the association is a relatively strong one and likely to be potentially available to affect consumer decisions. Associations later in the list, on the other hand, may be weaker and thus more likely to be overlooked during consumer decision making. Comparing associations with those elicited for competitive brands can also provide some indication of their relative uniqueness. Finally, even favorability, to some extent, may be discerned on the basis of how associations are stated and phrased.

Answers to these questions help marketers to clarify the range of possible associations and assemble a brand profile.[7] To better understand the favorability of associations, consumers can be asked follow-up questions as to the favorability of associations they listed or, more generally, what they like best about the brand. Similarly, consumers can also be asked direct follow-up questions as to the uniqueness of associations they listed or, more generally, what they find unique about the brand. Thus, useful questions include the following:

1. What do you like best about the brand? What are its positive aspects? What do you dislike? What are its disadvantages?
2. What do you find unique about the brand? How is it different from other brands? In what ways is it the same?

These simple, direct measures can be extremely valuable at determining core aspects of a brand image. To provide more structure and guidance, consumers can be asked further follow-up questions to describe what the brand means to them in terms of "who, what, when, where, why, and how" questions such as the following:

BRANDING BRIEF 9-2

Using Archetype Research to Gain Consumer Insights

According to medical anthropologist G. C. Rapaille, consumers often make purchase decisions based on factors that they are aware of only subconsciously. Conventional market research typically does not elicit responses that indicate these factors, so Rapaille employs the "archetype research" technique to uncover these hidden consumer motivations.

Rapaille believes that children experience a significant initial exposure to an element of their world called the "imprinting moment." The pattern that emerges when these imprinting moments are generalized for the entire population is the archetype. The archetype is a fundamental psychological association, shared by the members of the culture, with a given cultural object. For example, the American archetype for coffee is "home," because American children typically wake up to their mothers cooking breakfast and making coffee. Different cultures have dramatically different archetypes for the same objects. In France, the archetype for cheese is "alive" because age is its most important trait. By contrast, the American archetype for cheese is "dead"; it is wrapped in plastic ("a body-bag"), put in the refrigerator ("a morgue"), and pasteurized ("scientifically dead").

Rapaille uses relaxation exercises and visualization with consumers to find the imprinting moments appropriate to the product he is researching. For example, at a focus group he will dim the lights, play soothing music, and coax the subjects into a meditative state. He will then elicit stories about the product from the subjects, and analyze these stories to illuminate the archetype.

One of Rapaille's recent projects was the top-selling Chrysler PT Cruiser. He used archetype research to arrive at the conclusion that American car buyers wanted over-sized and rugged vehicles in order to feel safe-even intimidating—in the "jungle out there." These same car buyers, however, wanted the car's interior to resemble "the Ritz-Carlton." Based on these findings, Chrysler designers altered the PT Cruiser prototype to give it more exterior bulk and a more functional and accommodating interior. Consumers likened the PT Cruiser to a 1920s gangster car and a 1950s hot rod. The $16,000 car won accolades from the automobile industry, winning *Motor Trend*'s 2001 Car of the Year award. Demand for the PT Cruiser was so high that consumers paid $1,000 to $4,000 over the sticker price at some dealerships in order to obtain one.

Sources: Alexandra Harrington, "G.C. Rapaille: Finding the Keys in the Cultural Unconscious," *Response TV*, 1 September 2001; Jeffrey Ball, " 'But How Does It Make You Feel?' " *Wall Street Journal*, 3 May 1999; Jack Hitt, "Does the Smell of Coffee Brewing Remind You of Your Mother?" *New York Times Magazine*, 7 May 2000.

Focus Group Guidelines

When conducting qualitative research, consumer responses may be collected either in small groups called *focus groups* or individually, depending on the depth and nature of the task involved with the qualitative technique. Focus groups are a data collection tool that gathers the opinions of 6 to 10 people who are carefully selected based on certain demographic, psychographic, or other considerations and brought together to freely discuss various topics of interest at length. A professional research moderator provides questions and probes based on a discussion guide or agenda prepared by the responsible marketing managers to ensure that the right material gets covered. Moderators often, however, follow and lead the discussion at times to track down some potentially useful insight as they attempt to discern the real motivations of consumers and why they are saying and doing certain things. The sessions are typically taped in some fashion, and marketing managers often remain behind one-way mirrors in the room.

Focus groups, like any research technique, can be abused if not conducted carefully.[1] The key for marketers to successfully use any qualitative approaches in a focus group setting is to *listen*. Consumer responses must be interpreted, so it is critical that biases are eliminated as much as possible. On the positive side, many useful insights can emerge from thoughtfully run focus groups. On the negative side, there are questions as to their validity, especially in today's marketing environment. Some researchers believe that consumers have been so bombarded with ads that they unconsciously (or perhaps cynically) parrot what they have already heard rather than what they really think. There is also always a concern that participants are just trying to maintain their self-image and public persona or have a need to identify with the other members of the group. Participants may not be willing to admit in public—or may not even recognize—their behavior patterns and motivations. For all these reasons, participants must feel as relaxed and at ease as possible and feel a strong obligation to speak the truth.

Focus groups may create problems. Researchers at Hill, Holiday, Connors, Cosmopulos Inc. knew they had a problem when a fight broke out between participants at one of their sessions. As one executive noted, "we wondered why people always seemed grumpy and negative—people were resistant to any idea we showed them." The problem was the room itself: cramped, stifling, forbidding. "It was a cross between a hospital room and a police interrogation." To fix the problem, the agency employed the ancient Chinese practice of feng shui.[2]

There is always the "loud mouth" problem as well—when one highly opinionated person drowns out the rest of the group.[3] Moreover, it may be expensive to recruit qualified subjects ($3,000 to $5,000 per group). Even when multiple groups are involved, it may be difficult to generalize the results to a broader population. For example, within the United States, focus group findings often vary from region to region. One New York firm specializing in focus group research claimed that the best city in which to conduct focus groups was Minneapolis because one could get a fairly well-educated sample of people who were honest and forthcoming about their opinions. The firm maintained that other cities could be more useful, however, for special purposes; for example, focus group participants in Houston provided valuable information on underarm deodorants because they were used to having to contend with the relentless heat and humidity of that city. Many marketers interpret focus groups in New York and other Northeastern cities carefully because the people in this area tend to be highly critical and generally do not report that they like much.

[1]Sarah Stiansen, "How Focus Groups Can Go Astray," *Adweek*, 5 December 1988, FK 4–6.
[2]Jeffrey Kasner, "Fistfights and Feng Shui," *Boston Globe*, 21 July 2001, C1-C2.
[3]Leslie Kaufman, "Enough Talk," *Newsweek*, 18 August 1997, 48–49.

1. Who uses the brand? What kind of person?
2. When and where do they use the brand? What types of situations?
3. Why do people use the brand? What do they get out of using it?
4. How do they use the brand? What do they use it for?

Guidelines

The two main issues to consider in conducting free association tasks are how to set up the questions in terms of the types of probes to give to subjects, and how to code and interpret the resulting data. With regard to question structure, in order not to bias results, it is best to move from more general considerations to more specific considerations, as illustrated earlier. Thus, consumers can be asked first what they think of the brand as a whole without reference to any one particular category, followed by specific questions as to particular products and aspects of the brand image. As with many qualitative research techniques, consumers' responses to open-ended probes can be either oral or written. The advantage of oral responses is that subjects may be less deliberate and more spontaneous in their reporting. Figure 9-3 lists one researcher's broad set of guidelines for how to elicit brand associations from consumers.

In terms of coding the data, the protocols provided by each consumer can be divided into phrases and aggregated across consumers in categories. Figure 9-4 provides some examples of possible free associations for some popular brands. Because of their more focused nature, responses to specific probes and follow-up questions are naturally easier to code. In one quantitative approach, Henderson has used network analysis to represent consumer brand associations and uncover the knowledge structures of consumers.[8] Her approach employs a variety of methods to elicit brand associations, such as free elicitation or response and a modified Kelly repertory grid. As applied to branding, use of the Kelly repertory grid involves presenting consumers with a series of brand triads. For each triad, consumers are asked to identify which two brands are most alike, and thus different from the third brand, and then are probed for their reasoning. Consumer responses to these various methods form the dimensions upon which all brands are evaluated. Based on this information, matrices are created with brands and dimensions as both rows and columns. Entries in the matrix thus represent the relationship among and between brands and dimensions. Dimensions can reflect any type of brand association—for example, physical product attributes as well as people, places, and occasions. Network analysis can then be used to reveal a network of associations between all brands and all dimensions.

1. Include at least one visual technique (e.g., moodboard technique of selecting pictures from magazines or newspapers).
2. Include at least one object-projective technique (e.g., describing brand as a car, animal, fabric, vegetable, celebrity, etc.).
3. Probe for secondary associations (e.g., use primary associations as stimulus words for subsequent probing, such as "what do you associate with quality?").
4. Probe for relevant situations in which individuals have experienced the brand or drawn on knowledge about the brand.
5. Address sensory associations directly (e.g., evoke product-related associations of appearance, sound, taste, smell, or feel).
6. Use real stimuli when practically possible (e.g., let consumers sample products or be exposed to a broad set of brand elements).
7. Use established scales for emotional and personality associations.
8. Instruct respondents to take their time and create acceptance for pauses.
9. Assure confidential treatment of responses.
10. Use person-projective techniques (e.g., to mitigate censoring effects, have respondents report associations on behalf of some person or figure belonging to the same group as the respondent).
11. Validate minority associations on a subset of the majority (ensure that responses from verbal respondents are also valid for less verbal respondents by follow-up interview).
12. Criteria of salience and frequency should not be used uncritically (recognize that some words or phrases are easier to report and come to mind more quickly and that this may not always reflect the strength of brand associations).
13. Use a follow-up survey or other methods to determine relationships between strength, favorability, and uniqueness of associations.
14. Elicit associations from different types of customers and from the advertising people (e.g., heavy users, average users, light users, and nonusers).
15. Divide the sample into two and include both users and nonusers (i.e., avoid respondent fatigue and potential "halo" effects).
16. Start with thorough instructions and visual techniques (verbalizations may disrupt visualizations).
17. Adapt to individual differences in response styles and response attitudes (i.e., make sure that the measures fit the sample appropriately).

Source: Magne J. Supphellen, "Understanding Core Brand Equity: Guidelines for In-Depth Elicitation of Brand Associations," *International Journal of Market Research* 42, no. 3 (2001): 319–337.

FIGURE 9-3 Guidelines for In-Depth Elicitation of Brand Associations

Projective Techniques

Uncovering the sources of brand equity requires that consumers' brand knowledge structures be profiled as accurately and completely as possible. Unfortunately, under certain situations, consumers may feel that it would be socially unacceptable or undesirable to express their true feelings—especially to an interviewer who they don't even know! As a result, they may find it easier to fall back on stereotypical, pat answers that they believe would be acceptable or perhaps even expected by the interviewer. This unwillingness or inability to reveal true feelings may be particularly operative when

The North Face
Rugged
Young
Durable
Expert
Expensive
Trendy
Ubiquitous

ESPN
Sports highlights
Great anchors and commentary
Clever commercials
24 hours a day
For men
Extreme sports
Sports leader
Credible

Godiva
Luxury chocolates
Elegant hand-crafted design
Distinctive package
Exquisite taste
European heritage
Special treat
Indulgent
Great gift

Nantucket Nectars
Real juice
Healthy additives
Natural ingredients
High quality
Unique company philosophy
"The Juice Guys"—Tom & Tom
Not mainstream
Community involved
Honest, simple

These free associations are based on responses by students in brand management classes at the Amos Tuck School of Business at Dartmouth College.

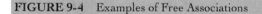

FIGURE 9-4   Examples of Free Associations

consumers are asked about brands characterized by a preponderance of imagery associations. For example, it may be difficult for consumers to admit that a certain brand name product has prestige and enhances their self-image. As a result, consumers may instead refer to some particular product feature as the reason why they like or dislike the brand. Alternatively, it may be that consumers find it difficult to identify and express their true feelings when asked directly *even if they attempt to do so*. For either of these reasons, an accurate portrayal of brand knowledge structures may be impossible without some rather unconventional research methods.

Projective techniques are diagnostic tools to uncover the true opinions and feelings of consumers when they are unwilling or otherwise unable to express themselves on these matters. The idea behind projective techniques is that consumers are presented with an incomplete stimulus and asked to complete it or are given an ambiguous stimulus that may not make sense in and of itself and asked to make sense of it. In doing so, the argument is that consumers will reveal some of their true beliefs and feelings. Thus, projective techniques can be especially useful when deeply rooted personal motivations or personally or socially sensitive subject matters may be involved.

In psychology, the most famous example of a projective technique is the *Rorschach test,* in which ink blots are presented to experimental subjects who are then asked what the ink blots remind them of. In responding, it is believed that subjects reveal certain facets of their own, perhaps subconscious, personality. Projective techniques have a long history in marketing, beginning with the motivation research of the late 1940s and 1950s.[9] A classic marketing example of projective techniques comes from an experiment exploring hidden feelings toward instant coffee conducted by Mason Haire in the late 1940s, summarized in Branding Brief 9-4.[10] Although projective techniques do not always yield as powerful results as in that example, they often provide useful insights that help to assemble a more complete picture of consumers and their relationships with brands. Many kinds of projective techniques are possible. A few are highlighted here.[11]

Completion and Interpretation Tasks

As mentioned previously, classic projective techniques use incomplete or ambiguous stimuli to elicit consumer thoughts and feelings. One such approach is with "bubble exercises" based on cartoons or photos in which different people are depicted buying or using certain products or services. Empty bubbles, as found in cartoons, are placed in the scenes to represent the thoughts, words, or actions of one or more of the participants in the scene. Consumers are then asked to figuratively "fill in the bubble" by indicating what they believe is happening or being said in the scene. The stories and conversations told through bubble exercises and picture interpretations can be especially useful to assess user and usage imagery for a brand. McCann-Erickson ad agency has used a variation of this approach involving figure drawings by consumers to discover hidden thoughts and feelings for different brands.[12]

American Express

In working on the agency's American Express account, McCann-Erickson researchers found in focus groups that consumers did not distinguish their perceptions of gold-card and green-card holders. Follow-up research instructing consumers to produce figure drawings, however, was more insightful. For example, one consumer portrayed a gold-card user as a broad-shouldered man standing in an active position. The green-card user, on the other hand, was drawn as a couch potato in front of a TV set. Based on this drawing and those of others, the agency decided to market the gold card as a "symbol of responsibility for people who have control over their lives and finances."

Comparison Tasks

Another technique that may be useful when consumers are not able to directly express their perceptions of brands is comparison tasks in which consumers are asked to convey their impressions by comparing brands to people, countries, animals, activities, fabrics, occupations, cars, magazines, vegetables, nationalities, or even other brands.[13] For example, consumers might be asked, "If Wheaties cereal were a car, which one would it be? If it were an animal, which one might it be? Looking at the people depicted in these pictures, which ones do you think would be most likely to eat Wheaties?" In each case, consumers could be asked a follow-up question as to why they made the comparison they did. The objects chosen to represent the brand and the reasons they were chosen can provide glimpses into the psyche of the consumer with respect to a brand. In particular, uncovering the types of associations or inferences that these choices reflect can be useful in understanding imagery associations for the brand.

Once Upon a Time . . . You Were What You Cooked

One of the most famous applications of psychographic techniques was by Mason Haire in the 1940s. The purpose of Mason Haire's experiment was to uncover consumers' true beliefs and feelings toward Nescafé instant coffee. The impetus to the experiment was the results of a survey conducted to determine why the initial sales of Nescafé instant coffee were so disappointing. The survey asked subjects if they used instant coffee and, if not, what they disliked about it. The majority of the people who reported that they didn't like the product stated that it was because they didn't like the flavor. On the basis of consumer taste tests, however, Nescafé's management knew that consumers found that the taste of instant coffee was acceptable when they didn't know what type of coffee they were drinking. Suspecting that consumers were not expressing their true feelings, Haire designed a clever experiment to discover what was really going on.

Haire set up two shopping lists containing the same six items. Shopping List 1 specified Maxwell House drip ground coffee, whereas Shopping List 2 specified Nescafé instant coffee, as follows:

Shopping List 1	**Shopping List 2**
Pound and a half of hamburger	Pound and a half of hamburger
2 loaves Wonder bread	2 loaves Wonder bread
Bunch of carrots	Bunch of carrots
1 can Rumford's Baking Powder	1 can Rumford's Baking Powder
Maxwell House coffee (drip ground)	Nescafé instant coffee
2 cans Del Monte peaches	2 cans Del Monte peaches
5 lbs. potatoes	5 lbs. potatoes

Two groups of matched subjects were each given one of the lists and asked to "Read the shopping list. . . . Try to project yourself into the situation as far as possible until you can more or less characterize the woman who bought the groceries." Subjects then wrote a brief description of the personality and character of that person.

After coding the responses into frequently mentioned categories, two starkly different profiles emerged:

	List 1 (Maxwell House)	List 2 (Nescafé)
Lazy	4%	48%
Fails to plan household purchases and schedules well	12%	48%
Thrifty	16%	4%
Not a good wife	0%	16%

Haire interpreted these results as indicating that instant coffee represented a departure from homemade coffee and traditions with respect to caring for one's family. In other words, at that time, the "labor-saving" aspect of instant coffee, rather than being an asset, was a *liability* in that it violated consumer traditions. Consumers were evidently reluctant to admit this fact when asked directly but were better able to express their true feelings when asked to project to another person.

The strategic implications of this new research finding were clear. Based on the original survey results, the obvious positioning for instant coffee with respect to regular coffee would have been to establish a point of difference on "convenience" and a point of parity on the basis of "taste." Based on the projective test findings, however, it was obvious that there also needed to be a point of parity on the basis of user imagery. As a result, a successful ad campaign was launched that promoted Nescafé coffee as a way for housewives to free up time so they could devote additional time for more important household activities.

For example, a Young & Rubicam study found that consumers had the following brand associations when asked to check adjectives and make comparisons based on various probes for four major brands:[14]

PROBE	KENTUCKY FRIED CHICKEN	HOLIDAY INN	BIRD'S EYE	OIL OF OLAY
Personality trait	Ordinary	Friendly	Reliable	Youthful
Animal	Zebra	Mink	Bat	Mink
Activity	Camping	Travel	Cooking	Swimming
Fabric	Denim	Polyester	Cotton	Silk
Occupation	Housewife	Trucker	Housewife	Secretary
Magazine	*TV Guide*	*Business Week*	*Woman's Daily*	*Vogue*

By examining the answers to these various probes, researchers may be better equipped to assemble a rich image for the brand, for example, identifying key brand personality associations.

One study that compared computers to automobile brands found that Dell and Gateway were seen to be the most like Honda, Compaq was most similar to BMW, Packard Bell was seen to be the most like Ford, and IBM was most strongly linked to Cadillac.[15] Branding Brief 9-5 outlines how hotel chain Joie de Vivre uses magazine imagery to clarify its brand positions.

Brand Personality and Values

As defined in Chapter 2, brand personality is the human characteristics or traits that can be attributed to a brand.[16] Brand personality can be measured in different ways. Perhaps the simplest and most direct way is to solicit open-ended responses to a probe such as the following:

> If the brand were to come alive as a person, what would it be like? What would it do? Where would it live? What would it wear? Who would it talk to if it went to a party (and what would it talk about)?

If consumers have difficulty getting started in their descriptions, they can be given an easily understood example or prompt as a guide. For example, consumers could be told

Finding the Good Life at Joie de Vivre

Joie de Vivre Hospitality Inc. operates a chain of boutique hotels, restaurants, and resorts in the San Francisco area. Chip Conley founded the company in 1987 when he purchased a rundown motel in a seedy area of San Francisco and converted it into the Phoenix, a fashionable destination popular among entertainment celebrities. In establishing Joie de Vivre, Conley's goal was "to create a company with hip hotel concepts that appealed to a younger consumer base."

Since the Phoenix, the company has added 19 boutique hotels, 5 restaurants and bars, a day spa, and a resort. Each property's unique décor, quirky amenities, and thematic style are loosely based on popular magazines. Conley explains the design choices for the hotels and resorts as follows:

> What we've learned over time is that people choose their hotels based on the brand as a mirror. So every time we create a new hotel, spa, or resort, we imagine a magazine that defines the hotel. We choose five words that define the magazine, and by doing that, we get the psychographic fit.

For example, the Phoenix is represented by *Rolling Stone*. The five words used by Conley to describe the magazine are "adventurous, hip, irreverent, funky, and young at heart." The Hotel del Sol—a converted motel bearing a yellow exterior and surrounded by palm trees wrapped with festive lights—is described as "kind of *Martha Stewart Living* meets *Islands* magazine." Costanoa, a luxury camping resort that features a lodge, cabins, and tent bungalows as well as room service, is characterized by "*Outside* magazine meets *Metropolitan Home*."

Joie de Vivre hotels strive to combine style and flavor with comfort and service. The boutique concept enables the hotels to offer personal touches for its clients, such as vitamins in place of chocolates on pillows, a standard at the Lambourne in Nob Hill. One of the company's Silicon Valley hotels offers guests high-speed Internet connections in their rooms and by the pool, and several other hotels offer complimentary evening wine hours. Other complimentary amenities at different Joie de Vivre hotels include CD/DVD players in rooms, billiards tables, and afternoon tea service.

In addition to providing comfort considerations, Joie de Vivre creates loyalty among its customers with a dedication to customer service. The company condenses all pertinent service information onto a small laminated card that all employees carry with them while they work. By way of introducing the staff to the guests, the company displays "Host Profiles" at the check-in desk that give useful and interesting information about the employees. Various hotel staff contributed to a set of 20 free guides to San Francisco that guests can use to find out about the city from a local's perspective. Joie de Vivre also developed a loyalty program, called Experience Rewards Club, whereby frequent guests earn redeemable points based on what they spend during each stay at one of the company's properties.

The personal touches and unique personality offered by Joie de Vivre hotels has helped the company build a loyal customer base (see Figure A). One repeat customer

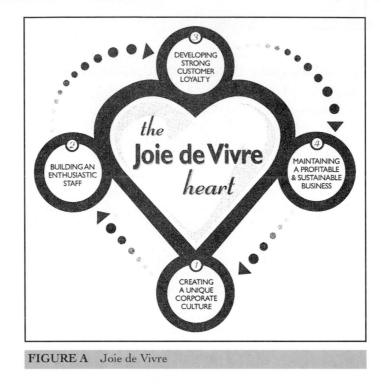

FIGURE A Joie de Vivre

referred to the company's Hotel Rex as "a home-away-from-home." Joie de Vivre now owns the largest number of independent hotel properties in the Bay Area.

Sources: Neal Templin, "Boutique-Hotel Group Thrives on Quirks," *Wall Street Journal*, 18 March 1999; Clifford Carlsen, "Joie de Vivre Resorts to New Hospitality Strategy," *San Francisco Business Times*, 18 June 1999; Chip Conley, *The Rebel Rules* (New York: Fireside, 2001).

that if Campbell's soup were to be described as a person, one possible response might be as follows:[17]

> Mrs. Campbell is a rosy-cheeked and plump grandmother who lives in a warm, cozy house and wears an apron as she cooks wonderful things for her grandchildren.

Other means are possible to capture consumers' points of view. For example, consumers could be given a variety of pictures or a stack of magazines and asked to assemble a profile of the brand. These pictures could be of celebrities or anything else. Along these lines, ad agencies often conduct "picture sorting" studies to clarify who are typical users of a brand. As Chapter 3 noted, brand personality and user imagery may not always agree. When *USA Today* was first introduced, a research study exploring consumer opinions of the newspaper indicated that the benefits of *USA Today* perceived by readers and nonreaders were highly consistent. Similarly, perceptions of the *USA Today* brand personality—as colorful, friendly, and simple—were also highly related. User imagery, however, differed dramatically: Nonreaders viewed a typical *USA Today* reader as a shallow "air head"; readers, on the other hand, saw a typical *USA Today* reader as a well-rounded person interested in a variety of issues. Based on these findings, an advertising campaign was introduced to appeal to nonreaders that showed how prominent people endorsed the newspaper.[18]

The Big Five

Brand personality can be assessed more definitively through adjective checklists or ratings. Stanford's Jennifer Aaker conducted a research project looking at brand personalities that provides an interesting glimpse into the personality of a number of well-known brands, as well as a methodological means to examine the personality of any one brand.[19] Based on an extensive data collection involving ratings of 114 personality traits on 37 brands in various product categories by over 600 individuals representative of the U.S. population, she created a reliable, valid, and generalizable scale of brand personality that reflected the following five factors (with underlying facets) of brand personality:

1. Sincerity (down-to-earth, honest, wholesome, and cheerful)
2. Excitement (daring, spirited, imaginative, and up-to-date)
3. Competence (reliable, intelligent, and successful)
4. Sophistication (upper class and charming)
5. Ruggedness (outdoorsy and tough)

Figure 9-5 depicts the specific trait items that make up the Aaker brand personality scale. Respondents in her study rated how descriptive each personality trait was for each brand according to a seven-point scale (1 = not at all descriptive; 7 = extremely descriptive); responses were then averaged to provide summary measures. Figure 9-6 contains the actual ratings of the 37 brands from the study on the five factors. Note that certain brands tended to be strong on one particular factor (e.g., Campbell's with "sincerity," MTV with "excitement," CNN with "competence," Revlon with "sophistication," and Levi's with "ruggedness"). Other brands (e.g., Hallmark) were high on more than one factor. Some brands (e.g., MCI) scored poorly on all factors. A cross-cultural study exploring the generalizability of this scale outside the United States found that three of the five factors applied in Japan and Spain, but that a "peacefulness" dimension replaced "ruggedness" both in Japan and Spain, and a "passion" dimension emerged in Spain instead of "competency."[20]

Experiential Methods

Increasingly, researchers are attempting to improve the effectiveness of their qualitative approaches as well as go beyond traditional qualitative techniques to research consumers in their natural environment.[21] The rationale is that no matter how clever the research design, consumers may not be able to fully express their true selves as part of a formalized research study. By tapping more directly into their actual home, work, or shopping behaviors, researchers might be able to elicit more meaningful responses from consumers. As markets become more competitive and many brand differences

FIGURE 9-5 Brand Personality Scale Measures

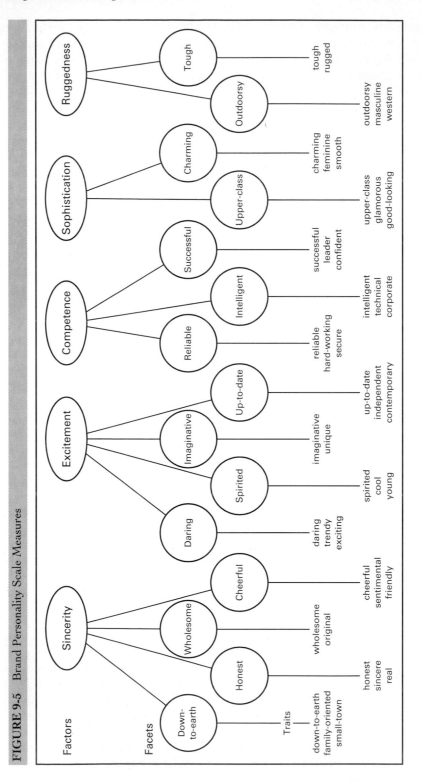

Indexed Profiles of 37 Brand Personalities: Based on the Five Factors

Factor (1–5)

	AT&T	Advil	AMEX	Apple	Avon	Campbell's	Charlie	Cheerios
Sincerity	1.06	.92	.83	.92	1.08	1.25	.83	1.14
Excitement	.91	.72	.83	.95	1.03	.87	.96	.77
Competence	1.15	.95	.99	1.07	1.01	1.01	.77	.88
Sophistication	.85	.75	.87	.86	1.22	.89	1.13	.76
Ruggedness	.94	.90	.83	.92	.92	.93	.77	.84

	CNN	Crest	Diet Coke	ESPN	Guess?	Hallmark	Hershey	IBM
Sincerity	.99	1.09	.94	.99	.88	1.27	1.11	.89
Excitement	1.02	.84	.93	1.10	1.15	1.21	.88	.91
Competence	1.18	.99	.85	1.04	.90	1.12	.89	1.10
Sophistication	.93	.87	.90	.89	1.24	1.31	.96	.84
Ruggedness	1.01	.94	.89	1.23	1.03	.95	.85	.91

	K-Mart	Kodak	LEGO	Lee	Levi's	Lexus	Mattel	McDonald's
Sincerity	1.07	1.10	1.11	1.14	1.20	.87	1.13	1.14
Excitement	.85	.99	1.10	1.00	1.11	1.12	1.10	.97
Competence	.97	1.08	1.01	.99	1.05	1.07	1.04	1.02
Sophistication	.78	.96	.87	1.09	1.13	1.27	.90	1.02
Ruggedness	.91	1.02	1.10	1.34	1.43	1.03	1.13	.90

	MCI	Mercedes	Michelin	MTV	Nike	Oil of Olay	Pepsi	Porsche
Sincerity	.81	.84	.96	.70	.98	1.00	1.02	.71
Excitement	.82	1.07	.86	1.27	1.17	.85	1.04	1.26
Competence	.90	1.06	1.03	.82	1.03	.94	.89	.95
Sophistication	.73	1.31	.82	1.02	1.05	1.17	.95	1.37
Ruggedness	.75	.99	1.20	.93	1.36	.76	.99	1.07

	Reebok	Revlon	Saturn	Sony	Visa			
Sincerity	.94	.96	.96	.87	.90			
Excitement	1.12	1.06	1.05	.94	.87			
Competence	.97	.98	.99	1.02	1.02			
Sophistication	1.00	1.31	1.08	.89	.87			
Ruggedness	1.30	.85	1.00	.90	.87			

FIGURE 9-6   Personality Ratings of Selected Brands

are threatened, any insight that helps to support a stronger brand positioning or create a stronger link to consumers is seen as indispensable (see Branding Brief 9-6).

Advocates of this approach have sent researchers to consumers' homes in the morning to see how they approach their days, have given business travelers Polaroid cameras and diaries to capture their feelings when in hotel rooms, and conducted "beeper studies" in which participants are instructed to write down what they're doing when they are paged.[22] Ogilvy & Mather's Discovery Group has sent researchers into homes with hand-held cameras to get an up-close picture of how people live. Hours of footage are then condensed into documentary-like 30-minute videos to help marketers

Making the Most of Consumer Insights

Marketers frequently emphasize the importance of a consumer focus in developing products and services. Consumer research plays a significant role in uncovering information valuable to consumer-focused companies. David Taylor, director of the Added Value Academy consultancy, cautions that not all findings from consumer research can be considered insights. He defines an insight as "a penetrating, discerning understanding that unlocks an opportunity." An insight holds far more potential than a finding. Using Microsoft as an example, Taylor draws the contrast between the finding that "people need to process more and more information and data" and the insight that "information is the key to power and freedom." This insight would seem to be able to be used by Microsoft to develop products that appeal to a larger consumer base than if the company relied solely on the finding.

Taylor developed a set of criteria to evaluate insights:

- *Fresh:* An insight might be obvious and, in fact, overlooked or forgotten as a result. Check again.
- *Relevant:* An insight when played back to other target consumers should strike a chord.
- *Enduring:* By building on a deep understanding of consumers' beliefs and needs, a true consumer insight should have potential to remain relevant over time.
- *Inspiring:* All the team should be excited by the insight and see different but consistent applications.

Insights can come from consumer research such as focus groups, but may also come from using what Taylor describes as the "core insight drills." A sample of these drills follows:

- How could the brand/category do more to help improve people's lives?
- What do people really value in the category, and what would they not miss?
- What conflicting needs do people have? How can these tradeoffs be solved?
- What bigger market is the brand really competing in from a consumer viewpoint? What could the brand do more of to better meet these "higher-order" needs?
- What assumptions do people make about the market that could be challenged?
- How do people think the product works, and how does it work in reality?
- How is the product used in reality? What other products are used instead of the brand, where the brand could do a better job?

These "drills" can help companies unearth consumer insights that lead to better products and services, and ultimately to stronger brands.

Source: David Taylor, "Drilling for Nuggets: How to Use Insight to Inspire Innovation," *Brand Strategy*, March 2000.

and the agency see how people communicate and interact in different real-life situations.[23] Other firms have adopted similar approaches.

Warner-Lambert

To find out what customers thought of Fresh Burst Listerine, a new mint-flavored product designed to compete with Scope, Warner-Lambert had 37 families set up cameras in their bathrooms to film their routines around the sink. Users of both brands said they rinsed with mouthwash to make their breath smell good, but they treated the products very differently. Scope users gave the product a quick swish and spit it out. Users of the new Listerine, on the other hand, felt obliged to keep the wash in their mouth for a lot longer. Warner-Lambert interpreted the evidence to suggest that Listerine still hadn't shaken its medicinal image.[24]

Red Lobster no longer relies exclusively on focus groups and management approval for new recipes: Chefs now also go into restaurants for up to a month, test new dishes on real customers, and get feedback from the people who cook and serve the meals (e.g., Asian-style lobster rolls were introduced as a result of one such study).[25] Other companies using observational or ethnographic research to study consumers include 3Com (to uncover hidden needs that might be served by an electronic home organizer), Best Western (to learn how seniors decide when and where to shop), and Moen (to observe over an extended time how customers really use their shower devices).[26]

Of special importance to many companies are lead or leading users. For example, some companies in Japan involve high school girls in the product design process because of their track record at being able to predict which products will be successful with consumers of all ages (as well as to create a buzz among teens). Warner-Lambert tapped into a research panel of 500 Japanese high school girls designated as "trend setters" to help choose a new gum flavor in 1995. The girls arrived at a flavor that became Trickle, now one of Japan's best-selling bubble gums.[27] Another company with close ties to leading-edge users is Burton Snowboards.

Burton Snowboards

The best-known snowboard brand, Burton Snowboards, saw its market share increase from 30 percent to 40 percent by focusing on one objective—providing the best equipment to the largest number of snowboarders (see Figure 9-7). To accomplish this goal, Burton's research approach is to focus on the 300 professional riders worldwide, 39 of whom are on its sponsored team. Staff members talk to the riders—on the slopes or on the phone—almost every day, and riders help to design virtually every Burton product. Company researchers immerse themselves in the riders' lives, watching where they shop, what they buy, and what they think about the sport and the equipment. To make sure it doesn't lose touch with its more rank-and-file consumers, however, the company makes sure at least 10 of its 22 U.S. sales representatives hit the slopes on the weekend to interact with amateur snowboarders. Moreover, at any given time, two 35-foot trailers are traveling in North America, six buses are criss-crossing Japan, and four trucks are rumbling through Europe, all with the purpose of testing gear on consumers. Burton also has the eTeam—an online community of 25,000 kids who provide real-time feedback in exchange for free product trials.[28]

FIGURE 9-7   Burton Snowboards

The Internet makes it easier for marketing executives to engage in dialogue with their most involved customers. Lincoln-Mercury's marketing head, Jim Rogers, regularly participates in chat sessions and bulletin board postings on his brand with interested customers, as evident by his following account:

> I began to monitor Edmunds [a leading car buying guide on the Web] about the time the Lincoln LS was launched. I did both monitoring and then later conversing with the participants. I built a relationship in many dimensions—especially when owners had trouble with the vehicle. One high-posting dissatisfied owner is a real problem; so when someone had an evident problem I would contact him or her and find a way to make it right. I ended up getting many cars fixed and even buying back cars in this way—and creating some very happy, loyal customers. Eventually I enlisted the group to help me find dealers who were putting vinyl tops on the LS—and they turned in about ten dealers! Dealers who were pretty surprised when the zone manager turned up the next day to check out the situation. . . . At the on-line group's request, we held a meeting for them in the Irvine CA headquarters in January 2001. We had fifty families turned out for the event. Some came from as far away as Long Island. This meeting spawned the Lincoln LS Owners Club (llsoc.com) which will be an important vehicle to create loyalty to the brand.[29]

Summary

Qualitative research techniques are a creative means of ascertaining consumer perceptions that may otherwise be difficult to uncover. The range of possible qualitative research techniques is limited only by the creativity of the marketing researcher.

Qualitative research also has drawbacks. The in-depth insights that emerge have to be tempered by the realization that the samples involved are often very small and may not necessarily generalize to broader populations. Moreover, given the qualitative nature of the data, there may be questions of interpretation. Different researchers examining the same results from a qualitative research study may draw different conclusions.

QUANTITATIVE RESEARCH TECHNIQUES

Although qualitative measures are useful to identify the range of possible associations to a brand and their characteristics in terms of strength, favorability, and uniqueness, a more definitive portrait of the brand often is desirable to permit more confident and defensible strategic and tactical recommendations. Whereas qualitative research typically elicits some type of verbal response from consumers, quantitative research typically employs various types of scale questions so that numerical representations and summaries can be made. Quantitative measures of brand knowledge can be employed to better assess the depth and breadth of brand awareness; the strength, favorability, and uniqueness of brand associations; the valence of brand responses and feelings; and the extent and nature of brand relationships. Quantitative measures are often the primary ingredient in tracking studies that monitor brand knowledge structures of consumers over time, as discussed in Chapter 8.

Awareness

Recall that brand awareness is related to the strength of the brand in memory, as reflected by consumers' ability to identify various brand elements (i.e., the brand name, logo, symbol, character, packaging, and slogan) under different conditions. Brand awareness relates to the likelihood that a brand will come to mind and the ease with which it does so given different types of cues.

Several measures of awareness of brand elements can be employed.[30] Choosing the appropriate measure depends on the relative importance of brand awareness for consumer behavior in the category and the resulting role it plays in the success of the marketing program for the brand, as discussed in Chapter 2. For example, if research reveals that many consumer decisions are made at the point of purchase, where the brand name, logo, packaging, and so on will be physically present and visible, then brand recognition will be important. If research reveals that consumer decisions are mostly made in settings away from the point of purchase, on the other hand, then brand recall will be more important. As a cautionary note, even though brand recall per se may be viewed as less important when consumer decisions are made at the point of purchase, consumers' brand evaluations and choices will still often depend on what *else* they recall about the brand given that they are able to recognize it there.

Recognition

In the abstract, recognition processes require that consumers be able to discriminate a stimulus—a word, object, image, or whatever—as something they have previously seen. Brand recognition relates to consumers' ability to identify the brand under a variety of circumstances and can involve identification of any of the brand elements. The most basic type of recognition procedure gives consumers a set of individual items visually or orally and asks them if they thought that they have previously seen or heard of these items. To provide a more sensitive test, it is often useful to include decoys or lures—items that consumers could not possibly have seen. In addition to "yes" or "no" responses, consumers can be asked to rate how confident they are in their recognition of an item.

A number of additional, somewhat more subtle, recognition measures involve "perceptually degraded" versions of the brand. In some cases, the brand element may be visually masked or distorted in some way or shown for extremely brief duration. For example, brand name recognition could be tested with missing letters. Figure 9-8 tests your ability to recognize brand names with less than full information. These more subtle measures may be particularly important for brands that have a high level of recognition to provide more sensitive assessments.

Brand recognition is especially important in terms of packaging, and some marketing researchers have used creative means to assess the visibility of package design. As

---

A brand name with a high level of awareness will be recognized under less than ideal conditions. Consider the following list of incomplete names (i.e., word fragments). Which ones do you recognize? Compare your answers to the answer key in the footnote to see how well you did.

1. D _ _ N E _
2. K O _ _ K
3. D U _ A C _ _ _
4. H Y _ T _
5. A D _ _ L
6. M _ T _ E L
7. D _ L T _
8. N _ Q U _ L
9. G _ L L _ T _ _
10. H _ _ S H _ Y
11. H _ L L _ _ R K
12. M _ C H _ _ I N
13. T _ P P _ R W _ _ E
14. L _ G _
15. N _ K _

Answers: (1) Disney; (2) Kodak; (3) Duracell; (4) Hyatt; (5) Advil; (6) Mattel; (7) Delta; (8) NyQuil; (9) Gillette; (10) Hershey; (11) Hallmark; (12) Michelin; (13) Tupperware; (14) Lego; (15) Nike.

FIGURE 9-8   Don't Tell Me, It's on the Tip of My Tongue

a starting point, they consider the benchmark or "best case" of the visibility of a package when a consumer (1) with 20–20 vision (2) is face-to-face with a package (3) at a distance of less than five feet (4) under ideal lighting conditions.

A key question then is whether the package design is robust enough to be still recognizable if one or more of these four conditions are not present. Because shopping is often not conducted under "ideal" conditions, such insights are important. For example, one research study indicated that one of six members of the population who wear eyeglasses do not wear them when shopping in a supermarket.[31] An important question then is whether a package is still able to effectively communicate to consumers under such conditions.

Research methods using tachistoscopes (T-scopes) and eye tracking techniques exist to test the effectiveness of alternative package designs according to a number of specific criteria:

➤ Degree of shelf impact
➤ Impact and recall of specific design elements
➤ Distance at which the package can first be identified
➤ Angle at which the package can first be identified
➤ Speed with which the package can be identified
➤ Perceived package size
➤ Copy visibility and legibility

These additional measures can provide more sensitive measures of recognition than simple "yes" or "no" tasks. By applying these direct and indirect measures of brand recognition, marketers can determine which brand elements exist in memory and, to some extent, the strength of their association. One advantage brand recognition measures have over recall measures is that they can be used in any modality. For example, because brand recognition is often visual in nature, visual recognition measures can be used. It may be difficult for consumers to describe a logo or symbol in a recall task either verbally or pictorially, but much easier for them to assess the same elements visually in a recognition task.

Nevertheless, brand recognition measures only provide an approximation of *potential* recallability. To determine whether the brand elements will actually be recalled under various circumstances, measures of brand recall are necessary.

Recall
Brand recall relates to consumers' ability to identify the brand under a variety of circumstances. With brand recall, consumers must retrieve the actual brand element from memory when given some related probe or cue. Thus, brand recall is a more demanding memory task than brand recognition because consumers are not just given a brand element and asked to identify or discriminate it as one they have or have not already seen.

Different measures of brand recall are possible depending on the type of cues provided to consumers. *Unaided recall* on the basis of "all brands" provided as a cue is likely to identify only the very strongest brands. *Aided recall* uses various types of cues to help consumer recall. One possible sequence of aided recall might use progressively narrower cues—such as product class, product category, and product type labels—to provide insight into the organization of consumers' brand knowledge structures. For example, if recall of the Porsche Boxster (a high-performance German sports car) in non-German markets was of interest, the recall probes could begin with "all cars" and move to more and more narrowly defined categories such as "sports cars," "foreign sports cars," or even "high-performance German sports cars." For example, consumers could be asked: "When you think of foreign sports cars, which brands come to mind?"

Other types of cues may be employed to measure brand recall. For example, consumers could be probed on the basis of product attributes (e.g., "When you think of chocolate, which brands come to mind?) or usage goals (e.g., "If you were thinking of having a healthy snack, which brands come to mind?"). Often, to capture the breadth of brand recall and to assess brand salience, it may be important to examine the context of the purchase decision or consumption usage situation. For example, consumers could be probed according to different purchase motivations as well as different times and places when the product could be used to see which brands came to mind (e.g., different times of the day, days of the week, or times of the year; at home, at work, or on vacation). The more that brands have strong associations to these nonproduct considerations, the more likely it is that they will be recalled when consumers are given those situational cues. Combined, measures of recall based on product attribute or category cues as well as situational or usage cues give an indication of breadth and depth of recall.

Brand recall also can provide some insight into category structure and brand positioning in consumers' minds. Past research has shown that brands tend to be recalled in categorical clusters when consumers are given a general probe. Certain brands are grouped together because they share certain associations and are thus likely to cue and remind consumers of each other if one is recalled.[32] Besides being judged as correctly recalled, brand recall can be further distinguished according to order, as well as latency or speed of recall. In many cases, people will recognize a brand when it is shown to them and will recall it if they are given a sufficient number of cues. Thus, potential recallability is high. The more important issue is the salience of the brand: Do consumers think of the brand under the right circumstances, for example, when they could be either buying or using the product? How quickly do they think of the brand? Is it automatically or easily recalled? Is it the first brand recalled?

Corrections for Guessing

Any research measure must consider the issue of consumers making up responses or guessing. That problem may be especially evident with certain types of aided awareness or recognition measures for the brand. *Spurious awareness* occurs when consumers erroneously claim that they recall something that they really don't and that maybe doesn't even exist. For example, one market research firm, Oxtoby-Smith, conducted a benchmark study of awareness of health and beauty products.[33] In the study, they asked consumers questions like this:

"The following is a list of denture adhesive brand names. Please answer yes if you've heard the name before and no if you haven't. Okay? Orafix? Fasteeth? Dentu-tight? Fixodent?"

Although 16 percent of the sample reported that they had heard of Dentu-Tight, there was one problem: It didn't really exist! Similarly high levels of reported recall were reported for plausible-sounding but fictitious brands such as Four O'Clock Tea (8 percent), Leone Pasta (16 percent), and Mrs. Smith's Cake Mix (31 percent). On the basis of this study, Oxtoby-Smith found that spurious awareness was around 8 percent for new health and beauty products and was even higher in some product categories. In one case, a proposed line extension was mistakenly thought to already exist by about 50 percent of the sample (a finding that no doubt sent a message to the company that they should go ahead and introduce the product!).

From a marketing perspective, the problem with spurious awareness is that it may send misleading signals about the proper strategic direction for a brand. For example, Oxtoby-Smith reported that one of its clients was struggling with a 5 percent market share despite the fact that 50 percent of survey respondents reported that they were aware of the brand. On the surface, it would seem that the recommended strategy would be to improve the image of the brand and attitudes toward it in some way. Upon further examination, it was determined that spurious awareness accounted for *almost half* of the survey respondents who reported brand awareness, suggesting that a more appropriate solution to the true problem would be to first build awareness to a greater degree. Marketers should be sensitive to the possibilities of misleading signals because of spurious brand awareness, especially with new brands or ones with plausible-sounding names.

Strategic Implications

The advantage of aided recall measures is that they yield insight into how brand knowledge is organized in memory and what kind of cues or reminders may be necessary for consumers to be able to retrieve the brand from memory. Understanding recall when different levels of product category specificity are used as cues is important because it has implications for how consideration sets are formed and product decisions are made by consumers.

For example, again take the case of the Porsche Boxster. Assume that consumer recall of this particular car model was fairly low when all cars were considered but very high when foreign sports cars were considered. In other words, consumers strongly categorized the Porsche Boxster as a prototypical sports car but tended to think of it in only that way. If that were the case, for more consumers to entertain the possibility of buying a Porsche Boxster, it might be necessary to broaden the meaning of Porsche so that it had a stronger association to cars in general. Of course, such a strategy would run the risk of alienating existing customers who had been initially attracted by the "purity" and strong identification of the Porsche Boxster as a sports car. Deciding on the appropriate strategy would depend on the relative costs and benefits of targeting the two different segments.

The important point to note is that the category structure that exists in consumers' minds—as reflected by brand recall performance—can have profound implications for consumer choice and marketing strategy, as demonstrated by the Science of Branding 9-2. The insights gleaned from measuring brand recall are also valuable for developing brand identity and integrated marketing communication programs, as Chapters 4 and 6 showed. For example, brand recall can be examined for each brand element to explore the extent to which any one brand element (the name, symbol, logo, etc.) suggests another brand element. In other words, is it the case that consumers are aware of all the different brand elements and understand how they relate?

In addition to obtaining a thorough understanding of brand awareness, it is important to gain a complete understanding of brand image, as covered in the following section.

THE SCIENCE OF BRANDING 9-2

Understanding Categorical Brand Recall

An experiment by Prakash Nedungadi provides a compelling demonstration of the importance of understanding the category structure that exists in consumer memory, as well as the value of strategies for increasing the recallability or accessibility of brands during choice situations.[1] As a preliminary step in his research study, Nedungadi first examined the category structure for fast food restaurants that existed in consumers' minds. He found that a "major subcategory" was "hamburger chains" and a "minor subcategory" was "sandwich shops." He also found, on the basis of usage and linking surveys, that within the major subcategory of national hamburger chains, a major brand was McDonald's and a minor brand was Wendy's, and within the minor subcategory of local sandwich shops, a major brand was Joe's Deli (a brand in his survey area) and a minor brand was Subway. Consistent with this reasoning, in an unaided recall and choice task, consumers were more likely to remember and select a brand from a major subcategory than from a minor subcategory and, within a subcategory, a major brand rather than a minor brand.

Nedungadi next looked at the effects of different brand "primes" on subsequent choices among the four fast food restaurants. Brands were primed by having subjects in the experiment first answer a series of seemingly unrelated questions—including some questions about the brand to be primed—before making their brand selections. Because of this initial exposure, a target brand was "primed" in memory and therefore potentially more accessible during the choice task. Two key findings emerged. First, a major brand that was primed was more likely to be selected in the later choice task even though the attitudes toward the brand were no different from those of a control group. In other words, merely making the brand more accessible in memory increased the likelihood that it would be chosen *independent of any differences in brand attitude.* Second, priming a minor brand in a minor subcategory actually benefited the *major* brand in that subcategory more. In other words, by drawing attention to the minor subcategory of sandwich shops—which could easily be overlooked—the minor brand, Subway, indirectly primed the major brand, Joe's Deli, in the subcategory. The implications of his research are that marketers must understand how consumers' memory is organized and, as much as possible, ensure that the proper cues and primes are evident to prompt brand recall.

---

[1] Prakash Nedungadi, "Recall and Consumer Consideration Sets: Influencing Choice without Altering Brand Evaluations," *Journal of Consumer Research* 17 (December 1990): 263–276.

Image

One vitally important aspect of the brand is its image, as reflected by the associations that consumers hold regarding the brand. Strong, favorable, and unique associations provide the foundation for customer-based brand equity. As noted earlier in this chapter, as well as in Chapter 2, brand associations come in many different forms and can be classified along many different dimensions. It is useful to make a distinction between lower-level considerations related to consumer perceptions of specific performance and imagery attributes and benefits versus higher-level considerations related to over-all judgments, feelings, attitudes, and behaviors. As noted in Chapter 2, there is an obvious relationship between the two levels because consumers' overall responses and relationship with a brand typically depend on perceptions of specific attributes and benefits of that brand. This section considers some issues in measuring lower-level brand performance and imagery associations.

Beliefs are descriptive thoughts that a person holds about something (e.g., a particular software package has many helpful features and menus and is easy to use).[34] Brand association beliefs are those specific attributes and beliefs linked to the brand and its competitors. Chapter 2 provided a structured set of measures to tap into performance and imagery associations. The qualitative research approaches described previously are useful in uncovering the different types of specific brand associations making up the brand image. To better understand their potential contribution to brand equity, the belief associations that are identified need to be assessed on the basis of one or more of the three key dimensions—strength, favorability, and uniqueness—making up the sources of brand equity.

As a first cut, open-ended measures could be employed, as noted earlier, that tap into the strength, favorability, and uniqueness of brand associations, as follows:

1. What are the strongest associations you have to the brand? What comes to mind when you think of the brand? (Strength)
2. What is good about the brand? What do you like about the brand? What is bad about the brand? What do you dislike about the brand? (Favorability)
3. What is unique about the brand? What characteristics or features does the brand share with other brands? (Uniqueness)

To provide more specific insights, these belief associations could be rated on scales according to strength, favorability, and uniqueness, as Figure 9-9 illustrates with Lipton iced tea.

Any potentially relevant association can and should be measured, including performance-related attributes and benefits—such as (where appropriate) primary characteristics and supplementary features; product reliability and durability; service effectiveness, efficiency, and empathy; style and design; and price—as well as imagery—related attributes and benefits related to user profiles; purchase and usage situations; brand personality and values; and history, heritage, and experiences. Indirect tests also can be employed to assess the derived importance and favorability of these brand associations (e.g., through multivariate regression techniques).

Scaling Considerations

There are many possible ways to ask these questions and actually scale these brand beliefs and perceptions. Generally, scales take the form of semantic differential (bipolar adjectives) or Likert-type scales, but all types are possible. Moreover, different scales can be constructed depending on the decisions taken with respect to a number of considerations, such as the following:

➤ Absolute or comparative scales
➤ Verbal, numerical, or spatial scales
➤ Number of points on the scale (e.g., whether they should be odd or even)

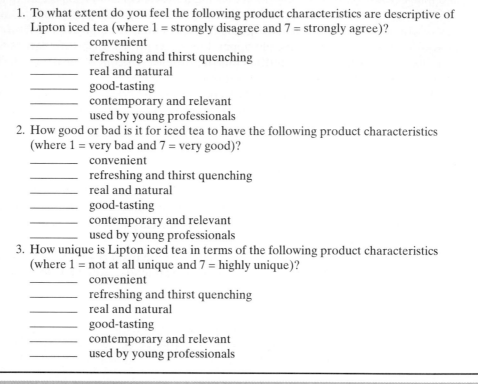

1. To what extent do you feel the following product characteristics are descriptive of
   Lipton iced tea (where 1 = strongly disagree and 7 = strongly agree)?
   _____ convenient
   _____ refreshing and thirst quenching
   _____ real and natural
   _____ good-tasting
   _____ contemporary and relevant
   _____ used by young professionals
2. How good or bad is it for iced tea to have the following product characteristics
   (where 1 = very bad and 7 = very good)?
   _____ convenient
   _____ refreshing and thirst quenching
   _____ real and natural
   _____ good-tasting
   _____ contemporary and relevant
   _____ used by young professionals
3. How unique is Lipton iced tea in terms of the following product characteristics
   (where 1 = not at all unique and 7 = highly unique)?
   _____ convenient
   _____ refreshing and thirst quenching
   _____ real and natural
   _____ good-tasting
   _____ contemporary and relevant
   _____ used by young professionals

FIGURE 9-9   Example of Brand Association Ratings in Terms of Strength, Favorability, and
Uniqueness

➤ Balanced or unbalanced scales
➤ Treatment of "no opinion" or "don't know" responses in the scale

Much research has considered the implications of these and other methodological
choices. For example, Barnard and Ehrenberg experimentally examined three different measures of consumer beliefs about different attributes:[35]

1. *Free choice:* On an attribute-by-attribute basis, subjects indicated which one or ones of a list
   of brands possessed the attribute.
2. *Scaling:* Subjects indicated the association of a brand with an attribute by ticking a box on a
   five-step scale from "agree a lot" to "disagree a lot," with a "no opinion" box provided.
3. *Ranking:* Subjects rank-ordered the different brands according to how closely associated
   they were with an attribute.

The researchers found that the three measurement approaches placed the brands in
roughly the same relative positions on each attribute dimension, suggesting that the
choice between absolute and comparative scales may not have been that critical in
measuring brand beliefs, at least in this particular context. For detailed discussion of
these more specific scaling or survey issues, however, it is necessary to consult a good
marketing research text.[36]

Other Approaches

A more complicated quantitative technique to assess overall brand uniqueness is multidimensional scaling, or perceptual maps. *Multidimensional scaling* (MDS) is a procedure for determining the perceived relative images of a set of objects, such as products or brands. MDS transforms consumer judgments of similarity or preference into distances represented in perceptual space. For example, if brands A and B are judged by respondents to be the most similar of a set of brands, the MDS algorithm will position brands A and B so that the distance between them in multidimensional space is smaller than the distance between any other two pairs of brands. Respondents may base their similarity between brands on any basis—tangible or intangible.[37]

European academic branding experts Kapferer and Laurent have proposed a related scale to measure the brand sensitivity of a product class as a whole.[38] They characterize brand sensitivity in terms of the relationship among brands for a given consumer in a given product class, particularly with respect to comparisons between national brands versus unbranded products or private labels in that product class. The types of items in their scale are displayed in Figure 9-10. According to their approach, the strength of a brand is reflected by the number of its customers who are brand sensitive. Brand sensitivity can be seen as a potential proxy for or measure of brand uniqueness. In other words, if consumers are not brand sensitive for a category as a whole, it is unlikely that any one specific brand will be unique.

FIGURE 9-10   Kapferer and Laurent's Brand Sensitivity Measure

---

Direct Questions
Forced choice between two items

1. For PRODUCT . . .
   "I prefer to buy a well known brand" or
   "I don't mind buying the store brand"

Four Likert items

2. "When I buy a PRODUCT, I look at the brand."
3. "I do not choose a PRODUCT according to the brand."
4. "For a PRODUCT, the brand name is not that important."
5. "When I buy a PRODUCT, I take account of the brand."

Indirect Measures

6. A dollarmetric measure involving three well-known brands: the last brand purchased by consumer in the product category and the first other two brands mentioned in a spontaneous brand awareness question. Would the consumer maintain his/her choice if the price differential increased by 10 percent, 25 percent, 50 percent between the chosen brand and the other two competitors?
7. A dollarmetric measure between the last brand bought by consumer and a private label or store brand in the product category.
8. A mini-information display board choice task. Five brands and five product attributes (including brand name and price) were included in a grid and consumers were asked to choose a brand. Brand sensitivity was indicated by usage of the brand name attribute in making the choice.

Brand Responses

The purpose of measuring more general, higher-level considerations is to find out how consumers combine all of the more specific, lower-level considerations about the brand in their minds to form different types of brand responses and evaluations. Chapter 2 provided examples of measures of key brand judgments (i.e., brand quality, credibility, consideration, and superiority) and feelings (i.e., warm, fun, exciting, sense of security, social approval, and self-respect). The Science of Branding 9-3 provides additional insight into brand attitudes and judgment.

Purchase Intentions

Another set of possible measures closely related to brand attitudes and consideration is purchase intentions.[39] Intention measures could focus on the likelihood of buying the brand or the likelihood of switching from the brand to another brand. Research in psychology suggests that purchase intentions are most likely to be predictive of actual purchase when there is correspondence between the two in the following categories:[40]

➤ Action (e.g., buying for own use or to give as a gift)
➤ Target (e.g., specific type of product and brand)
➤ Context (e.g., in what type of store based on what prices and other conditions)
➤ Time (e.g., within a week, month, or year)

In other words, when asking consumers to forecast their likely purchase of a product or a brand, it is important to specify *exactly* the circumstances involved—the purpose of the purchase, the location of the purchase, the time of the purchase, and so forth. For example, consumers could be asked,

"Assume your refrigerator broke down over the next weekend and could not be inexpensively repaired. If you went to your favorite appliance store and found all the different brands competitively priced, how likely would you be to buy a General Electric refrigerator?"

Consumers could indicate their purchase intention on a 11-point probability scale that ranges from 0 (definitely would not buy) to 10 (definitely would buy).

Brand Relationships

Chapter 2 characterized brand relationships in terms of brand resonance and offered possible measures for each of the four key dimensions: behavioral loyalty, attitudinal attachment, sense of community, and active engagement. This section considers several additional considerations with respect to those dimensions.

Behavioral Loyalty

To capture reported brand usage and behavioral loyalty, consumers could be asked several questions directly. Alternatively, consumers could be asked what percentage of their last purchases in the category went to the brand (past purchase history) and what

Understanding Brand Attitudes

There are several different ways to conceptualize or model attitudes. Two such ways with clear branding implications are highlighted here. One view takes the position that consumers form attitudes because they provide a function of some kind for a person. Daniel Katz, a social psychologist, developed a functional theory of attitudes to account for the different types of roles that attitudes can play.[1] He identified four main functions:

1. The *utilitarian function* deals with attitudes formed on the basis of rewards and punishments.
2. The *value-expressive function* deals with attitudes formed to express an individual's central value or self-concept.
3. The *ego-defensive function* deals with attitudes formed to protect an individual from either external threats or internal feelings of insecurity.
4. The *knowledge function* deals with attitudes formed to satisfy an individual's need for order, structure, and meaning.

Consumers thus form attitudes toward brands to provide the function they are seeking. In this way, they might like and use certain brands because they satisfy their needs (utilitarian function), allow themselves to express their personality (value-expressive function), bolster a perceived weakness they have (ego-defensive function), or simplify decision making (knowledge function).

Perhaps the most widely accepted approach to actually modeling attitudes is based on a multi-attribute formulation, in which brand attitudes are seen as a function of the associated attributes and benefits that are salient for the brand. Fishbein and Ajzen have proposed what has been probably the most influential multi-attribute model.[2] As applied to marketing, this *expectancy-value model* views brand attitudes as a multiplicative function of (1) the salient beliefs that a consumer has about the brand (i.e., the extent to which consumers think that the brand possesses certain attributes or benefits) and (2) the evaluative judgment regarding those beliefs (i.e., how good or bad it is that the brand possesses those attributes or benefits). Thus, overall brand attitudes depend on the strength of association between the brand and salient attributes or benefits and the favorability of those beliefs.

According to the multi-attribute model, belief strength can be measured by having consumers rate the probability that the brand possesses each of the salient attributes or benefits, as follows.

HOW LIKELY IS THAT COLGATE TOOTHPASTE FIGHTS TOOTH DECAY?

Extremely Unlikely   1 2 3 4 5 6 7   Extremely Likely

Similarly, belief evaluations can be measured by having consumers rate the favorability of the salient attributes or benefits.

HOW GOOD OR BAD IS IT THAT COLGATE TOOTHPASTE FIGHTS TOOTH DECAY?

Very Bad   -3 -2 -1 0 1 2 3   Very Good

Overall brand attitudes are then the sum of each attribute belief strength multiplied by its favorability. Fishbein and Ajzen also developed the theory of reasoned action to extend the multi-attribute model to include interpersonal, social effects. According to the theory, attitudes toward brands can also depend on consumers' beliefs about other people's opinions as well as consumers' motivation to comply with these other people's wishes.

Brand attitudes and judgments can vary in their strength. Attitude strength has been measured in psychology by the reaction time to evaluative queries about the attitude object: Individuals who can evaluate an attitude object quickly are assumed to have a highly accessible attitude.[3] Research has shown that attitudes formed from direct behavior or experience are more accessible than attitudes based on information or other indirect forms of behavior.[4] Highly accessible brand attitudes are more likely to be activated spontaneously upon exposure to the brand and to guide subsequent brand choices.[5]

Because of the embedded meaning that they contain, abstract associations such as attitudes, or even benefits to some extent, tend to be inherently more evaluative than attributes. Because of this evaluative nature, more abstract associations can be more durable and accessible in memory than the underlying attribute information.[6] Moreover, brand attitudes may be stored and retrieved in memory separately from the underlying attribute information.[7] In fact, Claremont's Peter Farquhar believes that one key element of brand equity is attitude accessibility.[8] Attitude accessibility can be measured on a microcomputer by seeing how long it takes a consumer to indicate his or her brand evaluation ratings. Although these differences may be in microseconds, they may still be significant managerially.

---

[1]Daniel Katz, "The Functional Approach to the Study of Attitudes," *Public Opinion Quarterly* 24 (1960): 163–204.

[2]Martin Fishbein and Icek Ajzen, *Belief, Attitude, Intention, and Behavior: An Introduction to Theory and Research* (Reading, MA: Addison-Wesley, 1975); Icek Ajzen and Martin Fishbein, *Understanding Attitudes and Predicting Social Behavior* (Englewood Cliffs, NJ: Prentice Hall, 1980).

[3]Russell H. Fazio, David M. Sanbonmatsu, Martha C. Powell, and Frank R. Kardes, "On the Automatic Activation of Attitudes," *Journal of Personality and Social Psychology* 50 (February 1986): 229–238.

[4]Russell H. Fazio and Mark Zanna, "Direct Experiences and Attitude Behavior Consistency," in *Advances in Experimental Social Psychology*, Vol. 14, ed. Leonard Berkowitz (New York: Academic Press, 1981), 161–202.

[5]Ida E. Berger and Andrew A. Mitchell, "The Effect of Advertising on Attitude Accessibility," *Journal of Consumer Research* 16 (December 1989): 280–288; Russell H. Fazio, Martha C. Powell, and Carol J. Williams, "The Role of Attitude Accessibility in the Attitude and Behavior Process," *Journal of Consumer Research* 16 (December 1989): 288–316.

[6]Amitava Chattopadhyay and Joseph W. Alba, "The Situational Importance of Recall and Inference in Consumer Decision Making," *Journal of Consumer Research* 15 (June 1988): 1–12.

[7]John G. Lynch Jr., Howard Mamorstein, and Michael Weigold, "Choices from Sets Including Remembered Brands: Use of Recalled Attributes and Prior Overall Evaluations," *Journal of Consumer Research* 15 (September 1988): 169–184.

[8]Peter H. Farquhar, "Managing Brand Equity," *Marketing Research* 1 (September 1989): 24–33.

---

percentage of their planned next purchases will go the brand (intended future purchases). For example, the marketers or brand managers of Fuji film might ask the following questions:

➤ Which brand of film do you usually buy?

➤ Which brand of film did you buy last time?

➤ Do you have any film on hand? Which brand?

➤ Which brands of film did you consider buying?

➤ Which brand of film will you buy next time?

➤ Do you expect to take pictures in the next two weeks?

➤ Have you taken any pictures in the last two weeks?

These types of questions can provide information on brand attitudes and usage for Fuji, including potential gaps with competitors and which other brands might be in the consideration set at the time of purchase.

These measures could be open ended, dichotomous (forcing consumers to choose a brand), or involve multiple choice or rating scales. The answers to these types of questions also could be compared with actual measures of consumer behavior to assess whether consumers are accurate in their predictions. For example, if 30 percent of consumers reported, on average, that they thought they would take pictures in the next two weeks, but only 15 percent of consumers reported two weeks later that they actually had taken pictures during that period, then Fuji brand managers might need to devise strategies to better convert intentions to actual behavior.

Brand Substitutability

Industry consultants Longman and Moran have developed a measure of *substitutability* related to brand behaviors that they see as a key source of brand equity.[41] Their measure is based on a scale produced by the answers to two questions:

1. Which brand did you buy last time?
2. If the brand had not been available, what would you have done (i.e., waited, gone to another store, or bought another brand—and, if another brand, which one)?

Based on their responses, consumers are placed into one of six segments, which are assumed to be of decreasing value for the brand:

1. People who bought your brand last time and who would have waited or gone to another store to buy your brand
2. People who bought your brand last time but would have accepted any other brand as a substitute
3. People who bought your brand last time but specified a particular other brand as a substitute
4. People who bought another brand last time but named your brand as a possible substitute
5. People who bought another brand last time and did not name your brand as a substitute
6. People who bought another brand last time and would have waited or gone to another store to buy that brand

Longman and Moran view repeat rate—how many of the people who bought a particular brand last time would buy it again this time—as a key indicator of brand equity: The higher the repeat rate, the greater the brand equity and the greater the marketing profitability; the less that people are willing to accept substitute brands, the more that they are likely to repeat buy.

Other Brand Resonance Dimensions

Although attitudinal attachment may require a fairly straightforward set of questions, both sense of community and active engagement could involve more varied measures because a more diverse set of issues may be involved. As marketing programs create more and more contact points with potential or existing customers, it will become increasingly important to assess how consumers are connecting or relating to the various elements of marketing programs.

For example, in terms of engagement, measures could explore word-of-mouth behavior, online behavior, and so forth in depth. For online behavior, measures could explore the extent of customer-initiated interactions versus firm-initiated interactions, the extent of learning and teaching by the customer versus the firm, the extent of customers teaching other customers, and so on.[42] The key to such metrics is the qualitative nature of the interaction and how it reflects intensity of feelings. One mistake made by many Internet firms was to put too much emphasis on "eyeballs" and "stickiness"—the number and duration of page views at a Web site, respectively. The depth of the underlying brand relationships of the customers making those visits, however, and the manner in which those relationships manifest themselves in brand-beneficial actions will typically be more important.

Review

According to the brand value chain, sources of brand equity arise from the customer mindset. In general, measuring sources of brand equity requires that the brand manager fully understand how customers shop for and use products and services and, most important, what customers know, think, and feel about various brands. In particular, measuring sources of customer-based brand equity requires measuring various aspects

I. Qualitative Research Techniques
  Free association
  Adjective ratings and checklists
  Projective techniques
  Photo sorts
  Bubble drawings
  Story telling
  Personification exercises
  Role playing
  Experiential methods
II. Quantitative Research Techniques
  A. Brand Awareness
    Direct and indirect measures of brand recognition
    Aided and unaided measures of brand recall
  B. Brand Image
    Open-ended and scale measures of specific brand attributes and benefits
      Strength
      Favorability
      Uniqueness
    Overall judgments and feelings
    Overall relationship measures
      Intensity
      Activity

FIGURE 9-11 Summary of Qualitative and Quantitative Measures

of brand awareness and brand image that potentially can lead to the differential customer response that creates brand equity.

This chapter described both qualitative and quantitative approaches to measure consumers' brand knowledge structures and identify potential sources of brand equity, that is, measures to capture the customer mindset. Qualitative research techniques are a means to identify possible brand associations. Quantitative research techniques are a means to better approximate the breadth and depth of brand awareness; the strength, favorability, and uniqueness of brand associations; the favorability of brand responses; and the nature of brand relationships. Because of their unstructured nature, qualitative measures are especially well suited to provide an in-depth glimpse of what brands and products means to consumers. To obtain more precise and generalizable information, however, quantitative scale measures are typically employed.

Figure 9-11 summarizes some of the different types of measures that were discussed in the chapter.

Discussion Questions

1. Pick a brand. Employ projective techniques to attempt to identify sources of its brand equity. Which measures work best? Why?
2. Run an experiment to see if you can replicate the Mason Haire instant coffee experiment (see Branding Brief 9-4). Do the same attributions still hold? If not, can you replace coffee with a brand combination from another product category that would produce pronounced differences?
3. Pick a product category. Can you profile the brand personalities of the leading brands in the category using Aaker's brand personality inventory?
4. Pick a brand. How would you best profile consumers' brand knowledge structures? How would you use quantitative measures?
5. Think of your brand relationships. Can you find examples of brands that fit into Fournier's different categories (see Brand Focus 9.0)?

Brand Focus 9 . 0

Harvard Research into Consumers and Brands

Researchers at the Harvard Business School have conducted path-breaking research into consumers and brands over the years. This appendix highlights two recent advances.

ZALTMAN METAPHOR ELICITATION TECHNIQUE

One interesting new approach to better understand how consumers view brands is the Zaltman Metaphor Elicitation Technique (ZMET).[43] ZMET is based on a belief that consumers often have subconscious motives for their purchasing behavior. "A lot goes on in our minds that we're not aware of," said Harvard Business School professor Jerry Zaltman. "Most of what influences what we say and do occurs below the level of awareness. That's why we need new techniques to get at hidden knowledge—to get at what people don't know they know." To access this hidden knowledge, he developed the Zaltman Metaphor Elicitation Technique. As worded in its U.S. patent, ZMET is "a technique for eliciting interconnected constructs that influence thought and behavior." The word *construct* refers to "an abstraction created by the researcher to capture common ideas, concepts, or themes expressed by customers." For example, the construct "ease of use" might capture the statements "simple to operate," "works without hassle," and "you don't really have to do anything."

ZMET stems from knowledge and research from varied fields such as "cognitive neuroscience, neurobiology, art critique, literary criticism, visual anthropology, visual sociology, semiotics, . . . art therapy, and psycholinguistics." The technique is based on the idea that "most social communication is nonverbal" and as a result approximately two-thirds of all stimuli received by the brain are visual. Using ZMET, Zaltman teases out consumers' hidden thoughts and feelings about a particular topic, which often can be expressed best using visual metaphors. Zaltman defines a metaphor as "a definition of one thing in terms of another, [which] people can use . . . to represent thoughts that are tacit, implicit, and unspoken."

A ZMET study starts with a group of participants who are asked in advance to select a minimum of 12 images from their own sources (e.g., magazines, catalogs, and family photo albums) that represent their thoughts and feelings about the research topic. The participants bring these images with them for a personal one-on-one interview with a study administrator who uses advanced interview techniques to explore the images with the participant and reveal hidden meanings through a "guided conversation." Finally, the participants use a computer program to create a collage with these images that communicates their subconscious thoughts and feelings about the topic. The findings are compiled in an interactive multimedia computer application. The guided conversation consists of a series of steps that includes some or all of the following:

1. *Story telling:* Participants describe the content of each picture.
2. *Missed images:* Participants describe the picture or pictures that he or she was unable to obtain and explain their relevance.

3. *Sorting task:* Participants sort pictures into meaningful groups and provide a label or description for each group.

4. *Construct elicitation:* Participants reveal basic constructs and their interconnections using images as stimuli through the Kelly repertory grid and laddering techniques (described in Chapter 3).

5. *The most representative picture:* Participants indicate which picture is most representative.

6. *Opposite images:* Participants indicate pictures that describe the opposite of the brand or the task that they were given.

7. *Sensory images:* Participants indicate what does and does not describe the concept in terms of color, emotion, sound, smell, taste, and touch.

8. *Mental map:* After reviewing all of the constructs discussed and asking participants if the constructs are accurate representations of what was meant and if any important ideas are missing, participants create a map or causal model connecting the constructs that have been elicited.

9. *Summary image:* Participants create a summary image or montage using their own images (sometimes augmented by images from an image bank) to express important issues. Digital imaging techniques may be employed to facilitate the creation of the image.

10. *Vignette:* Participants put together a vignette or short video to help communicate important issues.

Once the participants' interviews are completed, researchers identify key themes or constructs, code the data, and assemble a consensus map involving the most important constructs. Quantitative analyses of the data can provide information for advertising, promotions, and other marketing mix decisions. ZMET has been applied in a variety of different ways, including as a means to help understand consumers' images of brands, products, and companies. Marketers can employ ZMET for a variety of con-

sumer-insight research topics. Zaltman lists several of these:

> ZMET is useful in understanding consumers' images of brands, products, and companies, brand equity, product concepts and designs, product usage and purchase experiences, life experiences, consumption context, and attitudes toward business.

For example, DuPont enlisted Zaltman to research women's attitudes toward hosiery. Conventional research yielded the conclusion that "women mostly hated wearing pantyhose," but DuPont market researchers were not convinced that this conclusion provided a complete picture. Zaltman used ZMET with 20 subjects in order to uncover deeper answers to the question: "What are your thoughts and feelings about buying and wearing pantyhose?" He discovered that women had a "like-hate" relationship with pantyhose; they disliked the discomfort and run—proneness of pantyhose but liked the feel of elegance and sexiness they got from wearing it. This discovery prompted a number of hosiery manufacturers to include more sexy and alluring imagery in their advertising.

Zaltman also used ZMET to study a group of executives enrolled in an executive-education program, with the question "What are your thoughts and feelings about being customer-focused?" Beyond the anticipated results—that customer focus means "collecting information, analyzing data, anticipating customer needs"—the research revealed that customer focus also connotes integrity, trust, and authenticity. Other companies to employ ZMET include AT&T, Coca-Cola, Eastman Kodak, and Reebok. Figure 9-12 displays a consensus map that emerged from a study of intimate apparel.

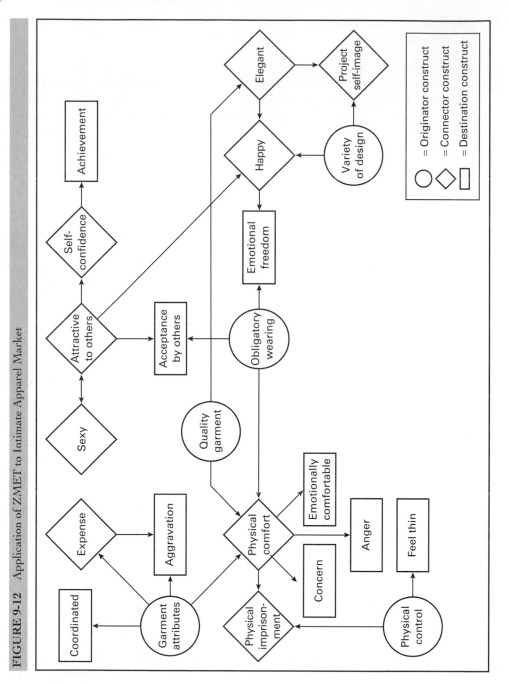

FIGURE 9-12   Application of ZMET to Intimate Apparel Market

BRAND RELATIONSHIPS

Taking the brand personality concept to the next level, and building upon momentum in marketing for the study of relationships, Harvard's Susan Fournier has reframed brand personality in relationship terms.[44] Fournier views brand personality not as a set of interpersonal attributes, but as the relationship role enacted by the brand in its partnership with the consumer. She has proposed a number of interesting ideas concerning brand equity by developing a framework for conceptualizing and understanding the relationships that consumers form with the brands they know and use.

Fournier argues that brands can and do serve as viable relationship partners, and suggests a reconceptualization of the notion of brand personality within this framework. Specifically, Fournier suggests that the everyday execution of marketing mix decisions constitutes a set of behaviors enacted on the part of the brand. These actions trigger a series of inferences regarding the implicit *contract* that appears to guide the engagement of the consumer and brand and, hence, the type of relationship that is formed. Brand personality as conceptualized within this framework concerns the *relationship role* enacted by the brand in its partnership capacity. For example, if the brand expresses behaviors that signal commitment to the consumer, and further if it sends gifts as symbols of affection, the consumer may infer a courtship or marriage type of engagement with the brand. Fournier identifies a typology of 15 different relationship types characterizing consumers' engagement with brands (see Figure 9-13). Fournier argues that this relationship role view of brand personality provides more actionable guidance to managers who wish to create and manage their brand personalities in line with marketing actions than does the trait-based view, which concerns general personality tendencies that might or might not be connected to marketing strategies and goals.

Fournier has conducted fascinating research that reframes the conceptualization and measurement of brand strength strictly in relationship terms. Here, a brand's strength is defined in terms of the strength, depth, and durability of the consumer-brand relational bond using the multifaceted concept of brand relationship quality, or BRQ. Extensive validation work supported a multifaceted hierarchical structure for the BRQ construct that includes six main dimensions of relationship strength, many with important subfacets. The main facets are (1) interdependence, (2) self-concept connection, (3) commitment, (4) love/passion, (5) intimacy, and (6) brand partner quality. Fournier argues that these facets and their subfacets (e.g., trust within the partner quality facet or consumer-to-firm and firm-to-consumer intimacy) have superior diagnostic value over competing strength measures, and she suggests they have greater managerial utility in their application. In her experience, BRQ measures have been successfully incorporated in brand tracking studies, where they provide profiles of brand strength vis-à-vis competitors, useful ties to marketplace performance indicators, and specific guidance for the enhancement and dilution of brand equity through managerial actions in the marketplace. Although brand relationship quality has many commonalities with brand resonance, it provides valuable additional perspectives and insights.

The six main facets of brand relationship quality are as follows.

➤ *Interdependence:* The degree to which the brand is ingrained in the consumer's daily course of living, both behaviorally (i.e., in terms of frequency, scope, and strength of interactions) and cognitively (i.e., in terms of longing for and preoccupation with anticipated brand interactions). Interdependence is often revealed through the presence

FIGURE 9-13 A Typology of Consumer-Brand Relationships

Relationship Form	Case Examples
Arranged marriage: Nonvoluntary union imposed by preferences of third party. Intended for long-term, exclusive commitment.	Karen's husband's preferred brands (e.g., Mop 'n Glo, Palmolive, Hellman's); Karen's Esteé Lauder, imposed through gift-giving; Jean's use of Murphy's Oil Soap as per manufacturer recommendation.
Casual friend/buddy: Friendship low in affect and intimacy, characterized by infrequent or sporadic engagement and few expectations of reciprocity or reward.	Karen and her household cleaning brands.
Marriage of convenience: Long-term, committed relationship precipitated by environmental influence rather than deliberate choice, and governed by satisficing rules.	Vicki's switch to regional Friend's Baked Beans brand from favored B&M brand left behind; Jean's loyalty to DeMoulas salad dressing brand left behind by client at the bar.
Committed partnership: Long-term, voluntarily imposed, socially supported union high in love, intimacy, trust, and commitment to stay together despite adverse circumstances. Adherence to exclusivity rules expected.	Jean and virtually all her cooking, cleaning, and household appliance brands; Karen and Gatorade.
Best friendship: Voluntary union based on reciprocity principle, the endurance of which is ensured through continued provision of positive rewards. Characterized by revelation of true self, honesty, and intimacy. Congruity in partner images and personal interests common.	Karen and Reebok running shoes.; Vicki and Crest or Ivory.
Compartmentalized friendship: Highly specialized, situationally confined, enduring friendship characterized by lower intimacy than other friendship forms but higher socio-emotional rewards and interdependence. Easy entry and exit.	Vicki and her stable of shampoos, perfumes, and lingerie brands.
Kinship: Nonvoluntary union with lineage ties.	Vicki's preferences for Tetley tea or Karen's for Ban, Joy, and Miracle Whip, all of which were inherited through their mothers.
Rebound relationship: Union precipitated by desire to replace prior partner, as opposed to attraction to replacement partner.	Karen's use of Comet, Gateway, and Success Rice.

(Continued)

FIGURE 9-15   *(Continued)*

Relationship Form	Case Examples
Childhood friendship: Infrequently engaged, affective relation reminiscent of childhood times. Yields comfort and security of past self.	Jean and Jell-O pudding.
Courtship: Interim relationship state on the road to commited partnership contract.	Vicki and her Musk scent brands.
Dependency: Obsessive, highly emotional, selfish attractions cemented by feeling that the other is irreplaceable. Separation from other yields anxiety. High tolerance of other's transgressions results.	Karen and Mary Kay; Vicki and Soft 'n Dry.
Fling: Short-term, time-bounded engagement of high emotional reward. Devoid entirely of commitment and reciprocity demands.	Vicki's trial-size shampoo brands.
Enmity: Intensely involving relationship characterized by negative affect and desire to inflict pain or revenge on the other.	Karen and her husband's brands, postdivorce; Jean and her other-recommended-but-rejected brands (e.g, ham, peanut butter, sinks).
Enslavement: Nonvoluntary relationship union governed entirely by desires of the relationship partner.	Karen and Southern Bell, Cable Vision. Vicki and Playtex, a bra for large-breasted women.
Secret affair: Highly emotive, privately held relationship considered risky if exposed to others.	Karen and the Tootsie Pops she sneaks at work.

of routinized behavioral rituals surrounding brand purchase and use and through separation anxiety experienced during periods of product deprivation. At its extremes, interdependence becomes dependency and addiction.

➤ *Self-concept connection:* The degree to which the brand delivers on important identity concerns, tasks, or themes, thereby expressing a significant part of the self-concept, both past (including nostalgic references and brand memories) and present, and personal as well as social. Grounding of the self provides feelings of comfort, connectedness, control, and security. In its extreme form, self-connection reflects integration of concepts of brand and self.

➤ *Commitment:* Dedication to continued brand association and betterment of the relationship, despite circumstances foreseen and unforeseen. Commitment includes professed faithfulness and loyalty to the other, often formalized through stated pledges and publicized intentions. Commitment is not defined solely by sunk costs and irretrievable investments that pose barriers to exit.

➤ *Love/Passion:* Affinity toward and adoration of the brand, particularly with respect to other available alternatives. The intensity of the emotional bonds joining relationship partners may range from feelings of warmth, caring, and affection to those of true passion. Love includes the belief that the brand is irreplaceable and uniquely qualified as a relationship partner.

➤ *Intimacy:* A sense of deep familiarity with and understanding of both the essence of the brand as a partner in the relationship and the nature of the consumer-brand relationship itself. Intimacy is revealed in the presence of a strong consumer-brand relationship culture, the sharing of little-known personal details of the self, and an elaborate brand memory containing significant experiences or associations. Intimacy is a two-dimensional concept: The consumer develops intimate knowledge of the brand, and also feels a sense of intimacy exhibited on the part of the brand toward the individual as a consumer.

➤ *Partner quality:* Perceived partner quality involves a summary judgment of the caliber of the role enactments performed by the brand in its partnership role. Partner quality includes three central components: (1) an empathic orientation toward the other (ability of the partner to make the other feel wanted, cared for, respected, noticed, and important; responsiveness to needs); (2) a character of reliability, dependability, and predictability in the brand; and (3) trust or faith in the belief that the brand will adhere to established relationship rules and be held accountable for its actions.

Notes

1. Burleigh B. Gardner and Sidney J. Levy, "The Product and the Brand," *Harvard Business Review* (March-April 1955): 35.

2. Some leading textbooks in this area are J. Paul Peter and Jerry C. Olson, *Consumer Behavior and Marketing Strategy*, 3rd ed. (Homewood, IL: Irwin, 1993); Wayne D. Hoyer and Deborah J. MacInnis, *Consumer Behavior*, 2nd ed. (Boston: Houghton Mifflin College, 2000); and Michael R. Solomon, *Consumer Behavior: Buying, Having, and Being*, 4th ed. (Upper Saddle River, NJ: Prentice-Hall, 1998).

3. John Motavalli, "Probing Consumer Minds," *Adweek*, 7 December 1987, 4–8.

4. Ernest Dichter, *Handbook of Consumer Motivations* (New York: McGraw-Hill, 1964).

5. H. Shanker Krishnan, "Characteristics of Memory Associations: A Consumer-Based Brand Equity Perspective," *International Journal of Research in Marketing* (October 1996): 389–405.

6. J. Wesley Hutchinson, "Expertise and the Structure of Free Recall," in *Advances in Consumer Research*, Vol. 10, eds. Richard P.

Bagozzi and Alice M. Tybout (Ann Arbor, MI: Association of Consumer Research, 1983), 585–589.

7. Yvan Boivin, "A Free Response Approach to the Measurement of Brand Perceptions," *International Journal of Research in Marketing* 3 (1986): 11–17.

8. Geraldine R. Henderson, Dawn Iacobucci, and Bobby J. Calder, "Brand Diagnostics: Mapping Branding Effects Using Consumer Associative Networks," *European Journal of Operations Research* 111, no. 2 (1998): 306–327.

9. Sydney J. Levy, "Dreams, Fairy Tales, Animals, and Cars," *Psychology and Marketing* 2, no. 2 (1985): 67–81.

10. Mason Haire, "Projective Techniques in Marketing Research, *Journal of Marketing* (April 1950): 649–656. Interestingly, a follow-up study conducted several decades later suggested that instant coffee users were no longer perceived as psychologically different from drip grind users. See Frederick E. Webster Jr. and Frederick Von Pechmann, "A Replication of the 'Shopping List' Study," *Journal of Marketing* 34 (April 1970): 61–63.

11. Levy, "Dreams, Fairy Tales."

12. Ronald Alsop, "Advertisers Put Consumers on the Couch," *Wall Street Journal*, 13 May 1988, 21.

13. Jeffrey Durgee and Robert Stuart, "Advertising Symbols and Brand Names That Best Represent Key Product Meanings," *Journal of Consumer Marketing* 4, no. 3 (1987): 15–24.

14. Jay Dean, "A Practitioner's Perspective or 15 Things I've Learned about Brand Personality" (paper presented at Society of Consumer Psychology annual meeting, February 1994).

15. Evan Ramstad, "If Market Surveys Were Carrots, This One Might Be a Bit Strained," *Wall Street Journal,* 26 November 1996, B1.

16. For an approach to brand personality based on narrative thought processes, see Jerry Olson and Doug Allen, "Building Bonds between the Brand and the Customer by Creating and Managing Brand Personality" (paper presented at Marketing Science Institute conference on Brand Equity and the Marketing Mix: Creating Customer Value, Tucson, AZ, March 2–3, 1995).

17. Jennifer Aaker, "Dimensions of Brand Personality," *Journal of Marketing Research* 34, no. 8 (1997): 347–356.

18. Jay Dean, "A Practitioner's Perspective on Brand Equity," in *Proceedings of the Society for Consumer Psychology*, eds. Wes Hutchinson and Kevin Lane Keller (Clemson, SC: CtC Press, 1994), 56–62.

19. Aaker, " Dimensions of Brand Personality." See also Jennifer Aaker, "The Malleable Self: The Role of Self-Expression in Persuasion," *Journal of Marketing Research* 36, no. 2 (1999): 45–57.

20. Jennifer L. Aaker, Veronica Benet-Martinez, and Jordi Garolera, "Consumption Symbols as Carriers of Culture: A Study of Japanese and Spanish Brand Personality Constructs," *Journal of Personality and Social Psychology* 81, no. 3 (2001): 492–508.

21. Yumiko Ono, "Marketers Seek the 'Naked Truth' in Consumer Psyches," *Wall Street Journal*, 30 May 1997, B1.

22. Melanie Wells, "New Ways to Get Into Our Heads," *USA Today*, 2 March 1999, B1–B2.

23. David Goetzel, "O&M Turns Reality TV into Research Tool," *Advertising Age*, 10 July 2000, 6.

24. Leslie Kaufman, "Enough Talk," *Newsweek*, 18 August 1997, 48–49.

25. Luisa Kroll, "Crawling Back," *Forbes*, 26 July 1999, 80.

26. Gerry Kermouch, "Consumers in the Mist," *Business Week*, 26 February 2001, 92–94.

27. Norihiko Shirouzu, "Japan's High-School Girls Excel in Art of Setting Trends," *Wall Street Journal*, 24 April 1998, B1, B6.

28. Rekha Balu, "Listen Up! (It Might Be Your Customer Talking)," *Fast Company*, May 2000, 304–316.

29. Jim Rogers, letter to author, September 2001.

30. Thomas K. Srull, "Methodological Techniques for the Study of Person Memory and Social Cognition," in *Handbook of Social Cognition*, Vol. 2, eds. Robert S. Wyer and Thomas K. Srull (Hillsdale, NJ: Lawrence Erlbaum, 1984), 1–72.

31. Bill Abrams and David P. Garino, "Package Design Gains Stature as Visual Competition Grows," *Wall Street Journal*, 6 August 1981, 25.

32. Joseph W. Alba and J. Wesley Hutchinson, "Dimensions of Consumer Expertise," *Journal of Consumer Research* 13 (March 1987): 411–454.

33. Raymond Gordon, "Phantom Products," *Forbes*, 21 May 1984, 202–204.

34. Philip Kotler, *Marketing Management: Analysis, Planning, Implementation, and Control,* 8th ed. (Upper Saddle River, NJ: Prentice-Hall, 1994).

35. Neil R. Barnard and Andrew S. C. Ehrenberg, "Robust Measures of Consumer Brand Beliefs," *Journal of Marketing Research* 26 (November 1990): 477–484.

36. For example, see Gilbert A. Churchill Jr., *Marketing Research*, 5th ed. (Chicago: Dryden, 1991); or David A. Aaker, *Marketing Research*, 5th ed. (New York: John Wiley & Son, 1993).

37. Joseph F. Hair Jr., Rolph E. Anderson, Ronald Tatham, and William C. Black, *Multivariate Data Analysis*, 4th ed. (Englewood Cliffs, NJ: Prentice-Hall, 1995).

38. Jean-Noel Kapferer and Gilles Laurent, "Consumers' Brand Sensitivity: A New Concept for Brand Management," (paper presented at the Annual Conference of the European Marketing Academy, 1985); Jean-Noel Kapferer and Gilles Laurent, "Consumer Brand Sensitivity: A Key to Measuring and Managing Brand Equity" (presentation at Marketing Science Institute conference on Defining, Measuring, and Managing Brand Equity, Austin, TX, March 1–3, 1988).

39. Vicki G. Morwitz, Joel H. Steckel, and Alok Gupta,"When Do Purchase Intentions Predict Sales?" working paper, Stern School of Business, New York University, 2002.

40. Icek Ajzen and Martin Fishbein, *Understanding Attitudes and Predicting Social Behavior* (Englewood Cliffs, NJ: Prentice-Hall, 1980).

41. "Longman-Moran Analytics," internal company document, unpublished.

42. Vikas Mittal and Mohanbir S. Sawhney, "Managing Customer Retention in the Attention Economy," working paper, University of Pittsburgh, 2001.

43. Gerald Zaltman and Robin Higie, "Seeing the Voice of the Customer: The Zaltman Metaphor Elicitation Technique," MSI Report 93–114 (Cambridge, MA: Marketing Science Institute, 1993); Gerald Zaltman and Robin Higie, "Seeing the Voice of the Customer: Metaphor-Based Advertising Research," *Journal of Advertising Research* (July/August 1995): 35–51; Daniel H. Pink, "Metaphor Marketing," *Fast Company*, April 1998; Gerald Zaltman, "Metaphorically Speaking," *Marketing Research* (Summer 1996); Ronald B. Leiber, "Storytelling: A New Way to Get Close to Your Customer," *Fortune*, 3 February 1997.

44. S.M. Fournier, "Consumers and Their Brands: Developing Relationship Theory in Consumer Research," *Journal of Consumer Research* 24, no. 3 (1998): 343–373; S. M. Fournier, "Dimensioning Brand Relationships Using Brand Relationship Quality" (paper presented at the Association for Consumer Research annual conference, Salt Lake City, UT, October 2000); S.M. Fournier, S. Dobscha, and S. Mick, "Preventing the Premature Death of Relationship Marketing," *Harvard Business Review* (January-February): 42–51; S.M. Fournier and J.L. Yao, "Reviving Brand Loyalty: A Reconceptualization Within the Framework of Consumer-Brand Relationships," *International Journal of Research in Marketing* 14 (1997): 451–472.

CHAPTER

10

Measuring Outcomes of Brand Equity: Capturing Market Performance

PREVIEW

Ideally, to measure brand equity, it would be possible to create a "brand equity index"—one easily calculated number that would summarize the "health" of the brand and completely capture its brand equity. But just as a thermometer measuring body temperature provides only one indication of how healthy a person is, so does any one measure of brand equity provide only one indication of the health of a brand. Brand equity is a multidimensional concept and complex enough that many different types of measures are required. Multiple measures increase the diagnostic power of marketing research and the likelihood that managers will better understand what is happening to their brands and, perhaps more important, why.

In arguing that researchers should employ multiple measures of brand equity, marketing executive Richard Chay draws an interesting comparison between measuring brand equity and determining the performance of an aircraft in flight:

> The pilot of the plane has to consider a number of indicators and gauges as the plane is flown. There is the fuel gauge, the altimeter, and a number of other important status indicators. All of these dials and meters tell the pilot different things about the health of the plane. There is no one gauge that summarizes everything about the plane. The plane needs the altimeter, compass, radar, and the fuel gauge. As the pilot looks at the instrument cluster, he has to take all of these critical indicators into account as he flies.[1]

Chay concludes by noting that the gauges on the plane, which together measure its health in flight, are analogous to the multiple measures of brand equity, which are necessary to collectively assess the health of a brand.

The previous chapter described different approaches for measuring brand knowledge structures and the customer mindset to be able to identify and quantify potential sources of brand equity. By applying these measurement techniques, marketers should be able to gain a good understanding of the depth and breadth of awareness; the strength, favorability, and uniqueness of associations; the valence of brand responses; and the nature of brand relationships for their brands. The customer-based brand equity model states that as a consequence of creating such knowledge structures, consumers will respond more favorably to the marketing activity for a brand than if the brand had not been identified to consumers. As described in Chapter 2, a product with positive brand equity can potentially enjoy the following seven important customer-related benefits:

1. Be perceived differently and produce different interpretations of product performance
2. Enjoy greater loyalty and be less vulnerable to competitive marketing actions
3. Command larger margins and have more inelastic responses to price increases and elastic responses to price decreases
4. Receive greater trade cooperation and support
5. Increase marketing communication effectiveness
6. Yield licensing opportunities
7. Support brand extensions

The CBBE model maintains that these benefits, and thus the ultimate value of a brand, depend on the underlying components of brand knowledge and sources of brand equity. As Chapter 9 described, these individual components can be measured; however, to provide more direct estimates, their resulting value still must be estimated in some way. This chapter examines measurement procedures to assess the effects of brand knowledge structures on these and other outcomes of interest to marketers—that is, measures that capture market performance for the brand. In doing so, marketers are able to get a much clearer picture of the value of the brand. The Science of Branding 10-1 describes how academic researchers have explored how branding affects the basic consumer behavior processes that underlie these benefits.

Understanding How Brands Affect Consumer Behavior

Academic researchers have identified a number of different theoretical mechanisms to explain why strong brands for which consumers have high brand knowledge receive a differential response from consumers. These explanations typically relate to assumptions concerning different aspects of consumer behavior in either a micro or macro sense. The mechanisms can be classified within three different stages of how brand knowledge is created and put to use by consumers: (1) *attention and learning,* that is, the building of brand knowledge structures; (2) *interpretation and evaluation* of marketing information or brand alternatives, that is, the use of brand knowledge; and (3) mechanisms that are thought to affect the *actual choice process,* that is, the application of brand knowledge. All through these three different stages of consumer behavior, advantages have been documented for strong brands.[1]

ATTENTION AND LEARNING

Strong brands can have a memory encoding and storage advantage over unknown or weak brands in building brand awareness and image. Consumers familiar with a brand have better encoding ability and better-developed procedural knowledge.[2] More elaborate memory structures can facilitate the formation of linkages of new associations.[3] Consumers also can develop a greater number of stronger links for familiar brands.[4]

Moreover, because strong brands have better developed brand knowledge structures in the minds of consumers, there is a greater likelihood that the links that make up this knowledge will be uniquely associated with the brand. When consumers have less developed knowledge structures, on the other hand, associations may end up being stored under the product category and not the specific brand. Along those lines, learning can decrease for brands that are late to enter into a market because they are seen as having less novel features.[5]

Consideration

Another advantage related to brand strength is differential inclusion of brands that are more accessible into consumers' consideration sets. The accessibility advantage for brands with a greater number of associations in a wide variety of contexts implies that strong brands are more likely to be in consumers' consideration sets.[6] Strong brands also receive an advantage when consumers begin their search with well-known and well-regarded brands that are seen as being more likely to satisfy their needs.[7]

Selective Attention

Strong brands may find the strength of their brand affected at an involuntary level to the extent that consumers automatically encode frequency information as they are exposed to brand names, symbols, slogans, and logos through various marketing activity.[8] Nonverbal information about the brand, such as symbols, slogans, and logos, may be more potent or meaningful than verbal cues.[9] Strong brands can also be given selectively more exposure, attention, comprehension, and retention by consumers.[10] Similarly, consumers may selectively allocate more attention to advertising for well-known brands.[11]

In short, it appears that information about strong brands is more easily noticed, and the frequency of advertising of strong brands may create favorable associations even in the absence of voluntary processing of the brand information. In addition, consumers may give more selective attention to strong brands than to other brands.

INTERPRETATION AND EVALUATION

There is evidence for both direct and indirect mechanisms operating to create differences in how consumers interpret and evaluate brands and related marketing information.

Direct effects occur when brand-related information is input directly into the decision process. For instance, one conceptual mechanism that is moderated by differences in brand knowledge is loss aversion.[12] With loss aversion, the losses of switching from a known brand loom larger than the potential gains from using another, lesser-known brand (e.g., as the result of a price reduction). Thus, the possibility of a potential loss leads to an advantage for strong brands. Consumers may rely on the affect associated with a familiar brand to aid in their decision making.[13] The halo effects related to the positive feelings regarding a strong brand can positively bias the evaluation of advertising of the brand.[14] Similarly, consumer confidence is another potential diagnostic cue that is derived from a well-developed knowledge structure. Consumer confidence is increased when consumers get more familiar in a domain.[15] In addition, consumer confidence may lead to greater use of favorable associations to facilitate decision making.[16] In summary, consumers are likely to *directly* use both the confidence associated with familiarity as well as affect transfer when evaluating and selecting strong brands.

Indirect effects are perhaps more common than direct effects and are driven by uncertainty or ambiguity in the decision process. After brand information has been acquired, consumers may interpret or evaluate the information. This evaluation and enhancement may be especially critical if there are ambiguities associated with brand-related information. In general, ambiguity in the decision-making process favors the incumbent or stronger brand.[17] For example, confirmation biases can lead to favorable evaluations in the presence of ambiguous information (e.g., as a result of advertising).[18] When evaluating ambiguous stimuli, the primary determinant of evaluative directionality is prior attitudes.[19] With prior positive evaluations, cognitive evaluations should be more receptive and less critical and richer for brands with which people have more experience in more contexts.[20] Finally, consumers may use brand names as a signal of the credibility of product claims.[21] Thus, evaluation advantages—through more elaboration—may help strong brands to *indirectly* create even stronger and more favorable associations.

CHOICE

Perhaps the most frequently cited advantage for strong brands at the choice stage is the notion of brand recognition or familiarity as a choice heuristic.[22] Essentially, when consumers have limited prior knowledge in a product category, the brand name may be the most accessible cue available.[23] In addition, using a familiar brand name as a diagnostic cue is thought to be a consumer strategy for dealing with risk and uncertainty, especially when consumers have limited prior experience.[24] The presence of a known brand can limit consumers' ability to detect differences in product quality across brands, even when they sample other brands.[25] Clearly, one of the most effective mechanisms that provide advantages to strong brands is their inherent familiarity.

[1]This summary is based on Steve Hoeffler and Kevin Lane Keller, "The Marketing Advantages of Strong Brands" working paper, University of North Carolina, 2002.

[2]Eric J. Johnson and J. Edward Russo, "Product Familiarity and Learning New Information," *Journal of Consumer Research* 11 (June 1984): 54–61.

[3]Joseph W. Alba and Wesley J. Hutchinson, "Dimensions of Consumer Expertise," *Journal of Consumer Research* 13 (March 1987): 411–455.

[4]Robert J. Kent and Chris T. Allen, "Competitive Interference Effects in Consumer Memory for Advertising: The Role of Brand Familiarity," *Journal of Marketing* 58 (July 1994): 97–105.

[5]Douglas Bowman and Hubert Gatignon, "Order of Entry as a Moderator of the Effect of the Marketing Mix on Market Share," *Marketing Science* 15, no. 3 (1996): 222–242.

[6]Donald R. Lehmann and Yigang Pan, "Context Effects, New Brand Entry, and Consideration Sets," *Journal of Marketing Research* 31 (August 1994): 364–374; Itamar Simonson, Joel Huber, and John Payne, "The Relationship between Prior Brand Knowledge and Information Acquisition Order," *Journal of Consumer Research* 14 (March 1988): 566–578.

[7]Simonson, Huber, and Payne, "Prior Brand Knowledge and Information Acquisition Order."

[8]Lynn Hasher and Rose T. Zacks, "Automatic and Effortful Processes in Memory," *Journal of Experimental Psychology* 108, no. 3 (1979): 356–388.

[9]Srinivas K. Reddy, Susan Holak, and Subodh Bhat, "To Extend or Not to Extend: Success Determinants of Line Extensions," *Journal of Marketing Research* 31, no. 5 (1994): 243–262.

[10]Gerard J. Tellis, "The Price Elasticity of Selective Demand: A Meta-analysis of Econometric Models of Sales," *Journal of Marketing Research* 25 (November 1988): 331–341.

[11]Kent and Allen, "Competitive Interference Effects."

[12]Ravi Dhar and Itamar Simonson, "The Effect of the Focus of Comparison on Consumer Preferences," *Journal of Marketing Research* 29 (November 1992): 430–440.

[13]Mary W. Sullivan, "How Brand Names Affect the Demand for Twin Automobiles," *Journal of Marketing Research* 35 (May 1998): 154–165.

[14]Steve P. Brown and Douglas M. Stayman, "Antecedents and Consequences of Attitude toward the Ad: A Meta-analysis," *Journal of Consumer Research* 19 (June 1992): 34–51.

[15]Michel Laroche, Chankon Kim, and Lianxi Zhou, "Brand Familiarity and Confidence as Determinants of Purchase Intention: An Empirical Test in a Multiple Brand Context," *Journal of Business Research* 37 (1996): 115–120.

[16]Peter A. Dacin and Daniel C. Smith, "The Effect of Brand Portfolio Characteristics on Consumer Evaluations of Brand Extensions," *Journal of Marketing Research* 31 (May 1994): 229–242.

[17]V. Muthukrishnan, "Decision Ambiguity and Incumbent Brand Advantage," *Journal of Consumer Research* 22 (June 1995): 98–109.

[18]Stephen J. Hoch and John Deighton, "Managing What Consumers Learn from Experience," *Journal of Marketing* 53 (April 1989): 1–20.

[19]Amitava Chattopadyay and Kunal Basu, "Humor in Advertising: The Moderating Role of Prior Brand Evaluation," *Journal of Marketing Research* 27 (November 1990): 466–476.

[20]Tellis, "Price Elasticity of Selective Demand."

[21]Tulin Erdem, "Brand Equity as a Signaling Phenomenon," *Journal of Consumer Psychology* 7, no. 2 (1998): 131–157.

[22]W. B. Dodds, K. B. Monroe, and D. Grewal, "Effects of Price, Brand, and Store Information on Buyers' Product Evaluations," *Journal of Marketing Research* 28 (August 1991): 307–319; Roger A. Kerin, Gurumurthy Kalyanaram, and Daniel J. Howard, "Product Hierarchy and Brand Strategy Influences on the Order of Entry Effect for Consumer Packaged Goods," *Journal of Product Innovation Management* 13 (1996): 21–34; Durairaj Maheswaran, Diane M. Mackie, and Shelly Chaiken, "Brand Name as a Heuristic Cue: The Effects of Task Importance and Expectancy Confirmation on Consumer Judgments," *Journal of Consumer Psychology* 1, no. 4 (1992): 317–336; Daniel C. Smith and C. Whan Park, "The Effects of Brand Extensions on Market Share and Advertising Efficiency," *Journal of Marketing Research* 29 (August 1992): 296–313.

[23]Jack M. Feldman and John G. Lynch Jr., "Self-Generated Validity and Other Effects of Measurement on Belief, Attitude, Intention, and Behavior," *Journal of Applied Psychology* 73 (August 1988): 421–435.

[24]Dodds, Monroe, and Grewal, "Effects of Price, Brand, and Store Information"; Kerin, Kalyanaram, and Howard, "Product Hierarchy and Brand Strategy Influences"; Smith and Park, "Effects of Brand Extensions."

[25]Wayne D. Hoyer and Steven P. Brown, "Effects of Brand Awareness on Choice for a Common, Repeat— Purchase Product," *Journal of Consumer Research* 17 (September 1990): 141–148.

This chapter first reviews comparative methods, which are means to better assess the effects of consumer perceptions and preferences on consumer response to various aspects of the marketing program and the specific benefits of brand equity. Next, it considers holistic methods, which attempt to come up with an estimate of the overall or summary value of a brand.[2]

COMPARATIVE METHODS

Comparative methods involve experiments that examine consumer attitudes and behavior toward a brand to directly estimate the benefits arising from having a high level of awareness and strong, favorable, and unique brand associations. There are two types of comparative methods. *Brand-based comparative approaches* use experiments in which one group of consumers responds to an element of the marketing program or some marketing activity when it is attributed to the target brand and another group responds to that same element or activity when it is attributed to a competitive or fictitiously named brand. *Marketing-based comparative approaches* use experiments in which consumers respond to changes in elements of the marketing program or marketing activity for the target brand or competitive brands.

The brand-based comparative approach holds the marketing program fixed and examines consumer response based on changes in brand identification, whereas the marketing-based comparative approach holds the brand fixed and examines consumer response based on changes in the marketing program. This section describes each of these two approaches in turn. Conjoint analysis is then described as a technique that, in effect, combines the two approaches.

Brand-Based Comparative Approaches

As a means of measuring the outcomes of brand equity, brand-based comparative approaches hold the marketing element or activity under consideration fixed and examine consumer response based on changes in brand identification. These measurement approaches typically employ experiments in which one group of consumers responds to questions about the product or some aspect of its marketing program when it is attributed to the brand and one or more groups of consumers respond to the same product or aspect of the marketing program when it is attributed to some other brand or brands, typically a fictitiously named or unnamed version of the product or service or one or more competitive brands. Comparing the responses of the two groups provides some useful insights into the equity of the brand. Consumer responses may be based on beliefs, attitudes, intentions, or actual behavior.

Competitive brands can be useful benchmarks in brand-based comparative approaches. Although consumers may interpret marketing activity for a fictitiously named or unnamed version of the product or service in terms of their general product category knowledge (e.g., by assuming prototypical product or service specifications and price, promotion, and distribution strategies for the anonymous entry in the category), they may also have a particular brand, or exemplar, in mind. This exemplar may be the category leader or some other brand that consumers feel is representative of the category (e.g., their most preferred brand). Inferences for any missing information may be made based on their knowledge of this particular brand in memory. Thus, it may be instructive to

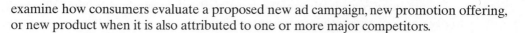

examine how consumers evaluate a proposed new ad campaign, new promotion offering, or new product when it is also attributed to one or more major competitors.

Applications

The classic example of the brand-based comparative approach is "blind testing" research studies in which consumers examine or use a product with or without brand identification. For example, recall the beer taste test results from Chapter 2, which showed how dramatically consumer perceptions differed depending on the presence or absence of brand identification. Thus, one natural application of the brand-based comparative approach is with product purchase or consumption, as long as the brand identification can be hidden in some way for the "unbranded" control group. Products could be existing ones or proposed new extensions. Brand-based comparative approaches are also useful to determine brand equity benefits related to price margins and premiums.

Premier Automobiles

When American Motors first tested the Renault Premier automobile (as it was called at the time), it conducted an experiment to come up with a financial value for the brand name.[3] One group of consumers was shown an unbranded model of the car. After visually inspecting the car, consumers in this group were asked what they would pay for it. For the unbranded version, consumers reported on average that they would pay about $10,000. Other groups of consumers went through the same inspection and measurement procedure when the car was identified as one of various other brand names. When the car was identified as the Renault Premier, consumers priced the car at around $13,000; when it was identified as a Chrysler, the average reservation price was slightly higher. After Chrysler subsequently bought American Motors, the car was later introduced as the Chrysler Eagle Premier, and the two models sold for $12,400 and $14,100.

Assessing customer-based brand equity with marketing communications presents a greater challenge for the brand-based comparative approach, for example, when evaluating consumer response to a proposed new advertising campaign. In this case, storyboards and animatic or photomatic versions of an ad could be used rather than a finished ad to allow for the necessary disguise of the brand. Although this approach should work well with informational-type ads, it probably would be less appropriate for transformational-type ads, in which production values are a critical ingredient in achieving communication goals. Also, such an approach would only capture the effects of brand knowledge on consumer response to creative and message strategies and not media weight.

Critique

The main advantage of a brand-based comparative approach is that because it holds all aspects of the marketing program fixed for the brand, it isolates the value of a brand in a very real sense. Understanding exactly how knowledge of the brand affects consumer responses to prices, advertising, and so forth is extremely useful in developing strategies in these different areas. At the same time, an almost infinite variety of marketing activities could potentially be studied, so the totality of what is learned will depend on how many different applications are examined.

Brand-based comparative methods are particularly applicable when the marketing activity under consideration represents a change from past marketing of the brand, for example, a new sales or trade promotion, ad campaign, or proposed brand extension. If the marketing activity under consideration is already strongly identified with the brand (e.g., an ad campaign that has been running for years), it may be difficult to attribute some aspect of the marketing program to a fictitiously named or unnamed version of the product or service in a believable fashion.

Thus, a crucial consideration with the brand-based comparative approach is the experimental realism that can be achieved when some aspect of the marketing program is attributed to a fictitiously named or unnamed version of the product or service. Some realism will need to be sacrificed to gain sufficient control for isolating the effects of brand knowledge. Detailed concept statements of the particular marketing activity under consideration can be employed in some situations when it may be otherwise difficult for consumers to examine or experience that element of the marketing program without being aware of the brand.

Thus, concept statements may be useful in assessing customer-based brand equity when consumers make some type of product evaluation or respond to a proposed price or distribution change. For example, consumers could be asked to judge a proposed new product when it is either introduced by the firm as a brand extension or introduced by an unnamed firm in that product market. Similarly, consumers could be asked acceptable price ranges and store locations for the brand name product or a hypothetical unnamed version. Nevertheless, a concern with brand-based comparative approaches is that the simulations and concept statements that are used may highlight those particular characteristics that are mentioned or featured and make them more salient than they would otherwise be, distorting the results.

Marketing-Based Comparative Approaches

Marketing-based comparative approaches hold the brand fixed and examine consumer response based on changes in the marketing program.

Applications

There is a long academic and industry tradition of exploring price premiums using marketing-based comparative approaches. In the mid-1950s, Edgar Pessemier developed a dollarmetric measure of brand commitment that involved a step-by-step increase of the price difference between the brand normally purchased and an alternative brand.[4] Pessemier plotted the percentage of consumers who switched from their regular brand as a function of the brand price increases to reveal brand-switching and loyalty patterns. Variations of this approach have been adopted by a number of marketing research suppliers to derive similar types of demand curves, and many firms now try to assess price sensitivity and thresholds for different brands. For example, Intel routinely surveys computer shoppers to find out how much of a discount they would require before switching to a personal computer that did not have an Intel microprocessor in it or, conversely, what premium they would be willing to pay to buy a personal computer with an Intel microprocessor in it. Branding Brief 10-1 describes the results of ad agency DDB Needham's pricing studies.

DDB Needham's Pricing Studies

James Crimmins reports that DDB Needham takes the consumer perspective to look at brand value.[1] He maintains that brand value has three dimensions:

1. The amount of value added by a brand name in a category
2. The breadth of the added value (i.e., the range of product categories in which the brand name can add value)
3. The content of the added value (i.e., the specific qualities implied by the brand name that serve as the reasons consumer choose the brands)

Crimmins argues that marketers often measure the content of the brand name but rarely measure the amount or breadth of brand value. He defines the amount of value added by a brand as the ratio of its price to its competitor's price when both products are equally desirable to consumers, minus 1. In other words, if brand A and brand B are equally desirable when brand A costs $1.20 and brand B costs $1.00, then the amount of relative value added by brand A is 20 percent, as follows:

$$\$1.20/\$1.00 - 1 = 20\%$$

DDB Needham implements this approach by offering consumers a series of choices among five or six brands in which only the price of the target brand is changed to become the lowest and highest in the choice set while all other prices stay constant.

In applying this methodology, DDB Needham has measured the value added by brand names in a wide range of categories. They found that across 13 categories, the median value added by the number one brand relative to a store brand was around 40 percent, although this number varied widely from a high of 113 percent to a low of 19 percent. It also examined the value added of the number one brand versus the number two brand across 14 product categories and found that a typical number one brand is worth approximately 10 percent more than its next biggest competitor.

---

[1] James C. Crimmins, "Better Management of Brand Value," *Journal of Advertising Research* (July/August 1992): 11–19.

Marketing-based comparative approaches can be applied in other ways. Consumer response to different advertising strategies, executions, or media plans can be assessed through multiple test markets. For example, IRI's electronic test markets (see The Science of Branding 6-1) and other such research methodologies can permit tests of different advertising weights or repetition schedules as well as ad copy tests. By controlling for other factors, the effects of the brand and product can be isolated. Recall from Chapter 2 how Anheuser-Busch conducted an extensive series of test markets that revealed that Budweiser beer had such a strong image with consumers that advertising could be cut, at least in the short run, without hurting sales performance.

Potential brand extensions can also be explored in this fashion by collecting consumer evaluations of a range of concept statements describing brand extension candidates. For example, Figure 10-1 displays the results of a consumer survey examining

Average Scale Rating[a]	Proposed Extensions
10	Peanuts
9	Snack mixes, nuts for baking
8	—
7	Pretzels, chocolate nut candy, caramel corn
6	Snack crackers, potato chips, nutritional granola bars
5	Tortilla chips, toppings (ice cream/dessert)
4	Lunchables/lunch snack packs, dessert mixes (cookie/cake/ brownie)
3	Ice cream/ice cream bars, toppings (salad/vegetable)
2	Cereal, toaster pastries, oriental entrees/sauces, stuffing mix, refrigerated dough, jams/jellies
1	Yogurt

[a]Consumers rated proposed extensions on an 11-point scale anchored by 0 (definitely would *not* expect Planter's to sell it) and 10 (definitely would expect Planter's to sell it).

FIGURE 10-1   Reactions to Proposed Planter's Extensions

reactions to possible extensions of the Planter's nuts brand (see also Figure 10-2). Contrasting those extensions of which consumers approve with those of which they disapprove provides some indication of the equity of the brand involved. In this example, the survey results would seem to suggest that consumers expect any Planter's brand extension to be "nut-related." Appropriate product characteristics for a possible Planter's brand extension would seem to be "crunchy," "sweet," "salty," "spicy," and "buttery." In terms of where in the store consumers would expect to find new Planter's products, the snack and candy sections seem most likely. On the other hand, consumers do not seem to expect to find new Planter's products in the breakfast food aisle, bakery product section, refrigerated section, or frozen food section.

Critique

The main advantage of the marketing-based comparative approach is the ease of implementation. Virtually any proposed set of marketing actions can be compared for the brand. At the same time, the main drawback of the comparative approach is that it may be difficult to discern whether consumer responses to changes in the marketing stimuli are being caused by brand knowledge or more generic product knowledge. In other words, it may be that for *any* brand in the product category, consumers would be willing or unwilling to pay certain prices, accept a particular brand extension, and so forth. One way to determine whether consumer response is specific to the brand is to conduct similar tests of consumer response with competitive brands. A statistical technique well suited to do just that is described next.

Conjoint Analysis

Conjoint analysis is a survey-based multivariate technique that enables marketers to profile the consumer decision process with respect to products and brands.[5] Specifically, by asking consumers to express preferences or make choices among a

FIGURE 10-2   Planter's Product Mix

number of different carefully designed product profiles, marketing researchers can determine the tradeoffs consumers are making between various brand attributes and thus the importance that consumers are attaching to those attributes.[6] Each profile shown to consumers is made up of a set of attribute levels. Particular attribute levels for any one profile are chosen on the basis of experimental design principles to satisfy certain mathematical properties. The value that consumers attach to each attribute level, as statistically derived by the conjoint formula, is called a *part worth.* The part worths can be used in various ways to estimate how consumers would value a new combination of the attribute levels.

In particular, one attribute that can be included is the brand name. The part worth for the "brand name" attribute would then reflect its value. One classic study of conjoint analysis was reported by Green and Wind.[7] This study concerned consumer evaluations of a spot-remover product. Five attributes were studied: package design, brand name, price, *Good Housekeeping* seal, and money-back guarantee. Figure 10-3 contains the 18 profiles that made up the experimental design. Figure 10-4 shows the results of the statistical analyses to determine the part worths.

Applications

Conjoint analysis has a number of different possible applications. Ogilvy & Mather ad agency has used a brand/price tradeoff methodology as a means of assessing advertising effectiveness and brand value.[8] Brand/price tradeoff is a simplified version of conjoint measurement with just two variables—brand and price. Consumers are faced with a series of simulated purchase choices between different combinations of brands and prices. Each choice triggers an increase in the price of the selected brand, forcing the consumer to trade off between choosing a preferred brand and paying less. In this

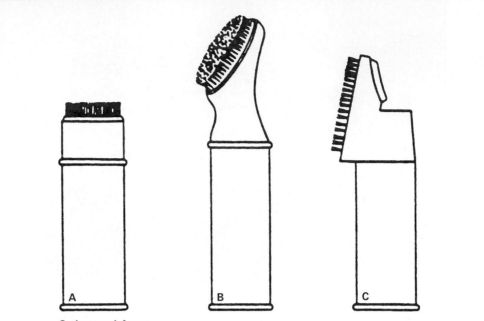

Orthogonal Array

	Package Design	Brand Name	Price	*Good Housekeeping* Seal?	Money-Back Guarantee?	Respondent's Evaluation (Rank Number)
1	A	K2R	$1.19	No	No	13
2	A	Glory	1.39	No	Yes	11
3	A	Bissell	1.59	Yes	No	17
4	B	K2R	1.39	Yes	Yes	2
5	B	Glory	1.59	No	No	14
6	B	Bissell	1.19	No	No	3
7	C	K2R	1.59	No	Yes	12
8	C	Glory	1.19	Yes	No	7
9	C	Bissell	1.39	No	No	9
10	A	K2R	1.59	Yes	No	18
11	A	Glory	1.19	No	Yes	8
12	A	Bissell	1.39	No	No	15
13	B	K2R	1.19	No	No	4
14	B	Glory	1.39	Yes	No	6
15	B	Bissell	1.59	No	Yes	5
16	C	K2R	1.39	No	No	10
17	C	Glory	1.59	No	No	16
18	C	Bissell	1.19	Yes	Yes	1*

*Highest ranked

FIGURE 10-3 Product Profiles for Conjoint Analysis Application

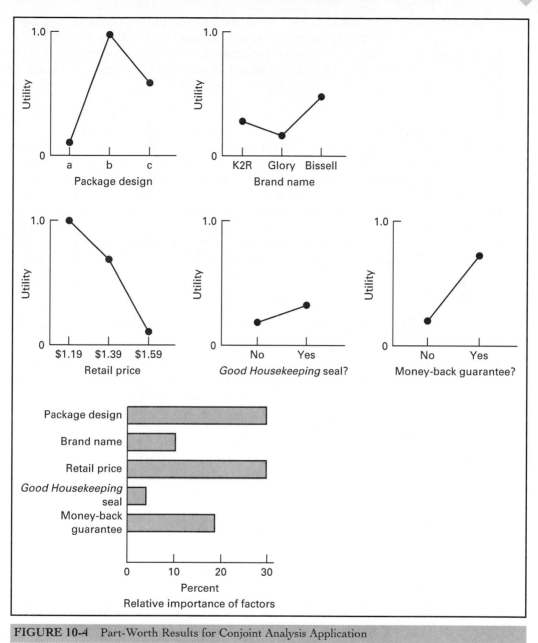

FIGURE 10-4   Part-Worth Results for Conjoint Analysis Application

way, consumers reveal how much their brand loyalty is worth and, conversely, which brands they would relinquish for a lower price.

Other variations and applications of conjoint analysis have been used by academic researchers with an interest in brand image and equity.[9] For example, academic researchers Rangaswamy, Burke, and Oliva use conjoint analysis to explore how brand names interact with physical product features to affect the extendability of brand names to new product categories.[10] Barich and Srinivasan apply conjoint analysis to corporate image programs to show how it can be used to determine the company attributes that are relevant to customers, rank the importance of those attributes, estimate the costs of making improvements (or correcting customer perceptions), and prioritize image goals so that the improvements in perceptions obtain the maximum benefit, in terms of customer value, for the resources spent.[11]

Critique

The main advantage of the conjoint-based approach is that it allows for different brands and different aspects of the product or marketing program (product composition, price, distribution outlets, etc.) to be studied simultaneously. Thus, information about consumers' responses to different marketing activities can be uncovered for both the focal and competing brands. One of the disadvantages of conjoint analysis is that marketing profiles may be presented to consumers that violate their expectations based on what they already know about brands. Thus, if conjoint analysis is employed, care must be taken that consumers do not evaluate unrealistic product profiles or scenarios.

HOLISTIC METHODS

Comparative methods attempt to approximate specific benefits of brand equity. *Holistic methods* attempt to place an overall value on the brand in either abstract utility terms or concrete financial terms. Thus, holistic methods attempt to "net out" various considerations to determine the unique contribution of the brand. The *residual approach* attempts to examine the value of the brand by subtracting consumers' preferences for the brand based on physical product attributes alone from their overall brand preferences. The *valuation approach* attempts to place a financial value on brand equity for accounting purposes, mergers and acquisitions, or other such reasons. This section describes each of these two approaches in turn.

Residual Approaches

The rationale behind residual approaches is the view that brand equity is what remains of consumer preferences and choices after subtracting physical product effects. A basic tenet behind these approaches is that it is possible to infer the relative valuation of brands through the observation of consumer preferences and choices *if* as many sources of measured attribute values are taken into account as possible. Specifically, several researchers have defined brand equity as the incremental preference over and above that which would result for the product without brand identification. According to this view, brand equity would then be calculated by attempting to subtract preferences for objective characteristics of the physical product from overall preference.[12]

Kamakura and Russell propose a measure that employs consumer purchase histories from supermarket scanner data to estimate brand equity through a residual approach.[13] Specifically, their model attempts to explain the choices observed from a panel of consumers as a function of the store environment (actual shelf prices, sales promotions, displays, etc.), the physical characteristics of available brands, and a residual term dubbed brand equity. By controlling for other aspects of the marketing mix, their approach attempts to estimate that aspect of brand preference that is unique to a brand and not currently duplicated by competitors. The outputs of their model are estimates of benefit segments, cross-price elasticities for segments and the entire market, and equity measures for each brand. They illustrate their approach with an application to the laundry detergent market. Their analysis shows that brand equity is closely related to order of entry of brands and their cumulative advertising expenditures.

Swait, Louviere, and colleagues have proposed a related approach to measuring brand equity that designs choice experiments that account for brand names, product attributes, brand image, and differences in consumer socio-demographic characteristics and brand usage.[14] They define the *equalization price* as the price that equates the utility of a brand to the utilities that could be attributed to a brand in the category where no brand differentiation occurred. Equalization price can be seen as a proxy for brand equity. They illustrate their approach with applications to the deodorant, athletic shoe, and jeans market.[15]

Park and Srinivasan have proposed a comprehensive residual methodology to measure brand equity based on the multi-attribute attitude model.[16] Their approach reveals the relative sizes of different bases of brand equity by dividing brand equity into two components: attribute based and non-attribute based. The *attribute-based component* of brand equity is the difference between subjectively perceived attribute values and objectively measured attribute values. Objectively measured attribute values are collected from independent testing services such as *Consumer Reports* or acknowledged experts in the field. The *non-attribute-based component* of brand equity is the difference between subjectively perceived attribute values and overall preference and reflects the consumer's configural appraisal of a brand that goes beyond the assessment of the utility of individual product attributes. They propose a survey procedure to collect information to estimate these different perception and preference measures.

To demonstrate their approach, they conducted a national survey of current users of toothpaste or mouthwashes. Objective attribute ratings were collected from a survey of 120 dentists. On the basis of this measurement procedure, the researchers concluded that Crest had a positive equity of 21.6 cents, whereas the baseline store brand had a negative equity of 33.4 cents. The researchers also concluded that the non-attribute-based component of brand equity showed larger variation across brands than the attribute-based components.

Critique

Residual approaches provide a useful benchmark for interpreting brand equity. In particular, they may be useful for situations in which approximations of brand equity are necessary and thus may also be valuable to researchers interested in a financially oriented perspective on brand equity. The disadvantage of these approaches is that they are most appropriate for brands characterized by a predominance of product-related attribute associations because they are unable to distinguish between different types of non-product-related attribute associations. Consequently, the residual approach's diagnostic value for strategic decision making in other cases is limited.

More generally, note that this approach takes a fairly static view of brand equity by attempting to identify sources of consumer preferences in order to uncover the contribution by the brand. This approach contrasts sharply with the "process" view advocated by the customer-based brand equity framework, as reflected by the brand-based and marketing-based comparative approaches, which stress looking at consumer response to the marketing of a brand and attempting to uncover the extent to which that *response* is affected by brand knowledge. Consumer response is defined in terms of perceptions, preferences, and behaviors and, most important, with respect to a variety of marketing activities. That is, the CBBE framework goes beyond attempting to dissect consumer preferences to the product itself to assess how consumers respond to the marketing of a brand and, especially, new marketing activity supporting it.

This distinction is also relevant for the issue of "separability" in brand valuation raised by various researchers. For example, Barwise and his colleagues note that marketing efforts to create an extended or augmented product (e.g., extra features or service plus other means to enhance brand value) "raise serious problems of separating the value of the brand name and trademark from the many other elements of the 'augmented' product."[17] According to customer-based brand equity, those efforts could affect the favorability, strength, and uniqueness of various brand associations, which would, in turn, affect consumer response to *future* marketing activities. For example, imagine that a brand becomes known for providing extraordinary customer service because of certain policies and favorable advertising, publicity, or word of mouth (e.g., as with Nordstrom department stores). These favorable perceptions of customer service and the favorable attitudes they engender could create customer-based brand equity by affecting consumer response to a price policy (e.g., a willingness to pay higher prices), a new ad campaign (e.g., the acceptance of an ad illustrating customer satisfaction), or a brand extension (e.g., interest in trying a new type of retail outlet).

Valuation Approaches

The ability to put a price tag on a brand's value may be useful for a number of reasons:

➤ *Mergers and acquisitions:* Both to evaluate possible purchases as well as to facilitate disposal
➤ *Brand licensing:* Internally for tax reasons and to third parties
➤ *Fund raising:* As collateral on loans or for sale or leaseback arrangements
➤ *Brand management decisions:* To allocate resources, develop brand strategy, or prepare financial reports

For example, many companies appear as attractive acquisition candidates because of the strong competitive positions of their brands and their reputation with consumers. Unfortunately, the value of the brand assets in many cases is largely excluded from the company's balance sheet and therefore of little use in determining overall value. As one commentator put it:

> The worth of a strong brand is rarely represented fully in a company's stock price. It doesn't appear on a balance sheet. But it's the motor behind the numbers, the fuel that drives consumers to the marketplace and helps them make choices.[18]

It has been argued that adjusting the balance sheet to reflect the true value of a company's brands permits a more realistic view and allows assessment of the purchase premium to book value that might be earned from the brands after acquisition. Such a calculation, however, would require estimates of capital required by brands and the expected after-acquisition return on investment (ROI) of a company.

Separating out the percentage of revenue or profits that is attributable to brand equity is a difficult task.[19] In the United States, there is no conventional accounting method for doing so. Thus, despite the fact that expert analysts estimate the value of the Coca-Cola name to approach $70 billion, it appears in the owner's books as only $25 *million*. Based on accounting rules, Coca-Cola's assets in 1999 were worth around $18 billion, but the stock market valued 2.5 billion shares at almost $70 a share, therefore pricing the company at nine times its assets. Clearly, market-based estimates of value can differ dramatically from those based on U.S. accounting conventions.[20] In other countries, however, there has been more movement in the direction of attempting to capture that value. How do you calculate the financial value of a brand? This section, after providing some accounting background and historical perspective, describes the leading brand valuation approach.

Accounting Background

The assets of a firm can be classified as either tangible or intangible. *Tangible assets* include property, plant, and equipment; current assets (inventories, marketable securities, and cash); and investments in stocks and bonds. The value of tangible assets can be estimated using accounting book values and reported estimates of replacement costs. *Intangible assets,* on the other hand, are defined as any factors of production or specialized resources that permit the company to earn cash flows in excess of the return on tangible assets. In other words, intangible assets augment the earning power of a firm's physical assets. Intangible assets are typically lumped by accountants under the heading of goodwill and include things such as patents, trademarks, and licensing agreements, as well as "softer" considerations such as the skill of the management and customer relations.

In an acquisition, the goodwill item often includes a premium paid to gain control, which, in certain instances, may even exceed the value of tangible and intangible assets. Despite these various types of intangibles being so disparate in nature, they are all swept together under the term *goodwill*. In Britain and certain other countries, it has been common to write off the goodwill element of an acquisition against reserves; tangible assets, on the other hand, are transferred straight to the acquiring company's balance sheet.

Historical Perspectives

Brand valuation's recent past started with Rupert Murdoch's News Corporation, which included a valuation of some of its magazines on its balance sheets in 1984, as permitted by Australian accounting standards. The rationale was that the goodwill element of publishing acquisitions—the difference in value between net assets and the price paid—was often enormous and negatively affecting the balance sheet. The recognition that the titles themselves contained much of the value of the acquisition was used to justify placing them on the balance sheet, improving the debt/equity ratio as a result and allowing News Corporation to get some much needed cash to finance the further acquisitions of some foreign media companies.

In the United Kingdom, Grand Metropolitan was one of the first British companies to place a monetary value on the brands it owned and to put that value on its balance sheet. When Grand Met acquired Heublin distributors, Pearle eye care, and Sambuca Romana liqueur in 1987, it placed the value of some of its brands—principally Smirnoff—on the balance sheet for roughly $1 billion. In doing so, Grand Met used one of two different methods. If a company consisted of primarily one brand, it figured that the value of the brand was 75 percent of the purchase price, whereas if the company had many brands, it used a multiple of an income figure.

British firms used brand values primarily to boost their balance sheets. By recording their brand assets, the firms maintained that they were attempting to bring their shareholder funds nearer to the market capitalization of the firm. In the United Kingdom, Rank Hovis McDougal (RHM) succeeded in putting the worth of the company's existing brands as a figure on the balance sheet to fight a hostile takeover bid in 1988. With the brand value information provided by Interbrand (via a method described later in this chapter), the RHM board was able to go back to investors and argue that the bid was too low, and eventually to repel it.

Accounting firms in favor of valuing brands argue that it is a way to strengthen the presentation of a company's accounts, to record hidden assets so that they are disclosed to company's shareholders, to enhance a company's shareholders' funds to improve its earnings ratios, to provide a realistic basis for management and investors to measure a company's performance, and to reveal detailed information on brand strengths so that management can formulate appropriate brand strategies. In practical terms, however, recording brand value as an intangible asset from the firm's perspective is a means to increase the asset value of the firm.

Actual practices have varied from country to country. Brand valuations have been accepted for inclusion in the balance sheets of companies in countries such as the United Kingdom, Australia, New Zealand, France, Sweden, Singapore, and Spain. When Grand Met acquired Pillsbury for $5.5 billion in January 1989, it revalued Pillsbury's intangible assets to add $2.4 billion to its intangible assets. Unlike a U.S. company, Grand Met did not intend to write down those intangible assets (unless permanently impaired). Grand Met also adjusted its goodwill account (separate from intangible assets) by a substantial amount as a result of the Pillsbury acquisition.[21]

In the United Kingdom, Martin Sorrell improved the balance sheet of WPP by attaching brand value to its primary assets, including J. Walter Thompson Company, Ogilvy & Mather, and Hill & Knowlton, stating in the annual report that:

> Intangible fixed assets comprise certain acquired separable corporate brand names. These are shown at a valuation of the incremental earnings expected to arise from the ownership of brands. The valuations have been based on the present value of notional royalty savings arising from [ownership] and on estimates of profits attributable to brand loyalty.[22]

In the United States, generally accepted accounting principles (blanket amortization principles) mean that placing a brand on the balance sheet would require amortization of that asset for up to 40 years. Such a charge would severely hamper firm profitability; as a result, firms avoid such accounting maneuvers. On the other hand, certain other countries (including Canada, Germany, and Japan) have gone beyond tax deductibility of brand equity to permit some or all of the goodwill arising from an acquisition to be deducted for tax purposes.

General Approaches

In determining the value of a brand in an acquisition or merger, three main approaches are possible: the cost, market, and income approaches.[23]

The cost approach maintains that brand equity is the amount of money that would be required to reproduce or replace the brand (including all costs for research and development, test marketing, advertising, etc.). One commonly noted criticism of approaches involving historic or replacement cost is that this rewards past performance in a way that may bear little relation to future profitability—for example, many brands with expensive introductions have been unsuccessful. On the other hand, for brands that have been around for decades (such as Heinz, Kellogg's, and Chanel), it would be virtually impossible to find out what the investment in brand development was—and largely irrelevant as well. Finally, it obviously is easier to estimate costs of tangible assets than intangible assets, but the latter often may lie at the heart of brand equity. Similar problems exist with a replacement cost approach; for example, the cost of replacing a brand depends a great deal on how quickly the process would take and what competitive, legal, and logistical obstacles might be encountered.

According to the market approach, brand equity can be thought of as the present value of the future economic benefits to be derived by the owner of the asset. In other words, it is the amount an active market would allow such that the asset would exchange between a willing buyer and willing seller. The main problems with this approach are the lack of open market transactions for brand name assets and the fact that the uniqueness of brands makes extrapolating from one market transaction to another problematic. The Science of Branding 10-2 reviews some considerations in the relationship of brand equity to the stock market.

The third approach to determining the value of a brand, the income approach, argues that brand equity is the discounted future cash flow from the future earnings stream for the brand. Three such income approaches are as follows:

1. Capitalizing royalty earnings from a brand name (when these can be defined)
2. Capitalizing the premium profits that are earned by a branded product (by comparing its performance with that of an unbranded product)
3. Capitalizing the actual profitability of a brand after allowing for the costs of maintaining it and the effects of taxation

As a very rough rule of thumb, Chevron's Lew Winters reports that accountants are inclined to price a brand at four to six times the annual profit realized from the sale of the product bearing the brand name to be acquired. The methodology described in the next section is largely based on an income approach.

Interbrand's Brand Valuation Methodology

Interbrand, probably the premier brand valuation firm, evaluated a number of different approaches in developing its brand valuation methodology. Its goal was to identify an approach that incorporated marketing, financial, and legal aspects; followed

Brand Equity and the Stock Market

An important topic, and one that has received increasing academic interest, is the relationship between brand equity valuations and stock market information and performance.

BRAND EQUITY ESTIMATES

Simon and Sullivan have developed a technique for estimating a firm's brand equity derived from financial market estimates of brand-related profits.[1] They define brand equity as the incremental cash flows that accrue to branded products over and above the cash flows that would result from the sale of unbranded products. To implement their approach, they begin by estimating the current market value of the firm. The market value of the firm's securities are then assumed to provide an unbiased estimate of the future cash flows that are attributable to all of the firm's assets. Their methodology attempts to extract the value of a firm's brand equity from the value of the firm's other assets. The result is an estimate of brand equity that is based on the financial market valuation of the firm's future cash flows.

Their rationale is as follows. They assume that the financial market value of a firm is based on the aggregate earning power of both tangible and intangible assets. They also make the "efficient-market" assumption that in a well-functioning capital market, securities prices provide the best available unbiased estimate of the value of a company's assets. In other words, the financial market's valuation of the firm incorporates the expected value of future cash flows and returns.

From these basic premises, Simon and Sullivan derive their methodology to extract the value of brand equity from the financial market value of the firm. The total asset value of the firm is defined as the sum of the market value of common stock, preferred stock, long-term debt, and short-term debt. The value of intangible assets is captured in the ratio of the market value of the firm to the replacement cost of its tangible assets. Three categories of intangible assets are defined: brand equity, nonbrand factors that reduce the firm's costs relative to competitors (e.g., R&D and patents), and industry-wide factors that permit monopoly profits, such as regulation. By considering factors such as the age of the brand, order of entry in the category, and current and past advertising share, Simon and Sullivan then provide estimates of brand equity.

Figure A displays their estimates of brand equity for some selected food companies. According to this analysis, the high estimated brand equity of Tootsie Roll suggests that even though it may be relatively easy to develop a "me-too" candy product, a considerable amount of the profits ascribed to Tootsie Roll accrue directly from its strong brand name. Simon and Sullivan conducted an in-depth analysis tracing the brand equity of Coca-Cola and Pepsi over three major events in the soft drink industry from 1982 to 1986—for example, showing how the introduction of Diet Coke increased the equity of Coca-Cola and decreased the equity of Pepsi.

Company	Brand Equity
Anheuser-Busch	35
Brown-Foreman	82
Cadbury Schweppes	44
Campbell	31
Dreyer's Ice Cream	151
General Mills	52
Heinz	62
Kellogg	61
Pillsbury	30
Quaker	59
Ralston Purina	40
Sara Lee	57
Seagram	73
Smucker	126
Tootsie Roll	148

FIGURE A   Simon and Sullivan's Measured Brand Equity for Food Product Companies (as a percentage of firm replacement value)

STOCK MARKET REACTIONS

Several researchers have studied how the stock market reacts to the brand equity for companies and products. For example, David Aaker and Robert Jacobson examined the association between yearly stock return and yearly brand changes (as measured by EquiTrend's perceived quality rating of brand equity) for 34 companies during the years 1989 to 1992.[2] They also compared the accompanying changes in current-term return on investment (ROI). They found that, as expected, stock market return was positively related to changes in ROI. Interestingly, they also uncovered a strong positive relationship between brand equity and stock return. Firms that experienced the largest gains in brand equity saw their stock return average 30 percent. Conversely, those firms with the largest losses in brand equity saw stock return average a negative 10 percent. The researchers concluded that investors can and do learn about changes in brand equity—not necessarily through EquiTrend studies (which may have little exposure to the financial community) but by learning about a company's plans and programs.

More recently, using data for firms in the computer industry in the 1990s, Aaker and Jacobson found that changes in brand attitude were associated contemporaneously with stock return and led accounting financial performance.[3] They also found five factors (new products, product problems, competitor actions, changes in top management, and legal actions) that were associated with significant changes in brand attitudes. Awareness that did not translate into more positive attitudes, however, did little to the stock price (e.g., Ameritrade, Juno, and Priceline). The authors conclude, "So it's not the brands customers know, but the brands customers respect, that are ultimately successful." Similarly, using *Financial World* estimates of brand equity, another comprehensive study found that brand equity was positively related to stock return and that this effect was incremental to other accounting variables such as the firm's net income.[4]

Adopting an event study methodology, Lane and Jacobson were able to show that stock market participants' response to brand extension announcements, consistent with the tradeoffs inherent in brand leveraging, depend interactively and nonmonoto-nically on brand attitude and familiarity.[5] Specifically, the stock market responded most favorably to extensions of high-esteem, high-familiarity brands (e.g., Hershey, Coke, Norton/Symantec) and to low-esteem, low-familiarity brands (in the latter case, presumably because there was little to risk and much to gain with extensions). The stock market reaction was less favorable (and sometimes even negative!) for extensions of brands for which consumer familiarity was disproportionately high compared with consumer regard and to extensions of brands for which consumer regard was disproportionately high compared with familiarity.

In another event study of 58 firms that changed their names in the 1980s, Horsky and Swyngedouw found that for most of the firms, name changes were associated with improved performance; the greatest improvement tended to occur in firms that produced industrial goods and whose performance prior to the change was relatively poor.[6] Not all changes, however, were successful. They interpret the act of a name change as a signal that other measures to improve performance (e.g., changes in product offerings and organizational changes) will be seriously and successfully undertaken.

[1]Carol J. Simon and Mary W. Sullivan, "Measurement and Determinants of Brand Equity: A Financial Approach," *Marketing Science* 12, no. 1 (Winter 1993): 28–52.

[2]David A. Aaker and Robert Jacobson, "The Financial Information Content of Perceived Quality," *Journal of Marketing Research* 31 (May 1994): 191–201.

[3]David A. Aaker and Robert Jacobson, "The Value Relevance of Brand Attitude in High-Technology Markets," *Journal of Marketing Research* 38 (November 2001): 485–493.

[4]M. E. Barth, M. Clement, G. Foster, and R. Kasznik, "Brand Values and Capital Market Valuation," *Review of Accounting Studies* 3 (1998): 41–68.

[5]Vicki Lane and Robert Jacobson, "Stock Market Reactions to Brand Extension Announcements: The Effects of Brand Attitude and Familiarity," *Journal of Marketing* 59 (January 1995): 63–77.

[6]Dan Horsky and Patrick Swyngedouw, "Does It Pay to Change Your Company's Name? A Stock Market Perspective," *Marketing Science* (Fall 1987): 320–335.

fundamental accounting concepts; allowed for regular revaluation on a consistent basis; and was suitable for acquired and home-grown brands.

Interbrand decided to approach the problem of brand valuation by assuming that the value of a brand, like the value of any other economic asset, was the present worth of the benefits of future ownership.[24] In other words, according to Interbrand, brand valuation is based on an assessment of what the value is today of the earnings or cash flow that the brand can be expected to generate in the future.

To estimate brand value, according to Interbrand, it is necessary to identify projected future earnings for the brand and the discount rate to adjust these earnings for inflation and risk. Based on all of these criteria, Interbrand has developed a two-step method of calculating brand value: (1) identifying the true brand earnings and cash flow and (2) capitalizing the earnings by applying a multiple to historic earnings as a discount rate to future cash flow.[25] Both steps require a number of different actions, as described next.

Brand Earnings   Interbrand believes that arriving at a measure of profitability is more complicated than merely applying a simple discount rate or multiplier to the post-tax profits of the brand-owning company. It maintains that not all of the profitability of a brand can necessarily be applied to the valuation of that brand. A brand may essentially be a commodity or derive much of its profitability from non-brand-related considerations (e.g., its distribution system). The elements of profitability that do not result from the brand's identity must therefore be excluded. In addition, because the valuation may be adversely affected by using a single, possibly unrepresentative, year's profit, a three-year weighted average of historical profit must be used.

A number of additional issues must be taken into consideration in calculating brand earnings: determining brand profits, eliminating private label production profits, remunerating capital, and so forth. In recognition of these considerations, brand earnings are calculated by subtracting a number of quantities from brand sales: costs of brand sales, marketing costs, variable and fixed overheads (including depreciation and central overhead allocation), remuneration of capital charge (a 5 percent to 10 percent rental charge on the replacement value of the capital employed in the line of production), and taxation.

Brand Strength   To adjust these earnings, Interbrand conducts an in-depth assessment of brand strength. Brand strength is reflected in a number of factors: historic and forecast, quantitative and qualitative, objective and subjective, and micro and macro. Assessing brand strength involves a detailed review of the brand, its positioning, the market in which it operates, competition, past performance, future plans, risks to the brand, and so forth. Specifically, to determine brand strength, Interbrand evaluates brands on the basis of the following seven factors and reasoning.[26]

1. *Leadership:* The brand's ability to influence its market and be a dominant force with a strong market share such that it can set price points, command distribution, and resist competitive invasions. A brand that leads its market or market sector is a more stable and valuable property than a brand lower down the order.

2. *Stability:* The ability of the brand to survive over a long period of time based on consumer loyalty and past history. Long-established brands that have become part of the fabric of their markets are particularly valuable.

3. *Market:* The brand's trading environment in terms of growth prospects, volatility, and barriers to entry. Brands in markets such as foods, drinks, and publishing are intrinsically more valuable than brands in, for example, high-tech or clothing areas because these latter markets are more vulnerable to technological or fashion changes.

4. *Geographic spread:* The ability of the brand to cross geographic and cultural borders. Brands that are international are inherently more valuable than national or regional brands due in part to their economies of scale.

5. *Trend:* The ongoing direction and ability of the brand to remain contemporary and relevant to consumers.

6. *Support:* The amount and consistency of marketing and communication activity. Those brand names that have received consistent investment and focused support must be regarded as more valuable than those that have not. Although the amount spent in supporting a brand is important, the quality of this support is equally significant.

7. *Protection:* The brand owner's legal titles. A registered trademark is a statutory monopoly in a name, device, or in a combination of these two. Other protection may exist in common law, at least in certain countries. The strength and breadth of the brand's protection is critical in assessing its worth.

Interbrand administers a detailed questionnaire to collect this information and may collect opinions from managers and customers, examine annual reports and other

Applications of Interbrand's Brand Valuation Methodology

Michael Birkin provides the following example of how four brands could be scored using Interbrand's brand valuation methodology.

Brand A This is a leading international toiletries brand operating in a mainstream and stable market sector. The brand has been established for many years and is a brand leader or a strong number two in all its major international markets.

Brand B This is a leading food brand that operates in a traditional and stable market, but one where tastes are slowly changing, with a move away from traditional products and toward convenience foods. The brand has limited export sales, and its trademark protection, though quite strong, is based mainly on common law rather than registered rights.

Brand C This is a secondary but aspiring national soft drink brand launched just five years ago. The market is very dynamic and growing strongly. The brand has been very heavily supported and much has been achieved; it is, however, still early days. Even though export sales are still very small, the brand name, "get up," and positioning have all been developed with international markets in mind. The brand still has some trademark registration problems in its home market.

Brand D This is an established but quite regional brand in a highly fragmented yet stable market.

Based on these profiles, the following scores might be given by Interbrand on the seven strength factors:

	Maximum Score	Brand A	Brand B	Brand C	Brand D
Leadership	25	18	19	9	6
Stability	15	11	10	7	11
Market	10	7	6	8	6
Internationality	25	17	5	2	0
Trend	10	6	6	7	5
Support	10	8	7	7	4
Protection	5	5	3	4	3
Total	100	72	56	44	35

Source: Michael Birkin, "Assessing Brand Value," in *Brand Power*, ed. Paul Stobart (Washington Square, NY: New York University Press, 1994).

printed materials, and even conduct inspection visits to distributors and retail outlets. Branding Brief 10-2 provides an example of how four different brands might be scored.

The brand strength is a composite of these seven factors, each of which is scored according to established guidelines (see Figure 10-5). The scores are weighted, and the resulting total, known as the brand strength score, is expressed as a percentage. This score is in turn converted to an earnings multiple to be used against the brand-related profits. Certain adjustments are made to created a weighted average of post-tax brand

Leadership (25%)
Market share
Awareness
Positioning
Competitor profile

Internationality (25%)
Geographic spread
International positioning
Relative market share
Prestige
Ambition

Stability (15%)
Longevity
Coherence
Consistency
Brand identity
Risks

Trend (10%)
Long-term market share performance
Projected brand performance
Sensibility of brand plans
Competitive actions

Market (10%)
What is the market?
Nature of the market (e.g., volatility)
Size of market
Market dynamics
Barriers to entry

Support (10%)
Consistency of message
Consistency of spending
Above vs. below line
Brand franchise

Protection (5%)
Trademark registration and registrability
Common law
Litigation/disputes

FIGURE 10-5   Interbrand's Brand Strength Attributes

profitability against which the brand multiplier is applied. Interbrand makes the comparison between the reciprocal of these multipliers and typical discount rates (or interest rates): A so-called perfect brand with a brand strength score of 100 would have a discount rate of 5 percent (1 over 20), which would be the typical return on a fairly low-risk investment; a weaker brand with a lower multiplier would have a higher discount rate to reflect the greater risk.

Interbrand notes that the relationship between brand strength and brand value follows a normal distribution and is represented by a classic S curve as a result of the following factors:[27]

➤ As a brand's strength increases from virtually zero (an unknown or new brand) to a position as the number three or four brand in a national market, the brand value increases gradually.

➤ As a brand moves into the number one or two position in its market or becomes internationally known, or both, there is an exponential effect on its brand value.

➤ Once a brand is established as a powerful world brand, its value no longer increases at the same exponential rate even if market share internationally is improved.

Branding Brief 10-3 describes how *Financial World* magazine applied the Interbrand methodology to value the Coke brand.

Financial World's Calculation of the Value of the Coca-Cola Brand

Although now defunct, *Financial World* magazine provided estimates of the brand equity of leading brands on the basis of a formula very similar to that of Interbrand. The magazine began its calculations with company sales and, based on expert estimates of margin, the resulting operating profits. Next, it deducted from operating profits an amount equal to what would have been earned on a basic unbranded or generic version of the product. For example, it estimated, again based on expert opinion, the amount of capital required to generate a brand's sales, multiplied that amount by the net return on that capital (e.g., it assumed a generic version of the product would generate a 5 percent net return on capital employed) and subtracted that figure from operating profits to determine the profit attributable to the brand name alone. After adjusting for taxes, the remainder was deemed net brand-related profits. Finally, it assigned a multiple based on Interbrand's seven-factor model of brand strength. The stronger the brand, the higher the multiple, ranging from 6 to 20.

For example, *Financial World* began its calculation of the value of the Coca-Cola brand in 1993 with the worldwide sales figure for the Coca-Cola brand family of $9 billion. Based on estimates of consultants and beverage experts, it assumed that Coke's operating margin was around 30 percent, resulting in operating profits for the Coke brand of $2.8 billion. Although Coke's extensive bottling and distribution system generated another $27 billion in revenues and $3 billion in operating profits, these numbers were not taken into consideration in valuing the Coca-Cola brand because they did not reflect the value added by Coke directly.

With Coke's product-related profits in place, *Financial World* next deducted from these operating profits an amount equal to what could have been expected to be earned on a basic or generic version of the product. To do so, it assumed, based on analysts' calculations, that it required on average 60 cents worth of capital (which is generally a little higher than net property, plant, and equipment plus net working capital) to produce each dollar of sales. Thus, *Financial World* calculated the capital used in production for Coke to be $5.5 billion. It next assumed that a 5 percent net return on employed capital after inflation could be expected from a similar nonbranded product and therefore deducted 5 percent of Coke's capital employed ($273 million) from the $2.7 billion in operating profits to obtain the profit attributable to the brand name alone.

The resulting adjusted operating profit figure was $2.4 billion. After adjusting for taxes, the remainder was deemed to be net brand-related profits. The final adjustment was made on the basis of brand strength. Brand strength was calculated based on Interbrand's definition and seven components. Consistent with Interbrand's approach, the brand strength multiplier takes on values ranging from 9 to 20. Coke was assigned the highest multiple, resulting in a brand value of $33.4 billion. Although *Financial World* ceased publication, Interbrand continues to rank top brands. In 2001, Coca-Cola's brand value figure rose to $68.95 billion, and it was deemed the world's most valuable brand.

Summary

Brand valuation and the "brands on the balance sheet" debate are controversial subjects.[28] The advantage of the Interbrand valuation approach is that it is very generalizable and can be applied to virtually any type of brand or product. Yet even Interbrand recognizes the complexities involved:

> The valuation of brands is still a relatively new concept. There is no active market in brands, as there is with stocks and shares or real estate. Brand valuation is without question partly art and partly science. Judgment is involved just as it is for any other valuation method for any other asset, tangible or intangible. Specialized knowledge of marketing, accounting and trade mark law is required to ensure that the correct blend of professional skills is present. Any brand valuation method has to take into account a wide variety of data, both factual and qualitative. Skilled professional judgment is needed to arrive at the right conclusions on the role of the brand, its strength and the underlying stream of cash flow it generates. All of the conclusions reached need to be supported as far as possible by independent research studies.[29]

Many marketing experts, however, feel it is impossible to reduce the richness of a brand to a single, meaningful number and that any formula is an abstraction and arbitrary. Thus, the primary disadvantage of valuation approaches is that they make a host of potentially oversimplified assumptions to arrive at one measure of brand equity. For example, Sir Michael Perry, chairman of Unilever, objects for philosophical reasons:

> The seemingly miraculous conjuring up of intangible asset values, as if from nowhere, only serves to reinforce the view of the consumer skeptics, that brands are just high prices and consumer exploitation. At Unilever, we have consistently rejected this approach.[30]

Wharton's Peter Fader points out a number of limitations of valuation approaches: They require much judgmental data and thus contain much subjectivity; intangible assets are not always synonymous with brand equity; the methods sometimes defy common sense and lack "face validity" (e.g., IBM's brand equity bounced around from number 3 or number 4 to as low as number 282 according to *Financial World* over just a few years); the financial measures generally ignore or downplay current investments in future equity (e.g., advertising or R&D); and the strength of the brand measures may be confounded with the strength of the company.[31]

At the heart of much of the criticism is the issue of separability that was identified earlier. An *Economist* editorial put it this way: "Brands can be awkward to separate as assets. With Cadbury's Dairy Milk, how much value comes from the name Cadbury?

How much from Dairy Milk? How much merely from the product's (replicable) contents or design?"[32] To make a sports analogy, extracting brand value may be as difficult as determining the value of the coach to a team's performance.

As a result of these criticisms, the climate regarding brand valuation has changed. In 1989, Britain's Accounting Standards Committee ruled that companies could only value brands if they were acquired in a takeover and only if they were then depreciated over 20 years against profits—adopting the more conservative American practice of gradually writing off goodwill (brands and all). The International Accounting Standards Committee is also grappling with the issue.

Review

This chapter considered the two main ways to measure the benefits or outcomes of brand equity: comparative methods (a means to better assess the effects of consumer perceptions and preferences on aspects of the marketing program) and holistic methods (attempts to come up with an estimate of the overall value of the brand). Figure 10-6 summarizes the different approaches, which can be seen as complementary. In fact, understanding the particular range of benefits for a brand on the basis of comparative methods may be useful as inputs in estimating the overall value of a brand by holistic methods.

Combining these outcome measures with the measures of sources of brand equity from Chapter 9 as part of the brand value chain can provide insight into the effectiveness of marketing actions. Nevertheless, assessing the ROI of marketing activities

FIGURE 10-6 Measures of Outcomes of Brand Equity

Comparative methods: Involve experiments that examine consumer attitudes and behavior toward a brand to more directly assess the benefits arising from having a high level of awareness and strong, favorable, and unique brand associations.

- *Brand-based comparative approaches:* Experiments in which one group of consumers responds to an element of the marketing program when it is attributed to the brand and another group responds to that same element when it is attributed to a competitive or fictitiously named brand.
- *Marketing-based comparative approaches:* Experiments in which consumers respond to changes in elements of the marketing program for the brand or competitive brands.
- *Conjoint analysis:* A survey-based multivariate technique that enables marketers to profile the consumer buying decision process with respect to products and brands.

Holistic methods: Attempt to place an overall value on the brand in either abstract utility terms or concrete financial terms. Thus, holistic methods attempt to "net out" various considerations to determine the unique contribution of the brand.

- *Residual approach:* Examines the value of the brand by subtracting out consumers' preferences for the brand based on physical product attributes alone from their overall brand preferences.
- *Valuation approach:* Places a financial value on the brand for accounting purposes, mergers and acquisitions, or other such reasons.

remains a challenge.[33] Four general guidelines can be offered for how to improve the ability to create and detect ROI from brand marketing activities:

1. *Spend wisely—focus and be creative.* To be able to measure ROI, there needs to be a return to begin with! By investing in distinctive and well-designed marketing activities, there is a greater chance that a more positive and discernible ROI will ensue.

2. *Look for benchmarks—examine competitive spending levels and historical company norms.* It is important to get the lay of the land in a market or category to understand the boundaries of what might be expected.

3. *Be strategic—apply brand equity models.* Use models such as the CBBE model and the brand value chain to provide discipline and a structured approach to planning, implementing, and interpreting marketing activity.

4. *Be observant—track both formally and informally.* Qualitative and quantitative insights can be used to better understand brand performance.

Perhaps the dominant theme of this and the previous chapter on measuring sources of brand equity is the importance of employing multiple measures and research methods to capture the richness and complexity of brand equity. No matter how well conducted, single measures of brand equity run the risk of missing important dimensions of brand equity. Recall the problems encountered by Coca-Cola from its overreliance on blind taste tests, described in Branding Brief 1-1. In explaining the New Coke debacle, marketing consultant Randy Scruggs makes an interesting analogy concerning the effects of Coca-Cola's focus on a single measure to assess consumer response, likening it to the interpretation that someone might give when viewing a pencil head-on from the end with the eraser.[34] From that perspective, a pencil might look like a circle. If one were to look through a magnifying glass—akin to Coke's 190,000 taste tests—one would be even more convinced that what one was looking at was a circle! Only if one were to look at the pencil from other angles and perspectives would it be clear that the object was multidimensional and had shape. Thus, as this analogy suggests, a single measure only provides at best a one- or two-dimensional view of a brand. To extend Scruggs's analogy, measuring the volume of a pencil may reveal something about its size but would say nothing about well the pencil writes, how comfortable it would be to hold, and so forth. Thus, any one measure of a multidimensional concept such as brand equity necessarily overlooks or distorts important information.

Consistent with this view and according to the definition of customer-based brand equity, no single number or measure fully captures brand equity.[35] Rather, brand equity should be thought of as a multidimensional concept that depends on what knowledge structures are present in the minds of consumers and what actions a firm takes to capitalize on the potential offered by these knowledge structures. Thus, there are many different sources of brand equity and many different possible outcomes of brand equity depending on the skill and ingenuity of the marketers involved. Different firms may be more or less able to maximize the potential value of a brand according to the type and nature of their marketing activities. Branding Brief 10-4 describes several brand acquisitions that turned out unsuccessfully for firms. As Wharton's Peter Fader says:

> The actual value of a brand depends on its fit with buyer's corporate structure and other assets. If the acquiring company has manufacturing or distribution capabilities that are synergistic with the brand, then it might be worth paying

Beauty Is in the Eye of the Beholder

Companies make acquisitions because they wish to grow and expand their business. In making acquisitions, a company has to determine what it feels that the acquiring brands are worth. In some instances, the hoped-for brand value has failed to materialize, serving as a reminder that the value of a brand is partly a function of what you do with it.

A classic example is Quaker Oats's $1.7 billion acquisition of Snapple in 1994. Snapple had become a popular national brand through powerful grassroots marketing and a willingness to distribute to small outlets and convenience stores. Quaker changed Snapple's ad campaign—abandoning the rotund and immensely popular Snapple Lady—and revamped its distribution system. Quaker also changed the packaging by updating the label and putting Snapple in 64-ounce bottles, moves that did not sit well with loyal customers. The results were disastrous: Snapple began losing money and market share, allowing a host of competitors to move in. Unable to revive the foundering brand, Quaker sold the company in 1997 for $300 million to Triarc, which owned other beverages such as Royal Crown Cola and Diet Rite.

Another unsuccessful acquisition occurred when Quality Dining bought Bruegger's Bagels in 1996 with $142 million in stock. Within one year, Quality Dining agreed to sell the bagel chain back to its original owners for $50 million after taking a $203 million charge on the acquisition. Experts blamed an overly ambitious expansion strategy. Quality Dining planned to expand to 2,000 stores within four years, despite the fact that before the acquisition, Bruegger's posted two consecutive annual losses due to its expansion to 339 stores. The new ownership also set the lofty goal of entering the top 60 domestic markets, which limited the amount of advertising and promotional support each market received. As Bruegger's fortunes turned, competitor Einstein/Noah Bagel overtook the company as the market leader in the United States. One franchisee commented, "[Quality Dining] would have had to stay up pretty late at night to screw up anything more than they did."

In 1996, Wells Fargo acquired competitor First Interstate Bancorp for $12.9 billion. The acquisition failed largely because the two banks had differing business styles. Wells Fargo focused on providing convenience for its customers, whereas First Interstate concentrated on offering customer service and support through its network of neighborhood branches. Following the merger, however, Wells Fargo alienated many First Interstate customers by failing to deliver on its promise that "it will be business as usual" for those customers. The bigger bank lost customers' deposits, bounced good checks, made balance errors, and answered customer complaints slowly or not at all. Many customers closed their accounts with Wells Fargo, causing non-California accounts to fall between 1 percent and 1.5 percent per month during 1997. The chairman and president of Wells Fargo apologized to bank customers in the 1997 annual report and admitted that "Overall, it was a sorry experience for far too many of our customers." Unfortunately for Wells Fargo, the customer exodus had a negative effect on earnings, and the bank was acquired in 1998 by Minneapolis-based Norwest.

Sources: "Cadbury Is Paying Triarc $1.45 Billion for Snapple Unit," *Baltimore Sun*, 19 September 2000; Thomas M. Burton, "The Profit Center of the Bagel Business Has Quite a Big Hole," *Wall Street Journal*, 6 October 1997; Jim Carlton, "Wells Fargo Discovers Getting Together Is Hard to Do," *Wall Street Journal*, 21 July 1997; David Olive, "Merger Track Record Spotty," *Financial Post*, 15 December 1998.

Loyalty

1. Price Premium
   - For a 17-ounce package of chocolate chip cookies, Nabisco is priced at $2.16. How much extra would you be willing to pay to obtain Pepperidge Farm instead of Nabisco?
   - Brand Y would have to cost _____ percent less than Brand X before I would switch brands.
   - For a 16-ounce package of chocolate chip cookies, would you prefer Nabisco at $2.16 or Pepperidge Farm at $2.29?
2. Satisfaction/Loyalty (among those who have used the brand)
   - Considering my recent use experience, I would say I was (dissatisfied, satisfied, delighted).
   - The brand met my expectations during the last use experience.
   - Would you buy the brand on the next opportunity?
   - Would you recommend the product or service to others?
   - The brand is (the only, one of two, one of three, one of more than three) brand(s) that I buy and use.

Perceived Quality and Leadership

3. Perceived Quality

In comparison with alternative brands, this brand is . . .
   - Very high quality
   - Consistently high quality
   - (The best, one of the best, one of the worst, the worst)
4. Leadership/Popularity

In comparison with alternative brands, this brand is . . .
   - Growing in popularity
   - A leading brand in the category
   - Respected for innovation

Esteem

In comparison with alternative brands, I
   - Hold this brand in high esteem
   - Highly respect this brand

Associations and Differentiation

5. Perceived Value
   - The brand is good value for the money.
   - There is a reason to buy this brand over others.
6. Personality
   - This brand has a personality.
   - This brand is interesting.
   - I have a clear image of the type of person who would use the brand.
   - This brand has a rich history.
7. Organization
   - This is a brand I would trust.
   - I admire the Brand X organization.
   - I would be proud to do business with the Brand X organization.

(Continued)

FIGURE 10-7 Aaker's Measures of Brand Equity across Products and Markets

Associations and Differentiation (cont.)

Differentiation
- This brand is different from other brands.
- This brand is basically the same as the other brands.

Awareness
8. Brand Awareness
- Name the brands in this product class.
- Have you heard of this brand?
- Do you have an opinion about this brand?
- Are you familiar with this brand?

Market Behavior
9. Market Share
- Market share based on market surveys of usage or syndicated data
10. Price and Distribution Indices
- Relative market price—the average price at which the brand was sold during the month, divided by the average price at which all brands were sold
- The percentage of stores carrying the brand
- The percentage of people who have access to the brand

FIGURE 10-7   *(Continued)*

a lot of money for it. Paul Feldwick, a British executive, makes the analogy between brands and properties on the Monopoly game board. You're willing to pay a lot more for Marvin Gardens if you already own Atlantic and Ventnor Avenues![36]

Accordingly, the customer-based brand equity framework emphasizes the importance of employing a range of research measures and methods to fully capture the multiple potential sources and outcomes of brand equity, as the next two chapters will consider. Figure 10-7 displays "The Brand Equity Ten"—a set of crucial brand equity and tracking measures according to leading branding guru David Aaker.[37]

Discussion Questions

1. Choose a product. Conduct a branded and unbranded experiment. What do you learn about the equity of the brands in that product class?
2. Can you identify any other advantages or disadvantages of the comparative methods?
3. Pick a brand and conduct an analysis similar to that done with the Planter's brand. What do you learn about its extendability as a result?
4. What do you think of the Interbrand methodology? What do you see as its main advantages and disadvantages?
5. What do you think of Young & Rubicam's BrandAsset Valuator (see Brand Focus 10.0)? What do you see as its main advantages and disadvantages?

Brand Focus 10.0

Young & Rubicam's BrandAsset Valuator

This appendix summarizes Young & Rubicam's presentation of its BrandAsset Valuator (BAV), the world's largest database of consumer-derived information on brands.[38] BAV measures brands on four fundamental measures of equity value and in terms of a broad array of perceptual dimensions. BAV provides comparative measures of the equity value of thousands of brands across hundreds of different categories, as well as a set of strategic brand management tools for planning brand extensions, joint branding ventures, and other strategies designed to maintain and grow brand value. BAV has now also been linked to a unique set of financial analytics, which allows determining a brand's contribution to a company's intangible value.

Since 1993 BAV has carried out research with almost 300,000 consumers in 40 countries. Consumers' perceptions of approximately 19,000 brands have been collected across the same set of 56 parameters.

BAV represents a unique brand equity research tool. Unlike most conventional brand image surveys, respondents evaluate brands from many different categories rather than just those within a narrowly defined category. BAV is thus able to follow truly global brand trends and to draw the broadest possible conclusions about how consumer-level brand equity is created and built—or lost. In the United States, data are now collected in quarterly waves, which allows short-term trends in branding to be followed.

In addition to the original measures, recent BAV surveys have included greater emphasis on brand usage and future usage intent, and have also built in a specially developed set of measures of brand loyalty.

FOUR PILLARS

There are four key components of brand health in BAV—the four pillars. Each pillar is derived from various measures that relate to different aspects of consumers' brand perceptions and that together trace the progression of a brand's development.

➤ *Differentiation* measures the degree to which a brand is seen as different from others. This is a necessary condition for profitable brand building.

➤ *Relevance* measures the breadth of a brand's appeal (the overall size of a brand's franchise) but not necessarily its profitability.

➤ *Esteem* measures how well the brand is regarded and respected—in short, how well it's liked.

➤ *Knowledge* measures how familiar and intimate consumers are with brand. Interestingly, high knowledge is inversely related to a brand's potential.

Leading Indicators of Brand Health: Brand Strength

Differentiation (the extent to which a brand has a distinctive meaning for the consumer and is able to gain consumer choice, preference, and loyalty) and relevance (which correlates with household penetration) combine to determine brand strength. These two pillars point to the brand's future value, rather than just reflecting its past.

Lagging Indicators of Brand Health: Brand Stature

Esteem and knowledge together create brand stature, which is a "report card" on a brand's past performance.

Pillar Patterns

The examination of the relationships between these four dimensions—a brand's "pillar pattern"—reveals much about a brand's current and future status. Examples of four typical pillar patterns are shown in Figure 10-8. New brands, just after they are launched, show low levels on all four pillars. Strong new brands tend to show higher levels of differentiation than relevance, while both esteem and knowledge are lower still. "Leadership" brands show high levels on all four pillars. Finally, declining brands show high knowledge—evidence of past performance—relative to a lower level of esteem, and even lower relevance and differentiation.

Comparison of pillar patterns between brands—in the same or different categories—permits the diagnosis of brands' relative strengths and weaknesses, whereas tracking changes in pillar patterns for the same brand over time traces the progress of the brand's consumer equity value.

THE POWERGRID

Young & Rubicam has integrated the two macrodimensions of brand strength (differ-

entiation and relevance) and brand stature (esteem and knowledge) into a visual analytical device known as the PowerGrid, illustrated in Figure 10-9. The PowerGrid depicts the stages in the cycle of brand development—each with its characteristic pillar patterns—in successive quadrants.

Brands generally begin their life in the lower left quadrant, where they first need to develop relevant differentiation and establish their reason for being.

Most often, the movement from there is "up" into the top left quadrant. Increased differentiation, followed by relevance, initiates a growth in brand strength. These developments occur before the brand has acquired esteem or is widely known. This quadrant represents two types of brands: For brands destined for a mass target, this is the stage of emerging potential, in which the brand's growing strength must be translated into stature. Specialist or narrowly targeted brands, however, tend to remain in this quadrant (when viewed from the perspective of a mass audience) and can use their strength to occupy a profitable niche. From the point of view of brand leaders, new potential competitors will emerge from this quadrant.

The upper right quadrant, the Leadership Quadrant, is populated by brand leaders—those that have both high levels of brand strength and brand stature. Both older and relatively new brands can be in this quadrant, meaning that brand leadership is truly a function of the pillar measures, not just of longevity, and that, when properly

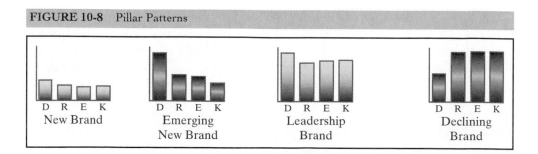

FIGURE 10-8   Pillar Patterns

D R E K	D R E K	D R E K	D R E K
New Brand	Emerging New Brand	Leadership Brand	Declining Brand

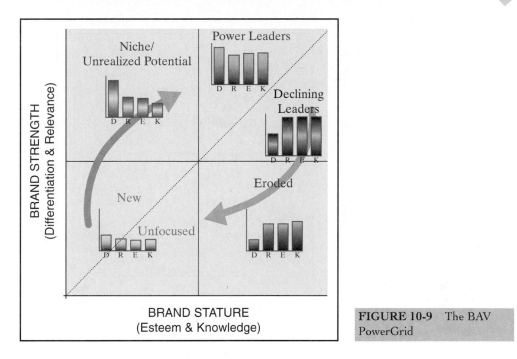

FIGURE 10-9   The BAV PowerGrid

managed, a brand can build and maintain a leadership position indefinitely. Although declining brand equity is not inevitable, brands whose strength has declined (usually driven by declining differentiation) can also be seen in this same quadrant. Brands whose strength has started to dip below the level of their stature display the first signs of weakness, which may well be masked by their still—buoyant sales and wide penetration.

Brands that fail to maintain their brand strength—their relevant differentiation— begin to fade and move "down" into the bottom right quadrant. These brands become vulnerable not just to existing competitors, but also to the depredations of discount price brands, and they frequently end up being drawn into heavy and continuous price promotion in order to defend their consumer franchise and market share. This process, if allowed to continue, takes its toll on brand stature, which also starts to decline. Figure 10-10 provides a recent depiction of brands in each of these quadrants, and Figure 10-11 shows how brand development may vary by different markets; for example, Coca-Cola has a much more uniform global image than, say, Apple Computer, Esteé Lauder, or American Express.

BRAND IMAGE ASSOCIATIONS

In addition to the pillar measures, BAV measures brands on a series of 48 brand image and brand personality attributes. Brand imagery can be analyzed in terms of all the single attributes or in terms of a reduced number of factor groupings. Because, like all BAV measures, the image attributes have been selected for their applicability to all categories, it is possible to compare the images of brands in widely differing categories. One very useful technique when trying to understand a brand's positioning is to determine which other brands its image is closest to. For example, for an Internet commerce site or computer brand, it is very helpful to know whether the

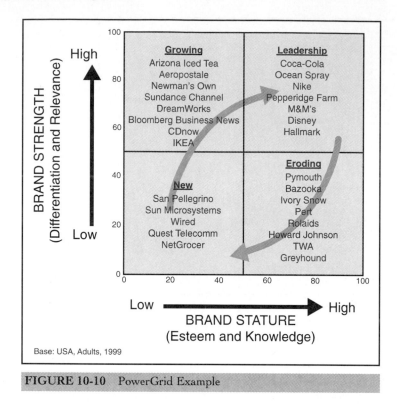

FIGURE 10-10   PowerGrid Example

brand's image has more in common with the Gap or with Macy's.

Drivers of Brand Strength and Stature

By analyzing the relationships between a brand's imagery on attributes and its position in the PowerGrid, it is possible to obtain a very precise understanding of the type of imagery that drives brand strength and brand stature.

Brand Elasticity

Because the BAV covers so many different categories, one of the key uses of the brand image component of BAV is to examine brand elasticity—the ease with which a brand can be "stretched" into a new category. According to BAV, the probability of success of such brand extensions depends on two criteria:

➤ Brand profile similarity: How similar— across all 48 attributes—is the image of the brand to the image of the brands in the target category? Does the brand have "permission to play"? Does its image match the lowest common denominator of the target category, the imagery shared by all brands in the category and which thus represents the minimum cost of entry?

➤ Does the brand have what it takes to stand out, to create differentiation in the new category? Although the image of the brand may have given it strong differentiation in its original category, this same imagery may not serve it so well in the new category. Does it also have necessary points of parity that would allow this differentiation to matter?

As shown in Figure 10-12, cross-analysis of these two criteria, according to Young & Rubicam, provides a clear prescription for alternative brand extension strategies.

If the brand's imagery satisfies the cost of entry for the category and also has the

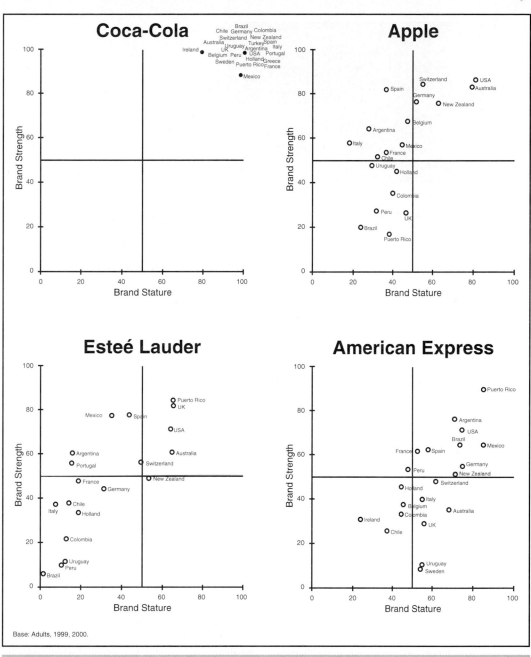

Base: Adults, 1999, 2000.

FIGURE 10-11 Global BAV PowerGrids for Four Leading Brands

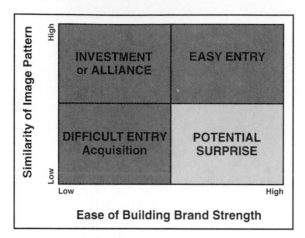

FIGURE 10-12   Brand Elasticity

ability to drive differentiation, this is the clearest green light for pushing ahead with the brand extension.

When a brand's imagery has what it takes to create differentiation in the new category but lacks the cost-of-entry image characteristics, then entry into that category will not be easy, but the brand may be able to achieve an "ambush" entry. If its differentiating characteristics are sufficient to overcome the barriers and gain it credibility, they will then propel it to a position of strength in the new category.

When the brand's image profile is dissimilar to the new category and its current imagery would not differentiate it in the new category, then the chances of a successful extension are low, and an entry into the category would be better accomplished via the acquisition either of an existing brand already in the category or of one whose imagery makes it more suitable for the job.

If a brand's imagery meets the cost-of-entry level for the new category but is lacking in drivers of differentiation, then it is clear that a successful entry can be achieved, but only with considerable investment. In this case, an alternative solution is to seek an alliance with another brand in the category: The two brands may be able to

reinforce each other's strengths and jointly create a stronger presence there.

Brand Alliances

In a recent addition to the BAV, the effect on individual brands of different types of brand alliances—from sweepstakes promotions through Web site links between brands—has been directly measured. The effects are various and unpredictable. For example:

➤ Alliances between Levi's and Wal-Mart produced an improvement of the brand strength of Wal-Mart, but left Levi's virtually unchanged.

➤ In contrast, Levi's did benefit from an alliance with Yahoo, growing differentiation and brand strength.

BRANDECONOMICS

BAV represents a potentially useful tool for brand valuation. By itself, BAV can be used to measure and track elements related to consumer-based brand equity. It has now been linked with a set of financial analytic tools that precisely measure the financial contribution of a company's brands to its balance sheet. As a consequence, the brand's economics can be better quantified.

Using these BrandEconomics tools (developed by Stern Stewart & Company) in conjunction with BAV, it is now possible to try to link the development of consumer-based brand equity—and the strategic brand management disciplines necessary to build and maintain it—with company financials. These metrics provide an insight into the value of the brand within the context of the current marketplace and company portfolio. Extensions of the BAV analytic tools, such as elasticity analysis, can then be used to quantify the relative costs and benefits of brand extension into new categories.

Intangible Value

Brand value contributes to a company's intangible value. When financial markets evaluate a firm's value, they evaluate its ability to generate returns over and above those necessary to "pay" for its use of tangible capital. Stern Stewart calls this "premium to tangible capital" the economic value added (EVA) of a company.[39] EVA is a measure of

profit less the cost of all capital employed.[40] EVA is also the spread between a company's return on and cost of capital, multiplied by invested capital. For example, if a $100,000 investment in a firm produces a 5 percent return whereas investments of similar risk elsewhere produce a 15 percent return, the EVA would be −$10,000.

As shown in Figure 10-13, a firm's total intangible value can be partitioned into its current EVA and expectations about its future growth value (FGV). Each company's brands—and the intangible value they represent—are key drivers of both current EVA and the company's future growth potential.

The relationship between brand value and company value is reflected in the PowerGrid. By applying the Brand-Economics analysis to brands in the BAV database and superimposing these analytics on the BAV PowerGrid, the relationship between brand and intangible value is revealed (see Figure 10-14). For the brands in

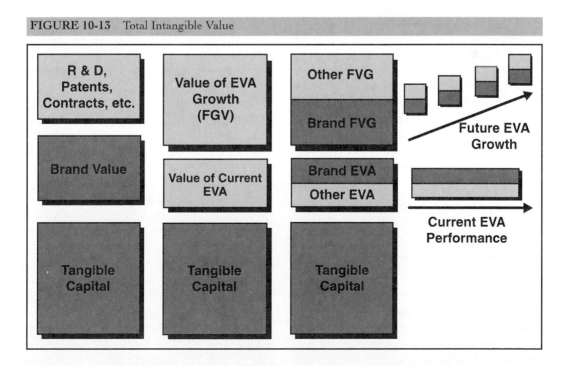

FIGURE 10-13   Total Intangible Value

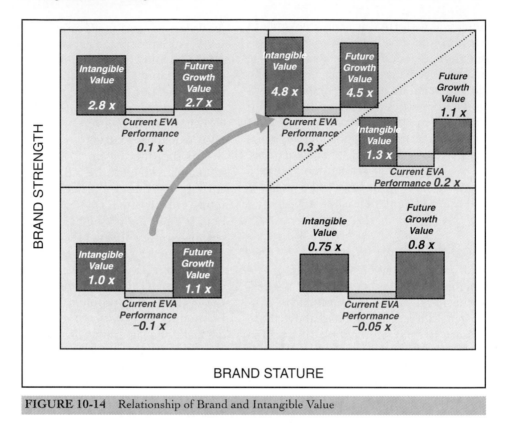

FIGURE 10-14 Relationship of Brand and Intangible Value

each quadrant of the PowerGrid, the average intangible value for the firms in each quadrant is calculated, while the core split of EVA and FGV from this intangible value is shown as multiples of sales. As reflected in these multiples, maximizing brand health garners greater intangible value multiples on average. In addition, the importance of FGV when measuring brand health is revealed. Across the board, brand value contributes most to a company's FGV portion of intangible value.

What Does This New Look at the PowerGrid Show?

Down in the new-brand territory (bottom left), the level of intangible value is not remarkable. The current EVA is actually slightly negative—these companies are not quite paying their shareholders for the use

of capital—while the FGV is just over 1. Brands do not play that significant a role in the valuation of a firm's intangible value in this quadrant.

As brands get stronger and move into the top left quadrant, the ratio of intangible value to sales jumps by a factor of almost 3. When examining the split between EVA and FGV, future growth potential remains the primary contributor to a firm's intangible value. Thus, the potential contained in these companies' brands has been recognized in the market's valuation of them, but this potential has yet to move to the bottom line. Brands are therefore emerging and gaining recognition, but are not leaders.

For leadership brand companies, the ratio of intangible value to sales is nearly 5, while for those in the same quadrant whose brand strength has begun to decline, the ratio is only 1.3—hardly better than those companies whose brands are just starting out. Leadership potential among brands is therefore related to stronger financial valuations, whereas eroding leadership status demarcates decline on both a brand and market valuation level.

Finally, for companies whose brands have seriously eroded, intangible value is less than their sales. Many Chapter 11 brands and firms are found in this quadrant. The financial metrics confirm this slip in the intangible value of these firms.

Thus, combining BrandEconomics with BAV closes the gap between company and brand valuation. These tools can be an integral component of strategic management. Not only does management possess the tools necessary for developing and maintaining healthy brands, but strategic investments in brands can now be evaluated in terms of their effect at the level of concern and on shareholder value.

SUMMARY

There is a lot of commonalty between the basic BAV model and the CBBE framework, as the four factors in the BAV model can easily be related to elements of the CBBE framework:

➤ BAV's knowledge relates to CBBE's brand awareness and familiarity

➤ BAV's esteem relates to CBBE's favorability of brand associations

➤ BAV's relevance relates to CBBE's strength of brand associations (as well as perhaps favorability)

➤ BAV's differentiation relates to CBBE's uniqueness of brand associations

Note that brand awareness and familiarity are handled differently in the two approaches. The CBBE framework maintains that awareness is a necessary *first* step in building brand equity. The BAV model treats familiarity in a more affective manner—almost in a warm feeling or friendship sense—and thus sees it as the *last* step in building brand equity.

The main advantage of the BAV model is that it provides rich descriptions and profiles of a numbers of brands. It also provides focus on four key branding dimensions. It provides a brand landscape in which marketers can see where their brands are located relative to other prominent brands or with respect to different markets. The descriptive nature of the BAV model does mean, however, that there is potentially less insight as to exactly *how* a brand could rate highly on those factors. Because the measures underlying the four factors have to be relevant across a very disparate range of product categories, the measures (and thus the factors) tend to be abstract in nature and not related directly to product attributes or benefits and more specific marketing concerns. Nevertheless, the BAV model represents a landmark study in terms of marketers' ability to better understand what drives top brands and where their brands fit in with other brands.

Notes

1. Richard F. Chay, "How Marketing Researchers Can Harness the Power of Brand Equity," *Marketing Research* 3, no. 2 (1991): 10–30.
2. Peter Farquhar and Yuji Ijiri make several other distinctions in classifying brand equity measurement procedures. Peter H. Farquhar, Julia W. Han, and Yuji Ijiri, "Recognizing and Measuring Brand Assets," *Marketing Science Institute Report* (1991): 91–119. They describe two broad classes of measurement approaches to brand equity: Separation approaches and integration approaches. *Separation approaches* view

brand equity as the value added to a product. Farquhar and Ijiri categorize separation approaches into residual methods and comparative methods. *Residual methods* determine brand equity by what remains after subtracting physical product effects. *Comparative methods* determine brand equity by comparing the branded product with an unbranded product or an equivalent benchmark.

    Integration approaches, on the other hand, typically define brand equity as a composition of basic elements. Farquhar and Ijiri categorize integration approaches into association and valuation methods. *Valuation methods* measure brand equity by its cost or value as an intangible asset for a particular owner and intended use. *Association methods* measure brand equity in terms of the favorableness of brand evaluations, the accessibility of brand attitudes, and the consistency of brand image with consumers.

    The previous chapter described techniques that could be considered association methods. This chapter considers techniques related to the other three categories of methods.

3. B. G. Yovovich, "What Is Your Brand Really Worth?" *Adweek's Marketing Week*, 8 August 1988, 18–24.

4. Edgar Pessemier, "A New Way to Determine Buying Decisions," *Journal of Marketing* 24 (1959): 41–46.

5. Paul E. Green and V. Srinivasan, "Conjoint Analysis in Consumer Research: Issues and outlook," *Journal of Consumer Research* 5 (1978): 103–123; Paul E. Green and V. Srinivasan, "Conjoint Analysis in Marketing: New Developments with Implications for Research and Practice," *Journal of Marketing*, 54 (1990): 3–19.

6. For more details see Betsy Sharkey, "The People's Choice," *Adweek*, 27 November 1989, MRC 8.

7. Paul E. Green and Yoram Wind, "New Ways to Measure Consumers' Judgments," *Harvard Business Review* 53 (July-August 1975): 107–111.

8. Max Blackstone, "Price Trade-Offs as a Measure of Brand Value," *Journal of*

Advertising Research (August/September 1990): RC3-RC6.

9. For some discussion, see Jordan Louviere and Richard Johnson, "Measuring Brand Image with Conjoint Analysis and Choice Models," in *Defining, Measuring, and Managing Brand Equity: A Conference Summary*, ed. Lance Leuthesser, MSI Report 88–104 (Cambridge, MA: Marketing Science Institute, 1988).

10. Arvind Rangaswamy, Raymond R. Burke, and Terence A. Oliva, "Brand Equity and the Extendibility of Brand Names," *International Journal of Research in Marketing* 10 (March 1993): 61–75. See also Moonkyu Lee, Jonathan Lee, and Wagner A. Kamakura, "Consumer Evaluations of Line Extensions: A Conjoint Approach," in *Advances in Consumer Research*, Vol. 23 (Ann Arbor, MI: Association of Consumer Research, 1996), 289–295.

11. Howard Barich and V. Srinivasan, "Prioritizing Marketing Image Goals under Resource Constraints," *Sloan Management Review* (Summer 1993): 69–76.

12. V. Srinivasan, "Network Models for Estimating Brand-Specific Effects in Multi-Attribute Marketing Models," *Management Science* 25 (January 1979): 11–21.

13. Wagner A. Kamakura and Gary J. Russell, "Measuring Brand Value with Scanner Data," *International Journal of Research in Marketing* 10 (1993): 9–22.

14. Joffre Swait, Tulin Erdem, Jordan Louviere, and Chris Dubelar, "The Equalization Price: A Measure of Consumer-Perceived Brand Equity," *International Journal of Research in Marketing* 10 (1993): 23–45.

15. See also Eric L. Almquist, Ian H. Turvill, and Kenneth J. Roberts, "Combining Economic Analysis for Breakthrough Brand Management," *Journal of Brand Management* 5, no. 4 (1998): 272–282.

16. Chan Su Park and V. Srinivasan, "A Survey-Based Method for Measuring and Understanding Brand Equity and its Extendability," *Journal of Marketing Research* 31 (May 1994): 271–288. See also Na Woon Bong, Roger Marshall, and Kevin Lane Keller, "Measuring Brand Power: Validating a Model for Optimizing Brand

Equity," *Journal of Product and Brand Management* 8, no. 3 (1999): 170–184.

17. Patrick Barwise (with Christopher Higson, Andrew Likierman, and Paul Marsh), "Brands as 'Separable Assets,'" *Business Strategy Review* (Summer 1990): 49.

18. Sharkey, "The People's Choice."

19. Joanne Lipman, "British Companies Value U.S. Brand Names—Literally," *Wall Street Journal*, 9 February 1989, B6; Laurel Wentz, "WPP Considers Brand Valuation," *Advertising Age*, 16 January 1989, 24.

20. Bernard Condon, "Gaps in GAAP," *Forbes*, 25 January 1999, 76–80.

21. David M. Fredricks, "Branded Assets: The Issue of Measurement" (paper presented at the ARF Fourth Annual Advertising and Promotion Workshop, February 12–13, 1992).

22. Quoted in "What's a Brand Worth? [editorial]," *Advertising Age*, 18 July 1994.

23. Lew Winters, "Brand Equity Measures: Some Recent Advances," *Marketing Research* (December 1991): 70–73; Gordon V. Smith, *Corporate Valuation: A Business and Professional Guide* (New York: John Wiley & Sons, 1988).

24. Michael Birkin, "Assessing Brand Value," in *Brand Power,* ed. Paul Stobart (Washington Square, NY: New York University Press, 1994).

25. Simon Mottram, "The Power of the Brand" (paper presented at the ARF Brand Equity Conference, February 15–16, 1994).

26. John Murphy, *Brand Valuation* (London: Hutchinson Business Books, 1989); Jean-Noel Kapferer, *Strategic Brand Management* (London: Kogan Page, 1992); Noel Penrose and Martin Moorhouse, "The Valuation of Brands," *Trademark World*, February 1989; Tom Blackett, "The Role of Brand Valuation in Marketing Strategy," *Marketing Research Today* 17, no. 4 (November 1989): 245–248.

27. Birkin, "Assessing Brand Value."

28. For some stimulating points of view, see the special issue on brand valuation of the *Journal of Brand Management* (Vol. 5, no. 4, 1998).

29. Susannah Hart and John Murphy, *Brands: The New Health Creators,* (New York: New York University Press, 1998).

30. Diane Summers, "IBM Plunges in Year to Foot of Brand Name Value League," *Financial Times*, 11 July 1994.

31. Peter Fader, Course notes, Wharton Business School, University of Pennsylvania, 1998.

32. "On the Brandwagon," *The Economist*, 20 January 1990.

33. Scott Davis and Jeff Smith, "Do You Know Your Brand ROBI?" *Management Review* (October 1998): 55–57.

34. Randy Scruggs, letter to author, 1996.

35. For an interesting empirical application, see Manoj K. Agarwal and Vithala Rao, "An Empirical Comparison of Consumer-Based Measures of Brand Equity," *Marketing Letters* 7, no. 3 (1996): 237)–247.

36. Fader, course notes.

37. David A. Aaker, *Building Strong Brands* (New York: Free Press, 1996).

38. This appendix benefited from contributions by Ed Lebar, Phil Buehler, Monika Sawicka, and Ryan Barker.

39. Justin Pettit, "EVA & Strategy," *EVAluation*, Stern Stewart Research, April 2000.

40. Bennett Stewart, *The Quest for Value* (New York: HarperCollins, 1991).

CHAPTER
11
Designing and Implementing Branding Strategies

PREVIEW

Parts II, III, and IV of this book examined strategies for building and measuring brand equity. Part V takes a broader perspective and considers how to create, maintain, and enhance brand equity under various situations and circumstances. Chapter 11 considers issues related to branding strategies and how brand equity can be maximized across all the different brands and products that might be sold by the firm. The branding strategy of a firm concerns which brand elements a firm chooses to apply across the products it offers for sale. As noted in Chapter 2, many firms employ complex branding strategies. For example, brand names may consist of multiple brand name elements (e.g., Toyota Camry V6 XLE) and may be applied across a range of products (e.g., Toyota cars and trucks). What is the best way to characterize a firm's branding strategy under such instances? What guidelines exist to choose the right combinations of brand names and other brand elements to optimally manage brand equity across the entire range of a firm's products? Branding strategy is critical because it is the means by which the firm can help consumers understand its products and services and organize them in their minds.

Chapter 11 begins by describing two important strategic tools. The brand-product matrix and the brand hierarchy help to characterize and formulate branding strategies by defining various relationships among brands and products. The chapter next suggests some guidelines as to how to best design branding strategies. Finally, it considers a number of different issues in implementing branding strategies, including designing the brand hierarchy and the supporting marketing program. Guidelines are provided concerning the number of levels of the hierarchy to use, how brands from different levels of the hierarchy can be combined, if at all, for any one particular product, and how any one brand can be linked, if at all, to multiple products. Brand Focus 11.0 devotes special attention to the topic of cause marketing. Subsequent chapters in Part V examine issues related to introducing and naming new products such as brand extensions (Chapter 12), managing brands over time (Chapter 13), and managing brands over geographic boundaries, cultures, and market segments (Chapter 14).

THE BRAND-PRODUCT MATRIX

To characterize the product and branding strategy of a firm, one useful tool is the *brand-product matrix,* a graphical representation of all the brands and products sold by the firm. The matrix (or grid) has the brands of a firm as rows and the corresponding products as columns (see Figure 11-1).

The rows of the matrix represent *brand-product relationships* and capture the brand extension strategy of the firm in terms of the number and nature of products sold under the firm's brands. A *brand line* consists of all products—original as well as line and category extensions—sold under a particular brand. Thus, a brand line would be one row of the matrix. As Chapter 12 discusses, a potential new product extension for a brand must be judged by how effectively it leverages existing brand equity from the parent brand to the new product, as well as how effectively the extension, in turn, contributes to the equity of the parent brand. In other words, what is the level of

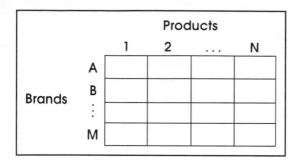

FIGURE 11-1 Brand-Product Matrix

awareness likely to be and what are the expected strength, favorability, and uniqueness of brand associations of the particular extension product? At the same time, how does the introduction of the brand extension affect the prevailing levels of awareness and the strength, favorability, and uniqueness of brand associations or overall responses (judgments and feelings) toward the parent brand as a whole?

The columns of the matrix, on the other hand, represent *product-brand relationships* and capture the brand portfolio strategy in terms of the number and nature of brands to be marketed in each category. The *brand portfolio* is the set of all brands and brand lines that a particular firm offers for sale to buyers in a particular category. Thus, a brand portfolio would be one particular column of the matrix. Different brands may be designed and marketed to appeal to different market segments. A brand portfolio must be judged on its ability to collectively maximize brand equity: Any one brand in the portfolio should not harm or decrease the equity of other brands in the portfolio. In other words, the optimal brand portfolio is one in which each brand maximizes equity in combination with all other brands in the portfolio. Branding Brief 11-1 describes the design of the Gap's brand portfolio.

One final set of definitions is useful.[1] A *product line* is a group of products within a product category that are closely related because they function in a similar manner, are sold to the same customer groups, are marketed through the same type of outlets, or fall within given price ranges. A product line may be composed of different brands or a single family brand or individual brand that has been line extended. A *product mix* (or product assortment) is the set of all product lines and items that a particular seller makes available to buyers. Thus, product lines represent different sets of columns in the brand-product matrix that, in total, make up the product mix. A *brand mix* (or brand assortment) is the set of all brand lines that a particular seller makes available to buyers.

The *branding strategy* for a firm reflects the number and nature of common and distinctive brand elements applied to the different products sold by the firm. In other words, branding strategy involves deciding which brand names, logos, symbols, and so forth should be applied to which products and the nature of new and existing brand elements to be applied to new products. A branding strategy for a firm can be characterized according to its *breadth* (i.e., in terms of brand-product relationships and brand extension strategy) and its *depth* (i.e., in terms of product-brand relationships and the brand portfolio or mix). For example, a branding strategy can be seen as both deep and broad if the firm has a large number of brands, many of which have been extended into various product categories. This chapter only briefly considers some basic issues concerning the breadth of a branding strategy and brand extensions; Chapter 12 is devoted

Bridging the Gap Brand

Donald Fisher founded The Gap in San Francisco in 1969 and named the store after the "generation gap." Fisher targeted baby boomers who had embraced jeans in general—and Levi's in particular—as the uniform of their generation. As the popularity of Gap stores increased, Fisher broadened the merchandising assortment by adding a limited number of Gap brand products and as many as 15 other national brands. To avoid shrinking margins and to tap into a more affluent market than students, Fisher decided to upgrade the Gap image starting in 1983.

In a bold move, new CEO Mickey Drexler dropped all non-Gap merchandise except for Levi's and introduced more colorful Gap sweaters, jerseys, and shirts to appeal to an increasingly older and affluent market. Eschewing trendy fashions, Gap brand clothing was positioned as casual, functional, and "basic with attitude." Gap sales grew through the 1980s, cracking the $1 billion mark in 1987. Its successful turnaround solidified its customer franchise—especially among women—and established its own brand equity, permitting further expansion. Gap expanded its clothing offerings to include new fashions and styles (including prints and plaids) and new fabrics, as well as new clothing categories such as blazers and outerwear, boxer shorts, footwear, swimsuits and swim trunks, hats, and handbags.

The Gap also expanded beyond its flagship stores through acquisitions and extensions. GapKids is a highly successful extension introduced in 1986. Riding the wave of the baby boom "echo" to successfully open more than 350 stores by 1995, GapKids accounted for approximately 16 percent of Gap's annual earnings that year. The Gap bought Banana Republic and its unique travel- and safari-themed stores and catalogs in 1983 and reformulated the clothing to reflect more urban tastes. In March 1994, Gap introduced Old Navy Clothing stores to sell Gap-like men's, women's, and children's apparel at lower prices in large warehouse-style outlets. Old Navy rapidly became popular with consumers, and the brand's contribution to Gap sales grew from 3 percent ($120 million) in 1994 to more than 30 percent ($4.3 billion) in 2000. Figure A displays the Gap's brand portfolio.

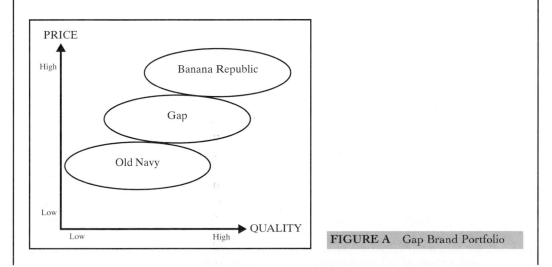

FIGURE A Gap Brand Portfolio

Old Navy encountered a drop-off in business following its half-decade of success. Back-to-school sales in August 2001 fell 17 percent, on top of a 14 percent decline the previous year. Adults began avoiding Old Navy because its styles were trended toward teens. The company planned to broaden its stylistic palette because, as CEO Mickey Drexler said, "This business is too big to focus on a narrow consumer segment."

Old Navy's woes, however, were not as serious as those of the Gap, which also saw customers abandon it in droves when it changed its styles to match the teen trends. In November 2001, the Gap recorded the nineteenth consecutive month of declines in same-store sales. CEO Mickey Drexler admitted, "We changed too much, too quickly, in ways that weren't consistent with our brands." A fashion industry consultant had stronger criticism: "Today there's no compelling reason to visit the Gap for fashion. It has fallen flat on its face."

Sources: Amy Merrick, "CEO Concedes Gap Made Errors, Promises Senior-Level Oversight," *Wall Street Journal*, 10 September 2001; Julie Creswell, "Confessions of a Fashion Victim," *Fortune,* 10 December 2001, 48–50.

to these topics. Following this brief discussion, the remainder of this section outlines some of the key issues associated with the depth of a branding strategy and the topic of brand portfolios.

Breadth of a Branding Strategy

The breadth of a branding strategy concerns the number and nature of different products linked to the brands sold by a firm. A number of considerations arise concerning the product mix and which products the firm should manufacture or sell. Strategic decisions have to be made concerning how many different product lines the company should carry (i.e., the breadth of the product mix), as well as how many variants should be offered in each product line (i.e., the depth of the product mix).

Breadth of Product Mix

Lehmann and Winer provide an in-depth consideration of factors affecting product category attractiveness.[2] They note that three main sets of factors determine the inherent attractiveness of a product category, as follows (see Figure 11-2).

1. *Aggregate market factors:* Descriptive characteristics of the market itself. All else being equal, a category is considered attractive if it is relatively large (as measured both in units and dollars); fast-growing (both in current and projected terms) and in the growth stage of the product life cycle; noncyclical and nonseasonal in sales patterns; and characterized by relatively high, steady profit margins.

2. *Category factors:* Underlying structural factors affecting the category. In general, a category is considered attractive if it is the case that the threat of new entrants is low (e.g., due to barriers of entry from economies of scale, product differentiation, capital requirements, switching costs, or distribution systems); bargaining power of buyers is low (e.g., when the product bought is a small percentage of buyers' costs or is sharply differentiated or when buyers are earning high profits, lack information about competitive offerings, or are unable to integrate backward); current category rivalry is low (e.g., when there are few or an imbalance of competitors in fast-growing markets); few close product substitutes exist in the eyes of consumers; and the market is operating at or near capacity.

Aggregate Market Factors
Market size
Market growth
Stage in product life cycle
Sales cyclicity
Seasonality
Profits

Category factors
Threat of new entrants
Bargaining power of buyers
Bargaining power of suppliers
Current category rivalry
Pressures from substitutes
Category capacity

Environmental Factors
Technological
Political
Economic
Regulatory
Social

FIGURE 11-2 Category Attractiveness Criteria

3. *Environmental factors:* External forces unrelated to the product's customers and competitors that affect marketing strategies. A host of technological, political, economic, regulatory, and social factors will affect the future prospects of a category and should be forecasted.

All of these factors relate in some way to consumers, competition, and the marketing environment and must be assessed to determine the inherent attractiveness of a product category or market. The ultimate decision for a firm to enter such markets, however, must also take into account fundamental considerations related to the firm's capabilities and abilities—its core competencies—as well as its strategic objectives and goals.

The actual names chosen for the products to enter these different markets will depend on the branding strategy adopted, as described in Chapter 12. For example, although Xerox felt the organizational and marketing imperative to move into office automation and computing, it chose to brand its first computers with the Xerox name. Because of the near-generic qualities of the name—virtually synonymous with photocopying—it is perhaps not surprising that consumers balked. Print ads announcing that "Here's a Xerox that does not even make a copy" may have raised questions in consumers' minds as to how—or even if—the computer worked.

Depth of Product Mix

Once broad decisions concerning appropriate product categories and markets in which to compete have been made, decisions concerning the optimal product line strategy must also be made. Product line analysis requires a clear understanding of the market and the cost interdependencies between products.[3] Specifically, product line analysis involves examining the percentage of sales and profits contributed by each item or member in the product line. The ability of each item in the product line to withstand competition and address consumer needs also must be assessed. At its simplest, a product line is too short if the manager can increase long-term profits by adding items; the line is too long if the manager can increase profits by dropping items.[4] Increasing the length of the product line by adding new variants or items typically expands market coverage and therefore market share but also increases costs. From a branding perspective, longer product lines may decrease the consistency of the associated brand image if the same brand is used.

> **Laura Ashley**
>
> Although a raging success in the 1980s, Laura Ashley found its sales wilting in the 1990s. The brand meant different things to different people, and, unfortunately, many of these people worked at Laura Ashley! Stores in the United States and Europe offered vastly different product lines. Designers and buyers were scattered all over the world and introduced hundreds of clothing styles, many of which clashed with the English country styles and flowery fashions for which Laura Ashley had become famous. The chain's vast range of product lines—which included adult clothes, children's clothes, and home furnishings—was filled with weak sellers and duplicate styles. Eighty-two percent of the company's sales came from just 22 percent of the merchandise. New management pared down the brands, eliminating 30 percent of the clothing styles and 20 percent of the home furnishing lines. They also consolidated design, buying, and merchandise and took steps to create a more common store design and format.[5] Having lost momentum, however, Laura Ashley found itself struggling in the marketplace as a succession of CEOs attempted to reenergize the brand.

Given that product policy has been set for a firm in terms of product boundaries (i.e., appropriate product categories and product lines), then the proper branding strategy must be decided upon in terms of which brand elements should be used for which products. Specifically, decisions must be made as to which products to attach to any one brand as well as how many brands to support in any one product category. The former decision concerns brand extensions and is discussed in detail in the next chapter; the latter decision concerns brand portfolios, which are addressed next. Branding Brief 11-2 describes Liz Claiborne's experiences in stretching its brand name and business.

Depth of a Branding Strategy

The depth of a branding strategy concerns the number and nature of different brands marketed in the product class sold by a firm. Why might a firm have multiple brands in the same product category? The primary reason relates to market coverage. Although multiple branding was originally pioneered by General Motors, Procter & Gamble is widely recognized as popularizing the practice. P&G became proponents of multiple brands after recognizing that introducing its Cheer detergent brand as an alternative to its already successful Tide detergent resulted in higher combined product category sales.

The main reason to adopt multiple brands is to pursue multiple market segments. These different market segments may be based on all types of considerations—different price segments, different channels of distribution, different geographic boundaries, and so forth. Figure 11-3 displays Seiko's different brands based on price segments. As another

Stretching the Liz Claiborne Brand

Liz Claiborne was founded in 1976 to make affordable and fashionable apparel for the working woman. Sales surpassed $1 billion in 1989 in the absence of any advertising support. In 1991, Liz Claiborne occupied over half of the women's apparel floor space in some department stores. Yet by this time, the brand's styles were becoming outdated and the merchandise was harder to sell without discounts. Liz Claiborne, who retired in 1989 to become a wildlife activist, criticized the brand's dowdiness, saying it had become "a mother's brand that didn't reach out to younger consumers. Here I am 70, and I don't want to wear those clothes." Concerned that Claiborne had achieved maximum penetration, the company sought to stretch the brand's range with a number of acquisitions and brand extensions to include products suitable for downscale retailers as well as up-market boutiques.

The company acquired faded brands Russ, Crazy Horse, and Villager from bankruptcy court in the early 1990s. These brands were originally positioned as second-tier department store brands, but were unable to compete with similarly priced private label brands. So Liz Claiborne marketed them in stores like JCPenney's, Kohl's, and Wal-Mart, where they flourished. In 1999 these brands, along with First Issue and Emma James, accounted for an estimated $250 million of Claiborne's $2.8 billion in sales.

FIGURE A   Liz Claiborne Brand Portfolio

Claiborne: Menswear and optical products
Crazy Horse: Affordable casual clothing
Dana Buchman: A top-end designer of women's business suits and sportswear
Elisabeth: Plus-size clothing for women
Emma James: Value-priced women's clothing
First Issue: Clothes, shoes, and optics sold exclusively at Sears
Laundry by Shelli Segal: Women's evening wear and sportswear, acquired in 1999
Liz Claiborne: Flagship brand, includes jeans, casual, swimwear, sportswear, golf apparel, intimate wear, and dresses
Lucky Brand: Hip jeanswear for men and women
Meg Allen: Casual clothing line sold exclusively at Target stores
Mexx: European mass merchandiser
Monet Group: Fashion jewelry
Russ: Budget brand found exclusively at Wal-Mart
Sigrid Olsen: Upscale women's clothing
Villager: Relaxed styles sold primarily at Kohl's stores

Licensed Brands

DKNY Jeans: Hip designer of jeanswear for teenagers (also licenses DKNY Active)
Kenneth Cole: Trendy women's lines Kenneth Cole New York and Reaction Kenneth Cole

During the 1990s, Claiborne added other brands to its portfolio and inked licensing deals with two fashion-forward brands, DKNY and Kenneth Cole (see Figure A). Referring to the depth and breadth of the Claiborne portfolio, the *Wall Street Journal* in 2000 declared the brand to be the "Procter & Gamble of fashion." In 2000, 20 percent of Claiborne's sales came from labels other than the namesake brand. Liz Claiborne CEO Paul Charron said, "Cannibalization is inevitable, but it's much better to steal market share from yourself than to sit back and let somebody else do it." In its 1999 annual report entitled "The Power of Our Brands," the company made the following observations:

> Five times every second of every day, someone buys a product created by Liz Claiborne Inc. Our current roster of brands is richer and more diversified than was the case a year ago. Our strategy recognizes that growth will come from offering brands that speak to different attitudes at different price points in different retail channels. Wherever consumers choose to shop, there is a brand from Liz Claiborne Inc. to meet their needs for fashion and value.

Sources: http://www.lizclaiborne.com; Teri Agins, "Claiborne Unveils Its First Big Campaign," *Wall Street Journal*, 26 September 1991, B1; Teri Agins, "Claiborne Patches Together an Empire," *Wall Street Journal*, 2 February 2002, B1.

example, as part of a plan to upgrade Holiday Inn Worldwide, the hotel chain broke its domestic hotels into five separate chains to tap into five different benefit segments: the upscale Crowne Plaza, the traditional Holiday Inn, the budget Holiday Inn Express, and the business-oriented Holiday Inn Select and Holiday Inn Suites & Rooms.[6] Different branded chains received different marketing programs and emphasis; for example, Holiday Inn Express has been advertised with the humorous "Stay Smart" advertising campaign showing the brilliant feats that ordinary people could attempt after staying at the chain. Posing as scientists, doctors, and even members of the rock group Kiss, these people always utter the same line when their identity and credentials are questioned, "No, but I did stay at a Holiday Inn Express." Marriott had adopted a very similar brand portfolio strategy at an earlier date, and other hotel chains have followed suit.

In many cases, multiple brands have to be introduced by a firm because any one brand is not viewed equally favorably by all the different market segments that the firm would like to target. Branding Brief 11-3 outlines Ford's brand portfolio strategy. Some other reasons for introducing multiple brands in a category include the following:[7]

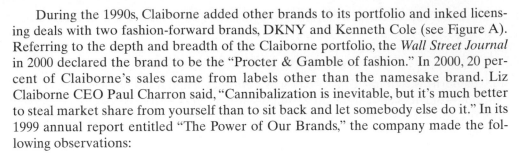

FIGURE 11-3 Seiko's Segmentation of the Watch Market

Segment	Seiko Brands
Luxury brands (e.g., Rolex, Piaget, Cartier)	Lassale
Up-market brands (e.g., Omega, Longines)	Credor, Seiko
Mid-price brands (e.g., Bulova, Tissot, Citizen)	Seiko, Pulsar
Mass-market brands (e.g., Swatch, Timex)	Pulsar, Lorus
Commodity watches (Hong Kong LCDs)	—

Source: Adapted from Helen Chase Kimball and Christine Pinson, "Swatch," Case 589-005 (Fontainbleau, France: INSEAD, 1987).

Ford's Brand Portfolio

Ford Motor Company, traditionally known for its American-made brands Ford, Lincoln, and Mercury, expanded in the past two decades with a string of foreign automaker acquisitions, beginning with the 1987 purchase of British luxury automaker Aston Martin. Over the next decade, Ford purchased Land Rover, Volvo, and Jaguar. These moves transformed Ford Motor Company into the world's number two seller by volume of luxury cars. (See Figure A.)

FIGURE A Ford Brand Portfolio

All told, Ford invested more than $12 billion in acquiring luxury brands in the 1980s and 1990s. Although Ford withholds financial results for its premium group, analysts estimate that the luxury unit had operating income of $1.3 billion in 2000, or 19 percent of Ford's total.

In 2000, Ford's luxury brands—Jaguar, Volvo, Land Rover, Aston Martin, and Lincoln—sold just under one million units worldwide. In contrast to competitors Lexus, BMW, and Mercedes, which sell a range of cars under a single brand, Ford's portfolio of luxury brands caters to different types of buyer. For example, Volvo attracts buyers interested in safety, Land Rover appeals to four-wheel-drive connoisseurs, and Jaguar represents tradition and British elegance. Victor H. Doolan, executive director for the premium auto group, explained the benefit of the portfolio: "We don't have to stretch our brands beyond their core values."

Ford aims to combine sales of all five luxury brands in a single dealership eventually. The single-dealership model would involve separate showrooms and sales staff for each brand, but combined service departments and administration. Each of the planned 10 dealerships includes a quarter-mile track where customers can take test drives. Doolan notes that since most luxury car buyers own three or more vehicles, the single dealership would enable customers to "fill all the needs of their garage."

On November 1, 1999, Ford launched its "Global Anthem" advertising campaign with a global "roadblock" created by showing a two-minute image ad at 9 P.M. local time on every major commercial television network in the world. The ad, which was shot on five continents and featured all of the automobile brands under the Ford Motor Company umbrella, reached a potential audience of 300 million, or roughly 75 percent of the global viewing population. Ford intended the Global Anthem ad to "add to people's regard for the company."

Following quality control problems in 2000 that cost Ford more than $1 billion, plus financial woes resulting from the Firestone and Explorer recall, Ford ousted CEO Jacques Nasser. In the wake of these problems, the company backed off the use of the Ford Motor Company umbrella brand to a great degree.

Sources: http://www.ford.com; Gregory L. White, "Ford Says Last Year's Quality Snafus Took Big Toll," *Wall Street Journal*, 12 January 2001, A3.

➤ To increase shelf presence and retailer dependence in the store
➤ To attract consumers seeking variety who may otherwise switch to another brand
➤ To increase internal competition within the firm
➤ To yield economies of scale in advertising, sales, merchandising, and physical distribution

In designing the optimal brand portfolio, marketers generally need to trade off market coverage and these other considerations with costs and profitability. As with a

---

FIGURE 11-4 Frito-Lay Brand Portfolio

	Fritos	**Doritos**	**Tostitos**
Name derivation	"Little fried bits" (Spanish)	"Little bits of gold" (Spanish)	"Little toasted bits" (Spanish)
Year introduced	1932	1964	1981
Main ingredients	Corn, vegetable oil, salt	Corn, vegetable oil, cheddar cheese, salt	White corn, vegetable oil, salt
Demographic Snack niche, according to Frito-Lay	33- to 51-year-old males "Hunger satisfaction"	Teens, skewing to males "Bold and daring snacking"	Upscale baby boomers "Casual interaction through friends and family . . . a social food that brings people together"
Advertising expenditure, Jan–June 2001	$360,000	$17.2 million	$6.7 million
Marketing campaign overview	One of the firm's oldest brands, it advertises in sports magazines such as *Sports Illustrated* and *ESPN*. Also sponsors *NASCAR* driver Jeff Gordon, who appears on Fritos.com, where you can download a demo of a racing video game.	Doritos advertises exclusively on television. Almost a quarter of its first-half budget was spent on cable-TV networks such as MTV and Comedy Central. Sponsorships include alternative music festival EdgeFest. On Doritos.com: "Doritos Sessions," interviews with pop stars such as Christina Aguilera.	Promoted as a "party" chip, Tostitos advertises heavily during televised sports events, especially college football. Magazine ad budget totals less than $100,000. Sponsors the Fiesta Bowl. On Tostitos.com: sweepstakes for football tickets and a Jeep Cherokee.
Slogan	Fuel Up with Fritos	Be Bold, Be Daring	Dig In, Kick Back
Spokesperson	Jeff Gordon, a three-time *Nascar* Winston Cup champion	Ali Landry, a former Miss USA whose role as the Doritos Girl landed her on *People* magazine's list of the 50 most beautiful people	Various sports stars, including Patrick Ewing and Marcus Camby
Brand valuation	$588 million	$1.1 billion	$981 million

Sources: Frito-Lay, Competitive Media Reporting, Houlihan Lokey Howard & Zukin, Publishers Information Bureau. Reprinted from Colleen Bazdarich, "Corn-ering the Market," *Business 2.0,* December 2001, 138.

product line, a portfolio is too big if profits can be increased by dropping brands; a portfolio is not big enough if profits can be increased by adding brands. In other words, any brand should be clearly differentiated and appealing to a sizable enough marketing segment to justify its marketing and production costs. Figure 11-4 characterizes some of Frito-Lay's brand portfolio. Brand lines with poorly differentiated brands are likely to be characterized by much cannibalization and require appropriate pruning.[8]

In general, the basic principle in designing a brand portfolio is to *maximize market coverage* so that no potential customers are being ignored, but to *minimize brand overlap* so that brands are not competing among themselves to gain the same customer's approval. Each brand should have a distinct target market and positioning.[9] For example, Nabisco announced that it was going to adopt a more cautious new product strategy after it appeared that the introduction of too many line extensions that consumers saw as offering too few differences depressed earnings. The firm also believed that an overreliance on new product extensions distracted it from providing adequate support to its tried and true brands such as Ritz crackers, Fig Newtons, and Oreo cookies.[10]

Besides these considerations, there are a number of specific roles that brands can play as part of a brand portfolio. Figure 11-5 summarizes some of the different functions and roles that brands might take.

Flankers

An increasingly important role for certain brands is as protective flanker or "fighter" brands. The purpose of flanker brands typically is to create stronger points of parity with competitors' brands so that more important (and more profitable) flagship brands can retain their desired positioning. In particular, as noted in Chapter 5, many firms are introducing discount brands as flanker brands to better compete with store brands and private labels and protect their higher-priced brand companions. For example, Philip Morris introduced a discount brand of cigarettes, Basic, which lived up to its name as a no-frills flanker brand designed to protect Marlboro and preserve its premium price position. Backed by the slogan "It tastes good. It costs less," one launch print ad showed a simple scene of the cigarette pack with a pair of blue jeans and the

---

FIGURE 11-5 Possible Special Roles of Brands in the Brand Portfolio

1. To attract a particular market segment not currently being covered by other brands of the firm.
2. To serve as a flanker and protect flagship brands.
3. To serve as a cash cow and be milked for profits.
4. To serve as a low-end entry-level product to attract new customers to the brand franchise.
5. To serve as a high-end prestige product to add prestige and credibility to the entire brand portfolio.
6. To increase shelf presence and retailer dependence in the store.
7. To attract consumers seeking variety who may otherwise have switched to another brand.
8. To increase internal competition within the firm.
9. To yield economies of scale in advertising, sales, merchandising, and physical distribution.

headline "Your basic fashion." Another introductory ad paired the cigarette with a Walkman-like personal stereo and the headline "Your basic concert."

In designing these fighter brands, marketers must walk a fine line. Fighter brands must not be designed to be so attractive that they take sales away from their higher-priced comparison brands or referents. At the same time, if fighter brands are seen as connected to other brands in the portfolio in any way (e.g., by virtue of a common branding strategy), then fighter brands must not be designed so cheaply that they reflect poorly on these other brands.

Cash Cows

Some brands may be kept around despite dwindling sales because they still manage to hold on to a sufficient number of customers and maintain their profitability with virtually no marketing support. These "cash cows" can be effectively milked by capitalizing on their reservoir of existing brand equity. For example, despite the fact that technological advances have moved much of its market to its newer Mach3 brand of razors, Gillette still sells its older Trac II, Atra, and Sensor brands. Because withdrawing these brands may not necessarily result in customers switching to another Gillette brand, it may be more profitable for Gillette to keep them in its brand portfolio than to discontinue them. Branding guru David Aaker notes how Unilever's Lux beauty bar, which hasn't been advertised in years, still is able to generate over $10 million in profits.[11]

Low-End Entry-Level or High-End Prestige Brands

Many brands introduce line extensions or brand variants in a certain product category that vary in price and quality. These sub-brands leverage associations from other brands while distinguishing themselves on the basis of their price and quality dimensions. In this case, the end points of the brand line often play a specialized role.

The role of a relatively low-priced brand in the brand portfolio often may be to attract customers to the brand franchise. Retailers like to feature these traffic builders because they often are able to "trade up" customers to a higher-priced brand. For example, BMW introduced certain models into its 3-series automobiles in part as a means of bringing new customers into its brand franchise with the hope of later moving them up to higher-priced models when they traded their cars in. Similarly, Mercedes is attempting to attract younger car buyers through its new A-Class, the smallest car it has ever made (although the sub-brand ran into some initial design and handling problems when launched in Europe).

On the other hand, the role of a relatively high-priced brand in the brand family often is to add prestige and credibility to the entire brand portfolio. For example, one analyst argued that the real value to Chevrolet of its Corvette high-performance sports car was in "its ability to lure curious customers into showrooms and at the same time help improve the image of other Chevrolet cars. It does not mean a hell of a lot for GM profitability, but there is no question that it is a traffic builder."[12] Corvette's technological image and prestige was hoped to cast a halo over the entire Chevrolet line.

Summary

In short, brands can play a number of different roles within the brand portfolio based on considerations related to consumers, the competition, and the company. Brands may expand coverage, provide protection, extend an image, or fulfill a variety of other roles for the firm. In all brand portfolio decisions, the basic criteria are simple,

Understanding Brands as Assets

Traditionally, marketers have thought of their brand portfolio as all the brands covered by the umbrella of the flagship brand or parent company. In this age of partnerships, however, it could be argued that the relationships between brands in a portfolio may involve more than just one company. For example, when Volkswagen and Trek partnered to bundle bicycles and cars, each company had to consider the marketing issues of the other company to ensure a proper fit. The relationship also affected future marketing decisions by both companies, since in the minds of consumers the brands were now linked. In their book *The Infinite Asset,* Sam Hill and Chris Lederer address this issue by redefining the concept of a brand portfolio. In their approach, *brand portfolio* takes on a much larger meaning, referring to "all the brands that factor into a consumer's decision to buy, whether or not the company owns them." The phrase *brand system* is used to refer to all the brands owned by a particular company.

Hill and Lederer developed a three-dimensional model called the *brand portfolio molecule* to represent their novel approach to brands. Each brand is assigned a representative atom, and the individual atoms (brands) are arranged to represent the consumer's view of them. For example, the Miller High Life brand molecule contains atoms for parent company Philip Morris, umbrella brand Miller, other Miller brands, and various events, organizations, and individuals sponsored by Miller (see Figure A). The size of each atom indicates the role of each brand. The largest atom represents the lead brand, the medium-sized atoms represent strategic brands, and the smallest atoms represent support brands. In the Miller High Life example, Miller is the lead

FIGURE A Brand Molecule for Miller High Life

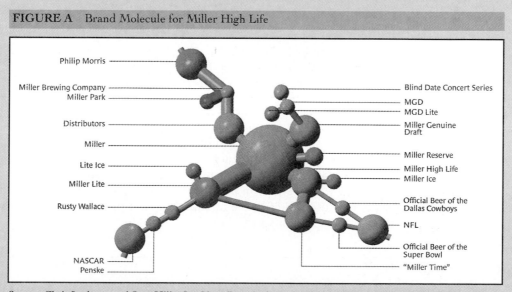

Source: Chris Lederer and Sam Hill, "See Your Brands through Your Customers' Eyes," *Harvard Business Review* (June 2001): 127.

brand, Miller Genuine Draft is a strategic brand, and endorser Rusty Wallace is a support brand.

Each atom receives a color depending on whether it exerts a positive influence (green), a negative influence (red), or a neutral influence (blue) on the purchase decision. The slogan "Miller Time" is positive because it creates a strong link to the brand. Miller Lite would be colored red because its image is not consistent with the hearty, full taste sought by Miller High Life drinkers.

An atom's position relative to another atom on a molecule indicates how the two relate. For example, Miller High Life is located near Miller Genuine Draft and Miller Reserve because they share similar positionings. Miller Lite has a different and distinct positioning, so its atom is further away from Miller High Life. A single link indicates a direct relationship. From the molecule, one notes that Miller High Life has a direct affiliation with the Dallas Cowboys, and through this relationship has an indirect link to the NFL. Finally, the width of the link indicates the degree of control one brand has over another, with thicker links indicating more control.

One can readily tell from looking at the model that Miller is the lead brand. Unfortunately, consumers make no distinction between Miller Beer and Miller High Life, even though they are two separate brands. Thus, the lead brand as defined by the company—on which Miller Brewing Company spends a proportionally larger amount of money to promote—is a source of confusion among consumers. Contrast this situation with that of Anheuser-Busch, which has a clear flagship brand in Budweiser, and one can see it is a major problem for Miller. Hill and Lederer recommend simplifying the relationship by combining the two brands into one: Miller High Life.

Another problem area is presented by the close proximity of the atoms for Miller Genuine Draft and Miller High Life. This indicates that consumers do not differentiate much between the two brands. The authors suggest officially changing the name of Miller Genuine Draft to MGD, because the shortened form will create further distance from Miller High Life. Ultimately, Hill and Lederer assert that the "Miller brand portfolio needs to create fewer, more differentiated brands—that is, simplify it and open it up."

Sources: Chris Lederer and Sam Hill, "See Your Brands Through Your Customer's Eyes," *Harvard Business Review* (June 2001): 125–133; Sam Hill and Chris Lederer, *The Infinite Asset* (Boston: Harvard Business School Press, 2001).

even though their application can be quite complicated: Each brand name product must have (1) a well-defined role of what it is supposed to do for the firm and, as such, (2) a well-defined positioning as to what benefits or promises it offers consumers, as encapsulated in the associations that the company would like it to own or represent in customers' minds. In that way, brands can maximize coverage and minimize overlap and thus optimize the portfolio. The Science of Branding 11-1 provides a provocative look at another way to think of brand portfolios.

BRAND HIERARCHY

The brand-product matrix helps to highlight the range of products and brands sold by a firm. As described, it assumes each product is given one brand name. In many cases, a firm may want to make connections across products and brands to show consumers how these products and brands may be related. As a result, brand names of products are typically not restricted to one name but often consist of a combination of multiple brand name elements. For example, an IBM ThinkPad A22M notebook personal computer consists of three different brand name elements, "IBM," "ThinkPad," and "A22M." Some of these brand name elements may be shared by many different products; other brand name elements are limited to a more restricted range of products. For example, whereas IBM uses its corporate name to brand many of its products, ThinkPad designates a certain type of computer (i.e., one that is portable as opposed to desktop), and A22M identifies a particular model of ThinkPad (i.e., one with a 1 GHz Intel Pentium III, 128 MB SDRAM, 30 GB EIDE hard disk, etc.).

A *brand hierarchy* is a means of summarizing the branding strategy by displaying the number and nature of common and distinctive brand elements across the firm's products, revealing the explicit ordering of brand elements. By capturing the potential branding relationships among the different products sold by the firm, a brand hierarchy is a useful means of graphically portraying a firm's branding strategy. Specifically, a brand hierarchy is based on the realization that a product can be branded in different ways depending on how many new and existing brand elements are used and how they are combined for any one product. Because certain brand elements are used to make more than one brand, a hierarchy can be constructed to represent how (if at all) products are nested with other products because of their common brand elements. Some brand elements may be shared by many products (e.g., Ford); other brand elements may be unique to certain products (e.g., F-series trucks). Figure 11-6 displays a simple characterization of ESPN's brand hierarchy.

FIGURE 11-6   ESPN Brand Hierarchy

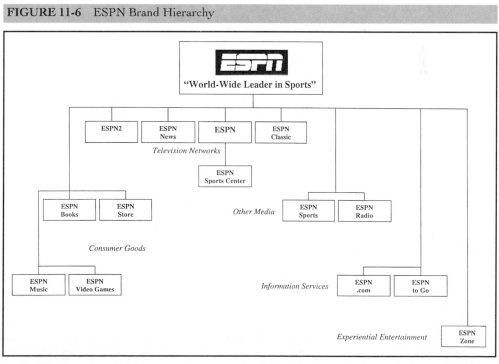

Source: 2000 Tuck Brand Audit Project

1. *Product brand:* Assign an exclusive name to a single product to accord the brand its own individual positioning (e.g., Procter & Gamble's Ariel, Tide, and Dash laundry detergents)
2. *Line brand:* Extend the specific concept across different products, allowing for cross-branding (e.g., Renault automobiles)
3. *Range brand:* Bestow a single name and promise on a group of products having the same ability (e.g., Green Giant foods)
4. *Umbrella brand:* Support products in different markets, each with its own communication and individual promise (e.g., Canon cameras, photocopiers, and office equipment)
5. *Source brand:* Similar to an umbrella brand, but the products are directly named (e.g., Yves Saint Laurent with Jazz perfumed deodorant and various brands of clothes)
6. *Endorsing brand:* Give approval to a wide diversity of products grouped under product brands, line brands, or range brands (e.g., General Motors cars)

Source: Jean-Noel Kapferer, *Strategic Brand Management* (London: Kogan-Page, 1992).

FIGURE 11-7   Kapferer's Branding System

As with any hierarchy, moving from the top level to the bottom level typically involves more entries at each succeeding level—in this case, more brands. There are different ways to define brand elements and levels of the hierarchy. For example, Figure 11-7 displays a classification system developed by one of Europe's leading branding experts, Jean-Noel Kapferer. Perhaps the simplest representation of possible brand elements and thus potential levels of a brand hierarchy—from top to bottom—might be as follows:

1. Corporate (or company) brand (e.g., *General Motors*)
2. Family brand (e.g., *Buick*)
3. Individual brand (e.g., *Park Avenue*)
4. Modifier (designating item or model) (e.g., *Ultra*)

The highest level of the hierarchy technically always involves one brand—the *corporate or company brand*. For legal reasons, the company or corporate brand is almost always present somewhere on the product or package, although it may be the case that the name of a company subsidiary may appear instead of the corporate name. For example, Fortune Brands owns many different companies, such as Titleist, Footjoy, Jim Beam, Master Lock, and Moen, but does not use its corporate name in any of its lines of business. For some firms, the corporate brand is virtually the only brand used (e.g., as with General Electric and Hewlett-Packard). Some other firms combine their corporate brand name with family brands or individual brands (e.g., conglomerate Siemens's varied electrical engineering and electronics business units are branded with descriptive modifiers, such as Siemens Transportation Systems). Finally, in some other cases, the company name is virtually invisible and, although technically part of the hierarchy, receives virtually no attention in the marketing program (e.g., Black & Decker does not use its name on its high-end DeWalt professional power tools, and Hewlett-Packard created a wholly owned subsidiary for its low-priced Apollo ink-jet printers).

At the next-lower level, a *family brand* is defined as a brand that is used in more than one product category but is not necessarily the name of the company or corporation itself. For example, ConAgra's Healthy Choice family brand is used to sell a wide spectrum of food products, including frozen microwave entrees, packaged cheeses, packaged meats, sauces, and ice cream. Other examples of family brands boasting over a billion dollars in annual sales include Seagram's Tropicana juices, PepsiCo's Gatorade thirst quencher, and Anheuser-Busch's Budweiser beer. Most firms typically only support a handful of family brands. If the corporate brand is applied to a range of products, then it functions as a family brand too, and the two levels collapse to one for those products.

An *individual brand* is defined as a brand that has been restricted to essentially one product category, although it may be used for several different product types within the category. For example, in the "salty snack" product class, Frito-Lay offers Fritos corn chips, Doritos tortilla chips, Lays and Ruffles potato chips, and Rold Gold pretzels. Each brand has a dominant position in its respective product category within the broader salty snack product class. A *modifier* is a means to designate a specific item or model type or a particular version or configuration of the product. Thus, many of Frito-Lay's snacks come in both full-flavor or low-fat "Better For You" forms. Similarly, Land O'Lakes offers "whipped," "unsalted," and "regular" versions of its butter. Yoplait yogurt comes as "light," "custard style," or "original" flavors.

Figure 11-8 displays an abridged version of a brand hierarchy that shows General Motors's branding strategy in 2001. It is important to note that, as this example suggests, different levels of the hierarchy may receive different emphasis in developing a branding strategy. For example, General Motors traditionally chose to downplay its corporate name in branding its cars, although the name recently has played a more important role in its supporting marketing activities. As will be discussed later in this chapter, such shifts in emphasis are an attempt by the firm to harness the positive associations and mitigate against the negative associations of different brands in different contexts, and there are a number of ways to place more or less emphasis on the different elements that combine to make up the brand.

FIGURE 11-8   General Motors's Brand Hierarchy

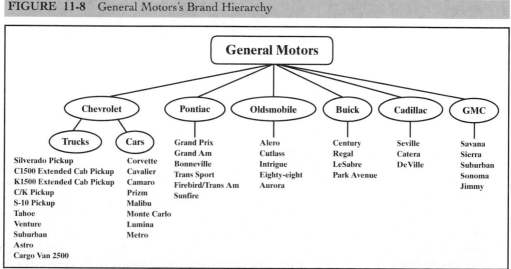

Source: 2001 Tuck Brand Audit Project

Akzo Nobel

A Netherlands-based maker of health care products, coatings, chemicals, and fibers, Akzo Nobel uses a four-tier brand hierarchy based on the following rationale:[13]

1. Use of the corporate brand only in some industrial markets for chemicals, coatings, and fibers where the company name establishes the product's reputation.
2. Use of the corporate brand plus a product brand in some industrial markets for chemicals, coatings, and fibers to add value or help position the product in relation to other brands.
3. Use of a prominent product brand endorsed by the corporate brand in some industrial markets for coating materials where the product brand is especially strong, but can still be helped by a corporate endorsement.
4. Use of only a product brand in pharmaceuticals and some coating products where marketing strategy makes this approach most desirable (but the corporate name might still appear on company stationery and signage).

Building Equity at Different Hierarchy Levels

Before considering how the brand hierarchy can help to formulate branding strategies, it is worthwhile to first examine some of the specific issues in building brand knowledge structures—and thus brand equity—at each of the different levels of the brand hierarchy.

Corporate or Company Brand Level

For simplicity, this chapter refers to corporate and company brands interchangeably, recognizing that consumers may not necessarily draw a distinction between the two or recognize that corporations may subsume multiple companies. A *corporate image* can be thought of as the associations that consumers have in memory to the company or corporation making the product or providing the service as a whole. Corporate image is a particularly relevant concern when the corporate or company brand plays a prominent role in the branding strategy adopted.

More generally, some marketing experts believe that a factor increasing in importance in consumer purchase decisions is consumer perceptions of a firm's whole role in society, for example, how a firm treats its employees, shareholders, local neighbors, and others. As the head of a large ad agency put it: "The only sustainable competitive advantage any business has is its reputation."[14] Consistent with this reasoning, a large national study of U.S. consumers indicated that 89 percent of the sample reported that the reputation of the company often determined which products they would buy. Moreover, 71 percent of the sample indicated that "the more they know about a company, the more favorable (they) feel toward it."[15] Similarly, a survey of 3,000 executives worldwide found that "knowing a company very well is a key reason to award new business."[16] In justifying their marketing investments, executives at Accenture maintain that a strong corporate image can also be an effective means to attract and motivate employees.

The realization that consumers and others may be interested in issues beyond product characteristics and associations has prompted much marketing activity to establish the proper corporate image. A corporate image will depend on a number of factors, such as the products a company makes, the actions it takes, and the manner in which it communicates to consumers. Barich and Kotler identify a host of specific determinants of company image (see Figure 11-9).[17] As the CEO at Johnson & Johnson once observed, "Reputations reflect behavior you exhibit day in and day out through a hundred small things. The way you manage your reputation is by always thinking and trying to do the right thing every day."[18]

Corporate brand equity can be defined as the differential response by consumers, customers, employees, other firms, or any relevant constituency to the words, actions, communications, products or services provided by an identified corporate brand entity. In other words, positive corporate brand equity occurs when a relevant constituency responds more favorably to a corporate ad campaign, a corporate-branded product or service, a corporate-issued PR release, and so on than if the same offering were to be attributed to an unknown or fictitious company. Corporate brand equity occurs when

FIGURE 11-9 Determinants of Corporate Image

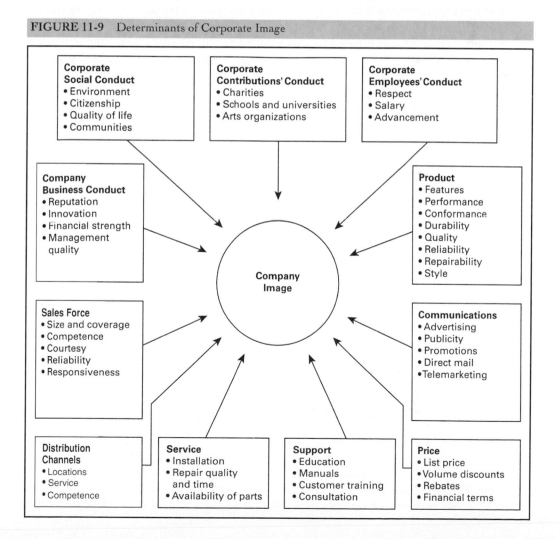

Corporate Social Conduct
• Environment
• Citizenship
• Quality of life
• Communities

Corporate Contributions' Conduct
• Charities
• Schools and universities
• Arts organizations

Corporate Employees' Conduct
• Respect
• Salary
• Advancement

Company Business Conduct
• Reputation
• Innovation
• Financial strength
• Management quality

Product
• Features
• Performance
• Conformance
• Durability
• Quality
• Reliability
• Repairability
• Style

Company Image

Sales Force
• Size and coverage
• Competence
• Courtesy
• Reliability
• Responsiveness

Communications
• Advertising
• Publicity
• Promotions
• Direct mail
• Telemarketing

Distribution Channels
• Locations
• Service
• Competence

Service
• Installation
• Repair quality and time
• Availability of parts

Support
• Education
• Manuals
• Customer training
• Consultation

Price
• List price
• Volume discounts
• Rebates
• Financial terms

relevant constituents hold strong, favorable, and unique associations about the corporate brand in memory. A corporate brand can be a powerful means for firms to express themselves in a way that is not tied to their specific products or services.

A corporate brand is distinct from a product brand in that it can encompass a much wider range of associations. That is, in establishing a corporate image, a corporate brand may evoke associations wholly different from an individual brand, which is identified only with a certain product or products. For example, a corporate brand name may be more likely to evoke associations of common products and their shared attributes or benefits; people and relationships; programs and values; and corporate credibility, as will be discussed in more detail in a later section of the chapter. These associations can have an important effect on the brand equity and market performance of individual products. For example, one research study revealed that consumers with a more favorable corporate image of DuPont were more likely to respond favorably to the claims made in an ad for Stainmaster carpet and therefore actually buy the product.[19]

Building and managing a strong corporate brand has additional requirements. For example, it necessitates that the firm keep a high public profile, especially in terms of influencing and shaping some of the more abstract types of associations. The chairman or managing director, if associated with a corporate brand, must be willing to maintain a more public profile to help to communicate news and information, as well as perhaps provide a symbol of current marketing activities. At the same time, by virtue of a more visible public profile, a firm must also be willing to be subject to more scrutiny and be more transparent in terms of its values, activities, and programs. Corporate brands thus have to be comfortable with a high level of openness.

A corporate brand offers a host of potential marketing advantages, but only if corporate brand equity is carefully built and nurtured—a challenging task. The evidence is mounting concerning the advantages of having a strong corporate brand. Many of the marketing winners in the coming years will therefore be those firms who properly build and manage corporate brand equity. It will take conviction, discipline, and focus on the part of senior management to make that happen, however. Branding Brief 11-4 describes a closely related concept—corporate reputation—and how it may be looked at from the perspective of consumers and other firms.[20] This chapter next considers brand image issues at the other three levels of the brand hierarchy.

Family Brand Level

Family brands, like corporate or company brands, are brands applied across a range of product categories. The main difference is that because a family brand may be distinct from the corporate or company brand, company-level associations may be less salient. Other authors sometimes refer to these types of brands as *range brands* or *umbrella brands*.

Family brands may be used instead of corporate brands for several reasons. As products become more dissimilar, it may be harder for the corporate brand to be used and still retain any product meaning or to effectively link the disparate products. As noted in Chapter 7, Beatrice was unable to create a meaningful corporate brand around its heterogeneous collection of products. Distinct family brands, on the other hand, can be circumscribed to evoke a specific set of associations across a group of related products. As with corporate brands, these associations may relate to common

Corporate Reputations: America's Most Admired Companies

Every year, *Fortune* magazine conducts a comprehensive survey of business perceptions of the companies with the best corporate reputations. The 2002 survey included the 1,000 largest U.S. companies (ranked by revenue) and the 25 largest U.S. subsidiaries of foreign-owned companies in 61 industry groups. More than 10,000 senior executives, outside directors, and financial analysts were asked to select the five companies they admired most, regardless of industry. To create industry lists, respondents rated companies in their industry by eight attributes: quality of management; quality of products or services; innovativeness; long-term investment value; financial soundness; ability to attract, develop, and keep talented people; responsibility to the community and the environment; and wise use of corporate assets. Interestingly, in ranking the eight attributes in terms of importance, respondents often listed "quality of management" and "quality of products and services" ahead of the three strictly financial measures.

Many of the same companies make the list year after year; for example, in 2002 General Electric was number 1 for the sixth year in the row. *Fortune* writers credited the stability of top companies to the fact that they had "mastered the art of maintaining continuity while fostering a state of perpetual renewal." They also cited these companies' ability to excel in tough times by consistently delivering value to shareholders, customers, and employees. *Fortune*'s Top Ten Most Admired companies in 2002 and their ratings are as follows:

Rank	Company	Rank	Company
1	General Electric	6	Home Depot
2	Southwest Airlines	7	Johnson & Johnson
3	Wal-Mart Stores	8	FedEx
4	Microsoft	9	Citigroup
5	Berkshire Hathaway	10	Intel

In an online survey of 26,011 consumers, Harris Interactive and the Reputation Institute determined the following to be the top 10 companies in terms of overall reputation of the 45 most visible companies in America.

Rank	Company	Rank	Company
1	Johnson & Johnson	6	Anheuser-Busch
2	Maytag	7	IBM
3	Sony	8	Disney
4	Home Depot	9	Microsoft
5	Intel	10	Procter & Gamble

Sources: Justin Fox, "America's Most Admired Companies," *Fortune*, 4 March 2002, 67; Ronald Alsop, "Survey Rates Companies' Reputations, and Many Are Found Wanting," *Wall Street Journal*, 7 February 2001, B1, B6.

product attributes, benefits, and attitudes and, perhaps to a lesser extent, people and relationships, programs and values, and corporate credibility.

Family brands thus can be an efficient means to link common associations to multiple, but distinct, products. The cost of introducing a related new product can be lower and the likelihood of acceptance can be higher when an existing family brand is used to brand a new product. On the other hand, if the products linked to the family brand and their supporting marketing programs are not carefully considered and designed, the associations to the family brand may become weaker and less favorable. Moreover, the failure of one product may have adverse ramifications on other products sold by the firm under the same brand by virtue of the common brand identification. These pros and cons must be assessed to determine whether an umbrella family brand (i.e., a "branded house") or a collection of individual brands (i.e., a "house of brands") is the more appropriate strategy.

Individual Brand Level

Individual brands are restricted to essentially one product category, although there may be multiple product types offered on the basis of different models, package sizes, flavors, and so forth. The main advantage of creating individual brands is that the brand and all its supporting marketing activity can be customized to meet the needs of a specific customer group. Thus, the name, logo, and other brand elements, as well as product design, marketing communication programs, and pricing and distribution strategies, can all be designed to focus on a certain target market. Moreover, if the brand runs into difficulty or fails, the risk to other brands and the company itself is minimized. The disadvantages of creating individual brands, however, are the difficulty, complexity, and expense involved in developing separate marketing programs to build sufficient levels of brand equity. Chapter 12 examines the pros and cons of individual brands versus corporate or family brands in the context of considering brand extensions.

Modifier Level

Regardless of whether corporate, family, or individual brands are employed, it is often necessary to further distinguish brands according to the different types of items or models involved. Adding a modifier often can signal refinements or differences in the brand related to factors such as quality levels (e.g., Johnnie Walker Red Label, Black Label, and Gold Label Scotch Whiskey), attributes (e.g., Wrigley's Spearmint, Doublemint, and Juicy Fruit flavors of chewing gum), functions (e.g., Kodak's 100, 200, and 400 speed film), and so forth.[21] Brand modifiers can play an important organizing role in communicating how different products within a category that share the same brand name differ on one or more significant attribute or benefit dimensions. Thus, one of the uses of brand modifiers is to show how one brand variation relates to others in the same brand family. As such, brand modifiers play an important role in ensuring market coverage within a category for the company as a whole. Modifiers help to make products more understandable and relevant to consumers or even the trade. Farquhar, Herr, and their colleagues note how modifiers can even become strong trademarks if they are able to develop a unique association with the parent brand, citing as examples the fact that only Uncle Ben has "Converted Rice" and only Orville Redenbacher sells "Gourmet Popping Corn."[22] Branding Brief 11-5 reviews some interesting recent developments in the use of brand modifiers.

Brand Modifiers

SMART AND LITE

The 1990 Nutrition Labeling and Education Act required foods labeled "light" to have half the fat content of the original product, making many products no longer worthy of the "light" moniker. For example, Procter & Gamble renamed its Pringles Light—which contain only one-third less fat than the original—as Pringles Right Crisps. Likewise, Kraft's Deliciously Light salad dressing became Deliciously Right, and Fleischmann's Light Margarine was transformed to Light Taste Margarine. In the year following the Nutrition Labeling and Education Act, only 3 percent of new foods contained the word *light,* compared with 7.4 percent in 1990.

One of the more popular modifiers, which has no government act regulating its usage, is *smart.* Products bearing the "smart" label include the Smart Broom, Smart Soup, Smart Manholes, Smart Gun, and Mr. Smart. In 1996, the U.S. Patent and Trademark Office received more than 1,000 applications for trademarks containing the word *smart,* up 2,600 percent from 35 in 1986.

SIZING

Smaller products became popular in the 1990s, but "they're never called tiny, they're called individual or one-time or disposable," according to one market research executive. Coffee shops avoid using traditional sizing. At Starbucks, the three sizes are short, tall, and grande. At Pasqua Coffee, espresso can be ordered as a single, double, or grande. Even more confusing: At Peet's Coffee, the double is called a doppio. McDonald's offers three sizes of soft drinks: regular, large, and super-size. "Nobody wants a small drink anymore," said a McDonald's spokesperson. Aside from the image considerations, there is an economic reason to develop larger sizes. Says a McDonald's executive, "The packaging and handling cost for a drink or french fries are a substantial part of the cost."

EXTENSIONS

Often marketers attach unorthodox modifiers to their brand extensions. For example, Curad brand bandages developed the "Curad Extreme Length," a bandage designed to wrap twice around a finger "for extra long hold." Marketers also may use similar-sounding modifiers to describe distinct brand extensions. Jergens introduced three new lotions in 2001, one that "nourishes and heals" called Replenishing Multi-Vitamin Lotion; one that "softens and heals," Ultra Healing Lotion; and one that "naturally softens," Soothing Aloe Lotion.

This brand proliferation may actually deter consumers. Mark Lepper, chairman of Stanford University's psychology department, concluded from the results of a study that greater product variety can induce shoppers to buy less. In the study, customers were offered free samples of jam and coupons for one dollar off if they purchased a jar. Half of the trials were done with 6 flavors, the other half with 24. A greater number of shoppers stopped for the samples when there were 24 of them, but only 3 percent eventually made a purchase. By comparison, 30 percent of shoppers made a purchase after encountering just the 6 flavors.

Sources: Cynthia Crossen, "Case of the Vanishing Medium: Perpetrator Is Large," *Wall Street Journal,* 26 February 1996; Yumiko Ono, "Let There Be 'Right.' Food Marketers Seek Appetizing Alternatives to 'Light,'" *Wall Street Journal,* 4 August 1994; J. Taylor Buckley, "Name Carries a Cachet for Product, Owner," *USA Today,* 16 January 1997; Laura Shanahan, "Designated Shopper," *Brandweek,* 26 March 2001, 46.

Product Descriptor

Although not considered a brand element per se, the product descriptor chosen for the actual branded product may be an important ingredient of branding strategy. The product descriptor helps consumers understand what the product is and does and also helps to define the relevant competition in consumers' minds. In some cases, it may be hard to actually describe succinctly what the product is, especially in the case of a new product with unusual functions.

Quicken

One of the branding challenges at Intuit, makers of the highly successful Quicken software package, is saying exactly what Quicken *is.* Although labeled as "personal financial software," this may not be a product category descriptor with which consumers have much familiarity. Consequently, a problem may arise if Intuit launches brand extensions under the Quicken name. Unless carefully differentiated, consumers could become confused as to what distinguishes different products sharing the same Quicken name and which product was the "original" one.

Introducing a truly new product with a familiar product name may facilitate basic familiarity and comprehension but perhaps at the expense of a richer understanding of how the new product is different from closely related, already-existing products.

Corporate Image Dimensions

Before considering some of the decisions needed to set up a brand hierarchy, it is worthwhile considering in more detail the types of associations that may exist at the corporate or company brand level—or perhaps even the family brand level—given their potential importance and relative lack of attention in the text up until now. This section highlights some of the different types of associations that are likely to be linked to a corporate brand and can potentially affect brand equity (see Figure 11-10).[23] The Science of Branding 11-2 describes some academic research into corporate branding.

Common Product Attributes, Benefits, or Attitudes

As with individual brands, a corporate or company brand may evoke performance or imagery attribute or benefit associations as well as judgment and feeling associations. Thus, a corporate brand may evoke a strong association with consumers to a

**Common Product Attributes,
Benefits, or Attitudes**
Quality
Innovativeness

People and Relationships
Customer orientation

Values and Programs
Concern with environment
Social responsibility

Corporate Credibility
Expertise
Trustworthiness
Likability

FIGURE 11-10   Some Important Corporate Image Associations

product attribute (e.g., Hershey with "chocolate"), type of user (e.g., BMW with "yuppies"), usage situation (e.g., Club Med with "fun times"), or overall judgment (e.g., Sony with "quality").

If a corporate brand is linked to products across diverse categories, then some of its strongest associations are likely to be those intangible attributes, abstract benefits, or attitudes that span each of the different product categories. For example, companies may be associated with products or services that solve particular problems (e.g., Black & Decker), bring excitement and fun to certain activities (e.g., Nintendo), are built with the highest quality standards (e.g., Motorola), contain advanced or innovative features (e.g., Rubbermaid), or represent market leadership (e.g., Hertz). Two specific product-related corporate image associations—high quality and innovation—deserve special attention.

A *high-quality corporate image association* involves the creation of consumer perceptions that a company makes products of the highest quality. A number of different organizations rate products (e.g., J.D. Power, *Consumer Reports,* and various trade publications for automobiles) and companies (e.g., the Malcolm Baldridge award) on the basis of quality. As Chapter 2 points out, consumer surveys often reveal that quality is one of the most important, if not *the* most important, decision factors for consumers.

An *innovative corporate image association* involves the creation of consumer perceptions of a company as developing new and unique marketing programs, especially with respect to product introductions or improvements. Being innovative is seen in part as being modern and up-to-date, investing in research and development, employing the most advanced manufacturing capabilities, and introducing the newest product features. An image priority for many Japanese companies—from consumer product companies such as Kao to more technically oriented companies such as Canon—is to be perceived as innovative.[24] Perceived innovativeness is also a key competitive weapon and priority for firms in other countries. In Europe, Michelin ("Driving Tire Science") has attempted to distinguish itself on its ability to innovate and successfully

Understanding the Corporate Brand

Several academic papers have considered issues surrounding the corporate brand. For example, Brown and Dacin distinguish between corporate associations related to corporate ability (i.e., expertise in producing and delivering product and/or service offerings) and corporate social responsibility (i.e., the character of the company with regard to important societal issues).[1]

Keller and Aaker experimentally showed how different corporate image strategies—being innovative, environmentally concerned, or community involved—could differentially affect corporate credibility and strategically benefit the firm by increasing the acceptance of brand extensions as a result.[2] Specifically, they showed how corporate images of being environmentally concerned and community involved affected consumer perceptions of corporate trustworthiness and likability but not corporate expertise. Interestingly, a company with an innovative corporate image was not only seen as expert but also as trustworthy and likable. Because only an innovative corporate image affected perceptions of corporate expertise, however, it was the only image type to affect perceptions of the fit and quality of a proposed extension. The other two image types, although perhaps useful in other contexts, were not as much of an asset in facilitating new product acceptance. The authors' findings also revealed that corporate marketing activity influenced evaluations even in the presence of advertising for the extension. In related research, Goldberg and Hartwick showed that consumers were more accepting of extreme ad claims (e.g., "best in the category") from companies with more credible reputations.[3]

In a qualitative study of 42 top managers at 11 Fortune 500 companies, Biehal and Sheinin examined three areas: the underlying dimensions of a corporate brand (CB) strategy, factors that influence the design of a CB strategy, and the influence of CB strategy on implementation.[4]

Their data indicated that managers considered scope, positioning, and locus of communication to be the three dimensions most relevant for designing a CB strategy. *Scope* was defined as the number of products in the portfolio that are subsumed by the corporate brand. *Positioning* was composed of two subdimensions: *diagnosticity* (the degree to which the CB positioning ties in with product positionings) and *variability* (the degree to which the CB positioning is allowed to vary across the defined scope). The third dimension, *locus of communication*, referred to whether the corporate brand was built primarily through corporate or product marketing activities, or a combination of the two.

Based on managers' comments, the authors proposed that three factors—market turbulence, the nature of the company's product portfolio, and the company's degree of organizational decentralization—were particularly important influences on the design of a CB strategy.

Finally, managers' comments suggested that decisions about the three CB strategy dimensions were particularly influential when it came to such implementation activities as organizational control, managerial coordination, and tactical marketing integration.

---

[1]T. J. Brown and P. Dacin, "The Company and the Product: Corporate Associations and Consumer Product Responses," *Journal of Marketing* 61 (January 1997): 68–84.

[2]Kevin Lane Keller and David A. Aaker, "The Effects of Sequential Introduction of Brand Extensions," *Journal of Marketing Research* 29 (February 1992): 35–50.

[3]Marvin E. Goldberg and Jon Hartwick, "The Effects of Advertiser Reputation and Extremity of Advertising Claim on Advertising Effectiveness," *Journal of Consumer Research* 17 (September 1990): 172–179.

[4]Gabriel J. Biehal and Daniel A. Sheinin, "Building Corporate Brands: An Exploratory Study," MSI Report 01–100 (Cambridge, MA: Marketing Science Institute, 2001).

invent new products. Branding Brief 11-6 describes how 3M has developed an innovative culture and image.

People and Relationships

Corporate image associations may reflect characteristics of the employees of the company. Although this is a natural positioning strategy for service firms such as airlines (e.g., Delta), rental cars (e.g., Avis), and hotels (e.g., Doubletree), manufacturing firms such as DuPont and others have also focused attention on their employees in communication programs. The rationale for such a positioning is that the traits exhibited by employees will directly or indirectly have implications for consumers concerning the products the firm makes or the services they provide.

Saturn

General Motors created an entire car division, Saturn, that advertises itself as a "Different Kind of Car Company" in an attempt to build unique relationships with consumers. According to then GM Chairman John Smale, Saturn's brand promise (and point of difference) was that it was the car to buy for consumers who "want a car built, sold, and serviced by people who really care—people whose No. 1 priority is to satisfy you and build and preserve a relationship with you, no matter what it takes." The entire marketing program created associations to Saturn as coming from a "dedicated and caring" car company.[25]

Retail stores also derive much brand equity from employees within the organization. For example, growing from its origins as a small shoe store, Seattle-based Nordstrom became one of the nation's leading fashion specialty stores through a commitment to quality, value, selection, and, especially, service. Legendary for its "personalized touch" and willingness to go to extraordinary lengths to satisfy its customers, Nordstrom creates brand equity in large part through the efforts of its salespeople and the relationships they develop with consumers.

Thus, a *customer-focused corporate image association* involves the creation of consumer perceptions of a company as being responsive to and caring about its customers. In such cases, consumers believe that their voice will be heard and that the company is not attempting to be exploitative. Thus, a company seen as customer focused is likely to be described as "listening" to customers and having their best interests in mind. Often this philosophy is reflected throughout the marketing program and communicated through advertising.

Values and Programs

Corporate image associations may reflect values and programs of the company that do not always directly relate to the products they sell. In many cases, these efforts are publicized through marketing communication campaigns. Firms can run corporate image ad campaigns as a means to describe to consumers, employees, and others the

Corporate Innovation at 3M

Minnesota Mining and Manufacturing (3M) has fostered a culture of innovation and improvisation evident in its very beginnings. In 1904, the company's directors were faced with a failed mining operation, but they turned the leftover grit and wastage into a revolutionary new product: sandpaper. Today 3M makes more than 60,000 products, including sandpaper, adhesives, computer disks, contact lenses, and optical films. Each year 3M launches scores of new products, and the company earns about 35 percent of revenues from products introduced within the past five years. The company regularly ranks among the top 10 U.S. companies each year in patents received. 3M has an annual R&D budget of $1 billion, which is a healthy portion of its annual $16.7 billion in sales.

3M has a long history of innovation. In addition to inventing sandpaper, the company has developed numerous products in its 99-year history that were the first of their kind. Here is a brief timeline:

1925: Scotch masking tape

1930: Scotch transparent tape

1939: First reflective traffic sign

1956: Scotchgard fabric protector

1962: Tartan Track, first synthetic running track

1979: Thinsulate thermal insulation

1980: Post-it Notes

1985: First refastening diaper tape

1995: First nonchlorofluorocarbon aerosol inhaler

2000: First laminating products that do not require heat

3M is able to consistently produce innovations in part because the company promotes a corporate environment that facilitates new discoveries. The following are some tactics the company uses to ensure its culture remains focused on innovation:

- 3M encourages everyone, not just engineers, to become "product champions." The company's "15 percent rule" allows all employees to spend up to 15 percent of their time working on projects of personal interest. Products such as Post-it Notes, masking tape, and the company's microreplication technology developed as a result of 15 percent rule activities.

- Each promising new idea is assigned to a multidisciplinary venture team headed by an "executive champion."

- 3M expects some failures and uses failed products as opportunities to learn how to make products that work. Its slogan is "You have to kiss a lot of frogs to find a prince."

- 3M hands out its Golden Step awards each year to the venture teams whose new products earned more than $2 million in U.S. sales or $4 million in worldwide sales within three years of commercial introduction.

In the late 1990s, 3M struggled as sales stalled and profits fell. The company restructured, shed several proprietary noncore businesses, and cut its workforce. As a result of

FIGURE A   3M Corporate Image Ad

these moves, 3M saw record sales and income in 2000. When 3M named former GE executive James McNerney as its new chairman and CEO that year, McNerney vowed he would continue to improve the company's bottom line while keeping its culture of innovation intact. Figure A displays a recent 3M corporate ad.

Sources: Philip Kotler, *Marketing Management*, 11 ed. (Upper Saddle River, NJ: Prentice-Hall, 2003); http://www.3m.com; 3M 2000 annual report.

philosophy and actions of the company with respect to organizational, social, political, or economic issues.

British Airways: Change For Good
British Airways partnered with UNICEF and developed a cause marketing campaign called Change For Good, in which travelers on British Airways flights are encouraged to donate leftover foreign currency from their travels. Since coins in particular are difficult to exchange at banks and currency exchanges, the program targets this loose change. The scheme is simple: Passengers deposit their surplus currency in envelopes provided by British Airways, which collects the deposits and donates them directly to UNICEF. British Airways advertises its program during an in-flight video, on the backs of seat cards, and with in-flight announcements. The company also developed a television advertisement that featured a child thanking British Airways for its contribution to UNICEF works.

For example, a focus of many recent corporate advertising campaigns has been company programs and activities designed to address environmental issues and communicate social responsibility. A *socially responsible corporate image association* involves creation of consumer perceptions of a company as contributing to community programs, supporting artistic and social activities, and generally attempting to improve the welfare of society as a whole. An *environmentally concerned corporate image association* involves the creation of consumer perceptions of a company as developing marketing programs to protect or improve the environment and make more effective use of scarce natural resources. Brand Focus 11.0 describes the broader issue of cause marketing.

Corporate Credibility

Besides all the associations noted previously, consumers may form more abstract judgments or even feelings about the company. For example, as Chapter 2 described with respect to an individual brand, consumers may form perceptions of the personality of a corporate brand. For example, one major public utility company was described by customers as "male, 35–40 years old, middle class, married with children, wearing a flannel shirt and khaki pants who would be reliable, competent, professional, intelligent, honest, ethical and business-oriented." On the downside, the company was also described by these same customers as "distant, impersonal, and self-focused," suggesting an important area for improvement in its corporate brand image.

A particularly important set of abstract associations to a corporate brand is corporate credibility. As defined in Chapter 2, *corporate credibility* refers to the extent to which consumers believe that a firm can design and deliver products and services that satisfy customer needs and wants. Thus, corporate credibility relates to the reputation that the firm has achieved in the marketplace. Corporate credibility, in turn, depends on three factors:

1. *Corporate expertise:* The extent to which a company is seen as able to competently make and sell its products or conduct its services
2. *Corporate trustworthiness:* The extent to which a company is seen as motivated to be honest, dependable, and sensitive to customer needs
3. *Corporate likability:* The extent to which a company is seen as likable, attractive, prestigious, dynamic, and so forth

A number of other characteristics can also be related to these three dimensions as consequences, for example, success and leadership. Creating a firm with a strong and credible reputation may offer benefits beyond the consumer response in the marketplace. A highly credible company may be treated more favorably by other external constituencies, such as government or legal officials. It also may be possible to attract better-qualified employees as a result. For example, Wendy's used the folksy image of its popular late CEO and advertising spokesperson, Dave Thomas, to attract employees. In-store signs solicited job applications by displaying his picture with a headline caption that read, "Would Dave Be Great to Work With or What?"

A highly credible company may also help motivate existing employees to be more productive and loyal. As one Shell Oil employee remarked as part of some internal corporate identity research, "If you're really proud of where you work, I think you put a little more thought into what you did to help get them there." A strong corporate reputation can help a firm survive a brand crisis and avert public outrage that could potentially depress sales, encourage unionism, or block expansion plans. As Harvard's Steve Greyser notes, "Corporate reputation . . . can serve as a capital account of favorable attitudes to help buffer corporate trouble."

L.L.Bean

A brand seen by its customers as highly credible, outdoors product retailer L.L.Bean attempts to earn consumer's trust every step of the way—providing prepurchase advice, secure transactions, best-in-class delivery, and easy returns and exchanges. Founded in 1912, L.L.Bean backs its efforts with a 100 percent Satisfaction Guarantee as well as its Golden Rule: "Sell good merchandise at a reasonable profit, treat your customers like human beings, and they will always come back for more." Now a billion dollar brand in sales, the company still retains its roots of being passionate about the outdoors with a profound belief in honesty, product quality, and customer service.

Summary

Many types of associations may become linked to a corporate brand that transcend physical product characteristics.[26] These intangible associations may provide valuable sources of brand equity and serve as critical points of parity or points of difference. Companies have a number of means—indirect or direct—of creating these associations. In doing so, it is important that companies talk the talk *and* walk the walk by communicating to consumers as well as backing up their claims with concrete programs that consumers can easily understand or even experience.

DESIGNING A BRANDING STRATEGY

Given the different possible levels of a branding hierarchy, a firm has a number of branding options available to it, depending on how each level is employed, if at all. There is no uniform agreement on the one type of branding strategy that should be adopted by all firms for all products. LaForet and Saunders conducted a content analysis of the branding strategies adopted by 20 key brands sold by each of 20 of the biggest suppliers of grocery products to Tesco and Sainsbury, Britain's two leading grocery chains.[27] They categorized the brand strategy adopted by each brand into a classification scheme that can be seen as essentially a refinement of the four-level brand hierarchy described earlier in this chapter. As Figure 11-11 shows, a variety of branding approaches were employed. The authors note how different companies within the same market could adopt sharply contrasting strategies, offering the following example:

> For a long time Cadbury, Mars, and Nestlé have competed in the confectionery market. They often match each other brand for brand but their branding strategies are quite different. While Cadbury led with the Cadbury name and colors across virtually all their products, such as Cadbury's Dairy Milk,

Branding Strategy	Percentage of Occurrence
Corporate Dominant	
Corporate brands: Corporate name used	5
House brands: Subsidiary name used	11
Mixed Brands	
Dual brands: Two or more names given equal prominence	38.5
Endorsed brands: Brand endorsed by corporate or house identity	13.5
Brand Dominant	
Mono brands: Single brand name used	19
Furtive brands: Single brand name used and corporate identity undisclosed	13

Source: Sylvie LaForet and John Saunders, "Managing Brand Portfolios: How the Leaders Do It," *Journal of Advertising Research* (September/October 1994): 64–76.

FIGURE 11-11   Breakdown of Brand Types

Cadbury's Milk Tray, Cadbury's Flake, etc. Mars led with their brands such as Mars Bars, Snickers, and Twix with no corporate endorsement. Until recently, Nestlé Rowntree pursued a branded approach like Mars, but now the Nestlé name has started to appear upon the once independently branded products.[28]

Even within any one firm, different branding strategies may be adopted for different products. For example, although Miller has used its name across its different types of beer over the years with various sub-brands (e.g., Miller High Life, Miller Lite, and Miller Genuine Draft), it carefully branded its no-alcohol beer substitute as Sharp's with no overt Miller identification. The assumption was that the corporate family brand name would not be relevant to and valued by the target market in question.

Thus, it is important to note that *the brand hierarchy may not be symmetric.* Because of considerations related to corporate objectives, consumer behavior, or competitive activity, there may sometimes be significant deviations in branding strategy and how the brand hierarchy is organized for different products or for different markets. Brand elements may receive more or less emphasis, or not be present at all, depending on the particular products and markets involved. For example, in appealing to an organizational market segment where the DuPont brand name may be more valuable, it might receive more emphasis than associated sub-brands. In appealing to a consumer market segment, a sub-brand such as Dacron may be more meaningful and thus receive relatively more emphasis. (See Figure 11-12.)

How does a firm use different levels of the brand hierarchy to build brand equity? Brand elements at each level of the hierarchy may contribute to brand equity through their ability to create awareness as well as foster strong, favorable, and unique brand associations and positive responses. Therefore, the challenge in setting up the brand hierarchy and arriving at a branding strategy is to (1) design the proper brand hierarchy

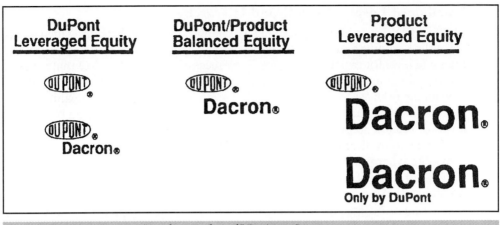

FIGURE 11-12 DuPont "Product-Endorsed" Business Strategy

in terms of the number and nature of brand elements to use at each level and (2) design the optimal supporting marketing program in terms of creating the desired amount of brand awareness and type of brand associations at each level. Specifically, designing a brand hierarchy and brand strategy involves decisions related to the following:

1. The number of levels of the hierarchy to use in general
2. Desired brand awareness and image at each level
3. How brand elements from different levels of the hierarchy are combined, if at all, for any one particular product
4. How any one brand element is linked, if at all, to multiple products

The following discussion reviews these decisions and can be summarized in terms of five guidelines that assist the design of brand hierarchies (see Figure 11-13).

FIGURE 11-13 Guidelines for Brand Hierarchy Decisions

1. Decide on the number of levels.
   - *Principle of simplicity:* Employ as few levels as possible.
2. Decide on the levels of awareness and types of associations to be created at each level.
   - *Principle of relevance:* Create abstract associations that are relevant across as many individual items as possible.
   - *Principle of differentiation:* Differentiate individual items and brands.
3. Decide on how to link brands from different levels for a product.
   - *Principle of prominence:* The relative prominence of brand elements affects perceptions of product distance and the type of image created for new products.
4. Decide on how to link a brand across products.
   - *Principle of commonality:* The more common elements shared by products, the stronger the linkages.

Number of Levels of the Brand Hierarchy

The first decision to make in defining a branding strategy is, broadly, which level or levels of the branding hierarchy should be used. In general, most firms choose to use more than one level for two main reasons. Each successive branding level that is used allows the firm to communicate additional, specific information about its products. Thus, developing brands at lower levels of the hierarchy allows the firm flexibility in communicating the uniqueness of its products. At the same time, developing brands at higher levels of the hierarchy such that the brand is applied across multiple products is obviously an economical means of communicating common or shared information and providing synergy across the company's operations, both internally and externally.

The practice of combining an existing brand with a new brand to brand a product is called *sub-branding* because the subordinate brand is a means of modifying the superordinate brand. Sub-branding often combines the company or family brand name with individual brands and even model types. Extending an earlier example, ThinkPad can be seen as a sub-brand to the IBM name, with A22M as a second-level sub-brand to further modify the meaning of the product. As suggested previously, a sub-brand, or hybrid branding, strategy offers two potential benefits in that it can both facilitate access to associations and attitudes regarding the company or family brand as a whole and, at the same time, allow for the creation of specific brand beliefs.

Thus, using the IBM name allows access to global associations that consumers may have toward the company (e.g., reliable, trustworthy, and good quality). Introducing different sub-brands—most recently NetVista (which replaced Aptiva and PS/1 as IBM's main business PCs) and ThinkPad (for its portable PCs)—allows IBM to develop distinct brand images at the same time.

Hershey's Kisses

Hershey's chocolate has a traditional, homespun image, as reflected by its 20-plus-year-old advertising slogan, "Hershey's. The Great American Candy Bar." As a result of a clever ad campaign that transforms the teardrop-shaped, foil-wrapped Hershey's Kisses into animate objects and places them in amusing, product-relevant situations, however, the Kisses sub-brand has a much more playful and fun brand image than the company brand. The successful Hershey's Kisses sub-brand led to a further extension, Hershey's Hugs (a Hershey's Kiss with an outside layer of white chocolate).

Sub-branding thus creates a stronger connection to the company or family brand and all the associations that come along with that. As an illustration, consider the cereal category, in which Kellogg has adopted a sub-branding strategy whereas other manufacturers (e.g., Post) have adopted an endorsement strategy. These different strategies have had profound implications on consumers' identification of and associations with certain cereal brands. For example, one research study revealed that when consumers were asked to identify the makers of each cereal from a list of ten cereals, Kellogg's cereals were mismatched or unidentified only 14 percent of the time, but Post cereals were not correctly matched 56 percent of the time. Moreover, when consumers were asked whether knowing the name of various manufacturers would have a positive, neutral, or negative effect on their likelihood of purchasing a new cereal product, over half of the sample claimed that the Kellogg's name would encourage them to make the purchase, but only a little over a quarter of the sample felt the same way about the Post name. Apparently, through its sub-branding strategy and marketing activities, Kellogg has done a more effective job than Post both in connecting its corporate name to its products and creating favorable associations to its corporate name. As a result, Kellogg's has become a strong umbrella brand for the company's individual products.

At the same time, developing sub-brands allows for the creation of brand-specific beliefs. This more detailed information can help customers better understand how products vary and which particular product may be the right one for them. Sub-brands also help to organize selling efforts so that salespeople and retailers have a clear picture as to how the product line is organized and how it might best be sold. For example, one of the main advantages to Nike of continually creating sub-brands in its basketball line (e.g., Air Jordan, Air Flight, Air Force, etc.) has been to generate retail interest and enthusiasm.

The *principle of simplicity* is based on the need to provide the right amount of branding information to consumers—no more and no less. In general, the desired number of levels of the brand hierarchy depends on the complexity of the product line or product mix associated with a brand and thus the combination of shared and separate brand associations that the company would like to link to any one product in its product line or mix. With relatively simple, low-involvement products—such as lightbulbs, batteries, and chewing gum—the branding strategy often consists of an individual or perhaps family brand combined with modifiers that describe differences in product features. For example, GE has two main brands of lightbulbs (Soft White and Enrich) combined with designations for functionality (e.g., 3-way, Super, and Miser) and performance (e.g., 40, 60, and 100 watts). For a complex set of products—such as cars, computers, or other durable goods—more levels of the hierarchy are necessary. Regardless of the complexity involved, it is difficult to brand a product with more than three levels of brand names without overwhelming or confusing consumers. In such cases, a better approach might be to introduce multiple brands at the same level (e.g., multiple family brands) and expand the depth of the branding strategy.

Desired Awareness and Image at Each Hierarchy Level

Once multiple brand levels are chosen, the question becomes, How much awareness and what types of associations are to be created for brand elements at each level? Achieving the desired level of awareness and strength, favorability, and uniqueness of brand associations may take some time and involve a considerable change in consumer perceptions. Marketing programs must be carefully designed, implemented, and evaluated. Assuming some type of sub-branding strategy is adopted involving two or more brand levels, two general principles—relevance and differentiation—should guide the brand knowledge creation process at each level.

The *principle of relevance* is based on the advantages of efficiency and economy. In general, it is desirable to create associations that are relevant to as many brands nested at the level below as possible, especially at the corporate or family brand level. The more it is the case that an association has some value in the marketing of products sold by the firm, the more efficient and economical it is to consolidate this meaning into one brand that becomes linked to all these products. For example, Nike's slogan ("Just Do It") reinforces a key point of difference for the brand—performance—that is relevant to virtually all the products it sells.

The more abstract the association, in general, the more likely it is to be relevant in different product settings. Thus, benefit associations are likely to be extremely advantageous associations because they potentially can cut across many product categories. Brands with strong product category and attribute associations, however, can find it difficult to create a robust enough brand image to permit successful extensions into new categories. For example, Blockbuster attempted to broaden its meaning from "a place to rent videos" to "your neighborhood entertainment center" to create a broader brand umbrella with greater relevance to more products.

The *principle of differentiation* is based on the disadvantages of redundancy. In general, it is desirable to distinguish brands at the same level as much as possible. If two brands cannot be easily distinguished, then it may be difficult for retailers or other channel members to justify supporting both brands. It may also be confusing for consumers to make choices between them. For example, Tropicana's sub-brands of orange juice have included its flagship Pure Premium (which comes in several flavors, including Ruby Red Orange), as well as the extensions Grovestand ("The Taste of Fresh Squeezed") and Season's Best (100 percent pure orange juice from concentrate with vitamins added); these extensions also come in different varieties and packaging. On the basis of the names and positionings, there would seem to be the potential for consumer confusion as to how the various juices differ and which Tropicana juice is the right product for them.

Although new products and brand extensions are critical to keeping a brand innovative and relevant, they must be introduced thoughtfully. Without restraint, brand variations can easily get out of control.[29] The typical grocery store now stocks 40,000 items, twice as many as a few years ago, which raises the question: Do consumers really need nine kinds of Kleenex tissues, Eggo waffles in 16 flavors, and 72 varieties of Pantene shampoo, all of which are potentially available at one point in time? To better control its inventory and avoid brand proliferation, Colgate-Palmolive has begun to discontinue one item for each it introduces.

Although the principle of differentiation is especially important at the individual brand or modifier levels, it is also valid at the family brand level. For example, one of the criticisms of marketing at General Motors is that the company has failed to adequately distinguish its family brands of automobiles (recall Branding Brief 8-5). The principle of differentiation also implies that not all products should receive the same emphasis at any level of the hierarchy. A key issue in designing a brand hierarchy thus concerns the relative emphasis received by different products making up the brand hierarchy. If a corporate or family brand is associated with multiple products, which product should be the core or flagship product? What should represent "the brand" to consumers? Which product do consumers think best represents or embodies the brand? Understanding these brand drivers is important in identifying sources of brand equity and therefore how to best fortify and leverage the brand.

Combining Brand Elements from Different Levels

If multiple brand elements from different levels of the brand hierarchy are combined to brand new products, it is necessary to decide how much emphasis should be given to each brand element. For example, if a sub-brand strategy is adopted, how much prominence should individual brands be given at the expense of the corporate or family brand?

When multiple brands are used, each brand element can vary in the relative emphasis it receives in the combined brand. The *prominence* of a brand element refers to its relative visibility compared with other brand elements. For example, the prominence of a brand name element depends on several factors, such as its order, size, and appearance, as well as its semantic associations. A name is generally more prominent when it appears first, is larger, and looks more distinctive. For example, assume PepsiCo has adopted a sub-branding strategy to introduce a new vitamin-fortified cola, combining its corporate family brand name with a new individual brand name (e.g., "Vitacola"). The Pepsi name could be made more prominent by placing it first and making it bigger: PEPSI *Vitacola*. On the other hand, the individual brand could be made more prominent by placing it first and making it bigger: Vitacola BY PEPSI.

Along these lines, Gray and Smeltzer define *corporate/product relationships* as the approach a firm follows in communicating the relationship of its products to one another and to the corporate entity. They identified five possible categories (with illustrative examples):[30]

1. *Single entity:* One product line or set of services is offered such that the image of the company and the product tend to be one and the same (e.g., Federal Express).
2. *Brand dominance:* The strategic decision is made not to relate brand and corporate names (e.g., Philip Morris makes little connection to Marlboro, Merit, and its other cigarettes).
3. *Equal dominance:* Separate images are maintained for products, but each is also associated with the corporation. Neither the corporate nor the individual brand names dominate (e.g., at the company level, General Motors with its different car divisions and individual brands—Buick LeSabre, Buick Electra, Buick Riviera, and so forth).
4. *Mixed dominance:* Sometimes the individual product brands are dominant and sometimes the corporate name is dominant, and in some cases, they are used together with equal emphasis (e.g., the German firm Bosch uses its corporate name on some of the products it manufactures but not on others, such as Blaupunkt radios).
5. *Corporate dominance:* The corporate name is supreme and applied across a range of product lines, and communications tend to reinforce the corporate image (e.g., Xerox).

The *principle of prominence* states that the relative prominence of brand elements affects perceptions of product distance and the type of image created for new products. That is, the relative prominence of the brand elements determines which element or elements become the primary one(s) and which element or elements become the secondary one(s). In general, primary brand elements should be chosen to convey the main product positioning and points of difference. Secondary brand elements are often chosen for a supporting role to convey a more restricted set of associations such as points of parity or perhaps an additional point of difference. A secondary brand element may also facilitate awareness. Thus, with the Canon Rebel 35mm camera, the primary brand element—through the use of the color red and a bold, prominent design—is the Rebel name, which reinforces the youthful, active lifestyle that makes up the desired user and usage imagery for the camera. The Canon name, on the other hand, is a secondary brand element that ideally conveys credibility, quality, and professionalism.

The relative prominence of the individual brand compared with the corporate brand should affect perceptions of product distance and the type of image created for the new product. If the corporate or family brand is made more prominent, then its associations are more likely to dominate. If the individual brand is made more prominent, on the other hand, then it should be easier to create a more distinctive brand image. In this case, the corporate or family brand is signaling to consumers that the new product is not as closely related to its other products that share that name. As a result, consumers should be less likely to transfer corporate or family brand associations. At the same time, the success or failure of the new product should, because of the greater perceived distance involved, be less likely to affect the image of the corporate or family brand. With a more prominent corporate or family brand, however, feedback effects are probably more likely to be evident. Chapter 12 discusses these issues in more detail.

To illustrate how relative prominence can affect the resulting image of a product, assume that in the Pepsi Vitacola example given earlier, Pepsi is the more prominent brand element. By making the corporate and family brand prominent, the new product would take on many of the associations common to other Pepsi-branded products (e.g., cola). If the Vitacola brand were more prominent, however, then the new product would most likely take on a more distinct positioning. In this case, the Pepsi name would function more for awareness and perhaps only transfer broader, more abstract associations, such as perceived quality or brand personality.

Finally, in some cases, the brand elements may not be explicitly linked at all. A *brand endorsement strategy* is when a brand element appears on the package, signage, or product appearance in some way but is not directly included as part of the brand name. Often this distinct brand element is the corporate brand name or logo. For example, General Mills places its "Big G" logo on its cereal packages but retains distinct brand names such as Cheerios, Wheaties, and so forth. As noted earlier, Kellogg, on the other hand, adopts a sub-brand strategy with its cereals that combines the corporate name with individual brands, e.g., Kellogg's Corn Flakes, Kellogg's Special K, and so on. The brand endorsement strategy presumably establishes the maximum distance between the corporate or family brand and the individual brands, suggesting that it would yield the smallest transfer of brand associations to the new product but, at the same time, minimize the likelihood of any negative feedback effects.

Linking Brand Elements to Multiple Products

The previous discussion highlighted how different brand elements can be applied to a particular product (i.e., "vertical" aspects of the brand hierarchy). Next, the chapter considers how any one brand element can be linked to multiple products (i.e., "horizontal" aspects of the brand hierarchy). There are many different ways to connect a brand element to multiple products. The *principle of commonality* states that the more common brand elements shared by products, the stronger the linkages between the products.

The simplest way to link products is to use the brand element "as is" across the different products involved. Other possibilities exist by adapting the brand, or some part of it, in some fashion to make the connection. For example, a common prefix or suffix of a brand name may be adapted to different products. Hewlett-Packard capitalized on its highly successful LaserJet computer printers to introduce a number of new products using the "Jet" suffix, for example, the DeskJet, PaintJet, ThinkJet, and OfficeJet printers. Sony has given its portable audio equipment a "man" suffix: Walkman personal stereos and Discman portable CD players. McDonald's has used its "Mc" prefix to introduce a number of products, such as Chicken McNuggets, Egg McMuffin, and the McRib sandwich. Initials can sometimes be used if multiple names make up the brand name, as with a designer name such as Donna Karan's DKNY brand, Calvin Klein's CK brand, and Ralph Lauren's Double RL brand.

A relationship between a brand and multiple products can also be made with common symbols. For example, corporate brands often place their corporate logo more prominently on their products than their name (e.g., Nabisco), creating a strong brand endorsement strategy.

Nestlé

Nestlé ran an advertising campaign in 1993 that attempted to create greater awareness and understanding of its corporate brand. The ads contained the slogan "makes the very best"—a subtle variation of its well-known "Nestlé's makes the very best chocolate" slogan—and prominently displayed a logo of a nest with a mother and two baby birds. Although the founder's name, Nestlé, in fact means "little nest," the company's hope in using the symbol was to communicate abstract associations of warmth, family, and shelter. The symbol was to be used on all packages as a means to unite a diversified set of products with vastly different names (see Figure 11-14).

FIGURE 11-14 Nestlé Corporate Brand Ad

ALL OVER THE WORLD THIS IS A SYMBOL FOR WARMTH, FAMILY AND SHELTER.

In 1867, a man named Henri Nestl began to build a food company.

His name, which means little nest, has since become synonymous with food, family and quality throughout the world.

Today, that symbol can be found on the back of many well-known products.

Great-tasting Nestl brands that include Stouffer s, Contadina, Libby s, Taster s Choice, Hills Bros, Carnation and more.

Finally, often it is desirable to have a logical ordering among brands in a product line to communicate how the different brands are related and to simplify consumer decision making. The relative ordering may be communicated to consumers though colors (e.g., American Express offers Green, Gold, and Platinum cards), numbers (e.g., BMW offers its 3-, 5-, and 7-series cars), or other means. Branding Brief 11-7 describes how Acura attempted to rename its product line to create more structure. Such a branding strategy is especially important in developing brand migration strategies for how customers should switch among the brands offered by the company, if at all, over their lifetime (see Chapter 13).

Adjustments to the Marketing Program

When a firm moves away from a simple "single brand—single product" branding strategy to adopt more complex branding strategies—perhaps involving multiple brand extensions, multiple brands, or multiple levels of the hierarchy used to brand any one product—certain adjustments may be necessary in the supporting marketing program. For example, as noted earlier, different brands can play different roles and therefore require quite different marketing mixes. Consequently, product design, pricing policies, distribution plans, and marketing communication campaigns may differ significantly depending on the role of the brand and its interdependencies with other brands. In general, many of the principles discussed in Chapters 5 to 7 for developing supporting marketing programs to build brand equity still apply. This section highlights some of the marketing communication adjustments that may be necessary in the supporting marketing program as a result of having interrelated brands and products.

Assuming that multiple levels of a branding hierarchy are employed, different levels of awareness and image may be desired at each level. In particular, if a sub-brand strategy is adopted, it may make sense to create a marketing communication campaign at the corporate, company, or family brand levels to complement more product-specific or individual brand marketing communication campaigns (as were reviewed in Chapter 6). As part of this higher-level campaign, companies may employ the full range of marketing communication options, including advertising, public relations, promotions, and sponsorship. Two potentially useful marketing communication strategies to build brand equity at the corporate brand or family brand level are discussed here.

Corporate Image Campaigns

Corporate image campaigns are designed to create associations to the corporate brand as a whole and, consequently, tend to ignore or downplay individual products or sub-brands in the process.[31] As would be expected, some of the biggest spenders on these kinds of campaigns are those well-known firms who prominently use their company or corporate name in their branding strategies, such as GE, Toyota, British Telecom, IBM, Novartis, Microsoft, Deutsche Bank, and Hewlett-Packard. For example, AT&T ran a $50 million television and print corporate advertising campaign in 2000 themed "Boundless" in a bid to reposition the company as a nimble, cutting-edge provider of digital broadband. Philip Morris ran a controversial campaign in the late 1990s to improve public perceptions of the often-criticized firm. More firms are now running these types of non-product-specific ads—especially retail and service brands that commonly use their corporate name—in part because so many products have become linked to their family or corporate brands over time.

Renaming the Acura Brand Portfolio

Honda grew from humble origins as a motorcycle manufacturer to become a top automobile import competitor in the United States. Recognizing that future sales growth would come from more upscale customers, Honda set out in the early 1980s to compete with European luxury cars. Deciding that the Honda image of dependable, functional, and economical cars did not have the cachet to appeal to luxury car buyers, Honda set up the new Acura division. Matching the quality, performance, and luxury of the European imports but costing thousands less, the $10,000 Acura Integra and the $20,000 Acura Legend were introduced in 1986. By the time Lexus and Infiniti (luxury brands from Toyota and Nissan, respectively) entered the market in 1989, Acura was selling 142,000 cars annually and receiving top marks in customer satisfaction.

Rapidly rising sticker prices—due in part to a strengthening yen—and increased competition eroded sales to the point at which Acura sales in the United States barely topped 100,000 cars in 1993. With its market leadership threatened and its customer base splintering (the average Integra buyer made $57,000 annually, or half of the average Legend owner), Honda felt it needed a dramatic marketing move. Research indicated that its Legend, Integra, and Vigor sub-brand names did not communicate luxury and order in the product line as well as the alphanumeric branding scheme of competitors BMW, Mercedes, Lexus, and Infiniti. Honda decided that the strength of the brand should lie in the Acura name. Thus, despite the fact that nearly $600 million had been spent on advertising those Acura sub-brands over the past eight years to build their equity, Honda announced a new alphanumeric branding scheme in the winter of 1995. The accompanying $100 million advertising campaign retained the upscale theme, "Some Things Are Worth the Price."

The new 2.5 TL and 3.2 TL (for Touring Luxury) sedan series, designed to replace the Vigor, was the first rebranded model available in 1995. The following year, Acura rolled out the 3.5 RL, a replacement for its top-of-the-line Legend model. At that time, Acura also introduced two new cars, called the 2.2 CL and 3.0 CL, priced in the mid-$20,000 range. The CL line was positioned below the TL but above the Integra, which had been renamed the RSX. In 1997, Honda estimated that up to 21 percent of Acura owners were switching to other brands that offered SUVs, so Acura introduced the SLX (later renamed the MDX) sport utility vehicle. The NSX sports car retained its name.

Acura spokesperson Mike Spencer said, "It used to be that people said they owned or drove a Legend. . . . Now they say they drive an Acura, and that's what we wanted." Acura's name awareness in 2001 was 25 percent higher than in 1996. Overall Acura sales rose 33 percent to 142,681 between 1996 and 2000.

Sources: David Kiley, "I'd Like to Buy a Vowel, Drivers Say," *USA Today*, 9 August 2000; Mark Rechtin, "Honda Hopes New CR-V Will Win Back Defectors," *Automotive News*, 3 February 1997; Stewart Toy, "The Selling of Acura—A Honda That's Not a Honda," *Business Week*, 17 March 1986, 93; Fara Werner, "Remaking of a Legend," *Brandweek*, 25 April 1994, 23–28; Neal Templin, "Japanese Luxury-Car Makers Unveiling Cheaper Models in Bid to Attract Buyers," *Wall Street Journal*, 9 February 1995; T. L. Stanley and Kathy Tryer, "Acura Plays Numbers Game to Fortify Future," *Brandweek*, 20 February 1995, 3; T. L. Stanley, "Acura Rolls TL, New Nameplate Position with $40M in Ad Fuel," *Brandweek*, 20 March 1995, 4.

Corporate image campaigns have been criticized by some in the past as an ego-stroking waste of time. Moreover, because these corporate brand-building marketing and management activities may be seen as not directly related to individual products, they may be more easily overlooked or ignored. One contention that can be made, however, is that a strong corporate brand can provide invaluable marketing and financial benefits by allowing the firm to express itself and embellish the meaning and associations for its individual products. To maximize the probability of success, however, objectives of a corporate image campaign must be clearly defined *and* results must be carefully measured against these objectives.[32] A number of different objectives are possible in a corporate brand campaign:[33]

➤ Build awareness of the company and the nature of its business
➤ Create favorable attitudes and perceptions of company credibility
➤ Link beliefs that can be leveraged by product-specific marketing
➤ Make a favorable impression on the financial community
➤ Motivate present employees and attract better recruits
➤ Influence public opinion on issues

In terms of building customer-based brand equity, the first three objectives are particularly critical. A corporate image campaign can enhance awareness and create a more positive image of the corporate brand that will influence consumer evaluations and increase the equity associated with individual products and any related sub-brands. In certain cases, however, the latter three objectives can take on greater importance.[34] Notable examples of the first three objectives—the ones most directly related to building customer-based brand equity—are highlighted in the following.

➤ *Building awareness of the company and the nature of its business.* Cingular Wireless launched a teaser corporate campaign to build brand recognition during the 2001 Super Bowl. Subsequently, it launched a $75 million ad campaign emphasizing self-expression as a means of differentiating itself from other wireless marketers.[35] Although clearly a mature brand, HP ran a corporate brand campaign themed "Expanding Possibilities" before later switching to one themed "Invent" as a means to emphasize its technological leadership, vision, and broad capabilities.

➤ *Building company trustworthiness and credibility.* Johnson & Johnson ran an ad campaign to promote the trustworthiness of the corporate brand. The commercials featured many "warm and fuzzy" shots of families. Johnson & Johnson products were not emphasized, although its baby powder, Band-Aids, and Reach toothbrush products were shown in passing. The ad concluded with the words: "Over the years, Johnson & Johnson has taken care of more families than anyone else." Similarly, to craft an image that transcended its products, Kraft ran a corporate brand campaign featuring its Kool-Aid, Philadelphia cream cheese, Post cereal, and Tombstone frozen pizza brands in a single TV spot or Sunday circular. The intent was to show that Kraft "got the importance of family values and made the kind of food that families with values ate."[36]

➤ *Creating corporate image associations that can be leveraged by product-specific marketing.* To solve a severe brand awareness problem, Philips Consumer Electronics launched a national corporate advertising campaign in 1998. Targeting young hipsters, the ads showcase cleverly designed Philips products as part of modern lifestyles. Featuring the Beatles song "Getting Better," the ads doubled awareness and improved the corporation's image, permitting much in-store product marketing.[37] Chase and DuPont are other companies that use their corporate brand to bolster all or most of their offerings.

Thus, corporate image campaigns focus on characteristics or aspects of the brand as a whole. These broader image campaigns may also be employed at the family brand level.

Brand Line Campaigns

A second marketing communication strategy to build brand equity at the corporate brand or family brand level is a brand line campaign. *Brand line campaigns* emphasize the breadth of products associated with the brand. Unlike a corporate image campaign that presents the brand in abstract terms with few, if any, references to specific products, brand line campaigns refer to the range of products associated with a brand line. By showing consumers the different uses or benefits of the multiple products offered by a brand, brand line ads may be particularly useful in building brand awareness, clarifying brand meaning, and suggesting additional usage applications. Brand line promotions can achieve similar goals.

Even when individual brands are used, umbrella ads that encompass multiple brands may serve a purpose. For example, in several advertising campaigns in 1995, Procter & Gamble promoted category-wide product benefits for its brands, such as the sanitary power of its dishwashing detergents and the waste-reduction advantages of "ultra" laundry detergents.[38] In both cases, the benefit is a point of difference (compared with lower-priced competitors) shared by all P&G brands in the category.

Review

A key aspect of managing brand equity is the proper branding strategy. Brand names of products typically do not consist of only one name but often consist of a combination of different names and other brand elements. A *branding strategy* for a firm identifies which brand elements a firm chooses to apply across the various products it sells. This chapter described two important tools to help formulate branding strategies: the brand-product matrix and the brand hierarchy. Combining these tools with customer, company, and competitive considerations can help a marketing manager formulate the optimal branding strategy.

The brand-product matrix is a graphical representation of all the brands and products sold by the firm. The matrix or grid has the brands for a firm as rows and the corresponding products as columns. The rows of the matrix represent brand-product relationships and capture the brand extension strategy of the firm with respect to a brand. Potential extensions must be judged by how effectively they leverage existing brand equity to a new product, as well as how effectively the extension, in turn, contributes to the equity of the existing parent brand. The columns of the matrix represent product-brand relationships and capture the brand portfolio strategy in terms of the number and nature of brands to be marketed in each category.

A branding strategy can be characterized according to its breadth (i.e., in terms of brand-product relationships and brand extension strategy) and its depth (i.e., in terms of product-brand relationships and the brand portfolio or mix). The breadth of the branding strategy concerns the product mix and which products the firm should manufacture or sell. The chapter considered issues concerning how many different product lines the company should carry (i.e., the breadth of the product mix), as well as how many variants should be offered in each product line (i.e., the depth of the product mix). The depth of the branding strategy concerns the brand portfolio and the set of all brands and brand lines that a particular seller offers to buyers. A firm may offer multiple brands in a category to attract different—and potentially mutually exclusive—market segments. Brands also can take on very specialized roles in the portfolio: as flanker brands to protect more valuable brands, as low-end entry-level brands to expand the customer franchise, as high-end prestige brands to enhance the worth of the entire brand line, or as cash cows to milk all potentially realizable profits. Companies must be careful to understand exactly what each brand should do for the firm and, more important, what they want it to do for the customer.

A brand hierarchy reveals an explicit ordering of all brand names by displaying the number and nature of common and distinctive brand name elements across the firm's products. By capturing the potential branding relationships among the different products sold by the firm, a brand hierarchy is a useful means to graphically portray a firm's branding strategy. One simple representation of possible brand elements and thus potential levels of a brand hierarchy is (from top to bottom): corporate (or company) brand, family brand, individual brand, and modifier.

A number of specific issues arise in designing the brand hierarchy. Brand elements at each level of the hierarchy may contribute to brand equity through their ability to create awareness and foster strong, unique, and favorable brand associations. The challenge in setting up the brand hierarchy and arriving at a branding strategy is (1) to design the proper brand hierarchy in terms of the number and nature of brand elements to use at each level and (2) to design the optimal supporting marketing program in terms of creating the desired amount of brand awareness and type of brand associations at each level.

In terms of designing a brand hierarchy, the number of different levels of brands that will be employed and the relative emphasis or prominence that brands at different levels will receive when combined to brand any one product must be defined. In general, the number of levels employed typically is two or three. One common strategy to brand a new product is to create a sub-brand, whereby an existing company or family brand is combined with a new individual brand. When multiple brand names are used, as with a sub-brand, the relative visibility of a brand element as compared with other brand elements determines its prominence. Brand visibility and prominence will depend on factors such as the order, size, color, and other aspects of the brand's physical appearance. To provide structure and content to the brand hierarchy, the specific means by which a brand is used across different products and, if different brands are used for different products, the relationships among those brands must be made clear to consumers.

In terms of designing the supporting marketing program in the context of a brand hierarchy, the desired awareness and image at each level of the brand hierarchy for each product must be defined. In a sub-branding situation, the desired awareness of a brand at any level will dictate the relative prominence of the brand and the extent to which associations linked to the brand will transfer to the product. In terms of building brand equity, determining which associations to link at any one level should be based on principles of relevance and differentiation. In general, it is desirable to create associations that are relevant to as many brands nested at the level below as possible and to distinguish any brands at the same level. Corporate or family brands can establish a number of valuable associations that can help to differentiate the brand, such as common product attributes, benefits, or attitudes; people and relationships; programs and values; and corporate credibility. A corporate image will depend on a number of factors, such as the products a company makes, the actions it takes, and the manner in which it communicates to consumers. Communications may focus on the corporate brand in the abstract or on the different products making up the brand line.

Discussion Questions

1. Pick a company. As completely as possible, characterize its brand portfolio and brand hierarchy. How would you improve the company's branding strategies?
2. Do you think the Nestlé corporate image campaign described in this chapter will be successful? Why or why not? What do you see as key success factors for a corporate image campaign?
3. Contrast the branding strategies and brand portfolios of market leaders in two different industries. For example, contrast the approach by Anheuser-Busch and its Budweiser brand with that of Kellogg in the ready-to eat cereal category.
4. What are some of the product strategies and communication strategies that General Motors could use to further enhance the level of perceived differentiation between its divisions?
5. Consider the companies listed in Branding Brief 11-4 as having strong corporate reputations. By examining their web sites, can you determine why they have such strong corporate reputations?

Brand   Focus   11.0

Using Cause Marketing
to Build Brand Equity

The 1980s saw the advent of cause marketing. Formally, *cause-related* (or *cause*) *marketing* has been defined as "the process of formulating and implementing marketing activities that are characterized by an offer from the firm to contribute a specified amount to a designated cause when customers engage in revenue-providing exchanges that satisfy organizational and individual objectives."[39] As Varadarajan and Menon note, the distinctive feature of cause marketing is the firm's contribution to a designated cause being linked to customers' engaging in revenue-producing transactions with the firm.

Many observers credit American Express for raising awareness of the mutual benefits of cause marketing through its 1983 campaign to help restore the Statue of Liberty. Donating a penny for every credit card transaction and a dollar for each new card issued, American Express gave $1.7 million to the Statue of Liberty—Ellis Island Foundation. In the process, transactions for American Express rose 30 percent, and the issuance of new cards increased by 15 percent during this period. In the next five years, American Express supported more than 70 different causes in 18 countries, ranging from the preservation of the national bird of Norway to the protection of the Italian coastline.

During this time, American Express's competitors followed suit: Visa created a transaction-based donation program to support the 1988 Olympics (see Chapter 7), and MasterCard tied use of its credit card to donations to six charitable organizations

with its "Make a Difference" campaign. Other companies became involved too, sponsoring charitable activities such as the Special Olympics, Live Aid, and Hands Across America. Despite some drop in interest during tighter economic times in the early 1990s, companies have begun again to look to cause marketing as a means of differentiating themselves. For example, in its first national media campaign for a philanthropic cause since its Statue of Liberty campaign, American Express initiated the "Charge Against Hunger" campaign in 1993. The campaign, which raised $5 million in its first year, contributed three cents to feed the hungry every time members used their American Express cards during the months of November and December.[40] American Express also supports the arts at the local community level, publicizing its efforts with ads praising the charitable cause while underscoring the convenience of using the American Express card.

ADVANTAGES OF CAUSE MARKETING

One reason for the rise in cause marketing is the positive response that it elicits from consumers.[41] Cone Communications, a firm that advises companies on cause-related marketing, revealed in the results of the 1999 Cone/Roper Cause Trends Report that 80 percent of Americans have a more positive image of companies that support a cause that they care about, nearly two-thirds of

Americans report that they would be likely to switch brands to one associated with a good cause, and almost three-quarters of Americans approve of cause programs as a business practice. The report also documented the positive impact on employees: 90 percent of employees felt proud of their companies' values when the companies had a cause program, and 87 percent of employees felt a strong sense of loyalty toward companies with cause programs. Not surprisingly, these already positive reactions increased dramatically after the tragic terrorist attack on the World Trade Center in New York City in September 2001.

Cause or corporate societal marketing (CSM) programs offer many potential benefits to a firm:

➤ *Building brand awareness.* Because of the nature of the brand exposure, CSM programs can be a means of improving recognition for a brand, although not necessarily recall. As with sponsorship and other indirect forms of brand-building communications, most CSM programs may be better suited to increasing exposure to the brand and less suited to tying the brand to specific consumption or usage situations, because it can be difficult or inappropriate to include product-related information. At the same time, exposure to the brand can literally be repeated or prominent as a result of the CSM program, facilitating brand recognition.

➤ *Enhancing brand image.* CSM offers several means of creating favorable brand differentiation. Because most CSM programs do not include much product-related information, they would not be expected to have much impact on more functional, performance-related considerations. On the other hand, two types of abstract or imagery-related associations can be linked to a brand via CSM: user profiles (e.g., CSM may allow consumers to develop a positive image of brand users to which they also may aspire in terms of being kind, generous, doing good things, etc.) and personality and values (e.g., CSM could clearly bolster the sincerity dimension of a brand's personality such that

consumers would think of the people behind the brand as caring and genuine).

➤ *Establishing brand credibility.* CSM could potentially affect all three dimensions of credibility because consumers may think of a firm that is willing to invest in CSM as caring more about customers and being more dependable than other firms, at least in a broad sense, as well as likable for "doing the right things."

➤ *Evoking brand feelings.* Two categories of brand feelings that seem particularly applicable to CSM are social approval and self-respect. In other words, CSM may help consumers to justify their self-worth to others or to themselves. To accentuate the former types of feelings, CSM programs may need to provide consumers with external symbols to explicitly "advertise" or signal their affiliation to others—for example, bumper stickers, ribbons, buttons, and T-shirts. In the case of the latter types of feelings, CSM programs can give people the notion that they are doing the right thing and that they should feel good about themselves for having done so. External symbols in this case may not be as important as the creation of "moments of internal reflection" during which consumers are able to experience these types of feelings. Communications that reinforce the positive outcomes associated with the cause program—and how consumer involvement contributed to that success—could help to trigger these types of experiences. To highlight the consumer contribution, it may be necessary to recommend certain actions or outcomes as targets for consumers (e.g., have consumers donate a certain percentage of income or a designated amount).

➤ *Creating a sense of brand community.* CSM and a well-chosen cause can serve as a rallying point for brand users and a means for them to connect to or share experiences with other consumers or employees of the company itself. One place where communities of like-minded users exist is online. Marketers may be able to tap into the many close-knit online groups that have been created around cause-related issues (e.g., medical concerns such as Alzheimer's, cancer, and autism). In some cases, the brand might even serve as the focal point or ally for these online efforts. As a result of these community-building initiatives, the brand may be seen in a more positive light.

➤ *Eliciting brand engagement.* Participating in a cause-related activity as part of a CSM program for a brand is certainly one means of eliciting active engagement. As part of any of these activities, customers themselves may become brand evangelists and ambassadors and help to communicate about the brand and strengthen the brand ties of others. A CSM program of "strategic volunteerism," whereby corporate personnel volunteer their time to help administer the nonprofit program, could be used to actively engage consumers with both the cause and the brand.

Perhaps the most important benefit of cause-related marketing is that by humanizing the firm, consumers may develop a strong, unique bond with the firm that transcends normal marketplace transactions. A dramatic illustration of such benefits is with McDonald's, whose franchises have long been required to stay close to local communities and whose 206 Ronald McDonald Houses for sick children in 19 countries concretely symbolize their "do-good" efforts. When whole blocks of businesses were burned and looted in the south central Los Angeles riots in 1992, one McDonald's executive observed, "We literally had people standing in front of some restaurants saying, 'No, don't throw rocks through this window—these are the good guys.'" When the dust cleared, all 60 McDonald's restaurants in the area were spared.

DESIGNING CAUSE MARKETING PROGRAMS

Cause marketing comes in many forms.[42] Although often associated with advertising and promotional activities, it may also involve product development. For example, Dannon launched a new line of yogurts that

tied in with the National Wildlife Federation, and Johnson & Johnson provides the World Wildlife Fund with a cut from sales of a special line of children's toiletries.

Some firms have used cause marketing very strategically to gain a marketing advantage.[43] Branding Brief 11-8 describes how the Body Shop adopted cause-related marketing as the essence of its brand positioning. Ben & Jerry's is another firm that has created a strong association as a "do-gooder" through various products (such as its rain forest crunch ice cream) and programs and its donation of 7.5 percent of its pretax profits to various causes. Toyota ran an extensive print ad campaign with the slogan "Investing in the Things We All Care About" to show how it has invested in local U.S. communities. For Toyota, this campaign may go beyond cause marketing and be seen as a means to help the brand create a vital point of parity with respect to domestic car companies on "country of origin."

A danger is that the promotional efforts behind a cause marketing program could backfire if cynical consumers question the link between the product and the cause and see the firm as being self-serving and exploitative as a result. The hope is that cause marketing strikes a chord with consumers and employees, improving the image of the company and energizing these constituents to act. With near-parity products, some marketers feel that a strongly held point of difference on the basis of community involvement and concern may in some cases be the best way—and perhaps the only way—to uniquely position a product.

To receive brand equity benefits, it is important that cause marketing efforts be branded in the right manner. In particular, it is important that consumers be able to make some kind of connection from the cause to the brand. Perhaps the classic example of doing so is McDonald's, which has effectively leveraged its Ronald McDonald character and its identification with children.

Image Management the Body Shop Way

In 1976, Anita Roddick opened the first Body Shop in Brighton, a little village on the south coast of England. In her first store, Anita offered some 25 natural body products. Now, the Body Shop has over 1,900 outlets in 50 countries, many of them franchised. The company offers over 400 naturally based body care products, over 550 sundry items, and customized care. Its colorful, fragrant products are based on natural ingredients, particularly fruits, vegetables, flowers, and herbs.

Since its early days, the Body Shop tried to avoid packaging excesses for its products. In the beginning, Roddick asked her customers to bring bottles back for refilling because the company didn't have a large bottle inventory. Today, the Body Shop has made refilling and recycling of bottles an integral part of the company's overall environmental stewardship program. The bottles, which were originally chosen for their simplicity and low cost, are still the primary packaging form today. In addition, the Body Shop has a number of subbrands, almost all of which are identified with new labeling and some new package forms as well.

The Body Shop has attempted to avoid the "narrow images" of "flawless beauty" portrayed in traditional cosmetic advertising. The Body Shop has followed a strategy of avoiding direct advertising and relying heavily on in-store promotion, word of mouth, and public relations or third-party reporting. Instore promotion is abundant. Bright, colorful posters announcing holidays, supporting AIDS protection, or promoting particular product lines are in all the display windows. All over the world the Body Shop stores "look and feel" the same. The typical outside "look" is a dark green wooden facade with large floor-to-ceiling display windows accented with bright, colorful, catchy campaign or promotional posters. The look inside is also consistent across all stores

The Body Shop became not only a successful natural body products company, but also an organization that has attempted to make a difference in the lives of humans and animals and the protection of the environment. In addition to the traditional "4 Ps" marketing mix, the Body Shop has a "Fifth P" in its marketing mix to build brand equity— their corporate philosophy of "Profits with Principles," also known as "Doing Good by Doing Well." To this end, the Body Shop is against animal testing, actively attempts to minimize the company's impact on the environment, engages in fair trading relationships, and encourages education, awareness, and community involvement among its staff.

Although initially quite successful, the Body Shop has struggled in recent years. Look-alike products from retailers (e.g., Bath and Body Works and Boots) and supermarkets (e.g., Tesco and Sainsbury) have chipped away at its market share, and its messages on social causes don't seem to arouse the same passion from customers. Body Shop stores became overstocked and cluttered with a poor product mix, and advertising efforts often missed the mark. In response to its troubles, Roddick chose to step down as head, and the firm underwent a radical makeover of its operations and management structure in a bid to cut costs and freshen its image.

Sources: This brief is based on published sources and a brand audit conducted as part of a Stanford Business School class project by Janet Kraus, Kathy Apruzzese, Maria Nunez, and Karen Reaudin.

Ronald McDonald House Charities provides comfort and care to children and their families by supporting Ronald McDonald Houses in communities around the world and by making grants to other not-for-profit organizations whose programs help children in need. Ronald McDonald House Charities has a network of over 174 local charities serving in 32 countries. This well-branded cause program enhances McDonald's reputation as caring and concerned for customers. Two other noteworthy programs are as follows:

➤ *The Avon Breast Cancer Crusade:* Founded in 1993, the Avon Breast Cancer Crusade is a U.S. initiative of Avon Products, Inc. Its mission has been to provide women, particularly those who are medically underserved, with direct access to breast cancer education and early detection screening services such as mammograms and clinical breast exams. In the United States, Avon is the largest corporate supporter of the breast cancer cause, with some $100 million generated since 1993. The Crusade raises funds to accomplish this mission in two ways: through the sale of special Crusade fund-raising (pink ribbon) products by Avon's nearly 500,000 independent sales representatives, and through the Avon Breast Cancer 3-Days, a series of three-day, 60-mile fund-raising walks.[44]

➤ *Liz Claiborne's Women's Work campaign against domestic violence:* In 1991, at a time when domestic violence was often a taboo or hot potato issue, Liz Claiborne developed its Women's Work campaign against domestic violence. Prior to starting the campaign, the company had conducted research that revealed that 96 percent of its customers believed that domestic violence was a problem and 91 percent of those same customers would have a positive opinion of a company that started an awareness campaign about the issue. The major fund-raising event is an annual charity shopping day every October at Liz Claiborne stores across the United States. The company donates 10 percent of sales to local organizations fighting domestic violence. Liz Claiborne also contributes proceeds from the sale of T-shirts, jewelry, and other products related to the campaign. Additionally, the company pays for public service campaigns that appear on television, radio, billboards, and bus shelters and distributes awareness posters, brochures, and mailings. Over the years, Liz Claiborne has also sponsored workshops, surveys, celebrity-endorsed awareness campaigns, and other events.[45]

GREEN MARKETING

A special case of cause marketing is green marketing. Concern for the environment is a growing social trend that is reflected in the attitudes and behavior of both consumers and corporations. For example, one survey found that 83 percent of American consumers said they prefer buying environmentally safe products.[46] Another survey found that 23 percent of American consumers now claim to make purchases based on environmental considerations.[47]

Although environmental issues have long affected marketing practices, especially in Europe, their salience has increased in recent years. The well-publicized Earth Day activities in the United States in April 1990 led to an explosion of "environmentally friendly" products and marketing programs. The *green marketing* movement was born, and firm after firm tried to capitalize on consumers' perceived increased sensitivity to environmental issues. On the corporate side, a host of marketing initiatives have been undertaken with environmental overtones. For example, Chevron's highly visible "People Do" ad campaign attempted to transform consumers' negative perceptions of oil companies and their effect on the environment by describing specific Chevron programs designed to save wildlife and preserve seashores.

McDonald's has introduced a number of well-publicized environmental initiatives through the years, such as moving to unbleached paper carry-out bags and replacing polystyrene foam sandwich clamshells with paper wraps and lightweight recyclable boxes. The company received the EPA WasteWise Partner of the Year award for its waste reduction efforts, which conserved 3,200 tons of paper and cardboard by eliminating sandwich containers and replacing them with single-layer flexible sandwich wraps; eliminated 1,100 tons of cardboard materials that would have been used for shipping by switching to light drink cups, and spent $355 million on recycled content products.

From a branding perspective, however, green marketing programs have not been entirely successful.[48] Despite reported public interest in greater environmental responsibility, many of these new products and programs were unsuccessful. What obstacles did the green marketing movement encounter?

Overexposure and Lack of Credibility

So many companies made environmental claims that the public became skeptical of their validity. Government investigations into some "green" claims (e.g., the degradability of trash bags) and media reports of the spotty environmental track records behind others only increased consumers' doubts. This backlash resulted in many consumers deeming environmental claims to be marketing gimmicks.

Consumer Behavior

As with many well-publicized social trends, the underlying reality is often fairly complex and does not always fully match public perceptions. Attitudes toward the environment are no exception. Several studies helped to put consumer attitudes toward the environment in perspective.

A 1991 Roper study found that the average price increases that consumers were willing to pay for otherwise identical products in six categories (gasoline, paper, plastics, aerosols, detergents, and autos) in order to buy products that would cause one-third less pollution was 6.6 percent. One-third of the sample was not willing to pay *anything* more. The study concluded that the products needed to achieve points of parity on quality and price and credible environmental claims for green marketing to work. A Syracuse University study also found that the proper price and quality were key to successful green marketing strategies. Two-thirds of their sample believed that the badge of "environmental correctness" should not result in higher prices—for example, "environmentally safe products shouldn't have to cost more because they use natural ingredients." The study revealed that environmental appeals were more likely to be effective for certain market segments (e.g., 31- to 45-year-old women) and in certain product categories (e.g., cleaners, detergents, fabric softeners, diapers, aerosol sprays, paints, and canned tuna).[49]

The main conclusion that could be drawn from these and other studies is that consumers as a whole may not be willing to pay a premium for environmental benefits, although there may be certain market segments that will. Most consumers appear unwilling to give up the benefits of other options to choose green products. For example, some consumers dislike the performance, appearance, or texture of recycled paper and household products. Similarly, some consumers are unwilling to give up the convenience of disposable products, such as diapers.

Poor Implementation

In jumping on the green marketing bandwagon, many firms did a poor job implementing their marketing program. Products were poorly designed in terms of their environmental worthiness, overpriced, and inappropriately promoted. For example, Starch, a well-known research supplier, surveyed thousands of magazine readers to study 300 "green" ads that appeared in 186 magazines since 1991. The analysis revealed that the main mistake with those ads that tested as "unpersuasive" was that they forgot to emphasize "what's in it for me" to the consumer—they failed to make the connection between what the company was doing for the environment and how it affected individual consumers. Starch's study conclusion was that firms should be specific about product benefits in their ads.[50]

Possible Solutions

The environmental movement in Europe or Japan has a longer history and firmer footing than that in the United States. In Europe, many of Procter & Gamble's basic household items, including cleaners and detergents, are available in refills that come in throw-away pouches. P&G says U.S. customers probably would not take to the pouches. In the United States, firms continue to strive to meet the wishes of consumers concerning the environmental benefits of their products, while maintaining necessary profitability. One expert in the field offers the following recommendations:[51]

> ➤ Green your product before forced to.
> ➤ Communicate environmental aspects of products, especially recycled content.
> ➤ Deliver on performance and price.
> ➤ Dramatize environmental benefits.
> ➤ Stress direct, tangible benefits.
> ➤ Be consistent and thorough.

Notes

1. Philip Kotler, *Marketing Management*, 11th ed. (Upper Saddle River, NJ: Prentice-Hall, 2003).
2. Donald R. Lehmann and Russell S. Winer, "Category Attractiveness Analysis" (Chapter 4) and "Market Potential and Forecasting" (Chapter 7), in *Product Management* (Burr Ridge, IL: Irwin, 1994).
3. Glen L. Urban and Steven H. Star, *Advanced Marketing Strategy: Phenomena, Analysis, and Decisions*. (Englewood Cliffs, NJ: Prentice-Hall, 1991).
4. Kotler, *Marketing Management*, 11th ed.
5. Tara Parker-Pope, "Laura Ashley's Chief Tries to Spruce Up Company That Isn't Dressing for Success," *Wall Street Journal*, 22 September 1995, B1.
6. David Greising, "Major Reservations," *Business Week*, 26 September 1994, 66.
7. Kotler, *Marketing Management*, 11th ed.; Patrick Barwise and Thomas Robertson, "Brand Portfolios," *European Management Journal* 10, no. 3 (September 1992): 277–285.
8. For a methodological approach for assessing the extent and nature of cannibalization, see Charlotte H. Mason and George R. Milne, "An Approach for Identifying Cannibalization within Product Line Extensions and Multi-brand Strategies," *Journal of Business Research* 31 (1994): 163–170.
9. Jack Trout, *Differentiate or Die: Survival in Our Era of Killer Competition* (New York: Wiley, 2000).
10. Yumiko Ono, "Nabisco Favors Tried and True Over New Lines," *Wall Street Journal*, 28 June 1996, B1–B3.
11. David A. Aaker, *Managing Brand Equity* (New York: Free Press, 1991).
12. Paul W. Farris, "The Chevrolet Corvette," Case UVA-M-320 (Charlottesville, VA: Darden Graduate Business School Foundation, University of Virginia, 1995).
13. Kathryn Troy, "Managing the Corporate Brand," Research Report 1214-98-RR (New York: The Conference Board, 1998).
14. Laurel Cutler, vice-chairman of FCB/Leber Katz Partners, a New York City advertising agency, quoted in Susan Caminit, "The Payoff from a Good Reputation," *Fortune*, 6 March 1995, 74.

15. Lydia Demworth, "Consumers Care about Corporate Images," *Psychology Today*, September 1989, 14.

16. "Corporate Advertising," *The Economist*, 21 March 1998, 82.

17. Howard Barich and Philip Kotler, "A Framework for Image Management," *Sloan Management Review* (Winter 1991): 94–104.

18. Kate Ballen, "America's Most Admired Corporations," *Fortune,* 10 February 1992, 40.

19. "DuPont: Corporate Advertising," Case 9-593-023 (Boston: Harvard Business School, 1992); John B. Frey, "Measuring Corporate Reputation and Its Value" (presentation given at Marketing Science Conference, Duke University, March 17, 1989).

20. Charles J. Fombrun, *Reputation* (Boston: Harvard Business School Press, 1996).

21. Much of this section—including examples— is based on an excellent article by Peter H. Farquhar, Julia Y. Han, Paul M. Herr, and Yuji Ijiri, "Strategies for Leveraging Master Brands," *Marketing Research* (September 1992): 32–43.

22. Farquhar, Han, Herr, and Ijiri, "Strategies for Leveraging Master Brands."

23. Several excellent reviews of corporate images are available. See, for example, Grahame R. Dowling, *Corporate Reputations* (Melbourne, Australia: Longman Professional, 1994); and James R. Gregory, *Marketing Corporate Image* (Lincolnwood, IL: NTC Business Books, 1991).

24. Masashi Kuga, "Kao's Strategy and Marketing Intelligence System," *Journal of Advertising Research* 30 (April/May 1990): 20–25.

25. John Smale, "Smale on Saturn—Don't Change What's Working," *Advertising Age,* 28 March 1994, S24.

26. Majken Schultz, Mary Jo Hatch, and Mogens Holten Larsen, eds., *The Expressive Organization: Linking Identity, Reputation, and the Corporate Brand* (New York: Oxford University Press, 2000); Mary Jo Hatch and Majken Schultz, "Are the Strategic Stars Aligned for your Corporate Brand?" *Harvard Business Review* (February 2001): 129–134; James Gregory, *Leveraging the Corporate Brand* (Chicago: NTC Press,

1997); Lynn B. Upshaw and Earl L. Taylor, *The Masterbrand Mandate* (New York: John Wiley & Sons, 2000).

27. Sylvie LaForet and John Saunders, "Managing Brand Portfolios: How the Leaders Do It," *Journal of Advertising Research* (September/ October 1994): 64–76. See also Sylvie LaForet and John Saunders, "Managing Brand Portfolios: Why Leaders Do What They Do," *Journal of Advertising Research* (January/February 1999): 51–65.

28. LaForet and Saunders, "Managing Brand Portfolios: How the Leaders Do It."

29. Emily Nelson, "Too Many Choices," *Wall Street Journal*, 20 April 2001, B1, B4.

30. Edmund Gray and Larry R. Smeltzer, "Corporate Image—An Integral Part of Strategy," *Sloan Management Review* (Summer 1985): 73–78.

31. For a review of current and past practices, see David W. Schumann, Jan M. Hathcote, and Susan West, "Corporate Advertising in America: A Review of Published Studies on Use, Measurement, and Effectiveness," *Journal of Advertising* 20, no. 3 (September 1991): 35–56.

32. David M. Bender, Peter Farquhar, and Sanford C. Schulert, "Growing from the Top: Corporate Advertising Nourishes the Brand Equity from which Profits Sprout," *Marketing Management* 4, no. 4 (1996): 10–19; Nicholas Ind, "An Integrated Approach to Corporate Branding," *Journal of Brand Management* 5, no. 5 (1998): 323–329; Cees B. M. Van Riel, Natasha E. Stroker, and Onno J. M. Maathuis, "Measuring Corporate Images," *Corporate Reputation Review* 1, no. 4 (1998): 313–326.

33. Gabriel J. Biehal and Daniel A. Shenin, "Managing the Brand in a Corporate Advertising Environment," *Journal of Advertising* 28, no. 2 (1998): 99–110.

34. Mary C. Gilly and Mary Wolfinbarger, "Advertising's Second Audience: Employee Reactions to Organizational Communications," MSI working paper 96–116 (Cambridge, MA: Marketing Science Institute, 1996).

35. Suzanne Vranica, "Cingular Ads Shift to Clear from Cryptic," *Wall Street Journal* 27 August 2001, B7.

36. Vanessa O'Connell, "Kraft Foods Plans 'Umbrella' Campaign," *Wall Street Journal*, 15 June 1998, B8.

37. Michael McCarthy, "Philips Can't Lose with Puppies, Beatles," *USA Today*, 15 January 2001, 7B.

38. Fara Warner, "P&G, Breaking with Tradition, Promotes Products as a Category," *Wall Street Journal*, 25 April 1995, B8.

39. P. Rajan Varadarajan and Anil Menon, "Cause-Related Marketing: A Coalignment of Marketing Strategy and Corporate Philanthropy," *Journal of Marketing* 52 (July 1988): 58–74.

40. Greg Goldin, "Cause-Related Marketing Grows Up," *Adweek*, 17 November 1987, 20–22; Ronald Alsop, "More Firms Push Promotion Aimed at Consumers' Hearts," *Wall Street Journal*, 29 August 1985, 23.

41. Sankar Sen and C. B. Bhattacharya, "Does Doing Good Always Lead to Doing Better? Consumer Reactions to Corporate Social Responsibility," *Journal of Marketing Research* 38 (May 2001): 225–243.

42. Yumiko Ono, "Do-Good Ads Aim for Sales That Do Better," *Wall Street Journal*, 2 September 1994, B8.

43. M. Drumwright, "Company Advertising with a Social Dimension: The Role of Noneconomic Criteria," *Journal of Marketing* 60 (October 1996): 71–87;

A. Menon and A. Menon, "Enviropreneurial Marketing Strategy: The Emergence of Corporate Environmentalism as Market Strategy," *Journal of Marketing* 61 (January 1997): 51–67.

44. Hamish Pringle and Marjorie Thompson, *Brand Spirit: How Cause Related Marketing Builds Brands* (Chichester, NY: Wiley, 1999).

45. Ibid.

46. Judann Dagnoli, "Consciously Green," *Advertising Age*, 19 September 1991, 14.

47. Lawrence E. Joseph, "The Greening of American Business," *Vis a Vis*, May 1991, 32.

48. Joanne Lipman, "Environmental Theme Hits Sour Notes," *Wall Street Journal*, 3 May 1990, B6.

49. Leah Rickard, "Natural Products Score Big on Image," *Advertising Age,* 8 August 1994, 26. Kevin Goldman, "Survey Asks Which 'Green' Ads Are for Real," *Wall Street Journal.* Lorne Manly, "It Doesn't Pay to Go Green When Consumers Are Seeing Red," *Adweek,* 23 March 1992, 32–33.

50. Leah Rickard, "Natural Products Score Big on Image," *Advertising Age,* 8 August 1994, 26. Kevin Goldman, "Survey Asks Which 'Green' Ads Are for Real," *Wall Street Journal.*

51. Jacquelyn A. Otman, "When It Comes to Green Marketing, Companies Are Finally Getting It Right," *Brandweek*, 17 April 1995.

CHAPTER

12

Introducing and Naming New Products and Brand Extensions

PREVIEW

Chapter 11 reviewed several key concepts for developing a corporate branding strategy. Two useful tools were introduced: the brand-product matrix—a graphical means of representing the products and brands marketed by a firm—and the brand hierarchy—a visual means to portray relationships among various brand elements. This chapter considers in more detail the role of product strategy in creating, maintaining, and enhancing brand equity. Specifically, it develops guidelines to facilitate the introduction and naming of new products and brand extensions.

To provide some historical perspective, for years firms tended to follow the lead of Procter & Gamble, Coca-Cola, and other major consumer goods marketers that essentially avoided introducing any new products using an existing brand name. Over time, tight economic conditions, a need for growth, and other factors forced firms to rethink their "one brand-one product" policies. Recognizing that one of their most valuable assets is their brands, many firms have since decided to leverage that asset by introducing a host of new products under some of their strongest brand names.

Because brand extensions have only recently become prevalent, to some extent "rules" guiding brand extension strategy are still emerging. Nevertheless, a flurry of academic research activity and some notable marketplace successes and failures are providing insight as to best management practices. The chapter begins by describing some basic brand extension issues and outlining the main advantages and disadvantages of brand extensions. It then presents a simple model of how consumers evaluate brand extensions and offers managerial guidelines concerning the proper means to introduce and name new products and brand extensions. The chapter concludes by extensively summarizing academic research findings on brand extensions. Brand Focus 12.0 addresses some important issues with respect to line extensions.

NEW PRODUCTS AND BRAND EXTENSIONS

As background, it is worthwhile to first consider the sources of growth for a firm. One useful perspective is offered by Ansoff's product/market expansion grid. As shown in Figure 12-1, growth strategies can be categorized according to whether they involve

	Current Products	New Products
Current Markets	Market Penetration Strategy	Product Development Strategy
New Markets	Market Development Strategy	Diversification Strategy

FIGURE 12-1   Ansoff's Growth Share Matrix

existing or new products and whether they target existing or new customers or markets. Branding Brief 12-1 describes McDonald's growth strategies along these lines. As evidenced by this framework, although existing products can be used to further penetrate existing customer markets or expand into new customer markets (the focus of Chapter 13), new product introductions are often vital to the long-run success of a firm.

As noted in Chapter 11, a number of factors related to consumer behavior, corporate capabilities, and competitive actions affect the successful development of a new product or market. The experience of Iridium, as summarized in Branding Brief 12-2, is a clear demonstration of how difficult it is to introduce new products and how new products must be carefully designed *and* marketed. A discussion of all of the issues involved in effectively managing the development and introduction of new products is beyond the scope of this chapter. This section, however, addresses some brand equity implications of new products.[1]

To facilitate the discussion, it is useful to establish some terminology. When a firm introduces a new product, it has three main choices as to how to brand it:

1. It can develop a new brand, individually chosen for the new product.
2. It can apply, in some way, one of its existing brands.
3. It can use a combination of a new brand with an existing brand.

A *brand extension* is when a firm uses an established brand name to introduce a new product (approaches 2 or 3). When a new brand is combined with an existing brand (approach 3), the brand extension can also be called a *sub-brand*. An existing brand that gives birth to a brand extension is referred to as the *parent brand*. As noted in Chapter 11, if the parent brand is already associated with multiple products through brand extensions, then it may also be called a *family brand*.

Brand extensions can be broadly classified into two general categories:[2]

➤ *Line extension:* The parent brand is used to brand a new product that targets a new market segment within a product category currently served by the parent brand. A line extension often involves a different flavor or ingredient variety, a different form or size, or a different application for the brand (e.g., Head & Shoulders Dry Scalp shampoo).

➤ *Category extension:* The parent brand is used to enter a different product category from that currently served by the parent brand (e.g., Swiss Army watches).

Growing the McDonald's Brand

McDonald's employs a number of different growth strategies in the pursuit of global brand leadership. In an attempt to further penetrate existing markets, McDonald's added a new element of service to its traditional menu in 2000 with the debut of its "Made for You" cooking system, which enables customers to order food how they like it and have it prepared fresh. This customized cooking system, modeled after Burger King's "Have it Your Way" program, provided existing customers with more choices.

McDonald's also developed new products in order to reach new customers. In the 1990s, McDonald's attempted to expand its menu to appeal to a broader set of customers with offerings such as pizza, breakfast bagels, and the Arch Deluxe sandwich. Only a few of these new items were successful. McDonald's launched its New Tastes menu in 2001 in order to offer a greater variety of products. The New Tastes menu enabled McDonald's franchises to rotate in groups of 4 as many as 64 new menu items, such as a chicken parmesan sandwich, a breakfast sandwich made from sausage and two pancakes, and a bacon, egg, and cheese bagel. Additionally, McDonald's began offering specialized menu items in different countries, such as the Teriyaki Burger in Japan, and Vegetable McNuggets in England. The company launched McDonald's ketchup in grocery stores in Germany in 2000 and amassed a 5 percent market share within months. The company also considered launching a line of McDonald's brand snacks and other packaged goods.

McDonald's expanded abroad aggressively during the 1990s. The company spent more than $1.5 billion between 1998 and 2001 to expand in the Asia-Pacific region. In 1997, McDonald's was growing overseas at a rate of almost five foreign outlets every day. McDonald's diversifies its product offerings according to regional tastes when it enters new markets. For example, when McDonald's entered India—where beef is not consumed because cows are sacred—in 1996, it introduced the Maharaja Mac made from mutton. The company also developed spicy sauces such as McMasala and McImli.

McDonald's extended its brand in 2001 with the opening of its first domestic McCafé, a gourmet coffee shop inspired by the success of Starbucks that debuted in Portugal and Austria. Another extension is McTreat, an ice cream and dessert shop. McDonald's also opened a McDonald's with the Diner Inside in Indiana, which featured 122 menu items such as meatloaf and chicken-fried steak. Another McDonald's extension was the McSnack Spot, a scaled-down version of the flagship McDonald's. The company developed a nonfood brand extension when it opened a Golden Arch Hotel in Switzerland. Said CEO Jack Greenberg, "Our passion for making a customer smile extends very naturally to the hotel sector."

Sources: Michael McCarthy, "McDonald's New Ads Aiming for Smiles All Around," *USA Today*, 9 October 2000; Bruce Horovitz, "McDonald's Tries a New Recipe to Revive Sales," *USA Today*, 10 July 2001; Margaret Studer and Jennifer Ordonez, "The Golden Arches: Burgers, Fries, and 4-Star Rooms," *Wall Street Journal*, 17 November 2000; Jennifer Ordonez, "Will Big Mac Find New Sizzle in Shoes, Videos?" *Wall Street Journal*, 14 April 2000, B1; "McDonald's to Spend $1.5 Billion to Expand in Asia-Pacific Region," *Wall Street Journal*, 10 April 1998; Richard Gibson and Matt Moffett, "Why You Won't Find Any Egg McMuffins for Breakfast in Brazil," *Wall Street Journal*, 23 October 1997.

"There's No Answer": Iridium Tries to Connect with Global Customers

The Iridium satellite phone was the brainchild of engineers at Motorola, which held an 18 percent stake in the consortium that controlled the company. Comprising a network of 66 satellites linked to 200 service providers in 90 countries, Iridium provided the coverage necessary to enable users to place a call from anywhere in the world. This technology was expensive: The Iridium system cost an estimated $7 billion to build, and when the phones were first launched, customers had to pay $3,000 for the phone and as much as $7 per minute for calls.

The phone was roughly the size of a brick, weighed nearly a pound, needed a thick antenna, and came with an array of accessories that required a small bag to carry. The phone could send and receive a signal from anywhere in the world—almost: It needed a direct line of sight to a satellite in order to function and did not work indoors or in moving cars. Concerns about the performance of the network led the original September 23, 1998, launch date to be pushed back to November 1 of that year.

The Iridium phone was launched with a $180 million global marketing campaign. Across the globe, the company developed print and television ads with a uniform look and different languages depending on the audience. In several cities, the company used lasers to beam Iridium's Big Dipper logo onto clouds. The company also published a quarterly magazine called *roam* that contained—aside from advertising for the product—content such as a how-to on subscribing to the service, an explanation of the Iridium logotype, and an article on amateur astronomers tracking Iridium satellites.

Except for the design and content of advertising and promotional materials, the marketing effort in individual markets was in the hands of 15 regional "gateway" partners. Some of these partners had little experience in telecommunications, and many fell behind schedule. The expected advanced sales of the phones never materialized, and though the company received over one million inquiries after the global marketing launch, few customers actually signed on. Iridium eventually attracted a mere 20,000 subscribers, well short of the estimated 500,000 accounts needed to offset the enormous cost of the system. Nine months after the delayed launch, Iridium filed for bankruptcy. A week after the filing, a headline in the *Wall Street Journal* summarized the company's problems with a headline: "Iridium's Downfall: The Marketing Took a Backseat to Science. Motorola and Partners Spent Billions on Satellite Links for a Phone Few Wanted." In March 2000, a judge ordered that the bankrupt system be shut down. The Iridium collapse was considered to be the most expensive nonmilitary product failure in history.

Sources: Jonathan Sidener, "Iridium's Adventure over Satellite Phone System Ordered Shut Down," *Arizona Republic*, 18 March 2000; Kevin Maney, "$3,000 Gadget Might Be Globe-Trotters Best Friend," *USA Today*, 17 September 1998; Leslie Cauley, "Iridium's Downfall," *Wall Street Journal*, 18 August 1999.

PT Cruiser

Chrysler revealed a new vehicle, the PT Cruiser, in 1999 (see Figure A). A *Wall Street Journal* writer described the PT Cruiser as "part 1920s gangster car, part 1950s hot rod and part London taxicab." The vehicle debuted with an eye-catching silver exterior that gave the car's retro styling a modern twist.

FIGURE A Pt Cruiser

The PT Cruiser was a "segment buster" that combined the practicality of a small car with the functionality of a minivan and the attitude of a sport utility vehicle. It was also an example of a "halo vehicle"—a niche model designed to make a buzz-generating splash and boost the bottom line.

Chrysler intended to stir up strong feelings from the car-buying public: It used an emerging market research process called archetype research to tap consumers' innermost thoughts and feelings about PT Cruiser prototypes (see Branding Brief 9–2). Chrysler's director of corporate market research approved of the consumer ambivalence, saying, "We have what we call a healthy level of dislike. We didn't make a generic vehicle."

The PT Cruiser exceeded all initial sales expectations.

Source: Jeffrey Ball, "But How Does It Make You Feel?" *Wall Street Journal*, 3 May 1999.

Most new products are line extensions—typically 80 percent to 90 percent in any one year. Moreover, many of the most successful new products, as rated by various sources, are extensions (e.g., Microsoft Xbox videogame system, Apple iPod digital music player, and BMW mini automobile). Nevertheless, many new products are introduced each year as new brands (e.g., Gleevec oncology drug, ReplayTV digital video recorders, and Harmony low-fat cereal). Branding Brief 12-3 describes the successful launch of the Chrysler PT Cruiser.

Brand extensions can come in all forms. One well-known branding expert, Edward Tauber, identifies the following seven general strategies for establishing a category—or what he calls a franchise—extension:[3]

1. *Introduce the same product in a different form.* Examples: Ocean Spray Cranberry Juice Cocktail and Jell-O Pudding Pops

2. *Introduce products that contain the brand's distinctive taste, ingredient, or component.* Examples: Philadelphia cream cheese salad dressing and Häagen-Dazs cream liqueur

3. *Introduce companion products for the brand.* Examples: Coleman camping equipment and Duracell Durabeam flashlights

4. *Introduce products relevant to the customer franchise of the brand.* Examples: Gerber insurance and Visa traveler's checks

5. *Introduce products that capitalize on the firm's perceived expertise.* Examples: Honda lawn mowers and Canon photocopy machines

6. *Introduce products that reflect the brand's distinctive benefit, attribute, or feature.* Example: Lysol's "deodorizing" household cleaning products and Ivory's "mild" cleaning products

7. *Introduce products that capitalize on the distinctive image or prestige of the brand.* Examples: Calvin Klein clothes and accessories and Porsche sunglasses

Brand extension strategies are considered more systematically later in this chapter. Next, however, some of the main advantages and disadvantages of brand extensions are outlined.

ADVANTAGES OF EXTENSIONS

For most firms, the question is not whether the brand should be extended, but when, where, and how the brand should be extended. Well-planned and well-implemented extensions offer a number of advantages to marketers. These advantages can broadly be categorized as those that facilitate new product acceptance and those that provide feedback benefits to the parent brand or company as whole (see Figure 12-2).

Facilitate New Product Acceptance

The high failure rate of new products is well documented. Marketing analysts estimate that perhaps only 2 of 10 new products will be successful, or maybe even as few as 1 of 10. As noted previously, new products can fail for a number of reasons. Robert McMath, who oversees a collection of over 75,000 once-new consumer products called the New Products Showcase and Learning Center in Ithaca, New York, identifies nine main reasons for product failure:[4]

1. The market was too small (insufficient demand for type of product).
2. The product was a poor match for the company.

Facilitate New Product Acceptance
Improve brand image
Reduce risk perceived by customers
Increase the probability of gaining distribution and trial
Increase efficiency of promotional expenditures
Reduce costs of introductory and follow-up marketing programs
Avoid cost of developing a new brand
Allow for packaging and labeling efficiencies
Permit consumer variety-seeking

Provide Feedback Benefits to the Parent Brand and Company
Clarify brand meaning
Enhance the parent brand image
Bring new customers into brand franchise and increase market coverage
Revitalize the brand
Permit subsequent extensions

FIGURE 12-2   Advantages of Brand Extension

3. The product was justified on inadequate or inaccurate marketing research, or the company ignored research results.
4. The company was too early or too late in researching the market (failure to capitalize on its marketing window).
5. The product provided insufficient return on investment (poor profit margins and high costs).
6. The product was not new or different (a poor idea that really offered nothing new).
7. The product did not go hand in hand with familiarity.
8. Credibility was not confirmed on delivery.
9. Consumers could not recognize the product.

Brand extensions can certainly suffer from some of the same shortcomings faced by any new product. Nevertheless, a new product introduced as a brand extension may be more likely to succeed, at least to some degree, because it offers the advantages described in the following subsections. Branding Brief 12-4 describes the successful launch of the Sony Playstation extension.

Improve Brand Image
As Chapter 2 noted, one of the advantages of a well-known and well-liked brand is that consumers form expectations over time concerning its performance. Similarly, with a brand extension, consumers can make inferences and form expectations as to the likely composition and performance of a new product based on what they already know about the brand itself and the extent to which they feel this information is relevant to the new product.[5] These inferences may improve the strength, favorability, and uniqueness of the extension's brand associations. For example, when Sony introduced a new personal computer tailored for multimedia applications, Vaio, consumers may have been more likely to feel comfortable with its anticipated performance because of

---

Sony PlayStation

Sony created one of the biggest electronics product sensations of all time with the advent of the PlayStation. Sony's first entry into the videogame market, PlayStation was an advanced videogame system designed to compete with the popular Nintendo and Sega game systems. Sony created Sony Computer Entertainment America to market and distribute the game system. It created a teaser ad campaign featuring the cryptic phrase "U R Not" followed by a red-colored "E," which meant "You are not ready." The product was an instant hit in the states, and the campaign took the 1997 Grand Effie award for advertising effectiveness awarded by the American Marketing Association.

During the first weekend of U.S. availability, Sony sold more than 100,000 units of the PlayStation. With an average selling price of $299 ($100 less than the average price for rival Sega's Saturn game system), Sony was likely losing money on each PlayStation sale. The low selling price was designed to enable PlayStation to quickly gain market share, and Sony expected to recover the losses with sales of higher-margin game software. In less than one year, PlayStation captured 20 percent of the U.S. console game market.

By mid-1998, Sony had sold 30 million PlayStations and captured 70 percent of the U.S. videogame market. At this time, Sony was developing the successor to PlayStation, called the PlayStation 2.

The PlayStation 2 launch was backed by a $150 million marketing campaign that included television, outdoor, interactive, and print advertising as well as viral marketing, direct marketing, and sponsorship. Due to production delays that kept almost 500,000 units off U.S. shelves for the holidays, the PlayStation 2 was one of the most coveted new products in the entertainment sector. Sony sold 5 million $299 PlayStation 2 machines in the United States during the first year of availability.

PlayStation was one of Sony's few bright spots in 2000. Though PlayStation contributes only 10 percent to Sony's total revenue, it makes up one-third of the company's profits. PlayStation 2 shipped more than 20 million units before the end of 2000.

Source: Benjamin Fulford, "Godzilla Needs Batteries," *Forbes,* 18 September 2000.

---

their experience with and knowledge of other Sony products than if the product had been branded by Sony as something completely new.

Reduce Risk Perceived by Customers

One research study examining factors affecting new product acceptance found that the most important factor for predicting initial trial of a new product was the extent to which a known family brand was involved.[6] Extensions from well-known corporate brands such as General Electric, Hewlett-Packard, Motorola, or others may communicate longevity and sustainability. Although corporate brands may lack specific product associations because of the breadth of products attached to their name, their established reputation for being able to introduce quality products and stand behind them may be an important risk-reducer for consumers.[7] Thus, perceptions of corporate credibility—in terms of expertise and trustworthiness—can be valuable associations in introducing brand extensions.[8] Similarly, although widely extended supermarket family brands such as Betty Crocker, Green Giant, Del Monte, and Pepperidge Farm may lack specific product meaning, they may still stand for product quality in the minds of consumers and, by reducing perceived risk, facilitate the adoption of brand extensions.

Increase the Probability of Gaining Distribution and Trial

Because of the potentially increased consumer demand resulting from introducing a new product as an extension, it may be easier to convince retailers to stock and promote a brand extension. For example, one study indicated that brand reputation was a key screening criteria of gatekeepers making new product decisions at supermarkets.[9]

Increase Efficiency of Promotional Expenditures

From a marketing communications perspective, one obvious advantage of introducing a new product as a brand extension is that the introductory campaign does not have to create awareness of both the brand and the new product but instead can concentrate on only the new product itself. In general, it should be easier to add a link from a brand already existing in memory to a new product than it is to first establish the brand in memory and then also link the new product to it.[10] As a dramatic illustration of the marketing communication efficiencies of brand extensions, when General Mills launched its fourth Cheerios extension, Frosted Cheerios, the brand was able to achieve a 0.44 percent market share in the extremely competitive cereal category in its very first week of sales with essentially *no* advertising or promotion. Solely on the basis of its name and product concept, demand for the sweetened oat cereal was so high that most supermarkets were forced to limit the number of boxes that could be purchased.

Several research studies document this extension benefit. One study of 98 consumer brands in 11 markets found that successful brand extensions spent less on advertising than did comparable new-name entries.[11] A comprehensive study by Indiana University's Dan Smith found similar results, indicating that the average advertising to sales ratio for brand extensions was 10 percent, compared with 19 percent for new brands. His study identified some underlying factors moderating this extension advantage. The difference in advertising efficiency between brand extensions and new brands was shown to increase as the fit with other products affiliated with the parent brand increased, as the new product's relative price compared with that of competitors increased, and as distribution intensity increased. On the other hand, the difference in advertising efficiency between brand extensions and new brands was shown to decrease when the new product was composed primarily of search attributes (i.e., when product quality could be judged through visual inspection), as the new product became established in the market, and as consumers' knowledge of the new product category increased.[12]

Reduce Costs of Introductory and Follow-Up Marketing Programs

Because of these push and pull considerations in distribution and promotion, it has been estimated that a firm can save 40 percent to 80 percent on the estimated $30 million to $50 million it can cost to launch a new supermarket product nationally in the United States. Moreover, other efficiencies can result after the launch. As one such example, when a brand becomes associated with multiple products, advertising can become more cost-effective for the family brand as a whole. For example, in 1988, Jaguar introduced its first substantially improved automobile model in 16 years, adopting new technology to improve reliability although still retaining the classic Jaguar look. The resulting marketing program, which included a lavish ad campaign, increased demand for *all* new Jaguars. Even older Jaguars found their resale market value enhanced.[13]

Avoid Cost of Developing a New Brand

As Chapter 4 indicated, developing new brand elements is an art and science. To conduct the necessary consumer research and employ skilled personnel to design high-quality brand names, logos, symbols, packages, characters, and slogans can be quite expensive, and there is no assurance of success. As the number of available— and appealing—brand names keeps shrinking, legal conflicts are more likely to result. Despite the fact that it had conducted a trademark search, Cosmair's L'Oreal division was successfully sued for $2.1 million when a court decided that the name it had chosen to introduce a new green and purple hair dye, Zazu, infringed on the name of a line of shampoos sold by a Hinsdale, Illinois, hairstyling salon called ZaZu Designs.[14]

Allow for Packaging and Labeling Efficiencies

Similar or virtually identical packages and labels for extensions can result in lower production costs and, if coordinated properly, more prominence in the retail store by creating a "billboard" effect. For example, Stouffer's offers a variety of frozen entrees with identical orange packaging that increases their visibility when stocked together in the freezer. A similar billboard effect is evident with other supermarket brands, such as Coca-Cola soft drinks and Campbell soup.

Permit Consumer Variety-Seeking

By offering consumers a portfolio of brand variants within a product category, consumers who need a change—because of boredom, satiation, or whatever—can switch to a different product type if they so desire without having to leave the brand family. Even without such underlying motivations, by offering a complement of line extensions, customers may be encouraged to use the brand to a greater extent or in different ways than otherwise might have been the case. Moreover, to even effectively compete in some categories, it may be necessary to have multiple items that together form a cohesive product line.

Suave

As an example of the benefits of expansive market coverage, consider the low-priced family brand Suave, sold by Helene Curtis. Suave includes a variety of personal care products, such as shampoo and conditioners, baby products, skin lotions, and antiperspirants and deodorants. Given the amount of brand switching and the large number of brands kept in inventory by consumers for personal care products in general and shampoos in particular, the ability of Suave to offer a full product line is a competitive advantage. By continually line extending, Suave keeps up with any new market trend or shift in consumer demand.[15] Helene Curtis has adopted a "follower" strategy: Whenever a new type of product becomes successful, the company introduces a similar version under the Suave name designed to match it. Suave's recent advertising slogan was "You Don't Have to Spend a

Lot to Get a Lot." Suave's well-defined brand image and branding strategy has resulted in high degrees of consumer loyalty and market share for the brand.

Provide Feedback Benefits to the Parent Brand

Besides facilitating acceptance of new products, brand extensions can also provide positive feedback to the parent brand in a number of ways, as described in the following subsections.

Clarify Brand Meaning

Extensions can help to clarify the meaning of a brand to consumers and define the kinds of markets in which it competes. Thus, through brand extensions, Hunts means "tomato," Clairol means "hair coloring," Gerber means "baby care," Nabisco means "baked cookies and crackers," and Chun King means "Chinese food" to consumers. Figure 12-3 shows how other brands that have introduced multiple brand extensions may have broadened their meaning with consumers.

Xerox

A fascinating example of attempting to broaden product meaning is Xerox.[16] Realizing that electronic copies of documents were increasingly replacing traditional paper copies (where the brand had originally made its name), Xerox expanded its product line from office copiers to include other products such as digital printers, scanners, and word processing software. Xerox embarked on an ambitious advertising and marketing campaign to change its image with consumers to better reflect its new capabilities. A new logo was designed for all Xerox advertising, marketing materials, and products. The new logo consisted of a stylized red "X" with squares missing from its upper right arm. The new logo was intended to convey a digital appearance and symbolize the company's commitment to technology. An accompanying ad campaign adopted the slogan "The Document Company" (see Figure 12-4). Despite the attempted new image, the company found it difficult financially to transform itself in the face of a new digital economy.

Broader brand meaning often is necessary so that firms avoid "marketing myopia" and do not mistakenly draw narrow boundaries around their brand and either miss

FIGURE 12-3   Expanding Brand Meaning through Extensions

Brand	Original Product	Extension Products	New Brand Meaning
Weight Watchers	Fitness centers	Low-calorie foods	Weight loss and maintenance
Sunkist	Oranges	Vitamins, juices	Good health
Crayola	Crayons	Markers, paints, pens, pencils, clay	Colorful crafts for kids
Aunt Jemima	Pancake mixes	Syrups, frozen waffles	Breakfast foods

FIGURE 12-4 Sample Xerox Ad

market opportunities or become vulnerable to well-planned competitive strategies. Thus, as Harvard's Ted Levitt pointed out in a pioneering article, railroads are not just in the "railroad" business but also the "transportation" business.[17] In other words, railroads do not necessarily compete with other railroads so much as with other forms of transportation (e.g., cars and planes). Thinking more broadly about product meaning can easily result in different marketing programs and new product opportunities. For example, Steelcase's one-time slogan, "A Smarter Way to Work," reflected the fact that the company defines its business not as manufacturing desks, chairs, file cabinets, and credenzas but as "helping to enhance office productivity." For some brands, creating broader meaning is critical and may be the only way to expand sales.

Ocean Spray

The growers cooperative Ocean Spray Cranberries, Inc., once found itself in such a position. During the 1960s and 1970s, it had been essentially associated with a single-purpose, single-usage product: Consumption of cranberries was almost entirely confined to the serving of cranberry sauce as a side dish with Thanksgiving and Christmas holiday dinners. After a pesticide scare one Thanksgiving drastically cut sales and almost put their growers out of business, the cooperative embarked on a program to diversify and create a year-round market by producing cranberry-based juice drinks and other products. After introducing Ocean Spray Cranberry Juice Cocktail and cranberry-flavored drinks such as Cranapple and Crangrape, it eventually introduced a line of grapefruit juices with *no* cranberry link at all. This ambitious brand extension program over a 20-year period has broadened the meaning of Ocean Spray to connote "good tasting fruit juice drinks that are good for you" (see Figure 12-5).[18]

In some cases, it is advantageous to establish a portfolio of related products that completely satisfy consumer needs in a certain area. For example, the $3 billion oral care market is characterized by a number of mega-brands (e.g., Colgate and Crest) that compete in multiple segments with multiple product offerings. Although these different brands were limited to a few specific products at one time, they have broadened their meaning through brand extensions to represent "complete oral care." Similarly, many specific-purpose cleaning products have broadened their meaning to become seen as multipurpose (e.g., Lysol, Comet).

Enhance the Parent Brand Image

According to the customer-based brand equity model, one desirable outcome of a successful brand extension is that it may enhance the parent brand image by strengthening an existing brand association, improving the favorability of an existing brand association, adding a new brand association, or a combination of these.

FIGURE 12-5   Ocean Spray Cranberry-based Brands

One common way that a brand extension affects the parent brand image is by helping to clarify its core brand values and associations. Core brand values, as defined in Chapter 3, are those attributes and benefits that come to characterize all the products in the brand line and, as a result, are those with which consumers often have the strongest associations. For example, Nike has expanded from running shoes to other athletic shoes, athletic clothing, and athletic equipment, strengthening its associations to "peak performance" and "sports" in the process.

Another type of association that may be improved by successful brand extensions is consumer perceptions of the credibility of the company behind the extension. For example, Keller and Aaker showed that a successful corporate brand extension led to improved perceptions of the expertise, trustworthiness, and likability of the company.[19] In the late 1990s, several firms chose to introduce online versions of their services under a separate brand name (e.g., Bank One chose to launch its online bank as Wingspan). Besides increasing the difficulty and expense of launching a new brand, such companies also lost the opportunity to modernize the parent brand image and improve its technological credentials. In many cases, these ventures failed and their capabilities were folded back into the parent organization.

Bring New Customers into the Brand Franchise and Increase Market Coverage

Line extensions can benefit the parent brand by expanding market coverage, for example, by offering a product benefit whose lack may have heretofore prevented consumers from trying the brand. For example, when Tylenol introduced a capsule form of its acetaminophen pain reliever, it was able to attract consumers who had difficulty swallowing tablets and therefore might have otherwise avoided the brand.

By creating "news" and bringing attention to the parent brand, its sales may also increase. For example, although the market share of regular powdered Tide—which once was at 27 percent—had slipped to 21 percent in the early 1980s, the introduction of Liquid Tide and Multi-Action Tide (a combined detergent, whitener, and fabric softener) resulted in market share increases of 2 percent to 4 percent for the flagship Tide parent brand by 1986. Remarkably, through the skillful introduction of extensions, Tide as a family brand has managed to maintain its market leadership and a market share of roughly 50 percent from the 1950s to the present.

Revitalize the Brand

Sometimes brand extensions can be a means to renew interest and liking for the brand.

Waterford

When Waterford Wedgewood, the well-known Irish maker of Waterford crystal and Wedgewood china, went through a sales slump in the late 1980s, the company's fortunes were turned around as the result of its first brand introduction in 200 years.[20] Marquis by Waterford, a new brand of crystal priced 20 percent less than traditional Waterford, was a calculated risk by the company to revitalize the brand. Company officials maintain that the key to the success of Marquis was keeping it sufficiently different from traditional Waterford while still allowing the new brand to benefit by association with the Waterford name. Therefore Marquis had to be seen as "cheaper" but not "cheap." The company gave Marquis a distinctively different design—one that was simpler and lighter-looking than traditional Waterford. Meanwhile, it freshened up the original Waterford products as well, introducing a series of new products, some of which reflected the company's Irish tradition. Marquis became the most successful new entry in the tabletop industry and the fourth-largest seller in the U.S. premium crystal segment. More important, Marquis did not detract from the flagship brand: Sales of traditional Waterford have continued to rise, and it is the top-selling premium brand.

Permit Subsequent Extensions

One benefit of a successful extension is that it may serve as the basis for subsequent extensions. For example, Goodyear's successful introduction of its Aquatred tires sub-brand led to the introduction of Eagle Aquatred for performance vehicles with either wider wheels (e.g., the Ford Mustang) or a luxury image (e.g., the Cadillac Seville).

Billabong

The Billabong brand was established in 1973 by Gordon Merchant, who wanted to create a brand that had "functional products for surfers to help us better enjoy our sport." During the 1970s and 1980s, Billabong established its brand credibility with the young surfing community as a designer and producer of quality surf apparel. In the early 1980s, Billabong began to sell its products in Japan, Europe, and the United States through licensees. In the late 1980s and early 1990s, the brand extended into other youth-oriented areas, such as snowboarding and skateboarding, sticking to its core brand proposition: contemporary, relevant, innovative products of consistent high quality. As a result of this strategic extension strategy, Billabong was ranked as the eighth most valuable brand in Australia, with an estimated value of $450 million.

DISADVANTAGES OF BRAND EXTENSIONS

Despite these potential advantages, brand extensions have a number of disadvantages (see Figure 12-6).

Can Confuse or Frustrate Consumers

As noted in Chapter 11, the different varieties of line extensions may confuse and perhaps even frustrate consumers as to which version of the product is the "right one" for them. As a result, they may reject new extensions for tried and true favorites or all-purpose versions that claim to supersede more specialized product versions. Moreover, because of the large number of new products and brands continually being introduced, many retailers do not have enough shelf or display space to stock them all. Consequently, some consumers may be disappointed when they are unable to find an advertised brand extension if a retailer is not able to or is unwilling to stock it. If a firm launches extensions that consumers deem inappropriate, they may question the integrity and competence of the brand.

Can confuse or frustrate consumers
Can encounter retailer resistance
Can fail and hurt parent brand image
Can succeed but cannibalize sales of parent brand
Can succeed but diminish identification with any
   one category
Can succeed but hurt the image of parent brand
Can dilute brand meaning
Can cause the company to forgo the chance to
   develop a new brand

FIGURE 12-6   Disadvantages of Brand Extension

Can Encounter Retailer Resistance

On average, the number of consumer packaged-goods stock-keeping units (SKUs) grew 16 percent each year from 1985 to 1992, whereas retail shelf space expanded only 1.5 percent each year during the same period. Many brands now come in a multitude of different forms. For example, Campbell has introduced a number of different lines of soup—including Condensed, Home Cookin', Chunky, Healthy Request, Select, Simply Home, and Ready-to-Serve Classic—and offers more than 100 flavors in all.

As a result, it has become virtually impossible for a grocery store or supermarket to offer *all* the different varieties available across *all* the different brands in any one product category. Moreover, retailers often feel that many line extensions are merely "me-too" products that duplicate existing brands in a product category and should not be stocked even if there were space. Attacking brand proliferation, a year-long Food Marketing Institute (FMI) study showed that retailers could reduce their SKUs by 5 percent to 25 percent in certain product categories without hurting sales or consumer perceptions of the variety offered by their stores.[21] The FMI "product variety" study recommended that retailers systematically identify duplicated and slow-moving items and eliminate them to maximize profitability.[22] The Science of Branding 12-1 summarizes one perspective on how to reduce brand proliferation and simplify marketing.

Can Fail and Hurt Parent Brand Image

The worst possible scenario with an extension is that not only does it fail, but it also harms the parent brand image somehow in the process. Unfortunately, these negative feedback effects can sometimes happen.

Consider General Motors's experience with the Cadillac Cimarron.[23] This model, introduced in the early 1980s, was a "relative" of models in other GM lines, such as the Pontiac 2000 and Chevrolet Cavalier. The target market was less-affluent buyers seeking a small luxury car who wanted, but could not really afford, a full-size Cadillac. Not only was the Cadillac Cimarron unsuccessful at generating new sales with this market segment, but existing Cadillac owners hated it. They felt it was inconsistent with the large size and prestige image they had expected from Cadillac. As a result, Cadillac sales dropped significantly in the mid-1980s. Looking back, one GM executive offered the following insights:

THE SCIENCE OF BRANDING 12-1

Simplicity Marketing

Today, consumers face an unprecedented number of choices. Supermarkets contain more than 40,000 products, up from only 7,000 products in the 1960s. Crest toothpaste comes in 42 varieties, Head & Shoulders shampoo boasts more than 30 varieties, and American Express customers can choose from among 20 different card types. Recently, per capita coupon distribution reached 1,000 in the United States, and telemarketing calls numbered more than 20 million daily in 1999. Consumers are often overwhelmed by this abundance of choice, and Steven M. Cristol and Peter Sealey, the authors of *Simplicity Marketing*, contend that "human capacity for choice is not an infinitely expandable commodity." In this climate of overchoice, "strong brands are simplifiers, the shortest, most efficient path to potential satisfaction and tension release."

According to the authors, since consumers are increasingly seeking simpler lives, brands that help them achieve this can win the loyalty of these consumers. The strategies of simplicity marketing can be summarized by the Four Rs: replace, repackage, reposition, and replenish.

- *Replace:* "Developing and positioning products as replacements either for multiple products, or for more complicated products or processes." Procter & Gamble's Pert Plus is a classic example of replacement. Shampoo and conditioner had always been sold separately until Pert Plus hit the shelves. Since these two products were typically used in tandem, Pert Plus added convenience by replacing two bottles with one. Conditioning shampoo now represents more than 30 percent of the total shampoo market.

- *Repackage:* "Bundling together a number of products or services that were previously only available from multiple sources (or as separate purchases from the same source), offering integrated solutions with a single point of contact for the customer." Bloomberg L.P. illustrates the repackaging concept. Bloomberg subscribers get global securities information; news, research, and analysis; real-time prices; and projections all delivered via a special terminal and custom keyboard. Today, Bloomberg is the leading financial information service and has extended the brand into television, radio, and the Internet.

- *Reposition:* "Directly positioning a brand on the promise of simplicity, or expanding a brand's positioning to reduce the number of brand relationships that a customer requires over time." In the late 1990s, Honda introduced a tag line that captured the repositioning concept: "Honda. We make it simple." This phrase distilled Honda's reputation for dependability and user-friendly design. Other simplified positionings included "Life Simplified" from Dasani mineral water, "Simplifies Your Life," for Safeway.com, and "The Power to Simplify," for both Delphi Automotive Systems and ALL-TELL Corporation.

- *Replenish:* "Providing a readily available continuous supply of zero-defect product or service to the existing customer base at acceptable price points." Crest offers its customers replenishment because users of the product are virtually guaranteed to find it on any retailer's shelves. Crest also delivers consistent product quality and familiar sizes, flavors, and formulations. If product quality slips or the products are out of stock, Crest runs the risk not only of disappointing loyal customers but also compounding decision-related stress as customers select alternatives.

Brands that consumers regard as complicating their lives, rather than simplifying them, run the risk of a consumer backlash. For example, research conducted by Pacific Bell prior to 1993 indicated that small business customers desired more contact with and attention from the company. Within two years, however, after heavy telemarketing by AT&T and MCI of their long-distance calling plans, Pacific Bell customers were expressing no desire to hear from Pacific Bell. The battle between AT&T and MCI had complicated the telephone service market, and Pacific Bell customers developed an aversion to calls of any type from telephone companies.

One result of this backlash is what Yankelovich Partners calls "one-think shopping," or making purchase decisions based solely on a product's brand. When faced with a complicated choice, the consumers essentially says, "I've hit my threshold for comparing all these features; this is the brand I want to do business with, based on my perception set, so let's just get on with it!" Simplifying brands are more likely to earn the trust, and repeated business, of these one-think shoppers. Amidst the proliferation of choice in today's cluttered markets, simplicity marketing aids consumers by making choices easier.

Source: Steven M. Cristol and Peter Sealey, *Simplicity Marketing* (New York: Free Press, 2000).

The decision was made purely on the basis of short-sighted profit and financial analysis, with no accounting for its effect on long-run customer loyalty or, if you will, equity. A typical financial analysis would argue that the Cimarron will rarely steal sales from Cadillac's larger cars, so any sale would be one that we wouldn't have gotten otherwise. The people who were most concerned with such long-range issues raised serious objections but the bean counters said, "Oh no, we'll get this many dollars for every model sold." There was no thinking about brand equity. We paid for the Cimarron down the road. Everyone now realizes that using the model to extend the name was a horrible mistake.

Even if an extension initially succeeds, by linking the brand to multiple products, the firm increases the risk that an unexpected problem or even tragedy with one product in the brand family can tarnish the image of some or all of the remaining products. For example, starting in 1986, the Audi 5000 car suffered from a tidal wave of negative publicity and word of mouth because it was alleged to have a "sudden acceleration" problem that resulted in an alarming number of sometimes fatal accidents. Even though there was little concrete evidence to support the claims (resulting in Audi, in a public relations disaster, attributing the problem to the clumsy way that Americans drove the car), Audi's U.S. sales declined from 74,000 in 1985 to 21,000 in 1989. As might be expected, the damage was most severe for sales of the Audi 5000, but the adverse publicity also spilled over to affect the 4000 model and, to a lesser extent, the Quattro model. The Quattro might have been relatively more insulated from negative repercussions because it was distanced from the 5000 by virtue of its more distinct branding and advertising strategy.[24]

Understanding when unsuccessful brand extensions may damage the parent brand is important, and this chapter later develops a conceptual model and describes some important findings to address the topic. On a more positive note, however, it should be recognized that one reason why an unsuccessful brand extension may not necessarily damage the parent brand is for the very reason that the extension may have been unsuccessful in the first place—hardly anyone may have even heard of it! Thus, the silver lining in the case when a brand extension fails as a result of an inability to secure adequate distribution or to achieve sufficient brand awareness is that the parent brand is more likely to survive relatively unscathed. Product failures in which the extension is found to be inadequate in some way on the basis of performance are more likely to negatively affect parent brand perceptions than these "market" failures.

Can Succeed but Cannibalize Sales of Parent Brand

Even if sales of a brand extension are high and meet targets, it is possible that this revenue may have merely resulted from consumers switching to the extension from existing product offerings of the parent brand—in effect cannibalizing the parent brand by decreasing its sales. Line extensions are often designed to establish points of parity with current offerings competing in the parent brand category, as well as to create additional points of difference in other areas (e.g., low-fat versions of foods). These types of line extensions may be particularly likely to result in cannibalization. Often, however, such intrabrand shifts in sales are not necessarily undesirable because they can be thought of as a form of "preemptive cannibalization." In other words, consumers might have switched to a competing brand instead of the line extension if it had not been introduced into the category.

For example, Diet Coke's point of parity of "good taste" and point of difference of "low calories" undoubtedly resulted in some of its sales coming from regular Coke drinkers. In fact, although U.S. sales of Coca-Cola's cola products have held steady since 1980, sales in 1980 came from Coke alone whereas sales today also receive significant contributions from Diet Coke, Cherry Coke, and uncaffeinated forms of Coke. Without the introduction of those extensions, however, some of Coke's sales might have gone to competing Pepsi products or other soft drinks or beverages instead.

Can Succeed but Diminish Identification with Any One Category

One risk of linking multiple products to a single brand is that the brand may not be strongly identified with any one product. Thus, brand extensions may obscure the identification of the brand with its original categories, reducing brand awareness.[25] For example, when Cadbury became linked in the United Kingdom to mainstream food products such as Smash instant potatoes, marketers of the brand may have run the risk of weakening its association to fine chocolates. Pepperidge Farm is another brand that has been accused by marketing critics of having been extended so much (e.g., into soups) that the brand has lost its original meaning as "delicious, high-quality cookies."

This potential drawback has been popularized by the vociferous business consultants Al Ries and Jack Trout, who in 1981 introduced the notion of the "line extension trap." They provide a number of examples of brands that, at the time, they believed had overextended.

One such example was Scott Paper, which Ries and Trout believe became overextended when its name was expanded to encompass ScotTowels paper towels, ScotTissue bath tissue, Scotties facial tissues, Scotkins, and Baby Scot diapers.[26] Interestingly, in the mid-1990s, Scott decided to attempt to unify its product line by renaming ScotTowels as Scott Towels and ScotTissue as Scott Tissue, adding a common look and logo (although some distinct colors) on both packages as well as their Scott Napkins. In perhaps a risky move, Scott also decided to phase out local brand names in 80 foreign countries where Scott garnered almost half its sales, including Andrex, its top-selling British bath tissue.[27] Scott's hope was that the advantages of brand consolidation and global branding would offset the disadvantages of losing local brand equity.

Some notable—and fascinating—counterexamples to these dilution effects exist, however, in terms of firms that have branded a heterogeneous set of products and still achieved a reasonable level of perceived quality in the minds of consumers for each product. As Chapter 11 noted, many Japanese firms have adopted a corporate branding strategy with a very broad product portfolio. For example, Yamaha has developed a strong reputation selling an extremely diverse brand line that includes motorcycles, guitars, and pianos. Mitsubishi uses its name to brand a bank, cars, and aircraft. Canon has successfully marketed cameras, photocopiers, and office equipment. In a similar vein, the founder of Virgin Records, Richard Branson, has conducted an ambitious, and perhaps risky, brand extension program (see Branding Brief 12-5). In all these cases, it seems as if the brand has been able to secure a dominant association to quality in the minds of consumers without strong product identification that might otherwise limit it.

Can Succeed but Hurt the Image of the Parent Brand

If the brand extension has attribute or benefit associations that are seen as inconsistent or perhaps even as conflicting with the corresponding associations for the parent brand, consumers may change their perceptions of the parent brand as a result. For example, Farquhar notes that when Domino's Pizza entered into a licensing agreement to sell fruit-flavored bubble gum a number of years ago, it ran the risk of creating a "chewiness" association that could negatively affect its flagship pizza products.[28]

As another example, Chapter 4 described Miller Brewing's difficulty in creating a "hearty" association to its flagship Miller High Life beer brand in part because of its clear bottle and other factors such as its advertising heritage as the "champagne of bottled beer." It has often been argued that the early success of the Miller Lite light beer extension-market share soared from 9.5 percent in 1978 to 19 percent in 1986—only exacerbated the tendency of consumers to think of Miller High Life as "watery" tasting and not a full-bodied beer. These unfavorable perceptions were thought to have helped to contribute to the sales decline of Miller High Life, whose market share slid from 21 percent to 12 percent during that same eight-year period.

Can Dilute Brand Meaning

The potential drawbacks from a lack of identification with any one category and a weakened image may be especially evident with high-quality or prestige brands.

Gucci

In its prime, the Gucci brand symbolized luxury, status, elegance, and quality. By the 1980s, however, the label had become tarnished from sloppy manufacturing, countless knockoffs, and even a family feud among the managing Gucci brothers. The product line consisted of 22,000 items, distributed extensively across all types of department stores. Not only were there too many items, but some items did not even fit the Gucci image, for example, a cheap canvas pocketbook with the double-G logo that was easily copied and

Are There Any Boundaries to the Virgin Brand Name?

Perhaps the most extensive brand extension program in recent years has been undertaken by Richard Branson with his Virgin brand. Branson founded the Virgin record label at the age of 21, and in 1984 he launched Virgin Atlantic Airways. Later, he made millions on the sale of his record label, his Virgin record retail chain, and his Virgin computer games business. After licensing the use of the Virgin name to European startup airlines who were flying the London/Athens and London/Dublin routes, Branson decided to expand the range of products carrying the Virgin brand. He has since licensed the Virgin name for use on personal computers and set up joint ventures in 1994 to market Virgin Vodka and Virgin Cola. In 1997, he took over six of the United Kingdom's government rail lines and established Virgin Rail. In 1999, Branson launched Virgin Mobile, a wireless company that provides cellular service through a partnership with Deutsche Telecom. Branson branched into e-commerce that same year with the debut of Virgin.com, a portal where consumers can purchase every product or service offered by the Virgin brand.

Today the Virgin Group spans three continents and contains more than 200 companies involving such diverse products as financial services, music stores, online auto sales, cola, cosmetics, utilities, mobile phones, bridal shops, and a variety of e-commerce ventures (see Figure A). Virgin had 1999 revenues of $5 billion, and Branson's personal fortune is estimated at $3.3 billion. Of the 11 highest-profile companies under the Virgin umbrella, however, only four (Virgin Travel, Virgin Entertainment Group, Virgin Rail, and Virgin Hotels) turned a profit in 1999.

Travel and Transport	**Leisure and Entertainment**
Virgin Atlantic	Virgin Active
Virgin Balloon Flights	Virgin Drinks
Virgin Bikes	Virgin Megastores
Virgin Blue	Virgin Mobile
Virgin Books	V.Shop
Virgin Cars	Virgin Space
Virgin Express	Virgin Student
Virgin Holidays	Virgin Wines
Virgin Limited Edition	V2 Music
Virgin.net	Radio Free Virgin
Virgin Trains	**Business and Finance**
Virgin Travelstore	Virgin Biz.net
House and Home	Virgin Direct
Virgin Bride	Virgin Money
Virgin Cosmetics	Virgin Incentives
Virgin Energy	
Virgin Wines	

Source: http://www.virgin.com.

FIGURE A   The Virgin Empire

FIGURE A   *(Continued)*

Virgin's recent financial troubles sparked debate about Branson's seemingly undisciplined extension of the brand. One branding expert criticized Virgin's rapid expansion: "Virgin makes no sense; it's completely unfocused." When Virgin ventures are poorly received, as Virgin Cola, Virgin Vodka, and Virgin Clothing were in recent years, experts worry about the cumulative negative effect of these unsuccessful brands on the company's overall equity. One marketing executive illustrated the risk of launching an unsuccessful brand by saying, "When I'm delayed on a Virgin train I start wondering about Virgin Atlantic. Every experience of a brand counts, and negative experiences count even more."

Some critics believe that Virgin consumer products will do little more than generate publicity for Virgin airlines. They also caution of overexposure, even with the young, hip audience the Virgin brand has attracted. For example, one advertising agency executive remarked, "I would imagine the risk is that the Virgin brand name can come to mean everything to everybody, which in turn means it becomes nothing to nobody." In Branson's view, as long as a new brand adds value for the consumer, then it strengthens the Virgin image: "If the consumer benefits, I see no reason why we should be frightened about launching new products."

Sources: Peter Fuhrman, "Brand-Name Branson," *Forbes*, 2 January 1995, 41–42; Tara Parker Pope, "Can the Virgin Name Sell Cola, Computers, Vodka and More?" *Wall Street Journal*, 14 October 1994, B3; Miriam Jordan, "Virgin's Air Chief to Offer 'Unreal' Cola in Hong Kong, Japan, China by Dec. 31," *Wall Street Journal*, 23 February 1988, 36; http://www.virgin.com; Melanie Wells, "Red Baron," *Forbes*, 3 July 2000; Quentin Sommerville, "High-Flying Brand Isn't All It Appears," *Scotland on Sunday*, 24 December 2000; Roger Crowe, "Global-A Brand Too Far?" *GlobalVue*, 28 October 1998.

sold on a counterfeit basis on the street for $35. Sales only recovered when Gucci refocused the brand, paring the product line to 7,000 high-end items and selling them through its own company-owned outlets.

Can Cause the Company to Forgo the Chance to Develop a New Brand

One easily overlooked disadvantage to brand extensions is that by introducing a new product as a brand extension, the company forgoes the chance to create a new brand with its own unique image and equity. For example, consider the advantages to Disney of having introduced Touchstone films, which attracted an audience interested in movies with more adult themes and situations than Disney's traditional family-oriented releases; to Levi's of having introduced Dockers pants, which attracted a customer segment interested in casual pants; to General Motors of having introduced Saturn, which attracted consumers weary of "the same old cars sold the same old way"; and to Black & Decker from having introduced DeWalt power tools, which attracted a higher-end, more skilled market segment.

Each of these brands created its own associations and image and tapped into markets completely different from those that currently existed for other brands sold by the company. Thus, introducing a new product as a brand extension can have significant and potentially hidden costs in terms of lost opportunities of creating a new brand franchise. Moreover, there may be a loss of flexibility in the brand positioning for the extension given that it has to live up to the parent brand promise and image. The positioning of a new brand could be introduced and updated in the most competitively advantageous way possible.

UNDERSTANDING HOW CONSUMERS EVALUATE BRAND EXTENSIONS

What determines whether a brand extension is able to capitalize on these potential advantages and avoid, or at least minimize, these potential disadvantages? Figure 12-7 displays some examples of successful and unsuccessful brand extensions through the years. The difficulty of introducing a brand extension can be recognized by noting how even leading marketing companies have failed, despite their best intentions, in launching a brand extension.

This section examines how consumers evaluate brand extensions. It develops some simple conceptual notions to help a marketing manager better forecast and improve the potential odds for success of a brand extension.[29]

Managerial Assumptions

In analyzing potential consumer response to a brand extension, it is useful to start with a baseline case in which it is assumed that consumers are evaluating the brand extension based *only* on what they already know about the parent brand and the extension category and before any advertising, promotion, or detailed product information is made available. This baseline case provides the cleanest test of the extension concept itself and provides managers with guidance as to whether to proceed with an extension concept and, if so, what type of marketing program might be necessary.

Successful Category Extensions	Unsuccessful Category Extensions
Ivory shampoo and conditioner	Campbell's tomato sauce
Vaseline Intensive Care skin lotion	LifeSavers chewing gum
Hershey chocolate milk	Cracker Jack cereal
Jell-O Pudding Pops	Harley-Davidson wine coolers
Visa traveler's checks	Hidden Valley Ranch frozen entrees
Sunkist orange soda	Bic perfumes
Colgate toothbrushes	Ben-Gay aspirin
Mars ice cream bars	Kleenex diapers
Arm & Hammer toothpaste	Clorox laundry detergent
Bic disposable lighters	Levi's Tailored Classics suits
Aunt Jemima pancake syrup	Nautilus athletic shoes
Honda lawn mowers	Domino's fruit-flavored bubble gum
	Smucker's ketchup
	Fruit of the Loom laundry detergent

FIGURE 12-7   Examples of Category Extensions

In evaluating a brand extension under these baseline conditions, consumers can be expected to use their existing brand knowledge, as well as what they know about the extension category, to try to infer what the extension product might be like. In order for these inferences to result in favorable consumer evaluations of an extension, four basic assumptions must generally hold true:

1. *Consumers have some awareness of and positive associations about the parent brand in memory.* Unless there exists some type of potentially beneficial consumer knowledge about the parent brand, it is difficult to expect consumers to form favorable expectations of an extension.

2. *At least some of these positive associations will be evoked by the brand extension.* As will be discussed shortly, a number of different factors will determine which parent brand associations are evoked when consumers evaluate an extension. In general, consumers are likely to infer associations similar in strength, favorability, and uniqueness to the parent brand when the brand extension is seen as being similar or close in fit to the parent brand.

3. *Negative associations are not transferred from the parent brand.* Ideally, any negative associations that do exist for the parent brand would be left behind and not play a prominent role in the evaluation of the extension.

4. *Negative associations are not created by the brand extension.* Finally, it must be the case that any attributes or benefits that are viewed positively—or at least neutrally—by consumers with respect to the parent brand are not seen as a negative in the extension context. Consumers must also not infer any new attribute or benefit associations that did not characterize the parent brand but which they see as a potential drawback to the extension.

The more that these four assumptions hold true, the more likely it is that consumers will form favorable attitudes toward an extension. The chapter next examines some factors that influence the validity of these assumptions and considers in more detail how a brand extension, in turn, affects brand equity.

Brand Extensions and Brand Equity

The ultimate success of an extension will depend on its ability to both achieve some of its own brand equity in the new category as well as contribute to the equity of the parent brand. This section examines each consideration in turn.

Creating Extension Equity

For the brand extension to create equity, it must have a sufficiently high level of awareness and some strong, favorable, and unique associations, just like any brand. Brand awareness will depend primarily on the marketing program and resources devoted to spreading the word about the extension. As Chapter 11 described, it will also obviously depend on the type of branding strategy adopted: The more prominently an existing brand that has already achieved a certain level of awareness and image is used to brand an extension, the easier it should be to create awareness of and an image for the extension in memory.

Initially, creating a positive image for an extension will depend primarily on three consumer-related factors:

1. How *salient* parent brand associations are in the minds of consumers in the extension context, that is, what information comes to mind about the parent brand when consumers think of the proposed extension and the *strength* of those associations.
2. How *favorable* any inferred associations are in the extension context, that is, whether this information is seen as suggestive of the type of product or service that the brand extension would be and whether or not these associations would be viewed as good or bad in the extension context.
3. How *unique* any inferred associations are in the extension category, that is, how these perceptions compare with those of competitors.

As with any brand, successful brand extensions must achieve desired points of parity and points of difference. Without powerful points of difference, the brand risks becoming an undistinguished "me-too" entry, vulnerable to well-positioned competitors.[30] Tauber refers to "competitive leverage" as the set of advantages that a brand conveys to an extended product in the new category, that is, "when the consumer, by simply knowing the brand, can think of important ways that they perceive that the new brand extension would be better than competing brands in the category."[31]

At the same time, it is also necessary to establish any required points of parity. The more dissimilar the extension product is to the parent brand, the more likely it is that points of parity will become a positioning priority. For example, when Johnson & Johnson test-marketed a brand of aspirin for babies, the product failed despite the fact that the Johnson & Johnson name is virtually synonymous with baby products. As it turned out, parents were just as concerned with getting fevers down quickly as they were with the safety and gentleness of an aspirin—Johnson & Johnson's key point-of-difference and core benefit association for their existing baby products. Thus, the lack of a necessary point-of-parity association doomed the product.

Contributing to Parent Brand Equity

To contribute to parent brand equity, an extension must strengthen or add favorable and unique associations to the parent brand as well as not diminish the strength, favorability, or uniqueness of any already existing associations for the parent brand. The effects of an extension on consumer brand knowledge will depend on four factors:

1. How *compelling* the evidence is concerning the corresponding attribute or benefit association in the extension context, that is, how attention getting and unambiguous or easily interpretable the information is concerning product performance or imagery for that association. Strong evidence is attention getting and unambiguous. Weak evidence—whether it is less attention getting or more ambiguous—may be ignored or discounted.

2. How *relevant* or diagnostic the extension evidence is concerning the attribute or benefit for the parent brand, that is, how much evidence on product performance or imagery in one category is seen as predictive of product performance or imagery for the brand in other categories. Evidence will only affect parent brand evaluations if consumers feel that extension performance is indicative, in some way, of the parent brand.

3. How *consistent* the extension evidence is with the corresponding parent brand associations. Consistent extension evidence is less likely to change the evaluation of existing parent brand associations. Inconsistent extension evidence creates the potential for change, with the direction and extent of change depending on the relative strength and favorability of the evidence. Note that highly inconsistent extension evidence, however, may be discounted or ignored if not viewed as relevant.[32]

4. How *strong* existing attribute or benefit associations are held in consumer memory for the parent brand, that is, how potentially easy an association might be to change.

According to these factors, feedback effects that change brand knowledge are most likely when consumers view information about the extension as equally revealing about the parent brand and when they only hold a weak and inconsistent association about the parent brand with respect to that information. The nature of the feedback effects will depend on the nature of the actual information: An unfavorable extension evaluation can lead to negative feedback effects, whereas a favorable extension evaluation can lead to positive feedback effects. Note that negative feedback effects are not restricted to product-related performance associations. As noted earlier, if a brand has a favorable "prestige" image association, then a vertical extension (e.g., offering a new version of the product at a lower price) may be viewed disapprovingly or even resented by the existing consumer franchise.

EVALUATING BRAND EXTENSION OPPORTUNITIES

Academic research and industry experience have revealed a number of principles concerning the proper way to introduce brand extensions. Brand extension strategies must be carefully considered by systematically following the steps listed in Figure 12-8. Managerial judgment *and* consumer research should be employed to help make *each* of these decisions.

Define Actual and Desired Consumer Knowledge about the Brand

Chapter 9 examined qualitative and quantitative measures of consumer brand knowledge structures in detail. In particular, it noted that it is critical to fully understand the depth and breadth of awareness of the parent brand and the strength, favorability, and uniqueness of its associations. Moreover, before any extension decisions are contemplated, it is important that the desired knowledge structures have been fully articulated. Specifically, what is to be the basis of positioning and core benefits satisfied by the brand? Profiling actual and desired knowledge structures helps to identify possible

1. Define actual and desired consumer knowledge about the brand (e.g., create mental map and identify key sources of equity).
2. Identify possible extension candidates on basis of parent brand associations and overall similarity or fit of extension to the parent brand.
3. Evaluate the potential of the extension candidate to create equity according to the three-factor model:
   - Salience of parent brand associations
   - Favorability of inferred extension associations
   - Uniqueness of inferred extension associations
4. Evaluate extension candidate feedback effects according to the four-factor model:
   - How compelling the extension evidence is
   - How relevant the extension evidence is
   - How consistent the extension evidence is
   - How strong the extension evidence is
5. Consider possible competitive advantages as perceived by consumers and possible reactions initiated by consumers.
6. Design marketing campaign to launch extension.
7. Evaluate extension success and effects on parent brand equity.

FIGURE 12-8   Steps in Successfully Introducing Brand Extensions

brand extensions as well as to guide decisions concerning their likely success. In evaluating an extension, a company must understand where it would like to take the brand in the long run. Because the introduction of an extension potentially changes brand meaning, consumer response to all subsequent marketing activity may be affected as a result (see Chapter 13).

Identify Possible Extension Candidates

Chapter 11 described a number of criteria related to the consumer, firm, and competition for choosing which products and markets a firm should enter. With respect to consumer factors when identifying potential brand extensions, marketers should consider parent brand associations—especially as they relate to brand positioning and core benefits—and product categories that might seem to fit with that brand image in the minds of consumers. Possible category extension candidates can be generated through managerial brainstorming sessions as well as consumer research. Although consumers are generally better able to react to an extension concept than to suggest one, it still may be instructive to ask consumers what products the brand should consider offering if it were to introduce a new product.

One or more associations can often serve as the basis of fit. Figure 12-9 displays an analysis by Ed Tauber of possible extensions of the Vaseline Intensive Care brand by recognizing the range of associations held by consumers. As another example, Beecham marketed Lucozade in Britain for years as a glucose drink to combat dehydration and other maladies of sick children. By introducing new flavor formulas, packaging formats, and so forth, Beecham was able to capitalize on the association of the brand as a "fluid replenisher" to transform its meaning to "a healthy

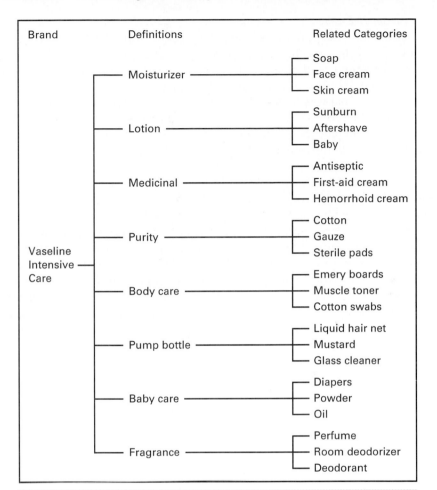

FIGURE 12-9   Possible Extensions of Vaseline Intensive Care Brand

sports drink for people of all ages." Reinforced by ads featuring the famous British Olympic decathlete Daley Thompson, sales and profits for the brand increased dramatically. Thus, by recognizing that Lucozade did not have to be just a pharmaceutical product but could be repositioned through brand extensions and other marketing activity as a healthy and nutritious drink, Beecham was able to credibly transform the brand.[33]

Evaluate the Potential of the Extension Candidate

In forecasting the success of a proposed brand extension, it is necessary to assess— through judgment and research—the likelihood that the extension would realize the advantages and avoid the disadvantages of brand extensions as summarized in Figures 12-2 and 12-6. As with any new product, analysis of consumer, corporate, and competitive factors can be useful.

Consumer Factors

Evaluating the potential success of a proposed brand extension requires an assessment of its ability to achieve its own brand equity, as well as the likelihood of it affecting the existing brand equity of the parent brand. First, marketers must forecast the strength, favorability, and uniqueness of *all* associations to the brand extension. In other words, what will be the salience, favorability, or uniqueness of parent brand associations in the proposed extension context? Similarly, what will be the strength, favorability, and uniqueness of any other inferred associations? The three-factor model of extension evaluations and four-factor model of extension feedback effects can provide guidance in studying consumer reactions.

To narrow down the list of possible extensions, consumer research is often needed (see Chapter 10 for a review). Consumers may be probed directly (e.g., "How well does the proposed extension fit with the parent brand?" or "Would you expect such a new product from the parent brand?"). Consumers may even be asked what products they believe are currently attached to the brand: If a majority of consumers believe a proposed extension product is already being sold under the brand, then there would seem to be little risk involved in introducing it, at least in terms of initial consumer reaction. To better understand consumers' perceptions of a proposed extension, consumer research is often employed using open-ended associations (e.g., "What comes into your mind when you think of the brand extension?" or "What are your first impressions on hearing that the parent brand is introducing the extension?") as well as ratings scales based on reactions to concept statements.

Several common pitfalls must be avoided when evaluating brand extension potential. One major mistake in evaluating extension opportunities is failing to take *all* of consumers' brand knowledge structures into account. Often marketers mistakenly focus on one or perhaps a few brand associations as a potential basis of fit and ignore other, possibly more important, brand associations in the process.

Bic

By emphasizing inexpensive, disposable products, the French company Société Bic was able to create markets for nonrefillable ballpoint pens in the late 1950s, disposable cigarette lighters in the early 1970s, and disposable razors in the early 1980s. It unsuccessfully tried the same strategy in marketing Bic perfumes in the United States and Europe in 1989. The perfumes—two for women ("Nuit" and "Jour") and two for men ("Bic for Men" and "Bic Sport for Men")—were packaged in quarter-ounce glass spray bottles that looked like fat cigarette lighters and sold for $5 each. The products were displayed on racks in plastic packages at checkout counters throughout Bic's extensive distribution channels, which included 100,000 or so drugstores, supermarkets, and other mass merchandisers. At the time, a Bic spokeswoman described the new products as extensions of the Bic heritage—"high quality at affordable prices, convenient to purchase, and convenient to use."[34] The brand extension was launched with a $20 million advertising and promotion campaign containing images of stylish people enjoying themselves with the perfume and using the tag line "Paris in Your Pocket." Nevertheless, Bic was unable to overcome its lack of cachet and negative image associations; by failing to achieve a critical point of parity, the extension was a failure.

Another major mistake in evaluating brand extensions is overlooking how literal consumers can be in evaluating brand extensions. Although consumers ultimately care about benefits, they often notice and evaluate attributes—especially concrete ones—in reacting to an extension. Brand managers, though, tend to focus on perceived benefits in predicting consumer reactions and, as a result, may overlook some potentially damaging attribute associations.

Bausch & Lomb Clear Choice

Bausch & Lomb acquired Interplak in 1988 and built it into a $100 million business by 1992, representing Bausch & Lomb's first move into dental care. Following this success, it chose to introduce Bausch & Lomb Clear Choice, a colorless, alcohol-free mouthwash, in 1992. This brand extension was thought to fit with Bausch & Lomb's strategy of marketing care products for "above-the-shoulders" orifices—the eyes, ears, nose, and throat. Bausch & Lomb supported Clear Choice with a $13 million advertising campaign that included TV spots developed in-house and print advertising. Analysts questioned, however, whether the Bausch & Lomb name, traditionally associated with contact lenses and eye care, could be transferred to sell mouthwash. Consumers were equally perplexed: Bausch & Lomb was never able to take a significant share of the market from leaders Scope and Listerine. Bausch & Lomb discontinued Clear Choice in 1995.[35]

Corporate and Competitive Factors

Marketers must not only take a consumer perspective in evaluating a proposed brand extension but must also take a broader corporate and competitive perspective. How effectively are the corporate assets leveraged in the extension setting? How relevant are existing marketing programs, perceived benefits, and target customers in the extension context? What are the competitive advantages to the extension as perceived by consumers and possible reactions initiated by competitors as a result?

Too many extension products and strongly entrenched competition can put a strain on company resources. For example, Church & Dwight in the 1980s decided to extend its Arm & Hammer baking soda brand and its familiar yellow box into a variety of new product categories—toothpaste, carpet deodorizer, air freshener, antiperspirant, and so forth. Despite some early successes, the company had one of its worst years ever in 1994 as earnings fell 77 percent from the previous year. What happened? The market share of two of its more promising product introductions—toothpaste and laundry detergent—fell sharply when, after observing increased consumer acceptance of baking soda-based products, packaged-goods giants such as Procter & Gamble, Unilever, and Colgate-Palmolive aggressively introduced their own baking soda versions of these products. Priced higher and with less advertising support, the market share of Arm & Hammer's products dropped. Church & Dwight management admitted that "it was too much for a company of our size to introduce so many new products in one year" and vowed to focus on existing products in the short run.

Too many new products have also been thought to pose a problem at times for PepsiCo.[36] In the early 1990s the company embarked on an aggressive multibrand strategy, expanding its brand offerings from 14 to 60 by introducing fruit juices (jointly with Ocean Spray), iced teas (jointly with Lipton), flavored waters, sports drinks (All Sport), and others. These brands met with mixed success. The company's one major line extension introduced in 1993, Crystal Pepsi, was a decided flop. A number of factors are thought to have contributed to its failure, such as wrong taste, wrong name, wrong packaging, and wrong advertising. Perhaps the biggest worry for PepsiCo during this episode was that its flagship cola brands lost market share to Coca-Cola, raising concerns that the flurry of new products had diverted Pepsi's attention from its core brands.

Design Marketing Programs to Launch Extension

Too often extensions are used as a shortcut means of introducing a new product, and insufficient attention is paid to developing a branding and marketing strategy that will maximize the equity of the brand extension as well as enhance the equity of the parent brand. As is the case with a new brand, building brand equity for a brand extension requires choosing brand elements, designing the optimal marketing program to launch the extension, and leveraging secondary associations.

Choosing Brand Elements

By definition, a brand extension retains one or more elements from an existing brand. Marketers should realize that brand extensions do not necessarily have to leverage only a brand name but can use other brand elements too. For example, companies such as Heinz and Campbell Soup have implemented package designs that attempt to distinguish different line extensions or brand types but reveal their common origin at the same time.[37]

In some cases, packaging is such a critical component of equity for the brand that it is hard to imagine an extension without the same package design elements. Brands in such cases are in a real dilemma because if they choose to use the same type of packaging, they run the risk that the extension will not be well distinguished. On the other hand, if they choose to use a different type of packaging, a key source of brand equity may be left behind. For example, Tanqueray gin has a distinctive green bottle with red trim, which had been the centerpiece of its print ads during the 1980s. To distinguish its new Tanqueray Sterling vodka extension, it chose to use a silver bottle, which, although stylish, failed to leverage its key packaging equities.

Kapferer describes the experiences of Kodak when it began marketing alkaline batteries under the Ultra Life brand name in 1985. Instead of using the familiar yellow and red colors for packaging, as with other Kodak products, the new battery had its own look and identity, with the Kodak name only appearing in small type. After disappointing sales, Kodak changed the packaging to give more emphasis to the Kodak name and return to the more familiar Kodak look, with an immediate increase in sales.[38]

Thus, a brand extension can retain or modify one or more brand elements from the parent brand as well as adopt its own brand elements. In creating new brand elements for an extension, the same guidelines of memorability, meaningfulness, likeability, protectability, adaptability, and transferability should be followed as were described in Chapter 4 for the development of any brand. New brand elements are often necessary to help to distinguish the brand extension from the parent brand to build its awareness and image. As Chapter 11 noted, the relative prominence of existing parent brand elements and new extension brand elements will dictate the strength of transfer from the parent brand to the extension as well as the feedback from the extension to the parent brand.

Designing Optimal Marketing Program

The marketing program for a brand extension must consider the same guidelines in building brand equity that were described in Chapters 5 and 6. In terms of designing the supporting marketing program, product-related and non-product-related associations often must be created, consumer perceptions of value must guide pricing decisions, distribution strategies must blend push and pull considerations, and marketing communications must be integrated by mixing and matching communication options.

In terms of properly positioning a brand extension, the less similar the extension is to the parent brand, the more important it typically is to establish necessary and competitive points of parity. The points of difference for a category extension in many cases directly follow from the points of difference for the parent brand and are easily perceived by consumers. Thus, when Ivory extended into shampoo and conditioners, its key "gentleness" point of difference presumably transferred easily. It would seem that the bigger challenge would have been to reach parity in the minds of consumers with category considerations related to glamour and how the shampoo made one look and feel. Thus, with category extensions, points of parity are often critical. With line extensions, on the other hand, it is often the case that a new association has to be created that can serve as an additional point of difference and help to distinguish the extension from the parent brand too.

For line extensions, it is important that consumers understand how the new product relates to existing products in order to minimize possible cannibalization or confusion. For example, in Australia, General Motors sells its cars under the Holden name. For some time, it marketed only one car, the Holden Gemini, in the small-car market segment there. When it decided to introduce a second car, the Holden Astra, consumers thought the car was intended to replace Holden's existing Gemini model. Without explicit communication as to the relationships among the products, consumers began to think of the Gemini as an outdated model.[39]

Miles Laboratories ran into a similar problem with its Alka-Seltzer Plus cold medicine. At first, consumers perceived it as simply a more potent form of regular Alka-Seltzer, resulting in less than effervescent sales. Consequently, the company shrank the Alka-Seltzer part of the name on the cold medicine package and began running more distinctive ads. Whereas regular Alka-Seltzer ads showed office workers suffering from stress huddled around a water cooler, the new Alka-Seltzer Plus ads featured testimonials from residents of frigid Winter Harbor, Maine. The brand's fortunes turned around as a result.

Leveraging Secondary Brand Associations

In general, brand extensions will often leverage the same secondary associations as the parent brand, although there may be instances in which competing in the extension category requires some additional fortification such that linking to other entities may be desirable. A brand extension differs in that, by definition, there is always some leveraging of another brand or company. The extent to which these other associations become linked to the extension, however, depends on the branding strategy that is adopted and how the extension is branded. As noted earlier, the more common the brand elements and the more prominence they receive, the more likely it is that parent brand associations will transfer.

Evaluate Extension Success and Effects on Parent Brand Equity

The final step in evaluating brand extension opportunities involves assessing the extent to which an extension is able to achieve its own equity as well as contribute to the equity of the parent brand. A number of decisions have to be made concerning the introduction of a brand extension, and a number of factors will affect the brand's success. To help interpret that success, brand tracking based on the customer-based brand equity model or other key measures of consumer response can be employed, centered on both the extension and the parent brand as a whole. Brand Focus 12.0 describes a perceptive analysis of line extensions by Quelch and Kenny.

EXTENSION GUIDELINES BASED ON ACADEMIC RESEARCH

Although the previous discussion provides some general insight into the effects of brand extensions on brand equity, more specific guidance is necessary. Fortunately, brand extension research has received much research attention from academics in recent years. Some of the important research conclusions that have emerged are summarized in Figure 12-10 and described in detail in this section.

Successful brand extensions occur when the parent brand is seen as having favorable associations and there is a perception of fit between the parent brand and the extension product. To better understand the process by which consumers evaluate a brand extension, many academic researchers have adopted a "categorization" perspective. Categorization research has its roots in psychological research that shows that people do not deliberately and individually evaluate each new stimulus to which they are exposed, but often evaluate a stimulus in terms of whether or not it can be classified as a member of a previously defined category, as illustrated by the following example.

Assume that you went to a party and found yourself in a conversation with an athletic-looking person who was casually dressed in sportswear and seemed to only want to talk about sports—what he or she read in the paper, saw on television, and was involved with as a participant. You might have a mental category of a "sports fanatic" as someone who looked like a "jock" and only read the sports section of the newspaper, watched sports on television, and talked sports with friends and family. As a result of this knowledge, you might quickly categorize that person as a "sports fanatic," and your evaluation of that person would probably depend on how you felt about the category of sports fanatics in general. As opposed to this "categorical processing," assume that you went up to another person at the party. This extremely pale person was dressed in a very fashionable "punk" manner yet, at the same time, also seemed to only want to talk about sports. Because of his or her appearance, this other person might not fit so neatly into your category of "sports fanatic," so you would have to form your evaluation in a more detailed fashion, that is, by "piecemeal processing" in which you constructed an attitude based on all the different considerations involved.

---

1. Successful brand extensions occur when the parent brand is seen as having favorable associations and there is a perception of fit between the parent brand and the extension product.
2. There are many bases of fit: product-related attributes and benefits as well as non-product-related attributes and benefits related to common usage situations or user types.
3. Depending on consumer knowledge of the product categories, perceptions of fit may be based on technical or manufacturing commonalities or more surface considerations such as necessary or situational complementarity.
4. High-quality brands stretch farther than average-quality brands, although both types of brands have boundaries.
5. A brand that is seen as prototypical of a product category can be difficult to extend outside the category.
6. Concrete attribute associations tend to be more difficult to extend than abstract benefit associations.
7. Consumers may transfer associations that are positive in the original product class but become negative in the extension context.
8. Consumers may infer negative associations about an extension, perhaps even based on other inferred positive associations.
9. It can be difficult to extend into a product class that is seen as easy to make.
10. A successful extension can not only contribute to the parent brand image but also enable a brand to be extended even farther.
11. An unsuccessful extension hurts the parent brand only when there is a strong basis of fit between the two.
12. An unsuccessful extension does not prevent a firm from backtracking and introducing a more similar extension.
13. Vertical extensions can be difficult and often require sub-branding strategies.
14. The most effective advertising strategy for an extension is one that emphasizes information about the extension (rather than reminders about the parent brand).

FIGURE 12-10   Brand Extension Guidelines Based on Academic Research

Applying categorization notions in a marketing context, it could be argued that consumers use their categorical knowledge of brands and products to simplify, structure, and interpret their marketing environment.[40] For example, it has been argued that consumers see brands as categories that over time have come to be associated with a number of specific attributes based on the attributes associated with the different products that represent individual members of the brand category. For example, Ivory might be associated with "soap," "mildness," and "quality" as a result of its soap, dishwashing liquid, laundry detergent, and shampoo and conditioner products.[41]

According to a categorization perspective, if a brand were to introduce an extension that was seen as closely related or similar to the brand category, then consumers could easily transfer their existing attitude about the parent brand to the extension. On the other hand, if consumers were not as sure about the similarity, then consumers might be expected to evaluate the extension in a more detailed, piecemeal fashion. In this case, the favorability of any specific associations that are inferred about the extension would be the primary determinant of extension evaluations.[42]

Thus, a categorization view considers consumers' evaluations of brand extensions to be a two-step process. First, consumers determine whether in their mind there is a match between what they know about the parent brand and what they believe to be true about the brand extension. Second, if the match is good, then consumers might be expected to transfer their existing parent brand attitudes to the extension. Otherwise, consumers might be more likely to evaluate the brand in a more piecemeal fashion. With this latter type of processing, consumer evaluations would depend on the strength, favorability, and uniqueness of salient brand associations in the extension context.

Consistent with these notions, Aaker and Keller collected consumer reactions to 20 proposed extensions from six well-known brands and found that both a perception of fit between the original and extension product categories and a perception of high quality for the parent brand led to more favorable extension evaluations.[43] A number of subsequent studies have explored the generalizability of these findings to markets outside the United States. Based on a comprehensive analysis of 131 brand extensions from seven such replication studies around the world, Bottomly and Holden concluded that this basic model clearly generalized, although cross-cultural differences influenced the relative importance attached to the model components.[44]

Thus, in general, brand extensions are more likely to be favorably evaluated by consumers if they see some bases of fit or similarity between the proposed extension and parent brand.[45] A lack of fit may doom a potentially successful brand extension.[46]

There are many bases of fit: product-related attributes and benefits, as well as non-product-related attributes and benefits related to common usage situations or user types. Any association held in memory by consumers about the parent brand may serve as a potential basis of fit. As Chapter 2 noted, many different types of associations may become linked to the brand. Therefore, brand extensions may be seen as similar or close in fit to the parent brand in many ways. Most academic researchers typically assume that similarity judgments are a function of salient shared associations between the parent brand and the extension product category. Specifically, the more common and fewer distinctive associations that exist, the greater the perception of overall similarity. These similarity judgments could be based on product-related attributes or benefits as well as non-product-related attributes or benefits.[47] Consumers may also use attributes for a prototypical brand or a particular exemplar as the standard of reference for the extension category and form their perceptions of fit with the parent brand on that basis.

To demonstrate how fit does not have to be based on product-related associations alone, Park, Milberg, and Lawson have distinguished between fit based on "product-feature similarity" (as described earlier) and "brand-concept consistency."[48] They define *brand concepts* as the brand-unique image associations that arise from a particular combination of attributes, benefits, and the marketing efforts used to translate these attributes into higher-order meanings (e.g., high status). *Brand-concept consistency* is defined in terms of how well the brand concept accommodates the extension product. The important point these researchers make is that different types of brand concepts from the same original product category may meet with varying degrees of acceptance regarding extending into the same category, even when product-feature similarity is high.

Park and his coauthors further distinguish between *function-oriented brands,* whose dominant associations relate to product performance (e.g., Timex watches), and *prestige-oriented brands,* whose dominant associations relate to consumers' expression of self-concepts or images (e.g., Rolex watches). Experimentally, they showed that the Rolex brand could more easily extend into categories such as grandfather clocks, bracelets, and rings than the Timex brand; however, Timex could more easily extend into categories such as stopwatches, batteries, and calculators than Rolex. In the former case, there was high brand-concept consistency for Rolex that overcame a lack of product-feature similarity; in the latter case, there was enough product-feature similarity to favor a function-oriented brand such as Timex. (See the Science of Branding 13-1 for further development of brand image types or concepts by Park and his coauthors.)

Broniarczyk and Alba provide another compelling demonstration of the importance of recognizing salient brand associations. They show that a brand that may not even be as favorably evaluated as a competing brand in its category may be more successfully extended into certain categories, depending on the particular parent brand associations involved. For example, although Close-Up toothpaste was not as well liked by their sample as Crest toothpaste, a proposed Close-Up breath mint extension was evaluated more favorably than one from Crest. Alternatively, a proposed Crest toothbrush extension was evaluated more favorably than one from Close-Up. Figure 12-11 displays some of their experimental results from other categories.[49]

Broniarczyk and Alba also showed that a perceived lack of fit between the parent brand's product category and the proposed extension category could be overcome if key parent brand associations were salient and relevant in the extension category. For example, Froot Loops cereal—which has strong brand associations to "sweet," "flavor," and "kids"—was better able to extend to dissimilar product categories such as lollipops and popsicles than to similar product categories such as waffles and hot cereal because of the relevance of its brand associations in the dissimilar extension category. The reverse was true for Cheerios cereal, however, which had a "healthy grain" association that was only relevant in similar extension product categories.

FIGURE 12-11   Role of Brand-Specific Associations in Determining Fit

Product Category	Preferred Brand and Focal Brand	Corresponding Favorably Evaluated Extensions[a]
Cereal	Cheerios	Oatmeal; waffles
	Froot Loops	Lollipops
Soap	Camay	Moisturizer; cleansing cream
	Irish Spring	Deodorant
Computer	Apple	Videogames
	IBM	Cellular phones
Beer	Coors	Wine coolers; bottled water
	Budweiser	Scotch

[a]The table should be interpreted as indicating that Cheerios was more successfully extended to oatmeal and waffles, whereas Froot Loops was more easily extended to lollipops, and so on.

Thus, extension fit is more than just the number of common and distinctive brand associations between the parent brand and the extension product category.[50] These research studies and others demonstrate the importance of taking a broader perspective of categorization and fit. For example, Bridges, Keller, and Sood refer to "category coherence." Coherent categories are those whose members "hang together" and "make sense." According to these authors, to understand the rationale for a grouping of products in a brand line, a consumer needs "explanatory links" that tie the products together and summarize their relationship. For example, the physically dissimilar toy, bath care, and car seat products in the Fisher-Price product line can be united by the link "products for children."[51] Similarly, Schmitt and Dubé proposed that brand extensions should be viewed as conceptual combinations.[52] A conceptual combination (e.g., "apartment dog") consists of a modifying concept, or "modifier" (e.g., *apartment*), and a modified concept, or "header" (e.g., *dog*). Thus, according to this view, a proposed brand extension such as McDonald's Theme Park would be interpreted as the original brand or company name (e.g., McDonald's) acting on the "header concept" of the extension category (e.g., theme parks) as a "modifier."

Finally, researchers have explored other, more specific, aspects of fit. Boush provides experimental data as to the context sensitivity of fit judgments.[53] Similarity judgments between pairs of product categories were found to be asymmetrical, and brand name associations could reverse the direction of asymmetry. For example, more subjects agreed with the statement "*Time* magazine is like *Time* books" than the statement that "*Time* books were like *Time* magazine," but without the brand names, the preferences were reversed. Smith and Andrews surveyed industrial goods marketers and found that the relationship between fit and new product evaluations was not direct but was mediated by customers' sense of certainty that a firm could provide a proposed new product.[54]

Depending on consumer knowledge of the product categories, perceptions of fit may be based on technical or manufacturing commonalities or more surface considerations such as necessary or situational complementarity. Fit perceptions can also be based on considerations other than attributes or benefits. Taking a demand-side and supply-side perspective of consumer perceptions, Aaker and Keller showed that perceived fit between the parent brand and extension product could be related to the economic notions of perceived substitutability and complementarity in product use (from a demand-side perspective), as well as to the perceived ability of the firm to have the skills and assets necessary to make the extension product (from a supply-side perspective). Thus, Honda's perceived expertise in making motors for lawn mowers and cars may help perceptions of fit for any other machinery with small motors that Honda might want to introduce. Similarly, expertise with small disposable products offers numerous opportunities for Bic. On the other hand, other extension examples have little manufacturing compatibility but greater usage complementarity, for example, Colgate's extension from toothpaste to toothbrushes or Duracell's extension from batteries to flashlights.

These perceptions of fit, however, may depend on how much consumers know about the product categories involved. As demonstrated by Muthukrishnan and Weitz, knowledgeable "expert" consumers are more likely to use technical or manufacturing commonalities to judge fit, considering similarity in terms of technology, design and fabrication, and the materials and components used in the manufacturing process. Less knowledgeable "novice" consumers, on the other hand, are more likely to use superficial, perceptual considerations such as common package, shape, color, size, and usage.[55] Specifically, they experimentally showed that less knowledgeable consumers were more likely to see a basis of fit between tennis racquets and tennis shoes than tennis racquets and golf clubs, despite the fact that the latter actually share more manufacturing commonalities. The effects for more knowledgeable consumers, on the other hand, were reversed because they recognized the technical synergies that would be involved in manufacturing tennis racquets and golf clubs.

Broniarczyk and Alba also showed that perceptions of fit on the basis of brand-specific associations were contingent on consumers having the necessary knowledge about the parent brand. Without such knowledge, consumers again tended to rely on more superficial considerations in forming extension evaluations, such as their level of awareness for the brand or their overall regard for the parent brand.[56]

High-quality brands stretch farther than average-quality brands, although both types of brands have boundaries. High-quality brands are often seen as more credible, expert, and trustworthy at what they do. As a result, even though consumers may still believe a relatively distant extension does not really fit with the brand, they may be more willing to give a high-quality brand the benefit of the doubt. When a brand is seen as more average in quality, however, such favorable source attributions may be less forthcoming, and consumers may be more likely to question the ability or motives of the company involved.[57] Thus, one important benefit of building a strong brand is that it can be extended more easily into more diverse categories.[58]

Regardless, all brands have boundaries, as a number of observers have persuasively argued by pointing out ridiculous, and even comical, hypothetical brand extension possibilities. For example, as Tauber states, few consumers would want Jell-O shoe laces or Tide frozen entrees!

A brand that is seen as prototypical of a product category can be difficult to extend outside the category. As a caveat to the previous conclusion, if a brand is seen as representing or exemplifying a category too much, it may be difficult for consumers to think of the brand in any other way. Numerous examples exist of category leaders that have failed in introducing brand extensions.[59] Bayer, a brand synonymous with aspirin, ran into a stumbling block introducing the Bayer Select line of specialized nonaspirin painkillers.[60] Chiquita was unsuccessful in its attempt to move beyond its strong "banana" association with its failed frozen juice bar extension.[61] Country Time could not overcome its "lemonade" association to introduce an apple cider. Perhaps the most extreme example of this caveat is brands that lost their trademark distinctiveness and became a generic term for the category, such as Thermos and Kleenex.

To illustrate the difficulty that a prototypical brand may have in extending, consider Clorox, a well-known brand whose name is virtually synonymous with bleach. In 1988, Clorox took on consumer goods giants Procter & Gamble and Unilever by introducing the first bleach with detergent. After pouring $225 million into the development and distribution of its detergent products over the next three years, Clorox was only able to achieve a 3 percent market share. Despite being beaten to market, P&G's subsequently introduced Tide with Bleach was able to achieve a 17 percent market share. Reluctantly, Clorox chose to exit the market. Although a number of factors may have driven that decision, Clorox's failure can certainly be attributed in part to the fact that consumers could only think of Clorox in a very limited sense as a bleach product. On the other hand, Clorox has successfully extended its brand into household cleaning products (e.g., toilet bowl cleaners), where the bleach ingredient is seen as more relevant.

Also note that Clorox's extension failure may have also been because in a combined "laundry detergent with bleach" product, laundry detergent is seen by consumers as the primary ingredient and bleach is seen as the secondary ingredient. As a result, a laundry detergent extension (such as Tide with Bleach) might be expected to have an advantage over a bleach extension (such as Clorox) when entering the combined laundry detergent with bleach category.[62] A similar type of interpretation might explain why Aunt Jemima was successful in introducing a pancake syrup extension from its well-liked pancake mix product but why Log Cabin was less successful in introducing a pancake mix extension from its well-regarded pancake syrup product: Pancake mix is seen as a more dominant ingredient than pancake syrup in breakfast pancakes. The Science of Branding 12-2 describes an interesting approach to dealing with this extendability challenge.

Concrete attribute associations tend to be more difficult to extend than abstract benefit associations. The limits to extension boundaries potentially faced by market leaders may be exacerbated by the fact that, in many cases, brands that are market leaders have strong concrete product attribute associations. In some cases, these attribute associations may even be reinforced by their name (e.g., Liquid Paper, Cheez Whiz, and Shredded Wheat).[63] La-Z-Boy, for example, has struggled to expand outside the narrow product line of recliners and its strong usage imagery.

In general, concrete attribute associations may not transfer as broadly to extension categories as more abstract attribute associations. For example, the Aaker and Keller study showed that consumers dismissed a hypothetical Heineken popcorn extension as potentially tasting bad or like beer; a hypothetical Vidal Sassoon perfume extension as having an undesirably strong shampoo scent; and a hypothetical Crest chewing gum extension as tasting like toothpaste or, more generally, tasting unappealing. In each case, consumers inferred a concrete attribute association for an extension that was technically feasible even though common sense might have suggested that a manufacturer logically would not be expected to introduce a product with such an attribute.

More abstract associations, on the other hand, may be seen as more relevant across a wide set of categories because of their intangible nature. For example, the Aaker and Keller study also showed that the Vuarnet brand had a remarkable ability to be exported to a disparate set of product categories, for example, sportswear, watches, wallets, and even skis. In these cases, complementarity may have led to an inference that the extension would have the "stylish" attribute associated with the Vuarnet name, and such an association was valued in the different extension contexts.

Several caveats should be noted, however, concerning the relative extendability of concrete and abstract associations. First, concrete attributes can be transferred to some product categories.[64] For example, if the parent brand has a concrete attribute association that is highly valued in the extension category because it creates a distinctive taste, ingredient, or component, an extension on that basis can often be successful. According to Farquhar and Herr, examples of such extensions might include Philadelphia cream cheese salad dressing, Tylenol sinus medication, Häagen-Dazs cream liqueur, Oreo cookies and cream ice cream, and Arm & Hammer carpet deodorizer.[65]

Second, abstract associations may not always transfer easily. This second caveat emerged from a study conducted by Bridges, Keller, and Sood who examined the rela-

Understanding Master Brands

Farquhar, Herr, and their colleagues have developed an intriguing approach to generating brand extension possibilities for prototypical brands and market leaders. They define a *master brand* as an established brand so dominant in customer's minds that it "owns" a particular association: The mention of a product attribute or category, a usage situation, or a customer benefit instantly brings a master brand to mind. Examples of master brands, according to these researchers, include Arm & Hammer baking soda, Band-Aid adhesive bandages, Bacardi rum, Alka-Seltzer antacid, Jell-O gelatin, Campbell's soup, Crayola crayons, Morton salt, Lionel toy trains, Philadelphia cream cheese, and Vaseline petroleum jelly.

Recognizing that the exceptionally strong associations of a master brand often make it difficult to extend it directly to other product categories, they propose strategies to extend master brands *indirectly* by leveraging alternative master brand associations that come from different parts of the brand hierarchies. Specifically, they describe the brand-leveraging compass to illustrate four principal directions for leveraging master brands:

1. *Sub-branding* introduces a new element into the brand hierarchy below the level of the master brand to refine or modify its meaning (e.g., DuPont Stainmaster carpet).

2. *Super-branding* adds new elements to an existing brand hierarchy above the level of the master brand, typically to suggest some product improvement (e.g., Eveready Energizer batteries).

3. *Brand bundling,* or "cross branding," fortifies a master brand through associations with other brands, including cooperative or co-branding (e.g., Citibank AAdvantage Visa card).

4. *Brand bridging* uses the master brand to endorse a new brand as the company attempts to move to a more distant product category (e.g., T/Gel therapeutic shampoo was initially endorsed by Neutrogena).

These strategies, all of which have been discussed in prior chapters, are suggested as different means to shield the parent or master brand by creating some distance to the extension and finding other ways to build brand equity for the extension by incorporating additional brands or brand elements. The authors note that marketing efforts can also "stay close to home" and fortify master brands by strengthening the brand's basic competencies, attracting new users, and developing new uses or expanding consumption among current users (as will be discussed in Chapter 13).

Source: Peter H. Farquhar, Julia Y. Han, Paul M. Herr, and Yuji Ijiri, "Strategies for Leveraging Master Brands," *Marketing Research* (September 1992): 32–43.

tive transferability of product-related brand information when it was represented either as an abstract brand association or as a concrete brand association.[66] For example, one such comparison contrasted the relative transferability of a watch characterized by dominant concrete attribute associations such as "water-resistant quartz movements, a time-keeping mechanism encased in shock proof steel covers, and shatterproof crystal" with that of a watch characterized by dominant abstract attribute associations such as "durable." Although these authors expected the abstract brand representation to fare better, they found that, for several reasons, the two types of brand images extended equally well into a dissimilar product category (e.g., handbags). Perhaps the most important reason was that consumers did not believe the abstract benefit would have the same meaning in the extension category (i.e., durability does not necessarily "transfer" because durability for a watch is not the same as durability for a handbag).

Finally, Joiner and Loken, in a demonstration of the "inclusion effect" in a brand extension setting, showed that consumers often generalized possession of an attribute from a specific category (e.g., Sony televisions) to a more general category (e.g., all Sony products) more readily than they generalized the attribute from the specific category (e.g., Sony televisions) to another specific category (e.g., Sony bicycles). This inclusion effect was attenuated when the specific extension category increased its typicality to the general category (e.g., Sony cameras versus Sony bicycles).[67]

Consumers may transfer associations that are positive in the original product class but become negative in the extension context. Because of different consumer motivations or product usage in the extension category, a brand association may not be as highly valued as it was in the original product context. For example, when Campbell test marketed a tomato sauce with the Campbell's name, it flopped. Apparently, Campbell's strong associations to soup signaled to consumers that the new product would be watery. To give the product more credibility, Campbell changed the name to the Italian-sounding "Prego," and the product has gone on to be a big success.

Consumers may infer negative associations about an extension, perhaps even based on other inferred positive associations. Even if consumers transfer positive associations from the parent brand to the extension, they may still infer other negative associations. For example, the Bridges, Keller, and Sood study showed that even if consumers thought that a proposed handbag extension from a hypothetical maker of durable watches also would be durable, they often assumed that it would not be fashionable, helping to contribute to low extension evaluations.[68]

It can be difficult to extend into a product class that is seen as easy to make. Some seemingly appropriate extensions may be dismissed because of the nature of the extension product involved. If the product is seen as comparatively easy to make—such that brand differences are hard to come by—then a high-quality brand may be seen as incongruous; alternatively, consumers may feel that the brand extension will attempt to command an unreasonable price premium and be too expensive.

For example, Aaker and Keller showed that hypothetical extensions such as Heineken popcorn, Vidal Sassoon perfume, Crest shaving cream, and Häagen-Dazs cottage cheese received relatively poor marks from experimental subjects in part because *all* brands in the extension category were seen as being about the same in quality, suggesting that the proposed brand extension was unlikely to be superior to existing products. The failure of designers such as Bill Blass and Gloria Vanderbilt to introduce certain products such as chocolates and perfume under their names may be in part a result of these perceptions of incongruity, lack of differentiation, and unwarranted price premiums.

When the extension category is seen as difficult to make, on the other hand, such that brands potentially vary a great deal in quality, there is a greater opportunity for a brand extension to differentiate itself, although consumers may also be less sure as to what exactly the quality level of the extension will be.[69]

A successful extension can not only contribute to the parent brand image but also enable a brand to be extended even farther. As noted earlier, a successful brand extension can change the meaning and image of a brand. An extension can help the image of the parent brand by improving the strength, favorability, or uniqueness of its associations. For example, Keller and Aaker showed that when consumers did not already have strongly held attitudes, the successful introduction of a brand extension improved evaluations of a parent brand that was originally perceived to be of only average quality. Finally, the associations that become linked to the parent brand by virtue of the extension product category may help clarify the basic core benefits for the brand. For example, one of Australia's leading cereal brands, Uncle Toby's, was able to broaden its meaning to be seen as a "healthy breakfast and snack food" by introducing muesli bars and other products.

If an extension changes the image and meaning of the brand, then subsequent brand extensions that otherwise might not have seemed appropriate to consumers may make more sense and be seen as a better fit. For example, Keller and Aaker showed that by taking little steps, that is, by introducing a series of closely related but increasingly distant extensions, it may be possible for a brand to ultimately enter product categories that would have been much more difficult, or perhaps even impossible, to have entered directly.[70]

The Dunhill brand provides an excellent example of gradually extending a brand to transform its meaning.[71] For all practical purposes, Dunhill started as a cigarette brand that was first extended into smoking accessories (e.g., pipes, pouches, and lighters). After establishing itself there, the brand was then extended into other male accessories (e.g., belts, desktop items, cufflinks, rings, and clothing). Most recently, the brand was extended yet again into male fragrances and mainstream fashion items. As a result of all of this extension activity, the Dunhill brand now not only represents a leading cigarette brand but also "luxury products and accessories for both men and women."

Boush and Loken found that far extensions from a "broad" brand were evaluated more favorably than from a "narrow" brand.[72] Relatedly, Dacin and Smith have shown that if the perceived quality levels of different members of a brand portfolio are more uniform, then consumers tend to make higher, more confident evaluations of a proposed new extension.[73] They also showed that a firm that had demonstrated little variance in quality across a diverse set of product categories was better able to overcome perceptions of lack of extension fit. In other words, it is as if consumers in this case think, "whatever the company does, it tends to do well."

In an empirical study of 95 brands in 11 nondurable consumer goods categories, Sullivan found that, in terms of stages of the product category life cycle, early-entering brand extensions did not perform as well, on average, as either early-entering new-name products or late-entering brand extensions.[74] DeGraba and Sullivan provided an economic analysis to help interpret this observation.[75] They posited that the major source of uncertainty in introducing a new product is the inability to know if it would be received by customers in a way that would allow it to be a commercial success. They further argued that this source of uncertainty could be mitigated by spending more time on the development process. Under such assumptions, they showed that the large spillover effects triggered by introducing a poorly received brand extension caused introducers of brand extensions to spend more time on the development process than did introducers of new-name products.

An unsuccessful extension hurts the parent brand only when there is a strong basis of fit between the two. The general rule of thumb emerging from academic research and industry experience is that an unsuccessful brand extension potentially can damage the parent brand only when there is a high degree of similarity or fit involved—for example, in the case of a failed line extension in the same category. Roedder John and Loken found that perceptions of quality for a parent brand in the health and beauty aids area decreased with the hypothetical introduction of a lower-quality extension in a similar product category (shampoo). Quality perceptions of the parent brand were unaffected, however, when the proposed extension was in a dissimilar product category (facial tissue).[76] Similarly, Keller and Aaker as well as Romeo found that unsuccessful extensions in dissimilar product categories did not affect evaluations of the parent brand.[77] When the brand extension is farther removed, it seems easier for consumers to compartmentalize the brand's products and disregard its performance in what is seen as an unrelated product category.

Additional research reinforces and amplifies this conclusion. Roedder John, Loken, and Joiner found that dilution effects were less likely to be present with flagship products and occurred with line extensions but were not always evident for more dissimilar category extensions.[78] Gürhan-Canli and Maheswaran extended the results of these studies by considering the moderating effect of consumer motivation and extension typicality.[79] In high-motivation conditions, they found that incongruent extensions were scrutinized in detail and led to the modification of family brand evaluations, regardless of the typicality of the extensions. In low-motivation conditions, however, brand evaluations were more extreme in the context of high (versus low) typicality. Because the less typical extension was considered an exception, its impact was reduced. Consistent with these high-motivation findings, Milberg and colleagues found that negative feedback effects were present when (1) extensions were perceived as belonging to product categories dissimilar from those associated with the family brand and (2) extension attribute information was inconsistent with image beliefs associated with the family brand.[80]

In terms of individual differences, Lane and Jacobson found some evidence of a negative reciprocal impact from brand extensions, especially for high-need-for-cognition subjects, but did not explore extension similarity differences.[81] Kirmani, Sood, and Bridges found dilution effects with owners of prestige-image automobiles when low-priced extensions were introduced but not with owners of nonprestige automobiles or with nonowners of either automobile.[82]

Finally, Morrin examined the impact of brand extensions on the strength of parent brand associations in memory. Two computer-based studies revealed that exposing consumers to brand extension information strengthened rather than weakened parent brand associations in memory, particularly for parent brands that were dominant in their original product category. Higher fit also resulted in greater facilitation, but only for nondominant parent brands. Moreover, improvements in memory for the parent brand due to the advertised introduction of an extension was not as great as when the same level of advertising directly promoted the parent brand.[83]

An unsuccessful extension does not prevent a firm from backtracking and introducing a more similar extension. The Keller and Aaker study also showed that unsuccessful extensions do not necessarily prevent a company from retrenching and later introducing a more similar extension. For example, in the early 1980s, Levi Strauss attempted to introduce a Tailored Classics line of men's suits. Levi's Tailored Classics was targeted to independent-thinking "clothes horses," dubbed by research as "Classic Individualists." Although the suit was not supposed to need tailoring, to allow for the better fit necessary for these demanding consumers, Levi Strauss designed the suit slacks and coat to be sold as separates. It chose to price these wool suits quite competitively and to distribute them through its existing department store accounts as opposed to specialty stores where the classic individualist traditionally shopped. Despite a determined marketing effort, the product failed to achieve its desired sales goals. This failure can probably be attributed to a number of factors (e.g., problems with the chosen target market, distribution channels, and product design), but perhaps the most fundamental problem was the lack of fit with the Levi's brand image and the image needed for the extension product and desired by the target market. Levi's had an informal, rugged, outdoor image that was inconsistent with the self-image of the classic individualist and the image the company sought from its suits.

Despite the ultimate withdrawal and failure of the product, Levi Strauss later was able to execute one of the most successful apparel launches ever-Dockers pants. As Levi Strauss's experiences with brand extensions illustrate, failure does not doom a firm to never be able to introduce any extensions—certainly not for a brand with as much equity as Levi's. An unsuccessful extension does, however, create a "perceptual boundary" of sorts in that it reveals the limits to the brand in the minds of consumers. It does not preclude a firm from later introducing an extension with a higher degree of fit, however, as was the case with Levi Strauss.

Vertical extensions can be difficult and often require sub-branding strategies. For market reasons or competitive considerations, it may be desirable for the firm to introduce a lower-priced version of a product. As noted earlier, such a product could be introduced as its own brand and function essentially as a fighter brand. Alternatively, the existing brand could be stretched downward by vertically extending. The danger with such an extension strategy, however, is that the parent brand image could be cheapened or tarnished in some way.

As a result, firms often adopt sub-branding strategies as a means to distinguish their lower-priced entries. For example, Gillette introduced the Good News brand as a line of inexpensive personal care products such as disposable razors. US Airways introduced US Airways Shuttle as an inexpensive short-haul carrier to compete with no-frills Southwest Airlines in the lucrative Eastern corridor market. Courtyard by Marriott was a lower-priced version of the regular Marriott and upscale Marriott Marquis hotel chains (see Branding Brief 12-6). Such extension introductions clearly must be handled carefully-typically, the parent brand plays a secondary role.

An even more difficult vertical extension is an upward brand stretch.[84] In general, it is difficult to sufficiently change people's impressions of the brand to justify a significant upward extension.

Expanding the Marriott Brand

Marriott International grew to an international hospitality giant from humble roots as a single root beer stand started by John and Alice Marriott in Washington, D.C., during the 1920s. The Marriotts added hot food to their root beer stand and renamed their business the Hot Shoppe, which they incorporated in 1929 when they began building a regional chain of restaurants. As the number of Hot Shoppes in the Southeast grew, Marriott expanded into in-flight catering by serving food on Eastern, American, and Capital Airlines beginning in 1937. In 1939, Hot Shoppes began its food service management business when it opened a cafeteria in the U.S. Treasury building. The company expanded into another hospitality sector in 1957, when Hot Shoppes opened its first hotel in Arlington, Virginia. Hot Shoppes, which was renamed Marriott Corporation in 1967, grew nationally and internationally by way of strategic acquisitions and entering new service categories; by 1977, sales topped $1 billion.

In the pursuit of continued growth, Marriott continued to diversify its business. Marriott's 1982 acquisition of Host International made it America's top operator of airport food and beverage facilities. Over the course of the following three years, Marriott added 1,000 food service accounts by purchasing three food service companies: Gladieux, Service Systems, and Saga Corporation. Determining that its high penetration in the traditional hotel market did not offer many opportunities for growth, the company initiated a segmented marketing strategy for its hotels by introducing the moderately priced Courtyard by Marriott hotels in 1983. Moderately priced hotels constituted the largest segment of the U.S. lodging industry, a segment filled with established competitors such as Holiday Inn, Ramada, and Quality Inn. Research conducted by Marriott registered the greatest consumer dissatisfaction in the moderately priced hotels, and Courtyard hotels were designed to offer travelers greater convenience and amenities, such as balconies and patios, large desks and sofas, and pools and spas (see Branding Brief 10-2).

Early success with Courtyard prompted Marriott to expand further. In 1984, Marriott entered the vacation timesharing business by acquiring American Resorts Group. The following year, the company purchased Howard Johnson company, selling the hotels and retaining the restaurants and rest stops. In 1987, Marriott added three new market segments: Marriott Suites, full-service suite accommodations; Residence Inn, extended-stay rooms for business travelers; and Fairfield Inn, an economy hotel brand. A company spokesman explained this rapid expansion: "There is a lot of segmentation that's going on in the hotel business. Travelers are sophisticated and have many wants and needs. In addition to that, we saw there would be a finite . . . ability to grow the traditional business."

Marriott Corporation split into two in 1993, forming Host Marriott to own the hotel properties and Marriott International primarily to engage in the more lucrative practice of governing them. In 1995, Marriott International bought a minority stake in the Ritz-Carlton luxury hotel group (Marriott purchased the remaining share in 1998). In 1996 the company acquired the Forum Group, an assisted living and health care services franchise, and merged it with Marriott Senior Living services. Marriott added a new hotel brand in 1998 with the introduction of SpringHill Suites, which provide moderate-priced suites that are 25 percent larger than standard hotel rooms. The following year, the company acquired corporate housing specialist ExecuStay Corporation and formed ExecuStay by Marriott. To capitalize on the online travel and accommodations boom, the company developed Marriott.com, which offers customized content to registered visitors, such as a vacation planner, golf course information, express reservations, and business content. In 2000, the company announced plans to join with rival Hyatt Corporation to launch a joint business-to-business e-commerce venture that will provide procurement services for the hospitality industry.

The last Hot Shoppe restaurant, located in a shopping mall in Washington, D.C., closed on December 2, 1999. This closing was fitting, since the tiny restaurant in no way resembled the multinational hospitality leader it spawned. Today, Marriott International is the largest hotel and resort company in America and one of the leading hospitality companies in the world, maintaining over 2,200 operating units in 59 countries that brought in $20 billion in global revenues in 2000.

Sources: http://www.marriot.com; Kim Clark, "Lawyers Clash on Timing of Marriot's Plan to Split," *Baltimore Sun,* 27 September 1994; Neil Henderson, "Marriott Gambles on Low-Cost, Classy Suburban Motels," *Washington Post,* 18 June 1994; Neil Henderson, "Marriott Bares Courtyard Plans," *Washington Post,* 12 June 1984; Elizabeth Tucker, "Marriot's Recipe for Corporate Growth," *Washington Post,* 1 June 1987; Paul Farhi, "Marriott to Sell 800 Restaurants," *Washington Post,* 19 December 1989.

Gallo

For years, Gallo stubbornly refused to put any other brand on the label of its better vintages besides its Gallo brand. Despite repeated ad campaigns that promised that some new varietal would "change the way you think about Gallo" (e.g., as when the winery introduced White Grenache), many consumers continued to think of the brand as they did before—as a relatively inexpensive jug wine.[85] In 1995, recognizing the boundaries that exist with even strong brands, Gallo spent heavily to launch the more upscale Turning Leaf (priced at $7 to $8 a bottle), which contained no mention of the Gallo name. Several years later, it launched Gallo of Sonoma (priced at $10 to $30 a bottle) to better compete in the premium wine segment, using the founder's grandchildren as spokespeople in an intensive push and pull campaign. With a hip, young, and fun image, case sales volume tripled to 680,000 in 1999.

Concern about the unwillingness of consumers to update their brand knowledge was what led Honda, Toyota, and Nissan to introduce their luxury car models as separate nameplates (Acura, Lexus, and Infiniti, respectively). As it turns out, product improvements to the upper ends of their brand lines since the introduction of these new car nameplates may have made it easier to bridge the gap with their brands into the luxury market.

At the same time, it is possible to use certain brand modifiers to signal a noticeable, although presumably not dramatic, quality improvement—for example, Ultra Dry Pampers, Extra Strength Tylenol, or PowerPro Dustbuster Plus. As noted earlier, Farquhar, Herr, and their colleagues state that this means of indirect extension, or "super-branding," may be less risky than direct extensions when moving a master brand up-market.[86] They recommend veiling the master brand from the customer's view. The idea would be for the new super-brand to draw attention to itself and the merits of the product and later unveil the super-brand's link to the "hidden master brand" to provide familiar reassurance to consumers. They caution that a premature connection with the master brand can generate skepticism and indecision, citing as supporting evidence Coleman's success at introducing up-market camping equipment first as Peak 1 and then only later making the Coleman connection.

Vertical extensions can be especially tricky for prestige brands. In such cases, firms must often maintain a balance between availability and scarcity such that people always aspire to be a customer and not feel excluded. By launching ambitious marketing campaigns with such offerings as "How to Buy a Diamond" and "Pearl Authority," the tony retail chain Tiffany's has attempted to convince buyers of the quality of its products and the fact that they are attainable. With an average retail price of goods sold of around $250, Tiffany's has managed to maintain its lofty image while also drawing a wider array of customers.[87]

Comparatively little empirical academic research, however, has been conducted on this topic. In an empirical study of the U.S. mountain bicycle industry, Randall, Ulrich, and Reibstein found that brand price premium was significantly positively correlated with the quality of the lowest-quality model in the product line for the lower-quality segments of the market; for the upper-quality segments of the market, brand price premium was also significantly positively correlated with the quality of the highest-quality model in the product line. They concluded that these results suggest that managers wishing to maximize the equity of their brands should offer only high-quality products and avoid offering low-quality products, although overall profit maximization could dictate a different strategy.[88]

Kirmani, Sood, and Bridges examined the "ownership effect"—whereby owners have more favorable responses than nonowners to brand extensions—in the context of brand line stretches. They found that the ownership effect occurred for upward and downward stretches of nonprestige brands (e.g., Acura) and for upward stretches of prestige brands (e.g., Calvin Klein and BMW). For downward stretches of prestige brands, however, the ownership effect did not occur because of owners' desires to maintain brand exclusivity. In this situation, a sub-branding strategy protected owners' parent brand attitudes from dilution.[89]

The most effective advertising strategy for an extension is one that emphasizes information about the extension (rather than reminders about the parent brand). A number of studies have shown that the information provided about brand extensions, by triggering selective retrieval from memory, may frame the consumer decision process and affect extension evaluations. In general, the most effective strategy appears to be one that recognizes the type of information that is already salient for the brand in the minds of consumers when they first consider the proposed extension and highlights additional information that would otherwise be overlooked or misinterpreted.

For example, Aaker and Keller found that cueing or reminding consumers about the quality of a parent brand did not improve evaluations for poorly rated extensions. Because the brands they studied were well known and well liked, such reminders may have been unnecessary. Elaborating briefly on specific extension attributes about which consumers were uncertain or concerned, however, did lead to more favorable evaluations. Bridges, Keller, and Sood found that providing information could improve perceptions of fit in the following two cases when consumers perceived low fit between the brand and the extension.

When the parent brand and the extension shared physical attributes but the parent brand image was non-product-related and based on abstract user characteristics, consumers tended to overlook an obvious explanatory link between the parent brand and extension on the basis of shared product features (e.g., a tennis shoe with a high-fashion image attempting to extend to work boots was not evaluated favorably). Information that raised the salience of the physical relationship relative to distracting non-product-related associations—a "relational" communication strategy—improved extension evaluations (e.g., when subjects were told the work boots would have leather uppers similar to those used in the tennis shoes).

When the parent brand and the extension only shared non-product-related associations and the parent brand image was product-related, consumers often made negative inferences on the basis of existing associations (e.g., a tennis shoe with an image for durability attempting to extend to swimsuits was seen as being unfashionable). In this case, providing information that established an explanatory link on an entirely new, "reassuring" association—an "elaborational" communication strategy—improved extension evaluations (e.g., when subjects were told the swimsuits would be similar in fashionability to the tennis shoes).[90]

Lane found that repetition of an ad that evoked primarily benefit brand associations could overcome negative perceptions of a highly incongruent brand extension. Moreover, for moderately incongruent brand extensions, even ads that evoked peripheral brand associations (e.g., brand packaging or character) could improve negative extension perceptions with sufficient repetition.[91] In a somewhat similar vein, Barone, Miniard, and Romeo experimentally demonstrated that positive mood primarily enhanced evaluations of extensions viewed as moderately similar (as opposed to very similar or dissimilar) to a favorably evaluated core brand.[92]

Research has also explored several other aspects of extension marketing programs. Keller and Sood found that "branding effects" in terms of inferences based on parent brand knowledge operated both in the absence and presence of product experience with an extension, although they were less pronounced or, in the case of an unambiguous negative experience, even nonexistent.[93] In considering the effects of retailer displays, Buchanan, Simmons, and Bickart found that evaluations of a "high-equity" brand could be diminished by an unfamiliar competitive brand when (1) a mixed display structure led consumers to believe that the competitive brand was diagnostic for judging the high-equity brand, (2) the precedence given to one brand over another in the display made expectations about brand differences or similarities accessible, and (3) the unfamiliar competitive brand disconfirmed these expectations.[94]

Review

This chapter examined the role of brand extensions in managing brand equity. Brand extensions are when a firm uses an established brand name to introduce a new product. Brand extensions can be distinguished by whether the new product is being introduced in a product category currently served by the parent brand (a line extension) or in a completely different product category (a category extension). Brand extensions can come in all forms. They offer many potential benefits but also can pose many problems. This chapter outlined these pros and cons and offered some simple conceptual guidelines to maximize the probability of extension success.

The basic assumptions regarding brand extensions are that consumers have some awareness of and positive associations about the parent brand in memory and that at least some of these positive associations will be evoked by the brand extension. Moreover, negative associations should not be transferred from the parent brand or created by the brand extension. The ability of the extension to establish its own equity will depend on the salience of parent brand associations in the minds of consumers in the extension context and the resulting favorability and uniqueness of any inferred associations. The ability of the extension to contribute to parent brand equity will depend on how compelling the evidence is concerning the corresponding attribute or benefit association in the extension context, how relevant or diagnostic the extension evidence is concerning the attribute or benefit for the parent brand, and how strong existing attribute or benefit associations are held in consumer memory for the parent brand.

The chapter also outlined a process to evaluate brand extension opportunities. It was argued that brand extension strategies need to be carefully considered by using managerial judgment and consumer research to systematically conduct the following steps: Define actual and desired consumer knowledge about the brand, identify possible extension candidates, evaluate the potential of extension candidates, design marketing programs to launch extensions, and evaluate extension success and effects on parent brand equity. Finally, a number of important research findings concerning brand extensions were summarized that dealt with factors affecting the acceptance of a brand extension as well as the nature of feedback to the parent brand.

Discussion Questions

1. Pick a brand extension. Use the models presented in the chapter to evaluate its ability to achieve its own equity as well as contribute to the equity of a parent brand. If you were the manager of that brand, what would you do differently?
2. Do you think a brand like Xerox will be able to transform its product meaning? What are the arguments for or against?
3. Porsche has announced that it will introduce a four-door, four-seat vehicle with a tailgate and four-wheel drive—in other words, a sports utility vehicle. Analyze the proposed extension in terms of the models in this chapter.
4. How successful do you predict these recently proposed extensions will be? Why?
   a. Johnnie Walker (famous for scotch) and upscale men's apparel (sweaters, coats, golf wear, and watches)
   b. Jockey (famous for underwear) and fitted sheets
   c. Victoria's Secret (famous for lingerie) and laundry detergent
   d. Victorinox (famous for Swiss Army knives) and computer cases, briefcases, and travel gear
5. In launching the new Jaguar X-series in February 2001, priced at $29,500 and dubbed the "Baby Jag," Jaguar's president commented, "We have always been aspirational; now we want to be accessible." Comment.

B r a n d   F o c u s   1 2 . 0

Guidelines for Profitable Line Extensions

In a perceptive and illuminating analysis, Quelch and Kenney persuasively argue that unchecked product-line expansion can weaken a brand's image, disturb trade relations, and disguise cost increases.[95] In describing the lure of line extensions, Quelch and Kenny began by noting seven factors that explain why so many companies have aggressively pursued such a strategy:

1. *Customer segmentation:* Line extensions are seen as a low-cost, low-risk way to meet the needs of target market segments, which can be increasingly refined due to sophisticated marketing research, advertising media, and direct marketing practices.

2. *Consumer desires:* More consumers than ever are switching brands and making in-store purchase decisions. A full brand line can offer "something for everyone" and attracts consumer attention.

3. *Pricing breadth:* Line extensions give marketers the opportunity to offer a broader range of price points in order to capture a wider audience.

4. *Excess capacity:* Many companies have added faster production lines without retiring older ones. These already existing manufacturing capabilities can often be easily modified to produce line extensions.

5. *Short-term gain:* Many managers believe line extensions offer immediate rewards with minimal risk. Similar to sales promotions, line extensions are seen as a dependable, quick fix to improve sales.

6. *Competitive intensity:* Many managers also believe that extensions can expand the retail shelf space for the category, or at least that amount devoted to the brand itself. Frequent line extensions are often used by major brands to raise the admission price to the category for newly branded or private

label competitors and to drain the limited resources of third- and fourth-place brands.

7. *Trade pressure:* The proliferation of different types of retail channels—often demanding their own special versions of the brand to suit their marketing needs or to reduce price-shopping by consumers—necessitates a more varied product line.

Quelch and Kenny continue by noting that although it is easy to understand why line extensions have been so widely embraced against such a backdrop, managers are also discovering problems and risks from brand proliferation.

➤ *Weaker line logic:* Because managers often extend a line without removing any existing items, the strategic role of each item becomes muddled. As a result, retailers may fail to stock the entire line or even appropriate items. A disorganized product line may result in consumers seeking out a simple, all-purpose product as a result.

➤ *Lower brand loyalty:* Although line extensions can help a single brand satisfy a consumer's diverse needs, they can also motivate customers to seek variety and hence indirectly encourage brand switching. If line extensions result in cannibalization, a suboptimal shift in marketing support, or a blurring in image, the long-term health of the brand franchise will be weakened.

➤ *Underexploited ideas:* Some important new products justify the creation of a new brand, and potential long-term profits may suffer if such products are introduced as an extension.

➤ *Stagnant category demand:* A review of several product categories (pet food, crackers and cookies, ketchup, coffee, shampoo and conditioner, cake mix and frosting, and spaghetti sauce) reveals that line extensions rarely expand total category demand.

➤ *Poorer trade relations:* An explosion of line extensions in virtually every product category has put a squeeze on available shelf space. As manufacturers' credibility has declined, retailers have allocated more shelf space to their own private label products. Competition among manufacturers for limited shelf space has escalated overall promotion expenditures and shifted margin to increasingly powerful retailers.

➤ *More competitor opportunities:* By spreading marketing efforts across a range of line extensions, some of the most popular entries in the brand line may be vulnerable to well-positioned and supported competitors.

➤ *Increased costs:* Although marketers can correctly anticipate many of the increased costs of extensions, other possible complications may be overlooked, such as fragmentation of the marketing effort and dilution of the brand image, increased production complexities resulting from shorter production runs and more frequent line changeovers, more errors in forecasting demand, increased logistics complexity, increased supplier costs, and distraction of the research and development group from new product development.

➤ *Hidden costs:* Although these increased costs may make it difficult for a line extension to increase demand enough or command a high enough margin to achieve profitability, they remain hidden for several reasons. Traditional cost accounting systems allocate overheads to items in proportion to their sales, which can overburden the high sellers and undercharge the slow movers. Moreover, because line extensions are added one at a time, it is easy to overlook broader cost considerations that may affect or be affected by the entire brand line.

Quelch and Kenny conclude their analysis by offering eight directives to help marketing managers improve their product-line strategies:

1. *Improve cost accounting.* Study, in detail, the absolute and incremental costs associated with the production and distribution of each stock-keeping unit (SKU) from the beginning to the end of the value chain, accounting for timing of demand. Target underperforming SKUs and consider the incremental sales, costs, and savings of adding a new SKU.

2. *Allocate resources to winners.* To avoid undersupporting new, up-and-coming SKUs and oversupporting long-established SKUs whose appeal may be weakening, use an accurate activity-based cost-accounting system combined with an annual zero-based appraisal of each SKU to ensure a focused product line that optimizes the company's use of manufacturing capacity, advertising and promotion dollars, sales force time, and available retail space.

3. *Research consumer behavior.* Make an effort to learn how consumers perceive and use each SKU, especially in terms of loyalty and switching patterns among SKUs. Identify core items that have a long-standing appeal to loyal heavy users and other items that reinforce and expand usage among existing customers. Consider a third set of SKUs to attract new customers or to persuade multi-brand users to buy more from the same line more often.

4. *Apply the line logic test.* Ensure that everyone who may affect the success of the marketing program (e.g., salespeople) is able to state in one sentence the strategic role that a given SKU plays in the brand line. Similarly, ensure that the consumer is able to understand quickly which SKU fits his or her needs.

5. *Coordinate marketing across the line.* Adopt consistent and logical pricing and packaging to simplify understanding of the brand line by salespeople, trade partners, customers, and others.

6. *Work with channel partners.* To improve trade relations and new product acceptance, set up multifunctional teams to screen new product ideas and arrange in-store testing with leading trade customers in order to research, in advance, the sales and cost effects of adding new SKUs to the brand line.

7. *Expect product-line turnover.* Foster a climate in which product-line deletions are not only accepted but also encouraged.

8. *Manage deletions.* If items identified as unprofitable cannot be quickly and easily restored to profitability, develop a deletion plan that addresses customers' needs while managing costs.

In related research, Reddy, Holak, and Bhat studied the determinants of line extension success using data on 75 line extensions of 34 cigarette brands over a 20-year period.[96] The major findings from their study reinforce many of the Quelch and Kenney conclusions, indicating that

➤ Line extensions of strong brands are more successful than extensions of weak brands.

➤ Line extensions of symbolic brands enjoy greater market success than those of less symbolic brands.

➤ Line extensions that receive strong advertising and promotional support are more successful than those extensions that receive meager support.

➤ Line extensions entering earlier into a product subcategory are more successful than extensions entering later, but only if they are extensions of strong brands.

➤ Firm size and marketing competencies also play a part in an extension's success.

➤ Earlier line extensions have helped in the market expansion of the parent brand.

➤ Incremental sales generated by line extensions may more than compensate for the loss in sales due to cannibalization

Notes

1. For a more comprehensive treatment, see Glen Urban and John Hauser, *Design and Marketing of New Products*, 2nd ed. (Upper Saddle River, NJ: Prentice-Hall, 1993).

2. Peter Farquhar, "Managing Brand Equity," *Marketing Research* 1 (September 1989): 24–33.

3. Edward M. Tauber, "Brand Leverage: Strategy for Growth in a Cost Controlled World," Journal of Marketing Research 28, (August/September 1988): 26–30.

4. Robert M. McMath, "The Vagaries of Brand Equity" (paper presented at the ARF Fourth Annual Advertising and Promotion Workshop, February 12-13, 1992).

5. Byung-Do Kim and Mary W. Sullivan, "The Effect of Brand Experience on Extension Choice Probabilities: An Empirical Analysis," working paper, University of Chicago Graduate School of Business, 1995.

6. Henry J. Claycamp and Lucien E. Liddy, "Prediction of New Product Performance: An Analytical Approach," *Journal of Marketing Research* (November 1969): 414–420.

7. Kevin Lane Keller and David A. Aaker, "The Effects of Sequential Introduction of Brand Extensions," *Journal of Marketing Research* 29 (February 1992): 35–50; John Milewicz and Paul Herbig, "Evaluating the Brand Extension Decision Using a Model of Reputation Building," *Journal of Product & Brand Management* 3, no. 1 (1994): 39–47.

8. See also Jonlee Andrews, "Rethinking the Effect of Perceived Fit on Customers' Evaluations of New Products," *Journal of the Academy of Marketing Science* 23, no. 1 (1995): 4–14.

9. David B. Montgomery, "New Product Distribution: An Analysis of Supermarket Buyer Decisions," *Journal of Marketing Research* 12, no. 3 (1978): 255–264.

10. David A. Aaker and Ziv Carmon, "The Effectiveness of Brand Name Strategies at Creating Brand Recall," working paper, University of California at Berkeley, 1992.

11. Mary W. Sullivan, "Brand Extensions: When to Use Them," *Management Science* 38, no. 6 (June 1992): 793–806.

12. Daniel C. Smith, "Brand Extension and Advertising Efficiency: What Can and Cannot Be Expected," *Journal of Advertising Research* (November/December 1992): 11–20. See also Daniel C. Smith and C. Whan

Park, "The Effects of Brand Extensions on Market Share and Advertising Efficiency," *Journal of Marketing Research* 29 (August 1992): 296–313.

13. Mary W. Sullivan, "Measuring Image Spillovers in Umbrella-branded Products," *Journal of Business* 63, no. 3 (1990): 309–329.

14. Ronald Alsop, "It's Slim Pickings in Product Name Game," *Wall Street Journal,* 29 November 1988, B1.

15. Laurie Freeman, "Helene Curtis Relies on Finesse," *Advertising Age*, 14 July 1986, 2.

16. Kevin Goldman, "Xerox Touts Array of Products to Broaden Image Beyond Copiers," *Wall Street Journal*, 4 August 1994, B12; Tim Smart, "Can Xerox Duplicate Its Glory Days?" *Business Week*, 4 October 1993, 56–58; Subrata N. Chakravarty, "Back in Focus," *Forbes*, 6 June 1994, 72–76.

17. Theodore Levitt, "Marketing Myopia," *Harvard Business Review* (July–August 1960): 45–46.

18. Harold Thorkilsen, "Manager's Journal: Lessons of the Great Cranberry Crisis," *Wall Street Journal*, 21 December 1987, 20.

19. Keller and Aaker, "Effects of Sequential Introduction of Brand Extensions."

20. Judith Valente, "A New Brand Restores Sparkle to Waterford," *Wall Street Journal*, 10 November 1994, B1, B4.

21. Ira Teinowitz and Jennifer Lawrence, "Brand Proliferation Attacked," *Advertising Age*, 10 May 1993, 1, 48. The product categories studied were spaghetti sauce, toilet tissue, pet food, salad dressing, cereal, and toothpaste.

22. For additional support, see Peter Boatwright and Joseph C. Nunes, "Reducing Assortment: An Attribute-Based Approach," *Journal of Marketing* 65 (July 2001): 50–63.

23. B. G. Yovovich, "Hit and Run: Cadillac's Costly Mistake," *Adweek's Marketing Week*, 8 August 1988, 24.

24. Sullivan, "Measuring Image Spillovers."

25. Maureen Morrin, "The Impact of Brand Extensions on Parent Brand Memory Structures and Retrieval Processes," *Journal of Marketing Research* 36, no. 4 (1999): 517–525.

26. Al Ries and Jack Trout, *Positioning: The Battle for Your Mind* (New York: McGraw-Hill, 1985).

27. Joseph Weber, "Scott Rolls Out a Risky Strategy," *Business Week*, 22 May 1995, 48.

28. Peter H. Farquhar, "Managing Brand Equity," *Marketing Research* 1 (September 1989): 24–33.

29. For a review of some of the early brand extension literature, see Elyette Roux and Frederic Lorange, "Brand Extension Research: A Typology," working paper DR 92033, CERESSEC (Centre d'Etudes et de Recherche de l'ESSEC), Cergy Pontoise Cedex, France, 1993.

30. Kalpesh Kaushik Desai, Wayne D. Hoyer, and Rajendra Srivastava, "Evaluation of Brand Extension Relative to the Extension Category Competition: The Role of Attribute Inheritance from Parent Brand and Extension Category," working paper, State University of New York at Buffalo, 1996.

31. Edward M. Tauber, "Brand Leverage: Strategy for Growth in a Cost-Control World," *Journal of Advertising Research* (August/September 1988): 26–30.

32. B. Loken and D. Roedder John, "Diluting Brand Beliefs. When Do Brand Extensions Have a Negative Impact?" *Journal of Marketing* 57, no. 7 (1993): 71–84.

33. John M. Murphy, *Brand Strategy* (New York: Prentice-Hall, 1990).

34. Andrea Rothman, "France's Bic Bets U.S. Consumers Will Go for Perfume on the Cheap," *Wall Street Journal*, 12 January 1989, B6.

35. Seema Nayyar, "In Your Face," *Brandweek*, 7 December 1992; Dave Kansas, "Mouthwash Makers See Sales Evaporate," *Wall Street Journal*, 1 December 1992; Jennifer Reingold, "Above the Neck," *FW*, 18 January 1994; "Oral Care Products: Mouthwashes," *OTC Update*, 1 September 1996.

36. Laura Zinn, "Does Pepsi Have Too Many Products?" *Business Week*, 14 February 1994, 64–68.

37. Murphy, *Brand Strategy*.

38. Jean-Noel Kapferer, *Strategic Brand Management* (London: Kogan Page, 1992).

39. Max Sutherland and Bruce Smith, "Communicating Kinship: Beware Mistaken

Identity in Brand Extensions," *Journal of Brand Management* 1, no. 2 (1993): 90–93.

40. Mita Sujan, "Nature and Structure of Product Categories," working paper, Pennsylvania State University; 1990 Joan Myers-Levy and Alice M. Tybout, "Schema Congruity as a Basis for Product Evaluation," *Journal of Consumer Research* 16 (June 1989): 39–54.

41. Deborah Roedder John and Barbara Loken, "Diluting Brand Equity: The Impact of Brand Extensions," *Journal of Marketing* (July 1993): 71–84.

42. David Boush and Barbara Loken, "A Process Tracing Study of Brand Extension Evaluations," *Journal of Marketing Research* 28 (February 1991): 16–28; Cathy L. Hartman, Linda L. Price, and Calvin P. Duncan, "Consumer Evaluation of Franchise Extension Products: A Categorization Processing Perspective," *Advances in Consumer Research*, Vol. 17 (Provo, UT: Association for Consumer Research, 1990): 120–126.

43. David A. Aaker and Kevin Lane Keller, "Consumer Evaluations of Brand Extensions," *Journal of Marketing* 54 (January 1990): 27–41.

44. P. A. Bottomly and Stephen Holden, "The Formation of Attitudes towards Brand Extensions: Empirical Generalizations Based on Secondary Analysis of Eight Studies," *Journal of Marketing Research* (November 2001): 494.

45. David Boush, Shannon Shipp, Barbara Loken, Ezra Gencturk, Susan Crockett, Ellen Kennedy, Betty Minshall, Dennis Misurell, Linda Rochford, and Jon Strobel, "Affect Generalization to Similar and Dissimilar Line Extensions," *Psychology and Marketing* 4 (Fall 1987): 225–241.

46. On the other hand, applying Mandler's congruity theory, Meyers-Levy and her colleagues showed that suggested products associated with moderately incongruent brand names could be preferred over ones that were associated with either congruent or extremely incongruent brand names. They interpreted this finding in terms of the ability of moderately incongruent brand extensions to elicit more processing from consumers that could be satisfactorily resolved (assuming consumers could identify a meaningful relationship between the brand name and the product). See J. Meyers-Levy, T. A. Louie, and M. T. Curren, "How Does the Congruity of Brand Names Affect Evaluations of Brand Name Extensions?" *Journal of Applied Psychology* 79, no. 1 (1994): 46–53.

47. Deborah MacInnis and Kent Nakamoto, "Cognitive Associations and Product Category Comparisons: The Role of Knowledge Structures and Context," working paper, University of Arizona, 1990.

48. C. Whan Park, Sandra Milberg, and Robert Lawson, "Evaluation of Brand Extensions: The Role of Product Level Similarity and Brand Concept Consistency," *Journal of Consumer Research* 18 (September 1991): 185–193.

49. Susan M. Broniarczyk and Joseph W. Alba, "The Importance of the Brand in Brand Extension," *Journal of Marketing Research* 31 (May 1994): 214–228. Incidentally, although a Crest toothbrush was not available at the time that this study was conducted, one was later in fact introduced as Crest Complete.

50. T. H. A. Bijmolt, M. Wedel, R. G. M. Pieters, and W. S. DeSarbo, "Judgments of Brand Similarity," *International Journal of Research in Marketing* 15 (1998): 249–268.

51. Sheri Bridges, Kevin Lane Keller, and Sanjay Sood, "Explanatory Links and the Perceived Fit of Brand Extensions: The Role of Dominant Parent Brand Associations and Communication Strategies," *Journal of Advertising* 29, no. 4 (2000): 1–11.

52. B. H. Schmitt and L. Dubé, "Contextualized Representations of Brand Extensions: Are Feature Lists or Frames the Basic Components of Consumer Cognition?" *Marketing Letters* 3, no. 2 (1992): 115–126.

53. D. M. Boush, "Brand Name Effects on Interproduct Similarity Judgments," *Marketing Letters* 8, no. 4 (1997): 419–427.

54. D. C. Smith and Jonlee Andrews, "Rethinking the Effect of Perceived Fit on Customers' Evaluations of New Products," *Journal of the Academy of Marketing Science* 23, no. 1 (1995): 4–14.

55. A. V. Muthukrishnan and Barton A. Weitz, "Role of Product Knowledge in Brand

Extensions," in *Advances in Consumer Research*, Vol. 18, eds. Rebecca H. Holman and Michael R. Solomon (Provo, UT: Association for Consumer Research, 1990), 407–413.

56. Broniarcysyk and Alba, "Importance of the Brand."

57. Keller and Aaker, "Effects of Sequential Introduction of Brand Extensions."

58. See also Arvind Rangaswamy, Raymond Burke, and Terence A. Oliva, "Brand Equity and the Extendibility of Brand Names," *International Journal of Research in Marketing* 10 (1993): 61–75.

59. See, for example, Peter H. Farquhar and Paul M. Herr, "The Dual Structure of Brand Associations," in *Brand Equity and Advertising: Advertising's Role in Building Strong Brands*, eds. David A. Aaker and Alexander L. Biel (Hillsdale, NJ: Lawrence Erlbaum Associates, 1993), 263–277.

60. Ian M. Lewis, "Brand Equity or Why the Board of Directors Needs Marketing Research" (paper presented at the ARF Fifth Annual Advertising and Promotion Workshop, February 1, 1993).

61. Stephen Phillips, "Chiquita May Be a Little Too Ripe," *Business Week*, 30 April 1990, 100.

62. Robert D. Hof, "A Washout for Clorox?" *Business Week*, 9 July 1990, 32–33; Alicia Swasy, "P&G and Clorox Wade into Battle over the Bleaches," *Wall Street Journal*, 16 January 1989, 5; Maria Shao, "A Bright Idea that Clorox Wishes It Never Had," *Business Week*, 24 June 1991, 118–119.

63. Peter H. Farquhar, Julia Y. Han, Paul M. Herr, and Yuji Ijiri, "Strategies for Leveraging Master Brands," *Marketing Research* (September 1992): 32–43.

64. P. M. Herr, P. H. Farquhar, and R. H. Fazio, "Impact of Dominance and Relatedness on Brand Extensions," *Journal of Consumer Psychology* 5, no. 2 (1996): 135–159.

65. Farquhar, Han, Herr, and Ijiri, "Strategies for Leveraging Master Brands."

66. Bridges, Keller, and Sood, "Explanatory Links."

67. C. Joiner and B. Loken, "The Inclusion Effect and Category-Based Induction: Theory and Application to Brand

Categories," *Journal of Consumer Psychology* 7, no. 2 (1998): 101–129.

68. Bridges, Keller, and Sood, "Explanatory Links and the Perceived Fit of Brand Extensions."

69. Frank Kardes and Chris Allen, "Perceived Variability and Inferences about Brand Extensions," in *Advances in Consumer Research*, Vol. 18, eds. Rebecca H. Holman and Michael R. Solomon (Provo, UT: Association for Consumer Research, 1990), 392–398.

70. See also Sandy D. Jap, "An Examination of the Effects of Multiple Brand Extensions on the Brand Concept," in *Advances in Consumer Research*, Vol. 20 (Provo, UT: Association for Consumer Research, 1993), 607–611.

71. Murphy, *Brand Strategy*.

72. Boush and Loken, "Process Tracing Study."

73. Peter Dacin and Daniel C. Smith, "The Effect of Brand Portfolio Characteristics on Consumer Evaluations of Brand Extensions," *Journal of Marketing Research* 31 (May 1994): 229–242. See also Boush and Loken, "Process Tracing Study"; and Niraj Dawar, "Extensions of Broad Brands: The Role of Retrieval in Evaluations of Fit," *Journal of Consumer Psychology* 5, no. 2 (1996): 189–207.

74. M. W. Sullivan, "Brand Extensions: When to Use Them," *Management Science* 38, no. 6 (1992): 793–806.

75. P. DeGraba and M. W. Sullivan, "Spillover Effects, Cost Savings, R&D and the Use of Brand Extensions," *International Journal of Industrial Organization* 13 (1995): 229–248.

76. Deborah Roedder John and Barbara Loken, "Diluting Brand Beliefs: When Do Brand Extensions Have a Negative Impact?" *Journal of Marketing* 57 (Summer 1993): 71.

77. Jean B. Romeo, "The Effect of Negative Information on the Evaluation of Brand Extensions and the Family Brand," in *Advances in Consumer Research*, Vol. 18, eds. Rebecca H. Holman and Michael R. Solomon (Provo, UT: Association for Consumer Research, 1990), 399–406.

78. D. Roedder John, B. Loken, and C. Joiner, "The Negative Impact of Extensions: Can Flagship Products Be Diluted?" *Journal of Marketing* 62 (January 1998): 19–32.

79. Z. Gürhan-Canli and D. Maheswaran, "The Effects of Extensions on Brand Name Dilution and Enhancement," *Journal of Marketing Research* 35, no. 11 (1998): 464–473.

80. S. J. Milberg, C. W. Park, and M. S. McCarthy, "Managing Negative Feedback Effects Associated with Brand Extensions: The Impact of Alternative Branding Strategies," *Journal of Consumer Psychology* 6, no. 2 (1997): 119–140.

81. V. R. Lane and R. Jacobson, "Stock Market Reactions to Brand Extension Announcements: The Effects of Brand Attitude and Familiarity," *Journal of Marketing* 59, no. 1 (1995): 63–77.

82. A. Kirmani, S. Sood, and S. Bridges, "The Ownership Effect in Consumer Responses to Brand Line Stretches," *Journal of Marketing* 63, no. 1 (1999): 88–101.

83. Maureen Morrin, "The Impact of Brand Extensions on Parent Brand Memory Structures and Retrieval Processes," *Journal of Marketing Research* 36, no. 4 (1999): 517–525.

84. For related research, see Carol M. Motely and Srinivas K. Reddy, "Moving Up or Down: An Investigation of Repositioning Strategies," working paper 93–363, University of Georgia, Athens, 1993; and Carol M. Motely, "Vertical Extensions: Strategies for Changing Brand Prestige," working paper, University of Georgia, Athens, 1993.

85. Joshua Levine, "Pride Goeth Before a Fall," *Forbes*, 29 May 1989, 306.

86. Farquhar, Han, Herr, and Ijiri, "Strategies for Leveraging Master Brands."

87. Lori Bongiorno, "How Tiffany's Took the Tarnish Off," *Business Week*, 26 August 1996, 67–69.

88. T. Randall, K. Ulrich, and D. Reibstein, "Brand Equity and Vertical Product Line Extent," *Marketing Science* 17, no. 4 (1998): 356–379.

89. Kirmani, Sood, and Bridges, "The Ownership Effect."

90. Bridges, Keller, and Sood, "Explanatory Links."

91. V. R. Lane, "The Impact of Ad Repetition and Ad Content on Consumer Perceptions of Incongruent Extensions," *Journal of Marketing* 64, no. 4 (2000): 80–91.

92. M. J. Barone, P. W. Miniard, and J. B. Romeo, "The Influence of Positive Mood on Brand Extension Evaluations," *Journal of Consumer Research* 26, no. 3 (2000): 386–400.

93. Kevin Lane Keller and Sanjay Sood, "The Effects of Product Experience and Branding Strategies on Brand Evaluations," working paper, University of California, Los Angeles, 2000.

94. L. Buchanan, C. J. Simmons, and B. A. Bickart, "Brand Equity Dilution: Retailer Display and Context Brand Effects," *Journal of Marketing Research* 36, no. 8 (1999): 345–355.

95. John A. Quelch and David Kenny, "Extend Profits, Not Product Lines," *Harvard Business Review* (September–October 1994): 153–160. See also the commentary on this article and the issue of product line management in "The Logic of Line Extensions," *Harvard Business Review* (November–December 1994): 53–62.

96. Srinivas K. Reddy, Susan L. Holak, and Sbodh Bhat, "To Extend or Not to Extend: Success Determinants of Line Extensions," *Journal of Marketing Research* 31 (May 1994): 243–262. For some conceptual discussion, see Kalpesh Kaushik Desai and Wayne D. Hoyer, "Line Extensions: A Categorization and an Information Processing Perspective," in *Advances in Consumer Research*, Vol. 20 (Provo, UT: Association for Consumer Research, 1993), 599–606.

CHAPTER

13

Managing Brands over Time

PREVIEW

As noted in Chapter 1, one of the challenges in managing brands is the many changes that have occurred in the marketing environment in recent years. Undoubtedly, the marketing environment will continue to evolve and change, often in very significant ways, in the coming years. Shifts in consumer behavior, competitive strategies,

government regulations, or other aspects of the marketing environment can profoundly affect the fortunes of a brand. Besides these external forces, the firm itself may
engage in a variety of activities and changes in strategic focus or direction that may
necessitate minor or major adjustments in the way that its brands are being marketed.
Consequently, effective brand management requires proactive strategies designed to at
least maintain—if not actually enhance—customer-based brand equity in the face of
all of these different forces.

This chapter considers how to best manage brands over time. Effective brand management requires taking a long-term view of marketing decisions. Any action that a
firm takes as part of its marketing program has the potential to change consumer
knowledge about the brand in terms of some aspect of brand awareness or brand
image. These changes in consumer brand knowledge will have an indirect effect on the
success of *future* marketing activities. Thus, from the perspective of customer-based
brand equity, it is important to consider how the changes in brand awareness and
image that could result from a particular marketing decision may help or hurt *subsequent* marketing decisions (see Figure 13-1). For example, the frequent use of sales promotions involving temporary price decreases may create or strengthen a "discount"
association to the brand, with potentially adverse implications on customer loyalty and

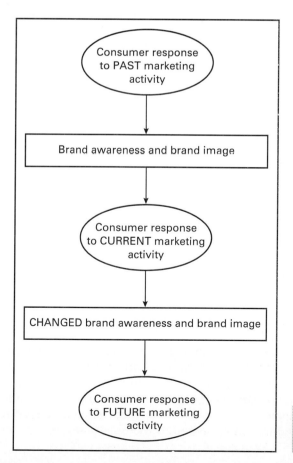

FIGURE 13-1   Understanding the
Long-Term Effects of Marketing Actions
on Brand Equity

responses to future price changes or non-price-oriented marketing communication efforts. Unfortunately, marketers may have a particularly difficult time trying to anticipate future consumer response: If the new knowledge structures that will influence future consumer response do not exist until the short-term marketing actions actually occur, how can future consumer response be realistically simulated to permit accurate predictions?

The main assertion of this chapter is that brand equity must be actively managed over time by reinforcing the brand meaning and, if necessary, by making adjustments to the marketing program to identify new sources of brand equity. In considering these two topics, this chapter examines a number of different issues, including the advantages of maintaining brand consistency, the importance of protecting sources of brand equity, tradeoffs between fortifying and leveraging brands, and different possible brand revitalization strategies. Brand Focus 13.0 considers how to change a corporate name.

REINFORCING BRANDS

How should brand equity be reinforced over time? How can marketers make sure that consumers have the desired knowledge structures such that their brands continue to have the necessary sources of brand equity? In a general sense, brand equity is reinforced by marketing actions that consistently convey the meaning of the brand to consumers in terms of brand awareness and brand image. Questions marketers should consider are as follows:

➤ *What products does the brand represent, what benefits does it supply, and what needs does it satisfy?* For example, Nutri-Grain has expanded from cereals into granola bars and other products, cementing its reputation as "makers of healthy breakfast and snack foods."

➤ *How does the brand make those products superior? What strong, favorable, and unique brand associations exist in the minds of consumers?* For example, through product development and the successful introduction of brand extensions, Black & Decker is now seen as offering "innovative designs" in its small appliance products.

Both of these issues—brand meaning in terms of products, benefits, and needs as well as in terms of product differentiation—depend on the firm's general approach to product development, branding strategies, and other strategic concerns, as was discussed in Chapters 11 and 12. This section reviews some other important considerations concerning brand reinforcement.

Maintaining Brand Consistency

Without question, the most important consideration in reinforcing brands is the consistency of the marketing support that the brand receives, both in terms of the amount and nature of that support. Brand consistency is critical to maintaining the strength and favorability of brand associations. Brands that receive inadequate support in terms of shrinking research and development and marketing communication budgets run the risk of becoming technologically disadvantaged—or even obsolete—as well as out-of-date, irrelevant, or forgotten.

Market Leaders and Failures

From the perspective of maintaining consumer loyalty, inadequate marketing support is an especially dangerous strategy when combined with price increases. An example of the consequences of failing to adequately support a brand occurred in the oil and gas industry. In the late 1970s, consumers had an extremely positive image of Shell Oil and saw clear differences between the brand and its major branded competitors. In the early 1980s, for various reasons, Shell went through a period of time during which it cut back considerably on its advertising and marketing support for the brand. As a result, Shell no longer enjoyed the same special status in the eyes of consumers and was seen as much more similar to other oil companies.

In terms of qualitative aspects of positioning, an even cursory examination of the brands that have maintained market leadership for the last 50 or 100 years or so is a testament to the advantages of staying consistent. Brands such as Budweiser, Coca-Cola, Hershey, and others have been remarkably consistent in their strategies once they achieved a preeminent market leadership position.

Marlboro

Philip Morris has single-mindedly focused its marketing communications for its Marlboro cigarette brand on a western cowboy image. Ironically, Marlboro was once a brand that was targeted to women. In the roaring '20s, Marlboro cigarettes were made with a rose-colored tip so that the red imprint of women's lipstick would not show. The brand at that time was backed by ads with the slogan "Mild as May." When filtered cigarettes became popular in the 1950s, Philip Morris decided to reposition the struggling brand. Packaging was redesigned to include the trademark red and white graphics and the innovative flip-top box. An authentic western image was achieved by using real cowboys from western ranches in its ads. Since the mid-1970s, Marlboro has been America's number one cigarette brand. The romantic images of the rugged cowboy have since been taken worldwide and even successfully transferred to billboards and print ads when cigarette commercials were banned from television and radio.[1]

Perhaps an even more compelling demonstration of the benefits of consistency is to consider the fortunes of those brands that have been inconsistent in their marketing program—for example, by constantly repositioning or changing ad agencies. One such brand is Burger King. Since its highly successful mid-1970s "Have It Your Way" campaign that touted the uniqueness and quality of its hamburgers, Burger King suffered through 20 years of false starts and wrong turns in brand support (see Figure 13-2). The disastrous $40 million Herb campaign in 1985—featuring a nerd-like character who was supposed to be the only person in America never to have tasted a Whopper—was pulled after only three months. While watching its market share of the total fast food market drop, Burger King went through four marketing chiefs and six presidents and CEOs from 1993 to 2001. Only in recent years, when Burger King advertising returned to perhaps the chain's greatest competitive strength—the popular Whopper hamburger and overall menu quality—did the company's fortunes revive, although it still continues to struggle to maintain consistency throughout its marketing program.

McDonald's has also employed many different slogans and ad campaigns over the years, but these advertising efforts all reflected the core values and associations for the

Years	Slogan
1974–1976	Have it your way.
1976–1978	America loves burgers and we're America's Burger King.
1978	Best darn burger.
1979–1982	Make it special, make it Burger King.
1982–1985	Battle of the burgers: Aren't you hungry for Burger King now?
1985	Search for Herb.
1986	This is a Burger King town.
1987	The best food for fast times.
1987–1989	We do it like you'd do it.
1989–1991	Sometimes you've gotta break the rules.
1991	Your way. Right away.
1992–1993	BK Tee Vee: I love this place.
1994–1999	Get your burger's worth.
2000	Got the urge?
2001	The Whopper says . . .

FIGURE 13-2   Burger King's Ad History

brand. For example, McDonald's 1995 ad theme, "Have You Had Your Break Today?" was a throwback to its 1970s ad campaign, "You Deserve a Break Today." The slogan was a clever way to capitalize on the good feelings and product meaning embedded in the old slogan—reminding consumers of the efficiency, convenience, and friendliness of McDonald's service—while providing a new twist and stronger call to action. In 2000, McDonald's adopted a new slogan, "Smile," with the refrain "We love to see you smile"—a similar evolution of its brand promise.

Consistency and Change

Consistency does *not* mean, however, that marketers should avoid making any changes in the marketing program. On the contrary, the opposite can be quite true: Being consistent in managing brand equity may require numerous tactical shifts and changes in order to maintain the strategic thrust and direction of the brand. As earlier chapters in the book described, brand awareness and brand image can be created, maintained, or improved in many ways through properly designed marketing programs. The tactics that may be most effective for a particular brand at any one time can certainly vary. As a consequence, prices may move up or down, product features may be added or dropped, ad campaigns may employ different creative strategies and slogans, different brand extensions may be introduced or withdrawn, and so on over time in order to create the *same* desired knowledge structures in consumer's minds. Nevertheless, despite these different types of changes in marketing programs, the strategic positioning of many leading brands has remained remarkably consistent over time. A contributing factor to the success of these brands is that despite these tactical changes, certain key elements of the marketing program are always retained and continuity has been preserved in brand meaning over time.

In fact, many brands have kept a key creative element in their marketing communication programs over the years and, as a result, have effectively created some "advertising equity." For example, Nestea iced tea has used the "Nestea Plunge" in ads and promotions for years. Jack Daniels bourbon whiskey has stuck with rural scenes of its Tennessee home and the slogan "Charcoal Mellowed Drop by Drop" literally for decades. Recognizing the latent value of past advertising, recent years have seen the return of such advertising icons as Colonel Sanders for KFC, Charlie the Tuna for StarKist tuna, American Tourister's luggage-thumping gorilla, the percolating Maxwell House coffee and sing-song Oscar Mayer wiener jingles, the Culligan lady who shouts "Hey, Culligan Man!" for the bottled water, the little girl in the Shake 'n' Bake coating ad who proudly proclaims "An' I Halped," and so on.

These ads should have a ring of familiarity to baby boom consumers, serving as a pleasant reminder of younger, perhaps simpler days. Dubbed *retro-branding* or *retro-advertising* by some marketing pundits, the tactic is a means to tie in with past advertising that was, and perhaps could still be, a key source of brand equity. Most important, it may activate and strengthen brand associations that would be virtually impossible to recreate with new advertising today. From an awareness standpoint, such efforts obviously make sense. At the same time, it is important to determine whether these old advertising elements have enduring meaning with older consumers and, at the same time, can be made to seem relevant to younger consumers. More generally, the entire marketing program should be examined to determine which elements are making a strong contribution to brand equity and therefore must be protected, as discussed next.

Protecting Sources of Brand Equity

Consistency therefore should be viewed in terms of strategic direction and not necessarily the particular tactics employed by the supporting marketing program for the brand at any point in time. Unless there is some change with either consumers, competition, or the company that makes the strategic positioning of the brand less powerful (e.g., changes that somehow make the points of difference or points of parity for the brand less desirable or deliverable), there is likely to be little need to deviate from a successful positioning. Although brands should always look for potentially powerful new sources of brand equity, a top priority under these circumstances is to preserve and defend those sources of brand equity that already exist, as illustrated by the examples of Cascade and Intel.

While rolling out its value-pricing initiative, Procter & Gamble made a minor change in the formulation of its Cascade automatic dishwashing detergent, primarily for cost-savings reasons. As a result, the product was not quite as effective as it previously had been under certain, albeit somewhat atypical, water conditions. After discovering the fact, one of P&G's chief competitors, Lever Brothers, began running comparative ads for its Sunlight brand featuring side-by-side glasses that claimed, "Sunlight Fights Spots Better Than Cascade." Since the consumer benefit of "virtually spotless" is a key brand association and source of brand equity for Cascade, P&G reacted swiftly. It immediately returned Cascade to its original formula and contacted Lever Brothers to inform that company of the change, effectively forcing it to stop running the new Sunlight ads on legal grounds. As this episode clearly demonstrates, Procter & Gamble fiercely defends the equity of its brands, perhaps explaining why so many of P&G's brands have had such longevity.

As another example, consider the public relations problems encountered by Intel Corporation with the "floating decimal" problem in its Pentium microprocessors in December 1994. Although the flaw in the chip resulted in miscalculation problems in only extremely unusual and rare instances, Intel was probably at fault—as company executives now admit—for not identifying the problem and proposing remedies to consumers more quickly. Once the problem became public, Intel endured an agonizing six-week period during which the company was the focus of media scrutiny and criticism for its reluctance to publicize the problem and its failure to offer replacement chips. Two key sources of brand equity for Intel microprocessors like the Pentium—emphasized throughout the company's marketing program—are "power" and "safety." Although consumers primarily think of safety in terms of upgradability, the perceptions of financial risk or other problems that might result from a potentially flawed chip certainly should have created a sense of urgency within Intel to protect one of its prize sources of brand equity. Eventually, Intel capitulated and offered a replacement chip. Perhaps not surprisingly, only a very small percentage of consumers (an estimated 1 percent to 3 percent) actually requested a replacement chip, suggesting that it was Intel's stubbornness to act and not the defect per se that rankled many consumers. Although it was a painful episode, Intel maintains it learned a lot about how to manage its brand in the process.

Ideally, key sources of brand equity are of enduring value. If so, these brand associations should be guarded and nurtured carefully. Unfortunately, their value can easily be overlooked as marketers attempt to expand the meaning of their brands and add new product-related or non-product-related brand associations. The next section considers these types of tradeoffs. Brand Focus 13.0 deals with the topic of corporate rebranding and name changes.

Fortifying versus Leveraging

As Chapters 4 to 7 described, there are a number of different ways to raise brand awareness and create strong, favorable, and unique brand associations in consumer memory to build customer-based brand equity. In managing brand equity, it is important to recognize tradeoffs between those marketing activities that attempt to fortify and further contribute to brand equity and those marketing activities that attempt to leverage or capitalize on existing brand equity to reap some financial benefit.

As noted in Chapter 2, the advantage of creating a brand with a high level of awareness and a positive brand image is that many benefits may accrue to the firm in terms of cost savings and revenue opportunities. Marketing programs can be designed that primarily attempt to capitalize on or perhaps even maximize these benefits—for example, by reducing advertising expenses, seeking increasingly higher price premiums, or introducing numerous brand extensions. The more that there is an attempt to realize or capitalize on brand equity benefits, however, the more likely it is that the brand and its sources of equity may become neglected and perhaps diminished in the process. In other words, marketing actions that attempt to leverage the equity of a brand in different ways may come at the expense of other activities that may help to fortify the brand by maintaining or enhancing its awareness and image.

At some point, failure to fortify the brand will diminish brand awareness and weaken brand image. Without these sources of brand equity, the brand itself may not continue to yield as valuable benefits. Recall the problems encountered by Shell from inconsistent advertising support noted earlier in the chapter.[2] Just as a failure to properly maintain a car eventually affects its performance, so too neglecting a brand, for whatever reason, can catch up with marketers.

Coors

As Coors Brewing devoted increasing attention in its marketing on growing the equity of less established brands (e.g., Coors Light beer) and introducing new products (e.g., Zima clear malt beverage), ad support for the flagship Coors beer slipped from a peak of about $43 million in 1985 to a meager $4 million by 1993. Perhaps not surprisingly, sales of Coors beer dropped in half from 1989 to 1993. In launching a new ad campaign to prop up sales, Coors returned to its iconoclastic, independent western image. Marketers at Coors now admit they did not give the brand the attention it deserves: "We've not marketed Coors as aggressively as we should have in the past 10 to 15 years."[3]

Fine-Tuning the Supporting Marketing Program

Although the specific tactics and supporting marketing program for the brand are more likely to change than the basic positioning and strategic direction for the brand, brand tactics also should only be changed when there is evidence that they are no longer making the desired contributions to maintaining or strengthening brand equity.

Dove

Unilever's Dove soap has been advertised in a remarkably consistent fashion over the years, even across geographic boundaries. Dove has been positioned as a beauty bar with one-quarter cleansing cream that "creams skin while it washes." Dove has consistently been positioned to consumers on a performance basis with the slogan "Dove Doesn't Dry Your Skin." For years, advertising has also been trial-oriented, using consumer testimonials to vouch for the quality of the product (e.g., "Take the 7-Day Dove Test").

Reinforcing brand meaning may depend on the nature of brand associations involved. The Science of Branding 13-1 outlines one perspective on different ways to manage brand concepts. Several specific considerations play a particularly important role in reinforcing brand meaning in terms of product-related performance and non-product-related imagery associations, as follows.

Product-Related Performance Associations.

For brands whose core associations are primarily product-related performance attributes or benefits, innovation in product design, manufacturing, and merchandising is especially critical to maintaining or enhancing brand equity. For example, after Timex watched brands such as Casio and Swatch gain significant market share by emphasizing digital technology and fashion (respectively) in their watches, it made a number of innovative marketing changes. Within a short period of time, Timex introduced Indiglo glow-in-the dark technology, showcased popular new models such as the Ironman in mass media advertising, and launched new Timex stores to showcase its products. Timex also bought the Guess and Monet watch brands to distribute through upscale department stores and expand its brand portfolio. These innovations in product design and merchandising have significantly revived the brand's fortunes.[4]

Brand Concept Management

In an award-winning academic article, C. W. Park, Bernard Jaworski, and Deborah MacInnis present a normative framework termed *brand concept management* (BCM) for selecting, implementing, and controlling brand image over time to enhance market performance.[1] The framework consists of a sequential process of selecting, introducing, elaborating, and fortifying a "brand concept." The brand concept guides positioning strategies, and hence the brand image, at each of these stages. The method for maintaining this concept-image linkage depends on whether the brand concept is functional, symbolic, or experiential.

Specifically, the authors define a brand concept in terms of firm-selected brand meaning derived from basic consumer needs. An important factor in influencing the selection of a brand concept is the different types of consumer needs that might prevail, as follows:

- *Functional benefits:* The more intrinsic advantages of product or service consumption, usually corresponding to product-related attributes. These benefits are often linked to fairly basic motivations (e.g., physiological and safety needs) and involve a desire to remove or avoid problems.[2] For example, functional benefits of a shampoo might be that it eliminates dandruff, removes greasiness, makes hair and scalp healthy, and gives hair moisture and body. Representative brands with strong functional benefit associations include Arm & Hammer, Ivory, Vaseline, Steelcase, and Timex. Functional needs are defined as those that involve the search for products that solve consumption-related problems (e.g., solve a current problem, prevent a potential problem, resolve conflict, or restructure a frustrating situation). A brand with a *functional concept* is defined as one designed to solve externally generated consumption needs.

- *Symbolic benefits:* The more extrinsic advantages of product or service consumption, usually corresponding to non-product-related attributes, especially user imagery. Symbolic benefits relate to underlying needs for social approval or personal expression and outer-directed self-esteem. Thus, consumers may value the prestige, exclusivity, or fashionability of a brand because of how it relates to their self-concept.[3] For example, symbolic benefits of a shampoo might be that it assures users that they are using a product only used by "beautiful people" who appreciate the "good things in life." Symbolic benefits should be especially relevant for socially visible, "badge" products. A *badge product* is one for which consumers believe that brand usage signals or conveys some information about the person to others. Representative brands with strong symbolic benefits include Brooks Bros., Calvin Klein, Lenox, Rolex, Gucci, Jaguar, and Tiffany. Symbolic needs are defined as desires for products that fulfill internally generated needs for self-enhancement, role position, group membership, or ego identification. A brand with a *symbolic concept* is one designed to associate the individual with a desired group, role, or self-image.

- *Experiential benefits:* What it feels like to use the product or service; can correspond to both product-related attributes as well as non-product-related attributes such as usage imagery. These benefits satisfy experiential needs such as sensory pleasure (sight, taste, sound, smell, or feel), variety, and cognitive stimulation. For example, experiential benefits of a shampoo might involve its scent and lather and the feelings of beauty and cleanliness from applying or using the product. Representative brands with strong experiential benefit associations include Disney, Kodak, Mountain Dew, Nike, and Carnival cruise lines. Experiential needs are defined as desires for products that provide sensory pleasure, variety, or cognitive stimulation. A brand with an *experiential concept* is designed to fulfill these internally generated needs for stimulation or variety.

Once a broad needs-based concept has been selected, according to these researchers, it can be used to guide positioning decisions. For each of the three management stages, positioning strategies need to be implemented that enable consumers to understand a brand image (introduction), perceive its steadily increasing value (elaboration), and generalize it to other products produced by the firm (fortification). Specifically, the *introductory stage* of BCM is defined as a set of activities designed to establish a brand image and position in the marketplace during the period of market entry. During the *elaboration stage,* positioning strategies focus on enhancing the value of the brand's image so that its perceived superiority in relation to competitors can be established or sustained. At the final stage of BCM, the *fortification stage,* the aim is to link an elaborated brand image to the image of other products produced by the firm in different product classes.

The specific positioning strategies implemented at the introduction, elaboration, and fortification stages depend on the concept type. Figure A displays examples of brands with different concepts and the implications for brand concept management.

[1]C. Whan Park, Bernard J. Jaworski, and Deborah J. MacInnis, "Strategic Brand Concept-Image Management," *Journal of Marketing* 50 (October 1986): 135–145.

[2]Abraham H. Maslow, *Motivation and Personality,* 2nd ed. (New York: Harper & Row, 1970); Geraldine Fennell, "Consumer's Perceptions of the Product-Use Situations," *Journal of Marketing* 42 (April 1978): 38–47; John R. Rossiter and Larry Percy, *Advertising and Promotion Management* (New York: McGraw-Hill, 1987).

[3]Michael R. Solomon, "The Role of Products as Social Stimuli: A Symbolic Interactionism Perspective," *Journal of Consumer Research* 10 (December 1983): 319–329.

FIGURE A   Examples of Brand Concept Management

Examples of Brands with Functional Concepts

Concept Introduction	*Concept Elaboration*	*Concept Forification*
Clorox Bleach (whiter and brighter clothes)		
In 1913 Clorox liquid bleach introduced to the market	Problem-solving generalization strategy[a]	Clorox Pre-Wash soil and stain remover used prior to laundering clothes
	Product usage extended from cottons to synthetic fibers	Tackle cleaner, a fresh-scented, all-purpose household cleaner[b]
Vaseline Petroleum Jelly (general-purpose medicinal cream)		
1869 Vaseline Petroleum Jelly introduced to the market as a lubricant and as a skin balm for burns	Problem-solving generalization strategy	Vaseline health- and beauty-related products:
	Produce usage extended to multiple-usage situations: preventing diaper rash, removing eye makeup, lip balm	Vaseline Intensive Care Lotion
		Intensive Care Bath Beads
		Vaseline Constant Care
		Vaseline Dermatology Formula
		Vaseline baby care products:
		Wipe 'N Dipes
		Vaseline Intensive Care Baby Lotion
		Vaseline Intensive Care Baby Shampoo

(Continued)

Examples of Brands with Functional Concepts

Concept Introduction	Concept Elaboration	Concept Forification
Vaseline Petroleum Jelly (cont.)		Vaseline baby care products *(cont.):* Vaseline Intensive Care Baby Powder

[a]Clorox did not follow this strategy. This strategy would be consistent with the proposed elaboration approach.

[b]Tackle cleaner should have been linked more clearly to the Clorox concept. One method to acccomplish this link would be to use family brand names.

Examples of Brands with Symbolic Concepts

Concept Introduction	Concept Elaboration	Concept Forification
Lenox China ("A World Apart," "Let It Express Your World") Almost a century ago, the Lenox Company introduced a line of fine china	Market shielding A tightly controlled marketing mix to preserve the status concept	Lenox crystal Lenox silverplated holloware Candles Jewelry
Brooks Brothers (attire for the conservative, professional gentleman) In 1818 Brooks Brothers introduced a "gentleman's suit"	Market shielding A tightly controlled marketing mix to shield the market (e.g., only 26 stores in the United States and carefully controlled in-store merchandising)	Brooks Brothers shoes Brooks Brothers cologne Brooks Brothers hats Brooks Brothers valet stands

Examples of Brands with Experiential Concepts

Concept Introduction	Concept Elaboration	Concept Fortification
Barbie Doll (the sophisticated teenager) Barbie Doll was introduced to the market in 1959	Brand accessory strategy Accessories like outfits, houses, furniture, cars, jewelry for Barbie, Ken	Barbie Magazine Barbie Game Barbie Boutique
Lego Building Blocks (unbreakable safe toy emphasizing creativity and imagination) Lego Building Blocks for 3- to 8-year-olds introduced in 1960	Brand accessory strategy Accessories like minifigures, trees, signs, idea books, storage cases	Do-it-yourself furniture[c] such as Lego chairs, couches, desks, bookshelves
	Accessories like large bricks for 1- to 5-year-olds that can link with the smaller bricks when the child gets older	
	Expert builder sets for ages 7–12 with items such as wheels, gears, axles, toggle joints, and connectors	

[c]Suggested; not actual fortification strategy for Lego.

FIGURE A *(Continued)*

Innovation for toy manufacturers is critical to their success. Hasbro is another company that has attempted to use product introductions and innovations to keep its brand lines fresh. Hasbro's formula for success is to take well-known but perhaps stagnant-selling brands (e.g., Cabbage Patch dolls, Nerf foam toys, and G.I. Joe action figures), spruce them up with new offerings and features, and step up its advertising support. New models such as Crimp N' Curl Cabbage Patch dolls; Nerf slingshots, bow-and-arrows, and footballs that whistle through the air; and a new 12-inch high, limited-edition "Hall of Fame" G.I. Joe helped to revitalize each of those brand franchises. At the same time, Hasbro also brings out new toy lines in hopes of finding the hot new hit. This diversification strategy of combining stable, dependable brands with exciting new ones is intended to yield a steadier profit picture for the company.[5] In a similar vein, Mattel found success in 2000 with the introduction of its new Diva Starz line of dolls while also benefiting from strong sales of its stalwart Barbie and Hot Wheels franchises. See Branding Brief 13-1 for a summary of how Gillette has built equity in its razor and blades categories through innovation.

Failure to innovate can have dire consequences. Smith Corona, after struggling to sell its typewriters and word processors in a booming personal computer market, finally filed for bankruptcy. As one industry expert observed, "Smith Corona never realized they were in the document business, not the typewriter business. If they had understood that, they would have moved into software."[6] London Fog rainwear found it sales slipping away when it faced sleek competition from the likes of Ralph Lauren and Liz Claiborne. London Fog revamped its products and launched a bold ad campaign to attempt to avoid bankruptcy.[7]

Schwinn

Schwinn Bicycle once owned the kids' bike market with famous models such as the Phantom (a 1950s workhorse with balloon tires) and the Varsity (a 10-speed stalwart of the 1970s). Unfortunately, its market share, which peaked at 25 percent in the 1960s, slipped to single digits by the early 1990s. The problem? In part, Schwinn was slow to adjust to changing consumer tastes and take aggressive new rivals seriously. While other companies won over biking enthusiasts with lighter, sleeker models in the early 1980s, Schwinn continued to crank out its durable, but bulky, standbys. As one custom bicycle dealer observed, "Schwinn never spent the money on research and development or planned for the long-term, like so many American companies. Except for their name, they really have nothing to sell."[8] Schwinn/GT filed voluntary petitions for reorganization under Chapter 11 on July 16, 2001.

Thus, product innovations are critical for performance-based brands whose sources of brand equity primarily rest in product-related associations. Branding Brief 13-2 describes the sales setbacks encountered by Bacardi from failing to innovate. In some cases, product advances may involve brand extensions based on a new or improved product ingredient or feature—for example, Hot & Spicy Spam, mini-Oreos, Ruffles potato chips with larger "Flavor Ridges," Tide Rapid Action Tablets, and Yoplait Go-Gurt.[9] In fact, in many categories, a strong family sub-brand has emerged from product innovations associated with brand extensions (e.g., Wilson Hammer wide-body tennis racquets). In other cases, product innovations may center on existing

Razor-Sharp Branding at Gillette

One of the strongest brands in the world is Gillette. The company owns roughly two-thirds of the U.S. blade and razor market and even more in Europe and Latin America. In fact, more than 70 percent of sales and profits come from overseas operations in 200 countries. Moreover, its 10 percent profit margin is substantially higher than at most packaged-goods companies. How has Gillette been so successful? The company's marketing and branding practices provide a number of useful lessons to marketers.

Fundamentally, Gillette continually innovates to produce a demonstrably superior product. More than 40 percent of Gillette's sales in the first half of the 1990s came from new products. Gillette's credo is to "increase spending in 'growth drivers'—R&D, plants and equipment, and advertising—at least as fast as revenues go up." As Gillette's former CEO Alfred Zeien proclaimed, "Good products come out of market research. Great products come from R&D." Gillette spent more than 2 percent of its annual sales—or over $200 million—on R&D during the late 1990s, double the average for most consumer products companies. Gillette also backs its products with strong advertising and promotional support. TV ads in the past often used a montage of slow-motion scenes of men shown in different roles interspersed with product shots

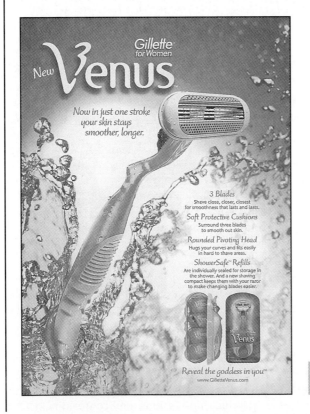

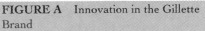

FIGURE A   Innovation in the Gillette Brand

with upbeat background music and the now-familiar tag line "The Best a Man Can Get." Thus, Gillette's marketing can be seen as creating both strong performance *and* imagery associations.

The following is a history of Gillette's product innovations during the last 30 years:

Trac II (1971): First twin-blade razor

Atra (1977): First twin-blade razor with a pivoting head

Good News (1976): Top-selling disposable twin-blade razor since introduction

Atra Plus (1985): Twin-blade razor with a lubricant strip

Sensor (1990): Individually mounted twin blades

Sensor for Women (1992): First razor designed specifically for women

Sensor Excel (1993): Fitted with microfins that stretch skin for closer shave

Mach3 (1998): First triple-blade razor

Gillette considered the Mach3 to the "most important new product" in its history, and invested more than $750 million in research and development and manufacturing expenses. Like its predecessor, the Sensor Excel, the Mach3 featured spring-mounted blades, flexible microfins, and a special coating that strengthens the blade. The major advancement of the Mach3 was the triple blade, each designed to shave progressively closer. The product was highly anticipated: Before the advertising campaign began, Mach3 generated more than 500 million media impressions. During the launch year for the Mach3, Gillette set a marketing budget of $300 million globally and $100 million in the United States. The Mach3, which cost 35 percent more than the Sensor Excel, captured a stunning 35 percent of the razor market within two weeks of its launch date. Mach3 surpassed the $1 billion sales mark only 15 months after its debut. In 2001, Gillette released a women's version of the Mach3 called the Venus. Gillette spent $150 million on marketing for the worldwide Venus launch (see Figure A).

Sources: Patricia Sellers, "Brands, It's Thrive or Die," *Fortune*, 23 August 1993, 52–56; Linda Grant, "Gillette Knows Shaving—and How to Turn Out Hot New Products," *Fortune*, 14 October 1996, 207–210; http://www.gillette.com; "Gillette to Launch Massive Atra Plus Advertising Campaign," PR Newswire, 14 December 1988; William C. Symonds, "Gillette's Edge," *Business Week*, 19 January 1998.

brands. For example, General Mills's "Big G" cereal division strives to improve at least a third of its nearly two dozen brand lines each year.[10]

At the same time, it is important not to change products too much, especially if the brand meaning to consumers is wrapped up in the product design or makeup. Recall the strong consumer resistance encountered by New Coke described in Chapter 1. As another example, Revlon also underestimated how passionately consumers can feel about well-established brands and how much they can resent any tampering with the products themselves. To better appeal to younger women, Revlon reformulated the heavy floral scent of its 30-year-old Intimate fragrance to a lighter, less sweet scent. Longtime customers protested, forcing the company to reintroduce the old formulation as "Intimate the Original" while continuing to market the reformulated Intimate.

In making product changes to a brand, it is important that loyal consumers feel that a reformulated product is a *better* product but not necessarily a *different* product. The timing of the announcement and introduction of a product improvement are also

Bacardi's Sour Sales Slide

Bacardi rum, although still the largest liquor brand in the United States in terms of sales, suffered one of the worst sales drop in modern spirits history, losing over two million cases in sales *in one year* as its sales decreased from 8.7 million cases in 1991 to 6.4 million cases in 1992. The reasons behind Bacardi's sales slide during this period provide a textbook example of how *not* to build brand equity over time.

Through the 1950s and 1960s, sales of Bacardi in the United States exploded as young drinkers adopted rum and Coke as an easy, fun alternative to the martinis and scotches drunk by their parents. Although the brand enjoyed uninterrupted growth for nearly three decades, there was little innovation in its supporting marketing program during that time. With an onset of "cola fatigue" and the growing popularity of juice-based drinks, however, Bacardi found it increasingly difficult to compete. Not only did rum lose the "mixable" crown to vodka, but Bacardi faced stiff competition in its own market. Seagram's Captain Morgan Spiced Rum, launched in 1983, successfully implemented the type of marketing program that Bacardi had avoided, infusing its drink with a sweeter taste and promoting the brand to young drinkers in popular nightspots with the Captain Morgan pirate character and his girlfriends the Morganettes. Other

FIGURE A   Bacardi's Limon Extension

competitors also introduced trendy, flavored products such as Absolut Kurant and Stolichnaya Ohranj (currant and orange vodkas, respectively) to entice young drinkers. Through it all, Bacardi stubbornly refused to expand its product portfolio. In addition to these developments, a series of price increases and a federal excise tax increase between 1988 and 1991 resulted in the price of a 750-milliliter (22.5 fluid ounce) bottle increasing from $7.50 to as much as $10.99, which contributed to the dismal sales performance in 1992.

To stop the slide in sales, Bacardi management aggressively cut prices, doubled spending to launch a new print ad campaign, began on-premise promotions in big-city bars, and introduced a new pre-mixed drink called Bacardi Breezer that came in 12-ounce bottles. The company also introduced a lemon-flavored rum (Bacardi Limon) in 1995 and a spiced rum (Bacardi Spice) in 1996. To capitalize on positive consumer response to the Limon introduction, Bacardi launched a $10 million new marketing campaign in 1998 with the tag line "Rocks. Tonic. Juice. Magic." Within two years, Bacardi Limon was selling 500,000 cases annually and helped halt Bacardi's sales decline (see Figure A).

Not ignoring its flagship brand, Bacardi also went after young adults in 1998 with the $15 million-plus lifestyle-focused print ad campaign "Bacardi by Night," promoting the diversity and uniqueness of its brand users. Bacardi management also expanded into other product categories with the 1998 acquisition of the Dewar's scotch and Bombay gin brands and new markets in Eastern Europe, Latin America, and the Far East. Bacardi remained the best-selling liquor in the United States, and sales of the flagship rum grew 5.2 percent to 7.5 million cases in 2000. The company continued to develop innovative products, and in 2001 Bacardi launched an orange-seasoned rum called Bacardi O. Now furiously playing catch-up, Bacardi hopes to transform itself from a traditional company to an industry-leading trend setter.

Source: Adapted from Suein L. Hwang, "As Rivals Innovate, Old-Line Bacardi Becomes a Chaser," *Wall Street Journal*, 6 July 1994, B4. See also Rich Brandes, "Liquor Holds Its Breath as Economy Teeters," *Beverage Industry*, 1 May 2001.

important: If the brand improvement is announced too soon, consumers may cease to buy existing products; if the brand improvement is announced too late, competitors may have already taken advantage of the market opportunity with their own introductions.

Non-Product-Related Imagery Associations

For brands whose core associations are primarily non-product-related attributes and symbolic or experiential benefits, relevance in user and usage imagery is critical. Because of their intangible nature, non-product-related associations may be potentially easier to change, for example, through a major new advertising campaign that communicates a different type of user or usage situation. Nevertheless, ill-conceived or too-frequent repositionings can blur the image of a brand and confuse or perhaps even alienate consumers.

In categories in which advertising plays a key role in building brand equity, imagery may be an important means of differentiation. For example, in the soft drinks category, millions of dollars in advertising are spent to craft an image for a brand. Consequently, ad campaigns have become a valuable branding tool in terms of crafting a brand image, as illustrated by the recent histories of the two competing cola giants, Coca-Cola and Pepsi.

Coca-Cola, as the market leader in soft drinks, is especially concerned with creating catchy, well-liked slogans that capture its brand equity.[11] Perhaps its most successful slogan, "It's the Real Thing," dates back to 1969. Since that time, the company has introduced several variations of this puffery-based slogan: "Coke Adds Life," "Have a Coke and a Smile," "Coke Is It," "Catch the Wave," "Can't Beat the Feeling," "Can't Beat the Real Thing," "Always Coca-Cola," and "Enjoy."

Pepsi-Cola's fresh, youthful appeal has been a key point of difference versus Coca-Cola. Pepsi-Cola has also used a number of slogans over the years from its original "Pepsi Generation," which evolved over time to "The Choice of a New Generation." Pepsi next launched a campaign with the slogan "Gotta Have It" during the 1992 Super Bowl. The ads, showing young and old Pepsi drinkers, was an attempt to expand the "Pepsi Generation" to include older age groups. With little indication of sales success, Pepsi returned to its more familiar and powerful positioning, introducing new ads with the snappy tag line "Be Young. Have Fun. Drink Pepsi."[12] After that, however, Pepsi ran the risk of again straying away from a key source of equity with the introduction of the broader-appealing ad theme "Nothing Else Is a Pepsi." More recently, it returned to the youth-appealing "Generation Next" before arriving at "The Joy of Cola."

During the 2000 Summer Olympics, Coke almost made the same mistake as Pepsi has sometimes made by straying from its advertising roots to launch a campaign that overly modernized its characteristic upbeat, "feel good" messages. For example, in one ad, a wheelchair-bound 102-year-old grandmother at a family reunion went ballistic and began knocking down tables upon learning that Coca-Cola was not available. After negative consumer reactions to the "ruined special moments" campaign, Coke marketers launched the more faithful and reverent "Life Tastes Good" campaign.[13]

Another example of a too hasty departure from advertising equity occurred with Miller Lite light beer. As described in Chapter 3, Miller Lite was advertised for years in humorous ads featuring famous retired athletes and the slogan "Tastes Great. Less Filling." In part to revive fading brand sales, a new ad campaign was launched in 1992. A dramatic departure from previous advertising, the new campaign, featuring fashionable young people, contained the slogans "C'mon, Let Me Show You Where It's At" and "It's It and That's That." When the slide in brand sales continued, Miller reversed field to create a new campaign that was more faithful to its original positioning. The "Combinations" campaign showed Miller Lite drinkers disagreeing over which of two completely different events to watch on TV. After the drinkers bang their TV set with a bottle of Lite beer, the two events become combined into one wacky spectator sport, such as "Sumo High Dive," "Recliner Chair Ski Jump," and "Big Lawyer Round-Up." The new ad tag line, echoing the past, was "Great Taste. Less Filling. Can Your Beer Do This?" More recently, Miller Lite adopted yet another slogan, "Life Is Good," although retaining some of the stylistic characteristics of the "Combinations" campaign. The return to advertising form saw a comeback in sales.

Dissatisfied with its progress, however, in 1997 Miller chose to introduce a quirky, controversial ad campaign featuring a fictitious copywriter, Dick. The ads failed to click with the 21- to 25-year-old male target and alienated older consumers at the same

Pick a Positioning! Brand Repositioning with Michelob

A brand that failed to turn around sales while enduring numerous repositionings is Michelob. Celebrating its 100th anniversary in 1996, Michelob has always been positioned as an upscale, superpremium beer. In the 1970s, Michelob ran ads featuring successful young professionals that confidently proclaimed, "Where You're Going, It's Michelob." Moving away from the strong user imagery of that campaign, the next ad campaign trumpeted, "Weekends Were Made for Michelob." Later, to bolster sagging sales, the ad theme was switched to "Put a Little Weekend in Your Week." In the mid-1980s, yet another campaign was launched—featuring laid-back rock music and stylish shots of beautiful people—that proclaimed "The Night Belongs to Michelob."

None of these campaigns could stop a sales slide. Sales in 1994 were 2.3 million barrels, compared with a 1980 peak of 8.1 million barrels. Finally, another ad campaign was introduced in that year, "Some Days Are Better Than Others," which explained to consumers that "A Special Day Requires a Special Beer." The slogan was later modified to "Some Days Were Made for Michelob." Pity the poor consumer! Previous ad campaigns just required that they look at a calendar or out a window to decide whether or not it was the right time to drink Michelob—now they had to figure out how well their day was going! After so many different messages, consumers could hardly be blamed if they had no idea when they were supposed to drink the beer. Through all of this, sales performance for Michelob continued to suffer.

Source: Kevin Goldman, "Michelob Tries to Rebottle Its Old Success," *Wall Street Journal*, 28 September 1995, B8.

time, sending the brand's sales into a tail spin. After the top executives and ad agency were all fired, a new management team developed a new campaign with a heavy dose of humor and sex appeal and the tag line "Grab a Miller Lite. It's Miller Time."

It is particularly dangerous to flip-flop between product-related performance and non-product-related imagery associations because of the fundamentally different marketing and advertising approaches each entails. Consider Heineken. Earlier ads showed simple scenes of the bottle or people peacefully drinking the beer, backed by the slogan "Just being the best is enough." Subsequent ads, in an attempt to make the brand more hip and contemporary, were much artier—featuring a bright red star logo—and had a more prominent lifestyle component. Perhaps as a result of being too much of a departure, the ads failed to really drive sales. A new, edgy campaign, "It's All about the Beer," was much more successful at communicating the quality message in a contemporary, humorous manner. In an ad titled "The Premature Pour," for example, a young guy spots a beautiful woman across a crowded bar. She gives him the eye while seductively pouring her beer. Although he tries to stay calm, he pours too fast and spills beer all over the place.

Significant repositionings may be dangerous for other reasons too. Brand images can be extremely sticky, and once consumers form strong brand associations, they may be difficult to change. Consumers may choose to ignore or simply be unable to

Freshening Walker's Crisps

Walker's, founded in 1948 in Leicester, England, sold crisps (potato chips) at a price premium because its product was fresher than the competition. The price premium enabled Walker's to spend more on advertising than the competition, which in turn drove the sales rate up. This model was predicated on the freshness of the product: As long as the crisps remained fresh, Walker's could charge the premium price and the advertising and sales would follow.

PepsiCo acquired Walker's in 1989 and immediately set about to expand the brand across the United Kingdom. PepsiCo invested significantly in manufacturing technology in order to change the packaging from see-through cellophane to foil packaging, which kept the product fresher longer. The old packaging kept the crisps fresh for 45 days, while the new wrapper ensured freshness for 70 days. This enabled PepsiCo to expand Walker's beyond a regional brand to a pan-U.K. one, while keeping the freshness-based business model intact. In blind taste tests conducted regularly by the company, Walker's earned consumer preference 60 percent of the time, compared with 40 percent for the competition. By 1994, Walker's was the biggest food brand in the United Kingdom in terms of unit sales, with per capita consumption averaging four units per week.

Seeking to grow further, the company enlisted British soccer hero Gary Lineker to appear as spokesperson in a campaign entitled "No More Mr. Nice Guy." Lineker was famous for his sportsmanship and fair play, and the ads inverted his persona by showing him in various humorous settings stealing crisps. Tracking studies revealed that the tongue-in-cheek ads resonated with both children and adults, helping volume sales rise 40 percent from 1996 to 1997. The campaign was hailed by the Millward Brown market research agency as "extraordinarily successful, contributing significantly to Walker's ambition to become part of the fabric of British life." In 1999, Walker's introduced a special edition of its popular Salt & Vinegar flavor called "Salt & Lineker" that led to a 27 percent sales increase in the quarter following the introduction. Later, Lineker was joined as a spokesperson by rising British soccer star, Michael Owen, who was given his own flavor, "cheese & onion," for their cheese and onion flavored crisps.

Walker's maintained its dominant market leader position in Walker's new century. In 2001, Walker's captured a U.K. market share of 60 percent. An estimated 11 million people ate a Walker's product every day that year. Walker's continued its strong financial performance as sales exceeded an estimated $700 million in 2000.

Sources: Dean Dawson, "Advalue: Walker's Snacks," *Marketing Week*, 7 March 1997; http://www.walker's.com; Jacqueline Wake, "Face of the Day," *The Herald*, 15 November 1999; Bill McLaughlin, PepsiCo, presentation at Dartmouth College, February 22, 1999.

remember the new positioning when strong, but different, brand associations already exist in memory.[14] Club Med has attempted for years to transcend its image as a vacation romp for swingers to attract a broader cross-section of people. Branding Brief 13-3 describes how Michelob's constant repositioning coincided with a steady sales decline.

For dramatic repositioning strategies to work, convincing new brand claims must be presented in a compelling fashion. One brand that successfully shifted from a primarily non-product-related image to a primarily product-related image is BMW. Uniformly decreed to be the quintessential "yuppie" vehicle of the 1980s, sales of the brand dropped almost in half from 1986 to 1991 as new Japanese competition emerged and a backlash to the "Greed Decade" set in. Convinced that high status was no longer a sufficiently desirable and sustainable position, marketing and advertising efforts switched the focus to BMW's product developments and improvements, such as the responsive performance, distinctive styling, and leading-edge engineering of the cars. These efforts, showcased in well-designed ads, helped to diminish the "yuppie" association, and by 1995 sales had approached their earlier peak.[15]

Summary

Reinforcing brand equity requires consistency in the amount and nature of the supporting marketing program for the brand. Although the specific tactics may change, the key sources of equity for the brand should be preserved and amplified where appropriate. Product innovation and relevance are paramount in maintaining continuity and expanding the meaning of the brand. Branding Brief 13-4 describes how the Walker's brand stayed fresh in the United Kingdom. The chapter next considers situations in which more drastic brand actions are needed.

REVITALIZING BRANDS

At the beginning of the chapter, it was noted that changes in consumer tastes and preferences, the emergence of new competitors or new technology, or any new development in the marketing environment can potentially affect the fortunes of a brand. In virtually every product category, there are examples of once prominent and admired brands that have fallen on hard times or, in some cases, even completely disappeared. Nevertheless, a number of these brands have managed to make impressive comebacks in recent years as marketers have breathed new life into their customer franchises. Brands such as *Reader's Digest,* Boston Market, Coach, and Bally have all seen their brand fortunes successfully turned around to varying degrees in recent years. Branding Brief 13-5 describes how RCA, Hush Puppies, and Adidas restored the status of their brands.

As these examples illustrate, brands sometimes have had to return to their roots to recapture lost sources of equity. In other cases, the meaning of the brand has had to fundamentally change to regain lost ground and recapture market leadership. Reversing a fading brand's fortunes thus requires either lost sources of brand equity to be recaptured or new sources of brand equity to be identified and established. Regardless of which approach is taken, brands on the comeback trail have to make more "revolutionary" changes than the "evolutionary" changes to reinforce brand meaning that were described earlier in this chapter.

Often, the first place to look in turning around the fortunes of a brand is the original sources of brand equity. As Ogilvy & Mather's Norman Berry once remarked:

The brands most likely to respond to revitalization efforts are those that have clear and relevant values that have been left dormant for a long time, have

Three Brand Comeback Stories

RCA

Radio Corporation of America (RCA) was the inventor of television on a commercial basis. For 40 years, RCA dominated the U.S. television market. Unfortunately, while the consumer electronics market exploded in size and diversity in the 1970s and 1980s, RCA failed to innovate. Missing the market in videocassette recorders and camcorders with young, affluent customers, RCA risked being left behind by well-designed, high-technology products. Consumers—especially younger ones—thought of the brand in terms of the ornate wooden cabinets in their grandparents' houses. RCA reinvigorated the brand through dramatic product innovations (e.g., RCA branded its larger-screen televisions "Home Theatre") and a modern-looking new ad campaign. Ads featured the longtime (over 100 years old!) RCA Dalmatian icon, "Nipper," providing break-through and instantaneous recognition. The new dimension of change was portrayed by giving Nipper a young son, "Chipper," in 1991 who could represent the forward-looking RCA, a clever means to build on—but distinguish itself from—past advertising efforts. Launching its ProScan high-end brand in 1990 and the RCA Satellite System featuring DirecTV programming in 1994 helped to further enhance the company's contemporary image.[1]

HUSH PUPPIES

Hush Puppies' suede shoes, symbolized by a cuddly, rumpled, droopy-eyed dog, were a kid's favorite in the 1950s and 1960s. Changes in fashion trends and a series of marketing mishaps, however, eventually resulted in an out-of-date image and diminished sales. Wolverine World Wide, makers of Hush Puppies, made a number of marketing changes in the early 1990s to reverse the sales slide. New product designs and numerous off-beat color combinations (e.g., bright shades of green, purple, and pink) enhanced the brand's fashion appeal. Increased expenditures backed an ad campaign featuring youthful, attractive people wearing the shoes and the tag line "We Invented Casuals." Popular designers began to use the shoes in their fashion shows. The brand even got a boost when the actor Tom Hanks wore a pair of old Hush Puppies in the final scene of *Forrest Gump*. As a result of all these developments and a concerted program to engage retailer interest, the brand reappeared in fashionable department stores with an increase in sales and profits.[2]

ADIDAS

The one-time standard of athletic footwear, Adidas saw its leading market position overtaken by rivals Nike and Reebok as the company suffered from unfocused marketing, a glut of products, poor channel relations, costly manufacturing procedures, and internal squabbles. After losing almost $100 million in 1992, new management began efforts to turn the brand around in 1993. Adidas decided to concentrate its efforts on the lucrative—but fickle—teenage market with the hope that this group might choose to reject brands adopted by their parents and others to create their own identity. Doubling their marketing spend to 11 percent of sales, management reduced the number of products, introduced new performance-oriented products, launched new advertising, and signed sponsors such as the NBA's Kobe Bryant, the WTA's Anna Kournikova, and the New York Yankees. Complementing this pull effort that targeted a young, urban audience, Adidas also attempted to increase its share of shelf space in stores. The three-stripe logo began to be seen as cool, appearing on rappers and other urban hipsters. As a result, Adidas U.S. footwear sales soared to $935 million in 1999 from $165 million in 1990, and the company increased its share of the $8 billion athletic shoe market to almost 14 percent from 2 percent in that same period of time.[3] In Europe, the brand was even stronger, amassing 40 percent of the performance footwear market.

----

[1]Nicholas Ind, "RCA Consumer Electronics: Making the Most of Your Heritage," in *Great Advertising Campaigns* (London: Kogan Page, 1993).

[2]Oscar Suris, "Ads Aim to Sell Hush Puppies to New Yuppies," *Wall Street Journal*, 28 July 1993, B1, B6; Keith Naughton, "Don't Step on My Blue Suede Hush Puppies," *Business Week*, 11 September 1995, 84–86; Cyndee Miller, "Hush Puppies: All of a Sudden They're Cool," *Marketing News*, 12 February 1996, 10.

[3]Kevin Goldman, "Adidas Tries to Fill Its Rivals' Big Shoes," *Wall Street Journal*, 17 March 1994, B5; Joshua Levine, "Adidas Flies Again," *Forbes*, 25 March 1996, 44–45.

----

not been well expressed in the marketing and communications recently, have been violated by product problems, cost reductions, and so on. *Where there is evidence that these values exist and that they were indeed a part of the brand's magnetism during healthier days, then chances of revitalization are good.* If you find that the brand really does not have any strong values, chances are that the product or business strength in the past was a function simply of performance and spending characteristics and that, in fact, according to our definition, it never really became a *true brand*. Bringing these brands back to life is more like starting from scratch. It really isn't revitalization.[16]

In profiling brand knowledge structures to guide repositioning, it is important to accurately and completely characterize the breadth and depth of brand awareness; the strength, favorability, and uniqueness of brand association and brand responses held in consumer memory; and the nature of consumer-brand relationships. A comprehensive brand equity measurement system as outlined in Chapter 8 should be able to help reveal the current status of these sources of brand equity. If not, or to provide additional insight, a special brand audit may be necessary. Of particular importance is the extent to which key brand associations are still adequately functioning as points of difference or points of parity to properly position the brand. Are positive associations losing their strength or uniqueness? Have negative associations become linked to the brand, for example, because of some type of change in the marketing environment?

Decisions must then be made as to whether to retain the same positioning or to create a new one and, if so, which positioning to adopt. The positioning considerations outlined in Chapter 3 can provide useful insights as to the desirability and deliverability of different possible positions based on company, consumer, and competitive considerations. Sometimes the positioning is still appropriate, but the marketing program is the source of the problem because it is failing to deliver on it. In these instances, a "back to basics" strategy may make sense. Branding Brief 13-6 describes how Harley-Davidson rode a back-to-basics strategy to icon status. In other cases, however, the old positioning is just no longer viable and a "reinvention" strategy is necessary. Branding Brief 13-7 describes how Mountain Dew completely overhauled its brand image to become a soft drink powerhouse. As that example illustrates, it is often easiest to revive a brand that has simply been forgotten.

Revitalization strategies obviously involve a continuum, with pure "back to basics" at one end and pure "reinvention" at the other end. Many revitalizations combine elements of both strategies. Finally, note that marketing failures, in which insufficient consumers are attracted to a brand, are typically much less damaging than product failures, in which the brand fundamentally fails to live up to its consumer promise. In the latter case, strong, negative associations may be difficult to overcome. For example, Boo.com, the poster child for Internet excesses, went out of business in early 2000 because it spent too much money on misguided marketing that failed to generate sales revenue. Given that few consumers actually had a negative experience with the brand, it was purchased by Fashionmall.com in June 2000 and relaunched later in the year.

With an understanding of the current and desired brand knowledge structures in hand, the customer-based brand equity framework again provides guidance as to how to best refresh old sources of brand equity or create new sources of brand equity to achieve the intended positioning. According to the model, two such approaches are possible:

1. Expand the depth or breadth of brand awareness, or both, by improving consumer recall and recognition of the brand during purchase or consumption settings.
2. Improve the strength, favorability, and uniqueness of brand associations making up the brand image. This approach may involve programs directed at existing or new brand associations.

By enhancing brand salience and brand meaning in these ways, more favorable responses and greater brand resonance can result. Strategically, lost sources of brand equity can be refurbished and new sources of brand equity can be established in the same three main ways that sources of brand equity are created to start with: by changing brand elements, changing the supporting marketing program, or leveraging new secondary associations. The remainder of this section considers several alternative strategies for affecting the awareness and image of an existing brand to refresh old sources or create new sources of brand equity.

Expanding Brand Awareness

With a fading brand, often it is not the *depth* of brand awareness that is a problem—consumers can still recognize or recall the brand under certain circumstances. Rather, the *breadth* of brand awareness is the stumbling block-consumers only tend to think of the brand in very narrow ways. Therefore, as was suggested in Chapter 3, one powerful means of building brand equity is to increase the breadth of brand awareness, making sure that consumers do not overlook the brand and that they will think of purchasing or consuming it in those situations in which the brand can satisfy consumers' needs and wants.

Harley-Davidson Motor Company

Harley-Davidson is one of the few companies in the world that can claim a legion of fans so dedicated to the brand that some of them get tattoos depicting the logo. Even more impressive is the fact that Harley-Davidson attracted such a loyal customer base with a minimum of advertising. Founded in 1903 in Milwaukee, Wisconsin, Harley-Davidson has twice narrowly escaped bankruptcy but is today one of the most-recognized motor vehicle brands in the world. Among consumers throughout the world, Harley enjoys 55 percent unaided awareness. Customers are willing to endure three-year waiting lists in order to get their hands on a Harley.

Before the 1980s, the company relied almost exclusively on word-of-mouth endorsements and the image of its user group to sell its motorcycles. In 1983 the company established an owners club, the Harley Owners Group (HOG), which sponsored bike rallies, charity rides, and other motorcycle events. Every Harley owner receives free admission into the group and can sign up at the www.hog.com Web site. In its first year, HOG had 33,000 members. By 2001, there were more than 600,000 HOG members in more than 1,200 chapters throughout the world.

Because of financial desperation, Harley-Davidson began to aggressively license its products in the 1980s. After some early missteps, including the ill-advised Harley-

FIGURE A   Revving Up the Harley-Davidson Brand

Davidson brand of cigarettes begun in 1985 and the "Scooter Juice" brand of wine coolers, the company licensed its name to such credible ventures as the Harley-Davidson Café chain. Other licensing agreements have led to the creation of a Harley Barbie doll, a Harley cologne, a Harley Visa card, a Ford F-150 Harley truck, and even a Harley state lottery game. Harley-Davidson licensed products bring in tens of millions in revenue annually.

The company realized that the Harley leather "uniform," while an important aspect of its core audience, was alienating potential customers. So Harley-Davidson created Harley-Davidson Motorclothes, which balanced aggressive leather riding gear with "cuter" items like women's underwear and baby clothes. Harley Motorclothes are a key facet of the company's general merchandise division, which had revenues grow 14 percent to $151 million in 2000.

Harley-Davidson continues to promote its brand with grassroots marketing efforts. For example, most executives at the company own Harleys and often ride them with customers. This customer intimacy makes traditional advertising almost unnecessary. In 1996, Harley spent no money on advertising. In 1997, Harley's total marketing budget was $20 million, only $1 million of which went to advertising. As ever, Harley's highly visible contingent of riders provides invaluable promotions and endorsements free of cost. Additionally, many marketers seek to borrow the Harley cachet and use the bikes in other ads, giving the company product placement gratis. The company continues to please customers and investors: In 2000 Harley-Davidson sold more than 131,000 bikes, which gave the company a 27 percent share of the U.S. motorcycle market.

Sources: Bill Tucker, Terry Keenan, and Daryn Kagan, "In the Money," *CNNfn,* 20 January 2000; "Harley-Davidson Extends MDI Entertainment License for Lotteries' Hottest Brand," *Business Wire,* 1 May 2001; Glenn Rifkin, "How Harley-Davidson Revs Its Brand," *Strategy & Business,* Fourth Quarter 1997.

This section considers strategies to increase usage of and find new uses for the brand. Assuming a brand has a reasonable level of consumer awareness and a positive brand image, perhaps the most appropriate starting point for creating new sources of brand equity is with ways that increase usage. In many cases, such approaches represent the path of least resistance because they do not involve potentially difficult and costly changes in brand image or positioning as much as potentially easier-to-implement changes in brand salience and awareness.

Usage can be increased by either increasing the level or quantity of consumption (i.e., how much the brand is used) or increasing the frequency of consumption (i.e., how often the brand is used).

In general, it is probably easier to increase the number of times a consumer uses the product than it is to actually change the amount used at any one time. Consumption amount is more likely to be a function of the particular beliefs that the consumer holds as to how the product is best consumed. A possible exception to that rule is for "impulse" consumption products whose usage increases when the product is made more available (e.g., soft drinks, snacks).

Increasing frequency of use, on the other hand, involves either identifying additional or new opportunities to use the brand in the same basic way or identifying completely new and different ways to use the brand. Increasing frequency of use is a particularly attractive option for brands with large market share that are leaders in

A New Morning for Mountain Dew

Mountain Dew was launched in 1969. PepsiCo initially marketed Mountain Dew with the countrified tag line "Yahoo Mountain Dew! It'll tickle your innards." Since then, the drink has outgrown its provincial roots. After an unsuccessful attempt in the early 1980s to bring urban teenage drinkers to the brand by advertising on MTV, the company switched its focus to using outdoors action scenes in its ads. In the late 1980s, Mountain Dew posted double-digit annual volume increases. This phenomenal growth continued through the 1990s, and Mountain Dew was the fastest-growing major soft drink in America for much of the decade. The brand's aggressive pursuit of young soda drinkers aided Mountain Dew's market share rise from 2.7 percent in 1980 to 7.2 percent in 2000, the year Mountain Dew briefly passed Diet Coke to become the number three soft drink in terms of market share.

Mountain Dew updated its outdoors image in the 1990s by using extreme sports such as skydiving, skateboarding, and snowboarding. Early ads featured athletes participating in extreme sports while consuming Mountain Dew products, accompanied by the tag line "Do the Dew." A more recent ad featured a man on a mountain bike chasing a cheetah to retrieve a can of Dew while another portrayed a man who butts heads with a ram in order to protect his Mountain Dew. To reach the urban demographic, which typically does not watch action sports competitions, Mountain Dew also developed a series of print, radio, and television ads featuring hip-hop superstar endorser Busta Rhymes.

Mountain Dew balances its high-profile nationally televised campaigns with grassroots marketing efforts such as sponsoring action-sports athletes and events such as the ESPN X-Games, offering samples from its branded Dew Hummer trucks and subway cars, and staging promotions at local skate parks. Another grassroots campaign involved a beeper promotion in which more than 50,000 teens bought reduced-price pagers with proofs of purchase, and received weekly discounts and prize offerings from Mountain Dew. The total marketing effort, from local event marketing to national television spots, contributes what PepsiCo executives call the brand's "mass intimacy" with consumers. PepsiCo recognizes that this mass intimacy must be carefully managed, lest Mountain Dew become too mass market and lose its feel of intimacy. Scott Moffitt, Mountain Dew's director of marketing, acknowledged the challenge of keeping Dew's marketing fresh, saying, "You can't preach to [our customers] or tell them what's cool."

Mountain Dew again proved the power of its marketing program in 2000 when it introduced Mountain Dew Code Red, its first line extension since Diet Mountain Dew debuted in 1988. The bright red cherry-flavored drink was supported by a national advertising campaign that employed grassroots marketing as well as high-profile media buys. The Code Red launch was an unqualified success (see Branding Brief 4–1).

Sources: Theresa Howard, "Being True to Dew," *Brandweek*, 24 April 2000; Greg Johnson, "Mountain Dew Hits New Heights to Help Pepsi Grab a New Generation," *Los Angeles Times*, 6 October 1999; Michael J. McCarthy, "Mountain Dew Goes Urban to Revamp Country Image," *Wall Street Journal*, 19 April 1989; "Top-10 U.S. Soft Drink Companies and Brands for 2000," *Beverage Digest*, 15 February 2001.

their product category. Both of these approaches to increasing the frequency of product usage are examined in turn.

Identifying Additional or New Usage Opportunities

In some cases, the brand may be seen as useful only in certain places and at certain times, especially if it has strong brand associations to particular usage situations or user types. In general, to identify additional or new opportunities for consumers to use the brand more—albeit in the same basic way—a marketing program should be designed to include both of the following:

➤ Communications to consumers as to the appropriateness and advantages of using the brand more frequently in existing situations or in new situations

➤ Reminders to consumers to actually use the brand as close as possible to those situations

For many brands, increasing usage may be as simple as improving top-of-mind awareness through reminder advertising (e.g., as with V-8 vegetable juice and its classic "Wow! I Could Have Had a V-8" ad campaign). In other cases, more creative types of retrieval cues may be necessary. These reminders may be critical because consumers often adopt "functional fixedness" with a brand such that it can be easily ignored in nontraditional consumption settings.

For example, some brands are seen as only appropriate for special occasions. An effective strategy for those brands may be to redefine what it means for something to be "special." For example, at one time Chivas Regal ran a print ad campaign for its Blended Scotch with the theme "What are you saving the Chivas for?" The ads, showing different people in different scenes, included headlines such as "Sometimes life begins when the baby-sitter arrives," "Your Scotch and soda is only as good as your Scotch and soda," and "If you think people might think you order Chivas to show off, maybe you're thinking too much." Similarly, Nabisco's strategy of making Grey Poupon mustard a premium brand—supported by popular TV commercials showing stuffy aristocrats passing the product through the windows of their Rolls-Royces—worked a little too well: Consumers tended to reserve it for special occasions. A follow-up ad campaign encouraging broader usage of the brand suggested "Poupon the Potato Salad" and "Class Up the Cold Cuts."[17] For these types of campaigns to work, however, it is essential that the brand be able to retain its "premium" brand association—a key source of equity—while consumers are convinced to adopt broader usage habits at the same time.

Another potential opportunity to increase frequency of use is when consumer's *perceptions* of their usage differ from the *reality* of their usage. For many products with relatively short life spans, consumers may fail to replace the product in a timely manner because of a tendency to underestimate the length of productive usage.[18] One strategy to speed up product replacement is to tie the act of replacing the product to a certain holiday, event, or time of year. For example, several brands have run promotions tied in with the spring-time switch to daylight savings time (e.g., Oral-B toothbrushes). Another strategy might be to provide consumers with better information as to either (1) when the product was first used or would need to be replaced or (2) the current level of product performance. For example, batteries offer built-in gauges that show how much power they have left, and toothbrushes have color indicators on their brushes to indicate when they are too worn.

Finally, perhaps the simplest way to increase usage is when actual usage of a product is less than the optimal or recommended usage. In this case, consumers must be persuaded of the merits of more regular usage, and any potential hurdles to increased usage must be overcome. In terms of the latter, product designs and packaging can make the product more convenient and easier to use.

Identifying New and Completely Different Ways to Use The Brand

The second approach for increasing frequency of use for a brand is to identify completely new and different usage applications. For example, food product companies have long advertised new recipes that use their branded products in entirely different ways. After years of sales declines of 3 percent to 4 percent annually, sales of Cheez-Whiz rose 35 percent when the brand was backed by a new ad campaign promoting the product as a cheese sauce accompaniment to be used in the microwave oven.[19] Perhaps the classic example of finding creative new usage applications for a product is Arm & Hammer baking soda, whose deodorizing and cleaning properties have led to a number of new uses for the brand.

Other brands have taken a page from Arm & Hammer's book: Clorox has run ads stressing the many benefits of its bleach, such as how it eliminates kitchen odors; Wrigley's chewing gum has run ads touting its product as a substitute for smoking; and Tums has run ads for its antacid that promote its benefits as a calcium substitute. New usage applications may require more than just new ad campaigns. Often, new uses can arise from new packaging. For example, Arm & Hammer introduced a "Fridge-Freezer Pack" (with "freshflo vents") for its natural baking soda that was specially designed to better freshen and deodorize refrigerators and freezers. Maxwell House Filter Pack Singles and Folgers Coffee Singles were both an attempt to accommodate consumers' desires to drink ground roast coffee without brewing an entire pot. The Science of Branding 13-2 describes a number of ways to expand usage.

Improving Brand Image

Although changes in brand awareness are probably the easiest means of creating new sources of brand equity, more fundamental changes are often necessary. A new marketing program may be necessary to improve the strength, favorability, and uniqueness of brand associations making up the brand image. As part of this repositioning—or recommitment to the existing positioning—any positive associations that have faded may need to be bolstered, any negative associations that have been created may have to be neutralized, and additional positive associations may have to be created.

Repositioning the Brand

In some cases, repositioning the brand requires establishing more compelling points of difference. This may simply require reminding consumers of the virtues of a brand that they have begun to take for granted. Recall how the New Coke debacle described in Chapter 1 accomplished just that in a round-about way. Along these lines, Kellogg's Corn Flakes ran a successful ad campaign with the slogan "Try Them Again for the First Time." Wonder Bread similarly tried to walk consumers down memory lane in its late-1990s "Remember the Wonder" ads. In some of these cases, a key point

Understanding Usage Expansion

University of Illinois professor Brian Wansink has studied various marketing and branding issues associated with product consumption. Wansink describes a number of different ways to identify and communicate new usage situations.[1] An obvious starting point for generating potential expansion opportunities is with brainstorming meetings or focus groups involving loyal or heavy users and less-loyal or light users. Contrasting the preferences and behaviors of the two groups can yield insights into potential barriers in perceptions and usage that must be overcome, as well as opportunities for further growth. Additionally, he notes how perceptions of potentially related products and situations can be uncovered through cluster analysis or other multivariate statistical approaches.

Wansink further argues that successful media strategies for expansion ad campaigns are often based on clever targeting and timing. He notes how small-share brands can more affordably target users of their brands by advertising new uses on their packages and labels. For example, Trix cereal used a side panel to note complementary products (e.g., ice cream, yogurt, trail mix, etc.) on which Trix could be sprinkled. Murphy's Oil Soap printed a series of different usage ideas under peel-off stickers that had been affixed to its spray bottles. Similarly, Roy Rogers restaurants used its paper placemats to advertise eight situations—parties, picnics, meetings, and so forth—in which customers could eat their carry-out chicken. In terms of timing, Wansink notes that advertising exposure ideally would coincide with situations in which brand choice has the highest likelihood of being made. For example, Campbell schedules radio ads for its soups to be broadcast just prior to lunch and dinner to be top-of-mind at the most opportune moment.

Wansink defines *usage variant products* as products that have elastic demand functions because they have a high degree of substitutability or because they are able to create their own demand when salient, such as food and household cleaning products.[2] For these types of products, marketing strategies to increase consumer stockpiling (e.g., promotions or changes in packaging) may increase the salience and thus usage of the product. For example, larger package sizes and price discounts, by lowering the perceived unit cost of the product, have been shown to accelerate usage.[3] Another potential way to increase the quantity used is to reduce the undesirable consequences of an increased usage level.[4] For example, a shampoo designed to be gentle enough for daily use may alleviate concerns from those consumers who believe that frequent hair washing is undesirable and therefore eliminate their tendency to conserve the amount of product they use.

---

[1] Brian Wansink, "Advertising Strategies to Increase Usage Frequency," *Journal of Marketing* 60, no. 1 (January 1996): 31–46; Brian Wansink and Jennifer Marie Gilmore, "New Uses That Revitalize Old Brands," *Journal of Advertising Research* (March–April 1999): 90–98.

[2] Brian Wansink, "Can Package Size Accelerate Usage Volume?" *Journal of Marketing* 60, no. 3 (July 1996): 1–14.

[3] Ibid.

[4] David A. Aaker, *Managing Brand Equity* (New York: Free Press, 1991).

of difference may turn out to be nostalgia and heritage rather than any product-related difference.

Other times a brand needs to be repositioned to establish a point of parity on some key image dimension. A common problem for established, mature brands is that they must be made more contemporary by creating relevant usage situations, a more contemporary user profile, or a more modern brand personality. Heritage brands that have been around for years may be seen as trustworthy but also boring, uninteresting, and not that likable. Updating a brand may involve some combination of new products, new advertising, new promotions, new packaging, and so forth. For example, the 170-year-old regional beer Yuengling saw its sales virtually double by introducing lighter and fuller-flavored versions; new labels that gave the beer an arty, nostalgic look; and new promotions that tapped into regional pride by focusing on the brewery's place in history. The new image permitted higher prices and allowed the brand to gain more high-end, on-premise accounts.[20]

Sometimes negative product-related associations emerge because of changes in consumer tastes. For example, Del Monte, makers of canned fruits and vegetables, found that its sales steadily declined after a peak in 1969. Even worse, their loyal buyers were aging—the typical buyer was a woman over the age of 55—and not being replaced by younger ones. The problem was that younger consumers saw Del Monte products as being old-fashioned, inconvenient, and laden with additives and preservatives. In 1994, the company launched its first ad campaign in 10 years to dispel negative associations that had been created. Attempting to make canned foods more relevant and contemporary, the campaign targeted "emerging families"—those consumers beginning a career, starting a household, getting married, and having children, who would presumably be more likely to reevaluate their eating habits.[21]

Changing Brand Elements

Often one or more brand elements must be changed to either convey new information or to signal that the brand has taken on new meaning because the product or some other aspect of the marketing program has changed. Although the brand name is typically the most important brand element, it is often the most difficult to change. Nevertheless, names can be dropped or combined into initials to reflect shifts in marketing strategy or to ease pronounceability and recall. Shortened names or initials also can disguise potentially negative product associations. For example, in an attempt to convey a healthier image, Kentucky Fried Chicken's name was abbreviated to the initials KFC. The company also introduced a new logo incorporating the character of Colonel Sanders as a means to maintain tradition but also modernize its appeal. Brand names may be changed for other reasons. Federal Express chose to officially shorten its name to FedEx and introduce a new logo in response to what consumers actually were calling the brand.[22]

Other brand elements are easier to change and may need to be, especially if they play an important awareness or image function. Chapter 4 described how packaging, logos, characters, and so forth could be modified and updated over time. An important point noted there is that changes generally should be moderate and evolutionary in nature, and great care should be taken to preserve the most salient aspects of the brand elements. For example, when General Electric decided it wanted to communicate a fresh, high-tech look to the public—but not lose the valuable equity it had accrued in its name—it chose to rename the company as GE with virtually no loss in equity. Brand Focus 13.0 considers in more detail issues concerning changing corporate names.

Entering New Markets

Positioning decisions require a specification of the target market and the nature of competition to set the competitive frame of reference. The target market or markets for a brand typically do not constitute all possible segments that make up the entire market. In some cases, the firm may have other brands that target these remaining market segments. In other cases, however, these market segments represent potential growth targets for the brand. Effectively targeting these other segments, however, typically requires some changes or variations in the marketing program, especially in advertising and other communications, and the decision as to whether to target these segments ultimately depends on a cost-benefit analysis. Chapter 3 introduced some basic segmentation issues, and Chapter 14 considers some specific segmentation issues in the context of global brands as well as geographic and other factors. This section highlights a few key segmentation issues as they relate to brand revitalization.

To grow the brand franchise, many firms have reached out to new customer groups to build brand equity. One classic example of this approach was executed by Procter & Gamble with its Ivory soap, which was revived by promoting it as a pure and simple product for adults instead of just for babies. Johnson & Johnson baby shampoo achieved success by virtue of a similar strategy in which the company promoted the gentleness and everyday applicability of its shampoo to an adult audience. After a century of fighting tooth and nail with archrival Arrow, Van Huesen finally was able to take over the top spot in the dress shirt market in 1991. By devoting half of its $8 million budget to advertise directly to women in women's magazines, Van Huesen was able to influence key decision makers: Women buy an estimated 60 percent to 70 percent of men's shirts. After seeing the success of this strategy, Arrow—which had earlier survived a difficult transformation to selling bolder colors and busier patterns at higher prices—also began a more aggressive advertising campaign to brand its shirts, especially with women.[23]

Segmenting on the basis of demographic variables or other means and identifying neglected segments is thus one viable brand revitalization option. In some cases, just retaining existing customers who might eventually move away from the brand or recapturing lost customers who no longer use the brand can be a means to increase sales. Brands such as Kellogg's Frosted Flakes cereal, Oreo cookies, and Keds tennis shoes have run ad campaigns targeting adults who presumably stopped using the product long ago. Some of these ads use themes and appeals to nostalgia or heritage. Others attempt to make the case that the product's enduring appeal is still relevant for users today. The importance of retaining current customers can be recognized by calculating the lifetime value of customers. One study noted that a purchaser of automobiles would spend more than $500,000 on cars during his or her lifetime, but that it costs five times as much to sell an automobile to a new customer as it does to sell to a satisfied existing customer.[24]

Attracting a new market segment can be deceptively difficult. Nike, Gillette, and other marketers have struggled for years to find the right blend of products and advertising to make their brands—which have more masculine-oriented images—appear relevant and appealing to women. Creating marketing programs to appeal to women has become a priority of makers of products from cars to computers. As described in Brand Focus 14.0, marketers have also introduced new marketing programs targeted to different racial groups (e.g., African Americans, Asian Americans, and Hispanic Americans), age groups, and income groups. Attracting emerging new market segments based on cultural dimensions may require different messages, creative strategies, and media.[25]

Of course, one strategic option for revitalizing a fading brand is simply to more or less abandon the consumer group that supported the brand in the past to target a completely new market segment. Gillette decided Dippity-Do hair gel carried too much negative baggage to appeal to those women who used it in the 1960s but who now associated it with out-of-fashion bouffant hairdos and flips. Rather than targeting middle-aged consumers, Gillette chose to start with a clean slate by targeting a new generation of active younger consumers and repositioning the brand as a fun, hip product.[26] Dippity-Do Sport was launched with new ads featuring Brian Griese, the Denver Broncos quarterback, and new packaging featuring cobalt-blue bottles with grab-and-go sport grips. Similarly, the hair conditioner Brylcreem, which gave teenagers the slicked-back look in the 1950s, saw its sales go limp in the 1960s when the Beatles popularized a "mop-top" look and bangs. To revive the brand, product packaging was modernized and a clear Brylcreem Power Gel introduced to appeal to a younger audience, at one point enlisting British soccer star David Beckham as its U.K. endorser.[27]

ADJUSTMENTS TO THE BRAND PORTFOLIO

Managing brand equity and the brand portfolio requires taking a long-term view of the brand. As part of this long-term perspective, it is necessary to carefully consider the role of different brands and the relationships among different brands in the portfolio over time. In particular, a brand migration strategy needs to be designed and implemented so that consumers understand how various brands in the portfolio can satisfy their needs as they potentially change over time or as the products and brands themselves change over time. Managing brand transitions is especially important in rapidly changing, technologically intensive markets. Branding Brief 13-8 describes some branding issues faced by the Palm PDA.

Migration Strategies

As noted in Chapter 11, brands can play special roles that facilitate the migration of customers within the brand portfolio. For example, entry-level brands are often critical in bringing in new customers and introducing them to the brand offerings. Ideally, brands would be organized in consumers' minds so that they at least implicitly know how they can switch among brands within the portfolio as their needs or desires change. For example, a corporate or family branding strategy in which brands are ordered in a logical manner could provide the hierarchical structure in consumers' minds to facilitate brand migration. Car companies are quite sensitive to this issue, and brands such as BMW with its 3-, 5- and 7-series numbering systems to denote increasingly higher levels of quality are good examples of such a strategy. Chrysler designated

---

Updating the Palm Brand Hierarchy

When it was founded in 1992, Palm Computing entered the personal digital assistant (PDA) category with a simplified product that combined pocket size with easy PC connectivity. The initial success of the Palm PDA attracted many imitators, including Sony, Compaq, and Microsoft, but the Palm remained the most popular product. By 2001, Palm captured 66 percent of the global hand-held market. This success came despite a frequently changing product naming scheme.

The company's first product was the Palm Computing Pilot 1000 Connected Organizer. This name conveyed the product's three key features: small size ("palm"), PC connectivity ("connected"), and personal organizer utility ("organizer"). Consumers began referring to the product as a "Palm Pilot," and this shorthand version has stuck with the product ever since. US Robotics acquired Palm in 1995.

Following its purchase of Palm, US Robotics continued to employ the "Pilot" name while eliminating the numeric naming system, developing products such as the Palm Pilot Professional Connected Organizer. Consumers rarely used the full name, preferring to shorten it to "Professional" or "Palm." 3Com purchased US Robotics in 1998 and promptly dropped the word "Pilot" from the product name, replacing it with a series of Roman numerals that indicated different platforms, such as Palm III and Palm V. The Palm III was the entry-level Palm, the Palm V was the "executive" Palm, and the Palm VII was the Palm that offered wireless access. Additionally, 3Com added the letters *e, x,* or *c* to the product name to indicate product extensions with additional features (e.g., Palm IIIc, with color display).

In March 2000, 3Com spun off Palm to create a new company, Palm Inc. Shortly thereafter, Palm unveiled another model that broke with the Roman-numeral naming trend: the Palm m100. The m100 was a low-end Palm device, designed to be lightweight and even simpler than the other models. The letter *m* connoted the intended mobility of the product and also served to set the m100 apart from the Roman-numeral series of Palms.

Confusing though Palm's portfolio may be, the company boasted over 5 million users in 2001.

Plymouth as its "starter" car line, such that Plymouth owners would then be expected to trade up in later years to higher-priced Chrysler models.

Acquiring New Customers

All firms face tradeoffs in their marketing efforts between attracting new customers and retaining existing ones. In mature markets, trial is generally less important than building loyalty and retaining existing customers. Nevertheless, some customers inevitably leave the brand franchise—even if only by natural causes. Consequently, it is imperative that firms proactively develop strategies to attract new customers, especially younger ones. The marketing challenge in acquiring new customers, however, lies in making a brand seem relevant to customers from potentially vastly different generations and cohort groups or lifestyles (see Figure 13-3). This challenge is exacerbated when the brand has strong personality or user image associations that tie the brand to one particular consumer group. Branding Brief 13-9 describes Volkswagen's highly successful appeals to younger drivers.

Unfortunately, even as younger consumers age, there is no guarantee they will have the same attitudes and behaviors of older consumers who preceded them. In

FIGURE 13-3   *Advertising Age's* Profiles of Generations

Generation	Birth Dates	Size	Experiences and Attitudes
GI Generation	1901–1924	16 million	• Survivors of the Depression and two World Wars • Conservative spenders • Civic-minded
Silent Generation	1925–1945	35 million	• Much like GIs before them, lived with specter of Depression and war, but were born too late to be war heroes • Conformists; raised families at young age • The grandparents of the Millennials are now involved in civic life and extended families in a bid to recapture lost youth
Baby Boomers	1946–1964	76 million	• Great acquisitors, unapologetic consumers • Now often newly liberated parents with high disposable income • Value-driven despite indulgences • Fearful of words related to aging
Generation X	1961–1981	57 million	• Cynical and media-savvy • Once rebellious, now a big economic force • Alienated, alternative, sexy
Generation Y	1976–1981 (a subset of Generation X)	32 million	• Edgy, focused on urban style • Moved toward more positive, retro style: swing dancing, big band, outdoor life • Total X and Y combined: 81 million people
Millennials	1982–2002	70 million	• Tech-savvy and educated • Multicultural • Bombarded by media messages; accustomed to sex, violence • Growing up in affluent society; big spending power

Volkswagen's Branding U-Turn

Volkswagen, the third-largest automaker in the world, was founded in 1937. With the help of creative and effective marketing, Volkswagen became a household name in America during the 1960s. Volkswagen's economy car—the classic Beetle—rapidly became a cult favorite, then a popular favorite, and eventually the number one selling car in history with over 22 million units sold. Sales of VW cars in America peaked, however, at 569,000 units in 1970. Cutthroat competition among compacts, especially from Japanese manufacturers, hurt Volkswagen's sales during the 1970s. The 1980s were not much better for the company, as sales continued to decline.

By 1990, U.S. sales had slipped to a mere 1.3 percent of the American market from a high of 7 percent in 1970. In an attempt to revitalize its business, Volkswagen unveiled an advertising campaign centered on the word *Fahrvergnugen,* German for "driving pleasure." The hard-to-pronounce word became an instant pop-culture buzzword, but U.S. sales dropped under 50,000 units in 1993. The company clarified its brand message under the umbrella of the "Drivers Wanted" slogan in 1995, and U.S. sales rose 18 percent to 135,907 cars in 1996. The "Drivers Wanted" campaign was designed to revitalize the company by appealing to the core customers willing to spend a little extra on a Volkswagen because they liked the car's German engineering, sportier image, and versatility, rather than appealing to the mass market. The voiceover on the introductory television spot identified the target audience by saying, "On the road of life, there are passengers and there are drivers."

In 1998, Volkswagen released a modernized version of its iconic Beetle. Ads for the New Beetle contained irreverent humor, with one ad reading "If you sold your soul in the '80s, here's your chance to buy it back." American buyers leapt at the chance to buy the classically influenced—but clearly modern—cars, often at well above sticker price. Waiting lists for the new cars, which sold more than 55,000 units in 1998, were common. Volkswagen sold out its inventory immediately. Said one dealer, "The New Beetle is like a magnet that draws people back to us." By bringing consumers into Volkswagen showrooms, the New Beetle helped the company achieve 50 percent growth in sales volume between 1998 and 1999.

In 2001, the company unveiled its latest retro offering, the Microbus, as a concept car. The car, not expected to be available to the American public until 2003, will likely set off another wave of nostalgia and help the company achieve further sales growth. Other new models slated for introduction include a sport utility vehicle and a luxury V-8 Passat sedan designed to compete with BMW and Mercedes.

Sources: Al Beeber, "Volkswagen Sets Stage for New Microbus," *Lethbridge Herald*, 14 June 2001; Rupert Spiegelberg, "If You Love Bug, Rejoice," *Houston Chronicle*, 29 June 1997; David Kiley, "VW Goes More Off Beat with 'Wanted' Ads," *Brandweek*, 28 April 1997; David Welch, "VW: Now That's How to Rebuild a Brand," *Business Week*, 19 June 2000; Keith Naughton, "Can You Say Fahrvergnugen?" *Detroit News*, 2 February 1990; Randall Rothenberg, "The Advertising Century," *Advertising Age*, 29 March 1999; "Volkswagen Sales Fall with Beetle's Demise," Reuters News Agency, 15 October 1982.

1996, the first wave of post-World War II baby boomers celebrated their 50th birthdays and officially entered the "senior market." Many experts forecast that this group will demand that companies embrace their own unique values in marketing their products and services. As one demographic expert says, "Nothing could be further from the truth than saying boomers will be like their parents." Because there can be no expectations that younger consumers will necessarily view brands and products in the same way as consumers who preceded them, proactive strategies must be put in place to both acquire new customers and retain existing ones.

The response to the challenge of marketing across generations and cohort groups has taken all forms. Some marketers have attempted to cut loose from the past.

Old Spice

Procter & Gamble's Old Spice has had to wrestle with the problem of being seen as "your father's aftershave" to young male consumers. As one P&G marketing executive notes, "We recognize the need to change and bring in a new generation of young users. At the same time, we don't want to alienate the users we already have." To revitalize the brand, a new campaign backed by heavy spending was launched in 1993. The new TV ads eliminated the trademark "whistling sailor" character to show—via rapid-fire editing—active, contemporary men. Old Spice also became a sponsor for several AVP volleyball tournaments. On the product side, P&G put heavy support behind its fast-selling and more youthfully positioned Old Spice High Endurance family of deodorants, including the Red Zone sub-brand.[28]

Other brands have attempted to develop more inclusive marketing strategies to encompass both new and old customers. Some alternative approaches that attempt to broaden the marketing program and attract new customers as well as retain existing ones are discussed in the following subsections.

Multiple Marketing Communication Programs

One approach to attract a new market segment for a brand and satisfy current segments is to create separate advertising campaigns and communication programs for each segment. For example, Dewars launched the "Authentic" and "Profiles" campaigns, each directed to a different market segment. The "Authentic" campaign focused on the brand heritage in terms of its product quality and Scottish roots and was focused on an older segment, including existing customers. The "Profiles" campaign took a completely different tact, literally profiling younger users of the brand to make the brand seem relevant and attractive to a younger audience. Different media buys then attempted to ensure that the appropriate campaign was seen by the relevant market segment.

Similar approaches have been adopted by beer companies. The increased effectiveness of targeted media makes multiple targets more and more feasible. The obvious drawback to this approach is the expense involved and the potential blurring of images if there is too much media overlap among target groups and if the respective ad positionings are seen as incompatible.

Brand Extensions and Sub-brands

Another approach to attract new customers to a brand and keep the brand modern and up-to-date is to introduce a line extension or establish a new sub-brand.

These new product offerings for the brand can incorporate new technology, features, and other attributes to satisfy the needs of new customers as well as satisfy the changing desires of existing customers. For example, Aqua Velva introduced its Ice Sport aftershave sub-brand to appeal to a younger audience while still selling classic Aqua Velva to a loyal cadre of older consumers. Kmart's online retail site, BlueLight.com, may be seen as a means to both attract new customers as well as reinvigorate the brand.

New Distribution Outlets

In some cases attracting a new market segment may be as simple as making the product more available to that group. For example, the sunglasses industry, which grew sales from $100 million in 1972 to $2.5 billion 15 years later, benefited from social and fashion trends but also a shift in distribution strategies. Sunglasses used to be sold mostly by opticians, but in the 1970s Sunglass Hut and other companies moved into malls, sporting goods stores, and campuses. A leader in specialty niche retailing, Sunglass Hut uses a wide variety of over 2,000 high-traffic shopping and tourist destinations to reach new audiences.

Retiring Brands

Because of dramatic or adverse changes in the marketing environment, some brands are just not worth saving. Their sources of brand equity may have essentially dried up or, even worse, damaging and difficult-to-change new associations may have been created. At some point, the size of the brand franchise—no matter how loyal—fails to justify the support of the brand. In the face of such adversity, decisive management actions are necessary to properly retire or milk the brand.

Several options are possible to deal with a fading brand. A first step in retrenching a fading brand is to reduce the number of its product types (e.g., package sizes or variations). Such actions reduce the cost of supporting the brand and allow the brand to put its best foot forward. Under these reduced levels of support, a brand may more easily hit profit targets. If a sufficiently large and loyal enough customer base exists, marketing support can be virtually eliminated altogether as a means to milk or harvest brand profits from these cash cows. An *orphan brand* has been defined as a once-popular brand with diminished equity that a parent company allows to decline by withdrawing marketing support. Typically these orphan brands have a customer base too small to warrant advertising and promotional expenditures. Coca-Cola's Tab brand might be seen as an example of an orphan. Tab, which was introduced in 1963 and was known as the "beautiful drink for beautiful people," has sold little more than a million cases annually since 1990 and commands less than a 1 percent market share. Coke gives Tab no marketing support and no brand manager, and keeps the brand alive mainly as a goodwill gesture to its small but loyal following. Said Doug Daft, Coca-Cola's CEO, "We want to make sure those who want Tab get Tab."

In some cases, the brand is beyond repair and more drastic measures have to be taken. One possible option for fading brands is to consolidate them into a stronger brand. For example, Procter & Gamble merged White Cloud and Charmin toilet paper, eliminating the White Cloud line in 1992. Ironically, Wal-Mart secured the rights to the White Cloud brand and used it to help successfully brand its own private label diapers. P&G also merged Solo and Bold detergents. With shelf space at a premium, brand consolidation will increasingly be seen as a necessary option to create a stronger brand, cut costs, and focus marketing efforts.[29]

Finally, a more permanent solution may be to discontinue the product altogether. The marketplace is littered with brands that either failed to establish an adequate level of brand equity or found their sources of brand equity disappear because of changes in the marketing environment. Companies sometimes spin off their orphan brands when sales shrink too low. Campbell spun off a number of labels, including Vlasic pickles and Swanson frozen dinners in 1998. Similarly, American Home Products spun off Chef Boyardee, Bumble Bee tuna, and Pam cooking spray. Other companies sell the orphans.

Oxydol

In 2000, Procter & Gamble sold its Oxydol laundry detergent to Redox Brands, a company headed by two former P&G executives, for an estimated $7 million. Annual sales of Oxydol, which is only available in grocery stores, had fallen from $80 million in 1992 to a mere $5 million in 2000. P&G had marketed Oxydol since 1927, but the brand was stocked by only 15 percent of U.S. stores by the year Redox purchased it. While focus groups revealed that older consumers exhibited more brand loyalty and were unlikely to switch to Oxydol, consumers in their twenties were less loyal and in fact wanted to buy different detergent than their parents. Redox repositioned Oxydol as an "extreme clean," updated the packaging by enlarging the letter X and using a green container, and launched a Web site (www.the-extreme-clean.com) boasting "We're proud that Oxydol kicks some mean bootie in the washing machine." By summer 2001, Oxydol was stocked in 70 percent of the retail outlets in the United States. Following the success of Oxydol, Redox purchased Biz bleach, another orphan from P&G. The two brands combined brought in an estimated $80 million in 2001.

FIGURE 13-4 Investment Decisions in a Declining Industry

Market Prospects
- Is the rate of decline orderly and predictable?
- Are there pockets of enduring demand?
- What are the reasons for the decline—is it temporary? Might it be reversed?

Competitive Intensity
- Are there dominant competitors with unique skills or assets?
- Are there many competitors unwilling to exit or contract gracefully?
- Are customers brand-loyal? Is there product differentiation?
- Are there price pressures?

Brand Strength and Organizational Capabilities
- Is the brand strong? Does it enjoy high recognition and positive, meaningful associations?
- What is the market share position and trend?
- Does the business have some key sustainable competitive advantages with respect to key segments?
- Can the business manage a milking strategy?
- Is there synergy with other businesses?
- Does the brand fit with the firm's current strategic thrust?
- What are the exit barriers?

Brand Migration at Unilever

Unilever, which was formed in 1929 by the merger of Dutch-owned Margarine Unie and the British-based Lever Brothers soap concern, owned more than 1,600 distinct brands in 2000. Some of Unilever's famed brands include Lipton tea, Snuggle fabric softener, Ragu pasta sauces, Birds Eye frozen foods, Close-Up toothpaste, Calvin Klein fragrances, and Dove personal care products. Unilever also has thousands of lesser-known brands that are not strong competitors in their markets. In an effort called "Path to Growth" designed to get the most value from its brand portfolio, the company announced in 1999 its intention of eliminating three-quarters of its brands by 2003.

Antony Burgmans, Unilever co-chairman, described the means of reducing the brand portfolio: "

Some [brands] we will try and fold into a power brand. . . . Another way of doing it is just letting [a brand] fade away and see where it stops. And some may be disposed of."

The company intended to retain its global brands such as Lipton, as well as its regional brands and "local jewels" such as Persil, the leading detergent in the United Kingdom. Unilever sold brands such as Batchelors and Elizabeth Arden, delisted brands including Blueband and Krona margarine, and merged second-tier brands like Radion into leading brands like Surf. Additionally, Unilever planned to reduce headcount by 25,000, or 10 percent of its workforce, in five years. The company also planned to close 100 of its 380 manufacturing sites.

While Unilever was reducing its brand portfolio, it was also making several high-profile acquisitions and expanding into services. Between 1996 and 2000, the company spent more than $28 billion on acquisitions. In 2000, the company acquired Slim-Fast Foods and Ben & Jerry's ice cream for a total of more than $2.6 billion. Since only 6 percent of Slim-Fast's sales came from outside North America, Unilever expected to use its global distribution network to significantly expand the brand. Ben & Jerry's gave Unilever a superpremium ice cream to compete against Häagen-Dazs, owned by rival General Mills's Pillsbury unit. Unilever also added a host of services in the "health, hygiene, and indulgence sectors." The company launched MyHome, a home-cleaning service available in the United Kingdom, and opened a chain of tea houses under the name Cha.

By the end of the first quarter in 2001, Unilever had significantly reduced its portfolio to 900 brands, and had another 250 brands "marked for disposal." Unilever expected to achieve $356 million in cost savings in 2001 from its brand reductions.

Sources: John Willman, "Leaner, Cleaner, and Healthier Is the Stated Aim," *Financial Times*, 23 February 2000; John Thornhill, "A Bad Time to Be in Consumer Goods," *Financial Times*, 28 September 2000; "Unilever's Goal: 'Power Brands,'" *Advertising Age*, 3 January 2000; "Unilever Axes 25,000 Jobs," *CNNfn*, 22 February 2000; "Unilever sees 395 mln eur Cost Savings This Yr from Brand Reduction," *AFX* (UK), 9 May 2001; "A Chat with Unilever's Niall FitzGerald," *Business Week Online*, 2 August 2001; Harriet Marsh, "Unilever A Year Down the 'Path,'" *Marketing*, 22 February 2001, 30.

Harvard University professor Nancy Koehn explains that old brands retain some value because consumers often remember them from childhood. "There's at least an unconscious link," says Koehn.[30] Perhaps this fact helps to explain why a Web site called www.hometownfavorites.com, which offers more than 400 exotic orphan brands such as Bre'r Rabbit Molasses and My-T-Fine Pudding, has revenue approaching $1 million. As long as orphan brands remain popular with a core audience, it seems that companies are willing to sell them.[31]

Obsoleting Existing Products

How do you decide which brands to attempt to revitalize (or at least milk) and which ones to obsolete? Beecham chose to abandon such dying brands as 5-Day deodorant pads, Rose Milk skin care lotion, and Serutam laxative but attempted to resurrect Aqua Velva aftershave, Geritol iron and vitamin supplement, and Brylcreem hair styling products. The decision to retire a brand depends on a number of factors. Aaker outlines a number of strategic questions that can be raised when considering whether to invest in a fading brand (see Figure 13-4).[32]

Fundamentally, the issue is the existing and latent equity of the brand. As the head of consumer packaged-goods giant Unilever commented in explaining his company's decision to review about 75 percent of its brands and lines of businesses for possible sell-offs, "If businesses aren't creating value, we shouldn't be in them. It's like having a nice garden that gets weeds. You have to clean it up, so the light and air get in to the blooms which are likely to grow the best."[33] Branding Brief 13-10 describes how Unilever is attempting to clean up its brand portfolio.

Review

Effective brand management requires taking a long-term view of marketing decisions. A long-term perspective of brand management recognizes that any changes in the supporting marketing program for a brand may, by changing consumer knowledge, affect the success of future marketing programs. Additionally, a long-term view necessitates proactive strategies designed to maintain and enhance customer-based brand equity over time in the face of external changes in the marketing environment and internal changes in a firm's marketing goals and programs. This chapter considered how to reinforce, revitalize, and retire brands and examined a number of specific topics in managing brands over time.

Brand equity is reinforced by marketing actions that consistently convey the meaning of the brand to consumers in terms of what products the brand represents, what core benefits it supplies, and what needs it satisfies and in terms of how the brand makes those products superior and which strong, favorable, and unique brand associations should exist in the minds of consumers. The most important consideration in reinforcing brands is the consistency of the marketing support that the brand receives, both in terms of the amount and nature of that support. Consistency does not mean that marketers should avoid making any changes in the marketing program; in fact, many tactical changes may be necessary to maintain the strategic thrust and direction of the brand. Unless there is some change in the marketing environment, however, there is little need to deviate from a successful positioning. In such cases, the critical points of parity and points of difference that represent sources of brand equity should be vigorously preserved and defended.

Reinforcing brand meaning depends on the nature of the brand association involved. For brands whose core associations are primarily product-related attributes and functional benefits, innovation in product design, manufacturing, and merchandising is especially critical to maintaining or enhancing brand equity. For brands whose core associations are primarily non-product-related attributes and symbolic or experiential benefits, relevance in user and usage imagery is especially critical to maintaining or enhancing brand equity. In managing brand equity, it is important to recognize the tradeoffs that exist between those marketing activities that fortify the brand and reinforce its meaning and those that attempt to leverage or borrow from its existing brand equity to reap some financial benefit. At some point, failure to fortify the brand will diminish brand awareness and weaken brand image. Without these sources of brand equity, the brand itself may not continue to yield valuable benefits. Figure 13-5 summarizes brand reinforcement strategies.

Revitalizing a brand requires either that lost sources of brand equity be recaptured or that new sources of brand equity be identified and established. According to the CBBE framework, two general approaches are possible: (1) Expand the depth or breadth (or both) of brand awareness by improving brand recall and recognition by consumers during purchase or consumption settings; and (2) improve the strength, favorability, and uniqueness of brand associations making up the brand image. This latter approach may involve programs directed at existing or new brand associations.

With a fading brand, the depth of brand awareness is often not as much of a problem as the breadth; that is, consumers tend to think of the brand in very narrow ways. Strategies to increase usage of and find new uses for the brand were reviewed. Although changing brand awareness is probably the easiest means of creating new sources of brand equity, a new marketing program often may have to be implemented to improve the strength, favorability, and uniqueness of brand associations. As part of this repositioning, new markets may have to be tapped. The challenge in all of these efforts to modify the brand image is to not destroy the equity that already exists. Figure 13-6 summarizes brand revitalization strategies.

As part of the long-term perspective in managing a brand portfolio, it is necessary to carefully consider the role of different brands and the relationships among different brands in the portfolio over time. In particular, a brand migration strategy needs to be designed and implemented so that consumers understand how various brands in the portfolio can satisfy their needs as they potentially change over time or as the products and brands themselves change over time. A number of different possible strategies designed to both acquire new customers and retain existing ones were reviewed. Different possible strategies to retire those brands whose sources of brand equity had essentially dried up or which had acquired damaging and difficult-to-change associations were also discussed.

In closing, the importance of the material in this chapter can be seen through the words of one marketing commentator who has an interesting view of how to think about managing brands over time:

> Brands are like ships. You could fill a book with analogies. One key common denominator is that brands, once they gain momentum, overtake agility. A brand heading in the right direction absorbs a lot of mishandling before it stops dead in the water, or goes off course. A brand heading south takes effort and time to turn around. Think through all of the similarities and you'll soon

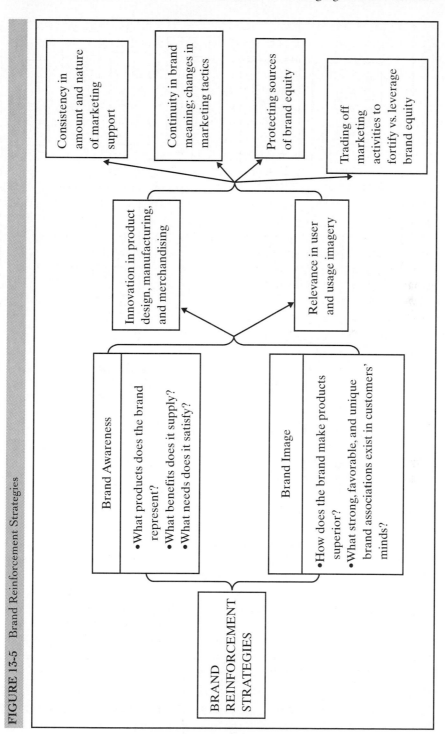

FIGURE 13-5   Brand Reinforcement Strategies

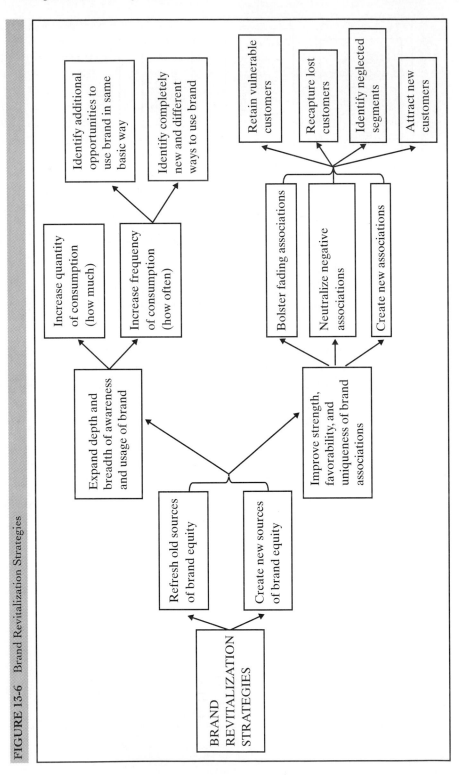

FIGURE 13-6 Brand Revitalization Strategies

find yourself wondering why brands aren't staffed like ships. True most brands have a captain, several admirals, and assorted crew to run the engines and polish the brass. But all too few brands have a navigator whose job is to keep the ship on course towards a destination that is far over the horizon. This is especially scary when you consider your USS Brand will undergo several complete crew changeovers before reaching anything remotely resembling a safe port, and that it sails in oceans studded with the perils of changing winds, tides, and currents, to say nothing of enemy subs and icebergs appearing out of the fog.[34]

Discussion Questions

1. Pick a brand. Assess its efforts to manage brand equity in the last five years. What actions has it taken to be innovative and relevant? Can you suggest any changes to its marketing program?

2. Pick a product category. Examine the histories of the leading brands in that category over the last decade. How would you characterize their efforts to reinforce or revitalize brand equity?

3. Identify a fading brand. What suggestions can you offer to revitalize its brand equity? Try to apply the different approaches suggested in this chapter. Which strategies would seem to work best?

4. Try to think of additional examples of brands that adopted either a "back to basics" or "reinvention" revitalization strategy. How well did the strategies work?

5. Conduct a review of the Unilever brand portfolio (see Branding Brief 13-10). How successful has the company been at reducing the number of brands? What lessons are to be learned from its strategies?

Brand   Focus   13 . 0

Corporate Rebranding and Name Changes

RATIONALE

As Chapter 11 noted, corporate brand names and corporate images can perform a variety of functions to multiple audiences or target markets. Consequently, corporate names may have to be changed for a number of different reasons. Hundreds of private and public companies change their names each year.

The main reason that corporations change their name is because of mergers and acquisitions with other businesses. In such cases, a completely new name may be chosen to signal new capabilities. For example, when Sperry and Burroughs merged they became Unisys (a Latin cognate that was designed to suggest information systems). In other cases, a new corporate name arising from a merger or acquisition may be based on some combination of the two existing corporate names. For example, when Glaxo and Burroughs Wellcome merged they became Glaxo Wellcome, and Lockheed and Martin Marrietta became Lockheed Martin. Finally, in some cases, the name with more potential inherent brand equity is chosen and the other name is relegated to a sub-brand role or eliminated altogether. For example, when Citicorp merged with Travelers, the latter's name was dropped, although its familiar red umbrella symbol was retained as part of the new Citigroup brand look. Deciding which is the appropriate strategy depends on the existing and potential brand equity associated with each brand in the context of the newly merged business.

Another reason that corporate names may need to be changed is because of divestitures, leveraged buyouts, or sale of assets. For example, when the 155-year-old farm equipment and truck maker International Harvester Company sold its agricultural equipment operations along with its name and the IH logo in 1984, it was legally required to change its name within five years. After much research, the new name Navistar was chosen, with "Navi" coming from the Latin word for leading or navigating and "star" signifying a heavenly body or outstanding performer. Although some critics criticized the name for sounding more like a company with interests in marine equipment or space flight than trucks, Navistar marketing executives note that the name was deliberately chosen to be flexible and permit room for growth in the future.

The corporate name may also need to be changed because of public misperceptions about the nature of the company's business. For example, Europe's third-largest food company, BSN, renamed the company after its Danone brand—a hugely successful fresh dairy products subsidiary, second only to Coca-Cola in terms of branded sales in Europe—because many consumers didn't know what the old name stood for. Moreover, BSN was already used by other companies in other countries: a bank in Spain, a textile firm in the United States, and a television station in Japan.[35]

Finally, significant shifts in corporate strategy may necessitate name changes. For example, US Steel changed its name to USX to downplay the importance of steel and metal in its product mix. Allegheny Airlines changed its name to USAir when it moved from a regional to a national carrier, and then later to USAirways when it wanted to be seen as an international carrier.

GUIDELINES

In changing the corporate name, the assumption is that the existing brand associations do not have the desired strength, favorability, and uniqueness and that a new name can be chosen—perhaps in combination with a corporate image campaign—that better conveys the desired brand image. Name changes are typically complicated, time-consuming, and expensive, however, and should only be undertaken when compelling marketing or financial considerations prevail and a proper supporting marketing program can be put into place. A new corporate name cannot hide product or other marketing deficiencies. A company with little consumer exposure may spend as much as $5 million on research, advertising, and other marketing costs (e.g., new signs, stationery, business cards, and so on) to change its identity, but a company with a high public profile may have to spend up to $100 million.[36]

Many of the same issues regarding choosing brand names that were discussed in Chapter 4 are relevant in choosing or changing a corporate name. Thus, candidate names should be evaluated in terms of memorability, meaningfulness, likability, protectability, adaptability, and transferability. The importance of the corporate name will depend on the corporate branding strategy that is adopted and the marketing objectives with respect to different target markets. If the financial community is a priority, a different name may be chosen than if the consumer market is the priority. For example, if the financial community is a priority, corporate names may be changed to highlight a particular brand or company (e.g., Consolidated Foods Corporation switched to Sara Lee Corporation; Castle & Cooke, Inc., switched to Dole Food Company; and United Brands Company switched to Chiquita Brands International). If the consumer market is the primary objective, names may be chosen to reflect or be suggestive of certain product characteristics, benefits, or values.

One of the biggest name-change fizzles ever occurred with UAL, the parent company of United Airlines. In 1987, UAL was no longer just an airline but a $9 billion business that owned Hertz car rental, as well as Westin and Hilton International hotels. It was decided that a new name was necessary to convey the identity of a travel company that offered one-stop shopping. After extensive research, the name "Allegis" was chosen, a compound of "allegiance" and "aegis." Public reaction was decidedly negative. Critics maintained that the name was difficult to pronounce, pretentious sounding, and had little connection with travel services. Real estate developer Donald Trump, formerly a major UAL shareholder, said the new name was "better suited to the next world class disease." After six weeks and $7 million in research and promotion expenditures, the company decided to shed its car rental and hotel businesses and rename the surviving company as United Airlines Inc.[37]

Many name changes seem to follow trends. One corporate identity specialist notes that although businesses took on exotic-sounding animal-like names in the 1950s and 1960s, high-tech names became popular in the 1970s and 1980s.[38] "Star" became a commonly used prefix, and names with "X" also became popular as a means to signal excellence. A new corporate brand name and other supporting brand elements, however, should be chosen systematically in the same careful way that any brand name is chosen. Moreover, once a new name is chosen, substantial efforts must be undertaken to sell the new name to employees, customers, suppliers, investors, and the public at large.[39] Because of a resistance to change, initial reaction to a new name is almost always negative. For example, when New York Telephone and New England Telephone changed their name to NYNEX, critics attacked the name as sounding too much like medicine or Ex-Lax (a well-known laxative).[40] Over time, though, if properly chosen and handled, new names gain familiarity and acceptance. Effective implementation requires guidelines that encourage uniformity and consistency in the appearance and usage of the brand; these rules should be included as part of a revised brand charter (see Chapter 8).

Notes

1. Ronald Alsop, "Enduring Brands Hold Their Allure by Sticking Close to Their Roots," *Wall Street Journal Centennial Edition*, 23 June 1989, B4.
2. For an empirical examination of the power of sustained advertising, see Cathy J. Cobb-Walgren, Cynthia A. Ruble, and Naveen Donthu, "Brand Equity, Brand Preference, and Purchase Intent," *Journal of Advertising* 24, no. 3 (Fall 1995): 25–40.
3. Marj Charlier, "Coors Pours on Western Themes to Revive Flagship Beer's Cachet," *Wall Street Journal*, 2 August 1994, B6.
4. Chris Roush, "At Timex, They're Positively Glowing," *Business Week*, 12 July 1993, 141.
5. Joseph Pereira, "Hasbro Enjoys Life Off the Toy-Market Roller Coaster," *Wall Street Journal*, 5 May 1992, B4; Keith H. Hammonds, "'Has-Beens Have Been Very Good to Hasbro," *Business Week*, 5 August 1991, 76–77.
6. Jonathan Auerbach, "Smith Corona Seeks Protection of Chapter 11," *Wall Street Journal*, 6 July 1995, A4.
7. Melanie Wells, "Foggy Bottom," *Forbes*, 28 May 2001, 155.
8. Timothy L. O'Brien, "Beleaguered Schwinn Seeks Partner to Regain Luster," *Wall Street Journal*, 20 May 1992, B2.
9. Peter H. Farquhar, "Managing Brand Equity," *Marketing Research* 1 (September 1989): 24–33.
10. Richard Gibson, "Classic Cheerios and Wheaties Reformulated," *Wall Street Journal*, 31 August 1994, B1.
11. Joanne Lipman, "Coca-Cola Is Close to Picking New Slogan," *Wall Street Journal*, 28 September 1992, B10; Kevin Goldman, "Diet Coke Loses Its Taste for Latest Slogan," *Wall Street Journal*, 13 July 1993, B5; Kevin Goldman, "Lintas's Campaign for Diet Coke Fizzles," *Wall Street Journal*, 28 May 1993, B3; Kevin Goldman, "Interpublic's Lintas Loses Diet Coke Job," *Wall Street Journal*, 6 October 1993, B10; Kevin Goldman, "Refreshment Bears Weight for Diet Coke," *Wall Street Journal*, 13 January 1994, B6.
12. Michael J. McCarthy, "Pepsi is Returning to Original Focus: Its Profitable Younger Generation," *Wall Street Journal*, 22 January 1993, B6.
13. Betsy McKay, "Coke Taps Ripken for Home-Run Pitch," *Wall Street Journal*, 7 September 2001, B6.
14. Susan Heckler, Kevin Lane Keller, and Michael J. Houston, "The Effects of Brand Name Suggestiveness on Advertising Recall," *Journal of Marketing* 62 (January 1998): 48–57.
15. Raymond Serafin, "BMW: From Yuppie-Mobile to Smart Car of the '90s," *Advertising Age*, 3 October 1994, S2.
16. Norman C. Berry, "Revitalizing Brands," *Journal of Consumer Marketing* 5, no. 3 (Summer 1988): 15–20.
17. Laura Bird, "Grey Poupon Tones Down Tony Image," *Wall Street Journal*, 22 July 1994, B3.
18. John D. Cripps, "Heuristics and Biases in Timing the Replacement of Durable Products," *Journal of Consumer Research* 21 (September 1994): 304–318.
19. Ronald Alsop, "Giving Fading Brands a Second Chance," *Wall Street Journal*, 24 January 1989, B1.
20. Marj Charlier, "Yuengling's Success Defies Convention," *Wall Street Journal*, 26 August 1993, B1.
21. Kevin Goldman, "Del Monte Tries to Freshen Its Market," *Wall Street Journal*, 20 October 1994, B4.

22. Tim Triplett, "Generic Fear to Xerox Is Brand Equity to FedEx," *Marketing News*, 15 August 1994, 12–13.

23. Teri Agins, "Women Help Van Heusen Collar Arrow," *Wall Street Journal*, 22 May 1992, B1.

24. David W. Stewart, "Advertising in a Slow-Growth Economy," *American Demographics* (September 1994): 40–46.

25. Ibid.

26. Alsop, "Giving Fading Brands a Second Chance."

27. Bruce Horovitz and Melanie Wells, "Long After Their Sales Stop Sizzling, Some Brand Names Linger in . . . Product Purgatory," *USA Today*, 2 May 1995, B1.

28. Kevin Goldman, "Old Spice's Familiar Sailor Is Lost at Sea," *Wall Street Journal*, 10 September 1993, B2.

29. Jennifer Reingold, "Darwin Goes Shopping," *Financial World*, 1 September 1993, 44.

30. Nancy F. Koehn, *Brand New: How Enterpreneurs Earned Consumers' Trust from Wedgwood to Dell,* (Boston: Harvard Business School Press, 2001).

31. Betsy McKay, "Why Coke Indulges (the Few) Fans of Tab," *Wall Street Journal*, 13 April 2001, B1; Devon Spurgeon, "Aurora Bet It Could Win by Fostering Neglected Foods," *Wall Street Journal*, 13 April 2001, B1; Jim Hopkins, "Partners Turn Decrepit Detergent into Boffo Start-Up," *USA Today*, 20 June 2001, 6B; Matthew Swibel, "Spin Cycle," *Forbes*, 2 April 2001, 118.

32. David A. Aaker, *Managing Brand Equity* (New York: Free Press, 1991).

33. Tara Parker-Pope, "Unilever Plans a Long-Overdue Pruning," *Wall Street Journal*, 3 September 1996, A13.

34. Brad Morgan, "Navigating Marketing Waters Is a Risky, Learning Process," *Brandweek,* 5 September 1994, 17.

35. "BSWho?" *The Economist*, 14 May 1994, 70.

36. Dottie Enrico, "Companies Play Name-Change Game," *USA Today*, 28 December 1994, 4B.

37. "Allegis: A $7 Million Name Is Grounded," *San Francisco Examiner*, 16 June 1987, C9.

38. Bernice Kanner, "The New Name Game," *New York*, 16 March 1987, 16, 19.

39. Amanda Bennett, "Firms Grapple to Find New Names as Images and Industries Change," *Wall Street Journal*, 17 November 1986, 36.

40. Kanner, "The New Name Game."

CHAPTER

14

Managing Brands over Geographic Boundaries and Market Segments

    4. Embrace Integrated Marketing Communications
        Advertising
        Promotion and Sponsorship
    5. Cultivate Brand Partnerships
    6. Balance Standardization and Customization
        Product Strategy
        Pricing Strategy
    7. Balance Global and Local Control
    8. Establish Operable Guidelines
    9. Implement a Global Brand Equity Measurement System
    10. Leverage Brand Elements
Review
Discussion Questions
Brand Focus 14.0   Building Brand Equity across Other Market Segments

PREVIEW

An important consideration in managing brand equity is recognizing and accounting for different types of consumers in developing brand marketing programs. Previous chapters have considered how and why marketers may need to (1) create brand portfolios to satisfy different market segments and (2) develop brand migration strategies to attract new customers and retain existing customers through brand and family life cycles. This chapter examines in more detail the implications of differences in consumer behavior and the existence of different types of market segments for managing brand equity. It pays particular attention to international issues and global branding strategies.

Specifically, after discussing the basic rationale for taking brands into new geographic markets, the chapter considers the broader issues in developing a global brand strategy. Some of the pros and cons of developing a standardized global marketing program for a brand are examined. The remainder of the chapter then concentrates on specific strategic and tactical issues in building global customer-based brand equity, organized around the concept of the "Ten Commandments of Global Branding." To illustrate these guidelines, particular emphasis is placed on global brand pioneers such as Coca-Cola, Nestlé, and Procter & Gamble. Brand Focus 14.0 addresses brand management issues over other types of market segments.

RATIONALE FOR GOING INTERNATIONAL

A number of well-known global brands have derived much of their sales and profits from nondomestic markets for years, for example, Coca-Cola, Shell, Bayer, Rolex, Marlboro, Pampers, and Mercedes-Benz to name a few. Brands such as Apple computers, L'Oreal cosmetics, and Nescafé instant coffee have become fixtures on the global landscape (see Branding Brief 14-1). The successes of these brands have provided encouragement to many firms to market their brands internationally. A number of other forces have also contributed to the growing interest in global marketing, including the following:

L'Oreal Colors the World

L'Oreal was founded in 1907 by French chemist Eugene Schueller, who developed a safe hair color formula named "Aureole." Today, L'Oreal is the largest and fastest-growing cosmetics company in the world. It markets more than 500 brands and over 2,000 products in all sectors of the beauty business.

Recently, L'Oreal has pursued an aggressive global growth strategy, prompting one business writer to christen the company "the United Nations of beauty." L'Oreal has a number of global mega-brands that cast a broad net over the global market. For example, Maybelline is the best-selling brand in many Asian markets, while eastern Europeans prefer L'Oreal's French brands, and African immigrants in Europe go for the American brand Dark & Lovely. At the same time, the company ensures its business remains sound on a local level by establishing national divisions. Gilles Weil, L'Oreal's head of luxury products, said, "You have to be local and as strong as the best locals but backed by an international image and strategy."

One of L'Oreal's global success stories started with the acquisition of struggling American cosmetics company Maybelline in 1996. With the help of a series of innovative product introductions, L'Oreal turned the brand into the number one makeup brand in the United States. The star product for the new Maybelline was Wondercurl, a mascara and brush that curls and thickens eyelashes. Wondercurl took off again when L'Oreal took control of Maybelline Japan in 1999 and quickly introduced the product. Within three months, Wondercurl captured 18 percent of the market and became Japan's leading mascara. Unit sales of Maybelline Japan rose from 5 million to 12 million within one year of L'Oreal's takeover.

Within national markets, L'Oreal devotes attention to serving different customer segments. For example, in 2000 L'Oreal captured 20 percent of the $1.2 billion American "ethnic hair care" market with separate acquisitions of Soft Sheen Products and Carson Products. The company considered the ethnic hair care market vital because African Americans account for 30 percent of total U.S. hair care expenditures despite the fact they comprise only 13 percent of the population. These acquisitions figured to add to L'Oreal's 49 percent share of the $1.3 billion U.S. hair color market.

Though the company keeps such statistics private, *Advertising Age* estimated that L'Oreal increased its global ad spending to $1.25 billion in 1998. Despite long-term problems in many foreign markets, L'Oreal's profits rose at a 15 percent compounded rate through 2000. As one analyst puts it, "L'Oreal is the only real global leader in every segment of the industry."

Sources: Richard C. Morais, "The Color of Beauty," *Forbes*, 27 November 2000, 170–176; Gail Edmondson, "L'Oreal: The Beauty of Global Branding," *Business Week*, 28 June 1999, 24.

➤ Perception of slow growth and increased competition in domestic markets
➤ Belief in enhanced overseas growth and profit opportunities
➤ Desire to reduce costs from economies of scale
➤ Need to diversify risk
➤ Recognition of global mobility of customers

In more and more product categories, the ability to establish a global profile is becoming virtually a prerequisite for success.[1] For example, with U.S. liquor consumption steadily declining, many American producers have stepped up their marketing efforts abroad, riding the fortunes of brands such as Jim Beam, Jack Daniels, and Southern Comfort in overseas markets. As one observer notes, "Spirits companies now view themselves as global marketers. If you want to be a player, you have to be in America, Europe, and the Far East. You must have world-class brands, a long-term perspective, and deep pockets."[2]

Ideally, the marketing program for a global brand would consist of one product formulation, one package design, one advertising program, one pricing schedule, one distribution plan, and so on that would turn out to be the most effective and efficient possible option for each and every country in which the brand was sold. Unfortunately, such a uniformly optimal strategy is rarely possible. Before considering the decisions to be made in developing a global marketing program for a brand and the factors affecting the tradeoff between standardization and customization, it is useful to first consider some of the main advantages and disadvantages of creating globally standardized marketing programs for brands.

ADVANTAGES OF GLOBAL MARKETING PROGRAMS

A number of potential advantages have been put forth concerning the development of a global marketing program (see Figure 14-1). In general, the more standardized the marketing program—that is, the less the marketing program varies from country to country—the greater the extent to which these different advantages will actually be realized.

Economies of Scale in Production and Distribution

From a supply-side or cost perspective, the primary advantage of a global marketing program is the manufacturing efficiencies and lower costs that derive from higher volumes in production and distribution. The more that strong experience curve effects

Economies of scale in production and distribution
Lower marketing costs
Power and scope
Consistency in brand image
Ability to leverage good ideas quickly and efficiently
Uniformity of marketing practices

FIGURE 14-1   Advantages of Global Marketing Programs

exist—such that the cost of making and marketing a product declines sharply with increases in cumulative production—the more economies of scale in production and distribution will be realized from a standardized global marketing program.

Lower Marketing Costs

Another set of cost advantages can be realized from uniformity in packaging, advertising, promotion, and other marketing communication activities. In particular, the more uniform the branding strategy adopted across countries, the more potential cost savings should prevail. Along these lines, a global corporate branding strategy (e.g., as with Sony) is perhaps the most efficient means of spreading marketing costs across both products and countries.

> ### ExxonMobil
> In 1999, ExxonMobil launched a $150 million marketing effort to promote its portfolio of brands (Exxon, Esso, Mobil, and General). To make sure the ads had the same look and feel regardless of the 100 or so countries in which they might appear, the company produced five hours of commercial footage to be used as a library by local markets. As many as six different casts acted out essentially the same story lines, and 25 different languages were used in the voiceovers. ExxonMobil's ad agency, DDB Worldwide, noted that the campaign, which carried the tag line "We Are Drivers Too," was tweaked to account for cultural differences (e.g., making sure actors ate with their right hands in some shots as is customary in some Muslim markets).[3] Management believed that this approach helped to save the company millions.

Power and Scope

A global brand profile may communicate credibility to consumers. Consumers may believe that selling in many diverse markets is an indication that a manufacturer has gained much expertise and acceptance. The fact that the brand is widely available may signal that the product is high quality and convenient to use. A prominent international profile may be especially important for certain service brands. For example, Avis assures their customers that they can receive the same high-quality service renting its cars anywhere in the world, further reinforcing a key benefit promise embodied in its slogan, "We Try Harder."

Consistency in Brand Image

Maintaining a common marketing platform all over the world helps to maintain the consistency of brand and company image. This consideration becomes particularly important in those markets where there is much customer mobility or where media exposure transmits images across national boundaries. For example, Gillette Mach3 sells "functional superiority" and "an appreciation of human character and aspirations" worldwide. Services often desire to convey a uniform image due to consumer movements. For example, American Express communicates the prestige and utility of its card and the convenience and ease of replacement of its traveler's checks worldwide.

Ability to Leverage Good Ideas Quickly and Efficiently

One global marketer notes that globalization also can result in increased sustainability and "facilitate continued development of core competencies with the organization . . . in manufacturing, in R&D, in Marketing and Sales, and in less talked about areas such as Competitive Intelligence . . . all of which enhance the company's ability to compete."[4]

Rank Xerox

Rank Xerox, an 80 percent-owned subsidiary of Xerox that sells billions of dollars worth of copiers, document processors, and services, initiated a "plug-and-play" benchmarking project in an attempt to spread best marketing practices. Gathering sales data and making country-by-country comparisons, it easily found eight cases in which one country outperformed the others and documented how it was being done. For example, France sold five times more color copiers than its sister divisions. By copying France's practices in selling color copiers—chiefly by improving sales training and making sure that color copiers were pushed through dealer channels as well as direct sales—Switzerland increased its unit sales of color copiers by 328 percent, Holland by 300 percent, Norway by 152 percent, and so on.[5]

Uniformity of Marketing Practices

Finally, a standardized global marketing program may simplify coordination and provide greater control of how the brand is being marketed in different countries. By keeping the core of the marketing program constant, greater attention can be paid to making refinements over markets and over time to improve its effectiveness.

Colgate Total

In 1992, an advertisement was developed to launch Colgate Total toothpaste in Europe featuring a "Brushing Man." The ad followed this man throughout his day, from after he brushed with Colgate Total in the early morning until he went to sleep at night. Every time the viewer saw him throughout his day, a brushing sound was evident, suggesting that Colgate Total was still working. The ad campaign was eventually used in over 100 countries to launch Colgate Total globally. It evolved over time, however, as certain elements were found to be stronger communicators and persuaders than others. For example, it was found that it was very important to have the Brushing Man interacting with people since knowledge that toothpaste was working in social situations turned out to be highly persuasive, and a clock needed to be shown throughout to show the passage of time and the conditions Colgate Total worked against.

DISADVANTAGES OF GLOBAL MARKETING PROGRAMS

A number of potential disadvantages of standardized global marketing programs have also been raised (see Figure 14-2). Perhaps the most compelling criticism is that standardized global marketing programs often ignore fundamental differences of various kinds across countries and cultures. Critics claim that designing one marketing program for all possible markets often results in unimaginative and ineffective strategies

Differences in consumer needs, wants, and usage patterns
   for products
Differences in consumer response to marketing mix
   elements
Differences in brand and product development and the
   competitive environment
Differences in the legal environment
Differences in marketing institutions
Differences in administrative procedures

FIGURE 14-2 Disadvantages of Global Marketing Programs

geared to the lowest common denominator. Possible differences across countries come in a host of forms, as discussed next.

Differences in Consumer Needs, Wants, and Usage Patterns for Products

Because of differences in cultural values, economic development, and other factors across nationalities, consumer behavior with respect to many product categories is fundamentally different. For example, marketing research at one time revealed that the French ate 4 times more yogurt than the British, the British consumed 8 times more chocolate than the Italians, and Americans drank 11 times more soft drinks than consumers abroad.[6] Product strategies that work in one country may not work in another. For example, when Disney entered a licensing agreement with Tupperware to sell in Japan, although marketing research suggested it was a good idea, the product failed miserably. Apparently the problem was in the politeness of the Japanese housewives. Although they said they would attend Tupperware parties—and did in fact come and buy products at parties—they resented the people who hosted the party and the company for putting them into that situation.

Differences in Consumer Response to Marketing Mix Elements

Consumers in different parts of the world can vary in their attitudes and opinions concerning marketing activity.[7] For example, countries vary in their general attitudes toward advertising as an institution. Research has shown that Americans, in general, tend to be fairly cynical toward advertising, whereas Japanese view it much more positively. Research has also shown differences in advertising style between the two countries: Japanese ads tend to be softer and more abstract in tone, whereas American ads tend to be richer in product information.

Price sensitivity, promotion responsiveness, sponsorship support, and other activities all may differ by the country involved. These differences in response to marketing activity may also be reflected in differences in consumer behavior and decision making. For example, in a comparative study of brand purchase intentions for Korean and U.S. consumers, the purchase intentions of Americans were twice as likely to be affected by their product beliefs and attitudes toward the brand itself, whereas Koreans were eight times more likely to be influenced by social normative beliefs and what they felt others would think about the purchase.[8]

Differences in Brand and Product Development and the Competitive Environment

Products may be at different stages of their life cycle in different countries. Moreover, the perceptions and positions of particular brands may also differ considerably across countries. Figure 14-3 shows the results of a comprehensive study of leading brands (of all kinds, including country brands) in different parts of the world by Young & Rubicam with its BrandAsset Valuator (see Brand Focus 10.0). Relatively few brands appear on all the lists, suggesting that, if nothing else, consumer perceptions of even top brands can vary significantly by geographic region. The nature of competition may also differ. Europeans tend to have more competitors because shipping products across borders is easy. For example, Procter & Gamble competes in France against Italian, Swedish, and Danish companies in many categories.[9]

Differences in the Legal Environment

Different kinds of regulatory hurdles exist in different countries. One of the challenges in developing a global ad campaign is the maze of constantly changing legal restrictions that exist from country to country. For example, at one time, laws in Venezuela, Canada, and Australia stipulated that commercials had to be physically produced in the native country. Poland required commercial lyrics to be sung in Polish. Advertising restrictions have been placed on the use of children in commercials in Austria, heroic figures in cigarette ads in the United Kingdom (e.g., prohibiting even the use of the Marlboro man), comparative ads in Singapore, and toy soldiers with either machine guns or tanks in Germany. Note the challenges posed by the following example.

> At the J. Walter Thompson ad agency, executives point to a 30-second cereal commercial produced for British TV to show how much regulations in Europe alone can sap an ad. References to iron and vitamins would have to be deleted in the Netherlands; a child wearing a Kellogg's T-shirt would be edited out in France where children are forbidden from endorsing products on TV. And in Germany, the line "Kellogg makes their corn flakes the best they've ever been" would be axed because of rules against making competitive claims. After the required changes, the commercial would be about 5 seconds long.[10]

Although some of these laws have been or are being relaxed, numerous legal differences still exist.

Differences in Marketing Institutions

Some of the basic marketing infrastructure may differ from country to country, making implementation of the same marketing strategy difficult. For example, channels of distribution, retail practices, media availability, and media costs all may vary significantly. Foreign companies have struggled for years to break into Japan's rigid distribution system that locks out many foreign goods. China's primitive logistics—poor roads, jammed rivers, and clogged railways—and inexperienced, indifferent, and often corrupt middlemen present a different kind of challenge.[11] The penetration of television

FIGURE 14-3 Global Brand Rankings

Rank	United States (1999)	United Kingdom (1999)	Germany (2000)	Brazil (1999)	Singapore (1999)	Japan (1997)	France (2000)
1	United States	England	Germany	Coca-Cola	Singapore	Disney	France
2	Disney	United Kingdom	Aldi	BomBril	Coca-Cola	Nike	ARTE
3	Hallmark	Cadbury	DM Deutsche Mark	OMO	Singapore Airlines	Mosburger	Coca-Cola
4	The Discovery Channel	Channel 4	Coca-Cola	Rede Globo	MRT	Sony	Nutella
5	PBS	Heinz	Nivea	Nestlé	TCS 5	Mister Donuts	Levi's
6	The Wonderful World of Disney	After Eight	ARD	Brastemp	Takashimaya	Torikkiri Konica	Scrabble
7	Coca-Cola	Toblerone	The Olympic Games	General Foods (Kibon)	Ikea	McDonald's	Tefal
8	Dr Pepper	BBC 2	Volkswagen	McDonald's	Ngee Ann City	Coca-Cola	LeTGV
9	Mickey Mouse	Coca-Cola	Milka	Guaraná Antarctica	TCS 8	Nintendo	Canal +
10	The Learning Channel	Nescafé	Mercedes	Sonho de Valsa	Suntec City	Mickey Mouse	Monopoly
11	Tupperware	BBC	LEGO	Sadia	Nokia	Asahi Super Dry	M6
12	Fox Network	Pringles	Ferrero	Havaianas	Microsoft	Sony PlayStation	Ferrero Rocher
13	M & Ms	BBC 1	Ikea	Dove Soap	Swatch	Honda	Suchard
14	Cotton (Fabric)	Disney	Mon Cheri	Estrela	Sentosa	Nissin Rao	Perrier
15	Oreo	Thorntons	Adidas	Nescau	Bugis Junction	Lawson	Apéricube

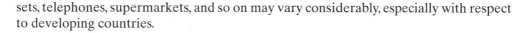

sets, telephones, supermarkets, and so on may vary considerably, especially with respect to developing countries.

Differences in Administrative Procedures

In practice, it may be difficult to achieve the control necessary to implement a standardized global marketing program. Local offices may resist having their autonomy threatened. Local managers may suffer from the "not invented here" syndrome and raise objections—rightly or wrongly—that the global marketing program misses some key dimension of the local market. Local managers who feel that their autonomy has been reduced may lose motivation and feel doomed to failure.

STANDARDIZATION VERSUS CUSTOMIZATION

As the previous discussion suggests, although firms are increasingly adopting an international marketing perspective to capitalize on market opportunities, a number of possible pitfalls exist. Before providing some strategic and tactical guidelines as to how to build global customer-based brand equity, it is worthwhile to examine more closely issues concerning standardization versus customization of brand marketing programs. In many ways, the most fundamental issue in developing a global marketing program is the extent to which the marketing program should be standardized across countries because it has such a deep impact on marketing structure and processes.

Perhaps the biggest proponent of standardization is the legendary Harvard professor Ted Levitt. In a controversial 1983 article, Levitt argued that companies needed to learn to operate as if the world were one large market, ignoring superficial regional and national differences:

> A thousand suggestive ways attest to the ubiquity of the desire for the most advanced things that the world makes and sells—goods of the best quality and reliability at the lowest price. The world's needs and desires have been irrevocably homogenized. This makes the multinational corporation obsolete and the global corporation absolute. . . .
>
> But although companies customize products for particular market segments, they know that success in a world with homogenized demand requires a search for sales opportunities in similar segments across the globe in order to achieve the economies of scale necessary to compete.[12]

According to Levitt, because the world is shrinking—due to leaps in technology, communication, and so forth—well-managed companies should shift their emphasis from customizing items to offering globally standardized products that are advanced, functional, reliable, and low-priced for all.

Levitt's strong position elicited an equally strong response. Carl Spielvogel, chairman and chief executive of ad agency Backer Spielvogel Bates Worldwide, replied, "There are about two products that lend themselves to global marketing—and one of them is Coca-Cola." Other critics pointed out that even Coca-Cola did not standardize its marketing and noted the lack of standardization in other leading global brands, such as McDonald's and Marlboro. The experiences of these top marketers have been shared by others who found out—in many cases, the hard way—that differences in consumer behavior still prevail across countries. Many firms have been forced to tailor products and marketing programs to different national markets as a result.

➤ When Pillsbury decided to introduce a canned sweet corn as a global launch of its Green Giant brand of vegetables, it was surprised to find that, instead of eating the corn as a hot side dish as intended, the French added it to salad and ate it cold, the British used it as a sandwich and pizza topping, and Japanese children ate it as an after-school treat.[13]

➤ When General Foods attempted to make its Tang powdered orange drink into a global brand, the company found that the Germans did not like the name, the British did not like the taste, and the French did not typically drink orange juice for breakfast. To crack those markets, it had to rename the drink Seefrisch in Germany, sell a tarter-tasting Tang in Britain, and reposition the product as an all-day, fun, family drink in France.[14]

➤ Heinz ketchup has a slightly sweet taste in the United States but is spicier in certain European countries, where it is available in hot, Mexican, and curry flavors. Ketchup usage varies by country too. In Greece, it is poured on pasta, eggs, and cuts of meat. In Japan, it is promoted as an ingredient to Western-style foods such as omelets, sausages, and pasta. Heinz has downplayed its American heritage in certain countries, for example, in Sweden, where ketchup is used to accompany traditional meatballs and fishballs. In fact, Swedes thought the brand was German because of the name. In Germany, however, American themes work well and have been used in advertising.[15]

In summary, it is difficult to identify any one company applying the global marketing concept in the *strict* sense—selling an identical brand exactly the same way, everywhere.

Standardization *and* Customization

Increasingly, marketers are blending global objectives with local or regional concerns. Coca-Cola's new global marketing mantra is "Think Local. Act Local."—an important twist on its old mantra, "Think Global. Act Local." Intended to get Coca-Cola back to the basics, the strategy involves hiring more local staff and allowing field managers to tailor marketing to their regions. Beyond trying to better connect the company to consumers in each market, the locally oriented strategy strives for more targeted marketing and faster decision making.[16] Branding Brief 14-2 describes some of the history of Coca-Cola's global branding efforts.

Similar to this approach, Procter & Gamble's strategy is to make global plans, replan for each region, and execute locally. Former P&G head of marketing Robert L. Wehling made the following comments concerning the company's global marketing efforts during the 1990s:

> To us, a global brand is one that has a clear and consistent equity—or identity—with consumers across geographies. It is generally positioned the same from one country to another. It has essentially the same product formulation, delivers the same benefits and uses a consistent advertising concept. That isn't to say there isn't room for local tailoring. In fact, there must be room to adapt to local needs. But where there's no justification for difference, the brand is the same in every part of the world.[17]

Coca-Cola Becomes the Quintessential Global Brand

The most recognized brand name in the world got its start in an Atlanta pharmacy, where it sold for five cents a glass. The name Coca-Cola was registered as a trademark on January 31, 1893. In its early days, when the drink contained a form of cocaine, a drug made from coca leave extracts, Coca-Cola was marketed as an "Esteemed Brain Tonic and Intellectual Beverage." The name was penned by Dr. Pemberton's business partner, Frank Robinson, in the unique flowing script that is famous world wide today. Mr. Robinson thought that the two Cs would look good in advertising. The company's first president, Asa Candler, was a savvy businessman who implemented numerous marketing strategies to increase consumption. At Candler's behest, the company printed coupons offering complimentary first tastes of Coca-Cola, and outfitted distributing pharmacists with clocks, calendars, and scales bearing the Coca-Cola brand. The drink soon became a national phenomenon; by 1895, the company had established syrup plants in Chicago, Dallas, and Los Angeles.

Coca-Cola expanded into numerous countries in the early 1900s, including Cuba, Puerto Rico, and France. In the 1920s, Coca-Cola pursued aggressive global branding, finding creative placements for its logo, such as on dogsleds in Canada and on the walls of bullfighting arenas in Spain. During World War II, the U.S. Army shipped bottles of the beverage and bottling plants abroad to supply American soldiers in Europe and Asia. Its popularity throughout the world was fueled by colorful and persuasive advertising that cemented its image as the "All-American" beverage. When the Vietnam War tarnished the American iconography somewhat, Coca-Cola developed more globally aware advertising. In 1971, Coca-Cola ran its legendary "I'd like to buy the world a Coke" television spot, in which a crowd of children sang the song from atop a hill in Italy. Coca-Cola's moves into formerly restricted markets, such as China in 1978 and the Soviet Union in 1979, bolstered its image as a global company. By 1988, Coca-Cola was voted the best known and most admired brand in the world.

Despite—or perhaps as a result of—this immense scope, Coca-Cola did not institute a uniform marketing program in each of its global markets. Rather, the company often tailored the flavor, packaging, price, and advertising to match the tastes in specific markets. For example, Coke's famous "Mean Joe" Green TV ad from the United States—in which the weary football star reluctantly accepts a Coke from an admiring young fan and then unexpectedly tosses the kid his jersey in appreciation—was replicated in a number of different regions using the same format but substituting famous athletes from those regions (e.g., ads in South America used the Argentine soccer star Maradona, while those in Asia used the Thai soccer star Niat). Additionally, local managers were assigned responsibility for sales and distribution programs of Coke products to reflect the marked differences in consumer behavior across countries. For example, in Spain, Coke has been used as a mixer with wine; in Italy, Coke has been served with meals in place of wine or cappuccino; in China, the beverage was served at special government occasions.

Perhaps the most standardized element of Coca-Cola is its product appearance. Coke essentially keeps the same basic look and packaging of the product everywhere (except in countries where laws dictate use of local language). For legal reasons, Diet

Coke is called Coca-Cola Light in Europe, and the particular artificial sweeteners and packaging used for Diet Coke can differ in various parts of the world too. The company simultaneously stresses that the brand be *relevant* and well positioned relative to competition. In trying to keep the brand relevant, Coca-Cola uses different advertising agencies in different countries in order to make the brand feel local. For example, in Australia the advertising appeals to the same "classic, original" ideals but in a very Australian fashion. Moreover, the marketing mix is designed in each country to stress that Coke is positioned positively on attributes relative to local competitive products. Hence, although Coke looks similar across the globe, its specific image may be very different, depending on what is considered "relevant" in each country. The advantage of this approach is that Coke becomes entwined with the cultural fabric of the country, just as it has in the United States. Over time this yields an advantage with younger generations who don't even think of Coke as an imported brand. An illustrative example that Coca-Cola recounts is of a Japanese family visiting the United States for the first time whose young son, upon passing a vending machine, joyfully exclaimed to his parents, "Look, they have Coke here too!"

Today, Coca-Cola conducts business with more than 230 brands in 200 countries. More than two-thirds of Coca-Cola's revenues come from outside the United States, a fact that makes the company vulnerable to downturns in international economies, as evidenced by the company's shallow earnings during the global economic upheaval in the late 1990s. In response to the depressed sales wrought by international recessions, the company pursued a restructuring plan that would recast the beverage giant as "a collection of smaller, locally run businesses." When Douglas Daft took over as chairman and CEO in 2000, he expressed his desire for Coca-Cola managers to adopt a new mantra: "Think locally and act locally."

Sources: "The Story of Coca-Cola," http://www.coca-cola.com; Betsy McKay, "Coca-Cola Restructuring Effort Has Yet to Prove Effective," *Asian Wall Street Journal*, 2 March 2001; Andrew Marshall, "Focus: Can They Still Sell the World a Coke?" *The Independent*, 20 June 1999.

From these perspectives, transferring products across borders may mean consistent positioning for the brand, but not necessarily the same brand name and marketing program in each market. Similarly, packaging may have the same overall look, but be tailored as required to fit the local populace and market needs. As brand consultant Robert Kahn notes, "Global branding does not mean having the same brand everywhere. It means having an overarching strategy that optimizes brand effectiveness in local, regional, and international markets." According to Kahn, one soap formula sold under different names can achieve global brand status as long as the marketing efforts are managed centrally.[18]

In short, centralized marketing strategies that preserve local customs and traditions can be a boon for products sold in more than one country—even in diverse cultures. Fortunately, firms have improved their capabilities to tailor products and programs to local conditions: "[New technologies] have the important attribute of allowing customized or tailored product offerings reflecting local conditions at much lower costs. The need to standardize products worldwide is diminishing."[19] The implication is that there is a decreasing concentration of activities made possible by flexible manufacturing technology, as well as an increasing ability for coordination made possible by advances in information systems and telecommunications.

You Can Have It Your Way:
McDonald's Adapts Its Global Marketing

Another famous global marketer is McDonald's, which has modified and adapted its successful formula of "food, fun, and families" in going overseas. Although the Big Mac and Ronald McDonald appear worldwide, McDonald's customizes other aspects of its marketing program. It serves beer in Germany, wine in France, and coconut, mango, and tropical mint shakes in Hong Kong. Hamburgers are made with different meat and spices in Japan, and McSpaghetti is offered in the Philippines. McDonald's joint venture partners, who typically run the franchises abroad, take much of the responsibility for their own local marketing.

Nevertheless, McDonald's fierce commitment to product and service standardization is one reason why the retail outlets are also so similar all over the world. To achieve such consistency, McDonald's handpicks its global partners one by one in order to find "compulsive achievers." Norman Sinclair, the first franchisee in Perth, Australia, had to put up cash, pass an extensive interview panel (to ensure a "family feeling"), attend school at Hamburger University (expanded to locations in Germany, Japan, England, and Australia), work five days in a local restaurant, and then volunteer for 800 hours of unpaid service. After such a rigorous qualification process, partners come to understand and appreciate McDonald's attention to detail. As a result, most partners strictly follow the operating manual. Meticulously detailed and as thick as a phone book, the rules cover everything from how often bathrooms should be cleaned to the temperature of the grease to fry potatoes. Countries such as Japan have embraced the rigid system of rules, which includes 19 steps to cook and bag fries. The end result is that a French fry in Tokyo tastes like one in Russia, which tastes like one in New York.

Sources: Joanne Lipman, "Marketers Turn Sour on Global Sales Pitch Harvard Guru Makes," *Wall Street Journal*, 12 May 1988, 1; Julie Skur Hill and Jospeh M. Winski, "Goodbye Global Ads," *Advertising Age*, 16 November 1987.

Many good examples exist of companies that have successfully blended standardization and customization. Branding Brief 14-3 describes the global marketing efforts and adaptations of McDonald's. As another example, Domino's tries to maintain the same delivery system everywhere but has to adapt the model to local customs. In Britain, customers think anybody knocking on the door is rude; in Kuwait, the delivery is just as likely to be made to a limousine as it is to a house; and in Japan, houses are not numbered sequentially, making finding a particular address difficult.

On the other hand, Disney has experienced some of the disadvantages of not balancing local with global. As one executive stated, "Not many companies do global branding well. . . . We don't." Disney has had a tendency to originate much of its marketing in Burbank and hasn't adapted its products and merchandising as much as it feels it should. Strong country managers have not existed. Each division has had separate organizations (e.g., Consumer Products, Japan; Home Video, Japan; and Theme

Parks, Japan). For example, television has been created in the States with U.S. sensibilities and is often shipped out "without a lot of thought." This lack of customization has resulted in some "totally wrong stuff" for some markets.[20]

Other notable examples of brands with differentiated global marketing strategies are Heineken and Nescafé. Although Heineken is seen as an everyday brand in the Netherlands, it is considered a "top-shelf" brand almost everywhere else. For example, a case of Heineken costs almost twice as much in the United States as a case of the most popular American beer, Budweiser.[21] For a long time, its slogan in the United Kingdom and other countries—"Heineken Refreshes the Parts Other Beers Can't Reach"—was different from its U.S. positioning. Although advertising for Nescafé, the world's largest brand of coffee, generally stresses the taste, aroma, and warmth of shared moments, the brand was successfully positioned in Thailand as a way to relax from the pressures of daily life.[22]

GLOBAL BRAND STRATEGY

With the preceding comments as background, the chapter turns to some basic strategic issues concerning global branding in this section before reviewing a set of specific tactical guidelines, "The Ten Commandments of Global Branding." The basic contention of this chapter is that in building brand equity, it is often necessary to create different marketing programs to satisfy different market segments. In terms of building global customer-based brand equity, strategically it is therefore necessary to do the following:

1. Identify differences in consumer behavior (i.e., how consumers purchase and use products and what they know and feel about brands) in each market.
2. Adjust the branding program accordingly (i.e., through the choice of brand elements, the nature of the supporting marketing program, and leverage of secondary associations).

Note that the third way to build global brand equity, leveraging secondary brand associations, is probably the most likely to *have* to be changed across countries. Because the various entities that may be linked to a brand may take on very different meanings in different countries, secondary associations may have to be leveraged differently in different countries. For example, American companies such as Coca-Cola, Levi Strauss, and Nike gain an important source of equity in going overseas by virtue of their American heritage, which is not as much of an issue or asset in their domestic market. Harley-Davidson has aggressively marketed its classic American image—customized for different cultures—to generate a quarter of its sales from abroad. Chapter 7 reviewed how country of origin, as in these cases, could be leveraged to build brand equity. Thus, in developing global brands, it is important to consider how secondary associations may vary in their strength, favorability, and uniqueness and may therefore play a different role in building brand equity.

Global Customer-Based Brand Equity

As explained in Chapter 2, to build customer-based brand equity, it is necessary to (1) establish breadth and depth of brand awareness; (2) create strong, favorable, and unique brand associations; (3) elicit positive, accessible brand responses; and (4) forge intense, active brand relationships. Achieving these four steps, in turn, involves establishing six core brand building blocks: brand salience, brand performance, brand imagery, brand judgments, brand feelings, and brand resonance. In each and every market in which the brand is sold, consideration must be given as to how to achieve these steps and create these building blocks. Some of the issues that come into play are discussed in the following subsections.

Creating Brand Salience

One of the most challenging aspects of building global brand equity for a widely extended, multiple-product brand is the order of product introduction. It is rare that the product rollout for a brand in new markets will duplicate the order of product introduction in the home market. Often, product introductions in the domestic market are done sequentially, stretched out over a longer period of time, as compared with the more simultaneous introductions that occur in overseas markets.

Nivea

Nivea's flagship product in its European home market has been its category leader, Nivea Creme. Although the company had introduced other skin care and personal care products, Nivea Creme was the product with the most history and heritage and reflected many of the key Nivea core brand values. In Asia, however, for cultural and climate reasons, the creme product was less well received and the facial skin care sub-brand, Nivea Visage, and creme line extension, Nivea Soft, were of greater strategic and market importance. Because these two product brands have slightly different images than the Creme brand, an important issue is what would be the impact on consumers' collective impressions of Nivea.

Different orders of introduction can have a very profound impact on consumer perceptions as to what the brand represents in terms of products offered, benefits supplied, and needs satisfied. Thus, the breadth and depth of recall need to be carefully examined to ensure that the proper brand salience and meaning exist along those lines.

Crafting Brand Image

To the extent that the actual composition of the product does not vary appreciably across markets, brand performance associations in terms of the basic benefits provided may not need to be that different. In other words, product functionality often will be held relatively fixed across markets even if some of the specific attributes may differ. Brand imagery associations, on the other hand, may be quite different, and one challenge in global marketing is to meaningfully refine the brand image across diverse markets. For example, the brand's history and heritage, which may be rich and a strong competitive advantage in the home market, may be virtually nonexistent in a new market. A desirable brand personality in one market may be less so in another.

Eliciting Brand Responses

Brand judgments must be positive in new markets such that consumers find the brand to be of good quality, credible, worthy of consideration, and superior. Crafting the right brand image will help to accomplish these outcomes. One of the challenges in global marketing, however, is to ensure that the proper balance and type of emotional responses and brand feelings are created. Blending inner (enduring and private) and outer (immediate experiential) emotions can be difficult given cultural differences across markets.

Cultivating Resonance

Finally, achieving brand resonance in new markets means that consumers must be given sufficient opportunities and incentives to buy and use the product, interact with other consumers and the company itself, and actively learn and experience the brand and its marketing. Clearly, interactive, online marketing can be advantageous as long as it can be designed to be accessible and relevant anywhere in the world. Nevertheless, digital efforts cannot completely replace grassroots marketing efforts that help to connect the consumer with the brand. In dealing with diverse international markets, simply exporting marketing programs, even with some adjustments, may be insufficient because consumers are at arm's length. As a result, they may not be able to develop the intense, active loyalty that characterizes brand resonance.

Global Brand Positioning

To best capture differences in consumer behavior and to guide efforts for revising the marketing program to build global customer-based brand equity, it is necessary to revisit the brand positioning in each market. Recall that developing the brand positioning in a market involves creating mental maps, defining core brand values, and identifying points of parity and points of difference. Accordingly, in developing a global brand positioning, three key sets of questions must be answered:

1. How valid is the mental map in the new market? How appropriate is the positioning? What is the existing level of awareness? How valuable are the core brand values, points of parity, and points of difference?

2. What changes need to be made to the positioning? Do any new associations need to be created? Should any existing associations *not* be created? Do existing associations need to be modified?

3. By what means should this new mental map be created? Can the same marketing activities still be employed? What changes need to be made? What new marketing activities are necessary?

Because the brand is often at an earlier stage of development when going abroad, it will often be necessary to first establish awareness and key points of parity. Once brand awareness and points-of-parity category considerations have been established, then additional competitive considerations may come into the picture. In effect, a hierarchy of brand associations must be defined in a global context that defines which associations are to be held by consumers in all countries and which are to be held only in certain countries. At the same time, decisions have to be made as to how these associations should be created in different markets to account for different consumer perceptions, tastes, and environments. Thus, marketers must be attuned to similarities *and* differences across markets. The remainder of this chapter provides a set of tactical guidelines to help fulfill these strategic imperatives.

BUILDING GLOBAL CUSTOMER-BASED BRAND EQUITY

The previous discussion provided a broad perspective of some of the pros and cons of creating standardized global marketing programs. In designing and implementing a marketing program to create a strong global brand, marketers attempt, in a general sense, to maximize the probability of realizing the advantages of a global marketing program while minimizing the probability of suffering from any potential disadvantages of globalization.[23] This section explores in more detail exactly how to best build strong global brands. Specifically, it shares some common themes or guidelines for success that have emerged in global branding, guidelines that are encapsulated as the "Ten Commandments of Global Branding" (see Figure 14-4).

1. Understand Similarities and Differences in the Global Branding Landscape

The first—and most fundamental—guideline is to recognize the fact that international markets can vary in terms of brand development, consumer behavior, marketing infrastructure, competitive activity, legal restrictions, and so on. As noted earlier, differences on any of these dimensions can have profound implications on building and managing brand equity across geographic boundaries. At the same, many countries do *not* vary much on one or more of these dimensions, suggesting that differences in marketing activity can create unnecessary or ineffective marketing activity. Recognition of this guideline is reflected by the fact that virtually every top global brand and company adjusts its marketing program in some way across some markets but holds the parameters fixed in other markets.

Indeed, one key to global success is to recognize and take advantage of local consumer behavior. As noted earlier, when Pillsbury launched its Green Giant vegetables in foreign markets, it discovered that product usage varied widely by country. After learning each variation of product usage, Green Giant decided to abandon a standardized advertising campaign in favor of local variations based on consumer behavior in that country. On the other hand, failures in standardized global marketing programs often result from a disconnect with the consumer.

FIGURE 14-4   The Ten Commandments of Global Branding

1. Understand similarities and differences in the global branding landscape.
2. Don't take shortcuts in brand building.
3. Establish marketing infrastructure.
4. Embrace integrated marketing communications.
5. Cultivate brand partnerships.
6. Balance standardization and customization.
7. Balance global and local control.
8. Establish operable guidelines.
9. Implement a global brand equity measurement system.
10. Leverage brand elements.

The soup category illustrates an interesting juxtaposition that reflects just how important consumer behavior can be to the success or failure of any brand, even dominant brands, when entering new markets. After enjoying decades as the leading soup in the United States, Campbell's soup experienced difficulty conquering Europe. As it turned out, Campbell had broken the first global branding commandment by neglecting differences in consumer behavior across markets. When it introduced its condensed soup into the United Kingdom in the late 1960s, Heinz's noncondensed soup was considered the category standard. Consumers there had to be convinced that adding liquid would not water the soup down. On the other hand, Knorr, the top-selling brand of soup in Europe, had trouble entering the U.S. market with its line of dry packaged soups. Although the initial advertising tried to educate American consumers about the advantages of dry soups relative to condensed soups such as Campbell's, the products failed to gain a widespread following. Today, Knorr soups are perceived to be for gourmets, and dehydrated soups represent a small niche in the U.S. soup category.

The best examples of global brands often retain a thematic consistency and alter specific elements of the marketing mix in accordance with consumer behavior and the competitive situation in each country. An effective example of custom-tailoring the marketing mix is illustrated by Unilever's Snuggle fabric softener.

Snuggle

The product was initially launched in Germany in 1970 as an economy brand in a category dominated by Procter & Gamble. To counteract the negative quality inferences associated with low price, Unilever emphasized softness as the product's key point of difference. The softness association was communicated through the name, Kuschelweich, which meant "enfolded in softness," and through a picture of a teddy bear on the package. When the product was launched in France, Unilever kept the brand positioning of economy and softness but changed the name to Cajoline, meaning softness in French. In addition, the teddy bear that had been inactive in Germany took center stage in the French advertising as the brand symbol for softness and quality. Success in France led to global expansion, and in each case the brand name was changed to connote softness in the local language, while the advertising featuring the teddy bear remained virtually identical across global markets. By the 1990s, Unilever was marketing the fabric softener around the globe with over a dozen brand names (e.g., Coccolino in Italy and Mimosin in Spain), all with the same product positioning and advertising support. More important, the fabric softener was generally the number one or number two brand in each market.[24]

The success of Snuggle reflects the importance of understanding similarities and differences in the branding landscape. Although marketers typically strive to keep the same brand name across markets, in this case the need for a common name was reduced since people generally do not buy fabric softener away from home. On the other hand, a common consumer desire for softness that transcended country boundaries could be effectively communicated by a teddy bear as the main character in a global ad campaign.

Developed versus Developing Markets

Perhaps the most basic distinction often made with global brands is between developing and developed markets (e.g., India and Germany, respectively). Typically, differences in consumer behavior, marketing infrastructure, competitive frame of reference, and so on are so profoundly different that distinct marketing programs have to be devised for each type of market. With developing markets, often the product category itself may not be well developed, so that the marketing program must operate at a very fundamental level. In China, for example, Procter & Gamble runs ads promoting its corporate image because consumers in that country are concerned about the reputation and trustworthiness of the companies behind the products.[25]

Changing Landscape for Global Brands

Finally, it should be noted that the landscape for global brands is dramatically changing, especially with respect to younger consumers. Because of increased consumer mobility, better communication capabilities, and expanding transnational entertainment options, lifestyles are fast becoming more similar across countries within sociodemographic segments than they are within countries across sociodemographic segments. Because of the growth of global media such as MTV, a teenager in Paris may have more in common with a teenager in London, New York, Sydney, or almost any other major city in the world than with his or her own parents. This younger generation may be more easily influenced by trends and broader cultural movements fueled by worldwide exposure to movies, television, and other media than ever before. Certainly one consequence of this trend is that those brands that are able to tap into the global sensibilities of the youth market may be better able to adopt a standardized branding program and marketing strategy.

2. Don't Take Shortcuts in Brand Building

In terms of building global customer-based brand equity, many of the basic tactics already discussed in Part II of the text still apply. In particular, it is necessary to create brand awareness and a positive brand image in each country in which the brand is sold. As noted previously, the means by which sources of brand equity are created may differ from country to country, or the actual sources of brand equity themselves may vary across countries in terms of the particular attribute or benefit associations that make up the points of parity and points of difference. Nevertheless, it is critically important in each country that there exist sufficient levels of brand awareness and strong, favorable, and unique brand associations to provide sources of brand equity.

The danger in entering new markets is that marketers will take shortcuts and fail to build the necessary sources of brand equity by inappropriately exporting marketing programs from other countries or markets in which the brand has already established a great deal of equity. Many companies have learned this lesson the hard way. For example, in 1990, Pepsi bought the rights to bottle and sell its soft drink to German retailers. Pepsi attempted to match Coke's high prices in the market without sufficient pull from brand-building activities and merchandising and without sufficient push from a strong distribution network with the right kind of trucks, coolers, and so forth. Pepsi so alienated two major German retailers, Tengelmann and Asko, that it actually lost distribution in those stores for a couple of years. The brand languished with a market share under 5 percent as a result and has only recently started to bounce back.[26]

Building a brand in new markets should be done from the bottom up, both strategically and tactically. Strategically, that means concentrating on building awareness first before the brand image (i.e., laying the foundation for the brand). Tactically, or operationally, that means determining how to best create sources of brand equity in new markets. In other words, the means by which a brand was built in one market (e.g., the particular product, distribution, communication, or pricing strategies and marketing activities) may not be appropriate in another market even if the same overall brand image may be desired.

Many times marketing programs have to be adjusted because the brand is at an earlier stage of development. In such situations, consumer education often accompanies brand development efforts.

Kellogg

When Kellogg first introduced its corn flakes into the Brazilian market in 1962, cereal was eaten as a dry snack by Brazilians (like Americans eat potato chips) because many Brazilians did not eat breakfast at all. As a result, the ads there centered on the family and breakfast table—much more so than in the United States. As in other Latin American countries where big breakfasts have not been part of the meal tradition, Kellogg's task was to inform consumers of the "proper" way to eat cereal with cold milk in the morning.[27] Similarly, Kellogg had to educate French consumers that corn flakes were meant to be eaten with cold instead of warm milk. Initial advertising showed milk being poured from transparent glass pitchers that were used for cold milk rather than opaque porcelain jugs that were used for warm milk. Similarly, a challenge to Kellogg in increasing the relatively low per capita consumption of ready-to-eat breakfast cereals in Asia was the low consumption of milk products and the positive distaste with which drinking milk was held in many Asian countries. Because cereal consumption and habits vary widely across countries, Kellogg has learned to build the brand from the bottom up in each market.

This guideline suggests having some patience because it implies possibly backtracking in terms of brand development to engage in a set of marketing programs and activities that the brand has long since moved beyond in its original markets. Although the time taken to build the brand in these other markets may be compressed because of greater financial resources and a keener understanding of effective strategies and tactics, it will still take some time. The temptation—and often mistake—is to export the current marketing program because it seems to "transfer" or "work." Although that may be the case, the fact that a marketing program can meet with acceptance or even some success does not mean that it is the proper marketing activity in terms of building strong, sustainable global brand equity. An important key to success is to understand each consumer, recognize what he or she knows or could potentially value about the brand, and tailor marketing programs to his or her desires.

In short, one of the major pitfalls that global markers can fall into is a mistaken belief that their strong position in a domestic market can easily—or even automatically—translate into a strong position in a foreign market, especially with respect to the brand associations held by consumers. Thus, they fail to realize that in their own country, they are building on a foundation of perhaps decades of carefully compiled associations in customers' minds. Observing that many large companies simply diluted formulas to make less expensive products, Hindustan Lever, an Indian subsidiary of Unilever, made a substantial commitment to R&D and innovation to better serve the Indian market. These efforts resulted in completely new products that were both affordable and uniquely suited to India's rural poor, including a high-quality combination soap and shampoo, that were backed by successful new sales and marketing tactics specifically developed to reach remote and highly dispersed populations.[28]

3. Establish Marketing Infrastructure

A critical success factor for many brands has been their manufacturing, distribution, and logistical advantages. This has involved creating the appropriate marketing infrastructure from scratch (if necessary), as well as adapting to capitalize on the existing marketing infrastructure in other countries.

Since international markets vary greatly in terms of existing infrastructure, companies have gone to great lengths to ensure consistency in product quality. In some case, distribution channels have to be built from scratch. For example, after 13 years of negotiations, Nestlé was finally invited into the Heilongjiang province of China in 1987 to boost milk production. Soon thereafter, Nestlé opened a powdered milk and baby cereal plant in China. The company deemed the overburdened local trains and roads undependable to collect milk and deliver finished goods. Nestlé chose to establish its own distribution network, known as "milk loads," between 27 villages in the region and factory collection points called "chilling centers" where farmers could push wheel barrows, pedal bicycles, or walk to have their milk weighed and analyzed. Production has exploded as a result.[29] Similarly, McDonald's gets over 90 percent of its raw materials from local suppliers and will even expend resources to create the necessary inputs if they are not locally available. Hence, investing to improve potato farms in Russia is standard practice because French fries are one of McDonald's core products and a key source of brand equity.

More often, however, companies have to adapt operations or invest in foreign partners, or both, in order to succeed abroad. In many cases, production and distribution are the keys to the success of a global marketing program. For example, General Motors's success in Brazil in the 1990s after years of mediocre performance can be attributed in part to its concerted efforts to develop a lean manufacturing program and a sound dealership strategy to create the proper marketing infrastructure.[30]

Companies often differ in their approach to distribution, and the results can be dramatic. For example, Coca-Cola's distribution strategy has been one key to its global success. Rather than leaving foreign operations in the control of fragmented local bottlers, Coca-Cola's anchor bottler model resulted in the company deciding to either use only large bottlers (e.g., Norway's Ringnes or Australia's Amatil) or take an equity stake in smaller bottlers in order to gain control of local management. At a more micro level, Coca-Cola's intensive deployment of vending machines in Japan was a key to success in that market. Overall, Coca-Cola invested over $3 billion internationally from 1981 to 1993 in infrastructure and marketing. PepsiCo, on the other hand, sold off some of its bottling investments during this time. Investing in expensive ad campaigns and diversifying into restaurants and snack foods, PepsiCo's global fortunes subsequently sagged relative to Coca-Cola, resulting in renewed efforts in recent years.

As in domestic markets, it is often desirable to blend push and pull strategies to build brand equity. This is certainly true in global markets and can present special challenges. Concerned about poor refrigeration in European stores, Häagen-Dazs ended up supplying thousands of free freezers to retailers across the continent.[31] Sometimes companies mistakenly adapt strategies that were critical factors to success, only to discover that these changes erode the brand's competitive advantage. For example, Dell Computer initially abandoned its direct distribution strategy in Europe and instead decided to establish a traditional retailer network through existing channels. The end result was a paltry 2.5 percent market share, and the company lost money for the first time ever in 1994. Ignoring critics who claimed that a direct distribution model would never work in Europe, Dell revamped its direct approach and relaunched its personal computer line with a new management team to execute the direct model that the company had pioneered in the United States. Since then the company has never looked back. In 1999, Dell's personal computer sales in Europe grew at an astronomical 49 percent rate, substantially outpacing other competitors in the industry.

4. Embrace Integrated Marketing Communications

A number of top global firms have introduced extensive integrated marketing communications programs. Overseas markets do not have the same advertising opportunities as in the extensive, well-developed American media market. As a result, U.S.-based marketers have had to embrace other forms of communication in those markets—such as sponsorship, promotions, public relations, merchandising activity, and so on—to a much greater extent in going global.

An important consideration is that the nontraditional form of advertising should be consistent with the brand's overall positioning and heritage. Disney's theme parks are not only huge profit generators (Tokyo Disneyland has been an overwhelming success with over 75 percent repeat visitors), but also serve as advertising vehicles that help solidify Disney's association with "fun family entertainment." eBay adopted a grassroots approach in its entry into Europe, shunning advertising just as it had done in the States. Besides costing less, eBay's approach seemed to produce better customers: Although chief competitor QXL had 50 percent more users than eBay, eBay users averaged 90 minutes a month on site compared with under 20 minutes for QXL.[32]

It is common for non-American companies to undertake smaller, local events that can also serve a brand-building purpose. For example, Guinness often partners with aspiring entrepreneurs to develop the Irish pub business concept in a variety of countries. In 1995, some of the best pubs in Ireland joined forces with some of the best pubs in Europe in what Guinness called the Twinning Initiative. These events had two-fold benefits in that they generated local publicity and interest as well as served to reinforce Guinness beer's Irish association.

Many opportunities exist to take advantage of idiosyncrasies in local markets. One of the more creative examples was when Ben & Jerry's leveraged the beef crisis in Britain by using cows that couldn't be sold on the open market as an advertising opportunity. The company draped these "mad cows" with the company logo. Since the grazing cows were in full view of the driving public, the campaign attracted a lot of attention and eventually made the major London newspapers. The company also later devised another clever promotion in this market.

To help make this quintessential Vermont brand more locally relevant, Ben & Jerry's ran a contest in Britain to create the "quintessential British ice cream flavor." Finalists covered the gamut of the British cultural spectrum and included references to royalty (e.g., Cream Victoria and Queen Yum Mum), rock and roll (e.g., John Lemon and

Ruby Chewsday), literature (e.g., Grape Expectations and Agatha Crispie) and Scottish heritage (e.g., Nessie's Nectar and Choc Ness Monster). Other finalists included Minty Python, Cashew Grant, and James Bomb. The winning flavor, Cool Britannia, was a play on the popular British military anthem "Rule Britannia" and consisted of vanilla ice cream, English strawberries, and chocolate-covered Scottish shortbread.[33]

Although some companies have managed to execute their global marketing program entirely with nontraditional forms of advertising (e.g., the Body Shop), traditional advertising options are often employed too, suggesting that issues concerning advertising, promotion, and sponsorship, among other marketing communications, need to be addressed.

Advertising

In going global, it is important to recognize that although the brand positioning may be the same in different countries, creative strategies in advertising may have to differ. Thus, even if a basic positioning is adopted everywhere, it may need to be adapted and translated as appropriate in local markets. For example, although Dove soap adopted the same basic positioning worldwide for years—based on the fact that it contains one-quarter cleansing cream—the company used testimonials in which pretty, 30ish women praised the brand's skin-softening virtues in their own language in countries such as Australia, France, Germany, and Italy.[34]

Different countries can be characterized as being more or less receptive to different creative styles. For example, humor is more common in U.S. and U.K. ads than, say, in German ads. European countries such as France and Italy are more tolerant of sex appeal and nudity in advertising. William Wells, former ad agency executive at DDB Needham, makes the general distinction in advertising response between *high-context* cultures, where the meaning of a message cannot be understood without its context, and *low-context* cultures, where the meaning of a message can be isolated from the context in which it occurs and understood as an independent entity, as follows:

> High context cultures—much of the Middle East, Asia, and Africa, for example—are relational, holistic, integrative, intuitive, and contemplative, while the low-context cultures found in North America and much of Western Europe are logical, analytical, linear, and action-oriented. In high context cultures, emphasis is placed on interpersonal relationships between communicators, nonverbal expression, physical setting, and social circumstances. Low-context cultures tend to stress clearly articulated spoken or written messages.[35]

Relatedly, Roth found that in countries with high individualism (e.g., European countries), brand images that emphasized functional needs, variety, novelty, or experiential needs were more effective than social image strategies that emphasized group membership and affiliation benefits. On the other hand, cultures with low individualism (e.g., Asian countries) were more amenable to social image strategies than sensory brand images. Roth also found that in low power-distance cultures (e.g., Germany, Netherlands, and Argentina) in which people are not highly focused on social roles and group affiliation, functional brand images that de-emphasize the social, symbolic, sensory, and experiential benefits of products were most appropriate. On the other hand, for countries with a high degree of power distance (e.g., China, France, and Belgium) in which people are more concerned with prestige, wealth, and class differences, Roth found that social and sensory needs were more appropriate.[36]

Camay

Procter & Gamble found that although its U.S. ads for Camay soap could be effectively adapted for other countries, they turned out to be a disaster in Japan. Specifically, Camay traditionally has been advertised as a luxury soap that makes a woman's skin feel soft and smell sweet, allowing her to feel more attractive as a result. Ads in other countries showed a beautiful woman bathing blissfully in a bathtub of suds. In ads for France, Italy, and Venezuela, her husband came into the bathroom and talked to her while she was bathing. In Japan, the ads also featured a man entering the bathroom and gently touching the woman's skin and complimenting her while she bathed. Although these ads might perhaps be seen as sensual in other countries, such behavior could be considered rude and in bad taste in Japan—even the idea of a man being in the same bathroom with a woman can be seen as taboo there. As a result of negative public reaction, the Japanese ad for Camay was changed to show a beautiful European-looking woman—alone—in a European-style bath.

Numerous advertising media options exist globally. Although commercial television time has been limited worldwide, the penetration of satellite and cable TV has expanded the broadcast media options available. As a result, it is easier to simultaneously air the same TV commercial in many different countries. American cable networks such as CNN, MTV, and the Cartoon Network and other networks such as Sky TV in Commonwealth countries and Star TV in Asia have increased advertisers' global reach. *Fortune*, *Time*, *Newsweek*, and other magazines have printed foreign editions in English for years. Increasingly, other publishers are starting or adding local-language editions, either by licensing their trademarks to local companies, entering into joint ventures, or creating wholly owned subsidiaries, for example, *Rolling Stone* in French, *Esquire* in Japanese, and *Fortune* in Italian.[37] *Elle* has 19 editions targeting the same demographic group but tailored to the country where each is published.

Each country has its own unique media challenges and opportunities. For example, when Colgate-Palmolive decided to further penetrate the market of the 630 million or so people that live in rural India, the company had to overcome the fact that more than half of all Indian villagers are illiterate and only one-third live in households with television sets. Its solution was to create half-hour infomercials carried through the countryside in video vans.[38] To sell Tampax tampons in Mexico, Procter & Gamble created in-home informational gatherings or "bonding sessions" akin to Tupperware parties led by company-designated counselors. Although about 70 percent of women in the United States, Canada, and Western Europe use tampons, just 2 percent of women in most of Latin America do so. To overcome cultural inhibitors, P&G developed its unorthodox approach.[39]

Promotion and Sponsorship

Chapters 6 and 7 described some of the issues in developing sponsorship programs. It was noted there that sponsorship programs have a long tradition in many countries outside the United States because of a historical lack of advertising media there. Increasingly, sponsorship can now be executed on a global basis. Entertainment and sports sponsorships can be an especially effective way to reach a younger audience. For example, Nestlé has run worldwide promotional tie-ins with Disney movies such as *Atlantis* and *Monsters, Inc.* Mars has become a worldwide sponsor of the World Cup and Olympics.

5. Cultivate Brand Partnerships

Most global brands have marketing partners of some form in their international markets, ranging from joint venture partners, licensees or franchisees, distributors, ad agencies, and other marketing support personnel.

One common reason for establishing brand partnerships is access to distribution. For example, Guinness has very strategically used partnerships to develop markets or provide expertise that the company lacked with its own personnel or capabilities. Joint venture partners, such as with Moet Hennessey, have provided access to distribution abroad that otherwise would have been hard to achieve within the same time constraints. These partnerships have been crucial for Guinness as it expands operations into developing markets (where almost half its profits are now derived). Similarly, Lipton increased its sales by 500 percent in the first four years of its partnership with PepsiCo to distribute the product. Lipton adds the power of its brand to the ready-to-drink iced tea market, while PepsiCo adds its contacts in global distribution. On the other hand, AOL struggled in entering the European market due to its initial failure to link up with either a media or telecommunications company.

Barwise and Robertson identify three alternative ways to enter a new global market:[40]

1. By exporting existing brands of the firm into the new market (i.e., introducing a "geographic extension")
2. By acquiring existing brands already sold in the new market but not owned by the firm
3. By creating some form of brand alliance with another firm (e.g., joint ventures, partnerships, or licensing agreements)

They also identify three key criteria—speed, control, and investment—by which the different entry strategies can be judged.

According to Barwise and Robertson, there are tradeoffs among the three criteria such that no one strategy dominates (see Figure 14-5). For example, the major problem with geographic extensions is speed. Because most firms do not have the necessary financial resources and marketing experience to roll out products to a large number of countries simultaneously, global expansion can be a slow, market-by-market process.

FIGURE 14-5   Tradeoffs in Market Entry Strategies

	Criteria for Evaluation		
Strategy	*Speed*	*Control*	*Investment*
Geographic extension	Slow	High	Medium
Brand acquisition	Fast	Medium	High
Brand alliance	Moderate	Low	Low

Brand acquisitions, on the other hand, can be expensive and often more difficult to control than is typically assumed. Brand alliances may offer even less control although are generally much less costly.

The choices among these different entry strategies depend in part on how the resources and objectives of the firm match up with the costs and benefits of each strategy. For example, Procter & Gamble typically first enters new markets in categories in which it excels (e.g., diapers, detergents, and sanitary pads), building its infrastructure and then bringing in other categories such as personal care or health care.[41] Similarly, in entering India, Pillsbury chose initially to forgo selling its high-margin products such as microwave pizzas that were important revenue generators in other parts of the world in favor of pitching a product that it had pretty much abandoned elsewhere— plain flour. Recognizing that it wouldn't make much money, Pillsbury's aim was to establish its reputation in the flour business and then later introduce new products. Even the Pillsbury Doughboy got a makeover in the process. In TV ads, he pressed his palms together and bowed in the traditional Indian greeting, speaking six different regional languages.[42]

Heineken's sequential strategy has been slightly different. The company first enters a new market by exporting to build brand awareness and image. If the market response is deemed satisfactory, the company will then license its brands to a local brewer in hopes of expanding volume. If that relationship is successful, Heineken may then take an equity stake or forge a joint venture. In doing so, Heineken piggybacks sales of its high-priced Heineken brand with an established local brand.[43] As a consequence of this strategy, Heineken now sells in more than 170 countries with a product portfolio of over 80 brands. With more than 110 breweries in over 50 countries and export activities all over the world, Heineken is the most international brewery group in the world.

Joint ventures are a common entry strategy and are often seen as a fast and convenient way to enter complex foreign markets. Fuji Xerox has been a highly successful joint venture in Japan that has even outperformed Xerox's U.S. parent company.

Fuji Xerox was initially a joint venture formed to give Xerox a foothold in Japan. Over time, however, Fuji Xerox has become a critical part of both parent companies and has been referred to as "Xerox's most important strategic asset." The company dominated the Japanese market in office equipment for years, but the partnership proved to be much more than just a sales office for photocopiers. Knowing that Xerox photocopiers were too large for many Japanese small businesses, Fuji Xerox developed a compact photocopier without permission from Xerox. The product turned out to be a huge success, and Fuji Xerox was granted more self-control by the parent companies. Today, Fuji Xerox makes and sells almost all of its own products, including almost all of the small and mid-sized copiers sold by Xerox corporate.

Joint ventures have been popular in Japan, where convoluted distribution systems, tightly knit supplier relationships, and close business—government cooperation have long encouraged foreign companies to link up with knowledgeable local partners.[44] Blockbuster entered Japan with a joint venture with one of that country's best-known retailers, Den Fujita, which also runs McDonald's (Japan) and has a stake in Toys"R"Us in Japan. Blockbuster also negotiated joint ventures in France, Germany, and Italy.[45] Pier 1 similarly expanded through joint ventures and licensing accords.[46] Pepsi has ownership positions via joint ventures and five outright acquisitions in 40 percent of its bottling networks outside North America.[47]

Finally, in some cases, mergers or acquisitions result from a desire to command a higher global profile. For example, U.S. baby food maker Gerber agreed to be acquired by Swiss drug maker Sandoz in part because of a need to establish a stronger presence in Europe and Asia, where Sandoz has a solid base.[48] Sandoz later merged with Ciba-Geigy and now is part of the Novartis group of companies.

As these examples illustrate, different entry strategies have been adopted by different firms, by the same firm in different countries, or even in combination by one firm in the same country. Branding Brief 14-4 describes how global brand powerhouse Nestlé enters new markets. These entry strategies also may evolve over time. For example, in Australia, Coca-Cola, through its licensee Coca-Cola Amatil, not only sells its global brands such as Coke, Fanta, and Sprite, but also sells local brands it has acquired such as Lift, Deep Spring, and Mount Franklin. One of Coca-Cola's objectives with these acquisitions is to slowly migrate demand from some of the local brands to global brands, thus capitalizing on economies of scale.

6. Balance Standardization and Customization

As noted earlier, one implication of the reality of similarities and differences across international markets is the need to blend local and global elements in marketing programs. The challenge, of course, is to determine the nature of this balance—which elements to customize or adapt and which to standardize. Customization may imply adjusting some aspect of the marketing program or the desired brand image or both (e.g., by the creation or deletion of brand associations).

Much has been written concerning the circumstances favoring standardization over customization when designing global marketing programs. Some of the commonly observed factors suggested as favoring the use of a more standardized global marketing program include the following:

➤ Common customer needs
➤ Global customers and channels
➤ Favorable trade policies and common regulations
➤ Compatible technical standards
➤ Transferable marketing skills

Similarly, one industry observer offered the following three criteria as essential for the development of a global brand:[49]

➤ Basic positioning and branding that can be applied globally
➤ Technology that can be applied globally, with local tailoring
➤ Capabilities for local implementation

Reinforcing these points, Ed Meyer, the long-time head of one of the world's largest ad agencies, Grey Advertising, asserted that there are two key considerations in implementing a global marketing program.[50] First, market development and the competitive environment must be at similar stages from country to country. New products thus often represent more promising candidates for standardization. Whereas mature products may have vastly different histories (or even positionings) in different markets, consumer knowledge for new products is generally the same everywhere because

Managing Global Nestlé Brands

For a roughly 10-year period starting in 1984, Nestlé spent $18 billion on acquisitions in different countries, including such major brands as Carnation dairy (and other) products (United States), Perrier mineral water (France), Stouffer's frozen foods (United States), Rowntree confectionery (United Kingdom), and Buitoni-Perugina pasta and chocolate (Italy). Thus, major acquisitions yield valuable economies of scale to Nestlé in developed markets. In less-developed markets, however, they adopt a different strategy. The company's entry strategy there is to manipulate ingredients or processing technology for local conditions and then apply the appropriate brand name, for example, existing brands like Nescafé coffee in some cases or new brands such as Bear brand condensed milk in Asia in other cases. Nestlé strives to get into markets first and is patient—the company negotiated for more than a decade to enter China. To limit risks and simplify its efforts in new markets, Nestlé attacks with a handful of labels, selected from a set of 11 strategic brand groups. Nestlé then concentrates its advertising and marketing money on just two or three brands.

Nestlé attempts to balance global and local control in managing its brands. Some decisions, such as branding, follow strict corporate guidelines. The company has 10 *worldwide corporate* strategic brands, including Nestlé, Nescafé, Maggi, and Carnation. There are 45 different strategic *worldwide product* brands, including Kit Kat, Coffeemate, and Crunch. There are 25 *regional corporate strategic* brands, including Perugina, Findus, and Stouffer's. There are 100 *regional product* brands, including Eskimo, Taster's Choice, and Go-Cat. Finally, there are 700 *local strategic* brands that are important to particular countries, including Brigadeiro in Brazil.

Most other decisions, however, are primarily decided by the local managers. Nestlé's policy is to recognize that it is a foreigner in any country outside Switzerland and to simply let the local managers run most of the business operations. For example, the company does not do corporate-level strategic planning. Instead, the top managers in each region tell headquarters what they plan to do, and a combination of bottom-up or top-down approaches are used to finalize a strategy. Headquarters meets once a year with each of the country managers to discuss strategic issues. The bottom line resides with headquarters, which has the power to force local managers to adopt a policy if necessary. This happened with ice cream in the United States. The country manager classified the product as a dairy product, whereas headquarters viewed it more strategically as a frozen confectionery. The country manager proposed machines and cones, and headquarters countered with self-manufacture and direct store delivery. Today, Nestlé is a strong number two in the ice cream impulse segment, and has invested in a 17 percent stake in Dreyer.

Source: Carla Rapoport, "Nestlé's Brand Building Machine," *Fortune,* 19 September 1994, 147–156.

perceptions have yet to be formed. For example, the "Intel Inside" campaign has transferred relatively easily across geographic boundaries because personal computers have been relatively new to each market they enter. As the head of another large ad agency noted:

> There is more hope for a brand yet to be developed going global than for taking current products and making them global brands, because you can't change the structure through which existing brands are being marketed. But you can create the structure for a brand that is in development. And it is that structure that determines the outcome, because without that, and a paralleling agency structure, you just have a marketing mess on your hands.[51]

The second key consideration according to Meyer is that consumer target markets should be alike, and consumers must share the same desires, needs, and uses for the product. Similarly, Harvard's Stephen Greyser claims, "The fulcrum of global marketing rests on whether the consumer or customer segment is similar across countries seeking the same values in physical performance or psychological satisfactions or both."[52] In other words, according to Greyser, brand image must be relevant to consumers in both a product-related and non-product-related sense. As the head of a large multinational advertising agency observed:

> It may sound simplistic but making the brand relevant can actually be particularly tricky when it comes to global marketing. Since brand perception alters according to past experience, a marketer needs to understand the likely perceptions and experiences of consumers in individual markets.[53]

What types of products are difficult to sell through standardized global marketing programs? Many experts note that foods and beverages that have years of tradition and entrenched preferences and tastes can be particularly difficult to sell in a standardized global fashion. For example, Unilever has found that standard preferences are more common across countries for cleaning products such as detergents and soaps than for food products. In addition, high-end products can also benefit from standardization because high quality or prestige often can be marketed similarly across countries. For example, Italian coffee maker illycafe maintains a "one brand, one blend" strategy, offering only a single blend of espresso made of 100 percent Arabica beans across the globe. As Andrea Illy, CEO of his family's business since 1994, states, "Our marketing strategy focuses on building quality consumer perceptions—no promotions, just differentiating ourselves from the competition by offering top quality, consistency and an image of excellence."

More generally, the following types of products and brands are often noted as likely candidates for global campaigns that are able to retain a similar marketing strategy worldwide:

➤ *High-technology products with strong functional images:* Examples are televisions, VCRs, watches, computers, cameras, and automobiles. Such products tend to be universally understood and are not typically part of the cultural heritage.

➤ *High-image products with strong associations to fashionability, sensuality, wealth, or status.* Examples are cosmetics, clothes, jewelry, and liquor. Such products can appeal to the same type of market worldwide.

➤ *Services and business-to-business products that emphasize corporate images in their global marketing campaigns.* Examples are airlines and banks.

➤ *Retailers that sell to upper-class individuals or that specialize in a salient but unfulfilled need.* For example, by offering a wide variety of toys at affordable prices, Toys"R"Us transformed the European toy market by getting Europeans to buy toys for children any time of the year, not just Christmas, and forcing competitors to level prices across countries.

➤ *Brands positioned primarily on the basis of their country of origin.* An example is Australia's Foster's beer.[54]

➤ *Products that do not need customization or other special products to be able to function properly.* ITT found that stand-alone products such as heart pacemakers could be sold easily the same way worldwide, but that integrated products such as telecommunications equipment have to be tailored to function within local phone systems.[55]

Tradeoffs between standardization and customization and issues concerning communication and distribution strategies were outlined earlier. It is useful, however, to consider some additional issues concerning product and pricing strategies.

Product Strategy

Many marketers believe that only certain products can be marketed similarly—in some places—and only after variables such as marketing mix and culture are fully analyzed, understood, and incorporated into the marketing program. One reason why so many companies ran into trouble initially going overseas is that they unknowingly—or perhaps even deliberately—overlooked differences in consumer behavior. Because of the relative expense and sometimes unsophisticated nature of the marketing research industry in smaller markets, many companies chose to forgo basic consumer research and put products on the shelf to see what would happen. As a result, they sometimes became aware of these consumer differences only after the fact. To better understand consumer preferences and avoid these types of mistakes, marketers may need to conduct research into local markets. For example, Japanese firms often hire local marketing experts to help design their products to better suit local tastes.[56]

In many cases, however, marketing research reveals that product differences are just not justified for certain countries. At one time, Palmolive soap was sold globally, although with 22 different fragrances, 17 different packages, 9 different shapes, and with numerous different positionings. After marketing analyses to reap the benefits of global marketing, the company now employs just 7 fragrances, 1 core packaging design, and 3 main shapes, all executed around two related positionings (one for developing markets and one for developed markets).[57] Branding Brief 14-5 describes how UPS has attempted to adapt its service for the European market.

From a corporate perspective, one obvious solution to the tradeoff between global and local brands is to sell both types of brands as part of the brand portfolio in a category. Even companies that have succeeded with global brands maintain that standardized international marketing programs work only with some products, in some places, and at some times, and will never totally replace brands and ads with local appeal.[58] For example, while Coca-Cola sells Coke to a growing group of consumers in Asia, it also sells local brands there such as the hugely successful Georgia canned ice coffee in

UPS's European Express

Over the last decade, United Parcel Service of America has spent $1 billion to buy 16 delivery businesses, put brown uniforms on 25,000 Europeans, and spray its brown paint on 10,000 delivery trucks in the process of becoming the largest delivery company in Europe. UPS had to overcome a number of obstacles along the way. French drivers were outraged that they could not have wine with lunch, British drivers protested when their dogs were banned from delivery trucks, Spaniards were dismayed when they realized the brown UPS trucks resembled the local hearses, and Germans were shocked when brown shirts were required for the first time since 1945.

Although UPS operations are basically the same, the company faces problems that may be less common or even nonexistent in the United States: truck restrictions on weekends and holidays, low bridges and tunnels, widely varying weight regulations, terrible traffic, and, in some places, limited highway systems, primitive airports, and night curfews. Also, the standard of service in Europe is typically well below what Americans have grown accustomed to. Another issue was that express delivery was not as popular in Europe as it was in the States. One industry analyst said, "Europeans are not as time-sensitive as the Americans are."

Hampering the spread of services and service-related jobs in Europe is the reluctance there to part with traditional ways of doing business, such as state-owned monopolies and rigid work practices (e.g., resisting part-time work and providing stronger employment protection and higher nonwage costs than for workers in the United States). The standards of service, like the techniques for providing it, are well below American levels. For example, Manpower Inc. virtually created the temporary help business in Europe and derives more than 40 percent of its worldwide revenues there.

UPS had difficulty building awareness, hampered by the fact that it has only been advertising for the last six years and has been using country-specific advertising. In 1997, UPS had only 15 percent of the European parcel delivery market, sales were growing at 15 percent annually, or half the U.S. growth rate, and the company's European operations had lost $500 million since its launch. UPS lost money on intra-European express shipping, mostly because more than 90 percent of European shipping is domestic.

To improve its share of European business, UPS spent an estimated $1.1 billion between 1995 and 2000 upgrading its European operations by purchasing vehicles, aircraft, buildings, and logistics systems. In 1999, the company flew 300 intercontinental flights daily and had 17,000 trucks driving on the ground. Yet UPS faces a future challenge when European postal bureaucracies lose their letter monopolies following EU deregulation in 2003, which will introduce a host of new competitors. UPS Europe president Randy Pulito said, "Europe is a tough market, but we're here for the long haul."

Sources: Adapted from Dana Milbank, "Can Europe Deliver?" *Wall Street Journal*, 30 September 1994, R15; Alan Saloman, "Delivering a Market Battle," *Advertising Age*; and William Echikson, "The Continent Is Still a Tough Neighborhood For UPS," *Business Week*, 29 September 1997.

Japan as well as new drinks in Japan such as Nagomi green tea, Fanta Asari Berry (a cola blending raspberry, blueberry, and gooseberry), and the honey-and-grapefruit drink Hachimittsu. In China, the company introduced Tian Yu Di ("heaven and earth"), a fruit juice and tea, and Xing Mu ("Smart"), a carbonated fruit-flavored drink in apple, grape, coconut, watermelon, and other flavors. In India, Coca-Cola's biggest selling cola is Thums Up, an indigenous variant it bought in 1993. This combination of local and global brands enables Coca-Cola to exploit the benefits of global branding and global trends in tastes while tapping into traditional domestic markets at the same time.[59] Thus, despite the trend toward globalization, it seems that there will always be opportunities for good local brands.

JCPenney

In entering the Brazilian market in 1999, JCPenney bought control of the 21-store regional brand Lojas Renner. Penney chose to keep local management and the Renner name. Renner had a strong reputation for customer service with its middle-class consumers, driven by practices such as its daily "enchantment meters," which customers completed by punching one of three buttons as they left the store; "pre-checkout checkout" attendants who scanned all purchased items while customers waited in line so that all they had to do was pay when reaching the cashier; and bells in fitting rooms to call an attendant if customers wanted to try on a different size or item. Penney focused its efforts on backroom operations and merchandise presentation (e.g., modernizing displays) while injecting funds for expansion (doubling the number of stores in the process). It also helped Renner develop private labels with English-language names (e.g., Blue Steel youth wear) while also letting it adopt a more rapidly evolving product mix in the fast fashion-moving country.[60]

Pricing Strategy

In designing a global pricing strategy, the value-pricing principle from Chapter 5 still generally applies. Thus, it is necessary to understand in each country what consumer perceptions of the value of the brand are, their willingness to pay, and their elasticities with respect to price changes. Sometimes differences in these considerations permit differences in pricing strategies. For example, brands such as Levi's, Heineken, and Perrier have been able to command a much higher price outside their domestic market because they have a distinctly different brand image—and thus sources of brand equity—in other countries that consumers place more value on. In addition to these consumer differences across countries, differences in distribution structures, competitive positions, and tax and exchange rates all may justify differences in prices.

Unfortunately, setting drastically different prices across countries is becoming more difficult.[61] Pressures for international price alignment have arisen, in part, because of the increasing numbers of legitimate imports and exports and the ability of retailers and suppliers to exploit price differences through "gray imports" across borders. This problem is especially acute in Europe, where price differences are often large (e.g., prices of identical car models may vary by 30 percent to 40 percent) and ample opportunity exists to ship or shop across national boundaries.

In such cases, Hermann Simon, a German expert on pricing, recommends creating an international "price corridor" that takes into account both the inherent differences between countries and alignment pressures. Specifically, the corridor is calculated by company headquarters and its country subsidiaries by considering market data for the individual countries, price elasticities in the countries, parallel imports resulting from price differentials, currency exchange rates, costs in countries and arbitrage costs between them, and data on competition and distribution. No country is then allowed to set its price outside the corridor: Countries with lower prices have to raise them, and countries with higher prices have to lower them. Another possible strategy suggested by Simon is to introduce different brands in high-price, high-income countries and in low-price, low-income countries, depending on the relative cost tradeoffs of standardization versus customization.

In Asia, many American brands command hefty premiums over inferior home-grown competitors because consumers in these countries strongly associate the United States with high-quality consumer products.[62] In assessing the viability of Asian markets, it is important not to just look at average income but to also consider the distribution of incomes because of the large consumer population involved. For example, although the average annual income in India is maybe only $330, some 60 million people can still afford the same types of products that might be sold to middle-class Europeans. In China, Gillette recently introduced Oral-B toothbrushes at 90 cents, compared with locally produced toothbrushes sold at 19 cents. Gillette's reasoning is that even if it only gained 10 percent of the Chinese market, it still would sell more toothbrushes there than they were currently selling in the U.S. market.

7. Balance Global and Local Control

Building brand equity in a global context must be a carefully designed and implemented process. A key decision in developing a global marketing program is choosing the most appropriate organizational structure for managing global brands. In general, there are three main approaches to organizing for a global marketing effort:

1. Centralization at home office or headquarters
2. Decentralization of decision making to local foreign markets
3. Some combination of centralization and decentralization

Companies vary as to which approach they adopt. In general, however, firms tend to adopt a combination of centralization and decentralization to better balance local adaptation and global standardization.

In many, if not most, markets, the cost savings of standardization may not outweigh the revenue potential from tailoring programs in some fashion to different groups of consumers.[63] Each aspect of the marketing program is a candidate for globalization. Which elements of the marketing program should be standardized, and to what degree? In a basic sense, cost and revenue considerations should be the primary considerations in deciding which elements of the marketing program should be adapted for which country. Riesenbeck and Freeling advocate a mixed strategy, standardizing the "core aspects" of the brand (i.e., those that provide its main competitive edge) but allowing local adaptation of "secondary aspects." According to their approach, branding, positioning, and product formulation are more likely to be standardized, and advertising and pricing less so; distribution is most often localized.[64] The Science of Branding 14-1

Customizing Global Marketing

John Quelch, with his coauthor Edward Hoff, wrote an insightful piece on how to develop global marketing strategies. The central tenet of their approach is that the big issue faced by marketers is not whether to go global but how to tailor the global marketing concept to fit each business and how to make it work.

> Too often, executives view global marketing as an either/or proposition—either full standardization or local control. But when a global approach can fall anywhere on a spectrum from tight worldwide coordination on programming details to loose agreement on a product idea, why the extreme view? In applying the global marketing concept and making it work, flexibility is essential. Managers need to tailor the approach they use to each element of the business system and marketing program.

Quelch and Hoff examine four dimensions of global marketing—business functions, products, marketing mix elements, and countries—in light of the degree of standardization or adaptation that is appropriate. In doing so, they make a number of valuable observations, such as the following:

- Marketing is usually one of the last functions to be centrally directed because it is difficult to measure its effectiveness.
- Products that enjoy high scale economies or are not highly culture bound are easier to market globally than others.
- For most products, the appropriate degree of standardization varies from one element of the marketing mix to another.
- Strategic elements like product positioning are more easily standardized than execution-sensitive elements like sales promotions.
- The extent to which a decentralized multinational wishes to pursue global marketing will often vary from one country to another.
- Because large markets with strong local management are often less willing to accept global programs, headquarters should make standard marketing programs reflect the needs of large rather than small markets.

Quelch and Hoff note that the challenge in implementing a global marketing program is the extent of the gap between the current and desired levels of program adaptation or standardization on the four dimensions. Although the urgency with which a gap must be closed depends on factors such as a company's strategy and financial performance, competitive pressures, technological change, and converging consumer values, Quelch and Hoff caution against moving forward too far too fast, describing how headquarters can intervene with local offices by informing, persuading, coordinating, approving, and directing. They conclude their recommendations by making five suggestions as to how to motivate and retain talented country managers when making the shift to global marketing:

1. Encourage field managers to generate ideas.
2. Ensure that the field participates in the development of the marketing strategies and programs for global brands.

3. Maintain a product portfolio that includes, where scale economies permit, local as well as regional and global brands.

4. Allow country managers continued control of their marketing budgets so they can respond to local customer needs and counter local competition.

5. Emphasize the general management responsibilities of country managers that extend beyond the marketing function.

Source: John A. Quelch and Edward J. Hoff, "Customizing Global Marketing," _Harvard Business Review_ (May–June 1986): 59–68.

describes how leading marketing strategists Quelch and Hoff believe global marketing should be customized.

Many global companies divide their markets into five or so regions, for example, Europe, Asia, Latin America, North America, and Africa/Middle East. In considering how these markets are managed internally, a key theme regarding organizational structures, entry strategies, and coordination processes and mechanisms is the need to balance global and local control. Coca-Cola, for example, distinguishes between local marketing activities that would appear to dilute brand equity and those that would not appear to be as efficacious as desired. Headquarters would stop the former from occurring but would not stop the latter, leaving it to the local manager's judgment of the activity's appropriateness but also holding him or her responsible for its success. Similarly, Levi Strauss balances global and local control with a "thermometer" model. Marketing elements below the "freezing point" are fixed: "Brand soul" (described shortly) and logos are standardized worldwide. Above the freezing point, product quality, pricing, advertising, distribution, and promotions are all fluid, meaning each international division can handle the marketing mix elements in any way that it feels is appropriate for its region.

One area of centralization is with advertising. As noted in Chapter 8, firms increasingly are consolidating their worldwide ad accounts and shifting most or all of their advertising billings to agencies with extensive global networks. Firms are making these moves as a means to reduce costs and increase efficiency and control. Nevertheless, Braun's and Levi Strauss's regional managers have been able to bar a global campaign from being run in their area. Unilever's regional managers who seek to substitute their own campaigns, however, must produce research showing that the global plan is inappropriate. Coke and Procter & Gamble take the middle ground, developing a global communications program but testing them and fine-tuning them in meetings with regional managers.[65]

8. Establish Operable Guidelines

Brand definitions and guidelines must be established, communicated, and properly enforced so that marketers in different regions have a good understanding of what they are expected to do and _not_ to do. The goal is to clearly set the rules for how the brand should be positioned and marketed. Hence, everyone within the organization understands the brand's meaning and can translate that meaning to satisfy local consumer preferences. Brand definition and communication often revolve around two related issues. First, some sort of document, such as a brand charter, should be developed that details what the brand is and what the brand is not. Second, the product line should reflect only those products that are consistent with the brand definition.

Coca-Cola has a strategy document that clearly articulates the company's strategy and how the brand positioning is manifested in various aspects of the marketing mix elements. This document sets out the parameters for the brand and therefore determines how much is left to chance. Similarly, McDonald's operating manual imposes rigorous worldwide controls (e.g., the 19 steps to cook and bag french fries). Nestlé ensures that branding decisions at least follow strict corporate guidelines.

Colgate-Palmolive

Colgate-Palmolive has been a highly successful global marketer for years because of its tight focus on marketing strategies and objectives.[66] Colgate's "bundle books" contain, down to the smallest details, everything that Colgate knows about any given brand—and that a country or regional manager needs to know. The books describe how to effectively market a particular product, including the product attributes, its formulas, ingredient sourcing information, market research, pricing positions, graphics, and even advertising, public relations, and point-of-sales materials. With a bundle book, a Colgate manager in any one of the 206 countries and territories where Colgate sells its products can project the Colgate brand exactly like every one of his or her counterparts. As one executive noted, "As the smallest among our major competitors, we are trying to make sure that we maximize our resources. By having tightly controlled brands, we can leverage across borders rapidly."

As an example of deriving product strategy from a brand definition, consider Disney. Everyone at Disney is exposed to the Disney brand mantra, "fun family entertainment" (see Branding Brief 3-8). To establish global guidelines, Disney's centralized marketing group worked with members of the consumer products group for months on virtually every possible product to assign them to one of three categories:

➤ Acceptable to license without permission (e.g., T-shirts)
➤ Not permissible to ever license (e.g., toilet paper)
➤ Requires validation from headquarters to license (about 20 categories—e.g., air fresheners)

Internationally, Disney has noticed that the "gray areas" grow larger and more numerous. The company also has been trying to identify which product groups may be more amenable to localizing than others. For example, movies cannot be tailored for the European market because it is difficult to determine what will be attractive to those consumers. On the other hand, certain items in the Disney store may sell well in Germany but not Japan.

Finally, for all of this to work, there must be effective lines of communication. Coca-Cola stresses the importance of having people on the ground who can effectively manage the brand in concert with headquarters in Atlanta. For example, to facilitate coordination, much training occurs in headquarters; a sophisticated e-mail and voice-mail system is in place; and global databases are available. The goal of this heavily integrated information system is to facilitate the local manager's ability to tap into what constitutes "relevance" in any particular country and then communicate those ideals to headquarters.

9. Implement a Global Brand Equity Measurement System

As suggested by the guidelines in Chapter 8, a global brand equity measurement system would be a set of research procedures designed to provide timely, accurate, and actionable information for marketers on brands so that they can make the best possible tactical decisions in the short run and strategic decisions in the long run in all relevant markets. As part of this, a global brand equity management system needs to be implemented that defines the brand equity charter in a global context, outlining how the brand positioning and resulting marketing program should be interpreted in different markets, as suggested by the previous commandment. With the global brand strategy template in place, brand tracking can assess the progress that is being made, especially in terms of creating the desired positioning, eliciting the proper responses, and developing brand resonance.

Levi Strauss

Levi Strauss is an example of a company that has fully implemented a global brand equity measurement system. Based on brand audits, Levi Strauss has defined what the "brand soul" is for each of its brands. The brand soul is a statement of brand values and how those brand values will be translated through marketing elements across the globe. The brand soul is described in terms of what the soul is today, what the company wants it to be in the future, and how to execute and achieve that goal by means of marketing mix activity. Each territory manager helps to define what the soul is based on current knowledge and input from marketing research and advertising agencies. The brand soul is then communicated to every employee, including the receptionist, so that even the music heard while on the phone reflects the brand value in some substantive way. Marketing research in the form of brand tracking is tailored to determine how each brand is stacking up against the tenets of the brand soul in each territory. A new global marketing group was established at headquarters to handle global issues in general and monitor progression to the brand soul objectives in particular.

The challenge is that the marketing research infrastructure may be found lacking in many countries. When DuPont set out to implement a global tracking system for its various brands, its efforts were hampered by the fact that the level of sophistication of local marketing research companies varied considerably for the 40 primary countries in which DuPont operated.

10. Leverage Brand Elements

Proper design and implementation of brand elements (i.e., the brand name and all related trademarked brand identifiers) can often be critical to the successful building of global brand equity. As Chapter 4 pointed out, in assembling the brand elements that make up the brand, an important consideration is their geographic transferability. As Figure 4-2 showed, a number of brands have encountered resistance because of difficulty in translating their name, packaging, slogans, or other brand elements to another culture.

In general, nonverbal brand elements such as logos, symbols, and characters are more likely to directly transfer effectively—at least as long as their meaning is visually clear—than verbal brand elements that may need to be translated into another language. Nonverbal brand elements are more likely to be helpful in creating brand awareness than brand image, however, which may require more explicit meaning and direct statements. If the meaning of a brand element is visually clear, it can be an invaluable source of brand equity worldwide. As the old saying goes, "A picture is worth a thousand words," so it is not surprising that choosing the right brand logo, symbol, or character can have a huge impact on global marketing effectiveness.

For example, the image of Ronald McDonald clearly communicates McDonald's association with kids without the need for words. Similarly, Mr. Peanut, the Apple logo, and the M&M characters need no translation. Other brand elements become synonymous with an association and also serve as effective communications tools without the use of words. Thus, brand logos and symbols also play an important role in global branding. The Nike swoosh connotes sports, Coke's contour bottle connotes refreshment, and the Mercedes star connotes status and prestige worldwide. Perhaps the most compelling example of the importance of brand symbols is the Marlboro man.

Marlboro

In repositioning the Marlboro brand, Philip Morris created the Marlboro man, a cowboy who is almost always depicted somewhere in the western United States among magnificent scenery deemed "Marlboro country." By 1975, Marlboro had become the best-selling cigarette in the United States. But the appeal of the Marlboro man extends far beyond the United States. Indeed, the cowboy imagery attracts consumers from all over the world in part by capturing an image that is uniquely American. Today the Marlboro man is used in over 150 countries, and Marlboro is the biggest-selling brand in Germany, Mexico, Switzerland, Saudi Arabia, Hong Kong, Argentina, and 11 other major global markets. The Marlboro brand is consistently ranked as one of the world's most valuable brands, due in large part to the widespread appeal of its brand character and personality.

Even nonverbal elements, however, can encounter translation problems. For example, certain colors have strong cultural meaning. Marketing campaigns using various shades of green in advertising, packaging, and other marketing programs ran into trouble in Malaysia, where these colors symbolize death and disease.[67] In some cases, verbal elements can be translated into native languages without much appreciable loss in meaning. For example, Coke's "Can't Beat the Feeling" slogan was translated to the equivalent of "I Feel Coke" in Japan, "Unique Sensation" in Italy, and "The Feeling of Life" in Chile. Germany proved a problem—no translation really worked—so the slogan was kept in English because of the relatively large bilingual audience there.

Because of a desire to standardize globally, however, many firms have attempted to create more uniform brand elements. Pursuing a global branding strategy, Mars chose to replace its Treets and Bonitos brands with the M&M's brand worldwide and changed the name of its third-largest U.K. brand—Marathon—to the Snickers name used in the rest of Europe and the United States.[68] To create a stronger global brand, PepsiCo pulled together its dozens of company-owned brands of potato chips—previously sold under different names—and began to market them all abroad under a more uniform Lay's logo. The company also boosted advertising and improved quality to enhance the brand image at the same time.[69]

Review

Increasingly, it is imperative that marketers properly define and implement a global branding strategy. A number of factors are encouraging firms to sell their products and services abroad. Some advantages of a global marketing program are economies of scale in production and distribution, lower marketing costs, communication of power and scope, consistency in brand image, an ability to leverage good ideas quickly and efficiently, and uniformity of marketing practices and thus greater competitiveness. The more standardized the marketing program, in general, the more that these different advantages will actually be realized. At the same time, the primary disadvantages of a standardized global marketing program are that it may potentially ignore important differences across countries in consumer needs, wants, and usage patterns for products; consumer response to marketing mix elements; product development and the competitive environment; the legal environment; marketing institutions; and administrative procedures.

In developing a global marketing program, marketers attempt to obtain as many of these advantages as possible while minimizing any of these possible disadvantages. Building global customer-based brand equity means creating brand awareness and a positive brand image in each country in which the brand is sold. A number of issues regarding creating a standardized marketing program were noted. It is difficult to identify any one company applying the global marketing concept in the strictest sense. Increasingly, marketers are blending global objectives with local or regional concerns. The means by which brand equity is built may differ from country to country, or the actual sources of brand equity themselves may vary across countries in terms of specific attribute or benefit associations. Nevertheless, there must be sufficient levels of brand awareness and strong, favorable, and unique brand associations in each country in which the brand is sold to provide sources of brand equity. It is necessary to identify differences in consumer behavior (i.e., how consumers purchase and use products and what they know and feel about brands) and adjust the branding program accordingly (i.e., through the choice of brand elements, nature of the supporting marketing program, and leverage of secondary associations).

The chapter reviewed material concerning how to best modify the branding program to adapt to differences in consumer behavior through different product features, prices, channels, and marketing communication programs. Figure 14-6 lists the "Ten Commandments of Global Branding" and a series of questions that can be asked to help guide effective global brand management. Brand Focus 14.0 concludes by considering other possible segmentation bases.

1. Understand similarities and differences in the global branding landscape.
   - Have you tried to find as many commonalities as possible across markets?
   - Have you identified what is unique about different markets?
   - Have you examined all aspects of the marketing environment (e.g., stages of brand development, consumer behavior, marketing infrastructure, competitive activity, legal restrictions)?
   - Have you reconciled these similarities and differences in the most cost-effective and brand-building manner possible?
2. Don't take shortcuts in brand building.
   - Have you ensured that the brand is being built from the bottom up strategically by creating brand awareness first before crafting the brand image?
   - Have you ensured that the brand is being built from the bottom up tactically by determining the appropriate marketing programs and activity for the brand in each market given the particular strategic goals?
3. Establish marketing infrastructure.
   - Have you created the appropriate marketing infrastructure—in terms of manufacturing, distribution, and logistics—from scratch if necessary?
   - Have you adapted to capitalize on the existing marketing infrastructure in other countries?
4. Embrace integrated marketing communications.
   - Have you considered nontraditional forms of communication that go beyond conventional advertising?
   - Have you ensured that all communications are integrated in each market and are consistent with the brand's desired positioning and heritage?
5. Cultivate brand partnerships.
   - Have you formed partnerships with global and local partners to improve possible deficiencies in your marketing programs?
   - Have you ensured that all partnerships avoid compromising the brand promise and do not harm brand equity in any way?
6. Balance standardization and customization.
   - Have you been careful to retain elements of marketing programs that are relevant and add value to the brand across all markets?
   - Have you sought to find local adaptations and additions that complement and supplement these global elements to achieve greater local appeal?
7. Balance global and local control.
   - Have you established clear managerial guidelines as to principles and actions that all global managers must adhere to?
   - Have you carefully delineated the areas in which local managers are given discretion and autonomy in their decision making?
8. Establish operable guidelines.
   - Have you explicated brand management guidelines in a clear and concise fashion in a document to be used by all global marketers?
   - Have you established means of seamless communication between headquarters and local and regional marketing organizations?
9. Implement a global brand equity measurement system.
   - Do you conduct brand audits when appropriate in overseas markets?
   - Have you devised a brand tracking system to provide timely, accurate, and actionable information on brands in relevant markets?

(Continued)

FIGURE 14-6   Self-Evaluation Ratings for the Ten Commandments of Global Branding

- Have you established a global brand equity management system with brand equity charters, brand equity reports, and brand equity overseers?
10. Leverage brand elements.
    - Have you checked the relevance of brand elements in global markets?
    - Have you established visual brand identities that transfer across market boundaries?

FIGURE 14-6   *(Continued)*

Discussion Questions

1. Pick a brand marketed in more than one country. Assess the extent to which the brand is marketed on a standardized versus customized basis.
2. How aware are you of the country of origin of different products you own? For which products do you care about the country of origin? Why? For those imported brands that you view positively, find out and critique how they are marketed in their home country.
3. Pick a product category. Consider the strategies of market leaders in different countries. How are they the same and how are they different?
4. Pick a product category. How are different leading brands targeting different demographic market segments?
5. Contrast Coca-Cola's and McDonald's global branding strategies. How are they similar and how are they different? Why are they so well respected?

Building Brand Equity
across Other Market Segments

The chapter discussion concentrated on market segmentation based on national boundaries. Many of the principles discussed concerning building brand equity are equally valid for market segments based on other criteria, such as those identified in Chapter 3. This appendix briefly consider several other segmentation plans and their implications for branding and marketing strategy.[70]

REGIONAL MARKET SEGMENTS

Regionalization is an important recent trend that, perhaps on the surface, seems to run counter to the globalization trend. Although marketers have developed different marketing programs for different geographic regions of a country for years, regional marketing received a boost in the United States with Campbell's well-publicized move to a regionalized marketing plan. Starting in the 1980s, Campbell began to tailor its soup products, advertising, promotion, and sales efforts to fit different regions of the country—and even individual neighborhoods within cities. The company divided the United States into 22 regions; a combined sales and marketing force received marketing strategy and media buying information and was given an ad and trade promotion budget.[71] Some examples of tailored Campbell's programs during this time included a car giveaway in Pittsburgh tied to a local TV station, short film spots for Campbell's dip soups and its brand name mushrooms in two Sacramento cinemas, soup billboards atop a ski lift in upstate New York, and a Spanish radio and giveaway campaign for V-8 juice in Northern California.[72] In a similar spirit, Pepsi divided its U.S. operations into four regional companies to gear its marketing locally.

Around the same time, Joel Garreau published *The Nine Nations of North America,* which argued that North America was divided into nine "nations," regions populated by people sharing distinct values, attitudes, and styles. These differences were found to manifest themselves in market behavior. As one observer noted:

> [P]eople are different in different parts of the country. For example, Northeasterners and Midwesterners prefer chicken noodle and tomato soups, but in California, cream of mushroom is number one. Pepper pot soup sells primarily in the Philadelphia area, and cream of vegetable on the West Coast. People in the Southwest drive more pickup trucks, people in the Northeast more vans, and Californians like high-priced imported cars such as BMWs and Mercedes Benzes. Texans drive big cars, New Yorkers like smaller ones. New Hampshirites drink more beer per capita

than other Americans. The anxious denizens of Atlanta consume more aspirin and antacids a head, and sweet toothed Mormons of Salt Lake City eat more candy bars and marshmallows.[73]

Interest in regional marketing has been driven by a number of factors: a realization that mass markets are splintering, an availability of computerized sales data from supermarket scanners that reveal pockets of sales strengths and weaknesses in different parts of the country, and an opportunity to employ marketing communications that now permit more focused targeting of consumer groups defined along virtually any lines. The shift from national advertising to sales promotions, in particular, necessitated more market-by-market planning. Different battles are now being fought between brands in different regions of the country. Anheuser-Busch and Miller Brewing have waged a fierce battle in Texas, where nearly 1 in 10 beers sold in the United States is drunk. Anheuser-Busch has made sizable inroads in recent years through special ad campaigns, displays, and sales strategies. As one observer noted, "Texans believe it's a whole different country down here. They don't want you to just slap an armadillo in a TV spot."[74]

Regional marketing must be done carefully and is not without its drawbacks.[75] Modifying products can lead to production headaches. For example, when Campbell set out to make a spicier version of its nacho cheese soup for the west and southwest United States, so many jalapeno peppers were added that it created a gas cloud during manufacturing that was virtually impossible for their factory workers to overcome! Marketing efficiency may suffer and costs may rise with regional marketing. Moreover, regional campaigns may force local producers to become more competitive or can blur a brand's national identity.

OTHER DEMOGRAPHIC AND CULTURAL SEGMENTS

Any market segment—however defined—may be considered as a candidate for a specialized marketing and branding program. For example, Chapter 3 noted how consumers may be categorized according to demographic dimensions such as age, income, gender, and race as well as psychographic considerations. These more descriptive factors often are related to more fundamental behavioral considerations as to how different types of consumers shop for products or think about brands. These differences in attitudes and behavior with respect to products and brands can often serve as the rationale for a separate branding and marketing program. The segmentation decision ultimately rests on cost and benefit considerations regarding the costs of customizing marketing efforts versus the benefits of a more targeted focus.

For example, Chapter 13 described how important it is for marketers to consider age segments and how younger consumers can be brought into the consumer franchise. As another example, the 2000 census revealed that Asian and Hispanic people in the United States accounted for 79 million out of 281 million Americans and combined represented an estimated $1 trillion in annual purchasing power. Various firms have created specialized marketing programs with different products, advertising, promotions, and so on to better reach and persuade this market. For example, Sears Roebuck & Company's most profitable stores were the ones near Hispanic neighborhoods that carried clothing and cosmetics specially designed for Hispanics. Bank of America prospered by targeting Asians in San Francisco with separate TV campaigns aimed at Chinese, Korean, and Vietnamese customers. When

Marketing to African Americans

Census and marketing surveys have revealed the buying power of the African American community. Representing approximately 12 percent of the population, their expenditures approach $300 billion in sales. Despite that fact, only $736 million was spent to specifically target the African American market in 1990, compared with $51 billion in total advertising dollars—only a little over 1 percent of the total. Although much marketing has targeted baby boomers, the elderly, and other demographic or psychographic groups, many critics argue that the African American market has not been effectively targeted by many companies. Marlene Rossman, author of *Multicultural Marketing*, makes the following argument:

> Whether it is a poverty myth, the fear of venturing into an unknown market, or just plain ignorance that holds back mainstream markets, the fact is not enough goods and services are being targeted to the African-American market and its segments. Many businesses that are struggling to stay afloat continue to target the same overtapped general market when going after black consumers could make the difference between breaking even and increased market share and profits.

Because almost all African Americans speak English as their first and primary language and watch much network television, many companies rely on their general marketing campaigns to reach these consumers. Black media executives such as Thomas Burrell, chairman of Burrell Advertising in Chicago, the largest black-owned agency in the United States, maintains that such an approach is a mistake: "Black people aren't dark-skinned white people. We have different preferences and customs, and we require special effort."

African Americans can be found in virtually every conceivable income, education, and geographic segment. At the same time, they often have unique attitudes and behaviors that distinguish them from other groups. Many observers note the important role of religion, church, and family for African Americans. As a result of their historical experiences, African Americans are often thought to exhibit a strong togetherness and pride in their heritage. In terms of buying habits, African Americans spend a disproportionate amount of their income on apparel, footwear, and home electronics. For example, recognizing that African Americans often prefer larger helpings of sugar, cream, or nondairy creamer in their coffee, CoffeeMate began marketing to African Americans more specifically through black radio, magazines, and billboards, with a corresponding increase in sales.

Alcohol and tobacco companies were some of the first firms to develop campaigns targeted specifically to African American consumers, in recognition of different product preferences held by these consumers (e.g., a disproportionate amount of purchases of menthol cigarettes, certain types of hard liquors—brandy, scotch, cognac—and malt liquor beers than the general population). The marketing efforts of some of these pioneers, however, were controversial. Colt 45's suggestive ad campaign that portrayed actor Billy Dee Williams romancing young women to drink the malt liquor while the tag line proclaimed, "The power of Colt 45. It works every time." was roundly criticized as being in poor taste.

Other marketing campaigns attempt to address African Americans through existing campaigns in some way. Several possible shortcomings have been noted by marketing critics. Ads may fall prey to what African Americans decry as "eleventh man black tokenism," such as when an African American is stuck in the back of a crowd in an ad in what is seen as a blatant appeal to the African American audience. Other mistakes pointed out by marketing critics are to simple-mindedly replace white actors with black actors or run the same ads in black media vehicles. For example, because a large proportion of its travelers are African Americans, Greyhound decided to promote its low cross-country fares on urban contemporary radio stations that appealed to that group. Because they used the same ad as was being run for the mass market, the music in the background was country and western, "turning off and tuning out" many of the black listeners. Similarly, Mattel several years ago put out a "black Barbie" in an attempt to attract African American consumers, but the doll was simply a "white Barbie" (e.g., same facial features) painted one shade of brown and with straight, brown hair.

In terms of building brand equity, the challenge is how to create relevant marketing programs and communication campaigns for African American consumers that accurately portray brand personality and user and usage imagery. Along these lines, one president of a black-owned agency asserted that the formula for marketing to blacks consists of relevance, recognition, and respect. According to author Marilyn Rossman, several guidelines should be adhered to.

First, it is important to recognize the diversity of the African American market—just as in the mass market, there is great variety in lifestyle across different geographic and psychographic segments in the African American market. For example, Cover Girl advertises its 10 different shades of makeup designed for African Americans, from Cappucino Cream to Rich Mahogany. Such understanding clearly requires properly conducting and interpreting marketing research.

Second, design marketing campaigns that are relevant to the lifestyles of African Americans and reflect their consumer sensibilities. One survey indicated that 60 percent of black consumers feel that most television and print ads "are designed only for white people." What types of messages should be sent? Rossman makes the following argument: "When marketing to African-Americans, keep in mind that they value self-image, style, and personal elegance. . . . African-Americans are trendsetters. . . . African-Americans often want to define their own style rather than follow what the establishment dictates."

Finally, explore media that specifically targets African Americans, such as cable's Black Entertainment Television (BET); *Ebony*, *Essence*, *Black Enterprise*, and other magazines and newspapers; and urban contemporary and other types of radio stations. Even general media should be bought differently. For example, through much of the 1990s, virtually none of the top 10 programs most watched by African Americans were on the list of the top 10 shows most watched by the general market.

The challenge is to target African Americans in a way that builds brand equity without fostering stereotypes, offending sensibilities, or lumping segments together. As with global brand programs, standardization and customization should be blended as appropriate.

Sources: Based on material from Marlene Rossman, *Multicultural Marketing: Selling to a Diverse America* (New York: AMACOM, 1994); and Barbara Lloyd, *Capitalizing on the American Dream: Marketing to America's Ethnic Minorities*, Stanford Business School independent study, 1990.

Frito-Lay introduced line extensions in 1997 targeted primarily to the U.S. Hispanic market, with zesty flavors such as Salsa Verde and Flamin' Hot Sarositos, sales topped $100 million. General Mills approached the Hispanic market with a cereal line, Para su Familia ("For Your Family"), that featured bilingual packaging and a strong nutritional message.[76] Branding Brief 14-6 describes marketing efforts to build brand equity with African Americans.

Beyond the expense involved, other challenges exist in targeting cultural groups. Data on media habits, buying behavior, and so on are difficult to obtain. For example, although Mott's Inc. managed to build a following among Hispanics for its Mott's Juice, Hawaiian Punch, and Clamato brands, the company admits that it had few numbers to use for guidance. Language problems can make surveys hard to conduct, especially in Asian households where a range of languages and dialects may prevail. One major concern raised by marketing critics about creating separate marketing campaigns for different demographic groups is that some consumers may not like the fact that they are being targeted because they are "different" as that only reinforces their image or stereotype as outsiders or a minority. Moreover, consumers *not* in the market segment targeted may feel more alienated or at least distanced from the company and brand as a result.[77]

Notes

1. Michael J. Thomas, Jack R. Bureau, and Narsingh Saxena, "The Relevance of Global Branding," *Journal of Brand Management* 2, no. 5 (1995): 299–307.
2. James S. Hirsch, "U.S. Liquor Makers Seek Tonic in Foreign Markets," *Wall Street Journal*, 24 October 1989, 1.
3. Vanessa O'Connell, "Exxon 'Centralizes' New Global Campaign," *Wall Street Journal*, 11 July 2001, B6.
4. Ian M. Lewis, "Key Issues in Globalizing Brands: Why There Aren't Any Global OTC Medicine Brands" (talk presented at the Third Annual Advertising and Promotion Workshop, Advertising Research Foundation, February 5–6, 1991).
5. Thomas A. Stewart, "Beat the Budget and Astound Your CFO," *Fortune*, 28 October 1996, 187–189.
6. Patricia Sellers, "Pepsi Opens a Second Front," *Fortune*, 8 August 1994, 70–76; Patrick Barwise and Thomas Robertson, "Brand Portfolios," *European Management Journal* 10, no. 3 (September 1992): 277–285.
7. Dawar and Parker, however, show how the use of brand name as an important signal of quality occurs in various countries. See Niraj Dawar and Philip Parker, "Marketing Universals: Consumers' Use of Brand Name, Price, Physical Appearance, and Retailer Reputation as Signals of Quality," *Journal of Marketing* 58 (April 1994): 81–95.
8. Choi Lee and Robert T. Green, "Cross-Cultural Examination of the Fishbein Behavioral Intentions Model," *Journal of International Business Studies*, (Second Quarter 1991): 289–305.
9. Dennis Chase, "A Global Comeback," *Advertising Age*, 20 August 1987, 142–214.
10. Ronald Alsop, "Countries Different Ad Rules Are Problem for Global Firms," *Wall Street Journal*, 27 September 1984, 33.
11. Craig S. Smith, "Doublemint in China: Distribution Isn't Double the Fun," *Wall Street Journal*, 5 December 1995, B1.
12. Theodore Levitt, "The Globalization of Markets," *Harvard Business Review* (May–June 1983): 92–102.
13. Joanne Lipman, "Marketers Turn Sour on Global Sales Pitch Harvard Guru Makes," *Wall Street Journal*, 12 May 1988, 1; Tara Parker-Pope, "Custom-Made. The Most Successful Companies Have to Realize a Simple Truth: All Consumer's Aren't Alike," *Wall Street Journal*, 26 September 1996, R22–R23.

14. George Anders, "Ad Agencies and Big Concerns Debate World Brands' Value," *Wall Street Journal*, 14 June 1984, 33.

15. Gabriella Stern, "Heinz Aims to Export Taste for Ketchup," *Wall Street Journal*, 20 November 1992, B1.

16. Theresa Howard, "Coca-Cola Hopes Taking New Path Leads to Success," *USA Today*, 6 March 2001, 6B.

17. Robert L. Wehling, "Even at P&G, Only 3 Brands Make Truly Global Grade So Far," *Advertising Age*, 1 January 1998, 8.

18. Shelly Branch, "ACNielsen Gives 43 Brands Global Status," *Wall Street Journal*, 31 October 2001, B8.

19. Michael Porter, *Competitive Advantage* (New York: Free Press, 1985), 4–5.

20. Laurie Lang, personal correspondence.

21. Julia Flynn, "Heineken's Battle to Stay Top Bottle," *Business Week*, 1 August 1994, 60–62.

22. Carla Rapoport, "Nestlé's Brand Building Machine," *Fortune*, 19 September 1994, 147–156.

23. For more information on global marketing strategies, see George S. Yip, *Total Global Strategy* (Englewood Cliffs, NJ: Prentice-Hall, 1996).

24. Asihish Banerjee, "Global Campaigns Don't Work; Multinationals Do," *Advertising Age*, 18 April 1994, 23.

25. Louise Lee, "P&G Wants to Be on Tip of Tongues in, Let's Say, Tianjin," *Wall Street Journal*, 24 August 1998, B2.

26. Sellers, "Pepsi Opens Second Front."

27. Julie Skur Hill and Joseph M. Winski, "Goodbye Global Ads," *Advertising Age*, 16 November 1987, 22.

28. Vijay Govindarajan and Christopher Trimble, "Serving the Need of the Poor—For Profit," *Across the Board*, December 2001.

29. Rapoport, "Nestlé's Brand Building Machine."

30. Peter Fritsch and Gregory L. White, "Even Rivals Concede GM Has Deftly Steered Road to Success in Brazil," *Wall Street Journal*, 25 February 1999, A1, A8.

31. Mark Maremont, "They're All Screaming for Häagen-Dazs," *Business Week*, 4 October 1991, 121.

32. Carol Matlack, "eBay Steams into Europe," *Business Week*, 6 November 2000, 116.

33. Tara Parker-Pope, "Minty Python and Cream Victoria? Ice Creams Leave Some Groaning," *Wall Street Journal*, 3 July 1996, B1.

34. Ken Wells, "Global Campaigns, After Many Missteps, Finally Pay Dividends," *Wall Street Journal*, 27 August 1992, A1.

35. William Wells, "Global Advertisers Should Pay Heed to Contextual Variations," *Marketing News*, 13 February 1987, 18.

36. Martin S. Roth, "The Effects of Culture and Socioeconomics on the Performance of Global Brand Image Strategies," *Journal of Marketing Research* 32 (May 1995): 163–175.

37. Joann S. Lublin, "More U.S. Magazines to Travel Abroad," *Wall Street Journal*, 18 January 1990, B1.

38. Miriam Jordan, "In Rural India, Video Vans Sell Toothpaste and Shampoo," *Wall Street Journal*, 10 January 1996, B1, B5.

39. Emily Nelson and Miriam Jordan, "Seeking New Markets for Tampons, P&G Faces Cultural Barrier," *Wall Street Journal*, 8 December 2000, A1, A8.

40. Patrick Barwise and Thomas Robertson, "Brand Portfolios," *European Management Journal* 10, no. 3 (September 1992): 277–285.

41. Jennifer Lawrence and Dagmar Mussey, "P&G Accelerates International Pace," *Advertising Age*, 21 March 1994, I3.

42. Miriam Jordan, "Pillsbury Presses Flour Power in India," *Wall Street Journal*, 5 May 1999, B1.

43. Flynn, "Heineken's Battle."

44. David P. Hamilton, "United It Stands. Fuji Xerox Is a Rarity in World Business: A Joint Venture That Works," *Wall Street Journal*, 26 September 1996, R19.

45. Gail DeGeorge, "They Don't Call It Blockbuster for Nothing," *Business Week*, 19 October 1992, 113–114.

46. Stephanie Anderson Forest, "A Pier 1 in Every Port?," *Business Week*, 31 May 1993, 81.

47. Sellers, "Pepsi Opens Second Front."

48. Richard Gibson, "Gerber Missed the Boat in Quest to Go Global, So It Turned to Sandoz," *Wall Street Journal*, 24 May 1994, A1, A4.

49. Lewis, "Key Issues in Globalizing Brands."

50. Edward H. Meyer, "Consumers around the World: Do They Have the Same Wants and

Needs?" *Management Review* (January 1985): 26–29.

51. Fred Gardner, "BBDO Thinks Beyond Global Options," *Marketing & Media Decisions* (December 1984): 52–53.

52. Stephen A. Greyser, "Let's Talk Sense about Global Marketing" (speech given to Asian Advertising Congress, Bangkok, July 1986).

53. Rebecca Fanin, "JWT's Global Mandate: Keep It Local," *Marketing & Media Decisions* (December 1984): 49–50.

54. Rebecca Fanin, "What Agencies Really Think of Global Theory," *Marketing & Media Decisions* (December 1984): 74–82.

55. Anders, "Ad Agencies and Big Concerns."

56. Douglas R. Sease, "Japanese Firms Use U.S. Designers to Tailor Products to Local Tastes," *Wall Street Journal*, 4 March 1986, 1.

57. Maureen Marston, "Transferring Equity across Border" (paper presented at the ARF Fourth Annual Advertising and Promotion Workshop, February 12–13, 1992).

58. Lipman, "Marketers Turn Sour."

59. Michael Flagg, "Coca-Cola Adopts Local-Drinks Strategy in Asia," *Wall Street Journal*, 30 July 2001.

60. Miriam Jordan, "Penney Blends Two Business Cultures," *Wall Street Journal*, 5 April 2001, A15.

61. Hermann Simon, "Pricing Problems in a Global Setting," *Marketing News*, 9 October 1995, 4.

62. Rahul Jacob, "Asia, Where Big Brands Are Blooming," *Business Week*, 23 August 1993, 55.

63. Hubert Gatignon and Piet Vanden Abeele, "To Standardize or Not to Standardize: Marketing Mix Effectiveness in Europe," MSI Report 95–109 (Cambridge, MA: Marketing Science Institute, 1995).

64. Hajo Riesenbeck and Anthony Freeling, "How Global Are Global Brands?" *McKinsey Quarterly* no. 4, 3–18, as referenced in Barwise and Robertson, "Brand Portfolios." See also Dennis M. Sandler and David Shani, "Brand Globally but Advertise Locally? An Empirical Investigation," *Journal of Product & Brand Management* 2, no. 2 (1993): 59–71; Gatignon and Vanden Abeele, "To Standardize or Not to Standardize"; Saeed Samiee and Kendall Roth, "The Influence of Global Marketing

Standardization on Performance," *Journal of Marketing* 56 (April 1992): 1–17; and David M. Szymanski, Sundar G. Bharadwaj, and P. Rajan Varadarajan, "Standardization versus Adaptation of International Marketing Strategy: An Empirical Investigation," *Journal of Marketing* 57 (October 1993): 1–17.

65. Wells, "Global Campaigns."

66. Sharen Kindel, "A Brush with Success: Colgate Palmolive Company," *Hemisphere*, September 1996, 15.

67. George E. Belch and Michael Belch, *Introduction to Advertising and Promotion Management: An Integrated Marketing Communications Perspective*, 3rd ed. (Chicago, Richard Irwin, 1995).

68. Barwise and Robertson, "Brand Portfolios."

69. Robert Frank, "Potato Chips to Go Global—Or So Pepsi Bets," *Wall Street Journal*, 30 November 1995, B1.

70. Gerry Kermouch, "An Almost-Invisible $1 Trillion Market," *Business Week*, 11 June 2001, 151.

71. Christine Dugas, "Marketing's New Look," *Business Week*, 26 January 1987, 64–69.

72. Peter Oberlink, "Regional Marketing Starts Taking Hold," *Adweek*, 6 April 1987, 36–37.

73. Thomas Moore, "Different Folks, Different Strokes," *Fortune*, 16 September 1985, 65, 68.

74. Michael J. McCarthy, "In Texas Beer Brawl, Anheuser and Miller Aren't Pulling Punches," *Wall Street Journal*, 5 December 1996, A1, A12.

75. Alix M. Freedman, "National Firms Find That Selling to Local Tastes Is Costly, Complex," *Wall Street Journal*, 9 February 1987, 1.

76. Roberta Bernstein, "Food for Thought," *American Demographics* (May 2000): 39–40.

77. Jennifer L. Aaker, Anne M. Brumbuagh, and Sonya A. Grier, "Nontarget Markets and Viewer Distinctiveness: The Impact of Target Marketing on Advertising Attitudes," *Journal of Consumer Psychology* 9, no. 3 (2000): 127–140; Sonya A. Grier and Rohit Deshpande, "Social Dimensions of Consumer Distinctiveness: The Influence of Social Status on Group Identity and Advertising Persuasion," *Journal of Marketing Research* 38 (May 2001): 216–224.

CHAPTER
15
Closing Observations

PREVIEW

After introducing branding and the concept of brand equity and outlining the customer-based brand equity framework in Parts I and II of the text, previous chapters addressed how to build (Part III), measure (Part IV), and manage (Part V) customer-based brand equity. Part VI considers some implications and applications of the CBBE framework. Specifically, this final chapter provides some closing observations concerning strategic brand management. It first briefly reviews the CBBE framework. Next, it highlights managerial guidelines and key themes that emerged in previous chapters and summarizes success factors for branding. Following up on some of the discussion from Chapter 1, it then considers some special topics by applying the CBBE framework to address specific strategic brand management issues for different types of products. The chapter concludes by considering the future of branding. Brand Focus 15.0 presents "The Brand Report Card" to help brand managers understand and rate their brands' performance on key branding dimensions.

STRATEGIC BRAND MANAGEMENT GUIDELINES

Summary of Customer-Based Brand Equity Framework

Strategic brand management involves the design and implementation of marketing programs and activities to build, measure, and manage brand equity. Before reviewing some guidelines for strategic brand management, it is useful to briefly summarize—one last time!—the customer-based brand equity framework.

The rationale behind the framework is to recognize the importance of the customer in the creation and management of brand equity. As one top marketing executive put it: "Consumers own brands and your brand is what consumers will permit you to have." Consistent with this view, customer-based brand equity was defined in Chapter 2 as the differential effect that consumers' brand knowledge has on their response to the marketing of that brand. A brand is said to have positive customer-based brand equity when customers react more favorably to a product and the way it is marketed when the brand is identified than when it is not (e.g., when it is attributed to a fictitiously named or unnamed version of the product).

The basic premise of customer-based brand equity is that the power of a brand lies in the minds of consumers and what they have experienced and learned about the brand over time. More formally, brand knowledge was described in Chapter 3 in terms of an associative network memory model in which the brand can be thought of as being a node in memory with a variety of different types of associations potentially linked to it. Brand knowledge can be characterized in terms of two components: brand awareness and brand image. *Brand awareness* is related to the strength of the brand node or trace in memory as reflected by consumers' ability to recall or recognize the brand under different conditions. Brand awareness can be characterized by depth and breadth. The depth of brand awareness relates to the likelihood that the brand can be recognized or recalled. The breadth of brand awareness relates to the variety of purchase and consumption situations in which the brand comes to mind. *Brand image* is defined as consumer perceptions of and preferences for a brand, as reflected by the various types of brand associations held in consumers' memory. Although brand associations come in many forms, a useful distinction can be made between performance-related versus imagery-related attributes and benefits.

Sources of Brand Equity

Customer-based brand equity occurs when the consumer has a high level of awareness and familiarity with the brand and holds some strong, favorable, and unique brand associations in memory. In some cases, brand awareness alone is sufficient to result in more favorable consumer response, for example, in low-involvement decision settings in which consumers lack motivation or ability and are willing to base their choices merely on familiar brands. In other cases, the strength, favorability, and uniqueness of the brand associations play a critical role in determining the differential response making up the brand equity. Conceptually, these three dimensions of brand associations are determined by the following factors:

1. *Strength:* The strength of a brand association is a function of both the amount, or quantity, of processing that information initially receives as well as the nature, or quality, of that processing. The more deeply a person thinks about brand information and relates it to existing brand knowledge, the stronger the resulting brand associations. Two factors facilitating the strength of association to any piece of brand information are the personal relevance of the information and the consistency with which this information is presented over time.

2. *Favorability:* Favorable associations for a brand are those associations that are desirable to customers and are successfully delivered by the product and conveyed by the supporting marketing program for the brand. Associations may relate to the product or other intangible, non-product-related aspects (e.g., usage or user imagery). Not all brand associations, however, will be deemed important and viewed favorably by consumers, nor will they be equally valued across different purchase or consumption situations.

3. *Uniqueness:* To create the differential response that leads to customer-based brand equity, it is important to associate unique, meaningful points of difference to the brand to provide a competitive advantage and a "reason why" consumers should buy it. For other brand associations, however, it may be sufficient that they are seen as comparable or roughly equal in favorability to competing brand associations. These associations function as points of parity in consumers' minds to establish category membership and negate potential points of difference for competitors. In other words, these associations are designed to provide consumers "no reason why not" to choose the brand.

Figure 15-1 summarizes these broad conceptual guidelines for creating desired brand knowledge structures. These guidelines can provide general motivation and direction in designing tactical programs and activities to build brand equity.

Outcomes of Brand Equity

Assuming that a positive brand image is created by marketing programs that are able to register the brand in memory and link it to strong, favorable, and unique associations, a number of benefits for the brand may be realized, as follows:

FIGURE 15-1   Determinants of Desired Brand Knowledge Structures

1. *Depth of brand awareness* is determined by the ease of brand recognition and recall.
2. *Breadth of brand awareness* is determined by the number of purchase and consumption situations for which the brand comes to mind.
3. *Strong brand associations* are created by marketing programs that convey relevant information to consumers in a consistent fashion at any one point in time, as well as over time.
4. *Favorable brand associations* are created when marketing programs effectively deliver product-related and non-product-related benefits that are desired by consumers.
5. *Unique brand associations* that are also strong and favorable create points of difference that distinguish the brand from other brands. Brand associations that are not unique, however, can create valuable points of parity to establish necessary category associations or to neutralize competitive points of difference.

> Greater loyalty
> Less vulnerability to competitive marketing actions
> Less vulnerability to marketing crises
> Larger margins
> More inelastic consumer response to price increases
> More elastic consumer response to price decreases
> Greater trade cooperation and support
> Increased marketing communication effectiveness
> Possible licensing opportunities
> Additional brand extension opportunities

Tactical Guidelines

Figures 1-14 to 1-16 summarized the chief ingredients of the CBBE framework in terms of how to build, measure, and manage brand equity. The specific themes and recommendations that were developed in subsequent chapters are as follows.

Building Brand Equity

Tactically, brand equity can be built in three major ways: (1) through the initial choice of the brand elements making up the brand, (2) through marketing activities and the design of the marketing program, and (3) through the leverage of secondary associations by linking the brand to other entities (e.g., a company, geographic region, other brand, person, event, and so on). Guidelines emerged in Chapters 4 to 7 for each of these three different types of approaches, as summarized in Figure 15-2.

FIGURE 15-2 Guidelines for Building Brand Equity

1. Mix and match brand elements—brand names, logos, symbols, characters, slogans, jingles, and packages—by choosing different brand elements to achieve different objectives and by designing brand elements to be as mutually reinforcing as possible.
2. Ensure a high level of perceived quality and create a rich brand image by linking tangible and intangible product-related and non-product-related associations to the brand.
3. Adopt value-based pricing strategies to set prices and guide discount pricing policies over time that reflect consumers' perceptions of value and willingness to pay a premium.
4. Consider a range of direct and indirect distribution options and blend brand-building push strategies for retailers and other channel members with brand-building pull strategies for consumers.
5. Mix marketing communication options by choosing a broad set of communication options based on their differential ability to affect brand awareness and create, maintain, or strengthen favorable and unique brand associations. Match marketing communication options by ensuring consistency and directly reinforcing some communication options with other communication options.
6. Leverage secondary associations to compensate for otherwise missing dimensions of the marketing program by linking the brand to other entities such as companies, channels of distribution, other brands, characters, spokespeople or other endorsers, or events that reinforce and augment the brand image.

Themes   A dominant theme across many of these different ways to build brand equity is the importance of complementarity and consistency. *Complementarity* involves choosing different brand elements and different supporting marketing activities and programs such that the potential contribution to brand equity of one particular brand element or marketing activity compensates for the shortcomings of other elements and activities. For example, some brand elements may be designed primarily to enhance awareness (e.g., through a memorable brand logo), whereas other brand elements may be designed primarily to facilitate the linkage of brand associations (e.g., via a meaningful brand name or a clever slogan). Similarly, an ad campaign may be designed primarily to create a certain point-of-difference association, whereas a retail promotion may be designed primarily to create a vital point-of-parity association. Finally, certain other entities may be linked to the brand to leverage secondary associations and provide otherwise missing sources of brand equity or further reinforce existing associations.

Thus, it is important that a varied set of brand elements and marketing activities and programs be strategically put into place to create the desired level of awareness and type of image to provide necessary sources of brand equity. At the same time, a high degree of consistency across these elements helps to create the highest level of awareness and the strongest and most favorable associations possible. *Consistency* involves ensuring that diverse brand and marketing mix elements share a common core meaning, perhaps in some cases literally containing or conveying the same information. For example, brand elements may be designed to convey a certain benefit association that is further reinforced by a highly integrated, well-branded marketing communications program.

Measuring Brand Equity

According to the definition of customer-based brand equity, brand equity can be measured indirectly, by measuring the potential sources of brand equity, and directly, by measuring the possible outcomes of brand equity. Measuring sources of customer-based brand equity requires measuring various aspects of brand awareness and brand image that potentially can lead to the differential customer response that creates brand equity: breadth and depth of brand awareness; the strength, favorability, and uniqueness of brand associations; the valence of brand responses; and the nature of brand relationships. Measuring outcomes of brand equity involves approximating the various benefits realized from creating these sources of brand equity. The brand value chain depicts this relationship more broadly by considering how marketing activity affects these sources of brand equity and how the resulting outcomes influence the investment community, as well as how various filters or multipliers intervene between the stages.

Organizationally, it is important to properly design and implement a brand equity measurement system. A *brand equity measurement system* was defined as a set of research procedures designed to provide timely, accurate, and actionable information for marketers about their brands so that they can make the best possible tactical decisions in the short run as well as strategic decisions in the long run. Implementing a brand equity measurement system involves three steps: (1) conducting brand audits, (2) designing brand tracking studies, and (3) establishing a brand equity management system.

Guidelines in each of these areas are summarized in Figure 15-3.

Themes   The dominant theme in measuring brand equity is the need to employ a full complement of research techniques and processes that capture as much as possible the

1. Formalize the firm's view of brand equity into a document, the brand equity charter, that provides relevant branding guidelines to marketing managers.
2. Conduct brand inventories to profile how all of the products sold by a company are branded and marketed and conduct brand exploratories to understand what consumers think and feel about a brand as part of periodic brand audits to assess the health of brands, understand their sources of brand equity, and suggest ways to improve and leverage that equity.
3. Conduct consumer tracking studies on a routine basis to provide current information as to how brands are performing with respect to the key sources and outcomes of brand equity as identified by the brand audit.
4. Assemble results of tracking survey and other relevant outcome measures into a brand equity report to be distributed on a regular basis to provide descriptive information as to what is happening with a brand as well as diagnostic information as to why it is happening.
5. Establish a person or department to oversee the implementation of the brand equity charter and brand equity reports to make sure that, as much as possible, product and marketing actions across divisions and geographic boundaries are done in a way that reflects the spirit of the charter and the substance of the report so as to maximize the long-term equity of the brand.

FIGURE 15-3   Guidelines for Measuring Brand Equity

richness and complexity of brand equity. Multiple techniques and measures are necessary to tap into all the various sources and outcomes of brand equity. Simplistic approaches to measuring brand equity—for example, by attempting to estimate the equity of a brand with only one number—are potentially fraught with error and lack diagnostic or prescriptive power. Multiple processes are necessary to help interpret brand equity research and ensure that actionable information is provided to the right people at the right time.

Managing Brand Equity

Finally, managing brand equity requires taking a broad, long-term perspective of brands. A broad view of brand equity is critically important, especially when firms are selling multiple products and multiple brands in multiple markets. In such cases, brand hierarchies must be created that define common and distinct brand elements among various nested products. New product and brand extension strategies also must be designed to determine optimal brand and product portfolios. Finally, these brands and products must be effectively managed over geographic boundaries and target market segments by creating brand awareness and a positive brand image in each market in which the brand is sold.

A long-term view of brand equity is necessary because of the implications that changes in current marketing programs and activities and the marketing environment have on consumers' brand knowledge structures and thus their response to future marketing programs and activities. Managing brands over time requires reinforcing the brand meaning and adjusting the branding program as needed. For brands whose equity has eroded over time, a number of revitalizing strategies are available.

Figure 15-4 highlights some important guidelines for managing brand equity.

Themes   The dominant themes in managing brand equity are the importance of balance in marketing activities and of making moderate levels of change in the marketing

1. Define the brand hierarchy in terms of the number of levels to use and the relative prominence that brands at different levels will receive when combined to brand any one product.
2. Create global associations relevant to as many brands nested at the level below in the hierarchy as possible but sharply differentiate brands at the same level of the hierarchy.
3. Introduce brand extensions that complement the product mix of the firm, leverage parent brand associations, and enhance parent brand equity.
4. Clearly establish the roles of brands in the brand portfolio, adding, deleting, and modifying brands as necessary.
5. Reinforce brand equity over time through marketing actions that consistently convey the meaning of the brand in terms of what products the brand represents, what benefits it supplies, what needs it satisfies, and why it is superior to competitive brands.
6. Enhance brand equity over time through innovation in product design, manufacturing, and merchandising and continued relevance in user and usage imagery.
7. Identify differences in consumer behavior in different market segments and adjust the branding program accordingly on a cost-benefit basis.

FIGURE 15-4 Guidelines for Managing Brand Equity

program over time. Without some modifications of the marketing program, a brand runs the risk of becoming obsolete or irrelevant to consumers. At the same time, dramatic shifts back and forth in brand strategies run the risk of confusing or alienating consumers. Thus, a consistent thread of meaning—which consumers can recognize—should run through the marketing program that reflects the key sources of equity for the brand and its core brand associations. In other words, changes in the product and how it is priced, advertised, promoted, or distributed may be needed to preserve or enhance sources of brand equity over time, but these changes should illuminate and not obscure key brand associations

WHAT MAKES A STRONG BRAND?

With the previous discussion as background, this section can provide some perspective on what makes a strong brand. To create a strong brand and maximize brand equity, marketing managers must do the following:

➤ Understand brand meaning and market appropriate products in an appropriate manner.
➤ Properly position the brand.
➤ Provide superior delivery of desired benefits.
➤ Employ a full range of complementary brand elements and supporting marketing activities.
➤ Embrace integrated marketing communications and communicate with a consistent voice.
➤ Measure consumer perceptions of value and develop a pricing strategy accordingly.
➤ Establish credibility and appropriate brand personality and imagery.
➤ Maintain innovation and relevance for the brand.
➤ Strategically design and implement a brand hierarchy and brand portfolio.
➤ Implement a brand equity management system to ensure that marketing actions properly reflect the brand equity concept.

On the flip side of the coin, what are the common branding mistakes that prevent firms from creating strong, powerful brands? In contrast to the previous list, some of the more common branding problems—the "seven deadly sins of brand management"—include the following (see Figure 15-5):[1]

1. *Failure to fully understand the meaning of the brand.* Given that consumers "own" brands, it is critical to understand what consumers think and feel about brands and then plan and implement marketing programs accordingly. Too often, managers convince themselves of the validity of marketing actions—for example, a new brand extension, ad campaign, or price hike—based on a mistaken belief of what consumers know or what marketers would like them to know about the brand. Relatedly, managers often ignore the full range of associations—both tangible and intangible—that may characterize the brand.

2. *Failure to live up to the brand promise.* A brand should be a promise and a commitment to consumers, but too often that promise is broken. A common mistake is to set brand expectations too high and then fail to live up to them in the marketing program. By overpromising and not delivering, a firm is worse off in many ways than if it had not set expectations at all.

3. *Failure to adequately support the brand.* Creating and maintaining brand knowledge structures requires marketing investments. Too often, managers want to get something for nothing by building brand equity without a willingness to provide proper marketing support or, once brand equity has been built, expecting the brand to remain strong despite the lack of further investments.

4. *Failure to be patient with the brand.* Brand equity must be carefully and patiently built from the ground up. A firm foundation for brand equity requires that consumers have the proper depth and breadth of awareness and strong, favorable, and unique associations in memory. Too often, managers want to take shortcuts and bypass more basic branding considerations—such as achieving the necessary level of brand awareness—to concentrate on flashier aspects of brand building related to its image.

5. *Failure to adequately control the brand.* Brand equity must be understood by all employees of the firm, and actions must be taken to reflect a broader corporate perspective as well as a more specific product perspective. Too often, decisions are made haphazardly without a true understanding of the current and desired brand equity and without a recognition of the impact of these decisions on other brands or brand-related activities.

6. *Failure to properly balance consistency and change with the brand.* Managing a brand necessitates striking the difficult, but crucial, balance between maintaining continuity in marketing activities and implementing changes to update the product or image of a brand. Too often, managers are left behind as a result of not making adjustments in their marketing

---

1. Failure to fully understand the meaning of the brand.
2. Failure to live up to the brand promise.
3. Failure to adequately support the brand.
4. Failure to be patient with the brand.
5. Failure to adequately control the brand.
6. Failure to properly balance consistency and change with the brand.
7. Failure to understand the complexity of brand equity measurement and management.

FIGURE 15-5 Seven Deadly Sins of Brand Management

program to reflect changes in the marketing environment; alternatively, they may make so many changes that the brand becomes a moving target without any meaning to consumers.

7. *Failure to understand the complexity of brand equity measurement and management.* Effective brand management requires discipline, creativity, focus, and the ability to make hundreds of decisions in the best possible manner. Unfortunately, sometimes marketers oversimplify the process and try to equate success in branding with one particular action or approach. By not realizing the many other actions that also have to occur, brand equity is not optimized as a result.

SPECIAL APPLICATIONS

Although conventional use of the term *product* might be seen as representing only physical goods, *product* was deliberately defined broadly in Chapter 1 to encompass not only physical goods but also services, retail stores, people, organizations, places, or ideas. Chapter 1 provided examples of how each of these different types of products could be branded. Accordingly, the term *product* was used throughout the text in a broad sense, and the themes and guidelines for building, measuring, and managing brand equity presented earlier in this chapter should be appropriate for virtually all types of products. Nevertheless, it is worthwhile to consider in greater detail some specific strategic brand management issues for some of these less conventional types of products. This section suggests additional guidelines for the following six special cases: industrial and business-to-business products, high-technology products, services, retailers, small businesses, and online brands.

Industrial and Business-to-Business Products

Because industrial goods usually involve business-to-business marketing practices, they sometimes involve some different branding practices.[2] Regardless of the particular type of industrial goods sold, some basic branding guidelines can be offered, as follows (see Figure 15-6). Branding Brief 15-1 describes how Siemens has attempted to create a strong corporate industrial brand.

Adopt a corporate or family branding strategy and create a well-defined brand hierarchy. Because companies selling industrial goods are often characterized by a large and complex number of product lines and variations, it is important that a logical and well-organized brand hierarchy be devised. In particular, because of the breadth and complexity of their product mix, companies selling industrial goods are more likely to emphasize corporate or family brands (e.g., as with GE, Hewlett-Packard, IBM, ABB,

---

FIGURE 15-6   Additional Guidelines for Industrial Products

1. Adopt a corporate or family branding strategy and create a well-defined brand hierarchy.
2. Link non-product-related imagery associations.
3. Employ a full range of marketing communication options.
4. Leverage equity of other companies that are customers.
5. Segment markets carefully and develop tailored branding and marketing programs.

Business-to-Business Branding at Siemens

Despite the fact that Siemens products have been available in the U.S. market since 1954, research indicated that only 12 percent of Americans are able to identify the company. Siemens employs over 80,000 American workers, turbines made by its Westinghouse division provide 40 percent of the power in the United States, and more than half the cars in America run using Siemens parts. Though it is not a high-visibility corporation in America, Siemens is a household name in most of the 192 other countries in which it competes.

Siemens began its first corporate advertising campaign in the United States in 1988. But in 2000, CEO Gerhard Schulmeyer expressed disappointment with his company's previous branding efforts in America:

"We get mad at ourselves. We haven't done the greatest job of branding. No letter could move in this country without our technology, but we never felt a need to tell the people this."

In 2001, the company set out to raise its image in the eyes of American consumers. This move represented the third step in a plan initiated in 1998 to reinvent Siemens as a high-profile brand using longtime competitor GE as a model. The company made the United States a primary target for a series of image advertisements that launched in April 2001. Siemens spent $25 million on U.S. media for the campaign, which was part of an estimated $500 million that the company earmarked for U.S. marketing through 2002. The series began with teaser print ads, which were followed by television spots. Aiming at increasing sales of its consumer goods, the ads featured Siemens mobile phones. One problem with the company's mobiles, however, was that they were based on European wireless standards different from the dominant standard in the U.S. market, so the company planned to hold back from mass marketing these phones until universal standards developed.

Total U.S. sales for Siemens in 2000 were $16 billion. That year, the United States overtook Germany to become Siemens's largest market. Siemens hoped to increase U.S. sales to $25 billion within five years.

Sources: James Cox, "Siemens Cultivates American Accent," *USA Today,* 5 March 2001; Sarah Ellison, "Siemens Woos Youth with New Attitude," *Wall Street Journal,* 15 February 2001; Alfred Kueppers, "Siemens's U.S. Debut Isn't Ideal," *Asian Wall Street Journal,* 19 March 2001, N1.

BASF, and John Deere). In completing the brand hierarchy for industrial goods, individual brands and modifiers often take on descriptive product meaning for clarity and differentiation. Thus, a particularly effective branding strategy for industrial goods is to create sub-brands by combining a well-known and respected corporate name with descriptive product modifiers.

Link non-product-related imagery associations. Developing supporting marketing programs to build brand equity for industrial goods can be different from consumer goods because given the nature of the organizational buying process, product-related associations may play a relatively more important role than non-product-related associations. Industrial brands often emphasize functionality and cost/benefit considerations. Nevertheless, even non-product-related associations can be useful in terms of other perceptions of the firm, such as the prestige or type of company that uses the firm's products.

It is especially important that these corporate or family brands convey credibility and possess favorable global associations. Corporate credibility is often a primary risk reduction heuristic adopted by industrial buyers. For years, one of the key sources of brand equity for IBM was the fact that a marketplace perception existed that "you'll never get fired for buying IBM." Once that special cachet faded, the brand found itself in a much more competitive situation. Creating a feeling of security for industrial buyers can thus be an important source of brand equity.

Many industrial firms distinguish themselves on the basis of the customer service they provide in addition to the quality of their products. For example, Premier Industrial Corporation charges up to 50 percent more than competitors for every one of the 250,00 industrial parts it stocks and distributes because of its strong commitment to customer service, as exemplified by the following anecdote:

> Early one afternoon in late 1988, Premier Industrial Corp. got a call from the manager of a Caterpillar Inc. tractor plant in Decatur, Illinois. A $10 electrical relay had broken down, idling an entire assembly line. A sales representative for Premier located a replacement at the company's Los Angeles warehouse and rushed it to a plane headed for St. Louis. By 10:30 that night, a Premier employee had delivered the part, and the line was up and running. "You can't build tractors if you can't move the line," remarked the Caterpillar purchasing analyst. "They really saved us a bundle of money."[3]

As further illustration, creative changes in customer service have similarly built brand equity and allowed Armstrong World Industries to charge higher prices for its floor tiles and Weyerhaeuser's wood-products division to command premiums for its commodity-like two-by-fours.

Employ a full range of marketing communication options. Another difference between industrial and consumer products is the manner by which they are sold: A different marketing communication mix exists with industrial products than with consumer products (see Figure 15-7). Because of the well-defined target market and complex nature of product decisions, marketing communications tend to convey more detailed product information in a more direct or face-to-face manner. Thus, personal selling plays an important role. At the same time, other communication options can be employed to enhance awareness or the formation of brand associations. One effective industrial marketing communication approach is thus to combine direct hard-sell messages with more indirect image-related messages that convey who and what the company is all about

Leverage equity of other companies that are customers. Secondary associations can be leveraged differently for industrial brands. For example, one commonly adopted means of communicating credibility is to identify other companies that are customers for the firm's products or services. The challenge in communicating this endorsement

Media advertising (TV, radio, newspaper, magazines)
Trade journal advertising
Directories
Direct mail
Brochures and sales literature
Audiovisual presentation tapes
Giveaways
Sponsorship or event marketing
Exhibitions, trade shows, and conventions
Publicity or public relations

FIGURE 15-7 Alternative Communication Options: Business-to-Business Market

through advertising, however, is ensuring that the other companies used as endorsers do not distract from the message about the advertised company and its brands. Even countries can be used in an endorsement strategy. For example, Interlock Industries— a New Zealand firm that specializes in window hardware—has used the fact that it is the only foreign company in its industry to sell in Japan as an endorsement strategy to sell its products to firms in other countries.

Segment customers carefully and develop tailored branding and marketing programs. Finally, as with any brand, it is important to understand how different customer segments view products and brands. For industrial goods, however, the different customer segments may exist within organizations as well as across organizations. Depending on the perceptions and preferences of the organizational segments involved—for example, engineers, brand or marketing managers, accountants or purchasing managers, and so forth—the particular associations that serve as sources of brand equity may differ. It may be particularly important to achieve points of parity with these different constituencies so that key points of difference can come into play. U.K. branding experts de Chernatony and McDonald put it this way:

> In consumer marketing, brands tend to be bought by individuals, while many people are involved in organizational purchasing. The brand marketer is faced with the challenge of not only identifying which managers are involved in the purchasing decision, but also what brand attributes are of particular concern to each of them. The various benefits of the brand, therefore, need to be communicated to all involved, stressing the relevant attributes to particular individuals. For example, the brand's reliable delivery may need to be stressed to the production manager, its low life-cycle costs to the accountant, and so on.[4]

Marketing programs must reflect the role of individuals in the buying center or process-initiator, influencer, purchaser, user, and so on. Some individuals within the organization may be more concerned with developing a deep relationship with the company and therefore place greater value on the trustworthiness dimension and corporate credibility; other individuals may seek merely to make transactions and therefore place greater value on product performance and expertise.

High-Tech Products

One special category of physical goods—potentially sold to both consumers and industrial customers—is technologically intensive or "high-tech" products. The main distinguishing feature of high-tech products is that the products themselves change rapidly over time because of technological innovations and R&D breakthroughs. It should be recognized that high-tech products are not restricted to computer- or microprocessor-related products. Technology has played an important role in the branding and marketing of products as diverse as razor blades for Gillette and athletic shoes for Nike. The short product life cycles for high-tech products have several significant branding implications (see Figure 15-8 for specific guidelines). Branding Brief 15-2 describes branding developments for Microsoft, one of the fastest-growing and most successful corporate brands of the past decade.

Establish brand awareness and a rich brand image. Many high-tech companies have learned the hard way the importance of branding their products and not relying on product specifications alone to drive their sales. Typically, it cannot be assumed that "if you build a great product, they will come." Well-designed and well-funded marketing programs need to be put into place that create brand awareness and a strong brand image. In doing so, non-product-related associations concerning brand personality or other imagery may be important, especially in distinguishing near-parity products.

Create corporate credibility associations. One implication of rapid product turnover is the need to create a corporate or family brand with strong credibility associations. Because of the often complex nature of high-tech products and the continual introduction of new products or modifications of existing products, consumer perceptions of the expertise and trustworthiness of the firm are particularly important. In a high-tech setting, trustworthiness also relates to consumers' perceptions of the firm's longevity and staying power. With technology companies, the president or CEO often is a key component of the brand and performs an important brand-building and communication function, in some cases as an advocate of the technology involved.

Leverage secondary associations of quality. Lacking the ability to judge the quality of high-tech products, consumers may use brand reputation as a means to reduce risk. This lack of ability by consumers to judge quality also means that it may be necessary to leverage secondary associations to better communicate product quality. Third-party endorsements from top companies, leading consumer magazines, or industry experts may help to achieve the necessary perceptions of product quality. To be able to garner these endorsements, however, will typically necessitate demonstrable differences in product performance, suggesting the importance of innovative product development over time.

Avoid overbranding products. One mistake made by many high-tech firms is to "overbrand" their products by using too many ingredient and endorser brands. For

---

1. Establish brand awareness and a rich brand image.
2. Create corporate credibility associations.
3. Leverage secondary associations of quality.
4. Avoid overbranding products.
5. Selectively introduce new products as new brands and clearly identify the nature of brand extensions.

FIGURE 15-8   Additional Guidelines for High-Tech Products

Building the Microsoft Brand

One of the more revered (and perhaps feared!) brands is Microsoft, which has become the undisputed personal computer software leader. Microsoft was founded in 1975 when Bill Gates left Harvard at age 19 to work with high school friend Paul Allen on a version of the BASIC programming language. After moving the company from Albuquerque, New Mexico, to Seattle in 1979, Gates and Allen began writing operating system software. What happened to the company since its founding is a well-known and oft-told story. Recognizing the importance of branding, Microsoft has engaged in a number of activities to enhance its brand equity and market value. Microsoft's software products are designed to be technologically advanced, reliable, easy to use, and reasonably priced. Microsoft has used classic packaged-goods marketing techniques—TV, print, and outdoor advertising, direct response with toll-free 800 numbers, specially designed packaging, and sophisticated merchandising—to sell its products. This brief highlights a few of the key strategies that enabled the company to achieve such remarkable growth in the competition-ridden computer industry.

PRODUCT INNOVATION

Microsoft achieved early success as a result of a single product innovation. In 1980, IBM contracted Microsoft to write the operating system for its new PCs, which led to the creation of Microsoft Disk Operating System (MS-DOS). Because other PC manufacturers desired compatibility with IBM machines, MS-DOS was soon adopted as the standard PC operating system. Another, even bigger innovation followed. In 1983 the company introduced the now-ubiquitous Windows, which was based on a graphical interface similar to Apple's Macintosh system. Because it was the first "windowing" software to work on PCs from any brand, Windows—like DOS before it—became the standard for personal computers. While Windows enabled the company to vault to unforeseen heights, the company continued to develop innovative software and other products. Microsoft's current big project is the development of a next-generation operating system called Microsoft.Net (pronounced "dot-net"), designed to merge Windows with the Internet directly. Microsoft .Net will allow multiple devices—PCs, wireless phones, pagers, digital cameras, PDAs, and other "smart devices"—to work together over Web connections with unprecedented ease.

BRAND-EXTENSION STRATEGY

Microsoft uses its strong brand name to launch new software products. Some examples include Microsoft Word, Microsoft Office, and Microsoft Internet Explorer. In 1989, Microsoft passed Lotus to become the world's largest seller of software worldwide. At that time, the company boasted the broadest array of software products and applications as well as the highest profit margin in the industry, at close to 25 percent.

HEAVY ADVERTISING

In the early years, Microsoft used advertising sparingly. In the mid-1990s, however, Microsoft began to advertise aggressively. In 1994, the company made two major moves: It hired the head of marketing and advertising from Procter & Gamble and developed its first global advertising campaign. The campaign doubled the company's ad budget to $100 million, and the following year that figure ballooned to $200 million for the Windows 95 launch. Today, it is common for the company to spend $50 million marketing a single product. Its global marketing budget for 2001 exceeded $500 million.

COMPETITIVE TOUGHNESS

Microsoft's aggressive competitive practices enabled the company to establish a leadership role in many product categories, but also led to legal battles. In one of the most publicized antitrust suits ever, the U.S. Justice Department charged Microsoft, claiming that it had limited consumer choice and stifled competition in part by bundling software, such as Internet Explorer, with its operating system. The presiding judge ruled to split Microsoft into two separate companies—an operating system company and an applications company—but the company continues to operate as a whole while its appeal is pending.

PRODUCT EXPANSION

Microsoft was quick to expand its business beyond operating systems into software applications for home and business PC users, educational software, and computer games. The company also expanded its operating system business. In 1993, the company introduced its Windows NT operating system, which was designed to compete with UNIX as the operating system of choice for large networks. After overcoming initial reluctance to embrace the Internet, Microsoft developed the Internet Explorer Web browser as an answer to Netscape, and developed the Web portal Microsoft Network (MSN) to compete with the likes of Yahoo and AOL. MSN was not successful and endured major alterations before being reborn as MSN.com.

The company also expanded into media development in the 1990s. It formed a joint venture with NBC to create the cable station MSNBC, which featured news, financial, and talk show programming. The company added another television venture in 1997 when it bought the set-top box system WebTV (later to become UltimateTV). In 2001, the company rolled out a videogame console called Xbox intended to compete with advanced game systems from Sony and Nintendo. Later that year, Microsoft introduced its latest operating system, Windows XP, and supported it with what the company described as "the biggest marketing [investment] in Microsoft history-doubling the investment of the Windows 95 launch in the first four months of product availability alone."

Sources: Tim Clark, "Microsoft Reboots Future Marketing," *Advertising Age,* 26 April 1994, 64; Don Clark, "Windows 95 Buzz Will Get Even Louder," *Wall Street Journal,* 18 August 1995, B1; Rebecca Buckman, "About Advertising: Microsoft Ad Campaign Touts Its Software for Big Business," *Wall Street Journal Europe,* 23 January 2001; "Windows of Opportunity," *Marketing Week,* 9 December 1994; "Microsoft Hires P&G Marketer," *Marketing Week,* 18 November 1994; http://www.microsoft.com; Lyndsey Erwin, "Great XPectations," *Point of Purchase,* 1 November 2001, 14.

example, in 1995 Silicon Graphics introduced its next-generation 3-D workstation, the Indigo^2 IMPACT, which was divided into performance categories with the following modifiers (in increasing order of performance): "High," "Solid," "Killer," and "Maximum." Given the length of the brand name, customers typically used the most specific modifier in the product name as a shorthand reference to the computer. For example, customers abbreviated the "Indigo^2 IMPACT Solid" to just "Solid." By overbranding in this way, brand equity slides down the hierarchy to lower levels at the expense of the family brand or company brand. Though the company made national headlines, the Silicon Graphics master brand was not necessarily as well known as its popular Indigo sub-brands, which became problematic as successors to Indigo were introduced.

Selectively introduce new products as new brands and clearly identify the nature of brand extensions. Another implication of the abbreviated nature of product life cycles is the importance of optimally designing brand portfolios and brand hierarchies. Several issues are relevant here. First, brand extensions are a common high-tech branding strategy. With new products continually emerging, it would be prohibitively expensive to brand them with new names in each case. Typically, names for new products are given modifiers from existing products—for example, numerical (Microsoft Word 6.0), time-based (Microsoft Windows 2000), or other schemes—unless they represent dramatic departures or marked product improvements for the brand, in which case a new brand name might be employed. Using a new name for a new product is a means to signal to consumers that this particular generation or version of a product is a major departure and significantly different from prior versions of the product.

Thus, family brands are an important means of grouping products. Individual items or products within those brand families must be clearly distinguished, however, and brand migration strategies must be defined that reflect product introduction strategies and consumer market trends. Other brand portfolio issues relate to the importance of retaining some brands. Too often, high-tech firms continually introduce totally new sub-brands, making it difficult for consumers to develop product or brand loyalty to any one brand.

Services

As noted in Chapter 1, although strong service brands have been around for years, the level of sophistication with branding has greatly increased in recent years, as suggested by the following guidelines (see Figure 15-9). Branding Brief 15-3 reviews how Charles Schwab built a strong services brand in the 1990s.

Maximize service quality by recognizing the myriad ways to affect consumer service perceptions. From a branding perspective, one challenge with services is their intangible nature. One consequence of this intangibility is that consumers may have difficulty forming their quality evaluations and may end up basing those evaluations on considerations other than factors directly related to their service experience. Researchers have identified a number of dimensions of service quality:[5]

➤ *Tangibles:* Physical facilities, equipment, and appearance of personnel
➤ *Reliability:* Ability to perform the promised service right the first time (standardized facilities and operations)
➤ *Responsiveness:* Willingness to help customers and provide customer service
➤ *Competence:* Knowledge and skill of employees

---

1. Maximize service quality by recognizing the myriad ways to affect consumer service perceptions.
2. Employ a full range of brand elements to enhance brand recall and signal more tangible aspects of the brand.
3. Create and communicate strong organizational associations.
4. Design corporate communication programs that augment consumers' service encounters and experiences.
5. Establish a brand hierarchy by creating distinct family brands or individual brands as well as meaningful ingredient brands.

FIGURE 15-9   Additional Guidelines for Services

➤ *Trustworthiness:* Believability and honesty (ability to convey trust and confidence)

➤ *Empathy:* Caring, individualized attention

➤ *Courtesy:* Friendliness of customer contact

➤ *Communication:* Keeping customers informed in language they can understand and listening to what they say

Thus, service quality perceptions depend on a number of specific associations that vary in how directly they relate to the actual service experience. In terms of creating service offerings that excel on these various dimensions, academic researchers Berry, Parasuraman, and Zeithaml offer ten recommendations that they maintain are essential for improving service quality across service industries (see Figure 15-10).[6]

Employ a full range of brand elements to enhance brand recall and signal more tangible aspects of the brand. Intangibility also has implications for the choice of brand elements. Because service decisions and arrangements are often made away from the actual service location itself (e.g., at home or at work), brand recall becomes critically important. In such cases, an easy-to-remember and easy-to-pronounce brand name may become critically important. Because a physical product does not exist, packaging in a literal sense is not really relevant, although the physical facilities of the service provider can perhaps be seen as the external "packaging" of a service (e.g., through its primary and secondary signage, environmental design and reception area, apparel, collateral material, and so on). Other brand elements—logos, symbols, characters, and slogans—must then pick up the slack and complement the brand name to build brand awareness and brand image. These other brand elements often attempt to make the service and some of its key benefits more tangible, concrete, and real—for example, the "friendly skies" of United, the "good hands" of Allstate, and the "bullish" nature of Merrill Lynch. All aspects of the service delivery process can be branded, which is why Allied Moving Lines is concerned about the appearance of its drivers and laborers, why UPS has developed such strong equity with the brown color of its trucks, and why Doubletree hotels offers warm, fresh-baked cookies as a means of symbolizing the company's care and friendliness.

Create and communicate strong organizational associations. Organizational associations, such as perceptions about the people who make up the organization and who provide the service, are likely to be particularly important brand associations that may affect evaluations of service quality directly or indirectly. Particularly important associations are company credibility and perceived expertise, trustworthiness, and likability.

BRANDING BRIEF 15-3

Branding a Step Ahead at Charles Schwab

Charles Schwab founded the discount brokerage named for him in 1974. The company's no-frills investment offerings were predicated on Charles Schwab's distaste for traditional brokers, who he labeled "hucksters of inside information, always trying to get me to buy this product or investment." Until 1993, Schwab's brokers were instructed not to offer investment advice, but rather to refer curious customers to publicly available research from Standard & Poor's or Morningstar.

Schwab benefited most from the online trading boom. Long before any of the traditional brokerage houses considered an e-commerce move, in 1997 Schwab was one of the first discount brokerages to offer online trading. It offered online trades at $29.95 for the first 1,000 shares, compared with per-trade fees that exceeded $100. Starting at zero in 1995, online trades accounted for 85 percent of all trades executed by Schwab by 2001. The company's retail assets grew threefold to almost $1 trillion during the same time period, putting it in the same league as the biggest brokerages in America. Between 1997 and 2000, daily trades rose 183 percent, while profits increased 112 percent.

Schwab's marketing activities helped the company become a household name synonymous with online trading. Early ads used real Schwab customers and employees in testimonial advertisements. In 1999, the company enlisted celebrity spokespersons to advertise its full-service online investing offerings. The humorous ads featured sports stars such as football player Shannon Sharpe and tennis star Anna Kournikova playing themselves as Schwab customers who surprised competitors with their knowledge of investing principles. The tag line served to reinforce Schwab's difference from online-only brokerages: "We've created a smarter kind of investing. We've created a smarter kind of investor." These ads were part of Schwab's $200 million marketing budget for 1999.

In 2001, as online trading slowed in the wake of the dot-com crash, Schwab sought to expand its business by providing its customers with a greater number of services. Rather than rely on a high volume of low-cost trades to drive revenues, Schwab began focusing on providing investment advice to its clients. In new brokerage offices, Schwab placed financial advisers from whom clients could seek investment tips and other services for a fee. Schwab also considered offering proprietary stock research for its customers. Industry experts expected these new services would recast Schwab in a role more similar to traditional brokerage houses. A former Schwab executive predicted, "Schwab will be a lot closer to Merrill Lynch than it is to the Schwab of yesterday."

Sources: John Gorman, "Charles Schwab, Version 4.0," *Forbes,* 8 January 2001, 89–95; Charles Gasparino and Ken Brown, "Schwab's Own Stock Suffers from Move into Online Trading," *Wall Street Journal,* 19 June 2001, A1; Rebecca Buckman and Kathryn Kranhold, "Schwab Serves Up Sports-Themed Ads," *Wall Street Journal,* 30 August 1999.

1. *Listening:* Understand what customers really want through continuous learning about the expectations and perceptions of customers and non-customers (e.g., by means of a service quality information system).
2. *Reliability:* Reliability is the single most important dimension of service quality and must be a service priority.
3. *Basic service:* Service companies must deliver the basics and do what they are supposed to do—keep promises, use common sense, listen to customers, keep customers informed, and be determined to deliver value to customers.
4. *Service design:* Develop a holistic view of the service while managing its many details.
5. *Recovery:* To satisfy customers who encounter a service problem, service companies should encourage customers to complain (and make it easy for them to do so), respond quickly and personally, and develop a problem resolution system.
6. *Surprising customers:* Although reliability is the most important dimension in meeting customers' service expectations, process dimensions (e.g., assurance, responsiveness, and empathy) are most important in exceeding customer expectations, such as by surprising customers with uncommon swiftness, grace, courtesy, competence, commitment, and understanding.
7. *Fair play:* Service companies must make special efforts to be fair and to demonstrate fairness to customers and employees.
8. *Teamwork:* Teamwork is what enables large organizations to deliver service with care and attentiveness by improving employee motivation and capabilities.
9. *Employee research:* Conduct research with employees to reveal why service problems occur and what companies must do to solve problems.
10. *Servant leadership:* Quality service comes from inspired leadership throughout the organization; from excellent service-system design; from the effective use of information and technology; and from a slow-to-change, invisible, all-powerful, internal force called corporate culture.

Source: Leonard L. Berry, A. Parasuraman, and Valarie A. Zeithaml, "Ten Lessons for Improving Service Quality," MSI Report 93–104 (Cambridge, MA: Marketing Science Institute, 1993).

FIGURE 15-10   Recommendations for Improving Service Quality

Fidelity's ad campaign in the early 2000s that featured Peter Lynch leveraged its famed analyst's equity in humorous ad executions in an attempt to create favorable perceptions on all three credibility dimensions.

Design communication programs that augment consumers' service encounters and experiences. Service firms must design marketing communication and information programs so that consumers learn more about the brand than the information they glean from their service encounters alone. These programs may involve advertising, direct mail, and other communications that may be particularly effective at helping the firm to develop the proper brand personality. The communication programs should be fully integrated and evolve over time. Surprisingly, Citigroup walked away from a strong credibility position for its retail brand when it dropped its "Citi Never Sleeps" ad campaign.

Establish a brand hierarchy by creating distinct family brands or individual brands as well as meaningful ingredient brands. Finally, services also must consider developing a brand hierarchy and brand portfolio that permit positioning and targeting of different market segments. Classes of service can be branded vertically on the basis of price and quality. Vertical extensions often require sub-branding strategies in which the corporate name is combined with an individual brand name or modifier. In the hotel and airlines industries, brand lines and portfolios have been created by brand extensions and introductions. For example, United airlines brands its business class service as Connoisseur Class, its frequent flier program as Mileage Plus, and its short-haul airlines as United Express. As another example, Hilton Hotel has introduced Hilton Garden Inns to target budget-conscious business travelers and compete with the popular Courtyard by Marriott chain.

Retailers

Chapters 5 and 7 reviewed a number of issues concerning how retailers and other channel intermediaries can affect the brand equity of the products they sell as well as how they can create their own brand equity. Fundamentally, retailers create their own brand equity by establishing awareness and associations to their product assortment (breadth and depth), pricing and credit policy, quality of service, and so on. For example, Wal-Mart has become perhaps the premier U.S. retail brand by becoming seen as the low-price, high-value provider of a host of everyday consumer products. Consumers may form these associations in many ways, such as on the basis of personal experience, word of mouth, or through advertisements or other indirect means. In building brand equity for a retailer, several guidelines are particularly relevant (see Figure 15-11). Branding Brief 15-4 describes the recent ascension of U.K. retailer Tesco.

Create a brand hierarchy by branding the store as a whole, as well as individual departments, classes of service, or any other noteworthy aspects of the retail service or shopping experience. Establishing a brand hierarchy helps to create synergies in brand development. Retailers also must consider brand portfolio issues and what other retail stores or chains should be introduced to provide more complete market coverage. For example, Wal-Mart introduced another retail chain, Sam's Club, to tap into the growing discount or warehouse retail market.

Similarly, individual departments can take on unique sets of associations that appeal to a particular target market. For example, Nordstrom has clothing

FIGURE 15-11   Additional Guidelines for Retailers

1. Create a brand hierarchy by branding the store as a whole, as well as individual departments, classes of service, or any other aspects of the retail service or shopping experience.
2. Enhance manufacturers' brand equity by communicating and demonstrating their points of difference and other strong, favorable, and unique brand associations.
3. Establish brand equity at all levels of the brand hierarchy by offering added value in the selection, purchase, or delivery of product offerings.
4. Create multichannel shopping experiences.
5. Avoid overbranding.

Branding Success at Tesco

British supermarket Tesco was the second-biggest grocery chain in the United Kingdom in the 1980s, behind the dominant Sainsbury chain. Tesco began upgrading its stores and product selection around 1983, but by 1990 the company had still been unable to take market share from Sainsbury. Tesco was still considered a "pile it high and sell it cheap" mass-market retailer and wanted to change this perception. In a brief to its advertising agency in 1989, Tesco expressed a desire "to develop an image campaign which will lift us out of the mold in our particular sector."

The company's first image campaign, called "Quest for Quality," ran from 1990 to 1992. It starred Dudley Moore as a Tesco employee who looked all over the globe for French free-range chickens and discovered en route other exotic products to add to Tesco shelves. The idea was to surprise consumers with the range of high-quality goods available at Tesco. An instant success, the ad peaked at 89 percent prompted awareness in tracking studies. During the time that the "Quest for Quality" ran, Tesco also invested heavily in improvements for the business by launching 114 initiatives that improved the overall shopping experience, such as baby-changing facilities, a frequent-shopper program, and a new value product range.

Tesco devised a new campaign featuring 20 commercials, each focusing on a different initiative, that were linked by the tag line "Every Little Helps." These ads conveyed Tesco's new customer-oriented approach of always "doing right by the customer." Prompted awareness of these ads reached 64 percent, and Tesco's revenues and market share rose steadily until Tesco surpassed Sainsbury as the U.K. market leader in 1995. Company research revealed that 1.3 million new customers started shopping at Tesco between 1990 and 1995.

Another Tesco advertising campaign that helped endear the company to customers is its Computers for Schools cause-related marketing campaign, started in 1992. It quickly became the best-known cause-related campaign in the United Kingdom, with prompted awareness levels near 50 percent. Customers receive vouchers from Tesco for every £10 spent, which they can donate to the school of their choosing. The chosen school exchanges the vouchers for new computer equipment. Parent-teacher associations and school governors joined together to maximize voucher collection, which further enhanced the community involvement in the program. Tesco capitalized on the link between its brand and the Computers for Schools program in 1998, when the company began selling computer hardware. Since the program began, Tesco Computers for Schools has delivered almost $90 million worth of computer equipment to schools in the United Kingdom.

Tesco's market share continued to rise, reaching 15.4 percent in 1999. In both 1998 and 1999, other British companies voted Tesco as Britain's most admired company. With the help of savvy and sustained marketing efforts, Tesco transformed itself from an also-ran into a market leader in less than a decade.

Sources: Ashleye Sharpe and Joanna Bamford, "Tesco Stores Ltd." (paper presented at Advertising Effectiveness Awards, 2000); Hamish Pringle and Marjorie Thompson, *Brand Spirit* (New York: John Wiley, 1999); "The Prime Minister Launches the 10th Tesco Computers for Schools Scheme," *M2 Presswire,* 26 January 2001.

departments such as Point of View, Brass Plum, Encore, and Individualist, each designed with distinct images and positions. These departments may be branded by the retailer or even as "ingredient brands," designed and supported by a national manufacturer (e.g., as with Polo shops in major department stores, which only sell that Ralph Lauren brand).

Enhance manufacturer's brand equity. As a second guideline, retailers should exploit as much as possible the brand equity of the manufacturer brands they sell by communicating and demonstrating their points of difference and other strong, favorable, and unique brand associations. Manufacturers often employ push strategies that involve various programs to encourage retailers to better support their brands. By cooperating with and perhaps even enhancing these programs to better communicate the value and equity of the brands sold, retailers should be able to sell these products at higher prices and margins, generating greater profits as a result. Consider the marketing push provided by DuPont to help out merchants in the very fragmented retail carpet market.

DuPont Stainmaster Carpet

When DuPont launched Stainmaster carpet, it provided intensive retail support. Dealers received a 12-page catalog describing what DuPont had to offer in merchandising DuPont Stainmaster carpet, as well as cards, brochures, cleaning instructions, and DuPont's *Complete Book of Carpeting*. Store and product identification for dealers comprised hanging mobiles with Stainmaster logos, large canvas banners that could be hung outside showrooms, in-store wall and window posters, carpet-identification medallions, sales tags, and photo boards depicting the Stainmaster TV commercials. A key feature was a demonstration unit that allowed customers to dip a toothbrush-like swizzle stick, which had one treated and one untreated group of tufts, into various stains and go through the simple stain-removal process to see for themselves how Stainmaster worked. Promotional activities encouraged dealers to hold special events or sales to promote Stainmaster (e.g., one chain ran a "Pet Parade" in Los Angeles that featured hundreds of animals—from cats to monkeys—strutting along a length of red carpet made with Stainmaster).

Establish brand equity at all levels of the brand hierarchy by offering added value in the selection, purchase, or delivery of product offerings. Retailers must create their own strong, favorable, and unique associations that go beyond the products they sell. Sharper Image has created a niche as a seller of creative, upscale products and gadgets. Victoria's Secret has gained notoriety as a provider of stylish, feminine clothing. Costco and Price Club created strong discount associations.

Some of the most successful retail brands in recent years have been warehouse stores or "category killers" that have created strong associations to a certain set of products. Home Depot captured a huge chunk of the home-improvement and hardware store business by selling thousands of items through skilled and helpful salespeople and a "no questions asked" return policy. Other category killers include retailers such as Toys"R"Us, Linens 'N Things, and Circuit City. One advantage these chains have is the sharp positioning they are able to create in the minds of consumers.

To communicate these broader associations, retail strategies are often reflected in image campaigns that focus on the advantages to consumers of shopping at and buying from the stores in general rather than on promotions for specific sale items. For example, Radio Shack now advertises that it is the "consumer-friendly" provider of electronic parts, accessories, and specialty equipment through a campaign with the slogan "You've Got Questions. We've Got Answers."

Land Rover Centres
According to the president of Land Rover North America, car buying is "literally the most horrible retail experience any customer can imagine—why not make it easy and why not make it fun?" Land Rover Centres feature safari-garbed salespeople who are trained to avoid high-pressure sales tactics. The Centres have a specialty store look. In addition to showcasing vehicles, they display Land Rover Gear such as a branded line of shirts, gloves, sweatshirts, and coats. Some Centres show videotapes of Rovers in the wilds of Africa or have an adjacent short off-road course with steep climbs and falls.[7]

Create multichannel shopping experiences. Increasingly, retailers are selling their wares in a variety of channels, such as physical stores, catalogs, and online Web sites. Office Depot recognized the importance of supplementing its 800-plus stores back in 1997 with a strong online and catalog presence. By offering service and convenience—and not cutting its prices—Office Depot has been able to maintain its market leadership. Regardless of the channel employed, it is important that consumers have rewarding shopping experiences in searching, choosing, paying for, and receiving products. In some case, these experiences may turn out to be valuable points of difference, or at least necessary points of parity, with respect to competitors.

Avoid overbranding. Finally, if a retailer is selling its own private labels, it is important not to employ too many brands. Retailers are particularly susceptible to "bottom-up branding," in which each department creates its own set of brands. For example, Nordstrom found itself in the position of having to support scores of different brands across its different departments, sometimes with little connection among them. Recall from Chapter 5 that one advantage of store brands, however, is that they often represent associations (e.g., value) that transfer across categories. The greater the extent to which an abstract association (value, fashionability, etc.) can be seen as desirable and deliverable across categories, the more likely it is that efficiencies can be gained by concentrating on a few major brands.

Small Businesses

Building brands for a small business is a challenge because of the limited resources and budgets typically involved. Unlike major brands that often have more resources at their disposal, small businesses usually do not have the luxury to make mistakes and must design and implement marketing programs much more carefully. Nevertheless, numerous success stories exist of entrepreneurs who have built their brands up essentially from scratch to become powerhouse brands. Through word of mouth—the company only spends 1 percent of revenues on advertising—Krispy Kreme has seen its sales explode. From humble origins in North Carolina, its sales more than doubled from 1997 to 2001.

SCIENCE OF BRANDING 15-1

How Smaller Can Be Better

Adam Morgan, in a fascinating book, *Eating the Big Fish: How Challenger Brands Can Compete Against Brand Leaders,* offers eight suggestions of how small brands can better compete:

1. *Break with your immediate past:* Don't be afraid to ask "dumb" questions to challenge convention and view your brand differently.

2. *Build a "lighthouse identity":* Establish values and communicate who and why you are (e.g., Apple).

3. *Assume thought leadership of the category:* Break convention in terms of representation (what you say about yourself), where you say it (medium), and experience (what you do beyond talk).

4. *Create symbols of reevaluation:* A rocket uses half of its fuel in the first mile to break loose from the gravitational pull—you may need to polarize people.

5. *Sacrifice:* Focus your target, message, reach and frequency, distribution, and line extensions and recognize that less can be more.

6. *Overcommit:* Although you may do fewer things, do "big" things when you do them.

7. *Use publicity and advertising to enter popular culture:* Unconventional communications can get people talking.

8. *Be idea centered, not consumer centered:* Sustain challenger momentum by not losing sight of what the brand is about and can be and redefine marketing support and the center of the company to reflect this vision.

―――――
Source: Adam Morgan, *Eating the Big Fish: How Challenger Brands Can Compete Against Brand Leaders* (New York: John Wiley & Sons, 1999).

In general, because limited resources may be placed behind the brand, both focus and consistency in marketing programs are critically important. To compensate for fewer funds, creativity is also paramount—finding new ways to market new ideas about products to consumers. The Science of Branding 15-1 contains some provocative notions as to how small brands can compete with big ones. Figure 15-12 displays some specific branding guidelines for small businesses, as follows. Branding Brief 15-5 describes how Green Mountain Coffee built a strong brand.

Emphasize building one or two strong brands. Given the reality of fewer resources, strategically, it may be necessary to emphasize building one or two strong brands. Along these lines, employing a corporate branding strategy can be an efficient means to build brand equity, although the focus may just be on a major family brand. For example, Intuit concentrated its marketing efforts on building the Quicken brand name of software.

Focus the marketing program on one or two key associations. Small businesses often must rely on only one or two key associations as points of difference. These associations must be consistently reinforced across the marketing program and over time. The

1. Emphasize building one or two strong brands.
2. Focus the marketing program on one or two key associations.
3. Employ a well-integrated set of brand elements that enhances both brand awareness and brand image.
4. Design creative brand-building push campaigns and consumer-involving pull campaigns that capture attention and generate demand.
5. Leverage as many secondary associations as possible.

FIGURE 15-12   Additional Guidelines for Small Businesses

College Kit, in Hanover, New Hampshire, "delivers products, services and marketing messages into the hands and minds of college consumers through creative, connected, sometimes outrageous and always entertaining programs." Thus, its key associations are to "creative," "well-targeted," "marketing programs for college students."

Employ a well-integrated set of brand elements. Tactically, it is important for small businesses to maximize the contribution of each of the three main ways to build brand equity. First, a distinctive, well-integrated set of brand elements should be developed that enhances both brand awareness and brand image, as suggested by the following example.

Rumba

Seattle's Wall Data made connectivity software between desktop and host computers (various mainframes) that allowed users to avoid rebooting or reconfiguring. In the mid 1990s, Wall Data cleverly branded its family of software products "Rumba" and combined that name with a symbol of a man and woman dancing cheek-to-cheek. It used the slogan "Get Connected" in advertising, promotional materials, and packaging. To further build awareness and image, the company even hosted rumba dance lessons at trade shows. The success of the Rumba product line permitted the later introduction of a new set of software products, branded "Salsa."

Brand elements ideally should be memorable and meaningful, with as much creative potential as possible. Innovative packaging can be a substitute for ad campaigns by capturing attention at the point of purchase. For example, Smartfood introduced its first product without any advertising by means of both a unique package that served as a strong visual symbol on the shelf as well as an extensive sampling program that encouraged trial. Proper names or family names, which often characterize small businesses, may provide some distinctiveness but suffer in terms of pronounceability, meaningfulness, memorability, or other branding considerations. If these deficiencies are too great, alternative brand elements should be explored.

Design creative brand-building push campaigns and consumer-involving pull campaigns that capture attention and generate demand. Small businesses must design creative push and pull programs that capture the attention of consumers and other channel members alike. Clearly, this is a sizable challenge on a limited budget. Unfortunately, without a strong pull campaign creating product interest, retailers may

---

Green Mountain Coffee Roasters

Bob Stiller founded Green Mountain Coffee Roasters in 1981 when he opened a small café in Waitsfield, Vermont. According to the company, it was not long before tourists who stopped in the café asked if they could receive Green Mountain Coffee at home, via mail. The company answered this demand by launching its mail-order business. Green Mountain sought out local customers by opening other retail locations in Vermont and Maine. In the company's early years, it used no advertising, instead engaging in extensive sampling.

Stiller took the company public in 1993 and used the proceeds to expand the mail-order operation and open additional retail stores. Green Mountain also invested in technological improvements for its roasting and packaging system, spending $500,000 on a system that removes oxygen from packages of coffee and improves shelf life.

Green Mountain closed its 12 retail locations in 1998 in order to focus on wholesale business. The company's wholesale customers include restaurants, convenience stores, office coffee distributors, and airlines. For at-home customers, Green Mountain retained its mail-order catalog and its Coffee Club home-delivery subscription service, and in 1998 it began selling coffee and other specialty products online at www.greenmountaincoffee.com. In addition to 60 varieties of Green Mountain Coffee, customers can order from a diverse assortment of products, including coffee grinders, mugs, chocolates, and gift baskets.

Green Mountain grew rapidly as its wholesale business brought it in contact with an ever-widening customer base. Between 1995 and 2000, sales increased at an average rate of 24 percent annually. In 2001, the company sold the equivalent of 10 million cups of coffee every day and maintained relationships with more than 7,000 wholesale customers. That same year, *Forbes* named Stiller as its first-ever "Entrepreneur of the Year." Additionally, Green Mountain Coffee improved to sixteenth in *Forbes*'s annual listing of the "200 Best Small Companies in America," up from nineteenth in 2000. Green Mountain gives 5 percent of its pretax profits to "socially responsible" causes.

S*ources:* http://www.greenmountaincoffee.com; Luisa Kroll, "Entrepreneur of the Year: Java Man," *Forbes,* 29 October 2001, 142; "Green Mountain Coffee, Inc. Founder, President and CEO Named Forbes First 'Entrepreneur of the Year,'" *Business Wire,* 16 October 2001.

---

not feel enough motivation to stock and support the brand. Conversely, without a strong push campaign that convinces retailers of the merits of the product, the brand may fail to achieve adequate support or may not even be stocked at all. Thus, push and pull marketing programs ideally would be creatively designed and integrated, employing the most cost-effective tools available, to increase the visibility of the brand and get both consumers and retailers talking about the brand.

Because small businesses often must rely on word of mouth to create strong, favorable, and unique brand associations, public relations and low-cost promotions and sponsorship can be inexpensive means to enhance brand awareness and brand image. For example, Noah Alper, co-founder of Noah's Bagels, reached out to the Jewish community and transplanted New Yorkers in Northern California through well-publicized events and appearances that promoted the "authentic" nature of the bagel chain. Marketers of the PowerBar, a nutrient-rich, low-fat "energy bar," used selective sponsorship of top marathon runners, cyclists, and tennis players and events like the Boston Marathon to raise awareness and improve image. Selective distribution that targets opinion leaders can also be a cost-effective means to implement a push strategy. For example, brands such as Perrier bottled water and Paul Mitchell and Nexus shampoo were initially introduced to a carefully selected set of outlets before broadening distribution.

Leverage as many secondary associations as possible. Finally, another way for small businesses to build brand equity is to leverage as many secondary associations as possible. Secondary associations are often a cost-effective, shortcut means to build brand equity. Any entity with potentially relevant associations should be considered, especially those that help to signal quality or credibility. Along those lines, to enhance perceptions of scope (i.e., make the company appear "bigger" than it really is), a well-designed Web site can be invaluable.

Online

Creating a brand online brings a special set of challenges. Many of the guidelines for business-to-business, high-tech, retailing, and small businesses may apply, depending on the nature of the online business. At the same time, there are a number of other guidelines worth reinforcing (as summarized in Figure 15-13). Branding Brief 15-6 outlines how eBay built one of the strongest online brands.

Don't forget the brand-building basics. With online brands, it is important to not forget brand-building basics such as establishing points of parity (e.g., in terms of convenience, price, and variety) and points of difference (e.g., in terms of customer service, credibility, and personality). As noted in earlier chapters, one mistake of many failed dot-com brands was to be impatient in building their brands and failing to build the brand from the bottom up. In research to understand online service quality, defined as the extent to which a Web site facilitates efficient and effective shopping, purchasing, and delivery, one study identified 11 dimensions of perceived e-service quality: access, ease of navigation, efficiency, flexibility, reliability, personalization, security/privacy, responsiveness, assurance/trust, site aesthetics, and price knowledge.[8] Land's End became a top-selling company online by treating its internet operations as a digital translation of its successful catalog, ensuring that merchandise was presented properly and that excellent customer service prevailed.

Create strong brand identity. Given that consumers aren't physically confronted by brands as they are in a store, brand awareness and recall are critical. Toward that goal, choosing the right URL is an important priority. Because the Internet revolution led to an explosion of .com name registrations, with over 17 million .com brands registered by the end of 2000, choosing the best new URL is difficult. URLs must be chosen with the

1. Don't forget the brand-building basics.
2. Create strong brand identity.
3. Generate strong consumer pull.
4. Selectively choose brand partnerships.
5. Maximize relationship marketing.

FIGURE 15-13 Additional Guidelines for Online Brands

Making the Sale at eBay

In a little over five years, eBay grew from a free trading network that tallied exactly no users during its first month of operation into the most popular shopping site on the Internet, as measured by total user minutes. Founder Pierre Omidyar started eBay (short for "electronic Bay Area" after the area in which Omidyar lived) so his wife could trade Pez candy dispensers online with collectors. eBay rapidly became a destination for traders and collectors of items of all description and amassed a loyal user base despite having no national advertising campaigns between 1995 and late 1998.

eBay was able to grow quickly without much advertising in part because the auction site had an inherent grassroots marketing engine in its user network. The trading of memorabilia, collectibles, and antiques fostered a strong sense of community. One user said, "eBay is not only a business, it's a place for all of us to bring back a part of our past and regain the memories of our childhood." Brian Swette, senior vice president for marketing and international at eBay, said, "From the beginning, community was integrated into our business. When you make a transaction on eBay, you have to make a ton of personal interactions with other users. It's built into the experience."

Once eBay started focusing on bigger-ticket items and more lucrative partnerships with larger vendors and companies such as Hasbro, General Motors, and Visa, longtime customers feared that the collectible nostalgia that drove the brand's growth in the early years would be marginalized. The company introduced the PowerSeller program, which provides additional customer support to large vendors. When eBay acquired San Francisco auction house Butterfield & Butterfield in 1999, one customer sniffed, "It seems that the 'junk' that brought Pierre [Omidyar] millions is just not good enough anymore."

As eBay grew, it developed satellite sites to better serve foreign customers. The company currently has country-specific sites in Austria, Australia, Canada, France, Germany, Ireland, Italy, Japan, Korea, New Zealand, Switzerland, and the United Kingdom. In order to assist customers buying and selling items not easily shipped, eBay developed local sites, such as eBay Pittsburgh, in over 60 markets in the United States. These sites feature items such as cars and tickets to local sporting events.

eBay, which was one of the earliest and few profitable dot-coms, continues to grow. In 2000, the eBay community included more than 22 million users, who traded goods worth more than $5 billion. At any given time that year, eBay listed more than 6 million items up for bid. In 2000, eBay added 5,000 new categories in order to continue its mission to be "The Internet's Marketplace." The company grew financially as well: Consolidated revenues increased 92 percent in 2000 to $431 million, and net profits totaled nearly $60 million.

Sources: Daniel Roth, "Meg Muscles eBay Uptown," *Fortune,* 5 July1999, 81; "eBay Rolls Out Additional Sites," *Wall Street Journal,* 7 December 1999, B7.

basic brand element criteria in mind, with perhaps greater emphasis on brand recall as an objective (e.g., 1-800-FLOWERS took its brand directly to the Web). A simple but evocative name can be useful in that regard, as with BabyCenter.com, an information and commerce Web site providing content on pregnancy and babies, an interactive community for parents and parents-to-be, and a store featuring thousands of baby products and supplies.

Generate strong consumer pull. An important lesson for online brands was the need to create demand off line to drive consumers online. One aspect of this strategy is to use a wide variety of sampling and other trial devices. For example, AOL conducted massive sampling and free giveaways of its CD-ROMs that eventually led to increased consumer adoptions. More broadly, online brands must introduce the best possible integrated marketing communication program, consisting of combinations of public relations; television, radio, and print advertising; sponsorship; and so on.

Selectively choose brand partnerships. Online brands can benefit from establishing a number of brand partners with which they can link. Such linkages can drive traffic, signal credibility, and help to enhance image. Partnerships must be entered selectively, however, to satisfy brand-building and profit criteria. For example, CDNOW has an active affiliate program with its Cosmic Credit program that targets low-volume, nonprofessional sites of music fans, but also has initiated a number of higher-profile strategic partnerships through the years by alliances with powerful online brands such as AOL and Excite.[9]

Maximize relationship marketing. Finally, some of the potential advantages of online brands are the customization and interactivity involved. It is especially important, then, to engage in one-to-one, participatory, experiential, and other forms of relationship marketing. Creating a strong online brand community between the consumer and the brand, as well as perhaps other consumers, can help to achieve brand resonance. For example, one marketing executive at Yahoo characterized its strategy by saying, "We've really focused our marketing efforts on attracting new users and providing an experience online that makes them stay."[10] Yahoo attempts to make the Internet experience as fun and entertaining as possible but also practical, useful, and convenient in its range of applications. Online brokerage Ameritrade provides detailed, timely, customized financial information to its clients. Online brands can offer much potentially relevant customer information; for example, Amazon provides professional and customer reviews; purchase circles and overall sales rankings; text samples; and personalized recommendations.

FUTURE BRAND PRIORITIES

The journey to better understand strategic brand management is about over, but it is worth considering a few final questions. How will branding change in the coming years? What are the biggest branding challenges? What will make a successful "twenty-first-century brand?" In a general sense, the importance of branding seems unlikely to change for one critical reason: It seems highly likely that consumers will continue to value the functions provided by brands. In a seemingly more and more complex world, well-managed brands can simplify, communicate, reassure, and provide important meaning to consumers. Using the principles reflected in the brand report card and avoiding the seven deadly sins of brand management reviewed earlier should help in the pursuit of brand management. This final section highlights several important considerations in building, measuring, and managing brand equity in the future and concludes by suggesting a broad theme for strategic brand management.

Building Brand Equity

Brand Elements

In a cluttered, competitive marketplace, the brand elements that make up the brand will have to do more and more of the selling job. In a time-compressed marketing world, the fact that a brand name can be noticed and its meaning registered or activated in memory within just a few seconds is a tremendous asset. Creating a powerful brand with inherent marketing value to build awareness and image, as well as serve as a strong foundation to link associations, can provide a firm with a strong competitive advantage.

Although general branding principles should apply in designing a twenty-first-century brand, what may change are some of the means of creating strong brands. For example, the brand elements that are chosen will increasingly involve verbal and visual elements that creatively and dramatically help to build brand equity. Meaningful brands with creative potential will benefit from multiple sensory presentations. Brands have long used auditory branding devices, for example, the three-note Nabisco jingle, the percolating Maxwell House jingle, and the NBC jingle. Movie studios have always been able to take advantage of their cinematic exposure to use sight, sound, and motion to present their brands (e.g., Universal's spinning globe, Paramount's mountain peak, and MGM's roaring lion). With increased technical abilities and improved special effects, marketers will now be able to create brand elements that come to life and capture consumer attention, an important quality given the need to communicate and sell through brands in current markets. Thus, the static images of brands with which marketers are used to dealing will be supplemented by multidimensional forms that play a more important role in audio and video presentations of the brand. A twenty-first-century brand will consider how to take advantage of different media to customize the brand presentation so that each brand element more effectively contributes to brand equity through enhanced awareness and image and brand elements more effectively reinforce each other so that they become more consistent and cohesive as a result.

Marketing Programs

Strong brands in the twenty-first century also will rise above other brands by better understanding the needs, wants, and desires of consumers and creating marketing programs that fulfill and even surpass consumer expectations. Successful brands will have a rich but internally cohesive brand image whose associations are highly valued by consumers. Marketing programs will seamlessly reinforce these associations through product, pricing, distribution, and communication strategies that consistently and creatively inform and remind consumers of what the brand has to offer. With these marketing programs, consumers will have a clear picture of what the brand represents and why it is special. Consumers will then view the brand as a "trusted friend" and value its dependability and superiority. Marketers will engage in dialogue with consumers, listening to their product joys and frustrations and establishing a rapport and relationship that will transcend mere commercial exchanges. Marketers will develop a deep understanding of what makes their brand successful, retaining enduring core elements while modifying peripheral elements that fail to add value or unnecessarily absorb costs.

Finally, smart marketers in the twenty-first century will attempt to find ways to make sure that strong brand associations are created to all possible marketing effects. In particular, it will be necessary to carefully and imaginatively consider how the brand itself will be effectively integrated into the marketing program to maximize its contribution to brand equity. In other words, the issue will not just be which brand elements are chosen to represent the brand but also how these brand elements will actually be used in the marketing program.

Measuring Brand Equity

Marketers of successful twenty-first-century brands will create formalized measurement approaches and processes that ensure that they continually and exhaustively monitor their sources of brand equity and those of competitors. As part of this process, managers will develop a greater understanding of how different marketing actions affect their sources and outcomes of brand equity. Thus, marketers of successful twenty-first-century brands will go beyond piecemeal research projects (e.g., periodic advertising campaign evaluations) to devise new and original ways to obtain accurate, comprehensive, and up-to-date information on the status of their brands. By maintaining close contact with the brand, managers will be better able to understand just what makes their brand tick. By achieving greater accountability in marketing activities and programs, it will be possible for managers to better optimize their brand investments, putting money behind the right brands at the right time and in the right ways.

Managing Brand Equity

It will be essential in building strong twenty-first-century brands to align internal and external brand management. *Internal brand management* involves activities that ensure that employees and marketing partners appreciate and understand basic branding notions and how they can affect the equity of brands. Brand management must not be perceived as a separate function within the organization but as the responsibility and obligation of all. For that to happen, however, it is important that the right structures, processes, incentives, and resources are put into place, for example, through brand equity charters, reports, and oversight.

Internal brand management is especially critical for a corporate brand, in which every employee directly or indirectly represents the brand and can therefore affect brand equity.[11] Internal brand management helps to ensure that external brand management is done properly. *External brand management* involves understanding the needs, wants, and desires of consumers and creating marketing programs for brands that fulfill and even surpass consumer expectations.

Companies must also align bottom-up and top-down marketing management. *Bottom-up brand management* requires that marketing managers primarily direct their marketing activities to maximize brand equity for individual products in particular markets, with relatively little regard for other brands and products sold by the firm or for other markets in which their brands and products may be sold. Although such close, detailed brand supervision can be advantageous, creating brand equity for every different possible product and market in this way can be an expensive and difficult process and, most important, ignores possible synergies that may be obtainable.

Top-down brand management, on the other hand, involves marketing activities that capture the big picture and recognize the possible synergies across products and markets to brand products accordingly. Such a top-down approach would seek to find common products and markets that could share marketing programs and activities for brands and only develop separate brands and marketing programs and activities as dictated by the consumer or competitive environment.

Unfortunately, if left unmanaged, firms tend to follow the bottom-up approach, resulting in many brands marketed inconsistently and incompatibly. Managing brands in a top-down fashion requires centralized and coordinated marketing guidance and actions from high-level marketing supervisors. Particular attention must be paid on how to best develop and leverage the corporate brand.

Both pairs of brand management activities can be complementary and mutually reinforcing: Successful brands will be those that effectively blend top-down versus bottom-up and internal versus external brand management activities. Ignoring one or more of these dimensions can put the brands of a firm in peril. In avoiding this pitfall, marketers of successful twenty-first-century brands will continually evolve and adapt every aspect of their marketing programs to enhance brand equity. These marketers will develop a deep understanding of what makes their brand successful, retaining enduring core elements while modifying peripheral elements that fail to add value or unnecessarily absorb costs. Marketers of successful twenty-first century brands also will appreciate how their brands fit in with respect to other brands sold by the firm. They will capitalize on and judiciously exploit the potential of their brand in product development and brand extensions while at the same time recognizing its limits and boundaries.

Achieving Marketing Balance

These potential brand management tradeoffs suggest a broader issue and challenge with marketing and brand management. In many ways, the most fundamental challenge of marketing and brand management is how to reconcile or address the many potential tradeoffs that exist in making marketing decisions.[12] Figure 15-14 lists a number of the different possible tradeoffs or conflicts that can occur in making strategic, tactical, financial, or organizational decisions for a brand. Clearly, tradeoffs are pervasive and must be made in the context of constrained—and often fairly limited—resources. To illustrate, recall from Chapter 3 the many negatively correlated attributes and benefits that exist in the minds of consumers and the challenge that these relationships presented for positioning.

FIGURE 15-14   Some Brand Marketing Tradeoffs

Strategic
Retaining customers vs. acquiring customers
Brand expansion vs. brand fortification
Product performance vs. brand image
Points of parity vs. points of difference

Tactical
Push vs. pull
Continuity vs. change
Classic vs. contemporary image
Independent vs. universal image

Financial
Short-run vs. long-run objectives
Sales-generating vs. brand-building activities
Accountable or measurable tactics vs. non-measurable tactics
Quality maximization vs. cost minimization

Organizational
Global vs. local
Top down vs. bottom up
Customization vs. standardization
Internal vs. external

One response to these tradeoffs is to adopt an extreme solution and maximize one of the two dimensions involved with the tradeoff. Many management gurus advocate positions that, in effect, lead to such a singular focus. Such approaches, however, obviously leave the brand vulnerable to whatever are the negative consequences of ignoring the other dimension. The reality is that for marketing success, both dimensions in each of these decision tradeoffs typically must be adequately addressed. Doing so involves achieving a more balanced marketing solution. Marketing balance occurs when marketers attempt to address all possible tradeoffs as much as possible in organizing, planning, and implementing their marketing programs.

There are three means or levels of achieving marketing balance, in increasing order of potential effectiveness:

1. *Alternate:* Identify and recognize the various tradeoffs, but attempt to emphasize one dimension at a time and try to alternate whichever dimension receives emphasis over time so that both dimensions are not completely ignored. Although potentially effective, the downside of this approach is that often the firm experiences a pendulum effect. There can be a tendency to overreact to a perceived imbalance in emphasis such that an imbalance in one direction leads to a subsequent imbalance in the other direction as a result.

2. *Divide:* Split the difference and do a little of both to cover all the bases. Again, although potentially effective, this approach may suffer if insufficient or inadequate resources are put against the two objectives such that critical mass is not achieved. Attempting to do a little of this and a little of that may be too wishy-washy and lack sufficient impact.

3. *Finesse:* Finesse the difference and achieve synergy between the two dimensions. Marketing balance in this way is achieved by shrewdly reconciling the decision tradeoffs—that is, by finessing the conflicting dimensions.

Hitting the marketing sweet spot thus may involve some well-thought-out moderation and balance throughout the marketing organization and its activities. For example, marketing balance can involve strategically creative advertising that entertains and sells products (e.g., as with the California Milk Processor Board's "Got Milk?" campaign). It can involve equity-building promotions such as Procter & Gamble's promotion for Ivory soap that reinforced a key attribute of "floating" and a key benefit of "purity" while also moving product. It can involve robust brand positions such as Apple's "The Power to Be Your Best," which reconciled the seemingly negatively correlated benefits of "easy to use" and "powerful" in the minds of consumers.

Marketing balance can actually be more difficult to achieve than more extreme solutions in that it can involve greater discipline, care, and thought. To use a golf analogy, the golfer with the smoothest swing is often the one who hits the ball farther and straighter. Marketing balance may not be as "exciting" as more radical proposed solutions, but can turn out to be much more productive. Marketing balance is all about making marketing work harder, be more versatile, and achieve more objectives. To realize marketing balance, it is necessary to create multiple meanings, multiple responses, and multiple effects with marketing activities.

Marketing balance does not imply that marketers should not take chances, should not do different things, or should not do things differently. It *does* imply an acceptance of the fact that marketing is multifaceted and involves multiple objectives, markets, and activities. Marketing balance recognizes the importance of avoiding oversimplification: Marketers must do many things and do them right. Fundamentally, to achieve marketing balance, marketers must understand and address marketing tradeoffs.

David Aaker's Brand Equity Model

One of branding's academic pioneers is Berkeley's David Aaker. Aaker defines brand equity as a set of five categories of brand assets and liabilities linked to a brand, its name, and symbol that add to or subtract from the value provided by a product or service to a firm or to that firm's customers, or both. These categories of brand assets are (1) brand loyalty, (2) brand awareness, (3) perceived quality, (4) brand associations,

FIGURE A   Aaker's Brand Equity Framework

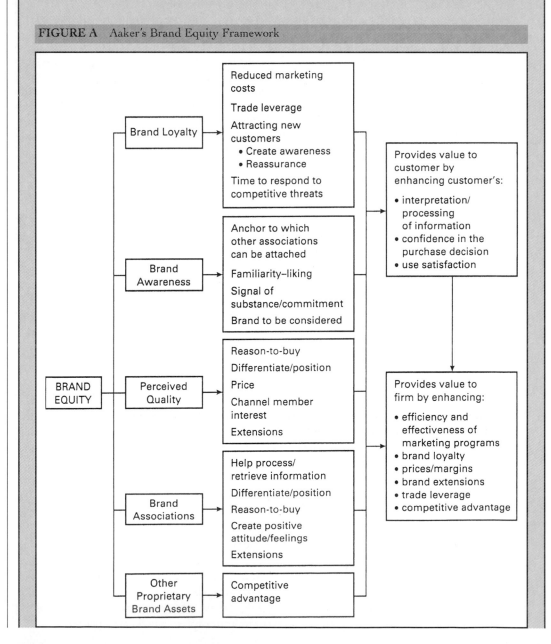

and (5) other proprietary assets (e.g., patents, trademarks, and channel relationships). These assets provide various benefits and value, as shown in Figure A.

Aaker describes a number of issues in building, measuring, and managing brand equity. A summary of guidelines emerging from his framework can be found in Figure B. According to Aaker, a particularly important concept for building brand equity is brand identity. Aaker defines *brand identity* as

a unique set of brand associations that the brand strategist aspires to create or maintain. These associations represent what the brand stands for and imply a promise to customers from the organization members. Brand identity should help establish a relationship between the brand and the customer by generating a value proposition involving functional, emotional, or self-expressive benefits.

FIGURE B Aaker's Ten Guidelines for Building Strong Brands

1. **Brand identity.** Have an identity for each brand. Consider the perspective of the brand-as-person, brand-as-organization, and brand-as-symbol, as well as the brand-as-product. Identify the core identity. Modify the identity as needed for different market segments and products. Remember that an image is how you are perceived, and an identity is how you aspire to be perceived.
2. **Value proposition.** Know the value proposition for each brand that has a driver role. Consider emotional and symbolic benefits as well as functional benefits. Know how endorser brands will provide credibility. Understand the customer/brand relationship.
3. **Brand position.** For each brand, have a brand position that will provide clear guidance to those implementing a communication program. Recall that a position is the part of the identity that is actively communicated.
4. **Execution.** Execute the communication program so that it not only is on target with the identity and position but achieves brilliance and durability. Generate alternatives and consider options beyond media advertising.
5. **Consistency over time.** Have as a goal a consistent identity, position, and execution over time. Maintain symbols, imagery, and metaphors that work. Understand and resist organizational biases toward changing the identity, position, and execution.
6. **Brand system.** Make sure the brands in the portfolio are consistent and synergistic. Know their roles. Have or develop silver bullets to help support brand identities and positions. Exploit branded features and services. Use sub-brands to clarify and modify. Know the strategic brands.
7. **Brand leverage.** Extend brands and develop co-branding programs only if the brand identity will be both used and reinforced. Identify range brands and, for each, develop an identity and specify how that identity will be different in disparate product contexts. If a brand is moved up or down, take care to manage the integrity of the resulting brand identity.
8. **Tracking brand equity.** Track brand equity over time, including brand awareness, perceived quality, brand loyalty, and especially brand associations. Have specific communication objectives. Especially note areas where the brand identity and positioning and communication objectives are not reflected in the perceptions of the brand.
9. **Brand responsibility.** Have someone in charge of the brand who will create the identity and positions and coordinate the execution over organizational units, media, and markets. Beware when a brand is being used in a business where it is not the cornerstone.
10. **Invest in brands.** Continue investing in brands even when the financial goals are not being met.

Brand identity consists of twelve dimensions organized around four perspectives—the brand-as-product (product scope, product attributes, quality/value, uses, users, country of origin), brand-as-organization (organizational attributes, local versus global), brand-as-person (brand personality, brand-customer relationships), and brand-as-symbol (visual imagery/metaphors and brand heritage).

Brand identity structure includes a core and extended identity. The core identity—the central, timeless essence of the brand—is most likely to remain constant as the brand travels to new markets and products. The extended identity includes brand identity elements, organized into cohesive and meaningful groups.

A particularly important concept for managing brand equity according to Aaker is that of brand systems. Aaker emphasizes that a key to managing brands in an environment of complexity is to consider them as not just individual performers but as members of a system of brands that must work together to support one another. He notes that the goals of the system are qualitatively different from the goals of individual brand identities and include exploiting commonalities to generate synergy, reducing brand identity damage, achieving clarity of product offerings, facilitating change and adaptation, and allocating resources. Aaker also notes that many brands within a system fall into a natural hierarchy and may play different roles in the system—for example, endorsers, drivers, strategic brands, silver bullets, branded benefits, and sub-brand roles.

Source: David A. Aaker, *Building Strong Brands* (New York: Free Press, 1995).

Review

The challenges and complexities of the modern marketplace make efficient and effective marketing an imperative. The concept of brand equity has been put forth as a means to focus marketing efforts. The businesses that win in the twenty-first century will be those that have marketers who successfully build, measure, and manage brand equity. This final chapter reviewed some of the important guidelines put forth in this text to help in that endeavor. Effective brand management requires consistent actions and applications of these guidelines across all aspects of the marketing program. Nevertheless, to some extent, rules are made to be broken, and these guidelines should be viewed only as a point of departure in the difficult process of creating a world-class brand. Each branding situation and application is unique and requires careful scrutiny and analysis as how best to apply, or perhaps in some cases ignore, these various recommendations and guidelines. Smart marketers will capitalize on every tool at their disposal—and devise ones that are not—in their relentless pursuit of achieving brand preeminence. To provide further stimulation, the Science of Branding 15-2 and 15-3 summarize some ideas from leading brand strategists David Aaker and Scott Bedbury.

Scott Bedbury's Eight Branding Principles

Scott Bedbury, one of the key brand architects behind both the Starbucks and Nike brands in the 1990s, offers his brand philosophy in his book *A New Brand World*. A strong proponent of a consumer-centric approach to branding, Bedbury outlines the following eight branding principles for brand leadership in the twenty-first century.

1. Relying on brand awareness has become marketing's fool's gold.
2. You have to know it before you grow it.
3. Remember the spandex rule of branding: Just because you can doesn't mean you should.
4. Transcend a product-only relationship with consumers.
5. Everything matters.
6. All brands need good parents.
7. Big doesn't have to be bad.
8. Relevance, simplicity, and humanity—rather than technology—will distinguish brands in the future.

Source: Scott Bedbury with Stephen Fenichell, *A New Brand World: Eight Principles for Achieving Brand Leadership in the 21st Century* (New York: Viking Press, 2002).

Discussion Questions

1. What do you think makes a strong brand? Can you add any criteria to the list provided?
2. What about deadly sins of brand management? Do you see anything missing from the list of seven in Figure 15-5?
3. Pick one of the special applications of branding and choose a representative brand within that category. How well do the five guidelines for that category apply? Can you think of others not listed?
4. What do you see as the future of branding? How will the roles of brands change? What different strategies might emerge as to how to build, measure, and manage brand equity in the coming years? What do you see as the biggest challenges?
5. Review the different tradeoffs identified as part of achieving marketing balance. Can you identify any other tradeoffs not listed? For each tradeoff, can you identify a company that has excelled in achieving balance on that tradeoff?

Brand Focus 15.0

The Brand Report Card

Rate your brand on a scale of 1 to 10 (1 = extremely poor; 10 = extremely good) for each characteristic below.[13] Create a similar report card for your major competitors. Compare and contrast the results with all the relevant participants in the management of your brand. Doing so should help you identify areas that need improvement, recognize areas in which you excel, and learn more about how your particular brand is configured. Be brutally honest in answering the questions—approach them as an outsider and from a consumer perspective.

SCORE

1. ____ Managers understand what the brand means to consumers.
   - Have you created detailed, research-driven mental maps of your target customers?
   - Have you attempted to define a brand mantra?
   - Have you outlined customer-driven boundaries for brand extensions and guidelines for marketing programs?

2. ____ The brand is properly positioned.
   - Have you established necessary and competitive points of parity?
   - Have you established desirable and deliverable points of difference?

3. ____ Customers receive superior delivery of the benefits they value most.
   - Have you attempted to uncover unmet consumer needs and wants?
   - Do you relentlessly focus on maximizing your customers' product and service experiences?

4. ____ The brand takes advantage of the full repertoire of branding and marketing activities available to build brand equity.
   - Have you strategically chosen and designed your brand name, logo, symbol, slogan packaging, signage, and so forth to build brand awareness and image?
   - Have you implemented integrated push and pull strategies that target intermediaries and end customers, respectively?

5. ____ Marketing and communications efforts are seamlessly integrated (or as close to it as humanly possible). The brand communicates with one voice.
   - Have you considered all the alternative ways to create brand awareness and link brand associations?
   - Have you ensured that common meaning is contained throughout your marketing communication program?
   - Have you capitalized on the unique capabilities of each communication option?
   - Have you been careful to preserve important brand values in your communications over time?

6. ____ The brand's pricing strategy is based on consumer perceptions of value.
   - Have you estimated the added value perceived by customers?
   - Have you optimized price, cost, and quality to meet or exceed consumer expectations?

7. ____ The brand uses appropriate imagery to support its personality.
   - Have you established credibility by ensuring that the brand and the people behind it are seen as expert, trustworthy, and likable?
   - Have you established appropriate user and usage imagery?
   - Have you crafted the right brand personality?

8. ____ The brand is innovative and relevant.
   - Have you invested in product improvements that provide improved benefits and better solutions for your customers?

- Have you stayed up-to-date and in touch with your customers?

9. ___ For a multiproduct, multibrand company, the brand hierarchy and brand portfolio are strategically sound.

- For the brand hierarchy, are associations at the highest levels relevant to as many products as possible at the next lower levels and are brands well differentiated at any one level?
- For the brand portfolio, do the brands maximize market coverage while minimizing their overlap at the same time?

10. ___ The company has in place a system to monitor brand equity and performance.

- Have you created a brand charter that defines the meaning and equity of the brand and how it should be treated?
- Do you conduct periodic brand audits to assess the health of your brands and to set strategic direction?
- Do you conduct routine tracking studies to evaluate current marketing performance?
- Do you regularly distribute brand equity reports that summarize all brand-relevant research and information to assist marketing decision making?
- Have you assigned people within the organization the responsibility of monitoring and preserving brand equity?

Notes

1. Based on Kevin Lane Keller, "The Brand Report Card," *Harvard Business Review* (Jan/Feb 2000): 147–157.
2. Kevin Lane Keller and Frederick E. Webster Jr., "Branding Industrial Products," working paper, Amos Tuck School of Business, Dartmouth College, 2002.
3. Stephen Philips and Amy Dunkin, "King Customer," *Business Week,* 12 March 1990, 88–94.
4. Leslie de Chernatony and Malcom H. B. McDonald, *Creating Powerful Brands* (Oxford: Butterworth-Heinemann, 1992).
5. A. Parasuraman, Valarie A. Zeithaml, and Leonard L. Berry, "A Conceptual Model of Service Quality and Its Implications for Future Research," *Journal of Marketing* (Fall 1985): 41–50
6. Leonard L. Berry, A. Parasuraman, and Valarie A. Zeithaml, "Ten Lessons for Improving Service Quality," MSI Report 93–104 (Cambridge, MA: Marketing Science Institute, 1993).
7. Keith Naughton, "The Ralph Lauren of Car Dealers," *Business Week*, 20 November 1995, 151.
8. Valarie A. Zeithaml, Parsu Parasuraman, and Arvind Malhotra, "Understanding e-Service Quality" (presentation made at MSI Board of Trustees Meeting entitled "Marketing Knowledge in the Age of e-Commerce," November 2000). See also Parasuraman, Zeithaml, and Berry, "Conceptual Model of Service Quality," as well as William Boulding, Ajay Kalra, and Richard Staelin, "A Dynamic Process Model of Service Quality: From Expectations to Behavioral Intentions," *Journal of Marketing Research* (February 1993): 7–27 for an important extension.
9. Donna L. Hoffman and Thomas P. Novak, "How to Acquire Customers on the Web," *Harvard Business Review* (May–June 2000): 179–188.
10. Debra Thompson, "Branding Hasn't Changed Much," *Marketing Computers,* April 2000.
11. Mary Jo Hatch and Majken Scultz, "Are the Corporate Stars Aligned for your Corporate Brand?" *Harvard Business Review* (February 2001): 129–134.
12. Kevin Lane Keller and Frederick E. Webster Jr. "Marketing Balance: Finessing Marketing Trade-Offs," working paper, Tuck School of Business, Dartmouth College, 2002.
13. Based on Kevin Lane Keller, "The Brand Report Card," *Harvard Business Review* (Jan/Feb 2000): 147–157.

Epilogue

When asked how he beat Jimmy Conners in the 1980 Master's tournament after losing to him in their 16 previous matches, Vitas Gerulatis quipped:

Hey, *nobody* beats Vitas Gerulatis 17 times in a row.

I guess you have to draw the line somewhere.

Life is short. Build strong brands.

Credits

Chapter 1

6: AP/Wide World Photos; 14: Courtesy of Intel Corporation; 18: © 2001 Southwest Airlines, Inc. Courtesy of Southwest Airlines; 24: AP/Wide World Photos; 27: Carsten Peter/NGS Image Collection—February 2002 cover; 29: AP/Wide World Photos.

Chapter 2

78: Frank LaBua, Pearson Education/PH College; 80: Teri Stratford; 85: © 2002 Abercrombie & Fitch; Bruce Weber, Photographer; 91: Hallmark Cards, Inc.

Chapter 3

121: Courtesy of Pepsi-Cola Company; 134: Frank LaBua, Pearson Education/PH College; 135: Courtesy of Miller Brewing Company; 136: Frank LaBua, Pearson Education/PH College; 140: Steve Marcus/Reuters/NewMedia, CORBIS; 146: © Apple, Inc. Used with permission.

Chapter 4

179: Courtesy of Pepsi-Cola Company; 193: Reproduced with permission of Yahoo! Inc. © 2000 by Yahoo! Inc. YAHOO! and the YAHOO! Logo are trademarks of Yahoo! Inc. Photograph © by Terry Husebye. All rights reserved; 198 (top): AP/Wide World Photos; 198 (bottom): Courtesy of Deere & Company; 200: Courtesy Lee Jeans; 240: AP/Wide World Photos; 205: General Mills/AP Wide World.

Chapter 5

239: Tim Boyle/Getty Images, Inc.; 265: Spongebob Squarepants provided by Nickelodeon; 267: 2000 Nike, Inc. All rights reserved. Reproduced by permission; 268: AP/Wide World Photos; 277: Loblaw Brands Limited.

Chapter 6

306: Courtesy Volvo Cars of North America, LLC; 316: AP/Wide World Photos; 323: Frank LaBua, Pearson Education/PH College; 326: Courtesy Ford Motor Company.

Chapter 7

365: Frank LaBua, Pearson Education/PH College.

Chapter 8

404: Michael Newman/PhotoEdit; 414: Frank LaBua, Pearson Education/PH College.

Chapter 9

446: AP/Wide World Photos; 452: AP/Wide World Photos.

Chapter 10
487: Frank LaBua, Pearson Education/PH College.

Chapter 11
549: Courtesy of 3M Corporation; 559: Courtesy of the Nestle Corporation.

Chapter 12
580: image courtesy of DaimlerChrysler Corporation. PT CRUISER is a trademark of Daimler Chrysler; 587: Courtesy of Xerox Corporation; 588: Frank LaBua, Pearson Education/PH College; 597: AP/Wide World Photos.

Chapter 13
644: Courtesy of the Gillette Company; 646: Frank LaBua, Pearson Education/PH College; 655: AP/Wide World Photos.

Index